THE BOOK OF MORMON

ANOTHER TESTAMENT
OF JESUS CHRIST

Journal Edition for Missionaries

**DESERET
BOOK**

SALT LAKE CITY, UTAH

Austin Garver

"The Book of Mormon is central to this work.
It declares the doctrine of the gathering.
It causes people to learn about Jesus Christ,
to believe His gospel, and to join His Church.
In fact, if there were no Book of Mormon, the
promised gathering of Israel would not occur."

—President Russell M. Nelson

"The Gathering of Scattered Israel,"
Ensign, November 2006

THE
BOOK OF MORMON

AN ACCOUNT WRITTEN BY

THE HAND OF MORMON

UPON PLATES
TAKEN FROM THE PLATES OF NEPHI

Wherefore, it is an abridgment of the record of the people of Nephi, and also of the Lamanites—Written to the Lamanites, who are a remnant of the house of Israel; and also to Jew and Gentile—Written by way of commandment, and also by the spirit of prophecy and of revelation—Written and sealed up, and hid up unto the Lord, that they might not be destroyed—To come forth by the gift and power of God unto the interpretation thereof—Sealed by the hand of Moroni, and hid up unto the Lord, to come forth in due time by way of the Gentile—The interpretation thereof by the gift of God.

An abridgment taken from the Book of Ether also, which is a record of the people of Jared, who were scattered at the time the Lord confounded the language of the people, when they were building a tower to get to heaven—Which is to show unto the remnant of the house of Israel what great things the Lord hath done for their fathers; and that they may know the covenants of the Lord, that they are not cast off forever—And also to the convincing of the Jew and Gentile that JESUS is the CHRIST, the ETERNAL GOD, manifesting himself unto all nations—And now, if there are faults they are the mistakes of men; wherefore, condemn not the things of God, that ye may be found spotless at the judgment-seat of Christ.

TRANSLATED BY JOSEPH SMITH, JUN.

ABBREVIATIONS

Old Testament

Gen.	Genesis
Ex.	Exodus
Lev.	Leviticus
Num.	Numbers
Deut.	Deuteronomy
Josh.	Joshua
Judg.	Judges
Ruth	Ruth
1 Sam.	1 Samuel
2 Sam.	2 Samuel
1 Kgs.	1 Kings
2 Kgs.	2 Kings
1 Chr.	1 Chronicles
2 Chr.	2 Chronicles
Ezra	Ezra
Neh.	Nehemiah
Esth.	Esther
Job	Job
Ps.	Psalms
Prov.	Proverbs
Eccl.	Ecclesiastes
Song	Song of Solomon
Isa.	Isaiah
Jer.	Jeremiah
Lam.	Lamentations
Ezek.	Ezekiel
Dan.	Daniel
Hosea	Hosea
Joel	Joel
Amos	Amos
Obad.	Obadiah
Jonah	Jonah
Micah	Micah
Nahum	Nahum
Hab.	Habakkuk
Zeph.	Zephaniah
Hag.	Haggai
Zech.	Zechariah
Mal.	Malachi

New Testament

Matt.	Matthew
Mark	Mark
Luke	Luke
John	John
Acts	Acts
Rom.	Romans
1 Cor.	1 Corinthians
2 Cor.	2 Corinthians
Gal.	Galatians
Eph.	Ephesians
Philip.	Philippians
Col.	Colossians
1 Thes.	1 Thessalonians
2 Thes.	2 Thessalonians
1 Tim.	1 Timothy
2 Tim.	2 Timothy
Titus	Titus
Philem.	Philemon
Heb.	Hebrews
James	James
1 Pet.	1 Peter
2 Pet.	2 Peter
1 Jn.	1 John
2 Jn.	2 John
3 Jn.	3 John
Jude	Jude
Rev.	Revelation

Book of Mormon

1 Ne.	1 Nephi
2 Ne.	2 Nephi
Jacob	Jacob
Enos	Enos
Jarom	Jarom
Omni	Omni
W of M	Words of Mormon
Mosiah	Mosiah
Alma	Alma
Hel.	Helaman
3 Ne.	3 Nephi
4 Ne.	4 Nephi
Morm.	Mormon
Ether	Ether
Moro.	Moroni

Doctrine and Covenants

D&C	Doctrine and Covenants
OD	Official Declaration

Pearl of Great Price

Moses	Moses
Abr.	Abraham
JS—M	Joseph Smith—Matthew
JS—H	Joseph Smith—History
A of F	Articles of Faith

Other Abbreviations and Explanations

JST	Joseph Smith Translation
TG	Topical Guide
BD	Bible Dictionary
HEB	An alternate translation from the Hebrew
GR	An alternate translation from the Greek
IE	An explanation of idioms and difficult wording
OR	Alternate words that clarify the meaning of an archaic expression

CONTENTS

INTRODUCTION

The Book of Mormon is a volume of holy scripture comparable to the Bible. It is a record of God's dealings with ancient inhabitants of the Americas and contains the fulness of the everlasting gospel.

The book was written by many ancient prophets by the spirit of prophecy and revelation. Their words, written on gold plates, were quoted and abridged by a prophet-historian named Mormon. The record gives an account of two great civilizations. One came from Jerusalem in 600 B.C. and afterward separated into two nations, known as the Nephites and the Lamanites. The other came much earlier when the Lord confounded the tongues at the Tower of Babel. This group is known as the Jaredites. After thousands of years, all were destroyed except the Lamanites, and they are among the ancestors of the American Indians.

The crowning event recorded in the Book of Mormon is the personal ministry of the Lord Jesus Christ among the Nephites soon after His resurrection. It puts forth the doctrines of the gospel, outlines the plan of salvation, and tells men what they must do to gain peace in this life and eternal salvation in the life to come.

After Mormon completed his writings, he delivered the account to his son Moroni, who added a few words of his own and hid up the plates in the Hill Cumorah. On September 21, 1823, the same Moroni, then a glorified, resurrected being, appeared to the Prophet Joseph Smith and instructed him relative to the ancient record and its destined translation into the English language.

In due course the plates were delivered to Joseph Smith, who translated them by the gift and power of God. The record is now published in many languages as a new and additional witness that Jesus Christ is the Son of the living God and that all who will come unto Him and obey the laws and ordinances of His gospel may be saved.

Concerning this record the Prophet Joseph Smith said: "I told the brethren that the Book of Mormon was the most correct of any book on earth, and the keystone of our religion, and a man would get nearer to God by abiding by its precepts, than by any other book."

In addition to Joseph Smith, the Lord provided for eleven others to see the gold plates for themselves and to be special witnesses of the truth and divinity of the Book of Mormon. Their written testimonies are included herewith as "The Testimony of Three Witnesses" and "The Testimony of Eight Witnesses."

We invite all men everywhere to read the Book of Mormon, to ponder in their hearts the message it contains, and then to ask God, the Eternal Father, in the name of Christ if the book is true. Those who pursue this course and ask in faith will gain a testimony of its truth and divinity by the power of the Holy Ghost. (See Moroni 10:3–5.)

Those who gain this divine witness from the Holy Spirit will also come to know by the same power that Jesus Christ is the Savior of the world, that Joseph Smith is His revelator and prophet in these last days, and that The Church of Jesus Christ of Latter-day Saints is the Lord's kingdom once again established on the earth, preparatory to the Second Coming of the Messiah.

[Handwritten margin notes:]

Joseph Smith recieved strength beyond his own to translate the Book of Mormon.

Revelation :
· ask
· faith
· listen to Holy Ghost

THE TESTIMONY OF THREE WITNESSES

Be it known unto all nations, kindreds, tongues, and people, unto whom this work shall come: That we, through the grace of God the Father, and our Lord Jesus Christ, have seen the plates which contain this record, which is a record of the people of Nephi, and also of the Lamanites, their brethren, and also of the people of Jared, who came from the tower of which hath been spoken. And we also know that they have been translated by the gift and power of God, for his voice hath declared it unto us; wherefore we know of a surety that the work is true. And we also testify that we have seen the engravings which are upon the plates; and they have been shown unto us by the power of God, and not of man. And we declare with words of soberness, that an angel of God came down from heaven, and he brought and laid before our eyes, that we beheld and saw the plates, and the engravings thereon; and we know that it is by the grace of God the Father, and our Lord Jesus Christ, that we beheld and bear record that these things are true. And it is marvelous in our eyes. Nevertheless, the voice of the Lord commanded us that we should bear record of it; wherefore, to be obedient unto the commandments of God, we bear testimony of these things. And we know that if we are faithful in Christ, we shall rid our garments of the blood of all men, and be found spotless before the judgment-seat of Christ, and shall dwell with him eternally in the heavens. And the honor be to the Father, and to the Son, and to the Holy Ghost, which is one God. Amen.

OLIVER COWDERY
DAVID WHITMER
MARTIN HARRIS

THE TESTIMONY OF EIGHT WITNESSES

Be it known unto all nations, kindreds, tongues, and people, unto whom this work shall come: That Joseph Smith, Jun., the translator of this work, has shown unto us the plates of which hath been spoken, which have the appearance of gold; and as many of the leaves as the said Smith has translated we did handle with our hands; and we also saw the engravings thereon, all of which has the appearance of ancient work, and of curious workmanship. And this we bear record with words of soberness, that the said Smith has shown unto us, for we have seen and hefted, and know of a surety that the said Smith has got the plates of which we have spoken. And we give our names unto the world, to witness unto the world that which we have seen. And we lie not, God bearing witness of it.

CHRISTIAN WHITMER   HIRAM PAGE
JACOB WHITMER   JOSEPH SMITH, SEN.
PETER WHITMER, JUN.   HYRUM SMITH
JOHN WHITMER   SAMUEL H. SMITH

THE TESTIMONY OF THE
PROPHET JOSEPH SMITH

The Prophet Joseph Smith's own words about the coming forth of the Book of Mormon are:

"On the evening of the . . . twenty-first of September [1823] . . . I betook myself to prayer and supplication to Almighty God. . . .

"While I was thus in the act of calling upon God, I discovered a light appearing in my room, which continued to increase until the room was lighter than at noonday, when immediately a personage appeared at my bedside, standing in the air, for his feet did not touch the floor.

"He had on a loose robe of most exquisite whiteness. It was a whiteness beyond anything earthly I had ever seen; nor do I believe that any earthly thing could be made to appear so exceedingly white and brilliant. His hands were naked, and his arms also, a little above the wrist; so, also, were his feet naked, as were his legs, a little above the ankles. His head and neck were also bare. I could discover that he had no other clothing on but this robe, as it was open, so that I could see into his bosom.

"Not only was his robe exceedingly white, but his whole person was glorious beyond description, and his countenance truly like lightning. The room was exceedingly light, but not so very bright as immediately around his person. When I first looked upon him, I was afraid; but the fear soon left me.

"He called me by name, and said unto me that he was a messenger sent from the presence of God to me, and that his name was Moroni; that God had a work for me to do; and that my name should be had for good and evil among all nations, kindreds, and tongues, or that it should be both good and evil spoken of among all people.

"He said there was a book deposited, written upon gold plates, giving an account of the former inhabitants of this continent, and the source from whence they sprang. He also said that the fulness of the everlasting Gospel was contained in it, as delivered by the Savior to the ancient inhabitants;

"Also, that there were two stones in silver bows—and these stones, fastened to a breastplate, constituted what is called the Urim and Thummim—deposited with the plates; and the possession and use of these stones were what constituted 'seers' in ancient or former times; and that God had prepared them for the purpose of translating the book. . . .

"Again, he told me, that when I got those plates of which he had spoken—for the time that they should be obtained was not yet fulfilled—I should not show them to any person; neither the breastplate with the Urim and Thummim; only to those to whom I should be commanded to show them; if I did I should be destroyed. While he was conversing with me about the plates, the vision was opened to my mind that I could see the place where the plates were deposited, and that so clearly and distinctly that I knew the place again when I visited it.

"After this communication, I saw the light in the room begin to gather immediately around the person of him who had been speaking to me, and it continued to do so until the room was again left dark, except just around him; when, instantly I saw, as it were, a conduit open right up into heaven, and he ascended till he entirely disappeared, and the room was left as it had been before this heavenly light had made its appearance.

"I lay musing on the singularity of the scene, and marveling greatly at what had been told to me by this extraordinary messenger; when, in the

Meditation/Ponder help you recognize revelation

Moroni added the Great Judgement

Each visit Moroni added more to the revelation.
• God may want us to make the next step and then he gives us more information

After receiving revelation you must go and obey

midst of <u>my meditation</u>, I suddenly discovered that my room was again beginning to get lighted, and in an instant, as it were, the same heavenly messenger was again by my bedside.

"He commenced, and again related the very same things which he had done at his first visit, without the least variation; which having done, he informed me of great judgments which were coming upon the earth, with great desolations by famine, sword, and pestilence; and that these grievous judgments would come on the earth in this generation. Having related these things, he again ascended as he had done before.

"By this time, so deep were the impressions made on my mind, that sleep had fled from my eyes, and I lay overwhelmed in astonishment at what I had both seen and heard. But what was my surprise when again I beheld the same messenger at my bedside, and heard him rehearse or repeat over again to me the same things as before; and added a caution to me, telling me that Satan would try to tempt me (in consequence of the indigent circumstances of my father's family), to get the plates for the purpose of getting rich. This he forbade me, saying that I must have no other object in view in getting the plates but to glorify God, and must not be influenced by any other motive than that of building his kingdom; otherwise I could not get them.

"After this third visit, he again ascended into heaven as before, and I was again left to ponder on the strangeness of what I had just experienced; when almost immediately after the heavenly messenger had ascended from me for the third time, the cock crowed, and I found that day was approaching, so that our interviews must have occupied the whole of that night.

"I shortly after arose from my bed, and, as usual, went to the necessary labors of the day; but, in attempting to work as at other times, I found my strength so exhausted as to render me entirely unable. My father, who was laboring along with me, discovered something to be wrong with me, and told me to go home. I started with the intention of going to the house; but, in attempting to cross the fence out of the field where we were, my strength entirely failed me, and I fell helpless on the ground, and for a time was quite unconscious of anything.

"The first thing that I can recollect was a voice speaking unto me, calling me by name. I looked up, and beheld the same messenger standing over my head, surrounded by light as before. He then again related unto me all that he had related to me the previous night, and commanded me to go to my father and tell him of the vision and commandments which I had received.

"<u>I obeyed</u>; I returned to my father in the field, and rehearsed the whole matter to him. He replied to me that it was of God, and told me to go and do as commanded by the messenger. I left the field, and went to the place where the messenger had told me the plates were deposited; and owing to the distinctness of the vision which I had had concerning it, I knew the place the instant that I arrived there.

"Convenient to the village of Manchester, Ontario county, New York, stands a hill of considerable size, and the most elevated of any in the neighborhood. On the west side of this hill, not far from the top, under a stone of considerable size, lay the plates, deposited in a stone box. This stone was thick and rounding in the middle on the upper side, and thinner towards the edges, so that the middle part of it was visible above the ground, but the edge all around was covered with earth.

"Having removed the earth, I obtained a lever, which I got fixed under the edge of the stone, and with a little exertion raised it up. I looked in, and there indeed did I behold the plates, the Urim and Thummim, and the breastplate, as stated by the messenger. The box in which they lay was formed by laying stones together in some kind of cement. In the bottom of the box were laid two stones crossways of the box, and on these stones lay the plates and the other things with them.

"I made an attempt to take them out, but was forbidden by the messenger, and was again informed that the time for bringing them forth had not yet arrived, neither would it, until four years from that time; but he told me that I should come to that place precisely in one year from that time, and that he would there meet with me, and that I should continue to do so until the time should come for obtaining the plates.

"Accordingly, as I had been commanded, I went at the end of each year, and at each time I found the same messenger there, and received instruction and intelligence from him at each of our interviews, respecting what the Lord was going to do, and how and in what manner his kingdom was to be conducted in the last days. . . .

"At length the time arrived for obtaining the plates, the Urim and Thummim, and the breastplate. On the twenty-second day of September, one thousand eight hundred and twenty-seven, having gone as usual at the end of another year to the place where they were deposited, the same heavenly messenger delivered them up to me with this charge: that I should be responsible for them; that if I should let them go carelessly, or through any neglect of mine, I should be cut off; but that if I would use all my endeavors to preserve them, until he, the messenger, should call for them, they should be protected.

"I soon found out the reason why I had received such strict charges to keep them safe, and why it was that the messenger had said that when I had done what was required at my hand, he would call for them. For no sooner was it known that I had them, than the most strenuous exertions were used to get them from me. Every stratagem that could be invented was resorted to for that purpose. The persecution became more bitter and severe than before, and multitudes were on the alert continually to get them from me if possible. But by the wisdom of God, they remained safe in my hands, until I had accomplished by them what was required at my hand. When, according to arrangements, the messenger called for them, I delivered them up to him; and he has them in his charge until this day, being the second day of May, one thousand eight hundred and thirty-eight."

For a more complete account, see Joseph Smith—History in the Pearl of Great Price.

The ancient record thus brought forth from the earth as the voice of a people speaking from the dust, and translated into modern speech by the gift and power of God as attested by Divine affirmation, was first published to the world in the year 1830 as THE BOOK OF MORMON.

A BRIEF EXPLANATION ABOUT
THE BOOK OF MORMON

The Book of Mormon is a sacred record of peoples in ancient America and was engraved upon metal plates. Sources from which this record was compiled include the following:

1. *The Plates of Nephi,* which were of two kinds: the small plates and the large plates. The former were more particularly devoted to spiritual matters and the ministry and teachings of the prophets, while the latter were occupied mostly by a secular history of the peoples concerned (1 Nephi 9:2–4). From the time of Mosiah, however, the large plates also included items of major spiritual importance.

2. *The Plates of Mormon,* which consist of an abridgment by Mormon from the large plates of Nephi, with many commentaries. These plates also contained a continuation of the history by Mormon and additions by his son Moroni.

3. *The Plates of Ether,* which present a history of the Jaredites. This record was abridged by Moroni, who inserted comments of his own and incorporated the record with the general history under the title "Book of Ether."

4. *The Plates of Brass* brought by the people of Lehi from Jerusalem in 600 B.C. These contained "the five books of Moses, . . . and also a record of the Jews from the beginning, . . . down to the commencement of the reign of Zedekiah, king of Judah; and also the prophecies of the holy prophets" (1 Nephi 5:11–13). Many quotations from these plates, citing Isaiah and other biblical and nonbiblical prophets, appear in the Book of Mormon.

The Book of Mormon comprises fifteen main parts or divisions, known, with one exception, as books, usually designated by the name of their principal author. The first portion (the first six books, ending with Omni) is a translation from the small plates of Nephi. Between the books of Omni and Mosiah is an insert called the Words of Mormon. This insert connects the record engraved on the small plates with Mormon's abridgment of the large plates.

The longest portion, from Mosiah through Mormon chapter 7, is a translation of Mormon's abridgment of the large plates of Nephi. The concluding portion, from Mormon chapter 8 to the end of the volume, was engraved by Mormon's son Moroni, who, after finishing the record of his father's life, made an abridgment of the Jaredite record (as the book of Ether) and later added the parts known as the book of Moroni.

In or about the year A.D. 421, Moroni, the last of the Nephite prophet-historians, sealed the sacred record and hid it up unto the Lord, to be brought forth in the latter days, as predicted by the voice of God through His ancient prophets. In A.D. 1823, this same Moroni, then a resurrected personage, visited the Prophet Joseph Smith and subsequently delivered the engraved plates to him.

About this edition: The original title page, immediately preceding the contents page, is taken from the plates and is part of the sacred text. Introductions in a non-italic typeface, such as in 1 Nephi and immediately preceding Mosiah chapter 9, are also part of the sacred text. Introductions in italics, such as in chapter headings, are not original to the text but are study helps included for convenience in reading.

Some minor errors in the text have been perpetuated in past editions of the Book of Mormon. This edition contains corrections that seem appropriate to bring the material into conformity with prepublication manuscripts and early editions edited by the Prophet Joseph Smith.

THE FIRST BOOK OF NEPHI

HIS REIGN AND MINISTRY

An account of Lehi and his wife Sariah, and his four sons, being called, (beginning at the eldest) Laman, Lemuel, Sam, and Nephi. The Lord warns Lehi to depart out of the land of Jerusalem, because he prophesieth unto the people concerning their iniquity and they seek to destroy his life. He taketh three days' journey into the wilderness with his family. Nephi taketh his brethren and returneth to the land of Jerusalem after the record of the Jews. The account of their sufferings. They take the daughters of Ishmael to wife. They take their families and depart into the wilderness. Their sufferings and afflictions in the wilderness. The course of their travels. They come to the large waters. Nephi's brethren rebel against him. He confoundeth them, and buildeth a ship. They call the name of the place Bountiful. They cross the large waters into the promised land, and so forth. This is according to the account of Nephi; or in other words, I, Nephi, wrote this record.

CHAPTER 1

Nephi begins the record of his people—Lehi sees in vision a pillar of fire and reads from a book of prophecy—He praises God, foretells the coming of the Messiah, and prophesies the destruction of Jerusalem—He is persecuted by the Jews. About 600 B.C.

I, NEPHI, having been ᵃborn of ᵇgoodly ᶜparents, therefore I was ᵈtaught somewhat in all the learning of my father; and having seen many ᵉafflictions in the course of my days, nevertheless, having been highly favored of the Lord in all my days; yea, having had a great knowledge of the goodness and the mysteries of God, therefore I make a ᶠrecord of my proceedings in my days.

2 Yea, I make a record in the ᵃlanguage of my father, which consists of the learning of the Jews and the language of the Egyptians.

3 And I know that the record which I make is ᵃtrue; and I make it with mine own hand; and I make it according to my knowledge.

4 For it came to pass in the commencement of the ᵃfirst year of the reign of ᵇZedekiah, king of Judah, (my father, Lehi, having dwelt at ᶜJerusalem in all his days); and in that same year there came many ᵈprophets, prophesying unto the people that they must ᵉrepent, or the great city ᶠJerusalem must be destroyed.

5 Wherefore it came to pass that my father, Lehi, as he went forth prayed unto the Lord, yea, even

---

1 1a TG Birthright.
  b Prov. 22:1.
  c Mosiah 1:2 (2–3);
    D&C 68:25 (25, 28).
    TG Honoring Father and
    Mother.
  d Enos 1:1.
    TG Education;
    Family, Children,
    Responsibilities toward;
    Family, Love within.
  e TG Affliction;
    Blessing;
    God, Gifts of.
  f TG Record Keeping;

Scriptures, Writing of.
2a Mosiah 1:4;
   Morm. 9:32 (32–33).
3a 1 Ne. 14:30;
   2 Ne. 25:20;
   Mosiah 1:6;
   Alma 3:12;
   Ether 5:3 (1–3).
4a 1 Ne. 2:4;
   Mosiah 6:4.
  b 2 Kgs. 24:18;
    2 Chr. 36:10;
    Jer. 37:1; 44:30; 49:34;
    52:3 (3–5);
    Omni 1:15.

c 1 Chr. 9:3;
  2 Chr. 15:9;
  Alma 7:10.
d 2 Kgs. 17:13 (13–15);
  2 Chr. 36:15 (15–16);
  Jer. 7:25; 26:20.
  TG Prophets, Mission of.
e TG Repent.
f Jer. 26:18 (17–19);
  2 Ne. 1:4;
  Hel. 8:20.
  TG Israel, Bondage of,
  in Other Lands;
  Jerusalem.

Revelation does not always come how we expect it and that can make it so we don't realize we are recieving revelation

with all his [a]heart, in behalf of his
people.
6 And it came to pass as he prayed
unto the Lord, there came a [a]pillar
of fire and dwelt upon a rock before
him; and he saw and heard much;
and because of the things which he
saw and heard he did [b]quake and
tremble exceedingly.
7 And it came to pass that he returned to his own house at Jerusalem; and he cast himself upon
his bed, being [a]overcome with the
Spirit and the things which he had
seen.
8 And being thus overcome with
the Spirit, he was carried away
in a [a]vision, even that he saw the
[b]heavens open, and he thought he
[c]saw God sitting upon his throne,
surrounded with numberless concourses of angels in the attitude
of singing and praising their God.
9 And it came to pass that he saw
One descending out of the midst
of heaven, and he beheld that his
[a]luster was above that of the sun
at noon-day.
10 And he also saw [a]twelve others
following him, and their brightness
did exceed that of the stars in the
firmament.
11 And they came down and went
forth upon the face of the earth; and
the first came and [a]stood before my
father, and gave unto him a [b]book,
and bade him that he should read.
12 And it came to pass that as he
read, he was filled with the [a]Spirit
of the Lord.
13 And he read, saying: Wo, wo,
unto Jerusalem, for I have seen
thine [a]abominations! Yea, and many
things did my father read concerning [b]Jerusalem—that it should be
destroyed, and the inhabitants
thereof; many should perish by the
sword, and many should be [c]carried
away captive into Babylon.
14 And it came to pass that when
my father had read and seen many
great and marvelous things, he did
exclaim many things unto the Lord;
such as: Great and marvelous are
thy works, O Lord God Almighty!
Thy throne is high in the heavens,
and thy [a]power, and goodness, and
mercy are over all the inhabitants
of the earth; and, because thou art
merciful, thou wilt not suffer those
who [b]come unto thee that they shall
perish!
15 And after this manner was
the language of my father in the
praising of his God; for his soul did
rejoice, and his whole heart was
filled, because of the things which
he had seen, yea, which the Lord
had shown unto him.
16 And now I, Nephi, do not make
a full account of the things which
my father hath written, for he hath
written many things which he saw
in [a]visions and in [b]dreams; and
he also hath written many things
which he [c]prophesied and spake

5*a* Jer. 29:13; James 5:16; 2 Ne. 4:24 (23–25).
6*a* Ex. 13:21; Hel. 5:24 (24, 43); D&C 29:12; JS—H 1:16, 30.
b Isa. 6:5 (1–5).
7*a* Dan. 8:27 (26–27); 10:8 (8–12); 1 Ne. 17:47; Alma 27:17; Moses 1:10 (9–10).
8*a* 1 Ne. 3:18 (17–18); 5:4. TG Vision.
b Ezek. 1:1; Acts 7:56 (55–56); 1 Ne. 11:14; Alma 36:22; Hel. 5:48 (45–49); D&C 137:1.
c TG God, Manifestations of; God, Privilege of Seeing.
9*a* JS—H 1:17 (16–17), 30 (30–32).
10*a* TG Apostles.
11*a* 1 Sam. 3:10; D&C 110:2 (2–3).
b Ezek. 2:9 (9–10); Rev. 10:9 (2–11).
12*a* Gen. 41:38; Mosiah 27:24; Alma 18:16.
13*a* 2 Kgs. 24:19; 2 Chr. 36:14; Jer. 13:27.
b 2 Kgs. 23:27; 24:2; Jer. 13:14; Ezek. 15:6 (6–8); 1 Ne. 2:13; 3:17.
c 2 Kgs. 20:17 (17–18); Jer. 52:15 (3–15); 2 Ne. 25:10; Omni 1:15. TG Babylon.
14*a* TG God, Power of.
b 2 Ne. 26:25 (24–28); Alma 5:34 (33–36); 3 Ne. 9:14 (13–14).
16*a* Ezek. 1:1; JS—H 1:24 (21–25).
b 1 Ne. 8:2 (2–38).
c 1 Ne. 7:1.

unto his children, of which I shall not make a full account.

17 But I shall make an account of my proceedings in my days. Behold, I make an *a*abridgment of the record of my *b*father, upon *c*plates which I have made with mine own hands; wherefore, after I have abridged the record of my *d*father then will I make an account of mine own life.

18 Therefore, I would that ye should know, that after the Lord had shown so many marvelous things unto my father, Lehi, yea, concerning the *a*destruction of Jerusalem, behold he went forth among the people, and began to *b*prophesy and to declare unto them concerning the things which he had both seen and heard.

19 And it came to pass that the *a*Jews did *b*mock because of the things which he testified of them; for he truly testified of their *c*wickedness and their abominations; and he testified that the things which he saw and heard, and also the things which he read in the book, manifested plainly of the coming of a *d*Messiah, and also the redemption of the world.

20 And when the Jews heard these things they were angry with him; yea, even as with the prophets of old, whom they had *a*cast out, and stoned, and slain; and they also *b*sought his life, that they might take it away. But behold, I, Nephi, will show unto you that the tender *c*mercies of the Lord are over all those whom he hath chosen, because of their faith, to make them mighty even unto the power of *d*deliverance.

CHAPTER 2

Lehi takes his family into the wilderness by the Red Sea—They leave their property—Lehi offers a sacrifice to the Lord and teaches his sons to keep the commandments—Laman and Lemuel murmur against their father—Nephi is obedient and prays in faith; the Lord speaks to him, and he is chosen to rule over his brethren. About 600 B.C.

FOR behold, it came to pass that the Lord spake unto my father, yea, even in a dream, and said unto him: Blessed art thou Lehi, because of the things which thou hast done; and because thou hast been faithful and declared unto this people the things which I commanded thee, behold, they seek to *a*take away thy *b*life.

2 And it came to pass that the Lord *a*commanded my father, even in a *b*dream, that he should *c*take his family and depart into the wilderness.

3 And it came to pass that he was *a*obedient unto the word of the Lord, wherefore he did as the Lord commanded him.

4 And it came to pass that he departed into the wilderness. And he left his house, and the land of his inheritance, and his gold, and his silver, and his precious things, and took nothing with him, save it

17a 1 Ne. 9:2 (2–5);
      Enos 1:13 (13, 15–18).
   TG Scriptures,
      Writing of.
  b 1 Ne. 6:1 (1–3);
      8:29 (29–30); 19:1 (1–6).
  c 1 Ne. 10:15.
  d 2 Ne. 4:14; 5:33 (29–33);
      D&C 10:42.
18a 2 Ne. 25:9;
      D&C 5:20.
  b TG Prophets, Mission of;
      Prophets, Rejection of.
19a TG Apostasy of Israel.
  b 2 Chr. 36:16;
      Jer. 25:4 (1–4);

      Ezek. 5:6;
      1 Ne. 2:13; 7:14.
  c 1 Ne. 17:22.
  d TG Jesus Christ,
      Prophecies about.
20a Jer. 13:11;
      Hel. 13:24 (24–28).
  b Jer. 11:19;
      1 Ne. 2:2 (1–4).
   TG Prophets,
      Rejection of.
  c Gen. 32:10;
      Alma 34:38;
      D&C 46:15.
  d TG Deliver.
2 1a TG Persecution.

   b 1 Ne. 7:14.
2a 1 Ne. 3:16; 4:34;
      5:8; 17:44;
      Mosiah 7:20;
      Alma 7:9.
   TG Called of God.
  b TG Dream.
  c Gen. 12:1; 19:12;
      1 Ne. 1:20 (18–20);
      2 Ne. 10:20;
      Ether 1:42;
      Abr. 2:3.
   TG Protection, Divine.
3a TG Commitment.

[Handwritten margin notes:]

render mercies of the Lord make me mighty even unto the power of deliverance. Nephi first promises of the strength we recieve from the Lord!

• Keeping Commandments
• obedience
• praying in faith
  Personal Revelation

Lehi immediately listened and followed the revelation he recieved

were his family, and provisions, and tents, and *a*departed into the wilderness.

5 And he came down by the borders near the shore of the *a*Red Sea; and he traveled in the wilderness in the borders which are nearer the Red Sea; and he did travel in the wilderness with his family, which consisted of my mother, Sariah, and my elder brothers, who were Laman, Lemuel, and Sam.

6 And it came to pass that when he had traveled three days in the wilderness, he pitched his tent in a *a*valley by the side of a *b*river of water.

7 And it came to pass that he built an *a*altar of *b*stones, and made an *c*offering unto the Lord, and gave *d*thanks unto the Lord our God.

8 And it came to pass that he called the name of the river, Laman, and it emptied into the Red Sea; and the valley was in the borders near the mouth thereof.

9 And when my father saw that the waters of the river emptied into the *a*fountain of the Red Sea, he spake unto Laman, saying: O that thou mightest be like unto this river, continually running into the fountain of all righteousness!

10 And he also spake unto Lemuel: O that thou mightest be like unto this valley, *a*firm and *b*steadfast, and immovable in keeping the commandments of the Lord!

11 Now this he spake because of the *a*stiffneckedness of Laman and

Lemuel; for behold they did *b*murmur in many things against their *c*father, because he was a *d*visionary man, and had led them out of the land of Jerusalem, to leave the land of their inheritance, and their gold, and their silver, and their precious things, to perish in the wilderness. And this they said he had done because of the foolish imaginations of his heart.

12 And thus Laman and Lemuel, being the eldest, did murmur against their *a*father. And they did *b*murmur because they *c*knew not the dealings of that God who had *d*created them.

13 Neither did they *a*believe that Jerusalem, that great city, could be *b*destroyed according to the words of the prophets. And they were like unto the Jews who were at Jerusalem, who sought to take away the life of my father.

14 And it came to pass that my father did speak unto them in the *a*valley of Lemuel, with *b*power, being filled with the Spirit, until their frames did *c*shake before him. And he did confound them, that they durst not utter against him; wherefore, they did as he commanded them.

15 And my father dwelt in a *a*tent.

16 And it came to pass that I, Nephi, being exceedingly young, nevertheless being large in stature, and also having great desires to know of the *a*mysteries of God,

4a 1 Ne. 10:4; 19:8.
5a 1 Ne. 16:14;
    D&C 17:1.
6a 1 Ne. 9:1.
  b Joel 1:20.
7a Gen. 12:7 (7–8); 26:25;
    Ex. 24:4;
    Abr. 2:17.
  b Ex. 20:25;
    Deut. 27:5 (5–6);
    Josh. 8:31 (30–31).
  c TG Sacrifice.
  d TG Thanksgiving.
9a IE fount, or source, like
    the Gulf of Akaba,
    which empties into the
    Red Sea.

10a IE like Ezion-geber, the
    Hebrew roots of which
    denote firmness and
    strength, or might of
    a man.
  b TG Dependability.
11a TG Stiffnecked.
  b 1 Ne. 17:17.
    TG Murmuring.
  c Prov. 20:20.
  d 1 Ne. 5:4 (2–4); 17:20.
12a Lam. 4:16 (16–17).
  b 1 Sam. 3:13;
    Mosiah 27:8 (7–37);
    Moses 5:16.
  c Moses 4:6.
  d Deut. 32:6;

    D&C 43:23.
    TG Man, Physical
    Creation of.
13a Ezek. 5:6;
    1 Ne. 1:19 (18–20).
  b Jer. 13:14;
    1 Ne. 1:13 (4–13).
14a 1 Ne. 9:1; 16:6 (6, 12).
  b TG Priesthood,
    Power of.
  c 1 Ne. 17:45.
15a Gen. 12:8;
    26:17 (17, 25);
    31:25 (25, 33);
    1 Ne. 4:38; 10:16.
16a TG Mysteries of
    Godliness.

Steps to follow to receive personal revelation

wherefore, I did cry unto the Lord; and behold he did ᵇvisit me, and did ᶜsoften my heart that I did ᵈbelieve all the words which had been spoken by my ᵉfather; wherefore, I did not ᶠrebel against him like unto my brothers.

17 And I spake unto Sam, making known unto him the things which the Lord had manifested unto me by his Holy Spirit. And it came to pass that he believed in my words.

18 But, behold, Laman and Lemuel would not hearken unto my words; and being ᵃgrieved because of the hardness of their hearts I cried unto the Lord for them.

19 And it came to pass that the Lord spake unto me, saying: Blessed art thou, Nephi, because of thy ᵃfaith, for thou hast sought me diligently, with lowliness of heart.

20 And inasmuch as ye shall keep my commandments, ye shall ᵃprosper, and shall be led to a ᵇland of promise; yea, even a land which I have prepared for you; yea, a land which is choice above all other lands.

21 And inasmuch as thy brethren shall rebel against thee, they shall be ᵃcut off from the presence of the Lord.

22 And inasmuch as thou shalt keep my commandments, thou shalt be made a ᵃruler and a teacher over thy brethren.

23 For behold, in that day that they shall ᵃrebel against me, I will ᵇcurse them even with a sore curse, and they shall have no power over thy seed except they shall ᶜrebel against me also.

24 And if it so be that they rebel against me, they shall be a ᵃscourge unto thy seed, to ᵇstir them up in the ways of remembrance.

CHAPTER 3

Lehi's sons return to Jerusalem to obtain the plates of brass—Laban refuses to give the plates up—Nephi exhorts and encourages his brethren—Laban steals their property and attempts to slay them—Laman and Lemuel smite Nephi and Sam and are reproved by an angel. About 600–592 B.C.

AND it came to pass that I, Nephi, returned from ᵃspeaking with the Lord, to the tent of my father.

2 And it came to pass that he spake unto me, saying: Behold I have dreamed a ᵃdream, in the which the Lord hath commanded me that thou and thy brethren shall ᵇreturn to Jerusalem.

3 For behold, Laban hath the record of the Jews and also a ᵃgenealogy of my forefathers, and they are ᵇengraven upon plates of brass.

4 Wherefore, the Lord hath commanded me that thou and thy brothers should go unto the house of Laban, and seek the records, and bring them down hither into the wilderness.

5 And now, behold thy brothers murmur, saying it is a hard thing which I have required of them; but behold I have not required it of

16b Ps. 8:4;
    1 Ne. 3:1; 19:11;
    Alma 17:10;
    D&C 5:16.
    TG Guidance, Divine.
  c 1 Kgs. 18:37;
    Alma 5:7.
  d 1 Ne. 11:5.
  e TG Honoring Father and
    Mother.
  f TG Family, Love within.
18a Alma 31:24;
    3 Ne. 7:16.
19a 1 Ne. 7:12 (9–13); 15:11.
20a Josh. 1:7;

    1 Ne. 4:14;
    Mosiah 1:7.
  b Deut. 33:13 (13–16);
    1 Chr. 28:8 (7–8);
    1 Ne. 5:5 (5, 22); 7:13;
    Moses 7:17 (17–18).
    TG Promised Lands.
21a Josh. 23:13;
    2 Ne. 5:20 (20–24);
    Alma 9:14 (13–15); 38:1.
22a Gen. 37:8 (8–11);
    1 Ne. 3:29.
    TG Authority.
23a Job 24:13.
  b Deut. 11:28;

    1 Ne. 12:22 (22–23);
    D&C 41:1.
    TG Curse.
  c Josh. 22:16;
    Mosiah 15:26.
24a Josh. 23:13;
    Judg. 2:22 (22–23).
  b 2 Ne. 5:25.
3 1a 1 Ne. 2:16.
 2a TG Dream.
  b 1 Ne. 2:4 (1–5); 7:3.
 3a 1 Ne. 3:12; 5:14.
  b Jer. 17:1;
    1 Ne. 3:24 (12, 19–24).

Holy Spirit manifests personal revelation

them, but it is a commandment of the Lord.

6 Therefore go, my son, and thou shalt be favored of the Lord, because thou hast ^anot ^bmurmured.

7 And it came to pass that I, Nephi, said unto my father: I ^awill go and do the things which the Lord hath commanded, for I know that the Lord giveth no ^bcommandments unto the children of men, save he shall ^cprepare a way for them that they may accomplish the thing which he commandeth them.

8 And it came to pass that when my father had heard these words he was exceedingly glad, for he knew that I had been blessed of the Lord.

9 And I, Nephi, and my brethren took our journey in the wilderness, with our tents, to go up to the land of Jerusalem.

10 And it came to pass that when we had gone up to the land of Jerusalem, I and my brethren did consult one with another.

11 And we ^acast lots—who of us should go in unto the house of Laban. And it came to pass that the lot fell upon Laman; and Laman went in unto the house of Laban, and he talked with him as he sat in his house.

12 And he desired of Laban the records which were engraven upon the plates of brass, which contained the ^agenealogy of my father.

13 And behold, it came to pass that Laban was angry, and thrust him out from his presence; and he would not that he should have the records. Wherefore, he said unto him: Behold thou art a robber, and I will slay thee.

14 But Laman fled out of his presence, and told the things which Laban had done, unto us. And we began to be exceedingly sorrowful, and my brethren were about to return unto my father in the wilderness.

15 But behold I said unto them that: ^aAs the Lord liveth, and as we live, we will not go down unto our father in the wilderness until we have ^baccomplished the thing which the Lord hath commanded us.

16 Wherefore, let us be faithful in keeping the commandments of the Lord; therefore let us go down to the land of our father's ^ainheritance, for behold he left gold and silver, and all manner of riches. And all this he hath done because of the ^bcommandments of the Lord.

17 For he knew that Jerusalem must be ^adestroyed, because of the wickedness of the people.

18 For behold, they have ^arejected the words of the prophets. Wherefore, if my father should dwell in the land after he hath been ^bcommanded to flee out of the land, behold, he would also perish. Wherefore, it must needs be that he flee out of the land.

19 And behold, it is wisdom in God that we should obtain these ^arecords, that we may preserve unto our children the language of our fathers;

20 And also that we may ^apreserve unto them the words which have been spoken by the mouth of all the holy ^bprophets, which have been delivered unto them by the Spirit and power of God, since the world began, even down unto this present time.

6a TG Sustaining Church Leaders.
 b TG Murmuring.
7a 1 Sam. 17:32;
   1 Kgs. 17:15 (11–15).
   TG Faith; Loyalty; Obedience.
 b TG Commandments of God.
 c Gen. 18:14; Philip. 4:13;
   1 Ne. 17:3, 50;
   D&C 5:34.

11a Neh. 10:34; Acts 1:26.
12a 1 Ne. 3:3; 5:14;
    Jarom 1:1.
15a TG Oath; Promise.
 b TG Commitment; Dedication.
16a 1 Ne. 2:4.
 b 1 Ne. 2:2; 4:34.
17a 2 Chr. 36:20 (16–20);
    Jer. 39:9 (1–9);
    1 Ne. 1:13.

18a Jer. 26:23 (21–24).
    TG Prophets, Rejection of.
 b 1 Ne. 5:21; 7:2; 16:8.
19a Omni 1:17;
    Mosiah 1:3 (2–6).
    TG Record Keeping.
20a TG Scriptures, Preservation of.
 b Zech. 7:12;
    Matt. 11:13;
    Mosiah 15:13.

21 And it came to pass that after this manner of language did I ᵃpersuade my brethren, that they might be faithful in keeping the commandments of God.

22 And it came to pass that we went down to the land of our inheritance, and we did gather together our ᵃgold, and our silver, and our precious things.

23 And after we had gathered these things together, we went up again unto the house of Laban.

24 And it came to pass that we went in unto Laban, and desired him that he would give unto us the records which were engraven upon the ᵃplates of brass, for which we would give unto him our gold, and our silver, and all our precious things.

25 And it came to pass that when Laban saw our property, and that it was exceedingly great, he did ᵃlust after it, insomuch that he thrust us out, and sent his servants to slay us, that he might obtain our property.

26 And ᵃit came to pass that we did flee before the servants of Laban, and we were obliged to leave behind our property, and it fell into the hands of Laban.

27 And it came to pass that we fled into the wilderness, and the servants of Laban did not overtake us, and we ᵃhid ourselves in the cavity of a rock.

28 And it came to pass that Laman was angry with me, and also with my father; and also was Lemuel, for he hearkened unto the words of Laman. Wherefore Laman and Lemuel did speak many ᵃhard words unto us, their younger brothers, and they did smite us even with a rod.

29 And it came to pass as they smote us with a rod, behold, an ᵃangel of the Lord came and stood before them, and he spake unto them, saying: Why do ye smite your younger brother with a rod? Know ye not that the Lord hath chosen him to be a ᵇruler over you, and this because of your iniquities? Behold ye shall go up to Jerusalem again, and the Lord will ᶜdeliver Laban into your hands.

30 And after the ᵃangel had spoken unto us, he departed.

31 And after the angel had departed, Laman and Lemuel again began to ᵃmurmur, saying: How is it possible that the Lord will deliver Laban into our hands? Behold, he is a mighty man, and he can command fifty, yea, even he can slay fifty; then why not us?

CHAPTER 4

Nephi slays Laban at the Lord's command and then secures the plates of brass by stratagem—Zoram chooses to join Lehi's family in the wilderness. About 600–592 B.C.

AND it came to pass that I spake unto my brethren, saying: Let us go up again unto Jerusalem, and let us be ᵃfaithful in keeping the commandments of the Lord; for behold he is mightier than all the earth, then why not ᵇmightier than Laban and his fifty, yea, or even than his tens of thousands?

2 Therefore let us go up; let us be ᵃstrong like unto Moses; for he truly spake unto the waters of the ᵇRed Sea and they divided hither and thither, and our fathers came through, out of captivity, on dry ground, and the armies of Pharaoh

[handwritten margin note: We should NOT complain after we recieve personal revelation]

21 a TG Family, Love within; Persuade.
22 a 1 Ne. 2:4.
24 a 1 Ne. 3:3; 4:24 (24, 38).
25 a TG Covet.
26 a 1 Ne. 4:11.
27 a Josh. 10:16 (16–17); 1 Sam. 13:6; Jer. 36:26; Ether 13:13 (13, 22).
28 a 1 Ne. 17:18.
29 a 1 Ne. 4:3; 7:10. TG Angels.
  b Gen. 41:43 (41–43); 1 Ne. 2:22.
  c 2 Kgs. 3:18; 3 Ne. 3:21.
30 a 1 Ne. 4:3; 16:38.
31 a TG Murmuring.
4 1 a TG Courage; Dependability; Faithful.
  b 1 Ne. 7:11. TG God, Power of.
2 a Deut. 11:8; Prov. 24:10 (10–12).
  b Ex. 14:21 (18–30); Josh. 2:10; 1 Ne. 17:26; Mosiah 7:19.

did follow and were drowned in the waters of the Red Sea.

3 Now behold ye know that this is true; and ye also know that an ªangel hath spoken unto you; wherefore can ye ᵇdoubt? Let us go up; the Lord is able to ᶜdeliver us, even as our fathers, and to destroy Laban, even as the Egyptians.

4 Now when I had spoken these words, they were yet wroth, and did still continue to murmur; nevertheless they did follow me up until we came without the walls of Jerusalem.

5 And it was by night; and I caused that they should hide themselves without the walls. And after they had hid themselves, I, Nephi, crept into the city and went forth towards the house of Laban.

6 And I was ªled by the Spirit, not ᵇknowing beforehand the things which I should do.

7 Nevertheless I went forth, and as I came near unto the house of Laban I beheld a man, and he had fallen to the earth before me, for he was ªdrunken with wine.

8 And when I came to him I found that it was Laban.

9 And I beheld his ªsword, and I drew it forth from the sheath thereof; and the hilt thereof was of pure gold, and the workmanship thereof was exceedingly fine, and I saw that the blade thereof was of the most precious steel.

10 And it came to pass that I was ªconstrained by the Spirit that I should kill Laban; but I said in my heart: Never at any time have I shed the blood of man. And I shrunk and would that I might not slay him.

11 And the Spirit said unto me again: Behold the ªLord hath ᵇdelivered him into thy hands. Yea, and I also knew that he had sought to take away mine own life; yea, and he would not hearken unto the commandments of the Lord; and he also had ᶜtaken away our property.

12 And it came to pass that the Spirit said unto me again: Slay him, for the Lord hath delivered him into thy hands;

13 Behold the Lord ªslayeth the ᵇwicked to bring forth his righteous purposes. It is ᶜbetter that one man should perish than that a nation should dwindle and perish in ᵈunbelief.

14 And now, when I, Nephi, had heard these words, I remembered the words of the Lord which he spake unto me in the wilderness, saying that: ªInasmuch as thy seed shall keep my ᵇcommandments, they shall ᶜprosper in the ᵈland of promise.

15 Yea, and I also thought that they could not keep the commandments of the Lord according to the ªlaw of Moses, save they should have the law.

16 And I also knew that the ªlaw was engraven upon the plates of brass.

17 And again, I knew that the Lord had delivered Laban into my hands for this cause—that I might obtain the records according to his commandments.

18 Therefore I did obey the voice of the Spirit, and took Laban by the hair of the head, and I smote off his head with his own ªsword.

19 And after I had smitten off his

3a 1 Ne. 3:30 (29–31); 7:10.
  b TG Doubt.
  c TG Deliver.
6a TG Guidance, Divine;
    Holy Ghost, Gifts of;
    Inspiration.
  b Heb. 11:8.
7a TG Drunkenness.
9a 2 Ne. 5:14;
    D&C 17:1.
10a 1 Sam. 15:3 (3–33).
11a Deut. 3:3;
    1 Sam. 17:46 (41–49).

b 1 Ne. 7:11.
c 1 Ne. 3:26.
13a Num. 25:17;
    Deut. 12:29;
    Ps. 139:19;
    1 Ne. 17:37 (33–38);
    D&C 98:32 (31–32).
  b TG Justice;
    Punish;
    Wickedness.
  c Alma 30:47.
    TG Life, Sanctity of.
  d TG Unbelief.

14a Omni 1:6;
    Mosiah 2:22;
    Ether 2:7 (7–12).
  b TG Commandments
    of God.
  c 1 Ne. 2:20.
  d 1 Ne. 17:13 (13–14);
    Jacob 2:12.
15a Mosiah 1:5 (1–6).
16a Josh. 1:8.
    TG Law of Moses.
18a 1 Sam. 17:51.

head with his own sword, I took the garments of Laban and put them upon mine own body; yea, even every whit; and I did gird on his armor about my loins.

20 And after I had done this, I went forth unto the treasury of Laban. And as I went forth towards the treasury of Laban, behold, I saw the ^aservant of Laban who had the keys of the treasury. And I commanded him in the voice of Laban, that he should go with me into the treasury.

21 And he supposed me to be his master, Laban, for he beheld the garments and also the sword girded about my loins.

22 And he spake unto me concerning the ^aelders of the Jews, he knowing that his master, Laban, had been out by night among them.

23 And I spake unto him as if it had been Laban.

24 And I also spake unto him that I should carry the engravings, which were upon the ^aplates of brass, to my elder brethren, who were without the walls.

25 And I also bade him that he should follow me.

26 And he, supposing that I spake of the ^abrethren of the ^bchurch, and that I was truly that Laban whom I had slain, wherefore he did follow me.

27 And he spake unto me many times concerning the elders of the Jews, as I went forth unto my brethren, who were without the walls.

28 And it came to pass that when Laman saw me he was exceedingly frightened, and also Lemuel and Sam. And they fled from before my presence; for they supposed it was Laban, and that he had slain me and had sought to take away their lives also.

29 And it came to pass that I called

after them, and they did hear me; wherefore they did cease to flee from my presence.

30 And it came to pass that when the servant of Laban beheld my brethren he began to tremble, and was about to flee from before me and return to the city of Jerusalem.

31 And now I, Nephi, being a man large in stature, and also having received much ^astrength of the Lord, therefore I did seize upon the servant of Laban, and held him, that he should not flee.

32 And it came to pass that I spake with him, that if he would hearken unto my words, as the Lord liveth, and as I live, even so that if he would hearken unto our words, we would spare his life.

33 And I spake unto him, even with an ^aoath, that he need not fear; that he should be a ^bfree man like unto us if he would go down in the wilderness with us.

34 And I also spake unto him, saying: Surely the Lord hath ^acommanded us to do this thing; and shall we not be diligent in keeping the commandments of the Lord? Therefore, if thou wilt go down into the wilderness to my father thou shalt have place with us.

35 And it came to pass that ^aZoram did take courage at the words which I spake. Now Zoram was the name of the servant; and he promised that he would go down into the wilderness unto our father. Yea, and he also made an oath unto us that he would tarry with us from that time forth.

36 Now we were desirous that he should tarry with us for this cause, that the Jews might not know concerning our flight into the wilderness, lest they should pursue us and destroy us.

37 And it came to pass that when

20*a* 2 Ne. 1:30.
22*a* 2 Sam. 17:15;
    Ezek. 8:1;
    Acts 25:15.
24*a* 1 Ne. 3:24 (12, 19–24);
    5:10 (10–22).
26*a* Ex. 2:11;

Num. 18:6;
   2 Sam. 19:41.
  b TG Church Organization.
31*a* TG Strength;
   Strengthen.
33*a* 2 Sam. 21:7.
  TG Oath.

  b TG Free.
34*a* 1 Ne. 2:2; 3:16.
35*a* 1 Ne. 16:7;
   2 Ne. 5:6 (5–6);
   Jacob 1:13;
   Alma 54:23;
   4 Ne. 1:36 (36–37).

Zoram had made an ᵃoath unto us, our ᵇfears did cease concerning him.

38 And it came to pass that we took the plates of brass and the servant of Laban, and departed into the wilderness, and journeyed unto the ᵃtent of our father.

CHAPTER 5

Sariah complains against Lehi—Both rejoice over the return of their sons—They offer sacrifices—The plates of brass contain writings of Moses and the prophets—The plates identify Lehi as a descendant of Joseph—Lehi prophesies concerning his seed and the preservation of the plates. About 600–592 B.C.

AND it came to pass that after we had come down into the wilderness unto our father, behold, he was filled with joy, and also my mother, Sariah, was exceedingly glad, for she truly had mourned because of us.

2 For she had supposed that we had perished in the wilderness; and she also had ᵃcomplained against my father, telling him that he was a ᵇvisionary man; saying: Behold thou hast led us forth from the land of our inheritance, and my sons are no more, and we perish in the wilderness.

3 And after this manner of language had my mother complained against my father.

4 And it had come to pass that my father spake unto her, saying: I know that I am a ᵃvisionary man; for if I had not seen the things of God in a ᵇvision I should not have known the goodness of God, but had tarried at Jerusalem, and had perished with my brethren.

5 But behold, I have ᵃobtained a ᵇland of promise, in the which things I do rejoice; yea, and I ᶜknow that the Lord will deliver my sons out of the hands of Laban, and bring them down again unto us in the wilderness.

6 And after this manner of language did my father, Lehi, ᵃcomfort my mother, Sariah, concerning us, while we journeyed in the wilderness up to the land of Jerusalem, to obtain the record of the Jews.

7 And when we had returned to the tent of my father, behold their joy was full, and my mother was comforted.

8 And she spake, saying: Now I know of a surety that the Lord hath ᵃcommanded my husband to ᵇflee into the wilderness; yea, and I also know of a surety that the Lord hath protected my sons, and delivered them out of the hands of Laban, and given them power whereby they could ᶜaccomplish the thing which the Lord hath commanded them. And after this manner of language did she speak.

9 And it came to pass that they did rejoice exceedingly, and did offer ᵃsacrifice and burnt offerings unto the Lord; and they gave ᵇthanks unto the God of Israel.

10 And after they had given thanks unto the God of Israel, my father, Lehi, took the records which were engraven upon the ᵃplates of brass, and he did search them from the beginning.

11 And he beheld that they did contain the five ᵃbooks of Moses, which gave an account of the creation of the world, and also of Adam and Eve, who were our first parents;

37a Ex. 22:11 (10–11);
   Josh. 9:19 (1–21).
   TG Oath;
   Vow.
  b TG Trustworthiness.
38a 1 Ne. 2:15.
5 2a TG Murmuring.
  b Gen. 37:19 (8, 19).
4a 1 Ne. 2:11; 17:20.
  b 1 Ne. 1:8 (8–13);
   3:18 (17–18).
   TG Vision.

5a Eph. 1:11;
   Heb. 6:15 (13–15).
  b 1 Ne. 2:20;
   18:8 (8, 22–23).
   TG Promised Lands.
  c TG Faith;
   Trust in God.
6a TG Comfort;
   Family, Love within.
8a 1 Ne. 2:2.
  b Gen. 19:14.
  c 1 Ne. 3:7.

9a 1 Ne. 7:22;
   Mosiah 2:3;
   3 Ne. 9:19.
   TG Law of Moses.
  b TG Thanksgiving.
10a 1 Ne. 4:24 (24, 38); 13:23.
11a Ex. 17:14;
   Deut. 31:9;
   Luke 16:29; 24:27;
   1 Ne. 19:23;
   Moses 1:41 (40–41).

12 And also a ªrecord of the Jews from the beginning, even down to the commencement of the reign of Zedekiah, king of Judah;

13 And also the prophecies of the holy prophets, from the beginning, even down to the commencement of the reign of ªZedekiah; and also many prophecies which have been spoken by the mouth of ᵇJeremiah.

14 And it came to pass that my father, Lehi, also found upon the ªplates of brass a ᵇgenealogy of his ᶜfathers; wherefore he knew that he was a descendant of ᵈJoseph; yea, even that Joseph who was the son of ᵉJacob, who was ᶠsold into Egypt, and who was ᵍpreserved by the hand of the Lord, that he might preserve his father, Jacob, and all his household from perishing with famine.

15 And they were also ªled out of captivity and out of the land of Egypt, by that same God who had preserved them.

16 And thus my father, Lehi, did discover the genealogy of his fathers. And Laban also was a descendant of ªJoseph, wherefore he and his fathers had kept the ᵇrecords.

17 And now when my father saw all these things, he was filled with the Spirit, and began to prophesy concerning his seed—

18 That these ªplates of brass should go forth unto all ᵇnations, kindreds, tongues, and people who were of his seed.

19 Wherefore, he said that these plates of brass should ªnever perish; neither should they be dimmed any more by time. And he prophesied many things concerning his seed.

20 And it came to pass that thus far I and my father had kept the commandments wherewith the Lord had commanded us.

21 And we had obtained the records which the Lord had commanded us, and searched them and found that they were desirable; yea, even of great ªworth unto us, insomuch that we could ᵇpreserve the commandments of the Lord unto our children.

22 Wherefore, it was wisdom in the Lord that we should carry them with us, as we journeyed in the wilderness towards the land of promise.

CHAPTER 6

Nephi writes of the things of God—Nephi's purpose is to persuade men to come unto the God of Abraham and be saved. About 600–592 B.C.

AND now I, Nephi, do not give the genealogy of my fathers in ªthis part of my record; neither at any time shall I give it after upon these ᵇplates which I am ᶜwriting; for it is given in the record which has been kept by my ᵈfather; wherefore, I do not write it in this work.

2 For it sufficeth me to say that we are descendants of ªJoseph.

3 And it mattereth not to me that I am particular to give a full account of all the things of my father, for they cannot be written upon ªthese

---

12ª 1 Chr. 9:1.
   TG Scriptures,
      Writing of.
13ª 2 Kgs. 24:18; Jer. 37:1.
   b Ezra 1:1;
      Jer. 36:32 (17–32);
      1 Ne. 7:14; Hel. 8:20.
14ª Mosiah 2:34.
   b 1 Ne. 3:3, 12; Jarom 1:1.
      TG Book of
         Remembrance.
   c TG Israel, Origins of.
   d 2 Ne. 3:4; Alma 10:3.
      TG Israel, Joseph,
         People of.
   e Gen. 25:26;

2 Ne. 20:21;
   Alma 7:25;
   D&C 27:10.
   f Gen. 37:36 (29–36).
   g TG Protection, Divine.
15ª Gen. 15:14 (13–14);
   Ex. 15:13;
   Amos 3:1 (1–2);
   1 Ne. 17:31 (23–31); 19:10;
   D&C 103:16 (16–18);
   136:22.
16ª 2 Chr. 15:9;
   1 Ne. 6:2.
   TG Israel, Joseph,
      People of.
   b TG Record Keeping.

18ª Alma 22:12.
   b JS—H 1:33.
19ª Alma 37:4.
21ª TG Scriptures, Value of.
   b TG Scriptures,
      Preservation of.
6 1ª 2 Ne. 4:15.
   b 1 Ne. 9:2.
   c TG Scriptures,
      Writing of.
   d 1 Ne. 1:17 (16–17);
      19:1 (1–6).
   2ª 1 Ne. 5:16 (14–16).
   3ª Jacob 7:27;
      Jarom 1:2 (2, 14);
      Omni 1:1, 30.

plates, for I desire the room that I may write of the things of God.

4 For the fulness of mine intent is that I may ^apersuade men to ^bcome unto the God of Abraham, and the God of Isaac, and the God of Jacob, and be saved.

5 Wherefore, the things which are ^apleasing unto the world I do not write, but the things which are pleasing unto God and unto those who are not of the world.

6 Wherefore, I shall give commandment unto my seed, that they shall not occupy these plates with things which are not of worth unto the children of men.

CHAPTER 7

Lehi's sons return to Jerusalem and invite Ishmael and his household to join them in their journey—Laman and others rebel—Nephi exhorts his brethren to have faith in the Lord—They bind him with cords and plan his destruction—He is freed by the power of faith—His brethren ask forgiveness—Lehi and his company offer sacrifice and burnt offerings. About 600–592 B.C.

AND now I would that ye might know, that after my father, Lehi, had made an end of ^aprophesying concerning his seed, it came to pass that the Lord spake unto him again, saying that it was not meet for him, Lehi, that he should take his family into the wilderness alone; but that his sons should take ^bdaughters to ^cwife, that they might raise up ^dseed unto the Lord in the land of promise.

2 And it came to pass that the Lord ^acommanded him that I, Nephi, and my brethren, should again return unto the land of Jerusalem, and bring down Ishmael and his family into the wilderness.

3 And it came to pass that I, Nephi, did ^aagain, with my brethren, go forth into the wilderness to go up to Jerusalem.

4 And it came to pass that we went up unto the house of Ishmael, and we did gain favor in the sight of Ishmael, insomuch that we did speak unto him the words of the Lord.

5 And it came to pass that the ^aLord did soften the heart of Ishmael, and also his household, insomuch that they took their journey with us down into the wilderness to the tent of our father.

6 And it came to pass that as we journeyed in the wilderness, behold Laman and Lemuel, and two of the ^adaughters of Ishmael, and the two ^bsons of Ishmael and their families, did ^crebel against us; yea, against me, Nephi, and Sam, and their father, Ishmael, and his wife, and his three other daughters.

7 And it came to pass in the which rebellion, they were desirous to return unto the land of Jerusalem.

8 And now I, Nephi, being ^agrieved for the hardness of their hearts, therefore I spake unto them, saying, yea, even unto Laman and unto Lemuel: Behold ye are mine elder brethren, and how is it that ye are so hard in your hearts, and so blind in your minds, that ye have need that I, your ^byounger brother, should speak unto you, yea, and set an ^cexample for you?

9 How is it that ye have not hearkened unto the word of the Lord?

10 How is it that ye have ^aforgotten that ye have seen an angel of the Lord?

4a Luke 1:4 (3–4);
　　John 20:31 (30–31).
　b 2 Ne. 9:41 (41, 45, 51).
5a Gal. 1:10;
　　1 Thes. 2:4;
　　Heb. 13:21;
　　W of M 1:4.
7 1a 1 Ne. 1:16.
　b 1 Ne. 16:7.

c TG Marriage, Marry.
d Ps. 127:3.
2a 1 Ne. 16:8.
3a 1 Ne. 3:2.
5a TG Guidance, Divine.
6a 1 Ne. 16:7 (7, 27).
　b 2 Ne. 4:10.
　c 1 Ne. 17:18 (17–55).
8a Mosiah 28:3;

Alma 31:2;
3 Ne. 17:14;
Moses 7:41.
b 1 Chr. 29:1;
　D&C 1:19 (19, 23).
c TG Example.
10a Deut. 4:9 (9–13);
　　1 Ne. 4:3.

11 Yea, and how is it that ye have forgotten what great things the Lord hath done for us, in ^adelivering us out of the hands of Laban, and also that we should obtain the record?

12 Yea, and how is it that ye have forgotten that the Lord is able to do all ^athings according to his will, for the children of men, if it so be that they exercise ^bfaith in him? Wherefore, let us be faithful to him.

13 And if it so be that we are faithful to him, we shall obtain the ^aland of promise; and ye shall know at some future period that the word of the Lord shall be fulfilled concerning the ^bdestruction of ^cJerusalem; for all things which the Lord hath spoken concerning the destruction of Jerusalem must be fulfilled.

14 For behold, the ^aSpirit of the Lord ^bceaseth soon to strive with them; for behold, they have ^crejected the prophets, and ^dJeremiah have they sought into prison. And they have sought to take away the ^elife of my father, insomuch that they have driven him out of the land.

15 Now behold, I say unto you that if ye will return unto Jerusalem ye shall also perish with them. And now, if ye have choice, go up to the land, and remember the words which I speak unto you, that if ye go ye will also perish; for thus the Spirit of the Lord constraineth me that I should speak.

16 And it came to pass that when I, Nephi, had spoken these words unto my brethren, they were angry with me. And it came to pass that they did lay their hands upon me, for behold, they were exceedingly wroth, and they did ^abind me with cords, for they sought to take away my life, that they might leave me in the wilderness to be devoured by wild beasts.

17 But it came to pass that I prayed unto the Lord, saying: O Lord, according to my faith which is in thee, wilt thou deliver me from the hands of my brethren; yea, even give me ^astrength that I may ^bburst these bands with which I am bound.

18 And it came to pass that when I had said these words, behold, the bands were loosed from off my hands and feet, and I stood before my brethren, and I spake unto them again.

19 And it came to pass that they were angry with me again, and sought to lay hands upon me; but behold, one of the ^adaughters of Ishmael, yea, and also her mother, and one of the sons of Ishmael, did plead with my brethren, insomuch that they did soften their hearts; and they did cease striving to take away my life.

20 And it came to pass that they were sorrowful, because of their wickedness, insomuch that they did bow down before me, and did plead with me that I would ^aforgive them of the thing that they had done against me.

21 And it came to pass that I did frankly ^aforgive them all that they had done, and I did exhort them that they would pray unto the Lord their God for ^bforgiveness. And it came to pass that they did so. And after they had done praying unto the Lord we did again travel on our journey towards the tent of our father.

22 And it came to pass that we did

11a 1 Ne. 4:1 (1–38).
12a Ps. 18:32 (32–40);
     1 Ne. 17:50;
     Alma 26:12.
  b 1 Ne. 2:19 (18–21); 15:11.
13a 1 Ne. 2:20.
     TG Promised Lands.
  b 2 Kgs. 25:4 (1–21).
  c 2 Ne. 6:8; 25:10;
     Omni 1:15;

       Hel. 8:21 (20–21).
14a TG God, Spirit of.
  b Ezek. 5:6;
     1 Ne. 1:19 (18–20); 2:13.
  c TG Prophets,
     Rejection of.
  d Jer. 37:15 (15–21).
  e 1 Ne. 2:1.
16a 1 Ne. 18:11 (11–15).
17a Judg. 14:6.

  b Jacob 4:6;
     Alma 14:28 (26–28);
     3 Ne. 28:20 (19–22).
19a 1 Ne. 16:7;
     18:19 (19–20).
20a TG Repent.
21a TG Family, Love within.
  b TG Forgive.

come down unto the tent of our father. And after I and my brethren and all the house of Ishmael had come down unto the tent of my father, they did give *a*thanks unto the Lord their God; and they did offer *b*sacrifice and burnt offerings unto him.

CHAPTER 8

Lehi sees a vision of the tree of life— He partakes of its fruit and desires his family to do likewise—He sees a rod of iron, a strait and narrow path, and the mists of darkness that enshroud men— Sariah, Nephi, and Sam partake of the fruit, but Laman and Lemuel refuse. About 600–592 B.C.

AND it came to pass that we had gathered together all manner of *a*seeds of every kind, both of grain of every kind, and also of the seeds of fruit of every kind.

2 And it came to pass that while my father tarried in the wilderness he spake unto us, saying: Behold, I have *a*dreamed a dream; or, in other words, I have *b*seen a *c*vision.

3 And behold, because of the thing which I have seen, I have reason to rejoice in the Lord because of *a*Nephi and also of Sam; for I have reason to suppose that they, and also many of their seed, will be saved.

4 But behold, *a*Laman and Lemuel, I fear exceedingly because of you; for behold, methought I saw in my dream, a dark and dreary wilderness.

5 And it came to pass that I saw a *a*man, and he was dressed in a white *b*robe; and he came and stood before me.

6 And it came to pass that he spake unto me, and bade me follow him.

7 And it came to pass that as I followed him I beheld myself that I was in a dark and dreary waste.

8 And after I had traveled for the space of many hours in darkness, I began to pray unto the Lord that he would have *a*mercy on me, according to the multitude of his tender mercies.

9 And it came to pass after I had prayed unto the Lord I beheld a large and spacious *a*field.

10 And it came to pass that I beheld a *a*tree, whose *b*fruit was desirable to make one *c*happy.

11 And it came to pass that I did go forth and partake of the *a*fruit thereof; and I beheld that it was most sweet, above all that I ever before tasted. Yea, and I beheld that the fruit thereof was white, to exceed all the *b*whiteness that I had ever seen.

12 And as I partook of the fruit thereof it filled my soul with exceedingly great *a*joy; wherefore, I began to be *b*desirous that my family should partake of it also; for I knew that it was *c*desirable above all other fruit.

13 And as I cast my eyes round about, that perhaps I might discover my family also, I beheld a *a*river of water; and it ran along, and it was near the tree of which I was partaking the fruit.

14 And I looked to behold from whence it came; and I saw the head thereof a little way off; and at the head thereof I beheld your mother Sariah, and Sam, and *a*Nephi; and they stood as if they knew not whither they should go.

15 And it came to pass that I

22*a* TG Thanksgiving.
   b 1 Ne. 5:9.
8 1*a* 1 Ne. 16:11.
  2*a* 1 Ne. 1:16; 10:2.
    TG Dream;
    Revelation;
    Vision.
   b 1 Ne. 14:29.
   c 1 Ne. 10:17.
  3*a* 1 Ne. 8:14 (14–18).
  4*a* 1 Ne. 8:35.
  5*a* Dan. 10:5 (2–12).

   b JS—H 1:31 (30–32).
  8*a* TG God, Mercy of.
  9*a* Matt. 13:38.
 10*a* Gen. 2:9;
    Rev. 2:7 (1–7);
    22:2 (1–16);
    1 Ne. 11:4, 8 (8–25).
   b 1 Ne. 8:24 (15, 20, 24);
    Alma 32:42 (41–43).
   c TG Happiness.
 11*a* 1 Ne. 15:36;
    Alma 5:34.

   b 1 Ne. 11:8.
 12*a* TG Joy.
   b Enos 1:9;
    Alma 36:24.
    TG Family, Love within.
   c Gen. 3:6;
    1 Ne. 15:36.
 13*a* 1 Ne. 12:16 (16–18);
    15:26–27 (26–29).
 14*a* 1 Ne. 8:3 (3–4).

beckoned unto them; and I also did say unto them with a loud voice that they should come unto me, and partake of the fruit, which was desirable above all other fruit.

16 And it came to pass that they did come unto me and partake of the fruit also.

17 And it came to pass that I was desirous that Laman and Lemuel should come and partake of the fruit also; wherefore, I cast mine eyes towards the head of the river, that perhaps I might see them.

18 And it came to pass that I saw them, but they would ᵃnot come unto me and partake of the fruit.

19 And I beheld a ᵃrod of iron, and it extended along the bank of the river, and led to the tree by which I stood.

20 And I also beheld a ᵃstrait and narrow path, which came along by the rod of iron, even to the tree by which I stood; and it also led by the head of the fountain, unto a large and spacious field, as if it had been a ᵇworld.

21 And I saw numberless concourses of people, many of whom were ᵃpressing forward, that they might obtain the ᵇpath which led unto the tree by which I stood.

22 And it came to pass that they did come forth, and commence in the path which led to the tree.

23 And it came to pass that there arose a ᵃmist of darkness; yea, even an exceedingly great mist of darkness, insomuch that they who had commenced in the path did lose their way, that they wandered off and were ᵇlost.

24 And it came to pass that I beheld others pressing forward, and they came forth and caught hold of the end of the rod of iron; and they did press forward through the mist of darkness, ᵃclinging to the rod of iron, even until they did come forth and partake of the ᵇfruit of the tree.

25 And after they had partaken of the fruit of the tree they did cast their eyes about as if they were ᵃashamed.

26 And I also cast my eyes round about, and beheld, on the ᵃother side of the river of water, a great and ᵇspacious building; and it stood as it were in the ᶜair, high above the earth.

27 And it was filled with people, both old and young, both male and female; and their manner of dress was exceedingly fine; and they were in the ᵃattitude of ᵇmocking and pointing their fingers towards those who had come at and were partaking of the fruit.

28 And after they had ᵃtasted of the fruit they were ᵇashamed, because of those that were ᶜscoffing at them; and they ᵈfell away into forbidden paths and were lost.

29 And now I, Nephi, do not speak ᵃall the words of my father.

30 But, to be short in writing, behold, he saw other multitudes pressing forward; and they came and caught hold of the end of the ᵃrod of iron; and they did press their way forward, continually holding

---

18a 2 Ne. 5:20 (20–25).
19a Ps. 2:9;
    Rev. 2:27; 12:5; 19:15;
    JST Rev. 19:15
    (Rev. 19:15 note a);
    1 Ne. 8:30; 11:25;
    15:23 (23–24).
20a Matt. 7:14;
    2 Ne. 31:18 (17–20).
  b Matt. 13:38.
21a D&C 123:12.
  b TG Objectives; Path;
    Way.
23a Matt. 13:19 (18–19);
    2 Pet. 2:17;

1 Ne. 12:17;
    15:24 (23–24).
  b TG Apostasy of
    Individuals.
24a TG Diligence;
    Perseverance.
  b 1 Ne. 8:10.
25a Rom. 1:16;
    2 Tim. 1:8;
    Alma 46:21;
    Morm. 8:38.
26a Luke 16:26.
  b 1 Ne. 11:35 (35–36);
    12:18.
  c Eph. 2:2 (1–3).

27a TG Haughtiness; Pride.
  b Matt. 9:24 (20–26).
    TG Mocking.
28a 2 Pet. 2:20 (19–22).
  b Mark 4:17 (14–20); 8:38;
    Luke 8:13 (11–15);
    John 12:43 (42–43);
    Rom. 3:3.
    TG Courage;
    Fearful.
  c TG Peer Influence.
  d TG Apostasy of
    Individuals.
29a 1 Ne. 1:17 (16–17).
30a 1 Ne. 8:19; 15:24 (23–24).

Personal Revelation helped them have an eternal perspective and desire to continually hold fast.

fast to the rod of iron, until they came forth and fell down and partook of the fruit of the tree.

31 And he also saw other ªmultitudes feeling their way towards that great and spacious building.

32 And it came to pass that many were drowned in the ªdepths of the ᵇfountain; and many were lost from his view, wandering in strange roads.

33 And great was the multitude that did enter into that strange building. And after they did enter into that building they did point the finger of ªscorn at me and those that were partaking of the fruit also; but we heeded them not.

34 These are the words of my father: For as many as ªheeded them, had fallen away.

35 And ªLaman and Lemuel partook not of the fruit, said my father.

36 And it came to pass after my father had spoken all the words of his dream or vision, which were many, he said unto us, because of these things which he saw in a vision, he exceedingly feared for Laman and Lemuel; yea, he feared lest they should be cast off from the presence of the Lord.

37 And he did ªexhort them then with all the feeling of a tender parent, that they would hearken to his words, that perhaps the Lord would be merciful to them, and not cast them off; yea, my father did preach unto them.

38 And after he had preached unto them, and also prophesied unto them of many things, he bade them to keep the commandments of the Lord; and he did cease speaking unto them.

CHAPTER 9

Nephi makes two sets of records—Each is called the plates of Nephi—The larger plates contain a secular history; the smaller ones deal primarily with sacred things. About 600–592 B.C.

AND all these things did my father see, and hear, and speak, as he dwelt in a tent, in the ªvalley of Lemuel, and also a great many more things, which cannot be written upon these plates.

2 And now, as I have spoken concerning these plates, behold they are not the plates upon which I make a full account of the history of my people; for the ªplates upon which I make a full account of my people I have given the name of Nephi; wherefore, they are called the plates of Nephi, after mine own name; and these plates also are called the plates of Nephi.

3 Nevertheless, I have received a commandment of the Lord that I should make these plates, for the special ªpurpose that there should be an account engraven of the ᵇministry of my people.

4 Upon the other plates should be engraven an account of the reign of the kings, and the wars and contentions of my people; wherefore these plates are for the more part of the ministry; and the ªother plates are for the more part of the reign of the kings and the wars and contentions of my people.

31 a Matt. 7:13.
32 a 1 Ne. 15:29 (26–29).
   b 1 Ne. 8:14 (13–14).
33 a Neh. 2:19;
     Alma 26:23.
     TG Persecution;
     Scorn;
     Scorner.
34 a Ex. 23:2;
     Prov. 19:27;
     Mosiah 2:37 (33, 37).
35 a 1 Ne. 8:4 (4, 17–18);

      2 Ne. 5:20 (19–24).
37 a TG Family, Children,
      Responsibilities
      toward.
9 1 a 1 Ne. 2:6 (4–6, 8, 14–15);
      16:6 (6, 12).
2 a IE the full account is on
      larger plates; the special
      account of his ministry
      is on the smaller plates
      of Nephi. See
      Jacob 3:13–14. See also

      1 Ne. 1:17 (16–17); 6:1;
      10:1; 19:2, 4;
      Omni 1:1;
      W of M 1:3 (2–11);
      D&C 10:38 (38–40).
3 a D&C 3:19.
   b 1 Ne. 6:3.
4 a 2 Ne. 4:14; 5:33 (29–33);
     Jacob 1:3 (2–4);
     Jarom 1:14;
     Omni 1:18;
     W of M 1:10.

5 Wherefore, the Lord hath commanded me to make these plates for a ^awise purpose in him, which purpose I know not.

6 But the Lord ^aknoweth all things from the beginning; wherefore, he prepareth a way to accomplish all his works among the children of men; for behold, he hath all ^bpower unto the fulfilling of all his words. And thus it is. Amen.

CHAPTER 10

Lehi predicts that the Jews will be taken captive by the Babylonians—He tells of the coming among the Jews of a Messiah, a Savior, a Redeemer—Lehi tells also of the coming of the one who should baptize the Lamb of God—Lehi tells of the death and resurrection of the Messiah—He compares the scattering and gathering of Israel to an olive tree—Nephi speaks of the Son of God, of the gift of the Holy Ghost, and of the need for righteousness. About 600–592 B.C.

AND now I, Nephi, proceed to give an account upon ^athese plates of my proceedings, and my reign and ministry; wherefore, to proceed with mine account, I must speak somewhat of the things of my father, and also of my brethren.

2 For behold, it came to pass after my father had made an end of speaking the words of his ^adream, and also of exhorting them to all diligence, he spake unto them concerning the Jews—

3 That after they should be destroyed, even that great city ^aJerusalem, and many be ^bcarried away captive into ^cBabylon, according to the own due time of the Lord, they should ^dreturn again, yea, even be brought back out of captivity; and after they should be brought back out of captivity they should possess again the land of their inheritance.

4 Yea, even ^asix hundred years from the time that my father left Jerusalem, a ^bprophet would the Lord God raise up among the ^cJews—even a ^dMessiah, or, in other words, a Savior of the world.

5 And he also spake concerning the prophets, how great a number had ^atestified of these things, concerning this Messiah, of whom he had spoken, or this Redeemer of the world.

6 Wherefore, all mankind were in a ^alost and in a ^bfallen state, and ever would be save they should rely on this Redeemer.

7 And he spake also concerning a ^aprophet who should come before the Messiah, to prepare the way of the Lord—

8 Yea, even he should go forth and cry in the wilderness: ^aPrepare ye the way of the Lord, and make his paths straight; for there standeth one among you whom ye know not; and he is mightier than I, whose shoe's latchet I am not worthy to unloose. And much spake my father concerning this thing.

9 And my father said he should

5a 1 Ne. 19:3;
    W of M 1:7;
    Alma 37:14 (2, 12, 14).
6a Isa. 48:3 (3–7);
    Moses 1:6, 35.
    TG God, Foreknowledge
    of; God, Intelligence of;
    God, Omniscience of.
  b Matt. 28:18.
10 1a 1 Ne. 9:2 (1–5);
    19:3 (1–6).
2a 1 Ne. 8:2 (2–36).
3a Esth. 2:6; 2 Ne. 6:8;
    Hel. 8:20 (20–21).
  b Ezek. 36:12 (8–15);
    2 Ne. 25:10.
    TG Israel, Bondage of,
    in Other Lands;

Israel, Scattering of.
  c Ezek. 24:2;
    1 Ne. 1:13;
    Omni 1:15.
    TG Babylon.
  d Neh. 12:1;
    Jer. 29:10 (9–10);
    2 Ne. 6:9 (8–9);
    Abr. 2:6.
4a 1 Ne. 19:8 (8–14);
    2 Ne. 25:19;
    Alma 13:25;
    3 Ne. 1:1.
  b 1 Ne. 22:21 (20–21).
  c TG Israel, Judah,
    People of.
  d Jacob 1:6.
    TG Jesus Christ,

Birth of;
    Jesus Christ, Messiah.
5a Jacob 7:11;
    Mosiah 13:33;
    Hel. 8:24 (19–24);
    3 Ne. 20:24 (23–24).
    TG Jesus Christ,
    Prophecies about.
6a Rom. 3:23;
    2 Ne. 2:5 (5–8).
  b TG Death, Spiritual,
    First.
7a 1 Ne. 11:27;
    2 Ne. 31:4 (4–18).
    TG Foreordination.
8a Isa. 40:3;
    Matt. 3:3 (1–3);
    D&C 84:26.

baptize in ^aBethabara, beyond Jordan; and he also said he should ^bbaptize with water; even that he should baptize the Messiah with water.

10 And after he had baptized the Messiah with water, he should behold and bear record that he had baptized the ^aLamb of God, who should take away the sins of the world.

11 And it came to pass after my father had spoken these words he spake unto my brethren concerning the gospel which should be preached among the Jews, and also concerning the ^adwindling of the Jews in ^bunbelief. And after they had ^cslain the Messiah, who should come, and after he had been slain he should ^drise from the dead, and should make himself ^emanifest, by the Holy Ghost, unto the Gentiles.

12 Yea, even my father spake much concerning the Gentiles, and also concerning the house of Israel, that they should be compared like unto an ^aolive tree, whose ^bbranches should be broken off and should be ^cscattered upon all the face of the earth.

13 Wherefore, he said it must needs be that we should be led with one accord into the ^aland of promise, unto the fulfilling of the word of the Lord, that we should be scattered upon all the face of the earth.

14 And after the house of ^aIsrael should be scattered they should be ^bgathered together again; or, in fine, after the ^cGentiles had received the fulness of the ^dGospel, the natural branches of the ^eolive tree, or the ^fremnants of the house of ^gIsrael, should be grafted in, or ^hcome to the knowledge of the true Messiah, their Lord and their Redeemer.

15 And after this manner of language did my father prophesy and speak unto my brethren, and also many more things which I do not write in this book; for I have written as many of them as were expedient for me in mine ^aother book.

16 And all these things, of which I have spoken, were done as my father dwelt in a ^atent, in the valley of Lemuel.

17 And it came to pass after I, Nephi, having heard all the ^awords of my father, concerning the things which he saw in a ^bvision, and also the things which he spake by the power of the Holy Ghost, which power he received by faith on the Son of God—and the Son of God was the ^cMessiah who should come—I, Nephi, was ^ddesirous also that I might see, and hear, and know of these things, by the power of the ^eHoly Ghost, which is the ^fgift of God unto ^gall those who diligently seek him, as well in times of ^hold

---

9a John 1:28.
  b TG Jesus Christ, Baptism of.
10a TG Jesus Christ, Lamb of God.
11a Rom. 11:1 (1–36); Jacob 4:15 (14–18).
  b Morm. 5:14 (14–20). TG Unbelief.
  c TG Jesus Christ, Crucifixion of; Jesus Christ, Prophecies about.
  d TG Jesus Christ, Resurrection.
  e 3 Ne. 15:23 (21–24). TG Holy Ghost, Mission of.
12a Gen. 49:22 (22–26);

1 Ne. 15:12; 2 Ne. 3:5 (4–5); Jacob 5:3 (3–77); 6:1 (1–7).
  TG Vineyard of the Lord.
  b TG Israel, Bondage of, in Other Lands.
  c Deut. 32:26; 1 Ne. 22:3 (3–8). TG Israel, Scattering of.
13a 1 Ne. 2:20. TG Promised Lands.
14a TG Israel, Ten Lost Tribes of.
  b TG Israel, Gathering of.
  c 1 Ne. 13:42; D&C 14:10.
  d TG Gospel.
  e 1 Ne. 15:7.

f TG Israel, Remnant of.
  g TG Israel, Twelve Tribes of.
  h 1 Ne. 19:15 (14–17).
15a 1 Ne. 1:17 (16–18).
16a 1 Ne. 2:15 (15–16).
17a Enos 1:3; Alma 36:17 (17–18).
  b 1 Ne. 8:2.
  c TG Jesus Christ, Messiah.
  d 2 Ne. 4:24.
  e 2 Pet. 1:21.
  f TG God, Gifts of; Holy Ghost, Gift of.
  g Moro. 7:36; 10:7 (4–5, 7, 19).
  h D&C 20:26.

as in the time that he should manifest himself unto the children of men.

18 For he is the *a*same yesterday, today, and forever; and the way is prepared for all men from the foundation of the world, if it so be that they repent and come unto him.

19 For he that diligently *a*seeketh shall find; and the *b*mysteries of God shall be unfolded unto them, by the power of the *c*Holy Ghost, as well in these times as in times of old, and as well in times of old as in times to come; wherefore, the *d*course of the Lord is one eternal round.

20 Therefore remember, O man, for all thy doings thou shalt be brought into *a*judgment.

21 Wherefore, if ye have sought to do *a*wickedly in the days of your *b*probation, then ye are found *c*unclean before the judgment-seat of God; and no unclean thing can dwell with God; wherefore, ye must be cast off forever.

22 And the Holy Ghost giveth *a*authority that I should speak these things, and deny them not.

CHAPTER 11

Nephi sees the Spirit of the Lord and is shown in vision the tree of life—He sees the mother of the Son of God and learns of the condescension of God—He sees the baptism, ministry, and crucifixion of the Lamb of God—He sees also the call and ministry of the Twelve Apostles of the Lamb. About 600–592 B.C.

FOR it came to pass after I had desired to know the things that my father had seen, and believing that the Lord was able to make them known unto me, as I sat *a*pondering in mine heart I was *b*caught away in the Spirit of the Lord, yea, into an exceedingly high *c*mountain, which I never had before seen, and upon which I never had before set my foot.

2 And the Spirit said unto me: Behold, what *a*desirest thou?

3 And I said: I desire to behold the things which my father *a*saw.

4 And the Spirit said unto me: *a*Believest thou that thy father saw the *b*tree of which he hath spoken?

5 And I said: Yea, thou knowest that I *a*believe all the words of my father.

6 And when I had spoken these words, the Spirit cried with a loud voice, saying: Hosanna to the Lord, the most high God; for he is God over all the *a*earth, yea, even above all. And blessed art thou, Nephi, because thou *b*believest in the Son of the most high God; wherefore, thou shalt behold the things which thou hast desired.

7 And behold this thing shall be given unto thee for a *a*sign, that after thou hast beheld the tree which bore the fruit which thy father tasted, thou shalt also behold a man descending out of heaven, and him shall ye witness; and after ye have witnessed him ye shall *b*bear record that it is the Son of God.

8 And it came to pass that the Spirit said unto me: Look! And I

18a Heb. 13:8;
   Morm. 9:9 (9–11);
   D&C 20:12.
   TG God, Perfection of.
19a TG Objectives.
   b TG Mysteries of
      Godliness.
   c TG Holy Ghost, Source
      of Testimony.
   d Alma 7:20; 37:12;
      D&C 3:2; 35:1.
   TG God, Eternal
      Nature of.
20a Eccl. 12:14;
   Ezek. 33:20.

TG Judgment, the Last.
21a Ezek. 33:9.
   b TG Probation.
   c 1 Cor. 6:9 (9–10);
      Morm. 7:7;
      D&C 76:62 (50–62);
      138:20, 37;
      Moses 6:57.
22a TG Holy Ghost,
      Mission of.
11 1a D&C 76:19.
   TG Meditation.
   b Dan. 8:2;
      2 Cor. 12:2 (1–4);
      Rev. 21:10;

2 Ne. 4:25; Moses 1:1.
   c Ex. 24:13 (12–13);
      Deut. 10:1; Ether 3:1.
2a Zech. 4:2 (1–6).
3a 1 Ne. 8:2.
4a Mosiah 5:1 (1–2).
   b 1 Ne. 8:10 (10–12);
      15:22 (21–22).
5a 1 Ne. 2:16.
6a Ex. 9:29; Deut. 10:14;
      2 Ne. 29:7; 3 Ne. 11:14;
      D&C 55:1; Moses 6:44.
   b TG Believe.
7a TG Signs.
   b TG Testimony; Witness.

looked and beheld a tree; and it was like unto the *a*tree which my father had seen; and the *b*beauty thereof was far beyond, yea, exceeding of all beauty; and the *c*whiteness thereof did exceed the whiteness of the driven snow.

9 And it came to pass after I had seen the tree, I said unto the Spirit: I behold thou hast shown unto me the tree which is *a*precious above all.

10 And he said unto me: What desirest thou?

11 And I said unto him: To know the *a*interpretation thereof—for I spake unto him as a man speaketh; for I beheld that he was in the *b*form of a man; yet nevertheless, I knew that it was the Spirit of the Lord; and he spake unto me as a man speaketh with another.

12 And it came to pass that he said unto me: Look! And I looked as if to look upon him, and I saw him not; for he had gone from before my presence.

13 And it came to pass that I looked and beheld the great city of Jerusalem, and also other cities. And I beheld the city of Nazareth; and in the city of *a*Nazareth I beheld a *b*virgin, and she was exceedingly fair and white.

14 And it came to pass that I saw the *a*heavens open; and an angel came down and stood before me; and he said unto me: Nephi, what beholdest thou?

15 And I said unto him: A virgin, most beautiful and fair above all other virgins.

16 And he said unto me: Knowest thou the *a*condescension of God?

17 And I said unto him: I know that he loveth his children; nevertheless, I do not know the meaning of all things.

18 And he said unto me: Behold, the *a*virgin whom thou seest is the *b*mother of the Son of God, after the manner of the flesh.

19 And it came to pass that I beheld that she was carried away in the Spirit; and after she had been carried away in the *a*Spirit for the space of a time the angel spake unto me, saying: Look!

20 And I looked and beheld the virgin again, bearing a *a*child in her arms.

21 And the angel said unto me: Behold the *a*Lamb of God, yea, even the *b*Son of the Eternal *c*Father! Knowest thou the meaning of the *d*tree which thy father saw?

22 And I answered him, saying: Yea, it is the *a*love of God, which *b*sheddeth itself abroad in the hearts of the children of men; wherefore, it is the *c*most desirable above all things.

23 And he spake unto me, saying: Yea, and the most *a*joyous to the soul.

24 And after he had said these words, he said unto me: Look! And I looked, and I beheld the Son of God *a*going forth among the children of men; and I saw many fall down at his feet and worship him.

25 And it came to pass that I beheld that the *a*rod of iron, which my father had seen, was the *b*word of God, which *c*led to the fountain of *d*living waters, or to the *e*tree of life;

8*a* 1 Ne. 8:10.
  b TG Beauty.
  c 1 Ne. 8:11.
9*a* 1 Ne. 11:22 (22–25).
11*a* Gen. 40:8.
  b TG Spirit Body.
13*a* Matt. 2:23.
  b Luke 1:27 (26–27);
     Alma 7:10.
14*a* Ezek. 1:1;
     1 Ne. 1:8 (6–11).
16*a* 1 Ne. 11:26.
     TG Jesus Christ,
     Condescension of.
18*a* Luke 1:34 (34–35).

TG Foreordination;
   Jesus Christ, Prophecies
   about.
  b Matt. 1:16;
     Mosiah 3:8;
     Alma 19:13.
     TG Jesus Christ, Birth of.
19*a* Matt. 1:20.
20*a* Luke 2:16.
21*a* TG Jesus Christ, Lamb
     of God.
  b TG Jesus Christ, Divine
     Sonship.
  c TG God the Father,
     Elohim.

d 1 Ne. 8:10; Alma 5:62.
22*a* TG God, Love of.
  b Moro. 8:26.
  c 1 Ne. 11:9.
23*a* TG Joy.
24*a* Luke 4:14 (14–21).
25*a* Rev. 2:27;
     JST Rev. 2:27 (Bible
     Appendix).
  b 1 Ne. 8:19.
  c TG Guidance, Divine.
  d TG Living Water.
  e Gen. 2:9;
     Prov. 11:30 (22–30);
     Moses 4:28 (28, 31).

which waters are a representation of the love of God; and I also beheld that the tree of life was a representation of the love of God.

26 And the angel said unto me again: Look and behold the ^acondescension of God!

27 And I looked and ^abeheld the Redeemer of the world, of whom my father had spoken; and I also beheld the ^bprophet who should prepare the way before him. And the Lamb of God went forth and was ^cbaptized of him; and after he was baptized, I beheld the heavens open, and the Holy Ghost come down out of heaven and abide upon him in the form of a ^ddove.

28 And I beheld that he went forth ministering unto the people, in ^apower and great glory; and the multitudes were gathered together to hear him; and I beheld that they cast him out from among them.

29 And I also beheld ^atwelve others following him. And it came to pass that they were ^bcarried away in the Spirit from before my face, and I saw them not.

30 And it came to pass that the angel spake unto me again, saying: Look! And I looked, and I beheld the heavens open again, and I saw ^aangels descending upon the children of men; and they did minister unto them.

31 And he spake unto me again, saying: Look! And I looked, and I beheld the Lamb of God going forth among the children of men. And I beheld multitudes of people who were ^asick, and who were afflicted with all manner of diseases, and with ^bdevils and ^cunclean spirits; and the angel spake and showed all these things unto me. And they were ^dhealed by the power of the Lamb of God; and the devils and the unclean spirits were cast out.

32 And it came to pass that the angel spake unto me, saying: Look! And I looked and beheld the Lamb of God, that he was ^ataken by the people; yea, the Son of the everlasting God was ^bjudged of the world; and I saw and bear record.

33 And I, Nephi, saw that he was ^alifted up upon the cross and ^bslain for the sins of the world.

34 And after he was slain I saw the multitudes of the earth, that they were gathered together to ^afight against the apostles of the Lamb; for thus were the twelve called by the angel of the Lord.

35 And the multitude of the earth was gathered together; and I beheld that they were in a large and spacious ^abuilding, like unto the building which my father saw. And the angel of the Lord spake unto me again, saying: Behold the world and the wisdom thereof; yea, behold the house of Israel hath gathered together to ^bfight against the twelve apostles of the Lamb.

36 And it came to pass that I saw and bear record, that the great and spacious building was the ^apride of the world; and it ^bfell, and the fall thereof was exceedingly great. And the angel of the Lord spake unto me

26a 1 Ne. 11:16.
     TG Jesus Christ,
     Condescension of.
27a 2 Ne. 25:13.
   b Mal. 3:1; Matt. 11:10;
     John 1:6 (6–7);
     1 Ne. 10:7 (7–10);
     2 Ne. 31:4 (4–18);
     D&C 35:4.
   c TG Jesus Christ,
     Baptism of.
   d TG Holy Ghost, Dove,
     Sign of.
28a D&C 138:26.
29a 1 Ne. 12:9;

13:40 (24–26, 40).
     TG Apostles.
   b 1 Ne. 14:30.
30a TG Angels.
31a TG Sickness.
   b Mark 5:15 (15–20); 7:30;
     Mosiah 3:6 (5–7);
     Morm. 9:24.
   c TG Spirits, Evil or
     Unclean.
   d TG Heal.
32a TG Jesus Christ,
     Betrayal of.
   b Mark 15:19 (17–20);
     Luke 9:44 (44–45).

33a Luke 18:31;
     2 Ne. 10:3;
     Mosiah 3:9 (9–10);
     3 Ne. 27:14.
   b TG Jesus Christ,
     Atonement through;
     Jesus Christ, Death of.
34a Mark 13:13;
     1 Cor. 4:9 (6–13).
35a 1 Ne. 8:26; 12:18.
   b Micah 3:5;
     D&C 121:38.
36a TG Pride.
   b TG Earth, Cleansing of;
     World, End of.

again, saying: Thus shall be the destruction of all nations, kindreds, tongues, and people, that shall fight against the twelve apostles of the Lamb.

CHAPTER 12

Nephi sees in vision the land of promise; the righteousness, iniquity, and downfall of its inhabitants; the coming of the Lamb of God among them; how the Twelve Disciples and the Twelve Apostles will judge Israel; and the loathsome and filthy state of those who dwindle in unbelief. About 600–592 B.C.

AND it came to pass that the angel said unto me: Look, and behold thy seed, and also the seed of thy brethren. And I looked and beheld the ªland of promise; and I beheld multitudes of people, yea, even as it were in number as many as the ᵇsand of the sea.

2 And it came to pass that I beheld multitudes gathered together to battle, one against the other; and I beheld ªwars, and rumors of wars, and great slaughters with the sword among my people.

3 And it came to pass that I beheld many generations pass away, after the manner of wars and contentions in the land; and I beheld many cities, yea, even that I did not number them.

4 And it came to pass that I saw a ªmist of ᵇdarkness on the face of the land of promise; and I saw lightnings, and I heard thunderings, and earthquakes, and all manner of tumultuous noises; and I saw the earth and the rocks, that they rent; and I saw mountains tumbling into pieces; and I saw the plains of the earth, that they were ᶜbroken up; and I saw many cities that they were ᵈsunk; and I saw many that they were burned with fire; and I saw many that did tumble to the earth, because of the quaking thereof.

5 And it came to pass after I saw these things, I saw the ªvapor of darkness, that it passed from off the face of the earth; and behold, I saw multitudes who had not fallen because of the great and terrible judgments of the Lord.

6 And I saw the heavens open, and the ªLamb of God descending out of heaven; and he came down and ᵇshowed himself unto them.

7 And I also saw and bear record that the Holy Ghost fell upon ªtwelve others; and they were ordained of God, and chosen.

8 And the angel spake unto me, saying: Behold the twelve disciples of the Lamb, who are chosen to minister unto thy seed.

9 And he said unto me: Thou rememberest the ªtwelve apostles of the Lamb? Behold they are they who shall ᵇjudge the twelve tribes of Israel; wherefore, the twelve ministers of thy seed shall be judged of them; for ye are of the house of Israel.

10 And these ªtwelve ministers whom thou beholdest shall judge thy seed. And, behold, they are righteous forever; for because of their faith in the Lamb of God their ᵇgarments are made white in his blood.

11 And the angel said unto me: Look! And I looked, and beheld ªthree generations pass away in

12 1a   TG Promised Lands.
    b   Gen. 22:17 (17–18);
      1 Kgs. 4:20.
   2a   Enos 1:24;
      Morm. 8:7 (7–8).
      TG War.
   4a   1 Ne. 19:12;
      Hel. 14:28 (20–28);
      3 Ne. 10:11.
    b   1 Ne. 19:10;
      2 Ne. 26:3.
    c   Gen. 7:11.

    d   3 Ne. 8:14.
   5a   3 Ne. 8:20.
   6a   2 Ne. 26:1 (1, 9);
      3 Ne. 11:8 (3–17).
    b   2 Ne. 32:6;
      Alma 7:8; 16:20.
   7a   3 Ne. 11:22; 12:1.
   9a   Matt. 10:1;
      Luke 6:13;
      John 6:70;
      1 Ne. 11:29;
      13:40 (24–26, 40).

    b   Matt. 19:28;
      D&C 29:12.
      TG Judgment, the Last.
  10a   3 Ne. 27:27;
      Morm. 3:18–19.
    b   Rev. 7:14; 19:8;
      Alma 5:21 (21–27);
      13:11 (11–13);
      3 Ne. 27:19 (19–20);
      D&C 88:85.
  11a   2 Ne. 26:9 (9–10);
      3 Ne. 27:32 (30–32).

righteousness; and their garments were white even like unto the Lamb of God. And the angel said unto me: These are made white in the blood of the Lamb, because of their faith in him.

12 And I, Nephi, also saw many of the ªfourth generation who passed away in righteousness.

13 And it came to pass that I saw the multitudes of the earth gathered together.

14 And the angel said unto me: Behold thy seed, and also the seed of thy brethren.

15 And it came to pass that I looked and beheld the people of my seed gathered together in multitudes ªagainst the seed of my brethren; and they were gathered together to battle.

16 And the angel spake unto me, saying: Behold the fountain of ªfilthy water which thy father saw; yea, even the ᵇriver of which he spake; and the depths thereof are the depths of ᶜhell.

17 And the ªmists of darkness are the temptations of the devil, which ᵇblindeth the eyes, and hardeneth the hearts of the children of men, and leadeth them away into ᶜbroad roads, that they perish and are lost.

18 And the large and spacious ªbuilding, which thy father saw, is vain ᵇimaginations and the ᶜpride of the children of men. And a great and a terrible ᵈgulf divideth them; yea, even the word of the ᵉjustice of the Eternal God, and the Messiah who is the Lamb of God, of whom the Holy Ghost beareth record, from the beginning of the world

until this time, and from this time henceforth and forever.

19 And while the angel spake these words, I beheld and saw that the seed of my brethren did contend against my seed, according to the word of the angel; and because of the pride of my seed, and the ªtemptations of the devil, I beheld that the seed of my brethren did ᵇoverpower the people of my seed.

20 And it came to pass that I beheld, and saw the people of the seed of my brethren that they had overcome my seed; and they went forth in multitudes upon the face of the land.

21 And I saw them gathered together in multitudes; and I saw ªwars and rumors of wars among them; and in wars and rumors of wars I saw ᵇmany generations pass away.

22 And the angel said unto me: Behold these shall ªdwindle in unbelief.

23 And it came to pass that I beheld, after they had dwindled in unbelief they became a ªdark, and loathsome, and a ᵇfilthy people, full of ᶜidleness and all manner of abominations.

CHAPTER 13

Nephi sees in vision the church of the devil set up among the Gentiles, the discovery and colonizing of America, the loss of many plain and precious parts of the Bible, the resultant state of gentile apostasy, the restoration of the gospel, the coming forth of latter-day scripture, and the building up of Zion. About 600–592 B.C.

12a 2 Ne. 26:9;
    Alma 45:12 (10–12);
    Hel. 13:10 (5, 9–10);
    3 Ne. 27:32;
    4 Ne. 1:14 (14–41).
15a Morm. 6:7 (1–22).
16a TG Filthiness.
  b 1 Ne. 8:13 (13–14);
    15:27 (26–29).
  c TG Hell.
17a 2 Pet. 2:17;
    1 Ne. 8:23; 15:24 (23–24).

  b TG Apostasy of
    Individuals.
  c Prov. 4:14;
    Luke 13:24.
18a 1 Ne. 8:26;
    11:35 (35–36).
  b Jer. 7:24; 9:14.
  c TG Haughtiness;
    Pride.
  d Luke 16:26;
    1 Ne. 15:28 (28–30).
  e TG God, Justice of.

19a TG Temptation.
  b Jarom 1:10;
    W of M 1:2 (1–2).
21a Morm. 8:8;
    Moro. 1:2.
  b 2 Ne. 1:18.
22a 1 Ne. 15:13;
    2 Ne. 26:15.
23a 2 Ne. 26:33.
  b 2 Ne. 5:22 (20–25).
    TG Filthiness.
  c TG Idleness.

AND it came to pass that the angel spake unto me, saying: Look! And I looked and beheld many nations and kingdoms.

2 And the angel said unto me: What beholdest thou? And I said: I behold many ᵃnations and kingdoms.

3 And he said unto me: These are the nations and kingdoms of the Gentiles.

4 And it came to pass that I saw among the nations of the ᵃGentiles the formation of a ᵇgreat church.

5 And the angel said unto me: Behold the formation of a ᵃchurch which is most abominable above all other churches, which ᵇslayeth the saints of God, yea, and tortureth them and bindeth them down, and yoketh them with a ᶜyoke of iron, and bringeth them down into captivity.

6 And it came to pass that I beheld this ᵃgreat and ᵇabominable church; and I saw the ᶜdevil that he was the founder of it.

7 And I also saw ᵃgold, and silver, and silks, and scarlets, and fine-twined ᵇlinen, and all manner of precious clothing; and I saw many harlots.

8 And the angel spake unto me, saying: Behold the gold, and the silver, and the silks, and the scarlets, and the fine-twined linen, and the precious clothing, and the harlots, are the ᵃdesires of this great and abominable church.

9 And also for the ᵃpraise of the world do they ᵇdestroy the saints of God, and bring them down into captivity.

10 And it came to pass that I looked and beheld many waters; and they divided the Gentiles from the seed of my brethren.

11 And it came to pass that the angel said unto me: Behold the wrath of God is upon the seed of thy brethren.

12 And I looked and beheld a man among the Gentiles, who was separated from the seed of my brethren by the many waters; and I beheld the Spirit of God, that it came down and ᵃwrought upon the man; and he went forth upon the many waters, even unto the seed of my brethren, who were in the promised land.

13 And it came to pass that I beheld the Spirit of God, that it wrought upon other Gentiles; and they went forth out of captivity, upon the many waters.

14 And it came to pass that I beheld many ᵃmultitudes of the Gentiles upon the ᵇland of promise; and I beheld the wrath of God, that it was upon the seed of my brethren; and they were ᶜscattered before the Gentiles and were smitten.

15 And I beheld the Spirit of the Lord, that it was upon the Gentiles, and they did prosper and ᵃobtain the ᵇland for their inheritance; and I beheld that they were white, and exceedingly fair and ᶜbeautiful, like unto my people before they were ᵈslain.

16 And it came to pass that I, Nephi, beheld that the Gentiles who had gone forth out of captivity did humble themselves before the Lord; and the power of the Lord was ᵃwith them.

17 And I beheld that their mother Gentiles were gathered together

13 2a TG Kings, Earthly;
        Nations.
    4a TG Gentiles.
     b 1 Ne. 13:26 (26, 34);
        14:10 (3, 9–17).
    5a 2 Ne. 10:16.
     b Rev. 17:6 (3–6); 18:24;
        1 Ne. 14:13.
     c Jer. 28:14 (10–14).
        TG Bondage, Spiritual.
    6a D&C 88:94.

     b TG Devil, Church of.
     c 1 Ne. 22:23 (22–23).
        TG Devil.
    7a Morm. 8:37 (36–38).
     b Ether 10:24.
    8a Rev. 18:19 (10–24);
        Morm. 8:37 (36–41).
    9a Morm. 8:38.
     b Rev. 13:7 (4–7).
   12a TG Guidance, Divine.
   14a 2 Ne. 1:11;

        Morm. 5:19 (19–20).
     b TG Promised Lands.
     c 1 Ne. 22:7.
        TG Israel, Scattering of.
   15a Morm. 5:19.
     b 2 Ne. 10:19.
     c 2 Ne. 5:21;
        4 Ne. 1:10;
        Morm. 9:6.
     d Morm. 6:19 (17–22).
   16a D&C 101:80.

upon the waters, and upon the land also, to battle against them.

18 And I beheld that the power of God was with them, and also that the wrath of God was upon all those that were gathered together ᵃagainst them to battle.

19 And I, Nephi, beheld that the Gentiles that had gone out of captivity were ᵃdelivered by the power of God out of the hands of all other nations.

20 And it came to pass that I, Nephi, beheld that they did prosper in the land; and I beheld a ᵃbook, and it was carried forth among them.

21 And the angel said unto me: Knowest thou the meaning of the book?

22 And I said unto him: I know not.

23 And he said: Behold it proceedeth out of the mouth of a Jew. And I, Nephi, beheld it; and he said unto me: The ᵃbook that thou beholdest is a ᵇrecord of the ᶜJews, which contains the covenants of the Lord, which he hath made unto the house of Israel; and it also containeth many of the prophecies of the holy prophets; and it is a record like unto the engravings which are upon the ᵈplates of brass, save there are not so many; nevertheless, they contain the covenants of the Lord, which he hath made unto the house of Israel; wherefore, they are of great worth unto the Gentiles.

24 And the angel of the Lord said unto me: Thou hast beheld that the ᵃbook proceeded forth from the mouth of a Jew; and when it proceeded forth from the mouth of a Jew it contained the fulness of the gospel of the Lord, of whom the twelve apostles bear record; and they bear record according to the truth which is in the Lamb of God.

25 Wherefore, these things go forth from the ᵃJews in purity unto the ᵇGentiles, according to the truth which is in God.

26 And after they go forth by the ᵃhand of the twelve apostles of the Lamb, from the Jews ᵇunto the Gentiles, thou seest the formation of that ᶜgreat and abominable ᵈchurch, which is most abominable above all other churches; for behold, they have ᵉtaken away from the gospel of the Lamb many parts which are ᶠplain and most precious; and also many covenants of the Lord have they taken away.

27 And all this have they done that they might pervert the right ways of the Lord, that they might blind the eyes and harden the hearts of the children of men.

28 Wherefore, thou seest that after the book hath gone forth through the hands of the great and abominable church, that there are many plain and ᵃprecious things taken away from the book, which is the book of the Lamb of God.

29 And after these plain and precious things were ᵃtaken away it goeth forth unto all the nations of the Gentiles; and after it goeth forth unto all the nations of the Gentiles, yea, even across the many waters which thou hast seen with the Gentiles which have gone forth out of captivity, thou seest—because of the many plain and precious things which have been taken out of the

18a 1 Ne. 17:35.
19a 2 Ne. 10:10 (10–14);
     3 Ne. 21:4;
     Ether 2:12.
20a 1 Ne. 13:41 (3–41); 14:23.
23a 1 Ne. 13:38;
     2 Ne. 29:6 (4–12).
  b TG Scriptures,
     Preservation of.
  c 2 Ne. 3:12.
  d 1 Ne. 5:10 (10–22); 19:22.

24a 2 Ne. 29:3.
25a 2 Ne. 29:4 (4–6);
     D&C 3:16.
  TG Israel, Judah,
     People of.
  b TG Gentiles.
26a Luke 1:1 (1–4);
     2 Tim. 4:13.
  b Matt. 21:43.
  c 1 Ne. 13:4 (4–6);
     14:10 (3, 9–17).

  d TG Apostasy of the Early
     Christian Church.
  e Morm. 8:33;
     Moses 1:41.
  TG False Doctrine;
     Scriptures, Lost.
  f 1 Ne. 14:21 (20–26);
     A of F 1:8.
28a 1 Ne. 14:23.
29a 2 Pet. 3:16.

book, which were plain unto the understanding of the children of men, according to the plainness which is in the Lamb of God—because of these things which are taken away out of the gospel of the Lamb, an exceedingly great many do stumble, yea, insomuch that Satan hath great power over them.

30 Nevertheless, thou beholdest that the Gentiles who have gone forth out of captivity, and have been lifted up by the power of God above all other nations, upon the face of the land which is choice above all other lands, which is the land that the Lord God hath covenanted with thy father that his seed should have for the ^aland of their inheritance; wherefore, thou seest that the Lord God will not suffer that the Gentiles will utterly destroy the ^bmixture of thy ^cseed, which are among thy brethren.

31 Neither will he suffer that the Gentiles shall ^adestroy the seed of thy brethren.

32 Neither will the Lord God suffer that the Gentiles shall forever remain in that awful state of blindness, which thou beholdest they are in, because of the plain and most precious parts of the gospel of the Lamb which have been kept back by that ^aabominable church, whose formation thou hast seen.

33 Wherefore saith the Lamb of God: I will be ^amerciful unto the Gentiles, unto the visiting of the remnant of the house of Israel in great judgment.

34 And it came to pass that the angel of the Lord spake unto me, saying: Behold, saith the Lamb of God, after I have ^avisited the ^bremnant of the house of Israel—and this remnant of whom I speak is the seed of thy father—wherefore, after I have visited them in judgment, and smitten them by the hand of the Gentiles, and after the Gentiles do ^cstumble exceedingly, because of the most plain and precious parts of the ^dgospel of the Lamb which have been kept back by that abominable church, which is the mother of harlots, saith the Lamb—I will be merciful unto the ^eGentiles in that day, insomuch that I will ^fbring forth unto them, in mine own power, much of my ^ggospel, which shall be plain and precious, saith the Lamb.

35 For, behold, saith the Lamb: I will manifest myself unto thy seed, that they shall write many things which I shall minister unto them, which shall be plain and precious; and after thy seed shall be destroyed, and dwindle in unbelief, and also the seed of thy brethren, behold, ^athese things shall be hid up, to come forth unto the Gentiles, by the gift and power of the Lamb.

36 And in them shall be written my ^agospel, saith the Lamb, and my ^brock and my salvation.

37 And ^ablessed are they who shall seek to bring forth my ^bZion at that day, for they shall have the ^cgift and the ^dpower of the Holy Ghost; and if they ^eendure unto the end they

---

30a TG Lands of Inheritance; Promised Lands.
  b 2 Ne. 29:12 (12–13); Alma 45:14 (10–14); D&C 3:17.
  c 2 Ne. 3:3.
31a 2 Ne. 4:7; 10:18 (18–19); Jacob 3:6 (5–9); Hel. 15:12 (10–17); 3 Ne. 16:8 (4–13); Morm. 5:20 (20–21).
32a TG Devil, Church of.
33a Isa. 42:1 (1, 3–4).
34a D&C 124:8; Abr. 1:17.
  b TG Israel, Joseph,

  People of.
  c 1 Ne. 14:1 (1–3); 2 Ne. 26:20.
  d TG Gospel.
  e TG Millennium, Preparing a People for.
  f TG Scriptures, Lost.
  g D&C 10:62. TG Restoration of the Gospel.
35a 1 Ne. 14:7; 22:8; 2 Ne. 27:26 (6–26); 29:1 (1–2). TG Book of Mormon.
36a 3 Ne. 27:21.

  b 3 Ne. 11:39 (38–39). TG Rock.
37a Jacob 5:75 (70–76); D&C 21:9. TG Israel, Mission of; Mission of Latter-day Saints.
  b TG Zion.
  c TG Holy Ghost, Gift of.
  d Luke 24:49; 1 Ne. 14:14; D&C 38:38 (32–38).
  e 3 Ne. 27:16. TG Endure; Perseverance; Steadfastness.

shall be ᶠlifted up at the last day, and shall be saved in the everlasting ᵍkingdom of the Lamb; and whoso shall ʰpublish peace, yea, tidings of great joy, how beautiful upon the mountains shall they be.

38 And it came to pass that I beheld the remnant of the seed of my brethren, and also the ᵃbook of the Lamb of God, which had proceeded forth from the mouth of the Jew, that it came forth from the Gentiles ᵇunto the remnant of the seed of my brethren.

39 And after it had come forth unto them I beheld ᵃother ᵇbooks, which came forth by the power of the Lamb, from the Gentiles unto them, unto the ᶜconvincing of the Gentiles and the remnant of the seed of my brethren, and also the Jews who were scattered upon all the face of the earth, that the records of the prophets and of the twelve apostles of the Lamb are ᵈtrue.

40 And the angel spake unto me, saying: These ᵃlast records, which thou hast seen among the Gentiles, shall ᵇestablish the truth of the ᶜfirst, which are of the ᵈtwelve apostles of the Lamb, and shall make known the plain and precious things which have been taken away from them; and shall make known to all kindreds, tongues, and people, that the Lamb of God is the Son of the Eternal Father, and the ᵉSavior of the world; and that all men must come unto him, or they cannot be saved.

41 And they must come according to the words which shall be established by the mouth of the Lamb; and the words of the Lamb shall be made known in the records of thy seed, as well as in the ᵃrecords of the twelve apostles of the Lamb; wherefore they both shall be established in ᵇone; for there is ᶜone God and one ᵈShepherd over all the earth.

42 And the time cometh that he shall manifest himself unto all nations, both unto the ᵃJews and also unto the Gentiles; and after he has manifested himself unto the Jews and also unto the Gentiles, then he shall manifest himself unto the Gentiles and also unto the Jews, and the ᵇlast shall be first, and the ᶜfirst shall be last.

CHAPTER 14

An angel tells Nephi of the blessings and cursings to fall upon the Gentiles—There are only two churches: the Church of the Lamb of God and the church of the devil—The Saints of God in all nations are persecuted by the great and abominable church—The Apostle John will write concerning the end of the world. About 600–592 B.C.

AND it shall come to pass, that if the ᵃGentiles shall hearken unto the Lamb of God in that day that he shall manifest himself unto them in word, and also in ᵇpower, in very deed, unto the ᶜtaking away of their ᵈstumbling blocks—

2 And harden not their hearts

37ᶠ James 4:10.
   g TG Kingdom of God, in Heaven.
   h Isa. 52:7 (7–10); Mark 13:10; 3 Ne. 20:40.
38ᵃ 1 Ne. 13:23; 2 Ne. 29:6 (4–6).
   b Morm. 5:15; 7:8 (8–9).
39ᵃ D&C 9:2.
   b TG Scriptures to Come Forth.
   c Ezek. 37:17 (15–20); 1 Ne. 14:2 (1–5).
   d 1 Ne. 14:30.
40ᵃ 2 Ne. 26:17 (16–17); 27:6 (6–26); 29:12.

   TG Book of Mormon.
   b TG Scriptures, Value of.
   c See the title page of the Book of Mormon.
   TG Bible.
   d 1 Ne. 11:29; 12:9.
   e Moses 1:6.
41ᵃ 1 Ne. 13:20 (20–28).
   b Ezek. 37:17.
   c Deut. 6:4; 2 Ne. 31:21.
   d TG Jesus Christ, Good Shepherd.
42ᵃ D&C 18:6, 26; 19:27; 21:12; 90:9 (8–9); 107:33; 112:4.
   b Jacob 5:63; Ether 13:12.

   c Luke 13:30; 1 Ne. 10:14; 15:13 (13–20); D&C 14:10.
14 1ᵃ 1 Ne. 22:9 (8–9); 2 Ne. 30:3; 3 Ne. 16:6 (6–13). TG Gentiles.
   b 1 Thes. 1:5; 1 Ne. 14:14; Jacob 6:2 (2–3).
   c Ether 12:27.
   d Isa. 57:14; Ezek. 7:19; 1 Cor. 1:23; 1 Ne. 13:34 (29, 34); 2 Ne. 26:20.

against the Lamb of God, they shall be numbered among the seed of thy father; yea, they shall be *a*numbered among the house of Israel; and they shall be a *b*blessed people upon the *c*promised land forever; they shall be no more brought down into captivity; and the house of Israel shall no more be confounded.

3 And that great *a*pit, which hath been digged for them by that great and abominable church, which was founded by the devil and his children, that he might lead away the souls of men down to hell— yea, that great pit which hath been digged for the destruction of men shall be filled by those who digged it, unto their utter destruction, saith the Lamb of God; not the destruction of the soul, save it be the casting of it into that *b*hell which hath no end.

4 For behold, this is according to the *a*captivity of the devil, and also according to the justice of God, upon all those who will work wickedness and abomination before him.

5 And it came to pass that the angel spake unto me, Nephi, saying: Thou hast beheld that if the Gentiles repent it shall be *a*well with them; and thou also knowest concerning the covenants of the Lord unto the house of Israel; and thou also hast heard that whoso *b*repenteth not must perish.

6 Therefore, *a*wo be unto the Gentiles if it so be that they harden their hearts against the Lamb of God.

7 For the time cometh, saith the Lamb of God, that I will work a great and a *a*marvelous work among the children of men; a *b*work which shall be everlasting, either on the one hand or on the other—either to the convincing of them unto *c*peace and *d*life eternal, or unto the deliverance of them to the hardness of their hearts and the blindness of their minds unto their being brought down into captivity, and also into destruction, both temporally and spiritually, according to the *e*captivity of the devil, of which I have spoken.

8 And it came to pass that when the angel had spoken these words, he said unto me: Rememberest thou the *a*covenants of the Father unto the house of Israel? I said unto him, Yea.

9 And it came to pass that he said unto me: Look, and behold that great and abominable church, which is the mother of abominations, whose founder is the *a*devil.

10 And he said unto me: Behold there are save *a*two churches only; the one is the church of the Lamb of God, and the *b*other is the church of the *c*devil; wherefore, *d*whoso belongeth not to the church of the Lamb of God belongeth to that great church, which is the mother of abominations; and she is the *e*whore of all the earth.

11 And it came to pass that I

2a Gal. 3:7 (7, 29);
   2 Ne. 10:18 (18–19);
   3 Ne. 16:13; 21:6 (6, 22);
   Abr. 2:10 (9–11).
 b 2 Ne. 6:12; 10:10 (8–14);
   3 Ne. 16 (6–7); 20:27;
   Morm. 5:19.
 c TG Israel, Deliver-
   ance of;
   Israel, Restoration of;
   Lands of Inheritance.
3a Ps. 57:6;
   Matt. 7:2 (1–2);
   1 Ne. 22:14 (13–14);
   D&C 10:26 (25–27);
   109:25.
 b Alma 19:29.

   TG Damnation; Hell.
4a TG Bondage, Spiritual.
5a 1 Ne. 13:39 (34–42);
   22:9.
 b TG Repent.
6a 2 Ne. 28:32.
7a Isa. 29:14;
   1 Ne. 13:35; 22:8;
   2 Ne. 27:26; 29:1 (1–2);
   D&C 4:1.
   TG Restoration of the
   Gospel.
 b TG God, Works of.
 c TG Peace;
   Peace of God.
 d Jer. 21:8.
   TG Eternal Life.

 e 2 Ne. 2:29 (26–29);
   Alma 12:11 (9–11).
8a TG Abrahamic Covenant;
   Israel, Mission of.
9a 1 Ne. 15:35;
   D&C 1:35.
   TG Devil, Church of.
10a 1 Ne. 22:23;
   2 Ne. 26:20;
   Morm. 8:28 (25–41).
   TG Church.
 b 1 Ne. 13:4 (4–6),
   26 (26, 34).
 c TG Devil, Church of;
   False Prophets.
 d 2 Ne. 10:16.
 e Rev. 17:15 (5, 15).

looked and beheld the whore of all the earth, and she sat upon many ^awaters; and she had dominion over ^ball the earth, among all nations, kindreds, tongues, and people.

12 And it came to pass that I beheld the church of the Lamb of God, and its numbers were ^afew, because of the wickedness and abominations of the whore who sat upon many waters; nevertheless, I beheld that the church of the Lamb, who were the saints of God, were also upon ^ball the face of the earth; and their dominions upon the face of the earth were small, because of the wickedness of the great whore whom I saw.

13 And it came to pass that I beheld that the great mother of abominations did gather together multitudes upon the face of all the earth, among all the nations of the Gentiles, to ^afight against the Lamb of God.

14 And it came to pass that I, Nephi, beheld the power of the Lamb of God, that it descended upon the saints of the church of the Lamb, and upon the covenant people of the Lord, who were scattered upon all the face of the earth; and they were ^aarmed with ^brighteousness and with the ^cpower of God in great glory.

15 And it came to pass that I beheld that the wrath of God was ^apoured out upon that great and abominable church, insomuch that there were wars and rumors of wars among all the ^bnations and kindreds of the earth.

16 And as there began to be ^awars and rumors of wars among all the nations which belonged to the mother of abominations, the angel spake unto me, saying: Behold, the wrath of God is upon the mother of harlots; and behold, thou seest all these things—

17 And when the ^aday cometh that the ^bwrath of God is poured out upon the mother of harlots, which is the great and abominable church of all the earth, whose founder is the devil, then, at that day, the ^cwork of the Father shall commence, in preparing the way for the fulfilling of his ^dcovenants, which he hath made to his people who are of the house of Israel.

18 And it came to pass that the angel spake unto me, saying: Look!

19 And I looked and beheld a man, and he was dressed in a white robe.

20 And the angel said unto me: Behold ^aone of the twelve apostles of the Lamb.

21 Behold, he shall ^asee and ^bwrite the ^cremainder of these things; yea, and also many things which have been.

22 And he shall also write concerning the end of the world.

23 Wherefore, the things which he shall write are just and true; and behold they are written in the ^abook which thou beheld proceeding out of the mouth of the Jew; and at the time they proceeded out of the mouth of the Jew, or, at the time the book proceeded out of the mouth of the Jew, the things which were written were plain and pure, and most ^bprecious and easy to the understanding of all men.

11a Jer. 51:13 (12–14).
   b D&C 35:11.
12a Matt. 7:14;
   Jacob 5:70;
   3 Ne. 14:14;
   D&C 138:26.
   b D&C 90:11.
13a Rev. 17:6 (1–6); 18:24;
   1 Ne. 13:5.
14a TG Mission of Latter-day
   Saints.
   b TG Deliver;
   Protection, Divine.
   c Luke 24:49;

1 Ne. 13:37; 14:1;
   Jacob 6:2 (2–3);
   D&C 38:38 (32–38).
15a D&C 115:6 (5–6).
   b Mark 13:8;
   D&C 87:6.
16a 1 Ne. 22:13 (13–14);
   Morm. 8:30.
   TG War.
17a TG Last Days.
   b 1 Ne. 21:26;
   22:16 (15–16);
   3 Ne. 20:20 (19–21).
   c 3 Ne. 21:26 (7, 20–29).

TG Israel, Restoration of.
   d Morm. 8:21 (21, 41).
   TG Abrahamic Covenant.
20a Rev. 1:1 (1–3);
   1 Ne. 14:27.
21a Rev. 1:1.
   b 1 Ne. 13:24 (20–40);
   A of F 1:8.
   c Rev. 4:1.
23a 1 Ne. 13:20 (20–24);
   Morm. 8:33;
   Ether 4:16.
   b 1 Ne. 13:28 (28–32).

24 And behold, the things which this [a]apostle of the Lamb shall write are many things which thou hast seen; and behold, the remainder shalt thou see.

25 But the things which thou shalt see hereafter thou shalt not write; for the Lord God hath ordained the apostle of the Lamb of God that he should [a]write them.

26 And also others who have been, to them hath he shown all things, and they have [a]written them; and they are [b]sealed up to come forth in their purity, according to the truth which is in the Lamb, in the own due time of the Lord, unto the house of Israel.

27 And I, Nephi, heard and bear record, that the name of the apostle of the Lamb was [a]John, according to the word of the angel.

28 And behold, I, Nephi, am forbidden that I should write the remainder of the things which I saw and heard; wherefore the things which I have written sufficeth me; and I have written but a small part of the things which I saw.

29 And I bear record that I saw the things which my [a]father saw, and the angel of the Lord did make them known unto me.

30 And now I make an end of speaking concerning the things which I saw while I was [a]carried away in the Spirit; and if all the things which I saw are not written, the things which I have written are [b]true. And thus it is. Amen.

CHAPTER 15

Lehi's seed are to receive the gospel from the Gentiles in the latter days—The gathering of Israel is likened unto an olive tree whose natural branches will be grafted in again—Nephi interprets the vision of the tree of life and speaks of the justice of God in dividing the wicked from the righteous. About 600–592 B.C.

AND it came to pass that after I, Nephi, had been carried away in the Spirit, and seen all these things, I returned to the tent of my father.

2 And it came to pass that I beheld my brethren, and they were disputing one with another concerning the things which my father had spoken unto them.

3 For he truly spake many great things unto them, which were hard to be [a]understood, save a man should inquire of the Lord; and they being hard in their hearts, therefore they did not look unto the Lord as they ought.

4 And now I, Nephi, was grieved because of the hardness of their hearts, and also, because of the things which I had seen, and knew they must unavoidably come to pass because of the great wickedness of the children of men.

5 And it came to pass that I was overcome because of my afflictions, for I considered that mine [a]afflictions were great above all, because of the [b]destruction of my people, for I had beheld their fall.

6 And it came to pass that after I had received [a]strength I spake unto my brethren, desiring to know of them the cause of their disputations.

7 And they said: Behold, we cannot understand the words which our father hath spoken concerning the natural branches of the [a]olive tree, and also concerning the Gentiles.

8 And I said unto them: Have ye [a]inquired of the Lord?

24a Ether 4:16.
25a John 20:30 (30–31);
   21:25;
   Rev. 1:19.
26a TG Scriptures,
   Writing of.
  b Dan. 12:9;
   2 Ne. 27:10 (6–23); 30:17;
   Ether 3:21 (21–27);
   4:5 (4–7); 12:21;

D&C 35:18;
   JS—H 1:65.
27a Rev. 1:1 (1–3).
29a 1 Ne. 8:2 (2–35).
30a 1 Kgs. 18:12;
   1 Ne. 11:29 (19, 29).
  b 1 Ne. 13:39;
   2 Ne. 25:20.
15 3a 1 Cor. 2:11 (10–12).
   TG Hardheartedness;

   Understanding.
5a Moses 7:44 (41–44).
  b Enos 1:13;
   Morm. 6:1.
6a Moses 1:10;
   JS—H 1:20, 48.
7a 1 Ne. 10:14 (2–15).
8a 2 Ne. 1:25 (24–27);
   Mosiah 10:14.
   TG Problem-Solving.

9 And they said unto me: *a*We have not; for the Lord maketh no such thing known unto us.

10 Behold, I said unto them: How is it that ye do not keep the commandments of the Lord? How is it that ye will *a*perish, because of the hardness of your hearts?

11 Do ye not remember the things which the Lord hath said?—If ye will not harden your hearts, and *a*ask me in *b*faith, believing that ye shall receive, with diligence in keeping my commandments, surely these things shall be made known unto you.

12 Behold, I say unto you, that the house of Israel was compared unto an olive tree, by the Spirit of the Lord which was in our father; and behold are we not broken off from the house of Israel, and are we not a *a*branch of the house of Israel?

13 And now, the thing which our father meaneth concerning the grafting in of the natural branches through the fulness of the Gentiles, is, that in the latter days, when our seed shall have *a*dwindled in unbelief, yea, for the space of many years, and many generations after the *b*Messiah shall be manifested in body unto the children of men, then shall the fulness of the *c*gospel of the Messiah come unto the Gentiles, and from the *d*Gentiles unto the remnant of our seed—

14 And at that day shall the remnant of our *a*seed *b*know that they are of the house of Israel, and that they are the *c*covenant people of the Lord; and then shall they know and

*d*come to the *e*knowledge of their forefathers, and also to the knowledge of the gospel of their Redeemer, which was ministered unto their fathers by him; wherefore, they shall come to the knowledge of their Redeemer and the very points of his doctrine, that they may know how to come unto him and be saved.

15 And then at that day will they not rejoice and give praise unto their everlasting God, their *a*rock and their salvation? Yea, at that day, will they not receive the strength and nourishment from the true *b*vine? Yea, will they not come unto the true fold of God?

16 Behold, I say unto you, Yea; they shall be remembered again among the house of Israel; they shall be *a*grafted in, being a natural branch of the olive tree, into the true olive tree.

17 And this is what our father meaneth; and he meaneth that it will not come to pass until after they are scattered by the Gentiles; and he meaneth that it shall come by way of the Gentiles, that the Lord may show his power unto the Gentiles, for the very cause that he shall be *a*rejected of the Jews, or of the house of Israel.

18 Wherefore, our father hath not spoken of our seed alone, but also of all the house of Israel, pointing to the covenant which should be fulfilled in the latter days; which covenant the Lord made to our father Abraham, saying: In thy *a*seed shall all the kindreds of the earth be *b*blessed.

9 *a* D&C 58:33.
10 *a* TG Apostasy of Individuals.
11 *a* James 1:5 (5–6). TG Prayer.
  b 1 Ne. 2:19 (18–21); 7:12 (9–13).
12 *a* Gen. 49:22 (22–26); 1 Ne. 10:12 (12–14); 19:24. TG Israel, Joseph, People of.
13 *a* 1 Ne. 12:22 (22–23); 2 Ne. 26:15.

b TG Jesus Christ, Messiah.
c TG Gospel; Mission of Latter-day Saints.
d 1 Ne. 13:42; 22:9 (5–10); D&C 14:10. TG Gentiles.
14 *a* 2 Ne. 10:2; 3 Ne. 5:23 (21–26); 21:7 (4–29).
  b 2 Ne. 3:12; 30:5; Morm. 7:9 (1, 9–10).
  c TG Abrahamic Covenant.
d Jacob 3:6.

e D&C 3:18 (16–20). See also title page of the Book of Mormon.
15 *a* TG Rock.
  b Gen. 49:11; John 15:1.
16 *a* Jacob 5:54 (1–77).
17 *a* TG Jesus Christ, Betrayal of; Jesus Christ, Crucifixion of.
18 *a* Gen. 12:3 (1–3); Abr. 2:11 (6–11). TG Seed of Abraham.
  b TG Israel, Mission of.

19 And it came to pass that I, Nephi, spake much unto them concerning these things; yea, I spake unto them concerning the ^arestoration of the Jews in the latter days.

20 And I did rehearse unto them the words of ^aIsaiah, who spake ^bconcerning the ^crestoration of the Jews, or of the house of Israel; and after they were restored they should no more be confounded, neither should they be scattered again. And it came to pass that I did speak many words unto my brethren, that they were pacified and did ^dhumble themselves before the Lord.

21 And it came to pass that they did speak unto me again, saying: What meaneth this thing which our father saw in a dream? What meaneth the ^atree which he saw?

22 And I said unto them: It was a representation of the ^atree of life.

23 And they said unto me: What meaneth the ^arod of iron which our father saw, that led to the tree?

24 And I said unto them that it was the ^aword of God; and whoso would hearken unto the word of God, and would ^bhold fast unto it, they would never perish; neither could the ^ctemptations and the fiery ^ddarts of the ^eadversary overpower them unto blindness, to lead them away to destruction.

25 Wherefore, I, Nephi, did exhort them to give ^aheed unto the word of the Lord; yea, I did exhort them with all the energies of my soul, and with all the ^bfaculty which I possessed, that they would give heed to the word of God and remember to keep his commandments always in all things.

26 And they said unto me: What meaneth the ^ariver of water which our father saw?

27 And I said unto them that the ^awater which my father saw was ^bfilthiness; and so much was his mind swallowed up in other things that he beheld not the filthiness of the water.

28 And I said unto them that it was an awful ^agulf, which separated the wicked from the tree of life, and also from the saints of God.

29 And I said unto them that it was a representation of that awful ^ahell, which the angel said unto me was prepared for the wicked.

30 And I said unto them that our father also saw that the ^ajustice of God did also divide the wicked from the righteous; and the brightness thereof was like unto the brightness of a flaming ^bfire, which ascendeth up unto God forever and ever, and hath no end.

31 And they said unto me: Doth this thing mean the torment of the body in the days of ^aprobation, or doth it mean the final state of the soul after the ^bdeath of the temporal body, or doth it speak of the things which are temporal?

32 And it came to pass that I said unto them that it was a representation of things both temporal and spiritual; for the day should come that they must be judged of their ^aworks, yea, even the works which were done by the temporal body in their days of ^bprobation.

19a Isa. 42:22 (22–23);
  1 Ne. 19:15.
  TG Israel, Gathering of;
  Israel, Judah, People of.
20a 1 Ne. 19:23.
  b Isa. 40:9.
  c TG Israel, Restoration of.
  d 1 Ne. 16:5 (5, 24, 39).
21a 1 Ne. 8:10 (10–12).
22a 1 Ne. 11:4;
  Moses 3:9.
23a 1 Ne. 8:19 (19–24).
24a 1 Ne. 8:19.
  TG Gospel.

  b Prov. 4:13.
  c 1 Ne. 8:23.
  TG Temptation.
  d Eph. 6:16;
  D&C 3:8; 27:17.
  e TG Devil.
25a D&C 11:2; 32:4;
  84:43 (43–44).
  TG Scriptures, Study of.
  b W of M 1:18.
26a 1 Ne. 8:13.
27a 1 Ne. 12:16 (16–18).
  b TG Filthiness.
28a Luke 16:26;

  1 Ne. 12:18;
  2 Ne. 1:13.
29a 1 Ne. 8:32 (13–14, 32).
  TG Hell.
30a TG God, Justice of;
  Justice.
  b Num. 11:1 (1, 10);
  2 Ne. 26:6.
31a TG Probation.
  b Alma 40:11 (6–26).
32a TG Good Works.
  b TG Probation.

33 Wherefore, if they should ᵃdie in their wickedness they must be ᵇcast off also, as to the things which are spiritual, which are pertaining to righteousness; wherefore, they must be brought to stand before God, to be ᶜjudged of their ᵈworks; and if their works have been filthiness they must needs be ᵉfilthy; and if they be filthy it must needs be that they cannot ᶠdwell in the kingdom of God; if so, the kingdom of God must be filthy also.

34 But behold, I say unto you, the kingdom of God is not filthy, and there cannot any unclean thing enter into the kingdom of God; wherefore there must needs be a place of ᵃfilthiness prepared for that which is filthy.

35 And there is a place prepared, yea, even that ᵃawful ᵇhell of which I have spoken, and the ᶜdevil is the preparator of it; wherefore the final state of the souls of men is to dwell in the kingdom of God, or to be cast out because of that ᵈjustice of which I have spoken.

36 Wherefore, the wicked are rejected from the righteous, and also from that ᵃtree of life, whose fruit is most precious and most ᵇdesirable above all other fruits; yea, and it is the ᶜgreatest of all the ᵈgifts of God. And thus I spake unto my brethren. Amen.

CHAPTER 16

The wicked take the truth to be hard— Lehi's sons marry the daughters of Ishmael—The Liahona guides their course in the wilderness—Messages from the Lord are written on the Liahona from time to time—Ishmael dies; his family murmurs because of afflictions. About 600–592 B.C.

AND now it came to pass that after I, Nephi, had made an end of speaking to my brethren, behold they said unto me: Thou hast declared unto us hard things, more than we are able to bear.

2 And it came to pass that I said unto them that I knew that I had spoken ᵃhard things against the wicked, according to the truth; and the righteous have I justified, and testified that they should be lifted up at the last day; wherefore, the ᵇguilty taketh the ᶜtruth to be hard, for it ᵈcutteth them to the very center.

3 And now my brethren, if ye were righteous and were willing to hearken to the truth, and give heed unto it, that ye might ᵃwalk uprightly before God, then ye would not murmur because of the truth, and say: Thou speakest hard things against us.

4 And it came to pass that I, Nephi, did exhort my brethren, with all diligence, to keep the commandments of the Lord.

5 And it came to pass that they did ᵃhumble themselves before the Lord; insomuch that I had joy and great hopes of them, that they would walk in the paths of righteousness.

6 Now, all these things were said

33a Ezek. 18:26;
    Mosiah 15:26;
    Moro. 10:26.
  b Alma 12:16; 40:26.
  c TG Jesus Christ, Judge;
    Judgment, the Last.
  d Ps. 33:15 (13–15);
    3 Ne. 27:25 (23–27).
  e 2 Ne. 9:16;
    D&C 88:35.
  f Ps. 15:1 (1–5); 24:3 (3–4);
    Mosiah 15:23;
    Alma 11:37;
    D&C 76:62 (50–70);
    Moses 6:57 (55–59).

34a TG Filthiness.
35a 2 Ne. 9:19;
    Mosiah 26:27.
  b TG Hell.
  c 1 Ne. 14:9;
    D&C 1:35.
  d TG Justice.
36a Gen. 2:9;
    1 Ne. 8:11;
    2 Ne. 2:15.
  b 1 Ne. 8:12.
  c Hel. 5:8.
  d D&C 14:7.
    TG God, Gifts of.
16 2a Acts 7:54;

    2 Ne. 33:5;
    Enos 1:23;
    W of M 1:17.
    TG Chastening.
  b John 3:20 (19–21); 7:7;
    Hel. 13:24 (24–27).
  c Prov. 15:10;
    2 Ne. 1:26; 9:40.
  d Acts 5:33;
    Mosiah 13:7;
    Moses 6:37.
3a D&C 5:21.
    TG Walking with God.
5a 1 Ne. 15:20;
    16:24 (24, 39); 18:4.

and done as my father dwelt in a tent in the ªvalley which he called Lemuel.

7 And it came to pass that I, Nephi, took one of the ªdaughters of Ishmael to ᵇwife; and also, my brethren took of the ᶜdaughters of Ishmael to wife; and also ᵈZoram took the eldest daughter of Ishmael to wife.

8 And thus my father had fulfilled all the ªcommandments of the Lord which had been given unto him. And also, I, Nephi, had been blessed of the Lord exceedingly.

9 And it came to pass that the voice of the Lord spake unto my father by night, and commanded him that on the morrow he should take his ªjourney into the wilderness.

10 And it came to pass that as my father arose in the morning, and went forth to the tent door, to his great astonishment he beheld upon the ground a round ªball of curious workmanship; and it was of fine brass. And within the ball were two spindles; and the one ᵇpointed the way whither we should go into the wilderness.

11 And it came to pass that we did gather together whatsoever things we should carry into the wilderness, and all the remainder of our provisions which the Lord had given unto us; and we did take ªseed of every kind that we might carry into the wilderness.

12 And it came to pass that we did take our tents and depart into the wilderness, across the river Laman.

13 And it came to pass that we traveled for the space of four days, nearly a south-southeast direction, and we did pitch our tents again; and we did call the name of the place ªShazer.

14 And it came to pass that we did take our bows and our arrows, and go forth into the wilderness to slay food for our families; and after we had slain food for our families we did return again to our families in the wilderness, to the place of Shazer. And we did go forth again in the wilderness, following the same direction, keeping in the most fertile parts of the wilderness, which were in the borders near the ªRed Sea.

15 And it came to pass that we did travel for the space of many days, ªslaying food by the way, with our bows and our arrows and our stones and our slings.

16 And we did follow the ªdirections of the ball, which led us in the more fertile parts of the wilderness.

17 And after we had traveled for the space of many days, we did pitch our tents for the space of a time, that we might again rest ourselves and obtain food for our families.

18 And it came to pass that as I, Nephi, went forth to slay food, behold, I did break my bow, which was made of fine ªsteel; and after I did break my bow, behold, my brethren were angry with me because of the loss of my bow, for we did obtain no food.

19 And it came to pass that we did return without food to our families, and being much fatigued, because of their journeying, they did suffer much for the want of food.

20 And it came to pass that Laman and Lemuel and the sons of Ishmael did begin to murmur exceedingly, because of their sufferings and afflictions in the wilderness; and also my father began to murmur against the Lord his God; yea, and they were all exceedingly sorrowful,

6a 1 Ne. 2:14 (8, 14); 9:1.
7a 1 Ne. 7:1 (1, 19);
  18:19 (19–20).
 b TG Marriage, Marry.
 c 1 Ne. 7:6.
 d 1 Ne. 4:35;
  2 Ne. 5:6 (5–6).
8a 1 Ne. 3:18; 5:21; 7:2.

9a Omni 1:16.
10a 1 Ne. 16:16;
  Alma 37:38 (38–47).
 b Ex. 13:21.
11a 1 Ne. 8:1; 18:6;
  Ether 1:41; 2:3.
13a HEB twisting,
  intertwining.

14a 1 Ne. 2:5; D&C 17:1.
15a Alma 17:7.
16a 1 Ne. 16:10 (10, 16, 26);
  18:12 (12, 21);
  2 Ne. 5:12;
  Alma 37:38 (38–47);
  D&C 17:1.
18a 2 Sam. 22:35; Ps. 18:34.

even that they did ^amurmur against the Lord.

21 Now it came to pass that I, Nephi, having been afflicted with my brethren because of the loss of my bow, and their bows having lost their ^asprings, it began to be exceedingly difficult, yea, insomuch that we could obtain no food.

22 And it came to pass that I, Nephi, did speak much unto my brethren, because they had hardened their hearts again, even unto ^acomplaining against the Lord their God.

23 And it came to pass that I, Nephi, did ^amake out of wood a bow, and out of a straight stick, an arrow; wherefore, I did arm myself with a bow and an arrow, with a sling and with stones. And I said unto my ^bfather: Whither shall I go to obtain food?

24 And it came to pass that he did ^ainquire of the Lord, for they had ^bhumbled themselves because of my words; for I did say many things unto them in the energy of my soul.

25 And it came to pass that the voice of the Lord came unto my father; and he was truly ^achastened because of his murmuring against the Lord, insomuch that he was brought down into the depths of sorrow.

26 And it came to pass that the voice of the Lord said unto him: Look upon the ball, and behold the things which are written.

27 And it came to pass that when my father beheld the things which were ^awritten upon the ball, he did fear and tremble exceedingly, and also my brethren and the sons of Ishmael and our wives.

28 And it came to pass that I, Nephi, beheld the pointers which were in the ball, that they did work according to the ^afaith and diligence and heed which we did give unto them.

29 And there was also written upon them a new writing, which was plain to be read, which did give us ^aunderstanding concerning the ways of the Lord; and it was written and changed from time to time, according to the faith and diligence which we gave unto it. And thus we see that by ^bsmall means the Lord can bring about great things.

30 And it came to pass that I, Nephi, did go forth up into the top of the mountain, according to the ^adirections which were given upon the ball.

31 And it came to pass that I did slay wild ^abeasts, insomuch that I did obtain food for our families.

32 And it came to pass that I did return to our tents, bearing the beasts which I had slain; and now when they beheld that I had obtained ^afood, how great was their joy! And it came to pass that they did humble themselves before the Lord, and did give thanks unto him.

33 And it came to pass that we did again take our journey, traveling nearly the same course as in the beginning; and after we had traveled for the space of many days we did pitch our tents again, that we might tarry for the space of a time.

34 And it came to pass that ^aIshmael died, and was buried in the place which was called ^bNahom.

35 And it came to pass that the daughters of Ishmael did ^amourn exceedingly, because of the loss of

20a TG Murmuring.
21a Gen. 49:24.
22a Ex. 16:8;
   Num. 11:1 (1–2);
   D&C 29:19.
23a TG Initiative.
   b TG Honoring Father and Mother.
24a TG Guidance, Divine; Prayer.
   b 1 Ne. 15:20; 16:5.

25a Ether 2:14.
   TG Chastening; Repent.
27a TG Warn.
28a Alma 37:40.
   TG Faith.
29a TG Understanding.
   b 2 Kgs. 5:13;
   James 3:4;
   Alma 37:6 (6–8, 41);
   D&C 123:16.

30a TG Guidance, Divine.
31a Gen. 9:3.
32a 2 Ne. 1:24.
   TG Food; Thanksgiving.
34a 1 Ne. 7:2 (2–6, 19).
   b HEB probably "consolation," from verb *naham*, "be sorry, console oneself."
35a TG Mourning.

their father, and because of their [b]afflictions in the wilderness; and they did [c]murmur against my father, because he had brought them out of the land of Jerusalem, saying: Our father is dead; yea, and we have wandered much in the wilderness, and we have suffered much affliction, hunger, thirst, and fatigue; and after all these sufferings we must perish in the wilderness with hunger.

36 And thus they did murmur against my father, and also against me; and they were desirous to [a]return again to Jerusalem.

37 And Laman said unto Lemuel and also unto the sons of Ishmael: Behold, let us [a]slay our father, and also our brother Nephi, who has taken it upon him to be our [b]ruler and our teacher, who are his elder brethren.

38 Now, he says that the Lord has talked with him, and also that [a]angels have ministered unto him. But behold, we know that he lies unto us; and he tells us these things, and he worketh many things by his cunning arts, that he may deceive our eyes, thinking, perhaps, that he may lead us away into some strange wilderness; and after he has led us away, he has thought to make himself a king and a ruler over us, that he may do with us according to his will and pleasure. And after this manner did my brother Laman [b]stir up their hearts to [c]anger.

39 And it came to pass that the Lord was with us, yea, even the voice of the Lord came and did speak many words unto them, and did [a]chasten them exceedingly; and after they were chastened by the voice of the Lord they did turn away their anger, and did repent of their sins,

insomuch that the Lord did bless us again with food, that we did not perish.

CHAPTER 17

Nephi is commanded to build a ship—His brethren oppose him—He exhorts them by recounting the history of God's dealings with Israel—Nephi is filled with the power of God—His brethren are forbidden to touch him, lest they wither as a dried reed. About 592–591 B.C.

AND it came to pass that we did again take our journey in the wilderness; and we did travel nearly eastward from that time forth. And we did travel and [a]wade through much affliction in the wilderness; and our [b]women did bear children in the wilderness.

2 And so great were the [a]blessings of the Lord upon us, that while we did live upon [b]raw [c]meat in the wilderness, our women did give plenty of suck for their children, and were strong, yea, even like unto the men; and they began to bear their journeyings without murmurings.

3 And thus we see that the commandments of God must be fulfilled. And if it so be that the children of men keep the commandments of God he doth nourish them, and [a]strengthen them, and provide means whereby they can accomplish the thing which he has commanded them; wherefore, he did [b]provide means for us while we did sojourn in the wilderness.

4 And we did sojourn for the space of many years, yea, even eight years in the wilderness.

5 And we did come to the land which we called [a]Bountiful, because

---

35b TG Affliction.
  c TG Murmuring.
36a Num. 14:4 (1–5).
37a 1 Ne. 17:44; 2 Ne. 1:24.
  TG Murder.
  b Gen. 37:10 (9–11);
    Num. 16:13;
    1 Ne. 2:22; 18:10.
38a 1 Ne. 3:30 (30–31); 4:3.

  b TG Provoking.
  c TG Anger.
39a TG Chastening.
17 1a Ps. 69:2 (1–2, 14).
  b TG Woman.
2a TG Blessing.
  b 1 Ne. 17:12.
  c Ex. 16:13 (12–13);
    1 Ne. 18:6.

  TG Meat.
3a Ex. 1:19;
    Ezra 8:22 (22–23);
    Isa. 45:24;
    Mosiah 2:41;
    Alma 26:12.
    TG Strength.
  b Gen. 18:14; 1 Ne. 3:7.
5a Alma 22:29 (29–33).

of its much fruit and also wild honey; and all these things were prepared of the Lord that we might not perish. And we beheld the sea, which we called Irreantum, which, being interpreted, is many waters.

6 And it came to pass that we did pitch our tents by the seashore; and notwithstanding we had suffered many ªafflictions and much difficulty, yea, even so much that we cannot write them all, we were exceedingly rejoiced when we came to the seashore; and we called the place Bountiful, because of its much fruit.

7 And it came to pass that after I, Nephi, had been in the land of Bountiful for the space of many days, the voice of the Lord came unto me, saying: ªArise, and get thee into the mountain. And it came to pass that I arose and went up into the mountain, and cried unto the Lord.

8 And it came to pass that the Lord spake unto me, saying: Thou shalt ªconstruct a ship, after the ᵇmanner which I shall show thee, that I may carry thy people across these waters.

9 And I said: Lord, whither shall I go that I may find ore to molten, that I may make ªtools to construct the ship after the manner which thou hast shown unto me?

10 And it came to pass that the Lord told me whither I should go to find ore, that I might make tools.

11 And it came to pass that I, Nephi, did make a bellows wherewith to ªblow the fire, of the skins of beasts; and after I had made a bellows, that I might have wherewith to blow the fire, I did smite two stones together that I might make fire.

12 For the Lord had not hitherto suffered that we should make much fire, as we journeyed in the wilderness; for he said: I will make thy food become sweet, that ye ªcook it not;

13 And I will also be your ªlight in the wilderness; and I will prepare the way before you, if it so be that ye shall keep my commandments; wherefore, inasmuch as ye shall keep my commandments ye shall be led towards the ᵇpromised land; and ye shall ᶜknow that it is by me that ye are led.

14 Yea, and the Lord said also that: After ye have arrived in the promised land, ye shall ªknow that I, the Lord, am ᵇGod; and that I, the Lord, did ᶜdeliver you from destruction; yea, that I did bring you out of the land of Jerusalem.

15 Wherefore, I, Nephi, did strive to keep the ªcommandments of the Lord, and I did ᵇexhort my brethren to faithfulness and diligence.

16 And it came to pass that I did ªmake tools of the ore which I did molten out of the rock.

17 And when my brethren saw that I was about to ªbuild a ship, they began to ᵇmurmur against me, saying: Our brother is a fool, for he thinketh that he can build a ship; yea, and he also thinketh that he can cross these great waters.

18 And thus my brethren did ªcomplain against me, and were desirous that they might not labor, for they did not ᵇbelieve that I could build a ship; neither would they

6a 2 Ne. 4:20.
7a Ezek. 3:22 (22–27).
8a Gen. 6:14 (14–16).
  b Ex. 25:40;
    1 Chr. 28:12 (11–12, 19);
    1 Ne. 18:2.
9a Deut. 8:9;
    1 Kgs. 6:7;
    1 Chr. 22:3 (3, 14);
    Job 28:2;
    Isa. 44:12.
11a Isa. 54:16.
12a 1 Ne. 17:2.

13a Alma 5:37 (37–38);
    D&C 88:66.
  b 1 Ne. 2:20; 4:14;
    Jacob 2:12.
  c Ex. 6:7; 13:21.
    TG Guidance, Divine.
14a 2 Ne. 1:4.
    TG God, Knowledge
    about;
    Testimony.
  b D&C 5:2.
  c TG Deliver.
15a 1 Kgs. 2:3;

    Prov. 7:2.
  b Acts 14:22;
    Titus 2:15;
    Heb. 3:13.
16a TG Skill.
17a 1 Ne. 17:49 (8, 49–51);
    18:1 (1–6).
  b TG Murmuring.
18a 1 Ne. 3:28; 7:6 (6–19);
    18:10 (9–22).
  b TG Unbelief.

believe that I was instructed of the Lord.

19 And now it came to pass that I, Nephi, was exceedingly sorrowful because of the hardness of their hearts; and now when they saw that I began to be sorrowful they were glad in their hearts, insomuch that they did [a]rejoice over me, saying: We knew that ye could not construct a ship, for we knew that ye were lacking in judgment; wherefore, thou canst not accomplish so great a work.

20 And thou art like unto our father, led away by the foolish [a]imaginations of his heart; yea, he hath led us out of the land of Jerusalem, and we have wandered in the wilderness for these many years; and our women have toiled, being big with child; and they have borne children in the wilderness and suffered all things, save it were death; and it would have been better that they had died before they came out of Jerusalem than to have suffered these afflictions.

21 Behold, these many years we have suffered in the wilderness, which time we might have enjoyed our possessions and the land of our inheritance; yea, and we might have been happy.

22 And we know that the people who were in the land of Jerusalem were a [a]righteous people; for they kept the statutes and judgments of the Lord, and all his commandments, according to the law of Moses; wherefore, we know that they are a righteous people; and our father hath judged them, and hath led us away because we would hearken unto his words; yea, and our brother is like unto him. And after this manner of language did my brethren murmur and complain against us.

23 And it came to pass that I, Nephi, spake unto them, saying: Do ye believe that our fathers, who were the children of Israel, would have been led away out of the hands of the [a]Egyptians if they had not hearkened unto the words of the Lord?

24 Yea, do ye suppose that they would have been led out of bondage, if the Lord had not commanded Moses that he should [a]lead them out of bondage?

25 Now ye know that the children of Israel were in [a]bondage; and ye know that they were laden with [b]tasks, which were grievous to be borne; wherefore, ye know that it must needs be a good thing for them, that they should be [c]brought out of bondage.

26 Now ye know that [a]Moses was commanded of the Lord to do that great work; and ye know that by his [b]word the waters of the Red Sea were divided hither and thither, and they passed through on dry ground.

27 But ye know that the Egyptians were [a]drowned in the Red Sea, who were the armies of Pharaoh.

28 And ye also know that they were fed with [a]manna in the wilderness.

29 Yea, and ye also know that Moses, by his word according to the power of God which was in him, [a]smote the rock, and there came

---

19a TG Mocking; Persecution.
20a 1 Ne. 2:11; 5:4 (2–4).
22a 1 Ne. 1:19 (4, 13, 18–20).
23a Ex. 20:2; Ps. 80:8; Moses 1:26.
24a Ex. 3:10 (2–10); Hosea 12:13 (12–14); 1 Ne. 19:10; 2 Ne. 3:9; 25:20.
25a Gen. 15:13 (13–14); Mosiah 11:21; D&C 101:79.

TG Israel, Bondage of, in Egypt.
b Ex. 1:11 (10–11); 2:11; 1 Ne. 20:10.
c Ex. 5:1.
26a Josh. 24:6; Jer. 2:2; Acts 7:27 (22–39).
b Ex. 14:21 (19–31); Josh. 2:10; Neh. 9:11; 1 Ne. 4:2; Mosiah 7:19; Hel. 8:11; D&C 8:3; Moses 1:25.

TG Israel, Deliverance of.
27a Josh. 24:6.
28a Ex. 16:15 (4, 14–15, 35); Num. 11:7 (7–8); Deut. 8:3; Neh. 9:20; Hosea 13:6 (5–8); John 6:49; Mosiah 7:19.
29a Ex. 17:6; Num. 20:11; Deut. 8:15; Neh. 9:15; 1 Ne. 20:21; 2 Ne. 25:20.

forth water, that the children of Israel might quench their thirst.

30 And notwithstanding they being led, the Lord their God, their Redeemer, going before them, [a]leading them by day and giving light unto them by night, and doing all things for them which were [b]expedient for man to receive, they hardened their hearts and blinded their minds, and [c]reviled against Moses and against the true and living God.

31 And it came to pass that according to his word he did [a]destroy them; and according to his word he did [b]lead them; and according to his word he did do all things for them; and there was not any thing done save it were by his word.

32 And after they had crossed the river Jordan he did make them mighty unto the [a]driving out of the children of the land, yea, unto the scattering them to destruction.

33 And now, do ye suppose that the children of this land, who were in the land of promise, who were driven out by our fathers, do ye suppose that they were righteous? Behold, I say unto you, Nay.

34 Do ye suppose that our fathers would have been more choice than they if they had been righteous? I say unto you, Nay.

35 Behold, the Lord esteemeth all [a]flesh in one; he that is [b]righteous is [c]favored of God. But behold, this [d]people had rejected every word of God, and they were ripe in iniquity; and the fulness of the wrath of God was upon them; and the Lord did curse the land against them, and bless it unto our fathers; yea, he did curse it against them unto their destruction, and he did bless it unto our fathers unto their obtaining power over it.

36 Behold, the Lord hath created the [a]earth that it should be [b]inhabited; and he hath created his children that they should possess it.

37 And he [a]raiseth up a righteous nation, and destroyeth the nations of the wicked.

38 And he leadeth away the righteous into precious [a]lands, and the wicked he [b]destroyeth, and curseth the land unto them for their sakes.

39 He ruleth high in the heavens, for it is his throne, and this earth is his [a]footstool.

40 And he loveth those who will have him to be their God. Behold, he loved our [a]fathers, and he [b]covenanted with them, yea, even Abraham, [c]Isaac, and [d]Jacob; and he remembered the covenants which he had made; wherefore, he did bring them out of the land of [e]Egypt.

41 And he did straiten them in the wilderness with his rod; for they [a]hardened their hearts, even as ye have; and the Lord straitened them because of their iniquity. He sent

---

30a Ex. 13:18 (18, 20).
  b D&C 18:18;
     88:64 (64–65).
  c Ex. 32:8;
     Num. 14:11 (11–12);
     Ezek. 20:13 (13–16);
     D&C 84:24 (23–25).
31a Num. 26:65.
  b Ex. 15:13;
     1 Ne. 5:15;
     D&C 103:16 (16–18).
32a Ex. 34:11;
     Num. 33:52 (52–53);
     Josh. 11:6; 24:8.
35a Acts 10:15 (15, 34);
     Rom. 2:11;
     2 Ne. 26:33 (23–33).
  b Ps. 55:22;
     John 15:10;
     1 Ne. 22:17.

  c 1 Sam. 2:30;
     1 Kgs. 2:3;
     Ps. 97:10; 145:20 (1–21);
     Alma 13:4; 28:13;
     D&C 82:10 (8–10).
  d Gen. 15:16;
     Ex. 23:31 (28–31);
     Deut. 7:10;
     Josh. 2:24.
36a Gen. 1:28 (26–28);
     Jer. 27:5;
     Moses 1:29.
     TG Earth, Purpose of;
     Man, a Spirit Child of
     Heavenly Father;
     Man, Physical
     Creation of.
  b Isa. 45:18.
37a Ps. 1:6;
     Prov. 14:34;

     Isa. 45:1 (1–3);
     1 Ne. 4:13;
     Ether 2:10;
     D&C 98:32 (31–32);
     117:6.
38a TG Lands of Inheritance.
  b Lev. 20:22.
39a Isa. 66:1;
     Lam. 2:1;
     D&C 38:17;
     Abr. 2:7.
40a TG Israel, Origins of.
  b TG Abrahamic
     Covenant.
  c Gen. 21:12;
     D&C 27:10.
  d Gen. 28:4 (1–5).
  e Deut. 4:37 (37–38).
41a 2 Kgs. 17:7 (7–23).

fiery flying [b]serpents among them; and after they were bitten he prepared a way that they might be [c]healed; and the labor which they had to perform was to look; and because of the [d]simpleness of the way, or the easiness of it, there were many who perished.

42 And they did harden their hearts from time to time, and they did [a]revile against [b]Moses, and also against God; nevertheless, ye know that they were led forth by his matchless power into the land of promise.

43 And now, after all these things, the time has come that they have become wicked, yea, nearly unto ripeness; and I know not but they are at this day about to be [a]destroyed; for I know that the day must surely come that they must be destroyed, save a few only, who shall be led away into captivity.

44 Wherefore, the Lord [a]commanded my father that he should depart into the wilderness; and the Jews also sought to take away his life; yea, and [b]ye also have sought to take away his life; wherefore, ye are murderers in your hearts and ye are like unto them.

45 Ye are [a]swift to do iniquity but slow to remember the Lord your God. Ye have seen an [b]angel, and he spake unto you; yea, ye have heard his voice from time to time; and he hath spoken unto you in a still small voice, but ye were [c]past feeling, that ye could not feel his words; wherefore, he has spoken unto you like unto the voice of thunder, which did cause the earth to shake as if it were to divide asunder.

46 And ye also know that by the [a]power of his almighty word he can cause the earth that it shall pass away; yea, and ye know that by his word he can cause the rough places to be made smooth, and smooth places shall be broken up. O, then, why is it, that ye can be so hard in your hearts?

47 Behold, my soul is rent with anguish because of you, and my heart is pained; I fear lest ye shall be cast off forever. Behold, I am [a]full of the Spirit of God, insomuch that my frame has [b]no strength.

48 And now it came to pass that when I had spoken these words they were angry with me, and were desirous to throw me into the depths of the sea; and as they came forth to lay their hands upon me I spake unto them, saying: In the name of the Almighty God, I command you that ye [a]touch me not, for I am filled with the [b]power of God, even unto the consuming of my flesh; and whoso shall lay his hands upon me shall [c]wither even as a dried reed; and he shall be as naught before the power of God, for God shall smite him.

49 And it came to pass that I, Nephi, said unto them that they should murmur no more against their father; neither should they withhold their labor from me, for God had commanded me that I should [a]build a ship.

50 And I said unto them: [a]If God had commanded me to do all things I could do them. If he should command me that I should say unto this water, be thou earth, it should be earth; and if I should say it, it would be done.

51 And now, if the Lord has such great power, and has wrought so

---

41b Num. 21:6 (4–9);
   Deut. 8:15;
   Alma 33:19 (18–22).
   c Hosea 11:3;
   John 3:14;
   2 Ne. 25:20.
   d Alma 37:46 (44–47);
   Hel. 8:15.
42a Ex. 32:23;
   Num. 14:2 (1–12).
   TG Reviling.
   b D&C 84:23.

43a Hosea 7:13.
   TG Israel, Scattering of.
44a 1 Ne. 2:2 (1–2).
   b 1 Ne. 16:37.
45a Mosiah 13:29.
   b 1 Ne. 4:3.
   c Acts 17:27;
   Eph. 4:19;
   1 Ne. 2:14.
46a Hel. 12:10 (6–18).
47a Micah 3:8.
   b Dan. 10:8 (8, 17);

1 Ne. 1:7; 19:20.
48a Mosiah 13:3.
   b 2 Ne. 1:27 (26–27).
   TG God, Power of;
   Priesthood, Power of.
   c 1 Kgs. 13:4 (4–7);
   Moses 1:11; 6:47.
49a 1 Ne. 17:17; 18:1 (1–6).
50a Philip. 4:13;
   1 Ne. 3:7;
   D&C 24:13.

many miracles among the children of men, how is it that he cannot *a*instruct me, that I should build a ship?

52 And it came to pass that I, Nephi, said many things unto my brethren, insomuch that they were *a*confounded and could not contend against me; neither durst they lay their hands upon me nor touch me with their fingers, even for the space of many days. Now they durst not do this lest they should wither before me, so powerful was the *b*Spirit of God; and thus it had wrought upon them.

53 And it came to pass that the Lord said unto me: Stretch forth thine hand again unto thy brethren, and they shall not wither before thee, but I will *a*shock them, saith the Lord, and this will I do, that they may know that I am the Lord their God.

54 And it came to pass that I stretched forth my hand unto my brethren, and they did not wither before me; but the Lord did shake them, even according to the word which he had spoken.

55 And now, they said: We know of a surety that the Lord is *a*with thee, for we know that it is the power of the Lord that has shaken us. And they fell down before me, and were about to *b*worship me, but I would not suffer them, saying: I am thy brother, yea, even thy younger brother; wherefore, worship the Lord thy God, and honor thy father and thy mother, that thy *c*days may be long in the land which the Lord thy God shall give thee.

CHAPTER 18

The ship is finished—The births of Jacob and Joseph are mentioned—The *company embarks for the promised land—The sons of Ishmael and their wives join in revelry and rebellion—Nephi is bound, and the ship is driven back by a terrible tempest—Nephi is freed, and by his prayer the storm ceases—The people arrive in the promised land. About 591–589 B.C.*

AND it came to pass that they did *a*worship the Lord, and did go forth with me; and we did work timbers of curious *b*workmanship. And the Lord did show me from time to time after what manner I should work the timbers of the *c*ship.

2 Now I, Nephi, did not work the timbers after the manner which was learned by men, neither did I build the ship after the manner of men; but I did build it after the manner which the Lord had shown unto me; wherefore, it was not after the manner of men.

3 And I, Nephi, did go into the mount oft, and I did *a*pray oft unto the Lord; wherefore the Lord *b*showed unto me *c*great things.

4 And it came to pass that after I had finished the ship, according to the word of the Lord, my brethren beheld that it was good, and that the workmanship thereof was exceedingly fine; wherefore, they did *a*humble themselves again before the Lord.

5 And it came to pass that the voice of the Lord came unto my father, that we should arise and go down into the ship.

6 And it came to pass that on the morrow, after we had prepared all things, much fruits and *a*meat from the wilderness, and honey in abundance, and provisions according to that which the Lord had commanded us, we did go down into the ship, with all our loading and our

51 *a* Gen. 6:14 (14–16);
   1 Ne. 18:1.
52 *a* IE ashamed, overawed.
  b TG God, Spirit of.
53 *a* IE cause to shake or
   tremble; see vv. 54–55.
55 *a* Ex. 3:12;
   Alma 38:4.

  b Dan. 2:46;
   Acts 14:15 (11–15).
  c Ex. 20:12;
   Prov. 9:11;
   Mosiah 14:10;
   Hel. 7:24;
   D&C 5:33.
18 1 *a* 1 Ne. 17:55.

  b TG Art.
  c 1 Ne. 17:49 (8, 17, 49–51).
3 *a* Jer. 33:3.
  b TG Guidance, Divine.
  c 2 Ne. 1:24.
4 *a* 1 Ne. 16:5.
6 *a* 1 Ne. 17:2.

[b]seeds, and whatsoever thing we had brought with us, every one according to his age; wherefore, we did all go down into the [c]ship, with our wives and our children.

7 And now, my father had begat two sons in the wilderness; the elder was called [a]Jacob and the younger [b]Joseph.

8 And it came to pass after we had all gone down into the ship, and had taken with us our provisions and things which had been commanded us, we did put forth into the [a]sea and were driven forth before the wind towards the [b]promised land.

9 And after we had been [a]driven forth before the wind for the space of many days, behold, my brethren and the sons of Ishmael and also their wives began to make themselves merry, insomuch that they began to dance, and to sing, and to speak with much [b]rudeness, yea, even that they did forget by what power they had been brought thither; yea, they were lifted up unto exceeding rudeness.

10 And I, Nephi, began to fear exceedingly lest the Lord should be angry with us, and smite us because of our iniquity, that we should be swallowed up in the depths of the sea; wherefore, I, Nephi, began to speak to them with much soberness; but behold they were [a]angry with me, saying: We will not that our younger brother shall be a [b]ruler over us.

11 And it came to pass that Laman and Lemuel did take me and [a]bind me with cords, and they did treat me with much harshness; nevertheless, the Lord did suffer it that he might show forth his power, unto the fulfilling of his word which he had [b]spoken concerning the wicked.

12 And it came to pass that after they had bound me insomuch that I could not move, the [a]compass, which had been prepared of the Lord, did cease to work.

13 Wherefore, they knew not whither they should steer the ship, insomuch that there arose a great [a]storm, yea, a great and terrible tempest, and we were [b]driven back upon the waters for the space of three days; and they began to be frightened exceedingly lest they should be drowned in the sea; nevertheless they did not loose me.

14 And on the fourth day, which we had been driven back, the tempest began to be exceedingly sore.

15 And it came to pass that we were about to be swallowed up in the depths of the sea. And after we had been driven back upon the waters for the space of four days, my brethren began to [a]see that the judgments of God were upon them, and that they must perish save that they should repent of their iniquities; wherefore, they came unto me, and loosed the bands which were upon my wrists, and behold they had swollen exceedingly; and also mine ankles were much swollen, and great was the soreness thereof.

16 Nevertheless, I did look unto my God, and I did [a]praise him all the day long; and I did not murmur against the Lord because of mine afflictions.

17 Now my father, Lehi, had said many things unto them, and also unto the sons of [a]Ishmael; but, behold, they did breathe out much

6b 1 Ne. 8:1; 16:11.
   c Gen. 7:7.
7a 2 Ne. 2:1.
   b 2 Ne. 3:1.
8a Ps. 8:8;
   2 Ne. 10:20.
   b 1 Ne. 2:20; 5:5 (5, 22).
   TG Promised Lands.
9a Ether 6:5.
   b 2 Ne. 1:2.
   TG Rioting and Reveling.

10a 1 Ne. 17:18 (17–55);
    2 Ne. 4:13 (13–14).
   b Gen. 37:10 (9–11);
    1 Ne. 16:37 (37–38);
    2 Ne. 1:25 (25–27).
11a 1 Ne. 7:16 (16–20).
   b Ex. 23:7;
    Ps. 37:9 (8–13);
    Alma 14:11.
12a 1 Ne. 16:16 (10, 16, 26);
    2 Ne. 5:12;

    Alma 37:38 (38–47);
    D&C 17:1.
13a Jonah 1:4; Matt. 8:24.
   b Mosiah 1:17.
15a Hel. 12:3.
16a Ezra 3:11 (11–13);
    2 Ne. 9:49;
    Mosiah 2:20 (20–21);
    Alma 36:28;
    D&C 136:28.
17a 1 Ne. 7:4 (4–20).

threatenings against anyone that should speak for me; and my parents being *b*stricken in years, and having *c*suffered much grief because of their *d*children, they were brought down, yea, even upon their sick-beds.

18 Because of their grief and much sorrow, and the iniquity of my brethren, they were brought near even to be carried out of this time to meet their God; yea, their *a*grey hairs were about to be brought down to lie low in the dust; yea, even they were near to be cast with sorrow into a watery grave.

19 And Jacob and Joseph also, being young, having need of much nourishment, were grieved because of the afflictions of their mother; and also *a*my wife with her tears and prayers, and also my children, did not soften the hearts of my brethren that they would loose me.

20 And there was nothing save it were the power of God, which threatened them with destruction, could soften their *a*hearts; wherefore, when they saw that they were about to be swallowed up in the depths of the sea they repented of the thing which they had done, insomuch that they loosed me.

21 And it came to pass after they had loosed me, behold, I took the compass, and it did work whither I desired it. And it came to pass that I *a*prayed unto the Lord; and after I had prayed the winds did cease, and the storm did cease, and there was a great calm.

22 And it came to pass that I, Nephi, did guide the ship, that we sailed again towards the promised land.

23 And it came to pass that after we had sailed for the space of many days we did arrive at the *a*promised land; and we went forth upon the land, and did pitch our tents; and we did call it the promised land.

24 And it came to pass that we did begin to till the earth, and we began to plant seeds; yea, we did put all our *a*seeds into the earth, which we had brought from the land of Jerusalem. And it came to pass that they did grow exceedingly; wherefore, we were blessed in abundance.

25 And it came to pass that we did find upon the land of promise, as we journeyed in the wilderness, that there were *a*beasts in the forests of every kind, both the cow and the ox, and the ass and the horse, and the goat and the wild goat, and all manner of wild animals, which were for the use of men. And we did find all manner of *b*ore, both of *c*gold, and of silver, and of copper.

CHAPTER 19

Nephi makes plates of ore and records the history of his people—The God of Israel will come six hundred years from the time Lehi left Jerusalem—Nephi tells of His sufferings and crucifixion—The Jews will be despised and scattered until the latter days, when they will return unto the Lord. About 588–570 B.C.

AND it came to pass that the Lord commanded me, wherefore I did make plates of ore that I might engraven upon them the *a*record of my people. And upon the plates which I made I did *b*engraven the record of my *c*father, and also our journeyings in the wilderness, and the prophecies of my father; and also many of mine own prophecies have I engraven upon them.

2 And I knew not at the time when I made them that I should be

---

17*b* Gen. 24:1.
  c TG Suffering.
  d TG Family, Children,
     Duties of;
     Honoring Father and
     Mother.
18*a* Gen. 42:38.
19*a* 1 Ne. 7:19; 16:7.

20*a* TG Hardheartedness.
21*a* Jonah 1:6.
23*a* Mosiah 10:13.
     TG Promised Lands.
24*a* 1 Ne. 8:1.
25*a* Enos 1:21.
  b 2 Ne. 5:15 (14–16).
  c Deut. 33:16 (13–17).

19 1*a* TG Plate;
         Record Keeping.
     b TG Scribe.
     c 1 Ne. 1:17 (16–17);
        6:1 (1–3);
        Jacob 7:26 (26–27).

commanded of the Lord to make ^athese plates; wherefore, the record of my father, and the genealogy of his fathers, and the more part of all our proceedings in the wilderness are engraven upon those first plates of which I have spoken; wherefore, the things which transpired before I made ^bthese plates are, of a truth, more particularly made mention upon the first plates.

3 And after I had made these plates by way of commandment, I, Nephi, received a commandment that the ministry and the prophecies, the more plain and precious parts of them, should be written upon ^athese plates; and that the things which were written should be kept for the instruction of my people, who should possess the land, and also for other ^bwise purposes, which purposes are known unto the Lord.

4 Wherefore, I, Nephi, did make a record upon the ^aother plates, which gives an account, or which gives a greater account of the wars and contentions and destructions of my people. And this have I done, and commanded my people what they should do after I was gone; and that these plates should be handed down from one generation to another, or from one prophet to another, until further commandments of the Lord.

5 And an account of my ^amaking these plates shall be given hereafter; and then, behold, I proceed according to that which I have spoken; and this I do that the more sacred things may be ^bkept for the knowledge of my people.

6 Nevertheless, I do not ^awrite anything upon plates save it be that I think it be ^bsacred. And now, if I do err, even did they err of old; not that I would excuse myself because of other men, but because of the ^cweakness which is in me, according to the flesh, I would excuse myself.

7 For the things which some men esteem to be of great worth, both to the body and soul, others set at ^anaught and trample under their feet. Yea, even the very God of Israel do men ^btrample under their feet; I say, trample under their feet but I would speak in other words—they set him at naught, and ^chearken not to the voice of his counsels.

8 And behold he ^acometh, according to the words of the angel, in ^bsix hundred years from the time my father left Jerusalem.

9 And the world, because of their iniquity, shall judge him to be a thing of naught; wherefore they scourge him, and he suffereth it; and they smite him, and he suffereth it. Yea, they ^aspit upon him, and he suffereth it, because of his loving ^bkindness and his ^clong-suffering towards the children of men.

10 And the ^aGod of our fathers, who were ^bled out of Egypt, out of bondage, and also were preserved in the wilderness by him, yea, the

---

2a 2 Ne. 5:30;
    Jacob 3:14.
  b 1 Ne. 9:2 (1–5);
    Omni 1:1.
3a 1 Ne. 10:1;
    Jacob 1:1 (1–4);
    3:13 (13–14); 4:1 (1–4).
  b 1 Ne. 9:5 (4–5);
    W of M 1:7;
    D&C 3:19 (19–20);
    10:38 (1–51).
4a 1 Ne. 9:4 (2–5);
    2 Ne. 5:33.
5a 2 Ne. 5:30 (28–33).
  b TG Scriptures,
    Preservation of.
6a TG Scriptures,
    Writing of.

  b See title page of the
    Book of Mormon.
    TG Sacred.
  c Morm. 8:17 (13–17);
    Ether 12:23 (23–28).
7a Num. 15:31 (30–31);
    2 Ne. 33:2;
    Jacob 4:14;
    D&C 3:7 (4–13).
  b Ezek. 34:19;
    D&C 76:35.
    TG Blaspheme;
    Sacrilege.
  c TG Disobedience;
    Prophets, Rejection of.
8a TG Jesus Christ,
    Betrayal of; Jesus Christ,
    Birth of; Jesus Christ,

      Prophecies about.
  b 1 Ne. 2:4; 10:4 (4–11);
    2 Ne. 25:19.
9a Isa. 50:6 (5–6);
    Matt. 27:30.
  b TG Kindness.
  c TG Forbear.
10a 2 Ne. 10:3; 26:12;
    Mosiah 7:27;
    27:31 (30–31);
    Alma 11:39 (38–39);
    3 Ne. 11:14 (14–15).
  b Gen. 15:14 (13–14);
    Ex. 3:10 (2–10); 6:6;
    1 Ne. 5:15;
    17:24 (24, 31, 40);
    2 Ne. 25:20;
    D&C 136:22.

*c*God of Abraham, and of Isaac, and the God of Jacob, *d*yieldeth himself, according to the words of the angel, as a man, into the hands of *e*wicked men, to be *f*lifted up, according to the words of *g*Zenock, and to be *h*crucified, according to the words of Neum, and to be buried in a *i*sepulchre, according to the words of *j*Zenos, which he spake concerning the three days of *k*darkness, which should be a sign given of his death unto those who should inhabit the isles of the sea, more especially given unto those who are of the *l*house of Israel.

11 For thus spake the prophet: The Lord God surely shall *a*visit all the house of Israel at that day, some with his *b*voice, because of their righteousness, unto their great joy and salvation, and others with the *c*thunderings and the lightnings of his power, by tempest, by fire, and by *d*smoke, and *e*vapor of *f*darkness, and by the opening of the *g*earth, and by *h*mountains which shall be carried up.

12 And *a*all these things must surely come, saith the prophet *b*Zenos. And the *c*rocks of the earth must rend; and because of the *d*groanings of the earth, many of the kings of the isles of the sea shall be wrought upon by the Spirit of God, to exclaim: The God of nature suffers.

13 And as for those who are at Jerusalem, saith the prophet, they shall be *a*scourged by all people, because they crucify the God of Israel, and turn their hearts aside, rejecting signs and wonders, and the power and glory of the God of Israel.

14 And because they turn their hearts aside, saith the prophet, and have *a*despised the Holy One of Israel, they shall wander in the flesh, and perish, and become a *b*hiss and a *c*byword, and be *d*hated among all nations.

15 Nevertheless, when that day cometh, saith the prophet, that they *a*no more *b*turn aside their hearts against the Holy One of Israel, then will he remember the *c*covenants which he made to their fathers.

16 Yea, then will he remember the *a*isles of the sea; yea, and all the people who are of the house of Israel, will I *b*gather in, saith the Lord, according to the words of the prophet Zenos, from the four quarters of the earth.

17 Yea, and all the earth shall *a*see the salvation of the Lord, saith the

10*c* Gen. 32:9;
  Matt. 22:32;
  Mosiah 7:19;
  D&C 136:21.
  TG Jesus Christ, Jehovah.
 d TG Jesus Christ,
  Condescension of.
 e TG Jesus Christ,
  Betrayal of.
 f 3 Ne. 27:14; 28:6.
 g BD Lost books. See also
  Alma 33:15; 34:7;
  Hel. 8:20 (19–20);
  3 Ne. 10:16 (15–16).
 h 2 Ne. 6:9;
  Mosiah 3:9.
  TG Jesus Christ,
  Crucifixion of.
 i Matt. 27:60;
  Luke 23:53;
  2 Ne. 25:13.
 j Jacob 5:1; 6:1;
  Hel. 15:11.

 k 1 Ne. 12:4 (4–5);
  Hel. 14:27 (20, 27);
  3 Ne. 8:19 (3, 19–23); 10:9.
 l 3 Ne. 16:1 (1–4).
11*a* D&C 5:16.
 b 3 Ne. 9:1 (1–22).
 c Hel. 14:21 (20–27);
  3 Ne. 8:6 (5–23).
 d Gen. 19:28;
  Ex. 19:18;
  Morm. 8:29 (29–30);
  D&C 45:41 (40–41).
 e 1 Ne. 12:5.
 f Luke 23:44 (44–45).
  TG Darkness, Physical.
 g Num. 16:32;
  2 Ne. 26:5.
 h 3 Ne. 10:13 (13–14).
12*a* Hel. 14:28 (20–28);
  3 Ne. 10:11.
 b Jacob 5:1.
 c Matt. 27:51 (51–54).
 d Moses 7:56 (48–56).

13*a* Matt. 23:38 (37–39);
  Luke 23:28 (27–30).
14*a* Ps. 22:6;
  Mosiah 14:3 (3–6).
 b Jer. 24:9;
  3 Ne. 29:8 (8–9).
  TG Israel, Bondage of,
  in Other Lands.
 c Deut. 28:37;
  1 Kgs. 9:7 (6–7);
  Joel 2:17;
  3 Ne. 16:9 (8–9).
 d 2 Ne. 10:6; 25:15.
  TG Hate.
15*a* 1 Ne. 15:19;
  22:12 (11–12).
 b TG Israel, Restoration of.
 c TG Abrahamic Covenant.
16*a* 1 Ne. 22:4;
  2 Ne. 10:21.
 b Isa. 49:22 (20–22); 60:4.
  TG Israel, Gathering of.
17*a* Isa. 40:5 (4–5).

prophet; every nation, kindred, tongue and people shall be blessed.

18 And I, Nephi, have written these things unto my people, that perhaps I might persuade them that they would *a*remember the Lord their Redeemer.

19 Wherefore, I speak unto all the house of Israel, if it so be that they should obtain *a*these things.

20 For behold, I have workings in the spirit, which doth *a*weary me even that all my joints are weak, for those who are at Jerusalem; for had not the Lord been merciful, to show unto me concerning them, even as he had prophets of old, I should have perished also.

21 And he surely did show unto the *a*prophets of old all things *b*concerning them; and also he did show unto many concerning us; wherefore, it must needs be that we know concerning them for they are written upon the plates of brass.

22 Now it came to pass that I, Nephi, did teach my brethren these things; and it came to pass that I did read many things to them, which were engraven upon the *a*plates of brass, that they might know concerning the doings of the Lord in other lands, among people of old.

23 And I did read many things unto them which were written in the *a*books of Moses; but that I might more fully persuade them to believe in the Lord their Redeemer I did read unto them that which was written by the prophet *b*Isaiah; for I did *c*liken all scriptures unto us, that it might be for our *d*profit and learning.

24 Wherefore I spake unto them, saying: Hear ye the words of the prophet, ye who are a *a*remnant of the house of Israel, a *b*branch who have been broken off; *c*hear ye the words of the prophet, which were written unto all the house of Israel, and liken them unto yourselves, that ye may have hope as well as your brethren from whom ye have been broken off; for after this manner has the prophet written.

CHAPTER 20

The Lord reveals His purposes to Israel—Israel has been chosen in the furnace of affliction and is to go forth from Babylon—Compare Isaiah 48. About 588–570 B.C.

*a*HEARKEN and hear this, O house of Jacob, who are called by the name of Israel, and are come forth out of the waters of Judah, or out of the waters of *b*baptism, who *c*swear by the name of the Lord, and make mention of the God of Israel, yet they swear *d*not in truth nor in righteousness.

2 Nevertheless, they call themselves of the *a*holy city, but they do *b*not stay themselves upon the God of Israel, who is the Lord of Hosts; yea, the Lord of Hosts is his name.

3 Behold, I have declared the *a*former things from the beginning; and they went forth out of my mouth, and I showed them. I did show them suddenly.

4 And I did it because I knew that thou art obstinate, and thy *a*neck is an iron sinew, and thy brow brass;

5 And I have even from the beginning declared to thee; before it came

---

18*a* Mosiah 13:29.
19*a* Enos 1:16;
   Morm. 5:12; 7:9 (9–10).
   TG Israel, Restoration of.
20*a* Dan. 10:8 (8–12);
   1 Ne. 1:7;
   Alma 27:17;
   Moses 1:10 (9–10).
21*a* 2 Kgs. 17:13;
   Amos 3:7.
   TG Prophets, Mission of.
   b 3 Ne. 10:16 (16–17).
22*a* 1 Ne. 13:23; 22:1.

23*a* Ex. 17:14; 1 Ne. 5:11;
   Moses 1:41 (40–41).
   b Isa. 1:1;
   1 Ne. 15:20;
   2 Ne. 25:5 (2–6);
   3 Ne. 23:1.
   c TG Scriptures, Value of.
   d 2 Ne. 4:15.
24*a* 2 Kgs. 19:31.
   b Gen. 49:22 (22–26);
   1 Ne. 15:12 (12, 16);
   2 Ne. 3:5 (4–5).
   c TG Scriptures, Study of.

20 1*a* Isa. 48:1 (1–22).
   b TG Baptism;
   Conversion.
   c Deut. 6:13.
   d Jer. 4:2; 5:2.
2*a* Isa. 52:1.
   TG Jerusalem.
   b TG Hypocrisy;
   Prophets, Rejection of.
3*a* Isa. 42:9; 46:10 (9–10).
   TG God, Foreknowledge of.
4*a* TG Stiffnecked.

to pass I ^ashowed them thee; and I showed them for fear lest thou shouldst say—Mine idol hath done them, and my graven image, and my molten image hath commanded them.

6 Thou hast seen and heard all this; and will ye ^anot declare them? And that I have showed thee new things from this time, even hidden things, and thou didst not know them.

7 They are created now, and not from the beginning, even before the day when thou heardest them not they were declared unto thee, lest thou shouldst say—Behold I knew them.

8 Yea, and thou heardest not; yea, thou knewest not; yea, from that time thine ear was not opened; for I knew that thou wouldst deal very treacherously, and wast called a ^atransgressor from the womb.

9 Nevertheless, for my ^aname's sake will I defer mine anger, and for my praise will I refrain from thee, that I cut thee not off.

10 For, behold, I have refined thee, I have chosen thee in the furnace of ^aaffliction.

11 For mine own sake, yea, for mine own sake will I do this, for I will not suffer my ^aname to be polluted, and I will ^bnot give my glory unto another.

12 Hearken unto me, O Jacob, and Israel my called, for I am he; I am the ^afirst, and I am also the last.

13 Mine hand hath also ^alaid the foundation of the earth, and my right hand hath spanned the heavens. I ^bcall unto them and they stand up together.

14 All ye, assemble yourselves, and hear; who among them hath declared these things unto them? The Lord hath loved him; yea, and he will ^afulfil his word which he hath declared by them; and he will do his pleasure on ^bBabylon, and his arm shall come upon the Chaldeans.

15 Also, saith the Lord; I the Lord, yea, I have spoken; yea, I have called ^ahim to declare, I have brought him, and he shall make his way prosperous.

16 Come ye near unto me; I have not spoken in ^asecret; from the beginning, from the time that it was declared have I spoken; and the Lord God, and his ^bSpirit, hath sent me.

17 And thus saith the Lord, thy ^aRedeemer, the Holy One of Israel; I have sent him, the Lord thy God who teacheth thee to profit, who ^bleadeth thee by the way thou shouldst go, hath done it.

18 O that thou hadst hearkened to my ^acommandments—then had thy ^bpeace been as a river, and thy righteousness as the waves of the sea.

19 Thy ^aseed also had been as the sand; the offspring of thy bowels like the gravel thereof; his name should not have been cut off nor destroyed from before me.

20 ^aGo ye forth of Babylon, flee ye from the ^bChaldeans, with a voice of singing declare ye, tell this, utter to the end of the earth; say ye: The

5a TG God, Omniscience of; Idolatry.
6a 1 Cor. 9:16.
8a Ps. 58:3.
9a 1 Sam. 12:22; Ps. 23:3; 1 Jn. 2:12.
10a Ex. 1:11 (10–11); 1 Ne. 17:25. TG Affliction.
11a Jer. 44:26.
  b Isa. 42:8; Moses 4:1 (1–4).
12a Rev. 1:17; 22:13.

TG Jesus Christ, Firstborn; Jesus Christ, Jehovah.
13a Ps. 102:25. TG God the Father, Jehovah; Jesus Christ, Creator.
  b Ps. 148:8 (5–10).
14a 1 Kgs. 8:56; D&C 64:31; 76:3.
  b TG Babylon.
15a Isa. 45:1 (1–4).
16a Isa. 45:19.
  b TG God, Spirit of.

17a TG Jesus Christ, Jehovah.
  b TG Guidance, Divine.
18a Eccl. 8:5.
  b TG Israel, Blessings of; Peace of God.
19a Gen. 22:17 (15–19); Isa. 48:19 (18–22); Hosea 1:10.
20a Jer. 51:6 (6, 44–45); D&C 133:5 (5–14).
  b TG Israel, Bondage of, in Other Lands.

Lord hath redeemed his ^cservant Jacob.

21 And they ^athirsted not; he led them through the deserts; he caused the waters to flow out of the ^brock for them; he clave the rock also and the waters gushed out.

22 And notwithstanding he hath done all this, and greater also, there is no ^apeace, saith the Lord, unto the wicked.

CHAPTER 21

The Messiah will be a light to the Gentiles and will free the prisoners—Israel will be gathered with power in the last days— Kings will be their nursing fathers— Compare Isaiah 49. About 588–570 B.C.

^aAND again: Hearken, O ye house of Israel, all ye that are broken off and are driven out because of the wickedness of the pastors of my people; yea, all ye that are broken off, that are scattered abroad, who are of my people, O house of Israel. Listen, O ^bisles, unto me, and hearken ye people from ^cfar; the Lord hath called me from the womb; from the bowels of my mother hath he made mention of my name.

2 And he hath made my mouth like a sharp sword; in the shadow of his hand hath he hid me, and made me a polished shaft; in his quiver hath he hid me;

3 And said unto me: Thou art my ^aservant, O Israel, in whom I will be glorified.

4 Then I said, I have labored in ^avain, I have spent my strength for naught and in vain; surely my judgment is with the Lord, and my work with my God.

5 And now, saith the Lord—that ^aformed me from the womb that I should be his servant, to bring Jacob again to him—though Israel be not gathered, yet shall I be glorious in the eyes of the Lord, and my God shall be my ^bstrength.

6 And he said: It is a light thing that thou shouldst be my servant to raise up the ^atribes of Jacob, and to restore the preserved of Israel. I will also give thee for a ^blight to the ^cGentiles, that thou mayest be my salvation unto the ends of the earth.

7 Thus saith the Lord, the Redeemer of Israel, his Holy One, to him whom man despiseth, to him whom the nations abhorreth, to servant of rulers: Kings shall see and arise, princes also shall worship, because of the Lord that is faithful.

8 Thus saith the Lord: In an acceptable time have I heard thee, O isles of the sea, and in a day of salvation have I helped thee; and I will preserve thee, and give thee ^amy servant for a covenant of the people, to establish the earth, to cause to inherit the desolate heritages;

9 That thou mayest say to the ^aprisoners: Go forth; to them that sit in ^bdarkness: Show yourselves. They shall feed in the ways, and their ^cpastures shall be in all high places.

10 They shall not hunger nor thirst, neither shall the heat nor the sun smite them; for he that hath mercy on them shall lead them, even by the springs of water shall he guide them.

11 And I will make all my mountains a way, and my ^ahighways shall be exalted.

20c Isa. 44:1 (1–2, 21); 45:4.
21a Ps. 107:33 (33–37); Isa. 41:18 (17–20).
  b Ex. 17:6; Num. 20:11; 1 Ne. 17:29; 2 Ne. 25:20; D&C 133:26 (26–30).
22a Rom. 3:17. TG Peace of God.
21 1a Isa. 49:1 (1–26).
  b 1 Ne. 22:4; 2 Ne. 10:21 (20–22).
  c D&C 1:1.

3a Lev. 25:55; Isa. 41:8; D&C 93:46 (45–46).
4a Isa. 55:2 (1–2).
5a Isa. 44:24.
  b TG Strength.
6a TG Israel, Twelve Tribes of.
  b Ezek. 5:5; D&C 103:9 (8–9); Abr. 2:11 (6–11).
  c 3 Ne. 21:11. TG Israel, Mission of.

8a 2 Ne. 3:11 (6–15); 3 Ne. 21:11 (8–11); Morm. 8:16 (16, 25).
9a TG Salvation for the Dead; Spirits in Prison.
  b 2 Ne. 3:5.
  c Ezek. 34:14; 1 Ne. 22:25.
11a Isa. 62:10; D&C 133:27 (23–32). TG Jesus Christ, Second Coming.

49

12 And then, O house of Israel, behold, ^athese shall come from far; and lo, these from the north and from the west; and these from the land of Sinim.

13 ^aSing, O heavens; and be joyful, O earth; for the feet of those who are in the east shall be established; and ^bbreak forth into singing, O mountains; for they shall be smitten no more; for the Lord hath comforted his people, and will have mercy upon his ^cafflicted.

14 But, behold, Zion hath said: The Lord hath forsaken me, and my Lord hath forgotten me—but he will show that he hath not.

15 For can a ^awoman forget her sucking child, that she should not have ^bcompassion on the son of her womb? Yea, they may ^cforget, yet will I not forget thee, O house of Israel.

16 Behold, I have graven thee upon the ^apalms of my hands; thy walls are continually before me.

17 Thy children shall make haste against thy destroyers; and they that made thee ^awaste shall go forth of thee.

18 Lift up thine eyes round about and behold; all these ^agather themselves together, and they shall come to thee. And as I live, saith the Lord, thou shalt surely clothe thee with them all, as with an ornament, and bind them on even as a bride.

19 For thy waste and thy desolate places, and the land of thy destruction, shall even now be too narrow by reason of the inhabitants; and they that swallowed thee up shall be far away.

20 The children whom thou shalt have, after thou hast lost the first, shall ^aagain in thine ears say: The place is too strait for me; give place to me that I may dwell.

21 Then shalt thou say in thine heart: Who hath begotten me these, seeing I have lost my children, and am ^adesolate, a captive, and removing to and fro? And who hath brought up these? Behold, I was left alone; these, where have they been?

22 Thus saith the Lord God: Behold, I will lift up mine hand to the ^aGentiles, and set up my ^bstandard to the people; and they shall bring thy sons in their ^carms, and thy daughters shall be carried upon their shoulders.

23 And ^akings shall be thy ^bnursing fathers, and their queens thy nursing mothers; they shall bow down to thee with their face towards the earth, and lick up the dust of thy feet; and thou shalt know that I am the Lord; for they shall not be ashamed that ^cwait for me.

24 For shall the prey be taken from the mighty, or the ^alawful captives delivered?

25 But thus saith the Lord, even the captives of the mighty shall be taken away, and the prey of the terrible shall be delivered; for I will contend with him that contendeth with thee, and I will save thy children.

26 And I will ^afeed them that

12a Isa. 43:5 (5–7).
13a Isa. 44:23.
  b TG Earth, Renewal of.
  c 2 Sam. 22:28;
    Ps. 18:27;
    Isa. 49:13.
15a TG Woman.
  b Ps. 103:13.
  c 2 Kgs. 17:38;
    Isa. 41:17 (15–17);
    Alma 46:8;
    D&C 61:36; 133:2.
16a Zech. 13:6.
17a 3 Ne. 21:13 (12–20).
18a Micah 4:11 (11–13).

20a TG Israel, Gathering of.
21a Isa. 54:1; Gal. 4:27.
22a Isa. 66:19 (18–20).
    TG Israel, Mission of.
  b Isa. 11:12 (10–12); 18:3;
    Zech. 9:16.
  c 1 Ne. 22:8;
    2 Ne. 10:8 (8–9).
23a Isa. 60:16 (14–16).
  b 1 Ne. 22:6.
  c Gen. 49:18;
    Prov. 27:18;
    2 Ne. 6:13;
    D&C 98:2;
    133:11 (10–11, 45).

24a IE the covenant people
    of the Lord. See also
    v. 25.
    JST Isa. 49:25 reads: "But
    thus saith the Lord;
    even the captives of the
    mighty shall be taken
    away, and the prey of
    the terrible shall be
    delivered; *for the mighty
    God shall deliver his
    covenant people . . .*"
26a 1 Ne. 14:17 (15–17);
    22:13 (13–14);
    2 Ne. 6:14 (14–18).

oppress thee with their own flesh; they shall be drunken with their own blood as with sweet wine; and all flesh shall ^bknow that I, the Lord, am thy ^cSavior and thy Redeemer, the ^dMighty One of Jacob.

CHAPTER 22

Israel will be scattered upon all the face of the earth—The Gentiles will nurse and nourish Israel with the gospel in the last days—Israel will be gathered and saved, and the wicked will burn as stubble—The kingdom of the devil will be destroyed, and Satan will be bound. About 588–570 B.C.

AND now it came to pass that after I, Nephi, had read these things which were engraven upon the ^aplates of brass, my brethren came unto me and said unto me: What ^bmeaneth these things which ye have read? Behold, are they to be understood according to things which are ^cspiritual, which shall come to pass according to the spirit and not the flesh?

2 And I, Nephi, said unto them: Behold they were ^amanifest unto the prophet by the voice of the ^bSpirit; for by the Spirit are all things made known unto the ^cprophets, which shall come upon the children of men according to the flesh.

3 Wherefore, the things of which I have read are things pertaining to things both ^atemporal and spiritual; for it appears that the house of Israel, sooner or later, will be ^bscattered upon all the face of the earth, and also ^camong all nations.

4 And behold, there are many who are already lost from the knowledge of those who are at Jerusalem. Yea, the more part of all the ^atribes have been ^bled away; and they are ^cscattered to and fro upon the ^disles of the sea; and whither they are none of us knoweth, save that we know that they have been led away.

5 And since they have been led away, these things have been prophesied concerning them, and also concerning all those who shall hereafter be scattered and be confounded, because of the Holy One of Israel; for against him will they ^aharden their hearts; wherefore, they shall be scattered among all nations and shall be ^bhated of all men.

6 Nevertheless, after they shall be ^anursed by the ^bGentiles, and the Lord has lifted up his hand upon the Gentiles and set them up for a standard, and their ^cchildren have been carried in their arms, and their daughters have been carried upon their shoulders, behold these things of which are spoken are temporal; for thus are the covenants of the Lord with our fathers; and it meaneth us in the days to come, and also all our brethren who are of the house of Israel.

7 And it meaneth that the time cometh that after all the house of Israel have been scattered and confounded, that the Lord God will raise up a mighty nation among the ^aGentiles, yea, even upon the face of this land; and by them shall our seed be ^bscattered.

8 And after our seed is scattered the

26b Ezek. 26:6;
   Mosiah 11:22 (20–22).
 c TG Jesus Christ, Savior.
 d TG Jesus Christ,
   Jehovah.
22 1a 1 Ne. 19:22;
   2 Ne. 4:2.
 b TG Interpretation.
 c TG Spiritual.
2a 2 Pet. 1:21 (19–21).
 b TG God, Spirit of.
 c TG Prophecy.

3a D&C 29:34 (31–34).
 b 1 Ne. 10:12 (12–14);
   2 Ne. 25:15 (14–16).
   TG Israel, Scattering of.
 c TG Inspiration.
4a TG Israel, Ten Lost
   Tribes of.
 b 2 Ne. 10:22.
 c Ps. 107:4;
   Zech. 2:6.
 d Isa. 51:5;
   1 Ne. 21:1;

2 Ne. 10:8 (8, 20).
5a TG Hardheartedness.
 b Luke 23:28–31;
   1 Ne. 19:14.
6a 1 Ne. 21:23.
 b TG Gentiles.
 c 1 Ne. 15:13;
   2 Ne. 30:3 (1–7).
7a 3 Ne. 20:27.
 b Isa. 18:7;
   1 Ne. 13:14 (12–14);
   2 Ne. 1:11.

Lord God will proceed to do a ^amarvelous work among the ^bGentiles, which shall be of great ^cworth unto our seed; wherefore, it is likened unto their being nourished by the ^dGentiles and being carried in their arms and upon their shoulders.

9 And it shall also be of ^aworth unto the Gentiles; and not only unto the Gentiles but ^bunto all the ^chouse of Israel, unto the making known of the ^dcovenants of the Father of heaven unto Abraham, saying: In thy ^eseed shall all the kindreds of the earth be ^fblessed.

10 And I would, my brethren, that ye should know that all the kindreds of the earth cannot be blessed unless he shall make ^abare his arm in the eyes of the nations.

11 Wherefore, the Lord God will proceed to make bare his arm in the eyes of all the ^anations, in bringing about his covenants and his gospel unto those who are of the house of Israel.

12 Wherefore, he will ^abring them again out of ^bcaptivity, and they shall be ^cgathered together to the lands of their ^dinheritance; and they shall be ^ebrought out of obscurity and out of ^fdarkness; and they shall know that the ^gLord is

their ^hSavior and their Redeemer, the ⁱMighty One of Israel.

13 And the blood of that great and ^aabominable church, which is the whore of all the earth, shall turn upon their own heads; for they shall ^bwar among themselves, and the sword of their ^cown hands shall fall upon their own heads, and they shall be drunken with their own blood.

14 And every ^anation which shall war against thee, O house of Israel, shall be turned one against another, and they shall ^bfall into the pit which they digged to ensnare the people of the Lord. And all that ^cfight against Zion shall be destroyed, and that great whore, who hath perverted the right ways of the Lord, yea, that great and abominable church, shall tumble to the ^ddust and great shall be the fall of it.

15 For behold, saith the prophet, the time cometh speedily that Satan shall have no more power over the hearts of the children of men; for the day soon cometh that all the proud and they who do wickedly shall be as ^astubble; and the day cometh that they must be ^bburned.

16 For the time soon cometh that the fulness of the ^awrath of God shall be poured out upon all the children

8 a Isa. 29:14;
  1 Ne. 14:7;
  2 Ne. 27:26.
  TG Restoration of the
   Gospel.
 b 2 Ne. 10:10;
  3 Ne. 16:6 (4–7);
  Morm. 5:19.
 c 1 Ne. 15:14 (13–18);
  Jacob 3:6;
  3 Ne. 5:23 (21–26);
  21:7 (4–29).
 d TG Mission of Latter-day
  Saints.
9 a 1 Ne. 14:5 (1–5);
  2 Ne. 28:2.
 b 1 Ne. 15:13 (13–17);
  2 Ne. 30:3 (1–7).
 c 2 Ne. 29:14 (13–14).
 d Deut. 4:31.
 e TG Abrahamic Covenant;
  Seed of Abraham.
 f Gen. 12:2;
  3 Ne. 20:25 (25, 27).

10 a Isa. 52:10.
11 a TG Israel, Mission of.
12 a Ps. 80:19 (17–19);
  D&C 35:25.
 b 1 Ne. 21:25 (24–25).
 c TG Israel, Gathering of.
 d TG Lands of Inheritance.
 e TG Israel, Restoration of.
 f TG Darkness, Spiritual.
 g 1 Ne. 19:15;
  2 Ne. 6:11 (10–15).
 h TG Jesus Christ,
  Prophecies about;
  Jesus Christ, Savior.
 i TG Jesus Christ, Jehovah.
13 a Rev. 17:16 (16–17).
  TG Devil, Church of.
 b 1 Ne. 14:16 (3, 15–17);
  2 Ne. 6:15.
  TG War.
 c 1 Ne. 21:26 (24–26).
14 a Luke 21:10.
 b Ps. 7:15;
  Prov. 26:27; 28:10;

  Isa. 60:12;
  Zech. 12:9;
  1 Ne. 14:3;
  2 Ne. 28:8;
  D&C 109:25.
 c 2 Ne. 10:13; 27:3 (2–3);
  Morm. 8:41 (40–41);
  D&C 136:36.
  TG Protection, Divine.
 d Isa. 25:12.
15 a Isa. 5:23–24;
  Nahum 1:10;
  Mal. 4:1;
  2 Ne. 15:24; 26:6 (4–6);
  D&C 64:24 (23–24);
  133:64.
 b Ps. 21:9 (8–10);
  3 Ne. 25:1;
  D&C 29:9.
  TG Earth, Cleansing of.
16 a 1 Ne. 14:17;
  3 Ne. 20:20 (19–21).

of men; for he will not suffer that the wicked shall destroy the righteous.

17 Wherefore, he will ^apreserve the ^brighteous by his power, even if it so be that the fulness of his wrath must come, and the righteous be preserved, even unto the destruction of their enemies by fire. Wherefore, the righteous need not fear; for thus saith the prophet, they shall be saved, even if it so be as by fire.

18 Behold, my brethren, I say unto you, that these things must shortly come; yea, even blood, and fire, and vapor of smoke must come; and it must needs be upon the face of this earth; and it cometh unto men according to the flesh if it so be that they will harden their hearts against the Holy One of Israel.

19 For behold, the righteous shall not perish; for the time surely must come that all they who fight against Zion shall be cut off.

20 And the Lord will surely ^aprepare a way for his people, unto the fulfilling of the words of Moses, which he spake, saying: A ^bprophet shall the Lord your God raise up unto you, like unto me; him shall ye hear in all things whatsoever he shall say unto you. And it shall come to pass that all those who will not hear that prophet shall be ^ccut off from among the people.

21 And now I, Nephi, declare unto you, that this ^aprophet of whom Moses spake was the Holy One of Israel; wherefore, he shall execute ^bjudgment in righteousness.

22 And the righteous need not fear, for they are those who shall not be confounded. But it is the kingdom of the devil, which shall be built up among the children of men, which kingdom is established among them which are in the flesh—

23 For the time speedily shall come that all ^achurches which are built up to get gain, and all those who are built up to get power over the flesh, and those who are built up to become ^bpopular in the eyes of the world, and those who seek the lusts of the flesh and the things of the world, and to do all manner of iniquity; yea, in fine, all those who belong to the kingdom of the ^cdevil are they who need fear, and tremble, and ^dquake; they are those who must be brought low in the dust; they are those who must be ^econsumed as stubble; and this is according to the words of the prophet.

24 And the time cometh speedily that the righteous must be led up as ^acalves of the stall, and the Holy One of Israel must reign in dominion, and might, and power, and great ^bglory.

25 And he ^agathereth his children from the four quarters of the earth; and he numbereth his ^bsheep, and they know him; and there shall be one fold and one shepherd; and he shall feed his sheep, and in him they shall find ^cpasture.

26 And because of the ^arighteousness of his people, ^bSatan has no power; wherefore, he cannot be loosed for the space of ^cmany years; for he hath no power over the hearts

---

17a 2 Ne. 30:10;
      3 Ne. 22:13 (13–17);
      Moses 7:61.
      TG Protection, Divine.
   b Ps. 55:22;
      1 Ne. 17:35 (33–38).
20a TG Millennium,
      Preparing a People for.
   b John 4:19; 7:40.
   c D&C 133:63.
21a Deut. 18:15 (15–19);
      Acts 3:22 (20–23);
      1 Ne. 10:4; 3 Ne. 20:23;
      Moses 1:6.
      TG Jesus Christ,

Prophecies about.
   b Ps. 98:9;
      Moses 6:57.
      TG Jesus Christ, Judge.
23a 1 Ne. 14:10 (9–10);
      2 Ne. 26:20.
      TG Covet; Priestcraft.
   b Luke 6:26; Alma 1:3.
   c 1 Ne. 13:6.
   d 2 Ne. 28:19.
   e Zeph. 1:2 (2–3);
      2 Ne. 26:6.
24a Amos 6:4; Mal. 4:2;
      3 Ne. 25:2.
   b TG Jesus Christ, Glory of.

25a Isa. 43:6 (5–7);
      Eph. 1:10.
      TG Israel, Gathering of.
   b TG Jesus Christ, Good
      Shepherd; Sheep;
      Shepherd.
   c 1 Ne. 21:9.
26a TG Millennium;
      Righteousness.
   b Rev. 20:2;
      Alma 48:17 (16–17);
      D&C 43:31; 45:55; 88:110;
      101:28.
      TG Devil.
   c Jacob 5:76.

of the people, for they dwell in righteousness, and the Holy One of Israel ^dreigneth.

27 And now behold, I, Nephi, say unto you that all these ^athings must come according to the flesh.

28 But, behold, all nations, kindreds, tongues, and people shall dwell safely in the Holy One of Israel if it so be that they will ^arepent.

29 And now I, Nephi, make an end; for I durst not speak further as yet concerning these things.

30 Wherefore, my brethren, I would that ye should consider that the things which have been written upon the ^aplates of brass are true; and they testify that a man must be obedient to the commandments of God.

31 Wherefore, ye need not suppose that I and my father are the only ones that have testified, and also taught them. Wherefore, if ye shall be obedient to the ^acommandments, and endure to the end, ye shall be saved at the last day. And thus it is. Amen.

THE SECOND BOOK OF NEPHI

An account of the death of Lehi. Nephi's brethren rebel against him. The Lord warns Nephi to depart into the wilderness. His journeyings in the wilderness, and so forth.

CHAPTER 1

Lehi prophesies of a land of liberty—His seed will be scattered and smitten if they reject the Holy One of Israel—He exhorts his sons to put on the armor of righteousness. About 588–570 B.C.

AND now it came to pass that after I, Nephi, had made an end of teaching my brethren, our ^afather, Lehi, also spake many things unto them, and rehearsed unto them, how great things the Lord had done for them in bringing them out of the land of Jerusalem.

2 And he spake unto them concerning their ^arebellions upon the waters, and the mercies of God in sparing their lives, that they were not swallowed up in the sea.

3 And he also spake unto them concerning the land of promise, which they had obtained—how ^amerciful the Lord had been in ^bwarning us that we should flee out of the land of Jerusalem.

4 For, behold, said he, I have ^aseen a ^bvision, in which I know that ^cJerusalem is ^ddestroyed; and had we remained in Jerusalem we should also have ^eperished.

5 But, said he, notwithstanding our afflictions, we have obtained a ^aland of promise, a land which is ^bchoice above all other lands; a land which the Lord God hath ^ccovenanted

---

26*d* TG Jesus Christ, Millennial Reign.
27*a* IE these things pertain to this mortal world.
28*a* TG Forgive; Repent.
30*a* 1 Ne. 19:22; 2 Ne. 4:2.
31*a* Matt. 19:17. TG Commandments of God.

[2 NEPHI]
1 1*a* TG Patriarch.
2*a* Isa. 65:2 (1–5); 1 Ne. 18:9 (9–20); Alma 18:38.
3*a* Gen. 19:16.
  b TG Warn.
4*a* 1 Ne. 17:14.
  b TG Vision.

c Jer. 26:18 (17–19); 1 Ne. 1:4 (4–18); Hel. 8:20. TG Jerusalem.
d Jer. 44:2.
e Alma 9:22.
5*a* TG Promised Lands.
  b Ether 2:10 (7–12).
  c TG Vow.

with me should be a land for the inheritance of my seed. Yea, the Lord hath ^dcovenanted this land unto me, and to my children forever, and also all those who should be ^eled out of other countries by the hand of the Lord.

6 Wherefore, I, Lehi, prophesy according to the workings of the Spirit which is in me, that there shall ^anone come into this land save they shall be brought by the hand of the Lord.

7 Wherefore, this ^aland is consecrated unto him whom he shall bring. And if it so be that they shall serve him according to the commandments which he hath given, it shall be a land of ^bliberty unto them; wherefore, they shall never be brought down into captivity; if so, it shall be because of iniquity; for if iniquity shall abound ^ccursed shall be the land for their sakes, but unto the righteous it shall be blessed forever.

8 And behold, it is wisdom that this land should be ^akept as yet from the knowledge of other ^bnations; for behold, many nations would overrun the land, that there would be no place for an inheritance.

9 Wherefore, I, Lehi, have obtained a ^apromise, that ^binasmuch as those whom the Lord God shall bring out of the land of Jerusalem shall keep his commandments, they shall ^cprosper upon the face of this land; and they shall be kept from all other nations, that they may possess this land unto themselves. And if it so be that they shall ^dkeep his commandments they shall be blessed upon the face of this land, and there shall

be none to molest them, nor to take away the land of their ^einheritance; and they shall dwell safely forever.

10 But behold, when the time cometh that they shall dwindle in ^aunbelief, after they have received so great blessings from the hand of the Lord—having a knowledge of the creation of the earth, and all men, knowing the great and marvelous works of the Lord from the creation of the world; having power given them to do all things by faith; having all the commandments from the beginning, and having been brought by his infinite goodness into this precious land of promise—behold, I say, if the day shall come that they will reject the Holy One of Israel, the true ^bMessiah, their Redeemer and their God, behold, the judgments of him that is ^cjust shall rest upon them.

11 Yea, he will bring ^aother nations unto them, and he will give unto them power, and he will take away from them the lands of their possessions, and he will cause them to be ^bscattered and smitten.

12 Yea, as one generation passeth to another there shall be ^abloodsheds, and great visitations among them; wherefore, my sons, I would that ye would remember; yea, I would that ye would hearken unto my words.

13 O that ye would awake; awake from a deep ^asleep, yea, even from the sleep of ^bhell, and shake off the awful ^cchains by which ye are bound, which are the chains which bind the children of men, that they are carried away captive down to the eternal ^dgulf of misery and woe.

5d TG Covenants.
  e Ezra 8:22.
6a 2 Ne. 10:22.
7a Mosiah 29:32;
    Alma 46:10 (10–28, 34).
  b 2 Ne. 10:11.
    TG Liberty.
  c Alma 45:16 (10–14, 16);
    Morm. 1:17;
    Ether 2:11 (8–12).
8a 3 Ne. 5:20.
  b TG Nations.

9a Jacob 1:5.
  b 2 Ne. 4:4;
    Alma 9:13.
  c Deut. 29:9; 30:9.
  d TG Obedience.
  e TG Inheritance.
10a TG Unbelief.
  b TG Jesus Christ, Messiah.
  c TG Justice.
11a 1 Ne. 13:14 (12–20);
    Morm. 5:19 (19–20).
  b 1 Ne. 22:7.

12a Morm. 1:11 (11–19);
    4:1 (1–23);
    D&C 87:6 (1–6).
13a TG Sleep.
  b TG Damnation.
  c Isa. 58:6;
    Alma 12:11 (9–11).
    TG Bondage, Spiritual.
  d 1 Ne. 12:18;
    15:28 (28–30);
    Alma 26:20 (19–20);
    Hel. 3:29.

14 Awake! and arise from the dust, and hear the words of a trembling ªparent, whose limbs ye must soon lay down in the cold and silent ᵇgrave, from whence no traveler can ᶜreturn; a few more ᵈdays and I go the ᵉway of all the earth.

15 But behold, the Lord hath ªredeemed my soul from hell; I have beheld his ᵇglory, and I am encircled about eternally in the ᶜarms of his ᵈlove.

16 And I desire that ye should remember to observe the ªstatutes and the judgments of the Lord; behold, this hath been the anxiety of my soul from the beginning.

17 My heart hath been weighed down with sorrow from time to time, for I have feared, lest for the hardness of your hearts the Lord your God should come out in the fulness of his ªwrath upon you, that ye be ᵇcut off and destroyed forever;

18 Or, that a ªcursing should come upon you for the space of ᵇmany generations; and ye are visited by sword, and by famine, and are hated, and are led according to the will and captivity of the ᶜdevil.

19 O my sons, that these things might not come upon you, but that ye might be a choice and a ªfavored people of the Lord. But behold, his will be done; for his ᵇways are righteousness forever.

20 And he hath said that: ªInas-much as ye shall keep my ᵇcommandments ye shall ᶜprosper in the land; but inasmuch as ye will not keep my commandments ye shall be cut off from my presence.

21 And now that my soul might have joy in you, and that my heart might leave this world with gladness because of you, that I might not be brought down with grief and sorrow to the grave, arise from the dust, my sons, and be ªmen, and be determined in ᵇone mind and in one heart, united in all things, that ye may not come down into captivity;

22 That ye may not be ªcursed with a sore cursing; and also, that ye may not incur the displeasure of a ᵇjust God upon you, unto the destruction, yea, the eternal destruction of both soul and body.

23 Awake, my sons; put on the armor of ªrighteousness. Shake off the ᵇchains with which ye are bound, and come forth out of obscurity, and arise from the dust.

24 Rebel no more against your brother, whose views have been ªglorious, and who hath kept the commandments from the time that we left Jerusalem; and who hath been an instrument in the hands of God, in bringing us forth into the land of promise; for were it not for him, we must have perished with ᵇhunger in the wilderness; nevertheless, ye sought to ᶜtake away his

14a TG Family, Love within.
  b TG Death.
  c Job 10:21.
  d Gen. 47:29 (28–29);
    Jacob 1:9.
  e Josh. 23:14;
    1 Kgs. 2:2.
15a Alma 36:28.
    TG Jesus Christ,
    Atonement through.
  b Ex. 24:16;
    Lev. 9:6 (6, 23);
    Ether 12:6 (6–18).
    TG Jesus Christ,
    Glory of.
  c Isa. 59:16; Jacob 6:5;
    Alma 5:33;
    3 Ne. 9:14.
  d Rom. 8:39.
    TG God, Love of.

16a Deut. 4:6 (5–8);
    Ezek. 20:11;
    2 Ne. 5:10 (10–11).
17a 1 Ne. 2:23;
    2 Ne. 5:21 (21–24);
    Alma 3:6 (6–19).
    TG God, Indignation of.
  b Gen. 6:13;
    1 Ne. 17:31;
    Mosiah 12:8;
    3 Ne. 9:9.
18a TG Curse.
  b 1 Ne. 12:21 (20–23).
  c Rev. 12:9 (7–9);
    Moses 1:12.
    TG Devil.
19a TG Peculiar People.
  b Hosea 14:9.
20a Jarom 1:9; Omni 1:6;
    Mosiah 1:7;

Alma 9:13 (13–14);
    36:30; 37:13;
    3 Ne. 5:22.
  b Lev. 26:3 (3–14);
    Joel 2:25 (23–26);
    Amos 5:4 (4–8);
    Mosiah 26:30.
  c Ps. 67:6;
    Prov. 22:4 (4–5);
    Mosiah 2:24 (21–25).
21a 1 Sam. 4:9; 1 Kgs. 2:2.
  b Moses 7:18.
22a TG Curse.
  b D&C 3:4.
    TG Justice.
23a TG Righteousness.
  b TG Bondage, Spiritual.
24a 1 Ne. 18:3.
  b 1 Ne. 16:32.
  c 1 Ne. 16:37.

life; yea, and he hath suffered much sorrow because of you.

25 And I exceedingly fear and tremble because of you, lest he shall suffer again; for behold, ye have [a]accused him that he sought power and [b]authority over you; but I know that he hath not sought for power nor authority over you, but he hath sought the glory of God, and your own eternal welfare.

26 And ye have murmured because he hath been plain unto you. Ye say that he hath used [a]sharpness; ye say that he hath been angry with you; but behold, his [b]sharpness was the sharpness of the power of the word of God, which was in him; and that which ye call anger was the truth, according to that which is in God, which he could not restrain, manifesting boldly concerning your iniquities.

27 And it must needs be that the [a]power of God must be with him, even unto his commanding you that ye must obey. But behold, it was not he, but it was the [b]Spirit of the Lord which was in him, which [c]opened his mouth to utterance that he could not shut it.

28 And now my son, Laman, and also Lemuel and Sam, and also my sons who are the sons of Ishmael, behold, if ye will hearken unto the voice of Nephi ye shall not perish. And if ye will hearken unto him I leave unto you a [a]blessing, yea, even my first blessing.

29 But if ye will not hearken unto him I take away my [a]first blessing, yea, even my blessing, and it shall rest upon him.

30 And now, Zoram, I speak unto you: Behold, thou art the [a]servant of Laban; nevertheless, thou hast been brought out of the land of Jerusalem, and I know that thou art a true [b]friend unto my son, Nephi, forever.

31 Wherefore, because thou hast been faithful thy seed shall be blessed [a]with his seed, that they dwell in prosperity long upon the face of this land; and nothing, save it shall be iniquity among them, shall harm or disturb their prosperity upon the face of this land forever.

32 Wherefore, if ye shall keep the commandments of the Lord, the Lord hath consecrated this land for the security of thy seed with the seed of my son.

CHAPTER 2

Redemption comes through the Holy Messiah—Freedom of choice (agency) is essential to existence and progression—Adam fell that men might be—Men are free to choose liberty and eternal life. About 588–570 B.C.

AND now, Jacob, I speak unto you: Thou art my [a]firstborn in the days of my tribulation in the wilderness. And behold, in thy childhood thou hast suffered afflictions and much sorrow, because of the rudeness of thy brethren.

2 Nevertheless, Jacob, my firstborn in the wilderness, thou knowest the greatness of God; and he shall consecrate thine [a]afflictions for thy gain.

3 Wherefore, thy soul shall be blessed, and thou shalt dwell safely with thy brother, Nephi; and thy days shall be [a]spent in the service of thy God. Wherefore, I know that thou art redeemed, because of the righteousness of thy Redeemer; for thou hast [b]beheld that in the [c]fulness

25a 1 Ne. 15:8 (8–11);
  Mosiah 10:14.
  b Gen. 37:10 (9–11);
  1 Ne. 2:22.
26a Prov. 15:10;
  1 Ne. 16:2.
  b W of M 1:17;
  Moro. 9:4;
  D&C 121:43 (41–43).

27a 1 Ne. 17:48.
  b D&C 121:43.
  c D&C 33:8.
28a TG Birthright.
29a Gen. 49:3 (3–4);
  D&C 68:17;
  Abr. 1:3.
30a 1 Ne. 4:20 (20, 35).
  b TG Friendship.

31a 2 Ne. 5:6.
2 1a 1 Ne. 18:7 (7, 19).
  2a Micah 4:13;
  2 Ne. 32:9.
  TG Affliction.
  3a Enos 1:1.
  b 2 Ne. 11:3.
  c TG Fulness.

of time he cometh to bring salvation unto men.

4 And thou hast ^abeheld in thy youth his glory; wherefore, thou art blessed even as they unto whom he shall minister in the flesh; for the Spirit is the same, yesterday, today, and forever. And the way is prepared from the fall of man, and ^bsalvation is ^cfree.

5 And men are instructed sufficiently that they ^aknow good from evil. And the ^blaw is given unto men. And by the law no flesh is ^cjustified; or, by the law men are ^dcut off. Yea, by the temporal law they were cut off; and also, by the spiritual law they perish from that which is good, and become miserable forever.

6 Wherefore, ^aredemption cometh in and through the ^bHoly ^cMessiah; for he is full of ^dgrace and truth.

7 Behold, he offereth himself a ^asacrifice for sin, to answer the ends of the law, unto all those who have a broken heart and a contrite spirit; and unto ^bnone else can the ^cends of the law be answered.

8 Wherefore, how great the importance to make these things known unto the inhabitants of the earth, that they may know that there is no flesh that can dwell in the presence of God, ^asave it be through the merits, and mercy, and grace of the Holy Messiah, who ^blayeth down his life according to the flesh, and taketh it again by the power of the Spirit, that he may bring to pass the ^cresurrection of the dead, being the first that should rise.

9 Wherefore, he is the firstfruits unto God, inasmuch as he shall make ^aintercession for all the children of men; and they that believe in him shall be saved.

10 And because of the intercession for ^aall, all men come unto God; wherefore, they stand in the presence of him, to be ^bjudged of him according to the truth and ^choliness which is in him. Wherefore, the ends of the law which the Holy One hath given, unto the inflicting of the ^dpunishment which is affixed, which punishment that is affixed is in opposition to that of the happiness which is affixed, to answer the ends of the ^eatonement—

11 For it must needs be, that there is an ^aopposition in all things. If not so, my firstborn in the wilderness, righteousness could not be brought to pass, neither wickedness, neither holiness nor misery, neither good nor bad. Wherefore, all things must needs be a compound in one;

4a 2 Ne. 11:3;
   Jacob 7:5.
   TG Jesus Christ,
   Appearances,
   Antemortal.
 b Jude 1:3.
 c TG Grace.
5a Moro. 7:16.
 b Gal. 2:16; 3:2;
   Mosiah 13:28 (27–28).
 c Rom. 3:20 (20–24); 7:5;
   2 Ne. 25:23;
   Alma 42:14 (12–16).
   TG Justification.
 d Lev. 7:20 (20–21);
   1 Ne. 10:6;
   2 Ne. 9:6 (6–38);
   Alma 11:42 (40–45);
   12:16 (16, 24, 36);
   42:7 (6–11);
   Hel. 14:16 (15–18).
6a 1 Ne. 10:6;
   2 Ne. 25:20;

Mosiah 16:5 (4–5);
   Alma 12:22 (22–25).
   TG Jesus Christ,
   Redeemer; Redemption.
 b TG Holiness.
 c TG Jesus Christ, Messiah.
 d John 1:17 (14, 17);
   Alma 13:9; Moses 1:6.
   TG Grace.
7a TG Jesus Christ,
   Atonement through;
   Sacrifice; Self-Sacrifice.
 b 1 Sam. 2:2 (1–10).
 c Rom. 10:4.
8a 2 Ne. 25:20; 31:21;
   Mosiah 4:8; 5:8;
   Alma 21:9; 38:9.
 b TG Jesus Christ,
   Prophecies about.
 c 1 Cor. 15:20;
   Mosiah 13:35;
   Alma 7:12; 12:25 (24–25);
   42:23.

TG Jesus Christ,
   Resurrection.
9a Isa. 53:12 (1–12);
   Mosiah 14:12; 15:8;
   Moro. 7:28 (27–28).
   TG Jesus Christ,
   Mission of.
10a Ps. 65:2.
   TG Jesus Christ,
   Redeemer.
 b TG Jesus Christ, Judge.
 c TG Holiness.
 d TG Punish.
 e 2 Ne. 9:26 (7, 21–22, 26);
   Alma 22:14; 33:22;
   34:9 (8–16).
   TG Jesus Christ,
   Atonement through.
11a Job 2:10; Matt. 5:45;
   D&C 29:39; 122:7 (5–9);
   Moses 6:55.
   TG Adversity; Agency;
   Mortality; Opposition.

wherefore, if it should be one body it must needs remain as dead, having no life neither death, nor corruption nor incorruption, happiness nor misery, neither sense nor insensibility.

12 Wherefore, it must needs have been created for a thing of naught; wherefore there would have been no *purpose in the end of its creation. Wherefore, this thing must needs destroy the wisdom of God and his eternal purposes, and also the power, and the mercy, and the *justice of God.

13 And if ye shall say there is *no law, ye shall also say there is no sin. If ye shall say there is no sin, ye shall also say there is no righteousness. And if there be no righteousness there be no happiness. And if there be no righteousness nor happiness there be no punishment nor misery. And if these things are not *there is no God. And if there is no God we are not, neither the earth; for there could have been no creation of things, neither to act nor to be acted upon; wherefore, all things must have vanished away.

14 And now, my sons, I speak unto you these things for your profit and *learning; for there is a God, and he hath *created all things, both the heavens and the earth, and all things that in them are, both things to act and things to be *acted upon.

15 And to bring about his eternal *purposes in the end of man, after he had *created our first parents, and the beasts of the field and the *fowls of the air, and in fine, all things which are created, it must needs be that there was an opposition; even the *forbidden *fruit in *opposition to the *tree of life; one being sweet and the other bitter.

16 Wherefore, the Lord God gave unto man that he should *act for himself. Wherefore, man could not *act for himself save it should be that he was *enticed by the one or the other.

17 And I, Lehi, according to the things which I have read, must needs suppose that an *angel of God, according to that which is written, had *fallen from heaven; wherefore, he became a *devil, having sought that which was evil before God.

18 And because he had fallen from heaven, and had become miserable forever, he *sought also the misery of all mankind. Wherefore, he said unto Eve, yea, even that old serpent, who is the devil, who is the father of all *lies, wherefore he said: Partake of the forbidden fruit, and ye shall not die, but ye shall be as God, *knowing good and evil.

19 And after Adam and Eve had *partaken of the forbidden fruit they were driven out of the garden of *Eden, to till the earth.

20 And they have brought forth

12a D&C 88:25.
   TG Earth, Purpose of.
  b TG God, Justice of.
13a Rom. 4:15; 5:13;
   2 Ne. 9:25; 11:7.
  b Alma 42:13.
14a TG Learn.
  b TG Creation;
   God, Creator;
   Jesus Christ, Creator.
  c D&C 93:30.
15a Isa. 45:18 (17–18);
   Matt. 5:48;
   Rom. 8:17 (14–21);
   Eph. 3:11 (7–12);
   Alma 42:26;
   D&C 29:43 (42–44);
   Moses 1:31, 39.
   TG Earth, Purpose of.
  b TG Man, Physical

Creation of.
  c Gen. 1:20.
  d Gen. 2:17 (16–17);
   Moses 3:17.
  e Gen. 3:6;
   Mosiah 3:26;
   Alma 12:22 (21–23).
  f TG Opposition.
  g Gen. 2:9;
   1 Ne. 15:36 (22, 28, 36);
   Alma 12:26 (21, 23, 26);
   32:40.
16a Alma 12:31.
   TG Initiative.
  b 2 Ne. 10:23.
   TG Agency.
  c D&C 29:39 (39–40).
17a TG Council in Heaven.
  b Isa. 14:12;
   2 Ne. 9:8;

Moses 4:3 (3–4);
   Abr. 3:28 (27–28).
   TG Sons of Perdition.
  c TG Adversary; Devil;
   Lucifer; Satan.
18a Luke 22:31;
   Rev. 13:7;
   2 Ne. 28:20 (19–23);
   3 Ne. 18:18;
   D&C 10:22 (22–27);
   50:3; 76:29.
  b 2 Ne. 28:8; Moses 4:4.
  c Gen. 3:5;
   Mosiah 16:3;
   Alma 29:5;
   Moro. 7:16 (15–19).
19a Gen. 2:17 (16–17);
   Alma 12:31.
   TG Fall of Man.
  b TG Eden.

children; yea, even the ᵃfamily of all the earth.

21 And the days of the children of ᵃmen were prolonged, according to the ᵇwill of God, that they might ᶜrepent while in the flesh; wherefore, their state became a state of ᵈprobation, and their time was lengthened, according to the commandments which the Lord God gave unto the children of men. For he gave commandment that all men must repent; for he showed unto all men that they were ᵉlost, because of the transgression of their parents.

22 And now, behold, if Adam had not transgressed he would not have fallen, but he would have remained in the garden of Eden. And all things which were created must have remained in the same state in which they were after they were created; and they must have remained forever, and had no end.

23 And they would have had no ᵃchildren; wherefore they would have remained in a state of innocence, having no ᵇjoy, for they knew no misery; doing no good, for they knew no ᶜsin.

24 But behold, all things have been done in the wisdom of him who ᵃknoweth all things.

25 ᵃAdam ᵇfell that men might be; and men ᶜare, that they might have ᵈjoy.

26 And the ᵃMessiah cometh in the fulness of time, that he may ᵇredeem the children of men from the fall. And because that they are ᶜredeemed from the fall they have become ᵈfree forever, knowing good from evil; to act for themselves and not to be acted upon, save it be by the punishment of the ᵉlaw at the great and last day, according to the commandments which God hath given.

27 Wherefore, men are ᵃfree according to the ᵇflesh; and ᶜall things are ᵈgiven them which are expedient unto man. And they are free to ᵉchoose ᶠliberty and eternal ᵍlife, through the great Mediator of all men, or to choose captivity and death, according to the captivity and power of the devil; for he seeketh that all men might be ʰmiserable like unto himself.

28 And now, my sons, I would that ye should look to the great ᵃMediator, and hearken unto his great commandments; and be faithful unto his words, and choose eternal life, according to the will of his Holy Spirit;

29 And not choose eternal death, according to the will of the flesh and the ᵃevil which is therein, which giveth the spirit of the devil power to ᵇcaptivate, to bring you down to ᶜhell, that he may reign over you in his own kingdom.

30 I have spoken these few words unto you all, my sons, in the last days of my probation; and I have

20a 1 Cor. 15:45 (45–48); D&C 27:11; 138:38; Moses 1:34. TG Adam.
21a Job 14:1; Alma 12:24; Moses 4:23 (22–25). b TG God, Will of. c Alma 34:32. TG Repent. d TG Mortality; Probation. e Jacob 7:12.
23a Gen. 3:16; Moses 5:11. TG Family; Marriage, Motherhood. b TG Joy. c TG Sin.
24a TG God, Foreknowledge of; God, Intelligence of; God, Omniscience of.
25a TG Adam. b Moses 6:48. TG Fall of Man. c TG Mortality. d Moses 5:10. TG Joy; Man, Potential to Become like Heavenly Father.
26a TG Jesus Christ, Messiah. b TG Salvation, Plan of. c TG Redemption. d Gal. 5:1; Alma 41:7; 42:27; Hel. 14:30. e TG God, Law of.
27a Gal. 5:1; Hel. 14:30 (29–30); Moses 6:56.
b TG Mortality. c 2 Ne. 26:24; Jacob 5:41; Alma 26:37. d Alma 29:8. TG Talents. e TG Initiative; Opposition. f TG Liberty. g Deut. 30:15. h D&C 10:22.
28a TG Jesus Christ, Mediator.
29a TG Evil; Sin. b Rom. 6:14 (14–18); 1 Ne. 14:7; Alma 12:11 (9–11). TG Bondage, Spiritual. c TG Hell.

chosen the good part, according to the words of the prophet. And I have none other object save it be the everlasting ªwelfare of your souls. Amen.

CHAPTER 3

Joseph in Egypt saw the Nephites in vision—He prophesied of Joseph Smith, the latter-day seer; of Moses, who would deliver Israel; and of the coming forth of the Book of Mormon. About 588–570 B.C.

AND now I speak unto you, Joseph, my ªlast-born. Thou wast born in the wilderness of mine afflictions; yea, in the days of my greatest sorrow did thy mother bear thee.

2 And may the Lord consecrate also unto thee this ªland, which is a most precious land, for thine inheritance and the inheritance of thy seed with thy brethren, for thy security forever, if it so be that ye shall keep the commandments of the Holy One of Israel.

3 And now, Joseph, my last-born, whom I have brought out of the wilderness of mine afflictions, may the Lord bless thee forever, for thy ªseed shall not utterly be ᵇdestroyed.

4 For behold, thou art the fruit of my loins; and I am a descendant of ªJoseph who was carried ᵇcaptive into Egypt. And great were the ᶜcovenants of the Lord which he made unto Joseph.

5 Wherefore, Joseph truly ªsaw our day. And he obtained a ᵇpromise of the Lord, that out of the fruit of his loins the Lord God would raise up a ᶜrighteous ᵈbranch unto the house of Israel; not the Messiah, but a branch which was to be broken off, nevertheless, to be remembered in the covenants of the Lord that the Messiah should be made ᵉmanifest unto them in the latter days, in the spirit of power, unto the bringing of them out of ᶠdarkness unto light—yea, out of hidden darkness and out of captivity unto freedom.

6 For Joseph truly testified, saying: A ªseer shall the Lord my God raise up, who shall be a choice seer unto the fruit of my ᵇloins.

7 Yea, Joseph truly said: Thus saith the Lord unto me: A choice ªseer will I ᵇraise up out of the fruit of thy loins; and he shall be esteemed highly among the fruit of thy loins. And unto him will I give commandment that he shall do a work for the fruit of thy loins, his brethren, which shall be of great worth unto them, even to the bringing of them to the ᶜknowledge of the covenants which I have made with thy fathers.

8 And I will give unto him a commandment that he shall do ªnone other work, save the work which I shall command him. And I will make him great in mine eyes; for he shall do my work.

9 And he shall be great like unto ªMoses, whom I have said I would raise up unto you, to ᵇdeliver my ᶜpeople, O house of Israel.

10 And ªMoses will I raise up, to deliver thy people out of the land of Egypt.

11 But a ªseer will I raise up out

---

30 a ᴛɢ Family, Children, Responsibilities toward.
3 1 a 1 Ne. 18:7 (7, 19).
2 a 1 Ne. 2:20.
  ᴛɢ Promised Lands.
3 a Gen. 45:7; 1 Ne. 13:30.
  b Amos 9:8;
    2 Ne. 9:53; 25:21.
4 a Gen. 39:2; 45:4;
    49:22 (22–26);
    Ps. 77:15;
    1 Ne. 5:14 (14–16).
  b Gen. 37:36 (29–36).
  c Amos 5:15.
5 a ᴊsᴛ Gen. 50:24–38 (Bible Appendix);

2 Ne. 3:22; 4:2 (1–32).
  b ᴛɢ Promise.
  c Jacob 2:25.
  d Gen. 45:7 (5–7);
    49:22 (22–26);
    1 Ne. 15:12 (12, 16); 19:24;
    2 Ne. 14:2.
  ᴛɢ Vineyard of the Lord.
  e 2 Ne. 6:14;
    D&C 3:18 (16–20).
  f Isa. 42:16;
    1 Jn. 2:8;
    1 Ne. 21:9.
6 a 3 Ne. 21:11 (8–11);
    Morm. 8:16 (16, 25);
    Ether 3:28 (21–28).

ᴛɢ Seer.
  b D&C 132:30.
7 a ᴛɢ Joseph Smith.
  b ᴛɢ Millennium,
    Preparing a People for.
  c ᴛɢ Book of Mormon.
8 a D&C 24:9 (8–9).
9 a Moses 1:41.
  b Ex. 3:10 (7–10);
    1 Ne. 17:24.
  c 2 Ne. 29:14.
10 a ᴛɢ Foreordination.
11 a 1 Ne. 21:8;
    3 Ne. 21:11 (8–11);
    Morm. 8:16 (16, 25).
  ᴛɢ Prophets, Mission of.

of the fruit of thy loins; and unto him will I give *b*power to *c*bring forth my word unto the seed of thy loins—and not to the bringing forth my word only, saith the Lord, but to the convincing them of my word, which shall have already gone forth among them.

12 Wherefore, the fruit of thy loins shall *a*write; and the fruit of the loins of *b*Judah shall *c*write; and that which shall be written by the fruit of thy loins, and also that which shall be written by the fruit of the loins of Judah, shall grow together, unto the *d*confounding of *e*false doctrines and laying down of contentions, and establishing *f*peace among the fruit of thy loins, and *g*bringing them to the *h*knowledge of their fathers in the latter days, and also to the knowledge of my covenants, saith the Lord.

13 And out of weakness he shall be made strong, in that day when my work shall commence among all my people, unto the restoring thee, O house of Israel, saith the Lord.

14 And thus prophesied Joseph, saying: Behold, that seer will the Lord bless; and they that seek to destroy him shall be confounded; for this promise, which I have obtained of the Lord, of the fruit of my loins, shall be fulfilled. Behold, I am sure of the fulfilling of this promise;

15 And his *a*name shall be called after me; and it shall be after the *b*name of his father. And he shall be *c*like unto me; for the thing, which the Lord shall bring forth by his hand,

by the power of the Lord shall bring *d*my people unto *e*salvation.

16 Yea, thus prophesied Joseph: I am sure of this thing, even as I am sure of the promise of Moses; for the Lord hath said unto me, I will *a*preserve thy seed forever.

17 And the Lord hath said: I will raise up a Moses; and I will give power unto him in a rod; and I will give judgment unto him in writing. Yet I will not loose his tongue, that he shall speak much, for I will not make him mighty in speaking. But I will *a*write unto him my law, by the finger of mine own hand; and I will make a *b*spokesman for him.

18 And the Lord said unto me also: I will raise up unto the fruit of thy loins; and I will make for him a spokesman. And I, behold, I will give unto him that he shall write the writing of the fruit of thy loins, unto the fruit of thy loins; and the spokesman of thy loins shall declare it.

19 And the words which he shall write shall be the words which are expedient in my wisdom should go forth unto the *a*fruit of thy loins. And it shall be as if the fruit of thy loins had cried unto them *b*from the dust; for I know their faith.

20 And they shall *a*cry from the *b*dust; yea, even repentance unto their brethren, even after many generations have gone by them. And it shall come to pass that their cry shall go, even according to the simpleness of their words.

21 Because of their faith their *a*words shall proceed forth out of

11*b* D&C 5:4 (3–4).
  c TG Scriptures to Come
     Forth.
12*a* TG Book of Mormon.
  b 1 Ne. 13:23 (23–29);
     2 Ne. 29:12.
  c TG Scriptures,
     Preservation of;
     Scriptures, Writing of.
  d Ezek. 37:17 (15–20);
     1 Ne. 13:39 (38–41);
     2 Ne. 29:8; 33:10 (10–11).
  e TG False Doctrine.
  f TG Peacemakers.

  g Moro. 1:4.
  h 1 Ne. 15:14;
     2 Ne. 30:5;
     3 Ne. 5:23;
     Morm. 7:9 (1, 5, 9–10).
15*a* D&C 18:8.
  b JS—H 1:3.
  c D&C 28:2.
  d Enos 1:13 (12–18);
     Alma 37:19 (1–20).
  e TG Scriptures, Value of.
16*a* Gen. 45:7 (1–8);
     D&C 107:42.
17*a* Deut. 10:2 (2, 4);

     Moses 2:1.
     TG Scriptures,
        Writing of.
  b Ex. 4:16 (14–16).
19*a* D&C 28:8.
  b Isa. 29:4;
     2 Ne. 27:13;
     33:13 (13–15);
     Morm. 9:30;
     Moro. 10:27.
20*a* 2 Ne. 26:16;
     Morm. 8:23 (23, 26).
  b TG Book of Mormon.
21*a* 2 Ne. 29:2.

my mouth unto their brethren who are the fruit of thy loins; and the weakness of their words will I make strong in their faith, unto the remembering of my covenant which I made unto thy fathers.

22 And now, behold, my son Joseph, after this manner did my father of old *prophesy.

23 Wherefore, because of this covenant thou art *blessed; for thy seed shall not be destroyed, for they shall *hearken unto the words of the book.

24 And there shall rise up *one mighty among them, who shall do much good, both in word and in deed, being an instrument in the hands of God, with exceeding faith, to work mighty wonders, and do that thing which is great in the sight of God, unto the bringing to pass much *restoration unto the house of Israel, and unto the seed of thy brethren.

25 And now, blessed art thou, Joseph. Behold, thou art little; wherefore hearken unto the words of thy brother, Nephi, and it shall be done unto thee even according to the words which I have spoken. Remember the words of thy dying father. Amen.

CHAPTER 4

Lehi counsels and blesses his posterity—He dies and is buried—Nephi glories in the goodness of God—Nephi puts his trust in the Lord forever. About 588–570 B.C.

AND now, I, Nephi, speak concerning the prophecies of which my father hath spoken, concerning *Joseph, who was carried into Egypt.

2 For behold, he truly prophesied concerning all his seed. And the *prophecies which he wrote, there are not many greater. And he prophesied concerning us, and our future generations; and they are written upon the *plates of brass.

3 Wherefore, after my father had made an end of speaking concerning the prophecies of Joseph, he called the children of Laman, his sons, and his daughters, and said unto them: Behold, my sons, and my daughters, who are the sons and the daughters of my *firstborn, I would that ye should give ear unto my words.

4 For the Lord God hath said that: *Inasmuch as ye shall keep my commandments ye shall prosper in the land; and inasmuch as ye will not keep my commandments ye shall be cut off from my presence.

5 But behold, my sons and my daughters, I cannot go down to my grave save I should leave a *blessing upon you; for behold, I know that if ye are *brought up in the *way ye should go ye will not depart from it.

6 Wherefore, if ye are *cursed, behold, I leave my blessing upon you, that the *cursing may be taken from you and be answered upon the *heads of your parents.

7 Wherefore, because of my blessing the Lord God will *not suffer that ye shall perish; wherefore, he will be *merciful unto you and unto your seed forever.

8 And it came to pass that after my father had made an end of speaking to the sons and daughters of Laman, he caused the sons and daughters of Lemuel to be brought before him.

9 And he spake unto them, saying:

22a 2 Ne. 3:5.
23a TG Birthright.
  b TG Obedience.
24a TG Joseph Smith.
  b TG Dispensations;
  Israel, Restoration of;
  Restoration of the
  Gospel.
4 1a Gen. 39:2.
2a 2 Ne. 3:5.
  b 1 Ne. 22:30;

2 Ne. 5:12.
3a TG Firstborn.
4a 2 Ne. 1:9;
  Alma 9:13.
5a TG Family, Patriarchal;
  Patriarchal Blessings.
  b TG Family, Children,
  Responsibilities
  toward.
c Prov. 22:6.
6a 1 Ne. 2:23.

b TG Curse.
c D&C 68:25 (25–29).
7a 1 Ne. 22:7 (7–8);
  2 Ne. 10:3 (3–6);
  Jacob 1:5.
  TG Book of Mormon.
  b 1 Ne. 13:31;
  2 Ne. 10:18 (18–19);
  Jacob 3:6 (5–9);
  Hel. 15:12 (10–17);
  Morm. 5:20 (20–21).

Behold, my sons and my daughters, who are the sons and the daughters of my second son; behold I leave unto you the same blessing which I left unto the sons and daughters of Laman; wherefore, thou shalt not utterly be destroyed; but in the end thy seed shall be blessed.

10 And it came to pass that when my father had made an end of speaking unto them, behold, he spake unto the sons of ^aIshmael, yea, and even all his household.

11 And after he had made an end of speaking unto them, he spake unto Sam, saying: Blessed art thou, and thy ^aseed; for thou shalt inherit the land like unto thy brother Nephi. And thy seed shall be numbered with his seed; and thou shalt be even like unto thy brother, and thy seed like unto his seed; and thou shalt be blessed in all thy days.

12 And it came to pass after my father, Lehi, had ^aspoken unto all his household, according to the feelings of his heart and the Spirit of the Lord which was in him, he waxed ^bold. And it came to pass that he died, and was buried.

13 And it came to pass that not many days after his death, Laman and Lemuel and the sons of Ishmael were ^aangry with me because of the admonitions of the Lord.

14 For I, Nephi, was constrained to speak unto them, according to his word; for I had spoken many things unto them, and also my father, before his death; many of which sayings are written upon mine ^aother plates; for a more history part are written upon mine other plates.

15 And upon ^athese I ^bwrite the things of my soul, and many of the scriptures which are engraven upon the plates of brass. For my soul ^cdelighteth in the scriptures, and my heart ^dpondereth them, and writeth them for the ^elearning and the profit of my children.

16 Behold, my ^asoul delighteth in the things of the Lord; and my ^bheart pondereth continually upon the things which I have seen and heard.

17 Nevertheless, notwithstanding the great ^agoodness of the Lord, in showing me his great and marvelous works, my heart exclaimeth: O ^bwretched man that I am! Yea, my heart ^csorroweth because of my flesh; my soul grieveth because of mine iniquities.

18 I am encompassed about, because of the temptations and the sins which do so easily ^abeset me.

19 And when I desire to rejoice, my heart groaneth because of my sins; nevertheless, I know in whom I have ^atrusted.

20 My God hath been my ^asupport; he hath led me through mine ^bafflictions in the wilderness; and he hath preserved me upon the waters of the great deep.

21 He hath filled me with his ^alove, even unto the ^bconsuming of my flesh.

22 He hath confounded mine ^aenemies, unto the causing of them to quake before me.

23 Behold, he hath heard my cry by

10a 1 Ne. 7:6.
11a Jacob 1:14 (12–14).
12a Gen. 49:1 (1–27).
  b TG Old Age.
13a 1 Ne. 7:6 (6–19);
    17:18 (17–55);
    18:10 (9–22);
    2 Ne. 5:2 (1–25).
    TG Anger.
14a 1 Ne. 1:17 (16–17); 9:4;
    2 Ne. 5:33 (29–33);
    D&C 10:42.
15a 1 Ne. 6:1 (1–6).
  b TG Scriptures,

Writing of.
  c Ps. 119:24;
    Moses 6:59.
  d TG Meditation;
    Scriptures, Study of.
  e 1 Ne. 19:23.
    TG Scriptures, Value of.
16a TG Spirituality;
    Thanksgiving.
  b TG Heart.
17a Ex. 34:6 (5–7);
    2 Ne. 9:10;
    D&C 86:11.
  b Rom. 7:24.

  c TG Poor in Spirit;
    Repent;
    Sorrow.
18a Rom. 7:21 (15–25);
    Heb. 12:1;
    Alma 7:15.
19a TG Trust in God.
20a 2 Cor. 4:16.
  b 1 Ne. 17:6.
    TG Affliction;
    Comfort.
21a TG God, Love of.
  b D&C 84:33.
22a Ps. 3:7 (7–8).

day, and he hath given me ªknowl-
edge by ᵇvisions in the night-time.

24 And by day have I waxed bold
in mighty ªprayer before him; yea,
my voice have I sent up on high;
and angels came down and ministered unto me.

25 And upon the wings of his Spirit
hath my body been ªcarried away
upon exceedingly high mountains.
And mine eyes have beheld great
things, yea, even too great for man;
therefore I was bidden that I should
not write them.

26 O then, if I have seen so great
things, if the Lord in his condescension unto the children of men hath
ªvisited men in so much ᵇmercy,
ᶜwhy should my ᵈheart weep and my
soul linger in the valley of sorrow,
and my flesh waste away, and my
strength slacken, because of mine
afflictions?

27 And why should I ªyield to
sin, because of my flesh? Yea, why
should I give way to ᵇtemptations,
that the evil one have place in my
heart to destroy my ᶜpeace and afflict my soul? Why am I ᵈangry because of mine enemy?

28 Awake, my soul! No longer
ªdroop in sin. Rejoice, O my heart,
and give place no more for the ᵇen-
emy of my soul.

29 Do not ªanger again because of
mine enemies. Do not slacken my
strength because of mine afflictions.

30 Rejoice, O my ªheart, and cry
unto the Lord, and say: O Lord, I
will praise thee forever; yea, my

soul will rejoice in thee, my God,
and the ᵇrock of my salvation.

31 O Lord, wilt thou ªredeem my
soul? Wilt thou deliver me out of
the hands of mine enemies? Wilt
thou make me that I may shake at
the appearance of ᵇsin?

32 May the gates of hell be shut
continually before me, because that
my ªheart is broken and my spirit
is contrite! O Lord, wilt thou not
shut the gates of thy righteousness
before me, that I may ᵇwalk in the
path of the low valley, that I may
be strict in the plain road!

33 O Lord, wilt thou encircle me
around in the robe of thy ªrighteousness! O Lord, wilt thou make
a way for mine escape before mine
ᵇenemies! Wilt thou make my path
straight before me! Wilt thou not
place a stumbling block in my way—
but that thou wouldst clear my way
before me, and hedge not up my
way, but the ways of mine enemy.

34 O Lord, I have ªtrusted in thee,
and I will ᵇtrust in thee forever. I
will not put my ᶜtrust in the arm
of flesh; for I know that cursed is
he that putteth his ᵈtrust in the
arm of flesh. Yea, cursed is he that
putteth his trust in man or maketh
flesh his arm.

35 Yea, I know that God will give
ªliberally to him that asketh. Yea,
my God will give me, if I ᵇask ᶜnot
amiss; therefore I will lift up my
voice unto thee; yea, I will cry
unto thee, my God, the ᵈrock of my
ᵉrighteousness. Behold, my voice

23ª TG Knowledge.
  ᵇ 2 Chr. 26:5.
    TG Dream; Vision.
24ª James 5:16;
    1 Ne. 1:5 (5–8); 10:17.
25ª 2 Cor. 12:2 (1–4);
    1 Ne. 11:1 (1–36);
    Moses 1:1.
26ª Ex. 3:16; Alma 9:21;
    Morm. 1:15.
  ᵇ TG Compassion;
    God, Mercy of.
  ᶜ Ps. 43:5.
  ᵈ TG Heart.
27ª Rom. 6:13 (10–16).
  ᵇ TG Temptation.

  ᶜ TG Contentment; Peace;
    Peace of God.
  ᵈ TG Self-Mastery.
28ª Ps. 42:11.
  ᵇ TG Adversary;
    Enemies.
29ª TG Anger.
30ª TG Heart.
  ᵇ 1 Cor. 3:11 (9–13).
    TG Rock.
31ª Ps. 16:10.
  ᵇ Rom. 12:9;
    Alma 13:12; 37:32.
    TG Sin.
32ª TG Contrite Heart.
  ᵇ TG Walking with God.

33ª TG Righteousness.
  ᵇ Lev. 26:7 (1–13);
    D&C 44:5.
34ª TG Trustworthiness.
  ᵇ TG Trust in God.
  ᶜ Ps. 33:16; 44:6 (6–8).
    TG Trust Not in the Arm
    of Flesh.
  ᵈ Prov. 14:16; Jer. 17:5;
    Morm. 3:9; 4:8.
35ª James 1:5.
    TG Abundant Life.
  ᵇ TG Prayer.
  ᶜ Hel. 10:5.
  ᵈ Deut. 32:4.
  ᵉ Ps. 4:1.

shall forever ascend up unto thee, my rock and mine everlasting God. Amen.

CHAPTER 5

The Nephites separate themselves from the Lamanites, keep the law of Moses, and build a temple—Because of their unbelief, the Lamanites are cut off from the presence of the Lord, are cursed, and become a scourge unto the Nephites. About 588–559 B.C.

BEHOLD, it came to pass that I, Nephi, did cry much unto the Lord my God, because of the ᵃanger of my brethren.

2 But behold, their ᵃanger did increase against me, insomuch that they did seek to take away my life.

3 Yea, they did murmur against me, saying: Our younger brother thinks to ᵃrule over us; and we have had much trial because of him; wherefore, now let us slay him, that we may not be afflicted more because of his words. For behold, we will not have him to be our ruler; for it belongs unto us, who are the elder brethren, to ᵇrule over this people.

4 Now I do not write upon these plates all the words which they murmured against me. But it sufficeth me to say, that they did seek to take away my life.

5 And it came to pass that the Lord did ᵃwarn me, that I, ᵇNephi, should depart from them and flee into the wilderness, and all those who would go with me.

6 Wherefore, it came to pass that I, Nephi, did take my family, and also ᵃZoram and his family, and Sam, mine elder brother and his family,

and Jacob and Joseph, my younger brethren, and also my sisters, and all those who would go with me. And all those who would go with me were those who believed in the ᵇwarnings and the revelations of God; wherefore, they did hearken unto my words.

7 And we did take our tents and whatsoever things were possible for us, and did journey in the wilderness for the space of many days. And after we had journeyed for the space of many days we did pitch our tents.

8 And my people would that we should call the name of the place ᵃNephi; wherefore, we did call it Nephi.

9 And all those who were with me did take upon them to call themselves the ᵃpeople of Nephi.

10 And we did observe to keep the judgments, and the ᵃstatutes, and the commandments of the Lord in all things, according to the ᵇlaw of Moses.

11 And the Lord was with us; and we did ᵃprosper exceedingly; for we did sow seed, and we did reap again in abundance. And we began to raise flocks, and herds, and animals of every kind.

12 And I, Nephi, had also brought the records which were engraven upon the ᵃplates of brass; and also the ᵇball, or ᶜcompass, which was prepared for my father by the hand of the Lord, according to that which is written.

13 And it came to pass that we began to prosper exceedingly, and to multiply in the land.

14 And I, Nephi, did take the ᵃsword of Laban, and after the manner

5 1 *a* 2 Ne. 4:13; Jacob 7:24;
      Enos 1:20;
      Mosiah 10:12, 15.
   2 *a* 1 Ne. 7:6 (6–19); 17:18
      (17–55); 18:10 (9–22);
      2 Ne. 4:13 (13–14).
   3 *a* Num. 16:13;
      1 Ne. 16:37 (37–38);
      Mosiah 10:15.
      b Alma 54:17.
   5 *a* TG Guidance, Divine.
      b Mosiah 10:13.

6 *a* 1 Ne. 4:35; 16:7;
      2 Ne. 1:31 (30–32).
      b TG Warn.
   8 *a* Omni 1:12 (12, 27);
      Mosiah 7:1 (1–7, 21);
      9:1 (1–6, 14); 28:1 (1, 5);
      Alma 2:24; 20:1;
      50:8 (8, 11).
   9 *a* Jacob 1:14.
  10 *a* Ezek. 20:11;
      2 Ne. 1:16 (16–17).
      b 2 Ne. 11:4.

TG Law of Moses.
  11 *a* Matt. 6:33.
  12 *a* 2 Ne. 4:2;
      Mosiah 1:3 (3–4).
      b Mosiah 1:16.
      c 1 Ne. 16:16 (10, 16, 26);
      18:12 (12, 21);
      Alma 37:38 (38–47);
      D&C 17:1.
  14 *a* 1 Ne. 4:9; Jacob 1:10;
      W of M 1:13;
      Mosiah 1:16; D&C 17:1.

of it did make many *b*swords, lest by any means the people who were now called Lamanites should come upon us and destroy us; for I knew their *c*hatred towards me and my children and those who were called my people.

15 And I did teach my people to *a*build buildings, and to *b*work in all *c*manner of wood, and of *d*iron, and of copper, and of *e*brass, and of steel, and of *f*gold, and of silver, and of precious ores, which were in great abundance.

16 And I, Nephi, did *a*build a *b*temple; and I did construct it after the manner of the temple of *c*Solomon save it were not built of so many *d*precious things; for they were not to be found upon the land, wherefore, it could not be built like unto Solomon's *e*temple. But the manner of the construction was like unto the temple of *f*Solomon; and the workmanship thereof was exceedingly fine.

17 And it came to pass that I, Nephi, did cause my people to be *a*industrious, and to *b*labor with their *c*hands.

18 And it came to pass that they would that I should be their *a*king. But I, Nephi, was desirous that they should have no king; nevertheless, I did for them according to that which was in my power.

19 And behold, the words of the Lord had been fulfilled unto my brethren, which he spake concerning them, that I should be their *a*ruler and their teacher. Wherefore, I had been their ruler and their *b*teacher, according to the commandments of the Lord, until the time they sought to take away my life.

20 Wherefore, the word of the Lord was fulfilled which he spake unto me, saying that: Inasmuch as they will *a*not hearken unto thy words they shall be *b*cut off from the presence of the Lord. And behold, they were *c*cut off from his presence.

21 And he had caused the *a*cursing to come upon them, yea, even a sore cursing, because of their iniquity. For behold, they had hardened their hearts against him, that they had become like unto a flint; wherefore, as they were white, and exceedingly fair and *b*delightsome, that they might not be *c*enticing unto my people the Lord God did cause a *d*skin of *e*blackness to come upon them.

22 And thus saith the Lord God: I will cause that they shall be *a*loathsome unto thy people, save they shall repent of their iniquities.

23 And cursed shall be the seed of him that *a*mixeth with their seed; for they shall be cursed even with the same cursing. And the Lord spake it, and it was done.

24 And because of their *a*cursing which was upon them they did become an *b*idle people, full of

---

14b Jarom 1:8; Mosiah 10:8;
   Alma 2:12; Hel. 1:14;
   3 Ne. 3:26.
  c TG Hate.
15a TG Skill.
  b TG Art.
  c Jarom 1:8.
  d Josh. 8:31; 1 Ne. 18:25;
    Jacob 2:12 (12–13);
    Hel. 6:9 (9–11);
    Ether 9:17; 10:23 (12, 23);
    Moses 5:46.
  e Gen. 4:22.
  f Ex. 31:4 (4–5);
    1 Kgs. 6:21 (21–22);
    D&C 124:26 (26–27).
16a 2 Chr. 3:1 (1–17);
    D&C 84:5 (5, 31);
    124:31 (25–55).

  b 1 Kgs. 5:5;
    Jacob 1:17;
    Mosiah 1:18; 7:17; 11:10;
    Alma 16:13;
    Hel. 3:14 (9, 14);
    3 Ne. 11:1.
    TG Temple.
  c 1 Kgs. 6:2.
  d 1 Kgs. 5:17.
  e 1 Kgs. 9:1.
  f 1 Chr. 18:8.
17a TG Industry;
    Work, Value of.
  b TG Labor.
  c Prov. 31:13.
18a 2 Ne. 6:2;
    Jacob 1:9 (9, 11, 15);
    Jarom 1:7 (7, 14);
    Mosiah 1:10.

19a 2 Ne. 1:25 (25–27).
  b TG Teacher.
20a 1 Ne. 8:18.
  b 1 Ne. 8:35 (35–36).
  c 1 Ne. 2:21;
    Alma 9:14 (13–15); 38:1.
21a TG Curse.
  b Gen. 24:16; 1 Ne. 13:15;
    4 Ne. 1:10; Morm. 9:6.
  c TG Marriage, Temporal.
  d 2 Ne. 30:6;
    3 Ne. 2:15 (14–16).
  e 2 Ne. 26:33;
    Moses 7:8.
22a 1 Ne. 12:23.
23a TG Marriage, Interfaith.
24a TG Curse.
  b Alma 22:28.
    TG Idleness.

mischief and subtlety, and did seek in the wilderness for beasts of prey.

25 And the Lord God said unto me: They shall be a scourge unto thy seed, to ^astir them up in remembrance of me; and inasmuch as they will not remember me, and hearken unto my words, they shall scourge them even unto destruction.

26 And it came to pass that I, Nephi, did ^aconsecrate Jacob and Joseph, that they should be ^bpriests and ^cteachers over the land of my people.

27 And it came to pass that we lived after the manner of ^ahappiness.

28 And thirty years had passed away from the time we left Jerusalem.

29 And I, Nephi, had kept the ^arecords upon my plates, which I had made, of my people thus far.

30 And it came to pass that the Lord God said unto me: ^aMake other plates; and thou shalt engraven many things upon them which are good in my sight, for the profit of thy people.

31 Wherefore, I, Nephi, to be obedient to the commandments of the Lord, went and made ^athese plates upon which I have engraven these things.

32 And I engraved that which is pleasing unto God. And if my people are pleased with the things of God they will be pleased with mine engravings which are upon these plates.

33 And if my people desire to know the more particular part of the history of my people they must search mine ^aother ^bplates.

34 And it sufficeth me to say that forty years had passed away, and we had already had wars and contentions with our brethren.

CHAPTER 6

Jacob recounts Jewish history: The Babylonian captivity and return; the ministry and crucifixion of the Holy One of Israel; the help received from the Gentiles; and the Jews' latter-day restoration when they believe in the Messiah. About 559–545 B.C.

THE ^awords of Jacob, the brother of Nephi, which he spake unto the people of Nephi:

2 Behold, my beloved brethren, I, Jacob, having been called of God, and ordained after the manner of his holy ^aorder, and having been consecrated by my brother Nephi, unto whom ye look as a ^bking or a protector, and on whom ye depend for safety, behold ye know that I have spoken unto you exceedingly many things.

3 Nevertheless, I speak unto you again; for I am desirous for the ^awelfare of your souls. Yea, mine anxiety is great for you; and ye yourselves know that it ever has been. For I have exhorted you with all diligence; and I have taught you the words of my father; and I have spoken unto you concerning all things which are ^bwritten, from the creation of the world.

4 And now, behold, I would speak unto you concerning things which are, and which are to come; wherefore, I will read you the words of ^aIsaiah. And they are the words which my brother has desired that I should speak unto you. And I speak unto you for your sakes, that ye may learn and glorify the name of your God.

5 And now, the words which I shall read are they which Isaiah spake concerning all the house of Israel;

25a 1 Ne. 2:24.
26a Lev. 16:32;
    Jacob 1:18 (18–19);
    Mosiah 23:17.
    TG Priesthood,
    Authority.
  b TG Priest, Melchizedek
    Priesthood.
  c TG Teacher.
27a Alma 50:23.

29a TG Record Keeping.
30a 1 Ne. 19:5 (1–6);
    Jacob 3:14.
31a 1 Ne. 19:3;
    Jacob 1:1.
33a 1 Ne. 1:17 (16–17);
    2 Ne. 4:14;
    D&C 10:42.
  b 1 Ne. 19:4; Jacob 1:3.
6 1a 2 Ne. 11:1; Jacob 2:1.

2a TG Priesthood,
    Melchizedek.
  b 2 Ne. 5:18;
    Jacob 1:9 (9, 11, 15);
    Jarom 1:7 (7, 14);
    Mosiah 1:10.
3a Jacob 2:3;
    Mosiah 25:11.
  b TG Scriptures, Value of.
4a 3 Ne. 23:1 (1–3).

wherefore, they may be ^alikened unto you, for ye are of the house of Israel. And there are many things which have been spoken by Isaiah which may be likened unto you, because ye are of the house of Israel.

6 And now, these are the words: ^aThus saith the Lord God: Behold, I will lift up mine hand to the Gentiles, and set up my ^bstandard to the people; and they shall bring thy sons in their arms, and thy daughters shall be carried upon their shoulders.

7 And ^akings shall be thy nursing fathers, and their queens thy nursing mothers; they shall bow down to thee with their faces towards the earth, and lick up the dust of thy feet; and thou shalt know that ^bI am the Lord; for they shall not be ashamed that ^cwait for me.

8 And now I, Jacob, would speak somewhat concerning these words. For behold, the Lord has shown me that those who were at ^aJerusalem, from whence we came, have been ^bslain and ^ccarried away captive.

9 Nevertheless, the Lord has shown unto me that they should ^areturn again. And he also has shown unto me that the Lord God, the Holy One of Israel, should manifest himself unto them in the flesh; and after he should manifest himself they should ^bscourge him and ^ccrucify him, according to the words of the angel who spake it unto me.

10 And after they have ^ahardened their hearts and ^bstiffened their necks against the Holy One of Israel, behold, the ^cjudgments of the Holy One of Israel shall come upon them. And the day cometh that they shall be smitten and afflicted.

11 Wherefore, after they are driven to and fro, for thus saith the angel, many shall be afflicted in the flesh, and shall not be suffered to ^aperish, because of the prayers of the faithful; they shall be scattered, and smitten, and hated; nevertheless, the Lord will be merciful unto them, that ^bwhen they shall come to the ^cknowledge of their Redeemer, they shall be ^dgathered together again to the ^elands of their inheritance.

12 And blessed are the ^aGentiles, they of whom the prophet has written; for behold, if it so be that they shall repent and fight not against Zion, and do not unite themselves to that great and ^babominable church, they shall be saved; for the Lord God will fulfil his ^ccovenants which he has made unto his children; and for this cause the prophet has written these things.

13 Wherefore, they that fight against Zion and the covenant people of the Lord shall lick up the dust of their feet; and the people of the Lord shall not be ^aashamed. For the people of the Lord are they who ^bwait for him; for they still wait for the coming of the Messiah.

5a IE applied.
6a Isa. 49:22 (22–23);
   2 Ne. 10:9.
 b TG Ensign.
7a Isa. 60:16.
 b Isa. 44:8;
   45:5 (5–22); 46:9;
   3 Ne. 24:6;
   Moses 1:6.
 c Lam. 3:25 (25–26);
   D&C 133:45.
8a Esth. 2:6;
   1 Ne. 7:13; 10:3;
   2 Ne. 25:6, 10;
   Omni 1:15;
   Hel. 8:20 (20–21).
 b Ezek. 23:25 (24–29).
 c 2 Kgs. 24:14 (10–16);
   25:11 (1–12);

   Jer. 13:19 (19, 24).
   TG Israel, Bondage of, in
   Other Lands.
9a Jer. 29:10 (9–10);
   1 Ne. 10:3.
 b TG Jesus Christ,
   Betrayal of.
 c 1 Ne. 19:10 (10, 13);
   Mosiah 3:9;
   3 Ne. 11:14 (14–15).
   TG Jesus Christ,
   Crucifixion of.
10a TG Hardheartedness.
 b TG Stiffnecked.
 c Matt. 27:25 (24–25).
11a Amos 9:8 (8–9);
   2 Ne. 20:20 (20–21).
 b 1 Ne. 22:12 (11–12);
   2 Ne. 9:2 (1–2).

 c Hosea 3:5;
   D&C 113:10.
   TG Israel, Restoration of.
 d TG Israel, Gathering of.
 e TG Lands of Inheritance.
12a 1 Ne. 14:2 (1–5);
   2 Ne. 10:10 (8–14, 18).
 b TG Devil, Church of.
 c TG Abrahamic Covenant.
13a Joel 2:26 (26–27);
   3 Ne. 22:4;
   D&C 90:17.
 b Gen. 49:18;
   Ps. 25:5;
   Prov. 20:22; 27:18;
   Isa. 40:31;
   1 Ne. 21:23;
   D&C 98:2; 133:11, 45.

14 And behold, according to the words of the prophet, the Messiah will set himself again the ^asecond time to recover them; wherefore, he will ^bmanifest himself unto them in power and great glory, unto the ^cdestruction of their enemies, when that day cometh when they shall believe in him; and none will he destroy that believe in him.

15 And they that believe not in him shall be ^adestroyed, both by ^bfire, and by tempest, and by earthquakes, and by ^cbloodsheds, and by ^dpestilence, and by ^efamine. And they shall know that the Lord is God, the Holy One of Israel.

16 ^aFor shall the prey be taken from the mighty, or the ^blawful captive delivered?

17 But thus saith the Lord: Even the captives of the mighty shall be taken away, and the prey of the terrible shall be delivered; ^afor the ^bMighty God shall ^cdeliver his covenant people. For thus saith the Lord: I will contend with them that contendeth with thee—

18 And I will feed them that oppress thee, with their own flesh; and they shall be drunken with their own blood as with sweet wine; and all flesh shall know that I the Lord am thy Savior and thy ^aRedeemer, the ^bMighty One of Jacob.

CHAPTER 7

Jacob continues reading from Isaiah: Isaiah speaks messianically—The Messiah will have the tongue of the learned—He will give His back to the smiters—He will not be confounded—Compare Isaiah 50. About 559–545 B.C.

^aYEA, for thus saith the Lord: Have I put thee away, or have I cast thee off forever? For thus saith the Lord: Where is the ^bbill of your mother's ^cdivorcement? To whom have I put thee away, or to which of my ^dcreditors have I ^esold you? Yea, to whom have I sold you? Behold, for your iniquities have ye sold yourselves, and for your transgressions is your mother put away.

2 Wherefore, when I came, there was no man; when I ^acalled, yea, there was none to answer. O house of Israel, is my hand shortened at all that it cannot redeem, or have I no power to deliver? Behold, at my rebuke I ^bdry up the ^csea, I make their ^drivers a wilderness and their ^efish to stink because the waters are dried up, and they die because of thirst.

3 I clothe the heavens with ^ablackness, and I make ^bsackcloth their covering.

4 The Lord God hath given me the ^atongue of the learned, that I should know how to speak a word in season unto thee, O house of Israel. When

14a 2 Ne. 21:11; 25:17; 29:1.
  b 2 Ne. 3:5;
    D&C 3:18 (16–20).
  c 1 Ne. 21:26 (24–26);
    22:13 (13–14).
15a 1 Ne. 22:13 (13–23);
    2 Ne. 10:16 (15–16);
    28:15 (15–32);
    3 Ne. 16:8 (8–15);
    Ether 2:9 (8–11).
    TG Last Days.
  b Joel 1:19 (19–20);
    Jacob 5:77; 6:3.
  c TG Blood, Shedding of.
  d Luke 21:11 (10–13);
    Mosiah 12:4;
    D&C 97:26 (22–26).
    TG Plague.
  e TG Drought.
16a Isa. 49:24 (24–26);

    2 Ne. 11:2.
  b HEB righteous captive;
    i.e., the covenant people
    of the Lord, as stated in
    v. 17.
17a 1 Ne. 21:25.
  b TG Jesus Christ, Jehovah.
  c 2 Kgs. 17:39;
    D&C 105:8.
    TG Jesus Christ,
    Prophecies about;
    Jesus Christ, Savior.
18a TG Jesus Christ,
    Redeemer.
  b Gen. 49:24;
    Ps. 132:2;
    Isa. 1:24; 60:16.
7 1a Isa. 50:1 (1–11);
    2 Ne. 8:1.
  b Jer. 3:8.

    c TG Divorce.
    d 2 Kgs. 4:1;
      Matt. 18:25.
    e Judg. 4:2;
      Isa. 52:3.
      TG Apostasy of Israel.
  2a Prov. 1:24 (24–27);
      Isa. 65:12;
      Alma 5:37.
    b Nahum 1:4.
    c Ex. 14:21 (1–31);
      Ps. 106:9;
      D&C 133:68.
    d Josh. 3:16 (15–16).
    e Ex. 7:21 (17–21).
  3a Ex. 10:21.
    b Rev. 6:12.
  4a Luke 21:15.

ye are weary he waketh morning by morning. He waketh mine ear to hear as the learned.

5 The Lord God hath opened mine [a]ear, and I was not rebellious, neither turned away back.

6 I gave my back to the [a]smiter, and my cheeks to them that plucked off the hair. I hid not my face from [b]shame and spitting.

7 For the Lord God will help me, therefore shall I not be confounded. Therefore have I set my face like a flint, and I know that I shall not be [a]ashamed.

8 And the Lord is near, and he [a]justifieth me. Who will contend with me? Let us stand together. Who is mine adversary? Let him come near me, and I will [b]smite him with the strength of my mouth.

9 For the Lord God will help me. And all they who shall [a]condemn me, behold, all they shall [b]wax old as a garment, and the moth shall eat them up.

10 Who is among you that feareth the Lord, that obeyeth the [a]voice of his servant, that [b]walketh in darkness and hath no light?

11 Behold all ye that kindle fire, that compass yourselves about with sparks, walk in the light of [a]your fire and in the sparks which ye have kindled. [b]This shall ye have of mine hand—ye shall lie down in sorrow.

CHAPTER 8

Jacob continues reading from Isaiah: In the last days, the Lord will comfort Zion and gather Israel—The redeemed will come to Zion amid great joy— Compare Isaiah 51 and 52:1–2. About 559–545 B.C.

[a]HEARKEN unto me, ye that follow after righteousness. Look unto the [b]rock from whence ye are hewn, and to the hole of the pit from whence ye are digged.

2 Look unto Abraham, your [a]father, and unto [b]Sarah, she that bare you; for I called him alone, and blessed him.

3 For the Lord shall [a]comfort [b]Zion, he will comfort all her waste places; and he will make her [c]wilderness like [d]Eden, and her desert like the garden of the Lord. Joy and gladness shall be found therein, thanksgiving and the voice of melody.

4 Hearken unto me, my people; and give ear unto me, O my nation; for a [a]law shall proceed from me, and I will make my judgment to rest for a [b]light for the people.

5 My righteousness is near; my [a]salvation is gone forth, and mine arm shall [b]judge the people. The [c]isles shall wait upon me, and on mine arm shall they trust.

6 Lift up your eyes to the [a]heavens, and look upon the earth beneath; for the heavens shall [b]vanish away like smoke, and the earth shall [c]wax old like a garment; and they that dwell therein shall die in like manner. But my salvation shall be forever, and my righteousness shall not be abolished.

7 Hearken unto me, ye that know righteousness, the people in whose heart I have written my law, [a]fear

---

5a D&C 58:1.
6a Isa. 53:4; Matt. 27:26;
    2 Ne. 9:5 (4–7).
  b TG Shame.
7a Rom. 9:33.
8a Rom. 8:33 (32–34).
  b Isa. 11:4.
9a Rom. 8:31.
  b Ps. 102:26.
10a D&C 1:38.
  b TG Walking in Darkness.
11a Deut. 12:8;
    Judg. 17:6.
  b D&C 133:70.

8 1a Isa. 51:1 (1–23);
    2 Ne. 7:1.
  b IE Abraham and Sarah;
    see v. 2.
    TG Rock.
2a Gen. 17:4 (1–8);
    D&C 109:64; 132:49.
  b Gen. 24:36.
3a TG Israel, Restoration of.
  b TG Zion.
  c Isa. 35:2 (1–2, 6–7).
    TG Israel, Blessings of.
  d TG Earth, Renewal of;
    Eden.

4a Isa. 2:3.
    TG God, Law of.
  b TG Light [noun].
5a TG Jesus Christ, Savior;
    Salvation.
  b TG Jesus Christ, Judge.
  c 2 Ne. 10:20.
6a 2 Pet. 3:10.
  b Isa. 13:13.
  c Ps. 102:26 (25–28).
7a Deut. 1:17;
    Ps. 56:4 (4, 11); 118:6;
    D&C 122:9.
    TG Peer Influence.

ye not the ᵇreproach of men, neither be ye afraid of their ᶜrevilings.

8 For the ᵃmoth shall eat them up like a garment, and the worm shall eat them like wool. But my righteousness shall be forever, and my salvation from generation to generation.

9 ᵃAwake, awake! Put on ᵇstrength, O arm of the Lord; awake as in the ancient days. Art thou not he that hath cut ᶜRahab, and wounded the ᵈdragon?

10 Art thou not he who hath dried the sea, the waters of the great deep; that hath made the depths of the sea a ᵃway for the ransomed to pass over?

11 Therefore, the ᵃredeemed of the Lord shall ᵇreturn, and come with ᶜsinging unto Zion; and everlasting joy and holiness shall be upon their heads; and they shall obtain gladness and joy; sorrow and ᵈmourning shall flee away.

12 ᵃI am he; yea, I am he that comforteth you. Behold, who art thou, that thou shouldst be ᵇafraid of man, who shall die, and of the son of man, who shall be made like unto ᶜgrass?

13 And ᵃforgettest the Lord thy maker, that hath ᵇstretched forth the heavens, and laid the foundations of the earth, and hast feared continually every day, because of the fury of the ᶜoppressor, as if he were ready to destroy? And where is the fury of the oppressor?

14 The ᵃcaptive exile hasteneth, that he may be loosed, and that he should not die in the pit, nor that his bread should fail.

15 But I am the Lord thy God, whose ᵃwaves roared; the Lord of Hosts is my name.

16 And I have ᵃput my words in thy mouth, and have covered thee in the shadow of mine hand, that I may plant the heavens and lay the foundations of the earth, and say unto Zion: Behold, thou art my ᵇpeople.

17 Awake, awake, stand up, O Jerusalem, which hast drunk at the hand of the Lord the ᵃcup of his ᵇfury—thou hast drunken the dregs of the cup of trembling wrung out—

18 And none to guide her among all the sons she hath brought forth; neither that taketh her by the hand, of all the sons she hath brought up.

19 These two ᵃsons are come unto thee, who shall be sorry for thee—thy desolation and destruction, and the famine and the sword—and by whom shall I comfort thee?

20 Thy sons have fainted, save these two; they lie at the head of all the streets; as a wild bull in a net, they are full of the fury of the Lord, the rebuke of thy God.

21 Therefore hear now this, thou afflicted, and ᵃdrunken, and not with wine:

22 Thus saith thy Lord, the Lord and thy God ᵃpleadeth the cause of his people; behold, I have taken out of thine hand the cup of trembling, the dregs of the cup of my fury; thou shalt no more drink it again.

23 But ᵃI will put it into the hand

7b TG Reproach.
  c TG Hate.
8a Isa. 50:9.
9a Isa. 52:1.
  b D&C 113:8 (7–8).
    TG Israel, Restoration of.
  c Ps. 89:10;
    Isa. 27:1.
  d Ezek. 29:3.
10a Isa. 35:8 (8–10).
11a TG Israel, Restoration of.
  b TG Israel, Gathering of.
  c Isa. 35:10;
    Jer. 31:12 (12–13).

d Rev. 21:4 (2–5).
12a D&C 133:47; 136:22.
  b Jer. 1:8 (7–8).
  c Isa. 40:6 (6–8);
    1 Pet. 1:24 (24–25).
13a Jer. 23:27 (27–39).
  b Job 9:8.
  c IE Israel's captors,
    typifying evil rulers
    who oppress the
    righteous; see v. 14.
    TG Oppression.
14a Isa. 52:2.
15a 1 Ne. 4:2.

16a TG Israel, Mission of;
    Prophets, Mission of.
  b 1 Kgs. 8:51;
    2 Ne. 3:9; 29:14.
17a Jer. 25:15.
  b Luke 21:24 (22–24).
19a Rev. 11:3 (3–12).
21a 2 Ne. 27:4.
22a Jer. 50:34.
23a Joel 3:16 (9–16);
    Zech. 12:9 (2–3, 8–9);
    14:12 (3, 12–15).

of them that afflict thee; who have said to thy soul: Bow down, that we may go over—and thou hast laid thy body as the ground and as the street to them that went over.

24 ^aAwake, awake, put on thy ^bstrength, O ^cZion; put on thy beautiful garments, O Jerusalem, the holy city; for henceforth there shall ^dno more come into thee the uncircumcised and the unclean.

25 Shake thyself from the dust; arise, sit down, O Jerusalem; loose thyself from the ^abands of thy neck, O captive daughter of Zion.

CHAPTER 9

Jacob explains that the Jews will be gathered in all their lands of promise—The Atonement ransoms man from the Fall—The bodies of the dead will come forth from the grave, and their spirits from hell and from paradise—They will be judged—The Atonement saves from death, hell, the devil, and endless torment—The righteous are to be saved in the kingdom of God—Penalties for sins are set forth—The Holy One of Israel is the keeper of the gate. About 559–545 B.C.

AND now, my beloved brethren, I have read these things that ye might know concerning the ^acovenants of the Lord that he has covenanted with all the house of Israel—

2 That he has spoken unto the Jews, by the mouth of his holy prophets, even from the beginning down, from generation to generation, until the time comes that they shall be

^arestored to the true church and fold of God; when they shall be ^bgathered home to the ^clands of their inheritance, and shall be established in all their lands of promise.

3 Behold, my beloved brethren, I speak unto you these things that ye may rejoice, and ^alift up your heads forever, because of the blessings which the Lord God shall bestow upon your children.

4 For I know that ye have searched much, many of you, to know of things to come; wherefore I know that ye know that our ^aflesh must waste away and die; nevertheless, in our ^bbodies we shall see God.

5 Yea, I know that ye know that in the body he shall show himself unto those at Jerusalem, from whence we came; for it is expedient that it should be among them; for it behooveth the great ^aCreator that he ^bsuffereth himself to become ^csubject unto man in the flesh, and ^ddie for ^eall men, that all men might become subject unto him.

6 For as ^adeath hath passed upon all men, to fulfil the merciful ^bplan of the great Creator, there must needs be a power of ^cresurrection, and the resurrection must needs come unto man by reason of the ^dfall; and the fall came by reason of ^etransgression; and because man became fallen they were ^fcut off from the ^gpresence of the Lord.

7 Wherefore, it must needs be an ^ainfinite ^batonement—save it should be an infinite atonement this

---

24a Isa. 52:1 (1–2).
  b D&C 113:8 (7–8).
    TG Strength.
  c TG Zion.
  d Joel 3:17;
    Zech. 14:21.
25a D&C 113:10 (9–10).
9 1a TG Abrahamic Covenant;
    Israel, Mission of.
2a 2 Ne. 6:11 (10–15);
    10:7 (5–9).
    TG Israel,
    Restoration of;
    Restoration of the
    Gospel.
  b TG Israel, Gathering of;
    Mission of Latter-day

Saints.
  c TG Lands of Inheritance.
3a Ps. 24:7 (7–10).
4a Gen. 6:3;
    Moses 8:17.
  b Job 19:26;
    Alma 11:41 (41–45);
    42:23;
    Hel. 14:15 (15–18);
    Morm. 9:13.
    TG Body, Sanctity of.
5a TG Jesus Christ, Creator.
  b 2 Ne. 7:6 (4–9).
  c Mark 10:44 (43–44).
  d TG Jesus Christ,
    Death of;
    Jesus Christ, Mission of.

  e John 12:32;
    2 Ne. 26:24;
    3 Ne. 27:14 (14–15).
6a Eccl. 8:8 (6–8).
  b TG Salvation, Plan of.
  c TG Jesus Christ,
    Resurrection.
  d TG Fall of Man.
  e TG Transgress.
  f 2 Ne. 2:5 (5–8);
    Alma 11:42 (40–45).
  g TG God, Presence of.
7a Alma 34:10.
  b Matt. 26:54 (52–56).
    TG Jesus Christ,
    Atonement through.

corruption could not put on incorruption. Wherefore, the ^cfirst judgment which came upon man must needs have ^dremained to an endless duration. And if so, this flesh must have laid down to rot and to crumble to its mother earth, to rise no more.

8 O the ^awisdom of God, his ^bmercy and ^cgrace! For behold, if the ^dflesh should rise no more our spirits must become subject to that angel who ^efell from before the presence of the Eternal God, and became the ^fdevil, to rise no more.

9 And our spirits must have become ^alike unto him, and we become devils, ^bangels to a ^cdevil, to be ^dshut out from the presence of our God, and to remain with the father of ^elies, in misery, like unto himself; yea, to that being who ^fbeguiled our first parents, who ^gtransformeth himself nigh unto an ^hangel of light, and ⁱstirreth up the children of men unto ^jsecret combinations of murder and all manner of secret works of darkness.

10 O how great the ^agoodness of our God, who prepareth a way for our ^bescape from the grasp of this awful monster; yea, that monster, ^cdeath and ^dhell, which I call the death of the body, and also the death of the spirit.

11 And because of the way of ^adeliverance of our God, the Holy One of Israel, this ^bdeath, of which I have spoken, which is the temporal, shall deliver up its dead; which death is the grave.

12 And this ^adeath of which I have spoken, which is the spiritual death, shall deliver up its dead; which spiritual death is ^bhell; wherefore, death and hell must ^cdeliver up their dead, and hell must deliver up its ^dcaptive ^espirits, and the grave must deliver up its captive ^fbodies, and the bodies and the ^gspirits of men will be ^hrestored one to the other; and it is by the power of the resurrection of the Holy One of Israel.

13 O how great the ^aplan of our God! For on the other hand, the ^bparadise of God must deliver up the spirits of the righteous, and the grave deliver up the body of the righteous; and the spirit and the body is ^crestored to itself again, and all men become incorruptible, and ^dimmortal, and they are living souls, having a ^eperfect ^fknowledge like unto us in the flesh, save it be that our knowledge shall be perfect.

14 Wherefore, we shall have a ^aperfect ^bknowledge of all our ^cguilt, and our ^duncleanness, and our ^enakedness; and the righteous shall

7c Mosiah 16:4 (4–7);
  Alma 11:45; 12:36;
  42:6 (6, 9, 14).
 d Mosiah 15:19.
8a Job 12:13 (7–25);
  Abr. 3:21.
  TG God, Wisdom of.
 b TG God, Mercy of.
 c TG Grace.
 d D&C 93:34.
 e Isa. 14:12;
  2 Ne. 2:17;
  Moses 4:3 (3–4);
  Abr. 3:28 (27–28).
 f TG Devil.
9a 3 Ne. 29:7.
 b Jacob 3:11;
  Alma 5:25, 39;
  Moro. 9:13.
 c 2 Cor. 11:14 (13–15).
 d Rev. 12:9 (7–9).
 e TG Lying.
 f Gen. 3:13 (1–13);

  Mosiah 16:3;
  Ether 8:25;
  Moses 4:19 (5–19).
 g Rev. 16:14 (13–14);
  Alma 30:53.
 h D&C 129:8.
 i TG Motivations.
 j TG Secret Combinations.
10a Ex. 34:6 (5–7);
  2 Ne. 4:17;
  D&C 86:11.
 b TG Death, Power over.
 c Mosiah 16:8 (7–8);
  Alma 42:15 (6–15).
 d TG Hell.
11a TG Deliver.
 b TG Death.
12a TG Death, Spiritual,
  First.
 b D&C 76:84.
 c D&C 138:18.
 d TG Bondage, Spiritual;
  Spirits in Prison.

  e TG Spirits, Disembodied.
 f TG Body, Sanctity of.
 g TG Spirit Body.
 h TG Resurrection.
13a TG Salvation, Plan of.
 b D&C 138:19.
  TG Paradise.
 c Alma 11:43; 40:23;
  41:4 (3–5);
  D&C 138:17.
 d TG Immortality.
 e TG Perfection.
 f Eccl. 9:10;
  D&C 130:18.
14a Mosiah 3:25.
 b Isa. 59:12;
  Alma 5:18; 11:43.
 c TG Guilt.
 d TG Uncleanness.
 e Gen. 2:25;
  Ex. 32:25;
  Moses 4:13 (13, 16–17).

have a perfect knowledge of their enjoyment, and their [f]righteousness, being [g]clothed with [h]purity, yea, even with the [i]robe of righteousness.

15 And it shall come to pass that when all men shall have passed from this first death unto life, insomuch as they have become immortal, they must appear before the [a]judgment-seat of the Holy One of Israel; and then cometh the [b]judgment, and then must they be judged according to the holy judgment of God.

16 And assuredly, as the Lord liveth, for the Lord God hath spoken it, and it is his eternal [a]word, which cannot [b]pass away, that they who are righteous shall be righteous still, and they who are [c]filthy shall be [d]filthy still; wherefore, they who are filthy are the [e]devil and his angels; and they shall go away into [f]everlasting fire, prepared for them; and their [g]torment is as a [h]lake of fire and brimstone, whose flame ascendeth up forever and ever and has no end.

17 O the greatness and the [a]justice of our God! For he executeth all his words, and they have gone forth out of his mouth, and his law must be [b]fulfilled.

18 But, behold, the [a]righteous, the [b]saints of the Holy One of Israel, they who have believed in the Holy One of Israel, they who have

endured the [c]crosses of the world, and despised the shame of it, they shall [d]inherit the [e]kingdom of God, which was prepared for them [f]from the foundation of the world, and their [g]joy shall be full [h]forever.

19 O the greatness of the mercy of our God, the Holy One of Israel! For he [a]delivereth his saints from that [b]awful monster the devil, and death, and [c]hell, and that lake of fire and brimstone, which is endless torment.

20 O how great the [a]holiness of our God! For he [b]knoweth [c]all things, and there is not anything save he knows it.

21 And he cometh into the world that he may [a]save all men if they will hearken unto his voice; for behold, he suffereth the pains of all men, yea, the [b]pains of every living creature, both men, women, and children, who belong to the family of [c]Adam.

22 And he suffereth this that the resurrection might pass upon all men, that all might stand before him at the great and judgment day.

23 And he commandeth all men that they must [a]repent, and be [b]baptized in his name, having perfect [c]faith in the Holy One of Israel, or they cannot be saved in the kingdom of God.

14f TG Righteousness.
  g Prov. 31:25.
  h TG Purity.
  i D&C 109:76.
15a TG Judgment, the Last.
  b Job 34:12;
    Ps. 19:9;
    2 Ne. 30:9.
16a 1 Kgs. 8:56;
    Ps. 33:11;
    D&C 1:38 (37–39);
    Moses 1:4.
  b D&C 56:11.
  c Prov. 22:8.
    TG Filthiness.
  d 1 Ne. 15:33 (33–35);
    Alma 7:21;
    Morm. 9:14;
    D&C 88:35.
  e TG Devil.
  f Mosiah 27:28.
  g TG Punish.

  h Rev. 19:20; 21:8;
    2 Ne. 28:23;
    D&C 63:17; 76:36.
17a TG God, Justice of;
    Justice.
  b Ezek. 24:14.
18a Ps. 5:12.
    TG Righteousness.
  b TG Saints.
  c Luke 14:27.
  d Col. 1:12;
    D&C 45:58 (57–58);
    84:38 (33–38).
  e TG Exaltation.
  f Alma 13:3 (3, 5, 7–9).
  g TG Matt. 5:12 (11–12).
  h TG Eternal Life.
19a Job 23:7;
    D&C 108:8.
  b 1 Ne. 15:35.
  c TG Hell.
20a TG Holiness.

  b Mosiah 24:12;
    Alma 26:35.
    TG God, Foreknowledge of; God, Intelligence of; God, Omniscience of.
  c Prov. 5:21;
    D&C 38:2 (1–2).
21a TG Salvation.
  b D&C 18:11;
    19:18 (15–18).
    TG Jesus Christ, Trials of.
  c D&C 107:54 (53–56);
    128:21.
    TG Adam.
23a TG Repent.
  b Mosiah 26:22;
    D&C 76:52 (50–52);
    84:74; 137:6.
    TG Baptism, Essential.
  c TG Baptism, Qualifications for; Faith.

24 And if they will not repent and believe in his ^aname, and be baptized in his name, and ^bendure to the end, they must be ^cdamned; for the Lord God, the Holy One of Israel, has spoken it.

25 Wherefore, he has given a ^alaw; and where there is ^bno ^claw given there is no ^dpunishment; and where there is no punishment there is no condemnation; and where there is no condemnation the mercies of the Holy One of Israel have claim upon them, because of the atonement; for they are delivered by the power of him.

26 For the ^aatonement satisfieth the demands of his ^bjustice upon all those who ^chave not the ^dlaw given to them, that they are ^edelivered from that awful monster, death and ^fhell, and the devil, and the lake of fire and brimstone, which is endless torment; and they are restored to that God who gave them ^gbreath, which is the Holy One of Israel.

27 But wo unto him that has all the ^alaw given, yea, that has all the commandments of God, like unto us, and that ^btransgresseth them, and that ^cwasteth the days of his ^dprobation, for awful is his state!

28 O that cunning ^aplan of the evil one! O the ^bvainness, and the frailties, and the ^cfoolishness of men! When they are ^dlearned they think they are ^ewise, and they ^fhearken not unto the ^gcounsel of God, for they set it aside, supposing they know of themselves, wherefore, their ^hwisdom is foolishness and it profiteth them not. And they shall perish.

29 But to be ^alearned is good if they ^bhearken unto the ^ccounsels of God.

30 But wo unto the ^arich, who are ^brich as to the things of the ^cworld. For because they are rich they despise the ^dpoor, and they persecute the meek, and their ^ehearts are upon their treasures; wherefore, their ^ftreasure is their god. And behold, their ^gtreasure shall perish with them also.

31 And wo unto the deaf that will not ^ahear; for they shall perish.

32 Wo unto the ^ablind that will not see; for they shall perish also.

33 Wo unto the ^auncircumcised of heart, for a knowledge of their

---

24a TG Jesus Christ, Taking the Name of.
  b TG Perseverance.
  c TG Damnation.
25a TG God, Law of.
  b Rom. 4:15; 5:13;
    2 Ne. 2:13.
  c John 15:22 (22–24);
    Acts 17:30; Rom. 5:13;
    James 4:17;
    Alma 42:17 (12–24).
    TG Accountability.
  d TG Punish.
26a Lev. 4:20; Neh. 10:33;
    2 Ne. 2:10.
    TG Jesus Christ,
    Atonement through.
  b TG God, Justice of;
    Justice.
  c Mosiah 3:11;
    Alma 9:16 (15–16); 42:21.
  d Mosiah 15:24;
    D&C 137:7.
    TG Ignorance.
  e TG Death, Power over.
  f TG Spirits in Prison.
  g Gen. 2:7; 6:17;
    Mosiah 2:21;

D&C 77:2; 93:33;
    Abr. 5:7 (7–8).
27a Luke 12:47 (47–48).
    TG God, Law of.
  b TG Disobedience.
  c TG Idleness;
    Procrastination; Waste.
  d TG Probation.
28a Alma 28:13.
  b Job 11:12 (11–12);
    Isa. 9:9 (9–10).
    TG Vanity.
  c Eccl. 4:5; 10:12 (1–3, 12);
    2 Ne. 19:17;
    D&C 35:7.
    TG Foolishness.
  d Luke 16:15;
    2 Ne. 26:20; 28:4 (4, 15).
    TG Education;
    Worldliness.
  e Prov. 14:6;
    Jer. 8:8 (8–9);
    Rom. 1:22.
    TG Pride; Wisdom.
  f TG Walking in Darkness.
  g Prov. 15:22; Jacob 4:10;
    Alma 37:12.
    TG Counsel.

h Prov. 23:4;
    Eccl. 8:17 (16–17);
    Ezek. 28:5 (4–5);
    D&C 76:9.
    TG Knowledge.
29a D&C 67:6.
    TG Learn.
  b 2 Ne. 28:26.
    TG Submissiveness.
  c Jacob 4:10.
    TG Counsel.
30a Jer. 17:11; Luke 12:34;
    D&C 56:16.
  b Matt. 19:23.
  c TG World.
  d TG Poor.
  e TG Hardheartedness.
  f TG Treasure.
  g Prov. 27:24.
31a Ezek. 33:31 (30–33);
    Matt. 11:15; 13:14;
    Heb. 5:11 (11–14);
    Mosiah 26:28;
    D&C 1:14 (2, 11, 14);
    Moses 6:27.
32a TG Apathy;
    Spiritual Blindness.
33a Rom. 2:29 (27–29).

iniquities shall smite them at the last day.

34 Wo unto the *a*liar, for he shall be thrust down to *b*hell.

35 Wo unto the *a*murderer who deliberately *b*killeth, for he shall *c*die.

36 Wo unto them who commit *a*whoredoms, for they shall be thrust down to hell.

37 Yea, wo unto those that *a*worship idols, for the devil of all devils delighteth in them.

38 And, in fine, wo unto all those who die in their *a*sins; for they shall *b*return to God, and behold his face, and remain in their sins.

39 O, my beloved brethren, remember the awfulness in *a*transgressing against that Holy God, and also the awfulness of yielding to the enticings of that *b*cunning one. Remember, to be *c*carnally-minded is *d*death, and to be *e*spiritually-minded is *f*life *g*eternal.

40 O, my beloved brethren, give ear to my words. Remember the greatness of the Holy One of Israel. Do not say that I have spoken hard things against you; for if ye do, ye will *a*revile against the *b*truth; for I have spoken the words of your Maker. I know that the words of truth are *c*hard against all *d*uncleanness; but the *e*righteous fear them not, for they love the truth and are not shaken.

41 O then, my beloved brethren, *a*come unto the Lord, the Holy One. Remember that his paths are righteous. Behold, the *b*way for man is *c*narrow, but it lieth in a straight course before him, and the keeper of the *d*gate is the Holy One of Israel; and he employeth no servant there; and there is none other way save it be by the gate; for he cannot be deceived, for the Lord God is his name.

42 And whoso *a*knocketh, to him will he open; and the *b*wise, and the learned, and they that are rich, who are puffed up because of their *c*learning, and their *d*wisdom, and their riches—yea, they are they whom he despiseth; and save they shall cast these things away, and consider themselves *e*fools before God, and come down in the depths of *f*humility, he will not open unto them.

43 But the things of the wise and the *a*prudent shall be *b*hid from them forever—yea, that happiness which is prepared for the saints.

44 O, my beloved brethren, remember my words. Behold, I take off my garments, and I shake them before you; I pray the God of my salvation that he view me with his

---

34*a* Prov. 19:9.
  TG Gossip; Honesty;
  Lying.
  b TG Hell.
35*a* Num. 35:16 (16–25).
  b Deut. 19:11;
  2 Sam. 12:9;
  Mosiah 13:21.
  c TG Capital Punishment.
36*a* 3 Ne. 12:27 (27–32).
  TG Chastity; Whore.
37*a* Isa. 41:24 (21–24).
  TG Idolatry.
38*a* Ezek. 18:24.
  TG Sin.
  b Alma 40:11.
39*a* TG Transgress.
  b 2 Ne. 28:21 (20–22); 32:8;
  Mosiah 2:32; 4:14;
  Alma 30:42 (42, 53).
  c Rom. 8:6.
  TG Carnal Mind.

  d TG Death; Death,
    Spiritual, First; Hell.
  e Prov. 15:24.
    TG Spirituality.
  f Prov. 11:19.
  g TG Eternal Life.
40*a* TG Reviling.
  b Prov. 15:10;
    Mosiah 13:7.
    TG Truth.
  c 1 Ne. 16:2;
    2 Ne. 28:28; 33:5.
  d TG Uncleanness.
  e Prov. 28:1.
41*a* 1 Ne. 6:4;
    Jacob 1:7;
    Omni 1:26 (25–26);
    Alma 29:2;
    3 Ne. 21:20;
    Morm. 9:27;
    Ether 5:5;
    Moro. 10:30 (30–32).

  b Ex. 33:13 (12–13);
    2 Ne. 31:21 (17–21);
    Alma 37:46;
    D&C 132:22 (22, 25).
  c Luke 13:24;
    2 Ne. 33:9;
    Jacob 6:11;
    Hel. 3:29 (29–30).
  d 2 Ne. 31:9 (9, 17–18);
    3 Ne. 14:14 (13–14);
    D&C 22:4; 43:7; 137:2.
42*a* TG Objectives; Study.
  b Matt. 11:25.
    TG Wisdom.
  c TG Knowledge; Learn;
    Worldliness.
  d Ezek. 28:5 (4–5).
  e 1 Cor. 3:18 (18–21).
  f TG Humility;
    Teachable.
43*a* TG Prudence.
  b 1 Cor. 2:14 (9–16).

ᵃall-searching eye; wherefore, ye shall know at the last day, when all men shall be judged of their works, that the God of Israel did witness that I ᵇshook your iniquities from my soul, and that I stand with brightness before him, and am ᶜrid of your blood.

45 O, my beloved brethren, turn away from your sins; shake off the ᵃchains of him that would bind you fast; come unto that God who is the ᵇrock of your salvation.

46 Prepare your souls for that glorious day when ᵃjustice shall be administered unto the righteous, even the day of ᵇjudgment, that ye may not shrink with awful fear; that ye may not remember your awful ᶜguilt in perfectness, and be constrained to exclaim: Holy, holy are thy judgments, O Lord God ᵈAlmighty—but I know my guilt; I transgressed thy law, and my transgressions are mine; and the devil hath ᵉobtained me, that I am a prey to his awful misery.

47 But behold, my brethren, is it expedient that I should awake you to an awful reality of these things? Would I harrow up your souls if your minds were pure? Would I be plain unto you according to the plainness of the truth if ye were freed from sin?

48 Behold, if ye were holy I would speak unto you of holiness; but as ye are not holy, and ye look upon me as a ᵃteacher, it must needs be expedient that I ᵇteach you the consequences of sin.

49 Behold, my soul abhorreth sin, and my heart ᵃdelighteth in righteousness; and I will ᵇpraise the holy name of my God.

50 Come, my brethren, every one that ᵃthirsteth, come ye to the ᵇwaters; and he that hath no ᶜmoney, come buy and eat; yea, come buy wine and milk without money and without price.

51 Wherefore, do not spend money for that which is of no worth, nor your ᵃlabor for that which cannot ᵇsatisfy. Hearken diligently unto me, and remember the words which I have spoken; and come unto the Holy One of Israel, and ᶜfeast upon that which perisheth not, neither can be corrupted, and let your soul delight in fatness.

52 Behold, my beloved brethren, remember the words of your God; pray unto him continually by day, and give ᵃthanks unto his holy name by night. Let your hearts ᵇrejoice.

53 And behold how great the ᵃcovenants of the Lord, and how great his ᵇcondescensions unto the children of men; and because of his greatness, and his ᶜgrace and ᵈmercy, he has promised unto us that our seed shall not utterly be destroyed, according to the flesh, but that he would ᵉpreserve them; and in future generations they shall become a righteous ᶠbranch unto the house of Israel.

54 And now, my brethren, I would speak unto you more; but on the morrow I will declare unto you the remainder of my words. Amen.

44ᵃ Jacob 2:10.
  b Jacob 1:19.
  c Jacob 2:2 (2, 16);
    Mosiah 2:28;
    D&C 61:34.
45ᵃ 2 Ne. 28:22;
    Alma 36:18.
  b TG Rock.
46ᵃ TG God, Justice of.
  b TG Judgment, the Last.
  c Mosiah 3:25.
  d Gen. 48:3;
    1 Ne. 1:14;
    3 Ne. 4:32;
    Moses 2:1.
  e TG Apostasy of

    Individuals.
48ᵃ 2 Ne. 5:26.
    TG Teacher;
    Teaching.
  b Deut. 33:10;
    2 Chr. 15:3 (1–4); 17:9.
    TG Prophets, Mission of.
49ᵃ TG Desire;
    Motivations.
  b Ezra 3:11 (11–13);
    1 Ne. 18:16;
    Alma 36:28.
50ᵃ Isa. 44:3; 55:1 (1–2).
  b TG Living Water.
  c Alma 5:34; 42:27.
51ᵃ Isa. 55:2.

    TG Work, Value of.
  b Eccl. 1:3.
  c Prov. 13:25;
    Enos 1:4;
    3 Ne. 12:6.
52ᵃ TG Thanksgiving.
  b Deut. 26:11.
53ᵃ TG Covenants.
  b TG Jesus Christ,
    Condescension of.
  c TG Grace.
  d TG Compassion;
    God, Mercy of.
  e TG Protection, Divine.
  f TG Vineyard of the
    Lord.

CHAPTER 10

Jacob explains that the Jews will crucify their God—They will be scattered until they begin to believe in Him—America will be a land of liberty where no king will rule—Reconcile yourselves to God and gain salvation through His grace. About 559–545 B.C.

AND now I, Jacob, speak unto you again, my beloved brethren, concerning this righteous ^abranch of which I have spoken.

2 For behold, the ^apromises which we have obtained are promises unto us according to the flesh; wherefore, as it has been shown unto me that many of our children shall perish in the flesh because of ^bunbelief, nevertheless, God will be merciful unto many; and our children shall be ^crestored, that they may come to that which will give them the true knowledge of their Redeemer.

3 Wherefore, as I said unto you, it must needs be expedient that Christ—for in the last night the ^aangel spake unto me that this should be his name—should ^bcome among the ^cJews, among those who are the more wicked part of the world; and they shall ^dcrucify him—for thus it behooveth our God, and there is none other nation on earth that would ^ecrucify their ^fGod.

4 For should the mighty ^amiracles be wrought among other nations they would repent, and know that he be their God.

5 But because of ^apriestcrafts and iniquities, they at Jerusalem will ^bstiffen their necks against him, that he be ^ccrucified.

6 Wherefore, because of their iniquities, destructions, famines, ^apestilences, and bloodshed shall come upon them; and they who shall not be destroyed shall be ^bscattered among all nations.

7 But behold, thus saith the ^aLord God: ^bWhen the day cometh that they shall believe in me, that I am Christ, then have I covenanted with their fathers that they shall be ^crestored in the flesh, upon the earth, unto the ^dlands of their inheritance.

8 And it shall come to pass that they shall be ^agathered in from their long dispersion, from the ^bisles of the sea, and from the four parts of the earth; and the nations of the Gentiles shall be great in the eyes of me, saith God, in ^ccarrying them forth to the lands of their inheritance.

9 ^aYea, the kings of the Gentiles shall be nursing fathers unto them, and their queens shall become nursing mothers; wherefore, the ^bpromises of the Lord are great unto the Gentiles, for he hath spoken it, and who can dispute?

10 But behold, this land, said God, shall be a land of thine inheritance, and the ^aGentiles shall be blessed upon the land.

11 And this land shall be a land of

10 1a 1 Ne. 15:12 (12–20);
2 Ne. 3:5;
Jacob 5:45 (43–45);
Alma 46:24 (24–25).
2a 1 Ne. 22:8 (8–12);
3 Ne. 5:23 (21–26);
21:7 (4–29).
TG Promise.
b TG Doubt.
c TG Restoration of the Gospel.
3a 2 Ne. 2:4; 11:3; 25:19;
Jacob 7:5; Moro. 7:22.
b TG Jesus Christ, Prophecies about.
c TG Israel, Judah, People of.
d Luke 18:31; 1 Ne. 11:33;

Mosiah 3:9 (9–10).
e TG Matt. 27:22;
Luke 22:2; 23:23 (20–24).
f 1 Ne. 19:10 (7, 10);
2 Ne. 26:12.
4a TG Miracle.
5a Matt. 27:20 (11–26);
Luke 22:2;
John 11:47 (47–53).
TG Apostasy of Israel;
Priestcraft.
b TG Stiffnecked.
c TG Jesus Christ, Crucifixion of.
6a TG Plague.
b 1 Ne. 19:14 (13–14);
2 Ne. 25:15.
TG Israel, Bondage of, in

Other Lands.
7a TG Jesus Christ, Lord.
b 2 Ne. 9:2 (1–2);
25:16 (16–17).
c Gen. 49:10.
TG Israel, Restoration of.
d TG Lands of Inheritance.
8a TG Israel, Gathering of.
b Isa. 51:5; 1 Ne. 22:4;
2 Ne. 29:7; D&C 133:8.
c Isa. 11:14;
1 Ne. 21:22; 22:8.
9a Isa. 49:22 (22–23);
2 Ne. 6:6.
b 1 Ne. 22:8 (1–9);
Alma 9:24; D&C 3:20.
10a 2 Ne. 6:12;
3 Ne. 16:6 (4–7).

*aliberty unto the Gentiles, and there shall be no *bkings upon the land, who shall raise up unto the Gentiles.

12 And I will fortify this land *aagainst all other nations.

13 And he that *afighteth against Zion shall *bperish, saith God.

14 For he that raiseth up a *aking against me shall perish, for I, the Lord, the *bking of heaven, will be their king, and I will be a *clight unto them forever, that hear my words.

15 Wherefore, for this cause, that my *acovenants may be fulfilled which I have made unto the children of men, that I will do unto them while they are in the flesh, I must needs destroy the *bsecret works of *cdarkness, and of murders, and of abominations.

16 Wherefore, he that *afighteth against *bZion, both Jew and Gentile, both bond and free, both male and female, *cshall perish; for *dthey are they who are the *ewhore of all the earth; for *fthey who are *gnot for me are *hagainst me, saith our God.

17 For I will *afulfil my *bpromises which I have made unto the children of men, that I will do unto them while they are in the flesh—

18 Wherefore, my beloved brethren, thus saith our God: I will afflict thy seed by the hand of the Gen-

tiles; nevertheless, I will *asoften the hearts of the *bGentiles, that they shall be like unto a father to them; wherefore, the Gentiles shall be *cblessed and *dnumbered among the house of Israel.

19 Wherefore, I will *aconsecrate this land unto thy seed, and them who shall be numbered among thy seed, forever, for the land of their inheritance; for it is a choice land, saith God unto me, above all other lands, wherefore I will have all men that dwell thereon that they shall worship me, saith God.

20 And now, my beloved brethren, seeing that our merciful God has given us so great knowledge concerning these things, let us remember him, and lay aside our sins, and not hang down our heads, for we are not cast off; nevertheless, we have been *adriven out of the land of our inheritance; but we have been led to a *bbetter land, for the Lord has made the sea our *cpath, and we are upon an *disle of the sea.

21 But great are the promises of the Lord unto them who are upon the *aisles of the sea; wherefore as it says isles, there must needs be more than this, and they are inhabited also by our brethren.

22 For behold, the Lord God has

11*a* TG Liberty.
  b 2 Ne. 1:7;
    Mosiah 29:32.
12*a* 1 Ne. 13:19.
13*a* 1 Ne. 22:14 (14, 19).
  b Isa. 60:12.
14*a* TG Kings, Earthly.
  b Josh. 2:11;
    Ps. 44:4;
    Matt. 2:2;
    Alma 5:50;
    D&C 20:17; 38:21 (21–22);
    128:22 (22–23);
    Moses 7:53.
  c TG Jesus Christ, Light of the World.
15*a* TG Abrahamic Covenant; Covenants.
  b Lev. 19:26;
    Hel. 3:23;
    7:25 (4–5, 21, 25).
    TG Secret Combinations.
  c TG Darkness, Spiritual.

16*a* TG Protection, Divine.
  b TG Zion.
  c Isa. 41:11 (11–12).
  d 1 Ne. 13:5.
  e TG Devil, Church of; Whore.
  f 1 Ne. 14:10.
  g 1 Ne. 22:13 (13–23);
    2 Ne. 6:15; 28:15 (15–32);
    3 Ne. 16:8 (8–15);
    Ether 2:9 (8–11).
  h Matt. 12:30.
17*a* 1 Kgs. 8:56;
    D&C 1:38; 101:64.
  b TG Promise.
18*a* 1 Ne. 13:31;
    2 Ne. 4:7;
    Jacob 3:6 (5–9);
    Hel. 15:12 (10–17);
    Morm. 5:20 (20–21).
  b Matt. 8:11 (11–12); 12:21;
    Luke 13:29 (28–30);
    Acts 10:45;

    D&C 45:9 (7–30).
  c Eph. 3:6 (1–7);
    2 Ne. 33:9;
    3 Ne. 21:14.
  d Gal. 3:7 (7, 29);
    1 Ne. 14:2;
    3 Ne. 16:13;
    21:6 (6, 22, 25); 30:2;
    Abr. 2:10 (9–11).
19*a* 1 Ne. 13:15.
20*a* 1 Ne. 1:20 (18–20);
    2:2 (1–4).
  b 1 Ne. 2:20.
    TG Promised Lands.
  c Ps. 8:8;
    1 Ne. 18:8 (5–23).
  d Isa. 11:11 (11–12);
    42:4; 51:5;
    Ezek. 26:15 (3, 6–7, 15);
    39:6;
    2 Ne. 8:5.
21*a* Isa. 49:1;
    1 Ne. 19:16; 21:1; 22:4.

[a]led away from time to time from the house of Israel, according to his will and pleasure. And now behold, the Lord remembereth all them who have been broken off, wherefore he remembereth us also.

23 Therefore, [a]cheer up your hearts, and remember that ye are [b]free to [c]act for yourselves—to [d]choose the way of everlasting death or the way of eternal life.

24 Wherefore, my beloved brethren, [a]reconcile yourselves to the [b]will of God, and not to the will of the devil and the flesh; and remember, after ye are reconciled unto God, that it is only in and through the [c]grace of God that ye are [d]saved.

25 Wherefore, may God [a]raise you from death by the power of the resurrection, and also from everlasting death by the power of the [b]atonement, that ye may be received into the [c]eternal kingdom of God, that ye may praise him through grace divine. Amen.

CHAPTER 11

Jacob saw his Redeemer—The law of Moses typifies Christ and proves He will come. About 559–545 B.C.

AND now, [a]Jacob spake many more things to my people at that time; nevertheless only these things have I caused to be [b]written, for the things which I have written sufficeth me.

2 And now I, Nephi, write [a]more of the words of [b]Isaiah, for my soul delighteth in his words. For I will liken his words unto my people, and I will send them forth unto all my children, for he verily [c]saw my [d]Redeemer, even as I have seen him.

3 And my brother, Jacob, also has [a]seen him as I have seen him; wherefore, I will send their words forth unto my children to prove unto them that my words are true. Wherefore, by the words of [b]three, God hath said, I will establish my word. Nevertheless, God sendeth more [c]witnesses, and he proveth all his words.

4 Behold, my soul delighteth in [a]proving unto my people the truth of the [b]coming of Christ; for, for this end hath the [c]law of Moses been given; and all things which have been given of God from the beginning of the world, unto man, are the [d]typifying of him.

5 And also my soul delighteth in the [a]covenants of the Lord which he hath made to our fathers; yea, my soul delighteth in his [b]grace, and in his justice, and power, and mercy in the great and eternal plan of [c]deliverance from death.

6 And my soul delighteth in proving unto my people that [a]save Christ should come all men must perish.

7 For if there be [a]no Christ there be no God; and if there be no God we

22a 1 Ne. 22:4 (4–5);
　　2 Ne. 1:6.
　　TG Israel,
　　Scattering of;
　　Israel, Ten Lost
　　Tribes of.
23a TG Cheerful.
　　b TG Agency.
　　c 2 Ne. 2:16.
　　d Deut. 30:19 (15, 19).
24a TG Reconciliation.
　　b TG God, Will of.
　　c TG Grace.
　　d TG Salvation;
　　　Salvation, Plan of.
25a TG Death, Power over;
　　　Resurrection.
　　b TG Jesus Christ,
　　　Atonement through.

　　c TG Eternity.
11 1a 2 Ne. 6:1 (1–10).
　　b 2 Ne. 31:1.
2a 2 Ne. 6:16 (16–18).
　　b 3 Ne. 23:1.
　　c 2 Ne. 16:1.
　　TG Jesus Christ,
　　　Appearances,
　　　Antemortal.
　　d TG Jesus Christ,
　　　Jehovah.
3a 2 Ne. 2:3 (3–4); 10:3;
　　Jacob 7:5.
　　TG God, Privilege of
　　　Seeing.
　　b 2 Ne. 27:12 (12–14);
　　　Ether 5:3 (2–4);
　　　D&C 5:11 (11, 15).
　　c TG Book of Mormon;

　　　Witness.
4a 2 Ne. 31:2.
　　b Jacob 4:5;
　　　Jarom 1:11;
　　　Alma 25:16 (15–16);
　　　Ether 12:19 (18–19).
　　c 2 Ne. 5:10.
　　d TG Jesus Christ, Types
　　　of, in Anticipation;
　　　Law of Moses.
5a TG Abrahamic Covenant.
　　b TG Benevolence;
　　　Grace.
　　c TG Deliver;
　　　Jesus Christ, Atonement
　　　through.
6a Mosiah 3:15.
7a 2 Ne. 2:13 (13–14).

are not, for there could have been no [b]creation. But there is a God, and [c]he is Christ, and he cometh in the fulness of his own time.

8 And now I write [a]some of the words of Isaiah, that whoso of my people shall see these words may lift up their hearts and rejoice for all men. Now these are the words, and ye may liken them unto you and unto all men.

CHAPTER 12

Isaiah sees the latter-day temple, gathering of Israel, and millennial judgment and peace—The proud and wicked will be brought low at the Second Coming— Compare Isaiah 2. About 559–545 B.C.

[a]THE word that Isaiah, the son of Amoz, saw concerning Judah and Jerusalem:

2 And it shall come to pass in the last days, [a]when the [b]mountain of the Lord's [c]house shall be established in the top of the [d]mountains, and shall be exalted above the hills, and all nations shall flow unto it.

3 And many [a]people shall go and say, Come ye, and let us go up to the [b]mountain of the Lord, to the [c]house of the God of Jacob; and he will teach us of his ways, and we will [d]walk in his paths; for out of Zion shall go forth the law, and the word of the Lord from Jerusalem.

4 And he shall [a]judge among the nations, and shall rebuke many people: and they shall beat their swords into plow-shares, and their spears into pruning-hooks—nation shall not lift up sword against nation, neither shall they learn war any more.

5 O house of Jacob, come ye and let us walk in the light of the Lord; yea, come, for ye have all [a]gone astray, every one to his [b]wicked ways.

6 Therefore, O Lord, thou hast forsaken thy people, the house of Jacob, because they be replenished from the east, and hearken unto [a]soothsayers like the [b]Philistines, and they please themselves in the children of strangers.

7 Their land also is full of silver and gold, neither is there any end of their [a]treasures; their land is also full of horses, neither is there any end of their chariots.

8 Their land is also full of [a]idols; they worship the work of their own hands, that which their own fingers have made.

9 And the mean man [a]boweth [b]not down, and the great man humbleth himself not, therefore, forgive him not.

10 O ye wicked ones, enter into the rock, and [a]hide thee in the dust, for the fear of the Lord and the glory of his majesty shall smite thee.

11 And it shall come to pass that the [a]lofty looks of man shall be humbled, and the haughtiness of men shall be bowed down, and the Lord alone shall be exalted in that day.

12 For the [a]day of the Lord of

7b Heb. 3:4 (3–4).
   TG Creation;
   God, Creator.
 c TG Jesus Christ,
   Jehovah.
8a See the Latter-day Saint
   edition of the King
   James Version of the
   Bible for other notes
   and cross-references
   on these chapters from
   Isaiah.
12 1a Isa. 2:1 (1–22).
 2a Comparison with the
   King James Bible in
   English shows that
   there are differences in

more than half of the
433 verses of Isaiah
quoted in the Book of
Mormon, while about
200 verses have the
same wording as KJV.
 b TG Zion.
 c 3 Ne. 24:1.
 d Gen. 49:26;
   D&C 49:25; 109:61;
   133:31 (29–31).
3a Zech. 8:22.
 b Joel 2:1;
   2 Ne. 30:15 (12–18);
   D&C 133:13.
 c Ps. 122:1.
 d TG Walking with God.

4a 2 Ne. 21:3 (2–5, 9).
5a 2 Ne. 28:14;
   Mosiah 14:6; Alma 5:37.
 b Isa. 53:6.
6a TG Sorcery.
 b Gen. 10:14.
7a TG Treasure.
8a Jer. 2:28.
   TG Idolatry.
9a Ex. 34:8; Isa. 2:9.
 b IE unto God; he
   worships idols instead.
10a Amos 9:3;
   Rev. 6:15 (15–16);
   Alma 12:14.
11a 2 Ne. 15:15 (15–16).
12a TG Day of the Lord.

Hosts soon cometh upon all nations, yea, upon every one; yea, upon the ^{b}proud and lofty, and upon every one who is lifted up, and he shall be brought low.

13 Yea, and the day of the Lord shall come upon all the ^{a}cedars of Lebanon, for they are high and lifted up; and upon all the oaks of Bashan;

14 And upon all the ^{a}high mountains, and upon all the hills, and upon all the nations which are lifted up, and upon every people;

15 And upon every ^{a}high tower, and upon every fenced wall;

16 And upon all the ships of the ^{a}sea, and upon all the ships of Tarshish, and upon all pleasant pictures.

17 And the loftiness of man shall be bowed down, and the ^{a}haughtiness of men shall be made low; and the Lord alone shall be exalted in ^{b}that day.

18 And the idols he shall utterly abolish.

19 And they shall go into the holes of the rocks, and into the caves of the earth, for the fear of the Lord shall come upon them and the ^{a}glory of his majesty shall smite them, when he ariseth to shake terribly the earth.

20 In that day a man shall cast his idols of silver, and his idols of gold, which he hath made for himself to worship, to the moles and to the bats;

21 To go into the clefts of the rocks, and into the tops of the ragged rocks, for the fear of the Lord shall come upon them and the majesty of his glory shall smite them, when he ariseth to shake terribly the earth.

22 Cease ye from man, whose breath is in his nostrils; for wherein is he to be accounted of?

CHAPTER 13

Judah and Jerusalem will be punished for their disobedience—The Lord pleads for and judges His people—The daughters of Zion are cursed and tormented for their worldliness—Compare Isaiah 3. About 559–545 B.C.

^{a}FOR behold, the Lord, the Lord of Hosts, doth take away from Jerusalem, and from Judah, the stay and the staff, the whole staff of bread, and the whole stay of water—

2 The ^{a}mighty man, and the man of ^{b}war, the judge, and the prophet, and the ^{c}prudent, and the ancient;

3 The captain of fifty, and the honorable man, and the counselor, and the cunning artificer, and the eloquent orator.

4 And I will give children unto them to be their princes, and babes shall rule over them.

5 And the people shall be ^{a}oppressed, every one by another, and every one by his neighbor; the child shall behave himself ^{b}proudly against the ancient, and the base against the honorable.

6 When a man shall take hold of his brother of the house of his father, and shall say: Thou hast clothing, be thou our ruler, and let not this ^{a}ruin come under thy hand—

7 In that day shall he swear, saying: I will not be a healer; for in my house there is neither bread nor clothing; make me not a ruler of the people.

8 For Jerusalem is ^{a}ruined, and Judah is ^{b}fallen, because their

---

12b Job 40:11;
Mal. 4:1;
2 Ne. 23:11;
D&C 64:24.
13a Isa. 37:24;
Ezek. 31:3;
Zech. 11:1 (1–2).
14a Isa. 30:25.
15a 3 Ne. 21:15 (15, 18).
16a The Greek (Septuagint) has "ships of the sea."

The Hebrew has "ships of Tarshish." The Book of Mormon has both, showing that the brass plates had lost neither phrase.
17a TG Haughtiness.
b IE the day of the Lord's coming in glory; see vv. 17–21.
19a TG Jesus Christ, Glory of.

13 1a Isa. 3:1 (1–26).
2a 2 Kgs. 24:14.
b 1 Chr. 28:3.
c TG Prudence.
5a TG Oppression.
b TG Haughtiness.
6a Isa. 3:6.
8a Isa. 1:7;
Jer. 9:11;
Ezek. 36:17 (16–20).
b Lam. 1:3 (1–3).

ctongues and their doings have been against the Lord, to dprovoke the eyes of his glory.

9 The show of their countenance doth witness against them, and doth declare their asin to be even as bSodom, and they cannot hide it. Wo unto their souls, for they have rewarded evil unto themselves!

10 Say unto the righteous that it is awell with them; for they shall beat the fruit of their doings.

11 Wo unto the wicked, for they shall perish; for the reward of their hands shall be upon them!

12 And my people, children are their oppressors, and women rule over them. O my people, they who alead thee cause thee to err and destroy the way of thy paths.

13 The Lord standeth up to aplead, and standeth to judge the people.

14 The Lord will enter into ajudgment with the ancients of his people and the princes thereof; for ye have eaten up the bvineyard and the spoil of the cpoor in your houses.

15 What mean ye? Ye abeat my people to pieces, and grind the faces of the poor, saith the Lord God of Hosts.

16 Moreover, the Lord saith: Because the daughters of Zion are ahaughty, and bwalk with stretched-forth necks and wanton eyes, walking and mincing as they go, and making a tinkling with their feet—

17 Therefore the Lord will smite with a ascab the crown of the head of the daughters of Zion, and the Lord will bdiscover their secret parts.

18 In that aday the Lord will take away the bravery of their tinkling ornaments, and cauls, and round tires like the moon;

19 The chains and the bracelets, and the mufflers;

20 The bonnets, and the ornaments of the legs, and the headbands, and the tablets, and the ear-rings;

21 The rings, and nose jewels;

22 The changeable suits of apparel, and the mantles, and the wimples, and the crisping-pins;

23 The glasses, and the fine linen, and hoods, and the veils.

24 And it shall come to pass, instead of sweet smell there shall be stink; and instead of a girdle, a rent; and instead of well set hair, abaldness; and instead of a stomacher, a girding of sackcloth; bburning instead of cbeauty.

25 Thy men shall fall by the sword and thy mighty in the war.

26 And her agates shall lament and bmourn; and she shall be desolate, and shall csit upon the ground.

CHAPTER 14

Zion and her daughters will be redeemed and cleansed in the millennial day— Compare Isaiah 4. About 559–545 B.C.

aAND in that day, seven women shall take hold of one man, saying: We will eat our own bread, and wear our own apparel; only let us be called by thy name to take away our breproach.

2 In that day shall the abranch of the Lord be beautiful and glorious; the fruit of the earth excellent and

8c Ps. 52:2.
  d TG Provoking.
9a TG Apostasy of Israel.
  b Gen. 18:20 (20–21);
    19:5, 24 (24–25);
    2 Ne. 23:19.
    TG Homosexual
    Behavior.
10a Deut. 12:28.
  b Ps. 128:2.
12a Isa. 9:16.
    TG Leadership.
13a Micah 6:2.

14a TG Jesus Christ, Judge.
  b Isa. 5:7.
  c Ezek. 18:12;
    2 Ne. 28:13 (12–13);
    Hel. 4:12 (11–13).
15a Micah 3:3 (2–3);
    2 Ne. 26:20.
16a TG Haughtiness.
  b TG Walking in Darkness.
17a Deut. 28:27.
  b Jer. 13:22;
    Nahum 3:5.
18a TG Day of the Lord.

24a Isa. 22:12;
    Micah 1:16.
  b 2 Ne. 14:4.
  c Lam. 1:6 (4–6).
26a Jer. 14:2.
  b Lam. 1:4 (4–6).
  c Lam. 2:10.
14 1a Isa. 4:1 (1–6).
  b TG Reproach.
 2a Isa. 60:21; 61:3;
    2 Ne. 3:5;
    Jacob 2:25.

comely to them that are escaped of Israel.

3 And it shall come to pass, they that are *left in Zion and remain in Jerusalem shall be called holy, every one that is written among the living in Jerusalem—

4 When the Lord shall have *washed away the filth of the daughters of Zion, and shall have purged the blood of Jerusalem from the midst thereof by the spirit of judgment and by the spirit of *burning.

5 And the *Lord will create upon every dwelling-place of mount Zion, and upon her assemblies, a *cloud and smoke by day and the shining of a flaming fire by night; for upon all the glory of Zion shall be a defence.

6 And there shall be a tabernacle for a shadow in the daytime from the heat, and for a place of *refuge, and a covert from storm and from rain.

CHAPTER 15

The Lord's vineyard (Israel) will become desolate, and His people will be scattered—Woes will come upon them in their apostate and scattered state—The Lord will lift an ensign and gather Israel—Compare Isaiah 5. About 559–545 B.C.

*AND then will I sing to my well-beloved a song of my beloved, touching his *vineyard. My well-beloved hath a vineyard in a very fruitful hill.

2 And he fenced it, and gathered out the stones thereof, and planted it with the choicest *vine, and built a tower in the midst of it, and also made a wine-press therein; and he looked that it should bring forth grapes, and it brought forth wild grapes.

3 And now, O inhabitants of Jerusalem, and men of Judah, judge, I pray you, betwixt me and my vineyard.

4 What could have been done more to my vineyard that I have not done in it? Wherefore, when I looked that it should bring forth grapes it brought forth wild grapes.

5 And now go to; I will tell you what I will do to my vineyard—I will *take away the hedge thereof, and it shall be eaten up; and I will break down the wall thereof, and it shall be trodden down;

6 And I will lay it waste; it shall not be pruned nor digged; but there shall come up *briers and thorns; I will also command the clouds that they *rain no rain upon it.

7 For the *vineyard of the Lord of Hosts is the house of Israel, and the men of Judah his pleasant plant; and he looked for *judgment, and behold, *oppression; for righteousness, but behold, a cry.

8 Wo unto them that join *house to house, till there can be no place, that they may be placed alone in the midst of the earth!

9 In mine ears, said the Lord of Hosts, of a truth many houses shall be desolate, and great and fair cities without inhabitant.

10 Yea, ten acres of vineyard shall yield one *bath, and the seed of a homer shall yield an ephah.

11 Wo unto them that rise up early in the morning, that they may *follow strong drink, that continue until night, and *wine inflame them!

12 And the harp, and the *viol, the tabret, and pipe, and wine are in their feasts; but they *regard not

---

3 a Matt. 13:43 (41–43).
4 a 2 Ne. 13:24 (16–26).
   TG Wash.
   b Mal. 3:2; 4:1.
5 a Isa. 60:20 (1–3, 19–21).
   TG God, Presence of.
   b Ex. 13:21;
   Zech. 2:5.
6 a Isa. 25:4.
   TG Refuge.

15 1 a Isa. 5:1 (1–30).
   b TG Vineyard of the Lord.
2 a Jer. 2:21.
5 a Ps. 80:12 (8–15).
6 a Isa. 7:23 (23–24); 32:13.
   b Lev. 26:4;
   Jer. 3:3.
7 a TG Vineyard of the Lord.
   b Amos 5:24.
   c TG Oppression.

8 a Micah 2:2.
10 a BD Weights and
   measures. See also
   Ezek. 45:11.
11 a Prov. 23:30 (29–32).
   b TG Drunkenness;
   Word of Wisdom.
12 a Amos 6:5 (5–6).
   b Ps. 28:5.
   TG Rebellion.

the work of the Lord, neither consider the operation of his hands.

13 Therefore, my people are gone into *a*captivity, because they have no *b*knowledge; and their honorable men are famished, and their multitude dried up with thirst.

14 Therefore, hell hath enlarged herself, and opened her mouth without measure; and their glory, and their multitude, and their pomp, and he that rejoiceth, shall descend into it.

15 And the mean man shall be *a*brought down, and the *b*mighty man shall be humbled, and the eyes of the *c*lofty shall be humbled.

16 But the Lord of Hosts shall be exalted in *a*judgment, and God that is holy shall be sanctified in righteousness.

17 Then shall the lambs feed after their manner, and the waste places of the *a*fat ones shall strangers eat.

18 Wo unto them that draw iniquity with cords of *a*vanity, and sin as it were with a cart rope;

19 That say: Let him *a*make speed, *b*hasten his work, that we may *c*see it; and let the counsel of the Holy One of Israel draw nigh and come, that we may know it.

20 Wo unto them that *a*call *b*evil good, and good evil, that put *c*darkness for light, and light for darkness, that put bitter for sweet, and sweet for bitter!

21 Wo unto the *a*wise in their own eyes and *b*prudent in their own sight!

22 Wo unto the mighty to drink *a*wine, and men of strength to mingle strong drink;

23 Who justify the wicked for *a*reward, and take away the righteousness of the righteous from him!

24 Therefore, as the *a*fire devoureth the *b*stubble, and the flame consumeth the *c*chaff, their *d*root shall be rottenness, and their blossoms shall go up as dust; because they have cast away the law of the Lord of Hosts, and *e*despised the word of the Holy One of Israel.

25 Therefore, is the *a*anger of the Lord kindled against his people, and he hath stretched forth his hand against them, and hath smitten them; and the hills did tremble, and their carcasses were torn in the midst of the streets. For all this his anger is not turned away, but his hand is stretched out still.

26 And he will lift up an *a*ensign to the *b*nations from far, and will hiss unto them from the *c*end of the earth; and behold, they shall *d*come with speed swiftly; none shall be weary nor stumble among them.

27 None shall slumber nor sleep; neither shall the girdle of their loins be loosed, nor the latchet of their shoes be broken;

28 Whose arrows shall be sharp, and all their bows bent, and their horses' hoofs shall be counted like flint, and their wheels like a whirlwind, their roaring like a lion.

29 They shall roar like young *a*lions; yea, they shall roar, and lay hold of the prey, and shall carry away safe, and none shall deliver.

30 And in that *a*day they shall roar against them like the roaring of the

13a Lam. 1:3 (1–3).
  b Isa. 1:3;
    Hosea 4:6.
    TG Knowledge.
15a Isa. 2:17 (11, 17).
  b 2 Ne. 12:11.
  c TG Haughtiness.
16a TG Jesus Christ, Judge.
17a Isa. 10:16.
18a TG Vanity.
19a Jer. 17:15.
  b TG Haste.
  c TG Sign Seekers.
20a D&C 64:16; 121:16.

  b Moro. 7:14 (14, 18).
  c 1 Jn. 1:6.
21a Prov. 3:7 (5–7);
    2 Ne. 28:15.
  b TG Prudence.
22a Prov. 31:4 (3–9).
23a TG Bribe.
24a Obad. 1:18;
    2 Ne. 20:17;
    3 Ne. 20:16.
  b Joel 2:5;
    1 Ne. 22:15 (15, 23);
    2 Ne. 26:6 (4, 6);
    D&C 64:24 (23–24);

    133:64.
  c Luke 3:17;
    Mosiah 7:30 (29–31).
  d Job 18:16 (16–21).
  e 2 Sam. 12:9 (7–9).
25a Deut. 32:21;
    D&C 63:32;
    Moses 6:27.
26a TG Ensign.
  b TG Nations.
  c 2 Ne. 29:2.
  d TG Israel, Gathering of.
29a 3 Ne. 21:12 (12–13).
30a TG Day of the Lord.

sea; and if they look unto the land, behold, darkness and sorrow, and the light is darkened in the heavens thereof.

CHAPTER 16

Isaiah sees the Lord—Isaiah's sins are forgiven—He is called to prophesy—He prophesies of the rejection by the Jews of Christ's teachings—A remnant will return—Compare Isaiah 6. About 559–545 B.C.

*a*IN the *b*year that king Uzziah died, I *c*saw also the Lord sitting upon a throne, high and lifted up, and his train filled the temple.

2 Above it stood the *a*seraphim; each one had six wings; with twain he covered his face, and with twain he covered his feet, and with twain he did fly.

3 And one cried unto another, and said: Holy, holy, holy, is the Lord of Hosts; the whole earth is full of his *a*glory.

4 And the posts of the door moved at the voice of him that cried, and the house was filled with smoke.

5 Then said I: Wo is unto me! for I am undone; because I am a man of unclean lips; and I dwell in the midst of a people of unclean lips; for mine eyes have *a*seen the King, the Lord of Hosts.

6 Then flew one of the seraphim unto me, having a live coal in his hand, which he had taken with the tongs from off the altar;

7 And he laid it upon my mouth, and said: Lo, this has touched thy lips; and thine *a*iniquity is taken away, and thy sin purged.

8 Also I heard the voice of the Lord, saying: *a*Whom shall I send, and who will go for us? Then I said: Here am I; send me.

9 And he said: Go and tell this people—Hear ye indeed, but they understood not; and see ye indeed, but they perceived not.

10 Make the heart of this people fat, and make their ears heavy, and shut their eyes—lest they see with their eyes, and *a*hear with their ears, and understand with their *b*heart, and be converted and be healed.

11 Then said I: Lord, how long? And he said: Until the cities be wasted without inhabitant, and the houses without man, and the land be utterly desolate;

12 And the Lord have *a*removed men far away, for there shall be a great forsaking in the midst of the land.

13 But yet there shall be a tenth, and they shall return, and shall be eaten, as a teil tree, and as an oak whose substance is in them when they cast their leaves; so the *a*holy seed shall be the substance thereof.

CHAPTER 17

Ephraim and Syria wage war against Judah—Christ will be born of a virgin—Compare Isaiah 7. About 559–545 B.C.

*a*AND it came to pass in the days of *b*Ahaz the son of *c*Jotham, that the son of Uzziah, king of Judah, that *d*Rezin, king of Syria, and *e*Pekah the son of Remaliah, king of Israel, went up toward Jerusalem to war against it, but could not prevail against it.

2 And it was told the house of David, saying: Syria is confederate with Ephraim. And his heart was moved, and the heart of his people, as the trees of the wood are moved with the wind.

3 Then said the Lord unto Isaiah: Go forth now to meet Ahaz, thou

---

16 1*a* Isa. 6:1 (1–13).
   b IE about 750 B.C.
   c John 12:41; 2 Ne. 11:2.
  2*a* TG Cherubim.
    BD Seraphim.
  3*a* Ps. 72:19 (19–20).
    TG Jesus Christ, Glory of.
  5*a* TG Jesus Christ, Appearances,

    Antemortal.
  7*a* TG Cleanse;
    Remission of Sins.
  8*a* TG Called of God.
 10*a* Matt. 13:14 (14–15);
    John 12:40;
    Acts 28:26–27;
    Rom. 11:8.
   b Prov. 2:2.

 12*a* 2 Kgs. 17:18 (18, 20);
    25:21.
 13*a* Ezra 9:2.
17 1*a* Isa. 7:1 (1–25).
   b 2 Kgs. 16:5;
    2 Chr. 28:5 (5–6).
   c 2 Kgs. 15:32.
   d 2 Kgs. 15:37 (36–38).
   e 2 Kgs. 15:25.

and Shearjashub thy son, at the end of the ^aconduit of the upper pool in the highway of the fuller's field;

4 And say unto him: Take heed, and be quiet; fear not, neither be faint-hearted for the two tails of these smoking firebrands, for the fierce anger of Rezin with Syria, and of the son of Remaliah.

5 Because Syria, Ephraim, and the son of Remaliah, have taken evil counsel against thee, saying:

6 Let us go up against Judah and vex it, and let us make a breach therein for us, and set a king in the midst of it, yea, the son of Tabeal.

7 Thus saith the Lord God: ^aIt shall not stand, neither shall it come to pass.

8 For the head of Syria is Damascus, and the head of Damascus, Rezin; and within threescore and five years shall Ephraim be ^abroken that it be not a people.

9 And the head of Ephraim is Samaria, and the head of Samaria is Remaliah's son. If ye will ^anot believe surely ye shall not be established.

10 Moreover, the Lord spake again unto Ahaz, saying:

11 Ask thee a ^asign of the Lord thy God; ask it either in the depths, or in the heights above.

12 But Ahaz said: I will not ask, neither will I ^atempt the Lord.

13 And he said: Hear ye now, O house of David; is it a small thing for you to weary men, but will ye weary my God also?

14 Therefore, the Lord himself shall give you a sign—Behold, a ^avirgin shall conceive, and shall bear a son, and shall call his name ^bImmanuel.

15 Butter and ^ahoney shall he eat, that he may know to refuse the evil and to choose the good.

16 For ^abefore the child shall know

to refuse the evil and choose the good, the land that thou abhorrest shall be forsaken of ^bboth her kings.

17 The Lord shall ^abring upon thee, and upon thy people, and upon thy father's house, days that have not come from the day that ^bEphraim departed from Judah, the king of Assyria.

18 And it shall come to pass in that day that the Lord shall hiss for the fly that is in the uttermost part of Egypt, and for the bee that is in the land of Assyria.

19 And they shall come, and shall rest all of them in the desolate valleys, and in the holes of the rocks, and upon all thorns, and upon all bushes.

20 In the same day shall the Lord shave with a ^arazor that is hired, by them beyond the river, by the king of Assyria, the head, and the hair of the feet; and it shall also consume the beard.

21 And it shall come to pass in that day, a man shall nourish a young cow and two sheep;

22 And it shall come to pass, for the abundance of milk they shall give he shall eat butter; for butter and honey shall every one eat that is left in the land.

23 And it shall come to pass in that day, every place shall be, where there were a thousand vines at a thousand silverlings, which shall be for briers and thorns.

24 With arrows and with bows shall men come thither, because all the land shall become briers and thorns.

25 And all hills that shall be digged with the mattock, there shall not come thither the fear of briers and thorns; but it shall be for the sending forth of oxen, and the treading of lesser cattle.

3*a* 2 Kgs. 18:17;
    Isa. 36:2.
7*a* Prov. 21:30;
    Isa. 8:10 (9–10).
8*a* TG Israel, Scattering of.
9*a* 2 Chr. 20:20.
    TG Unbelief.

11*a* Judg. 6:39 (36–40).
    TG Signs.
12*a* IE test, try, or prove.
14*a* Isa. 7:14.
    b Isa. 8:8;
    2 Ne. 18:8, 10.
15*a* 2 Sam. 17:29.

16*a* Isa. 8:4;
    2 Ne. 18:4.
    b 2 Kgs. 15:30; 16:9.
17*a* 2 Chr. 28:19 (19–21).
    b 1 Kgs. 12:19 (16–19).
20*a* 2 Kgs. 16:7 (7–8);
    2 Chr. 28:20 (20–21).

CHAPTER 18

*Christ will be as a stone of stumbling
and a rock of offense—Seek the Lord,
not peeping wizards—Turn to the law
and to the testimony for guidance—
Compare Isaiah 8. About 559–545 B.C.*

MOREOVER, the word of the Lord
said unto me: Take thee a great ªroll,
and write in it with a man's pen,
concerning ᵇMaher-shalal-hash-baz.

2 And I took unto me faithful
ªwitnesses to record, Uriah the
priest, and Zechariah the son of
Jeberechiah.

3 And I went unto the prophetess;
and she conceived and bare a son.
Then said the Lord to me: ªCall his
name, Maher-shalal-hash-baz.

4 For behold, ªthe child shall ᵇnot
have knowledge to cry, My father,
and my mother, before the riches
of Damascus and the ᶜspoil of ᵈSa-
maria shall be taken away before
the king of ᵉAssyria.

5 The Lord spake also unto me
again, saying:

6 Forasmuch as this people refus-
eth the waters of ªShiloah that go
softly, and rejoice in ᵇRezin and
Remaliah's son;

7 Now therefore, behold, the Lord
bringeth up upon them the waters
of the river, strong and many, even
the king of ªAssyria and all his glory;
and he shall come up over all his
channels, and go over all his banks.

8 And he shall pass through Judah; he shall overflow and go over,
he shall ªreach even to the neck;
and the stretching out of his wings
shall fill the breadth of thy land,
O Immanuel.

9 ªAssociate yourselves, O ye
people, and ye shall be broken in
pieces; and give ear all ye of far
countries; gird yourselves, and ye
shall be broken in pieces; gird yourselves, and ye shall be broken in
pieces.

10 Take counsel together, and it
shall come to naught; speak the
word, and it shall not stand; for
God is with us.

11 For the Lord spake thus to me
with a strong hand, and instructed
me that I should not walk in the
way of this people, saying:

12 Say ye not, A confederacy, to
all to whom this people shall say, A
ªconfederacy; neither fear ye their
fear, nor be afraid.

13 Sanctify the Lord of Hosts himself, and let him be your fear, and
let him be your dread.

14 And he shall be for a sanctuary;
but for a ªstone of ᵇstumbling, and
for a ᶜrock of ᵈoffense to both the
houses of Israel, for a gin and a ᵉsnare
to the inhabitants of Jerusalem.

15 And many among them shall
ªstumble and fall, and be broken,
and be snared, and be taken.

16 ªBind up the testimony, seal the
law among my disciples.

17 And I will wait upon the Lord,
that ªhideth his face from the house
of Jacob, and I will look for him.

18 Behold, I and the children
whom the Lord hath given me are
for ªsigns and for wonders in Israel from the Lord of Hosts, which
dwelleth in Mount Zion.

19 And when they shall say unto
you: Seek unto them that have
ªfamiliar spirits, and unto ᵇwizards

18 1a Isa. 8:1 (1–22).
  b HEB To speed to the
    spoil, he hasteneth
    the prey.
 2a TG Witness.
 3a 2 Ne. 18:18.
 4a 2 Ne. 17:16.
  b Isa. 8:4.
  c 2 Kgs. 15:29 (29–30).
  d 2 Kgs. 17:6.
  e 2 Kgs. 16:7 (7–18);
    2 Ne. 20:12.
    TG Israel, Scattering of.

 6a Neh. 3:15;
    John 9:7.
  b Isa. 7:1 (1–6).
 7a Isa. 10:12.
 8a Isa. 30:28.
 9a Joel 3:9 (9–14).
 12a Isa. 31:1 (1–3).
 14a Rom. 9:33 (32–33).
    TG Cornerstone;
    Jesus Christ, Prophecies
    about.
  b Isa. 8:14 (13–15);
    Luke 2:34;

    1 Pet. 2:8 (4–8);
    Jacob 4:15.
  c TG Rock.
  d Luke 7:23.
  e Mosiah 7:29.
 15a Matt. 21:44.
 16a Dan. 12:9.
 17a Isa. 54:8.
 18a 2 Ne. 18:3 (1–3).
 19a Moro. 10:30.
    TG Sorcery.
  b Lev. 20:6.

that peep and mutter—^cshould not a people seek unto their God for the living to hear from the dead?

20 To the ^alaw and to the testimony; and if they speak not according to this word, it is because there is no light in them.

21 And they shall pass through it hardly bestead and hungry; and it shall come to pass that when they shall be hungry, they shall fret themselves, and curse their king and their God, and look upward.

22 And they shall look unto the earth and behold trouble, and ^adarkness, dimness of anguish, and shall be driven to darkness.

CHAPTER 19

Isaiah speaks messianically—The people in darkness will see a great light— Unto us a child is born—He will be the Prince of Peace and will reign on David's throne—Compare Isaiah 9. About 559–545 B.C.

^aNEVERTHELESS, the dimness shall not be such as was in her vexation, when at first he lightly afflicted the ^bland of ^cZebulun, and the land of ^dNaphtali, and afterwards did more grievously afflict by the way of the Red Sea beyond Jordan in Galilee of the nations.

2 The people that walked in darkness have seen a great light; they that dwell in the land of the shadow of death, upon them hath the light shined.

3 Thou hast multiplied the nation, and ^aincreased the joy—they joy before thee according to the joy in harvest, and as men rejoice when they divide the spoil.

4 For thou hast broken the yoke of ^ahis burden, and the staff of his shoulder, the rod of his ^boppressor.

5 For every battle of the warrior is with confused noise, and garments rolled in blood; but ^athis shall be with burning and fuel of fire.

6 For unto us a ^achild is born, unto us a son is given; and the ^bgovernment shall be upon his shoulder; and his name shall be called, Wonderful, Counselor, The ^cMighty God, The ^dEverlasting Father, The Prince of ^ePeace.

7 Of the increase of ^agovernment and peace ^bthere is no end, upon the throne of ^cDavid, and upon his kingdom to order it, and to establish it with judgment and with justice from henceforth, even forever. The zeal of the Lord of Hosts will perform this.

8 The Lord sent his word unto Jacob and it hath lighted upon Israel.

9 And all the people shall know, even Ephraim and the inhabitants of Samaria, that say in the pride and stoutness of heart:

10 The bricks are fallen down, but we will build with hewn ^astones; the sycamores are cut down, but we will change them into ^bcedars.

11 Therefore the Lord shall set up the adversaries of ^aRezin against him, and join his enemies together;

12 The Syrians before and the Philistines behind; and they shall ^adevour Israel with open mouth. For all this his ^banger is not turned away, but his hand is stretched out still.

13 For the people turneth not unto ^ahim that smiteth them, neither do they seek the Lord of Hosts.

14 Therefore will the Lord cut off

19c 1 Sam. 28:11 (8–20).
20a Luke 16:29 (29–31).
22a Isa. 5:30.
19 1a Isa. 9:1 (1–21).
   b Matt. 4:15 (15–16).
   c Josh. 19:10 (10–16).
   d Josh. 19:33 (32–39).
3a Isa. 9:3.
4a IE Israel, the nation
   mentioned in v. 3.
   b TG Oppression.
5a Mal. 4:1.

6a Isa. 7:14;
   Luke 2:11.
   b Matt. 28:18.
   c Titus 2:13;
   Mosiah 7:27.
   TG Jesus Christ, Jehovah;
   Jesus Christ, Power of.
   d 2 Ne. 26:12;
   Mosiah 3:5;
   Alma 11:39 (38–39, 44);
   Moro. 7:22; 8:18.
   e Micah 5:5;

   D&C 27:16; 111:8.
7a TG Kingdom of God,
   on Earth.
   b Dan. 2:44.
   c Ezek. 37:24.
10a 1 Kgs. 5:17.
   b 1 Kgs. 5:6.
11a 2 Kgs. 16:9 (7–9).
12a 2 Kgs. 17:6 (1–18).
   b Isa. 5:25; 10:4;
   Jer. 4:8.
13a Amos 4:10 (6–12).

from Israel head and tail, branch and rush ªin one day.

15 The ªancient, he is the head; and the prophet that teacheth lies, he is the tail.

16 For the ªleaders of this people cause them to err; and they that are ᵇled of them are destroyed.

17 Therefore the Lord shall have no joy in their young men, neither shall have ªmercy on their fatherless and ᵇwidows; for ᶜevery one of them is a hypocrite and an ᵈevildoer, and every mouth speaketh ᵉfolly. For all this his anger is not turned away, but his ᶠhand is stretched out still.

18 For ªwickedness burneth as the fire; it shall devour the briers and thorns, and shall kindle in the thickets of the forests, and they shall mount up like the lifting up of smoke.

19 Through the wrath of the Lord of Hosts is the ªland darkened, and the people shall be as the fuel of the fire; ᵇno man shall spare his brother.

20 And he ªshall snatch on the right hand and be hungry; and he shall ᵇeat on the left hand and they shall not be satisfied; they shall eat every man the flesh of his own arm—

21 Manasseh, ªEphraim; and Ephraim, Manasseh; they together shall be against ᵇJudah. For all this his anger is not turned away, but his hand is stretched out still.

CHAPTER 20

The destruction of Assyria is a type of the destruction of the wicked at the Second Coming—Few people will be left after the Lord comes again—The remnant of Jacob will return in that day—Compare Isaiah 10. About 559–545 B.C.

ªWo unto them that decree ᵇunrighteous decrees, and that write grievousness which they have prescribed;

2 To turn away the needy from judgment, and to take away the right from the ªpoor of my people, that ᵇwidows may be their prey, and that they may rob the fatherless!

3 And what will ye do in the day of visitation, and in the desolation which shall come from far? to whom will ye flee for help? and where will ye leave your glory?

4 Without me they shall bow down under the prisoners, and they shall fall under the slain. For all this his anger is not turned away, but his hand is stretched out still.

5 O Assyrian, the rod of mine anger, and the staff in their hand is ªtheir indignation.

6 I will send him ªagainst a hypocritical nation, and against the people of my wrath will I give him a charge to take the spoil, and to take the prey, and to tread them down like the mire of the streets.

7 Howbeit he meaneth not so, neither doth his heart think so; but in his heart it is to destroy and cut off nations not a few.

8 For he saith: Are not my ªprinces altogether kings?

9 Is not ªCalno as ᵇCarchemish? Is not Hamath as Arpad? Is not Samaria as ᶜDamascus?

10 As ªmy hand hath founded the

14a Isa. 10:17.
15a Isa. 9:15.
16a Isa. 1:23.
    TG Leadership.
  b TG Trust Not in the Arm of Flesh.
17a TG Mercy.
  b TG Widows.
  c Micah 7:2 (2–3).
  d Prov. 1:16;
    D&C 64:16.
  e Eccl. 10:12 (1–3, 12);
    2 Ne. 9:28 (28–29);

D&C 35:7.
  f 2 Ne. 28:32;
    Jacob 5:47; 6:4.
18a Mal. 4:1.
19a Isa. 8:22.
  b Micah 7:2 (2–6).
20a Lev. 26:26 (26, 29).
  b Deut. 28:53 (53–57).
21a TG Israel, Joseph, People of.
  b TG Israel, Judah, People of.
20 1a Isa. 10:1 (1–34).

  b TG Injustice.
2a Amos 4:1.
  b TG Widows.
5a Isa. 10:5.
6a IE against Israel.
    TG Hypocrisy.
8a 2 Kgs. 18:33 (33–35);
    19:10 (10–13).
9a Amos 6:2 (1–2).
  b 2 Chr. 35:20.
  c 2 Kgs. 16:9.
10a IE the king of Assyria's hand (vv. 10–11).

kingdoms of the idols, and whose graven images did excel them of Jerusalem and of Samaria;

11 Shall I not, as I have done unto Samaria and her ªidols, so do to Jerusalem and to her idols?

12 Wherefore it shall come to pass that when the Lord hath performed his whole work upon Mount Zion and upon Jerusalem, I will punish the fruit of the stout heart of the king of ªAssyria, and the glory of his high looks.

13 For ªhe saith: By the strength of ᵇmy hand and by my wisdom I have done these things; for I am prudent; and I have moved the borders of the people, and have robbed their treasures, and I have put down the inhabitants like a valiant man;

14 And my hand hath found as a nest the riches of the people; and as one gathereth eggs that are left have I gathered all the earth; and there was none that moved the wing, or opened the mouth, or peeped.

15 Shall the ªax boast itself against him that heweth therewith? Shall the saw magnify itself against him that shaketh it? As if the rod should shake itself against them that lift it up, or as if the staff should lift up itself as if it were no wood!

16 Therefore shall the Lord, the Lord of Hosts, send among his fat ones, leanness; and under his glory he shall kindle a burning like the burning of a fire.

17 And the light of Israel shall be for a ªfire, and his Holy One for a flame, and shall burn and shall devour his thorns and his briers in one day;

18 And shall consume the glory of his forest, and of his fruitful field, both soul and body; and they shall be as when a standard-bearer fainteth.

19 And the ªrest of the trees of his forest shall be few, that a child may write them.

20 And it shall come to pass in that day, that the remnant of Israel, and such as are escaped of the ªhouse of Jacob, shall no more again ᵇstay upon him that smote them, but shall stay upon the Lord, the Holy One of Israel, in truth.

21 The ªremnant shall return, yea, even the remnant of Jacob, unto the mighty God.

22 For though thy people ªIsrael be as the sand of the sea, yet a remnant of them shall ᵇreturn; the ᶜconsumption decreed shall overflow with righteousness.

23 For the Lord God of Hosts shall make a ªconsumption, even determined in all the land.

24 Therefore, thus saith the Lord God of Hosts: O my people that dwellest in Zion, ªbe not afraid of the Assyrian; he shall smite thee with a rod, and shall lift up his staff against thee, after the ᵇmanner of Egypt.

25 For yet a very little while, and the ªindignation shall cease, and mine anger in their destruction.

26 And the Lord of Hosts shall ªstir up a scourge for him according to the slaughter of ᵇMidian at the rock of Oreb; and as his rod was upon the sea so shall he lift it up after the manner of ᶜEgypt.

11a Ezek. 36:18 (16–20).
12a 2 Kgs. 16:7 (7–18);
    Zeph. 2:13;
    2 Ne. 18:4 (4–7).
13a IE the king of Assyria
    (vv. 13–14).
  b Isa. 37:24 (24–38).
15a IE Can the king
    prosper against God?
17a Obad. 1:18;
    2 Ne. 15:24;
    3 Ne. 20:16.
19a IE the remnants of the

army of Assyria.
20a Amos 9:8 (8–9);
    2 Ne. 6:11 (10–11).
  b IE depend upon.
    2 Kgs. 16:8 (7–9);
    2 Chr. 28:21 (20–21).
21a Isa. 11:11.
    TG Israel, Remnant of.
22a Gen. 22:17;
    Rom. 9:27.
  b TG Israel, Gathering of.
  c Isa. 28:22.
    TG World, End of.

23a Dan. 9:27.
24a Isa. 37:6 (6–7).
  b TG Israel, Bondage of,
    in Egypt;
    Israel, Bondage of, in
    Other Lands.
25a Isa. 10:25;
    Dan. 11:36.
26a 2 Kgs. 19:35.
  b Gen. 25:2 (1–6);
    Judg. 7:25;
    Isa. 9:4.
  c Ex. 14:27 (26–27).

27 And it shall come to pass in that day that his ^aburden shall be taken away from off thy shoulder, and his yoke from off thy neck, and the yoke shall be destroyed because of the ^banointing.

28 ^aHe is come to Aiath, he is passed to Migron; at Michmash he hath laid up his carriages.

29 They are gone over the ^apassage; they have taken up their lodging at ^bGeba; Ramath is afraid; ^cGibeah of Saul is fled.

30 Lift up the voice, O daughter of ^aGallim; cause it to be heard unto Laish, O poor ^bAnathoth.

31 Madmenah is removed; the inhabitants of Gebim gather themselves to flee.

32 As yet shall he remain at ^aNob that day; he shall shake his hand against the mount of the daughter of Zion, the hill of Jerusalem.

33 Behold, the Lord, the Lord of Hosts shall lop the bough with terror; and the ^ahigh ones of stature shall be ^bhewn down; and the ^chaughty shall be humbled.

34 And he shall cut down the thickets of the forests with iron, and Lebanon shall fall by a mighty one.

CHAPTER 21

The stem of Jesse (Christ) will judge in righteousness—The knowledge of God will cover the earth in the Millennium—The Lord will raise an ensign and gather Israel—Compare Isaiah 11. About 559–545 B.C.

^aAND there shall ^bcome forth a rod out of the ^cstem of Jesse, and a ^dbranch shall grow out of his roots.

2 And the ^aSpirit of the Lord shall rest upon him, the spirit of ^bwisdom and ^cunderstanding, the spirit of counsel and might, the spirit of knowledge and of the fear of the Lord;

3 And shall make him of quick understanding in the fear of the Lord; and he shall not ^ajudge after the sight of his eyes, neither reprove after the hearing of his ears.

4 But with ^arighteousness shall he ^bjudge the poor, and reprove with equity for the ^cmeek of the earth; and he shall ^dsmite the earth with the ^erod of his mouth, and with the breath of his lips shall he slay the wicked.

5 And ^arighteousness shall be the girdle of his loins, and faithfulness the girdle of his reins.

6 The ^awolf also shall dwell with the lamb, and the leopard shall lie down with the kid, and the calf and the young lion and fatling together; and a little child shall lead them.

7 And the cow and the bear shall feed; their young ones shall lie down together; and the lion shall eat straw like the ox.

8 And the sucking child shall play on the hole of the asp, and the weaned child shall put his hand on the cockatrice's den.

9 They shall ^anot hurt nor ^bdestroy in all my holy mountain, for the ^cearth shall be full of the ^dknowledge

---

27a Isa. 14:25.
  b TG Jesus Christ, Messiah.
28a IE The Assyrian invasion forces introduced in v. 5 progress toward Jerusalem, vv. 28–32.
29a 1 Sam. 13:23.
  b Neh. 11:31.
  c 1 Sam. 11:4.
30a 1 Sam. 25:44.
  b Josh. 21:18.
32a 1 Sam. 21:1; 22:19; Neh. 11:32.
33a Obad. 1:3 (3–4); Hel. 4:12 (12–13); D&C 101:42.

  b Ezek. 17:24; Amos 2:9; D&C 112:8 (3–8).
  c Ps. 18:27; 3 Ne. 25:1; D&C 29:9.
21 1a Isa. 11:1 (1–16).
  b Isa. 53:2; Rev. 5:5.
  c D&C 113:2 (1–2).
  d TG Jesus Christ, Davidic Descent of.
2a Isa. 61:1 (1–3).
  b 1 Kgs. 3:28.
  c 1 Kgs. 3:11 (10–11).
3a 2 Ne. 12:4.
4a Ps. 50:6;

Mosiah 29:12.
  b Ps. 72:4 (2–4).
  TG Jesus Christ, Judge.
  c TG Meek.
  d Ps. 2:9.
  e 2 Thes. 2:8; Rev. 19:15.
5a TG Jesus Christ, Millennial Reign.
6a Isa. 65:25.
9a Isa. 2:4.
  b TG War.
  c Hab. 2:14.
  d Ps. 66:4; D&C 88:104. TG Knowledge; Millennium.

of the Lord, as the waters cover the sea.

10 And in that day there shall be a ^aroot of Jesse, which shall stand for an ensign of the people; to it shall the ^bGentiles seek; and his ^crest shall be glorious.

11 And it shall come to pass in that day that the Lord shall set his hand again the ^asecond time to recover the remnant of his people which shall be left, from ^bAssyria, and from Egypt, and from Pathros, and from Cush, and from Elam, and from ^cShinar, and from Hamath, and from the islands of the sea.

12 And he shall set up an ^aensign for the nations, and shall assemble the ^boutcasts of Israel, and ^cgather together the dispersed of Judah from the four corners of the earth.

13 The ^aenvy of Ephraim also shall depart, and the adversaries of Judah shall be cut off; Ephraim shall not ^benvy ^cJudah, and Judah shall not vex Ephraim.

14 But they shall fly upon the shoulders of the ^aPhilistines towards the west; they shall spoil them of the east together; they shall lay their hand upon ^bEdom and ^cMoab; and the children of Ammon shall obey them.

15 And the Lord shall utterly ^adestroy the tongue of the Egyptian sea; and with his mighty wind he shall shake his hand over the river, and shall smite it in the seven streams, and make men go over ^bdry shod.

16 And there shall be a ^ahighway for the remnant of his people which shall be left, from Assyria, like as it was to Israel in the day that he came up out of the land of Egypt.

CHAPTER 22

In the millennial day all men will praise the Lord—He will dwell among them—Compare Isaiah 12. About 559–545 B.C.

^aAND in that day thou shalt say: O Lord, I will praise thee; though thou wast angry with me thine anger is turned away, and thou comfortedst me.

2 Behold, God is my salvation; I will ^atrust, and not be afraid; for the Lord ^bJEHOVAH is my ^cstrength and my ^dsong; he also has become my salvation.

3 Therefore, with joy shall ye draw ^awater out of the wells of salvation.

4 And in that day shall ye say: ^aPraise the Lord, call upon his name, declare his doings among the people, make mention that his name is exalted.

5 ^aSing unto the Lord; for he hath done excellent things; this is known in all the earth.

6 ^aCry out and shout, thou inhabitant of Zion; for great is the Holy One of Israel in the midst of thee.

CHAPTER 23

The destruction of Babylon is a type of the destruction at the Second Coming—It will be a day of wrath and vengeance

---

10a Rom. 15:12;
　　D&C 113:5 (5–6).
　b D&C 45:9 (9–10).
　c D&C 19:9.
　　TG Earth, Renewal of.
11a 2 Ne. 6:14; 25:17; 29:1.
　b Zech. 10:10.
　c Gen. 10:10.
12a TG Ensign.
　b 3 Ne. 15:15; 16:1 (1–4).
　c Neh. 1:9;
　　1 Ne. 22:12 (10–12);
　　D&C 45:25 (24–25).
　　TG Israel, Gathering of.
13a Jer. 3:18.
　b Ezek. 37:22 (16–22).

TG Envy.
　c TG Israel, Joseph,
　　People of;
　　Israel, Judah, People of.
14a Obad. 1:19 (18–19).
　b Lam. 4:21.
　c Gen. 19:37 (30–38).
15a Zech. 10:11.
　b Rev. 16:12.
16a Isa. 11:16; 19:23;
　　35:8 (8–10);
　　D&C 133:27.
　　TG Earth, Renewal of.
22 1a Isa. 12:1 (1–6).
　2a Ps. 36:7 (7–8);
　　Mosiah 4:6;

Hel. 12:1.
　b Ex. 15:2;
　　Ps. 83:18.
　　TG Jesus Christ, Jehovah.
　c TG Strength.
　d TG Singing.
3a TG Living Water.
4a TG Praise;
　　Thanksgiving.
5a Ps. 57:7 (7–11);
　　108:1 (1–5);
　　Alma 26:8;
　　D&C 136:28.
6a Isa. 54:1 (1–8);
　　Zeph. 3:14 (14–20);
　　Zech. 2:10 (10–13).

—Babylon (the world) will fall forever—
Compare Isaiah 13. About 559–545 B.C.

^aTHE burden of ^bBabylon, which Isaiah the son of Amoz did see.

2 Lift ye up a banner upon the high mountain, exalt the voice unto them, ^ashake the hand, that they may go into the gates of the nobles.

3 I have commanded my sanctified ones, I have also called my ^amighty ones, for mine anger is not upon them that rejoice in my highness.

4 The noise of the multitude in the mountains like as of a great people, a tumultuous noise of the ^akingdoms of nations ^bgathered together, the Lord of Hosts mustereth the hosts of the battle.

5 They come from a far country, from the end of heaven, yea, the Lord, and the weapons of his indignation, to destroy the whole land.

6 Howl ye, for the ^aday of the Lord is at hand; it shall come as a destruction from the Almighty.

7 Therefore shall all hands be faint, every man's heart shall ^amelt;

8 And they shall be afraid; pangs and sorrows shall take hold of them; they shall be amazed one at another; their faces shall be as flames.

9 Behold, the day of the Lord cometh, cruel both with wrath and fierce anger, to lay the land desolate; and he shall ^adestroy the sinners thereof out of it.

10 For the ^astars of heaven and the ^bconstellations thereof shall not give their ^clight; the ^dsun shall be darkened in his going forth, and the moon shall not cause her light to shine.

11 And I will ^apunish the world for evil, and the ^bwicked for their iniquity; I will cause the arrogancy of the ^cproud to cease, and will lay down the haughtiness of the terrible.

12 I will make a ^aman more precious than fine gold; even a man than the golden wedge of Ophir.

13 Therefore, I will ^ashake the heavens, and the earth shall ^bremove out of her place, in the wrath of the Lord of Hosts, and in the day of his fierce anger.

14 And it shall be as the chased roe, and as a sheep that no man taketh up; and they shall every man turn to his own people, and flee every one into his own ^aland.

15 Every one that is proud shall be thrust through; yea, and every one that is ^ajoined to the wicked shall fall by the sword.

16 Their ^achildren also shall be ^bdashed to pieces before their eyes; their houses shall be spoiled and their wives ravished.

17 Behold, I will stir up the ^aMedes against them, which shall not regard silver and gold, nor shall they delight in it.

18 Their bows shall also dash the young men to pieces; and they shall have no ^apity on the fruit of the womb; their eyes shall not spare children.

19 And ^aBabylon, the glory of kingdoms, the beauty of the Chaldees' excellency, shall be as when God overthrew ^bSodom and Gomorrah.

---

23 1a Isa. 13:1 (1–22).
  b TG Babylon.
 2a IE wave the hand, give a signal.
 3a Joel 3:11.
 4a Joel 3:14 (11, 14);
    Zeph. 3:8;
    Zech. 14:2 (2–3).
  b Zech. 12:3 (2–9).
 6a TG Day of the Lord.
 7a Jer. 9:7;
    D&C 133:41.
 9a TG Earth, Cleansing of.
10a Isa. 24:23;

Ezek. 32:7 (7–8);
    Rev. 6:13 (12–13).
  b TG Astronomy.
  c Joel 3:15.
  d TG World, End of.
11a Isa. 24:6;
    Mal. 4:1.
  b Ex. 34:7;
    Prov. 21:12.
  c Job 40:11;
    2 Ne. 12:12;
    D&C 64:24.
12a Isa. 4:1 (1–4).
13a Hag. 2:6 (6–7);

Heb. 12:26.
  b TG Earth, Renewal of.
14a TG Lands of Inheritance.
15a Lam. 2:9;
    Alma 59:6 (5–6).
16a Job 27:14 (13–15).
  b Ps. 137:9 (8–9).
17a Isa. 21:2.
18a Lam. 2:2 (2, 17, 21).
19a Isa. 14:15 (4–27).
  b Gen. 19:24 (24–25);
    Deut. 29:23;
    Jer. 49:18;
    2 Ne. 13:9.

20 It shall never be ªinhabited, neither shall it be dwelt in from generation to generation: neither shall the Arabian pitch tent there; neither shall the shepherds make their fold there.

21 But ªwild beasts of the desert shall lie there; and their houses shall be full of doleful creatures; and owls shall dwell there, and satyrs shall dance there.

22 And the wild beasts of the islands shall cry in their desolate houses, and dragons in their pleasant palaces; and her time is near to come, and her day shall not be prolonged. For I will destroy her speedily; yea, for I will be merciful unto my people, but the wicked shall perish.

CHAPTER 24

Israel will be gathered and will enjoy millennial rest—Lucifer was cast out of heaven for rebellion—Israel will triumph over Babylon (the world)—Compare Isaiah 14. About 559–545 B.C.

ªFOR the Lord will have mercy on Jacob, and will yet ᵇchoose Israel, and set them in their own land; and the ᶜstrangers shall be joined with them, and they shall cleave to the house of Jacob.

2 And the people shall take them and bring them to their place; yea, from far unto the ends of the earth; and they shall return to their ªlands of promise. And the house of Israel shall ᵇpossess them, and the land of the Lord shall be for ᶜservants and handmaids; and they shall take them captives unto whom they were captives; and they shall ᵈrule over their oppressors.

3 And it shall come to pass in that day that the Lord shall give thee ªrest, from thy sorrow, and from thy fear, and from the hard bondage wherein thou wast made to serve.

4 And it shall come to pass in that day, that thou shalt take up this proverb ªagainst the king of ᵇBabylon, and say: How hath the oppressor ceased, the golden city ceased!

5 The Lord hath broken the staff of the ªwicked, the scepters of the rulers.

6 ªHe who smote the people in wrath with a continual stroke, he that ruled the nations in anger, is persecuted, and none hindereth.

7 The whole earth is at ªrest, and is quiet; they break forth into ᵇsinging.

8 Yea, the fir trees rejoice at thee, and also the cedars of Lebanon, saying: Since thou art laid down no feller is come up against us.

9 ªHell from beneath is moved for thee to meet thee at thy coming; it stirreth up the ᵇdead for thee, even all the chief ones of the earth; it hath raised up from their thrones all the kings of the nations.

10 All they shall speak and say unto thee: Art thou also become weak as we? Art thou become like unto us?

11 Thy pomp is brought down to the grave; the noise of thy viols is not heard; the worm is spread under thee, and the worms cover thee.

12 ªHow art thou fallen from heaven, O ᵇLucifer, son of the morning! Art thou cut down to the ground, which did weaken the nations!

13 For thou hast said in thy heart: ªI will ascend into heaven, I will

---

20a Jer. 50:39 (3, 39–40);
  51:29 (29, 62).
21a Isa. 34:14 (11–15).
24 1a Isa. 14:1 (1–32).
  b Zech. 1:17; 2:12.
  c Isa. 60:3 (3–5, 10).
    TG Stranger.
  2a TG Promised Lands.
  b Amos 9:12.
  c Isa. 60:14 (10–12, 14).
  d TG Kingdom of God, on

Earth.
3a Josh. 1:13;
  D&C 84:24.
4a Hab. 2:6 (6–8).
  b TG Babylon.
5a TG Earth, Cleansing of;
    Wickedness.
6a IE Babylon.
7a TG Earth, Renewal of.
  b Isa. 55:12 (12–13).
9a Ezek. 32:21.

TG Hell.
  b TG Spirits in Prison.
12a IE The fallen king of
    Babylon is typified by
    the fallen "son of the
    morning," Lucifer in
    vv. 12–15.
    D&C 76:26.
  b TG Devil.
13a Moses 4:1 (1–4).

exalt my throne above the stars of God; I will sit also upon the mount of the congregation, in the sides of the north;

14 *a*I will ascend above the heights of the clouds; I will be like the Most High.

15 Yet thou shalt be brought down to hell, to the sides of the *a*pit.

16 They that see thee shall narrowly look upon thee, and shall consider thee, and shall say: Is this the man that made the earth to tremble, that did shake kingdoms?

17 And made the world as a wilderness, and destroyed the cities thereof, and opened not the house of his prisoners?

18 All the kings of the nations, yea, all of them, lie in glory, every one of them in his own house.

19 But thou art cast out of thy grave like an abominable branch, and the remnant of those that are slain, thrust through with a sword, that go down to the stones of the pit; as a carcass trodden under feet.

20 Thou shalt not be joined with them in burial, because thou hast destroyed thy land and slain thy people; the *a*seed of *b*evil-doers shall never be renowned.

21 Prepare slaughter for his children for the *a*iniquities of their fathers, that they do not rise, nor possess the land, nor fill the face of the world with cities.

22 For I will rise up against them, saith the Lord of Hosts, and cut off from Babylon the *a*name, and remnant, and son, and *b*nephew, saith the Lord.

23 I will also make it a *a*possession for the bittern, and pools of water; and I will sweep it with the besom of destruction, saith the Lord of Hosts.

24 The Lord of Hosts hath sworn, saying: Surely as I have thought, so shall it come to pass; and as I have purposed, so shall it stand—

25 That I will bring the Assyrian in my land, and upon my mountains tread him under foot; then shall his *a*yoke depart from off them, and his burden depart from off their shoulders.

26 This is the purpose that is purposed upon the whole earth; and this is the hand that is stretched out upon all nations.

27 For the Lord of Hosts hath purposed, and who shall disannul? And his hand is stretched out, and who shall turn it back?

28 In the year that king *a*Ahaz died was this burden.

29 Rejoice not thou, whole Palestina, because the rod of him that *a*smote thee is broken; for out of the serpent's root shall come forth a cockatrice, and his *b*fruit shall be a *c*fiery flying serpent.

30 And the firstborn of the poor shall feed, and the needy shall lie down in safety; and I will kill thy root with famine, and he shall slay thy remnant.

31 Howl, O gate; cry, O city; thou, whole Palestina, art dissolved; for there shall come from the north a smoke, and none shall be alone in his appointed times.

32 What shall then answer the messengers of the nations? That the Lord hath founded *a*Zion, and the *b*poor of his people shall trust in it.

CHAPTER 25

Nephi glories in plainness—Isaiah's prophecies will be understood in the last days—The Jews will return from Babylon, crucify the Messiah, and be scattered and scourged—They will be restored when they believe in the

14*a* 2 Thes. 2:4.
15*a* Ps. 28:1; 88:4;
    1 Ne. 14:3.
20*a* Ps. 21:10 (10–11); 37:28;
    109:13.
  b TG Wickedness.
21*a* Ex. 20:5.

22*a* Prov. 10:7;
    Jer. 51:62.
  b Job 18:19.
23*a* Isa. 34:11 (11–15).
25*a* Isa. 10:27.
28*a* 2 Kgs. 16:20.
29*a* 2 Chr. 26:6.

  b 2 Kgs. 18:8 (1, 8).
  c TG Jesus Christ, Types
    of, in Anticipation.
32*a* TG Zion.
  b Zeph. 3:12.

Messiah—*He will first come six hundred years after Lehi left Jerusalem—The Nephites keep the law of Moses and believe in Christ, who is the Holy One of Israel. About 559–545* B.C.

Now I, Nephi, do speak somewhat concerning the words which I have written, which have been spoken by the mouth of Isaiah. For behold, Isaiah spake many things which were *a*hard for many of my people to understand; for they know not concerning the manner of prophesying among the Jews.

2 For I, Nephi, have not taught them many things concerning the manner of the Jews; for their *a*works were works of darkness, and their doings were doings of abominations.

3 Wherefore, I write unto my people, unto all those that shall receive hereafter these things which I write, *a*that they may know the judgments of God, that they come upon all nations, according to the word which he hath spoken.

4 Wherefore, hearken, O my people, which are of the house of Israel, and give ear unto my words; for because the words of Isaiah are not plain unto you, nevertheless they are plain unto all those that are filled with the *a*spirit of *b*prophecy. But I give unto you a *c*prophecy, according to the spirit which is in me; wherefore I shall prophesy according to the *d*plainness which hath been with me from the time that I came out from Jerusalem with my father; for behold, my soul delighteth in *e*plainness unto my people, that they may learn.

5 Yea, and my soul delighteth in the words of *a*Isaiah, for I came out from Jerusalem, and mine eyes hath beheld the things of the *b*Jews, and I know that the Jews do *c*understand the things of the prophets, and there is none other people that understand the things which were spoken unto the Jews like unto them, save it be that they are taught after the manner of the things of the Jews.

6 But behold, I, Nephi, have not taught my children after the manner of the Jews; but behold, I, of myself, have dwelt at Jerusalem, wherefore I know concerning the regions round about; and I have made mention unto my children concerning the judgments of God, which *a*hath come to pass among the Jews, unto my children, according to all that which Isaiah hath spoken, and I do not write them.

7 But behold, I proceed with mine own prophecy, according to my *a*plainness; in the which I *b*know that no man can err; nevertheless, in the days that the prophecies of Isaiah shall be fulfilled men shall know of a surety, at the times when they shall come to pass.

8 Wherefore, they are of *a*worth unto the children of men, and he that supposeth that they are not, unto them will I speak particularly, and confine the words unto mine *b*own people; for I know that they shall be of great worth unto them in the *c*last days; for in that day shall they understand them; wherefore, for their good have I written them.

9 And as one generation hath been *a*destroyed among the Jews because of iniquity, even so have they been destroyed from generation to

25 1a Jacob 4:14.
      TG Symbolism.
   2a 2 Kgs. 17:13–20.
   3a TG God, Knowledge
      about;
      Prophets, Mission of;
      Scriptures, Value of.
   4a TG Holy Ghost, Source
      of Testimony.
    b TG Prophecy.
    c 2 Ne. 31:1.

   d 2 Ne. 31:3; 33:5;
      Jacob 2:11; 4:13.
   e TG Communication;
      Plainness.
   5a 1 Ne. 19:23.
    b TG Israel, Judah,
      People of.
    c Matt. 13:11 (10–17).
   6a 2 Ne. 6:8;
      Hel. 8:20 (20–21).
   7a 2 Ne. 32:7;

      Alma 13:23;
      Ether 12:39.
    b Ezek. 12:23 (21–25).
   8a TG Scriptures, Value of.
    b 2 Ne. 27:6;
      Enos 1:16 (13–16);
      Morm. 5:12;
      D&C 3:20 (16–20).
    c TG Last Days.
   9a Lam. 1–5;
      Matt. 23:37.

generation according to their iniquities; and never hath any of them been destroyed save it were *b*foretold them by the prophets of the Lord.

10 Wherefore, it hath been told them concerning the destruction which should come upon them, immediately after my father left *a*Jerusalem; nevertheless, they *b*hardened their hearts; and according to my prophecy they have been destroyed, save it be those which are *c*carried away *d*captive into Babylon.

11 And now this I speak because of the *a*spirit which is in me. And notwithstanding they have been carried away they shall return again, and possess the land of Jerusalem; wherefore, they shall be *b*restored again to the *c*land of their inheritance.

12 But, behold, they shall have *a*wars, and rumors of wars; and when the day cometh that the *b*Only Begotten of the Father, yea, even the Son of heaven and of earth, shall *c*manifest himself unto them in the flesh, behold, they will reject him, because of their iniquities, and the hardness of their hearts, and the stiffness of their necks.

13 Behold, they will *a*crucify him; and after he is laid in a *b*sepulchre for the space of *c*three days he shall *d*rise from the dead, with healing in his wings; and all those who shall believe on his name shall be saved

in the kingdom of God. Wherefore, my soul delighteth to prophesy concerning him, for I have *e*seen his day, and my heart doth magnify his holy name.

14 And behold it shall come to pass that after the *a*Messiah hath risen from the dead, and hath manifested himself unto his people, unto as many as will believe on his name, behold, Jerusalem shall be *b*destroyed again; for *c*wo unto them that fight against God and the people of his *d*church.

15 Wherefore, the *a*Jews shall be *b*scattered among all nations; yea, and also *c*Babylon shall be destroyed; wherefore, the Jews shall be scattered by other nations.

16 And after they have been *a*scattered, and the Lord God hath scourged them by other nations for the space of many generations, yea, even down from generation to generation until they shall be persuaded to *b*believe in Christ, the Son of God, and the atonement, which is infinite for all mankind—and when that day shall come that they shall believe in Christ, and worship the Father in his name, with pure hearts and *c*clean hands, and look not forward any more for *d*another Messiah, then, at that time, the day will come that it must needs be expedient that they should believe these things.

17 And the Lord will set his hand

9*b* Ezek. 4:3;
   Amos 3:7;
   D&C 5:20.
10*a* 1 Ne. 7:13;
   2 Ne. 6:8;
   Omni 1:15;
   Hel. 8:21 (20–21).
   b TG Hardheartedness.
   c 2 Kgs. 24:14 (14–15);
   Jer. 52:15 (3–15);
   1 Ne. 1:13; 10:3.
   d Lam. 1:3 (1–3).
11*a* TG Teaching with the
   Spirit.
   b Jer. 24:6 (5–7).
   c TG Lands of Inheritance.
12*a* TG War.
   b TG Jesus Christ, Divine
   Sonship.

   c TG Jesus Christ, Birth of.
13*a* TG Jesus Christ,
   Crucifixion of.
   b Luke 23:53;
   John 19:41 (41–42);
   1 Ne. 19:10.
   c Mosiah 3:10.
   d Mal. 4:2.
   TG Jesus Christ,
   Prophecies about;
   Jesus Christ,
   Resurrection;
   Resurrection.
   e 1 Ne. 11:27 (13–34).
14*a* TG Jesus Christ, Messiah.
   b Matt. 24:2 (1–2);
   Luke 21:24.
   c Ps. 83:17 (2–17);
   D&C 71:7;

   Moses 7:15 (14–16).
   d TG Jesus Christ, Head of
   the Church.
15*a* TG Israel, Judah,
   People of.
   b Neh. 1:8 (7–9);
   2 Ne. 10:6;
   3 Ne. 16:8.
   TG Israel, Bondage of, in
   Other Lands;
   Israel, Scattering of.
   c TG Babylon.
16*a* Ezek. 34:12;
   Morm. 5:14.
   b 2 Ne. 10:7 (5–9);
   30:7 (7–8).
   c Job 17:9;
   D&C 88:86.
   d TG False Christs.

again the second time to ^arestore his people from their lost and fallen state. Wherefore, he will proceed to do a ^bmarvelous work and a wonder among the children of men.

18 Wherefore, he shall bring forth ^ahis ^bwords unto them, which words shall ^cjudge them at the last day, for they shall be given them for the purpose of ^dconvincing them of the true Messiah, who was rejected by them; and unto the convincing of them that they need not look forward any more for a Messiah to come, for there should not any come, save it should be a ^efalse Messiah which should deceive the people; for there is save one ^fMessiah spoken of by the prophets, and that Messiah is he who should be rejected of the Jews.

19 For according to the words of the prophets, the ^aMessiah cometh in ^bsix hundred years from the time that my father left Jerusalem; and according to the words of the prophets, and also the word of the ^cangel of God, his ^dname shall be Jesus Christ, the ^eSon of God.

20 And now, my brethren, I have spoken plainly that ye cannot err. And as the Lord God liveth that ^abrought Israel up out of the land of Egypt, and gave unto Moses power that he should ^bheal the nations after they had been bitten by the poisonous serpents, if they would cast their eyes unto the ^cserpent which he did raise up before them, and also gave him power that he should smite the ^drock and the water should come forth; yea, behold I say unto you, that as these things are ^etrue, and as the Lord God liveth, there is none other ^fname given under heaven save it be this Jesus Christ, of which I have spoken, whereby man can be saved.

21 Wherefore, for this cause hath the Lord God promised unto me that these things which I ^awrite shall be kept and preserved, and handed down unto my seed, from generation to generation, that the promise may be fulfilled unto Joseph, that his seed should never ^bperish as long as the earth should stand.

22 Wherefore, these things shall go from generation to generation as long as the earth shall stand; and they shall go according to the will and pleasure of God; and the nations who shall possess them shall be ^ajudged of them according to the words which are written.

23 For we labor diligently to write, to ^apersuade our children, and also our brethren, to believe in Christ, and to be reconciled to God; for we

17a Gen. 49:10;
  2 Ne. 21:11; 29:1.
  TG Israel, Gathering of;
  Israel, Restoration of;
  Restoration of the
  Gospel.
 b Isa. 29:14;
  2 Ne. 27:26;
  3 Ne. 28:32 (31–33).
18a 3 Ne. 16:4.
 b 2 Ne. 29:11;
  33:14 (11, 14–15);
  W of M 1:11;
  3 Ne. 27:25 (23–27);
  Ether 5:4.
 c TG Judgment, the Last.
 d 2 Ne. 26:12;
  Morm. 3:21.
 e TG False Christs.
 f TG Jesus Christ,
  Messiah.

19a TG Jesus Christ,
  Betrayal of;
  Jesus Christ, Birth of.
 b 1 Ne. 10:4; 19:8;
  3 Ne. 1:1.
 c 2 Ne. 10:3.
 d TG Jesus Christ,
  Prophecies about.
 e TG Jesus Christ, Divine
  Sonship.
20a Ex. 3:10 (2–10);
  1 Ne. 17:24 (24, 31, 40);
  19:10.
 b John 3:14;
  1 Ne. 17:41.
 c 2 Kgs. 18:4;
  Alma 33:19;
  Hel. 8:14 (14–15).
 d Ex. 17:6;
  Num. 20:11;
  Neh. 9:15;

  1 Ne. 17:29; 20:21.
 e 1 Ne. 14:30;
  Mosiah 1:6.
 f Hosea 13:4;
  Acts 4:12;
  1 Jn. 3:23 (19–24);
  1 Ne. 10:6;
  2 Ne. 2:6 (5–8);
  Mosiah 16:5 (4–5);
  Alma 12:22 (22–25).
  TG Jesus Christ, Savior.
21a 2 Ne. 27:6.
 b Amos 5:15;
  Alma 46:24 (24–27).
22a 2 Ne. 29:11;
  33:15 (10–15);
  3 Ne. 27:25 (23–27);
  Ether 4:10 (8–10).
23a TG Family, Children,
  Responsibilities
  toward.

know that it is by ^bgrace that we are saved, after all we can ^cdo.

24 And, notwithstanding we believe in Christ, we ^akeep the law of Moses, and look forward with steadfastness unto Christ, until the law shall be fulfilled.

25 For, for this end was the ^alaw given; wherefore the law hath become ^bdead unto us, and we are made alive in Christ because of our faith; yet we keep the law because of the commandments.

26 And we ^atalk of Christ, we rejoice in Christ, we preach of Christ, we ^bprophesy of Christ, and we write according to our prophecies, that our ^cchildren may know to what source they may look for a ^dremission of their sins.

27 Wherefore, we speak concerning the law that our children may know the deadness of the law; and they, by knowing the deadness of the law, may look forward unto that life which is in Christ, and know for what end the law was given. And after the law is fulfilled in Christ, that they need not harden their hearts against him when the law ought to be done away.

28 And now behold, my people, ye are a ^astiffnecked people; wherefore, I have spoken plainly unto you, that ye cannot misunderstand. And the words which I have spoken shall stand as a ^btestimony against you; for they are sufficient to ^cteach any man the ^dright way; for the right way is to believe in Christ and deny him not; for by denying ye also deny the prophets and the law.

29 And now behold, I say unto you that the right way is to believe in Christ, and deny him not; and Christ is the Holy One of Israel; wherefore ye must bow down before him, and ^aworship him with all your ^bmight, mind, and strength, and your whole soul; and if ye do this ye shall in nowise be cast out.

30 And, inasmuch as it shall be expedient, ye must keep the ^aperformances and ^bordinances of God until the law shall be fulfilled which was given unto Moses.

CHAPTER 26

Christ will minister to the Nephites—Nephi foresees the destruction of his people—They will speak from the dust—The Gentiles will build up false churches and secret combinations—The Lord forbids men to practice priestcrafts. About 559–545 B.C.

AND after Christ shall have ^arisen from the dead he shall ^bshow himself unto you, my children, and my beloved brethren; and the words which he shall speak unto you shall be the ^claw which ye shall do.

2 For behold, I say unto you that I have beheld that many generations shall pass away, and there shall be great wars and contentions among my people.

3 And after the Messiah shall come there shall be ^asigns given unto my people of his ^bbirth, and also of his ^cdeath and resurrection; and great and terrible shall that day be unto the wicked, for they shall perish; and they perish because they cast

23 b Ps. 130:4 (3–4);
  Rom. 3:20 (20–24); 7:5;
  2 Ne. 2:5 (4–10);
  Mosiah 13:32;
  Alma 42:14 (12–16);
  D&C 20:30; 138:4.
  TG Grace.
  c James 2:24 (14–26).
  TG Good Works.
24 a TG Law of Moses.
25 a TG Law of Moses.
  b Rom. 7:4 (4–6);
  D&C 74:5 (2–6).
26 a Jacob 4:12; Jarom 1:11;

Mosiah 3:13; 16:6.
  b Luke 10:24 (23–24).
  c TG Family, Children,
  Responsibilities toward.
  d TG Remission of Sins.
28 a Mosiah 3:14; Alma 9:31.
  TG Stiffnecked.
  b TG Testimony.
  c 1 Kgs. 8:36; 2 Ne. 33:10.
  TG Teaching.
  d 1 Sam. 12:23; Isa. 45:19;
  2 Pet. 2:15.
29 a TG Worship.
  b Deut. 6:5;

Mark 12:30 (29–31).
30 a 4 Ne. 1:12.
  b TG Ordinance.
26 1 a 3 Ne. 11:8 (1–12).
  TG Jesus Christ,
  Resurrection.
  b 1 Ne. 11:7; 12:6.
  c 3 Ne. 15:9 (2–10).
3 a 1 Ne. 12:4 (4–6).
  TG Signs.
  b TG Jesus Christ,
  Birth of.
  c TG Jesus Christ,
  Death of.

out the ^dprophets, and the saints, and stone them, and slay them; wherefore the cry of the ^eblood of the saints shall ascend up to God from the ground against them.

4 Wherefore, all those who are proud, and that do wickedly, the day that cometh shall ^aburn them up, saith the Lord of Hosts, for they shall be as stubble.

5 And they that kill the ^aprophets, and the saints, the depths of the earth shall ^bswallow them up, saith the Lord of Hosts; and ^cmountains shall cover them, and whirlwinds shall carry them away, and buildings shall fall upon them and crush them to pieces and grind them to powder.

6 And they shall be visited with thunderings, and lightnings, and earthquakes, and all manner of destructions, for the ^afire of the anger of the Lord shall be kindled against them, and they shall be as stubble, and the day that cometh shall consume them, saith the Lord of Hosts.

7 ^aO the pain, and the anguish of my soul for the loss of the slain of my people! For I, Nephi, have seen it, and it well nigh consumeth me before the presence of the Lord; but I must cry unto my God: Thy ways are ^bjust.

8 But behold, the righteous that hearken unto the words of the prophets, and destroy them not, but look forward unto Christ with ^asteadfast-

ness for the signs which are given, notwithstanding all ^bpersecution— behold, they are they which shall ^cnot perish.

9 But the Son of Righteousness shall ^aappear unto them; and he shall ^bheal them, and they shall have ^cpeace with him, until ^dthree generations shall have passed away, and many of the ^efourth generation shall have passed away in righteousness.

10 And when these things have passed away a speedy ^adestruction cometh unto my people; for, notwithstanding the pains of my soul, I have seen it; wherefore, I know that it shall come to pass; and they sell themselves for naught; for, for the reward of their pride and their ^bfoolishness they shall reap destruction; for because they yield unto the devil and ^cchoose works of ^ddarkness rather than light, therefore they must go down to ^ehell.

11 For the Spirit of the Lord will not always ^astrive with man. And when the Spirit ^bceaseth to strive with man then cometh speedy destruction, and this grieveth my soul.

12 And as I spake concerning the ^aconvincing of the ^bJews, that Jesus is the ^cvery Christ, it must needs be that the Gentiles be convinced also that Jesus is the Christ, the ^dEternal ^eGod;

13 And that he ^amanifesteth himself unto all those who believe in

---

3d TG Prophets,
    Rejection of.
  e Gen. 4:10;
    2 Ne. 28:10;
    Morm. 8:27.
4a 3 Ne. 8:14 (14–24);
    9:3 (3–9).
5a Ps. 105:15.
  b Num. 16:32;
    1 Ne. 19:11;
    3 Ne. 10:14.
  c Hosea 10:8; Alma 12:14.
6a 3 Ne. 8:8; 9:3–11.
7a Morm. 6:17 (17–22).
  b Rom. 3:5;
    Alma 42:1 (1, 13–25).
8a TG Steadfastness.
  b TG Persecution.
  c 3 Ne. 10:12 (12–13).

9a Alma 16:20.
  b John 12:40;
    3 Ne. 9:13 (13–14); 18:32;
    D&C 112:13.
  c TG Peace.
  d 1 Ne. 12:11 (11–12);
    3 Ne. 27:32 (30–32).
  e Alma 45:12 (10–12);
    Hel. 13:10 (5, 9–10).
10a Mosiah 12:8;
    Alma 45:11 (9–14);
    Hel. 13:6 (5–6).
  b TG Foolishness.
  c TG Agency.
  d Job 38:15;
    John 3:19.
  e Job 24:24 (17–24).
    TG Hell.
11a Gen. 6:3; Ether 2:15;

    Moses 8:17.
  b TG Holy Ghost, Loss of.
12a 2 Ne. 25:18.
  b 2 Ne. 30:7 (7–8);
    Morm. 5:14 (12–14);
    D&C 19:27.
    TG Israel, Judah,
    People of.
  c Morm. 3:21.
  d 2 Ne. 19:6;
    Mosiah 3:5;
    Alma 11:39 (38–39, 44);
    Moro. 7:22; 8:18.
  e 1 Ne. 19:10 (7, 10);
    2 Ne. 10:3;
    Mosiah 7:27;
    27:31 (30–31);
    3 Ne. 11:14.
13a TG God, Access to.

him, by the power of the ^bHoly Ghost; yea, unto every nation, kindred, tongue, and people, working mighty ^cmiracles, signs, and wonders, among the children of men according to their ^dfaith.

14 But behold, I prophesy unto you concerning the ^alast days; concerning the days when the Lord God shall ^bbring these things forth unto the children of men.

15 After my seed and the seed of my brethren shall have ^adwindled in unbelief, and shall have been smitten by the Gentiles; yea, after the Lord God shall have ^bcamped against them round about, and shall have laid siege against them with a mount, and raised forts against them; and after they shall have been brought down low in the dust, even that they are not, yet the words of the righteous shall be written, and the ^cprayers of the faithful shall be heard, and all those who have ^ddwindled in unbelief shall not be forgotten.

16 For those who shall be destroyed shall ^aspeak unto them out of the ground, and their speech shall be low out of the dust, and their voice shall be as one that hath a familiar spirit; for the Lord God will give unto him power, that he may whisper concerning them, even as it were out of the ground; and their speech shall whisper out of the dust.

17 For thus saith the Lord God: They shall ^awrite the things which shall be done among them, and they shall be written and ^bsealed up in a book, and those who have dwindled in ^cunbelief shall not have them, for they ^dseek to destroy the things of God.

18 Wherefore, as those who have been destroyed have been destroyed speedily; and the multitude of their ^aterrible ones shall be as ^bchaff that passeth away—yea, thus saith the Lord God: It shall be at an instant, suddenly—

19 And it shall come to pass, that those who have dwindled in unbelief shall be ^asmitten by the hand of the Gentiles.

20 And the Gentiles are lifted up in the ^apride of their eyes, and have ^bstumbled, because of the greatness of their ^cstumbling block, that they have built up many ^dchurches; nevertheless, they ^eput down the power and miracles of God, and preach up unto themselves their own wisdom and their own ^flearning, that they may get gain and ^ggrind upon the face of the poor.

21 And there are many churches built up which cause ^aenvyings, and ^bstrifes, and ^cmalice.

22 And there are also secret ^acombinations, even as in times of old, according to the combinations of the ^bdevil, for he is the founder of

---

13b TG Holy Ghost,
  Mission of.
  c TG Miracle.
  d TG Faith.
14a TG Last Days.
  b TG Restoration of the
  Gospel.
15a 1 Ne. 12:22 (22–23);
  15:13.
  b Isa. 29:3.
  c Ex. 3:9 (7, 9);
  Mosiah 21:15;
  D&C 109:49.
  d D&C 3:18.
16a Isa. 29:4;
  2 Ne. 3:20; 33:13;
  Morm. 8:23 (23, 26); 9:30;
  Moro. 10:27.
  TG Book of Mormon.

17a 1 Ne. 13:40 (39–42);
  2 Ne. 27:6 (6–26); 29:12.
  b TG Scriptures,
  Preservation of.
  c TG Unbelief.
  d Enos 1:14;
  Morm. 6:6.
18a Isa. 29:5.
  b Hosea 13:3 (1–4);
  Morm. 5:16 (16–18).
19a 1 Ne. 13:14;
  3 Ne. 16:8 (8–9);
  20:27 (27–28);
  Morm. 5:9.
20a Prov. 11:2;
  D&C 38:39.
  TG Pride.
  b 1 Ne. 13:34 (29, 34);
  14:1 (1–3).

  TG Apostasy of the Early
  Christian Church.
  c Ezek. 3:20; 14:4 (3–7).
  d 1 Ne. 14:10 (9–10); 22:23;
  Morm. 8:28 (25–41).
  e 2 Ne. 28:5 (4–6);
  Morm. 9:26 (7–26).
  f 1 Tim. 6:20;
  2 Ne. 9:28; 28:4 (4, 15);
  D&C 1:19.
  TG Learn.
  g Isa. 3:15;
  2 Ne. 13:15.
21a TG Envy.
  b Rom. 16:17 (17–18).
  TG Strife.
  c TG Malice.
22a TG Secret Combinations.
  b 2 Ne. 28:21.

all these things; yea, the founder of murder, and ^cworks of darkness; yea, and he leadeth them by the neck with a flaxen cord, until he bindeth them with his strong cords forever.

23 For behold, my beloved brethren, I say unto you that the Lord God worketh not in ^adarkness.

24 He doeth not ^aanything save it be for the benefit of the world; for he ^bloveth the world, even that he layeth down his own life that he may draw ^call men unto him. Wherefore, he commandeth none that they shall not partake of his salvation.

25 Behold, doth he cry unto any, saying: Depart from me? Behold, I say unto you, Nay; but he saith: ^aCome unto me all ye ^bends of the earth, ^cbuy milk and honey, without money and without price.

26 Behold, hath he commanded any that they should ^adepart out of the synagogues, or out of the houses of worship? Behold, I say unto you, Nay.

27 Hath he commanded any that they should not partake of his ^asalvation? Behold I say unto you, Nay; but he hath ^bgiven it free for all men; and he hath commanded his people that they should persuade all men to ^crepentance.

28 Behold, hath the Lord commanded any that they should not partake of his goodness? Behold I say unto you, Nay; but ^aall men are privileged the one ^blike unto the other, and none are forbidden.

29 He commandeth that there shall be no ^apriestcrafts; for, behold, priestcrafts are that men preach and set ^bthemselves up for a light unto the world, that they may get ^cgain and ^dpraise of the world; but they seek not the ^ewelfare of Zion.

30 Behold, the Lord hath forbidden this thing; wherefore, the Lord God hath given a commandment that all men should have ^acharity, which ^bcharity is ^clove. And except they should have charity they were nothing. Wherefore, if they should have charity they would not suffer the laborer in Zion to perish.

31 But the ^alaborer in ^bZion shall labor for Zion; for if they labor for ^cmoney they shall perish.

32 And again, the Lord God hath ^acommanded that men should not murder; that they should not lie; that they should not ^bsteal; that they should not take the name of the Lord their God in ^cvain; that they should not ^denvy; that they should not have ^emalice; that they should not contend one with another; that they should not commit ^fwhoredoms; and that they should do none of these things; for whoso doeth them shall perish.

33 For none of these iniquities come of the Lord; for he doeth that which is good among the children of men; and he doeth nothing save it be plain unto the children of men; and he ^ainviteth them ^ball to ^ccome unto him and partake of his goodness; and he ^ddenieth none that come

22c Lev. 19:26.
23a Isa. 48:16 (16–18).
24a 2 Ne. 2:27;
    Jacob 5:41;
    Alma 26:37.
  b John 3:16.
  c John 12:32;
    2 Ne. 9:5.
25a 1 Ne. 1:14;
    Alma 5:34 (33–36);
    3 Ne. 9:14 (13–14).
  b Mark 16:15–16.
  c Isa. 55:1.
26a Mark 9:39 (38–40).
27a TG Salvation.
  b Eph. 2:8.
  c TG Repent.

28a Rom. 2:11;
    Alma 13:5.
  b 1 Ne. 17:35 (33–35).
29a Acts 8:9;
    Alma 1:12;
    3 Ne. 16:10.
    TG Priestcraft.
  b TG Unrighteous
    Dominion.
  c Ezek. 22:27.
  d D&C 58:39;
    121:35 (34–37).
  e Ezek. 34:3.
30a TG Charity.
  b Moro. 7:47 (47–48).
  c TG God, Love of;
    Love.

31a TG Industry.
  b TG Zion.
  c Jacob 2:18 (17–19);
    D&C 11:7; 38:39.
32a TG Commandments of
    God; Law of Moses.
  b TG Stealing.
  c TG Profanity.
  d TG Envy.
  e TG Malice.
  f TG Chastity;
    Whore.
33a Jude 1:3.
  b Alma 19:36.
  c TG God, Access to.
  d Acts 10:28 (9–35, 44).
    TG Justice.

unto him, black and white, [e]bond and free, male and female; and he remembereth the [f]heathen; and all are alike unto God, both Jew and Gentile.

CHAPTER 27

Darkness and apostasy will cover the earth in the last days—The Book of Mormon will come forth—Three witnesses will testify of the book—The learned man will say he cannot read the sealed book—The Lord will do a marvelous work and a wonder—Compare Isaiah 29. About 559–545 B.C.

BUT, behold, in the [a]last days, or in the days of the Gentiles—yea, behold all the nations of the Gentiles and also the Jews, both those who shall come upon this land and those who shall be upon other lands, yea, even upon all the lands of the earth, behold, they will be [b]drunken with iniquity and all manner of abominations—

2 And when that day shall come they shall be [a]visited of the Lord of Hosts, with thunder and with earthquake, and with a great noise, and with storm, and with tempest, and with the [b]flame of devouring fire.

3 And all the [a]nations that [b]fight against Zion, and that distress her, shall be as a dream of a night vision; yea, it shall be unto them, even as unto a hungry man which dreameth, and behold he eateth but he awaketh and his soul is empty; or like unto a thirsty man which dreameth, and behold he drinketh but he awaketh and behold he is faint, and his soul

hath appetite; yea, even so shall the multitude of all the nations be that fight against Mount Zion.

4 For behold, all ye that doeth iniquity, stay yourselves and wonder, for ye shall cry out, and cry; yea, ye shall be [a]drunken but not with wine, ye shall stagger but not with strong drink.

5 For behold, the Lord hath poured out upon you the spirit of deep sleep. For behold, ye have closed your [a]eyes, and ye have [b]rejected the prophets; and your rulers, and the seers hath he covered because of your iniquity.

6 And it shall come to pass that the Lord God shall bring forth unto [a]you the words of a [b]book, and they shall be the words of them which have slumbered.

7 And behold the book shall be [a]sealed; and in the book shall be a [b]revelation from God, from the beginning of the world to the [c]ending thereof.

8 Wherefore, because of the things which are [a]sealed up, the things which are sealed shall not be delivered in the day of the wickedness and abominations of the people. Wherefore the book shall be kept from them.

9 But the book shall be delivered unto a man, and he shall deliver the words of the book, which are the words of those who have slumbered in the dust, and he shall deliver these words unto [a]another;

10 But the words which are [a]sealed he shall not deliver, neither shall he deliver the book. For the book shall

33e Rom. 2:11;
  1 Ne. 17:35 (35–40).
  f Jonah 4:11 (10–11);
  2 Ne. 29:12;
  Alma 26:37 (27, 37).
  TG Heathen.
27 1a TG Last Days.
  b Isa. 29:9.
  TG Abomination;
  Iniquity; Wickedness.
  2a Isa. 29:6 (6–10);
  Morm. 8:29.
  b Isa. 24:6; 66:16;
  Jacob 6:3; 3 Ne. 25:1.

3a Isa. 29:7 (7–8).
  b 1 Ne. 22:14.
  TG Protection, Divine.
4a Rev. 17:6 (1–6);
  2 Ne. 8:21.
5a TG Spiritual Blindness.
  b 2 Chr. 24:19;
  Jer. 26:5; 37:15;
  Zech. 1:4 (2–5).
6a Jarom 1:2;
  Morm. 5:12 (12–13).
  b 2 Ne. 26:17 (16–17);
  29:12.
  TG Book of Mormon.

7a Isa. 29:11 (11–12);
  Ether 3:27.
  TG Seal.
  b Mosiah 8:19;
  Ether 3:25 (20–28); 4:4.
  c Ether 1:2–4; 13:1–13.
8a 3 Ne. 26:9 (7–12, 18);
  Ether 4:5; 5:1;
  D&C 17:6.
9a JS—H 1:64.
10a Dan. 12:9;
  1 Ne. 14:26;
  D&C 35:18;
  JS—H 1:65.

be sealed by the power of God, and the revelation which was sealed shall be kept in the book until the own due time of the Lord, that they may come forth; for behold, they *b*reveal all things from the foundation of the world unto the end thereof.

11 And the day cometh that the words of the book which were sealed shall be read upon the house tops; and they shall be read by the power of Christ; and all things shall be *a*revealed unto the children of men which ever have been among the children of men, and which ever will be even unto the end of the earth.

12 Wherefore, at that day when the book shall be delivered unto the man of whom I have spoken, the book shall be hid from the eyes of the world, that the eyes of none shall behold it save it be that *a*three *b*witnesses shall behold it, by the power of God, besides him to whom the book shall be delivered; and they shall testify to the truth of the book and the things therein.

13 And there is *a*none other which shall view it, save it be a few according to the will of God, to bear testimony of his word unto the children of men; for the Lord God hath said that the words of the faithful should speak as if it were *b*from the dead.

14 Wherefore, the Lord God will proceed to bring forth the words of the book; and in the mouth of as many witnesses as seemeth him good will he establish his word; and wo be unto him that *a*rejecteth the word of God!

15 But behold, it shall come to pass that the Lord God shall say unto him to whom he shall deliver the book: Take these words which are not sealed and deliver them to another, that he may show them unto the learned, saying: *a*Read this, I pray thee. And the learned shall say: Bring hither the book, and I will read them.

16 And now, because of the glory of the world and to get *a*gain will they say this, and not for the glory of God.

17 And the man shall say: I cannot bring the book, for it is sealed.

18 Then shall the learned say: I cannot read it.

19 Wherefore it shall come to pass, that the Lord God will *a*deliver again the book and the words thereof to him that is not learned; and the man that is not learned shall say: I am not learned.

20 Then shall the Lord God say unto him: The learned shall not read them, for they have rejected them, and I am *a*able to do mine own work; wherefore thou shalt read the words which I shall give unto thee.

21 *a*Touch not the things which are sealed, for I will bring them forth in mine own due time; for I will show unto the children of men that I am able to do mine own work.

22 Wherefore, when thou hast read the words which I have commanded thee, and obtained the *a*witnesses which I have promised unto thee, then shalt thou seal up the book again, and hide it up unto me, that I may preserve the words which thou hast not read, until I shall see fit in mine own *b*wisdom to *c*reveal all things unto the children of men.

23 For behold, I am God; and I am a God of *a*miracles; and I will show

---

10*b* Ether 4:15.
    TG God, Omniscience of.
11*a* Luke 12:3;
    Morm. 5:8;
    D&C 121:26–31.
12*a* 2 Ne. 11:3;
    Ether 5:3 (2–4);
    D&C 5:11 (11, 15); 17:1.
    b Deut. 19:15.
13*a* D&C 5:14 (3, 14).

b 2 Ne. 3:19 (19–20);
    33:13 (13–15);
    Morm. 9:30;
    Moro. 10:27.
14*a* 2 Ne. 28:29 (29–30);
    Ether 4:8.
15*a* Isa. 29:11.
16*a* TG Priestcraft.
19*a* Isa. 29:12.
20*a* Ex. 4:11 (11–12);

Jer. 1:7 (7–9).
21*a* Ether 5:1.
22*a* TG Witness.
    b TG God, Wisdom of.
    c Ether 4:7 (6–7).
    TG Mysteries of
    Godliness.
23*a* TG Marvelous;
    Miracle.

unto the [b]world that I am the same yesterday, today, and forever; and I [c]work not among the children of men save it be [d]according to their faith.

24 And again it shall come to pass that the Lord shall say unto him that shall read the words that shall be delivered him:

25 [a]Forasmuch as this people draw near unto me with their mouth, and with their lips do [b]honor me, but have removed their [c]hearts far from me, and their fear towards me is taught by the [d]precepts of men—

26 Therefore, I will proceed to do a [a]marvelous work among this people, yea, a [b]marvelous work and a wonder, for the [c]wisdom of their wise and [d]learned shall perish, and the [e]understanding of their [f]prudent shall be hid.

27 And [a]wo unto them that seek deep to hide their [b]counsel from the Lord! And their works are in the [c]dark; and they say: Who seeth us, and who knoweth us? And they also say: Surely, your turning of things upside down shall be esteemed as the [d]potter's clay. But behold, I will show unto them, saith the Lord of Hosts, that I [e]know all their works. For shall the work say of him that made it, he made me not? Or shall the thing framed say of him that framed it, he had no understanding?

28 But behold, saith the Lord of Hosts: I will show unto the children of men that it is yet a very little while and Lebanon shall be turned into a fruitful field; and the [a]fruitful field shall be esteemed as a forest.

29 [a]And in that day shall the [b]deaf hear the words of the book, and the eyes of the blind shall see out of obscurity and out of darkness.

30 And the [a]meek also shall increase, and their [b]joy shall be in the Lord, and the poor among men shall rejoice in the Holy One of Israel.

31 For assuredly as the Lord liveth they shall see that the [a]terrible one is brought to naught, and the scorner is consumed, and all that watch for iniquity are cut off;

32 And they that make a man an [a]offender for a word, and lay a snare for him that reproveth in the [b]gate, and [c]turn aside the just for a thing of naught.

33 Therefore, thus saith the Lord, who redeemed Abraham, concerning the house of Jacob: Jacob shall [a]not now be ashamed, neither shall his face now wax pale.

34 But when he [a]seeth his children, the work of my hands, in the midst of him, they shall sanctify my name, and sanctify the Holy One of Jacob, and shall fear the God of Israel.

35 They also that [a]erred in spirit shall come to understanding, and they that murmured shall [b]learn doctrine.

CHAPTER 28

Many false churches will be built up in the last days—They will teach false, vain, and foolish doctrines—Apostasy will abound because of false teachers—The devil will rage in the hearts of men—He will teach all manner of false doctrines. About 559–545 B.C.

AND now, behold, my brethren, I have spoken unto you, according

23b TG World.
  c W of M 1:7.
  d Heb. 11;
    Ether 12:12 (7–22).
25a Isa. 29:13 (13–24).
  b Matt. 15:8 (7–9).
    TG Honor;
    Respect.
  c TG Hardheartedness.
  d 2 Ne. 28:31.
26a 1 Ne. 22:8;
    2 Ne. 29:1 (1–2).
    TG Restoration of the
    Gospel.

  b Isa. 29:14; 2 Ne. 25:17.
  c TG Wisdom.
  d TG Learn.
  e TG Knowledge.
  f TG Prudence.
27a Isa. 29:15 (15–16).
  b TG Conspiracy;
    Counsel.
  c TG Secret Combinations.
  d Jer. 18:6.
  e TG God, Omniscience of.
28a TG Earth, Renewal of.
29a Isa. 29:18.
  b TG Deaf.

30a TG Meek.
  b D&C 101:36.
31a Isa. 29:20.
32a Luke 11:54 (53–54);
    Acts 22:22.
    TG Offense.
  b Amos 5:10 (7, 10).
  c 2 Ne. 28:16.
33a TG Israel,
    Restoration of.
34a Isa. 29:23.
35a 2 Ne. 28:14;
    D&C 33:4.
  b Dan. 12:4 (4–10).

as the Spirit hath constrained me; wherefore, I know that they must surely come to pass.

2 And the things which shall be written out of the ^abook shall be of great ^bworth unto the children of men, and especially unto our seed, which is a ^cremnant of the house of Israel.

3 For it shall come to pass in that day that the ^achurches which are built up, and not unto the Lord, when the one shall say unto the other: Behold, I, I am the Lord's; and the others shall say: I, I am the Lord's; and thus shall every one say that hath built up ^bchurches, and not unto the Lord—

4 And they shall contend one with another; and their priests shall contend one with another, and they shall teach with their ^alearning, and deny the ^bHoly Ghost, which giveth utterance.

5 And they ^adeny the ^bpower of God, the Holy One of Israel; and they say unto the people: Hearken unto us, and hear ye our precept; for behold there is ^cno God today, for the Lord and the Redeemer hath done his work, and he hath given his power unto men;

6 Behold, hearken ye unto my precept; if they shall say there is a miracle wrought by the hand of the Lord, believe it not; for this day he is not a God of ^amiracles; he hath done his work.

7 Yea, and there shall be many which shall say: ^aEat, drink, and be merry, for tomorrow we die; and it shall be well with us.

8 And there shall also be many which shall say: ^aEat, drink, and be ^bmerry; nevertheless, fear God—he will ^cjustify in committing a little ^dsin; yea, ^elie a little, take the advantage of one because of his words, dig a ^fpit for thy neighbor; there is ^gno harm in this; and do all these things, for tomorrow we die; and if it so be that we are guilty, God will beat us with a few stripes, and at last we shall be saved in the kingdom of God.

9 Yea, and there shall be many which shall teach after this manner, ^afalse and vain and ^bfoolish ^cdoctrines, and shall be puffed up in their hearts, and shall seek deep to hide their counsels from the Lord; and their works shall be in the dark.

10 And the ^ablood of the saints shall cry from the ground against them.

11 Yea, they have all gone out of the ^away; they have become ^bcorrupted.

12 Because of ^apride, and because of ^bfalse teachers, and ^cfalse doctrine, their churches have become corrupted, and their churches are lifted up; because of pride they are puffed up.

13 They ^arob the ^bpoor because of their fine sanctuaries; they rob the poor because of their fine clothing;

28 2*a* TG Book of Mormon;
         Restoration of the
         Gospel.
     b 1 Ne. 13:39 (34–42);
         14:5 (1–5); 22:9;
         2 Ne. 30:3; 3 Ne. 21:6.
     c TG Israel, Remnant of.
   3*a* 1 Cor. 1:13 (10–13);
         1 Ne. 22:23;
         4 Ne. 1:26 (25–29);
         Morm. 8:28 (28, 32–38).
     b TG False Doctrine.
   4*a* 2 Ne. 9:28; 26:20.
     b 1 Cor. 2:4 (1–9).
   5*a* 2 Ne. 26:20;
         Morm. 9:26 (7–26).
     b 2 Tim. 3:5.
     c Alma 30:28.
   6*a* 3 Ne. 29:7;
         Morm. 8:26; 9:15 (15–26).

   7*a* Prov. 16:25;
         1 Cor. 15:32;
         Alma 30:17 (17–18).
   8*a* Isa. 22:13.
     b TG Worldliness.
     c Morm. 8:31.
     d Mal. 2:17.
     e D&C 10:25;
         Moses 4:4.
         TG Lying.
     f Job 6:27; Prov. 26:27;
         1 Ne. 14:3; 22:14;
         D&C 109:25.
     g Alma 30:17.
   9*a* TG False Doctrine.
     b Ezek. 13:3; Hel. 13:29.
     c Matt. 15:9;
         Col. 2:22 (18–22).
  10*a* Gen. 4:10;
         Rev. 6:10 (9–11);

         18:24 (22–24); 19:2;
         2 Ne. 26:3;
         Morm. 8:27;
         Ether 8:22 (22–24);
         D&C 87:7.
  11*a* Hel. 6:31;
         D&C 132:25 (22–25).
     b Morm. 8:28 (28–41);
         D&C 33:4.
  12*a* Prov. 28:25.
         TG Pride.
     b Jer. 23:21 (21–32); 50:6;
         3 Ne. 14:15.
         TG False Prophets.
     c TG False Doctrine.
  13*a* Ezek. 34:8;
         Morm. 8:37 (37–41).
     b Ether 8:12;
         2 Ne. 13:14 (14–15);
         Hel. 4:12 (11–13).

and they persecute the meek and the poor in heart, because in their ^cpride they are puffed up.

14 They wear ^astiff necks and high heads; yea, and because of pride, and wickedness, and abominations, and ^bwhoredoms, they have all ^cgone astray save it be a ^dfew, who are the humble followers of Christ; nevertheless, they are ^eled, that in many instances they do ^ferr because they are taught by the precepts of men.

15 O the ^awise, and the learned, and the rich, that are puffed up in the ^bpride of their ^chearts, and all those who preach ^dfalse doctrines, and all those who commit ^ewhoredoms, and pervert the right way of the Lord, ^fwo, wo, wo be unto them, saith the Lord God Almighty, for they shall be thrust down to hell!

16 Wo unto them that ^aturn aside the just for a thing of naught and ^brevile against that which is good, and say that it is of no worth! For the day shall come that the Lord God will speedily visit the inhabitants of the earth; and in that day that they are ^cfully ripe in iniquity they shall perish.

17 But behold, if the inhabitants of the earth shall repent of their wickedness and abominations they shall not be destroyed, saith the Lord of Hosts.

18 But behold, that great and ^aabominable church, the ^bwhore of all the earth, must ^ctumble to the earth, and great must be the fall thereof.

19 For the kingdom of the devil must ^ashake, and they which belong to it must needs be stirred up unto repentance, or the ^bdevil will grasp them with his everlasting ^cchains, and they be stirred up to anger, and perish;

20 For behold, at that day shall he ^arage in the ^bhearts of the children of men, and stir them up to anger against that which is good.

21 And others will he ^apacify, and lull them away into carnal ^bsecurity, that they will say: All is well in Zion; yea, Zion prospereth, all is well—and thus the ^cdevil ^dcheateth their souls, and leadeth them away carefully down to hell.

22 And behold, others he ^aflattereth away, and telleth them there is no ^bhell; and he saith unto them: I am no devil, for there is none—and thus he whispereth in their ears, until he grasps them with his awful ^cchains, from whence there is no deliverance.

23 Yea, they are grasped with death, and hell; and death, and hell, and the devil, and all that have been seized therewith must stand before the throne of God, and be ^ajudged according to their works, from whence they must go into the place prepared for them, even a ^blake of fire and brimstone, which is endless torment.

24 Therefore, wo be unto him that is at ^aease in Zion!

13c Alma 5:53;
    Morm. 8:36 (36–39).
14a Prov. 21:4.
    TG Stiffnecked.
  b TG Whore.
  c 2 Ne. 12:5;
    Mosiah 14:6;
    Alma 5:37.
  d Morm. 8:36.
  e 2 Pet. 3:17.
  f Matt. 22:29;
    2 Ne. 27:35 (34–35);
    D&C 33:4.
15a Prov. 3:7 (5–7);
    2 Ne. 15:21.
  b TG Pride.
  c TG Hardheartedness.
  d Matt. 5:19.

  e Mosiah 11:2.
  f 3 Ne. 29:5 (4–7);
    Morm. 9:26.
16a 2 Ne. 27:32.
  b Mal. 2:17.
    TG Reviling.
  c Ether 2:10 (8–11).
18a TG Devil, Church of.
  b Rev. 19:2.
  c 1 Ne. 14:3 (3, 17).
19a 1 Ne. 22:23 (22–23).
  b Alma 34:35.
  c Mosiah 23:12;
    Alma 12:11.
    TG Chain.
20a Rev. 13:7; 2 Ne. 2:18;
    D&C 10:27; 76:29.
  b Alma 8:9;

    D&C 10:20.
21a Jacob 3:11;
    Alma 5:7 (6–7);
    Morm. 8:31.
  b TG Apathy.
  c 2 Ne. 9:39; 32:8;
    Alma 30:42 (42, 53).
  d Rev. 13:14 (11–18).
22a TG Flatter.
  b Mal. 2:17.
  c 2 Ne. 9:45;
    Alma 36:18.
    TG Bondage, Spiritual.
23a TG Jesus Christ, Judge.
  b Rev. 19:20; 21:8;
    2 Ne. 9:16 (8–19, 26);
    Jacob 6:10.
24a Amos 6:1.

25 Wo be unto him that crieth: All is well!

26 Yea, wo be unto him that [a]hearkeneth unto the precepts of men, and denieth the power of God, and the gift of the Holy Ghost!

27 Yea, wo be unto him that saith: We have received, and we [a]need no more!

28 And in fine, wo unto all those who tremble, and are [a]angry because of [b]the truth of God! For behold, he that is built upon the [c]rock [d]receiveth it with gladness; and he that is built upon a sandy foundation trembleth lest he shall fall.

29 Wo be unto him that shall say: We have received the word of God, and we [a]need [b]no more of the word of God, for we have enough!

30 For behold, thus saith the Lord God: I will give unto the children of men line upon line, [a]precept upon precept, here a little and there a little; and blessed are those who hearken unto my precepts, and lend an ear unto my counsel, for they shall learn [b]wisdom; for unto him that [c]receiveth I will give [d]more; and from them that shall say, We have enough, from them shall be taken away even that which they have.

31 Cursed is he that putteth his [a]trust in man, or maketh flesh his arm, or shall hearken unto the [b]precepts of men, save their precepts shall be given by the power of the Holy Ghost.

32 [a]Wo be unto the Gentiles, saith the Lord God of Hosts! For notwith-

standing I shall lengthen out mine arm unto them from day to day, they will deny me; nevertheless, I will be merciful unto them, saith the Lord God, if they will repent and [b]come unto me; for mine [c]arm is lengthened out all the day long, saith the Lord God of Hosts.

CHAPTER 29

Many Gentiles will reject the Book of Mormon—They will say, We need no more Bible—The Lord speaks to many nations—He will judge the world out of the books which will be written. About 559–545 B.C.

BUT behold, there shall be many— at that day when I shall proceed to do a [a]marvelous work among them, that I may remember my [b]covenants which I have made unto the children of men, that I may set my hand again the [c]second time to recover my people, which are of the house of Israel;

2 And also, that I may remember the promises which I have made unto thee, Nephi, and also unto thy father, that I would remember your seed; and that the [a]words of your seed should proceed forth out of my mouth unto your seed; and my words shall [b]hiss forth unto the [c]ends of the earth, for a [d]standard unto my people, which are of the house of Israel;

3 And because my words shall hiss forth—many of the Gentiles shall say: A [a]Bible! A Bible! We have

---

26a 2 Ne. 9:29.
27a Alma 12:10 (10–11);
    3 Ne. 26:10 (9–10);
    Ether 4:8.
28a 2 Ne. 9:40; 33:5.
    TG Rebellion.
  b Matt. 7:25.
  c TG Rock.
  d TG Teachable.
29a 2 Ne. 29:10 (3–10).
  b 2 Ne. 27:14;
    Ether 4:8.
30a Prov. 2:9 (9–11);
    Isa. 28:13 (9–13);
    D&C 98:12.
  b Prov. 14:8.

TG Wisdom.
  c Luke 8:18.
  d Alma 12:10;
    D&C 50:24.
31a D&C 1:19 (19–20).
    TG Trust Not in the
    Arm of Flesh.
  b 2 Ne. 27:25.
32a 1 Ne. 14:6;
    3 Ne. 16:8.
  b TG God, Access to.
  c 2 Ne. 19:17 (17–21);
    Jacob 5:47; 6:4;
    D&C 133:67.
29 1a 2 Ne. 27:26.
    TG Restoration of the

Gospel.
  b TG Abrahamic
    Covenant.
  c 2 Ne. 6:14; 21:11; 25:17.
    TG Israel, Gathering of;
    Israel, Restoration of.
2a 2 Ne. 3:21.
  b Isa. 5:26;
    Moro. 10:28.
  c 2 Ne. 15:26.
  d Ps. 60:4.
    TG Ensign.
3a 1 Ne. 13:24 (23–24).
    TG Bible;
    Book of Mormon.

got a Bible, and there cannot be any more Bible.

4 But thus saith the Lord God: O fools, they shall have a ^a Bible; and it shall proceed forth from the ^b Jews, mine ancient covenant people. And what ^c thank they the ^d Jews for the Bible which they receive from them? Yea, what do the Gentiles mean? Do they remember the travails, and the labors, and the pains of the Jews, and their diligence unto me, in bringing forth salvation unto the Gentiles?

5 O ye Gentiles, have ye remembered the Jews, mine ancient covenant people? Nay; but ye have ^a cursed them, and have ^b hated them, and have not sought to recover them. But behold, I will return all these things upon your own heads; for I the Lord have not forgotten my people.

6 Thou fool, that shall say: A ^a Bible, we have got a Bible, and we need no more Bible. Have ye obtained a Bible save it were by the Jews?

7 Know ye not that there are more ^a nations than one? Know ye not that I, the Lord your God, have created all men, and that I remember those who are upon the ^b isles of the sea; and that I rule in the heavens above and in the ^c earth beneath; and I bring forth my ^d word unto the children of men, yea, even upon all the nations of the earth?

8 Wherefore murmur ye, because that ye shall receive more of my word? Know ye not that the ^a testi-mony of ^b two nations is a ^c witness unto you that I am God, that I remember one ^d nation like unto another? Wherefore, I speak the same words unto one nation like unto another. And when the two ^e nations shall run together the testimony of the two nations shall run together also.

9 And I do this that I may prove unto many that I am the ^a same yesterday, today, and forever; and that I speak forth my ^b words according to mine own pleasure. And because that I have spoken one ^c word ye need not suppose that I cannot speak another; for my ^d work is not yet finished; neither shall it be until the end of man, neither from that time henceforth and forever.

10 Wherefore, because that ye have a Bible ye need not suppose that it contains all my ^a words; neither ^b need ye suppose that I have not caused more to be written.

11 For I command ^a all men, both in the east and in the west, and in the north, and in the south, and in the islands of the sea, that they shall ^b write the words which I speak unto them; for out of the ^c books which shall be written I will ^d judge the world, every man according to their works, according to that which is written.

12 For behold, I shall speak unto the ^a Jews and they shall ^b write it; and I shall also speak unto the

4a Rom. 3:2 (1–3).
  b Neh. 1:10;
    1 Ne. 13:25 (23–25);
    D&C 3:16.
  c TG Ingratitude;
    Thanksgiving.
  d TG Israel, Judah,
    People of.
5a Micah 6:16.
  TG Curse.
  b 3 Ne. 29:8.
  TG Hate.
6a 1 Ne. 13:23, 38.
7a TG Jesus Christ, Creator;
  Man, Physical
  Creation of;
  Nations.
  b Isa. 51:5;
    1 Ne. 22:4;

2 Ne. 10:8 (8, 20);
  D&C 133:8.
  c Deut. 10:14;
    1 Ne. 11:6;
    D&C 55:1;
    Moses 6:44.
  d D&C 5:6.
8a TG Testimony.
  b Ezek. 37:17 (15–20);
    1 Ne. 13:39 (38–41);
    2 Ne. 3:12;
    33:10 (10–11).
  c Matt. 18:16.
  d 2 Sam. 7:23;
    Alma 9:20.
  e Hosea 1:11.
9a Heb. 13:8.
  b TG Word of God;
    Word of the Lord.

c TG Revelation.
  d Moses 1:4.
10a TG Scriptures to Come
  Forth.
  b 2 Ne. 28:29.
11a Alma 29:8.
  b 2 Tim. 3:16;
    Moses 1:40.
  TG Scriptures,
    Preservation of;
    Scriptures, Writing of.
  c TG Book of Life.
  d 2 Ne. 25:22 (18, 22);
    33:14 (11, 14–15).
  TG Jesus Christ, Judge.
12a 1 Ne. 13:23 (23–29);
    2 Ne. 3:12.
  b TG Scriptures, Lost.

Nephites and they shall ^cwrite it; and I shall also speak unto the other tribes of the house of Israel, which I have led away, and they shall write it; and I shall also speak unto ^dall nations of the earth and they shall write it.

13 And it shall come to pass that the ^aJews shall have the words of the Nephites, and the Nephites shall have the words of the Jews; and the Nephites and the Jews shall have the words of the ^blost tribes of Israel; and the lost tribes of Israel shall have the words of the Nephites and the Jews.

14 And it shall come to pass that my people, which are of the ^ahouse of Israel, shall be gathered home unto the ^blands of their possessions; and my word also shall be gathered in ^cone. And I will show unto them that fight against my word and against my ^dpeople, who are of the ^ehouse of Israel, that I am God, and that I ^fcovenanted with ^gAbraham that I would remember his ^hseed ⁱforever.

CHAPTER 30

Converted Gentiles will be numbered with the covenant people—Many Lamanites and Jews will believe the word and become delightsome—Israel will be restored and the wicked destroyed. About 559–545 B.C.

AND now behold, my beloved brethren, I would speak unto you; for I, Nephi, would not suffer that ye should suppose that ye are more righteous than the Gentiles shall be. For behold, except ye shall keep the commandments of God ye shall all likewise ^aperish; and because of the words which have been spoken ye need not suppose that the Gentiles are utterly destroyed.

2 For behold, I say unto you that as many of the Gentiles as will repent are the ^acovenant people of the Lord; and as many of the ^bJews as will not repent shall be ^ccast off; for the Lord ^dcovenanteth with none save it be with them that ^erepent and believe in his Son, who is the Holy One of Israel.

3 And now, I would prophesy somewhat more concerning the Jews and the Gentiles. For after the book of which I have spoken shall come forth, and be written unto the Gentiles, and sealed up again unto the Lord, there shall be many which shall ^abelieve the words which are written; and ^bthey shall carry them forth unto the ^cremnant of our seed.

4 And then shall the remnant of our seed know concerning us, how that we came out from Jerusalem, and that they are descendants of the Jews.

5 And the gospel of Jesus Christ shall be declared among ^athem; wherefore, ^bthey shall be restored unto the ^cknowledge of their fathers, and also to the knowledge of Jesus Christ, which was had among their fathers.

12c 1 Ne. 13:40 (39–42);
      2 Ne. 26:17 (16–17);
      27:6 (6–26).
  d 2 Ne. 26:33;
      Alma 29:8.
13a Morm. 5:14 (13–14).
  b TG Israel, Ten Lost
      Tribes of.
14a Jer. 3:18 (17–19).
  b TG Israel, Gathering of;
      Lands of Inheritance.
  c Ezek. 37:17 (16–17).
  d 1 Kgs. 8:51;
      2 Ne. 3:9; 8:16.
  e 1 Ne. 22:9;
      2 Ne. 30:7 (7–8).
  f Gen. 12:2 (1–3);
      1 Ne. 17:40;

    3 Ne. 20:27;
      Abr. 2:9.
      TG Abrahamic
      Covenant.
  g Micah 7:20 (18–20).
  h Ps. 102:28;
      D&C 132:30;
      Moses 7:52 (50–53).
      TG Seed of Abraham.
  i Gen. 17:7 (5–7).
30 1a Luke 13:3 (1–5).
  2a Gal. 3:29 (26–29);
      Abr. 2:10 (9–11).
  b Matt. 8:12.
      TG Israel, Judah,
      People of.
  c Luke 3:9 (3–9);
      Rom. 9:6;

    Jacob 5:6.
  d Rom. 3:29.
  e TG Repent.
3a 2 Ne. 28:2;
      3 Ne. 16:6 (6–13).
  b 1 Ne. 22:9 (5–10);
      3 Ne. 5:25 (20–26).
  c 2 Ne. 4:7 (7–11);
      Jacob 1:5.
      TG Israel, Remnant of.
5a 3 Ne. 21:5 (3–7, 24–26);
      Morm. 5:15.
  b D&C 3:20.
  c 1 Ne. 15:14;
      2 Ne. 3:12;
      Morm. 7:9 (1, 9–10).

6 And then shall they rejoice; for they shall ^aknow that it is a blessing unto them from the hand of God; and their ^bscales of darkness shall begin to fall from their eyes; and many generations shall not pass away among them, save they shall be a pure and a ^cdelightsome people.

7 And it shall come to pass that the ^aJews which are scattered also shall ^bbegin to believe in Christ; and they shall begin to gather in upon the face of the land; and as many as shall believe in Christ shall also become a delightsome people.

8 And it shall come to pass that the Lord God shall commence his work among all nations, kindreds, tongues, and people, to bring about the ^arestoration of his people upon the earth.

9 And with righteousness shall the ^aLord God ^bjudge the poor, and reprove with equity for the ^cmeek of the earth. And he shall smite the earth with the rod of his mouth; and with the breath of his lips shall he slay the wicked.

10 For the ^atime speedily cometh that the Lord God shall cause a great ^bdivision among the people, and the wicked will he ^cdestroy; and he will ^dspare his people, yea, even if it so be that he must ^edestroy the wicked by fire.

11 And ^arighteousness shall be the girdle of his loins, and faithfulness the girdle of his reins.

12 ^aAnd then shall the wolf dwell with the lamb; and the leopard shall lie down with the kid, and the calf, and the young lion, and the fatling, together; and a little child shall lead them.

13 And the cow and the bear shall feed; their young ones shall lie down together; and the lion shall eat straw like the ox.

14 And the sucking child shall play on the hole of the asp, and the weaned child shall put his hand on the cockatrice's den.

15 They shall not hurt nor destroy in all my holy ^amountain; for the earth shall be full of the ^bknowledge of the Lord as the waters cover the sea.

16 Wherefore, the things of ^aall nations shall be made known; yea, all things shall be made ^bknown unto the children of men.

17 There is nothing which is secret save it shall be ^arevealed; there is no work of darkness save it shall be made manifest in the light; and there is nothing which is sealed upon the earth save it shall be loosed.

18 Wherefore, all things which have been revealed unto the children of men shall at that ^aday be revealed; and Satan shall have power over the hearts of the children of men ^bno more, for a long time. And now, my beloved brethren, I make an end of my sayings.

CHAPTER 31

Nephi tells why Christ was baptized—Men must follow Christ, be baptized, receive the Holy Ghost, and endure to the end to be saved—Repentance and

---

6a Alma 3:14.
 b TG Darkness, Spiritual;
   Spiritual Blindness.
 c W of M 1:8;
   D&C 49:24; 109:65.
7a 2 Ne. 29:14 (13–14);
   3 Ne. 5:25 (23–26).
   TG Israel, Judah,
   People of.
 b 2 Ne. 25:16 (16–17).
8a TG Israel, Restoration of;
   Millennium, Preparing a
   People for.
9a Isa. 11:4 (4–9).
 b Ps. 19:9;

2 Ne. 9:15.
 c TG Meek.
10a Jacob 5:29; 6:2.
   TG Last Days.
 b D&C 63:54.
 c Ps. 73:17 (3–17);
   D&C 29:17;
   JS—M 1:55.
 d 1 Ne. 22:17 (15–22);
   3 Ne. 22:13 (13–17);
   Moses 7:61.
 e 1 Ne. 22:23 (15–17, 23);
   Jacob 5:69.
   TG Earth, Cleansing of.
11a Isa. 11:5 (5–9).

TG Righteousness.
12a Isa. 65:25.
   TG Earth, Renewal of.
15a Joel 2:1.
 b TG God, Knowledge
   about.
16a D&C 101:32 (32–35);
   121:28 (26–32).
 b Ether 4:7 (6–7, 13–17).
17a Luke 12:2 (2–3);
   D&C 1:3 (1–3).
18a Acts 3:21.
 b Rev. 20:2 (2–3);
   Ether 8:26.

baptism are the gate to the strait and narrow path—Eternal life comes to those who keep the commandments after baptism. About 559–545 B.C.

AND now I, Nephi, make an end of my ^aprophesying unto you, my beloved brethren. And I cannot write but a few things, which I know must surely come to pass; neither can I write but a few of the ^bwords of my brother Jacob.

2 Wherefore, the things which I have written sufficeth me, save it be a few words which I ^amust speak concerning the doctrine of Christ; wherefore, I shall speak unto you plainly, according to the plainness of my prophesying.

3 For my soul delighteth in ^aplainness; for after this manner doth the Lord God work among the children of men. For the Lord God giveth light unto the ^bunderstanding; for he speaketh unto men according to their ^clanguage, unto their understanding.

4 Wherefore, I would that ye should remember that I have spoken unto you concerning that ^aprophet which the Lord showed unto me, that should baptize the ^bLamb of God, which should take away the sins of the world.

5 And now, if the Lamb of God, he being ^aholy, should have need to be ^bbaptized by water, to fulfil all righteousness, O then, how much more need have we, being unholy, to be ^cbaptized, yea, even by water!

6 And now, I would ask of you, my beloved brethren, wherein the Lamb of God did fulfil all righteousness in being baptized by water?

7 Know ye not that he was holy? But notwithstanding he being holy, he showeth unto the children of men that, according to the flesh he humbleth himself before the Father, and witnesseth unto the Father that he would be ^aobedient unto him in keeping his commandments.

8 Wherefore, after he was baptized with water the Holy Ghost descended upon him in the ^aform of a ^bdove.

9 And again, it showeth unto the children of men the straitness of the path, and the narrowness of the ^agate, by which they should enter, he having set the ^bexample before them.

10 And he said unto the children of men: ^aFollow thou me. Wherefore, my beloved brethren, can we ^bfollow Jesus save we shall be willing to keep the commandments of the Father?

11 And the Father said: Repent ye, repent ye, and be baptized in the name of my Beloved Son.

12 And also, the voice of the Son came unto me, saying: He that is baptized in my name, to him will the Father ^agive the Holy Ghost, like unto me; wherefore, ^bfollow me, and do the things which ye have seen me do.

13 Wherefore, my beloved brethren, I know that if ye shall ^afollow the Son, with full purpose of heart, acting no ^bhypocrisy and no deception before God, but with real ^cintent, repenting of your sins, witnessing unto the Father that ye are ^dwilling to take upon you the ^ename

31 1*a* 2 Ne. 25:4 (1–4).
  b 2 Ne. 11:1.
 2*a* 2 Ne. 11:4 (4–6).
 3*a* 2 Ne. 25:7 (7–8); 32:7.
  b TG Understanding.
  c D&C 1:24.
    TG Language.
 4*a* 1 Ne. 10:7; 11:27.
  b TG Jesus Christ, Lamb of God.
 5*a* 1 Jn. 3:3.
  b Matt. 3:11 (11–17).
    TG Jesus Christ, Baptism of.

  c TG Baptism, Essential.
 7*a* John 5:30.
    TG Obedience.
 8*a* 1 Ne. 11:27.
  b TG Holy Ghost, Dove, Sign of.
 9*a* 2 Ne. 9:41;
    3 Ne. 14:14 (13–14);
    D&C 22:4; 43:7.
  b TG Example.
10*a* Matt. 4:19; 8:22; 9:9.
  b Matt. 8:19; Moro. 7:11;
    D&C 56:2.
12*a* TG Holy Ghost, Gift of.

  b Matt. 16:24 (24–26);
    Luke 9:59 (57–62);
    John 12:26; 1 Jn. 2:6.
    TG God, the Standard of Righteousness.
13*a* TG Jesus Christ, Exemplar.
  b TG Hypocrisy.
  c TG Integrity; Sincere.
  d TG Agency; Commitment.
  e TG Jesus Christ, Taking the Name of.

of Christ, by ᶠbaptism—yea, by following your Lord and your Savior down into the water, according to his word, behold, then shall ye receive the Holy Ghost; yea, then cometh the ᵍbaptism of fire and of the Holy Ghost; and then can ye speak with the ʰtongue of angels, and shout praises unto the Holy One of Israel.

14 But, behold, my beloved brethren, thus came the voice of the Son unto me, saying: After ye have repented of your sins, and witnessed unto the Father that ye are willing to keep my commandments, by the baptism of water, and have received the baptism of fire and of the Holy Ghost, and can speak with a new tongue, yea, even with the tongue of angels, and after this should ᵃdeny me, it would have been ᵇbetter for you that ye had not known me.

15 And I heard a voice from the Father, saying: Yea, the ᵃwords of my Beloved are true and faithful. He that ᵇendureth to the ᶜend, the same shall be saved.

16 And now, my beloved brethren, I know by this that unless a man shall ᵃendure to the end, in following the ᵇexample of the Son of the living God, he cannot be saved.

17 Wherefore, do the things which I have told you I have seen that your Lord and your Redeemer should do; for, for this cause have they been shown unto me, that ye might know the gate by which ye should enter. For the gate by which ye should enter is repentance and ᵃbaptism by water; and then cometh a ᵇremission of your sins by fire and by the Holy Ghost.

18 And then are ye in this ᵃstrait and narrow ᵇpath which leads to eternal life; yea, ye have entered in by the gate; ye have done according to the commandments of the Father and the Son; and ye have received the Holy Ghost, which ᶜwitnesses of the ᵈFather and the Son, unto the fulfilling of the promise which he hath made, that if ye entered in by the way ye should receive.

19 And now, my beloved brethren, after ye have gotten into this strait and narrow ᵃpath, I would ask if all is ᵇdone? Behold, I say unto you, Nay; for ye have not come thus far save it were by the word of Christ with unshaken ᶜfaith in him, ᵈrelying wholly upon the merits of him who is mighty to ᵉsave.

20 Wherefore, ye must press forward with a ᵃsteadfastness in Christ, having a perfect brightness of ᵇhope, and a ᶜlove of God and of all men. Wherefore, if ye shall press forward, feasting upon the word of Christ, and ᵈendure to the end, behold, thus saith the Father: Ye shall have ᵉeternal life.

21 And now, behold, my beloved brethren, this is the ᵃway; and there

13f Gal. 3:27 (26–27).
  g TG Holy Ghost,
    Baptism of.
  h 2 Ne. 32:2 (2–3).
    TG Holy Ghost, Gifts of.
14a Matt. 10:33 (32–33);
    Rom. 1:16 (15–18);
    2 Tim. 2:12 (10–15);
    Alma 24:30;
    D&C 101:5 (1–5).
    TG Holy Ghost,
    Unpardonable Sin
    against.
  b Heb. 6:4 (4–6);
    2 Pet. 2:21.
15a D&C 64:31; 66:11.
  b Jacob 6:11 (7–11).
    TG Endure;
    Steadfastness.
  c Alma 5:13.

16a Mark 13:13; Alma 38:2;
    D&C 20:29; 53:7.
  b TG Example;
    Jesus Christ, Exemplar.
17a Mosiah 18:10.
    TG Baptism.
  b TG Holy Ghost,
    Mission of;
    Remission of Sins.
18a 1 Ne. 8:20.
  b Prov. 4:18.
    TG Gate; Path; Way.
  c TG Holy Ghost, Mission
    of; Holy Ghost, Source
    of Testimony.
  d 3 Ne. 28:11;
    Moses 6:66.
19a Hosea 14:9 (8–9).
  b Mosiah 4:10.
  c TG Faith.

  d Moro. 6:4; D&C 3:20;
    Moses 7:53.
  e TG Jesus Christ,
    Atonement through.
20a TG Commitment;
    Dedication;
    Perseverance;
    Steadfastness;
    Walking with God.
  b TG Hope.
  c TG God, Love of; Love.
  d James 5:8 (7–11);
    Rev. 2:25 (25–26);
    3 Ne. 15:9.
  e 1 Jn. 2:25; 5:13 (10–21).
    TG Objectives.
21a Ex. 33:13 (12–13);
    Acts 4:12; 2 Ne. 9:41;
    Alma 37:46;
    D&C 132:22 (22, 25).

is ^bnone other way nor ^cname given under heaven whereby man can be saved in the kingdom of God. And now, behold, this is the ^ddoctrine of Christ, and the only and true doctrine of the ^eFather, and of the Son, and of the Holy Ghost, which is ^fone God, without end. Amen.

CHAPTER 32

Angels speak by the power of the Holy Ghost—Men must pray and gain knowledge for themselves from the Holy Ghost. About 559–545 B.C.

AND now, behold, my beloved brethren, I suppose that ye ponder somewhat in your hearts concerning that which ye should do after ye have entered in by the way. But, behold, why do ye ponder these things in your hearts?

2 Do ye not remember that I said unto you that after ye had ^areceived the Holy Ghost ye could speak with the ^btongue of angels? And now, how could ye speak with the tongue of angels save it were by the Holy Ghost?

3 ^aAngels speak by the power of the Holy Ghost; wherefore, they speak the words of Christ. Wherefore, I said unto you, ^bfeast upon the ^cwords of Christ; for behold, the words of Christ will ^dtell you all things what ye should do.

4 Wherefore, now after I have spoken these words, if ye cannot understand them it will be because ye ^aask not, neither do ye knock; wherefore, ye are not brought into

the light, but must perish in the dark.

5 For behold, again I say unto you that if ye will enter in by the way, and receive the Holy Ghost, it will ^ashow unto you all things what ye should do.

6 Behold, this is the doctrine of Christ, and there will be no more doctrine given until after he shall ^amanifest himself unto you in the flesh. And when he shall manifest himself unto you in the flesh, the things which he shall say unto you shall ye observe to do.

7 And now I, Nephi, cannot say more; the Spirit stoppeth mine utterance, and I am left to mourn because of the ^aunbelief, and the wickedness, and the ignorance, and the ^bstiffneckedness of men; for they will ^cnot search ^dknowledge, nor understand great knowledge, when it is given unto them in ^eplainness, even as plain as word can be.

8 And now, my beloved brethren, I perceive that ye ponder still in your hearts; and it grieveth me that I must speak concerning this thing. For if ye would hearken unto the ^aSpirit which teacheth a man to ^bpray, ye would know that ye must ^cpray; for the ^devil spirit teacheth not a man to pray, but teacheth him that he must not pray.

9 But behold, I say unto you that ye must ^apray always, and not faint; that ye must not perform any thing unto the Lord save in the first place ye shall ^bpray unto the Father in

---

21b 2 Ne. 25:20;
     Mosiah 3:17.
   c TG Jesus Christ, Taking
     the Name of.
   d Matt. 7:28;
     John 7:16.
   e TG Godhead.
   f Deut. 6:4; Gal. 3:20;
     1 Ne. 13:41;
     3 Ne. 28:10;
     Morm. 7:7.
     TG Unity.
32 2a Alma 36:24;
     3 Ne. 9:20.
   b 2 Ne. 31:13.
  3a TG Angels.
   b Jer. 15:16.

         TG Bread of Life; Study.
       c Col. 3:16.
       d Ex. 4:15.
         TG Problem-Solving.
      4a TG Ask.
      5a 3 Ne. 16:6;
         Ether 4:11 (11–12);
         D&C 28:15;
         Moses 8:24.
         TG Holy Ghost, Gifts of;
         Revelation.
      6a 1 Ne. 12:6.
      7a TG Doubt; Unbelief.
       b TG Stiffnecked.
       c 2 Pet. 3:5.
       d TG Knowledge.
       e 2 Ne. 25:7 (7–8); 31:3;

         Jacob 4:13;
         Alma 13:23;
         Ether 12:39.
      8a TG Discernment,
         Spiritual.
       b TG Prayer.
       c Jacob 3:1.
       d 2 Ne. 9:39;
         28:21 (20–22);
         Mosiah 2:32; 4:14;
         Alma 30:42 (42, 53).
         TG Spirits, Evil or
         Unclean.
      9a Mosiah 26:39;
         3 Ne. 20:1;
         D&C 75:11.
       b 3 Ne. 18:19.

the ᶜname of Christ, that he will ᵈconsecrate thy performance unto thee, that thy performance may be for the ᵉwelfare of thy soul.

CHAPTER 33

Nephi's words are true—They testify of Christ—Those who believe in Christ will believe Nephi's words, which will stand as a witness before the judgment bar. About 559–545 B.C.

AND now I, Nephi, cannot write all the things which were taught among my people; neither am I ᵃmighty in writing, like unto speaking; for when a man ᵇspeaketh by the power of the Holy Ghost the power of the Holy Ghost carrieth it unto the hearts of the children of men.

2 But behold, there are many that ᵃharden their ᵇhearts against the ᶜHoly Spirit, that it hath no place in them; wherefore, they cast many things away which are written and esteem them as things of naught.

3 But I, Nephi, have written what I have written, and I esteem it as of great ᵃworth, and especially unto my people. For I ᵇpray continually for them by day, and mine ᶜeyes water my pillow by night, because of them; and I cry unto my God in faith, and I know that he will hear my cry.

4 And I know that the Lord God will consecrate my prayers for the gain of my people. And the words which I have written in weakness will be made strong unto them; for it ᵃpersuadeth them to do good; it maketh known unto them of their fathers; and it speaketh of Jesus, and persuadeth them to believe in him, and to endure to the end, which is life ᵇeternal.

5 And it speaketh ᵃharshly against sin, according to the ᵇplainness of the truth; wherefore, no man will be angry at the words which I have written save he shall be of the spirit of the devil.

6 I ᵃglory in ᵇplainness; I glory in truth; I glory in my Jesus, for he hath ᶜredeemed my soul from hell.

7 I have ᵃcharity for my people, and great faith in Christ that I shall meet many souls spotless at his judgment-seat.

8 I have charity for the ᵃJew—I say Jew, because I mean them from whence I came.

9 I also have charity for the Gentiles. But behold, for none of ᵃthese can I hope except they shall be ᵇreconciled unto Christ, and enter into the ᶜnarrow ᵈgate, and ᵉwalk in the ᶠstrait path which leads to life, and continue in the path until the end of the day of ᵍprobation.

10 And now, my beloved brethren, and also ᵃJew, and all ye ends of the earth, hearken unto these words and ᵇbelieve in Christ; and if ye believe not in these words believe in Christ.

9c Col. 3:17;
   Moses 5:8.
d Micah 4:13;
   2 Ne. 2:2.
e Alma 34:27.
33 1a Ether 12:23 (23–27).
   b Rom. 10:17 (13–17);
     D&C 100:8 (7–8).
     TG Holy Ghost, Gifts of.
2a Num. 15:31 (30–31);
   1 Ne. 19:7;
   Jacob 4:14;
   D&C 3:7 (4–13).
   TG Hardheartedness.
   b TG Spiritual Blindness.
   c TG Holy Ghost, Loss of.
3a TG Scriptures, Value of.
   b Gen. 20:7;
     Num. 21:7;

1 Sam. 7:5;
   Jer. 42:4;
   Enos 1:9 (9–12);
   W of M 1:8;
   Moro. 9:22.
   c Ps. 6:6; Jer. 13:17;
     Acts 20:19.
4a Ether 8:26;
   Moro. 7:13 (12–17).
   b TG Eternal Life.
5a 1 Ne. 16:2 (1–3);
   2 Ne. 9:40; 28:28;
   Enos 1:23;
   W of M 1:17.
   b 2 Ne. 25:4;
     Jacob 2:11; 4:13.
6a Ps. 44:8 (4–8);
   D&C 76:61.

b 2 Ne. 31:3.
   c Enos 1:27.
7a TG Charity.
8a TG Israel, Judah,
   People of.
   BD Judah, Kingdom of.
9a Eph. 3:6 (1–7);
   2 Ne. 10:18;
   3 Ne. 21:14.
   b TG Reconciliation.
   c 2 Ne. 9:41;
     Hel. 3:29 (29–30).
   d Matt. 7:14.
   e TG Walking with God.
   f D&C 132:22.
   g TG Probation.
10a TG Israel, Judah,
   People of.
   b TG Believe.

And if ye shall ^cbelieve in Christ ye will believe in these ^dwords, for they are the ^ewords of Christ, and he hath given them unto me; and they ^fteach all men that they should do good.

11 And if they are not the words of Christ, judge ye—for Christ will show unto you, with ^apower and great ^bglory, that they are his words, at the last day; and you and I shall stand face to face before his bar; and ye shall know that I have been commanded of him to write these things, notwithstanding my weakness.

12 And I pray the Father in the name of Christ that many of us, if not all, may be saved in his ^akingdom at that great and last day.

13 And now, my beloved brethren, all those who are of the house of Israel, and all ye ends of the earth, I speak unto you as the voice of one ^acrying from the dust: Farewell until that great day shall come.

14 And you that will not partake of the goodness of God, and respect the words of the ^aJews, and also my ^bwords, and the words which shall proceed forth out of the mouth of the Lamb of God, behold, I bid you an everlasting farewell, for these words shall ^ccondemn you at the last day.

15 For what I seal on earth, shall be brought against you at the ^ajudgment bar; for thus hath the Lord commanded me, and I must ^bobey. Amen.

THE BOOK OF JACOB

THE BROTHER OF NEPHI

The words of his preaching unto his brethren. He confoundeth a man who seeketh to overthrow the doctrine of Christ. A few words concerning the history of the people of Nephi.

CHAPTER 1

Jacob and Joseph seek to persuade men to believe in Christ and keep His commandments—Nephi dies—Wickedness prevails among the Nephites. About 544–421 B.C.

FOR behold, it came to pass that fifty and five years had passed away from the time that Lehi left Jerusalem; wherefore, Nephi gave me, Jacob, a ^acommandment concerning the ^bsmall plates, upon which these things are engraven.

2 And he gave me, Jacob, a commandment that I should ^awrite upon ^bthese plates a few of the things which I considered to be most precious; that I should not touch, save it were lightly, concerning the history of this people which are called the people of Nephi.

3 For he said that the history of his

10c John 8:47.
  d TG Book of Mormon.
  e Isa. 51:16;
    Moro. 10:27 (27–29);
    D&C 1:24.
  f 1 Kgs. 8:36;
    2 Ne. 25:28.
11a Ether 5:4 (4–6);
    Moro. 7:35.
  b TG Jesus Christ,
    Glory of.
12a TG Kingdom of God,

in Heaven;
Kingdom of God,
on Earth.
13a Isa. 29:4;
    2 Ne. 27:13;
    Morm. 8:26.
14a TG Bible.
  b TG Book of Mormon.
  c 2 Ne. 29:11;
    W of M 1:11.
15a 2 Ne. 25:22;
    3 Ne. 27:25 (23–27);

Ether 4:10 (8–10).
  b TG Obedience.

[JACOB]

1 1a Jacob 7:27;
    Jarom 1:15 (1–2, 15);
    Omni 1:3.
  b 2 Ne. 5:31 (28–33);
    Jacob 3:13 (13–14).
2a TG Scribe;
    Scriptures, Writing of.
  b 1 Ne. 6:6.

people should be engraven upon his ^aother plates, and that I should ^bpreserve these plates and hand them down unto my seed, from generation to generation.

4 And if there were preaching which was ^asacred, or revelation which was great, or prophesying, that I should engraven the ^bheads of them upon these plates, and touch upon them as much as it were possible, for Christ's sake, and for the sake of our people.

5 For because of faith and great anxiety, it truly had been made manifest unto us concerning our people, what things should ^ahappen unto them.

6 And we also had many revelations, and the spirit of much prophecy; wherefore, we knew of ^aChrist and his kingdom, which should come.

7 Wherefore we labored diligently among our people, that we might persuade them to ^acome unto Christ, and partake of the goodness of God, that they might enter into his ^brest, lest by any means he should swear in his wrath they should not ^center in, as in the ^dprovocation in the days of temptation while the children of Israel were in the ^ewilderness.

8 Wherefore, we would to God that we could persuade all men ^anot to rebel against God, to ^bprovoke him to anger, but that all men would believe in Christ, and view his death, and suffer his ^ccross and bear the shame of the world; wherefore, I,

Jacob, take it upon me to fulfil the commandment of my brother Nephi.

9 Now Nephi began to be old, and he saw that he must soon ^adie; wherefore, he ^banointed a man to be a king and a ruler over his people now, according to the reigns of the ^ckings.

10 The people having loved Nephi exceedingly, he having been a great protector for them, having wielded the ^asword of Laban in their defence, and having labored in all his days for their welfare—

11 Wherefore, the people were desirous to retain in remembrance his name. And whoso should reign in his stead were called by the people, second Nephi, third Nephi, and so forth, according to the reigns of the kings; and thus they were called by the people, let them be of whatever name they would.

12 And it came to pass that Nephi died.

13 Now the people which were not ^aLamanites were Nephites; nevertheless, they were called Nephites, Jacobites, Josephites, ^bZoramites, Lamanites, Lemuelites, and Ishmaelites.

14 But I, Jacob, shall not hereafter distinguish ^athem by these names, but I shall ^bcall them Lamanites that seek to destroy the people of Nephi, and those who are friendly to Nephi I shall call ^cNephites, or the ^dpeople of Nephi, according to the reigns of the kings.

3a 2 Ne. 5:33 (29–33);
    Jacob 3:13 (13–14).
  b TG Scriptures,
    Preservation of.
4a TG Sacred.
  b IE the dominant,
    important items.
5a See 1 Ne. 12–15. See also
    1 Ne. 22:7 (7–8);
    2 Ne. 1:9 (5–10);
    4:7 (7–11); 30:3 (3–6).
6a 1 Ne. 10:4 (4–11);
    19:8 (8–14).
7a 2 Ne. 9:41 (41, 45, 51);
    Omni 1:26 (25–26);
    Moro. 10:32.
  b TG Rest.
  c Num. 14:23;

      Deut. 1:35 (35–37);
      D&C 84:24 (23–25).
    d Heb. 3:8.
    e Num. 26:65;
      1 Ne. 17:31 (23–31).
  8a TG Loyalty;
      Rebellion.
    b Num. 14:11 (11–12);
      1 Kgs. 16:33;
      1 Ne. 17:30 (23–31);
      Alma 12:37 (36–37);
      Hel. 7:18.
    c Luke 14:27.
  9a Gen. 47:29 (28–29);
      2 Ne. 1:14.
    b TG Anointing.
    c 2 Ne. 6:2;
      Jarom 1:7 (7, 14).

 10a 1 Ne. 4:9;
      2 Ne. 5:14;
      W of M 1:13;
      Mosiah 1:16;
      D&C 17:1.
 13a Enos 1:13;
      Alma 23:17;
      D&C 3:18.
    b 1 Ne. 4:35;
      Alma 54:23;
      4 Ne. 1:36 (36–37).
 14a W of M 1:16.
    b Mosiah 25:12;
      Alma 2:11.
    c 2 Ne. 4:11.
    d 2 Ne. 5:9.

15 And now it came to pass that the people of Nephi, under the reign of the second king, began to grow hard in their hearts, and indulge themselves somewhat in wicked practices, such as like unto David of old desiring many *a*wives and *b*concubines, and also Solomon, his son.

16 Yea, and they also began to search much *a*gold and silver, and began to be lifted up somewhat in pride.

17 Wherefore I, Jacob, gave unto them these words as I taught them in the *a*temple, having first obtained mine *b*errand from the Lord.

18 For I, Jacob, and my brother Joseph had been *a*consecrated priests and *b*teachers of this people, by the hand of Nephi.

19 And we did *a*magnify our office unto the Lord, taking upon us the *b*responsibility, answering the sins of the people upon our own heads if we did not *c*teach them the word of God with all diligence; wherefore, by laboring with our might their *d*blood might not come upon our garments; otherwise their blood would come upon our garments, and we would not be found spotless at the last day.

CHAPTER 2

Jacob denounces the love of riches, pride, and unchastity—Men may seek riches to help their fellowmen—The Lord commands that no man among the Nephites may have more than one wife—The Lord delights in the chastity of women. About 544–421 B.C.

THE *a*words which Jacob, the brother of Nephi, spake unto the people of Nephi, after the death of Nephi:

2 Now, my beloved brethren, I, Jacob, according to the *a*responsibility which I am under to God, to *b*magnify mine office with *c*soberness, and that I might *d*rid my garments of your sins, I come up into the temple this day that I might declare unto you the word of God.

3 And ye yourselves know that I have hitherto been diligent in the office of my calling; but I this day am weighed down with much more desire and anxiety for the *a*welfare of your souls than I have hitherto been.

4 For behold, as yet, ye have been obedient unto the word of the Lord, which I have given unto you.

5 But behold, hearken ye unto me, and know that by the help of the all-powerful Creator of heaven and earth I can tell you concerning your *a*thoughts, how that ye are beginning to labor in sin, which sin appeareth very abominable unto me, yea, and abominable unto God.

6 Yea, it grieveth my soul and causeth me to shrink with shame before the presence of my Maker, that I must testify unto you concerning the wickedness of your hearts.

7 And also it grieveth me that I must use so much *a*boldness of speech concerning you, before your wives and your children, many of whose feelings are exceedingly tender and *b*chaste and delicate

15*a* Deut. 17:17;
   1 Sam. 25:43 (42–43);
   D&C 132:38 (38–39).
  b 2 Sam. 20:3;
   1 Chr. 3:9.
16*a* Mosiah 2:12.
17*a* 2 Ne. 5:16;
   Alma 16:13;
   Hel. 3:14 (9, 14);
   3 Ne. 11:1.
   TG Temple.
  b TG Called of God.
18*a* 2 Ne. 5:26.
   TG Delegation of
   Responsibility;

   Setting Apart.
  b TG Teacher.
19*a* Jacob 2:2;
   D&C 24:3.
   TG Leadership;
   Priesthood, Magnifying
   Callings within.
  b Ezek. 34:10.
   TG Accountability;
   Stewardship.
  c 1 Sam. 8:9; Moro. 9:6.
  d Lev. 20:27; Acts 20:26;
   2 Ne. 9:44; Mosiah 2:27;
   D&C 88:85; 112:33.
 2 1*a* 2 Ne. 6:1.

 2*a* TG Stewardship.
  b Rom. 11:13;
   Jacob 1:19;
   D&C 24:3.
  c TG Sincere.
  d Mosiah 2:28.
 3*a* 2 Ne. 6:3;
   Mosiah 25:11.
 5*a* Amos 4:13;
   Alma 12:3 (3–7);
   D&C 6:16.
   TG God, Omniscience of.
 7*a* Lev. 19:17;
   D&C 121:43.
  b TG Chastity.

before God, which thing is pleasing unto God;

8 And it supposeth me that they have come up hither to hear the pleasing ᵃword of God, yea, the word which healeth the wounded soul.

9 Wherefore, it burdeneth my soul that I should be constrained, because of the strict commandment which I have received from God, to ᵃadmonish you according to your crimes, to enlarge the wounds of those who are already wounded, instead of consoling and healing their wounds; and those who have not been wounded, instead of feasting upon the pleasing word of God have daggers placed to pierce their souls and wound their delicate minds.

10 But, notwithstanding the greatness of the task, I must do according to the strict ᵃcommands of God, and tell you concerning your wickedness and abominations, in the presence of the pure in heart, and the broken heart, and under the glance of the ᵇpiercing eye of the Almighty God.

11 Wherefore, I must tell you the truth according to the ᵃplainness of the ᵇword of God. For behold, as I inquired of the Lord, thus came the word unto me, saying: Jacob, get thou up into the temple on the morrow, and declare the word which I shall give thee unto this people.

12 And now behold, my brethren, this is the word which I declare unto you, that many of you have begun to search for gold, and for silver, and for all manner of precious ᵃores, in the which this land, which is a ᵇland of promise unto you and to your seed, doth abound most plentifully.

13 And the hand of providence hath smiled upon you most pleasingly, that you have obtained many riches; and because some of you have obtained more abundantly than that of your brethren ye are ᵃlifted up in the pride of your hearts, and wear stiff necks and high heads because of the costliness of your apparel, and persecute your brethren because ye suppose that ye are better than they.

14 And now, my brethren, do ye suppose that God justifieth you in this thing? Behold, I say unto you, Nay. But he condemneth you, and if ye persist in these things his judgments must speedily come unto you.

15 O that he would show you that he can pierce you, and with one glance of his ᵃeye he can smite you to the dust!

16 O that he would rid you from this iniquity and abomination. And, O that ye would listen unto the word of his commands, and let not this ᵃpride of your hearts destroy your souls!

17 Think of your ᵃbrethren like unto yourselves, and be familiar with all and free with your ᵇsubstance, that ᶜthey may be rich like unto you.

18 But ᵃbefore ye seek for ᵇriches, seek ye for the ᶜkingdom of God.

19 And after ye have obtained a hope in Christ ye shall obtain riches, if ye seek them; and ye will seek them for the intent to ᵃdo good—

8a Micah 2:7;
   Alma 31:5; 36:26;
   Hel. 3:29 (29–30).
   TG Gospel.
9a TG Warn.
10a TG Commandments
   of God.
   b 2 Ne. 9:44.
   TG God, Omniscience of.
11a 2 Ne. 25:4; 33:5;
   Jacob 4:13.
   b Jacob 7:5.
12a 1 Ne. 18:25;
   2 Ne. 5:15 (14–16);
   Hel. 6:9 (9–11);

Ether 9:17; 10:23 (12, 23).
   b 1 Ne. 4:14;
   17:13 (13–14).
   TG Promised Lands.
13a 2 Kgs. 14:10;
   Alma 1:32; 31:25;
   Morm. 8:28 (28, 36–40).
15a TG God, Indignation of;
   God, Omniscience of.
16a TG Pride.
17a James 5:3 (1–6).
   TG Love.
   b TG Almsgiving;
   Generosity;
   Welfare.

c Alma 4:12; 5:55;
   4 Ne. 1:3 (3, 24–26).
18a Mark 10:24 (17–27).
   b 1 Kgs. 3:11 (11–13);
   Prov. 27:24 (24–27);
   2 Ne. 26:31;
   Alma 39:14;
   D&C 6:7.
   TG Worldliness.
   c Luke 12:31 (22–31).
19a Mosiah 4:26;
   3 Ne. 12:42;
   4 Ne. 1:3.
   TG Good Works.

to clothe the naked, and to feed the hungry, and to liberate the captive, and administer relief to the sick and the afflicted.

20 And now, my brethren, I have spoken unto you concerning pride; and those of you which have afflicted your neighbor, and persecuted him because ye were proud in your hearts, of the things which God hath given you, what say ye of it?

21 Do ye not suppose that such things are abominable unto him who created all flesh? And the one being is as precious in his sight as the other. And all flesh is of the dust; and for the selfsame end hath he created them, that they should keep his *commandments and glorify him forever.

22 And now I make an end of speaking unto you concerning this pride. And were it not that I must speak unto you concerning a grosser crime, my heart would rejoice exceedingly because of you.

23 But the word of God burdens me because of your grosser crimes. For behold, thus saith the Lord: This people begin to wax in iniquity; they understand not the scriptures, for they seek to excuse themselves in committing *whoredoms, because of the things which were written concerning David, and Solomon his son.

24 Behold, David and *Solomon truly had many *wives and concubines, which thing was *abominable before me, saith the Lord.

25 Wherefore, thus saith the Lord, I have led this people forth out of the land of Jerusalem, by the power of mine arm, that I might raise up

unto me a *righteous branch from the fruit of the loins of Joseph.

26 Wherefore, I the Lord God will not suffer that this people shall do like unto them of old.

27 Wherefore, my brethren, hear me, and hearken to the word of the Lord: For there shall not any *man among you have save it be *one *wife; and concubines he shall have none;

28 For I, the Lord God, delight in the *chastity of women. And *whoredoms are an abomination before me; thus saith the Lord of Hosts.

29 Wherefore, this people shall keep my commandments, saith the Lord of Hosts, or *cursed be the land for their sakes.

30 For if I will, saith the Lord of Hosts, raise up *seed unto me, I will command my people; otherwise they shall hearken unto these things.

31 For behold, I, the Lord, have seen the sorrow, and heard the mourning of the daughters of my people in the land of Jerusalem, yea, and in all the lands of my people, because of the wickedness and *abominations of their *husbands.

32 And I will not suffer, saith the Lord of Hosts, that the cries of the fair daughters of this people, which I have led out of the land of Jerusalem, shall come up unto me against the men of my people, saith the Lord of Hosts.

33 For they shall not lead away captive the daughters of my people because of their tenderness, save I shall visit them with a sore curse, even unto destruction; for they shall not commit *whoredoms, like

21a D&C 11:20;
    Abr. 3:25 (25–26).
23a TG Whore.
24a 1 Kgs. 11:1;
    Neh. 13:26 (25–27).
  b Deut. 17:17 (14–17);
    2 Sam. 5:13;
    D&C 132:39 (38–39).
  c Deut. 7:3 (1–4);
    1 Kgs. 11:3;
    Ezra 9:2 (1–2).
25a Gen. 49:22 (22–26);

Ezek. 17:22 (22–24);
Amos 5:15;
2 Ne. 3:5; 14:2;
Alma 26:36.
TG Israel, Joseph,
  People of.
27a TG Marriage, Husbands.
  b Jacob 3:5 (5–7);
    D&C 49:16.
    TG Marriage, Plural.
  c TG Marriage, Wives.
28a TG Chastity.

  b TG Sexual Immorality;
    Whore.
29a Ether 2:11 (8–12).
    TG Curse.
30a Mal. 2:15;
    D&C 132:63 (61–66).
31a TG Family, Children,
    Responsibilities toward.
  b TG Marriage, Husbands.
33a Ezek. 16:25 (20–34).
    TG Sensuality.

unto them of old, saith the Lord of Hosts.

34 And now behold, my brethren, ye know that these commandments were given to our *a*father, Lehi; wherefore, ye have known them before; and ye have come unto great condemnation; for ye have done these things which ye ought not to have done.

35 Behold, ye have done *a*greater iniquities than the Lamanites, our brethren. Ye have broken the hearts of your tender wives, and lost the confidence of your children, because of your bad examples before them; and the sobbings of their hearts ascend up to God against you. And because of the *b*strictness of the word of God, which cometh down against you, many hearts died, pierced with deep wounds.

CHAPTER 3

The pure in heart receive the pleasing word of God—Lamanite righteousness exceeds that of the Nephites—Jacob warns against fornication, lasciviousness, and every sin. About 544–421 B.C.

BUT behold, I, Jacob, would speak unto you that are pure in heart. Look unto God with firmness of mind, and *a*pray unto him with exceeding faith, and he will *b*console you in your *c*afflictions, and he will plead your cause, and send down *d*justice upon those who seek your destruction.

2 O all ye that are pure in heart, lift up your heads and receive the pleasing word of God, and feast upon his *a*love; for ye may, if your *b*minds are *c*firm, forever.

3 But, wo, wo, unto you that are not pure in heart, that are filthy this day before God; for except ye repent the land is *a*cursed for your sakes; and the Lamanites, which are not *b*filthy like unto you, nevertheless they are *c*cursed with a sore cursing, shall scourge you even unto destruction.

4 And the time speedily cometh, that except ye repent they shall possess the land of your inheritance, and the Lord God will *a*lead away the righteous out from among you.

5 Behold, the Lamanites your brethren, whom ye hate because of their filthiness and the cursing which hath come upon their skins, are more righteous than you; for they have not *a*forgotten the commandment of the Lord, which was given unto our father—that they should have save it were *b*one wife, and *c*concubines they should have none, and there should not be *d*whoredoms committed among them.

6 And now, this commandment they observe to keep; wherefore, because of this observance, in keeping this commandment, the Lord God will not destroy them, but will be *a*merciful unto them; and one day they shall *b*become a blessed people.

7 Behold, their *a*husbands *b*love their *c*wives, and their wives love their husbands; and their husbands and their wives love their children; and their *d*unbelief and their hatred towards you is because of the iniquity of their fathers; wherefore,

34*a* 1 Ne. 1:16 (16–17).
35*a* Jacob 3:5 (5–7).
  b Gen. 2:24.
3 1*a* 2 Ne. 32:8.
  b TG Comfort;
    Consolation;
    Purity.
  c TG Affliction.
  d TG Deliver;
    Protection, Divine.
2*a* TG God, Love of.
  b TG Steadfastness.

  c Alma 57:27.
3*a* TG Earth, Curse of.
  b TG Filthiness.
  c 1 Ne. 12:23.
4*a* Omni 1:12 (5–7, 12–13).
5*a* Jacob 2:35.
  b Jacob 2:27.
  c Mosiah 11:2 (2–14);
    Ether 10:5.
  d TG Chastity.
6*a* 1 Ne. 13:31;
    2 Ne. 4:7; 10:18 (18–19);

  Hel. 15:12 (10–17);
    Morm. 5:20 (20–21).
  b 1 Ne. 15:14 (13–18);
    22:8.
7*a* TG Marriage, Husbands.
  b TG Family, Love within;
    Marriage, Continuing
    Courtship in.
  c TG Marriage, Wives.
  d D&C 3:18.
    TG Unbelief.

how much better are you than they, in the sight of your great Creator?

8 O my brethren, I fear that unless ye shall repent of your sins that their skins will be ªwhiter than yours, when ye shall be brought with them before the throne of God.

9 Wherefore, a commandment I give unto you, which is the word of God, that ye ªrevile no more against them because of the darkness of their skins; neither shall ye revile against them because of their filthiness; but ye shall remember your own filthiness, and remember that their filthiness came because of their fathers.

10 Wherefore, ye shall remember your ªchildren, how that ye have grieved their hearts because of the ᵇexample that ye have set before them; and also, remember that ye may, because of your filthiness, bring your children unto destruction, and their sins be heaped upon your heads at the last day.

11 O my brethren, hearken unto my words; ªarouse the faculties of your souls; shake yourselves that ye may ᵇawake from the slumber of death; and loose yourselves from the pains of ᶜhell that ye may not become ᵈangels to the devil, to be cast into that lake of fire and brimstone which is the second ᵉdeath.

12 And now I, Jacob, spake many more things unto the people of Nephi, ªwarning them against ᵇfornication and ᶜlasciviousness, and every kind of sin, telling them the awful consequences of them.

13 And a hundredth part of the proceedings of this people, which now began to be numerous, cannot be written upon ªthese plates;

but many of their proceedings are written upon the ᵇlarger plates, and their wars, and their contentions, and the reigns of their kings.

14 ªThese plates are called the plates of Jacob, and they were ᵇmade by the hand of Nephi. And I make an end of speaking these words.

CHAPTER 4

All the prophets worshiped the Father in the name of Christ—Abraham's offering of Isaac was in similitude of God and His Only Begotten—Men should reconcile themselves to God through the Atonement—The Jews will reject the foundation stone. About 544–421 B.C.

Now behold, it came to pass that I, Jacob, having ministered much unto my people in word, (and I cannot write but a ªlittle of my words, because of the ᵇdifficulty of engraving our words upon plates) and we know that the things which we write upon plates must remain;

2 But whatsoever things we write upon anything save it be upon ªplates must perish and vanish away; but we can write a few words upon plates, which will give our children, and also our beloved brethren, a small degree of knowledge concerning us, or concerning their fathers—

3 Now in this thing we do rejoice; and we labor diligently to engraven these words upon plates, hoping that our beloved brethren and our children will receive them with thankful hearts, and look upon them that they may learn with joy and not with sorrow, neither with contempt, concerning their first ªparents.

8a 3 Ne. 2:15.
9a TG Reviling.
10a TG Family, Children,
    Responsibilities toward;
    Family, Love within.
  b TG Example.
11a TG Apathy.
  b 2 Ne. 28:21;
    Alma 5:7 (6–7).
  c TG Hell.

d 2 Ne. 9:9 (8–9).
  TG Spirits, Evil or
    Unclean.
  e TG Death, Spiritual,
    Second.
12a TG Warn.
  b TG Fornication.
  c TG Lust.
13a Jacob 1:1 (1–4);
    4:1 (1–4).

b Jarom 1:14.
14a Jarom 1:2 (1–2).
  b 1 Ne. 19:2 (2–3).
4 1a 1 Ne. 6:6;
    Jarom 1:14;
    Omni 1:30.
  b Ether 12:24 (23–26).
2a TG Scriptures,
    Preservation of.
3a TG Scriptures, Value of.

4 For, for this intent have we written these things, that they may know that we ^aknew of Christ, and we had a hope of his ^bglory many hundred years before his coming; and not only we ourselves had a hope of his glory, but also all the holy ^cprophets which were before us.

5 Behold, they believed in Christ and ^aworshiped the Father in his name, and also we worship the Father in his ^bname. And for this intent we ^ckeep the ^dlaw of Moses, it ^epointing our souls to him; and for this cause it is sanctified unto us for righteousness, even as it was accounted unto Abraham in the wilderness to be obedient unto the commands of God in offering up his son Isaac, which is a ^fsimilitude of God and his ^gOnly Begotten Son.

6 Wherefore, we search the prophets, and we have many revelations and the spirit of ^aprophecy; and having all these ^bwitnesses we obtain a hope, and our faith becometh unshaken, insomuch that we truly can ^ccommand in the ^dname of Jesus and the very trees obey us, or the mountains, or the waves of the sea.

7 Nevertheless, the Lord God showeth us our ^aweakness that we may know that it is by his ^bgrace, and his great condescensions unto the children of men, that we have power to do these things.

8 Behold, great and marvelous are the ^aworks of the Lord. How ^bunsearchable are the depths of the ^cmysteries of him; and it is impossible that man should find out all his ways. And no man ^dknoweth of his ^eways save it be revealed unto him; wherefore, brethren, despise not the ^frevelations of God.

9 For behold, by the power of his ^aword ^bman came upon the face of the earth, which earth was ^ccreated by the power of his word. Wherefore, if God being able to speak and the world was, and to speak and man was created, O then, why not able to command the ^dearth, or the workmanship of his hands upon the face of it, according to his will and pleasure?

10 Wherefore, brethren, seek not to ^acounsel the Lord, but to take counsel from his hand. For behold, ye yourselves know that he counseleth in ^bwisdom, and in justice, and in great mercy, over all his works.

11 Wherefore, beloved brethren, be ^areconciled unto him through the ^batonement of Christ, his ^cOnly

4a TG Jesus Christ,
   Prophecies about;
   Testimony.
  b TG Jesus Christ, Glory of.
  c Luke 24:27;
   1 Pet. 1:11;
   Jacob 7:11 (11–12);
   Mosiah 13:33 (33–35);
   D&C 20:26.
5a Moses 5:8.
  b Gen. 4:26;
   Hel. 8:16 (16–20).
   TG Name of the Lord.
  c 2 Ne. 25:24;
   Jacob 7:7;
   Mosiah 13:30.
  d Jarom 1:11;
   Alma 25:15 (15–16).
   TG Law of Moses.
  e Gal. 3:24;
   Ether 12:19 (18–19).
  f TG Jesus Christ, Types
   of, in Anticipation.
  g Gen. 22:2 (1–14);
   John 3:16 (16–21);

Heb. 11:17.
   TG Jesus Christ, Divine
   Sonship.
6a TG Prophecy.
  b TG Witness.
  c 3 Ne. 28:20 (19–22).
   TG God, Power of.
  d Acts 3:6 (6–16);
   3 Ne. 8:1.
7a Ether 12:27;
   D&C 66:3.
  b TG Grace.
8a Ps. 106:2.
  b Rom. 11:34 (33–36);
   Mosiah 4:9.
  c D&C 19:10;
   76:114 (114–16).
   TG Mysteries of
   Godliness.
  d Dan. 1:17;
   1 Cor. 2:11 (9–16);
   Alma 26:21 (21–22).
   TG God, Knowledge
   about.
  e Isa. 55:8 (8–9).

f D&C 3:7.
9a Morm. 9:17;
   Moses 1:32.
  b TG Man, Physical
   Creation of.
  c TG Creation;
   God, Creator;
   Jesus Christ, Creator.
  d Hel. 12:16 (8–17).
10a Josh. 9:14;
   Prov. 15:22;
   Isa. 45:9;
   2 Ne. 9:28–29;
   Alma 37:12, 37;
   D&C 3:4, 13; 22:4.
  b TG God, Justice of;
   God, Wisdom of.
11a Lev. 6:30.
   TG Jesus Christ,
   Mission of;
   Reconciliation.
  b TG Jesus Christ,
   Atonement through.
  c TG Jesus Christ, Divine
   Sonship.

Begotten Son, and ye may obtain a ^dresurrection, according to the ^epower of the resurrection which is in Christ, and be presented as the ^ffirst-fruits of Christ unto God, having faith, and obtained a good hope of glory in him before he manifesteth himself in the flesh.

12 And now, beloved, marvel not that I tell you these things; for why not ^aspeak of the atonement of Christ, and attain to a perfect knowledge of him, as to attain to the knowledge of a resurrection and the world to come?

13 Behold, my brethren, he that prophesieth, let him prophesy to the understanding of men; for the ^aSpirit speaketh the ^btruth and lieth not. Wherefore, it speaketh of things as they really ^care, and of things as they really will be; wherefore, these things are manifested unto us ^dplainly, for the salvation of our souls. But behold, we are not witnesses alone in these things; for God also ^espake them unto prophets of old.

14 But behold, the Jews were a ^astiffnecked people; and they ^bdespised the words of ^cplainness, and ^dkilled the prophets, and sought for things that they could not understand. Wherefore, because of their ^eblindness, which ^fblindness came by looking beyond the ^gmark, they must needs fall; for God hath taken away his plainness from them, and delivered unto them many things which they ^hcannot understand, be-

cause they desired it. And because they desired it God hath done it, that they may ⁱstumble.

15 And now I, Jacob, am led on by the Spirit unto prophesying; for I perceive by the workings of the Spirit which is in me, that by the ^astumbling of the ^bJews they will ^creject the ^dstone upon which they might build and have safe foundation.

16 But behold, according to the scriptures, this ^astone shall become the great, and the last, and the only sure ^bfoundation, upon which the Jews can build.

17 And now, my beloved, how is it possible that these, after having rejected the sure foundation, can ^aever build upon it, that it may become the head of their corner?

18 Behold, my beloved brethren, I will unfold this mystery unto you; if I do not, by any means, get shaken from my firmness in the Spirit, and stumble because of my over anxiety for you.

CHAPTER 5

Jacob quotes Zenos relative to the allegory of the tame and wild olive trees— They are a likeness of Israel and the Gentiles—The scattering and gathering of Israel are prefigured—Allusions are made to the Nephites and Lamanites and all the house of Israel—The Gentiles will be grafted into Israel—Eventually the vineyard will be burned. About 544–421 B.C.

11*d* TG Resurrection.
  e TG God, Power of.
  f Mosiah 15:21 (21–23);
    18:9;
    Alma 40:16 (16–21).
12*a* 2 Ne. 25:26.
13*a* TG Holy Ghost,
    Mission of.
  b John 17:17.
    TG Honesty.
  c D&C 93:24.
  d Neh. 8:8;
    Jacob 2:11;
    Alma 13:23.
  e TG Witness of the
    Father.
14*a* Deut. 9:13;

  Neh. 9:16;
  2 Ne. 25:2.
  TG Stiffnecked.
  b Num. 15:31 (30–31);
    Ezek. 20:13 (13–16);
    1 Ne. 17:30 (30–31); 19:7;
    2 Ne. 33:2;
    D&C 3:7 (4–13).
  c 2 Cor. 11:3.
  d Zech. 1:4 (2–5).
  e Isa. 44:18.
  f Rom. 11:25.
    TG Spiritual Blindness.
  g John 7:47 (45–53).
  h 2 Ne. 25:1.
  i Isa. 57:14.
15*a* Isa. 8:14 (13–15);

  1 Cor. 1:23;
  2 Ne. 18:14 (13–15).
  b TG Israel, Judah,
    People of.
  c Rom. 11:1, 20 (1–36);
    1 Ne. 10:11;
    Morm. 5:14 (14–20).
  d TG Cornerstone;
    Jesus Christ,
    Prophecies about;
    Rock.
16*a* Ps. 118:22 (22–23).
  b Isa. 28:16 (14–17);
    Hel. 5:12.
17*a* Matt. 19:30;
    Jacob 5:63 (62–64);
    D&C 29:30.

BEHOLD, my brethren, do ye not remember to have read the words of the prophet ^aZenos, which he spake unto the house of Israel, saying:

2 Hearken, O ye house of Israel, and hear the words of me, a prophet of the Lord.

3 For behold, thus saith the Lord, I will liken thee, O house of ^aIsrael, like unto a tame ^bolive tree, which a man took and nourished in his ^cvineyard; and it grew, and waxed old, and began to ^ddecay.

4 And it came to pass that the master of the vineyard went forth, and he saw that his olive tree began to decay; and he said: I will ^aprune it, and dig about it, and nourish it, that perhaps it may shoot forth young and tender branches, and it perish not.

5 And it came to pass that he ^apruned it, and digged about it, and nourished it according to his word.

6 And it came to pass that after many days it began to put forth somewhat a little, young and tender branches; but behold, the main ^atop thereof began to perish.

7 And it came to pass that the master of the vineyard saw it, and he said unto his ^aservant: It grieveth me that I should lose this tree; wherefore, go and pluck the branches from a ^bwild olive tree, and bring them hither unto me; and we will pluck off those main branches which are beginning to wither away, and we will cast them into the fire that they may be burned.

8 And behold, saith the Lord of the vineyard, I take ^aaway many of these young and tender branches, and I will graft them ^bwhithersoever I will; and it mattereth not that if it so be that the root of this tree will perish, I may preserve the fruit thereof unto myself; wherefore, I will take these young and tender branches, and I will graft them whithersoever I will.

9 Take thou the branches of the wild olive tree, and graft them in, in the ^astead thereof; and these which I have plucked off I will cast into the fire and burn them, that they may not cumber the ground of my vineyard.

10 And it came to pass that the servant of the Lord of the vineyard did according to the word of the Lord of the vineyard, and grafted in the branches of the ^awild olive tree.

11 And the Lord of the vineyard caused that it should be digged about, and pruned, and nourished, saying unto his servant: It grieveth me that I should lose this tree; wherefore, that perhaps I might preserve the roots thereof that they perish not, that I might preserve them unto myself, I have done this thing.

12 Wherefore, go thy way; watch the tree, and nourish it, according to my words.

13 And these will I ^aplace in the nethermost part of my vineyard, whithersoever I will, it mattereth not unto thee; and I do it that I may preserve unto myself the natural branches of the tree; and also, that I may lay up fruit thereof against the season, unto myself; for it grieveth me that I should lose this tree and the fruit thereof.

14 And it came to pass that the Lord of the vineyard went his way, and hid the natural ^abranches of the tame olive tree in the nethermost

5 1 *a* 1 Ne. 19:12 (12, 16);
  Jacob 6:1.
  TG Scriptures, Lost.
 3 *a* TG Israel, Twelve
  Tribes of.
 b Ezek. 36:8 (8–15);
  Rom. 11:21 (1–36);
  1 Ne. 10:12;
  Jacob 6:1 (1–7).
  TG Israel, Mission of;
  Vineyard of the Lord.

 c Matt. 21:33 (33–41);
  D&C 101:44.
 d TG Apostasy of Israel.
 4 *a* TG Prophets, Mission of.
 5 *a* 2 Kgs. 17:13 (13–18).
 6 *a* Luke 3:9 (8–9);
  2 Ne. 30:2.
  TG Chief Priest.
 7 *a* TG Servant.
 b Rom. 11:17 (17, 24).
 8 *a* TG Israel, Scattering of.

 b Ezek. 17:22 (4–10, 22).
 9 *a* Acts 9:15; 14:27;
  Rom. 1:13;
  Gal. 3:14.
10 *a* TG Gentiles.
13 *a* Hosea 8:8;
  1 Ne. 10:12.
14 *a* TG Israel, Bondage of, in
  Other Lands.

parts of the vineyard, some in one and some in another, according to his will and pleasure.

15 And it came to pass that a long time passed away, and the Lord of the vineyard said unto his servant: Come, let us go down into the vineyard, that we may ^alabor in the vineyard.

16 And it came to pass that the Lord of the vineyard, and also the servant, went down into the vineyard to labor. And it came to pass that the servant said unto his master: Behold, look here; behold the tree.

17 And it came to pass that the Lord of the vineyard looked and beheld the tree in the which the wild olive branches had been grafted; and it had sprung forth and begun to bear ^afruit. And he beheld that it was good; and the fruit thereof was like unto the natural fruit.

18 And he said unto the servant: Behold, the branches of the wild tree have taken hold of the moisture of the root thereof, that the root thereof hath brought forth much strength; and because of the much strength of the root thereof the wild branches have brought forth tame fruit. Now, if we had not grafted in these branches, the tree thereof would have perished. And now, behold, I shall lay up much fruit, which the tree thereof hath brought forth; and the fruit thereof I shall lay up against the season, unto mine own self.

19 And it came to pass that the Lord of the vineyard said unto the servant: Come, let us go to the nethermost part of the vineyard, and behold if the natural branches of the tree have not brought forth much fruit also, that I may lay up of the fruit thereof against the season, unto mine own self.

20 And it came to pass that they went forth whither the master had hid the natural branches of the tree, and he said unto the servant: Behold these; and he beheld the ^afirst that it had ^bbrought forth much fruit; and he beheld also that it was good. And he said unto the servant: Take of the fruit thereof, and lay it up against the season, that I may preserve it unto mine own self; for behold, said he, this long time have I nourished it, and it hath brought forth much fruit.

21 And it came to pass that the servant said unto his master: How comest thou hither to plant this tree, or this branch of the tree? For behold, it was the poorest spot in all the land of thy vineyard.

22 And the Lord of the vineyard said unto him: Counsel me not; I knew that it was a poor spot of ground; wherefore, I said unto thee, I have nourished it this long time, and thou beholdest that it hath brought forth much fruit.

23 And it came to pass that the Lord of the vineyard said unto his servant: Look hither; behold I have planted another branch of the tree also; and thou knowest that this spot of ground was poorer than the first. But, behold the tree. I have nourished it this long time, and it hath brought forth much fruit; therefore, gather it, and lay it up against the season, that I may preserve it unto mine own self.

24 And it came to pass that the Lord of the vineyard said again unto his servant: Look hither, and behold another ^abranch also, which I have planted; behold that I have nourished it also, and it hath brought forth fruit.

25 And he said unto the servant: Look hither and behold the last. Behold, this have I planted in a ^agood spot of ground; and I have

---

15a TG Millennium,
    Preparing a People for.
17a Matt. 12:33;
    John 15:16;
    Gal. 3:9 (7–9, 29);

Col. 1:6 (3–8).
20a Jacob 5:39.
   b TG Israel,
    Restoration of.
24a Ezek. 17:22 (22–24);

Alma 16:17.
25a Ezek. 17:8;
    1 Ne. 2:20;
    Jacob 5:43.

nourished it this long time, and only a [b]part of the tree hath brought forth tame fruit, and the [c]other part of the tree hath brought forth wild fruit; behold, I have nourished this tree like unto the others.

26 And it came to pass that the Lord of the vineyard said unto the servant: Pluck off the branches that have not brought forth good [a]fruit, and cast them into the fire.

27 But behold, the servant said unto him: Let us prune it, and dig about it, and nourish it a little [a]longer, that perhaps it may bring forth good fruit unto thee, that thou canst lay it up against the season.

28 And it came to pass that the Lord of the vineyard and the servant of the Lord of the vineyard did nourish all the fruit of the vineyard.

29 And it came to pass that a [a]long time had passed away, and the Lord of the vineyard said unto his [b]servant: Come, let us go down into the vineyard, that we may labor again in the vineyard. For behold, the time draweth near, and the [c]end soon cometh; wherefore, I must lay up fruit against the season, unto mine own self.

30 And it came to pass that the Lord of the vineyard and the servant went down into the vineyard; and they came to the tree whose natural branches had been broken off, and the wild branches had been grafted in; and behold all [a]sorts of fruit did cumber the tree.

31 And it came to pass that the Lord of the vineyard did [a]taste of the fruit, every sort according to its number. And the Lord of the vineyard said: Behold, this long time have we nourished this tree, and I have laid up unto myself against the season much fruit.

32 But behold, this time it hath brought forth much [a]fruit, and there is [b]none of it which is good. And behold, there are all kinds of bad fruit; and it profiteth me nothing, notwithstanding all our labor; and now it grieveth me that I should lose this tree.

33 And the Lord of the vineyard said unto the servant: What shall we do unto the tree, that I may preserve again good fruit thereof unto mine own self?

34 And the servant said unto his master: Behold, because thou didst graft in the branches of the wild olive tree they have nourished the roots, that they are alive and they have not perished; wherefore thou beholdest that they are yet good.

35 And it came to pass that the Lord of the vineyard said unto his servant: The tree profiteth me nothing, and the roots thereof profit me nothing so long as it shall bring forth evil fruit.

36 Nevertheless, I know that the roots are good, and for mine own purpose I have preserved them; and because of their much strength they have hitherto brought forth, from the wild branches, good fruit.

37 But behold, the wild branches have grown and have [a]overrun the roots thereof; and because that the wild branches have overcome the roots thereof it hath brought forth much evil fruit; and because that it hath brought forth so much evil fruit thou beholdest that it beginneth to perish; and it will soon become ripened, that it may be cast into the fire, except we should do something for it to preserve it.

38 And it came to pass that the Lord of the vineyard said unto his servant: Let us go down into the nethermost parts of the vineyard, and behold if the natural branches have also brought forth evil fruit.

39 And it came to pass that they

25b Hel. 15:3 (3–4).
  c Alma 26:36.
26a Matt. 7:19 (15–20);
     Alma 5:36;
     D&C 97:7.
27a Jacob 5:50 (50–51);

Alma 42:4.
29a TG Last Days.
  b D&C 101:55; 103:21.
  c 2 Ne. 30:10;
     Jacob 6:2.
30a TG Apostasy of Israel.

31a TG Jesus Christ, Judge;
     Judgment.
32a Hosea 10:1.
  b JS—H 1:19.
37a D&C 45:30.

went down into the nethermost parts of the vineyard. And it came to pass that they beheld that the fruit of the natural branches had become corrupt also; yea, the *a*first and the second and also the last; and they had all become corrupt.

40 And the *a*wild fruit of the last had overcome that part of the tree which brought forth good fruit, even that the branch had withered away and died.

41 And it came to pass that the Lord of the vineyard wept, and said unto the servant: *a*What could I have done more for my vineyard?

42 Behold, I knew that all the fruit of the vineyard, save it were these, had become *a*corrupted. And now these which have once brought forth good fruit have also become corrupted; and now all the trees of my vineyard are good for nothing save it be to be *b*hewn down and cast into the fire.

43 And behold this last, whose branch hath withered away, I did plant in a *a*good spot of ground; yea, even that which was choice unto me above all other parts of the land of my vineyard.

44 And thou beheldest that I also cut down that which *a*cumbered this spot of ground, that I might plant this tree in the stead thereof.

45 And thou beheldest that a *a*part thereof brought forth good fruit, and a part thereof brought forth wild fruit; and because I plucked not the branches thereof and cast them into the fire, behold, they have overcome the good branch that it hath withered away.

46 And now, behold, notwithstanding all the care which we have taken of my vineyard, the trees thereof have become corrupted, that they bring forth no good *a*fruit; and these I had hoped to preserve, to have laid up fruit thereof against the season, unto mine own self. But, behold, they have become like unto the wild olive tree, and they are of no worth but to be *b*hewn down and cast into the fire; and it grieveth me that I should lose them.

47 But *a*what could I have done more in my vineyard? Have I slackened mine hand, that I have not nourished it? Nay, I have nourished it, and I have digged about it, and I have pruned it, and I have dunged it; and I have *b*stretched forth mine *c*hand almost all the day long, and the *d*end draweth nigh. And it grieveth me that I should hew down all the trees of my vineyard, and cast them into the fire that they should be burned. Who is it that has corrupted my vineyard?

48 And it came to pass that the servant said unto his master: Is it not the *a*loftiness of thy vineyard—have not the branches thereof overcome the roots which are good? And because the branches have overcome the roots thereof, behold they grew faster than the strength of the roots, *b*taking strength unto themselves. Behold, I say, is not this the cause that the trees of thy vineyard have become corrupted?

49 And it came to pass that the Lord of the vineyard said unto the servant: Let us go to and hew down the trees of the vineyard and cast them into the fire, that they shall not cumber the ground of my vineyard, for I have done all. What could I have done more for my vineyard?

50 But, behold, the servant said unto the Lord of the vineyard: Spare it a little *a*longer.

39a Jacob 5:20 (20, 23, 25).
40a Hel. 15:4 (3–4).
41a Isa. 5:4;
    2 Ne. 2:27; 26:24;
    Jacob 5:47;
    Alma 26:37.
42a TG Apostasy of Israel.
  b Matt. 3:10.
43a Ezek. 17:8;

Jacob 5:25.
44a Moro. 9:23.
45a 1 Ne. 15:12 (12–17);
    2 Ne. 3:5; 10:1;
    Alma 46:24 (24–25).
46a Luke 3:9.
  b Alma 5:52;
    3 Ne. 27:11.
47a Jacob 5:41 (41, 49).

  b Isa. 9:12 (12, 17, 21).
  c 2 Ne. 19:17 (17–21); 28:32;
    Jacob 6:4.
  d TG World, End of.
48a TG Haughtiness; Pride.
  b D&C 121:39.
    TG Unrighteous
    Dominion.
50a Jacob 5:27.

51 And the Lord said: Yea, I will spare it a little longer, for it grieveth me that I should lose the trees of my vineyard.

52 Wherefore, let us take of the ᵃbranches of these which I have planted in the nethermost parts of my vineyard, and let us graft them into the tree from whence they came; and let us pluck from the tree those branches whose fruit is most bitter, and graft in the natural branches of the tree in the stead thereof.

53 And this will I do that the tree may not perish, that, perhaps, I may preserve unto myself the roots thereof for mine ᵃown purpose.

54 And, behold, the roots of the natural branches of the tree which I planted whithersoever I would are yet alive; wherefore, that I may preserve them also for mine own purpose, I will take of the ᵃbranches of this tree, and I will ᵇgraft them in unto them. Yea, I will graft in unto them the branches of their mother tree, that I may preserve the roots also unto mine own self, that when they shall be sufficiently strong perhaps they may bring forth good fruit unto me, and I may yet have glory in the fruit of my vineyard.

55 And it came to pass that they took from the natural tree which had become wild, and grafted in unto the natural trees, which also had become wild.

56 And they also took of the natural trees which had become wild, and ᵃgrafted into their mother tree.

57 And the Lord of the vineyard said unto the servant: Pluck not the wild branches from the trees, save it be those which are most bitter; and in them ye shall graft according to that which I have said.

58 And we will nourish again the trees of the vineyard, and we will trim up the ᵃbranches thereof; and we will pluck from the trees those branches which are ripened, that must perish, and cast them into the fire.

59 And this I do that, perhaps, the roots thereof may take strength because of their goodness; and because of the change of the branches, that the good may ᵃovercome the evil.

60 And because that I have preserved the natural branches and the roots thereof, and that I have grafted in the natural branches again into their mother tree, and have preserved the roots of their mother tree, that, perhaps, the trees of my vineyard may bring forth again good ᵃfruit; and that I may have joy again in the fruit of my vineyard, and, perhaps, that I may rejoice exceedingly that I have preserved the roots and the branches of the first fruit—

61 Wherefore, go to, and call ᵃservants, that we may ᵇlabor diligently with our might in the vineyard, that we may ᶜprepare the way, that I may bring forth again the natural fruit, which natural fruit is good and the most precious above all other fruit.

62 Wherefore, let us go to and labor with our might this last time, for behold the end draweth nigh, and this is for the last time that I shall ᵃprune my vineyard.

63 Graft in the branches; begin at the ᵃlast that they may be first, and that the first may be ᵇlast, and dig about the trees, both old and young, the first and the last; and the last and the first, that all may be nourished once again for the last time.

64 Wherefore, dig about them,

52a TG Israel, Gathering of;
    Israel, Restoration of.
53a Ex. 19:6;
    Isa. 49:6.
54a 3 Ne. 21:6 (5–6);
    Morm. 5:15.
  b 1 Ne. 15:16.
56a Jer. 24:6.

58a Isa. 27:11.
59a TG Triumph.
60a Isa. 27:6.
61a Jacob 6:2.
  b D&C 24:19; 39:17; 95:4.
  c TG Millennium,
    Preparing a People for.
62a D&C 75:2.

63a Matt. 20:16;
    Mark 10:31;
    Luke 13:30;
    1 Ne. 13:42;
    Ether 13:12 (10–12).
  b Matt. 19:30;
    Jacob 4:17;
    D&C 29:30.

and prune them, and dung them once more, for the last time, for the end draweth nigh. And if it be so that these last grafts shall grow, and bring forth the natural fruit, then shall ye prepare the way for them, that they may grow.

65 And as they begin to grow ye shall [a]clear away the branches which bring forth bitter fruit, according to the strength of the good and the size thereof; and ye shall not clear away the bad thereof all at once, lest the roots thereof should be too strong for the graft, and the graft thereof shall perish, and I lose the trees of my vineyard.

66 For it grieveth me that I should lose the trees of my vineyard; wherefore ye shall clear away the bad according as the good shall grow, that the root and the top may be equal in strength, until the good shall overcome the bad, and the bad be hewn down and cast into the fire, that they cumber not the ground of my vineyard; and thus will I sweep away the bad out of my vineyard.

67 And the branches of the natural tree will I graft in again into the natural tree;

68 And the branches of the natural tree will I graft into the natural branches of the tree; and thus will I bring them together again, that they shall bring forth the natural [a]fruit, and they shall be one.

69 And the bad shall be [a]cast away, yea, even out of all the land of my vineyard; for behold, only this once will I prune my vineyard.

70 And it came to pass that the Lord of the vineyard sent his [a]servant; and the servant went and did as the Lord had commanded him, and brought other [b]servants; and they were [c]few.

71 And the Lord of the vineyard said unto them: Go to, and [a]labor in the vineyard, with your might. For behold, this is the [b]last time that I shall [c]nourish my vineyard; for the end is nigh at hand, and the season speedily cometh; and if ye labor with your might with me ye shall have joy in the fruit which I shall lay up unto myself against the time which will soon come.

72 And it came to pass that the servants did go and labor with their mights; and the Lord of the vineyard labored also with them; and they did obey the commandments of the Lord of the vineyard in all things.

73 And there began to be the natural fruit again in the vineyard; and the natural branches began to grow and thrive exceedingly; and the wild branches began to be plucked off and to be cast away; and they did keep the root and the top thereof equal, according to the strength thereof.

74 And thus they labored, with all diligence, according to the commandments of the Lord of the vineyard, even until the bad had been cast away out of the vineyard, and the Lord had preserved unto himself that the trees had become again the natural fruit; and they became like unto [a]one body; and the fruits were equal; and the Lord of the vineyard had preserved unto himself the natural fruit, which was most precious unto him from the beginning.

75 And it came to pass that when the [a]Lord of the vineyard saw that his fruit was good, and that his vineyard was no more corrupt, he called up his servants, and said unto them: Behold, for this last time have we nourished my vineyard; and thou beholdest that I have done according to my will; and I have preserved the natural fruit, that it

---

65a D&C 86:6 (6–7).
68a TG Israel, Mission of.
69a 1 Ne. 22:23 (15–17, 23);
    2 Ne. 30:10 (9–10).
70a D&C 101:55; 103:21.
  b Matt. 9:37 (36–38).

  c 1 Ne. 14:12.
71a Matt. 21:28;
    Jacob 6:2 (2–3);
    D&C 33:3 (3–4).
  b D&C 39:17;
    43:28 (28–30).

  c TG Millennium,
    Preparing a People for.
74a D&C 38:27.
75a TG Jesus Christ,
    Millennial Reign.

is good, even like as it was in the beginning. And *b*blessed art thou; for because ye have been diligent in laboring with me in my vineyard, and have kept my commandments, and have brought unto me again the *c*natural fruit, that my vineyard is no more corrupted, and the bad is cast away, behold ye shall have *d*joy with me because of the fruit of my vineyard.

76 For behold, for a *a*long time will I lay up of the fruit of my vineyard unto mine own self against the season, which speedily cometh; and for the last time have I nourished my vineyard, and pruned it, and dug about it, and dunged it; wherefore I will lay up unto mine own self of the fruit, for a long time, according to that which I have spoken.

77 And when the time cometh that evil fruit shall again come into my vineyard, then will I cause the *a*good and the bad to be gathered; and the good will I preserve unto myself, and the bad will I cast away into its own place. And then cometh the *b*season and the end; and my vineyard will I cause to be *c*burned with *d*fire.

CHAPTER 6

The Lord will recover Israel in the last days—The world will be burned with fire—Men must follow Christ to avoid the lake of fire and brimstone. About 544–421 B.C.

AND now, behold, my brethren, as I said unto you that I would prophesy, behold, this is my prophecy—that the things which this prophet *a*Zenos spake, concerning the house of Israel, in the which he likened them unto a tame *b*olive tree, must surely come to pass.

2 And the day that he shall set his hand again the second time to *a*recover his people, is the day, yea, even the last time, that the *b*servants of the Lord shall go forth in his *c*power, to *d*nourish and prune his *e*vineyard; and after that the *f*end soon cometh.

3 And how *a*blessed are they who have labored *b*diligently in his vineyard; and how *c*cursed are they who shall be cast out into their own place! And the *d*world shall be *e*burned with fire.

4 And how merciful is our God unto us, for he remembereth the house of *a*Israel, both roots and branches; and he stretches forth his *b*hands unto them all the day long; and they are a *c*stiffnecked and a gainsaying people; but as many as will not harden their hearts shall be saved in the kingdom of God.

5 Wherefore, my beloved brethren, I beseech of you in words of soberness that ye would repent, and come with full purpose of heart, and *a*cleave unto God as he cleaveth unto you. And while his *b*arm of mercy is extended towards you in

75*b* 1 Ne. 13:37;
   D&C 21:9.
 c TG Israel, Restoration of.
 d D&C 6:31; 18:15 (15–16).
76*a* 1 Ne. 22:26.
77*a* D&C 86:7.
 b Rev. 20:3 (3–10);
   D&C 29:22;
   43:31 (30–31);
   88:111 (110–12).
 c TG World, End of.
 d Joel 1:19 (19–20);
   2 Ne. 6:15 (14–15);
   Jacob 6:3.
6 1*a* Jacob 5:1;
   Alma 33:13 (13–15).
   TG Scriptures, Lost.
 b Rom. 11:21 (1–36);
   1 Ne. 10:12;

   Jacob 5:3 (3–77).
2*a* 1 Ne. 22:12 (10–12);
   D&C 110:11; 137:6.
   TG Israel, Gathering of;
   Israel, Restoration of.
 b Jacob 5:61.
 c 1 Ne. 14:1, 14.
 d Jacob 5:71;
   D&C 101:56.
 e Jer. 12:10;
   D&C 138:56.
   TG Vineyard of the Lord.
 f 2 Ne. 30:10;
   Jacob 5:29;
   D&C 43:17 (17–20, 28).
3*a* Jacob 5:71.
 b TG Diligence;
   Perseverance.
 c D&C 41:1.

 d TG World.
 e Isa. 24:6;
   2 Ne. 27:2;
   Jacob 5:77;
   3 Ne. 25:1.
   TG World, End of.
4*a* 2 Sam. 7:24.
 b Neh. 9:19 (18–26);
   2 Ne. 19:17 (17–21); 28:32;
   Jacob 5:47.
 c TG Stiffnecked.
5*a* Deut. 10:20;
   Josh. 23:8;
   2 Kgs. 18:6;
   Hel. 4:25;
   D&C 11:19.
 b Isa. 59:16; 2 Ne. 1:15;
   Alma 5:33;
   3 Ne. 9:14.

the light of the day, harden not your hearts.

6 Yea, today, if ye will hear his voice, harden not your hearts; for why will ye [a]die?

7 For behold, after ye have been nourished by the good [a]word of God all the day long, will ye bring forth evil fruit, that ye must be [b]hewn down and cast into the fire?

8 Behold, will ye reject these words? Will ye reject the words of the [a]prophets; and will ye reject all the words which have been spoken concerning Christ, after so many have spoken concerning him; and [b]deny the good word of Christ, and the power of God, and the [c]gift of the Holy Ghost, and quench the Holy Spirit, and make a [d]mock of the great plan of redemption, which hath been laid for you?

9 Know ye not that if ye will do these things, that the power of the redemption and the resurrection, which is in Christ, will bring you to stand with [a]shame and [b]awful [c]guilt before the bar of God?

10 And according to the power of [a]justice, for justice cannot be denied, ye must go away into that [b]lake of fire and brimstone, whose flames are unquenchable, and whose smoke ascendeth up forever and ever, which lake of fire and brimstone is [c]endless [d]torment.

11 O then, my beloved brethren, repent ye, and enter in at the [a]strait gate, and [b]continue in the way which is narrow, until ye shall obtain eternal life.

12 O be [a]wise; what can I say more?

13 Finally, I bid you farewell, until I shall meet you before the [a]pleasing bar of God, which bar striketh the wicked with [b]awful dread and fear. Amen.

CHAPTER 7

Sherem denies Christ, contends with Jacob, demands a sign, and is smitten of God—All of the prophets have spoken of Christ and His Atonement—The Nephites lived out their days as wanderers, born in tribulation, and hated by the Lamanites. About 544–421 B.C.

AND now it came to pass after some years had passed away, there came a man among the people of Nephi, whose name was [a]Sherem.

2 And it came to pass that he began to preach among the people, and to declare unto them that there should be [a]no Christ. And he preached many things which were flattering unto the people; and this he did that he might [b]overthrow the doctrine of Christ.

3 And he labored diligently that he might lead away the hearts of the people, insomuch that he did lead away many hearts; and he knowing that I, Jacob, had faith in Christ who should come, he sought much opportunity that he might come unto me.

4 And he was [a]learned, that he had a perfect knowledge of the language of the people; wherefore, he could use much [b]flattery, and much power of speech, according to the [c]power of the devil.

5 And he had hope to shake me from the faith, notwithstanding the many [a]revelations and the many things which I had seen concerning

---

6a Ezek. 18:28 (26–28, 32).
7a Ps. 119:28.
  b Alma 5:52;
    3 Ne. 27:11 (11–12).
8a Jer. 26:5.
  b TG Holy Ghost, Loss of.
  c TG Holy Ghost, Gift of.
  d TG Sacrilege.
9a TG Shame.
  b Jacob 7:19;
    Mosiah 15:26.
  c TG Guilt;
    Judgment, the Last.

10a TG God, Justice of;
    Justice.
  b Rev. 19:20;
    2 Ne. 28:23;
    Mosiah 3:27.
    TG Hell.
  c Mosiah 2:33;
    D&C 19:11 (10–12).
  d TG Damnation.
11a 2 Ne. 9:41.
  b 2 Ne. 31:15.
    TG Commitment.
12a Matt. 10:16;

    Morm. 9:28.
13a Moro. 10:34.
  b Alma 40:14.
7 1a TG False Prophets.
2a Alma 21:8;
    30:12 (12, 22).
  b TG False Doctrine.
4a TG Learn.
  b TG Flatter.
  c TG False Priesthoods.
5a 2 Ne. 10:3; 11:3;
    Jacob 2:11.

these things; for I truly had seen [b]angels, and they had ministered unto me. And also, I had [c]heard the voice of the Lord speaking unto me in very word, from time to time; wherefore, I could not be shaken.

6 And it came to pass that he came unto me, and on this wise did he speak unto me, saying: Brother Jacob, I have sought much opportunity that I might speak unto you; for I have heard and also know that thou goest about much, preaching that which ye call the [a]gospel, or the doctrine of Christ.

7 And ye have led away much of this people that they pervert the right way of God, and [a]keep not the law of Moses which is the right way; and convert the law of Moses into the worship of a being which ye say shall come many hundred years hence. And now behold, I, Sherem, declare unto you that this is [b]blasphemy; for no man knoweth of such things; for he cannot [c]tell of things to come. And after this manner did Sherem contend against me.

8 But behold, the Lord God poured in his [a]Spirit into my soul, insomuch that I did [b]confound him in all his words.

9 And I said unto him: Deniest thou the Christ who shall come? And he said: If there should be a Christ, I would not deny him; but I know that there is no Christ, neither has been, nor ever will be.

10 And I said unto him: Believest thou the scriptures? And he said, Yea.

11 And I said unto him: Then ye do not understand them; for they truly testify of Christ. Behold, I say unto you that none of the [a]prophets have written, nor [b]prophesied, save they have spoken concerning this Christ.

12 And this is not all—it has been made manifest unto me, for I have heard and seen; and it also has been made manifest unto me by the [a]power of the Holy Ghost; wherefore, I know if there should be no atonement made all mankind must be [b]lost.

13 And it came to pass that he said unto me: Show me a [a]sign by this power of the Holy Ghost, in the which ye know so much.

14 And I said unto him: What am I that I should [a]tempt God to show unto thee a sign in the thing which thou knowest to be [b]true? Yet thou wilt deny it, because thou art of the [c]devil. Nevertheless, not my will be done; but if God shall smite thee, let that be a [d]sign unto thee that he has power, both in heaven and in earth; and also, that Christ shall come. And thy will, O Lord, be done, and not mine.

15 And it came to pass that when I, Jacob, had spoken these words, the power of the Lord came upon him, insomuch that he fell to the earth. And it came to pass that he was nourished for the space of many days.

16 And it came to pass that he said unto the people: Gather together on the morrow, for I shall die; wherefore, I desire to speak unto the people before I shall die.

17 And it came to pass that on the morrow the multitude were gathered together; and he spake plainly unto them and denied the things which he had taught them, and confessed the Christ, and the power

---

5b 2 Ne. 2:4.
  c Ex. 19:9 (9–13).
6a 2 Ne. 31:2.
7a Jacob 4:5.
  b TG Blaspheme.
  c Alma 30:13.
8a TG God, Spirit of;
    Holy Ghost, Mission of.
  b Ps. 97:7.
    TG Confound.
11a 1 Ne. 10:5;

3 Ne. 20:24 (23–24).
  TG Jesus Christ,
    Prophecies about.
  b 1 Pet. 1:11;
    Rev. 19:10;
    Jacob 4:4;
    Mosiah 13:33 (33–35);
    D&C 20:26.
12a TG Holy Ghost, Gifts of.
  b 2 Ne. 2:21 (10–30).
13a John 6:30;

Alma 30:43 (43–60);
  D&C 46:9 (8–9).
  TG Sign Seekers.
14a TG Test.
  b Mosiah 12:30;
    Alma 30:42 (41–42).
  c Alma 30:53.
  d Num. 26:10;
    D&C 124:53 (50–53).

of the Holy Ghost, and the ministering of angels.

18 And he spake plainly unto them, that he had been *a*deceived by the power of the *b*devil. And he spake of hell, and of *c*eternity, and of eternal *d*punishment.

19 And he said: I *a*fear lest I have committed the *b*unpardonable sin, for I have lied unto God; for I denied the Christ, and said that I believed the scriptures; and they truly testify of him. And because I have thus lied unto God I greatly fear lest my case shall be *c*awful; but I confess unto God.

20 And it came to pass that when he had said these words he could say no more, and he *a*gave up the *b*ghost.

21 And when the multitude had witnessed that he spake these things as he was about to give up the ghost, they were astonished exceedingly; insomuch that the power of God came down upon them, and they were *a*overcome that they fell to the earth.

22 Now, this thing was pleasing unto me, Jacob, for I had requested it of my Father who was in heaven; for he had heard my cry and answered my prayer.

23 And it came to pass that peace and the *a*love of God was restored again among the people; and they *b*searched the scriptures, and hearkened no more to the words of this wicked man.

24 And it came to pass that many means were devised to *a*reclaim and restore the Lamanites to the knowledge of the truth; but it all was *b*vain, for they delighted in *c*wars and *d*bloodshed, and they had an eternal *e*hatred against us, their brethren. And they sought by the power of their arms to destroy us continually.

25 Wherefore, the people of Nephi did fortify against them with their arms, and with all their might, trusting in the God and *a*rock of their salvation; wherefore, they became as yet, conquerors of their enemies.

26 And it came to pass that I, Jacob, began to be old; and the record of this people being kept on the *a*other plates of Nephi, wherefore, I conclude this record, declaring that I have written according to the best of my knowledge, by saying that the time passed away with us, and also our *b*lives passed away like as it were unto us a *c*dream, we being a *d*lonesome and a solemn people, *e*wanderers, cast out from Jerusalem, born in tribulation, in a wilderness, and hated of our brethren, which caused wars and contentions; wherefore, we did mourn out our days.

27 And I, Jacob, saw that I must soon go down to my grave; wherefore, I said unto my son *a*Enos: Take these *b*plates. And I told him the things which my brother Nephi had *c*commanded me, and he promised obedience unto the commands. And I make an end of my writing upon these plates, which writing has been *d*small; and to the reader I bid farewell, hoping that many of my brethren may read my words. Brethren, adieu.

18a Gal. 3:1 (1–4);
   Alma 30:53 (53, 60).
 b TG Deceit; Devil.
 c TG Eternity.
 d TG Punish.
19a TG Despair.
 b TG Holy Ghost,
   Unpardonable Sin
   against;
   Sons of Perdition.
 c Jacob 6:9;
   Mosiah 15:26.
20a Jer. 28:16 (15–17);
   Alma 30:59 (12–60).

 b Gen. 49:33; Hel. 14:21.
21a Alma 19:6 (1–36).
23a TG God, Love of.
 b Alma 17:2.
   TG Scriptures, Study of.
24a Enos 1:20.
 b Enos 1:14.
 c Mosiah 1:5;
   10:12 (11–18);
   Alma 3:8; 9:16;
   D&C 93:39.
 d Jarom 1:6;
   Alma 26:24 (23–25).
 e 2 Ne. 5:1 (1–3);

   Mosiah 28:2.
   TG Malice.
25a TG Rock.
26a 1 Ne. 19:1 (1–6);
   Jarom 1:14 (1, 14–15).
 b James 4:14.
 c 1 Chr. 29:15; Ps. 144:4.
 d Alma 13:23.
 e Alma 26:36.
27a Enos 1:1.
 b Omni 1:3.
 c Jacob 1:1 (1–4).
 d 1 Ne. 6:3 (1–6);
   Jarom 1:2 (2, 14).

THE BOOK OF ENOS

Enos prays mightily and gains a re-
mission of his sins—The voice of the
Lord comes into his mind, promising
salvation for the Lamanites in a future
day—The Nephites sought to reclaim
the Lamanites—Enos rejoices in his
Redeemer. About 420 B.C.

BEHOLD, it came to pass that
I, *a*Enos, knowing my father
that *b*he was a just man—for
he *c*taught me in his language, and
also in the *d*nurture and admoni-
tion of the Lord—and blessed be
the name of my God for it—

2 And I will tell you of the *a*wres-
tle which I had before God, before
I received a *b*remission of my sins.

3 Behold, I went to hunt beasts in
the forests; and the words which I
had often heard my father speak
concerning eternal life, and the *a*joy
of the saints, *b*sunk deep into my
heart.

4 And my soul *a*hungered; and I
*b*kneeled down before my Maker,
and I *c*cried unto him in mighty
*d*prayer and supplication for mine
own soul; and all the day long did
I cry unto him; yea, and when the
night came I did still raise my voice
high that it reached the heavens.

5 And there came a *a*voice unto me,
saying: Enos, thy sins are *b*forgiven
thee, and thou shalt be blessed.

6 And I, Enos, knew that God
*a*could not lie; wherefore, my guilt
was swept away.

7 And I said: Lord, how is it done?

8 And he said unto me: *a*Because
of thy *b*faith in Christ, whom thou
hast never before heard nor seen.
And many years pass away before
he shall manifest himself in the
flesh; wherefore, go to, thy faith
hath made thee *c*whole.

9 Now, it came to pass that when
I had heard these words I began to
feel a *a*desire for the *b*welfare of my
brethren, the Nephites; wherefore,
I did *c*pour out my whole soul unto
God for them.

10 And while I was thus strug-
gling in the spirit, behold, the voice
of the Lord came into my *a*mind
again, saying: I will visit thy brethren according to their diligence in
keeping my commandments. I have
*b*given unto them this land, and it
is a holy land; and I *c*curse it not
save it be for the cause of iniquity;
wherefore, I will visit thy brethren according as I have said; and
their *d*transgressions will I bring
down with sorrow upon their own
heads.

11 And after I, Enos, had heard
these words, my *a*faith began to
be *b*unshaken in the Lord; and I
*c*prayed unto him with many long

1 1*a* Jacob 7:27.
  b 2 Ne. 2:3 (2–4).
  c 1 Ne. 1:1;
    Mosiah 1:2.
  d Eph. 6:4.
  2*a* Gen. 32:24 (24–32);
    Alma 8:10.
    TG Repent.
  b TG Remission of Sins.
  3*a* TG Joy.
  b 1 Ne. 10:17 (17–19);
    Alma 36:17.
    TG Teachable.
  4*a* 2 Ne. 9:51;
    3 Ne. 12:6.
    TG Meditation;
    Motivations.
  b TG Reverence.

  c Ps. 138:3.
    TG Perseverance.
  d TG Prayer.
  5*a* TG Revelation.
  b TG Forgive.
  6*a* TG God, the Standard of
    Righteousness.
  8*a* Ether 3:13 (12–13).
  b TG Faith.
  c Matt. 9:22.
    TG Man, New, Spiritually
    Reborn;
    Steadfastness.
  9*a* 1 Ne. 8:12;
    Alma 36:24.
  b Alma 19:29.
    TG Benevolence.
  c Num. 21:7;

    1 Sam. 1:15; 7:5;
    Jer. 42:4;
    2 Ne. 33:3;
    Alma 34:26 (26–27).
  10*a* TG Inspiration;
    Mind.
  b 1 Ne. 2:20.
  c Gen. 8:21 (20–22);
    Ether 2:9 (7–12).
  d TG Transgress.
  11*a* TG Faith.
  b TG Steadfastness.
  c Gen. 20:7;
    1 Sam. 7:5;
    2 Ne. 33:3;
    W of M 1:8.

ᵈstrugglings for my brethren, the Lamanites.

12 And it came to pass that after I had ᵃprayed and labored with all diligence, the Lord said unto me: I will grant unto thee according to thy ᵇdesires, because of thy faith.

13 And now behold, this was the desire which I desired of him—that if it should so be, that my people, the Nephites, should fall into transgression, and by any means be ᵃdestroyed, and the Lamanites should not be ᵇdestroyed, that the Lord God would ᶜpreserve a record of my people, the Nephites; even if it so be by the power of his holy arm, that it might be ᵈbrought forth at some future day unto the Lamanites, that, perhaps, they might be ᵉbrought unto salvation—

14 For at the present our strugglings were ᵃvain in restoring them to the true faith. And they swore in their wrath that, if it were possible, they would ᵇdestroy our records and us, and also all the traditions of our fathers.

15 Wherefore, I, knowing that the Lord God was able to ᵃpreserve our records, I cried unto him continually, for he had said unto me: Whatsoever thing ye shall ask in faith, believing that ye shall receive in the name of Christ, ye shall receive it.

16 And I had faith, and I did cry unto God that he would ᵃpreserve the ᵇrecords; and he covenanted with me that he would ᶜbring ᵈthem forth unto the Lamanites in his own due time.

17 And I, Enos, ᵃknew it would be according to the covenant which he had made; wherefore my soul did rest.

18 And the Lord said unto me: Thy fathers have also required of me this thing; and it shall be done unto them according to their faith; for their faith was like unto thine.

19 And now it came to pass that I, Enos, went about among the people of Nephi, prophesying of things to come, and testifying of the things which I had heard and seen.

20 And I bear record that the people of Nephi did seek diligently to ᵃrestore the Lamanites unto the true faith in God. But our ᵇlabors were vain; their ᶜhatred was fixed, and they were led by their evil nature that they became wild, and ferocious, and a ᵈblood-thirsty people, full of ᵉidolatry and ᶠfilthiness; feeding upon beasts of prey; dwelling in ᵍtents, and wandering about in the wilderness with a short skin girdle about their loins and their heads shaven; and their skill was in the ʰbow, and in the cimeter, and the ax. And many of them did eat nothing save it was raw meat; and they were continually seeking to destroy us.

21 And it came to pass that the people of Nephi did till the land, and ᵃraise all manner of grain, and of fruit, and ᵇflocks of herds, and flocks of all manner of cattle of every kind, and goats, and wild goats, and also many horses.

22 And there were exceedingly

11d Eph. 6:18.
12a Morm. 5:21;
    8:25 (24–26);
    9:36 (36–37).
  b Ps. 37:4; 1 Ne. 7:12;
    Hel. 10:5.
13a 1 Ne. 15:5; Morm. 6:1.
  b Lev. 26:44.
  c W of M 1:7 (6–11);
    Alma 37:2.
  d 2 Ne. 3:15; Jacob 1:13;
    Alma 37:19;
    Morm. 7:9 (8–10);
    Ether 12:22; D&C 3:18.
  e Alma 9:17; Hel. 15:16.

14a Jacob 7:24.
  b 2 Ne. 26:17;
    Morm. 6:6.
15a TG Scriptures,
    Preservation of.
16a 3 Ne. 5:14 (13–15);
    D&C 3:19 (16–20);
    10:47 (46–50).
  b TG Book of Mormon.
  c 2 Ne. 25:8; 27:6;
    Morm. 5:12.
  d 1 Ne. 19:19.
    TG Israel,
    Restoration of.
17a TG Trust in God.

20a Jacob 7:24.
  b Moro. 9:6.
  c 2 Ne. 5:1.
    TG Hate.
  d Jarom 1:6.
  e Mosiah 9:12.
    TG Idolatry.
  f TG Filthiness.
  g Gen. 25:27.
  h Mosiah 10:8;
    Alma 3:5 (4–5);
    43:20 (18–21).
21a 1 Ne. 8:1; Mosiah 9:9.
  b 1 Ne. 18:25;
    Ether 9:19 (18–19).

many *a*prophets among us. And the people were a *b*stiffnecked people, hard to understand.

23 And there was nothing save it was exceeding *a*harshness, *b*preaching and prophesying of wars, and contentions, and destructions, and continually *c*reminding them of death, and the duration of eternity, and the judgments and the power of God, and all these things—stirring them up *d*continually to keep them in the fear of the Lord. I say there was nothing short of these things, and exceedingly great plainness of speech, would keep them from going down speedily to destruction. And after this manner do I write concerning them.

24 And I saw *a*wars between the Nephites and Lamanites in the course of my days.

25 And it came to pass that I began to be old, and an hundred and seventy and nine years had passed away from the time that our father Lehi *a*left Jerusalem.

26 And I saw that I *a*must soon go down to my grave, having been wrought upon by the power of God that I must preach and prophesy unto this people, and declare the word according to the truth which is in Christ. And I have declared it in all my days, and have rejoiced in it above that of the world.

27 And I soon go to the place of my *a*rest, which is with my Redeemer; for I know that in him I shall *b*rest. And I rejoice in the day when my *c*mortal shall put on *d*immortality, and shall stand before him; then shall I see his face with pleasure, and he will say unto me: Come unto me, ye blessed, there is a place prepared for you in the *e*mansions of my Father. Amen.

THE BOOK OF JAROM

The Nephites keep the law of Moses, look forward to the coming of Christ, and prosper in the land—Many prophets labor to keep the people in the way of truth. About 399–361 B.C.

NOW behold, I, Jarom, write a few words according to the commandment of my father, Enos, that our *a*genealogy may be kept.

2 And as *a*these plates are *b*small, and as these things are *c*written for the intent of the benefit of our brethren the *d*Lamanites, wherefore, it must needs be that I write a little; but I shall not write the things of my prophesying, nor of my revelations. For what could I write more than my fathers have written? For have not they revealed the plan of salvation? I say unto you, Yea; and this sufficeth me.

3 Behold, it is expedient that much

22*a* W of M 1:16.
  b Jarom 1:3.
23*a* 1 Ne. 16:2 (1–3);
    2 Ne. 33:5;
    W of M 1:17.
  b TG Preaching.
  c Hel. 12:3.
  d Jarom 1:12;
    Alma 4:19; 31:5.
24*a* 1 Ne. 12:2 (2–3);
    Morm. 8:7 (7–8).
  TG War.

25*a* 1 Ne. 2:2 (2–4).
26*a* 1 Cor. 9:16;
    Ether 12:2.
  TG Duty.
27*a* TG Rest.
  b 2 Ne. 33:6.
  c TG Mortality.
  d TG Immortality.
  e Ps. 65:4;
    John 14:2 (2–3);
    Ether 12:32 (32–34);
    D&C 72:4; 98:18.

[JAROM]
1 1*a* 1 Ne. 3:12; 5:14.
  2*a* Jacob 3:14 (13–14);
    Omni 1:1.
  b 1 Ne. 6:3 (1–6);
    Jacob 7:27.
  c TG Scriptures,
    Writing of.
  d 2 Ne. 27:6;
    Morm. 5:12 (12–13).

should be done among this people, because of the hardness of their hearts, and the deafness of their ears, and the blindness of their minds, and the ªstiffness of their necks; nevertheless, God is exceedingly merciful unto them, and has not as yet ᵇswept them off from the face of the land.

4 And there are many among us who have many ªrevelations, for they are not all ᵇstiffnecked. And as many as are not stiffnecked and have faith, have ᶜcommunion with the Holy Spirit, which maketh manifest unto the children of men, according to their faith.

5 And now, behold, two hundred years had passed away, and the people of Nephi had waxed strong in the land. They observed to ªkeep the law of Moses and the ᵇsabbath day holy unto the Lord. And they ᶜprofaned not; neither did they ᵈblaspheme. And the ᵉlaws of the land were exceedingly strict.

6 And they were scattered upon ªmuch of the face of the land, and the Lamanites also. And they were exceedingly more ᵇnumerous than were they of the Nephites; and they loved ᶜmurder and would drink the ᵈblood of beasts.

7 And it came to pass that they came many times against us, the Nephites, to battle. But our ªkings and our ᵇleaders were mighty men in the faith of the Lord; and they taught the people the ways of the Lord; wherefore, we withstood the Lamanites and swept them away out of ᶜour lands, and began to fortify our cities, or whatsoever place of our inheritance.

8 And we multiplied exceedingly, and spread upon the face of the land, and became exceedingly rich in ªgold, and in silver, and in precious things, and in fine ᵇworkmanship of wood, in buildings, and in ᶜmachinery, and also in iron and copper, and brass and steel, making all manner of tools of every kind to till the ground, and ᵈweapons of war—yea, the sharp pointed arrow, and the quiver, and the dart, and the javelin, and all preparations for war.

9 And thus being prepared to meet the Lamanites, they did not prosper against us. But the word of the Lord was verified, which he spake unto our fathers, saying that: ªInasmuch as ye will keep my commandments ye shall ᵇprosper in the land.

10 And it came to pass that the prophets of the Lord did threaten the people of Nephi, according to the word of God, that if they did not keep the commandments, but should fall into transgression, they should be ªdestroyed from off the face of the land.

11 Wherefore, the prophets, and the priests, and the ªteachers, did labor diligently, exhorting with all long-suffering the people to ᵇdiligence; teaching the ᶜlaw of Moses, and the intent for which it was given; persuading them to ᵈlook forward unto the Messiah, and believe in him to come ᵉas though he

3ª Enos 1:22 (22–23).
  b Ether 2:8 (8–10).
4ª Alma 26:22;
    Hel. 11:23;
    D&C 107:19 (18–19).
  b TG Stiffnecked.
  c TG Holy Ghost;
    Revelation.
5ª 2 Ne. 25:24;
    Mosiah 2:3;
    Alma 30:3; 34:14 (13–14).
  b Ex. 35:2.
    TG Sabbath.
  c TG Profanity.
  d TG Blaspheme.

  e Alma 1:1.
6ª Hel. 11:20 (19–20).
  b Alma 2:27.
  c Jacob 7:24;
    Enos 1:20;
    Alma 26:24 (23–25).
  d TG Blood, Eating of.
7ª 2 Ne. 5:18; 6:2;
    Jacob 1:9 (9, 11, 15);
    Mosiah 1:10.
  b TG Leadership.
  c W of M 1:14.
8ª 2 Ne. 5:15.
  b TG Art.
  c TG Skill.

  d 2 Ne. 5:14;
    Mosiah 10:8.
9ª 2 Ne. 1:20;
    Omni 1:6.
  b Josh. 1:7; Ps. 122:6.
10ª 1 Ne. 12:19 (19–20);
    Omni 1:5.
11ª TG Teacher.
   b TG Diligence.
   c Jacob 4:5;
     Alma 25:15 (15–16).
   d 2 Ne. 11:4;
     Ether 12:19 (18–19).
   e 2 Ne. 25:26 (24–27);
     Mosiah 3:13; 16:6.

already was. And after this manner did they teach them.

12 And it came to pass that by so doing they kept them from being *destroyed upon the face of the land; for they did *prick their hearts with the word, *continually stirring them up unto repentance.

13 And it came to pass that two hundred and thirty and eight years had passed away—after the manner of wars, and *contentions, and dissensions, for the space of *much of the time.

14 And I, Jarom, do not write more, for the plates are *small. But behold, my brethren, ye can go to the *other plates of Nephi; for behold, upon them the records of our wars are engraven, according to the writings of the *kings, or those which they caused to be written.

15 And I deliver these plates into the hands of my son Omni, that they may be kept according to the *commandments of my fathers.

THE BOOK OF OMNI

Omni, Amaron, Chemish, Abinadom, and Amaleki, each in turn, keep the records—Mosiah discovers the people of Zarahemla, who came from Jerusalem in the days of Zedekiah—Mosiah is made king over them—The descendants of Mulek at Zarahemla had discovered Coriantumr, the last of the Jaredites—King Benjamin succeeds Mosiah—Men should offer their souls as an offering to Christ. About 323–130 B.C.

BEHOLD, it came to pass that I, Omni, being commanded by my father, Jarom, that I should write somewhat upon *these plates, to preserve our genealogy—

2 Wherefore, in my days, I would that ye should know that I fought much with the sword to preserve my people, the Nephites, from falling into the hands of their enemies, the Lamanites. But behold, I of myself *am a wicked man, and I have not kept the statutes and the commandments of the Lord as I ought to have done.

3 And it came to pass that two hundred and seventy and six years had passed away, and we had many seasons of peace; and we had many *seasons of serious war and bloodshed. Yea, and in fine, two hundred and eighty and two years had passed away, and I had kept these plates according to the *commandments of my *fathers; and I *conferred them upon my son Amaron. And I make an end.

4 And now I, Amaron, write the things whatsoever I write, which are few, in the book of my father.

5 Behold, it came to pass that three hundred and twenty years had passed away, and the more wicked part of the Nephites were *destroyed.

6 For the Lord would not suffer, after he had led them out of the land of Jerusalem and kept and preserved them from falling into the hands of their enemies, yea, he would not suffer that the words should not be verified, which he

---

12*a* Ether 2:10 (8–10).
  b Alma 31:5.
  c Enos 1:23.
13*a* TG Contention.
  b Omni 1:3.
14*a* Jacob 4:1 (1–2);
    Omni 1:30.
  b Jacob 7:26 (26–27);
    W of M 1:3.

  c Omni 1:11;
    W of M 1:10.
15*a* Jacob 1:1 (1–4);
    Omni 1:3.

[OMNI]
 1 1*a* Jarom 1:2 (1–2);
      Omni 1:9.
   2*a* TG Confession;

      Honesty;
      Humility.
 3*a* Jarom 1:13.
   b Jacob 1:1 (1–4); 7:27;
      Jarom 1:15 (1–2, 15).
   c TG Patriarch.
   d TG Delegation of
      Responsibility.
 5*a* Jarom 1:10.

spake unto our fathers, saying that: [a]Inasmuch as ye will not keep my commandments ye shall not [b]prosper in the land.

7 Wherefore, the Lord did visit them in great judgment; nevertheless, he did spare the righteous that they should not perish, but did deliver them out of the hands of their enemies.

8 And it came to pass that I did deliver the plates unto my brother Chemish.

9 Now I, Chemish, write what few things I write, in the same book with my brother; for behold, I saw the last which he wrote, that he wrote it with his own hand; and he wrote it in the day that he delivered them unto me. And after this manner we keep the [a]records, for it is according to the commandments of our fathers. And I make an end.

10 Behold, I, Abinadom, am the son of Chemish. Behold, it came to pass that I saw much war and contention between my people, the Nephites, and the Lamanites; and I, with my own sword, have taken the lives of many of the Lamanites in the defence of my brethren.

11 And behold, the [a]record of this people is engraven upon plates which is had by the [b]kings, according to the generations; and I know of no revelation save that which has been written, neither prophecy; wherefore, that which is sufficient is written. And I make an end.

12 Behold, I am Amaleki, the son of Abinadom. Behold, I will speak unto you somewhat concerning [a]Mosiah, who was made king over the [b]land of Zarahemla; for behold, he being [c]warned of the Lord that he should

[d]flee out of the [e]land of [f]Nephi, and as many as would hearken unto the voice of the Lord should also [g]depart out of the land with him, into the wilderness—

13 And it came to pass that he did according as the Lord had commanded him. And they departed out of the land into the wilderness, as many as would hearken unto the voice of the Lord; and they were led by many preachings and prophesyings. And they were admonished continually by the word of God; and they were led by the power of his [a]arm, through the wilderness until they came down into the land which is called the [b]land of Zarahemla.

14 And they discovered a [a]people, who were called the people of Zarahemla. Now, there was great rejoicing among the people of Zarahemla; and also Zarahemla did rejoice exceedingly, because the Lord had sent the people of Mosiah with the [b]plates of brass which contained the record of the Jews.

15 Behold, it came to pass that Mosiah discovered that the people of [a]Zarahemla came out from Jerusalem at the time that [b]Zedekiah, king of Judah, was carried away captive into Babylon.

16 And they [a]journeyed in the wilderness, and were brought by the hand of the Lord across the great waters, into the land where Mosiah discovered them; and they had dwelt there from that time forth.

17 And at the time that Mosiah discovered them, they had become exceedingly numerous. Nevertheless, they had had many wars and serious contentions, and had fallen by the sword from time to time; and

---

6a Jarom 1:9;
Mosiah 1:7.
b Deut. 28:29.
9a Omni 1:1.
TG Record Keeping.
11a W of M 1:10.
b Jarom 1:14.
12a Omni 1:19.
b Alma 4:1.
c TG Warn.

d Mosiah 11:13.
e Omni 1:27;
W of M 1:13.
f 2 Ne. 5:8;
Mosiah 7:6 (6–7).
g Jacob 3:4.
13a Isa. 33:2;
Mosiah 12:24.
b Mosiah 1:1; 2:4.
14a Mosiah 1:10.

b 1 Ne. 3:3 (3, 19–20);
5:10 (10–22).
15a Ezek. 17:22 (22–23);
Mosiah 25:2 (2–4).
b Jer. 39:4 (1–10);
52:11 (9–11);
Hel. 8:21.
16a 1 Ne. 16:9.

their ^alanguage had become corrupted; and they had brought no
^brecords with them; and they de-
nied the being of their Creator; and
Mosiah, nor the people of Mosiah,
could understand them.

18 But it came to pass that Mosiah
caused that they should be taught
in his ^alanguage. And it came to
pass that after they were taught in
the language of Mosiah, Zarahemla
gave a genealogy of his fathers, according to his memory; and they
are written, but ^bnot in these plates.

19 And it came to pass that the
people of Zarahemla, and of Mosiah,
did ^aunite together; and ^bMosiah was
appointed to be their king.

20 And it came to pass in the days
of Mosiah, there was a large ^astone
brought unto him with engravings
on it; and he did ^binterpret the
engravings by the gift and power
of God.

21 And they gave an account of
one ^aCoriantumr, and the slain of
his people. And Coriantumr was
discovered by the people of Zarahemla; and he dwelt with them for
the space of nine moons.

22 It also spake a few words concerning his fathers. And his first
parents came out from the ^atower,
at the time the Lord ^bconfounded
the language of the people; and the
severity of the Lord fell upon them
according to his judgments, which
are just; and their ^cbones lay scattered in the land northward.

23 Behold, I, Amaleki, was born in
the days of Mosiah; and I have lived
to see his death; and ^aBenjamin, ^bhis
son, reigneth in his stead.

24 And behold, I have seen, in the
days of king Benjamin, a serious war
and much bloodshed between the
Nephites and the Lamanites. But
behold, the Nephites did obtain
much advantage over them; yea,
insomuch that king Benjamin did
drive them out of the land of Zarahemla.

25 And it came to pass that I began
to be old; and, having no seed, and
knowing king ^aBenjamin to be a just
man before the Lord, wherefore, I
shall ^bdeliver up ^cthese plates unto
him, exhorting all men to come
unto God, the Holy One of Israel,
and believe in prophesying, and in
revelations, and in the ministering
of angels, and in the gift of speaking with tongues, and in the gift of
interpreting languages, and in all
things which are ^dgood; for there is
nothing which is good save it comes
from the Lord: and that which is
evil cometh from the devil.

26 And now, my beloved brethren,
I would that ye should ^acome unto
Christ, who is the Holy One of Israel,
and partake of his salvation, and
the power of his redemption. Yea,
come unto him, and ^boffer your
whole souls as an ^coffering unto him,
and continue in ^dfasting and praying, and endure to the end; and as
the Lord liveth ye will be saved.

27 And now I would speak some-
what concerning a certain ^anumber
who went up into the wilderness to
^breturn to the ^cland of Nephi; for
there was a large number who were
desirous to possess the land of their
inheritance.

28 Wherefore, they went up into

17a 1 Ne. 3:19.
  TG Language.
  b Mosiah 1:3 (2–6).
18a Mosiah 24:4.
  b 1 Ne. 9:4;
    W of M 1:10.
19a Mosiah 25:13.
  b Omni 1:12.
20a Mosiah 21:28 (27–28);
    28:13.
  b Mosiah 8:13 (13–19);
    28:17.
    TG Urim and Thummim.

21a Ether 12:1 (1–2);
    13:20 (13–31); 15:32.
22a Ether 1:3 (1–6).
  b Gen. 11:7 (6–9);
    Mosiah 28:17;
    Ether 1:33.
  c Mosiah 8:8 (8–12).
23a W of M 1:3.
  b Mosiah 2:11.
25a W of M 1:18 (17–18);
    Mosiah 29:13.
  b W of M 1:10.
  c 1 Ne. 10:1.

  d Alma 5:40;
    Ether 4:12;
    Moro. 7:16 (15–17).
26a Jacob 1:7;
    Alma 29:2;
    Moro. 10:32.
  b TG Commitment;
    Self-Sacrifice.
  c 3 Ne. 9:20.
  d TG Fast, Fasting.
27a Mosiah 9:3 (1–4).
  b Mosiah 7:1.
  c Omni 1:12.

the wilderness. And their leader being a strong and mighty man, and a stiffnecked man, wherefore he caused a contention among them; and they were *all slain, save fifty, in the wilderness, and they returned again to the land of Zarahemla.

29 And it came to pass that they also took others to a considerable number, and took their journey again into the wilderness.

30 And I, Amaleki, had a brother, who also went with them; and I have not since known concerning them. And I am about to lie down in my grave; and *these plates are full. And I make an end of my speaking.

THE WORDS OF MORMON

Mormon abridges the large plates of Nephi—He puts the small plates with the other plates—King Benjamin establishes peace in the land. About A.D. 385.

AND now I, Mormon, being about to deliver up the *record which I have been making into the hands of my son Moroni, behold I have witnessed almost all the destruction of my people, the Nephites.

2 And it is *many hundred years after the coming of Christ that I deliver these records into the hands of my son; and it supposeth me that he will witness the entire *destruction of my people. But may God grant that he may survive them, that he may write somewhat concerning them, and somewhat concerning Christ, that perhaps some day it may *profit them.

3 And now, I speak somewhat concerning that which I have written; for after I had made an *abridgment from the *plates of Nephi, down to the reign of this king Benjamin, of whom Amaleki spake, I searched among the *records which had been delivered into my hands, and I found these plates, which contained this small account of the prophets, from Jacob down to the reign of this king *Benjamin, and also many of the words of Nephi.

4 And the things which are upon these plates *pleasing me, because of the prophecies of the coming of Christ; and my fathers knowing that many of them have been fulfilled; yea, and I also know that as many things as have been *prophesied concerning us down to this day have been fulfilled, and as many as go beyond this day must surely come to pass—

5 Wherefore, I chose *these things, to finish my *record upon them, which remainder of my record I shall take from the *plates of Nephi; and I cannot write the *hundredth part of the things of my people.

6 But behold, I shall take these

28a Mosiah 9:2 (1–4).
30a 1 Ne. 6:3 (3–6);
    Jacob 4:1 (1–2);
    Jarom 1:14.

[WORDS OF MORMON]
1 1a 3 Ne. 5:12 (9–12);
    Morm. 1:4 (1–4);
    2:17 (17–18);
    8:5 (1, 4–5, 14).
2a Morm. 6:5 (5–6).

b 1 Ne. 12:19.
c D&C 3:19 (16–20).
3a 1 Ne. 1:17 (16–17);
    D&C 10:44.
b Jarom 1:14;
    W of M 1:10;
    D&C 10:38 (38–40).
c Mosiah 1:6 (2–6);
    Hel. 3:13 (13–15);
    Morm. 4:23.
d Omni 1:23 (23–25).

4a 1 Ne. 6:5 (3–6).
b TG Jesus Christ,
    Prophecies about.
5a IE the things pleasing to
    him, mentioned in v. 4.
b 3 Ne. 5:17 (14–18);
    Morm. 1:1.
c 1 Ne. 9:2.
d Alma 13:31;
    3 Ne. 5:8 (8–11);
    26:6 (6–12).

plates, which contain these prophesyings and revelations, and put them with the remainder of my record, for they are choice unto me; and I know they will be choice unto my brethren.

7 And I do this for a *a*wise *b*purpose; for thus it whispereth me, according to the workings of the Spirit of the Lord which is in me. And now, I do not know all things; but the Lord *c*knoweth all things which are to come; wherefore, he *d*worketh in me to do according to his *e*will.

8 And my *a*prayer to God is concerning my brethren, that they may once again come to the knowledge of God, yea, the redemption of Christ; that they may once again be a *b*delightsome people.

9 And now I, Mormon, proceed to finish out my record, which I take from the plates of Nephi; and I make it according to the knowledge and the *a*understanding which God has given me.

10 Wherefore, it came to pass that after Amaleki had *a*delivered up these plates into the hands of king Benjamin, he took them and put them with the *b*other plates, which contained records which had been handed down by the *c*kings, from generation to generation until the days of king Benjamin.

11 And they were handed down from king Benjamin, from generation to generation until they have fallen into *a*my hands. And I, Mormon, pray to God that they may be preserved from this time henceforth. And I know that they will

be preserved; for there are great things written upon them, out of which *b*my people and their brethren shall be *c*judged at the great and last day, according to the word of God which is written.

12 And now, concerning this king Benjamin—he had somewhat of contentions among his own people.

13 And it came to pass also that the armies of the Lamanites came down out of the *a*land of Nephi, to battle against his people. But behold, king Benjamin gathered together his armies, and he did stand against them; and he did fight with the strength of his own arm, with the *b*sword of Laban.

14 And in the *a*strength of the Lord they did contend against their enemies, until they had slain many thousands of the Lamanites. And it came to pass that they did contend against the Lamanites until they had driven them out of all the lands of their *b*inheritance.

15 And it came to pass that after there had been false *a*Christs, and their mouths had been shut, and they punished according to their crimes;

16 And after there had been *a*false prophets, and false preachers and teachers among the people, and all these having been punished according to their crimes; and after there having been much contention and many dissensions away *b*unto the Lamanites, behold, it came to pass that king Benjamin, with the assistance of the holy *c*prophets who were among his people—

17 For behold, king Benjamin was

7a 1 Ne. 9:5; 19:3;
   Enos 1:13 (13–18);
   Alma 37:2;
   D&C 3:19 (9–20);
   10:34 (1–19, 30–47).
 b D&C 10:40 (20–46).
 c TG God, Foreknowledge of;
   God, Intelligence of;
   God, Omniscience of.
 d 2 Ne. 27:23.
 e TG God, Will of.
8a 2 Ne. 33:3;
   Enos 1:11 (11–12);

Moro. 9:22.
 b 2 Ne. 30:6.
9a TG Understanding.
10a Omni 1:25 (25, 30).
 b 1 Ne. 9:4;
   Omni 1:11, 18;
   W of M 1:3;
   Mosiah 28:11.
 c Jarom 1:14.
11a 3 Ne. 5:12 (8–12);
   Morm. 1:4 (1–5).
 b Hel. 15:3 (3–4).
 c 2 Ne. 25:18; 29:11;
   33:14 (11, 14–15);

3 Ne. 27:25 (23–27);
   Ether 5:4.
13a Omni 1:12.
 b 1 Ne. 4:9;
   2 Ne. 5:14;
   Jacob 1:10;
   Mosiah 1:16;
   D&C 17:1.
14a TG Strength.
 b Jarom 1:7.
15a TG False Christs.
16a TG False Prophets.
 b Jacob 1:14 (13–14).
 c Enos 1:22.

a ^aholy man, and he did reign over his people in righteousness; and there were many holy men in the land, and they did speak the word of God with ^bpower and with authority; and they did use much ^csharpness because of the stiffneckedness of the people—

18 Wherefore, with the help of these, king ^aBenjamin, by laboring with all the might of his body and the ^bfaculty of his whole soul, and also the prophets, did once more establish peace in the land.

THE BOOK OF MOSIAH

CHAPTER 1

King Benjamin teaches his sons the language and prophecies of their fathers—Their religion and civilization have been preserved because of the records kept on the various plates—Mosiah is chosen as king and is given custody of the records and other things. About 130–124 B.C.

AND now there was no more contention in all the ^aland of Zarahemla, among all the people who belonged to king Benjamin, so that king Benjamin had continual peace all the remainder of his days.

2 And it came to pass that he had three ^asons; and he called their names Mosiah, and Helorum, and Helaman. And he caused that they should be ^btaught in all the ^clanguage of his fathers, that thereby they might become men of understanding; and that they might know concerning the prophecies which had been spoken by the mouths of their fathers, which were delivered them by the hand of the Lord.

3 And he also taught them concerning the records which were engraven on the ^aplates of brass, saying: My sons, I would that ye should remember that were it not for these ^bplates, which contain these records and these commandments, we must have suffered in ^cignorance, even at this present time, not knowing the mysteries of God.

4 For it were not possible that our father, Lehi, could have remembered all these things, to have taught them to his children, except it were for the help of these plates; for he having been taught in the ^alanguage of the Egyptians therefore he could read these engravings, and teach them to his children, that thereby they could teach them to their children, and so fulfilling the commandments of God, even down to this present time.

5 I say unto you, my sons, ^awere it not for these things, which have been kept and ^bpreserved by the hand of God, that we might ^cread and understand of his ^dmysteries, and have his ^ecommandments always

17a Ex. 22:31;
  Alma 13:26;
  D&C 49:8; 107:29.
  b Alma 17:3 (2–3).
  TG God, Power of.
  c Enos 1:23; Moro. 9:4;
  D&C 121:43 (41–43).
18a Omni 1:25;
  Mosiah 29:13.
  b 1 Ne. 15:25.

[MOSIAH]

1 1a Omni 1:13;

  Alma 2:15.
2a 1 Ne. 1:1;
  D&C 68:25 (25, 28).
  b Enos 1:1;
  Mosiah 4:15 (14–15).
  c Morm. 9:32.
3a 2 Ne. 5:12;
  Mosiah 1:16; 28:20.
  b 1 Ne. 3:19 (19–20);
  Omni 1:17.
  c Alma 37:8.
4a 1 Ne. 1:2; 3:19;
  Morm. 9:32 (32–33);

  JS—H 1:64.
5a Alma 37:9.
  b TG Scriptures,
  Preservation of.
  c Deut. 6:6 (6–8);
  2 Chr. 34:21;
  1 Ne. 15:24 (23–24).
  TG Scriptures, Value of.
  d TG Mysteries of
  Godliness.
  e 1 Ne. 4:15.

before our eyes, that even our fathers would have dwindled in unbelief, and we should have been like unto our brethren, the Lamanites, who know nothing concerning these things, or even do not believe them when they are taught them, because of the [f]traditions of their fathers, which are not correct.

6 O my sons, I would that ye should remember that these sayings are true, and also that these records are [a]true. And behold, also the plates of Nephi, which contain the records and the sayings of our fathers from the time they left Jerusalem until now, and they are true; and we can know of their surety because we have them before our eyes.

7 And now, my sons, I would that ye should remember to [a]search them diligently, that ye may profit thereby; and I would that ye should [b]keep the commandments of God, that ye may [c]prosper in the land according to the [d]promises which the Lord made unto our fathers.

8 And many more things did king Benjamin teach his sons, which are not written in this book.

9 And it came to pass that after king Benjamin had made an end of teaching his sons, that he waxed [a]old, and he saw that he must very soon go the way of all the earth; therefore, he thought it expedient that he should confer the kingdom upon one of his sons.

10 Therefore, he had Mosiah brought before him; and these are the words which he spake unto him, saying: My son, I would that ye should make a proclamation throughout all this land among all this [a]people, or the people of Zarahemla, and the people of Mosiah who dwell in the land, that thereby they may be gathered together; for on the morrow I shall proclaim unto this my people out of mine own mouth that thou art a [b]king and a ruler over this people, whom the Lord our God hath given us.

11 And moreover, I shall give this people a [a]name, that thereby they may be distinguished above all the people which the Lord God hath brought out of the land of Jerusalem; and this I do because they have been a [b]diligent people in keeping the commandments of the Lord.

12 And I give unto them a name that never shall be blotted out, except it be through [a]transgression.

13 Yea, and moreover I say unto you, that if this highly favored people of the Lord should fall into [a]transgression, and become a wicked and an adulterous people, that the Lord will deliver them up, that thereby they become [b]weak like unto their brethren; and he will no more [c]preserve them by his matchless and marvelous power, as he has hitherto preserved our fathers.

14 For I say unto you, that if he had not extended his arm in the preservation of our fathers they must have fallen into the hands of the Lamanites, and become victims to their hatred.

15 And it came to pass that after king Benjamin had made an end of these sayings to his son, that he gave him [a]charge concerning all the affairs of the kingdom.

16 And moreover, he also gave him charge concerning the records which

---

5f Jacob 7:24;
  Mosiah 10:12 (11–17).
6a 1 Ne. 1:3; 14:30;
  2 Ne. 25:20;
  Alma 3:12;
  Ether 5:3 (1–3).
7a TG Scriptures, Study of.
  b Lev. 25:18 (18–19);
  Mosiah 2:22;
  Alma 50:20 (20–22).
  c Josh. 1:7;

Ps. 1:3 (2–3); 122:6;
  1 Ne. 2:20.
  d Omni 1:6;
  Alma 9:13 (13–14).
9a TG Old Age.
10a Omni 1:14;
  Mosiah 27:35.
  b Gen. 41:43 (41–43);
  Jarom 1:7 (7, 14);
  Mosiah 2:30.
11a Mosiah 5:8 (8–12).

TG Jesus Christ, Taking
  the Name of.
  b TG Diligence.
12a TG Transgress.
13a Heb. 6:6 (4–6).
  b Jer. 46:15 (15–17);
  Hel. 4:24 (24, 26).
  c D&C 103:8.
15a 1 Kgs. 2:1;
  Ps. 72:1 (1–4).

were engraven on the ªplates of brass; and also the plates of Nephi; and also, the ᵇsword of Laban, and the ᶜball or director, which led our fathers through the wilderness, which was prepared by the hand of the Lord that thereby they might be led, every one according to the heed and diligence which they gave unto him.

17 Therefore, as they were ªunfaithful they did not prosper nor progress in their journey, but were ᵇdriven back, and incurred the displeasure of God upon them; and therefore they were smitten with famine and sore ᶜafflictions, to stir them up in ᵈremembrance of their duty.

18 And now, it came to pass that Mosiah went and did as his father had commanded him, and proclaimed unto all the people who were in the land of Zarahemla that thereby they might gather themselves together, to go up to the ªtemple to hear the words which his father should speak unto them.

CHAPTER 2

King Benjamin addresses his people—He recounts the equity, fairness, and spirituality of his reign—He counsels them to serve their Heavenly King—Those who rebel against God will suffer anguish like unquenchable fire. About 124 B.C.

AND it came to pass that after Mosiah had done as his father had commanded him, and had made a proclamation throughout all the land, that the people ªgathered themselves together throughout all the land, that they might go up to the ᵇtemple to ᶜhear the ᵈwords which king Benjamin should speak unto them.

2 And there were a great number, even so many that they did not number them; for they had multiplied exceedingly and waxed great in the land.

3 And they also took of the ªfirstlings of their flocks, that they might offer ᵇsacrifice and ᶜburnt ᵈofferings ᵉaccording to the law of Moses;

4 And also that they might give thanks to the Lord their God, who had brought them out of the land of Jerusalem, and who had delivered them out of the hands of their enemies, and had ªappointed just men to be their ᵇteachers, and also a just man to be their king, who had established peace in the ᶜland of Zarahemla, and who had taught them to ᵈkeep the commandments of God, that they might rejoice and be filled with ᵉlove towards God and all men.

5 And it came to pass that when they came up to the temple, they pitched their tents round about, every man according to his ªfamily, consisting of his wife, and his sons, and his daughters, and their sons, and their daughters, from the eldest down to the youngest, every family being separate one from another.

6 And they pitched their tents round about the temple, every man having his ªtent with the door thereof towards the temple, that thereby they might remain in their tents and hear the words which king Benjamin should speak unto them;

16a Mosiah 1:3.
  b Jacob 1:10;
    W of M 1:13; D&C 17:1.
  c 2 Ne. 5:12.
17a TG Disobedience.
  b 1 Ne. 18:13 (12–13).
  c Lam. 1:5.
    TG Affliction.
  d Judg. 13:1;
    Hel. 12:3 (2–3).
18a 2 Ne. 5:16; Mosiah 2:1.
2 1a TG Assembly for
    Worship.

  b Mosiah 1:18.
  c 2 Chr. 34:30 (29–33).
  d Mosiah 26:1.
3a Gen. 4:4 (2–7);
    Ex. 13:12 (12–13);
    Deut. 12:6;
    Moses 5:20 (5, 19–23).
  b Ezra 6:10.
    TG Sacrifice.
  c Lev. 1:3 (2–9);
    Deut. 33:10.
  d Ezra 3:2 (2–5);
    1 Ne. 5:9.

  e 2 Ne. 25:24;
    Jarom 1:5;
    Alma 30:3;
    34:14 (13–14).
4a TG Called of God.
  b Mosiah 18:18 (18–22).
  c Omni 1:13 (12–15).
  d John 15:10;
    D&C 95:12.
  e Deut. 11:1.
    TG Love.
5a TG Family, Patriarchal.
6a Ex. 33:8 (8–10).

7 For the multitude being so great that king Benjamin could not teach them all within the walls of the temple, therefore he caused a ^atower to be erected, that thereby his people might hear the words which he should speak unto them.

8 And it came to pass that he began to speak to his people from the tower; and they could not all hear his words because of the greatness of the multitude; therefore he caused that the words which he spake should be written and sent forth among those that were not under the sound of his voice, that they might also receive his words.

9 And these are the words which he ^aspake and caused to be written, saying: My brethren, all ye that have assembled yourselves together, you that can hear my words which I shall speak unto you this day; for I have not commanded you to come up hither to ^btrifle with the words which I shall speak, but that you should ^chearken unto me, and open your ears that ye may hear, and your ^dhearts that ye may understand, and your ^eminds that the ^fmysteries of God may be unfolded to your view.

10 I have not commanded you to come up hither that ye should fear ^ame, or that ye should think that I of myself am more than a mortal man.

11 But I am like as yourselves, subject to all manner of infirmities in body and mind; yet I have been chosen by this people, and ^aconsecrated by ^bmy father, and was suffered by the hand of the Lord that I should be a ruler and a king over this people; and have been kept and preserved by his matchless power, to serve you with all the might, mind and strength which the Lord hath granted unto me.

12 I say unto you that as I have been suffered to ^aspend my days in your service, even up to this time, and have not sought ^bgold nor silver nor any manner of riches of you;

13 Neither have I suffered that ye should be confined in dungeons, nor that ye should make slaves one of another, nor that ye should murder, or plunder, or steal, or commit adultery; nor even have I suffered that ye should commit any manner of wickedness, and have taught you that ye should keep the commandments of the Lord, in all things which he hath commanded you—

14 And even I, myself, have ^alabored with mine own ^bhands that I might serve you, and that ye should not be ^claden with taxes, and that there should nothing come upon you which was grievous to be borne—and of all these things which I have spoken, ye yourselves are witnesses this day.

15 Yet, my brethren, I have not done these things that I might ^aboast, neither do I tell these things that thereby I might accuse you; but I tell you these things that ye may know that I can answer a clear ^bconscience before God this day.

16 Behold, I say unto you that because I said unto you that I had spent my days in your service, I do not desire to boast, for I have only been in the service of God.

17 And behold, I tell you these things that ye may learn ^awisdom; that ye may learn that when ye are in the ^bservice of your ^cfellow beings

---

7a Gen. 35:21;
  Neh. 8:4 (4–5);
  Mosiah 11:12 (12–13).
9a Mosiah 8:3.
  b D&C 6:12; 32:5.
  TG Mocking.
  c TG Teachable.
  d Prov. 8:5; Mosiah 12:27;
  3 Ne. 19:33.
  e TG Mind.
  f TG Mysteries of
  Godliness.

10a TG Humility.
11a TG Setting Apart.
  b Omni 1:23 (23–24).
  TG Serve; Service.
12a 1 Sam. 12:2 (1–25).
  b 2 Kgs. 5:16;
  Acts 20:33 (33–34);
  Jacob 1:16.
14a Deut. 17:17;
  Neh. 5:14 (14–15);
  1 Cor. 9:18 (4–18).
  TG Self-Sacrifice;

Work, Value of.
  b Acts 20:34 (33–35).
  c Ezek. 46:18.
15a TG Boast.
  b TG Conscience.
17a TG Wisdom.
  b Matt. 25:40;
  D&C 42:31 (30–31).
  TG Service.
  c TG Brotherhood and
  Sisterhood; Fellowshipping; Neighbor.

ye are only in the service of your God.

18 Behold, ye have called me your king; and if I, whom ye call your king, do labor to ^aserve you, then ought not ye to labor to serve one another?

19 And behold also, if I, whom ye call your king, who has spent his days in your service, and yet has been in the service of God, do merit any thanks from you, O how you ought to ^athank your heavenly ^bKing!

20 I say unto you, my brethren, that if you should render all the ^athanks and ^bpraise which your whole soul has power to possess, to that God who has created you, and has kept and ^cpreserved you, and has caused that ye should ^drejoice, and has granted that ye should live in peace one with another—

21 I say unto you that if ye should ^aserve him who has created you from the beginning, and is ^bpreserving you from day to day, by lending you ^cbreath, that ye may live and move and do according to your own ^dwill, and even supporting you from one moment to another—I say, if ye should serve him with all your ^ewhole souls yet ye would be ^funprofitable servants.

22 And behold, all that he ^arequires of you is to ^bkeep his commandments; and he has ^cpromised you that if ye would keep his commandments ye should prosper in the land; and he never doth ^dvary from that which he hath said; therefore, if ye do ^ekeep his ^fcommandments he doth bless you and prosper you.

23 And now, in the first place, he hath created you, and granted unto you your lives, for which ye are indebted unto him.

24 And secondly, he doth ^arequire that ye should do as he hath commanded you; for which if ye do, he doth immediately ^bbless you; and therefore he hath paid you. And ye are still indebted unto him, and are, and will be, forever and ever; therefore, of what have ye to boast?

25 And now I ask, can ye say aught of yourselves? I answer you, Nay. Ye cannot say that ye are even as much as the dust of the earth; yet ye were ^acreated of the ^bdust of the earth; but behold, it ^cbelongeth to him who created you.

26 And I, even I, whom ye call your king, am ^ano better than ye yourselves are; for I am also of the dust. And ye behold that I am old, and am about to yield up this mortal frame to its mother earth.

27 Therefore, as I said unto you that I had ^aserved you, ^bwalking with a clear conscience before God, even so I at this time have caused that ye should assemble yourselves together, that I might be found blameless, and that your ^cblood should not come upon me, when I shall stand to be judged of God of the things whereof he hath commanded me concerning you.

28 I say unto you that I have caused that ye should assemble yourselves together that I might

---

18a Luke 22:26.
19a 1 Chr. 16:8.
   TG Thanksgiving.
 b TG Kingdom of God,
   in Heaven.
20a Job 1:21;
   Ps. 34:1 (1–3);
   D&C 59:21; 62:7; 78:19.
 b 1 Sam. 12:24;
   1 Ne. 18:16;
   D&C 136:28.
 c D&C 63:3.
 d Neh. 12:43.
21a Job 22:3 (3–4).
 b Neh. 9:6.
 c 2 Ne. 9:26.
 d TG Agency.

 e TG Dedication.
 f Luke 17:10 (7–10);
   Rom. 3:12.
22a TG God, the Standard of
   Righteousness.
 b Gen. 4:7;
   Lev. 25:18 (18–19);
   Mosiah 1:7;
   Alma 50:20 (20–22).
 c 1 Ne. 4:14;
   Omni 1:6;
   Ether 2:7 (7–12).
 d TG God, Perfection of.
 e Ps. 19:11 (9–11);
   2 Ne. 1:20;
   D&C 14:7; 58:2.
 f TG Commandments

   of God.
24a TG Duty.
 b Prov. 22:4 (4–5);
   2 Ne. 1:20.
25a TG Man, Physical
   Creation of.
 b Jacob 2:21;
   Alma 42:2;
   Hel. 12:7 (7–8);
   Morm. 9:17.
 c 1 Chr. 29:12;
   Mosiah 4:22.
26a TG Equal.
27a TG Serve;
   Service.
 b TG Walking with God.
 c Jacob 1:19.

[a]rid my garments of your blood, at this period of time when I am about to go down to my grave, that I might go down in peace, and my immortal [b]spirit may join the [c]choirs above in singing the praises of a just God.

29 And moreover, I say unto you that I have caused that ye should assemble yourselves together, that I might declare unto you that I can no longer be your teacher, nor your king;

30 For even at this time, my whole frame doth tremble exceedingly while attempting to speak unto you; but the Lord God doth support me, and hath suffered me that I should speak unto you, and hath commanded me that I should declare unto you this day, that my son Mosiah is a [a]king and a ruler over you.

31 And now, my brethren, I would that ye should do as ye have hitherto done. As ye have kept my commandments, and also the commandments of my father, and have prospered, and have been kept from falling into the hands of your enemies, even so if ye shall keep the commandments of my son, or the commandments of God which shall be delivered unto you by him, ye shall prosper in the land, and your enemies shall have no power over you.

32 But, O my people, beware lest there shall arise [a]contentions among you, and ye [b]list to [c]obey the evil spirit, which was spoken of by my father Mosiah.

33 For behold, there is a wo pronounced upon him who listeth to

[a]obey that spirit; for if he listeth to obey him, and remaineth and dieth in his [b]sins, the same drinketh [c]damnation to his own soul; for he receiveth for his wages an [d]everlasting [e]punishment, having transgressed the law of God contrary to his own knowledge.

34 I say unto you, that there are not any among you, except it be your little children that have not been taught concerning these things, but what knoweth that ye are eternally [a]indebted to your heavenly Father, to render to him [b]all that you have and are; and also have been taught concerning the [c]records which contain the prophecies which have been spoken by the holy prophets, even down to the time our father, Lehi, left Jerusalem;

35 And also, all that has been spoken by our fathers until now. And behold, also, they spake that which was commanded them of the Lord; therefore, they are [a]just and true.

36 And now, I say unto you, my brethren, that after ye have known and have been taught all these things, if ye should transgress and go [a]contrary to that which has been spoken, that ye do [b]withdraw yourselves from the Spirit of the Lord, that it may have no place in you to guide you in wisdom's paths that ye may be blessed, prospered, and preserved—

37 I say unto you, that the man that doeth this, the same cometh out in open [a]rebellion against God; therefore he [b]listeth to obey the evil spirit, and becometh an enemy to

28a 2 Ne. 9:44;
      Jacob 2:2 (2, 16);
      D&C 61:34.
  b TG Spirit Body.
  c Morm. 7:7.
30a Mosiah 1:10; 6:3 (3–4).
      TG Kings, Earthly.
32a Eph. 4:27 (26–27);
      3 Ne. 11:29.
      TG Contention.
  b Alma 3:27 (26–27);
      5:42 (41–42); 30:60;
      D&C 29:45.

  c 2 Ne. 32:8;
      Mosiah 4:14;
      Alma 5:20.
33a TG Agency.
  b TG Accountability.
  c TG Damnation.
  d Jacob 6:10;
      D&C 19:11 (10–12).
  e TG Punish.
34a Philip. 3:8 (7–10).
      TG Debt.
  b Rom. 12:1 (1–2).
  c 1 Ne. 5:14;

      Alma 33:2.
35a Rom. 7:12;
      Rev. 15:3.
36a TG Disobedience.
  b TG Holy Ghost, Loss of.
37a Mosiah 3:12;
      Hel. 8:25 (24–25).
      TG Holy Ghost,
      Unpardonable Sin
      against;
      Rebellion.
  b Prov. 19:27;
      1 Ne. 8:34 (33–34).

all righteousness; therefore, the Lord has no place in him, for he dwelleth not in ^cunholy temples.

38 Therefore if that man ^arepenteth not, and remaineth and dieth an enemy to God, the demands of divine ^bjustice do awaken his immortal soul to a lively sense of his own ^cguilt, which doth cause him to shrink from the ^dpresence of the Lord, and doth fill his breast with guilt, and ^epain, and ^fanguish, which is like an unquenchable ^gfire, whose flame ascendeth up forever and ever.

39 And now I say unto you, that ^amercy hath no claim on that man; therefore his final doom is to endure a never-ending ^btorment.

40 O, all ye ^aold men, and also ye young men, and you little children who can understand my words, for I have spoken plainly unto you that ye might understand, I pray that ye should awake to a ^bremembrance of the awful situation of those that have fallen into transgression.

41 And moreover, I would desire that ye should consider on the blessed and ^ahappy state of those that keep the commandments of God. For behold, they are ^bblessed in all things, both temporal and spiritual; and if they hold out ^cfaithful to the end they are received into ^dheaven, that thereby they may dwell with God in a state of never-ending happiness. O remember, remember that these things are true; for the Lord God hath spoken it.

CHAPTER 3

King Benjamin continues his address—The Lord Omnipotent will minister among men in a tabernacle of clay—Blood will come from every pore as He atones for the sins of the world—His is the only name whereby salvation comes—Men can put off the natural man and become Saints through the Atonement—The torment of the wicked will be as a lake of fire and brimstone. About 124 B.C.

AND again my brethren, I would call your attention, for I have somewhat more to speak unto you; for behold, I have things to tell you concerning that which is to come.

2 And the things which I shall tell you are made known unto me by an ^aangel from God. And he said unto me: ^bAwake; and I awoke, and behold he stood before me.

3 And he said unto me: Awake, and hear the words which I shall tell thee; for behold, I am come to declare unto you the ^aglad tidings of great ^bjoy.

4 For the Lord hath heard thy prayers, and hath judged of thy ^arighteousness, and hath sent me to declare unto thee that thou mayest rejoice; and that thou mayest declare unto thy people, that they may also be filled with joy.

5 For behold, the time cometh, and is not far distant, that with power, the ^aLord ^bOmnipotent who ^creigneth, who was, and is from all ^deternity to all eternity, shall come down from heaven among the

37c Alma 7:21; 34:36;
      Hel. 4:24.
38a TG Repent.
    b TG God, Justice of.
    c Mosiah 27:29 (25–29).
      TG Guilt.
    d TG God, Presence of.
    e TG Pain.
    f TG Sorrow.
    g TG Hell.
39a TG Mercy.
    b TG Damnation;
      Punish.
40a TG Old Age.
    b Alma 5:18 (7–18).

41a Matt. 11:29 (28–30);
      Alma 50:23;
      4 Ne. 1:16 (15–18).
      TG Happiness;
      Joy.
    b Gen. 39:3 (1–6);
      Ps. 37:25;
      Matt. 6:33;
      1 Ne. 17:3 (1–5, 12–14).
    c Ps. 31:23;
      Ether 4:19;
      D&C 6:13; 63:47.
    d TG Heaven.
3 2a Mosiah 4:1; 5:5.
      TG Angels.

    b Zech. 4:1 (1–2).
3a Isa. 52:7 (7–10);
      Luke 2:10 (10–11);
      Rom. 10:15;
      D&C 31:3.
    b TG Joy.
4a TG Righteousness.
5a TG Jesus Christ, Jehovah.
    b Rev. 1:8 (7–8).
      TG Jesus Christ,
      Power of.
    c TG Jesus Christ,
      Authority of.
    d 2 Ne. 26:12;
      Mosiah 16:15.

children of men, and shall dwell in a ᵉtabernacle of clay, and shall go forth amongst men, working mighty ᶠmiracles, such as healing the sick, raising the dead, causing the lame to walk, the ᵍblind to receive their sight, and the deaf to hear, and curing all manner of diseases.

6 And he shall cast out ᵃdevils, or the ᵇevil spirits which dwell in the hearts of the children of men.

7 And lo, he shall ᵃsuffer ᵇtemptations, and pain of body, ᶜhunger, thirst, and fatigue, even more than man can ᵈsuffer, except it be unto death; for behold, ᵉblood cometh from every pore, so great shall be his ᶠanguish for the wickedness and the abominations of his people.

8 And he shall be called ᵃJesus ᵇChrist, the ᶜSon of God, the ᵈFather of heaven and earth, the ᵉCreator of all things from the beginning; and his ᶠmother shall be called Mary.

9 And lo, he cometh unto his own, that ᵃsalvation might come unto the children of men even through ᵇfaith on his name; and even after all this they shall consider him a man, and say that he hath a ᶜdevil,

and shall ᵈscourge him, and shall ᵉcrucify him.

10 And he shall ᵃrise the ᵇthird day from the dead; and behold, he standeth to ᶜjudge the world; and behold, all these things are done that a righteous judgment might come upon the children of men.

11 For behold, and also his ᵃblood ᵇatoneth for the sins of those who have ᶜfallen by the transgression of Adam, who have died not knowing the ᵈwill of God concerning them, or who have ᵉignorantly sinned.

12 But wo, wo unto him who knoweth that he ᵃrebelleth against God! For salvation cometh to none such except it be through repentance and faith on the ᵇLord Jesus Christ.

13 And the Lord God hath sent his holy ᵃprophets among all the children of men, to declare these things to every kindred, nation, and tongue, that thereby whosoever should believe that Christ should come, the same might receive ᵇremission of their sins, and rejoice with exceedingly great joy, even ᶜas though he had already come among them.

5e Mosiah 7:27; 15:2 (1–7); Alma 7:9 (9–13).
 f Matt. 4:24 (23–24); 9:35; Acts 2:22; 1 Ne. 11:31. TG Death, Power over; Heal; Miracle.
 g Matt. 9:28 (28–31); 20:30 (30–34); John 9:1 (1–4); 3 Ne. 17:9 (7–10); D&C 84:69.
6a Mark 1:34 (32–34); 1 Ne. 11:31.
 b TG Spirits, Evil or Unclean.
7a Luke 12:50. TG Suffering.
 b TG Jesus Christ, Temptation of; Temptation.
 c Matt. 4:2 (1–2).
 d D&C 19:16 (15–18).
 e Matt. 26:39 (38–39); Luke 22:44.
 f Isa. 53:4 (4–5).
8a TG Foreordination;

Jesus Christ, Prophecies about.
 b TG Jesus Christ, Messiah.
 c Mosiah 15:3; Alma 7:10; 3 Ne. 1:14.
 d Mosiah 15:4; Hel. 14:12; 3 Ne. 9:15; Ether 4:7.
 e TG Jesus Christ, Creator.
 f Matt. 1:16; 1 Ne. 11:18 (14–21).
9a TG Jesus Christ, Mission of.
 b TG Faith.
 c Luke 11:15 (14–22); John 8:48; 12:37; Hel. 13:26 (26–27).
 d Luke 18:33; 1 Ne. 11:33; 2 Ne. 10:3.
 e 1 Ne. 19:10 (10, 13); 2 Ne. 6:9; 3 Ne. 11:14 (14–15, 33). TG Jesus Christ, Crucifixion of.
10a TG Jesus Christ,

Resurrection.
 b 2 Ne. 25:13; Hel. 14:20 (20–27).
 c TG Jesus Christ, Judge.
11a TG Blood, Symbolism of.
 b TG Jesus Christ, Redeemer; Redemption.
 c TG Fall of Man.
 d TG God, Will of.
 e Lev. 4:13 (13–35); Num. 15:27 (2–29); 2 Ne. 9:26 (25–26); Alma 9:16 (15–16); 42:21; 3 Ne. 6:18. TG Accountability; Ignorance.
12a Mosiah 2:37 (36–38); Hel. 8:25 (24–25). TG Rebellion.
 b TG Jesus Christ, Lord.
13a TG Prophets, Mission of.
 b TG Remission of Sins.
 c 2 Ne. 25:26 (24–27); Jarom 1:11; Mosiah 16:6.

14 Yet the Lord God saw that his people were a *a*stiffnecked people, and he appointed unto them a *b*law, even the *c*law of Moses.

15 And many signs, and wonders, and *a*types, and shadows showed he unto them, concerning his coming; and also holy prophets spake unto them concerning his coming; and yet they *b*hardened their hearts, and understood not that the *c*law of Moses availeth nothing *d*except it were through the *e*atonement of his blood.

16 And even if it were possible that little *a*children could sin they could not be saved; but I say unto you they are *b*blessed; for behold, as in Adam, or by nature, they fall, even so the blood of Christ *c*atoneth for their sins.

17 And moreover, I say unto you, that there shall be *a*no other name given nor any other way nor means whereby *b*salvation can come unto the children of men, only in and through the name of Christ, the *c*Lord Omnipotent.

18 For behold he judgeth, and his judgment is just; and the infant perisheth not that dieth in his infancy; but men drink *a*damnation to their own souls except they humble themselves and *b*become as little children, and believe that *c*salvation was, and is, and is to come, in and through the *d*atoning blood of Christ, the Lord Omnipotent.

19 For the *a*natural *b*man is an *c*enemy to God, and has been from the *d*fall of Adam, and will be, forever and ever, unless he *e*yields to the enticings of the *f*Holy Spirit, and *g*putteth off the *h*natural man and becometh a *i*saint through the atonement of Christ the Lord, and becometh as a *j*child, *k*submissive, meek, humble, patient, full of love, willing to submit to all things which the Lord seeth fit to inflict upon him, even as a child doth submit to his father.

20 And moreover, I say unto you, that the time shall come when the *a*knowledge of a *b*Savior shall spread throughout *c*every nation, kindred, tongue, and people.

21 And behold, when that time cometh, none shall be found *a*blameless before God, except it be little children, only through repentance and faith on the name of the Lord God Omnipotent.

22 And even at this time, when thou shalt have taught thy people the things which the Lord thy God hath commanded thee, even then

---

14*a* 2 Ne. 25:28; Alma 9:31.
  TG Stiffnecked.
  b Josh. 1:8;
     Mosiah 13:29 (29–32);
     Alma 25:15 (15–16);
     D&C 41:5 (4–5).
  c TG Law of Moses.
15*a* TG Jesus Christ, Types of, in Anticipation; Passover; Symbolism.
  b TG Hardheartedness.
  c Heb. 10:1;
     Mosiah 12:31;
     13:28 (27–32);
     Alma 25:16.
  d 2 Ne. 11:6.
  e Lev. 4:20;
     Matt. 26:54 (51–56).
16*a* TG Conceived in Sin.
  b TG Salvation of Little Children.
  c Moro. 8:8 (8–9);
     Moses 6:54 (54–56).

TG Jesus Christ, Atonement through.
17*a* Acts 4:12 (10–12);
     2 Ne. 31:21;
     Mosiah 4:8 (7–8);
     3 Ne. 9:17.
  b Matt. 7:14 (13–14).
     TG Jesus Christ, Savior; Salvation, Plan of.
  c TG Jesus Christ, Lord.
18*a* 1 Cor. 11:29.
  b Matt. 18:3.
  c TG Salvation.
  d Mosiah 4:2; Hel. 5:9.
19*a* Gen. 8:21;
     1 Cor. 2:14 (11–14);
     2 Pet. 2:12; Mosiah 16:3;
     Alma 41:11; Ether 3:2.
     TG Man, Natural, Not Spiritually Reborn; Worldliness.
  b TG Mortality.
  c James 4:4.

TG Enemies.
  d TG Fall of Man.
  e 2 Chr. 30:8;
     Rom. 6:13 (12–14).
  f Rom. 8:4 (1–9).
     TG Guidance, Divine.
  g Alma 19:6.
  h Col. 3:9; D&C 67:12.
  i Luke 22:32 (31–38).
     TG Man, New, Spiritually Reborn; Saints; Spirituality.
  j Matt. 18:3;
     1 Pet. 2:2 (1–3);
     3 Ne. 9:22.
  k TG Self-Mastery; Submissiveness.
20*a* D&C 3:16.
  b TG Jesus Christ, Savior.
  c Mosiah 16:1.
     TG Missionary Work.
21*a* Col. 1:22; D&C 4:2.
     TG Accountability.

are they found no more blameless in the sight of God, only according to the words which I have spoken unto thee.

23 And now I have spoken the words which the Lord God hath commanded me.

24 And thus saith the Lord: They shall stand as a bright testimony against this people, at the judgment day; whereof they shall be judged, every man according to his ᵃworks, whether they be good, or whether they be evil.

25 And if they be evil they are consigned to an awful ᵃview of their own guilt and abominations, which doth cause them to shrink from the presence of the Lord into a state of ᵇmisery and ᶜendless torment, from whence they can no more return; therefore they have drunk damnation to their own souls.

26 Therefore, they have drunk out of the ᵃcup of the wrath of God, which justice could no more deny unto them than it could deny that ᵇAdam should fall because of his partaking of the forbidden ᶜfruit; therefore, ᵈmercy could have claim on them no more forever.

27 And their ᵃtorment is as a ᵇlake of fire and brimstone, whose flames are unquenchable, and whose smoke ascendeth up ᶜforever and ever. Thus hath the Lord commanded me. Amen.

CHAPTER 4

King Benjamin continues his address—Salvation comes because of the Atonement—Believe in God to be saved—Retain a remission of your sins through faithfulness—Impart of your substance to the poor—Do all things in wisdom and order. About 124 B.C.

AND now, it came to pass that when king Benjamin had made an end of speaking the words which had been delivered unto him by the ᵃangel of the Lord, that he cast his eyes round about on the multitude, and behold they had ᵇfallen to the earth, for the ᶜfear of the Lord had come upon them.

2 And they had ᵃviewed themselves in their own ᵇcarnal state, even ᶜless than the dust of the earth. And they all cried aloud with one voice, saying: O have mercy, and apply the ᵈatoning blood of Christ that we may receive forgiveness of our sins, and our hearts may be ᵉpurified; for we believe in Jesus Christ, the Son of God, who ᶠcreated heaven and earth, and all things; who shall come down among the children of men.

3 And it came to pass that after they had spoken these words the Spirit of the Lord came upon them, and they were filled with joy, having received a ᵃremission of their sins, and having peace of ᵇconscience, because of the exceeding ᶜfaith which they had in Jesus Christ who should come, according to the ᵈwords which king Benjamin had spoken unto them.

4 And king Benjamin again opened his mouth and began to speak unto them, saying: My friends and my brethren, my kindred and my people, I would again call your attention, that ye may hear and

24a TG Good Works.
25a 2 Ne. 9:14, 46;
     Alma 5:18; 11:43;
     12:15 (14–15).
  b Rom. 3:16;
     Morm. 8:38.
  c TG Punish.
26a Ps. 75:8;
     Jer. 25:15;
     Lam. 4:21.
  b Morm. 9:12;
     Moro. 8:8.
  c Gen. 3:6;
     2 Ne. 2:15 (15–19);

       Alma 12:22 (21–23).
  d TG Mercy.
27a TG Hell.
  b 2 Ne. 9:16;
     Jacob 6:10;
     Alma 12:17;
     D&C 76:36.
  c Mosiah 5:5.
4 1a 1 Chr. 21:18;
     Mosiah 3:2.
  b Neh. 8:9;
     Alma 19:17.
  c Jer. 36:16;
     Heb. 12:28.

     TG Reverence.
2a TG Poor in Spirit.
  b Neh. 9:1 (1–3).
     TG Carnal Mind.
  c Gen. 18:27.
  d Mosiah 3:18;
     Hel. 5:9.
  e TG Purification.
  f TG Jesus Christ, Creator.
3a TG Remission of Sins.
  b TG Conscience.
  c TG Faith.
  d Neh. 8:12.

understand the remainder of my words which I shall speak unto you.

5 For behold, if the knowledge of the goodness of God at this time has awakened you to a sense of your [a]nothingness, and your worthless and fallen state—

6 I say unto you, if ye have come to a [a]knowledge of the goodness of God, and his matchless power, and his wisdom, and his patience, and his long-suffering towards the children of men; and also, the [b]atonement which has been prepared from the [c]foundation of the world, that thereby salvation might come to him that should put his [d]trust in the Lord, and should be diligent in keeping his commandments, and continue in the faith even unto the end of his life, I mean the life of the mortal body—

7 I say, that this is the man who receiveth salvation, through the atonement which was prepared from the foundation of the world for all mankind, which ever were since the [a]fall of Adam, or who are, or who ever shall be, even unto the end of the world.

8 And this is the means whereby salvation cometh. And there is [a]none other salvation save this which hath been spoken of; neither are there any conditions whereby man can be saved except the conditions which I have told you.

9 Believe in [a]God; believe that he is, and that he [b]created all things, both in heaven and in earth; believe that he has all [c]wisdom, and all power, both in heaven and in earth;

believe that man doth not [d]comprehend all the things which the Lord can comprehend.

10 And again, believe that ye must [a]repent of your sins and forsake them, and humble yourselves before God; and ask in [b]sincerity of heart that he would [c]forgive you; and now, if you [d]believe all these things see that ye [e]do them.

11 And again I say unto you as I have said before, that as ye have come to the knowledge of the glory of God, or if ye have known of his goodness and have [a]tasted of his love, and have received a [b]remission of your sins, which causeth such exceedingly great joy in your souls, even so I would that ye should remember, and always retain in remembrance, the greatness of God, and your own [c]nothingness, and his [d]goodness and long-suffering towards you, unworthy creatures, and humble yourselves even in the depths of [e]humility, [f]calling on the name of the Lord daily, and standing [g]steadfastly in the faith of that which is to come, which was spoken by the mouth of the angel.

12 And behold, I say unto you that if ye do this ye shall always rejoice, and be filled with the [a]love of God, and always [b]retain a remission of your sins; and ye shall grow in the [c]knowledge of the glory of him that created you, or in the knowledge of that which is just and true.

13 And ye will not have a [a]mind to injure one another, but to live [b]peaceably, and to render to every

---

5a Moses 1:10.
6a TG God, Knowledge about; God, Perfection of.
  b TG Jesus Christ, Atonement through.
  c Mosiah 15:19; 18:13.
  d Ps. 36:7 (7–8); 2 Ne. 22:2; Hel. 12:1. TG Trust in God.
7a TG Fall of Man.
8a Acts 4:12; 2 Ne. 31:21; Mosiah 3:17.
9a Deut. 4:39.
  b TG God, Creator; Jesus Christ, Creator.

c Rom. 11:34 (33–36); Jacob 4:8 (8–13). TG God, Perfection of.
  d Isa. 55:9.
10a TG Repent.
  b TG Sincere.
  c Ps. 41:4; D&C 61:2.
  d Matt. 7:24 (24–27); Acts 16:31 (30–31).
  e 2 Ne. 31:19 (19–21).
11a Ps. 34:8; Alma 36:24 (24–26).
  b TG Remission of Sins.
  c Rom. 5:8 (6–8); Moses 1:10.

d Ex. 34:6 (5–7); Moro. 8:3.
  e TG Humility.
  f TG Prayer.
  g TG Steadfastness.
12a TG God, Love of.
  b Mosiah 4:26; Alma 4:14 (13–14); 5:26 (26–35); D&C 20:32 (31–34).
  c TG God, Knowledge about.
13a TG Man, New, Spiritually Reborn.
  b TG Peacemakers.

man according to that which is his due.

14 And ye will not suffer your ᵃchildren that they go hungry, or naked; neither will ye ᵇsuffer that they transgress the laws of God, and fight and ᶜquarrel one with another, and serve the devil, who is the master of sin, or who is the ᵈevil spirit which hath been spoken of by our fathers, he being an enemy to all righteousness.

15 But ye will ᵃteach them to ᵇwalk in the ways of truth and ᶜsoberness; ye will teach them to ᵈlove one another, and to serve one another.

16 And also, ye yourselves will ᵃsuccor those that stand in need of your succor; ye will administer of your substance unto him that standeth in need; and ye will not suffer that the ᵇbeggar putteth up his petition to you in vain, and turn him out to perish.

17 Perhaps thou shalt ᵃsay: The man has brought upon himself his misery; therefore I will stay my hand, and will not give unto him of my food, nor impart unto him of my substance that he may not suffer, for his punishments are just—

18 But I say unto you, O man, whosoever doeth this the same hath great cause to repent; and except he repenteth of that which he hath done he perisheth forever, and hath no interest in the kingdom of God.

19 For behold, are we not all ᵃbeggars? Do we not all depend upon the same Being, even God, for all the substance which we have, for both food and raiment, and for gold, and for silver, and for all the riches which we have of every kind?

20 And behold, even at this time, ye have been calling on his name, and begging for a ᵃremission of your sins. And has he suffered that ye have begged in vain? Nay; he has poured out his ᵇSpirit upon you, and has caused that your hearts should be filled with ᶜjoy, and has caused that your mouths should be stopped that ye could not find utterance, so exceedingly great was your joy.

21 And now, if God, who has created you, on whom you are dependent for your lives and for all that ye have and are, doth grant unto you whatsoever ye ask that is right, in faith, believing that ye shall receive, O then, how ye ought to ᵃimpart of the substance that ye have one to another.

22 And if ye ᵃjudge the man who putteth up his petition to you for your substance that he perish not, and condemn him, how much more just will be your ᵇcondemnation for withholding your substance, which doth not belong to you but to God, to whom also your life ᶜbelongeth; and yet ye put up no petition, nor repent of the thing which thou hast done.

23 I say unto you, wo be unto that man, for his substance shall perish with him; and now, I say these things unto those who are ᵃrich as pertaining to the things of this world.

24 And again, I say unto the poor, ye who have not and yet have sufficient, that ye remain from day to day; I mean all you who deny

14a 1 Tim. 5:8;
  D&C 83:4.
  TG Marriage,
  Fatherhood.
 b Prov. 13:24.
 c TG Contention.
 d 2 Ne. 32:8;
  Mosiah 2:32.
15a Mosiah 1:2;
  Moses 6:58 (58–63).
  TG Family, Children,
  Responsibilities toward.
 b TG Walking with God.
 c TG Sincere.

 d 1 Sam. 18:1;
  Mosiah 18:21.
  TG Family, Love within.
16a Prov. 19:17.
  TG Charity;
  Service;
  Welfare.
 b Prov. 21:13;
  Isa. 10:2;
  Luke 3:11;
  D&C 38:16.
17a Prov. 17:5.
19a Prov. 22:2;
  1 Cor. 4:7.

20a Rom. 2:4 (1–4).
 b TG God, Spirit of.
 c TG Joy.
21a Dan. 4:27.
  TG Generosity;
  Welfare.
22a Matt. 7:2 (1–2);
  John 7:24.
 b 1 Jn. 3:17.
 c Mosiah 2:25.
23a Luke 21:1 (1–4);
  D&C 56:16.

the beggar, because ye have not; I would that ye say in your hearts that: I *a*give not because I *b*have not, but if I had I would *c*give.

25 And now, if ye say this in your hearts ye remain guiltless, otherwise ye are *a*condemned; and your condemnation is just for ye covet that which ye have not received.

26 And now, for the sake of these things which I have spoken unto you—that is, for the sake of retaining a remission of your sins from day to day, that ye may *a*walk guiltless before God—I would that ye should *b*impart of your substance to the *c*poor, every man according to that which he hath, such as *d*feeding the hungry, clothing the naked, visiting the sick and administering to their relief, both spiritually and temporally, according to their wants.

27 And see that all these things are done in wisdom and *a*order; for it is not requisite that a man should run *b*faster than he has strength. And again, it is expedient that he should be diligent, that thereby he might win the prize; therefore, all things must be done in order.

28 And I would that ye should remember, that whosoever among you *a*borroweth of his neighbor should return the thing that he borroweth, according as he doth agree, or else thou shalt commit sin; and perhaps thou shalt cause thy neighbor to commit sin also.

29 And finally, I cannot tell you all the things whereby ye may commit sin; for there are divers ways and means, even so many that I cannot number them.

30 But this much I can tell you, that if ye do not *a*watch yourselves, and your *b*thoughts, and your *c*words, and your deeds, and observe the commandments of God, and *d*continue in the faith of what ye have heard concerning the coming of our Lord, even unto the end of your lives, ye must perish. And now, O man, remember, and perish not.

CHAPTER 5

The Saints become the sons and daughters of Christ through faith—They are then called by the name of Christ—King Benjamin exhorts them to be steadfast and immovable in good works. About 124 B.C.

AND now, it came to pass that when king Benjamin had thus spoken to his people, he sent among them, desiring to know of his people if they *a*believed the words which he had spoken unto them.

2 And they all cried with one voice, saying: Yea, we believe all the words which thou hast spoken unto us; and also, we know of their surety and truth, because of the Spirit of the Lord Omnipotent, which has wrought a mighty *a*change in us, or in our hearts, that we have no more disposition to do *b*evil, but to do good continually.

3 And we, ourselves, also, through the infinite *a*goodness of God, and the manifestations of his Spirit, have great views of that which is to come; and were it expedient, we could prophesy of all things.

4 And it is the faith which we have had on the things which our king has spoken unto us that has brought

24*a* Deut. 16:17.
  b Acts 3:6 (5–7).
  c Mark 12:44.
25*a* D&C 56:17.
26*a* TG Walking with God.
  b Jacob 2:19 (17–19);
     Mosiah 21:17;
     Alma 35:9.
  c Job 29:12;
     Zech. 7:10;
     Luke 18:22; Alma 1:27.
     TG Almsgiving.

  d Isa. 58:10 (9–11);
     Alma 4:12 (12–13);
     3 Ne. 12:42.
27*a* TG Order.
  b Eccl. 9:11;
     Alma 1:26;
     D&C 10:4.
28*a* TG Borrow; Debt;
     Honesty.
30*a* Deut. 4:9;
     Alma 12:14.
     TG Watch.

  b Matt. 5:28 (27–28);
     Mark 7:23 (15–23).
  c Matt. 15:18 (18–20).
     TG Gossip.
  d TG Steadfastness.
5 1*a* 1 Ne. 11:4 (1–5).
2*a* Rom. 8:2 (1–4);
     Alma 5:14; 13:12.
     TG Man, New, Spiritually
     Reborn.
  b Alma 19:33.
3*a* Ex. 34:6 (5–7).

us to this great knowledge, whereby we do rejoice with such exceedingly great joy.

5 And we are willing to enter into a ^acovenant with our God to do his will, and to be obedient to his commandments in all things that he shall command us, all the remainder of our days, that we may not bring upon ourselves a ^bnever-ending torment, as has been spoken by the ^cangel, that we may not drink out of the cup of the wrath of God.

6 And now, these are the words which king Benjamin desired of them; and therefore he said unto them: Ye have spoken the words that I desired; and the covenant which ye have made is a righteous covenant.

7 And now, because of the covenant which ye have made ye shall be called the ^achildren of Christ, his sons, and his daughters; for behold, this day he hath spiritually begotten you; for ye say that your hearts are ^bchanged through faith on his name; therefore, ye are ^cborn of him and have become his ^dsons and his daughters.

8 And under this head ye are made ^afree, and there is ^bno other head whereby ye can be made free. There is no other ^cname given whereby salvation cometh; therefore, I would that ye should ^dtake upon you the name of Christ, all you that have entered into the covenant with God that ye should be obedient unto the end of your lives.

9 And it shall come to pass that whosoever doeth this shall be found at the right hand of God, for he shall know the name by which he is called; for he shall be called by the name of Christ.

10 And now it shall come to pass, that whosoever shall not take upon him the name of Christ must be called by some ^aother name; therefore, he findeth himself on the ^bleft hand of God.

11 And I would that ye should remember also, that this is the ^aname that I said I should give unto you that never should be blotted out, except it be through transgression; therefore, take heed that ye do not transgress, that the name be not blotted out of your hearts.

12 I say unto you, I would that ye should remember to ^aretain the name written always in your hearts, that ye are not found on the left hand of God, but that ye hear and know the voice by which ye shall be called, and also, the name by which he shall call you.

13 For how ^aknoweth a man the master whom he has not served, and who is a stranger unto him, and is far from the thoughts and intents of his heart?

14 And again, doth a man take an ass which belongeth to his neighbor, and keep him? I say unto you, Nay; he will not even suffer that he shall feed among his flocks, but will drive him away, and cast him out. I say unto you, that even so shall it be among you if ye know not the name by which ye are called.

15 Therefore, I would that ye should be steadfast and immovable, always abounding in ^agood works, that Christ, the ^bLord God Omnipotent,

5a 2 Chr. 15:12 (12–15);
    Neh. 10:29;
    Mosiah 6:3.
    TG Commitment.
  b Mosiah 3:27 (25–27).
  c Mosiah 3:2.
7a 1 Jn. 2:12;
    Mosiah 15:2;
    27:25 (24–26);
    Moses 6:68 (64–68).
  b TG Sanctification.
  c John 1:13 (12–13);
    Mosiah 15:10.

TG Man, New, Spiritually
    Reborn.
  d Matt. 12:49 (49–50);
    D&C 11:30.
8a Rom. 6:18 (14–22);
    1 Cor. 7:22;
    Gal. 5:1; D&C 88:86.
  b Acts 4:12;
    Mosiah 4:8; Alma 21:9.
  c Gal. 3:27;
    Mosiah 1:11; 26:18.
  d Acts 11:26;
    Alma 46:15.

10a Alma 5:39 (38–42).
  b Matt. 25:33.
11a Mosiah 1:11 (11–12).
    TG Jesus Christ, Taking
    the Name of.
12a Num. 6:27;
    Ps. 119:55;
    D&C 18:25.
13a Jer. 4:22;
    Mosiah 26:25 (24–27).
15a TG Good Works.
  b TG Jesus Christ, Jehovah;
    Jesus Christ, Lord.

may ^cseal you his, that you may be brought to heaven, that ye may have everlasting salvation and eternal life, through the wisdom, and power, and justice, and mercy of him who ^dcreated all things, in heaven and in earth, who is God above all. Amen.

CHAPTER 6

King Benjamin records the names of the people and appoints priests to teach them—Mosiah reigns as a righteous king. About 124–121 B.C.

AND now, king Benjamin thought it was expedient, after having finished speaking to the people, that he should ^atake the names of all those who had entered into a covenant with God to keep his commandments.

2 And it came to pass that there was not one soul, except it were little children, but who had entered into the covenant and had taken upon them the name of Christ.

3 And again, it came to pass that when king Benjamin had made an end of all these things, and had consecrated his son ^aMosiah to be a ruler and a king over his people, and had given him all the charges concerning the kingdom, and also had ^bappointed ^cpriests to ^dteach the people, that thereby they might hear and know the commandments of God, and to stir them up in remembrance of the ^eoath which they had made, he dismissed the multitude, and they returned, every one, according to their ^ffamilies, to their own houses.

4 And Mosiah began to reign in his father's stead. And he began to reign in the thirtieth year of his age, making in the whole, about four hundred and seventy-six

years from the ^atime that Lehi left Jerusalem.

5 And king Benjamin lived three years and he died.

6 And it came to pass that king Mosiah did ^awalk in the ways of the Lord, and did observe his judgments and his statutes, and did keep his commandments in all things whatsoever he commanded him.

7 And king Mosiah did cause his people that they should till the earth. And he also, himself, did till the earth, that thereby he might ^anot become burdensome to his people, that he might do according to that which his father had done in all things. And there was no contention among all his people for the space of three years.

CHAPTER 7

Ammon finds the land of Lehi-Nephi, where Limhi is king—Limhi's people are in bondage to the Lamanites—Limhi recounts their history—A prophet (Abinadi) had testified that Christ is the God and Father of all things—Those who sow filthiness reap the whirlwind, and those who put their trust in the Lord will be delivered. About 121 B.C.

AND now, it came to pass that after king Mosiah had had continual peace for the space of three years, he was desirous to know concerning the people who ^awent up to dwell in the land of ^bLehi-Nephi, or in the city of Lehi-Nephi; for his people had heard nothing from them from the time they left the land of ^cZarahemla; therefore, they wearied him with their teasings.

2 And it came to pass that king Mosiah granted that sixteen of their strong men might go up to the land of Lehi-Nephi, to inquire concerning their brethren.

15*c* TG Election.
   d Col. 1:16;
     Mosiah 4:2;
     Alma 11:39.
6 1*a* D&C 128:8.
  3*a* Mosiah 1:10; 2:30.
   b TG Priesthood,

     Ordination.
   c Mosiah 29:42.
   d Alma 4:7.
   e Mosiah 5:5 (5–7).
   f Num. 1:2;
     Ether 1:41;
     D&C 48:6.

  4*a* 1 Ne. 1:4; 2:4.
  6*a* TG Walking with God.
  7*a* 2 Cor. 11:9.
7 1*a* Omni 1:27 (27–30).
   b 2 Ne. 5:8;
     Mosiah 9:6.
   c Omni 1:13.

3 And it came to pass that on the morrow they started to go up, having with them one ^aAmmon, he being a strong and mighty man, and a ^bdescendant of Zarahemla; and he was also their leader.

4 And now, they knew not the course they should travel in the wilderness to go up to the land of Lehi-Nephi; therefore they wandered many days in the wilderness, even ^aforty days did they wander.

5 And when they had wandered forty days they came to a ^ahill, which is north of the land of ^bShilom, and there they pitched their tents.

6 And ^aAmmon took three of his brethren, and their names were Amaleki, Helem, and Hem, and they went down into the land of ^bNephi.

7 And behold, they met the king of the people who were in the land of Nephi, and in the land of ^aShilom; and they were surrounded by the king's guard, and were ^btaken, and were ^cbound, and were committed to ^dprison.

8 And it came to pass when they had been in prison two days they were again brought before the king, and their bands were loosed; and they stood before the king, and were permitted, or rather ^acommanded, that they should answer the questions which he should ask them.

9 And he said unto them: Behold, I am ^aLimhi, the son of Noah, who was the son of Zeniff, who came up out of the ^bland of Zarahemla to inherit this land, which was the land of their fathers, who was made a ^cking by the ^dvoice of the people.

10 And now, ^aI desire to know the cause whereby ye were so bold as to come near the walls of the city, when I, myself, was with my guards without the ^bgate?

11 And now, for this cause have I suffered that ye should be preserved, that I might inquire of you, or else I should have caused that my guards should have put you to death. Ye are permitted to speak.

12 And now, when Ammon saw that he was permitted to speak, he went forth and ^abowed himself before the king; and rising again he said: O king, I am very thankful before God this day that I am yet alive, and am permitted to speak; and I will endeavor to speak with boldness;

13 For I am assured that if ye had known me ye would not have suffered that I should have worn these bands. For I am Ammon, and am a ^adescendant of Zarahemla, and have come up out of the ^bland of Zarahemla to inquire concerning our brethren, whom ^cZeniff brought up out of that land.

14 And now, it came to pass that after Limhi had heard the words of Ammon, he was exceedingly ^aglad, and said: Now, I know of a surety that my brethren who were in the land of Zarahemla are ^byet alive. And now, I will rejoice; and on the morrow I will cause that my people shall rejoice also.

15 For behold, we are in bondage to the Lamanites, and are ^ataxed with a tax which is grievous to be borne. And now, behold, our brethren will deliver us out of our ^bbondage, or out of the hands of the

3 a Mosiah 8:2.
  b Omni 1:14.
4 a Num. 13:25 (17–25).
5 a Mosiah 11:13.
  b Mosiah 9:14 (6, 8, 14);
    11:12 (12–13); 22:11 (8, 11);
    Alma 23:12.
6 a Mosiah 21:22, 26.
  b 2 Ne. 5:8;
    Omni 1:12 (12, 27);
    Mosiah 9:1 (1, 3–4, 14);

28:1 (1, 5);
    Alma 50:8 (8, 11).
7 a Mosiah 22:8.
  b Mosiah 21:21.
  c Alma 17:20.
  d Mosiah 21:23 (22–24).
8 a Alma 14:19.
9 a Mosiah 11:1; 19:16.
  b Omni 1:13.
  c TG Kings, Earthly.
  d Mosiah 19:26.

10 a Mosiah 21:23 (23–24).
  b Josh. 20:4.
12 a Alma 47:22 (22–23).
13 a Omni 1:14.
  b Omni 1:13.
  c Mosiah 8:2; 9:1.
14 a Mosiah 21:24.
  b Mosiah 21:25 (25–26).
15 a Mosiah 19:15.
  b TG Bondage, Physical.

Lamanites, and we will be their ᶜslaves; for it is better that we be slaves to the Nephites than to pay tribute to the king of the Lamanites.

16 And now, king Limhi commanded his guards that they should no more bind Ammon nor his brethren, but caused that they should go to the hill which was north of Shilom, and bring their brethren into the city, that thereby they might eat, and drink, and rest themselves from the labors of their journey; for they had suffered many things; they had suffered hunger, thirst, and fatigue.

17 And now, it came to pass on the morrow that king Limhi sent a proclamation among all his people, that thereby they might gather themselves together to the ᵃtemple, to hear the words which he should speak unto them.

18 And it came to pass that when they had gathered themselves together that he ᵃspake unto them in this wise, saying: O ye, my people, lift up your heads and be comforted; for behold, the time is at hand, or is not far distant, when we shall no longer be in subjection to our enemies, notwithstanding our many strugglings, which have been in vain; yet I trust there ᵇremaineth an effectual struggle to be made.

19 Therefore, lift up your heads, and rejoice, and put your ᵃtrust in ᵇGod, in that God who was the God of Abraham, and Isaac, and Jacob; and also, that God who ᶜbrought the children of ᵈIsrael out of the land of Egypt, and caused that they should walk through the ᵉRed Sea on dry ground, and fed them with ᶠmanna that they might not perish in the wilderness; and many more things did he do for them.

20 And again, that same God has brought our fathers ᵃout of the land of Jerusalem, and has kept and preserved his people even until now; and behold, it is ᵇbecause of our iniquities and abominations that he has brought us into bondage.

21 And ye all are witnesses this day, that Zeniff, who was made king over this people, he being ᵃoverzealous to inherit the land of his fathers, therefore being deceived by the cunning and craftiness of king Laman, who having entered into a treaty with king Zeniff, and having yielded up into his hands the possessions of a part of the land, or even the city of Lehi-Nephi, and the city of Shilom; and the land round about—

22 And all this he did, for the sole purpose of ᵃbringing this people into subjection or into bondage. And behold, we at this time do pay ᵇtribute to the king of the Lamanites, to the amount of one half of our corn, and our barley, and even all our grain of every kind, and one half of the increase of our flocks and our herds; and even one half of all we have or possess the king of the Lamanites doth exact of us, or our lives.

23 And now, is not this grievous to be borne? And is not this, our affliction, great? Now behold, how great reason we have to ᵃmourn.

24 Yea, I say unto you, great are the reasons which we have to ᵃmourn; for behold how many of our brethren have been slain, and their blood has been spilt in vain, and all because of iniquity.

25 For if this people had not fallen into transgression the Lord would not have suffered that this great evil should come upon them. But behold,

15c TG Slavery.
17a 2 Ne. 5:16.
18a Mosiah 8:1.
  b Mosiah 22:1 (1–16).
19a TG Trust in God.
  b Ex. 3:6 (2–10);
    1 Ne. 19:10;
    D&C 136:21.
  c Ex. 12:51; 1 Ne. 17:40;

Mosiah 12:34;
    Alma 36:28.
  d TG Israel, Origins of.
  e Josh. 2:10;
    1 Ne. 4:2; 17:26.
  f Ex. 16:15, 35;
    Num. 11:7 (7–8);
    Josh. 5:12;
    John 6:49;

1 Ne. 17:28.
20a 1 Ne. 2:2 (1–4).
  b Deut. 28:15 (1–2, 15–68).
21a Mosiah 9:3 (1–3).
22a Mosiah 9:10; 10:18.
  b TG Tribute.
23a Prov. 29:2.
24a Ezek. 24:23;
    Hel. 9:22.

they would not hearken unto his words; but there arose contentions among them, even so much that they did shed blood among themselves.

26 And a *a*prophet of the Lord have they *b*slain; yea, a chosen man of God, who told them of their wickedness and abominations, and prophesied of many things which are to come, yea, even the coming of Christ.

27 And because he said unto them that Christ was the *a*God, the Father of all things, and said that he should take upon him the *b*image of man, and it should be the *c*image after which man was created in the beginning; or in other words, he said that man was created after the image of *d*God, and that God should come down among the children of men, and take upon him flesh and blood, and go forth upon the face of the earth—

28 And now, because he said this, they did *a*put him to death; and many more things did they do which brought down the wrath of God upon them. Therefore, who wondereth that they are in bondage, and that they are smitten with sore afflictions?

29 For behold, the Lord hath said: I will not *a*succor my people in the day of their transgression; but I will hedge up their ways that they prosper not; and their doings shall be as a *b*stumbling block before them.

30 And again, he saith: If my people shall sow *a*filthiness they shall *b*reap the *c*chaff thereof in the whirlwind; and the effect thereof is poison.

31 And again he saith: If my

people shall sow filthiness they shall reap the *a*east wind, which bringeth immediate destruction.

32 And now, behold, the promise of the Lord is fulfilled, and ye are smitten and afflicted.

33 But if ye will *a*turn to the Lord with full purpose of heart, and put your trust in him, and serve him with all *b*diligence of mind, if ye do this, he will, according to his own will and pleasure, deliver you out of bondage.

CHAPTER 8

Ammon teaches the people of Limhi— He learns of the twenty-four Jaredite plates—Ancient records can be translated by seers—No gift is greater than seership. About 121 B.C.

AND it came to pass that after king Limhi had made an end of *a*speaking to his people, for he spake many things unto them and only a few of them have I written in this book, he told his people all the things concerning their brethren who were in the land of Zarahemla.

2 And he caused that Ammon should stand up before the multitude, and rehearse unto them all that had happened unto their brethren from the time that *a*Zeniff went up out of the land even until the time that he *b*himself came up out of the land.

3 And he also rehearsed unto them the last words which king Benjamin had *a*taught them, and explained them to the people of king Limhi, so that they might understand all the words which he spake.

26a Mosiah 17:20 (12–20).
  b TG Prophets, Rejection of.
27a Isa. 9:6;
    2 Ne. 26:12;
    Mosiah 27:31 (30–31).
  b TG God, Body of, Corporeal Nature.
  c Gen. 1:26 (26–28);
    Ether 3:15 (14–17);
    D&C 20:18 (17–18).
  d Mosiah 13:34; 15:2 (1–7);
    Alma 7:9 (9–13).

28a Mosiah 17:13.
29a Josh. 24:20;
    1 Sam. 12:15;
    2 Chr. 24:20.
  b Jer. 6:21.
30a TG Filthiness.
  b Hosea 8:7;
    Gal. 6:8 (7–8);
    D&C 6:33.
    TG Harvest.
  c Luke 3:17;
    2 Ne. 15:24.
31a Gen. 41:23;

    Jer. 18:17;
    Ezek. 27:26;
    Jonah 4:8;
    Mosiah 12:6.
33a Deut. 30:10;
    Lam. 5:21;
    Morm. 9:6;
    D&C 98:47.
  b TG Diligence.
8 1a Mosiah 7:18 (18–33).
  2a Mosiah 7:13.
  b Mosiah 7:3.
  3a Mosiah 2:9.

4 And it came to pass that after he had done all this, that king Limhi dismissed the multitude, and caused that they should return every one unto his own house.

5 And it came to pass that he caused that the ªplates which contained the ᵇrecord of his people from the time that they left the ᶜland of Zarahemla, should be brought before Ammon, that he might read them.

6 Now, as soon as Ammon had read the record, the king inquired of him to know if he could ªinterpret languages, and Ammon told him that he could not.

7 And the king said unto him: Being grieved for the afflictions of my people, I caused that ªforty and three of my people should take a journey into the wilderness, that thereby they might find the land of Zarahemla, that we might appeal unto our brethren to deliver us out of bondage.

8 And they were lost in the wilderness for the space of ªmany days, yet they were diligent, and found not the land of Zarahemla but returned to this land, having traveled in a land among many waters, having discovered a land which was covered with ᵇbones of men, and of beasts, and was also covered with ruins of buildings of every kind, having discovered a land which had been peopled with a people who were as numerous as the hosts of Israel.

9 And for a testimony that the things that they had said are true they have brought ªtwenty-four plates which are filled with engravings, and they are of pure gold.

10 And behold, also, they have brought ªbreastplates, which are large, and they are of ᵇbrass and of copper, and are perfectly sound.

11 And again, they have brought swords, the hilts thereof have perished, and the blades thereof were cankered with rust; and there is no one in the land that is able to interpret the language or the engravings that are on the plates. Therefore I said unto thee: Canst thou translate?

12 And I say unto thee again: Knowest thou of any one that can translate? For I am desirous that these records should be translated into our language; for, perhaps, they will give us a knowledge of a remnant of the people who have been destroyed, from whence these records came; or, perhaps, they will give us a knowledge of this very people who have been destroyed; and I am desirous to know the cause of their destruction.

13 Now Ammon said unto him: I can assuredly tell thee, O king, of a man that can ªtranslate the records; for he has wherewith that he can look, and translate all records that are of ancient date; and it is a gift from God. And the things are called ᵇinterpreters, and no man can look in them except he be commanded, lest he should look for that he ought not and he should perish. And whosoever is commanded to look in them, the same is called ᶜseer.

14 And behold, the king of the people who are in the land of Zarahemla is the man that is commanded to do these things, and who has this high gift from God.

15 And the king said that a ªseer is greater than a prophet.

16 And Ammon said that a seer is a revelator and a prophet also; and a gift which is greater can no man

---

5a See Mosiah 9–22.
  b Mosiah 9:1; 22:14.
  c Omni 1:13.
6a 1 Cor. 12:10;
    Mosiah 21:28.
7a Mosiah 21:25.
8a Alma 50:29;
    Hel. 3:4 (3–4);

Morm. 6:4.
  b Omni 1:22;
    Mosiah 21:26 (26–27).
9a Mosiah 21:27; 22:14.
10a Ex. 25:7;
    Ether 15:15.
  b Ether 10:23.
13a Dan. 5:16;

Omni 1:20 (20–22);
    Mosiah 28:17 (11–17).
  b Ex. 28:30;
    Mosiah 21:28 (27–28).
    TG Urim and Thummim.
  c TG Seer.
15a 1 Sam. 9:9;
    D&C 21:1.

have, except he should possess the power of God, which no man can; yet a man may have great power given him from God.

17 But a seer can know of things which are past, and also of things which are to come, and by them shall all things be revealed, or, rather, shall secret things be made manifest, and hidden things shall come to light, and things which are not known shall be made known by them, and also things shall be made known by them which otherwise could not be known.

18 Thus God has provided a means that man, through faith, might work mighty miracles; therefore he becometh a great benefit to his fellow beings.

19 And now, when Ammon had made an end of speaking these words the king rejoiced exceedingly, and gave thanks to God, saying: Doubtless a *great mystery is contained within these plates, and these interpreters were doubtless prepared for the purpose of unfolding all such mysteries to the children of men.

20 O how marvelous are the works of the Lord, and how long doth he suffer with his people; yea, and how *blind and impenetrable are the understandings of the children of men; for they will not seek wisdom, neither do they desire that *she should rule over them!

21 Yea, they are as a wild flock which fleeth from the shepherd, and scattereth, and are driven, and are devoured by the beasts of the forest.

THE RECORD OF ZENIFF—An account of his people, from the time they left the land of Zarahemla until the time that they were delivered out of the hands of the Lamanites.

Comprising chapters 9 through 22.

CHAPTER 9

Zeniff leads a group from Zarahemla to possess the land of Lehi-Nephi—The Lamanite king permits them to inherit the land—There is war between the Lamanites and Zeniff's people. About 200–187 B.C.

*I, *ZENIFF, having been taught in all the language of the Nephites, and having had a knowledge of the land of *Nephi, or of the land of our fathers' first inheritance, and having been sent as a spy among the Lamanites that I might spy out their forces, that our army might come upon them and destroy them—but when I saw that which was good among them I was desirous that they should not be destroyed.

2 Therefore, I contended with my brethren in the wilderness, for I would that our ruler should make a treaty with them; but he being an austere and a blood-thirsty man commanded that I should be slain; but I was rescued by the shedding of much blood; for father fought against father, and brother against brother, until the greater number of our army was destroyed in the wilderness; and we returned, those of us that were spared, to the land of Zarahemla, to relate that tale to their wives and their children.

3 And yet, I being *over-zealous to inherit the land of our fathers, collected as many as were desirous to go up to possess the land, and started again on our *journey into the wilderness to go up to the land; but we were smitten with famine and sore afflictions; for we were slow to remember the Lord our God.

4 Nevertheless, after many days' wandering in the wilderness we pitched our tents in the place where our brethren were slain, which was near to the land of our fathers.

5 And it came to pass that I went again with four of my men into the

---

19a Ether 3:26 (21–28); 4:4 (1–8).
20a TG Spiritual Blindness.
  b IE Wisdom, a feminine noun in Hebrew and Greek.

Prov. 9:1; Matt. 11:19.
9 1a Mosiah 8:5; 22:14.
  b Mosiah 7:13.
  c 2 Ne. 5:8; Omni 1:12 (12, 27);

Mosiah 7:6 (6–7); 28:1 (1, 5).
3a Omni 1:27 (27–29); Mosiah 7:21.
  b Mosiah 25:5.

city, in unto the king, that I might know of the disposition of the king, and that I might know if I might go in with my people and possess the land in peace.

6 And I went in unto the king, and he covenanted with me that I might possess the ^aland of Lehi-Nephi, and the land of Shilom.

7 And he also commanded that his people should depart out of the land, and I and my people went into the land that we might possess it.

8 And we began to build buildings, and to repair the walls of the city, yea, even the walls of the city of Lehi-Nephi, and the city of Shilom.

9 And we began to till the ground, yea, even with all manner of ^aseeds, with seeds of corn, and of wheat, and of barley, and with neas, and with sheum, and with seeds of all manner of fruits; and we did begin to multiply and prosper in the land.

10 Now it was the cunning and the craftiness of king ^aLaman, to ^bbring my people into bondage, that he yielded up the land that we might possess it.

11 Therefore it came to pass, that after we had dwelt in the land for the space of twelve years that king Laman began to grow uneasy, lest by any means my people should ^awax strong in the land, and that they could not overpower them and bring them into bondage.

12 Now they were a ^alazy and an ^bidolatrous people; therefore they were desirous to bring us into bondage, that they might glut themselves with the labors of our hands; yea, that they might feast themselves upon the flocks of our fields.

13 Therefore it came to pass that king Laman began to stir up his people that they should contend with my people; therefore there began to be wars and contentions in the land.

14 For, in the thirteenth year of my reign in the land of Nephi, away on the south of the land of ^aShilom, when my people were watering and ^bfeeding their flocks, and tilling their lands, a numerous host of Lamanites came upon them and began to slay them, and to take off their flocks, and the corn of their fields.

15 Yea, and it came to pass that they fled, all that were not overtaken, even into the city of Nephi, and did call upon me for protection.

16 And it came to pass that I did arm them with bows, and with arrows, with swords, and with cimeters, and with clubs, and with slings, and with all manner of weapons which we could invent, and I and my people did go forth against the Lamanites to battle.

17 Yea, in the ^astrength of the Lord did we go forth to battle against the Lamanites; for I and my people did cry mightily to the Lord that he would ^bdeliver us out of the hands of our enemies, for we were awakened to a remembrance of the deliverance of our fathers.

18 And God did ^ahear our cries and did answer our prayers; and we did go forth in his might; yea, we did go forth against the Lamanites, and in one day and a night we did slay three thousand and forty-three; we did slay them even until we had driven them out of our land.

19 And I, myself, with mine own hands, did help to bury their dead. And behold, to our great sorrow and lamentation, two hundred and seventy-nine of our brethren were slain.

6a 2 Ne. 5:8;
　　Mosiah 7:1 (1–4, 21).
9a 1 Ne. 8:1; Enos 1:21;
　　Mosiah 10:4.
10a Mosiah 24:3.
　b Mosiah 7:22; 10:18.
11a Ex. 1:9 (9–10).

12a TG Laziness.
　b Enos 1:20.
　　TG Idolatry.
14a Mosiah 7:5;
　　11:12 (12–13).
　b Mosiah 10:21.
17a TG Strength.

　b Josh. 21:44;
　　Alma 46:7.
18a Ex. 2:24 (23–24);
　　Ps. 4:1 (1, 3);
　　Dan. 10:12;
　　D&C 35:3;
　　Abr. 1:15 (15–16).

CHAPTER 10

King Laman dies—His people are wild and ferocious and believe in false traditions—Zeniff and his people prevail against them. About 187–160 B.C.

AND it came to pass that we again began to establish the kingdom and we again began to possess the land in peace. And I caused that there should be *a*weapons of war made of every kind, that thereby I might have weapons for my people against the time the Lamanites should come up again to war against my people.

2 And I set guards round about the land, that the Lamanites might not come upon us again unawares and destroy us; and thus I did guard my people and my flocks, and keep them from falling into the hands of our enemies.

3 And it came to pass that we did inherit the land of our fathers for many years, yea, for the space of twenty and two years.

4 And I did cause that the men should till the ground, and raise all manner of *a*grain and all manner of fruit of every kind.

5 And I did cause that the women should spin, and toil, and work, and work all manner of fine linen, yea, and *a*cloth of every kind, that we might clothe our nakedness; and thus we did prosper in the land— thus we did have continual peace in the land for the space of twenty and two years.

6 And it came to pass that king *a*Laman died, and his son began to reign in his stead. And he began to stir his people up in rebellion against my people; therefore they began to prepare for war, and to come up to battle against my people.

7 But I had sent my spies out round about the land of *a*Shemlon, that I might discover their preparations, that I might guard against them, that they might not come upon my people and destroy them.

8 And it came to pass that they came up upon the north of the land of Shilom, with their numerous hosts, men *a*armed with *b*bows, and with arrows, and with swords, and with cimeters, and with stones, and with slings; and they had their heads shaved that they were naked; and they were girded with a leathern girdle about their loins.

9 And it came to pass that I caused that the women and children of my people should be hid in the wilderness; and I also caused that all my old men that could bear arms, and also all my young men that were able to bear arms, should gather themselves together to go to battle against the Lamanites; and I did place them in their ranks, every man according to his age.

10 And it came to pass that we did go up to battle against the Lamanites; and I, even I, in my old age, did go up to battle against the Lamanites. And it came to pass that we did go up in the *a*strength of the Lord to battle.

11 Now, the Lamanites knew nothing concerning the Lord, nor the strength of the Lord, therefore they depended upon their own strength. Yet they were a strong people, as to the *a*strength of men.

12 They were a *a*wild, and ferocious, and a blood-thirsty people, believing in the *b*tradition of their fathers, which is this—Believing that they were driven out of the land of Jerusalem because of the iniquities of their fathers, and that they were *c*wronged in the wilderness by their brethren, and they were also wronged while crossing the sea;

13 And again, that they were

---

10 1*a* TG Weapon.
   4*a* Mosiah 9:9.
   5*a* Alma 1:29; Hel. 6:13.
      TG Clothing.
   6*a* Mosiah 9:10 (10–11);
      24:3.
   7*a* Mosiah 11:12.

8*a* 2 Ne. 5:14;
   Jarom 1:8;
   Alma 2:12.
   b Enos 1:20;
   Alma 3:5 (4–5).
10*a* TG Strength;
   Trust in God.

11*a* TG Trust Not in the Arm
   of Flesh.
12*a* Alma 17:14.
   b 2 Ne. 5:1 (1–3);
   Mosiah 1:5;
   Alma 3:8.
   c TG Injustice.

wronged while in the land of their ^afirst inheritance, after they had crossed the sea, and all this because that Nephi was more faithful in keeping the commandments of the Lord—therefore ^bhe was favored of the Lord, for the Lord heard his prayers and answered them, and he took the lead of their journey in the wilderness.

14 And his brethren were ^awroth with him because they ^bunderstood not the dealings of the Lord; they were also wroth with him upon the waters because they hardened their hearts against the Lord.

15 And again, they were ^awroth with him when they had arrived in the promised land, because they said that he had taken the ^bruling of the people out of their hands; and they sought to kill him.

16 And again, they were wroth with him because he departed into the wilderness as the Lord had commanded him, and took the ^arecords which were engraven on the plates of brass, for they said that he ^brobbed them.

17 And thus they have taught their children that they should hate them, and that they should murder them, and that they should rob and plunder them, and do all they could to destroy them; therefore they have an eternal hatred towards the children of Nephi.

18 For this very cause has king Laman, by his ^acunning, and lying craftiness, and his fair promises, deceived me, that I have brought this my people up into this land, that they may destroy them; yea, and we have suffered these many years in the land.

19 And now I, Zeniff, after having told all these things unto my people

concerning the Lamanites, I did stimulate them to go to battle with their might, putting their trust in the Lord; therefore, we did contend with them, face to face.

20 And it came to pass that we did drive them again out of our land; and we slew them with a great slaughter, even so many that we did not number them.

21 And it came to pass that we returned again to our own land, and my people again began to ^atend their flocks, and to till their ground.

22 And now I, being old, did confer the kingdom upon one of my sons; therefore, I say no more. And may the Lord ^abless my people. Amen.

CHAPTER 11

King Noah rules in wickedness—He revels in riotous living with his wives and concubines—Abinadi prophesies that the people will be taken into bondage—His life is sought by King Noah. About 160–150 B.C.

AND now it came to pass that Zeniff conferred the kingdom upon Noah, one of his sons; therefore Noah began to reign in his stead; and he did not walk in the ways of his father.

2 For behold, he did not keep the commandments of God, but he did walk after the desires of his own heart. And he had many wives and ^aconcubines. And he did ^bcause his people to commit sin, and do that which was ^cabominable in the sight of the Lord. Yea, and they did commit ^dwhoredoms and ^eall manner of wickedness.

3 And he laid a ^atax of one fifth part of all they possessed, a fifth part of their gold and of their silver,

---

13a 1 Ne. 18:23.
  b 2 Ne. 5:5 (5–9).
14a 1 Ne. 18:10 (10–11).
  b 1 Ne. 15:8 (8–11);
    2 Ne. 1:25 (24–27).
15a 2 Ne. 5:1.
  b 2 Ne. 5:3 (1–4).
16a 2 Ne. 5:12;

Mosiah 28:11.
  b Alma 20:10 (10, 13).
18a Mosiah 9:10;
    19:28 (26, 28).
21a Mosiah 9:14 (9, 14).
22a Num. 6:24 (22–27).
11 2a Jacob 3:5; Ether 10:5.
  b 1 Kgs. 14:16; 15:26;

  16:2; 21:22;
    2 Kgs. 21:2 (1–9);
    Mosiah 23:12; 29:31.
  c Mosiah 29:18.
  d 2 Ne. 28:15.
  e Mosiah 23:9.
3a Gen. 47:24;
    Ether 10:5 (5–6).

and a fifth part of their [b]ziff, and of their copper, and of their brass and their iron; and a fifth part of their fatlings; and also a fifth part of all their grain.

4 And all this did he take to [a]support himself, and his wives and his [b]concubines; and also his priests, and their wives and their concubines; thus he had changed the affairs of the kingdom.

5 For he put down all the priests that had been consecrated by his father, and consecrated new [a]ones in their stead, such as were lifted up in the pride of their hearts.

6 Yea, and thus they were supported in their laziness, and in their idolatry, and in their whoredoms, by the taxes which king Noah had put upon his people; thus did the people labor exceedingly to support iniquity.

7 Yea, and they also became idolatrous, because they were deceived by the vain and flattering words of the king and priests; for they did speak flattering things unto them.

8 And it came to pass that king Noah built many elegant and spacious buildings; and he ornamented them with fine work of wood, and of all manner of [a]precious things, of gold, and of silver, and of iron, and of brass, and of ziff, and of copper;

9 And he also built him a spacious palace, and a throne in the midst thereof, all of which was of fine wood and was ornamented with gold and silver and with precious things.

10 And he also caused that his workmen should work all manner of fine work within the walls of the [a]temple, of fine wood, and of copper, and of brass.

11 And the seats which were set apart for the [a]high priests, which were above all the other seats, he did ornament with pure gold; and he caused a breastwork to be built before them, that they might rest their bodies and their arms upon while they should speak lying and vain words to his people.

12 And it came to pass that he built a [a]tower near the temple; yea, a very high tower, even so high that he could stand upon the top thereof and overlook the land of [b]Shilom, and also the land of [c]Shemlon, which was possessed by the Lamanites; and he could even look over all the land round about.

13 And it came to pass that he caused many buildings to be built in the land Shilom; and he caused a great tower to be built on the [a]hill north of the land Shilom, which had been a resort for the children of Nephi at the time they [b]fled out of the land; and thus he did do with the riches which he obtained by the taxation of his people.

14 And it came to pass that he placed his heart upon his riches, and he spent his time in [a]riotous living with his wives and his concubines; and so did also his priests spend their time with harlots.

15 And it came to pass that he planted vineyards round about in the land; and he built wine-presses, and made [a]wine in abundance; and therefore he became a wine-bibber, and also his people.

16 And it came to pass that the Lamanites began to come in upon his people, upon small numbers, and to slay them in their fields, and while they were tending their flocks.

17 And king Noah sent guards round about the land to keep them

---

3 b HEB related words:
    adjective, "shining";
    verb, "to overlay or plate
    with metal."
4 a Prov. 29:3.
  b TG Concubine.
5 a 1 Kgs. 12:31;
    2 Chr. 11:14 (13–14);
    Mosiah 11:11;

12:25 (17, 25).
8 a Esth. 1:4.
10 a 2 Ne. 5:16.
11 a Mosiah 11:5 (5, 14);
    12:17.
12 a Gen. 35:21;
    Mosiah 2:7 (7–8);
    19:5 (5–6).
  b Mosiah 9:14 (6, 8, 14);

22:11 (8, 11).
  c Mosiah 10:7.
13 a Mosiah 7:5.
  b Omni 1:12 (12–13).
14 a TG Rioting and
    Reveling.
15 a TG Drunkenness;
    Wine.

off; but he did not send a sufficient number, and the Lamanites came upon them and killed them, and drove many of their flocks out of the land; thus the Lamanites began to destroy them, and to exercise their hatred upon them.

18 And it came to pass that king Noah sent his armies against them, and they were driven back, or they drove them back for a time; therefore, they returned rejoicing in their spoil.

19 And now, because of this great victory they were lifted up in the pride of their hearts; they did ªboast in their own strength, saying that their fifty could stand against thousands of the Lamanites; and thus they did boast, and did delight in blood, and the shedding of the blood of their brethren, and this because of the wickedness of their king and priests.

20 And it came to pass that there was a man among them whose name was ªAbinadi; and he went forth among them, and began to prophesy, saying: Behold, thus saith the Lord, and thus hath he commanded me, saying, Go forth, and say unto this people, thus saith the Lord— Wo be unto this people, for I have seen their abominations, and their wickedness, and their whoredoms; and except they repent I will ᵇvisit them in mine anger.

21 And except they repent and turn to the Lord their God, behold, I will deliver them into the hands of their enemies; yea, and they shall be brought into ªbondage; and they shall be afflicted by the hand of their enemies.

22 And it shall come to pass that they shall ªknow that I am the Lord their God, and am a ᵇjealous God, visiting the iniquities of my people.

23 And it shall come to pass that except this people repent and turn unto the Lord their God, they shall be brought into bondage; and none shall ªdeliver them, except it be the Lord the Almighty God.

24 Yea, and it shall come to pass that when they shall ªcry unto me I will be ᵇslow to hear their cries; yea, and I will suffer them that they be smitten by their enemies.

25 And except they repent in ªsackcloth and ashes, and cry mightily to the Lord their God, I will not ᵇhear their prayers, neither will I deliver them out of their afflictions; and thus saith the Lord, and thus hath he commanded me.

26 Now it came to pass that when Abinadi had spoken these words unto them they were wroth with him, and sought to take away his life; but the Lord ªdelivered him out of their hands.

27 Now when king Noah had heard of the words which Abinadi had spoken unto the people, he was also wroth; and he said: ªWho is Abinadi, that I and my people should be judged of him, or ᵇwho is the Lord, that shall bring upon my people such great affliction?

28 I command you to bring Abinadi hither, that I may slay him, for he has said these things that he might ªstir up my people to anger one with another, and to raise contentions among my people; therefore I will slay him.

29 Now the eyes of the people were ªblinded; therefore they ᵇhardened their hearts against the words of

---

19a Amos 6:13;
    D&C 3:4.
    TG Boast.
20a See accounts of Abinadi
    in Mosiah 11–17.
  b TG Punish; Reproof.
21a Mosiah 12:2;
    D&C 101:79.
22a Ezek. 26:6;
    1 Ne. 21:26 (25–26);

    D&C 43:25.
  b Ex. 20:5;
    Deut. 6:15; 32:21;
    Mosiah 13:13.
23a Hosea 13:10 (4, 10).
24a Micah 3:4.
  b Ps. 10:1;
    Jer. 2:27;
    Mosiah 21:15.
25a TG Sackcloth.

    b Isa. 1:15 (15–17); 59:2.
26a TG Prophets, Rejection
    of; Protection, Divine.
27a Alma 9:6 (5–6).
  b Ex. 5:2;
    Mosiah 12:13.
28a TG Provoking.
29a 1 Kgs. 15:26 (26–34).
    TG Spiritual Blindness.
  b TG Hardheartedness.

Abinadi, and they sought from that time forward to take him. And king Noah hardened his heart against the word of the Lord, and he did not repent of his evil doings.

CHAPTER 12

Abinadi is imprisoned for prophesying the destruction of the people and the death of King Noah—The false priests quote the scriptures and pretend to keep the law of Moses—Abinadi begins to teach them the Ten Commandments. About 148 B.C.

AND it came to pass that after the space of two years that Abinadi came among them in disguise, that they knew him not, and began to ^aprophesy among them, saying: Thus has the Lord commanded me, saying— Abinadi, go and prophesy unto this my people, for they have hardened their hearts against my words; they have repented not of their evil doings; therefore, I will ^bvisit them in my anger, yea, in my fierce anger will I visit them in their iniquities and abominations.

2 Yea, wo be unto this generation! And the Lord said unto me: Stretch forth thy hand and prophesy, saying: Thus saith the Lord, it shall come to pass that this generation, because of their iniquities, shall be brought into ^abondage, and shall be smitten on the ^bcheek; yea, and shall be driven by men, and shall be slain; and the vultures of the air, and the dogs, yea, and the wild beasts, shall devour their ^cflesh.

3 And it shall come to pass that the ^alife of king Noah shall be valued even as a garment in a hot ^bfurnace; for he shall know that I am the Lord.

4 And it shall come to pass that I will smite this my people with sore afflictions, yea, with famine and with ^apestilence; and I will cause that they shall ^bhowl all the day long.

5 Yea, and I will cause that they shall have ^aburdens lashed upon their backs; and they shall be driven before like a dumb ass.

6 And it shall come to pass that I will send forth ^ahail among them, and it shall smite them; and they shall also be smitten with the ^beast wind; and ^cinsects shall pester their land also, and devour their grain.

7 And they shall be smitten with a great pestilence—and all this will I do because of their ^ainiquities and abominations.

8 And it shall come to pass that except they repent I will utterly ^adestroy them from off the face of the earth; yet they shall leave a ^brecord behind them, and I will preserve them for other nations which shall possess the land; yea, even this will I do that I may discover the abominations of this people to other nations. And many things did Abinadi prophesy against this people.

9 And it came to pass that they were angry with him; and they took him and carried him bound before the king, and said unto the king: Behold, we have brought a man before thee who has prophesied evil concerning thy people, and saith that God will destroy them.

10 And he also prophesieth evil concerning thy ^alife, and saith that thy life shall be as a garment in a furnace of fire.

11 And again, he saith that thou shalt be as a stalk, even as a dry stalk

---

12 1*a* TG Missionary Work.
  b Isa. 65:6 (6–7, 11);
    Jer. 9:9.
 2*a* 1 Kgs. 8:46;
    Mosiah 11:21; 20:21.
  b Lam. 3:30;
    Mosiah 21:3 (3–4, 13).
  c Deut. 28:26.
 3*a* Amos 7:11 (10–11);
    Mosiah 12:10 (10–12).

  b Mosiah 19:20.
 4*a* Luke 21:11 (10–13);
    2 Ne. 6:15;
    D&C 97:26 (22–26).
  b Mosiah 21:9 (1–15).
 5*a* Mosiah 21:3.
 6*a* Ex. 9:18 (13–35);
    Ezek. 13:13.
  b Jer. 18:17;
    Ezek. 27:26;

    Mosiah 7:31.
  c Ex. 10:4 (1–12).
 7*a* D&C 3:18.
 8*a* Gen. 6:13;
    Isa. 42:14 (14–15);
    2 Ne. 26:10 (10–11);
    Alma 45:11 (9–14).
  b Morm. 8:14 (14–16).
10*a* Amos 7:11 (10–11);
    Mosiah 12:3.

of the field, which is run over by the beasts and trodden under foot.

12 And again, he saith thou shalt be as the blossoms of a thistle, which, when it is fully ripe, if the wind bloweth, it is driven forth upon the face of the land. And he pretendeth the Lord hath spoken it. And he saith all this shall come upon thee except thou repent, and this because of thine iniquities.

13 And now, O king, what great evil hast thou done, or what great sins have thy people committed, that we should be ªcondemned of God or judged of this man?

14 And now, O king, behold, we are ªguiltless, and thou, O king, hast not sinned; therefore, this man has ᵇlied concerning you, and he has prophesied in vain.

15 And behold, we are strong, we shall not come into bondage, or be taken captive by our enemies; yea, and thou hast prospered in the land, and thou shalt also prosper.

16 Behold, here is the man, we deliver him into thy hands; thou mayest do with him as seemeth thee good.

17 And it came to pass that king Noah caused that Abinadi should be cast into prison; and he commanded that the ªpriests should gather themselves together that he might hold a council with them what he should do with him.

18 And it came to pass that they said unto the king: Bring him hither that we may question him; and the king commanded that he should be brought before them.

19 And they began to question him, that they might cross him, that thereby they might have wherewith to ªaccuse him; but he answered them boldly, and withstood all their questions, yea, to their astonish-

ment; for he did ᵇwithstand them in all their questions, and did confound them in all their words.

20 And it came to pass that one of them said unto him: ªWhat meaneth the words which are written, and which have been taught by our fathers, saying:

21 ªHow beautiful upon the mountains are the feet of him ᵇthat bringeth good tidings; that publisheth peace; that bringeth good tidings of good; that publisheth salvation; that saith unto Zion, Thy God reigneth;

22 ªThy watchmen shall lift up the voice; with the voice together shall they sing; for they shall see eye to eye when the Lord shall bring again Zion;

23 Break forth into joy; sing together ye waste places of Jerusalem; for the Lord hath comforted his people, he hath redeemed Jerusalem;

24 The Lord hath made bare his holy ªarm in the eyes of all the nations, and all the ends of the earth shall see the salvation of our God?

25 And now Abinadi said unto them: Are you ªpriests, and pretend to teach this people, and to understand the spirit of prophesying, and yet desire to know of me what these things mean?

26 I say unto you, wo be unto you for perverting the ways of the Lord! For if ye understand these things ye have not taught them; therefore, ye have perverted the ways of the Lord.

27 Ye have not applied your ªhearts to ᵇunderstanding; therefore, ye have not been wise. Therefore, what teach ye this people?

28 And they said: We teach the law of Moses.

29 And again he said unto them:

13a Mosiah 11:27.
14a Jer. 2:35;
    Alma 21:6.
  b Hel. 13:26 (24–28).
17a Mosiah 11:11.
19a John 8:6.
  b D&C 100:5 (5–6).

20a Mosiah 13:3.
21a Isa. 52:7 (7–10);
    Nahum 1:15.
  b Mosiah 15:14;
    27:37 (36–37).
22a Mosiah 15:29.
24a Isa. 33:2;

    Omni 1:13.
25a John 3:10 (7–10);
    Mosiah 11:5.
27a Prov. 8:5;
    Mosiah 2:9.
  b TG Understanding.

If ye teach the ^alaw of Moses why do ye not keep it? Why do ye set your hearts upon ^briches? Why do ye commit whoredoms and ^cspend your strength with harlots, yea, and cause this people to commit sin, that the Lord has cause to send me to prophesy against this people, yea, even a great evil against this people?

30 Know ye not that I speak the ^atruth? Yea, ye know that I speak the truth; and you ought to tremble before God.

31 And it shall come to pass that ye shall be smitten for your iniquities, for ye have said that ye teach the law of Moses. And what know ye concerning the law of Moses? ^aDoth salvation come by the law of Moses? What say ye?

32 And they answered and said that salvation did come by the law of Moses.

33 But now Abinadi said unto them: I know if ye ^akeep the commandments of God ye shall be saved; yea, if ye keep the commandments which the Lord delivered unto Moses in the mount of ^bSinai, saying:

34 ^aI am the Lord thy God, who hath ^bbrought thee out of the land of Egypt, out of the house of bondage.

35 Thou shalt have no ^aother God before me.

36 ^aThou shalt not make unto thee any graven image, or any likeness of any thing in heaven above, or things which are in the earth beneath.

37 Now Abinadi said unto them, Have ye done all this? I say unto you, Nay, ye have not. And have ye ^ataught this people that they should do all these things? I say unto you, Nay, ye have not.

CHAPTER 13

Abinadi is protected by divine power—He teaches the Ten Commandments—Salvation does not come by the law of Moses alone—God Himself will make an atonement and redeem His people. About 148 B.C.

AND now when the king had heard these words, he said unto his priests: Away with this fellow, and slay him; for what have we to do with him, for he is ^amad.

2 And they stood forth and attempted to lay their hands on him; but he withstood them, and said unto them:

3 ^aTouch me not, for God shall smite you if ye lay your hands upon me, for I have not delivered the message which the Lord sent me to deliver; neither have I told you that which ye ^brequested that I should tell; therefore, God will not suffer that I shall be destroyed at this time.

4 But I must fulfil the commandments wherewith God has commanded me; and because I have told you the truth ye are angry with me. And again, because I have spoken the word of God ye have judged me that I am mad.

5 Now it came to pass after Abinadi had spoken these words that the people of king Noah durst not lay their hands on him, for the Spirit of the Lord was upon him; and his face ^ashone with exceeding luster, even as Moses' did while in the mount of Sinai, while speaking with the Lord.

6 And he spake with ^apower and authority from God; and he continued his words, saying:

7 Ye see that ye have not power to

29a TG Law of Moses.
  b Jer. 48:7.
  c TG Sexual Immorality.
30a Jacob 7:14;
   Alma 30:42 (41–42).
31a Mosiah 3:15;
   13:28 (27–32);
   Alma 25:16.
33a Deut. 27:1;

Neh. 9:13;
   3 Ne. 25:4.
  b Ex. 19:18 (9, 16–20);
   Mosiah 13:5.
34a Ex. 20:2 (2–4).
  b Ex. 12:51; 1 Ne. 17:40;
   Mosiah 7:19.
35a Hosea 13:4.
   TG Idolatry.

36a Mosiah 13:12.
37a Mosiah 13:25 (25–26).
13 1a John 10:20 (19–20).
  3a 1 Ne. 17:48.
  b Mosiah 12:20 (20–24).
  5a Ex. 34:29 (29–35).
  6a TG Priesthood,
   Power of; Teaching
   with the Spirit.

slay me, therefore I finish my ªmessage. Yea, and I perceive that it cuts you to your hearts because I tell you the truth concerning your iniquities.

8 Yea, and my words fill you with wonder and amazement, and with anger.

9 But I finish my message; and then it ªmatters not whither I go, if it so be that I am saved.

10 But this much I tell you, what you ªdo with me, after this, shall be as a ᵇtype and a shadow of things which are to come.

11 And now I read unto you the remainder of the ªcommandments of God, for I perceive that they are not written in your hearts; I perceive that ye have studied and taught ᵇiniquity the most part of your lives.

12 And now, ye remember that I ªsaid unto you: Thou shalt not make unto thee any graven image, or any likeness of things which are in heaven above, or which are in the earth beneath, or which are in the water under the earth.

13 And again: Thou shalt not ªbow down thyself unto them, nor serve them; for I the Lord thy God am a jealous God, visiting the iniquities of the fathers upon the children, unto the third and fourth generations of them that hate me;

14 And showing mercy unto thousands of them that love me and keep my commandments.

15 Thou shalt not take the name of the Lord thy God in vain; for the Lord will not hold him ªguiltless that taketh his name in vain.

16 Remember the ªsabbath day, to keep it holy.

17 Six days shalt thou labor, and do all thy work;

18 But the seventh day, the sabbath of the Lord thy God, thou shalt not do any work, thou, nor thy son, nor thy daughter, thy manservant, nor thy maid-servant, nor thy cattle, nor thy stranger that is within thy gates;

19 For in ªsix days the Lord made heaven and earth, and the sea, and all that in them is; wherefore the Lord blessed the sabbath day, and hallowed it.

20 ªHonor thy ᵇfather and thy mother, that thy days may be long upon the land which the Lord thy God giveth thee.

21 Thou shalt not ªkill.

22 Thou shalt not commit ªadultery. Thou shalt not ᵇsteal.

23 Thou shalt not bear ªfalse witness against thy neighbor.

24 Thou shalt not ªcovet thy neighbor's house, thou shalt not covet thy neighbor's wife, nor his manservant, nor his maid-servant, nor his ox, nor his ass, nor anything that is thy neighbor's.

25 And it came to pass that after Abinadi had made an end of these sayings that he said unto them: Have ye ªtaught this people that they should observe to do all these things for to keep these commandments?

26 I say unto you, Nay; for if ye had, the Lord would not have caused me to come forth and to prophesy evil concerning this people.

27 And now ye have said that salvation cometh by the law of Moses. I say unto you that it is expedient that ye should ªkeep the law of Moses as yet; but I say unto you,

7a Prov. 15:10;
  1 Ne. 16:2 (1–3);
  2 Ne. 9:40.
9a Dan. 3:16 (16–18).
10a Alma 25:10.
  b Jer. 26:14;
  Mosiah 17:18 (13–19).
11a Ex. 20:1 (1–17).
  b Micah 2:1 (1–2).
12a Mosiah 12:36.
13a Ex. 20:5.

15a Ex. 20:7;
  Morm. 7:7;
  D&C 58:30.
16a Mosiah 18:23.
  TG Sabbath.
19a Gen. 1:31;
  Ex. 20:11.
20a TG Honoring Father and
  Mother.
  b Prov. 20:20.
21a Ex. 20:13;

  Deut. 5:17;
  Matt. 5:21 (21–37);
  3 Ne. 12:21 (21–37);
  D&C 42:18.
22a TG Adulterer.
  b TG Stealing.
23a Prov. 24:28.
24a TG Covet.
25a Mosiah 12:37.
27a 2 Ne. 25:24.

that the time shall come when it shall ᵇno more be expedient to keep the law of Moses.

28 And moreover, I say unto you, that ᵃsalvation doth not come by the ᵇlaw alone; and were it not for the ᶜatonement, which God himself shall make for the sins and iniquities of his people, that they must unavoidably perish, notwithstanding the law of Moses.

29 And now I say unto you that it was expedient that there should be a law given to the children of Israel, yea, even a very ᵃstrict law; for they were a stiffnecked people, ᵇquick to do iniquity, and slow to remember the Lord their God;

30 Therefore there was a ᵃlaw given them, yea, a law of performances and of ᵇordinances, a law which they were to ᶜobserve strictly from day to day, to keep them in remembrance of God and their duty towards him.

31 But behold, I say unto you, that all these things were ᵃtypes of things to come.

32 And now, did they ᵃunderstand the law? I say unto you, Nay, they did not all understand the law; and this because of the hardness of their hearts; for they understood not that there could not any man be saved ᵇexcept it were through the redemption of God.

33 For behold, did not Moses prophesy unto them concerning the coming of the Messiah, and that God should redeem his people? Yea, and even ᵃall the prophets who have prophesied ever since the world began—have they not spoken more or less concerning these things?

34 Have they not said that ᵃGod himself should come down among the children of men, and take upon him the form of man, and go forth in mighty power upon the face of the earth?

35 Yea, and have they not said also that he should bring to pass the ᵃresurrection of the dead, and that he, himself, should be oppressed and afflicted?

CHAPTER 14

Isaiah speaks messianically—The Messiah's humiliation and sufferings are set forth—He makes His soul an offering for sin and makes intercession for transgressors—Compare Isaiah 53. About 148 B.C.

YEA, even doth not Isaiah say: Who hath ᵃbelieved our report, and to whom is the arm of the Lord revealed?

2 For he shall grow up before him as a tender plant, and as a root out of dry ground; he hath no form nor comeliness; and when we shall see him there is no beauty that we should desire him.

3 He is ᵃdespised and rejected of men; a man of sorrows, and acquainted with grief; and we hid as it were our faces from him; he was despised, and we esteemed him not.

4 Surely he has ᵃborne our ᵇgriefs, and carried our sorrows; yet we did esteem him stricken, smitten of God, and afflicted.

27 b 3 Ne. 9:19 (19–20);
       15:4 (2–10).
28 a Gal. 2:16;
       Mosiah 12:31;
       Alma 25:16.
       TG Redemption;
       Salvation, Plan of.
    b Rom. 7:4 (4–25);
       Gal. 2:21; 3:2;
       Heb. 10:1; 2 Ne. 2:5;
       Mosiah 3:15 (14–15).
    c TG Jesus Christ,
       Atonement through.
29 a Josh. 1:8;
       Heb. 9:10 (8–10);

Mosiah 3:14 (14–15);
       Alma 25:15 (15–16);
       D&C 41:5 (4–5).
    b 1 Ne. 17:45;
       Alma 46:8.
30 a Rom. 7:1 (1–3).
    b TG Ordinance.
    c 2 Ne. 25:24; Jacob 4:5.
31 a Mosiah 16:14;
       Alma 25:15 (15–16).
       TG Jesus Christ, Types
       of, in Anticipation;
       Symbolism.
32 a Ps. 111:10.
    b 2 Ne. 25:23 (23–25).

33 a 1 Pet. 1:11; 1 Ne. 10:5;
       Jacob 4:4; 7:11 (11–12);
       Alma 25:16 (10–16);
       30:44.
       TG Jesus Christ,
       Prophecies about.
34 a Mosiah 7:27; 15:1; 17:8;
       Alma 10:21.
       TG Jesus Christ,
       Jehovah.
35 a Isa. 26:19; 2 Ne. 2:8.
14 1 a Isa. 53:1 (1–12).
    3 a Ps. 22:6; 1 Ne. 19:14.
    4 a Alma 7:11.
    b Matt. 8:17.

5 But he was ^awounded for our ^btransgressions, he was bruised for our iniquities; the chastisement of our peace was upon him; and with his stripes we are ^chealed.

6 All we, like ^asheep, have gone astray; we have turned every one to his own way; and the Lord hath laid on him the iniquities of us all.

7 He was oppressed, and he was afflicted, yet he ^aopened not his mouth; he is brought as a ^blamb to the slaughter, and as a sheep before her shearers is dumb so he opened not his mouth.

8 He was taken from prison and from judgment; and who shall declare his generation? For he was cut off out of the land of the living; for the transgressions of my people was he stricken.

9 And he made his grave with the wicked, and with the ^arich in his death; because he had done no ^bevil, neither was any deceit in his mouth.

10 Yet it pleased the Lord to ^abruise him; he hath put him to grief; when thou shalt make his soul an offering for sin he shall see his ^bseed, he shall prolong his days, and the pleasure of the Lord shall prosper in his hand.

11 He shall see the travail of his soul, and shall be satisfied; by his knowledge shall my righteous servant justify many; for he shall ^abear their iniquities.

12 Therefore will I divide him a portion with the ^agreat, and ^bhe shall divide the spoil with the strong; because he hath poured out his soul unto death; and he was numbered with the transgressors; and he bore the sins of many, and made ^cintercession for the transgressors.

CHAPTER 15

How Christ is both the Father and the Son—He will make intercession and bear the transgressions of His people— They and all the holy prophets are His seed—He brings to pass the Resurrection—Little children have eternal life. About 148 B.C.

AND now Abinadi said unto them: I would that ye should understand that ^aGod himself shall ^bcome down among the children of men, and shall ^credeem his people.

2 And because he ^ddwelleth in ^bflesh he shall be called the ^cSon of God, and having subjected the flesh to the ^dwill of the ^eFather, being the Father and the Son—

3 The Father, ^abecause he was ^bconceived by the power of God; and the Son, because of the flesh; thus becoming the Father and Son—

5a TG Jesus Christ, Crucifixion of.
 b Mosiah 15:9; Alma 11:40.
 c 1 Pet. 2:24 (24–25).
6a Matt. 9:36; 2 Ne. 12:5; 28:14; Alma 5:37.
7a Isa. 53:7 (7–8); Mark 15:3 (2–14); John 19:9 (9–10); 1 Pet. 2:23 (22–23); Mosiah 15:6. TG Jesus Christ, Trials of.
 b Jer. 11:19. TG Passover.
9a Matt. 27:57 (57–60); Mark 15:46 (27, 43–46). TG Jesus Christ, Death of.

 b John 19:4.
10a Gen. 3:15; Rom. 16:20.
 b Mosiah 15:10 (10–13).
11a Lev. 16:22 (21–22); 1 Pet. 3:18; D&C 19:16 (16–19).
12a Luke 24:26.
 b Mosiah 15:12.
 c 2 Ne. 2:9; Mosiah 15:8; Moro. 7:28 (27–28).
15 1a Isa. 54:5; 1 Tim. 3:16; Mosiah 13:34 (33–34).
 b TG God, Manifestations of.
 c TG Jesus Christ, Mission of.
2a Mosiah 3:5; 7:27; Alma 7:9 (9–13).

 b TG Jesus Christ, Condescension of.
 c John 19:7. TG Jesus Christ, Divine Sonship.
 d TG God, Will of.
 e Isa. 9:6; 64:8; John 10:30; 14:10 (8–10); Mosiah 5:7; Alma 11:39 (38–39); Ether 3:14.
3a D&C 93:4.
 b Luke 1:32 (31–33); Mosiah 3:8 (8–9); Alma 7:10; 3 Ne. 1:14. TG Jesus Christ, Divine Sonship.

4 And they are ^aone God, yea, the very ^bEternal ^cFather of heaven and of earth.

5 And thus the flesh becoming subject to the Spirit, or the Son to the Father, being one God, ^asuffereth temptation, and yieldeth not to the temptation, but suffereth himself to be mocked, and ^bscourged, and cast out, and disowned by his ^cpeople.

6 And after all this, after working many mighty miracles among the children of men, he shall be led, yea, even ^aas Isaiah said, as a sheep before the shearer is dumb, so he ^bopened not his mouth.

7 Yea, even so he shall be led, ^acrucified, and slain, the ^bflesh becoming subject even unto death, the ^cwill of the Son being swallowed up in the will of the Father.

8 And thus God breaketh the ^abands of death, having gained the ^bvictory over death; giving the Son power to make ^cintercession for the children of men—

9 Having ascended into heaven, having the bowels of mercy; being filled with compassion towards the children of men; standing betwixt them and justice; having broken the bands of death, taken upon ^ahimself their iniquity and their transgressions, having redeemed them, and ^bsatisfied the demands of justice.

10 And now I say unto you, who shall declare his ^ageneration? Behold, I say unto you, that when his soul has been made an offering for ^bsin he shall see his ^cseed. And now what say ye? And who shall be his seed?

11 Behold I say unto you, that whosoever has heard the words of the ^aprophets, yea, all the holy prophets who have prophesied concerning the coming of the Lord—I say unto you, that all those who have hearkened unto their words, and believed that the Lord would redeem his people, and have looked forward to that day for a remission of their sins, I say unto you, that these are his seed, or they are the heirs of the ^bkingdom of God.

12 For these are they whose sins ^ahe has borne; these are they for whom he has died, to redeem them from their transgressions. And now, are they not his seed?

13 Yea, and are not the ^aprophets, every one that has opened his mouth to prophesy, that has not fallen into transgression, I mean all the holy prophets ever since the world began? I say unto you that they are his seed.

14 And these are ^athey who have published peace, who have brought good ^btidings of good, who have ^cpublished salvation; and said unto Zion: Thy God reigneth!

4a Deut. 6:4.
   TG Godhead.
  b Alma 11:39.
  c Mosiah 3:8;
    Hel. 14:12;
    3 Ne. 11:14;
    Ether 4:7.
5a Luke 4:2;
    Heb. 4:15.
    TG Jesus Christ,
    Temptation of.
  b John 19:1.
  c Matt. 21:42;
    Mark 8:31;
    Luke 17:25; 23:38.
6a Isa. 53:7.
  b Luke 23:9;
    John 19:9 (9–10);
    Mosiah 14:7.
    TG Jesus Christ, Trials of.

7a TG Jesus Christ,
    Crucifixion of.
  b Isa. 53:10.
  c Luke 22:42;
    John 6:38;
    3 Ne. 11:11.
8a Alma 5:7.
  b Hosea 13:14;
    1 Cor. 15:57 (55–57);
    Mosiah 16:7.
  c 2 Ne. 2:9;
    Mosiah 14:12;
    Moro. 7:28 (27–28).
9a Mosiah 14:5 (5–12).
    TG Self-Sacrifice.
  b TG Jesus Christ,
    Mission of.
10a Isa. 53:8.
  b Lev. 6:25 (25–26).
  c Isa. 53:10;

    Mosiah 5:7; 27:25;
    Moro. 7:19.
    TG God the Father,
    Jehovah.
11a Luke 10:16;
    D&C 84:36 (36–38).
  b TG Kingdom of God, in
    Heaven; Kingdom of
    God, on Earth.
12a Mosiah 14:12;
    Alma 7:13; 11:40 (40–41).
13a Zech. 7:12;
    Matt. 11:13;
    1 Ne. 3:20.
    TG Sons and Daughters
    of God.
14a Mosiah 12:21 (21–24);
    27:37.
  b Isa. 52:7.
  c TG Missionary Work.

15 And O how beautiful upon the mountains were their feet!

16 And again, how beautiful upon the mountains are the feet of those that are still publishing peace!

17 And again, how beautiful upon the mountains are the feet of those who shall hereafter publish peace, yea, from this time henceforth and forever!

18 And behold, I say unto you, this is not all. For O how beautiful upon the mountains are the ^afeet of him that bringeth good tidings, that is the founder of ^bpeace, yea, even the Lord, who has redeemed his people; yea, him who has granted salvation unto his people;

19 For were it not for the redemption which he hath made for his people, which was prepared from the ^afoundation of the world, I say unto you, were it not for this, all mankind must have ^bperished.

20 But behold, the bands of death shall be broken, and the Son reigneth, and hath power over the dead; therefore, he bringeth to pass the resurrection of the dead.

21 And there cometh a resurrection, even a ^afirst resurrection; yea, even a resurrection of those that have been, and who are, and who shall be, even until the resurrection of Christ—for so shall he be called.

22 And now, the resurrection of all the prophets, and all those that have believed in their words, or all those that have kept the commandments of God, shall come forth in the first resurrection; therefore, they are the first resurrection.

23 They are raised to ^adwell with God who has redeemed them; thus they have eternal life through Christ, who has ^bbroken the bands of death.

24 And these are those who have part in the first resurrection; and these are they that have died before Christ came, in their ignorance, not having ^asalvation declared unto them. And thus the Lord bringeth about the restoration of these; and they have a part in the first resurrection, or have eternal life, being redeemed by the Lord.

25 And little ^achildren also have eternal life.

26 But behold, and ^afear, and tremble before God, for ye ought to tremble; for the Lord redeemeth none such that ^brebel against him and ^cdie in their sins; yea, even all those that have perished in their sins ever since the world began, that have wilfully rebelled against God, that have known the commandments of God, and would not keep them; ^dthese are they that have ^eno part in the first ^fresurrection.

27 Therefore ought ye not to tremble? For salvation cometh to none such; for the Lord hath redeemed none such; yea, neither can the Lord redeem such; for he cannot deny himself; for he cannot deny ^ajustice when it has its claim.

28 And now I say unto you that the time shall come that the ^asalvation of the Lord shall be declared to every nation, kindred, tongue, and people.

29 Yea, Lord, ^athy ^bwatchmen shall lift up their voice; with the voice together shall they sing; for

18a Nahum 1:15;
      3 Ne. 20:40;
      D&C 128:19.
  b Micah 5:5 (4–7);
      John 16:33.
      TG Peace of God.
19a Mosiah 4:6.
  b 2 Ne. 9:7 (6–13).
21a Jacob 4:11;
      Alma 40:16 (16–21).
      TG Resurrection.
23a Ps. 15:1 (1–5); 24:3 (3–4);
      1 Ne. 15:33 (33–36);

      D&C 76:62 (50–70).
  b TG Death, Power over.
24a 2 Ne. 9:26 (25–26);
      D&C 137:7.
25a D&C 29:46; 137:10.
      TG Salvation of Little
      Children.
26a Deut. 5:29;
      Jacob 6:9; 7:19.
  b Josh. 22:16;
      Job 24:13;
      Ps. 5:10;
      1 Ne. 2:23 (21–24).

  c Ezek. 18:26;
      1 Ne. 15:33 (32–33);
      Moro. 10:26.
  d Alma 40:19.
  e D&C 76:85.
  f TG Telestial Glory.
27a Alma 12:32;
      34:16 (15–16); 42:1.
28a Ps. 67:2 (1–2).
      TG Missionary Work.
29a Isa. 52:8 (8–10);
      Mosiah 12:22 (22–24).
  b TG Watchman.

they shall see eye to eye, when the Lord shall bring again Zion.

30 Break forth into joy, sing together, ye waste places of Jerusalem; for the Lord hath comforted his people, he hath redeemed Jerusalem.

31 The Lord hath made bare his holy arm in the eyes of all the nations; and all the ends of the earth shall see the [a]salvation of our God.

CHAPTER 16

God redeems men from their lost and fallen state—Those who are carnal remain as though there were no redemption—Christ brings to pass a resurrection to endless life or to endless damnation. About 148 B.C.

AND now, it came to pass that after Abinadi had spoken these words he stretched forth his hand and said: The time shall come when all shall see the [a]salvation of the Lord; when [b]every nation, kindred, tongue, and people shall see eye to eye and shall [c]confess before God that his [d]judgments are just.

2 And then shall the [a]wicked be [b]cast out, and they shall have cause to howl, and [c]weep, and wail, and gnash their teeth; and this because they would not [d]hearken unto the voice of the Lord; therefore the Lord redeemeth them not.

3 For they are [a]carnal and devilish, and the devil has power over them; yea, even that old serpent that did [b]beguile our first parents, which was the [c]cause of their fall; which was the cause of [d]all mankind becoming carnal, sensual, devilish, [e]knowing evil from good, [f]subjecting themselves to the devil.

4 Thus all mankind were [a]lost; and behold, they would have been endlessly lost were it not that God redeemed his people from their lost and fallen state.

5 But remember that he that persists in his own [a]carnal nature, and goes on in the ways of sin and rebellion against God, remaineth in his fallen state and the [b]devil hath all power over him. Therefore he is as though there was no [c]redemption made, being an enemy to God; and also is the [d]devil an enemy to God.

6 And now if Christ had not come into the world, speaking of things to come [a]as though they had already come, there could have been no redemption.

7 And if Christ had not risen from the dead, or have broken the bands of death that the grave should have no victory, and that death should have no [a]sting, there could have been no resurrection.

8 But there is a [a]resurrection, therefore the grave hath no victory, and the sting of [b]death is swallowed up in Christ.

9 He is the [a]light and the life of the world; yea, a light that is endless,

31a TG Salvation.
16 1a TG Salvation.
  b Mosiah 3:20 (20–21).
  c Mosiah 27:31;
    D&C 88:104.
  d TG Justice.
2a Ps. 91:8; Jer. 12:1;
    D&C 1:9 (9–10).
  b Ps. 52:5; D&C 63:54.
  c Matt. 13:42 (41–42);
    Luke 13:28;
    Alma 40:13;
    Moses 1:22.
  d Jer. 44:16;
    Ether 11:13.
3a Gal. 5:19 (16–26);
    Mosiah 3:19.
  b Gen. 3:13; 2 Ne. 9:9;
    Ether 8:25;

Moses 4:19 (5–19).
  c Moses 5:13.
  d Ps. 14:3.
    TG Man, Natural, Not
    Spiritually Reborn.
  e Gen. 3:5;
    2 Ne. 2:18 (18, 26);
    Alma 29:5;
    Moro. 7:16 (15–19).
  f Alma 5:41 (41–42);
    D&C 29:40.
4a 2 Ne. 9:7;
    Alma 11:45; 12:36;
    42:6 (6, 9, 14).
    TG Fall of Man.
5a TG Carnal Mind;
    Man, Natural, Not
    Spiritually Reborn.
  b TG Bondage, Spiritual.

c 1 Ne. 10:6;
    2 Ne. 2:6 (5–8); 25:20;
    Alma 12:22 (22–25).
  d TG Devil.
6a 2 Ne. 25:26 (24–27);
    Jarom 1:11;
    Mosiah 3:13.
7a Hosea 13:14;
    Mosiah 15:8 (8, 20).
8a 2 Ne. 9:10;
    Alma 42:15 (6–15).
  b Isa. 25:8;
    1 Cor. 15:54–55;
    Morm. 7:5.
9a Ether 3:14;
    Moro. 7:18;
    D&C 88:13 (7–13).
    TG Jesus Christ, Light of
    the World.

that can never be darkened; yea, and also a life which is endless, that there can be no more death.

10 Even this mortal shall put on ^aimmortality, and this ^bcorruption shall put on incorruption, and shall be brought to ^cstand before the bar of God, to be judged of him according to their works whether they be good or whether they be evil—

11 If they be good, to the resurrection of ^aendless life and ^bhappiness; and if they be evil, to the resurrection of ^cendless damnation, being delivered up to the devil, who hath subjected them, which is damnation—

12 Having gone according to their own carnal wills and desires; having never called upon the Lord while the arms of mercy were extended towards them; for the arms of mercy were extended towards them, and they would ^anot; they being warned of their iniquities and yet they would not depart from them; and they were commanded to repent and yet they would not repent.

13 And now, ought ye not to tremble and repent of your sins, and remember that only in and through Christ ye can be saved?

14 Therefore, if ye teach the ^alaw of Moses, also teach that it is a ^bshadow of those things which are to come—

15 Teach them that redemption cometh through Christ the Lord, who is the very ^aEternal Father. Amen.

CHAPTER 17

Alma believes and writes the words of Abinadi—Abinadi suffers death by fire—He prophesies disease and death by fire upon his murderers. About 148 B.C.

AND now it came to pass that when Abinadi had finished these sayings, that the king commanded that the ^apriests should take him and cause that he should be put to ^bdeath.

2 But there was one among them whose name was ^aAlma, he also being a descendant of Nephi. And he was a young man, and he ^bbelieved the words which Abinadi had spoken, for he knew concerning the iniquity which Abinadi had testified against them; therefore he began to plead with the king that he would not be angry with Abinadi, but suffer that he might depart in peace.

3 But the king was more wroth, and caused that Alma should be cast out from among them, and sent his servants after him that they might slay him.

4 But he fled from before them and ^ahid himself that they found him not. And he being concealed for many days did ^bwrite all the words which Abinadi had spoken.

5 And it came to pass that the king caused that his guards should surround Abinadi and take him; and they bound him and cast him into prison.

6 And after three days, having counseled with his ^apriests, he caused that he should again be brought before him.

7 And he said unto him: Abinadi, we have found an accusation against thee, and thou art worthy of death.

8 For thou hast said that ^aGod himself should come down among

10a Alma 40:2.
  TG Immortality.
 b 1 Cor. 15:42.
 c 3 Ne. 26:4.
  TG Jesus Christ, Judge.
11a Dan. 12:2 (2–3);
  John 5:29 (28–29).
 b TG Happiness.
 c Alma 9:11.
  TG Damnation.

12a TG Prophets,
  Rejection of.
14a TG Law of Moses.
 b Mosiah 13:31;
  Alma 25:15 (15–16).
  TG Jesus Christ, Types
  of, in Anticipation.
15a Mosiah 3:8.
17 1a TG False Priesthoods.
 b Jer. 26:11.

2a Mosiah 23:9.
 b Mosiah 26:15;
  Alma 5:11.
4a 1 Kgs. 17:3 (1–16);
  Ether 13:13 (13, 22).
 b TG Scriptures,
  Writing of.
6a Mosiah 11:5.
8a Mosiah 7:27; 13:34.

the children of men; and now, for this cause thou shalt be put to death unless thou wilt recall all the words which thou hast spoken evil concerning me and my people.

9 Now Abinadi said unto him: I say unto you, I will ªnot recall the words which I have spoken unto you concerning this people, for they are true; and that ye may know of their surety I have suffered myself that I have fallen into your hands.

10 Yea, and I will ªsuffer even until death, and I will not recall my words, and they shall stand as a ᵇtestimony against you. And if ye slay me ye will shed ᶜinnocent blood, and this shall also stand as a testimony against you at the last day.

11 And now king Noah was about to release him, for he feared his word; for he feared that the judgments of God would come upon him.

12 But the ªpriests lifted up their voices against him, and began to accuse him, saying: He has reviled the king. Therefore the king was stirred up in ᵇanger against him, and he delivered him up that he might be slain.

13 And it came to pass that they took him and bound him, and ªscourged his skin with faggots, yea, even unto ᵇdeath.

14 And now when the flames began to scorch him, he cried unto them, saying:

15 Behold, even as ye have done unto me, so shall it come to pass that thy ªseed shall cause that many shall suffer the pains that I do suffer, even the pains of ᵇdeath by fire; and this because they believe in the salvation of the Lord their God.

16 And it will come to pass that ye shall be afflicted with all manner of ªdiseases because of your iniquities.

17 Yea, and ye shall be smitten on every hand, and shall be driven and scattered to and fro, even as a wild flock is driven by wild and ferocious beasts.

18 And in that day ye shall be ªhunted, and ye shall be taken by the hand of your enemies, and then ye shall suffer, as I suffer, the pains of ᵇdeath by fire.

19 Thus God executeth ªvengeance upon those that destroy his people. O God, ᵇreceive my soul.

20 And now, when ªAbinadi had said these words, he fell, having suffered death by fire; yea, having been put to death because he would not deny the commandments of God, having sealed the truth of his words by his ᵇdeath.

CHAPTER 18

Alma preaches in private—He sets forth the covenant of baptism and baptizes at the waters of Mormon—He organizes the Church of Christ and ordains priests—They support themselves and teach the people—Alma and his people flee from King Noah into the wilderness. About 147–145 B.C.

AND now, it came to pass that Alma, who had fled from the servants of king Noah, ªrepented of his sins and iniquities, and went about privately among the people, and began to teach the words of Abinadi—

2 Yea, concerning that which was to come, and also concerning the resurrection of the dead, and the ªredemption of the people, which was to be brought to pass through the

9a TG Courage;
  Integrity.
10a TG Persecution.
  b TG Testimony.
  c Jer. 26:15 (14–15);
  Lam. 4:13;
  Alma 14:11; 60:13.
12a Mosiah 11:5;
  12:25 (17, 25).
  b Prov. 20:2.

13a Dan. 3:6;
  James 5:10 (10–11);
  Alma 14:26 (20–27).
  b Mosiah 7:28; 21:30;
  Alma 25:11.
15a Mosiah 13:10;
  Alma 25:12 (7–12).
  b Alma 25:5.
16a Deut. 28:60 (25–60).
18a Alma 25:8.

  b Mosiah 13:10; 19:20;
  Alma 25:11 (7–12).
19a Ps. 125:3.
  b Luke 23:46;
  Acts 7:59.
20a Mosiah 7:26.
  b Heb. 9:16 (16–17).
18 1a Mosiah 23:9.
2a TG Jesus Christ,
  Redeemer.

power, and sufferings, and *b*death of Christ, and his resurrection and ascension into heaven.

3 And as many as would hear his word he did teach. And he taught them privately, that it might not come to the knowledge of the king. And many did believe his words.

4 And it came to pass that as many as did believe him did go forth to a *a*place which was called Mormon, having received its name from the king, being in the *b*borders of the land having been infested, by times or at seasons, by wild beasts.

5 Now, there was in Mormon a fountain of pure water, and Alma resorted thither, there being near the water a thicket of small trees, where he did hide himself in the daytime from the searches of the king.

6 And it came to pass that as many as believed him went thither to hear his words.

7 And it came to pass after many days there were a goodly number gathered together at the place of Mormon, to hear the words of Alma. Yea, all were gathered together that believed on his word, to hear him. And he did *a*teach them, and did preach unto them repentance, and redemption, and faith on the Lord.

8 And it came to pass that he said unto them: Behold, here are the waters of Mormon (for thus were they called) and now, as ye are *a*desirous to come into the *b*fold of God, and to be called his people, and are willing to bear one another's burdens, that they may be light;

9 Yea, and are *a*willing to mourn with those that *b*mourn; yea, and

comfort those that stand in need of comfort, and to stand as *c*witnesses of God at all times and in all things, and in all places that ye may be in, even until death, that ye may be redeemed of God, and be numbered with those of the *d*first resurrection, that ye may have eternal life—

10 Now I say unto you, if this be the desire of your hearts, what have you against being *a*baptized in the *b*name of the Lord, as a witness before him that ye have entered into a *c*covenant with him, that ye will serve him and keep his commandments, that he may pour out his Spirit more abundantly upon you?

11 And now when the people had heard these words, they clapped their hands for joy, and exclaimed: This is the desire of our hearts.

12 And now it came to pass that Alma took Helam, he being one of the first, and went and stood forth in the water, and cried, saying: O Lord, pour out thy Spirit upon thy servant, that he may do this work with holiness of heart.

13 And when he had said these words, the *a*Spirit of the Lord was upon him, and he said: Helam, I baptize thee, having *b*authority from the Almighty God, as a testimony that ye have entered into a *c*covenant to serve him until you are dead as to the mortal body; and may the Spirit of the Lord be poured out upon you; and may he grant unto you eternal life, through the redemption of Christ, whom he has prepared from the *d*foundation of the world.

14 And after Alma had said these words, both Alma and Helam were

2 b TG Jesus Christ, Ascension of; Jesus Christ, Death of.
4 a Alma 5:3; 3 Ne. 5:12.
 b Mosiah 18:31.
7 a Alma 5:13.
8 a D&C 20:36–37, 77.
 b TG Brotherhood and Sisterhood; Conversion.

9 a TG Baptism, Qualifications for.
 b TG Comfort; Compassion.
 c TG Missionary Work; Witness.
 d Jacob 4:11.
10 a 2 Ne. 31:17; Alma 4:4.
 b TG Jesus Christ, Taking the Name of.

 c Neh. 10:29.
  TG Commitment.
13 a TG Holy Ghost, Mission of.
 b Mosiah 21:33; Alma 5:3; 3 Ne. 11:25.
 c Mosiah 21:31.
  TG Covenants.
 d Mosiah 4:6; Alma 12:30 (25, 30).

ªburied in the water; and they arose and came forth out of the water rejoicing, being filled with the Spirit.

15 And again, Alma took another, and went forth a second time into the water, and baptized him according to the first, only he did not bury ªhimself again in the water.

16 And after this manner he did baptize every one that went forth to the place of Mormon; and they were in number about two hundred and four souls; yea, and they were ªbaptized in the waters of Mormon, and were filled with the ᵇgrace of God.

17 And they were called the church of God, or the ªchurch of Christ, from that time forward. And it came to pass that whosoever was baptized by the power and authority of God was added to his church.

18 And it came to pass that Alma, having ªauthority from God, ᵇordained priests; even one priest to every fifty of their number did he ordain to preach unto them, and to ᶜteach them concerning the things pertaining to the kingdom of God.

19 And he commanded them that ªthey should ᵇteach nothing save it were the things which he had taught, and which had been spoken by the mouth of the holy prophets.

20 Yea, even he commanded them that they should ªpreach nothing save it were repentance and faith on the Lord, who had redeemed his people.

21 And he commanded them that there should be no ªcontention one with another, but that they should look forward with ᵇone eye, having one faith and one baptism, having their hearts ᶜknit together in unity and in love one towards another.

22 And thus he commanded them to preach. And thus they became the ªchildren of God.

23 And he commanded them that they should observe the ªsabbath day, and keep it holy, and also every day they should give thanks to the Lord their God.

24 And he also commanded them that the priests whom he had ordained ªshould ᵇlabor with their own hands for their support.

25 And there was ªone day in every week that was set apart that they should ᵇgather themselves together to teach the people, and to worship the Lord their God, and also, as often as it was in their power, to ᶜassemble themselves together.

26 And the priests were not to depend upon the people for their support; but for their labor they were to receive the ªgrace of God, that they might wax strong in the Spirit, having the ᵇknowledge of God, that they might teach with power and authority from God.

27 And again Alma commanded that the people of the church should impart of their substance, ªevery one according to that which he had; if he have more abundantly he should impart more abundantly; and of him that had but little, but

14a TG Baptism, Immersion.
15a JS—H 1:71 (70–71).
16a Mosiah 25:18.
   b TG Grace.
17a Mosiah 21:34;
   25:22 (18–23); 26:4;
   Alma 4:5 (4–5);
   3 Ne. 26:21.
   TG Jesus Christ, Head of
   the Church.
18a Mosiah 23:16.
   TG Priesthood,
   Authority.
   b TG Priesthood,
   History of.
   c Mosiah 2:4; 23:14;

24:4 (4–8).
19a Mosiah 23:14.
   b D&C 5:10.
20a TG Preaching;
   Repent.
21a TG Contention.
   b Matt. 6:22;
   Morm. 8:15;
   D&C 4:5; 88:68.
   c 1 Sam. 18:1;
   Rom. 15:5 (1–7);
   Mosiah 4:15; 23:15.
22a Moses 6:68.
23a Ex. 35:2;
   Mosiah 13:16 (16–19).
24a Acts 20:34 (33–35);

Mosiah 27:5 (3–5);
   Alma 1:3, 26.
   b 1 Cor. 9:18 (16–19);
   Alma 30:32.
25a Alma 32:11.
   b TG Meetings.
   c TG Assembly for
   Worship.
26a TG Blessing;
   Reward;
   Wages.
   b Neh. 10:28 (28–31).
   TG God, Knowledge
   about.
27a Alma 16:16;
   4 Ne. 1:3.

little should be required; and to him that had not should be given.

28 And thus they should impart of their ^asubstance of their own free will and good desires towards God, and to those priests that stood in need, yea, and to every needy, naked soul.

29 And this he said unto them, having been commanded of God; and they did ^awalk uprightly before God, imparting to one another both temporally and spiritually according to their needs and their wants.

30 And now it came to pass that all this was done in Mormon, yea, by the ^awaters of Mormon, in the forest that was near the waters of Mormon; yea, the place of Mormon, the waters of Mormon, the forest of Mormon, how beautiful are they to the eyes of them who there came to the knowledge of their Redeemer; yea, and how blessed are they, for they shall ^bsing to his praise forever.

31 And these things were done in the ^aborders of the land, that they might not come to the knowledge of the king.

32 But behold, it came to pass that the king, having discovered a movement among the people, sent his servants to watch them. Therefore on the day that they were assembling themselves together to hear the word of the Lord they were discovered unto the king.

33 And now the king said that Alma was stirring up the people to rebellion against him; therefore he sent his ^aarmy to destroy them.

34 And it came to pass that Alma and the people of the Lord were ^aapprised of the coming of the king's army; therefore they took their tents and their families and ^bdeparted into the wilderness.

35 And they were in number about ^afour hundred and fifty souls.

CHAPTER 19

Gideon seeks to slay King Noah—The Lamanites invade the land—King Noah suffers death by fire—Limhi rules as a tributary monarch. About 145–121 B.C.

AND it came to pass that the ^aarmy of the king returned, having searched in vain for the people of the Lord.

2 And now behold, the forces of the king were small, having been reduced, and there began to be a division among the remainder of the people.

3 And the lesser part began to ^abreathe out threatenings against the king, and there began to be a great contention among them.

4 And now there was a man among them whose name was Gideon, and he being a strong man and an enemy to the king, therefore he drew his sword, and swore in his wrath that he would slay the king.

5 And it came to pass that he fought with the king; and when the king saw that he was about to overpower him, he fled and ran and got upon the ^atower which was near the temple.

6 And Gideon pursued after him and was about to get upon the tower to slay the king, and the king cast his eyes round about towards the land of ^aShemlon, and behold, the army of the Lamanites were within the borders of the land.

7 And now the king cried out in the anguish of his soul, saying: Gideon, ^aspare me, for the Lamanites are upon us, and they will destroy us; yea, they will destroy my people.

8 And now the king was not so much concerned about his people as

---

28a TG Generosity;
   Initiative.
29a TG Walking with God;
   Welfare.
30a Mosiah 26:15.
  b TG Praise;

     Singing.
31a Mosiah 18:4.
33a Mosiah 19:1.
34a Mosiah 23:1.
  b Mosiah 21:30; 23:13, 36.
35a Mosiah 23:10.

19 1a Mosiah 18:33.
  3a Acts 9:1.
  5a Judg. 9:51 (50–55);
    Mosiah 11:12.
  6a Mosiah 10:7; 11:12; 20:1.
  7a Deut. 13:8 (6–9).

he was about his ^aown life; nevertheless, Gideon did spare his life.

9 And the king commanded the people that they should flee before the Lamanites, and he himself did go before them, and they did flee into the wilderness, with their women and their children.

10 And it came to pass that the Lamanites did pursue them, and did overtake them, and began to slay them.

11 Now it came to pass that the king commanded them that all the men should ^aleave their wives and their children, and flee before the Lamanites.

12 Now there were many that would not leave them, but had rather stay and perish with them. And the rest left their wives and their children and fled.

13 And it came to pass that those who tarried with their wives and their children caused that their fair daughters should stand forth and plead with the Lamanites that they would not slay them.

14 And it came to pass that the Lamanites had compassion on them, for they were charmed with the beauty of their women.

15 Therefore the Lamanites did spare their lives, and took them captives and carried them back to the land of Nephi, and granted unto them that they might possess the land, under the conditions that they would deliver up king Noah into the hands of the Lamanites, and deliver up their property, even ^aone half of all they possessed, one half of their gold, and their silver, and all their precious things, and thus they should pay tribute to the king of the Lamanites from year to year.

16 And now there was one of the sons of the king among those that were taken captive, whose name was ^aLimhi.

17 And now Limhi was desirous that his father should not be destroyed; nevertheless, Limhi was not ignorant of the iniquities of his father, he himself being a just man.

18 And it came to pass that Gideon sent men into the wilderness secretly, to search for the king and those that were with him. And it came to pass that they met the people in the wilderness, all save the king and his priests.

19 Now they had sworn in their hearts that they would return to the land of Nephi, and if their ^awives and their children were slain, and also those that had tarried with them, that they would seek revenge, and also perish with them.

20 And the king commanded them that they should not return; and they were angry with the king, and caused that he should suffer, even unto ^adeath by fire.

21 And they were about to take the priests also and ^aput them to death, and they fled before them.

22 And it came to pass that they were about to return to the land of Nephi, and they met the men of Gideon. And the men of Gideon told them of all that had happened to their wives and their children; and that the Lamanites had granted unto them that they might possess the land by paying a tribute to the Lamanites of one half of all they possessed.

23 And the people told the men of ^aGideon that they had slain the king, and his ^bpriests had fled from them farther into the wilderness.

24 And it came to pass that after they had ended the ceremony, that they returned to the land of Nephi, rejoicing, because their wives and their children were not slain; and they told Gideon what they had done to the king.

25 And it came to pass that the

---

8 a TG Selfishness.
11 a Mosiah 19:19 (19–23).
15 a Mosiah 7:15.
16 a Mosiah 7:9; 11:1.

19 a Mosiah 19:11.
20 a Mosiah 12:3; 13:10;
17:18 (13–19);
Alma 25:11 (7–12).

21 a Mosiah 20:3.
23 a Mosiah 20:17.
b Mosiah 17:12 (1, 6, 12–18);
20:23 (3, 18, 23).

king of the Lamanites made an ᵃoath unto them, that his people should not slay them.

26 And also Limhi, being the son of the king, having the kingdom conferred upon him ᵃby the people, made ᵇoath unto the king of the Lamanites that his people should pay ᶜtribute unto him, even one half of all they possessed.

27 And it came to pass that Limhi began to establish the kingdom and to establish ᵃpeace among his people.

28 And the king of the Lamanites set ᵃguards round about the land, that he might ᵇkeep the people of Limhi in the land, that they might not depart into the wilderness; and he did support his guards out of the tribute which he did receive from the Nephites.

29 And now king Limhi did have continual peace in his kingdom for the space of two years, that the Lamanites did not molest them nor seek to destroy them.

CHAPTER 20

Some Lamanite daughters are abducted by the priests of Noah—The Lamanites wage war upon Limhi and his people—The Lamanite hosts are repulsed and pacified. About 145–123 B.C.

Now there was a place in ᵃShemlon where the daughters of the Lamanites did gather themselves together to sing, and to ᵇdance, and to make themselves merry.

2 And it came to pass that there was one day a small number of them gathered together to sing and to dance.

3 And now the priests of king Noah, being ashamed to return to the city of Nephi, yea, and also fearing that the people would ᵃslay them, therefore they durst not return to their wives and their ᵇchildren.

4 And having tarried in the wilderness, and having discovered the daughters of the Lamanites, they laid and watched them;

5 And when there were but few of them gathered together to dance, they came forth out of their secret places and took them and carried them into the wilderness; yea, twenty and four of the ᵃdaughters of the Lamanites they carried into the wilderness.

6 And it came to pass that when the Lamanites found that their daughters had been missing, they were angry with the people of Limhi, for they thought it was the people of Limhi.

7 Therefore they sent their armies forth; yea, even the king himself went before his people; and they went up to the land of Nephi to destroy the people of Limhi.

8 And now Limhi had discovered them from the ᵃtower, even all their preparations for war did he discover; therefore he gathered his people together, and laid wait for them in the fields and in the forests.

9 And it came to pass that when the Lamanites had come up, that the people of Limhi began to fall upon them from their waiting places, and began to slay them.

10 And it came to pass that the battle became exceedingly sore, for they fought like lions for their prey.

11 And it came to pass that the people of Limhi began to drive the Lamanites before them; yet they were not half so numerous as the Lamanites. But they ᵃfought for their lives, and for their ᵇwives, and for their children; therefore they exerted themselves and like dragons did they fight.

12 And it came to pass that they found the king of the Lamanites

25a Mosiah 21:3.
26a Mosiah 7:9.
  b Mosiah 20:14, 22.
  c Mosiah 22:7.
27a TG Peacemakers.
28a Mosiah 21:5;

22:6 (6–10).
  b Mosiah 7:22; 9:10.
20 1a Mosiah 19:6.
  b Judg. 21:21.
3a Mosiah 19:21.
  b Mosiah 25:12.

5a Mosiah 21:20;
  23:33 (30–35).
8a Mosiah 11:12.
11a Alma 43:45.
  b Alma 46:12.

among the number of their dead; yet he was not dead, having been wounded and left upon the ground, so speedy was the flight of his people.

13 And they took him and bound up his wounds, and brought him before Limhi, and said: Behold, here is the king of the Lamanites; he having received a wound has fallen among their dead, and they have left him; and behold, we have brought him before you; and now let us slay him.

14 But Limhi said unto them: Ye shall not slay him, but bring him hither that I may see him. And they brought him. And Limhi said unto him: What cause have ye to come up to war against my people? Behold, my people have not broken the ªoath that I made unto you; therefore, why should ye break the oath which ye made unto my people?

15 And now the king said: I have broken the oath because thy people did carry away the daughters of my people; therefore, in my anger I did cause my people to come up to war against thy people.

16 And now Limhi had heard nothing concerning this matter; therefore he said: I will search among my people and whosoever has done this thing shall perish. Therefore he caused a search to be made among his people.

17 Now when ªGideon had heard these things, he being the king's captain, he went forth and said unto the king: I pray thee forbear, and do not search this people, and lay not this thing to their charge.

18 For do ye not remember the priests of thy father, whom this people sought to destroy? And are they not in the wilderness? And are not they the ones who have stolen the daughters of the Lamanites?

19 And now, behold, and tell the king of these things, that he may

tell his people that they may be pacified towards us; for behold they are already preparing to come against us; and behold also there are but few of us.

20 And behold, they come with their numerous hosts; and except the king doth pacify them towards us we must perish.

21 For are not the words of Abinadi ªfulfilled, which he prophesied against us—and all this because we would not hearken unto the words of the Lord, and turn from our iniquities?

22 And now let us pacify the king, and we fulfil the ªoath which we have made unto him; for it is better that we should be in bondage than that we should lose our ᵇlives; therefore, let us put a stop to the shedding of so much blood.

23 And now Limhi told the king all the things concerning his father, and the ªpriests that had fled into the wilderness, and attributed the carrying away of their daughters to them.

24 And it came to pass that the king was pacified towards his people; and he said unto them: Let us go forth to meet my people, without arms; and I swear unto you with an ªoath that my people shall not slay thy people.

25 And it came to pass that they followed the king, and went forth without arms to meet the Lamanites. And it came to pass that they did meet the Lamanites; and the king of the Lamanites did bow himself down before them, and did plead in behalf of the people of Limhi.

26 And when the Lamanites saw the people of Limhi, that they were without arms, they had ªcompassion on them and were pacified towards them, and returned with their king in peace to their own land.

14a Mosiah 19:26 (25–26).
17a Mosiah 19:23 (4–8, 23);
    22:3;
    Alma 1:8 (8–9).
21a Mosiah 12:2 (1–8); 21:4.
22a Mosiah 19:26.
  b TG Life, Sanctity of.
23a Mosiah 19:23 (21, 23);
23:9 (9, 12, 31).
24a Mosiah 21:3.
26a TG Compassion.

CHAPTER 21

Limhi's people are smitten and defeated by the Lamanites—Limhi's people meet Ammon and are converted—They tell Ammon of the twenty-four Jaredite plates. About 122–121 B.C.

AND it came to pass that Limhi and his people returned to the city of Nephi, and began to dwell in the land again in peace.

2 And it came to pass that after many days the Lamanites began again to be stirred up in anger against the Nephites, and they began to come into the borders of the land round about.

3 Now they durst not slay them, because of the ^aoath which their king had made unto Limhi; but they would smite them on their ^bcheeks, and exercise authority over them; and began to put heavy ^cburdens upon their backs, and drive them as they would a dumb ass—

4 Yea, all this was done that the ^aword of the Lord might be ^bfulfilled.

5 And now the afflictions of the Nephites were great, and there was no way that they could deliver themselves out of their hands, for the Lamanites had ^asurrounded them on every side.

6 And it came to pass that the people began to murmur with the king because of their afflictions; and they began to be desirous to go against them to battle. And they did afflict the king sorely with their complaints; therefore he granted unto them that they should do according to their desires.

7 And they gathered themselves together again, and put on their armor, and went forth against the Lamanites to drive them out of their land.

8 And it came to pass that the Lamanites did beat them, and drove them back, and ^aslew many of them.

9 And now there was a great ^amourning and lamentation among the people of Limhi, the widow mourning for her husband, the son and the daughter mourning for their father, and the brothers for their brethren.

10 Now there were a great many ^awidows in the land, and they did cry mightily from day to day, for a great fear of the Lamanites had come upon them.

11 And it came to pass that their continual cries did stir up the remainder of the people of Limhi to anger against the Lamanites; and they went again to battle, but they were driven back again, suffering much loss.

12 Yea, they went again even the third time, and suffered in the like manner; and those that were not slain returned again to the city of Nephi.

13 And they did humble themselves even to the dust, subjecting themselves to the ^ayoke of bondage, ^bsubmitting themselves to be smitten, and to be driven to and fro, and burdened, according to the desires of their enemies.

14 And they did ^ahumble themselves even in the depths of humility; and they did cry mightily to God; yea, even all the day long did they cry unto their God that he would ^bdeliver them out of their afflictions.

15 And now the Lord was ^aslow to hear their cry because of their iniquities; nevertheless the Lord

---

21 3 *a* Mosiah 19:25; 20:24.
    b Lam. 3:30;
      Mosiah 12:2.
    c Ex. 1:11 (10–11);
      Mosiah 12:5; 24:9.
  4 *a* D&C 3:19.
    b Mosiah 20:21.
  5 *a* Mosiah 19:28;

      22:6 (6–10).
  8 *a* Mosiah 21:29.
  9 *a* Mosiah 12:4.
    TG Mourning.
 10 *a* TG Widows.
 13 *a* Mosiah 19:28 (26, 28);
      21:36.
    b TG Submissiveness.

 14 *a* Mosiah 29:20.
    b TG Deliver;
      Protection, Divine.
 15 *a* 1 Sam. 8:18;
      Prov. 15:29;
      Mosiah 11:24 (23–25);
      D&C 101:7 (7–9).

did hear their [b]cries, and began to soften the hearts of the Lamanites that they began to ease their burdens; yet the Lord did not see fit to deliver them out of bondage.

16 And it came to pass that they began to prosper by degrees in the land, and began to raise grain more abundantly, and flocks, and herds, that they did not suffer with hunger.

17 Now there was a great number of women, more than there was of men; therefore king Limhi commanded that every man should [a]impart to the support of the [b]widows and their children, that they might not perish with hunger; and this they did because of the greatness of their number that had been slain.

18 Now the people of Limhi kept together in a body as much as it was possible, and secured their grain and their flocks;

19 And the king himself did not trust his person without the walls of the city, unless he took his guards with him, fearing that he might by some means fall into the hands of the Lamanites.

20 And he caused that his people should watch the land round about, that by some means they might take those priests that fled into the wilderness, who had stolen the [a]daughters of the Lamanites, and that had caused such a great destruction to come upon them.

21 For they were desirous to take them that they might [a]punish them; for they had come into the land of Nephi by night, and carried off their grain and many of their precious things; therefore they laid wait for them.

22 And it came to pass that there was no more disturbance between the Lamanites and the people of Limhi, even until the time that [a]Ammon and his brethren came into the land.

23 And the king having been without the gates of the city with his guard, [a]discovered Ammon and his brethren; and supposing them to be priests of Noah therefore he caused that they should be taken, and bound, and cast into [b]prison. And had they been the priests of Noah he would have caused that they should be put to death.

24 But when he found that they were not, but that they were his brethren, and had come from the [a]land of Zarahemla, he was filled with exceedingly great joy.

25 Now king Limhi had sent, previous to the coming of Ammon, a [a]small number of men to [b]search for the land of Zarahemla; but they could not find it, and they were lost in the wilderness.

26 Nevertheless, they did find a land which had been peopled; yea, a land which was covered with dry [a]bones; yea, a land which had been peopled and which had been destroyed; and they, having supposed it to be the land of Zarahemla, returned to the land of Nephi, having arrived in the borders of the land not many days before the [b]coming of Ammon.

27 And they brought a [a]record with them, even a record of the people whose bones they had found; and it was engraven on plates of ore.

28 And now Limhi was again filled with joy on learning from the mouth of Ammon that king Mosiah had a [a]gift from God, whereby he could [b]interpret such engravings; yea, and Ammon also did rejoice.

29 Yet Ammon and his brethren were filled with sorrow because so

15b Ex. 3:9 (7, 9);
   2 Ne. 26:15;
   D&C 109:49.
17a Mosiah 4:26 (16, 26).
   b TG Widows.
20a Mosiah 20:5.
21a Mosiah 7:7 (7–11).
22a Mosiah 7:6 (6–13).

23a Mosiah 7:10.
   b Mosiah 7:7 (6–8);
     Hel. 5:21.
24a Omni 1:13.
25a Mosiah 8:7.
   b Mosiah 7:14.
26a Mosiah 8:8;
     Hel. 3:6 (3–12).

   b Mosiah 7:6 (6–11).
27a Mosiah 8:9; 28:11.
28a Omni 1:20 (20–22);
     Mosiah 28:13 (11–19).
   TG God, Gifts of.
   b 1 Cor. 12:10;
     Mosiah 8:6 (6, 12–13).

many of their brethren had been ªslain;

30 And also that king Noah and his priests had caused the people to commit so many sins and iniquities against God; and they also did mourn for the ªdeath of Abinadi; and also for the ᵇdeparture of Alma and the people that went with him, who had formed a church of God through the strength and power of God, and faith on the words which had been spoken by Abinadi.

31 Yea, they did mourn for their departure, for they knew not whither they had fled. Now they would have gladly joined with them, for they themselves had entered into a ªcovenant with God to serve him and keep his commandments.

32 And now since the coming of Ammon, king Limhi had also entered into a covenant with God, and also many of his people, to serve him and keep his commandments.

33 And it came to pass that king Limhi and many of his people were desirous to be baptized; but there was none in the land that had ªauthority from God. And Ammon declined doing this thing, considering himself an unworthy servant.

34 Therefore they did not at that time form themselves into a ªchurch, waiting upon the Spirit of the Lord. Now they were desirous to become even as Alma and his brethren, who had fled into the wilderness.

35 They were desirous to be baptized as a witness and a testimony that they were willing to serve God with all their hearts; nevertheless they did prolong the time; and an account of their baptism shall be ªgiven hereafter.

36 And now all the study of Ammon and ªhis people, and king Limhi and his people, was to deliver themselves out of the hands of the Lamanites and from ᵇbondage.

CHAPTER 22

Plans are made for the people to escape from Lamanite bondage—The Lamanites are made drunk—The people escape, return to Zarahemla, and become subject to King Mosiah. About 121–120 B.C.

AND now it came to pass that Ammon and king Limhi began to consult with the people how they should ªdeliver themselves out of bondage; and even they did cause that all the people should gather themselves together; and this they did that they might have the voice of the people concerning the matter.

2 And it came to pass that they could find no way to deliver themselves out of bondage, except it were to take their women and children, and their flocks, and their herds, and their tents, and depart into the wilderness; for the Lamanites being so numerous, it was impossible for the people of Limhi to contend with them, thinking to deliver themselves out of bondage by the sword.

3 Now it came to pass that ªGideon went forth and stood before the king, and said unto him: Now O king, thou hast hitherto hearkened unto my words many times when we have been contending with our brethren, the Lamanites.

4 And now O king, if thou hast not found me to be an unprofitable servant, or if thou hast hitherto listened to my words in any degree, and they have been of service to thee, even so I desire that thou wouldst listen to my words at this time, and I will be thy servant and deliver this people out of bondage.

5 And the king granted unto him that he might speak. And Gideon said unto him:

6 Behold the back pass, through the back wall, on the back side of the city. The Lamanites, or the

---

29ª Mosiah 21:8 (7–14); 25:9.
30ª Mosiah 17:13 (12–20).
  ᵇ Mosiah 18:34 (34–35).
31ª Mosiah 18:13.
33ª TG Baptism, Essential;

Priesthood, Authority.
34ª Mosiah 18:17.
35ª Mosiah 25:18 (17–18).
36ª Mosiah 7:3 (2–3).
  ᵇ Mosiah 21:13.

22 1ª Mosiah 7:18.
  3ª Mosiah 20:17;
    Alma 1:8 (8–9).

[a]guards of the Lamanites, by night are [b]drunken; therefore let us send a proclamation among all this people that they gather together their flocks and herds, that they may drive them into the wilderness by night.

7 And I will go according to thy command and pay the last [a]tribute of wine to the Lamanites, and they will be [b]drunken; and we will pass through the secret pass on the left of their camp when they are drunken and asleep.

8 Thus we will depart with our women and our children, our flocks, and our herds into the wilderness; and we will travel around the land of [a]Shilom.

9 And it came to pass that the king hearkened unto the words of Gideon.

10 And king Limhi caused that his people should gather their flocks together; and he sent the tribute of wine to the Lamanites; and he also sent more wine, as a present unto them; and they did drink freely of the wine which king Limhi did send unto them.

11 And it came to pass that the people of king Limhi did [a]depart by night into the wilderness with their flocks and their herds, and they went round about the land of [b]Shilom in the wilderness, and bent their course towards the land of Zarahemla, being led by Ammon and his brethren.

12 And they had taken all their gold, and silver, and their precious things, which they could carry, and also their provisions with them, into the wilderness; and they pursued their journey.

13 And after being many days in the wilderness they [a]arrived in the land of Zarahemla, and joined Mosiah's people, and became his subjects.

14 And it came to pass that Mosiah [a]received them with joy; and he also received their [b]records, and also the [c]records which had been found by the people of Limhi.

15 And now it came to pass when the Lamanites had found that the people of Limhi had departed out of the land by night, that they sent an [a]army into the wilderness to pursue them;

16 And after they had pursued them two days, they could no longer follow their tracks; therefore they were lost in the wilderness.

An account of Alma and the people of the Lord, who were driven into the wilderness by the people of King Noah.

Comprising chapters 23 and 24.

CHAPTER 23

Alma refuses to be king—He serves as high priest—The Lord chastens His people, and the Lamanites conquer the land of Helam—Amulon, leader of King Noah's wicked priests, rules subject to the Lamanite monarch. About 145–121 B.C.

Now Alma, having been [a]warned of the Lord that the armies of king Noah would come upon them, and having made it known to his people, therefore they gathered together their flocks, and took of their grain, and [b]departed into the wilderness before the armies of king Noah.

2 And the Lord did strengthen them, that the people of king Noah could not overtake them to destroy them.

3 And they fled [a]eight days' journey into the wilderness.

4 And they came to a land, yea, even a very beautiful and pleasant land, a land of pure water.

5 And they pitched their tents, and began to till the ground, and

---

6a Mosiah 19:28; 21:5.
  b Alma 55:14 (8–17).
7a Mosiah 19:26.
  b TG Drunkenness.
8a Mosiah 7:7 (5–16).
11a Mosiah 25:8.

b Mosiah 11:12 (12–13);
    Alma 23:12.
13a Mosiah 25:5.
14a Mosiah 24:25.
  b Mosiah 8:5; 9:1.
  c Mosiah 8:9.

15a Mosiah 23:30 (30–39).
23 1a Mosiah 18:34;
    Alma 5:4.
  TG Warn.
  b Mosiah 27:16.
3a Mosiah 24:25.

began to build buildings; yea, they were *industrious, and did labor exceedingly.

6 And the people were desirous that Alma should be their *king, for he was beloved by his people.

7 But he said unto them: Behold, it is not expedient that we should have a king; for thus saith the Lord: Ye shall *not esteem one flesh above another, or one man shall not think himself above another; therefore I say unto you it is not expedient that ye should have a king.

8 Nevertheless, if it *were possible that ye could always have just men to be your *kings it would be well for you to have a king.

9 But remember the *iniquity of king Noah and his *priests; and I myself was *caught in a snare, and did many things which were abominable in the sight of the Lord, which caused me sore *repentance;

10 Nevertheless, *after much *tribulation, the Lord did hear my cries, and did answer my prayers, and has made me an *instrument in his hands in bringing *so many of you to a knowledge of his truth.

11 Nevertheless, in this I do not glory, for I am unworthy to glory of myself.

12 And now I say unto you, ye have been *oppressed by king Noah, and have been in bondage to him and his priests, and have been *brought into iniquity by them; therefore ye were bound with the *bands of iniquity.

13 And now as ye have been delivered by the power of God out of these bonds; yea, even out of the *hands of king Noah and his people, and also from the *bonds of iniquity, even so I desire that ye should *stand fast in this *liberty wherewith ye have been made free, and that ye trust *no man to be a king over you.

14 And also trust no one to be your *teacher nor your minister, except he be a man of God, walking in his ways and keeping his commandments.

15 Thus did Alma teach his people, that every man should *love his *neighbor *as himself, that there should be no *contention among them.

16 And now, Alma was their *high priest, he being the founder of their church.

17 And it came to pass that none received *authority to preach or to teach except it were by him from God. Therefore he *consecrated all their priests and all their teachers; and none were consecrated except they were just men.

18 Therefore they did watch over their people, and did *nourish them with things pertaining to righteousness.

19 And it came to pass that they began to prosper exceedingly in the land; and they called the land *Helam.

20 And it came to pass that they did multiply and prosper exceedingly in the land of Helam; and they built a city, which they called the city of Helam.

21 Nevertheless the Lord seeth fit

5a TG Industry;
    Work, Value of.
6a 1 Sam. 8:5;
    3 Ne. 6:30.
7a Mosiah 27:3 (3–5).
8a Mosiah 29:13.
  b TG Governments.
9a Prov. 16:12;
    Mosiah 11:2 (1–15);
    29:17 (17–19).
  b Mosiah 17:12
    (1, 6, 12–18).
  c Mosiah 17:2 (1–4).
  d Mosiah 18:1.
10a D&C 58:4.

  b TG Tribulation.
  c Alma 17:9 (9–11); 26:3.
  d Mosiah 18:35.
12a TG Oppression;
    Unrighteous Dominion.
  b Mosiah 11:2 (1–15).
  c Isa. 58:6;
    2 Ne. 28:19 (19–22);
    Alma 12:11.
13a Mosiah 18:34 (34–35).
  b TG Bondage, Spiritual.
  c Gal. 5:1.
  d TG Liberty.
  e Mosiah 29:13 (5–36).
14a Mosiah 2:4; 18:18 (18–22).

15a TG Love.
  b TG Neighbor.
  c Mosiah 18:21.
  d 3 Ne. 11:29 (28–29).
16a Mosiah 18:18; 26:7.
17a TG Priesthood,
    Authority.
  b Lev. 16:32;
    2 Ne. 5:26.
18a Eph. 6:4;
    1 Tim. 4:6.
19a Mosiah 27:16;
    Alma 24:1.

to ^achasten his people; yea, he trieth their ^bpatience and their faith.

22 Nevertheless—whosoever putteth his ^atrust in him the same shall be ^blifted up at the last day. Yea, and thus it was with this people.

23 For behold, I will show unto you that they were brought into ^abondage, and none could deliver them but the Lord their God, yea, even the God of Abraham and Isaac and of Jacob.

24 And it came to pass that he did deliver them, and he did show forth his mighty power unto them, and great were their rejoicings.

25 For behold, it came to pass that while they were in the land of Helam, yea, in the city of Helam, while tilling the land round about, behold an army of the Lamanites was in the borders of the land.

26 Now it came to pass that the brethren of Alma fled from their fields, and gathered themselves together in the city of Helam; and they were much frightened because of the appearance of the Lamanites.

27 But Alma went forth and stood among them, and exhorted them that they should not be frightened, but that they should remember the Lord their God and he would deliver them.

28 Therefore they hushed their fears, and began to cry unto the Lord that he would soften the hearts of the Lamanites, that they would spare them, and their wives, and their children.

29 And it came to pass that the Lord did soften the hearts of the Lamanites. And Alma and his brethren went forth and delivered themselves up into their hands; and the Lamanites took possession of the land of Helam.

30 Now the ^aarmies of the Lamanites, which had followed after the people of king Limhi, had been lost in the wilderness for many days.

31 And behold, they had found those priests of king Noah, in a place which they called ^aAmulon; and they had begun to possess the land of Amulon and had begun to till the ground.

32 Now the name of the leader of those priests was ^aAmulon.

33 And it came to pass that Amulon did plead with the Lamanites; and he also sent forth their wives, who were the ^adaughters of the Lamanites, to plead with their brethren, that they should not destroy their husbands.

34 And the Lamanites had ^acompassion on Amulon and his brethren, and did not destroy them, because of their wives.

35 And ^aAmulon and his brethren did join the Lamanites, and they were traveling in the wilderness in search of the land of Nephi when they discovered the land of Helam, which was possessed by Alma and his brethren.

36 And it came to pass that the Lamanites promised unto Alma and his brethren, that if they would show them the ^away which led to the land of Nephi that they would grant unto them their lives and their liberty.

37 But after Alma had shown them the way that led to the land of Nephi the Lamanites would not keep their promise; but they set ^aguards round about the land of Helam, over Alma and his brethren.

38 And the remainder of them went to the land of Nephi; and a part of them returned to the land of Helam, and also brought with them the wives and the children of the guards who had been left in the land.

21a Deut. 11:2 (1–8);
    Hel. 12:3;
    D&C 98:21.
    TG Chastening.
  b TG Patience.
22a TG Trust in God.
  b 1 Ne. 13:37;
      Alma 26:7.
23a Alma 36:2.
30a Mosiah 22:15.
31a Mosiah 24:1;
      Alma 23:14.
32a Mosiah 24:8.
33a Mosiah 20:5; 25:12.
34a TG Compassion.
35a Alma 25:4.
36a Mosiah 18:34.
37a Mosiah 24:9 (8–15);
      Alma 5:5.

39 And the king of the Lamanites had granted unto Amulon that he should be a king and a ruler over his people, who were in the land of Helam; nevertheless he should have no power to do anything contrary to the will of the king of the Lamanites.

CHAPTER 24

Amulon persecutes Alma and his people—They are to be put to death if they pray—The Lord makes their burdens seem light—He delivers them from bondage, and they return to Zarahemla. About 145–120 B.C.

AND it came to pass that Amulon did gain favor in the eyes of the king of the Lamanites; therefore, the king of the Lamanites granted unto him and his brethren that they should be appointed teachers over his people, yea, even over the people who were in the land of Shemlon, and in the land of Shilom, and in the *a*land of Amulon.

2 For the Lamanites had taken possession of all these lands; therefore, the king of the Lamanites had appointed kings over all these lands.

3 And now the name of the king of the Lamanites was *a*Laman, being called after the name of his father; and therefore he was called king Laman. And he was king over a numerous people.

4 And he appointed *a*teachers of the *b*brethren of Amulon in every land which was possessed by his people; and thus the *c*language of Nephi began to be taught among all the people of the Lamanites.

5 And they were a people friendly one with another; nevertheless they knew not God; neither did the brethren of Amulon teach them anything concerning the Lord their God, neither the law of Moses; nor did they teach them the words of Abinadi;

6 But they taught them that they should keep their record, and that they might write one to another.

7 And thus the Lamanites began to increase in riches, and began to *a*trade one with another and wax great, and began to be a cunning and a wise people, as to the wisdom of the world, yea, a very cunning people, delighting in all manner of wickedness and plunder, except it were among their own brethren.

8 And now it came to pass that *a*Amulon began to exercise *b*authority over Alma and his brethren, and began to persecute him, and cause that his children should persecute their children.

9 For Amulon knew Alma, that he had been *a*one of the king's priests, and that it was he that believed the words of Abinadi and was driven out before the king, and therefore he was wroth with him; for he was subject to king Laman, yet he exercised authority over them, and put *b*tasks upon them, and put *c*taskmasters over them.

10 And it came to pass that so great were their afflictions that they began to cry mightily to God.

11 And Amulon commanded them that they should stop their cries; and he *a*put guards over them to watch them, that whosoever should be found calling upon God should be put to death.

12 And Alma and his people did not raise their voices to the Lord their God, but did pour out their *a*hearts to him; and he did know the *b*thoughts of their hearts.

13 And it *a*came to pass that the voice of the Lord came to them in their afflictions, saying: Lift up

---

24 1*a* Mosiah 23:31;
    Alma 21:3 (2–4).
  3*a* Mosiah 9:10 (10–11);
    10:6.
  4*a* Mosiah 2:4;
    18:18 (18–22); 23:14.
   b Mosiah 23:9 (9, 12, 31).

   c Omni 1:18.
  7*a* Gen. 34:10 (10–21);
    4 Ne. 1:46.
  8*a* Mosiah 23:32.
   b D&C 121:39.
  9*a* Mosiah 17:2 (1–4); 23:9.
   b Mosiah 21:3 (3–6).

   c Mosiah 23:37 (37–39).
 11*a* Dan. 6:7 (7–27).
 12*a* TG Prayer.
   b Ps. 139:2;
    Matt. 12:25.
 13*a* Jer. 33:3 (1–3);
    Matt. 6:6.

your heads and be of good comfort, for I know of the covenant which ye have made unto me; and I will covenant with my people and deliver them out of bondage.

14 And I will also ease the *burdens which are put upon your shoulders, that even you cannot feel them upon your backs, even while you are in bondage; and this will I do that ye may stand as *witnesses for me hereafter, and that ye may know of a surety that I, the Lord God, do visit my people in their *afflictions.

15 And now it came to pass that the burdens which were laid upon Alma and his brethren were made light; yea, the Lord did *strengthen them that they could bear up their *burdens with ease, and they did submit cheerfully and with *patience to all the will of the Lord.

16 And it came to pass that so great was their faith and their patience that the voice of the Lord came unto them again, saying: Be of good comfort, for on the morrow I will deliver you out of bondage.

17 And he said unto Alma: Thou shalt go before this people, and I will go *with thee and deliver this people out of *bondage.

18 Now it came to pass that Alma and his people in the night-time gathered their flocks together, and also of their grain; yea, even all the night-time were they gathering their flocks together.

19 And in the morning the Lord caused a *deep sleep to come upon the Lamanites, yea, and all their task-masters were in a profound sleep.

20 And Alma and his people departed into the wilderness; and when they had traveled all day they pitched their tents in a valley, and they called the valley Alma, because he led their way in the wilderness.

21 Yea, and in the valley of Alma they poured out their *thanks to God because he had been merciful unto them, and eased their *burdens, and had delivered them out of bondage; for they were in bondage, and none could deliver them except it were the Lord their God.

22 And they gave *thanks to God, yea, all their men and all their women and all their children that could speak lifted their voices in the praises of their God.

23 And now the Lord said unto Alma: Haste thee and get thou and this people out of this land, for the Lamanites have awakened and do pursue thee; therefore get thee out of this land, and I will stop the Lamanites in this valley that they come no further in pursuit of this people.

24 And it came to pass that they departed out of the valley, and took their journey into the wilderness.

25 And after they had been in the wilderness *twelve days they arrived in the land of Zarahemla; and king Mosiah did also *receive them with joy.

CHAPTER 25

The descendants of Mulek at Zarahemla become Nephites—They learn of the people of Alma and of Zeniff—Alma baptizes Limhi and all his people— Mosiah authorizes Alma to organize the Church of God. About 120 B.C.

AND now king Mosiah caused that all the people should be gathered together.

2 Now there were not so many of the children of Nephi, or so many of those who were descendants of

---

14*a* Isa. 46:4 (3–4).
  b TG Witness.
  c TG Adversity;
      Affliction.
15*a* Matt. 11:28 (28–30).
  b Alma 31:38; 33:23.
  c 2 Cor. 4:16;

D&C 54:10.
  TG Patience.
17*a* Ex. 3:12;
      1 Ne. 17:55;
      Alma 38:4.
  b Mosiah 25:10.
  TG Bondage, Physical.

19*a* 1 Sam. 26:12;
      Alma 55:15 (15–16).
21*a* TG Thanksgiving.
  b Ps. 81:6 (5–6).
22*a* TG Thanksgiving.
25*a* Mosiah 23:3.
  b Mosiah 22:14.

Nephi, as there were of the ^apeople of Zarahemla, who was a descendant of ^bMulek, and those who came with him into the wilderness.

3 And there were not so many of the people of Nephi and of the people of Zarahemla as there were of the Lamanites; yea, they were not half so numerous.

4 And now all the people of Nephi were assembled together, and also all the people of Zarahemla, and they were gathered together in two bodies.

5 And it came to pass that Mosiah did read, and caused to be read, the records of Zeniff to his people; yea, he read the records of the people of Zeniff, from the time they ^aleft the land of Zarahemla until they ^breturned again.

6 And he also read the account of Alma and his brethren, and all their afflictions, from the time they left the land of Zarahemla until the time they returned again.

7 And now, when Mosiah had made an end of reading the records, his people who tarried in the land were struck with wonder and amazement.

8 For they knew not what to think; for when they beheld those that had been delivered ^aout of bondage they were filled with exceedingly great joy.

9 And again, when they thought of their brethren who had been ^aslain by the Lamanites they were filled with sorrow, and even shed many tears of sorrow.

10 And again, when they thought of the immediate goodness of God, and his power in delivering Alma and his brethren out of the hands of the Lamanites and of ^abondage, they did raise their voices and give thanks to God.

11 And again, when they thought upon the Lamanites, who were their brethren, of their sinful and ^apolluted state, they were filled with ^bpain and anguish for the ^cwelfare of their souls.

12 And it came to pass that those who ^awere the children of Amulon and his brethren, who had taken to wife the ^bdaughters of the Lamanites, were displeased with the conduct of their fathers, and they would no longer be called by the names of their fathers, therefore they took upon themselves the name of Nephi, that they might be called the children of Nephi and be numbered among those who were ^ccalled Nephites.

13 And now all the people of Zarahemla were ^anumbered with the Nephites, and this because the kingdom had been conferred upon none but those who were descendants of Nephi.

14 And now it came to pass that when Mosiah had made an end of speaking and reading to the people, he desired that Alma should also speak to the people.

15 And Alma did speak unto them, when they were assembled together in large bodies, and he went from one body to another, preaching unto the people repentance and faith on the Lord.

16 And he did exhort the people of Limhi and his brethren, all those that had been delivered out of bondage, that they should remember that it was the Lord that did deliver them.

17 And it came to pass that after Alma had taught the people many things, and had made an end of speaking to them, that king Limhi was desirous that he might be baptized; and all his people were

---

25 2a Hel. 6:10.
     b Ezek. 17:22 (22–23);
       Omni 1:15 (14–19).
   5a Mosiah 9:3 (3–4).
     b Mosiah 22:13.
   8a Mosiah 22:11 (11–13).
   9a Mosiah 21:29 (8, 29).

10a Mosiah 24:17; 27:16.
11a TG Pollution.
     b Mosiah 28:3 (3–4);
       Alma 13:27.
     c 2 Ne. 6:3;
       Jacob 2:3.
       TG Worth of Souls.

12a Mosiah 20:3 (3–5).
     b Mosiah 23:33.
     c Jacob 1:14 (13–14);
       Alma 2:11.
13a Omni 1:19.

desirous that they might be baptized also.

18 Therefore, Alma did go forth into the water and did ᵃbaptize them; yea, he did baptize them after the manner he did his brethren in the ᵇwaters of Mormon; yea, and as many as he did baptize did belong to the church of God; and this because of their belief on the words of Alma.

19 And it came to pass that king Mosiah granted unto Alma that he might establish ᵃchurches throughout all the land of Zarahemla; and gave him power to ᵇordain ᶜpriests and ᵈteachers over every church.

20 Now this was done because there were so many people that they could not all be governed by one teacher; neither could they all hear the word of God in one assembly;

21 Therefore they did ᵃassemble themselves together in different bodies, being called churches; every church having their priests and their teachers, and every priest preaching the word according as it was delivered to him by the mouth of Alma.

22 And thus, notwithstanding there being many churches they were all one ᵃchurch, yea, even the church of God; for there was nothing preached in all the churches except it were repentance and faith in God.

23 And now there were seven churches in the land of Zarahemla. And it came to pass that whosoever were desirous to take upon them the ᵃname of Christ, or of God, they did join the churches of God;

24 And they were called the ᵃpeople of God. And the Lord did pour out his ᵇSpirit upon them, and they were blessed, and prospered in the land.

CHAPTER 26

Many members of the Church are led into sin by unbelievers—Alma is promised eternal life—Those who repent and are baptized gain forgiveness—Church members in sin who repent and confess to Alma and to the Lord will be forgiven; otherwise, they will not be numbered among the people of the Church. About 120–100 B.C.

Now it came to pass that there were many of the rising generation that could not understand the ᵃwords of king Benjamin, being little children at the time he spake unto his people; and they did ᵇnot believe the tradition of their fathers.

2 They did not believe what had been said concerning the resurrection of the dead, neither did they believe concerning the coming of Christ.

3 And now because of their ᵃunbelief they could not ᵇunderstand the word of God; and their hearts were hardened.

4 And they would not be baptized; neither would they join the ᵃchurch. And they were a separate people as to their faith, and remained so ever after, even in their ᵇcarnal and sinful state; for they would not call upon the Lord their God.

5 And now in the reign of Mosiah they were not half so numerous as the people of God; but because of the ᵃdissensions among the brethren they became more numerous.

6 For it came to pass that they did ᵃdeceive many with their ᵇflattering words, who were in the church, and did cause them to commit many sins; therefore it became expedient

---

18a Mosiah 21:35.
  b Mosiah 18:16 (8–17).
19a Mosiah 26:17.
  b TG Priesthood.
  c TG Priest, Melchizedek Priesthood.
  d TG Teacher.
21a TG Church.
22a Mosiah 18:17; 26:4.
23a TG Jesus Christ, Taking

the Name of.
24a TG Sons and Daughters of God.
  b TG God, Spirit of; Prosper.
26 1a Mosiah 2:1.
  b TG Family, Children, Duties of.
3a TG Unbelief.
  b TG Understanding.

4a Mosiah 25:22 (18–23); Alma 4:5 (4–5).
  b TG Man, Natural, Not Spiritually Reborn.
5a TG Apostasy of Individuals.
6a Col. 2:18 (16–23). TG Deceit.
  b TG Flatter.

that those who committed sin, that were in the church, should be ^cadmonished by the church.

7 And it came to pass that they were brought before the priests, and delivered up unto the ^apriests by the teachers; and the priests brought them before Alma, who was the ^bhigh priest.

8 Now king Mosiah had given Alma the ^aauthority over the ^bchurch.

9 And it came to pass that Alma did not know concerning them; but there were many ^awitnesses against them; yea, the people stood and testified of their iniquity in abundance.

10 Now there had not any such thing happened before in the church; therefore Alma was troubled in his spirit, and he caused that they should be brought before the king.

11 And he said unto the king: Behold, here are many whom we have brought before thee, who are accused of their brethren; yea, and they have been taken in divers iniquities. And they do not repent of their iniquities; therefore we have brought them before thee, that thou mayest judge them according to their crimes.

12 But king Mosiah said unto Alma: Behold, I judge them not; therefore I ^adeliver them into thy hands to be judged.

13 And now the spirit of Alma was again troubled; and he went and inquired of the Lord what he should do concerning this matter, for he feared that he should do wrong in the sight of God.

14 And it came to pass that after

he had poured out his whole soul to God, the ^avoice of the Lord came to him, saying:

15 Blessed art thou, Alma, and blessed are they who were baptized in the ^awaters of Mormon. Thou art blessed because of thy exceeding ^bfaith in the words alone of my servant Abinadi.

16 And blessed are they because of their exceeding faith in the words alone which thou hast spoken unto them.

17 And blessed art thou because thou hast established a ^achurch among this people; and they shall be established, and they shall be my people.

18 Yea, blessed is this people who are willing to bear my ^aname; for in my ^bname shall they be called; and they are mine.

19 And because thou hast inquired of me concerning the transgressor, thou art blessed.

20 Thou art my servant; and I covenant with thee that thou shalt have ^aeternal life; and thou shalt serve me and go forth in my name, and shalt gather together my sheep.

21 And he that will hear my voice shall be my ^asheep; and him shall ye receive into the church, and him will I also receive.

22 For behold, ^athis is my ^bchurch; whosoever is ^cbaptized shall be baptized unto repentance. And whomsoever ye receive shall ^dbelieve in my name; and him will I freely ^eforgive.

23 For it is I that taketh upon me the ^asins of the world; for it is I that hath ^bcreated them; and it is I that granteth unto him that believeth

6c Alma 5:57 (57–58); 6:3.
  TG Warn.
7a TG Priest, Melchizedek Priesthood.
  b Mosiah 23:16; 29:42.
8a TG Delegation of Responsibility.
  b TG Church Organization.
9a TG Witness.
12a D&C 42:87 (78–93).
14a TG Guidance, Divine.

15a Mosiah 18:30.
  b Mosiah 17:2; D&C 46:14.
  TG Faith.
17a Mosiah 25:19 (19–24).
18a Mosiah 1:11; 5:8.
  TG Jesus Christ, Taking the Name of.
  b Deut. 28:10.
20a TG Election.
21a TG Jesus Christ, Good

Shepherd.
22a Mosiah 27:13.
  b TG Jesus Christ, Head of the Church.
  c 2 Ne. 9:23.
  d TG Baptism, Qualifications for.
  e TG Remission of Sins.
23a TG Jesus Christ, Redeemer.
  b TG Jesus Christ, Creator.

unto the end a place at my right hand.

24 For behold, in my name are they called; and if they [a]know me they shall come forth, and shall have a place eternally at my right hand.

25 And it shall come to pass that when the [a]second trump shall sound then shall they that never [b]knew me come forth and shall stand before me.

26 And then shall they know that I am the Lord their God, that I am their Redeemer; but they would not be redeemed.

27 And then I will confess unto them that I never [a]knew them; and they shall [b]depart into [c]everlasting fire prepared for the devil and his angels.

28 Therefore I say unto you, that he that will not [a]hear my voice, the same shall ye not receive into my church, for him I will not receive at the last day.

29 Therefore I say unto you, Go; and whosoever transgresseth against me, him shall ye [a]judge [b]according to the sins which he has committed; and if he [c]confess his sins before thee and me, and [d]repenteth in the sincerity of his heart, him shall ye [e]forgive, and I will forgive him also.

30 Yea, and [a]as often as my people [b]repent will I forgive them their trespasses against me.

31 And ye shall also [a]forgive one another your trespasses; for verily I say unto you, he that forgiveth not his [b]neighbor's trespasses when he says that he repents, the same

hath brought himself under condemnation.

32 Now I say unto you, Go; and whosoever will [a]not repent of his sins the same shall not be numbered among my people; and this shall be observed from this time forward.

33 And it came to pass when Alma had heard these words he [a]wrote them down that he might have them, and that he might judge the people of that church according to the commandments of God.

34 And it came to pass that Alma went and judged those that had been taken in iniquity, according to the [a]word of the Lord.

35 And whosoever repented of their sins and did [a]confess them, them he did number among the people of the church;

36 And those that would not confess their sins and repent of their iniquity, the same were not numbered among the people of the church, and their names were [a]blotted out.

37 And it came to pass that Alma did regulate all the affairs of the church; and they began again to have peace and to prosper exceedingly in the affairs of the church, walking circumspectly before God, receiving many, and baptizing many.

38 And now all these things did Alma and his [a]fellow laborers do who were over the church, [b]walking in all diligence, teaching the word of God in all things, suffering all manner of afflictions, being persecuted by all those who did not belong to the church of God.

39 And they did admonish their

24a John 17:3.
25a Dan. 12:2 (1–2).
  b 3 Ne. 14:23 (21–23);
    D&C 76:85 (81–86);
    112:26.
27a Matt. 7:23 (21–23).
  b Luke 13:27.
  c 1 Ne. 15:35 (32–36).
28a 2 Ne. 9:31;
    D&C 1:14 (2, 11, 14);
    Moses 6:27.
29a TG Judgment.
  b TG Accountability.
  c Num. 5:7 (6–10);

Alma 17:4;
  3 Ne. 1:25.
  TG Confession.
  d TG Repent.
  e TG Forgive.
30a Moro. 6:8.
  b Ezek. 33:11 (11, 15–16);
    Amos 5:4 (4–8);
    Acts 3:19 (19–20);
    2 Ne. 1:20;
    Mosiah 29:20.
31a Col. 3:13 (12–14);
    3 Ne. 13:14 (14–15);
    D&C 64:10 (9–10).

b TG Neighbor.
32a Alma 1:24.
    TG Excommunication.
33a TG Scriptures,
    Writing of.
34a 2 Ne. 33:14 (13–15).
35a TG Confession.
36a Ex. 32:33;
    Ps. 9:5; 109:13;
    Alma 1:24.
    TG Book of Life.
38a TG Church Organization.
  b TG Walking with God.

brethren; and they were also ᵃadmonished, every one by the word of God, according to his sins, or to the sins which he had committed, being commanded of God to ᵇpray without ceasing, and to give ᶜthanks in all things.

CHAPTER 27

Mosiah forbids persecution and enjoins equality—Alma the younger and the four sons of Mosiah seek to destroy the Church—An angel appears and commands them to cease their evil course—Alma is struck dumb—All mankind must be born again to gain salvation—Alma and the sons of Mosiah declare glad tidings. About 100–92 B.C.

AND now it came to pass that the persecutions which were inflicted on the church by the unbelievers became so great that the church began to murmur, and complain to their leaders concerning the matter; and they did complain to Alma. And Alma laid the case before their king, Mosiah. And Mosiah ᵃconsulted with his priests.

2 And it came to pass that king Mosiah sent a proclamation throughout the land round about that there should not any unbeliever ᵃpersecute any of those who belonged to the church of God.

3 And there was a strict command throughout all the churches that there should be no ᵃpersecutions among them, that there should be an ᵇequality among all men;

4 That they should let no pride nor haughtiness disturb their ᵃpeace; that every man should ᵇesteem his ᶜneighbor as himself, ᵈlaboring with their own hands for their support.

5 Yea, and all their priests and teachers ᵃshould ᵇlabor with their own hands for their support, in all cases save it were in sickness, or in much want; and doing these things, they did abound in the ᶜgrace of God.

6 And there began to be much peace again in the land; and the people began to be very numerous, and began to scatter abroad upon the face of the earth, yea, on the north and on the south, on the east and on the west, building large cities and villages in all quarters of the land.

7 And the Lord did ᵃvisit them and ᵇprosper them, and they became a large and wealthy people.

8 Now the sons of Mosiah were numbered among the ᵃunbelievers; and also one of the sons of Alma was numbered among them, he being called Alma, after his father; nevertheless, he became a very wicked and an ᵇidolatrous man. And he was a man of many words, and did speak much ᶜflattery to the people; therefore he ᵈled many of the people to do after the manner of his ᵉiniquities.

9 And he became a great hinderment to the prosperity of the church of God; ᵃstealing away the hearts of the people; causing much dissension among the people; giving a chance for the enemy of God to exercise his ᵇpower over them.

10 And now it came to pass that while he was going about to ᵃdestroy the church of God, for he did go about secretly with the sons of Mosiah seeking to destroy the church,

39*a* TG Warn.
  b 2 Ne. 32:9 (8–9).
  c TG Thanksgiving.
27 1*a* TG Counsel.
  2*a* TG Persecution.
  3*a* TG Malice.
  b Mosiah 23:7; 29:32;
    Alma 30:11.
  4*a* TG Peace.
  b TG Love.
  c TG Neighbor.
  d TG Industry;

    Labor.
5*a* Mosiah 18:24 (24, 26);
    Alma 1:3, 26.
  b TG Work, Value of.
  c TG Grace.
7*a* Ex. 3:16.
  b TG Prosper.
8*a* 1 Sam. 3:13;
    1 Ne. 2:12 (12–13);
    Moses 5:16.
    TG Unbelief.
  b TG Idolatry.

  c TG Flatter.
  d TG Peer Influence.
  e Mal. 2:8.
9*a* 2 Sam. 12:14 (1–14);
    15:6 (1–6).
    TG Apostasy of
    Individuals.
  b D&C 50:7;
    93:39 (37, 39).
10*a* Acts 8:3;
    Mosiah 28:4 (3–4).

and to lead astray the people of the Lord, contrary to the commandments of God, or even the king—

11 And as I said unto you, as they were going about *a*rebelling against God, behold, the *b*angel of the Lord *c*appeared unto them; and he descended as it were in a *d*cloud; and he spake as it were with a voice of thunder, which caused the earth to shake upon which they stood;

12 And so great was their astonishment, that they fell to the earth, and understood not the words which he spake unto them.

13 Nevertheless he cried again, saying: Alma, arise and stand forth, for why persecutest thou the church of God? For the Lord hath said: *a*This is my church, and I will establish it; and nothing shall *b*overthrow it, save it is the transgression of my people.

14 And again, the angel said: Behold, the Lord hath *a*heard the prayers of his people, and also the *b*prayers of his servant, Alma, who is thy father; for he has *c*prayed with much faith concerning thee that thou mightest be brought to the *d*knowledge of the truth; therefore, for this purpose have I come to *e*convince thee of the power and authority of God, that the *f*prayers of his servants might be answered according to their faith.

15 And now behold, can ye dispute the power of God? For behold, doth not my voice shake the earth? And can ye not also *a*behold me before you? And I am sent from God.

16 Now I say unto thee: Go, and remember the captivity of thy fathers in the land of *a*Helam, and in the land of Nephi; and remember how great things he has done for them; for they were in *b*bondage, and he has *c*delivered them. And now I say unto thee, Alma, go thy way, and seek to destroy the church no more, that their prayers may be answered, and this even if thou wilt of *d*thyself be *e*cast off.

17 And now it came to pass that these were the last words which the angel spake unto Alma, and he departed.

18 And now Alma and those that were with him fell again to the earth, for great was their astonishment; for with their own eyes they had beheld an *a*angel of the Lord; and his voice was as thunder, which *b*shook the earth; and they knew that there was nothing save the power of God that could shake the earth and cause it to tremble as though it would part asunder.

19 And now the astonishment of Alma was so great that he became *a*dumb, that he could not open his mouth; yea, and he became weak, even that he could not move his hands; therefore he was taken by those that were with him, and carried helpless, even until he was laid before his father.

20 And they rehearsed unto his father all that had happened unto them; and his father rejoiced, for he knew that it was the power of God.

21 And he caused that a multitude should be gathered together that they might witness what the Lord

11 a TG Disobedience; Rebellion.
  b Alma 21:5.
  c Acts 9:3 (1–9); Mosiah 27:15; Alma 8:15; 17:2.
  d Ex. 19:9 (9, 16).
13 a Mosiah 26:22. TG Jesus Christ, Head of the Church.
  b Hosea 13:9. TG Apostasy of

Individuals.
14 a Dan. 10:12; Abr. 1:16 (15–16).
  b 2 Cor. 1:11; Alma 10:22.
  c TG Family, Love within.
  d Hosea 4:6.
  e Alma 29:10.
  f Alma 19:17; Morm. 9:36 (36–37).
15 a Mosiah 27:11.
16 a Mosiah 23:19;

Alma 24:1.
  b Mosiah 25:10; Alma 5:5 (5–6).
  c Mosiah 23:1 (1–4).
  d Alma 30:47.
  e Micah 3:6 (1–7); Matt. 8:12 (11–12).
18 a TG Angels.
  b Isa. 6:4; Alma 36:7.
19 a Dan. 10:15; Luke 1:20 (20–22).

had done for his son, and also for those that were with him.

22 And he caused that the priests should assemble themselves together; and they began to fast, and to pray to the Lord their God that he would open the mouth of Alma, that he might speak, and also that his limbs might receive their strength—that the eyes of the people might be opened to see and know of the goodness and glory of God.

23 And it came to pass after they had fasted and prayed for the space of ªtwo days and two nights, the limbs of Alma received their strength, and he stood up and began to speak unto them, bidding them to be of good comfort:

24 For, said he, I have repented of my sins, and have been ªredeemed of the Lord; behold I am born of the Spirit.

25 And the Lord said unto me: Marvel not that all mankind, yea, men and women, all nations, kindreds, tongues and people, must be ªborn again; yea, ᵇborn of God, ᶜchanged from their carnal and ᵈfallen state, to a state of righteousness, being redeemed of God, becoming his ᵉsons and daughters;

26 And thus they become new creatures; and unless they do this, they can in ªnowise inherit the kingdom of God.

27 I say unto you, unless this be the case, they must be cast off; and this I know, because I was like to be cast off.

28 Nevertheless, after ªwading through much ᵇtribulation, repenting nigh unto death, the Lord in mercy hath seen fit to snatch me out of an ᶜeverlasting burning, and I am born of God.

29 My soul hath been ªredeemed from the gall of bitterness and ᵇbonds of iniquity. I was in the darkest abyss; but now I behold the marvelous light of God. My soul was ᶜracked with eternal torment; but I am snatched, and my soul is ᵈpained no more.

30 I rejected my Redeemer, and denied that which had been spoken of by our fathers; but now that they may foresee that he will come, and that he remembereth every creature of his creating, he will make himself manifest unto ªall.

31 Yea, ªevery knee shall bow, and every tongue confess before him. Yea, even at the last day, when all men shall stand to be ᵇjudged of him, then shall they confess that he is ᶜGod; then shall they confess, who live ᵈwithout God in the world, that the judgment of an everlasting punishment is just upon them; and they shall quake, and tremble, and shrink beneath the glance of his ᵉall-searching eye.

32 And now it came to pass that Alma began from this time forward to teach the people, and those who were with Alma at the time the angel appeared unto them, traveling round about through all the land, publishing to all the people the things which they had heard and seen, and preaching the word of God in much tribulation, being greatly persecuted by those who were unbelievers, being smitten by many of them.

23 a Alma 36:10.
24 a Ps. 49:15;
     Alma 27:25;
     A of F 1:3.
25 a Rom. 6:3 (3–11).
     TG Conversion;
     Man, New, Spiritually
     Reborn.
   b Mosiah 5:7;
     Alma 5:14 (14, 49).
   c Moses 6:65.

   d TG Man, Natural, Not
     Spiritually Reborn.
   e Mosiah 15:10;
     Moro. 7:19.
26 a John 3:5.
28 a Alma 7:5.
   b TG Tribulation.
   c 2 Ne. 9:16.
29 a Isa. 38:17.
   b Isa. 58:6.
   c Mosiah 2:38.

   d TG Pain.
30 a D&C 84:46 (45–46).
31 a Philip. 2:10 (9–11);
     Mosiah 16:1 (1–2);
     D&C 88:104; 138:23.
   b TG Jesus Christ, Judge.
   c Mosiah 7:27;
     Alma 11:39 (38–39).
   d Eph. 2:12;
     Alma 41:11.
   e TG God, Omniscience of.

33 But notwithstanding all this, they did impart much consolation to the church, confirming their faith, and exhorting them with long-suffering and much travail to keep the commandments of God.

34 And four of them were the ªsons of Mosiah; and their names were Ammon, and Aaron, and Omner, and Himni; these were the names of the sons of Mosiah.

35 And they traveled throughout all the land of Zarahemla, and among all the ªpeople who were under the reign of king Mosiah, ᵇzealously striving to repair all the injuries which they had done to the church, ᶜconfessing all their sins, and publishing all the things which they had seen, and explaining the prophecies and the scriptures to all who desired to hear them.

36 And thus they were instruments in the hands of God in bringing many to the knowledge of the truth, yea, to the knowledge of their Redeemer.

37 And how blessed are they! For they did ªpublish ᵇpeace; they did publish good tidings of good; and they did declare unto the people that the Lord reigneth.

CHAPTER 28

The sons of Mosiah go to preach to the Lamanites—Using the two seer stones, Mosiah translates the Jaredite plates. About 92 B.C.

Now it came to pass that after the ªsons of Mosiah had done all these things, they took a small number with them and returned to their father, the king, and desired of him that he would grant unto them that they might, with these whom they had ᵇselected, go up to the land of ᶜNephi that they might preach the things which they had heard, and that they might impart the word of God to their brethren, the Lamanites—

2 ªThat perhaps they might bring them to the knowledge of the Lord their God, and convince them of the iniquity of their fathers; and that perhaps they might cure them of their ᵇhatred towards the Nephites, that they might also be brought to rejoice in the Lord their God, that they might become friendly to one another, and that there should be no more contentions in all the land which the Lord their God had given them.

3 Now they were desirous that salvation should be declared to every creature, for they could not ªbear that any human ᵇsoul should ᶜperish; yea, even the very thoughts that any soul should endure ᵈendless torment did cause them to quake and ᵉtremble.

4 And thus did the Spirit of the Lord work upon them, for they were the very ªvilest of sinners. And the Lord saw fit in his infinite ᵇmercy to spare them; nevertheless they suffered much anguish of soul because of their iniquities, suffering much and fearing that they should be cast off forever.

5 And it came to pass that they did plead with their father many days that they might go up to the land of Nephi.

6 And king Mosiah went and ªinquired of the Lord if he should let his sons go up among the Lamanites to preach the word.

34a Mosiah 28:1; 29:3;
     Alma 17:1.
35a Mosiah 1:10; 28:18.
   b TG Zeal.
   c Alma 39:13.
37a Mosiah 12:21;
     15:14 (14–17).
   b TG Peace of God.
28 1a Mosiah 27:34.
    b Alma 17:8.
    c Mosiah 9:1 (1, 3–4, 14);

     Alma 50:8 (8, 11).
2a Alma 17:16.
  b Jacob 7:24;
     Mosiah 1:5;
     Alma 26:9.
3a 1 Ne. 7:8;
     Mosiah 25:11;
     Alma 13:27 (27–30); 31:2;
     3 Ne. 17:14;
     Moses 7:41.
  b TG Worth of Souls.

     c Matt. 18:14.
     d Jacob 6:10;
       Moro. 8:21;
       D&C 19:12 (10–12).
     e 1 Cor. 2:3.
4a Mosiah 27:10;
     Alma 26:18 (17–18).
   b TG God, Mercy of.
6a Ex. 18:15;
     Alma 43:23.

7 And the Lord said unto Mosiah: Let them go up, for many shall believe on their words, and they shall have eternal life; and I will ^adeliver thy sons out of the hands of the Lamanites.

8 And it came to pass that Mosiah granted that they might go and do according to their request.

9 And they ^atook their journey into the wilderness to go up to preach the word among the Lamanites; and I shall give an ^baccount of their proceedings hereafter.

10 Now king Mosiah had no one to confer the kingdom upon, for there was not any of his sons who ^awould accept of the kingdom.

11 Therefore he took the records which were engraven on the plates of ^abrass, and also the plates of ^bNephi, and all the things which he had kept and preserved according to the commandments of God, after having translated and caused to be written the records which were on the ^cplates of gold which had been found by the people of Limhi, which were delivered to him by the hand of Limhi;

12 And this he did because of the great anxiety of his people; for they were desirous beyond measure to know concerning those people ^awho had been destroyed.

13 And now he translated them by the means of those two ^astones which were fastened into the two rims of a bow.

14 Now these things were prepared from the beginning, and were handed down from generation to generation, for the purpose of interpreting languages;

15 And they have been kept and preserved by the hand of the Lord, that he should discover to every creature who should possess the land the iniquities and abominations of his people;

16 And whosoever has these things is called ^aseer, after the manner of old times.

17 Now after Mosiah had finished ^atranslating these ^brecords, behold, it gave an account of the people who were ^cdestroyed, from the time that they were destroyed back to the building of the ^dgreat tower, at the time the Lord ^econfounded the language of the people and they were scattered abroad upon the face of all the earth, yea, and even from that time back until the creation of Adam.

18 Now this account did cause the people of Mosiah to mourn exceedingly, yea, they were filled with sorrow; nevertheless it gave them much knowledge, in the which they did rejoice.

19 And this account shall be ^awritten hereafter; for behold, it is expedient that all people should know the things which are written in this account.

20 And now, as I said unto you, that after king Mosiah had done these things, he took the plates of ^abrass, and all the things which he had kept, and ^bconferred them upon Alma, who was the son of Alma; yea, all the records, and also the ^cinterpreters, and conferred them upon him, and commanded him that he should keep and ^dpreserve them, and also keep a record of the people, handing them down from

7 a Alma 17:35; 19:23 (22–23).
9 a Alma 17:6 (6–9); 26:1.
  b IE in Alma 17–26.
10 a Mosiah 29:3 (1–3).
11 a Mosiah 10:16.
  b W of M 1:10.
  c Mosiah 21:27;
     Alma 37:21 (21–31).
12 a Mosiah 8:8.
13 a Ex. 28:30;
     Mosiah 21:28 (27–28);

Abr. 3:1;
  JS—H 1:35.
16 a Mosiah 8:13 (13–18).
     TG Seer.
17 a Omni 1:20;
     Alma 9:21.
  b TG Scriptures,
     Writing of.
  c Mosiah 8:8 (7–12);
     Alma 22:30.
  d Ether 1:3 (1–5).

e Gen. 11:7 (6–9);
  Omni 1:22.
19 a Ether 1:1.
20 a Mosiah 1:3 (3–4);
     Alma 37:3 (3–12).
  b Mosiah 37:1.
  c TG Urim and Thummim.
  d TG Scriptures,
     Preservation of.

one generation to another, even as they had been handed down from the time that Lehi left Jerusalem.

CHAPTER 29

Mosiah proposes that judges be chosen in place of a king—Unrighteous kings lead their people into sin—Alma the younger is chosen chief judge by the voice of the people—He is also the high priest over the Church—Alma the elder and Mosiah die. About 92–91 B.C.

Now when Mosiah had done this he sent out throughout all the land, among all the people, desiring to know their will concerning who should be their king.

2 And it came to pass that the voice of the people came, saying: We are desirous that Aaron thy son should be our king and our ruler.

3 Now Aaron had gone up to the land of Nephi, therefore the king could not confer the kingdom upon him; *a*neither would Aaron take upon him the kingdom; neither were any of the *b*sons of Mosiah *c*willing to take upon them the kingdom.

4 Therefore king Mosiah sent again among the people; yea, even a written word sent he among the people. And these were the words that were written, saying:

5 Behold, O ye my people, or my brethren, for I esteem you as such, I desire that ye should consider the cause which ye are called to *a*consider—for ye are desirous to have a king.

6 Now I declare unto you that he to whom the kingdom doth rightly belong has declined, and will not take upon him the kingdom.

7 And now if there should be another appointed in his stead, behold I fear there would rise *a*contentions among you. And who knoweth but what my son, to whom the kingdom doth belong, should turn to be angry and *b*draw away a part of this people after him, which would cause wars and contentions among you, which would be the cause of shedding much blood and perverting the way of the Lord, yea, and destroy the souls of many people.

8 Now I say unto you let us be wise and consider these things, for we have no right to destroy my son, neither should we have any right to destroy another if he should be appointed in his stead.

9 And if my son should turn again to his pride and vain things he would recall the things which he had said, and claim his right to the kingdom, which would cause him and also this people to commit much sin.

10 And now let us be wise and look forward to these things, and do that which will make for the peace of this people.

11 Therefore I will be your king the remainder of my days; nevertheless, let *a*us appoint *b*judges, to judge this people according to our law; and we will newly arrange the affairs of this people, for we will appoint wise men to be judges, that will judge this people according to the commandments of God.

12 Now it is better that a man should be *a*judged of God than of man, for the judgments of God are always just, but the judgments of man are not always just.

13 Therefore, *a*if it were possible that you could have *b*just men to be your kings, who would establish the *c*laws of God, and judge this people according to his commandments,

29 3*a* Alma 17:6.
  b Mosiah 27:34.
  c Mosiah 28:10.
 5*a* 1 Sam. 8:9 (9–19).
 7*a* TG Contention.
  b Judg. 8:23; 9:2 (1–55).
 11*a* Mosiah 29:25
   (25–27, 41).

  b Ex. 18:13;
   Deut. 16:18;
   Ezra 7:25;
   Alma 46:4;
   D&C 107:74 (74, 78).
 12*a* 2 Sam. 23:3;
   2 Chr. 1:10;
   Ps. 50:6; 75:7;

   2 Ne. 21:4;
   D&C 98:9;
   Moses 6:57.
   TG God, Justice of.
 13*a* Mosiah 23:8, 13.
  b 1 Kgs. 15:14 (11–14).
  c Ex. 18:21;
   Neh. 7:2.

yea, if ye could have men for your kings who would do even as my father *d*Benjamin did for this people—I say unto you, if this could always be the case then it would be expedient that ye should always have kings to rule over you.

14 And even I myself have labored with all the power and faculties which I have possessed, to teach you the commandments of God, and to establish peace throughout the land, that there should be no wars nor contentions, no stealing, nor plundering, nor murdering, nor any manner of iniquity;

15 And whosoever has committed iniquity, him have I *a*punished according to the crime which he has committed, according to the law which has been given to us by our fathers.

16 Now I say unto you, that because all men are not just it is not expedient that ye should have a *a*king or kings to rule over you.

17 For behold, how much *a*iniquity doth one *b*wicked king cause to be committed, yea, and what great destruction!

18 Yea, remember king Noah, his *a*wickedness and his abominations, and also the wickedness and abominations of his people. Behold what great destruction did come upon them; and also because of their iniquities they were brought into *b*bondage.

19 And were it not for the interposition of their all-wise Creator, and this because of their sincere repentance, they must unavoidably remain in bondage until now.

20 But behold, he did deliver them because they did *a*humble themselves before him; and because they *b*cried mightily unto him he did deliver them out of bondage; and thus doth the Lord work with his power in all cases among the children of men, extending the arm of *c*mercy towards them that put their *d*trust in him.

21 And behold, now I say unto you, ye cannot dethrone an iniquitous *a*king save it be through much contention, and the shedding of much blood.

22 For behold, he has his *a*friends in iniquity, and he keepeth his guards about him; and he teareth up the laws of those who have reigned in righteousness before him; and he trampleth under his feet the commandments of God;

23 And he enacteth laws, and sendeth them forth among his people, yea, laws after the manner of his own wickedness; and whosoever doth not obey his laws he *a*causeth to be destroyed; and whosoever doth rebel against him he will send his armies against them to war, and if he can he will destroy them; and thus an unrighteous *b*king doth pervert the ways of all righteousness.

24 And now behold I say unto you, it is not expedient that such abominations should come upon you.

25 Therefore, choose you by the *a*voice of this people, judges, that ye may be *b*judged according to the *c*laws which have been given you by our fathers, which are correct, and which were given them by the hand of the Lord.

26 Now it is not common that the *a*voice of the people desireth

13 *d* Omni 1:25;
   W of M 1:18 (17–18).
15 *a* Alma 1:32.
16 *a* 1 Sam. 8:5 (4–22).
   TG Kings, Earthly.
17 *a* 1 Kgs. 16:26 (25–26);
   Alma 46:9.
   b Prov. 16:12;
   Mosiah 23:9 (8–10).
18 *a* Mosiah 11:2 (1–15).
   b 1 Sam. 8:11 (10–18);
   Mosiah 12:2 (2–8);

   Ether 6:23.
20 *a* Mosiah 21:14.
   b Ex. 2:23 (23–25);
   Alma 43:49 (49–50).
   c Ezek. 33:11 (11, 15–16);
   Mosiah 26:30.
   d TG Trust in God.
21 *a* 1 Sam. 8:9;
   Prov. 25:5 (4–5).
22 *a* 1 Kgs. 12:8 (8–15).
23 *a* TG Tyranny;
   Unrighteous Dominion.

   b TG Kings, Earthly.
25 *a* Mosiah 29:11;
   Alma 2:3 (3–7).
   TG Citizenship.
   b Ex. 18:22 (19–27).
   c Deut. 4:8;
   Alma 34:11.
26 *a* 1 Sam. 8:7;
   Alma 29:4;
   D&C 26:2.
   TG Common Consent.

anything ᵇcontrary to that which is right; but it is common for the lesser part of the ᶜpeople to desire that which is not right; therefore this shall ye observe and make it your law—to do your business by the voice of the people.

27 And ᵃif the time comes that the voice of the people doth choose iniquity, then is the time that the judgments of God will come upon you; yea, then is the time he will visit you with great destruction even as he has hitherto visited this land.

28 And now if ye have judges, and they do not ᵃjudge you according to the law which has been given, ye can cause that they may be judged of a higher judge.

29 If your higher judges do not judge righteous judgments, ye shall cause that a small number of your lower judges should be gathered together, and they shall judge your higher judges, according to the voice of the people.

30 And I command you to do these things in the fear of the Lord; and I command you to do these things, and that ye have no king; that if these people commit sins and iniquities they shall be answered upon their own heads.

31 For behold I say unto you, the sins of many people have been ᵃcaused by the iniquities of their kings; therefore their iniquities are answered upon the heads of their kings.

32 And now I desire that this ᵃinequality should be no more in this land, especially among this my people; but I desire that this land be a land of ᵇliberty, and ᶜevery man may enjoy his rights and privileges alike, so long as the Lord sees fit that we may live and inherit the land, yea,

even as long as any of our posterity remains upon the face of the land.

33 And many more things did king Mosiah write unto them, unfolding unto them all the trials and ᵃtroubles of a righteous king, yea, all the travails of soul for their people, and also all the murmurings of the people to their king; and he explained it all unto them.

34 And he told them that these things ought not to be; but that the burden should come upon all the people, that every man might ᵃbear his part.

35 And he also unfolded unto them all the disadvantages they labored under, by having an unrighteous ᵃking to rule over them;

36 Yea, all ᵃhis iniquities and abominations, and all the wars, and contentions, and bloodshed, and the stealing, and the plundering, and the committing of whoredoms, and all manner of iniquities which cannot be enumerated—telling them that these things ought not to be, that they were expressly repugnant to the commandments of God.

37 And now it came to pass, after king Mosiah had sent these things forth among the people they were ᵃconvinced of the truth of his words.

38 Therefore they relinquished their desires for a king, and became exceedingly anxious that every man should have an equal ᵃchance throughout all the land; yea, and every man expressed a willingness to answer for his own sins.

39 Therefore, it came to pass that they assembled themselves together in bodies throughout the land, to cast in their ᵃvoices concerning who should be their ᵇjudges, to judge them according to the ᶜlaw which had been given them; and they were

26 b ᴛɢ Disobedience.
  c ᴛɢ Governments.
27 a Alma 2:4 (3–7); 10:19; Hel. 4:21 (20–24); 5:2.
28 a Deut. 17:8 (8–9).
31 a 1 Kgs. 14:16; 15:26; 16:2; 21:22; Mosiah 29:36.

32 a Mosiah 27:3; Alma 30:11. ᴛɢ Injustice.
  b 2 Ne. 1:7; 10:11; Alma 46:17 (10–28, 34). ᴛɢ Liberty.
  c Alma 27:9.
33 a ᴛɢ Stewardship.

34 a ᴛɢ Accountability.
35 a ᴛɢ Kings, Earthly.
36 a Mosiah 29:31.
37 a 1 Sam. 8:19.
38 a ᴛɢ Agency.
39 a ᴛɢ Common Consent.
  b Alma 62:47.
  c Alma 1:14.

exceedingly rejoiced because of the ^dliberty which had been granted unto them.

40 And they did wax strong in love towards Mosiah; yea, they did esteem him more than any other man; for they did not look upon him as a ^atyrant who was seeking for gain, yea, for that ^blucre which doth ^ccorrupt the soul; for he had not exacted riches of them, neither had he delighted in the shedding of blood; but he had established ^dpeace in the land, and he had granted unto his people that they should be delivered from all manner of bondage; therefore they did esteem him, yea, exceedingly, beyond measure.

41 And it came to pass that they did ^aappoint ^bjudges to rule over them, or to judge them according to the law; and this they did throughout all the land.

42 And it came to pass that Alma was appointed to be the first ^achief judge, he being also the ^bhigh priest, his father having conferred the office upon him, and having given him the charge concerning all the affairs of the church.

43 And now it came to pass that Alma did ^awalk in the ways of the Lord, and he did keep his commandments, and he did judge righteous judgments; and there was continual peace through the land.

44 And thus commenced the ^areign of the judges throughout all the land of Zarahemla, among all the people who were called the Nephites; and Alma was the first and chief judge.

45 And now it came to pass that his father died, being eighty and two years old, having lived to fulfil the commandments of God.

46 And it came to pass that Mosiah ^adied also, in the thirty and third year of his reign, being ^bsixty and three years old; making in the whole, five hundred and nine years from the time Lehi left Jerusalem.

47 And thus ended the reign of the kings over the people of Nephi; and thus ended the days of Alma, who was the founder of their church.

THE BOOK OF ALMA

THE SON OF ALMA

The account of Alma, who was the son of Alma, the first and chief judge over the people of Nephi, and also the high priest over the Church. An account of the reign of the judges, and the wars and contentions among the people. And also an account of a war between the Nephites and the Lamanites, according to the record of Alma, the first and chief judge.

CHAPTER 1

Nehor teaches false doctrines, establishes a church, introduces priestcraft, and slays Gideon—Nehor is executed for his crimes—Priestcrafts and persecutions spread among the people—The priests support themselves, the people care for the poor, and the Church prospers. About 91–88 B.C.

39 *d* TG Liberty.
40 *a* TG Tyranny.
  b Titus 1:11.
  c TG Bribe.
  d TG Peacemakers.

41 *a* Alma 11:4.
  b Judg. 2:16;
    Mosiah 29:11.
42 *a* Alma 2:16; 7:1.
  b Mosiah 26:7;

    Alma 4:4.
43 *a* TG Walking with God.
44 *a* Alma 17:6.
46 *a* Alma 1:1.
  b Mosiah 6:4.

NOW it came to pass that in the first year of the reign of the judges over the people of Nephi, from this time forward, king Mosiah having [a]gone the way of all the earth, having warred a good warfare, walking uprightly before God, leaving none to reign in his stead; nevertheless he had established [b]laws, and they were acknowledged by the people; therefore they were obliged to abide by the [c]laws which he had made.

2 And it came to pass that in the first year of the reign of Alma in the judgment-seat, there was a [a]man brought before him to be judged, a man who was large, and was noted for his much strength.

3 And he had gone about among the people, preaching to them that which he [a]termed to be the word of God, bearing down [b]against the church; declaring unto the people that every priest and teacher ought to become [c]popular; and they ought [d]not to labor with their hands, but that they ought to be supported by the people.

4 And he also testified unto the people that [a]all mankind should be saved at the last day, and that they [b]need not fear nor tremble, but that they might lift up their heads and rejoice; for the Lord had [c]created all men, and had also [d]redeemed [e]all men; and, in the end, all men should have eternal life.

5 And it came to pass that he did teach these things so much that many did believe on his words, even so many that they began to support him and give him [a]money.

6 And he began to be lifted up in the pride of his heart, and to wear very costly [a]apparel, yea, and even began to [b]establish a [c]church after the manner of his preaching.

7 And it came to pass as he was going, to preach to those who believed on his word, he met a man who belonged to the church of God, yea, even one of their [a]teachers; and he began to contend with him sharply, that he might lead away the people of the church; but the man withstood him, admonishing him with the [b]words of God.

8 Now the name of the man was [a]Gideon; and it was he who was an instrument in the hands of God in delivering the people of Limhi out of bondage.

9 Now, because Gideon withstood him with the words of God he was wroth with Gideon, and drew his sword and began to smite him. Now Gideon being [a]stricken with many years, therefore he was not able to withstand his blows, therefore he was [b]slain by the sword.

10 And the man who slew him was taken by the people of the church, and was brought before Alma, to be [a]judged according to the crimes which he had committed.

11 And it came to pass that he stood before Alma and pled for himself with much boldness.

12 But Alma said unto him: Behold, this is the first time that [a]priestcraft has been introduced among this people. And behold, thou art not only guilty of priestcraft, but hast endeavored to enforce it by the sword; and were

1 1a Mosiah 29:46.
   b Jarom 1:5;
    Alma 4:16; 8:17;
    Hel. 4:22.
   c TG Citizenship.
  2a Alma 1:15.
  3a Ezek. 13:3 (1–4).
   b TG Antichrist.
   c Luke 6:26;
    1 Ne. 22:23.
   d Mosiah 18:24 (24, 26);
    27:5 (3–5).
  4a Alma 15:15; 21:6; 30:17;

Morm. 8:31.
   b TG Humility; Meek.
   c TG Jesus Christ, Creator;
    Man, Physical
    Creation of.
   d TG Jesus Christ,
    Redeemer;
    Redemption.
   e Moses 4:1 (1–4).
  5a Acts 8:18 (17–23).
  6a TG Apparel.
   b TG Unrighteous
    Dominion.

   c TG Devil, Church of.
  7a TG Teacher.
   b TG Word of God;
    Word of the Lord.
  8a Mosiah 20:17; 22:3;
    Alma 2:1.
  9a Gen. 24:1;
    1 Ne. 18:17.
   b Alma 6:7.
 10a Mosiah 29:42.
 12a 2 Ne. 26:29;
    Alma 2:20; 14:16.
    TG Priestcraft.

*b*priestcraft to be enforced among this people it would prove their entire destruction.

13 And thou hast shed the *a*blood of a righteous man, yea, a man who has done much good among this people; and were we to spare thee his blood would come upon us for *b*vengeance.

14 Therefore thou art condemned to *a*die, according to the *b*law which has been given us by Mosiah, our last king; and it has been *c*acknowledged by this people; therefore this people must *d*abide by the law.

15 And it came to pass that they took him; and his name was *a*Nehor; and they carried him upon the top of the hill Manti, and there he was caused, or rather did acknowledge, between the heavens and the earth, that what he had taught to the people was contrary to the word of God; and there he suffered an ignominious *b*death.

16 Nevertheless, this did not put an end to the spreading of priestcraft through the land; for there were many who loved the vain things of the world, and they went forth preaching *a*false doctrines; and this they did for the sake of *b*riches and honor.

17 Nevertheless, they durst not *a*lie, if it were known, for fear of the law, for liars were punished; therefore they pretended to preach according to their belief; and now the law could have no power on any man for *b*his belief.

18 And they durst not *a*steal, for fear of the law, for such were punished; neither durst they rob, nor

murder, for he that *b*murdered was punished unto *c*death.

19 But it came to pass that whosoever did not belong to the church of God began to persecute those that did belong to the church of God, and had taken upon them the name of Christ.

20 Yea, they did persecute them, and afflict them with all manner of words, and this because of their humility; because they were not proud in their own eyes, and because they did impart the word of God, one with another, without *a*money and without price.

21 Now there was a strict law among the people of the church, that there should *a*not any man, belonging to the church, arise and persecute those that did not belong to the church, and that there should be no persecution among themselves.

22 Nevertheless, there were many among them who began to be proud, and began to contend warmly with their adversaries, even unto blows; yea, they would smite one another with their *a*fists.

23 Now this was in the second year of the reign of Alma, and it was a cause of much affliction to the church; yea, it was the cause of much trial with the church.

24 For the hearts of many were hardened, and their names were *a*blotted out, that they were remembered no more among the people of God. And also many *b*withdrew themselves from among them.

25 Now this was a great trial to those that did stand fast in the faith; nevertheless, they were *a*steadfast

12*b* Alma 21:4.
13*a* Prov. 28:17.
    TG Blood, Shedding of.
  b Luke 18:7;
    D&C 121:5.
    TG Vengeance.
14*a* TG Capital Punishment.
  b Mosiah 29:39.
  c Hel. 1:8.
  d TG Citizenship.
15*a* Alma 1:2; 2:1 (1, 20).
  b Deut. 13:5 (1–9).
16*a* TG False Doctrine.

  b TG Riches;
    Vanity.
17*a* TG Honesty;
    Lying.
  b Alma 30:7 (7–12);
    A of F 1:11.
18*a* Alma 30:10.
    TG Stealing.
  b TG Murder.
  c TG Capital Punishment.
20*a* Isa. 55:1 (1–2).
21*a* Alma 4:8.
    TG Persecution.

22*a* Ex. 21:18 (18–19);
    Isa. 58:4.
24*a* Ex. 32:33;
    Mosiah 26:32, 36;
    Alma 6:3.
    TG Excommunication.
  b Alma 46:7.
    TG Apostasy of
    Individuals.
25*a* TG Commitment;
    Steadfastness.

and immovable in keeping the commandments of God, and they bore with [b]patience the persecution which was heaped upon them.

26 And when the priests left their [a]labor to impart the word of God unto the people, the people also left their labors to hear the word of God. And when the priest had imparted unto them the word of God they all returned again diligently unto their labors; and the priest, not esteeming himself above his hearers, for the preacher was no better than the hearer, neither was the teacher any better than the learner; and thus they were all equal, and they did all labor, every man [b]according to his strength.

27 And they did [a]impart of their substance, every man according to that which he had, to the [b]poor, and the needy, and the sick, and the afflicted; and they did not wear costly [c]apparel, yet they were neat and comely.

28 And thus they did establish the affairs of the church; and thus they began to have continual peace again, notwithstanding all their persecutions.

29 And now, because of the steadiness of the church they began to be exceedingly [a]rich, having abundance of all things whatsoever they stood in need—an abundance of flocks and herds, and fatlings of every kind, and also abundance of grain, and of gold, and of silver, and of precious things, and abundance of [b]silk and fine-twined linen, and all manner of good homely [c]cloth.

30 And thus, in their [a]prosperous circumstances, they did not send away any who were [b]naked, or that were hungry, or that were athirst, or that were sick, or that had not been nourished; and they did not set their hearts upon [c]riches; therefore they were [d]liberal to all, both old and young, both bond and free, both male and female, whether out of the church or in the church, having no [e]respect to persons as to those who stood in need.

31 And thus they did [a]prosper and become far more wealthy than those who did not belong to their church.

32 For those who did not belong to their church did indulge themselves in [a]sorceries, and in [b]idolatry or [c]idleness, and in [d]babblings, and in [e]envyings and [f]strife; wearing costly apparel; being [g]lifted up in the pride of their own eyes; persecuting, lying, thieving, robbing, committing whoredoms, and murdering, and all manner of wickedness; nevertheless, the law was put in force upon all those who did transgress it, inasmuch as it was possible.

33 And it came to pass that by thus exercising the law upon them, every man suffering according to that which he had done, they became more still, and durst not commit any wickedness if it were known; therefore, there was much peace among the people of Nephi until the fifth year of the reign of the judges.

CHAPTER 2

Amlici seeks to be king and is rejected by the voice of the people—His followers make him king—The Amlicites

---

25b TG Patience.
26a Mosiah 18:24 (24, 26);
    27:5 (3–5).
  b Mosiah 4:27;
    D&C 10:4.
27a TG Almsgiving;
    Consecration.
  b Luke 18:22;
    Acts 20:35 (33–35);
    Mosiah 4:26;
    D&C 42:30 (29–31).
  c TG Vanity.
29a TG Riches;

Treasure.
  b Alma 4:6.
  c Mosiah 10:5;
    Hel. 6:13.
    TG Clothing.
30a 2 Cor. 8:14;
    Jacob 2:19 (17–19).
  b TG Poor.
  c Job 31:25.
    TG Wealth.
  d TG Generosity.
  e Deut. 10:17;
    Alma 16:14;

D&C 1:35.
31a TG Prosper.
32a TG Sorcery.
  b TG Idolatry.
  c TG Laziness.
  d TG Gossip.
  e TG Envy.
  f TG Strife.
  g 2 Kgs. 14:10;
    Jacob 2:13;
    Alma 31:25;
    Morm. 8:28.
    TG Pride.

make war on the Nephites and are defeated—The Lamanites and Amlicites join forces and are defeated—Alma slays Amlici. About 87 B.C.

AND it came to pass in the commencement of the fifth year of their reign there began to be a contention among the people; for a certain ^aman, being called Amlici, he being a very cunning man, yea, a wise man as to the wisdom of the world, he being after the order of the man that slew ^bGideon by the sword, who was executed according to the law—

2 Now this Amlici had, by his cunning, ^adrawn away much people after him; even so much that they began to be very powerful; and they began to endeavor to establish Amlici to be a king over the people.

3 Now this was alarming to the people of the ^achurch, and also to all those who had not been drawn away after the persuasions of Amlici; for they knew that according to their law that such things must be established by the ^avoice of the people.

4 Therefore, if it were possible that Amlici should gain the voice of the people, he, being a wicked man, would ^adeprive them of their rights and privileges of the church; for it was his intent to destroy the church of God.

5 And it came to pass that the people assembled themselves together throughout all the land, every man according to his mind, whether it were for or against Amlici, in separate bodies, having much dispute and wonderful ^acontentions one with another.

6 And thus they did assemble themselves together to cast in their ^avoices concerning the matter; and they were laid before the judges.

7 And it came to pass that the ^avoice of the people came against Amlici, that he was not made king over the people.

8 Now this did cause much joy in the hearts of those who were against him; but Amlici did stir up those who were in his favor to anger against those who were not in his favor.

9 And it came to pass that they gathered themselves together, and did ^aconsecrate Amlici to be their king.

10 Now when Amlici was made king over them he commanded them that they should take up arms against their brethren; and this he did that he might subject them to him.

11 Now the people of Amlici were distinguished by the name of Amlici, being called ^aAmlicites; and the remainder were ^bcalled Nephites, or the people of God.

12 Therefore the people of the Nephites were aware of the intent of the Amlicites, and therefore they did prepare to meet them; yea, they did arm themselves with swords, and with cimeters, and with bows, and with arrows, and with stones, and with slings, and with all manner of ^aweapons of war, of every kind.

13 And thus they were prepared to meet the Amlicites at the time of their coming. And there were appointed ^acaptains, and higher captains, and chief captains, according to their numbers.

14 And it came to pass that Amlici did arm his men with all manner of weapons of war of every kind; and he also appointed rulers and leaders over his people, to lead them to war against their brethren.

15 And it came to pass that the

---

2 1*a* Alma 1:15; 16:11;
        24:28 (28–30).
    b Alma 1:8.
  2*a* 2 Sam. 15:6 (1–10).
  3*a* Mosiah 29:25 (25–27);
        Alma 4:16 (16–17).
  4*a* Mosiah 29:27;

Alma 10:19;
  Hel. 5:2.
5*a* 3 Ne. 11:29.
6*a* TG Common Consent.
7*a* Mosiah 29:25 (25–27).
9*a* TG Unrighteous
  Dominion.

11*a* Alma 3:4.
    b Jacob 1:14 (13–14);
        Mosiah 25:12;
        Alma 3:11 (11, 17).
12*a* Mosiah 10:8;
        Hel. 1:14.
13*a* Alma 16:5.

Amlicites came upon the hill Amnihu, which was east of the [a]river Sidon, which ran by the [b]land of Zarahemla, and there they began to make war with the Nephites.

16 Now Alma, being the [a]chief judge and the [b]governor of the people of Nephi, therefore he went up with his people, yea, with his captains, and chief captains, yea, at the head of his armies, against the Amlicites to battle.

17 And they began to slay the Amlicites upon the hill east of Sidon. And the Amlicites did contend with the Nephites with great strength, insomuch that many of the Nephites did fall before the Amlicites.

18 Nevertheless the Lord did strengthen the hand of the Nephites, that they slew the Amlicites with great slaughter, that they began to flee before them.

19 And it came to pass that the Nephites did pursue the Amlicites all that day, and did slay them with much slaughter, insomuch that there were [a]slain of the Amlicites twelve thousand five hundred thirty and two souls; and there were slain of the Nephites six thousand five hundred sixty and two souls.

20 And it came to pass that when Alma could pursue the Amlicites no longer he caused that his people should pitch their tents in the [a]valley of Gideon, the valley being called after that Gideon who was slain by the hand of [b]Nehor with the sword; and in this valley the Nephites did pitch their tents for the night.

21 And Alma sent spies to follow the remnant of the Amlicites, that he might know of their plans and their plots, whereby he might guard himself against them, that he might preserve his people from being destroyed.

22 Now those whom he had sent out to watch the camp of the Amlicites were called Zeram, and Amnor, and Manti, and Limher; these were they who went out with their men to watch the camp of the Amlicites.

23 And it came to pass that on the morrow they returned into the camp of the Nephites in great haste, being greatly astonished, and struck with much fear, saying:

24 Behold, we followed the [a]camp of the [b]Amlicites, and to our great astonishment, in the land of Minon, above the land of Zarahemla, in the course of the land of [c]Nephi, we saw a numerous host of the Lamanites; and behold, the Amlicites have joined them;

25 And they are upon our brethren in that land; and they are fleeing before them with their flocks, and their wives, and their children, towards our city; and except we make haste they obtain possession of our city, and our fathers, and our wives, and our children be slain.

26 And it came to pass that the people of Nephi took their tents, and departed out of the valley of Gideon towards their [a]city, which was the city of [b]Zarahemla.

27 And behold, as they were crossing the river Sidon, the Lamanites and the Amlicites, being as [a]numerous almost, as it were, as the sands of the sea, came upon them to destroy them.

28 Nevertheless, the Nephites being [a]strengthened by the hand of the Lord, having prayed mightily to him that he would deliver them out of the hands of their enemies, therefore the Lord did hear their cries, and did strengthen them, and the Lamanites and the Amlicites did fall before them.

29 And it came to pass that Alma fought with Amlici with the sword,

15a Alma 3:3.
  b Omni 1:13;
    Mosiah 1:1.
16a Mosiah 29:42.
  b Mosiah 1:10.
19a Alma 3:1 (1–2, 26); 4:2.

20a Alma 6:7; 8:1.
  b Alma 1:12 (7–15);
    14:16.
24a Alma 3:20.
  b Alma 3:4 (4, 13–18).
  c 2 Ne. 5:8;

    Alma 20:1.
26a Alma 6:4.
  b Omni 1:14 (14, 18).
27a Jarom 1:6.
28a Deut. 31:6.

face to face; and they did contend mightily, one with another.

30 And it came to pass that Alma, being a man of God, being exercised with much ᵃfaith, cried, saying: O Lord, have mercy and ᵇspare my life, that I may be an instrument in thy hands to save and preserve this people.

31 Now when Alma had said these words he contended again with Amlici; and he was strengthened, insomuch that he slew Amlici with the sword.

32 And he also contended with the king of the Lamanites; but the king of the Lamanites fled back from before Alma and sent his guards to contend with Alma.

33 But Alma, with his guards, contended with the guards of the king of the Lamanites until he slew and drove them back.

34 And thus he cleared the ground, or rather the bank, which was on the west of the river Sidon, throwing the bodies of the Lamanites who had been slain into the waters of Sidon, that thereby his people might have room to cross and contend with the Lamanites and the Amlicites on the west side of the river Sidon.

35 And it came to pass that when they had all crossed the river Sidon that the Lamanites and the Amlicites began to flee before them, notwithstanding they were so numerous that they could not be numbered.

36 And they fled before the Nephites towards the wilderness which was west and north, away beyond the borders of the land; and the Nephites did pursue them with their might, and did slay them.

37 Yea, they were met on every hand, and slain and driven, until they were scattered on the west, and on the north, until they had reached the wilderness, which was called Hermounts; and it was that part of the wilderness which was infested by wild and ravenous beasts.

38 And it came to pass that many died in the wilderness of their wounds, and were devoured by those beasts and also the vultures of the air; and their bones have been found, and have been heaped up on the earth.

CHAPTER 3

The Amlicites had marked themselves according to the prophetic word—The Lamanites had been cursed for their rebellion—Men bring their own curses upon themselves—The Nephites defeat another Lamanite army. About 87–86 B.C.

AND it came to pass that the Nephites who were not ᵃslain by the weapons of war, after having buried those who had been slain—now the number of the slain were not numbered, because of the greatness of their number—after they had finished burying their dead they all returned to their lands, and to their houses, and their wives, and their children.

2 Now many women and children had been slain with the sword, and also many of their flocks and their herds; and also many of their fields of grain were destroyed, for they were trodden down by the hosts of men.

3 And now as many of the Lamanites and the Amlicites who had been slain upon the bank of the river Sidon were cast into the ᵃwaters of Sidon; and behold their bones are in the depths of the ᵇsea, and they are many.

4 And the ᵃAmlicites were distinguished from the Nephites, for they had ᵇmarked themselves with red in their foreheads after the manner of the Lamanites; nevertheless they had not shorn their heads like unto the Lamanites.

5 Now the heads of the Lamanites were shorn; and they were ᵃnaked,

---

30a TG Faith.
  b Alma 3:22.
3 1a Alma 2:19; 4:2.
  3a Alma 2:15; 4:4.

b Alma 44:22.
4a Alma 2:11, 24.
  b Alma 3:13 (13–19).
5a Enos 1:20;

Mosiah 10:8;
Alma 43:20 (18–21).

save it were skin which was girded about their loins, and also their armor, which was girded about them, and their bows, and their arrows, and their stones, and their slings, and so forth.

6 And the skins of the Lamanites were dark, according to the mark which was set upon their fathers, which was a ^acurse upon them because of their transgression and their rebellion against their brethren, who consisted of Nephi, Jacob, and Joseph, and Sam, who were just and holy men.

7 And their brethren sought to destroy them, therefore they were cursed; and the Lord God set a ^amark upon them, yea, upon Laman and Lemuel, and also the sons of Ishmael, and Ishmaelitish women.

8 And this was done that their seed might be distinguished from the seed of their brethren, that thereby the Lord God might preserve his people, that they might not ^amix and believe in incorrect ^btraditions which would prove their destruction.

9 And it came to pass that whosoever did mingle his seed with that of the Lamanites did bring the same curse upon his seed.

10 Therefore, whosoever suffered himself to be led away by the Lamanites was called under that head, and there was a mark set upon him.

11 And it came to pass that whosoever would not believe in the ^atradition of the Lamanites, but believed those records which were brought out of the land of Jerusalem, and also in the tradition of their fathers, which were correct, who believed in the commandments of God and kept them, were ^bcalled the Nephites, or the people of Nephi, from that time forth—

12 And it is they who have kept the records which are ^atrue of their people, and also of the people of the Lamanites.

13 Now we will return again to the Amlicites, for they also had a ^amark set upon them; yea, they set the mark upon themselves, yea, even a mark of red upon their foreheads.

14 Thus the word of God is fulfilled, for these are the words which he said to Nephi: Behold, the Lamanites have I cursed, and I will set a mark on them that they and their seed may be ^aseparated from thee and thy seed, from this time henceforth and forever, except they repent of their wickedness and ^bturn to me that I may have mercy upon them.

15 And again: I will set a mark upon him that mingleth his seed with thy brethren, that they may be cursed also.

16 And again: I will set a mark upon him that fighteth against thee and thy seed.

17 And again, I say he that departeth from thee shall no more be called thy seed; and I will bless thee, and whomsoever shall be called thy seed, henceforth and forever; and these were the promises of the Lord unto Nephi and to his seed.

18 Now the Amlicites knew not that they were fulfilling the words of God when they began to mark themselves in their foreheads; nevertheless they had come out in open ^arebellion against God; therefore it was expedient that the curse should fall upon them.

19 Now I would that ye should see that they brought upon themselves the ^acurse; and even so doth every man that is cursed bring

6a 2 Ne. 5:21; 26:33.
   TG Curse.
7a 1 Ne. 12:23.
8a TG Marriage, Interfaith;
   Separation.
 b Mosiah 10:12 (11–18);
   Alma 9:16.

11a Alma 17:9 (9–11).
  b Alma 2:11.
12a Mosiah 1:6;
   Ether 4:11 (6–11).
13a Alma 3:4.
14a TG Separation.
  b 2 Ne. 30:6 (4–7).

18a Josh. 22:18;
   4 Ne. 1:38.
   TG Rebellion.
19a 2 Ne. 5:21 (21–25);
   Alma 17:15.

upon himself his own condemnation.

20 Now it came to pass that not many days after the battle which was fought in the land of Zarahemla, by the Lamanites and the Amlicites, that there was another army of the Lamanites came in upon the people of Nephi, in the ᵃsame place where the first army met the Amlicites.

21 And it came to pass that there was an army sent to drive them out of their land.

22 Now Alma himself being afflicted with a ᵃwound did not go up to battle at this time against the Lamanites;

23 But he sent up a numerous army against them; and they went up and slew many of the Lamanites, and drove the remainder of them out of the borders of their land.

24 And then they returned again and began to establish peace in the land, being troubled no more for a time with their enemies.

25 Now all these things were done, yea, all these wars and contentions were commenced and ended in the fifth year of the reign of the judges.

26 And in one year were thousands and tens of thousands of souls sent to the eternal world, that they might reap their ᵃrewards according to their works, whether they were good or whether they were bad, to reap eternal happiness or eternal misery, according to the spirit which they listed to obey, whether it be a good spirit or a bad one.

27 For every man receiveth ᵃwages of him whom he listeth to ᵇobey, and this according to the words of the spirit of prophecy; therefore let it be according to the truth. And thus

endeth the fifth year of the reign of the judges.

CHAPTER 4

Alma baptizes thousands of converts—Iniquity enters the Church, and the Church's progress is hindered—Nephihah is appointed chief judge—Alma, as high priest, devotes himself to the ministry. About 86–83 B.C.

Now it came to pass in the sixth year of the reign of the judges over the people of Nephi, there were no contentions nor wars in the ᵃland of Zarahemla;

2 But the people were afflicted, yea, greatly afflicted for the loss of their brethren, and also for the ᵃloss of their flocks and herds, and also for the loss of their fields of grain, which were trodden under foot and destroyed by the Lamanites.

3 And so great were their afflictions that every soul had cause to mourn; and they believed that it was the judgments of God sent upon them because of their wickedness and their abominations; therefore they were ᵃawakened to a remembrance of their duty.

4 And they began to establish the ᵃchurch more fully; yea, and many were ᵇbaptized in the ᶜwaters of Sidon and were joined to the church of God; yea, they were baptized by the hand of Alma, who had been consecrated the ᵈhigh priest over the people of the church, by the hand of his father Alma.

5 And it came to pass in the seventh year of the reign of the judges there were about three thousand five hundred souls that united themselves to the ᵃchurch of God and were baptized. And thus ended the seventh year of the reign of the judges over the people

---

20ᵃ Alma 2:24.
22ᵃ Alma 2:30 (29–33).
26ᵃ Ps. 7:16.
　　TG Agency;
　　Reward.
27ᵃ Mosiah 2:32 (32–33);
　　Alma 5:42 (41–42).
　　TG Wages.

　ᵇ Rom. 6:16 (14–18);
　　Hel. 14:31 (29–31).
4 1ᵃ Omni 1:12 (12–19).
　2ᵃ Alma 2:19;
　　3:1 (1–2, 26).
　3ᵃ 1 Cor. 15:34 (33–34).
　4ᵃ TG Church Organization.
　　ᵇ Mosiah 18:10 (10–17).

　ᶜ Alma 3:3; 6:7.
　ᵈ Mosiah 29:42.
　　TG High Priest,
　　Melchizedek Priesthood.
　5ᵃ Mosiah 25:22 (18–23);
　　3 Ne. 26:21.

of Nephi; and there was continual peace in all that time.

6 And it came to pass in the eighth year of the reign of the judges, that the people of the church began to wax proud, because of their exceeding ªriches, and their ᵇfine silks, and their fine-twined linen, and because of their many flocks and herds, and their gold and their silver, and all manner of precious things, which they had obtained by their ᶜindustry; and in all these things were they lifted up in the pride of their eyes, for they began to wear very costly ᵈapparel.

7 Now this was the cause of much affliction to Alma, yea, and to many of the people whom Alma had consecrated to be ªteachers, and ᵇpriests, and ᶜelders over the church; yea, many of them were sorely grieved for the wickedness which they saw had begun to be among their people.

8 For they saw and beheld with great sorrow that the people of the church began to be lifted up in the pride of their eyes, and to set their ªhearts upon riches and upon the vain things of the world, that they began to be scornful, one towards another, and they began to persecute those that did ᵇnot believe according to their own will and pleasure.

9 And thus, in this eighth year of the reign of the judges, there began to be great ªcontentions among the people of the church; yea, there were ᵇenvyings, and ᶜstrife, and malice, and persecutions, and pride, even to exceed the pride of those who did not belong to the church of God.

10 And thus ended the eighth year of the reign of the judges; and the wickedness of the church was a great ªstumbling-block to those who did not belong to the church; and thus the church began to fail in its progress.

11 And it came to pass in the commencement of the ninth year, Alma saw the wickedness of the church, and he saw also that the ªexample of the church began to lead those who were unbelievers on from one piece of iniquity to another, thus bringing on the destruction of the people.

12 Yea, he saw great inequality among the people, some lifting themselves up with their pride, despising others, turning their backs upon the ªneedy and the naked and those who were ᵇhungry, and those who were athirst, and those who were sick and afflicted.

13 Now this was a great cause for lamentations among the people, while others were abasing themselves, succoring those who stood in need of their succor, such as imparting their substance to the ªpoor and the needy, feeding the hungry, and suffering all manner of ᵇafflictions, for Christ's ᶜsake, who should come according to the spirit of prophecy;

14 Looking forward to that day, thus ªretaining a ᵇremission of their sins; being filled with great ᶜjoy because of the resurrection of the dead, according to the will and power and ᵈdeliverance of Jesus Christ from the bands of death.

15 And now it came to pass that Alma, having seen the afflictions of the humble followers of God, and

---

6a TG Riches.
 b Alma 1:29.
 c TG Industry.
 d TG Apparel.
7a Mosiah 6:3.
   TG Teacher.
 b TG Church Organization.
 c Alma 4:16.
   TG Elder.
8a TG Pride;
   Vanity;
   Worldliness.

 b Alma 1:21.
9a TG Contention.
 b TG Envy.
 c Alma 16:18.
   TG Strife.
10a TG Stumblingblock.
11a 2 Sam. 12:14;
    Alma 39:11.
    TG Example.
12a Isa. 3:14;
    Ezek. 22:12 (6–13);
    Amos 3:10;

    Jacob 2:17.
 b Mosiah 4:26.
13a TG Almsgiving.
 b TG Affliction.
 c 2 Cor. 12:10.
14a Mosiah 4:12;
    Alma 5:26 (26–35);
    D&C 20:32 (31–34).
 b TG Justification.
 c TG Joy.
 d TG Deliver.

the persecutions which were heaped upon them by the remainder of his people, and seeing all their *a*inequality, began to be very sorrowful; nevertheless the Spirit of the Lord did not fail him.

16 And he selected a wise man who was among the *a*elders of the church, and gave him power according to the *b*voice of the people, that he might have power to enact *c*laws according to the laws which had been given, and to put them in force according to the wickedness and the crimes of the people.

17 Now this man's name was *a*Nephihah, and he was appointed *b*chief judge; and he sat in the judgment-seat to judge and to govern the people.

18 Now Alma did not grant unto him the office of being *a*high priest over the church, but he retained the office of high priest unto himself; but he delivered the judgment-seat unto *b*Nephihah.

19 And this he did that he *a*himself might go forth among his people, or among the people of Nephi, that he might *b*preach the *c*word of God unto them, to *d*stir them up in *e*remembrance of their duty, and that he might pull down, by the word of God, all the pride and craftiness and all the contentions which were among his people, seeing no way that he might reclaim them save it were in bearing down in pure *f*testimony against them.

20 And thus in the commencement of the ninth year of the reign of the judges over the people of Nephi, Alma delivered up the judgment-seat to *a*Nephihah, and confined himself

wholly to the *b*high priesthood of the holy order of God, to the *c*testimony of the word, according to the spirit of revelation and prophecy.

The words which Alma, the High Priest according to the holy order of God, delivered to the people in their cities and villages throughout the land.

Beginning with chapter 5.

CHAPTER 5

To gain salvation, men must repent and keep the commandments, be born again, cleanse their garments through the blood of Christ, be humble and strip themselves of pride and envy, and do the works of righteousness—The Good Shepherd calls His people—Those who do evil works are children of the devil—Alma testifies of the truth of his doctrine and commands men to repent—The names of the righteous will be written in the book of life. About 83 B.C.

Now it came to pass that Alma began to *a*deliver the word of *b*God unto the people, first in the land of Zarahemla, and from thence throughout all the land.

2 And these are the words which he spake to the people in the church which was established in the city of Zarahemla, according to his own record, saying:

3 I, Alma, having been *a*consecrated by my father, Alma, to be a *b*high priest over the church of God, he having power and *c*authority from God to do these things, behold, I say unto you that he began to

---

15*a* 2 Cor. 8:14;
  D&C 49:20.
16*a* Alma 4:7.
  b Alma 2:3 (3–7); 50:39.
  c Alma 1:1 (1, 14, 18).
17*a* Alma 27:20.
  b Alma 30:29; 50:37.
18*a* TG High Priest,
  Melchizedek Priesthood.
  b Alma 7:2.
19*a* Alma 7:1.

b Alma 5:1.
  c Alma 31:5;
  D&C 11:2.
  d Enos 1:23.
  e 2 Chr. 35:6;
  Alma 16:16;
  D&C 108:7.
  f TG Testimony.
20*a* Alma 8:12.
  b Mosiah 29:42;
  Alma 5:3 (3, 44, 49).

c TG Preaching.
5 1*a* Alma 4:19.
  b Alma 5:61.
3*a* TG Priesthood,
  Authority.
  b Alma 4:20 (4, 18, 20);
  8:23 (11, 23).
  c Mosiah 18:13;
  3 Ne. 11:25.

establish a church in the [d]land which was in the borders of Nephi; yea, the land which was called the land of Mormon; yea, and he did baptize his brethren in the waters of Mormon.

4 And behold, I say unto you, they were [a]delivered out of the hands of the people of king Noah, by the mercy and power of God.

5 And behold, after that, they were brought into [a]bondage by the hands of the Lamanites in the wilderness; yea, I say unto you, they were in captivity, and again the Lord did deliver them out of [b]bondage by the power of his word; and we were brought into this land, and here we began to establish the church of God throughout this land also.

6 And now behold, I say unto you, my brethren, you that belong to this church, have you sufficiently retained in [a]remembrance the captivity of your fathers? Yea, and have you sufficiently retained in remembrance his mercy and long-suffering towards them? And moreover, have ye sufficiently retained in remembrance that he has [b]delivered their souls from hell?

7 Behold, he changed their hearts; yea, he awakened them out of a deep sleep, and they awoke unto God. Behold, they were in the midst of darkness; nevertheless, their souls were illuminated by the light of the everlasting word; yea, they were encircled about by the [a]bands of death, and the [b]chains of hell, and an everlasting destruction did await them.

8 And now I ask of you, my brethren, were they destroyed?

Behold, I say unto you, Nay, they were not.

9 And again I ask, were the bands of death broken, and the [a]chains of hell which encircled them about, were they loosed? I say unto you, Yea, they were loosed, and their souls did expand, and they did [b]sing redeeming love. And I say unto you that they are saved.

10 And now I ask of you on what conditions are they [a]saved? Yea, what grounds had they to hope for salvation? What is the cause of their being loosed from the bands of death, yea, and also the chains of hell?

11 Behold, I can tell you—did not my father Alma believe in the words which were delivered by the [a]mouth of Abinadi? And was he not a holy prophet? Did he not speak the words of God, and my father Alma believe them?

12 And according to his faith there was a mighty [a]change wrought in his heart. Behold I say unto you that this is all true.

13 And behold, he [a]preached the word unto your fathers, and a mighty change was also wrought in their hearts, and they humbled themselves and put their [b]trust in the true and [c]living God. And behold, they were faithful until the [d]end; therefore they were saved.

14 And now behold, I ask of you, my brethren of the church, have ye [a]spiritually been [b]born of God? Have ye received his image in your countenances? Have ye experienced this mighty [c]change in your hearts?

15 Do ye exercise faith in the

3d Mosiah 18:4;
   3 Ne. 5:12.
4a Mosiah 23:1 (1–3).
5a Mosiah 23:37 (37–39);
   24:9 (8–15).
 b Mosiah 24:17;
   25:10; 27:16.
6a 2 Pet. 3:1 (1–2).
 b TG Deliver.
7a Mosiah 15:8.
   TG Bondage, Spiritual;
   Man, Natural, Not

Spiritually Reborn.
 b Alma 12:11 (9–11);
   D&C 138:23.
   TG Hell.
9a Alma 12:6.
 b Ps. 147:1 (1–7).
10a TG Save.
11a Mosiah 17:2 (2–4).
12a TG Conversion.
13a Mosiah 18:7 (1–31).
 b TG Trust in God.
 c 1 Sam. 17:26;

Ps. 42:2;
   Morm. 9:28;
   D&C 20:19.
 d 2 Ne. 31:15.
14a TG Spirituality.
 b Mosiah 27:25 (24–27);
   Alma 22:15.
 c Rom. 7:22; 8:11 (11–17);
   Col. 3:10 (9–10);
   Mosiah 5:2;
   Moses 6:65.
   TG Sanctification.

redemption of him who ^acreated you? Do you look forward with an eye of faith, and view this mortal body raised in immortality, and this corruption ^braised in incorruption, to stand before God to be ^cjudged according to the deeds which have been done in the mortal body?

16 I say unto you, can you imagine to yourselves that ye hear the voice of the Lord, saying unto you, in that day: Come unto me ye ^ablessed, for behold, your works have been the works of righteousness upon the face of the earth?

17 Or do ye ^aimagine to yourselves that ye can lie unto the Lord in that day, and ^bsay—Lord, our works have been righteous works upon the face of the earth—and that he will save you?

18 Or otherwise, can ye imagine yourselves brought before the tribunal of God with your souls filled with guilt and remorse, having a remembrance of all your guilt, yea, a perfect ^aremembrance of all your wickedness, yea, a remembrance that ye have set at defiance the commandments of God?

19 I say unto you, can ye look up to God at that day with a pure heart and clean hands? I say unto you, can you look up, having the ^aimage of God engraven upon your countenances?

20 I say unto you, can ye think of being saved when you have yielded yourselves to become ^asubjects to the devil?

21 I say unto you, ye will know at that day that ye cannot be ^asaved;

for there can no man be saved except his ^bgarments are washed white; yea, his garments must be ^cpurified until they are cleansed from all stain, through the blood of him of whom it has been spoken by our fathers, who should come to redeem his people from their sins.

22 And now I ask of you, my brethren, how will any of you feel, if ye shall stand before the bar of God, having your garments stained with ^ablood and all manner of ^bfilthiness? Behold, what will these things testify against you?

23 Behold will they not ^atestify that ye are murderers, yea, and also that ye are ^bguilty of all manner of wickedness?

24 Behold, my brethren, do ye suppose that such an one can have a place to sit down in the kingdom of God, with ^aAbraham, with Isaac, and with Jacob, and also all the holy prophets, whose garments are cleansed and are spotless, pure and white?

25 I say unto you, Nay; except ye make our Creator a liar from the beginning, or suppose that he is a liar from the beginning, ye cannot suppose that such can have place in the kingdom of heaven; but they shall be cast out for they are the ^achildren of the kingdom of the devil.

26 And now behold, I say unto you, my brethren, if ye have experienced a ^achange of heart, and if ye have felt to sing the ^bsong of redeeming love, I would ask, ^ccan ye feel so now?

15a TG Jesus Christ, Creator.
  b TG Immortality;
    Redemption;
    Resurrection.
  c TG Jesus Christ, Judge;
    Judgment, the Last.
16a Matt. 25:34 (31–46).
17a Alma 7:3.
  b 3 Ne. 14:22 (21–23).
18a Ezek. 20:43;
    2 Ne. 9:14;
    Mosiah 2:40; 3:25;

    Alma 11:43.
19a 1 Jn. 3:2 (1–3).
20a Mosiah 2:32.
21a TG Salvation, Plan of.
  b 1 Ne. 12:10;
    Alma 13:11 (11–13);
    3 Ne. 27:19 (19–20).
  c D&C 138:59.
    TG Purification.
22a Isa. 59:3.
  b TG Filthiness.
23a Isa. 59:12.

  b TG Guilt.
24a Luke 13:28.
25a Deut. 32:5;
    2 Ne. 9:9.
26a TG Change;
    Conversion;
    Man, New, Spiritually
    Reborn.
  b Alma 26:13.
  c Mosiah 4:12;
    Alma 4:14 (13–14);
    D&C 20:32 (31–34).

27 Have ye walked, keeping yourselves [a]blameless before God? Could ye say, if ye were called to die at this time, within yourselves, that ye have been sufficiently [b]humble? That your garments have been [c]cleansed and made white through the blood of Christ, who will come to [d]redeem his people from their sins?

28 Behold, are ye stripped of [a]pride? I say unto you, if ye are not ye are not prepared to meet God. Behold ye must prepare quickly; for the kingdom of heaven is soon at hand, and such an one hath not eternal life.

29 Behold, I say, is there one among you who is not stripped of [a]envy? I say unto you that such an one is not prepared; and I would that he should prepare [b]quickly, for the hour is close at hand, and he knoweth not when the time shall come; for such an one is not found guiltless.

30 And again I say unto you, is there one among you that doth make a [a]mock of his brother, or that heapeth upon him persecutions?

31 Wo unto such an one, for he is not prepared, and the [a]time is at hand that he must repent or he cannot be saved!

32 Yea, even wo unto all ye [a]workers of iniquity; repent, repent, for the Lord God hath spoken it!

33 Behold, he sendeth an invitation unto [a]all men, for the [b]arms of mercy are extended towards them, and he saith: Repent, and I will receive you.

34 Yea, he saith: [a]Come unto me and ye shall partake of the [b]fruit of the tree of life; yea, ye shall eat and drink of the [c]bread and the waters of life [d]freely;

35 Yea, come unto me and bring forth works of righteousness, and ye shall not be hewn down and cast into the fire—

36 For behold, the time is at hand that whosoever [a]bringeth forth not good fruit, or whosoever doeth not the works of righteousness, the same have cause to wail and mourn.

37 O ye workers of iniquity; ye that are [a]puffed up in the vain things of the world, ye that have professed to have known the ways of righteousness nevertheless have gone [b]astray, as [c]sheep having no [d]shepherd, notwithstanding a shepherd hath [e]called after you and is still calling after you, but ye will not [f]hearken unto his voice!

38 Behold, I say unto you, that the good [a]shepherd doth call you; yea, and in his own name he doth call you, which is the name of Christ; and if ye will not [b]hearken unto the voice of the [c]good shepherd, to the [d]name by which ye are called, behold, ye are not the sheep of the good shepherd.

39 And now if ye are not the [a]sheep of the good shepherd, of what fold are ye? Behold, I say unto you, that the [b]devil is your shepherd, and ye are of his fold; and now,

---

27a 1 Jn. 3:21 (19–24).
  TG Justification.
  b TG Humility.
  c Rev. 19:8.
  d 1 Cor. 15:3.
  TG Jesus Christ,
  Mission of.
28a TG Pride.
29a TG Envy.
  b TG Procrastination.
30a TG Backbiting;
  Mocking.
31a TG Procrastination.
32a Ps. 5:5 (4–6).
33a Alma 19:36;
  3 Ne. 18:25.
  b Isa. 59:16;
  2 Ne. 1:15;

Jacob 6:5;
  3 Ne. 9:14.
34a 1 Ne. 1:14;
  2 Ne. 26:25 (24–28);
  3 Ne. 9:14 (13–14).
  b 1 Ne. 8:11; 15:36.
  c TG Bread of Life.
  d 2 Ne. 9:50 (50–51);
  Alma 42:27.
36a Matt. 3:10; 7:19 (15–20);
  Jacob 5:26 (26–60);
  3 Ne. 14:19;
  D&C 97:7.
37a TG Worldliness.
  b 2 Ne. 12:5; 28:14;
  Mosiah 14:6.
  c Matt. 9:36.
  d TG Shepherd.

e Prov. 1:24 (24–27);
  Isa. 65:12;
  1 Ne. 17:13;
  2 Ne. 7:2.
  f 2 Chr. 33:10;
  Jer. 26:4;
  Alma 10:6 (5–6).
38a TG Jesus Christ, Good
  Shepherd.
  b Lev. 26:14 (14–20);
  D&C 101:7.
  c 3 Ne. 15:24; 18:31.
  d Mosiah 5:8;
  Alma 34:38.
39a Matt. 6:24;
  Luke 16:13.
  b Mosiah 5:10.
  TG Devil, Church of.

who can deny this? Behold, I say unto you, whosoever denieth this is a ᶜliar and a ᵈchild of the devil.

40 For I say unto you that whatsoever is ᵃgood cometh from God, and whatsoever is ᵇevil cometh from the devil.

41 Therefore, if a man bringeth forth ᵃgood works he hearkeneth unto the voice of the good shepherd, and he doth follow him; but whosoever bringeth forth evil works, the same becometh a ᵇchild of the devil, for he hearkeneth unto his voice, and doth follow him.

42 And whosoever doeth this must receive his ᵃwages of him; therefore, for his ᵇwages he receiveth ᶜdeath, as to things pertaining unto righteousness, being dead unto all good works.

43 And now, my brethren, I would that ye should hear me, for I speak in the ᵃenergy of my soul; for behold, I have spoken unto you plainly that ye cannot err, or have spoken according to the commandments of God.

44 For I am called to speak after this manner, according to the ᵃholy order of God, which is in Christ Jesus; yea, I am commanded to stand and testify unto this people the things which have been spoken by our fathers concerning the things which are to come.

45 And this is not all. Do ye not suppose that I ᵃknow of these things myself? Behold, I testify unto you that I do know that these things whereof I have spoken are true. And how do ye suppose that I know of their surety?

46 Behold, I say unto you they are made ᵃknown unto me by the Holy Spirit of God. Behold, I have ᵇfasted and prayed many days that I might know these things of myself. And now I do know of myself that they are true; for the Lord God hath made them manifest unto me by his Holy Spirit; and this is the spirit of ᶜrevelation which is in me.

47 And moreover, I say unto you that it has thus been revealed unto me, that the words which have been spoken by our fathers are true, even so according to the spirit of prophecy which is in me, which is also by the manifestation of the Spirit of God.

48 I say unto you, that I know of myself that whatsoever I shall say unto you, concerning that which is to come, is true; and I say unto you, that I know that Jesus Christ shall come, yea, the Son, the Only Begotten of the Father, full of grace, and mercy, and truth. And behold, it is he that cometh to take away the sins of the world, yea, the sins of every man who steadfastly believeth on his name.

49 And now I say unto you that this is the ᵃorder after which I am called, yea, to preach unto my beloved brethren, yea, and every one that dwelleth in the land; yea, to preach unto all, both old and young, both bond and free; yea, I say unto you the aged, and also the middle aged, and the rising generation; yea, to cry unto them that they must repent and be ᵇborn again.

50 Yea, thus saith the Spirit: Repent, all ye ends of the earth, for the kingdom of heaven is soon at hand; yea, the Son of God cometh in his ᵃglory, in his might, majesty, power,

39c 1 Jn. 2:22.
  d 2 Ne. 9:9.
40a Ezra 3:11;
     Ps. 85:12;
     Omni 1:25;
     Ether 4:12;
     Moro. 7:16 (15–17).
  b Isa. 45:7;
     Amos 3:6;
     Moro. 7:12.
41a 3 Ne. 14:17 (16–20).

TG Good Works.
  b Mosiah 16:3 (3–5);
     Alma 11:23.
42a Alma 3:27 (26–27);
     D&C 29:45.
  b Rom. 6:23.
  c Hel. 14:18 (16–18).
43a Alma 7:5.
44a Mosiah 29:42.
45a Alma 36:4.
46a 1 Cor. 2:10 (9–16).

  b Alma 10:7.
  c Rev. 19:10.
49a TG Called of God;
     Priesthood.
  b TG Man, New, Spiritually
     Reborn.
50a Ps. 24:8; 72:19.
     TG Jesus Christ,
     Glory of.

and dominion. Yea, my beloved brethren, I say unto you, that the Spirit saith: Behold the glory of the *b*King of all the earth; and also the King of heaven shall very soon shine forth among all the children of men.

51 And also the Spirit saith unto me, yea, crieth unto me with a mighty voice, saying: Go forth and say unto this people—Repent, for except ye repent ye can in nowise inherit the *a*kingdom of *b*heaven.

52 And again I say unto you, the Spirit saith: Behold, the *a*ax is laid at the root of the tree; therefore every tree that bringeth not forth good fruit shall be *b*hewn down and cast into the fire, yea, a fire which cannot be consumed, even an unquenchable fire. Behold, and remember, the Holy One hath spoken it.

53 And now my beloved brethren, I say unto you, can ye withstand these sayings; yea, can ye lay aside these things, and *a*trample the Holy One under your feet; yea, can ye be *b*puffed up in the pride of your hearts; yea, will ye still persist in the wearing of *c*costly apparel and setting your hearts upon the vain things of the world, upon your *d*riches?

54 Yea, will ye persist in supposing that ye are better one than another; yea, will ye persist in the persecution of your brethren, who humble themselves and do walk after the holy order of God, wherewith they have been brought into this church, having been *a*sanctified by the Holy Spirit, and they do bring forth works which are meet for repentance—

55 Yea, and will you persist in turning your backs upon the *a*poor, and the needy, and in withholding your substance from them?

56 And finally, all ye that will persist in your wickedness, I say unto you that these are they who shall be hewn down and cast into the fire except they speedily repent.

57 And now I say unto you, all you that are desirous to follow the voice of the *a*good shepherd, come ye out from the wicked, and be ye *b*separate, and touch not their unclean things; and behold, their names shall be *c*blotted out, that the names of the wicked shall not be numbered among the names of the righteous, that the word of God may be fulfilled, which saith: The names of the wicked shall not be mingled with the names of my people;

58 For the names of the righteous shall be written in the *a*book of life, and unto them will I grant an inheritance at my right hand. And now, my brethren, what have ye to say against this? I say unto you, if ye speak against it, it matters not, for the word of God must be fulfilled.

59 For what shepherd is there among you having many sheep doth not watch over them, that the wolves enter not and devour his flock? And behold, if a wolf enter his *a*flock doth he not drive him out? Yea, and at the last, if he can, he will destroy him.

60 And now I say unto you that the good shepherd doth call after you; and if you will hearken unto his voice he will bring you into his

---

50b Ps. 74:12; 149:2;
  Matt. 2:2;
  Luke 23:2;
  2 Ne. 10:14;
  D&C 38:21 (21–22);
  128:22 (22–23);
  Moses 7:53.
  TG Jesus Christ, King;
  Kingdom of God, on Earth.
51a TG Kingdom of God, in Heaven.
  b TG Heaven.

52a Luke 3:9;
  D&C 97:7.
  b Jacob 5:46; 6:7;
  3 Ne. 27:11 (11–12).
53a TG Sacrilege.
  b 1 Cor. 5:2.
  c 2 Ne. 28:13 (11–14);
  Morm. 8:36 (36–39).
  d Ps. 62:10;
  D&C 56:16 (16–18).
54a TG Sanctification.
55a Ps. 109:16 (15–16);
  Jacob 2:17;

  Hel. 6:39 (39–40);
  D&C 56:16.
57a TG Jesus Christ, Good Shepherd.
  b Ezra 6:21; 9:1;
  Neh. 9:2;
  2 Thes. 3:6;
  D&C 133:5 (5, 14).
  c Deut. 29:20;
  Ps. 109:13.
58a TG Book of Life.
59a Prov. 27:23.

fold, and ye are his sheep; and he commandeth you that ye suffer no ravenous wolf to enter among you, that ye may not be destroyed.

61 And now I, Alma, do command you in the language of ªhim who hath commanded me, that ye observe to do the words which I have spoken unto you.

62 I speak by way of command unto you that belong to the church; and unto those who do not belong to the church I speak by way of invitation, saying: Come and be baptized unto repentance, that ye also may be partakers of the fruit of the ªtree of life.

CHAPTER 6

The Church in Zarahemla is cleansed and set in order—Alma goes to Gideon to preach. About 83 B.C.

AND now it came to pass that after Alma had made an end of speaking unto the people of the church, which was established in the city of Zarahemla, he ªordained ᵇpriests and elders, by laying on his ᶜhands according to the order of God, to preside and ᵈwatch over the church.

2 And it came to pass that whosoever did not belong to the church who ªrepented of their sins were baptized unto repentance, and were received into the church.

3 And it also came to pass that whosoever did belong to the church that did not ªrepent of their wickedness and humble themselves before God—I mean those who were lifted up in the ᵇpride of their hearts—the same were rejected, and their names were ᶜblotted out, that their names were not numbered among those of the righteous.

4 And thus they began to establish the order of the church in the ªcity of Zarahemla.

5 Now I would that ye should understand that the word of God was liberal unto all, that none were deprived of the privilege of assembling themselves together to hear the word of God.

6 Nevertheless the children of God were commanded that they should gather themselves together oft, and join in ªfasting and mighty prayer in behalf of the welfare of the souls of those who knew not God.

7 And now it came to pass that when Alma had made these regulations he departed from them, yea, from the church which was in the city of Zarahemla, and went over upon the east of the ªriver Sidon, into the ᵇvalley of Gideon, there having been a city built, which was called the city of Gideon, which was in the valley that was called Gideon, being called after the man who was ᶜslain by the hand of Nehor with the sword.

8 And Alma went and began to declare the word of God unto the church which was established in the valley of Gideon, according to the revelation of the truth of the word which had been spoken by his fathers, and according to the spirit of prophecy which was in him, according to the ªtestimony of Jesus Christ, the Son of God, who should come to redeem his people from their sins, and the holy order by which he was called. And thus it is written. Amen.

The words of Alma which he delivered to the people in Gideon, according to his own record.

Comprising chapter 7.

61a Alma 5:1 (1, 44).
62a 1 Ne. 8:10;
       11:21 (21–23).
6 1a TG Ordain;
       Priesthood.
   b TG Elder;
       Priest, Melchizedek
       Priesthood.

c TG Hands, Laying on of.
d D&C 52:39.
2a TG Baptism,
       Qualifications for.
3a Mosiah 26:6.
   b 1 Cor. 5:2.
   c Ex. 32:33;
       Mosiah 26:36;

Alma 1:24; 5:57 (57–58).
       TG Excommunication.
4a Alma 2:26.
6a TG Fast, Fasting.
7a Alma 4:4; 8:3.
   b Alma 2:20.
   c Alma 1:9.
8a Rev. 19:10.

CHAPTER 7

Christ will be born of Mary—He will loose the bands of death and bear the sins of His people—Those who repent, are baptized, and keep the commandments will have eternal life—Filthiness cannot inherit the kingdom of God—Humility, faith, hope, and charity are required. About 83 B.C.

BEHOLD my beloved brethren, seeing that I have been permitted to come unto you, therefore I attempt to address you in my language; yea, by my ᵃown mouth, seeing that it is the first time that I have spoken unto you by the words of my mouth, I having been wholly confined to the ᵇjudgment-seat, having had much business that I could not come unto you.

2 And even I could not have come now at this time were it not that the judgment-seat hath been ᵃgiven to another, to reign in my stead; and the Lord in much mercy hath granted that I should come unto you.

3 And behold, I have come having great hopes and much desire that I should find that ye had humbled yourselves before God, and that ye had continued in the supplicating of his grace, that I should find that ye were blameless before him, that I should find that ye were not in the awful ᵃdilemma that our brethren were in at Zarahemla.

4 But blessed be the name of God, that he hath given me to know, yea, hath given unto me the exceedingly great joy of knowing that they are established again in the way of his righteousness.

5 And I trust, according to the Spirit of God which is in me, that I shall also have joy over you; nevertheless I do not desire that my joy over you should come by the cause of so much afflictions and sorrow which I have had for the brethren at Zarahemla, for behold, my joy cometh over them after wading through much affliction and sorrow.

6 But behold, I trust that ye are not in a state of so much unbelief as were your brethren; I trust that ye are not lifted up in the pride of your hearts; yea, I trust that ye have not set your hearts upon riches and the vain things of the world; yea, I trust that you do not worship ᵃidols, but that ye do worship the true and the ᵇliving God, and that ye look forward for the remission of your sins, with an everlasting faith, which is to come.

7 For behold, I say unto you there be many things to come; and behold, there is one thing which is of more importance than they all— for behold, the ᵃtime is not far distant that the Redeemer liveth and cometh among his people.

8 Behold, I do not say that he will come among us at the ᵃtime of his dwelling in his mortal tabernacle; for behold, the Spirit hath not said unto me that this should be the case. Now as to this thing I do not know; but this much I do know, that the Lord God hath power to do all things which are according to his word.

9 But behold, the Spirit hath said this much unto me, saying: Cry unto this people, saying—ᵃRepent ye, and prepare the way of the Lord, and walk in his paths, which are straight; for behold, the kingdom of heaven is at hand, and the Son of God ᵇcometh upon the face of the earth.

10 And behold, he shall be ᵃborn of Mary, at ᵇJerusalem which is the ᶜland of our forefathers, she being a ᵈvirgin, a precious and chosen

---

7 1a Alma 4:19.
  b Mosiah 29:42.
 2a Alma 4:18 (16–18).
 3a Alma 5:17 (16–17).
 6a 2 Ne. 9:37;
    Hel. 6:31.
  b Dan. 6:26.

 7a Alma 9:26.
 8a 1 Ne. 12:6 (4–8);
    Alma 16:20.
 9a Matt. 3:2 (2–3);
    Alma 9:25 (25–26).
  b Mosiah 3:5; 7:27;
    15:2 (1–7).

10a Isa. 7:14; Luke 1:27;
    Mosiah 3:8.
  b Luke 2:4.
  c 1 Chr. 9:3;
    2 Chr. 15:9;
    1 Ne. 1:4; 3 Ne. 20:29.
  d 1 Ne. 11:13 (13–21).

vessel, who shall be overshadowed and [e]conceive by the power of the Holy Ghost, and bring forth a son, yea, even the Son of God.

11 And he shall go forth, suffering pains and [a]afflictions and [b]temptations of every kind; and this that the word might be fulfilled which saith he will [c]take upon him the pains and the sicknesses of his people.

12 And he will take upon him [a]death, that he may [b]loose the bands of death which bind his people; and he will take upon him their infirmities, that his bowels may be filled with mercy, according to the flesh, that he may know according to the flesh how to [c]succor his people according to their infirmities.

13 Now the Spirit [a]knoweth all things; nevertheless the Son of God suffereth according to the [b]flesh that he might [c]take upon him the sins of his people, that he might blot out their transgressions according to the power of his deliverance; and now behold, this is the testimony which is in me.

14 Now I say unto you that ye must [a]repent, and be born again; for the Spirit saith if ye are not born again ye cannot inherit the kingdom of heaven; therefore come and be baptized unto repentance, that ye may be washed from your sins, that ye may have faith on the Lamb of God, who taketh away the sins of the world, who is mighty to save and to cleanse from all unrighteousness.

15 Yea, I say unto you come and fear not, and lay aside every sin, which easily doth [a]beset you, which doth bind you down to destruction, yea, come and go forth, and show unto your God that ye are willing to repent of your sins and enter into a covenant with him to keep his commandments, and witness it unto him this day by going into the waters of baptism.

16 And whosoever doeth this, and keepeth the commandments of God from thenceforth, the same will [a]remember that I say unto him, yea, he will remember that I have said unto him, he shall have eternal life, according to the testimony of the Holy Spirit, which testifieth in me.

17 And now my beloved brethren, do you believe these things? Behold, I say unto you, yea, I know that ye believe them; and the way that I know that ye believe them is by the manifestation of the Spirit which is in me. And now because your faith is strong concerning that, yea, concerning the things which I have spoken, great is my joy.

18 For as I said unto you from the beginning, that I had much desire that ye were not in the state of [a]dilemma like your brethren, even so I have found that my desires have been gratified.

19 For I perceive that ye are in the paths of righteousness; I perceive that ye are in the path which leads to the kingdom of God; yea, I perceive that ye are making his [a]paths straight.

20 I perceive that it has been made known unto you, by the testimony of his word, that he cannot [a]walk in crooked paths; neither doth he vary from that which he hath said; neither hath he a shadow of turning from the right to the left, or from that which is right to that which is wrong; therefore, his course is one eternal round.

10e Matt. 1:20;
    Mosiah 15:3.
11a Isa. 53:5 (3–5).
  b TG Jesus Christ,
    Temptation of.
  c Mosiah 14:4 (3–5).
12a TG Jesus Christ,
    Death of.
  b Ps. 116:16 (15–16);

2 Ne. 2:8;
  Alma 12:25 (24–25);
  42:23.
c Heb. 2:18; 4:15;
  D&C 62:1.
13a TG God, Omniscience of.
  b TG Jesus Christ,
    Condescension of.
  c Mosiah 15:12.

14a TG Purification.
15a 2 Ne. 4:18.
16a Ether 12:4;
    Moro. 7:3.
18a James 1:8.
19a Matt. 3:3.
20a 1 Ne. 10:19;
    Alma 37:12;
    D&C 3:2.

21 And he doth not dwell in ᵃunholy temples; neither can filthiness or anything which is unclean be received into the kingdom of God; therefore I say unto you the time shall come, yea, and it shall be at the last day, that he who is ᵇfilthy shall remain in his filthiness.

22 And now my beloved brethren, I have said these things unto you that I might awaken you to a sense of your duty to God, that ye may walk blameless before him, that ye may walk after the holy order of God, after which ye have been received.

23 And now I would that ye should be ᵃhumble, and be ᵇsubmissive and gentle; easy to be entreated; full of patience and long-suffering; being temperate in all things; being diligent in keeping the commandments of God at all times; asking for whatsoever things ye stand in need, both spiritual and temporal; always returning thanks unto God for whatsoever things ye do receive.

24 And see that ye have ᵃfaith, hope, and charity, and then ye will always abound in good works.

25 And may the Lord bless you, and keep your garments spotless, that ye may at last be brought to sit down with ᵃAbraham, Isaac, and Jacob, and the holy prophets who have been ever since the world began, having your garments ᵇspotless even as their garments are spotless, in the kingdom of heaven to go no more out.

26 And now my beloved brethren, I have spoken these words unto you according to the Spirit which testifieth in me; and my soul doth exceedingly rejoice, because of the exceeding diligence and heed which ye have given unto my word.

27 And now, may the ᵃpeace of God rest upon you, and upon your houses and lands, and upon your flocks and herds, and all that you possess, your women and your children, according to your faith and good works, from this time forth and forever. And thus I have spoken. Amen.

CHAPTER 8

Alma preaches and baptizes in Melek—He is rejected in Ammonihah and leaves—An angel commands him to return and cry repentance unto the people—He is received by Amulek, and the two of them preach in Ammonihah. About 82 B.C.

AND now it came to pass that Alma returned from the ᵃland of Gideon, after having taught the people of Gideon many things which cannot be written, having established the ᵇorder of the church, according as he had before done in the land of Zarahemla, yea, he returned to his own house at Zarahemla to rest himself from the labors which he had performed.

2 And thus ended the ninth year of the reign of the judges over the people of Nephi.

3 And it came to pass in the commencement of the tenth year of the reign of the judges over the people of Nephi, that Alma departed from thence and took his journey over into the land of ᵃMelek, on the west of the ᵇriver Sidon, on the west by the borders of the wilderness.

4 And he began to teach the people in the land of Melek according to the ᵃholy order of God, by which he had been called; and he began to teach the people throughout all the land of Melek.

5 And it came to pass that the people came to him throughout all

---

21a 1 Cor. 3:17 (16–17); 6:19;
    Mosiah 2:37;
    Alma 34:36.
  b 1 Ne. 15:33 (33–35);
    2 Ne. 9:16;
    Morm. 9:14;
    D&C 88:35.

23a Prov. 18:12.
  b TG Submissiveness.
24a 1 Cor. 13:13 (1–13);
    Ether 12:31 (30–35);
    Moro. 7:44 (33–48).
25a D&C 27:10.
  b 2 Pet. 3:14.

27a TG Peace of God.
8 1a Alma 2:20; 6:7.
  b TG Church Organization.
3a Alma 31:6.
  b Alma 6:7; 16:6 (6–7).
4a D&C 107:3 (2–4).
  TG Priesthood.

the borders of the land which was by the wilderness side. And they were baptized throughout all the land;

6 So that when he had finished his work at Melek he departed thence, and traveled three days' journey on the north of the land of Melek; and he came to a city which was called ^aAmmonihah.

7 Now it was the custom of the people of Nephi to call their lands, and their cities, and their villages, yea, even all their small villages, after the ^aname of him who first possessed them; and thus it was with the land of Ammonihah.

8 And it came to pass that when Alma had come to the city of Ammonihah he began to preach the word of God unto them.

9 Now Satan had gotten great ^ahold upon the hearts of the people of the city of Ammonihah; therefore they would not hearken unto the words of Alma.

10 Nevertheless Alma ^alabored much in the spirit, ^bwrestling with God in ^cmighty prayer, that he would pour out his Spirit upon the people who were in the city; that he would also grant that he might baptize them unto repentance.

11 Nevertheless, they hardened their hearts, saying unto him: Behold, we know that thou art Alma; and we know that thou art high priest over the church which thou hast established in many parts of the land, according to your tradition; and we are not of thy church, and we do not believe in such foolish traditions.

12 And now we know that because we are not of thy church we know that thou hast no power over us; and thou hast delivered up the judgment-seat unto ^aNephihah; therefore thou art not the chief judge over us.

13 Now when the people had said this, and withstood all his words, and ^areviled him, and spit upon him, and caused that he should be ^bcast out of their city, he departed thence and took his journey towards the city which was called Aaron.

14 And it came to pass that while he was journeying thither, being weighed down with sorrow, wading through much ^atribulation and anguish of soul, because of the wickedness of the people who were in the city of Ammonihah, it came to pass while Alma was thus weighed down with sorrow, behold an ^bangel of the Lord appeared unto him, saying:

15 Blessed art thou, Alma; therefore, lift up thy head and rejoice, for thou hast great cause to rejoice; for thou hast been faithful in keeping the commandments of God from the time which thou receivedst thy first message from him. Behold, I am he that ^adelivered it unto you.

16 And behold, I am sent to ^acommand thee that thou return to the city of Ammonihah, and preach again unto the people of the city; yea, preach unto them. Yea, say unto them, except they repent the Lord God will ^bdestroy them.

17 For behold, they do study at this time that they may destroy the liberty of thy people, (for thus saith the Lord) which is contrary to the ^astatutes, and judgments, and commandments which he has given unto his people.

18 Now it came to pass that after Alma had received his message from the angel of the Lord he returned speedily to the land of Ammonihah. And he entered the city by another way, yea, by the way which is on the south of the city of Ammonihah.

19 And as ^ahe entered the city he

6a Alma 9:1.
7a Ether 2:13.
9a 2 Ne. 28:20 (19–22);
    D&C 10:20.
10a Alma 17:5.
  b Enos 1:2 (1–12).
  c 3 Ne. 27:1;
    D&C 5:24; 29:2.

12a Alma 4:20.
13a 1 Cor. 4:12.
  b Alma 8:24.
14a TG Tribulation.
  b Mosiah 3:2 (2–3);
    Alma 10:20 (7–10, 20).
15a Mosiah 27:11 (11–16).
16a Gal. 2:2;

    Hel. 13:3.
  b Alma 9:12 (4, 12, 18, 24).
17a Alma 1:1 (1, 14).
    TG Commandments
    of God.
19a Alma 10:8.

was an hungered, and he said to a man: Will ye give to an humble servant of God something to eat?

20 And the man said unto him: I am a Nephite, and I know that thou art a holy prophet of God, for thou art the man whom an ^aangel said in a vision: Thou shalt receive. Therefore, go with me into my house and I will impart unto thee of my ^bfood; and I know that thou wilt be a blessing unto me and my house.

21 And it came to pass that the man received him into his house; and the man was called Amulek; and he brought forth bread and meat and set before Alma.

22 And it came to pass that Alma ate bread and was filled; and he ^ablessed Amulek and his house, and he gave thanks unto God.

23 And after he had eaten and was filled he said unto Amulek: I am Alma, and am the ^ahigh priest over the church of God throughout the land.

24 And behold, I have been called to preach the word of God among all this people, according to the spirit of revelation and prophecy; and I was in this land and they would not receive me, but they ^acast me out and I was about to set my back towards this land forever.

25 But behold, I have been commanded that I should turn again and prophesy unto this people, yea, and to testify against them concerning their iniquities.

26 And now, Amulek, because thou hast fed me and taken me in, thou art blessed; for I was an hungered, for I had fasted many days.

27 And Alma ^atarried many days with Amulek before he began to preach unto the people.

28 And it came to pass that the people did wax more gross in their iniquities.

29 And the word came to Alma,

saying: Go; and also say unto my servant ^aAmulek, go forth and prophesy unto this people, saying—Repent ye, for thus saith the Lord, except ye repent I will visit this people in mine anger; yea, and I will not turn my ^bfierce anger away.

30 And Alma went forth, and also Amulek, among the people, to declare the words of God unto them; and they were filled with the Holy Ghost.

31 And they had ^apower given unto them, insomuch that they could not be confined in dungeons; neither was it possible that any man could slay them; nevertheless they did not exercise their ^bpower until they were bound in bands and cast into prison. Now, this was done that the Lord might show forth his power in them.

32 And it came to pass that they went forth and began to preach and to prophesy unto the people, according to the spirit and power which the Lord had given them.

The words of Alma, and also the words of Amulek, which were declared unto the people who were in the land of Ammonihah. And also they are cast into prison, and delivered by the miraculous power of God which was in them, according to the record of Alma.

Comprising chapters 9 through 14.

CHAPTER 9

Alma commands the people of Ammonihah to repent—The Lord will be merciful to the Lamanites in the last days—If the Nephites forsake the light, they will be destroyed by the Lamanites—The Son of God will come soon—He will redeem those who repent, are baptized, and have faith in His name. About 82 B.C.

20a Alma 10:7 (7–9).
  b 1 Kgs. 17:11 (8–13).
22a Alma 10:11.
23a Alma 5:3 (3, 44, 49);
  13:1 (1–20).
24a Alma 8:13.
27a Alma 10:10.
29a Alma 10:1.
  b Alma 9:12, 18.
31a Alma 14:10.
  b Alma 14:25 (17–29).

AND again, I, Alma, having been commanded of God that I should take Amulek and go forth and preach again unto this people, or the people who were in the city of ^aAmmonihah, it came to pass as I began to preach unto them, they began to contend with me, saying:

2 Who art thou? Suppose ye that we shall believe the testimony of ^aone man, although he should preach unto us that the earth should pass away?

3 Now they understood not the words which they spake; for they knew not that the earth should pass away.

4 And they said also: We will not believe thy words if thou shouldst prophesy that this great city should be destroyed in ^aone day.

5 Now they knew not that God could do such marvelous ^aworks, for they were a hard-hearted and a stiffnecked people.

6 And they said: ^aWho is God, that sendeth ^bno more authority than one man among this people, to declare unto them the truth of such great and marvelous things?

7 And they stood forth to lay their hands on me; but behold, they did not. And I stood with boldness to declare unto them, yea, I did boldly testify unto them, saying:

8 Behold, O ye wicked and perverse ^ageneration, how have ye forgotten the ^btradition of your fathers; yea, how soon ye have forgotten the commandments of God.

9 Do ye not remember that our father, Lehi, was brought out of Jerusalem by the ^ahand of God? Do ye not remember that they were all led by him through the wilderness?

10 And have ye forgotten so soon how many times he ^adelivered our fathers out of the hands of their enemies, and preserved them from being destroyed, even by the hands of their own brethren?

11 Yea, and if it had not been for his matchless power, and his mercy, and his ^along-suffering towards us, we should unavoidably have been cut off from the face of the earth long before this period of time, and perhaps been consigned to a state of ^bendless misery and woe.

12 Behold, now I say unto you that he commandeth you to repent; and except ye repent, ye can in nowise inherit the kingdom of God. But behold, this is not all—he has commanded you to repent, or he will utterly ^adestroy you from off the face of the earth; yea, he will visit you in his ^banger, and in his ^cfierce anger he will not turn away.

13 Behold, do ye not remember the words which he spake unto Lehi, saying that: ^aInasmuch as ye shall keep my commandments, ye shall prosper in the land? And again it is said that: Inasmuch as ye will not keep my commandments ye shall be cut off from the presence of the Lord.

14 Now I would that ye should remember, that inasmuch as the Lamanites have not kept the commandments of God, they have been ^acut off from the presence of the Lord. Now we see that the word of the Lord has been verified in this thing, and the Lamanites have been cut off from his presence, from the beginning of their transgressions in the land.

15 Nevertheless I say unto you, that it shall be more ^atolerable for them in the day of judgment than for you, if ye remain in your sins,

9 1a Alma 8:6.
  2a Deut. 17:6.
  4a Alma 16:10 (9–10).
  5a TG God, Works of.
  6a Ex. 5:2;
     Mosiah 11:27;
     Moses 5:16.
   b Alma 10:12.
  8a Matt. 3:7;

     Alma 10:17 (17–25).
   b TG Birthright.
  9a 1 Ne. 2:2 (1–7).
 10a TG Deliver.
 11a TG Long-Suffering.
   b Mosiah 16:11.
 12a Alma 8:16;
     10:27 (19, 23, 27).
   b Jer. 18:10 (6–10).

     c Alma 8:29.
 13a 2 Ne. 1:20;
     Mosiah 1:7;
     Alma 37:13.
 14a 2 Ne. 5:20 (20–24);
     Alma 38:1.
 15a Matt. 11:22 (22, 24).

yea, and even more tolerable for them in this life than for you, except ye repent.

16 For there are many promises which are ᵃextended to the Lamanites; for it is because of the ᵇtraditions of their fathers that caused them to remain in their state of ᶜignorance; therefore the Lord will be merciful unto them and ᵈprolong their existence in the land.

17 And at some period of time they will be ᵃbrought to believe in his word, and to know of the incorrectness of the traditions of their fathers; and many of them will be saved, for the Lord will be merciful unto all who ᵇcall on his name.

18 But behold, I say unto you that if ye persist in your wickedness that your days shall not be ᵃprolonged in the land, for the ᵇLamanites shall be sent upon you; and if ye repent not they shall come in a time when you know not, and ye shall be visited with ᶜutter destruction; and it shall be according to the fierce ᵈanger of the Lord.

19 For he will not suffer you that ye shall live in your iniquities, to ᵃdestroy his people. I say unto you, Nay; he would rather suffer that the Lamanites might destroy all his people who are called the people of Nephi, if it were possible that they could ᵇfall into sins and transgressions, after having had so much light and so much knowledge given unto them of the Lord their God;

20 Yea, after having been such a highly favored people of the Lord; yea, after having been favored above every other ᵃnation, kindred,

tongue, or people; after having had all things ᵇmade known unto them, according to their desires, and their faith, and prayers, of that which has been, and which is, and which is to come;

21 Having been ᵃvisited by the Spirit of God; having conversed with angels, and having been spoken unto by the voice of the Lord; and having the spirit of prophecy, and the spirit of revelation, and also many gifts, the gift of speaking with tongues, and the gift of preaching, and the gift of the Holy Ghost, and the gift of ᵇtranslation;

22 Yea, and after having been ᵃdelivered of God out of the land of Jerusalem, by the hand of the Lord; having been ᵇsaved from famine, and from sickness, and all manner of diseases of every kind; and they having waxed strong in battle, that they might not be destroyed; having been brought out of ᶜbondage time after time, and having been kept and preserved until now; and they have been prospered until they are rich in all manner of things—

23 And now behold I say unto you, that if this people, who have received so many blessings from the hand of the Lord, should transgress ᵃcontrary to the light and knowledge which they do have, I say unto you that if this be the case, that if they should fall into transgression, it would be far more ᵇtolerable for the Lamanites than for them.

24 For behold, the ᵃpromises of the Lord are extended to the Lamanites, but they are not unto you if ye transgress; for has not the Lord expressly

16a Alma 17:15.
  b Alma 3:8; 17:15.
  c 2 Ne. 9:26 (25–26);
    Mosiah 3:11;
    Alma 42:21.
  d Deut. 11:9 (8–9); 32:47;
    Hel. 15:11 (10–11);
    D&C 5:33.
17a Enos 1:13.
  b Ps. 81:7;
    Alma 38:5;
    D&C 3:8.
18a Deut. 6:2.
  b Alma 16:3.
  c Alma 16:9.
  d Alma 8:29.
19a 1 Ne. 12:19 (15, 19–20);
    Alma 45:11 (10–14).
  b Alma 24:30.
20a 2 Sam. 7:23;
    Abr. 2:9.
  b TG Prophets, Mission of.
21a Ex. 3:16;
    2 Ne. 4:26;
    Morm. 1:15.
  b Omni 1:20;
    Mosiah 8:13 (13–19);
    28:17 (11–17).
22a 2 Ne. 1:4.
  b TG Protection, Divine.
  c Mosiah 27:16.
23a TG Disobedience.
  b Matt. 11:22 (22–24).
24a 2 Ne. 30:6 (4–7);
    D&C 3:20.

promised and firmly decreed, that if ye will rebel against him that ye shall [b]utterly be destroyed from off the face of the earth?

25 And now for this cause, that ye may not be destroyed, the Lord has sent his angel to visit many of his people, declaring unto them that they must go forth and cry mightily unto this people, saying: [a]Repent ye, for the kingdom of heaven is nigh at hand;

26 And [a]not many days hence the Son of God shall come in his [b]glory; and his glory shall be the glory of the Only Begotten of the Father, full of [c]grace, equity, and truth, full of patience, [d]mercy, and long-suffering, quick to [e]hear the cries of his people and to answer their prayers.

27 And behold, he cometh to [a]redeem those who will be [b]baptized unto repentance, through faith on his name.

28 Therefore, prepare ye the way of the Lord, for the time is at hand that all men shall reap a [a]reward of their [b]works, according to that which they have been—if they have been righteous they shall [c]reap the salvation of their souls, according to the power and deliverance of Jesus Christ; and if they have been evil they shall reap the [d]damnation of their souls, according to the power and captivation of the devil.

29 Now behold, this is the voice of the angel, crying unto the people.

30 And now, my [a]beloved brethren, for ye are my brethren, and ye ought to be beloved, and ye ought to bring forth works which are meet for repentance, seeing that your hearts have been grossly hardened against the word of God, and see-

ing that ye are a [b]lost and a fallen people.

31 Now it came to pass that when I, Alma, had spoken these words, behold, the people were wroth with me because I said unto them that they were a hard-hearted and a [a]stiffnecked people.

32 And also because I said unto them that they were a lost and a fallen people they were angry with me, and sought to lay their hands upon me, that they might cast me into prison.

33 But it came to pass that the Lord did not suffer them that they should take me [a]at that time and cast me into prison.

34 And it came to pass that Amulek went and stood forth, and began to preach unto them also. And now the [a]words of Amulek are not all written, nevertheless a part of his words are written in this book.

CHAPTER 10

Lehi descended from Manasseh—Amulek recounts the angelic command that he care for Alma—The prayers of the righteous cause the people to be spared—Unrighteous lawyers and judges lay the foundation of the destruction of the people. About 82 B.C.

Now these are the [a]words which [b]Amulek preached unto the people who were in the land of Ammonihah, saying:

2 I am Amulek; I am the son of Giddonah, who was the son of Ishmael, who was a descendant of Aminadi; and it was that same Aminadi who interpreted the [a]writing which was upon the wall of the temple, which was written by the finger of God.

24b Alma 16:9 (2–9);
     Morm. 6:15 (15–22).
25a Matt. 3:2 (2–3);
     Alma 7:9;
     Hel. 5:32.
26a Alma 7:7.
   b TG Jesus Christ,
     Glory of.
   c TG Grace.
   d TG God, Mercy of.

 e Deut. 26:7;
   Isa. 65:24.
27a TG Redemption.
  b TG Baptism, Essential.
28a TG Reward.
  b Job 34:11;
    D&C 1:10; 6:33.
  c Ps. 7:16.
  d TG Damnation.
30a 1 Jn. 4:11.

 b Alma 12:22.
31a 2 Ne. 25:28;
    Mosiah 3:14.
33a Alma 14:17 (17–18).
34a Alma 10:1 (1–11).
10 1a Alma 9:34.
   b Alma 8:29 (21–29).
   2a Dan. 5:16.

3 And Aminadi was a descendant of Nephi, who was the son of Lehi, who came out of the land of Jerusalem, who was a descendant of ^aManasseh, who was the son of ^bJoseph who was ^csold into Egypt by the hands of his brethren.

4 And behold, I am also a man of no small ^areputation among all those who know me; yea, and behold, I have many kindreds and ^bfriends, and I have also acquired much riches by the hand of my ^cindustry.

5 Nevertheless, after all this, I never have known much of the ways of the Lord, and his ^amysteries and marvelous power. I said I never had known much of these things; but behold, I mistake, for I have seen much of his mysteries and his marvelous power; yea, even in the preservation of the lives of this people.

6 Nevertheless, I did harden my heart, for I was ^acalled many times and I would not ^bhear; therefore I knew concerning these things, yet I would not know; therefore I went on rebelling ^cagainst God, in the wickedness of my heart, even until the fourth day of this seventh month, which is in the tenth year of the reign of the judges.

7 As I was journeying to see a very near kindred, behold an ^aangel of the Lord appeared unto me and said: Amulek, return to thine own house, for thou shalt feed a prophet of the Lord; yea, a holy man, who is a chosen man of God; for he has ^bfasted many days because of the sins of this people, and he is an hungered, and thou shalt ^creceive him into thy house and feed him, and he shall bless thee and thy house;

and the blessing of the Lord shall rest upon thee and thy house.

8 And it came to pass that I obeyed the voice of the angel, and returned towards my house. And as I was going thither I found the ^aman whom the angel said unto me: Thou shalt receive into thy house—and behold it was this same man who has been speaking unto you concerning the things of God.

9 And the angel said unto me he is a ^aholy man; wherefore I know he is a holy man because it was said by an angel of God.

10 And again, I know that the things whereof he hath testified are true; for behold I say unto you, that as the Lord liveth, even so has he sent his ^aangel to make these things manifest unto me; and this he has done while this Alma hath ^bdwelt at my house.

11 For behold, he hath ^ablessed mine house, he hath blessed me, and my women, and my children, and my father and my kinsfolk; yea, even all my kindred hath he blessed, and the blessing of the Lord hath rested upon us according to the words which he spake.

12 And now, when Amulek had spoken these words the people began to be astonished, seeing there was ^amore than one witness who testified of the things whereof they were accused, and also of the things which were to come, according to the spirit of prophecy which was in them.

13 Nevertheless, there were some among them who thought to question them, that by their cunning ^adevices they might catch them in their words, that they might ^bfind

3a Gen. 41:51;
    Josh. 17:1;
    1 Chr. 7:14; 9:3;
    1 Ne. 5:14.
  b TG Israel, Joseph,
    People of.
  c Gen. 37:36 (29–36).
4a Acts 5:34 (34–39).
  b Alma 15:16.
  c TG Industry;
    Work, Value of.

5a TG Mysteries of
    Godliness.
6a 2 Chr. 33:10;
    Isa. 50:2;
    Alma 5:37.
  b D&C 39:9.
  c Acts 9:5.
7a Alma 8:20.
  b Alma 5:46; 6:6.
  c Acts 10:30 (30–35).
    TG Hospitality.

8a Alma 8:19 (19–21).
9a TG Holiness.
10a Mosiah 3:2 (2–3);
    Alma 11:31.
  b Alma 8:27.
11a 1 Sam. 2:20; Alma 8:22.
12a Alma 9:6.
13a Jer. 11:19;
    Lam. 3:62 (60–62);
    Alma 11:21.
  b Mark 14:55 (55–60).

witness against them, that they might deliver them to their judges that they might be judged according to the law, and that they might be slain or cast into prison, according to the crime which they could make appear or witness against them.

14 Now it was those men who sought to destroy them, who were ᵃlawyers, who were hired or appointed by the people to administer the law at their times of trials, or at the trials of the crimes of the people before the judges.

15 Now these lawyers were learned in all the arts and ᵃcunning of the people; and this was to enable them that they might be skilful in their profession.

16 And it came to pass that they began to question Amulek, that thereby they might make him ᵃcross his words, or contradict the words which he should speak.

17 Now they knew not that Amulek could ᵃknow of their designs. But it came to pass as they began to question him, he ᵇperceived their thoughts, and he said unto them: O ye wicked and perverse ᶜgeneration, ye lawyers and hypocrites, for ye are laying the foundations of the devil; for ye are laying ᵈtraps and snares to catch the holy ones of God.

18 Ye are laying plans to ᵃpervert the ways of the righteous, and to bring down the wrath of God upon your heads, even to the utter destruction of this people.

19 Yea, well did Mosiah say, who was our last king, when he was about to deliver up the kingdom, having no one to confer it upon, causing that this people should be governed by their own voices—yea, well did he say that if the time should come that the voice of this people should ᵃchoose iniquity, that is, if the time should come that this people should fall into transgression, they would be ripe for destruction.

20 And now I say unto you that well doth the Lord ᵃjudge of your iniquities; well doth he cry unto this people, by the voice of his ᵇangels: Repent ye, repent, for the kingdom of heaven is at hand.

21 Yea, well doth he cry, by the voice of his angels that: ᵃI will come down among my people, with equity and justice in my hands.

22 Yea, and I say unto you that if it were not for the ᵃprayers of the righteous, who are now in the land, that ye would even now be visited with utter destruction; yet it would not be by ᵇflood, as were the people in the days of ᶜNoah, but it would be by famine, and by pestilence, and the ᵈsword.

23 But it is by the ᵃprayers of the righteous that ye are spared; now therefore, if ye will ᵇcast out the righteous from among you then will not the Lord stay his hand; but in his fierce anger he will come out against you; then ye shall be smitten by famine, and by pestilence, and by the sword; and the ᶜtime is soon at hand except ye repent.

24 And now it came to pass that the people were more angry with Amulek, and they cried out, saying: This man doth revile against our laws which are just, and our wise ᵃlawyers whom we have selected.

25 But Amulek stretched forth his hand, and cried the mightier unto them, saying: O ye wicked and

14a Alma 10:24; 11:21 (20–37);
        14:18 (18, 23);
        3 Ne. 6:11.
15a Luke 20:23.
16a Mark 12:13.
17a Luke 5:22.
    b Alma 12:3;
        D&C 6:16.
    c Matt. 3:7;
        Alma 9:8.
    d D&C 10:25 (21–27).

18a Acts 13:10.
19a Mosiah 29:27;
        Alma 2:4 (3–7);
        Hel. 5:2.
20a TG Jesus Christ, Judge.
    b Alma 8:14 (14–16, 20);
        13:22.
21a Mosiah 13:34 (28–35).
22a 1 Sam. 7:9 (7–10);
        Mosiah 27:14 (14–16).
    b Gen. 8:21;

        3 Ne. 22:9 (8–10).
        TG Flood.
    c TG Earth, Cleansing of.
    d Deut. 32:25;
        JS—H 1:45.
23a TG Prayer.
    b 2 Chr. 13:9;
        Moro. 9:14.
    c TG Procrastination.
24a Alma 10:14.

perverse generation, why hath Satan got such great hold upon your hearts? Why will ye yield yourselves unto him that he may have power over you, to ^ablind your eyes, that ye will not understand the words which are spoken, according to their truth?

26 For behold, have I testified against your law? Ye do not understand; ye say that I have spoken against your law; but I have not, but I have spoken in favor of your law, to your condemnation.

27 And now behold, I say unto you, that the foundation of the ^adestruction of this people is beginning to be laid by the ^bunrighteousness of your ^clawyers and your judges.

28 And now it came to pass that when Amulek had spoken these words the people cried out against him, saying: Now we know that this man is a ^achild of the devil, for he hath ^blied unto us; for he hath spoken against our law. And now he says that he has not spoken against it.

29 And again, he has reviled against our lawyers, and our judges.

30 And it came to pass that the lawyers put it into their hearts that they should remember these things against him.

31 And there was one among them whose name was Zeezrom. Now he was the foremost to ^aaccuse Amulek and Alma, he being one of the most expert among them, having much business to do among the people.

32 Now the object of these lawyers was to get gain; and they got gain ^aaccording to their employ.

CHAPTER 11

The Nephite monetary system is set forth—Amulek contends with Zeez- rom—*Christ will not save people in their sins—Only those who inherit the kingdom of heaven are saved—All men will rise in immortality—There is no death after the Resurrection. About 82 B.C.*

Now it was in the law of Mosiah that every man who was a judge of the law, or those who were appointed to be judges, should receive ^awages ^baccording to the time which they labored to judge those who were brought before them to be judged.

2 Now if a man owed another, and he would not ^apay that which he did owe, he was complained of to the judge; and the judge executed authority, and sent forth officers that the man should be brought before him; and he judged the man according to the law and the evidences which were brought against him, and thus the man was compelled to pay that which he owed, or be stripped, or be cast out from among the people as a thief and a robber.

3 And the judge received for his wages ^aaccording to his time—a ^bsenine of gold for a day, or a senum of silver, which is equal to a senine of gold; and this is according to the law which was given.

4 Now these are the names of the different pieces of their gold, and of their silver, according to their value. And the names are given by the Nephites, for they did not reckon after the ^amanner of the Jews who were at Jerusalem; neither did they measure after the manner of the Jews; but they altered their reckoning and their measure, according to the minds and the circumstances of the people, in every generation, until the reign of the judges, they having been ^bestablished by king Mosiah.

25a 2 Cor. 4:4 (3–4);
     Alma 14:6;
     Moses 6:27.
27a Alma 8:16;
     9:12 (4, 12, 18, 24).
  b TG Injustice.
  c Luke 11:46 (45–52);

     2 Ne. 28:16.
28a John 7:20.
  b Alma 14:2.
31a Alma 11:21 (20–36).
32a Alma 11:1 (1–3).
11 1a TG Wages.
  b Alma 10:32.

2a TG Justice.
3a Alma 10:32.
  b Alma 30:33;
     3 Ne. 12:26.
4a BD Money.
  b Mosiah 29:41 (40–44).

5 Now the reckoning is thus—a senine of gold, a seon of gold, a shum of gold, and a limnah of gold.

6 A senum of silver, an amnor of silver, an ezrom of silver, and an onti of silver.

7 A senum of silver was equal to a senine of gold, and either for a measure of barley, and also for a measure of every kind of grain.

8 Now the amount of a seon of gold was twice the value of a senine.

9 And a shum of gold was twice the value of a seon.

10 And a limnah of gold was the value of them all.

11 And an amnor of silver was as great as two senums.

12 And an ezrom of silver was as great as four senums.

13 And an onti was as great as them all.

14 Now this is the value of the lesser numbers of their reckoning—

15 A shiblon is half of a senum; therefore, a shiblon for half a measure of barley.

16 And a shiblum is a half of a shiblon.

17 And a leah is the half of a shiblum.

18 Now this is their number, according to their reckoning.

19 Now an antion of gold is equal to three shiblons.

20 Now, it was for the sole purpose to get ^again, because they received their wages according to their ^bemploy, therefore, they did ^cstir up the people to ^driotings, and all manner of disturbances and wickedness, that they might have more employ, that they might ^eget ^fmoney according to the suits which were brought before them; therefore they did stir up the people against Alma and Amulek.

21 And this Zeezrom began to question Amulek, saying: Will ye answer me a few questions which I shall ask you? Now Zeezrom was a man who was ^aexpert in the ^bdevices of the devil, that he might destroy that which was good; therefore, he said unto Amulek: Will ye answer the questions which I shall put unto you?

22 And Amulek said unto him: Yea, if it be according to the ^aSpirit of the Lord, which is in me; for I shall say nothing which is contrary to the Spirit of the Lord. And Zeezrom said unto him: Behold, here are six onties of silver, and all these will I ^bgive thee if thou wilt deny the existence of a Supreme Being.

23 Now Amulek said: O thou ^achild of hell, why ^btempt ye me? Knowest thou that the righteous yieldeth to no such temptations?

24 Believest thou that there is no God? I say unto you, Nay, thou knowest that there is a God, but thou lovest that ^alucre more than him.

25 And now thou hast lied before God unto me. Thou saidst unto me—Behold these six onties, which are of great worth, I will give unto thee—when thou hadst it in thy heart to retain them from me; and it was only thy desire that I should deny the true and living God, that thou mightest have cause to destroy me. And now behold, for this great evil thou shalt have thy reward.

26 And Zeezrom said unto him: Thou sayest there is a true and living God?

27 And Amulek said: Yea, there is a true and living God.

28 Now Zeezrom said: Is there more than one God?

20a TG Selfishness.
  b Prov. 28:8.
  c TG Provoking.
  d TG Rioting and
    Reveling.
  e Alma 10:32.
  f Luke 11:52 (45–54).
21a Alma 10:31;

14:7 (6–7, 18, 23).
  b Lam. 3:62 (60–62);
    Alma 10:13.
22a TG God, Spirit of;
    Holy Ghost, Mission of.
  b TG Bribe.
23a Acts 13:10 (8–12);
    Alma 5:41.

  b TG Temptation;
    Test.
24a Luke 16:14;
    John 12:43 (42–43);
    Acts 19:27 (27, 36–38);
    Titus 1:11.

29 And he answered, No.

30 Now Zeezrom said unto him again: How knowest thou these things?

31 And he said: An ^aangel hath made them known unto me.

32 And Zeezrom said again: Who is he that shall come? Is it the Son of God?

33 And he said unto him, Yea.

34 And Zeezrom said again: Shall he save his people ^ain their sins? And Amulek answered and said unto him: I say unto you he shall not, for it is impossible for him to deny his word.

35 Now Zeezrom said unto the people: See that ye remember these things; for he said there is but one God; yet he saith that the Son of God shall come, but he shall ^anot save his people—as though he had authority to command God.

36 Now Amulek saith again unto him: Behold thou hast ^alied, for thou sayest that I spake as though I had authority to command God because I said he shall not save his people in their sins.

37 And I say unto you again that he cannot save them in their ^asins; for I cannot deny his word, and he hath said that ^bno unclean thing can inherit the ^ckingdom of heaven; therefore, how can ye be saved, except ye inherit the kingdom of heaven? Therefore, ye cannot be saved in your sins.

38 Now Zeezrom saith again unto him: Is the Son of God the very Eternal Father?

39 And Amulek said unto him: Yea, he is the very ^aEternal Father

of heaven and of earth, and ^ball things which in them are; he is the beginning and the end, the first and the last;

40 And he shall come into the ^aworld to ^bredeem his people; and he shall ^ctake upon him the transgressions of those who believe on his name; and these are they that shall have eternal life, and salvation cometh to none else.

41 Therefore the wicked remain as though there had been ^ano redemption made, except it be the loosing of the bands of death; for behold, the day cometh that ^ball shall rise from the dead and stand before God, and be ^cjudged according to their works.

42 Now, there is a death which is called a temporal death; and the death of Christ shall loose the ^abands of this temporal death, that all shall be raised from this temporal death.

43 The spirit and the body shall be ^areunited again in its ^bperfect form; both limb and joint shall be restored to its proper frame, even as we now are at this time; and we shall be brought to stand before God, ^cknowing even as we know now, and have a bright ^drecollection of all our ^eguilt.

44 Now, this restoration shall come to all, both old and young, both bond and free, both male and female, both the wicked and the righteous; and even there shall not so much as a hair of their heads be lost; but every thing shall be ^arestored to its perfect frame, as it is now, or in the body, and shall be

31a Alma 10:10.
34a Hel. 5:10 (10–11).
35a Alma 14:5.
36a Alma 12:1.
37a 1 Cor. 6:9 (9–10).
  b 1 Ne. 15:33;
    Alma 40:26;
    3 Ne. 27:19.
    TG Uncleanness.
  c TG Kingdom of God, in
    Heaven.
39a Isa. 9:6; 64:8;
    Mosiah 15:4 (2–4);

Moro. 7:22; 8:18.
  b Col. 1:16;
    Mosiah 4:2.
40a TG World.
  b Luke 2:34;
    Rom. 11:26 (26–27).
  c Ex. 34:7;
    1 Jn. 2:2;
    Mosiah 14:5 (5, 8); 15:12;
    D&C 19:17 (16–18); 29:17.
41a Alma 12:18;
    D&C 88:33.
  b Rev. 20:13 (12–13);

Alma 28:12; 42:23.
  c TG Judgment, the Last.
42a Alma 12:16 (16, 24, 36).
43a 2 Ne. 9:13;
    Alma 40:23.
  b TG Perfection.
  c D&C 130:18.
  d 2 Ne. 9:14;
    Mosiah 3:25;
    Alma 5:18.
  e Matt. 12:36 (36–37).
    TG Guilt.
44a Rev. 20:12 (12–15).

brought and be arraigned before the bar of Christ the Son, and God the *b*Father, and the Holy Spirit, which is *c*one Eternal God, to be *d*judged according to their works, whether they be good or whether they be evil.

45 Now, behold, I have spoken unto you concerning the *a*death of the mortal body, and also concerning the *b*resurrection of the mortal body. I say unto you that this mortal body is *c*raised to an *d*immortal body, that is from death, even from the first death unto life, that they can *e*die no more; their spirits uniting with their bodies, never to be divided; thus the whole becoming *f*spiritual and immortal, that they can no more see corruption.

46 Now, when Amulek had finished these words the people began again to be astonished, and also Zeezrom began to tremble. And thus ended the words of Amulek, or this is all that I have written.

CHAPTER 12

Alma speaks to Zeezrom—The mysteries of God can be given only to the faithful—Men are judged by their thoughts, beliefs, words, and works—The wicked will suffer a spiritual death—This mortal life is a probationary state—The plan of redemption brings to pass the Resurrection and, through faith, a remission of sins—The repentant have a claim on mercy through the Only Begotten Son. About 82 B.C.

Now Alma, seeing that the words of Amulek had silenced Zeezrom, for he beheld that Amulek had caught him in his *a*lying and deceiving to destroy him, and seeing that he began to tremble under a *b*consciousness

of his guilt, he opened his mouth and began to speak unto him, and to establish the words of Amulek, and to explain things beyond, or to unfold the scriptures beyond that which Amulek had done.

2 Now the words that Alma spake unto Zeezrom were heard by the people round about; for the multitude was great, and he spake on this wise:

3 Now Zeezrom, seeing that thou hast been taken in thy lying and craftiness, for thou hast not lied unto men only but thou hast lied unto God; for behold, he knows all thy *a*thoughts, and thou seest that thy *b*thoughts are made known unto us by his Spirit;

4 And thou seest that we know that thy plan was a very *a*subtle plan, as to the subtlety of the devil, for to lie and to deceive this people that thou mightest set them against us, to *b*revile us and to cast us out—

5 Now this was a plan of thine *a*adversary, and he hath exercised his power in thee. Now I would that ye should remember that what I say unto thee I say unto all.

6 And behold I say unto you all that this was a *a*snare of the adversary, which he has laid to catch this people, that he might bring you into subjection unto him, that he might encircle you about with his *b*chains, that he might chain you down to everlasting destruction, according to the power of his captivity.

7 Now when Alma had spoken these words, Zeezrom began to tremble more exceedingly, for he was convinced more and more of the power of God; and he was also

---

44*b* TG Godhead.
 c 3 Ne. 11:27 (27–28, 36).
  TG God, Eternal
  Nature of.
 d 2 Pet. 2:9.
  TG Jesus Christ, Judge.
45*a* Alma 12:12.
 b Alma 40:23;
  D&C 88:16.

 c TG Death, Power over.
 d TG Immortality.
 e Rev. 21:4;
  Alma 12:18 (18, 20);
  D&C 63:49; 88:116.
 f 1 Cor. 15:44.
12 1*a* Alma 11:36 (20–38).
 b Alma 62:45;
  D&C 6:11; 18:44.

  TG Conscience.
3*a* Jacob 2:5;
  D&C 6:16.
 b Alma 10:17.
4*a* D&C 123:12.
 b TG Slander.
5*a* TG Devil.
6*a* Prov. 29:6 (3–8).
 b Alma 5:9 (7–10).

convinced that Alma and Amulek had a knowledge of him, for he was convinced that they [a]knew the thoughts and intents of his heart; for power was given unto them that they might know of these things according to the spirit of prophecy.

8 And Zeezrom began to inquire of them diligently, that he might know more concerning the kingdom of God. And he said unto Alma: What does this mean which Amulek hath spoken concerning the resurrection of the dead, that all shall rise from the dead, both the [a]just and the unjust, and are brought to stand before God to be [b]judged according to their works?

9 And now Alma began to expound these things unto him, saying: It is given unto many to [a]know the [b]mysteries of God; nevertheless they are laid under a strict command that they shall not impart [c]only according to the portion of his word which he doth grant unto the children of men, according to the heed and diligence which they give unto him.

10 And therefore, he that will [a]harden his heart, the same receiveth the [b]lesser portion of the word; and he that will [c]not harden his heart, to him is [d]given the greater portion of the word, until it is given unto him to know the mysteries of God until he know them in full.

11 And they that will harden their hearts, to them is given the lesser [a]portion of the word until they [b]know nothing concerning his mysteries;

and then they are taken captive by the devil, and led by his will down to destruction. Now this is what is meant by the [c]chains of [d]hell.

12 And Amulek hath spoken plainly concerning [a]death, and being raised from this mortality to a state of immortality, and being brought before the bar of God, to be [b]judged according to our works.

13 Then if our hearts have been hardened, yea, if we have hardened our hearts against the word, insomuch that it has not been found in us, then will our state be awful, for then we shall be condemned.

14 For our [a]words will condemn us, yea, all our works will condemn us; we shall not be found spotless; and our thoughts will also condemn us; and in this awful state we shall not dare to look up to our God; and we would fain be glad if we could command the rocks and the [b]mountains to fall upon us to [c]hide us from his presence.

15 But this cannot be; we must come forth and stand before him in his glory, and in his power, and in his might, majesty, and dominion, and acknowledge to our everlasting [a]shame that all his [b]judgments are just; that he is just in all his works, and that he is merciful unto the children of men, and that he has all power to save every man that believeth on his name and bringeth forth fruit meet for repentance.

16 And now behold, I say unto you then cometh a death, even a second [a]death, which is a spiritual death;

7a Alma 14:2.
8a Dan. 12:2.
  b TG Judgment, the Last.
9a Dan. 1:17.
  b Alma 26:22.
    TG Mysteries of
    Godliness.
  c John 16:12;
    Alma 29:8;
    3 Ne. 26:10 (6–11);
    Ether 4:7 (1–7).
10a 2 Ne. 28:27;
    3 Ne. 26:10 (9–10);
    Ether 4:8.
  b D&C 93:39.

  c TG Teachable.
  d Dan. 2:21; 2 Ne. 28:30;
    D&C 50:24; 71:5.
11a Matt. 25:29 (29–30).
  b TG Apostasy of
    Individuals.
  c Prov. 5:22;
    John 8:34 (31–36);
    2 Ne. 28:19 (19–22);
    Mosiah 23:12;
    Alma 26:14.
    TG Bondage, Spiritual.
  d Prov. 9:18; 1 Ne. 14:7;
    2 Ne. 2:29 (26–29).
    TG Hell.

12a Alma 11:45 (41–45).
  b TG Judgment, the Last.
14a Prov. 18:21; Matt. 12:36;
    James 3:6 (1–13);
    Mosiah 4:30 (29–30).
  b Hosea 10:8;
    2 Ne. 26:5.
  c Job 34:22; Amos 9:3;
    2 Ne. 12:10.
15a Mosiah 3:25.
    TG Shame.
  b 2 Pet. 2:9.
    TG Justice.
16a TG Death, Spiritual,
    Second.

then is a time that whosoever dieth in his sins, as to a temporal *b*death, shall also *c*die a spiritual death; yea, he shall die as to things pertaining unto righteousness.

17 Then is the time when their torments shall be as a *a*lake of fire and brimstone, whose flame ascendeth up forever and ever; and then is the time that they shall be chained down to an everlasting destruction, according to the power and captivity of Satan, he having subjected them according to his will.

18 Then, I say unto you, they shall be as though there had been *a*no redemption made; for they cannot be redeemed according to God's justice; and they cannot *b*die, seeing there is no more corruption.

19 Now it came to pass that when Alma had made an end of speaking these words, the people began to be more astonished;

20 But there was one Antionah, who was a chief ruler among them, came forth and said unto him: What is this that thou hast said, that man should rise from the dead and be changed from this mortal to an *a*immortal state, that the soul can never die?

21 What does the scripture mean, which saith that God placed *a*cherubim and a flaming sword on the east of the garden of *b*Eden, lest our first parents should enter and partake of the fruit of the tree of life, and live forever? And thus we see that there was no possible chance that they should live forever.

22 Now Alma said unto him: This is the thing which I was about to explain. Now we see that Adam did *a*fall by the partaking of the forbidden *b*fruit, according to the word of God; and thus we see, that by his fall, all mankind became a *c*lost and fallen people.

23 And now behold, I say unto you that if it had been possible for Adam to have *a*partaken of the fruit of the tree of life at that time, there would have been no death, and the word would have been void, making God a liar, for he said: *b*If thou eat thou shalt surely die.

24 And we see that *a*death comes upon mankind, yea, the death which has been spoken of by Amulek, which is the temporal death; nevertheless there was a space granted unto *b*man in which he might repent; therefore this life became a *c*probationary state; a time to *d*prepare to meet God; a time to prepare for that endless state which has been spoken of by us, which is after the resurrection of the dead.

25 Now, if it had not been for the plan of redemption, which was laid from the foundation of the world, there could have been no *a*resurrection of the dead; but there was a plan of *b*redemption laid, which shall bring to pass the resurrection of the dead, of which has been spoken.

26 And now behold, if it were possible that our first parents could have gone forth and partaken of the *a*tree of life they would have been forever miserable, having no preparatory state; and thus the *b*plan

---

16*b* Alma 11:42 (40–45).
  c 1 Ne. 15:33;
       Alma 40:26.
17*a* Rev. 19:20; 21:8;
       Mosiah 3:27;
       Alma 14:14.
18*a* Alma 11:41.
  b Rev. 21:4;
       Alma 11:45;
       D&C 63:49; 88:116.
20*a* TG Immortality.
21*a* Gen. 3:24;
       Alma 42:2;
       Moses 4:31.

       TG Cherubim.
  b TG Eden.
22*a* TG Fall of Man.
  b Gen. 3:6;
       2 Ne. 2:15 (15–19);
       Mosiah 3:26.
  c Mosiah 16:5 (4–5);
       Alma 9:30 (30–32).
23*a* Alma 42:5 (2–9).
  b Gen. 2:17.
24*a* TG Death.
  b 2 Ne. 2:21;
       Moses 5:8–12.
  c 1 Pet. 2:20 (20–21).

       TG Earth, Purpose of;
       Probation.
  d Alma 34:32 (32–35).
25*a* 2 Ne. 2:8;
       Alma 7:12; 42:23.
  b TG Redemption.
26*a* Gen. 2:9;
       1 Ne. 15:36 (22, 28, 36);
       2 Ne. 2:15;
       Alma 32:40.
  b Alma 34:9 (8–16);
       42:8 (6–28);
       Moses 6:62.

of redemption would have been frustrated, and the word of God would have been void, taking none effect.

27 But behold, it was not so; but it was ᵃappointed unto men that they must die; and after death, they must come to ᵇjudgment, even that same judgment of which we have spoken, which is the end.

28 And after God had appointed that these things should come unto man, behold, then he saw that it was expedient that man should know concerning the things whereof he had appointed unto them;

29 Therefore he sent ᵃangels to converse with them, who caused men to behold of his glory.

30 And they began from that time forth to call on his name; therefore God ᵃconversed with men, and made known unto them the ᵇplan of redemption, which had been prepared from the ᶜfoundation of the world; and this he made known unto them according to their faith and repentance and their ᵈholy works.

31 Wherefore, he gave ᵃcommandments unto men, they having first transgressed the ᵇfirst commandments as to things which were temporal, and becoming as gods, ᶜknowing good from evil, placing themselves in a state to ᵈact, or being placed in a state to act according to their wills and pleasures, whether to do evil or to do good—

32 Therefore God gave unto them commandments, after having made ᵃknown unto them the plan of redemption, that they should not do

evil, the penalty thereof being a second ᵇdeath, which was an everlasting ᶜdeath as to things pertaining unto righteousness; for on such the plan of redemption could have no power, for the works of ᵈjustice could not be destroyed, according to the supreme ᵉgoodness of God.

33 But God did call on men, in the name of his Son, (this being the ᵃplan of redemption which was laid) saying: If ye will ᵇrepent, and harden not your hearts, then will I have mercy upon you, through mine Only Begotten Son;

34 Therefore, whosoever repenteth, and hardeneth not his heart, he shall have claim on ᵃmercy through mine Only Begotten Son, unto a ᵇremission of his sins; and these shall enter into my ᶜrest.

35 And whosoever will harden his heart and will do ᵃiniquity, behold, I swear in my wrath that he shall not enter into my rest.

36 And now, my brethren, behold I say unto you, that if ye will harden your hearts ye shall not enter into the rest of the Lord; therefore your iniquity ᵃprovoketh him that he sendeth down his ᵇwrath upon you as in the ᶜfirst provocation, yea, according to his word in the last provocation as well as the first, to the everlasting ᵈdestruction of your souls; therefore, according to his word, unto the last death, as well as the first.

37 And now, my brethren, seeing we know these things, and they are true, let us repent, and harden not

27a Job 7:1;
     Heb. 9:27;
     D&C 42:48; 121:25.
   b TG Judgment, the Last.
29a Moro. 7:25 (25, 31);
     D&C 29:42.
30a Moses 1:1; 5:4 (4–5);
     6:51 (4, 51–68).
   b TG Salvation, Plan of.
   c Gen. 2:16 (16–17);
     Mosiah 18:13;
     Alma 13:3 (3, 5, 7–8);
     Abr. 3:26 (24–26).
   d Luke 8:15 (14–15).
31a TG Commandments

   of God.
  b Gen. 2:17 (16–17);
     2 Ne. 2:19 (18–19).
  c Gen. 3:22; Moses 4:11.
  d 2 Ne. 2:16.
     TG Agency.
32a Moses 5:9 (4–9).
  b TG Death, Spiritual,
     Second.
  c TG Damnation.
  d Mosiah 15:27;
     Alma 34:16 (15–16); 42:15.
  e TG Goodness.
33a TG Salvation, Plan of.
  b Moses 5:8.

34a 2 Cor. 4:1.
  b TG Remission of Sins.
  c D&C 84:24.
     TG Rest.
35a Moses 5:15.
36a 1 Kgs. 16:33.
     TG Provoking.
  b TG God, Indignation of.
  c Heb. 3:8;
     2 Ne. 9:7;
     Jacob 1:7 (7–8);
     Mosiah 16:4 (4–7);
     Alma 11:45;
     42:6 (6, 9, 14).
  d TG Damnation.

our hearts, that we ^aprovoke not the Lord our God to pull down his wrath upon us in these his second commandments which he has given unto us; but let us enter into the ^brest of God, which is prepared according to his word.

CHAPTER 13

Men are called as high priests because of their exceeding faith and good works— They are to teach the commandments— Through righteousness they are sanctified and enter into the rest of the Lord—Melchizedek was one of these—Angels are declaring glad tidings throughout the land—They will declare the actual coming of Christ. About 82 B.C.

AND again, my brethren, I would cite your minds forward to the time when the Lord God gave these commandments unto his children; and I would that ye should remember that the Lord God ^aordained priests, after his holy order, which was after the order of his Son, to teach these things unto the people.

2 And those priests were ordained after the ^aorder of his Son, in a ^bmanner that thereby the people might know in what manner to look forward to his Son for redemption.

3 And this is the manner after which they were ordained—being ^acalled and ^bprepared from the ^cfoundation of the world according to the ^dforeknowledge of God, on account of their exceeding faith and good works; in the first place being left to ^echoose good or evil; therefore they having chosen good, and

exercising exceedingly great ^ffaith, are ^gcalled with a holy calling, yea, with that holy calling which was prepared with, and according to, a preparatory redemption for such.

4 And thus they have been ^acalled to this holy calling on account of their faith, while others would reject the Spirit of God on account of the hardness of their hearts and ^bblindness of their minds, while, if it had not been for this they might have had as great ^cprivilege as their brethren.

5 Or in fine, in the first place they were on the ^asame standing with their brethren; thus this holy calling being prepared from the foundation of the world for such as would not harden their hearts, being in and through the atonement of the Only Begotten Son, who was prepared—

6 And thus being called by this holy calling, and ordained unto the high priesthood of the holy order of God, to teach his commandments unto the children of men, that they also might enter into his ^arest—

7 This high priesthood being after the order of his Son, which order was from the foundation of the world; or in other words, being ^awithout beginning of days or end of years, being prepared from ^beternity to all eternity, according to his ^cforeknowledge of all things—

8 Now they were ^aordained after this manner—being called with a holy calling, and ordained with a holy ordinance, and taking upon them the high priesthood of the holy order, which calling, and ordinance,

37*a* Num. 14:11 (11–12);
    1 Ne. 17:30 (23–31);
    Jacob 1:8;
    Hel. 7:18.
  b Alma 13:6 (6–29); 16:17;
    D&C 84:24.
13 1*a* Alma 8:23 (11, 23);
    D&C 84:17 (17–19);
    Moses 6:7;
    Abr. 2:9 (9, 11).
  2*a* D&C 107:3 (2–4).
  b Alma 13:16.
  3*a* D&C 127:2.
    TG Election;

    Foreordination.
  b D&C 138:56.
  c Alma 12:30 (25, 30);
    22:13.
    TG Man, Antemortal
    Existence of.
  d TG God, Foreknowledge of.
  e TG Agency.
  f TG Priesthood,
    Qualifying for.
  g TG Called of God.
  4*a* Ether 12:10.
  b TG Spiritual Blindness.

  c 1 Ne. 17:35 (32–35).
  5*a* Rom. 2:11;
    2 Ne. 26:28.
  6*a* Alma 12:37; 16:17.
    TG Rest.
  7*a* Heb. 7:3;
    Abr. 1:3 (2–4).
  b TG Eternity.
  c TG God, Foreknowledge of; God, Omniscience of.
  8*a* TG Priesthood,
    Melchizedek;
    Priesthood, Oath and
    Covenant.

and high priesthood, is without beginning or end—

9 Thus they become ^ahigh priests forever, after the order of the Son, the Only Begotten of the Father, who is without beginning of days or end of years, who is full of ^bgrace, equity, and truth. And thus it is. Amen.

10 Now, as I said concerning the holy order, or this ^ahigh priesthood, there were many who were ordained and became high priests of God; and it was on account of their exceeding ^bfaith and ^crepentance, and their righteousness before God, they choosing to repent and work righteousness rather than to perish;

11 Therefore they were called after this holy order, and were ^asanctified, and their ^bgarments were washed white through the blood of the Lamb.

12 Now they, after being ^asanctified by the ^bHoly Ghost, having their garments made white, being ^cpure and spotless before God, could not look upon ^dsin save it were with ^eabhorrence; and there were many, exceedingly great many, who were made pure and entered into the rest of the Lord their God.

13 And now, my brethren, I would that ye should humble yourselves before God, and bring forth ^afruit meet for repentance, that ye may also enter into that rest.

14 Yea, humble yourselves even as the people in the days of ^aMelchizedek, who was also a high priest after this same order which I have

spoken, who also took upon him the high priesthood forever.

15 And it was this same Melchizedek to whom Abraham paid ^atithes; yea, even our father Abraham paid tithes of one-tenth part of all he possessed.

16 Now these ^aordinances were given after this ^bmanner, that thereby the people might look forward on the Son of God, it being a ^ctype of his order, or it being his order, and this that they might look forward to him for a remission of their sins, that they might enter into the rest of the Lord.

17 Now this Melchizedek was a king over the land of Salem; and his people had waxed strong in iniquity and abomination; yea, they had all gone astray; they were full of all manner of wickedness;

18 But Melchizedek having exercised mighty faith, and received the office of the high priesthood according to the ^aholy order of God, did preach repentance unto his people. And behold, they did repent; and Melchizedek did establish peace in the land in his days; therefore he was called the prince of peace, for he was the king of Salem; and he did reign under his father.

19 Now, there were ^amany before him, and also there were many afterwards, but ^bnone were greater; therefore, of him they have more particularly made mention.

20 Now I need not rehearse the matter; what I have said may suffice. Behold, the ^ascriptures are

9a TG High Priest, Melchizedek Priesthood.
 b John 1:17 (14, 17); 2 Ne. 2:6; Moses 1:6. TG Grace.
10a D&C 84:18 (6–22); 107:53 (40–55).
 b TG Priesthood, Magnifying Callings within.
 c TG Spirituality.
11a Lev. 8:30; Moses 6:60 (59–60).
 b 1 Ne. 12:10; Alma 5:21 (21–27); 3 Ne. 27:19 (19–20).

12a Rom. 8:1 (1–9); D&C 11:12 (12–13). TG Sanctification.
 b TG Holy Ghost, Baptism of.
 c TG Purity.
 d Rom. 12:9; 2 Ne. 4:31; Mosiah 5:2; Alma 19:33.
 e Prov. 8:13; Alma 37:29.
13a Luke 3:8.
14a JST Gen. 14:25–40 (Bible Appendix); D&C 84:14. TG Priesthood, History of.

15a Gen. 14:20 (18–20); Mal. 3:10 (8–10). TG Tithing.
16a A of F 1:5. TG Ordinance.
 b Alma 13:2.
 c TG Jesus Christ, Types of, in Anticipation.
18a TG Priesthood.
19a TG Priesthood; D&C 84:14 (6–16); 107:53 (40–55).
 b D&C 107:2 (1–4).
20a Alma 14:1 (1, 8, 14). TG Scriptures, Value of.

before you; if ye will *b*wrest them it shall be to your own destruction.

21 And now it came to pass that when Alma had said these words unto them, he stretched forth his hand unto them and cried with a mighty voice, saying: *a*Now is the time to repent, for the day of salvation draweth nigh;

22 Yea, and the voice of the Lord, by the *a*mouth of angels, doth declare it unto all nations; yea, doth declare it, that they may have glad tidings of great joy; yea, and he doth sound these glad tidings among all his people, yea, even to them that are scattered abroad upon the face of the earth; wherefore they have come unto us.

23 And they are made known unto us in *a*plain terms, that we may understand, that we cannot err; and this because of our being *b*wanderers in a strange land; therefore, we are thus highly favored, for we have these glad tidings declared unto us in all parts of our vineyard.

24 For behold, *a*angels are declaring it unto many at this time in our land; and this is for the purpose of preparing the hearts of the children of men to receive his word at the time of his coming in his glory.

25 And now we only wait to hear the joyful news declared unto us by the mouth of angels, of his coming; for the time cometh, we *a*know not how soon. Would to God that it might be in my day; but let it be sooner or later, in it I will rejoice.

26 And it shall be made known unto *a*just and holy men, by the mouth of angels, at the time of his coming,

that the words of our fathers may be fulfilled, according to that which they have spoken concerning him, which was according to the spirit of prophecy which was in them.

27 And now, my brethren, I *a*wish from the inmost part of my heart, yea, with great *b*anxiety even unto pain, that ye would hearken unto my words, and cast off your sins, and not *c*procrastinate the day of your repentance;

28 But that ye would humble yourselves before the Lord, and call on his holy name, and *a*watch and pray continually, that ye may not be *b*tempted above that which ye can bear, and thus be *c*led by the Holy Spirit, becoming humble, *d*meek, submissive, patient, full of love and all long-suffering;

29 *a*Having faith on the Lord; having a hope that ye shall receive eternal life; having the *b*love of God always in your hearts, that ye may be lifted up at the last day and enter into his *c*rest.

30 And may the Lord grant unto you repentance, that ye may not bring down his wrath upon you, that ye may not be *a*bound down by the chains of *b*hell, that ye may not suffer the second *c*death.

31 And Alma spake many more words unto the people, which are not written in *a*this book.

CHAPTER 14

Alma and Amulek are imprisoned and smitten—The believers and their holy scriptures are burned by fire— These martyrs are received by the Lord

---

20*b* 2 Pet. 3:16;
   Alma 41:1.
21*a* TG Procrastination.
22*a* Alma 10:20 (7–10, 20).
23*a* 2 Ne. 25:7 (7–8);
   31:3; 32:7;
   Jacob 4:13;
   Ether 12:39.
   b Jacob 7:26.
24*a* Alma 10:10; 39:19.
25*a* 1 Ne. 10:4;
   3 Ne. 1:1.
26*a* Ex. 22:31;

   Amos 3:7;
   W of M 1:17;
   D&C 49:8; 107:29.
27*a* Mosiah 28:3 (3–4).
   b Mosiah 25:11.
   c TG Apathy;
   Procrastination.
28*a* TG Prayer; Watch.
   b Rom. 7:23 (23–24);
   1 Cor. 10:13;
   D&C 64:20.
   c Alma 22:1;
   Morm. 5:17.

   d TG Forbear;
   Love; Meek.
29*a* Alma 7:24.
   b Ps. 18:1;
   D&C 20:31; 76:116.
   TG God, Love of.
   c D&C 84:24.
30*a* TG Bondage, Spiritual.
   b TG Damnation; Hell.
   c TG Death, Spiritual,
   Second.
31*a* W of M 1:5;
   3 Ne. 5:9 (8–12).

in glory—The prison walls are rent and fall—Alma and Amulek are delivered, and their persecutors are slain. About 82–81 B.C.

AND it came to pass after he had made an end of speaking unto the people many of them did believe on his words, and began to repent, and to search the ^ascriptures.

2 But the more part of them were desirous that they might destroy Alma and Amulek; for they were angry with Alma, because of the ^aplainness of his words unto Zeezrom; and they also said that Amulek had ^blied unto them, and had reviled against their law and also against their lawyers and judges.

3 And they were also angry with Alma and Amulek; and because they had ^atestified so plainly against their wickedness, they sought to ^bput them away privily.

4 But it came to pass that they did not; but they took them and bound them with strong cords, and took them before the chief judge of the land.

5 And the people went forth and witnessed against them—testifying that they had reviled against the law, and their lawyers and judges of the land, and also of all the people that were in the land; and also testified that there was but one God, and that he should send his Son among the people, but he should ^anot save them; and many such things did the people testify against Alma and Amulek. Now this was done before the chief judge of the land.

6 And it came to pass that Zeezrom was astonished at the words which had been spoken; and he also knew concerning the ^ablindness of the minds, which he had caused among the people by his ^blying

words; and his soul began to be ^charrowed up under a ^dconsciousness of his own guilt; yea, he began to be encircled about by the pains of hell.

7 And it came to pass that he began to cry unto the people, saying: Behold, I am ^aguilty, and these men are spotless before God. And he began to plead for them from that time forth; but they reviled him, saying: Art thou also possessed with the devil? And they spit upon him, and ^bcast him out from among them, and also all those who believed in the words which had been spoken by Alma and Amulek; and they cast them out, and sent men to cast stones at them.

8 And they brought their wives and children together, and whosoever believed or had been taught to believe in the word of God they caused that they should be ^acast into the fire; and they also brought forth their records which contained the holy scriptures, and cast them into the fire also, that they might be ^bburned and destroyed by fire.

9 And it came to pass that they took Alma and Amulek, and carried them forth to the place of ^amartyrdom, that they might witness the destruction of those who were consumed by fire.

10 And when Amulek saw the pains of the women and children who were consuming in the fire, he also was pained; and he said unto Alma: How can we witness this awful scene? Therefore let us stretch forth our hands, and exercise the ^apower of God which is in us, and save them from the flames.

11 But Alma said unto him: The Spirit constraineth me that I must not stretch forth mine hand; for behold the Lord receiveth them up

---

14 1*a* 2 Kgs. 22:11 (8–13);
　　　Acts 17:2 (2–3, 11);
　　　Alma 13:20.
　　2*a* Alma 12:7 (3–7).
　　　b Alma 10:28 (24–32).
　　3*a* Prov. 26:26;
　　　Alma 37:21.

　　　b Acts 23:12 (12–15).
　　5*a* Alma 11:35 (33–37).
　　6*a* TG Spiritual Blindness.
　　　b Alma 10:31 (25–31).
　　　c Alma 15:5.
　　　d TG Conscience.
　　7*a* Alma 10:31;

　　　11:21 (21–36); 15:3.
　　　b Alma 15:1.
　　8*a* Alma 15:2.
　　　b Jer. 36:23 (21–28).
　　9*a* TG Martyrdom.
　　10*a* Alma 8:31 (30–31).

unto himself, in ªglory; and he doth suffer that they may do this thing, or that the people may do this thing unto them, according to the hardness of their hearts, that the ᵇjudgments which he shall exercise upon them in his wrath may be just; and the ᶜblood of the ᵈinnocent shall stand as a witness against them, yea, and cry mightily against them at the last day.

12 Now Amulek said unto Alma: Behold, perhaps they will burn us also.

13 And Alma said: Be it according to the will of the Lord. But, behold, our work is not finished; therefore they burn us not.

14 Now it came to pass that when the bodies of those who had been cast into the fire were consumed, and also the records which were cast in with them, the chief judge of the land came and stood before Alma and Amulek, as they were bound; and he smote them with his hand upon their ªcheeks, and said unto them: After what ye have seen, will ye preach again unto this people, that they shall be cast into a ᵇlake of fire and brimstone?

15 Behold, ye see that ye had not power to save those who had been cast into the fire; neither has God saved them because they were of thy faith. And the judge smote them again upon their cheeks, and asked: What say ye for yourselves?

16 Now this judge was after the order and faith of ªNehor, who slew Gideon.

17 And it came to pass that Alma and Amulek answered him ªnothing; and he smote them again, and delivered them to the officers to be ᵇcast into prison.

18 And when they had been cast into prison three days, there came many ªlawyers, and judges, and priests, and teachers, who were of the profession of Nehor; and they came in unto the prison to see them, and they questioned them about many words; but they answered them nothing.

19 And it came to pass that the judge stood before them, and said: Why do ye not answer the words of this people? Know ye not that I have ªpower to deliver you up unto the flames? And he ᵇcommanded them to speak; but they answered nothing.

20 And it came to pass that they departed and went their ways, but came again on the morrow; and the judge also smote them again on their cheeks. And many came forth also, and smote them, saying: Will ye stand again and judge this people, and condemn our law? If ye have such great power why do ye not ªdeliver yourselves?

21 And many such things did they say unto them, gnashing their teeth upon them, and spitting upon them, and saying: How shall we look when we are damned?

22 And many such things, yea, all manner of such things did they say unto them; and thus they did ªmock them for many days. And they did withhold food from them that they might hunger, and water that they might thirst; and they also did take from them their clothes that they were naked; and thus they were ᵇbound with strong cords, and confined in ᶜprison.

23 And it came to pass after they had thus suffered for many days, (and it was on the twelfth day, in the tenth month, in the tenth year of the reign of the judges over the

11a ᴛɢ Exaltation.
  b Ex. 23:7; Ps. 37:9 (8–13); Alma 60:13; D&C 103:3. ᴛɢ Justice.
  c ᴛɢ Cruelty; Martyrdom.
  d Lam. 4:13; Mosiah 17:10.
14a 1 Kgs. 22:24 (14–27).

  b Alma 12:17. ᴛɢ Damnation.
16a Alma 1:12 (7–15); 2:20; 21:4.
17a Matt. 27:12 (12–14).
  b Alma 9:33.
18a Alma 10:14; 11:21 (20–37).

19a John 19:10 (9–10).
  b Mosiah 7:8.
20a Matt. 27:40 (39–43).
22a ᴛɢ Mocking.
  b Acts 16:23 (23–40); D&C 122:6.
  c Gen. 39:20; Mosiah 7:7.

people of Nephi) that the chief judge over the land of ᵃAmmonihah and many of their teachers and their lawyers went in unto the prison where Alma and Amulek were bound with cords.

24 And the chief judge stood before them, and smote them again, and said unto them: If ye have the ᵃpower of God deliver yourselves from these bands, and then we will believe that the Lord will destroy this people according to your words.

25 And it came to pass that they all went forth and smote them, saying the same words, even until the last; and when the last had spoken unto them the ᵃpower of God was upon Alma and Amulek, and they rose and stood upon their feet.

26 And Alma cried, saying: How long shall we suffer these great ᵃafflictions, O Lord? O Lord, ᵇgive us strength according to our faith which is in Christ, even unto ᶜdeliverance. And they broke the cords with which they were bound; and when the people saw this, they began to flee, for the fear of destruction had come upon them.

27 And it came to pass that so great was their fear that they fell to the earth, and did not obtain the outer door of the ᵃprison; and the earth shook mightily, and the walls of the prison were rent in twain, so that they fell to the earth; and the chief judge, and the lawyers, and priests, and teachers, who smote upon Alma and Amulek, were slain by the fall thereof.

28 And Alma and Amulek came forth out of the prison, and they were not hurt; for the Lord had granted unto them ᵃpower, according to their faith which was in Christ.

And they straightway came forth out of the prison; and they were ᵇloosed from their ᶜbands; and the prison had fallen to the earth, and every soul within the walls thereof, save it were Alma and Amulek, was slain; and they straightway came forth into the city.

29 Now the people having heard a great noise came running together by multitudes to know the cause of it; and when they saw Alma and Amulek coming forth out of the prison, and the walls thereof had fallen to the earth, they were struck with great fear, and fled from the presence of Alma and Amulek even as a goat fleeth with her young from two lions; and thus they did flee from the presence of Alma and Amulek.

CHAPTER 15

Alma and Amulek go to Sidom and establish a church—Alma heals Zeezrom, who joins the Church—Many are baptized, and the Church prospers—Alma and Amulek go to Zarahemla. About 81 B.C.

AND it came to pass that Alma and Amulek were commanded to depart out of that city; and they departed, and came out even into the land of Sidom; and behold, there they found all the people who had departed out of the land of ᵃAmmonihah, who had been ᵇcast out and stoned, because they believed in the words of Alma.

2 And they related unto them all that had happened unto their ᵃwives and children, and also concerning themselves, and of their ᵇpower of deliverance.

3 And also Zeezrom lay sick at Sidom, with a burning fever, which was caused by the great tribulations

---

23a Alma 8:6; 15:1 (1, 15–16).
24a TG Sign Seekers.
25a Alma 8:31.
26a James 5:10 (10–11);
    Mosiah 17:13 (10–20);
    JS—H 1:22.
   b Ps. 69:14 (1–2, 14);
    D&C 121:3.

c TG Deliver.
27a Acts 12:4 (4–6); 16:26;
    Hel. 5:21 (21–50);
    3 Ne. 28:19 (19–20);
    4 Ne. 1:30;
    Ether 12:13.
28a Alma 15:2.
   b 1 Ne. 7:17 (17–18);

    Jacob 4:6;
    3 Ne. 28:20 (19–22).
   c Alma 36:27.
15 1a Alma 14:23;
    16:2 (2–3, 9, 11).
   b Alma 14:7.
2a Alma 14:8 (8–14).
   b Alma 14:28 (26–29).

of his mind on account of his *wickedness, for he supposed that Alma and Amulek were no more; and he supposed that they had been slain because of his iniquity. And this great sin, and his many other sins, did harrow up his mind until it did become exceedingly sore, having no deliverance; therefore he began to be scorched with a burning heat.

4 Now, when he heard that Alma and Amulek were in the land of Sidom, his heart began to take courage; and he sent a message immediately unto them, desiring them to come unto him.

5 And it came to pass that they went immediately, obeying the message which he had sent unto them; and they went in unto the house unto Zeezrom; and they found him upon his bed, sick, being very low with a burning fever; and his mind also was *exceedingly sore because of his iniquities; and when he saw them he stretched forth his hand, and besought them that they would heal him.

6 And it came to pass that Alma said unto him, taking him by the hand: *Believest thou in the power of Christ unto salvation?

7 And he answered and said: Yea, I believe all the words that thou hast taught.

8 And Alma said: If thou believest in the redemption of Christ thou canst be *healed.

9 And he said: Yea, I believe according to thy words.

10 And then Alma cried unto the Lord, saying: O Lord our God, have *mercy on this man, and *heal him according to his faith which is in Christ.

11 And when Alma had said these words, *Zeezrom leaped upon his feet, and began to walk; and this was done to the great astonishment of all the people; and the knowledge of this went forth throughout all the land of Sidom.

12 And Alma baptized Zeezrom unto the Lord; and he began from that time forth to preach unto the people.

13 And Alma established a church in the land of Sidom, and consecrated *priests and *teachers in the land, to baptize unto the Lord whosoever were desirous to be baptized.

14 And it came to pass that they were many; for they did flock in from all the region round about Sidom, and were baptized.

15 But as to the people that were in the land of Ammonihah, they yet remained a hard-hearted and a stiffnecked people; and they repented not of their sins, *ascribing all the power of Alma and Amulek to the devil; for they were of the profession of *Nehor, and did not believe in the repentance of their sins.

16 And it came to pass that Alma and Amulek, Amulek having *forsaken all his gold, and silver, and his precious things, which were in the land of Ammonihah, for the word of God, he being *rejected by those who were once his friends and also by his father and his kindred;

17 Therefore, after Alma having established the church at Sidom, seeing a great *check, yea, seeing that the people were checked as to the pride of their hearts, and began to *humble themselves before God, and began to assemble themselves together at their *sanctuaries to *worship God before the *altar, *watching and praying continually, that they might be delivered from Satan, and from *death, and from destruction—

3 *a* Alma 14:7 (6–7).
5 *a* Alma 14:6.
6 *a* Mark 9:23.
8 *a* TG Administrations to the Sick; Heal.
10 *a* TG Mercy.
   b Mark 2:11 (1–12).
11 *a* Acts 3:8 (1–11).

13 *a* Alma 4:20 (7, 16, 18, 20); 16:18.
   b TG Teacher.
15 *a* Matt. 12:24 (24–27).
   b Alma 1:15 (2–15).
16 *a* Luke 14:33; Alma 10:4.
   b TG Prophets, Rejection of.

17 *a* Alma 16:21.
   b Ezra 10:1 (1–5).
   c Ps. 150:1; Alma 16:13.
   d TG Worship.
   e Ex. 27:1 (1–8).
   f TG Watch.
   g TG Death, Spiritual, First.

18 Now as I said, Alma having seen all these things, therefore he took Amulek and came over to the land of Zarahemla, and took him to his ᵃown house, and did administer unto him in his tribulations, and ᵇstrengthened him in the Lord.

19 And thus ended the tenth year of the reign of the judges over the people of Nephi.

CHAPTER 16

The Lamanites destroy the people of Ammonihah—Zoram leads the Nephites to victory over the Lamanites—Alma and Amulek and many others preach the word—They teach that after His Resurrection Christ will appear to the Nephites. About 81–77 B.C.

AND it came to pass in the eleventh year of the reign of the judges over the people of Nephi, on the fifth day of the second month, there having been much peace in the land of Zarahemla, there having been no wars nor contentions for a certain number of years, even until the fifth day of the second month in the eleventh year, there was a cry of war heard throughout the land.

2 For behold, the armies of the Lamanites had come in upon the wilderness side, into the borders of the land, even into the city of ᵃAmmonihah, and began to slay the people and destroy the city.

3 And now it came to pass, before the Nephites could raise a sufficient army to drive them out of the land, they had ᵃdestroyed the people who were in the city of Ammonihah, and also some around the borders of Noah, and taken others captive into the wilderness.

4 Now it came to pass that the Nephites were desirous to obtain those who had been carried away captive into the wilderness.

5 Therefore, he that had been appointed chief captain over the armies of the Nephites, (and his name was Zoram, and he had two sons, Lehi and Aha)—now Zoram and his two sons, knowing that Alma was high priest over the church, and having heard that he had the spirit of prophecy, therefore they went unto him and desired of him to know whither the Lord would that they should go into the wilderness in search of their brethren, who had been taken captive by the Lamanites.

6 And it came to pass that Alma ᵃinquired of the Lord concerning the matter. And Alma returned and said unto them: Behold, the Lamanites will cross the river Sidon in the south wilderness, away up beyond the borders of the land of ᵇManti. And behold there shall ye meet them, on the east of the river Sidon, and there the Lord will deliver unto thee thy brethren who have been taken captive by the Lamanites.

7 And it came to pass that Zoram and his sons crossed over the river Sidon, with their armies, and marched away beyond the borders of Manti into the south wilderness, which was on the east side of the river Sidon.

8 And they came upon the armies of the Lamanites, and the Lamanites were scattered and driven into the wilderness; and they took their brethren who had been taken captive by the Lamanites, and there was not one soul of them had been lost that were taken captive. And they were brought by their brethren to possess their own lands.

9 And thus ended the eleventh year of the judges, the Lamanites having been driven out of the land, and the people of Ammonihah were ᵃdestroyed; yea, ᵇevery living soul

---

18a Alma 27:20.
  b Zech. 10:12 (11–12).
16 2a Alma 15:1 (1, 15–16);
    49:3 (1–15).
  3a Alma 9:18.

6a 2 Kgs. 6:8–12;
    Alma 43:23 (23–24);
    48:16;
    3 Ne. 3:20 (18–21).
  b Alma 17:1; 22:27; 56:14.

9a Alma 8:16;
    9:24 (18–24);
    Morm. 6:15 (15–22).
  b Alma 14:11.

of the Ammonihahites was ᶜdestroyed, and also their ᵈgreat city, which they said God could not destroy, because of its greatness.

10 But behold, in ᵃone day it was left desolate; and the ᵇcarcasses were mangled by dogs and wild beasts of the wilderness.

11 Nevertheless, after many days their ᵃdead bodies were heaped up upon the face of the earth, and they were covered with a shallow covering. And now so great was the scent thereof that the people did not go in to possess the land of Ammonihah for many years. And it was called Desolation of ᵇNehors; for they were of the profession of Nehor, who were slain; and their lands remained desolate.

12 And the Lamanites did not come again to war against the Nephites until the fourteenth year of the reign of the judges over the people of Nephi. And thus for three years did the people of Nephi have continual peace in all the land.

13 And Alma and Amulek went forth preaching repentance to the people in their ᵃtemples, and in their ᵇsanctuaries, and also in their ᶜsynagogues, which were built after the manner of the Jews.

14 And as many as would hear their words, unto them they did impart the word of God, without any ᵃrespect of persons, continually.

15 And thus did Alma and Amulek go forth, and also many more who had been chosen for the work, to preach the word throughout all the land. And the establishment of the church became general throughout the land, in all the region round about, among all the people of the Nephites.

16 And there was ᵃno inequality among them; the Lord did pour out his Spirit on all the face of the land to prepare the minds of the children of men, or to prepare their ᵇhearts to receive the word which should be taught among them at the time of his coming—

17 That they might not be hardened against the word, that they might not be unbelieving, and go on to destruction, but that they might receive the word with joy, and as a ᵃbranch be grafted into the true vine, that they might enter into the ᵇrest of the Lord their God.

18 Now those ᵃpriests who did go forth among the people did preach against all ᵇlyings, and ᶜdeceivings, and ᵈenvyings, and ᵉstrifes, and malice, and revilings, and stealing, robbing, plundering, murdering, committing adultery, and all manner of lasciviousness, crying that these things ought not so to be—

19 Holding forth things which must shortly come; yea, holding forth the ᵃcoming of the Son of God, his sufferings and death, and also the resurrection of the dead.

20 And many of the people did inquire concerning the place where the Son of God should come; and they were taught that he would ᵃappear unto them ᵇafter his resurrection; and this the people did hear with great joy and gladness.

21 And now after the church had been established throughout all the land—having got the ᵃvictory over

9c Alma 25:2.
  d Alma 49:3.
10a Alma 9:4.
  b Jer. 19:7.
11a Alma 28:11.
  b Alma 1:15; 2:1 (1, 20);
    24:28 (28–30).
13a 2 Ne. 5:16;
    Hel. 3:14 (9, 14).
  b Alma 15:17; 21:6.
  c Alma 21:20 (4–6, 20).
14a Deut. 10:17;

Alma 1:30.
16a Mosiah 18:27 (19–29);
    4 Ne. 1:3.
  b Acts 16:14.
    TG Teachable.
17a Jacob 5:24.
    TG Vineyard of the Lord.
  b Alma 12:37; 13:6 (6–29).
18a Alma 15:13;
    30:20 (20–23, 31).
  b 3 Ne. 30:2.
  c TG Deceit.

  d TG Envy.
  e Alma 4:9 (8–9).
    TG Strife.
19a TG Jesus Christ,
    Prophecies about.
20a 2 Ne. 26:9;
    3 Ne. 11:8 (7–14).
  b 1 Ne. 12:6 (4–8);
    Alma 7:8.
21a Alma 15:17.

the devil, and the word of God being preached in its purity in all the land, and the Lord pouring out his blessings upon the people—thus ended the fourteenth year of the reign of the judges over the people of Nephi.

An account of the sons of Mosiah, who rejected their rights to the kingdom for the word of God, and went up to the land of Nephi to preach to the Lamanites; their sufferings and deliverance—according to the record of Alma.

Comprising chapters 17 through 27.

CHAPTER 17

The sons of Mosiah have the spirit of prophecy and of revelation—They go their several ways to declare the word to the Lamanites—Ammon goes to the land of Ishmael and becomes the servant of King Lamoni—Ammon saves the king's flocks and slays his enemies at the water of Sebus. Verses 1–3, about 77 B.C.; verse 4, about 91–77 B.C.; and verses 5–39, about 91 B.C.

AND now it came to pass that as Alma was journeying from the land of Gideon southward, away to the land of *a*Manti, behold, to his astonishment, he *b*met with the *c*sons of Mosiah journeying towards the land of Zarahemla.

2 Now these sons of Mosiah were with Alma at the time the angel *a*first appeared unto him; therefore Alma did rejoice exceedingly to see his brethren; and what added more to his joy, they were still his brethren in the Lord; yea, and they had waxed strong in the knowledge of the truth; for they were men of a sound understanding and they had *b*searched the scriptures diligently, that they might know the word of God.

3 But this is not all; they had given themselves to much prayer, and *a*fasting; therefore they had the spirit of prophecy, and the spirit of revelation, and when they taught, they taught with *b*power and authority of God.

4 And they had been teaching the word of God for the space of fourteen years among the Lamanites, having had much *a*success in bringing many to the *b*knowledge of the truth; yea, by the power of their words many were brought before the altar of God, to call on his name and *c*confess their sins before him.

5 Now these are the circumstances which attended them in their journeyings, for they had many afflictions; they did suffer much, both in body and in mind, such as hunger, thirst and fatigue, and also much *a*labor in the spirit.

6 Now these were their journeyings: Having *a*taken leave of their father, Mosiah, in the *b*first year of the judges; having *c*refused the kingdom which their father was desirous to confer upon them, and also this was the minds of the people;

7 Nevertheless they departed out of the land of Zarahemla, and took their swords, and their spears, and their bows, and their arrows, and their slings; and this they did that they might *a*provide food for themselves while in the wilderness.

8 And thus they departed into the wilderness with their numbers which they had *a*selected, to go up to the land of Nephi, to preach the word of God unto the Lamanites.

9 And it came to pass that they

---

17 1a Alma 16:6.
   b Alma 27:16.
   c Mosiah 27:34.
  2a Mosiah 27:11 (11–17).
   b Jacob 7:23;
     D&C 84:85.
     TG Scriptures, Study of.
  3a TG Fast, Fasting.

   b W of M 1:17.
     TG Authority;
     Teaching with the
     Spirit.
  4a Alma 29:14.
   b TG Missionary Work.
   c Num. 5:7 (6–10);
     Mosiah 26:29 (29, 35);

     3 Ne. 1:25.
  5a Alma 8:10.
  6a Mosiah 28:9 (1, 5–9);
     Alma 26:1.
   b Mosiah 29:44 (41–44).
   c Mosiah 29:3.
  7a 1 Ne. 16:15 (15–32).
  8a Mosiah 28:1.

journeyed many days in the wilderness, and they fasted much and ^aprayed much that the Lord would grant unto them a portion of his Spirit to go with them, and abide with them, that they might be an ^binstrument in the hands of God to bring, if it were possible, their brethren, the Lamanites, to the knowledge of the truth, to the knowledge of the baseness of the ^ctraditions of their fathers, which were not correct.

10 And it came to pass that the Lord did ^avisit them with his ^bSpirit, and said unto them: Be ^ccomforted. And they were comforted.

11 And the Lord said unto them also: Go forth among the Lamanites, thy brethren, and establish my word; yet ye shall be ^apatient in long-suffering and afflictions, that ye may show forth good ^bexamples unto them in me, and I will make an instrument of thee in my hands unto the salvation of many souls.

12 And it came to pass that the hearts of the sons of Mosiah, and also those who were with them, took courage to go forth unto the Lamanites to declare unto them the word of God.

13 And it came to pass when they had arrived in the borders of the land of the Lamanites, that they ^aseparated themselves and departed one from another, trusting in the Lord that they should meet again at the close of their ^bharvest; for they supposed that great was the work which they had undertaken.

14 And assuredly it was great, for they had undertaken to preach the word of God to a ^awild and a hardened and a ferocious people; a people who delighted in murdering the Nephites, and robbing and plundering them; and their hearts were set upon riches, or upon gold

and silver, and precious stones; yet they sought to obtain these things by murdering and plundering, that they might not labor for them with their own hands.

15 Thus they were a very indolent people, many of whom did worship idols, and the ^acurse of God had fallen upon them because of the ^btraditions of their fathers; notwithstanding the promises of the Lord were extended unto them on the conditions of repentance.

16 Therefore, this was the ^acause for which the sons of Mosiah had undertaken the work, that perhaps they might bring them unto repentance; that perhaps they might bring them to know of the plan of redemption.

17 Therefore they separated themselves one from another, and went forth among them, every man alone, according to the word and power of God which was given unto him.

18 Now Ammon being the chief among them, or rather he did administer unto them, and he departed from them, after having ^ablessed them according to their several stations, having imparted the word of God unto them, or administered unto them before his departure; and thus they took their several journeys throughout the land.

19 And Ammon went to the land of ^aIshmael, the land being called after the sons of ^bIshmael, who also became Lamanites.

20 And as Ammon entered the land of Ishmael, the Lamanites took him and ^abound him, as was their custom to bind all the Nephites who fell into their hands, and carry them before the king; and thus it was left to the pleasure of the king to slay them, or to retain them in captivity,

---

9a Alma 25:17.
   TG Guidance, Divine.
  b Mosiah 23:10;
   Alma 26:3.
  c Alma 3:11.
10a 1 Ne. 2:16;
   D&C 5:16.
  b TG God, Spirit of.

  c Alma 26:27.
11a Alma 20:29; 26:27.
   TG Forbear; Patience.
  b TG Example.
13a Alma 21:1.
  b Matt. 9:37.
14a Mosiah 10:12.
15a Alma 3:19 (6–19);

  3 Ne. 2:15 (15–16).
  b Alma 9:16 (16–24); 18:5.
16a Mosiah 28:2 (1–3).
18a TG Blessing.
19a Alma 21:18 (18, 20);
   22:1 (1, 4); 25:13.
  b 1 Ne. 7:6 (4–6).
20a Mosiah 7:7 (7–10).

or to cast them into prison, or to cast them out of his land, according to his will and pleasure.

21 And thus Ammon was carried before the king who was over the land of Ishmael; and his name was Lamoni; and he was a descendant of Ishmael.

22 And the king inquired of Ammon if it were his desire to dwell in the land among the Lamanites, or among his people.

23 And Ammon said unto him: Yea, I desire to ^adwell among this people for a time; yea, and perhaps until the day I die.

24 And it came to pass that king Lamoni was much pleased with Ammon, and caused that his bands should be loosed; and he would that Ammon should take one of his daughters to wife.

25 But Ammon said unto him: Nay, but I will be thy servant. Therefore Ammon became a ^aservant to king Lamoni. And it came to pass that he was set among other servants to watch the flocks of Lamoni, according to the custom of the Lamanites.

26 And after he had been in the service of the king three days, as he was with the Lamanitish servants going forth with their flocks to the place of ^awater, which was called the water of Sebus, and all the Lamanites drive their flocks hither, that they may have water—

27 Therefore, as Ammon and the servants of the king were driving forth their flocks to this place of water, behold, a certain number of the Lamanites, who had been with their flocks to water, stood and ^ascattered the flocks of Ammon and the servants of the king, and they scattered them insomuch that they fled many ways.

28 Now the servants of the king began to murmur, saying: Now the king will slay us, as he has our brethren because their flocks were scattered by the wickedness of these men. And they began to weep exceedingly, saying: Behold, our flocks are scattered already.

29 Now they wept because of the fear of being slain. Now when Ammon saw this his heart was swollen within him with joy; for, said he, I will show forth my power unto these my fellow-servants, or the power which is in me, in restoring these flocks unto the king, that I may win the hearts of these my fellow-servants, that I may lead them to ^abelieve in my words.

30 And now, these were the thoughts of Ammon, when he saw the afflictions of those whom he termed to be his brethren.

31 And it came to pass that he flattered them by his words, saying: My brethren, be of good cheer and let us go in search of the flocks, and we will gather them together and bring them back unto the place of water; and thus we will preserve the flocks unto the king and he will not slay us.

32 And it came to pass that they went in search of the flocks, and they did follow Ammon, and they rushed forth with much swiftness and did head the flocks of the king, and did gather them together again to the place of water.

33 And those men again stood to scatter their flocks; but Ammon said unto his brethren: Encircle the flocks round about that they flee not; and I go and contend with these men who do scatter our flocks.

34 Therefore, they did as Ammon commanded them, and he went forth and stood to contend with those who stood by the waters of Sebus; and they were in number not a few.

35 Therefore they did not fear Ammon, for they supposed that one of their men could slay him according to their pleasure, for they knew not that the Lord had

---

23a Alma 19:19.
25a Alma 21:19.
26a Ex. 2:17 (15–20).
27a Alma 18:3 (3–7);
    19:21 (20–21).
29a 2 Kgs. 5:8.
35a Mosiah 28:7;
    Alma 19:23 (22–23).

promised Mosiah that he would ^adeliver his sons out of their hands; neither did they know anything concerning the Lord; therefore they delighted in the destruction of their brethren; and for this cause they stood to scatter the flocks of the king.

36 But ^aAmmon stood forth and began to cast stones at them with his sling; yea, with mighty power he did sling stones amongst them; and thus he slew a ^bcertain number of them insomuch that they began to be astonished at his power; nevertheless they were angry because of the slain of their brethren, and they were determined that he should fall; therefore, seeing that they ^ccould not hit him with their stones, they came forth with clubs to slay him.

37 But behold, every man that lifted his club to smite Ammon, he smote off their arms with his sword; for he did withstand their blows by smiting their arms with the edge of his sword, insomuch that they began to be astonished, and began to flee before him; yea, and they were not few in number; and he caused them to flee by the strength of his arm.

38 Now six of them had fallen by the sling, but he ^aslew none save it were their leader with his sword; and he smote off as many of their arms as were lifted against him, and they were not a few.

39 And when he had driven them afar off, he returned and they watered their flocks and returned them to the pasture of the king, and then went in unto the king, bearing the arms which had been smitten off by the sword of Ammon, of those who sought to slay him; and they were carried in unto the king for a testimony of the things which they had done.

CHAPTER 18

King Lamoni supposes that Ammon is the Great Spirit—Ammon teaches the king about the Creation, God's dealings with men, and the redemption that comes through Christ—Lamoni believes and falls to the earth as if dead. About 90 B.C.

AND it came to pass that king Lamoni caused that his ^aservants should stand forth and testify to all the things which they had seen concerning the matter.

2 And when they had all testified to the things which they had seen, and he had learned of the faithfulness of Ammon in preserving his flocks, and also of his ^agreat power in contending against those who sought to slay him, he was astonished exceedingly, and said: Surely, this is more than a man. Behold, is not this the Great Spirit who doth send such great punishments upon this people, because of their murders?

3 And they answered the king, and said: Whether he be the Great Spirit or a man, we know not; but this much we do know, that he ^acannot be slain by the enemies of the king; neither can they ^bscatter the king's flocks when he is with us, because of his expertness and ^cgreat strength; therefore, we know that he is a friend to the king. And now, O king, we do not believe that a man has such great power, for we know he cannot be slain.

4 And now, when the king heard these words, he said unto them: Now I know that it is the Great Spirit; and he has come down at this time to preserve your lives, that I might not ^aslay you as I did your brethren. Now this is the Great Spirit of whom our fathers have spoken.

5 Now this was the ^atradition of Lamoni, which he had received

---

36a Ether 12:15.
 b Alma 18:16 (16, 20).
 c Alma 18:3.
38a Alma 19:22.

18 1a Alma 19:15.
 2a Alma 22:9 (9–11).
 3a Alma 17:36 (34–38).
 b Alma 17:27;

 19:21 (20–21).
 c Alma 22:20.
4a Alma 17:28 (28–31).
5a Alma 17:15; 60:32.

from his father, that there was a ᵇGreat Spirit. Notwithstanding they believed in a Great Spirit, they supposed that ᶜwhatsoever they did was right; nevertheless, Lamoni began to fear exceedingly, with fear lest he had done wrong in slaying his servants;

6 For he had slain many of them because their brethren had scattered their flocks at the place of water; and thus, because they had had their flocks scattered they were slain.

7 Now it was the practice of these Lamanites to stand by the ᵃwaters of Sebus to scatter the flocks of the people, that thereby they might drive away many that were scattered unto their own land, it being a practice of plunder among them.

8 And it came to pass that king Lamoni inquired of his servants, saying: Where is this man that has such great power?

9 And they said unto him: Behold, he is feeding thy ᵃhorses. Now the king had commanded his servants, previous to the time of the watering of their flocks, that they should prepare his horses and chariots, and conduct him forth to the land of Nephi; for there had been a ᵇgreat ᶜfeast appointed at the land of Nephi, by the father of Lamoni, who was king over all the land.

10 Now when king Lamoni heard that Ammon was preparing his horses and his ᵃchariots he was more astonished, because of the faithfulness of Ammon, saying: Surely there has not been any servant among all my servants that has been so faithful as this man; for even he doth remember all my commandments to execute them.

11 Now I surely know that this is the Great Spirit, and I would desire

him that he come in unto me, but I durst not.

12 And it came to pass that when Ammon had made ready the horses and the chariots for the king and his servants, he went in unto the king, and he saw that the ᵃcountenance of the king was changed; therefore he was about to return out of his presence.

13 And one of the king's servants said unto him, ᵃRabbanah, which is, being interpreted, powerful or great king, considering their kings to be powerful; and thus he said unto him: Rabbanah, the king desireth thee to stay.

14 Therefore Ammon turned himself unto the king, and said unto him: What wilt thou that I should do for thee, O king? And the king answered him not for the space of an ᵃhour, according to their time, for he knew not what he should say unto him.

15 And it came to pass that Ammon said unto him again: What desirest thou of me? But the king answered him not.

16 And it came to pass that Ammon, being filled with the ᵃSpirit of God, therefore he perceived the ᵇthoughts of the king. And he said unto him: Is it because thou hast heard that I defended thy servants and thy flocks, and slew ᶜseven of their brethren with the sling and with the sword, and smote off the arms of others, in order to defend thy flocks and thy servants; behold, is it this that causeth thy marvelings?

17 I say unto you, what is it, that thy marvelings are so great? Behold, I am a ᵃman, and am thy servant; therefore, whatsoever thou desirest which is right, that will I do.

18 Now when the king had heard

5 b Alma 19:25 (25–27).
    TG God, Knowledge about.
  c Alma 30:17.
7 a Alma 17:26;
    19:20 (20–21).
9 a Enos 1:21;

    Alma 20:6.
  b Alma 20:9 (9, 12).
  c Esth. 1:3.
10 a Alma 20:6;
    3 Ne. 3:22.
12 a Dan. 5:6.
13 a John 20:16.

14 a 3 Ne. 8:19.
16 a Gen. 41:38;
    1 Ne. 1:12;
    Mosiah 27:24.
  b Alma 12:3.
  c Alma 17:36.
17 a Dan. 2:30.

these words, he marveled again, for he beheld that Ammon could ᵃdiscern his thoughts; but notwithstanding this, king Lamoni did open his mouth, and said unto him: Who art thou? Art thou that Great Spirit, who ᵇknows all things?

19 Ammon answered and said unto him: I am not.

20 And the king said: How knowest thou the thoughts of my heart? Thou mayest speak boldly, and tell me concerning these things; and also tell me by what power ye slew and smote off the arms of my brethren that scattered my flocks—

21 And now, ᵃif thou wilt tell me concerning these things, whatsoever thou desirest I will give unto thee; and if it were needed, I would guard thee with my armies; but I know that thou art more powerful than all they; nevertheless, whatsoever thou desirest of me I will grant it unto thee.

22 Now Ammon being ᵃwise, yet harmless, he said unto Lamoni: Wilt thou hearken unto my words, if I tell thee by what power I do these things? And this is the thing that I desire of thee.

23 And the king answered him, and said: Yea, I ᵃwill believe all thy words. And thus he was caught with ᵇguile.

24 And Ammon began to speak unto him with ᵃboldness, and said unto him: Believest thou that there is a God?

25 And he answered, and said unto him: I do not know what that meaneth.

26 And then Ammon said: Believest thou that there is a ᵃGreat Spirit?

27 And he said, Yea.

28 And Ammon said: This is God.

And Ammon said unto him again: Believest thou that this Great Spirit, who is God, created all things which are in heaven and in the earth?

29 And he said: Yea, I believe that he created all things which are in the earth; but I do not know the heavens.

30 And Ammon said unto him: The heavens is a place where God dwells and all his holy angels.

31 And king Lamoni said: Is it above the earth?

32 And Ammon said: Yea, and he looketh down upon all the children of men; and he ᵃknows all the thoughts and ᵇintents of the heart; for by his hand were they all created from the beginning.

33 And king Lamoni said: I believe all these things which thou hast spoken. Art thou ᵃsent from God?

34 Ammon said unto him: I am a ᵃman; and man in the beginning was created after the image of God, and I am called by his ᵇHoly Spirit to teach these things unto this people, that they may be brought to a knowledge of that which is just and true;

35 And a portion of that ᵃSpirit dwelleth in me, which giveth me ᵇknowledge, and also power according to my faith and desires which are in God.

36 Now when Ammon had said these words, he began at the creation of the world, and also the creation of Adam, and told him all the things concerning the fall of man, and ᵃrehearsed and laid before him the ᵇrecords and the holy scriptures of the people, which had been spoken by the ᶜprophets, even down to the time that their father, Lehi, left Jerusalem.

37 And he also rehearsed unto

18a ᴛɢ Discernment,
     Spiritual.
  b ᴛɢ God, Omniscience of.
21a Dan. 5:16.
22a Gen. 41:39;
     Alma 48:11 (11–17).
23a Alma 18:40.
  b Josh. 9:22.
24a Alma 38:12.

26a Alma 22:9 (9–10).
32a ᴛɢ God, Omniscience of.
  b Amos 4:13;
     3 Ne. 28:6.
33a 2 Chr. 24:19.
34a Mosiah 7:27;
     Ether 3:15 (13–16).
  b ᴛɢ Teaching with the
     Spirit.

35a ᴛɢ Inspiration.
  b ᴛɢ Knowledge.
36a Mosiah 1:4;
     Alma 22:12; 36:1; 37:9;
     Hel. 5:13 (1–13);
     Moses 6:58.
  b Alma 63:12.
     ᴛɢ Scriptures, Value of.
  c Acts 3:18 (18–21); 28:23.

them (for it was unto the king and to his servants) all the journeyings of their fathers in the wilderness, and all their sufferings with hunger and thirst, and their travail, and so forth.

38 And he also rehearsed unto them concerning the ªrebellions of Laman and Lemuel, and the sons of Ishmael, yea, all their rebellions did he relate unto them; and he expounded unto them all the ᵇrecords and scriptures from the time that Lehi left Jerusalem down to the present time.

39 But this is not all; for he ªexpounded unto them the ᵇplan of redemption, which was prepared from the foundation of the world; and he also made known unto them concerning the coming of Christ, and all the works of the Lord did he make known unto them.

40 And it came to pass that after he had said all these things, and expounded them to the king, that the king ªbelieved all his words.

41 And he began to cry unto the Lord, saying: O Lord, have mercy; according to thy abundant ªmercy which thou hast had upon the people of Nephi, have upon me, and my people.

42 And now, when he had said this, he ªfell unto the earth, ᵇas if he were dead.

43 And it came to pass that his ªservants took him and carried him in unto his wife, and laid him upon a bed; and he lay as if he were dead for the space of two days and two nights; and his wife, and his sons, and his daughters mourned over him, after the manner of the Lamanites, greatly lamenting his loss.

CHAPTER 19

Lamoni receives the light of everlasting life and sees the Redeemer—His house-

hold falls into a trance, and many see angels—Ammon is preserved miraculously—He baptizes many and establishes a church among them. About 90 B.C.

AND it came to pass that after two days and two nights they were about to take his ªbody and lay it in a sepulchre, which they had made for the purpose of burying their dead.

2 Now the queen having heard of the fame of Ammon, therefore she sent and desired that he should come in unto her.

3 And it came to pass that Ammon did as he was commanded, and went in unto the queen, and desired to know what she would that he should do.

4 And she said unto him: The ªservants of my husband have made it known unto me that thou art a ᵇprophet of a holy God, and that thou hast ᶜpower to do many mighty works in his name;

5 Therefore, if this is the case, I would that ye should go in and see my husband, for he has been laid upon his bed for the space of two days and two nights; and some say that he is not dead, but others say that he is dead and that he ªstinketh, and that he ought to be placed in the sepulchre; but as for myself, to me he doth not stink.

6 Now, this was what Ammon desired, for he knew that king Lamoni was under the power of God; he knew that the dark ªveil of ᵇunbelief was being cast away from his mind, and the ᶜlight which did light up his mind, which was the light of the glory of God, which was a marvelous light of his goodness—yea, this light had infused such joy into his soul, the cloud of darkness having been dispelled, and that the light of everlasting life was lit up in

38a 2 Ne. 1:2.
  b 1 Ne. 9:2.
39a Alma 19:31.
   TG Missionary Work.
  b TG Salvation, Plan of.
40a Alma 18:23.
41a TG God, Mercy of.

42a Alma 19:1 (1, 5–12).
  b Alma 22:18.
43a Alma 19:4 (4–5).
19 1a Alma 18:42 (42–43).
  4a Alma 18:43.
  b TG Prophets, Mission of.

 c D&C 3:4.
5a John 11:39.
6a 2 Cor. 4:4 (3–4).
   TG Veil.
  b TG Unbelief.
  c TG Light [noun].

his soul, yea, he knew that this had ^dovercome his natural frame, and he was carried away in God—

7 Therefore, what the queen desired of him was his only desire. Therefore, he went in to see the king according as the queen had desired him; and he saw the king, and he knew that he was not dead.

8 And he said unto the queen: He is not dead, but he sleepeth in God, and on the morrow he shall rise again; therefore bury him not.

9 And Ammon said unto her: ^aBelievest thou this? And she said unto him: I have had no witness save thy word, and the word of our servants; nevertheless I ^bbelieve that it shall be according as thou hast said.

10 And Ammon said unto her: Blessed art thou because of thy exceeding faith; I say unto thee, woman, there has not been such great faith among all the people of the ^aNephites.

11 And it came to pass that she watched over the bed of her husband, from that time even until that time on the morrow which Ammon had appointed that he should rise.

12 And it came to pass that he arose, according to the words of Ammon; and as he arose, he stretched forth his hand unto the woman, and said: Blessed be the name of God, and blessed art thou.

13 For as sure as thou livest, behold, I have ^aseen my Redeemer; and he shall come forth, and be ^bborn of a ^cwoman, and he shall redeem all mankind who believe on his name. Now, when he had said these words, his heart was swollen within him, and he sunk again with joy; and the queen also sunk down, being overpowered by the Spirit.

14 Now Ammon seeing the Spirit of the Lord poured out according to his ^aprayers upon the Lamanites, his brethren, who had been the cause of so much mourning among the Nephites, or among all the people of God because of their iniquities and their ^btraditions, he fell upon his knees, and began to pour out his soul in prayer and thanksgiving to God for what he had done for his brethren; and he was also overpowered with ^cjoy; and thus they all three had ^dsunk to the earth.

15 Now, when the servants of the king had seen that they had fallen, they also began to cry unto God, for the fear of the Lord had come upon them also, for it was ^athey who had stood before the king and testified unto him concerning the great power of Ammon.

16 And it came to pass that they did call on the name of the Lord, in their might, even until they had all fallen to the earth, save it were one of the Lamanitish ^awomen, whose name was Abish, she having been converted unto the Lord for many years, on account of a remarkable vision of her father—

17 Thus, having been converted to the Lord, and never having made it ^aknown, therefore, when she saw that all the servants of Lamoni had ^bfallen to the earth, and also her mistress, the queen, and the king, and Ammon lay ^cprostrate upon the earth, she knew that it was the power of God; and supposing that this opportunity, by making known unto the people what had happened among them, that by beholding this scene it would ^dcause them to believe in the power of God, therefore she ran forth from house to house, making it known unto the people.

18 And they began to assemble themselves together unto the house

6d Jacob 7:21;
  Mosiah 3:19.
9a John 11:26 (22–45).
  b Mosiah 26:15 (15–16).
10a Luke 7:9.
13a TG God, Privilege of
  Seeing;

Jesus Christ, Appearances, Antemortal.
  b TG Jesus Christ, Birth of.
  c 1 Ne. 11:18 (13–21).
14a D&C 42:14.
  b Mosiah 1:5.
  c TG Joy.

  d Alma 27:17.
15a Alma 18:1 (1–2).
16a Alma 19:28.
17a JS—H 1:74.
  b Mosiah 4:1.
  c Moses 1:9 (9–10).
  d Mosiah 27:14.

of the king. And there came a multitude, and to their astonishment, they beheld the king, and the queen, and their servants prostrate upon the earth, and they all lay there as though they were dead; and they also saw Ammon, and behold, he was a Nephite.

19 And now the people began to murmur among themselves; some saying that it was a great evil that had come upon them, or upon the king and his house, because he had suffered that the Nephite should ᵃremain in the land.

20 But others rebuked them, saying: The king hath brought this evil upon his house, because he slew his servants who had had their flocks scattered at the ᵃwaters of Sebus.

21 And they were also rebuked by those men who had stood at the waters of Sebus and ᵃscattered the flocks which belonged to the king, for they were angry with Ammon because of the number which he had slain of their brethren at the waters of Sebus, while defending the flocks of the king.

22 Now, one of them, whose brother had been ᵃslain with the sword of Ammon, being exceedingly angry with Ammon, drew his sword and went forth that he might let it fall upon Ammon, to slay him; and as he lifted the sword to smite him, behold, he fell dead.

23 Now we see that Ammon could not be slain, for the ᵃLord had said unto Mosiah, his father: I will spare him, and it shall be unto him according to thy faith—therefore, Mosiah ᵇtrusted him unto the Lord.

24 And it came to pass that when the multitude beheld that the man had fallen dead, who lifted the sword to slay Ammon, ᵃfear came upon them all, and they durst not put forth their hands to touch him

or any of those who had fallen; and they began to marvel again among themselves what could be the cause of this great power, or what all these things could mean.

25 And it came to pass that there were many among them who said that Ammon was the ᵃGreat Spirit, and others said he was sent by the Great Spirit;

26 But others rebuked them all, saying that he was a ᵃmonster, who had been sent from the Nephites to torment them.

27 And there were some who said that Ammon was sent by the Great Spirit to afflict them because of their iniquities; and that it was the Great Spirit that had always attended the Nephites, who had ever delivered them out of their hands; and they said that it was this Great Spirit who had destroyed so many of their brethren, the Lamanites.

28 And thus the contention began to be exceedingly sharp among them. And while they were thus contending, the ᵃwoman servant who had caused the multitude to be gathered together came, and when she saw the contention which was among the multitude she was exceedingly sorrowful, even unto tears.

29 And it came to pass that she went and took the queen by the ᵃhand, that perhaps she might raise her from the ground; and as soon as she touched her hand she arose and stood upon her feet, and cried with a loud voice, saying: O blessed Jesus, who has saved me from an ᵇawful hell! O blessed God, have ᶜmercy on this people!

30 And when she had said this, she clasped her hands, being filled with joy, speaking many words which were not understood; and when she had done this, she took the king,

19a Alma 17:23 (22–23).
20a Alma 17:26; 18:7.
21a Alma 17:27; 18:3.
22a Alma 17:38.
23a Mosiah 28:7;
    Alma 17:35.

b TG Family, Love within;
    Trust in God.
24a Luke 7:16;
    Moses 6:39 (37–40).
25a Alma 18:5 (2–5).
26a Moses 6:38 (37–39).

28a Alma 19:16.
29a Alma 22:22.
 b 1 Ne. 14:3.
 c Enos 1:9;
    Alma 36:24.

Lamoni, by the hand, and behold he arose and stood upon his feet.

31 And he, immediately, seeing the contention among his people, went forth and began to rebuke them, and to teach them the ^awords which he had heard from the mouth of Ammon; and as many as heard his words believed, and were converted unto the Lord.

32 But there were ^amany among them who would not hear his words; therefore they went their way.

33 And it came to pass that when Ammon arose he also administered unto them, and also did all the servants of Lamoni; and they did all declare unto the people the selfsame thing—that their hearts had been ^achanged; that they had no more desire to do ^bevil.

34 And behold, many did declare unto the people that they had seen ^aangels and had conversed with them; and thus they had told them things of God, and of his righteousness.

35 And it came to pass that there were many that did ^abelieve in their words; and as many as did believe were baptized; and they became a righteous people, and they did establish a church among them.

36 And thus the work of the Lord did commence among the Lamanites; thus the Lord did begin to pour out his ^aSpirit upon them; and we see that his arm is extended to ^ball people who will repent and believe on his name.

CHAPTER 20

The Lord sends Ammon to Middoni to deliver his imprisoned brethren—Ammon and Lamoni meet Lamoni's father, who is king over all the land—Ammon compels the old king to approve the release of his brethren. About 90 B.C.

AND it came to pass that when they had established a church in that ^aland, that king Lamoni desired that Ammon should go with him to the land of Nephi, that he might show him unto his father.

2 And the voice of the Lord came to Ammon, saying: Thou shalt not go up to the land of Nephi, for behold, the king will seek thy life; but thou shalt go to the land of ^aMiddoni; for behold, thy brother Aaron, and also Muloki and Ammah are in prison.

3 Now it came to pass that when Ammon had heard this, he said unto Lamoni: Behold, my brother and brethren are in prison at Middoni, and I go that I may deliver them.

4 Now Lamoni said unto Ammon: I know, in the ^astrength of the Lord thou canst do all things. But behold, I will go with thee to the land of Middoni; for the king of the land of Middoni, whose name is Antiomno, is a friend unto me; therefore I go to the land of Middoni, that I may flatter the king of the land, and he will cast thy brethren out of ^bprison. Now Lamoni said unto him: Who told thee that thy brethren were in prison?

5 And Ammon said unto him: No one hath told me, save it be God; and he said unto me—Go and deliver thy brethren, for they are in prison in the land of Middoni.

6 Now when Lamoni had heard this he caused that his servants should make ready his ^ahorses and his chariots.

7 And he said unto Ammon: Come, I will go with thee down to the land of Middoni, and there I will plead with the king that he will cast thy brethren out of prison.

8 And it came to pass that as Ammon and Lamoni were journeying

31a Alma 18:39 (36–39).
32a John 12:37 (35–37).
33a TG Man, New, Spiritually Reborn.
  b Jonah 3:8;
    Mosiah 5:2;
    Alma 13:12;
    3 Ne. 20:26.
34a TG Angels;
    Vision.
35a TG Baptism,
    Qualifications for.
36a TG God, Spirit of.
  b 2 Ne. 26:33;
    Alma 5:33;
    3 Ne. 18:25.
20 1a 2 Ne. 5:8;
    Alma 2:24.
  2a Alma 21:12 (12–13, 18);
    23:10.
  4a TG Strength.
  b Alma 20:22; 22:2.
  6a Alma 18:9.

thither, they met the father of Lamoni, who was king ^aover all the land.

9 And behold, the father of Lamoni said unto him: Why did ye ^anot come to the ^bfeast on that great day when I made a feast unto my sons, and unto my people?

10 And he also said: Whither art thou going with this Nephite, who is one of the children of a ^aliar?

11 And it came to pass that Lamoni rehearsed unto him whither he was going, for he feared to offend him.

12 And he also told him all the cause of his tarrying in his own kingdom, that he did not go unto his father to the feast which he had prepared.

13 And now when Lamoni had rehearsed unto him all these things, behold, to his astonishment, his father was angry with him, and said: Lamoni, thou art going to deliver these Nephites, who are sons of a liar. Behold, he robbed our fathers; and now his children are also come amongst us that they may, by their cunning and their lyings, deceive us, that they again may rob us of our property.

14 Now the father of Lamoni commanded him that he should slay Ammon with the sword. And he also commanded him that he should not go to the land of Middoni, but that he should return with him to the land of ^aIshmael.

15 But Lamoni said unto him: I will not slay Ammon, neither will I return to the land of Ishmael, but I go to the land of Middoni that I may release the brethren of Ammon, for I know that they are just men and holy prophets of the true God.

16 Now when his father had heard these words, he was angry with him, and he drew his sword that he might smite him to the earth.

17 But Ammon stood forth and said unto him: Behold, thou shalt not slay thy son; nevertheless, it were ^abetter that he should fall than thee, for behold, he has ^brepented of his sins; but if thou shouldst fall at this time, in thine anger, thy soul could not be saved.

18 And again, it is expedient that thou shouldst forbear; for if thou shouldst ^aslay thy son, he being an innocent man, his blood would cry from the ground to the Lord his God, for vengeance to come upon thee; and perhaps thou wouldst lose thy ^bsoul.

19 Now when Ammon had said these words unto him, he answered him, saying: I know that if I should slay my son, that I should shed innocent blood; for it is thou that hast sought to destroy him.

20 And he stretched forth his hand to slay Ammon. But Ammon withstood his blows, and also smote his arm that he could not use it.

21 Now when the king saw that Ammon could slay him, he began to plead with Ammon that he would spare his life.

22 But Ammon raised his sword, and said unto him: Behold, I will smite thee except thou wilt grant unto me that my brethren may be ^acast out of prison.

23 Now the king, fearing he should lose his life, said: If thou wilt spare me I will grant unto thee whatsoever thou wilt ask, even to half of the kingdom.

24 Now when Ammon saw that he had wrought upon the old king according to his desire, he said unto him: If thou wilt grant that my brethren may be cast out of prison, and also that Lamoni may retain his kingdom, and that ye be not displeased with him, but grant that he may do according to his own desires in ^awhatsoever thing he thinketh,

8a Alma 22:1.
9a 1 Sam. 20:27.
  b Alma 18:9.
10a Mosiah 10:16 (12–17).
14a Alma 17:19.
17a Alma 48:23.
  b Alma 22:6.
18a TG Murder.
  b D&C 42:18.
22a Alma 20:4.
24a Alma 21:21 (21–22);
    22:1.

then will I spare thee; otherwise I will smite thee to the earth.

25 Now when Ammon had said these words, the king began to rejoice because of his life.

26 And when he saw that Ammon had no desire to destroy him, and when he also saw the great *a*love he had for his son Lamoni, he was astonished exceedingly, and said: Because this is all that thou hast desired, that I would *b*release thy brethren, and suffer that my son Lamoni should retain his kingdom, behold, I will grant unto you that my son may retain his kingdom from this time and forever; and I will govern him no more—

27 And I will also grant unto thee that thy brethren may be cast out of prison, and thou and thy brethren may come unto me, in my kingdom; for I shall greatly desire to see thee. For the king was greatly astonished at the words which he had spoken, and also at the words which had been spoken by his son Lamoni, therefore he was *a*desirous to learn them.

28 And it came to pass that Ammon and Lamoni proceeded on their journey towards the land of Middoni. And Lamoni found favor in the eyes of the king of the land; therefore the brethren of Ammon were brought forth out of prison.

29 And when Ammon did meet them he was exceedingly sorrowful, for behold they were naked, and their skins were worn exceedingly because of being bound with strong cords. And they also had *a*suffered hunger, thirst, and all kinds of afflictions; nevertheless they were *b*patient in all their sufferings.

30 And, as it happened, it was their lot to have fallen into the hands of a more hardened and a more *a*stiffnecked people; therefore they would not hearken unto their words, and

they had cast them out, and had smitten them, and had driven them from house to house, and from place to place, even until they had arrived in the land of Middoni; and there they were taken and cast into prison, and bound with *b*strong cords, and kept in prison for many days, and were delivered by Lamoni and Ammon.

An account of the preaching of Aaron, and Muloki, and their brethren, to the Lamanites.

Comprising chapters 21 through 25.

CHAPTER 21

Aaron teaches the Amalekites about Christ and His Atonement—Aaron and his brethren are imprisoned in Middoni—After their deliverance, they teach in the synagogues and make many converts—Lamoni grants religious freedom to the people in the land of Ishmael. About 90–77 B.C.

Now when Ammon and his brethren *a*separated themselves in the borders of the land of the Lamanites, behold Aaron took his journey towards the land which was called by the Lamanites, *b*Jerusalem, calling it after the land of their fathers' nativity; and it was away joining the borders of Mormon.

2 Now the Lamanites and the Amalekites and the people of *a*Amulon had built a great city, which was called Jerusalem.

3 Now the Lamanites of themselves were sufficiently hardened, but the Amalekites and the Amulonites were still harder; therefore they did cause the Lamanites that they should harden their hearts, that they should wax strong in wickedness and their abominations.

4 And it came to pass that Aaron came to the city of Jerusalem, and

---

26a 2 Sam. 1:26.
    TG Loyalty.
  b Alma 22:2.
27a TG Teachable.
29a Alma 21:14.

    b Alma 17:11.
30a TG Stiffnecked.
  b Alma 26:29.
21 1a Alma 17:13 (13, 17).
  b Alma 24:1;

    3 Ne. 9:7.
2a Mosiah 23:31; 24:1;
    Alma 24:1 (1, 28–30);
    25:7 (4–9).

first began to preach to the Amalekites. And he began to preach to them in their ªsynagogues, for they had built synagogues after the ᵇorder of the Nehors; for many of the Amalekites and the Amulonites were after the order of the Nehors.

5 Therefore, as Aaron entered into one of their ªsynagogues to preach unto the people, and as he was speaking unto them, behold there arose an Amalekite and began to contend with him, saying: What is that thou hast testified? Hast thou seen an ᵇangel? Why do not angels appear unto us? Behold ᶜare not this people as good as thy people?

6 Thou also sayest, except we repent we shall perish. How knowest thou the thought and intent of our hearts? How knowest thou that we have cause to repent? How knowest thou that we are not a ªrighteous people? Behold, we have built ᵇsanctuaries, and we do assemble ourselves together to worship ᶜGod. We do believe that God will save all men.

7 Now Aaron said unto him: Believest thou that the Son of God shall come to redeem mankind from their sins?

8 And the man said unto him: We do not ªbelieve that thou knowest any such thing. We do not believe in these foolish traditions. We do not believe that thou knowest of things to come, neither do we believe that thy fathers and also that our fathers did know concerning the things which they spake, of that which is to come.

9 Now Aaron began to open the ªscriptures unto them concerning the coming of Christ, and also concerning the resurrection of the dead, and that there could be ᵇno redemption for mankind ᶜsave it were through the ᵈdeath and sufferings of Christ, and the atonement of his blood.

10 And it came to pass as he began to expound these things unto them they were angry with him, and began to ªmock him; and they would not hear the words which he spake.

11 Therefore, when he saw that they would not hear his words, he departed out of their synagogue, and came over to a village which was called Ani-Anti, and there he found Muloki preaching the word unto them; and also Ammah and his brethren. And they contended with many about the word.

12 And it came to pass that they saw that the people would harden their hearts, therefore they departed and came over into the land of ªMiddoni. And they did preach the word unto many, and ᵇfew believed on the words which they taught.

13 Nevertheless, Aaron and a certain number of his brethren were taken and cast into ªprison, and the remainder of them fled out of the land of Middoni unto the regions round about.

14 And those who were cast into prison ªsuffered many things, and they were delivered by the hand of Lamoni and Ammon, and they were fed and clothed.

15 And they went forth again to declare the word, and thus they were delivered for the first time out of prison; and thus they had suffered.

16 And they went forth whithersoever they were led by the ªSpirit of the Lord, preaching the word of God in every synagogue of the Amalekites, or in every assembly of the Lamanites where they could be admitted.

17 And it came to pass that the

4a D&C 66:7.
  b Alma 1:12 (2–15);
    14:16; 24:28.
5a Alma 16:13.
  b Mosiah 27:11 (11–15).
  c Moses 8:21.
6a Jer. 2:35;
    Mosiah 12:14 (9–15).

  b Alma 15:17; 16:13; 23:2;
    Hel. 3:14 (9, 14).
  c Alma 1:4.
8a Jacob 7:2 (1–7).
9a Alma 25:6.
  b Alma 22:14 (13–14).
  c Mosiah 5:8; Alma 38:9.
  d TG Jesus Christ,

    Death of.
10a TG Mocking.
12a Alma 23:10.
  b Matt. 7:14.
13a Alma 20:2.
14a Alma 20:29.
16a Acts 16:6;
    Alma 22:1 (1–4).

Lord began to bless them, insomuch that they brought many to the knowledge of the truth; yea, they did *a*convince many of their sins, and of the traditions of their fathers, which were not correct.

18 And it came to pass that Ammon and Lamoni returned from the land of Middoni to the land of *a*Ishmael, which was the land of their inheritance.

19 And king Lamoni would not suffer that Ammon should serve him, or be his *a*servant.

20 But he caused that there should be *a*synagogues built in the land of Ishmael; and he caused that his people, or the people who were under his reign, should assemble themselves together.

21 And he did rejoice over them, and he did teach them many things. And he did also declare unto them that they were a people who were under him, and that they were a *a*free people, that they were free from the oppressions of the king, his father; for that his father had granted unto him that he might reign over the people who were in the land of Ishmael, and in all the land round about.

22 And he also declared unto them that they might have the *a*liberty of worshiping the Lord their God according to their desires, in whatsoever place they were in, if it were in the land which was under the reign of king Lamoni.

23 And Ammon did preach unto the people of king Lamoni; and it came to pass that he did teach them all things concerning things pertaining to righteousness. And he did exhort them daily, with all diligence; and they gave heed unto his word, and they were *a*zealous for keeping the commandments of God.

CHAPTER 22

Aaron teaches Lamoni's father about the Creation, the Fall of Adam, and the plan of redemption through Christ—The king and all his household are converted—The division of the land between the Nephites and the Lamanites is explained. About 90–77 B.C.

Now, as Ammon was thus teaching the people of Lamoni continually, we will return to the account of Aaron and his brethren; for after he departed from the land of Middoni he was *a*led by the Spirit to the land of Nephi, even to the house of the king which was *b*over all the land *c*save it were the land of Ishmael; and he was the father of Lamoni.

2 And it came to pass that he went in unto him into the king's palace, with his brethren, and bowed himself before the king, and said unto him: Behold, O king, we are the brethren of Ammon, whom thou hast *a*delivered out of *b*prison.

3 And now, O king, if thou wilt spare our lives, we will be thy servants. And the king said unto them: Arise, for I will grant unto you your lives, and I will not suffer that ye shall be my servants; but I will insist that ye shall administer unto me; for I have been somewhat *a*troubled in mind because of the *b*generosity and the greatness of the words of thy brother Ammon; and I desire to know the cause why he has not come up out of Middoni with thee.

4 And Aaron said unto the king: Behold, the Spirit of the Lord has called him another way; he has gone *a*to the land of Ishmael, to teach the people of Lamoni.

5 Now the king said unto them: What is this that ye have said concerning the Spirit of the Lord?

17*a* Alma 62:45;
　　 D&C 18:44.
18*a* Alma 17:19;
　　 22:1 (1, 4); 25:13.
19*a* Alma 17:25.
20*a* Alma 16:13.
21*a* Alma 20:24; 22:1.

22*a* Luke 4:8;
　　 D&C 93:19; 134:4 (1–4);
　　 A of F 1:11.
　　 TG Liberty.
23*a* TG Zeal.
22 1*a* Gen. 24:27; Acts 16:6;
　　 Alma 21:16 (16–17).

　 b Alma 20:8.
　 c Alma 20:24; 21:21 (21–22).
2*a* Alma 20:26.
　 b Alma 20:4.
3*a* Acts 2:37 (37–38).
　 b Alma 20:26.
4*a* Alma 21:18.

Behold, this is the thing which doth trouble me.

6 And also, what is this that Ammon said—"If ye will repent ye shall be saved, and if ye will not repent, ye shall be cast off at the last day?

7 And Aaron answered him and said unto him: Believest thou that there is a God? And the king said: I know that the Amalekites say that there is a God, and I have granted unto them that they should build sanctuaries, that they may assemble themselves together to worship him. And if now thou sayest there is a God, behold I will "believe.

8 And now when Aaron heard this, his heart began to rejoice, and he said: Behold, assuredly as thou livest, O king, there is a God.

9 And the king said: Is God that "Great Spirit that brought our fathers out of the land of Jerusalem?

10 And Aaron said unto him: Yea, he is that Great Spirit, and he "created all things both in heaven and in earth. Believest thou this?

11 And he said: Yea, I believe that the Great Spirit created all things, and I desire that ye should tell me concerning all these things, and I will "believe thy words.

12 And it came to pass that when Aaron saw that the king would believe his words, he began from the creation of Adam, "reading the scriptures unto the king—how God "created man after his own image, and that God gave him commandments, and that because of transgression, man had fallen.

13 And Aaron did expound unto him the scriptures from the "creation of Adam, laying the fall of man

before him, and their carnal state and also the "plan of "redemption, which was prepared "from the foundation of the world, through Christ, for all whosoever would believe on his name.

14 And since man had "fallen he could not "merit anything of himself; but the sufferings and "death of Christ "atone for their sins, through faith and repentance, and so forth; and that he breaketh the bands of death, that the "grave shall have no victory, and that the sting of death should be swallowed up in the hopes of glory; and Aaron did expound all these things unto the king.

15 And it came to pass that after Aaron had expounded these things unto him, the king said: "What shall I do that I may have this eternal life of which thou hast spoken? Yea, what shall I do that I may be "born of God, having this wicked spirit "rooted out of my breast, and receive his Spirit, that I may be filled with joy, that I may not be cast off at the last day? Behold, said he, I will give up "all that I possess, yea, I will forsake my kingdom, that I may receive this great joy.

16 But Aaron said unto him: If thou desirest this thing, if thou wilt "bow down before God, yea, if thou wilt repent of all thy sins, and will bow down before God, and call on his name in faith, believing that ye shall receive, then shalt thou receive the "hope which thou desirest.

17 And it came to pass that when Aaron had said these words, the king did "bow down before the Lord, upon his knees; yea, even he did

6a Alma 20:17 (17–18).
7a D&C 46:14 (13–14).
9a Alma 18:2, 26 (18–28).
10a TG Creation.
11a TG Believe.
12a 1 Ne. 5:18 (10–18);
    Alma 18:36; 37:9.
  b TG Man, Physical
    Creation of.
13a Gen. 1:26 (26–28); 2:7.
  b TG Salvation, Plan of.

c TG Redemption.
d 2 Ne. 9:18;
  Alma 13:3 (3, 5, 7–9).
14a TG Fall of Man.
  b Eph. 2:8 (8–9);
    Alma 42:14 (10–25).
  c TG Jesus Christ,
    Death of.
  d 2 Ne. 2:10;
    Alma 33:22; 34:9 (8–16).
  e Isa. 25:8;

1 Cor. 15:55 (34–57).
15a TG Acts 2:37.
  b Alma 5:14 (14, 49);
    36:23 (23, 26).
  c Rom. 7:18.
  d Matt. 13:46 (44–46);
    19:21 (16–22).
16a TG Conversion.
  b Ether 12:4.
17a D&C 5:24.

prostrate himself upon the earth, and cried [b]mightily, saying:

18 O God, Aaron hath told me that there is a God; and if there is a God, and if thou art God, wilt thou make thyself known unto me, and I will give away all my sins to know thee, and that I may be raised from the dead, and be saved at the last day. And now when the king had said these words, he was struck [a]as if he were dead.

19 And it came to pass that his servants ran and told the queen all that had happened unto the king. And she came in unto the king; and when she saw him lay as if he were dead, and also Aaron and his brethren standing as though they had been the cause of his fall, she was angry with them, and commanded that her servants, or the servants of the king, should take them and slay them.

20 Now the servants had seen the cause of the king's fall, therefore they durst not lay their hands on Aaron and his brethren; and they pled with the queen saying: Why commandest thou that we should slay these men, when behold one of them is [a]mightier than us all? Therefore we shall fall before them.

21 Now when the queen saw the fear of the servants she also began to fear exceedingly, lest there should some evil come upon her. And she commanded her servants that they should go and call the people, that they might slay Aaron and his brethren.

22 Now when Aaron saw the determination of the queen, he, also knowing the hardness of the hearts of the people, feared lest that a multitude should assemble themselves together, and there should be a great contention and a disturbance among them; therefore he put forth his [a]hand and raised the king from the earth, and said unto him: Stand. And he stood upon his feet, receiving his strength.

23 Now this was done in the presence of the queen and many of the servants. And when they saw it they greatly marveled, and began to fear. And the king stood forth, and began to [a]minister unto them. And he did minister unto them, insomuch that his [b]whole household were [c]converted unto the Lord.

24 Now there was a multitude gathered together because of the commandment of the queen, and there began to be great murmurings among them because of Aaron and his brethren.

25 But the king stood forth among them and administered unto them. And they were [a]pacified towards Aaron and those who were with him.

26 And it came to pass that when the king saw that the people were pacified, he caused that Aaron and his brethren should stand forth in the midst of the multitude, and that they should preach the word unto them.

27 And it came to pass that the king sent a [a]proclamation throughout all the land, amongst all his people who were in all his land, who were in all the regions round about, which was bordering even to the sea, on the east and on the [b]west, and which was divided from the land of [c]Zarahemla by a narrow strip of wilderness, which ran from the sea east even to the sea west, and round about on the borders of the seashore, and the borders of the wilderness which was on the north by the land of Zarahemla, through the borders of [d]Manti, by the head of the [e]river Sidon, running from the east towards the west—and thus were the Lamanites and the Nephites divided.

17b TG Prayer.
18a Alma 18:42 (42–43).
20a Alma 18:3 (1–3).
22a Alma 19:29.
23a TG Minister;
   Ministration;

   Ministry.
 b Alma 23:3.
 c TG Conversion.
25a TG Peace;
   Peacemakers.
27a Alma 23:1 (1–4).

 b Hel. 3:8; 11:20.
 c Omni 1:13.
 d Alma 17:1; 56:14.
 e Alma 16:6 (6–7);
   43:22 (22–53).

28 Now, the more ^aidle part of the Lamanites lived in the wilderness, and dwelt in tents; and they were spread through the wilderness on the west, in the land of Nephi; yea, and also on the west of the land of Zarahemla, in the borders by the seashore, and on the west in the land of Nephi, in the place of their fathers' first inheritance, and thus bordering along by the seashore.

29 And also there were many Lamanites on the east by the seashore, whither the Nephites had driven them. And thus the Nephites were nearly surrounded by the Lamanites; nevertheless the Nephites had taken possession of all the northern parts of the land bordering on the wilderness, at the head of the river Sidon, from the east to the west, round about on the wilderness side; on the north, even until they came to the land which they called ^aBountiful.

30 And it bordered upon the land which they called ^aDesolation, it being so far northward that it came into the land which had been peopled and been destroyed, of whose ^bbones we have spoken, which was discovered by the ^cpeople of Zarahemla, it being the place of their ^dfirst landing.

31 And they came from there ^aup into the south wilderness. Thus the ^bland on the northward was called ^cDesolation, and the land on the southward was called Bountiful, it being the wilderness which is filled with all manner of wild animals of every kind, a part of which had come from the land northward for food.

32 And now, it was only the ^adistance of a day and a half's journey for a Nephite, on the line Bountiful and the land Desolation, from the east to the west sea; and thus the land of Nephi and the land of Zarahemla were nearly surrounded by water, there being a small ^bneck of land between the land northward and the land southward.

33 And it came to pass that the Nephites had inhabited the land Bountiful, even from the east unto the west sea, and thus the Nephites in their wisdom, with their guards and their armies, had hemmed in the Lamanites on the south, that thereby they should have no more possession on the north, that they might not overrun the land northward.

34 Therefore the Lamanites could have no more possessions only in the land of Nephi, and the wilderness round about. Now this was wisdom in the Nephites—as the Lamanites were an enemy to them, they would not suffer their afflictions on every hand, and also that they might have a country whither they might flee, according to their desires.

35 And now I, after having said this, return again to the account of Ammon and Aaron, Omner and Himni, and their brethren.

CHAPTER 23

Religious freedom is proclaimed—The Lamanites in seven lands and cities are converted—They call themselves Anti-Nephi-Lehies and are freed from the curse—The Amalekites and the Amulonites reject the truth. About 90–77 B.C.

BEHOLD, now it came to pass that the king of the Lamanites sent a ^aproclamation among all his people, that they should not lay their hands on Ammon, or Aaron, or Omner, or Himni, nor either of their brethren who should go forth preaching the word of God, in whatsoever place

---

28a 2 Ne. 5:24 (22–25).
29a Alma 52:9, 17, 27; 63:5.
30a Alma 46:17; 50:34;
    Morm. 3:5 (5, 7);
    4:3 (1–3).

b Mosiah 8:8 (7–12);
  28:17 (11–19).
c Omni 1:21 (20–22).
d Ether 6:12; 7:6.
31a Hel. 6:10.

b Alma 46:17; 63:4.
c Hel. 3:6 (5–6).
32a Hel. 4:7.
  b Alma 50:34; 52:9.
23 1a Alma 22:27.

they should be, in any part of their land.

2 Yea, he sent a decree among them, that they should not lay their hands on them to bind them, or to cast them into prison; neither should they spit upon them, nor smite them, nor cast them out of their *synagogues, nor scourge them; neither should they cast stones at them, but that they should have free access to their houses, and also their temples, and their *sanctuaries.

3 And thus they might go forth and preach the word according to their desires, for the king had been converted unto the Lord, and *all his *household; therefore he sent his proclamation throughout the land unto his people, that the word of God might have no obstruction, but that it might go forth throughout all the land, that his people might be convinced concerning the wicked *traditions of their fathers, and that they might be convinced that they were all brethren, and that they ought not to murder, nor to plunder, nor to steal, nor to commit adultery, nor to commit any manner of wickedness.

4 And now it came to pass that when the king had sent forth this proclamation, that Aaron and his brethren went forth from *city to city, and from one house of worship to another, establishing churches, and consecrating *priests and teachers throughout the land among the Lamanites, to preach and to teach the word of God among them; and thus they began to have great success.

5 And *thousands were brought to the knowledge of the Lord, yea, thousands were brought to believe in the *traditions of the Nephites; and they were taught the *records and prophecies which were handed down even to the present time.

6 And as sure as the Lord liveth, so sure as many as believed, or as many as were brought to the knowledge of the truth, through the preaching of Ammon and his brethren, according to the spirit of revelation and of prophecy, and the power of God working *miracles in them—yea, I say unto you, as the Lord liveth, as many of the Lamanites as believed in their preaching, and were *converted unto the Lord, *never did fall away.

7 For they became a righteous people; they did lay down the weapons of their rebellion, that they did not fight against God any more, neither against any of their brethren.

8 Now, these are *they who were converted unto the Lord:

9 The people of the Lamanites who were in the land of Ishmael;

10 And also of the people of the Lamanites who were in the land of *Middoni;

11 And also of the people of the Lamanites who were in the city of Nephi;

12 And also of the people of the Lamanites who were in the land of *Shilom, and who were in the land of Shemlon, and in the city of Lemuel, and in the city of Shimnilom.

13 And these are the names of the cities of the Lamanites which were *converted unto the Lord; and these are they that laid down the weapons of their rebellion, yea, all their weapons of war; and they were all Lamanites.

14 And the Amalekites were not

2a Alma 21:20 (4–6, 20); 26:29.
  b Hel. 3:14 (9, 14).
3a Alma 22:23.
  b Gen. 18:19.
  c Alma 26:24.
4a Luke 8:1;
    D&C 66:5; 75:18.

  b Alma 30:31.
5a Alma 26:4.
  b Alma 37:19.
  c Alma 63:12.
    TG Scriptures, Value of.
6a Ex. 8:19;
    1 Ne. 19:22;
    D&C 84:3; 121:12.

  b TG Commitment;
    Conversion.
  c Alma 27:27.
8a Alma 26:3, 31.
10a Alma 20:2;
    21:12 (12–13, 18).
12a Mosiah 22:11 (8, 11).
13a Alma 53:10.

^aconverted, save only one; neither were any of the ^bAmulonites; but they did harden their hearts, and also the hearts of the Lamanites in that part of the land wheresoever they dwelt, yea, and all their villages and all their cities.

15 Therefore, we have named all the cities of the Lamanites in which they did repent and come to the knowledge of the truth, and were converted.

16 And now it came to pass that the king and those who were converted were desirous that they might have a name, that thereby they might be distinguished from their brethren; therefore the king consulted with Aaron and many of their priests, concerning the name that they should take upon them, that they might be distinguished.

17 And it came to pass that they called their names ^aAnti-Nephi-Lehies; and they were called by this name and were no more called ^bLamanites.

18 And they began to be a very ^aindustrious people; yea, and they were friendly with the Nephites; therefore, they did ^bopen a correspondence with them, and the ^ccurse of God did no more follow them.

CHAPTER 24

The Lamanites come against the people of God—The Anti-Nephi-Lehies rejoice in Christ and are visited by angels—They choose to suffer death rather than to defend themselves—More Lamanites are converted. About 90–77 B.C.

AND it came to pass that the Amalekites and the Amulonites and the Lamanites who were in the land of ^aAmulon, and also in the land of ^bHelam, and who were in the land of ^cJerusalem, and in fine, in all the land round about, who had not been converted and had not taken upon them the name of ^dAnti-Nephi-Lehi, were stirred up by the Amalekites and by the Amulonites to anger against their brethren.

2 And their hatred became exceedingly sore against them, even insomuch that they began to rebel against their king, insomuch that they would not that he should be their king; therefore, they took up arms against the people of Anti-Nephi-Lehi.

3 Now the king conferred the kingdom upon his son, and he called his name Anti-Nephi-Lehi.

4 And the king died in that selfsame year that the Lamanites began to make preparations for war against the people of God.

5 Now when Ammon and his brethren and all those who had come up with him saw the preparations of the Lamanites to destroy their brethren, they came forth to the land of Midian, and there Ammon met all his brethren; and from thence they came to the land of Ishmael that they might hold a ^acouncil with Lamoni and also with his brother Anti-Nephi-Lehi, what they should do to defend themselves against the Lamanites.

6 Now there was not one soul among all the people who had been converted unto the Lord that would take up arms against their brethren; nay, they would not even make any preparations for war; yea, and also their king commanded them that they should not.

7 Now, these are the words which he said unto the people concerning the matter: I thank my God, my beloved people, that our great God has in goodness sent these our brethren, the Nephites, unto us to

14a Alma 24:29.
  b Mosiah 23:31 (31–39).
17a Alma 24:1 (1–3, 5, 20).
  b Jacob 1:13.
18a TG Industry.
  b Alma 24:8.

  c 1 Ne. 2:23;
    2 Ne. 30:6 (5–6);
    3 Ne. 2:15 (14–16).
24 1a Alma 21:3 (2–4);
     25:7 (4–9).
   b Mosiah 23:19; 27:16.

  c Alma 21:1.
  d Alma 23:17;
    25:13 (1, 13).
5a Alma 27:4.

preach unto us, and to convince us of the ᵃtraditions of our wicked fathers.

8 And behold, I thank my great God that he has given us a portion of his Spirit to soften our hearts, that we have ᵃopened a correspondence with these brethren, the Nephites.

9 And behold, I also thank my God, that by opening this correspondence we have been convinced of our ᵃsins, and of the many murders which we have committed.

10 And I also thank my God, yea, my great God, that he hath granted unto us that we might repent of these things, and also that he hath ᵃforgiven us of those our many sins and murders which we have committed, and taken away the ᵇguilt from our hearts, through the merits of his Son.

11 And now behold, my brethren, since it has been all that we could do (as we were the most lost of all mankind) to repent of all our sins and the many murders which we have committed, and to get God to ᵃtake them away from our hearts, for it was all we could do to repent sufficiently before God that he would take away our stain—

12 Now, my best beloved brethren, since God hath taken away our stains, and our swords have become bright, then let us stain our swords no more with the blood of our brethren.

13 Behold, I say unto you, Nay, let us retain our swords that they be not stained with the blood of our brethren; for perhaps, if we should stain our swords ᵃagain they can no more be ᵇwashed bright through the blood of the Son of our great God, which shall be shed for the atonement of our sins.

14 And the great God has had mercy on us, and made these things known unto us that we might not perish; yea, and he has made these things known unto us beforehand, because he loveth our ᵃsouls as well as he loveth our children; therefore, in his mercy he doth visit us by his angels, that the ᵇplan of salvation might be made known unto us as well as unto future generations.

15 Oh, how merciful is our God! And now behold, since it has been as much as we could do to get our stains taken away from us, and our swords are made bright, let us ᵃhide them away that they may be kept bright, as a testimony to our God at the last day, or at the day that we shall be brought to stand before him to be judged, that we have not stained our swords in the blood of our brethren since he imparted his word unto us and has made us ᵇclean thereby.

16 And now, my brethren, if our brethren seek to destroy us, behold, we will hide away our swords, yea, even we will bury them deep in the earth, that they may be kept bright, as a testimony that we have never used them, at the last day; and if our brethren destroy us, behold, we will ᵃgo to our God and shall be saved.

17 And now it came to pass that when the king had made an end of these sayings, and all the people were assembled together, they took their swords, and all the weapons which were used for the shedding of man's blood, and they did ᵃbury them up deep in the earth.

18 And this they did, it being in their view a testimony to God, and also to men, that they ᵃnever would use weapons again for the shedding of man's blood; and this they did, vouching and ᵇcovenanting with God, that rather than shed the

7a Mosiah 1:5.
8a Alma 23:18.
9a Micah 3:8;
   Hel. 13:26;
   D&C 18:44.
10a Dan. 9:9.
  b TG Guilt.

11a Isa. 53:6 (4–6).
13a D&C 42:26.
  b Rev. 1:5.
14a TG Worth of Souls.
  b TG Jesus Christ,
     Prophecies about;
     Salvation, Plan of.

15a Alma 25:14; 26:32.
  b TG Purification.
16a Alma 40:11 (11–15).
17a Hel. 15:9.
18a Alma 53:11.
  b TG Covenants.

blood of their brethren they would ^cgive up their own lives; and rather than take away from a brother they would give unto him; and rather than spend their days in idleness they would labor abundantly with their hands.

19 And thus we see that, when these Lamanites were brought to ^abelieve and to know the truth, they were ^bfirm, and would suffer even unto death rather than commit sin; and thus we see that they buried their weapons of peace, or they buried the weapons of war, for peace.

20 And it came to pass that their brethren, the Lamanites, made preparations for war, and came up to the land of Nephi for the purpose of destroying the king, and to place ^aanother in his stead, and also of destroying the people of Anti-Nephi-Lehi out of the land.

21 Now when the people saw that they were coming against them they went out to meet them, and ^aprostrated themselves before them to the earth, and began to call on the name of the Lord; and thus they were in this attitude when the Lamanites began to fall upon them, and began to slay them with the sword.

22 And thus without meeting any resistance, they did slay a ^athousand and five of them; and we know that they are blessed, for they have gone to dwell with their God.

23 Now when the Lamanites saw that their brethren would not flee from the sword, neither would they turn aside to the right hand or to the left, but that they would lie down and ^aperish, and ^bpraised God even in the very act of perishing under the sword—

24 Now when the Lamanites saw

this they did ^aforbear from slaying them; and there were many whose hearts had ^bswollen in them for those of their brethren who had fallen under the sword, for they repented of the things which they had done.

25 And it came to pass that they threw down their weapons of war, and they would not take them again, for they were stung for the murders which they had committed; and they came down even as their brethren, relying upon the mercies of those whose arms were lifted to slay them.

26 And it came to pass that the people of God were joined that day by more than the number who had been slain; and those who had been slain were righteous people, therefore we have no reason to doubt but what they were ^asaved.

27 And there was not a wicked man slain among them; but there were more than a thousand brought to the knowledge of the truth; thus we see that the Lord worketh in many ^aways to the salvation of his people.

28 Now the greatest number of those of the Lamanites who slew so many of their brethren were Amalekites and Amulonites, the greatest number of whom were after the ^aorder of the ^bNehors.

29 Now, among those who joined the people of the Lord, there were ^anone who were Amalekites or Amulonites, or who were of the order of Nehor, but they were actual descendants of Laman and Lemuel.

30 And thus we can plainly discern, that after a people have been once ^aenlightened by the ^bSpirit of God, and have had great ^cknowledge of things pertaining to righteousness, and then have ^dfallen away into

---

18c TG Self-Sacrifice.
19a TG Faith.
  b TG Integrity.
20a Isa. 7:6.
21a Alma 27:3.
22a Alma 26:34.
23a Alma 26:32.
  b Mosiah 16:7.
24a Alma 25:1.
  b TG Compassion;

Repent.
26a Isa. 57:1;
     Rev. 14:13.
27a 2 Kgs. 5:15;
     Isa. 55:8 (8–9);
     Alma 37:7 (6–7).
28a Alma 21:4.
  b Alma 1:15; 2:1 (1, 20);
     16:11.
29a Alma 23:14.

30a Matt. 12:45.
  b TG God, Spirit of.
  c Heb. 10:26 (26–27);
     Alma 47:36.
  d 2 Ne. 31:14;
     Alma 9:19; 31:8;
     D&C 93:19.
     TG Apostasy of
     Individuals;
     Holy Ghost, Loss of.

sin and transgression, they become more *e*hardened, and thus their state becomes *f*worse than though they had never known these things.

CHAPTER 25

Lamanite aggressions spread—The seed of the priests of Noah perish as Abinadi prophesied—Many Lamanites are converted and join the people of Anti-Nephi-Lehi—They believe in Christ and keep the law of Moses. About 90–77 B.C.

AND behold, now it came to pass that those Lamanites were more angry because they had slain their brethren; therefore they swore vengeance upon the Nephites; and they did *a*no more attempt to slay the people of *b*Anti-Nephi-Lehi at that time.

2 But they took their armies and went over into the borders of the land of Zarahemla, and fell upon the people who were in the land of Ammonihah and *a*destroyed them.

3 And after that, they had *a*many battles with the Nephites, in the which they were driven and slain.

4 And among the Lamanites who were slain were almost all the *a*seed of Amulon and his brethren, who were the priests of Noah, and they were slain by the hands of the Nephites;

5 And the remainder, having fled into the east wilderness, and having usurped the power and *a*authority over the Lamanites, caused that many of the Lamanites should *b*perish by fire because of their belief—

6 For many of *a*them, after having suffered much loss and so many afflictions, began to be stirred up in remembrance of the *b*words which Aaron and his brethren had

preached to them in their land; therefore they began to disbelieve the *c*traditions of their fathers, and to believe in the Lord, and that he gave great power unto the Nephites; and thus there were many of them converted in the wilderness.

7 And it came to pass that those rulers who were the remnant of the children of *a*Amulon caused that they should be put to *b*death, yea, all those that believed in these things.

8 Now this martyrdom caused that many of their brethren should be stirred up to anger; and there began to be contention in the wilderness; and the Lamanites began to *a*hunt the seed of Amulon and his brethren and began to slay them; and they fled into the east wilderness.

9 And behold they are hunted at this day by the Lamanites. Thus the words of Abinadi were brought to pass, which he said concerning the seed of the priests who caused that he should suffer death by fire.

10 For he said unto them: What ye shall *a*do unto me shall be a type of things to come.

11 And now Abinadi was the first that suffered *a*death by fire because of his belief in God; now this is what he meant, that many should suffer death by fire, according as he had suffered.

12 And he said unto the priests of Noah that their seed should cause many to be put to death, in the like manner as he was, and that they should be scattered abroad and slain, even as a sheep having no shepherd is driven and slain by wild beasts; and now behold, these words were verified, for they were driven by the Lamanites, and they were hunted, and they were smitten.

13 And it came to pass that when

30*e* TG Hardheartedness.
   f 2 Chr. 33:9;
      Ezek. 5:6;
      2 Pet. 2:20 (20–21).
25 1*a* Alma 24:24 (20–25).
   b Alma 27:2.
   2*a* Alma 8:16; 16:9.

3*a* Alma 27:1.
4*a* Mosiah 23:35.
5*a* TG Authority.
   b Mosiah 17:15.
6*a* IE the Lamanites.
   b Alma 21:9 (5–12).
   c Alma 26:24.

7*a* Alma 21:3 (2–4);
      24:1 (1, 28–30).
   b TG Martyrdom.
8*a* Mosiah 17:18.
10*a* Mosiah 13:10.
11*a* Mosiah 17:13 (13–20).

the Lamanites saw that they could not overpower the Nephites they returned again to their own land; and many of them came over to dwell in the land of [a]Ishmael and the land of Nephi, and did join themselves to the people of God, who were the people of [b]Anti-Nephi-Lehi.

14 And they did also [a]bury their weapons of war, according as their brethren had, and they began to be a righteous people; and they did walk in the ways of the Lord, and did observe to keep his commandments and his statutes.

15 Yea, and they did keep the law of Moses; for it was expedient that they should keep the law of Moses as yet, for it was not all fulfilled. But notwithstanding the [a]law of Moses, they did look forward to the coming of Christ, considering that the law of Moses was a [b]type of his coming, and believing that they must keep those [c]outward [d]performances until the time that he should be revealed unto them.

16 Now they did not suppose that [a]salvation came by the [b]law of Moses; but the law of Moses did serve to strengthen their faith in Christ; and thus they did retain a [c]hope through faith, unto eternal salvation, relying upon the spirit of prophecy, which spake of those things to come.

17 And now behold, Ammon, and Aaron, and Omner, and Himni, and their brethren did rejoice exceedingly, for the success which they had had among the Lamanites, seeing that the Lord had granted unto them according to their [a]prayers, and that he had also verified his word unto them in every particular.

CHAPTER 26

Ammon glories in the Lord—The faithful are strengthened by the Lord and are given knowledge—By faith men may bring thousands of souls unto repentance—God has all power and comprehends all things. About 90–77 B.C.

AND now, these are the words of Ammon to his brethren, which say thus: My brothers and my brethren, behold I say unto you, how great reason have we to rejoice; for could we have supposed when we [a]started from the land of Zarahemla that God would have granted unto us such great blessings?

2 And now, I ask, what great blessings has he bestowed upon us? Can ye tell?

3 Behold, I answer for you; for our brethren, the Lamanites, were in darkness, yea, even in the darkest abyss, but behold, how [a]many of them are brought to behold the marvelous light of God! And this is the blessing which hath been bestowed upon us, that we have been made [b]instruments in the hands of God to bring about this great work.

4 Behold, [a]thousands of them do rejoice, and have been brought into the fold of God.

5 Behold, the [a]field was ripe, and blessed are ye, for ye did thrust in the [b]sickle, and did reap with your might, yea, all the day long did ye labor; and behold the number of your [c]sheaves! And they shall be

13a Alma 22:1 (1, 4).
  b Alma 24:1 (1–3, 5, 20);
     27:21 (2, 21, 25).
14a Alma 24:15; 26:32.
15a Jacob 4:5;
     Jarom 1:11.
  b Mosiah 16:14.
     TG Jesus Christ, Types
     of, in Anticipation.
  c Josh. 1:8;
     Mosiah 3:14 (14–15);
     13:29 (29–32);

D&C 41:5 (4–5).
  d TG Ordinance.
16a Mosiah 3:15; 12:31;
     13:28 (27–33).
  b 2 Ne. 11:4;
     Jacob 4:5;
     Jarom 1:11;
     Ether 12:19 (18–19).
  c Alma 33:22 (19–23);
     37:46 (45–46).
17a Alma 17:9 (7–11).
26 1a Mosiah 28:9;

Alma 17:6 (6–11).
3a Alma 23:8 (8–13).
  b 2 Cor. 4:5;
     Mosiah 23:10.
4a Alma 23:5; 26:31.
5a John 4:35;
     D&C 4:4.
  b Joel 3:13.
  c D&C 33:9; 75:5.
     TG Reward.

gathered into the garners, that they are not wasted.

6 Yea, they shall not be beaten down by the storm at the last day; yea, neither shall they be harrowed up by the whirlwinds; but when the ^astorm cometh they shall be gathered together in their place, that the storm cannot penetrate to them; yea, neither shall they be driven with fierce winds whithersoever the enemy listeth to carry them.

7 But behold, they are in the hands of the Lord of the ^aharvest, and they are his; and he will ^braise them up at the last day.

8 ^aBlessed be the name of our God; let us ^bsing to his praise, yea, let us give ^cthanks to his holy name, for he doth work righteousness forever.

9 For if we had not come up out of the land of Zarahemla, these our dearly beloved brethren, who have so dearly beloved us, would still have been racked with ^ahatred against us, yea, and they would also have been ^bstrangers to God.

10 And it came to pass that when Ammon had said these words, his brother Aaron rebuked him, saying: Ammon, I fear that thy joy doth carry thee away unto boasting.

11 But Ammon said unto him: I do not ^aboast in my own strength, nor in my own wisdom; but behold, my ^bjoy is full, yea, my heart is brim with ^cjoy, and I will rejoice in my God.

12 Yea, I know that I am ^anothing; as to my strength I am weak; therefore I will ^bnot boast of myself, but I will ^cboast of my God, for in

his ^dstrength I can do all ^ethings; yea, behold, many mighty miracles we have wrought in this land, for which we will praise his name forever.

13 Behold, how many thousands of our brethren has he loosed from the pains of ^ahell; and they are brought to ^bsing redeeming love, and this because of the power of his word which is in us, therefore have we not great reason to rejoice?

14 Yea, we have reason to praise him forever, for he is the Most High God, and has loosed our brethren from the ^achains of hell.

15 Yea, they were encircled about with everlasting ^adarkness and destruction; but behold, he has brought them into his everlasting ^blight, yea, into everlasting salvation; and they are encircled about with the matchless bounty of his love; yea, and we have been instruments in his hands of doing this great and marvelous work.

16 Therefore, let us ^aglory, yea, we will ^bglory in the Lord; yea, we will rejoice, for our joy is full; yea, we will praise our God forever. Behold, who can glory too much in the Lord? Yea, who can say too much of his great power, and of his ^cmercy, and of his long-suffering towards the children of men? Behold, I say unto you, I cannot say the smallest part which I feel.

17 Who could have supposed that our God would have been so merciful as to have snatched us from our awful, sinful, and ^apolluted state?

18 Behold, we went forth even in

6a Hel. 5:12;
   3 Ne. 14:25 (25, 27).
7a TG Harvest.
  b Mosiah 23:22;
   Alma 36:28.
8a Ps. 41:13.
  b Ps. 57:7 (7–11);
   108:1 (1–5);
   2 Ne. 22:5 (5–6).
  c TG Thanksgiving.
9a Mosiah 28:2.
  b TG Stranger.
11a 2 Cor. 7:14 (13–16).

  b 1 Thes. 3:9;
   D&C 18:16 (14–16).
  c TG Joy.
12a TG Poor in Spirit.
  b Alma 29:9.
  c Jer. 9:24;
   Rom. 15:17.
  d Isa. 45:24;
   Philip. 4:13 (12–13);
   1 Ne. 17:3.
  e Ps. 18:32 (32–40);
   1 Ne. 7:12.
13a TG Hell.

  b Alma 5:26.
14a Alma 12:11.
15a Prov. 20:20.
  b TG Light [noun].
16a Rom. 15:17;
   1 Cor. 1:31.
  b Ps. 44:8 (4–8);
   2 Cor. 10:17 (15–18);
   D&C 76:61.
  c Ps. 36:5 (5–6);
   Morm. 6:22;
   D&C 97:6.
17a TG Pollution.

wrath, with mighty threatenings to ᵃdestroy his church.

19 Oh then, why did he not consign us to an awful destruction, yea, why did he not let the sword of his justice fall upon us, and doom us to eternal ᵃdespair?

20 Oh, my soul, almost as it were, fleeth at the thought. Behold, he did not exercise his justice upon us, but in his great mercy hath brought us over that everlasting ᵃgulf of death and misery, even to the salvation of our souls.

21 And now behold, my brethren, what ᵃnatural man is there that knoweth these things? I say unto you, there is ᵇnone that ᶜknoweth these things, save it be the penitent.

22 Yea, he that ᵃrepenteth and exerciseth faith, and bringeth forth good ᵇworks, and prayeth continually without ceasing—unto such it is given to know the ᶜmysteries of God; yea, unto such it shall be ᵈgiven to ᵉreveal things which never have been revealed; yea, and it shall be given unto such to bring thousands of souls to repentance, even as it has been given unto us to bring these our brethren to repentance.

23 Now do ye remember, my brethren, that we said unto our brethren in the land of Zarahemla, we go up to the land of Nephi, to preach unto our brethren, the Lamanites, and they ᵃlaughed us to scorn?

24 For they said unto us: Do ye suppose that ye can bring the Lamanites to the knowledge of the truth? Do ye suppose that ye can convince the Lamanites of the ᵃincorrectness of the ᵇtraditions of their fathers,

as ᶜstiffnecked a people as they are; whose hearts delight in the ᵈshedding of blood; whose days have been spent in the grossest iniquity; whose ways have been the ways of a transgressor from the beginning? Now my brethren, ye remember that this was their language.

25 And moreover they did say: Let us take up arms against them, that we destroy them and their iniquity out of the land, lest they overrun us and destroy us.

26 But behold, my beloved brethren, we came into the wilderness not with the intent to destroy our brethren, but with the intent that perhaps we might save some few of their souls.

27 Now when our hearts were depressed, and we were about to ᵃturn back, behold, the Lord ᵇcomforted us, and said: Go amongst thy brethren, the Lamanites, and bear with ᶜpatience thine ᵈafflictions, and I will give unto you success.

28 And now behold, we have come, and been forth amongst them; and we have been patient in our sufferings, and we have suffered every privation; yea, we have traveled from house to house, relying upon the mercies of the world—not upon the mercies of the world alone but upon the mercies of God.

29 And we have entered into their houses and taught them, and we have taught them in their streets; yea, and we have taught them upon their hills; and we have also entered into their temples and their ᵃsynagogues and taught them; and we have been cast out, and mocked, and spit upon, and smote upon our

---

18a Mosiah 27:10;
    28:4 (3–4);
    Alma 36:6 (6–11).
19a TG Despair.
20a 2 Ne. 1:13;
    Hel. 3:29.
21a TG Man, Natural, Not
    Spiritually Reborn.
  b Alma 36:5.
  c 1 Cor. 2:11 (9–16);
    Jacob 4:8 (8–10, 13).
22a TG Repent.

  b TG Good Works.
  c Luke 8:10;
    Alma 12:9.
    TG Mysteries of
    Godliness.
  d Dan. 2:22 (19–22, 28).
  e Jarom 1:4;
    Hel. 11:23;
    D&C 107:19 (18–19).
23a 2 Chr. 30:10;
    Neh. 2:19; Luke 8:53.
    TG Laughter.

24a Mosiah 1:5; 28:2.
  b Alma 23:3; 25:6.
  c TG Stiffnecked.
  d Jacob 7:24;
    Jarom 1:6.
27a Hel. 13:2 (2–3).
  b Alma 17:10.
  c Alma 17:11.
    TG Patience.
  d Alma 7:5.
    TG Affliction.
29a Alma 23:2 (2, 4).

cheeks; and we have been *b*stoned, and taken and bound with *c*strong cords, and cast into prison; and through the power and wisdom of God we have been delivered again.

30 And we have suffered all manner of afflictions, and all this, that perhaps we might be the means of saving some soul; and we supposed that our *a*joy would be full if perhaps we could be the means of saving some.

31 Now behold, we can look forth and see the *a*fruits of our labors; and are they few? I say unto you, Nay, they are *b*many; yea, and we can witness of their sincerity, because of their love towards their brethren and also towards us.

32 For behold, they had rather *a*sacrifice their lives than even to take the life of their enemy; and they have *b*buried their weapons of war deep in the earth, because of their love towards their brethren.

33 And now behold I say unto you, has there been so great love in all the land? Behold, I say unto you, Nay, there has not, even among the Nephites.

34 For behold, they would take up arms against their brethren; they would not suffer themselves to be slain. But behold how *a*many of these have laid down their lives; and we know that they have gone to their God, because of their love and of their hatred to sin.

35 Now have we not reason to rejoice? Yea, I say unto you, there never were men that had so great reason to rejoice as we, since the world began; yea, and my joy is carried away, even unto boasting in my God; for he has all *a*power, *b*all wisdom, and all understanding; he comprehendeth all things, and

he is a *c*merciful Being, even unto salvation, to those who will repent and believe on his name.

36 Now if this is *a*boasting, even so will I boast; for this is my life and my light, my joy and my salvation, and my redemption from everlasting wo. Yea, blessed is the name of my God, who has been mindful of this people, who are a *b*branch of the tree of Israel, and has been *c*lost from its body in a strange land; yea, I say, blessed be the name of my God, who has been mindful of us, *d*wanderers in a strange land.

37 Now my brethren, we see that God is *a*mindful of every *b*people, whatsoever land they may be in; yea, he numbereth his people, and his bowels of mercy are over all the earth. Now this is my joy, and my great thanksgiving; yea, and I will give thanks unto my God forever. Amen.

CHAPTER 27

The Lord commands Ammon to lead the people of Anti-Nephi-Lehi to safety—Upon meeting Alma, Ammon's joy exhausts his strength—The Nephites give the Anti-Nephi-Lehies the land of Jershon—They are called the people of Ammon. About 90–77 B.C.

NOW it came to pass that when those Lamanites who had gone to war against the Nephites had found, after their *a*many struggles to destroy them, that it was in vain to seek their destruction, they returned again to the land of Nephi.

2 And it came to pass that the Amalekites, because of their loss, were exceedingly angry. And when they saw that they could not seek revenge from the Nephites, they began to *a*stir up the people in anger

29*b* 2 Cor. 11:23 (23–29).
  c Alma 20:30 (29–30).
30*a* D&C 18:15 (15–16).
31*a* Acts 21:19 (19–20).
  b Alma 23:8 (8–13); 26:4.
32*a* Alma 24:23 (20–24).
  b Alma 24:15; 25:14.
34*a* Alma 24:22.
35*a* TG God, Intelligence of;

God, Perfection of;
God, Wisdom of.
  b D&C 88:41.
  c TG God, Mercy of.
36*a* Rom. 3:27.
  b Gen. 49:22 (22–26);
Ezek. 17:22;
Jacob 2:25.
  c Jacob 5:25 (25, 40–45).

d Jacob 7:26.
37*a* 2 Ne. 2:27; 26:24;
Jacob 5:41.
  b Jonah 4:11 (10–11);
Acts 10:35 (9–35, 44);
2 Ne. 26:33.
27 1*a* Alma 25:3.
  2*a* Acts 13:50.

against their [b]brethren, the people of [c]Anti-Nephi-Lehi; therefore they began again to destroy them.

3 Now this people [a]again refused to take their arms, and they suffered themselves to be slain according to the desires of their enemies.

4 Now when Ammon and his brethren saw this work of destruction among those whom they so dearly beloved, and among those who had so dearly beloved them—for they were treated as though they were angels sent from God to save them from everlasting destruction—therefore, when Ammon and his brethren saw this great work of destruction, they were moved with compassion, and they [a]said unto the king:

5 Let us gather together this people of the Lord, and let us go down to the land of Zarahemla to our brethren the Nephites, and flee out of the hands of our enemies, that we be not destroyed.

6 But the king said unto them: Behold, the Nephites will destroy us, because of the many murders and sins we have committed against them.

7 And Ammon said: I will go and inquire of the Lord, and if he say unto us, go down unto our brethren, will ye go?

8 And the king said unto him: Yea, if the Lord saith unto us go, we will go down unto our brethren, and we will be their slaves until we repair unto them the many murders and sins which we have committed against them.

9 But Ammon said unto him: It is against the law of our brethren, which was established by my father, that there should be any [a]slaves among them; therefore let us go down and rely upon the mercies of our brethren.

10 But the king said unto him: Inquire of the Lord, and if he saith unto us go, we will go; otherwise we will perish in the land.

11 And it came to pass that Ammon went and inquired of the Lord, and the Lord said unto him:

12 Get this people [a]out of this land, that they perish not; for Satan has great hold on the hearts of the Amalekites, who do stir up the Lamanites to anger against their brethren to slay them; therefore get thee out of this land; and blessed are this people in this generation, for I will [b]preserve them.

13 And now it came to pass that Ammon went and told the king all the words which the Lord had said unto him.

14 And they gathered together all their people, yea, all the people of the Lord, and did gather together all their flocks and herds, and departed out of the land, and came into the wilderness which divided the land of Nephi from the land of Zarahemla, and came over near the borders of the land.

15 And it came to pass that Ammon said unto them: Behold, I and my brethren will go forth into the land of Zarahemla, and ye shall remain here until we return; and we will [a]try the hearts of our brethren, whether they will that ye shall come into their land.

16 And it came to pass that as Ammon was going forth into the land, that he and his brethren met Alma, over in the [a]place of which has been spoken; and behold, this was a joyful meeting.

17 Now the [a]joy of Ammon was so great even that he was full; yea, he was swallowed up in the joy of his God, even to the [b]exhausting of his strength; and he fell [c]again to the earth.

---

2 b Alma 43:11.
  c Alma 25:1.
3 a Alma 24:21 (21–26).
4 a Alma 24:5 (3–5).
9 a Mosiah 29:32 (32, 38, 40).

12 a TG Separation.
  b TG Protection, Divine.
15 a Judg. 7:4.
16 a Alma 17:1 (1–4).
17 a TG Joy.

  b Dan. 10:8 (8–12);
    1 Ne. 1:7.
  c Alma 19:14 (14, 17).

18 Now was not this *exceeding joy? Behold, this is joy which none receiveth save it be the truly penitent and humble seeker of *happiness.

19 Now the joy of Alma in meeting his *brethren was truly great, and also the joy of Aaron, of Omner, and Himni; but behold their joy was not that to exceed their strength.

20 And now it came to pass that Alma conducted his brethren back to the land of Zarahemla; even to his *own house. And they went and told the *chief judge all the things that had happened unto them in the land of Nephi, among their brethren, the Lamanites.

21 And it came to pass that the chief judge sent a proclamation throughout all the land, desiring the voice of the people concerning the admitting their brethren, who were the people of *Anti-Nephi-Lehi.

22 And it came to pass that the voice of the people came, saying: Behold, we will give up the *land of *Jershon, which is on the east by the sea, which joins the land Bountiful, which is on the south of the land Bountiful; and this land Jershon is the land which we will give unto our brethren for an inheritance.

23 And behold, we will set our armies between the land Jershon and the land Nephi, that we may *protect our brethren in the land Jershon; and this we do for our brethren, on account of their fear to take up arms against their brethren lest they should commit sin; and this their great fear came because of their sore repentance which they had, on account of their many murders and their awful wickedness.

24 And now behold, this will we do unto our brethren, that they may inherit the land Jershon; and we will guard them from their enemies with our armies, on condition that they will give us a *portion of their substance to assist us that we may maintain our armies.

25 Now, it came to pass that when Ammon had heard this, he returned to the people of Anti-Nephi-Lehi, and also Alma with him, into the wilderness, where they had pitched their tents, and made known unto them all these things. And Alma also related unto them his *conversion, with Ammon and Aaron, and his brethren.

26 And it came to pass that it did cause great joy among them. And they went down into the land of Jershon, and took possession of the land of Jershon; and they were called by the Nephites the *people of Ammon; therefore they were distinguished by that name ever after.

27 And they were among the people of Nephi, and also numbered among the people who were of the church of God. And they were also distinguished for their *zeal towards God, and also towards men; for they were perfectly *honest and upright in all things; and they were *firm in the faith of Christ, even unto the end.

28 And they did look upon shedding the blood of their brethren with the greatest abhorrence; and they never could be prevailed upon to take up arms against their brethren; and they never did look upon death with any degree of terror, for their hope and views of Christ and the resurrection; therefore, death was swallowed up to them by the victory of Christ over it.

29 Therefore, they would suffer

18a Alma 28:8.
  b TG Happiness;
    Objectives.
19a TG Friendship.
20a Alma 15:18.
  b Alma 4:17 (16–18).
21a Alma 25:13 (1, 13);

43:11.
22a Alma 43:12.
  b Alma 28:1 (1, 8).
23a Alma 43:12.
24a Alma 43:13.
25a Mosiah 27:24 (10–25).
26a Alma 30:1.

27a TG Zeal.
  b Prov. 19:1;
    D&C 124:20 (15, 20).
    TG Honesty.
  c Alma 23:6;
    Hel. 15:8 (6–10).

[a]death in the most aggravating and distressing manner which could be inflicted by their brethren, before they would take the sword or cimeter to smite them.

30 And thus they were a zealous and beloved people, a highly favored people of the Lord.

CHAPTER 28

The Lamanites are defeated in a tremendous battle—Tens of thousands are slain—The wicked are consigned to a state of endless woe; the righteous attain a never-ending happiness. About 77–76 B.C.

AND now it came to pass that after the people of Ammon were established in the land of [a]Jershon, and a church also established in the land of Jershon, and the armies of the Nephites were set round about the land of Jershon, yea, in all the borders round about the land of Zarahemla; behold the armies of the Lamanites had followed their brethren into the wilderness.

2 And thus there was a tremendous battle; yea, even such an one as never had been known among all the people in the land from the time Lehi left Jerusalem; yea, and tens of thousands of the Lamanites were slain and scattered abroad.

3 Yea, and also there was a tremendous slaughter among the people of Nephi; nevertheless, the Lamanites were [a]driven and scattered, and the people of Nephi returned again to their land.

4 And now this was a time that there was a great [a]mourning and lamentation heard throughout all the land, among all the people of Nephi—

5 Yea, the cry of [a]widows mourning for their husbands, and also of fathers mourning for their sons,

and the daughter for the brother, yea, the brother for the father; and thus the cry of mourning was heard among all of them, mourning for their kindred who had been slain.

6 And now surely this was a sorrowful day; yea, a time of solemnity, and a time of much [a]fasting and prayer.

7 And thus endeth the fifteenth year of the reign of the judges over the people of Nephi;

8 And [a]this is the account of Ammon and his brethren, their journeyings in the land of Nephi, their sufferings in the land, their sorrows, and their afflictions, and their [b]incomprehensible joy, and the reception and safety of the brethren in the land of Jershon. And now may the Lord, the Redeemer of all men, bless their souls forever.

9 And this is the account of the wars and contentions among the Nephites, and also the wars between the Nephites and the Lamanites; and the fifteenth year of the reign of the judges is ended.

10 And from the [a]first year to the fifteenth has brought to pass the destruction of many thousand lives; yea, it has brought to pass an awful scene of bloodshed.

11 And the bodies of many thousands are laid low in the earth, while the bodies of many thousands are [a]moldering in heaps upon the face of the earth; yea, and many thousands are [b]mourning for the loss of their kindred, because they have reason to fear, according to the promises of the Lord, that they are consigned to a state of endless wo.

12 While many thousands of others truly [a]mourn for the loss of their kindred, yet they rejoice and exult in the hope, and even know, according to the [b]promises of the Lord, that

---

29a Alma 24:23 (20–23).
28 1a Alma 27:22;
   30:19 (1, 19).
  3a Alma 30:1.
  4a TG Mourning.
  5a TG Widows.

6a Matt. 5:4; Alma 30:2;
   3 Ne. 12:4.
8a IE the account covered
   in Alma 17–28.
  b Alma 27:18 (16–19).
10a IE the years recounted

   in Alma 1–28.
11a Alma 16:11.
  b Alma 48:23;
   D&C 42:45.
12a Gen. 50:10.
  b Alma 11:41.

they are raised to dwell at the right hand of God, in a state of never-ending ᶜhappiness.

13 And thus we see how great the ᵃinequality of man is because of sin and ᵇtransgression, and the power of the devil, which comes by the cunning ᶜplans which he hath devised to ensnare the hearts of men.

14 And thus we see the great call of ᵃdiligence of men to labor in the vineyards of the Lord; and thus we see the great reason of sorrow, and also of rejoicing—sorrow because of death and destruction among men, and joy because of the ᵇlight of Christ unto life.

CHAPTER 29

Alma desires to cry repentance with angelic zeal—The Lord grants teachers for all nations—Alma glories in the Lord's work and in the success of Ammon and his brethren. About 76 B.C.

O THAT I were an angel, and could have the wish of mine heart, that I might go forth and speak with the ᵃtrump of God, with a voice to shake the earth, and cry repentance unto every people!

2 Yea, I would declare unto every soul, as with the voice of thunder, repentance and the plan of redemption, that they should repent and ᵃcome unto our God, that there might not be more sorrow upon all the face of the earth.

3 But behold, I am a man, and do sin in my wish; for I ought to be content with the things which the Lord hath allotted unto me.

4 I ought not to harrow up in my desires the firm decree of a just God,

for I know that he granteth unto men according to their ᵃdesire, whether it be unto death or unto life; yea, I know that he allotteth unto men, yea, decreeth unto them decrees which are unalterable, according to their ᵇwills, whether they be unto salvation or unto destruction.

5 Yea, and I know that good and evil have come before all men; he that knoweth not good from evil is ᵃblameless; but he that ᵇknoweth good and evil, to him it is given according to his desires, whether he desireth good or evil, life or death, joy or remorse of ᶜconscience.

6 Now, seeing that I know these things, why should I desire more than to ᵃperform the work to which I have been called?

7 Why should I desire that I were an angel, that I could speak unto all the ends of the earth?

8 For behold, the Lord doth ᵃgrant unto ᵇall nations, of their own nation and ᶜtongue, to teach his word, yea, in wisdom, all that he ᵈseeth fit that they should have; therefore we see that the Lord doth counsel in wisdom, according to that which is just and true.

9 I know that which the Lord hath commanded me, and I glory in it. I do ᵃnot ᵇglory of myself, but I glory in that which the Lord hath commanded me; yea, and this is my glory, that perhaps I may be an instrument in the hands of God to bring some soul to repentance; and this is my joy.

10 And behold, when I see many of my brethren truly penitent, and coming to the Lord their God, then is my soul filled with joy; then do I remember ᵃwhat the Lord has done

---

12c Alma 56:11.
13a 1 Ne. 17:35.
  b TG Transgress.
  c 2 Ne. 9:28.
14a TG Diligence;
    Vineyard of the Lord.
  b TG Light of Christ.
29 1a Isa. 58:1;
     D&C 29:4.
  2a Omni 1:26 (25–26);
     3 Ne. 21:20.

4a Ps. 21:2; 37:4.
  b TG Agency.
5a TG Accountability.
  b Gen. 3:5;
    2 Ne. 2:18 (18, 26);
    Mosiah 16:3;
    Moro. 7:16 (15–19).
    TG Discernment,
    Spiritual.
  c Job 27:6.
    TG Conscience.

6a TG Stewardship.
8a 3 Ne. 26:8 (7–10);
    D&C 11:22.
  b 2 Ne. 2:27; 29:12.
  c D&C 90:11.
  d Alma 12:9 (9–11).
9a Alma 26:12.
  b TG Glory.
10a Mosiah 27:14 (11–31).

for me, yea, even that he hath heard my prayer; yea, then do I remember his merciful arm which he extended towards me.

11 Yea, and I also remember the captivity of my fathers; for I surely do know that the ^aLord did deliver them out of bondage, and by this did establish his church; yea, the Lord God, the God of Abraham, the God of Isaac, and the God of Jacob, did deliver them out of bondage.

12 Yea, I have always remembered the captivity of my fathers; and that same God who ^adelivered them out of the hands of the Egyptians did deliver them out of ^bbondage.

13 Yea, and that same God did establish his church among them; yea, and that same God hath called me by a ^aholy calling, to ^bpreach the word unto this people, and hath given me much success, in the which my joy is full.

14 But I do not joy in my own ^asuccess alone, but my joy is more full because of the success of my brethren, who have been up to the land of Nephi.

15 Behold, they have labored exceedingly, and have brought forth much fruit; and how great shall be their reward!

16 Now, when I think of the success of these my brethren my soul is carried away, even to the separation of it from the body, as it were, so great is my ^ajoy.

17 And now may God grant unto these, my brethren, that they may sit down in the kingdom of God; yea, and also all those who are the fruit of their labors that they may go no more out, but that they may praise him forever. And may God grant that it may be done according to my words, even as I have spoken. Amen.

CHAPTER 30

Korihor, the anti-Christ, ridicules Christ, the Atonement, and the spirit of prophecy—He teaches that there is no God, no fall of man, no penalty for sin, and no Christ—Alma testifies that Christ will come and that all things denote there is a God—Korihor demands a sign and is struck dumb—The devil had appeared to Korihor as an angel and taught him what to say—Korihor is trodden down and dies. About 76–74 B.C.

BEHOLD, now it came to pass that after the ^apeople of Ammon were established in the land of Jershon, yea, and also after the Lamanites were ^bdriven out of the land, and their dead were buried by the people of the land—

2 Now their dead were not numbered because of the greatness of their numbers; neither were the dead of the Nephites numbered—but it came to pass after they had buried their dead, and also after the days of ^afasting, and ^bmourning, and prayer, (and it was in the sixteenth year of the reign of the judges over the people of Nephi) there began to be continual peace throughout all the land.

3 Yea, and the people did observe to keep the commandments of the Lord; and they were strict in observing the ^aordinances of God, according to the law of Moses; for they were taught to ^bkeep the law of Moses until it should be fulfilled.

4 And thus the people did have no disturbance in all the sixteenth year of the reign of the judges over the people of Nephi.

5 And it came to pass that in the commencement of the seventeenth year of the reign of the judges, there was continual peace.

6 But it came to pass in the latter end of the seventeenth year, there came a man into the land of

11*a* Ex. 3:6;
        Alma 36:2.
12*a* Micah 6:4.
    b Alma 5:5 (5–6);
        36:29 (2, 29).
13*a* Alma 5:3.

    b TG Preaching.
14*a* Alma 17:4 (1–4).
16*a* TG Joy.
30 1*a* Alma 27:26.
    b Alma 28:3 (2–3).
2*a* Alma 28:6.

    b TG Mourning.
3*a* TG Ordinance.
    b 2 Ne. 25:24;
        Jarom 1:5;
        Mosiah 2:3;
        Alma 34:14 (13–14).

Zarahemla, and he was ªAnti-Christ, for he began to preach unto the people ᵇagainst the prophecies which had been spoken by the prophets, concerning the coming of Christ.

7 Now there was no law against a ªman's ᵇbelief; for it was strictly contrary to the commands of God that there should be a law which should bring men on to unequal grounds.

8 For thus saith the scripture: ªChoose ye this day, whom ye will serve.

9 Now if a man desired to serve God, it was his privilege; or rather, if he believed in God it was his privilege to serve him; but if he did not believe in him there was no law to punish him.

10 But if he ªmurdered he was punished unto ᵇdeath; and if he ᶜrobbed he was also punished; and if he stole he was also punished; and if he committed ᵈadultery he was also punished; yea, for all this wickedness they were punished.

11 For there was a law that men should be judged according to their crimes. Nevertheless, there was no law against a man's belief; therefore, a man was punished only for the crimes which he had done; therefore all men were on ªequal grounds.

12 And this ªAnti-Christ, whose name was Korihor, (and the law could have no hold upon him) began to preach unto the people that there should be ᵇno Christ. And after this manner did he preach, saying:

13 O ye that are bound down under a ªfoolish and a vain hope, why do ye yoke yourselves with such foolish things? Why do ye look for a Christ? For no man can ᵇknow of anything which is to come.

14 Behold, these things which ye call prophecies, which ye say are handed down by holy prophets, behold, they are foolish traditions of your fathers.

15 How do ye know of their surety? Behold, ye cannot know of things which ye do not ªsee; therefore ye cannot know that there shall be a Christ.

16 Ye look forward and say that ye see a remission of your sins. But behold, it is the effect of a ªfrenzied mind; and this derangement of your minds comes because of the traditions of your fathers, which lead you away into a belief of things which are not so.

17 And many more such things did he say unto them, telling them that there could be no atonement made for the sins of men, but every man ªfared in this life according to the management of the creature; therefore every man prospered according to his genius, and that every man conquered according to his strength; and ᵇwhatsoever a man did was ᶜno crime.

18 And thus he did preach unto them, leading away the hearts of many, causing them to lift up their heads in their wickedness, yea, leading away many women, and also men, to commit whoredoms—telling them that when a man was dead, that was the end thereof.

19 Now this man went over to the land of ªJershon also, to preach these things among the people of Ammon, who were once the people of the Lamanites.

20 But behold they were more wise than many of the Nephites; for they took him, and bound him, and carried him before Ammon, who was a ªhigh priest over that people.

6a TG Antichrist;
    False Prophets.
  b TG False Doctrine;
    Prophets, Rejection of.
7a Alma 1:17.
  b Acts 18:13.
8a Josh. 24:15.
    TG Agency.
10a TG Murder.
  b TG Capital Punishment.

  c Alma 1:18.
  d TG Adulterer.
11a Mosiah 27:3; 29:32.
12a TG Antichrist.
  b Jacob 7:2 (2, 9);
    Alma 31:16 (16, 29); 34:5.
13a 1 Cor. 1:25 (18–25).
  b Jacob 7:7.
15a Hel. 16:20;
    Ether 12:5 (5–6, 19).

    TG Spiritual Blindness.
16a Acts 26:24 (24–25).
17a Prov. 16:25;
    2 Ne. 28:7 (5–9).
  b Alma 18:5.
  c Alma 1:4;
    Morm. 8:31.
19a Alma 28:1 (1, 8); 31:3.
20a Alma 46:38.

21 And it came to pass that he caused that he should be carried out of the land. And he came over into the land of Gideon, and began to preach unto them also; and here he did not have much success, for he was taken and bound and carried before the high priest, and also the chief judge over the land.

22 And it came to pass that the high priest said unto him: Why do ye go about perverting the ways of the Lord? Why do ye teach this people that there shall be no Christ, to interrupt their rejoicings? Why do ye speak against all the prophecies of the holy prophets?

23 Now the high priest's name was Giddonah. And Korihor said unto him: Because I do not teach the foolish traditions of your fathers, and because I do not teach this people to bind themselves down under the foolish ordinances and performances which are laid down by ancient priests, to usurp power and authority over them, to keep them in ignorance, that they may not lift up their heads, but be brought down according to thy words.

24 Ye say that this people is a free people. Behold, I say they are in bondage. Ye say that those ancient prophecies are true. Behold, I say that ye do not know that they are true.

25 Ye say that this people is a guilty and a fallen people, because of the transgression of a parent. Behold, I say that a child is not guilty because of its parents.

26 And ye also say that Christ shall come. But behold, I say that ye do not know that there shall be a Christ. And ye say also that he shall be slain for the *a*sins of the world—

27 And thus ye lead away this people after the foolish traditions of your fathers, and according to your own desires; and ye keep them

down, even as it were in bondage, that ye may glut yourselves with the labors of their hands, that they durst not look up with boldness, and that they durst not enjoy their rights and privileges.

28 Yea, they durst not make use of that which is their own lest they should offend their priests, who do yoke them according to their desires, and have brought them to believe, by their traditions and their dreams and their whims and their visions and their pretended mysteries, that they should, if they did not do according to their words, offend some unknown being, who they say is God—a being who *a*never has been seen or known, who *b*never was nor ever will be.

29 Now when the high priest and the *a*chief judge saw the hardness of his heart, yea, when they saw that he would *b*revile even against God, they would not make any reply to his words; but they caused that he should be bound; and they delivered him up into the hands of the officers, and sent him to the land of Zarahemla, that he might be brought before Alma, and the chief judge who was governor over all the land.

30 And it came to pass that when he was brought before Alma and the chief judge, he did go on in the same manner as he did in the land of Gideon; yea, he went on to *a*blaspheme.

31 And he did rise up in great *a*swelling words before Alma, and did revile against the *b*priests and teachers, accusing them of leading away the people after the silly traditions of their fathers, for the sake of glutting on the labors of the people.

32 Now Alma said unto him: Thou knowest that we do not glut ourselves upon the labors of this people; for behold I have *a*labored even from

---

26a Isa. 53:6 (4–12).
28a 2 Ne. 28:5.
  b Alma 30:53.
29a Alma 4:17.

  b TG Reviling.
30a TG Blaspheme.
31a Hel. 13:22.
  TG Boast.

  b Alma 23:4.
32a TG Labor;
  Self-Sacrifice.

the commencement of the reign of the judges until now, with mine ^bown hands for my support, notwithstanding my many travels round about the land to declare the word of God unto my people.

33 And notwithstanding the many labors which I have performed in the church, I have never received so much as even one ^asenine for my labor; neither has any of my brethren, save it were in the judgment-seat; and then we have received only according to law for our time.

34 And now, if we do not receive anything for our labors in the church, what doth it profit us to labor in the church save it were to declare the truth, that we may have rejoicings in the ^ajoy of our brethren?

35 Then why sayest thou that we preach unto this people to get gain, when thou, of thyself, knowest that we receive no gain? And now, believest thou that we deceive this people, that ^acauses such joy in their hearts?

36 And Korihor answered him, Yea.

37 And then Alma said unto him: Believest thou that there is a God?

38 And he answered, Nay.

39 Now Alma said unto him: Will ye deny again that there is a God, and also deny the Christ? For behold, I say unto you, I know there is a God, and also that Christ shall come.

40 And now what evidence have ye that there is no ^aGod, or that Christ cometh not? I say unto you that ye have none, save it be your word only.

41 But, behold, I have all things as a ^atestimony that these things are true; and ye also have all things as a testimony unto you that they are true; and will ye deny them? Believest thou that these things are true?

42 Behold, I know that thou ^abelievest, but thou art possessed with a ^blying spirit, and ye have put ^coff the Spirit of God that it may have no place in you; but the devil has power over you, and he doth carry you about, working devices that he may destroy the children of God.

43 And now Korihor said unto Alma: If thou wilt show me a ^asign, that I may be convinced that there is a God, yea, show unto me that he hath power, and then will I be convinced of the truth of thy words.

44 But Alma said unto him: Thou hast had signs enough; will ye tempt your God? Will ye say, Show unto me a sign, when ye have the testimony of ^aall these thy brethren, and also all the holy prophets? The scriptures are laid before thee, yea, and all things denote there is a God; yea, even the ^bearth, and ^call things that are upon the face of it, yea, and its ^dmotion, yea, and also all the ^eplanets which move in their regular form do witness that there is a Supreme Creator.

45 And yet do ye go about, leading away the hearts of this people, testifying unto them there is no God? And yet will ye deny against all these ^awitnesses? And he said: Yea, I will deny, except ye shall show me a sign.

46 And now it came to pass that Alma said unto him: Behold, I am grieved because of the hardness of your heart, yea, that ye will still resist the spirit of the truth, that thy soul may be destroyed.

47 But behold, it is ^abetter that thy

32b Acts 20:34 (33–35);
  1 Thes. 2:9;
  Mosiah 18:24.
33a Alma 11:3.
34a TG Joy.
35a Matt. 7:16.
40a Ps. 14:1.
41a TG Testimony.
42a Acts 26:27;
  Jacob 7:14;

Mosiah 12:30;
  Alma 30:52.
 b Jer. 27:10;
  Rom. 3:3–4;
  Mosiah 2:32.
 c 1 Sam. 16:14.
43a John 6:30;
  Jacob 7:13 (13–21);
  D&C 46:9 (8–9).
  TG Sign Seekers.

44a Mosiah 13:33 (33–34).
 b Job 12:8 (7–10).
  TG Nature, Earth.
 c D&C 88:47.
 d Hel. 12:15 (11–15).
 e Moses 6:63.
  TG Astronomy.
45a TG Witness.
47a 1 Ne. 4:13.

soul should be [b]lost than that thou shouldst be the means of bringing many souls down to destruction, by thy lying and by thy flattering words; therefore if thou shalt deny again, behold God shall smite thee, that thou shalt become dumb, that thou shalt never open thy mouth any more, that thou shalt not deceive this people any more.

48 Now Korihor said unto him: I do not deny the existence of a God, but I do not believe that there is a God; and I say also, that ye do not know that there is a God; and except ye show me a sign, I will not believe.

49 Now Alma said unto him: This will I give unto thee for a sign, that thou shalt be [a]struck dumb, according to my words; and I say, that in the name of God, ye shall be struck dumb, that ye shall no more have utterance.

50 Now when Alma had said these words, Korihor was struck dumb, that he could not have utterance, according to the words of Alma.

51 And now when the chief judge saw this, he put forth his hand and wrote unto Korihor, saying: Art thou convinced of the power of God? In whom did ye desire that Alma should show forth his sign? Would ye that he should afflict others, to show unto thee a sign? Behold, he has showed unto you a sign; and now will ye dispute more?

52 And Korihor put forth his hand and wrote, saying: I know that I am dumb, for I cannot speak; and I know that nothing save it were the [a]power of God could bring this upon me; yea, and I always [b]knew that there was a God.

53 But behold, the devil hath [a]deceived me; for he [b]appeared unto me in the [c]form of an angel, and said unto me: Go and reclaim this people, for they have all gone astray after an unknown God. And he said unto me: There is [d]no God; yea, and he taught me that which I should say. And I have taught his words; and I taught them because they were pleasing unto the [e]carnal mind; and I taught them, even until I had much success, insomuch that I verily believed that they were true; and for this cause I withstood the truth, even until I have brought this great [f]curse upon me.

54 Now when he had said this, he besought that Alma should pray unto God, that the [a]curse might be taken from him.

55 But Alma said unto him: If this curse should be taken from thee thou wouldst again lead away the hearts of this people; therefore, it shall be unto thee even as the Lord will.

56 And it came to pass that the curse was not taken off of Korihor; but he was [a]cast out, and went about from house to house begging for his food.

57 Now the knowledge of what had happened unto Korihor was immediately published throughout all the land; yea, the proclamation was sent forth by the chief judge to all the people in the land, declaring unto those who had believed in the words of Korihor that they must speedily repent, [a]lest the same judgments would come unto them.

58 And it came to pass that they were all convinced of the wickedness of Korihor; therefore they were all converted again unto the Lord; and this put an end to the iniquity after the manner of Korihor. And Korihor did go about from house to house, begging food for his support.

59 And it came to pass that as he went forth among the people, yea, among a people who had separated themselves from the Nephites and called themselves [a]Zoramites, being

47b Mosiah 27:16.
49a Luke 1:20;
    Acts 13:11 (8–12).
52a 2 Chr. 13:20.
  b Alma 30:42 (41–42).
53a Jacob 7:14 (14, 18).
  b 2 Ne. 9:9.
  c 2 Cor. 11:14.
  d Ps. 10:4 (2–11);
    Alma 30:28.
  e TG Carnal Mind.
  f TG Curse.
54a Num. 12:13 (9–15).
56a Dan. 5:21.
57a John 5:14.
59a Alma 31:7 (7–8).

led by a man whose name was Zoram—and as he went forth amongst them, behold, he was run upon and trodden down, even until he was *b*dead.

60 And thus we see the end of him who *a*perverteth the ways of the Lord; and thus we see that the devil will not *b*support his children at the last day, but doth speedily drag them down to *c*hell.

CHAPTER 31

Alma heads a mission to reclaim the apostate Zoramites—The Zoramites deny Christ, believe in a false concept of election, and worship with set prayers—The missionaries are filled with the Holy Spirit—Their afflictions are swallowed up in the joy of Christ. About 74 B.C.

Now it came to pass that after the end of Korihor, Alma having received tidings that the Zoramites were perverting the ways of the Lord, and that Zoram, who was their leader, was leading the hearts of the people to *a*bow down to dumb *b*idols, his heart again began to *c*sicken because of the iniquity of the people.

2 For it was the cause of great *a*sorrow to Alma to know of iniquity among his people; therefore his heart was exceedingly *b*sorrowful because of the separation of the Zoramites from the Nephites.

3 Now the Zoramites had gathered themselves together in a land which they called *a*Antionum, which was east of the land of Zarahemla, which lay nearly bordering upon the seashore, which was south of the land of *b*Jershon, which also bordered upon the wilderness south, which wilderness was full of the Lamanites.

4 Now the Nephites greatly feared that the Zoramites would enter into a *a*correspondence with the Lamanites, and that it would be the means of great loss on the part of the Nephites.

5 And now, as the *a*preaching of the *b*word had a great tendency to *c*lead the people to do that which was just—yea, it had had more powerful effect upon the minds of the people than the sword, or anything else, which had happened unto them—therefore Alma thought it was expedient that they should try the virtue of the word of God.

6 Therefore he took Ammon, and Aaron, and Omner; and Himni he did leave in the church in Zarahemla; but the former three he took with him, and also *a*Amulek and Zeezrom, who were at *b*Melek; and he also took two of his sons.

7 Now the eldest of his sons he took not with him, and his name was Helaman; but the names of those whom he took with him were *a*Shiblon and *b*Corianton; and these are the names of those who went with him among the *c*Zoramites, to preach unto them the word.

8 Now the Zoramites were *a*dissenters from the Nephites; therefore they had had the word of God preached unto them.

9 But they had *a*fallen into great errors, for they would not observe to keep the commandments of God,

---

59*b* Jer. 28:16 (15–17);
　　Jacob 7:20 (1–20).
60*a* TG Lying.
　　b Alma 3:27 (26–27);
　　　5:42 (41–42);
　　　D&C 29:45.
　　c TG Hell.
31 1*a* Ex. 20:5;
　　Mosiah 13:13.
　　b 2 Ne. 9:37.
　　TG Idolatry.
　　c Alma 35:15.
2*a* 1 Ne. 7:8;
　　Mosiah 28:3;

3 Ne. 17:14; Moses 7:41.
　　b Isa. 22:4.
3*a* Alma 43:5 (5, 15, 22).
　　b Alma 27:22.
4*a* TG Conspiracy.
5*a* Ex. 24:7; Jonah 3:5;
　　Rom. 10:17;
　　Enos 1:23;
　　Alma 4:19.
　　TG Preaching.
　　b 2 Kgs. 22:11;
　　Heb. 4:12; Jacob 2:8;
　　Alma 36:26.
　　c Jarom 1:12;

Alma 45:21;
Hel. 5:51 (50–52);
D&C 11:2.
TG Gospel.
6*a* Hel. 5:41.
　　b Alma 8:3; 35:13; 45:18.
7*a* Alma 31:32; 35:14.
　　b Alma 39:1.
　　c Alma 30:59; 38:3.
8*a* Alma 24:30; 53:8;
Hel. 1:15;
D&C 93:19.
9*a* TG Apostasy of
Individuals.

and his statutes, according to the law of Moses.

10 Neither would they observe the ªperformances of the church, to continue in prayer and supplication to God daily, that they might not enter into temptation.

11 Yea, in fine, they did pervert the ways of the Lord in very many instances; therefore, for this cause, Alma and his brethren went into the land to preach the word unto them.

12 Now, when they had come into the land, behold, to their astonishment they found that the Zoramites had built synagogues, and that they did gather themselves together on one day of the week, which day they did call the day of the Lord; and they did ªworship after a manner which Alma and his brethren had never beheld;

13 For they had a place built up in the center of their synagogue, a place for standing, which was high above the head; and the top thereof would only admit one person.

14 Therefore, whosoever desired to ªworship must go forth and stand upon the top thereof, and stretch forth his hands towards heaven, and cry with a loud voice, saying:

15 Holy, holy God; we believe that thou art God, and we believe that thou art holy, and that thou wast a ªspirit, and that thou art a spirit, and that thou wilt be a spirit forever.

16 Holy God, we believe that thou hast separated us from our brethren; and we do not believe in the tradition of our brethren, which was handed down to them by the childishness of their fathers; but we believe that thou hast ªelected us to be thy ᵇholy children; and also thou hast made it known unto us that ᶜthere shall be ᵈno Christ.

17 But thou art the same yesterday, today, and forever; and thou hast ªelected us that we shall be saved, whilst all around us are elected to be cast by thy wrath down to hell; for the which holiness, O God, we thank thee; and we also thank thee that thou hast elected us, that we may not be led away after the foolish traditions of our brethren, which doth ᵇbind them down to a belief of Christ, which doth lead their hearts to wander far from thee, our God.

18 And again we thank thee, O God, that we are a chosen and a holy people. Amen.

19 Now it came to pass that after Alma and his brethren and his sons had heard these prayers, they were astonished beyond all measure.

20 For behold, every man did go forth and offer up these same ªprayers.

21 Now the place was called by them Rameumptom, which, being interpreted, is the holy stand.

22 Now, from this stand they did offer up, every man, the selfsame prayer unto God, thanking their God that they were chosen of him, and that he did not lead them away after the tradition of their brethren, and that their hearts were not stolen away to believe in things to come, which they knew nothing about.

23 Now, after the people had all offered up thanks after this manner, they returned to their homes, ªnever speaking of their God again until they had assembled themselves together again to the holy stand, to offer up thanks after their manner.

24 Now when Alma saw this his heart was ªgrieved; for he saw that they were a wicked and a perverse people; yea, he saw that their hearts were set upon gold, and upon silver, and upon all manner of fine goods.

10ª TG Ordinance.
12ª TG Worship.
14ª Matt. 6:5 (1–7).
15ª Alma 18:4 (4–5).
16ª Luke 18:11;
    Alma 38:14 (13–14).

ᵇ Isa. 65:5 (1–5).
ᶜ Alma 34:5.
ᵈ Jacob 7:2 (2, 9);
    Alma 30:12 (12, 22).
17ª TG Conceit;
    Pride.

ᵇ TG False Doctrine.
20ª Matt. 6:7.
23ª James 1:22 (21–25).
24ª Gen. 6:6;
    1 Ne. 2:18.

25 Yea, and he also saw that their hearts were ªlifted up unto great boasting, in their pride.

26 And he lifted up his voice to heaven, and ªcried, saying: O, how long, O Lord, wilt thou suffer that thy servants shall dwell here below in the flesh, to behold such gross wickedness among the children of men?

27 Behold, O God, they ªcry unto thee, and yet their hearts are swallowed up in their pride. Behold, O God, they cry unto thee with their mouths, while they are ᵇpuffed up, even to greatness, with the vain things of the ᶜworld.

28 Behold, O my God, their costly apparel, and their ringlets, and their ªbracelets, and their ornaments of gold, and all their precious things which they are ornamented with; and behold, their hearts are set upon them, and yet they cry unto thee and say—We thank thee, O God, for we are a chosen people unto thee, while others shall perish.

29 Yea, and they say that thou hast made it known unto them that there shall be no Christ.

30 O Lord God, how long wilt thou suffer that such wickedness and infidelity shall be among this people? O Lord, wilt thou give me strength, that I may ªbear with mine infirmities. For I am infirm, and such wickedness among this people doth pain my soul.

31 O Lord, my heart is exceedingly sorrowful; wilt thou comfort my soul ªin Christ. O Lord, wilt thou grant unto me that I may have strength, that I may suffer with patience these ᵇafflictions which shall come upon me, because of the iniquity of this people.

32 O Lord, wilt thou comfort my soul, and give unto me success, and also my fellow laborers who are with me—yea, Ammon, and Aaron, and Omner, and also ªAmulek and Zeezrom, and also my ᵇtwo sons—yea, even all these wilt thou comfort, O Lord. Yea, wilt thou comfort their souls in Christ.

33 Wilt thou grant unto them that they may have strength, that they may ªbear their afflictions which shall come upon them because of the iniquities of this people.

34 O Lord, wilt thou grant ªunto us that we may have success in bringing them again unto thee in Christ.

35 Behold, O Lord, their ªsouls are precious, and many of them are our brethren; therefore, give unto us, O Lord, power and wisdom that we may bring these, our brethren, again unto thee.

36 Now it came to pass that when Alma had said these words, that he ªclapped his ᵇhands upon all them who were with him. And behold, as he clapped his hands upon them, they were filled with the Holy Spirit.

37 And after that they did separate themselves one from another, ªtaking no thought for themselves what they should eat, or what they should drink, or what they should put on.

38 And the Lord provided for them that they should hunger not, neither should they thirst; yea, and he also gave them strength, that they should suffer no manner of ªafflictions, save it were swallowed up in the joy of Christ. Now this was according to the prayer of Alma; and this because he prayed in ᵇfaith.

25a 2 Kgs. 14:10;
     Jacob 2:13;
     Alma 1:32.
26a Moses 7:44 (41–58).
27a Isa. 29:13.
   TG Hypocrisy.
   b TG Pride; Selfishness.
   c TG Worldliness.
28a Isa. 3:19 (16–24).

30a Num. 11:14.
31a John 16:33.
   TG Comfort;
     Peace of God.
   b TG Affliction.
32a Alma 8:21; 34:1.
   b Alma 31:7.
33a Rom. 15:1.
34a 2 Ne. 26:33.

35a TG Worth of Souls.
36a 3 Ne. 18:37.
   b TG Hands, Laying on of.
37a Matt. 6:25 (25–34);
     3 Ne. 13:25 (25–34).
38a Matt. 5:10 (10–12);
     Mosiah 24:15 (13–15);
     Alma 33:23.
   b TG Faith.

CHAPTER 32

Alma teaches the poor whose afflictions had humbled them—Faith is a hope in that which is not seen which is true—Alma testifies that angels minister to men, women, and children—Alma compares the word unto a seed—It must be planted and nourished—Then it grows into a tree from which the fruit of eternal life is picked. About 74 B.C.

AND it came to pass that they did go forth, and began to preach the word of God unto the people, entering into their synagogues, and into their houses; yea, and even they did preach the word in their streets.

2 And it came to pass that after much labor among them, they began to have success among the ^apoor class of people; for behold, they were cast out of the synagogues because of the coarseness of their apparel—

3 Therefore they were not permitted to enter into their synagogues to worship God, being esteemed as filthiness; therefore they were poor; yea, they were esteemed by their brethren as ^adross; therefore they were ^bpoor as to things of the world; and also they were poor in heart.

4 Now, as Alma was teaching and speaking unto the people upon the hill ^aOnidah, there came a great ^bmultitude unto him, who were those of whom we have been speaking, of whom were ^cpoor in heart, because of their poverty as to the things of the world.

5 And they came unto Alma; and the one who was the foremost among them said unto him: Behold, ^awhat shall these my brethren do, for they are ^bdespised of all men because of their poverty, yea, and more especially by our priests; for they have ^ccast us out of our synagogues which we have labored abundantly to build with our own hands; and they have cast us out because of our exceeding poverty; and we have ^dno place to worship our God; and behold, ^ewhat shall we do?

6 And now when Alma heard this, he turned him about, his face immediately towards him, and he beheld with great joy; for he beheld that their ^aafflictions had truly ^bhumbled them, and that they were in a ^cpreparation to hear the word.

7 Therefore he did say no more to the other multitude; but he stretched forth his hand, and cried unto those whom he beheld, who were truly penitent, and said unto them:

8 I behold that ye are ^alowly in heart; and if so, blessed are ye.

9 Behold thy brother hath said, What shall we do?—for we are cast out of our synagogues, that we cannot worship our God.

10 Behold I say unto you, do ye suppose that ye ^acannot worship God save it be in your synagogues only?

11 And moreover, I would ask, do ye suppose that ye must not worship God only ^aonce in a week?

12 I say unto you, it is well that ye are cast out of your synagogues, that ye may be humble, and that ye may learn ^awisdom; for it is necessary that ye should learn wisdom; for it is because that ye are cast out, that ye are despised of your brethren because of your exceeding ^bpoverty, that ye are brought to a lowliness of heart; for ye are necessarily brought to be humble.

---

32 2a Luke 6:20; 7:22.
    TG Poor.
  3a Luke 18:9.
    b Alma 34:40.
  4a Alma 47:5.
    b TG Assembly for
      Worship.
    c TG Poor in Spirit.
  5a Prov. 18:23.

    b TG Oppression.
    c Alma 33:10.
    d Alma 33:2.
    e Acts 2:37 (37–38);
      Alma 34:3.
  6a TG Adversity.
    b TG Humility;
      Teachable.
    c Prov. 16:1;

      Alma 16:16 (16–17);
      D&C 101:8.
  8a Matt. 5:5 (3–5).
 10a TG Worship.
 11a Mosiah 18:25.
 12a Eccl. 4:13.
    b Prov. 16:8; 28:11.

13 And now, because ye are compelled to be humble blessed are ye; for a man sometimes, if he is compelled to be humble, seeketh ᵃrepentance; and now surely, whosoever repenteth shall find mercy; and he that findeth mercy and ᵇendureth to the end the same shall be saved.

14 And now, as I said unto you, that because ye were compelled to be ᵃhumble ye were blessed, do ye not suppose that they are more blessed who truly humble themselves because of the word?

15 Yea, he that truly humbleth himself, and repenteth of his sins, and endureth to the end, the same shall be blessed—yea, much more blessed than they who are compelled to be humble because of their exceeding poverty.

16 Therefore, blessed are they who ᵃhumble themselves without being ᵇcompelled to be humble; or rather, in other words, blessed is he that believeth in the word of God, and is baptized without ᶜstubbornness of heart, yea, without being brought to know the word, or even compelled to know, before they will believe.

17 Yea, there are many who do say: If thou wilt show unto us a ᵃsign from heaven, then we shall know of a surety; then we shall believe.

18 Now I ask, is this faith? Behold, I say unto you, Nay; for if a man knoweth a thing he hath no cause to ᵃbelieve, for he knoweth it.

19 And now, how much ᵃmore ᵇcursed is he that ᶜknoweth the ᵈwill of God and doeth it not, than he that only believeth, or only hath cause to believe, and falleth into ᵉtransgression?

20 Now of this thing ye must judge.

Behold, I say unto you, that it is on the one hand even as it is on the other; and it shall be unto every man according to his work.

21 And now as I said concerning faith—ᵃfaith is not to have a perfect knowledge of things; therefore if ye have faith ye ᵇhope for things which are ᶜnot seen, which are true.

22 And now, behold, I say unto you, and I would that ye should remember, that God is ᵃmerciful unto all who believe on his name; therefore he desireth, in the first place, that ye should believe, yea, even on his word.

23 And now, he imparteth his word by angels unto men, yea, ᵃnot only men but women also. Now this is not all; little ᵇchildren do have words given unto them many times, which ᶜconfound the wise and the learned.

24 And now, my beloved brethren, as ye have desired to know of me what ye shall do because ye are afflicted and cast out—now I do not desire that ye should suppose that I mean to judge you only according to that which is true—

25 For I do not mean that ye all of you have been compelled to humble yourselves; for I verily believe that there are some among you who ᵃwould humble themselves, let them be in whatsoever circumstances they might.

26 Now, as I said concerning faith—that it was not a perfect knowledge—even so it is with my words. Ye cannot know of their surety at first, unto perfection, any more than faith is a perfect knowledge.

27 But behold, if ye will awake and arouse your faculties, even to an experiment upon my words, and

13a TG Objectives.
  b Alma 38:2;
    3 Ne. 15:9; 27:6 (6–17).
    TG Perseverance;
    Steadfastness.
14a 2 Kgs. 22:19.
16a TG Humility.
  b TG Initiative.
  c TG Stubbornness.
17a TG Signs;
    Sign Seekers.

18a Luke 16:30 (27–31);
    Ether 12:12 (12, 18).
19a D&C 41:1.
  b TG Curse.
  c John 15:24 (22–24).
  d TG God, Will of.
  e TG Transgress.
21a John 20:29;
    Heb. 11:1 (1–40).
  b TG Hope.
  c Ether 12:6.

22a TG God, Mercy of.
23a Joel 2:29 (28–29).
  b Matt. 11:25;
    Luke 10:21;
    3 Ne. 26:14 (14–16);
    D&C 128:18.
  c D&C 133:58.
25a TG Initiative;
    Sincere.

exercise a particle of faith, yea, even if ye can no more than ^adesire to believe, let this desire work in you, even until ye believe in a manner that ye can give place for a portion of my words.

28 Now, we will compare the word unto a ^aseed. Now, if ye give place, that a ^bseed may be planted in your ^cheart, behold, if it be a true seed, or a good seed, if ye do not cast it out by your ^dunbelief, that ye will resist the Spirit of the Lord, behold, it will begin to swell within your breasts; and when you feel these swelling motions, ye will begin to say within yourselves—It must needs be that this is a good seed, or that the word is good, for it beginneth to enlarge my soul; yea, it beginneth to ^eenlighten my ^funderstanding, yea, it beginneth to be delicious to me.

29 Now behold, would not this increase your faith? I say unto you, Yea; nevertheless it hath not grown up to a perfect knowledge.

30 But behold, as the seed swelleth, and sprouteth, and beginneth to grow, then you must needs say that the seed is good; for behold it swelleth, and sprouteth, and beginneth to grow. And now, behold, will not this strengthen your faith? Yea, it will strengthen your faith: for ye will say I know that this is a good seed; for behold it sprouteth and beginneth to grow.

31 And now, behold, are ye sure that this is a good seed? I say unto you, Yea; for every seed bringeth forth unto its own ^alikeness.

32 Therefore, if a seed groweth it is good, but if it groweth not, behold it is not good, therefore it is cast away.

33 And now, behold, because ye have tried the experiment, and planted the seed, and it swelleth and sprouteth, and beginneth to grow, ye must needs know that the seed is good.

34 And now, behold, is your ^aknowledge ^bperfect? Yea, your knowledge is perfect in that thing, and your ^cfaith is dormant; and this because you know, for ye know that the word hath swelled your souls, and ye also know that it hath sprouted up, that your understanding doth begin to be enlightened, and your ^dmind doth begin to expand.

35 O then, is not this real? I say unto you, Yea, because it is ^alight; and whatsoever is light, is ^bgood, because it is discernible, therefore ye must know that it is good; and now behold, after ye have tasted this light is your knowledge perfect?

36 Behold I say unto you, Nay; neither must ye lay aside your faith, for ye have only exercised your faith to plant the seed that ye might try the experiment to know if the seed was good.

37 And behold, as the tree beginneth to grow, ye will say: Let us nourish it with great care, that it may get root, that it may grow up, and bring forth fruit unto us. And now behold, if ye nourish it with much care it will get root, and grow up, and bring forth fruit.

38 But if ye ^aneglect the tree, and take no thought for its nourishment, behold it will not get any root; and when the heat of the sun cometh and scorcheth it, because it hath no root it withers away, and ye pluck it up and cast it out.

39 Now, this is not because the seed was not good, neither is it because the fruit thereof would not be desirable; but it is because your ^aground is ^bbarren, and ye will not nourish the tree, therefore ye cannot have the fruit thereof.

27a TG Motivations; Teachable.
28a Alma 33:1.
  b Luke 8:11 (11–15).
  c TG Heart.
  d TG Doubt; Unbelief.
  e TG Discernment, Spiritual; Edification.
  f TG Intelligence; Testimony; Understanding.
31a Gen. 1:12 (11–12).
34a TG Knowledge.
  b Ps. 19:7.
  c Ether 3:19.
  d TG Mind.
35a TG Light [noun].
  b Gen. 1:4.
38a TG Apostasy of Individuals.
39a Matt. 13:5 (3–8).
  b TG Barren.

40 And thus, if ye will not nourish the word, looking forward with an eye of faith to the fruit thereof, ye can never pluck of the fruit of the *a*tree of life.

41 But if ye will nourish the word, yea, nourish the tree as it beginneth to grow, by your faith with great diligence, and with *a*patience, looking forward to the fruit thereof, it shall take root; and behold it shall be a tree *b*springing up unto everlasting life.

42 And because of your *a*diligence and your faith and your patience with the word in nourishing it, that it may take root in you, behold, by and by ye shall pluck the *b*fruit thereof, which is most precious, which is sweet above all that is sweet, and which is white above all that is white, yea, and pure above all that is pure; and ye shall feast upon this fruit even until ye are filled, that ye hunger not, neither shall ye thirst.

43 Then, my brethren, ye shall *a*reap the *b*rewards of your faith, and your diligence, and patience, and long-suffering, waiting for the tree to bring forth *c*fruit unto you.

CHAPTER 33

Zenos taught that men should pray and worship in all places, and that judgments are turned away because of the Son— Zenock taught that mercy is bestowed because of the Son—Moses had lifted up in the wilderness a type of the Son of God. About 74 B.C.

Now after Alma had spoken these words, they sent forth unto him desiring to know whether they should believe in *a*one God, that they might obtain this fruit of which he had spoken, or *b*how they should plant the *c*seed, or the word of which he had spoken, which he said must be planted in their hearts; or in what manner they should begin to exercise their faith.

2 And Alma said unto them: Behold, ye have said that ye *a*could not *b*worship your God because ye are cast out of your synagogues. But behold, I say unto you, if ye suppose that ye cannot worship God, ye do greatly err, and ye ought to search the *c*scriptures; if ye suppose that they have taught you this, ye do not understand them.

3 Do ye remember to have read what *a*Zenos, the prophet of old, has said concerning prayer or *b*worship?

4 For he said: Thou art merciful, O God, for thou hast heard my prayer, even when I was *a*in the wilderness; yea, thou wast merciful when I prayed concerning those who were mine *b*enemies, and thou didst turn them to me.

5 Yea, O God, and thou wast merciful unto me when I did cry unto thee in my *a*field; when I did cry unto thee in my prayer, and thou didst hear me.

6 And again, O God, when I did turn to my house thou didst hear me in my prayer.

7 And when I did turn unto my *a*closet, O Lord, and prayed unto thee, thou didst hear me.

8 Yea, thou art merciful unto thy children when they cry unto thee, to be heard of thee and not of men, and thou *a*wilt hear them.

9 Yea, O God, thou hast been merciful unto me, and heard my cries in the midst of thy congregations.

40a Gen. 2:9;
      1 Ne. 15:36 (22, 28, 36).
41a TG Patience.
  b Alma 33:23;
      D&C 63:23.
42a TG Diligence.
  b Matt. 13:23;
      Col. 1:6;
      1 Ne. 8:10 (10–18);
      3 Ne. 14:16;
      D&C 52:34 (18, 34).

43a TG Harvest.
  b TG Reward.
  c Alma 33:23.
33 1a 2 Ne. 31:21;
      Mosiah 15:4;
      Alma 11:28 (28–35).
  b Alma 33:23.
  c Alma 32:28 (28–43).
 2a Alma 32:5.
  b TG Worship.
  c Mosiah 2:34;

      Alma 37:8 (3–10).
      TG Prayer.
 3a Alma 34:7.
      TG Scriptures, Lost.
  b TG Worship.
 4a 1 Kgs. 8:47 (44–52).
  b Matt. 5:44.
 5a Alma 34:20 (20–25).
 7a Matt. 6:6 (5–6);
      Alma 34:26 (17–27).
 8a TG God, Access to.

10 Yea, and thou hast also heard me when I have been ᵃcast out and have been despised by mine enemies; yea, thou didst hear my cries, and wast angry with mine enemies, and thou didst ᵇvisit them in thine anger with speedy destruction.

11 And thou didst hear me because of mine afflictions and my ᵃsincerity; and it is because of thy Son that thou hast been thus merciful unto me, therefore I will cry unto thee in all mine ᵇafflictions, for in thee is my joy; for thou hast turned thy judgments away from me, ᶜbecause of thy Son.

12 And now Alma said unto them: Do ye ᵃbelieve those scriptures which have been written by them of old?

13 Behold, if ye do, ye must believe what ᵃZenos said; for, behold he said: Thou hast turned away thy judgments because of thy Son.

14 Now behold, my brethren, I would ask if ye have read the scriptures? If ye have, how can ye ᵃdisbelieve on the Son of God?

15 For it is ᵃnot written that Zenos alone spake of these things, but ᵇZenock also spake of these things—

16 For behold, he said: Thou art angry, O Lord, with this people, because they ᵃwill not understand thy mercies which thou hast bestowed upon them because of thy Son.

17 And now, my brethren, ye see that a second prophet of old has testified of the Son of God, and because the people would not understand his words they ᵃstoned him to death.

18 But behold, this is not all; these are not the only ones who have spoken concerning the Son of God.

19 Behold, he was spoken of by ᵃMoses; yea, and behold a ᵇtype was ᶜraised up in the wilderness, that whosoever would look upon it might live. And many did look and live.

20 But few understood the meaning of those things, and this because of the hardness of their hearts. But there were many who were so hardened that they would not look, therefore they perished. Now the reason they would not look is because they did not believe that it would ᵃheal them.

21 O my brethren, if ye could be healed by merely casting about your eyes that ye might be healed, would ye not behold quickly, or would ye rather harden your hearts in ᵃunbelief, and be ᵇslothful, that ye would not cast about your eyes, that ye might perish?

22 If so, wo shall come upon you; but if not so, then cast about your eyes and ᵃbegin to believe in the Son of God, that he will come to redeem his people, and that he shall suffer and die to ᵇatone for their sins; and that he shall ᶜrise again from the dead, which shall bring to pass the ᵈresurrection, that all men shall stand before him, to be ᵉjudged at the last and judgment day, according to their ᶠworks.

23 And now, my brethren, I desire that ye shall ᵃplant this word in your hearts, and as it beginneth to swell even so nourish it by your faith. And behold, it will become a tree, ᵇspringing up in you unto ᶜeverlasting

10a Alma 32:5.
  b Ps. 3:7; 18:17.
11a TG Sincere.
  b TG Affliction.
  c TG Jesus Christ,
     Atonement through.
12a TG Scriptures, Value of.
13a Jacob 6:1; Alma 34:7.
14a John 5:39.
15a Jacob 4:4;
     Mosiah 15:11 (11–13).
  b 1 Ne. 19:10;
     Alma 34:7.
16a 2 Pet. 3:5 (4–5).

17a TG Martyrdom.
19a Deut. 18:15 (15, 18);
     Alma 34:7.
  b Num. 21:9;
     1 Ne. 17:41;
     2 Ne. 25:20.
     TG Jesus Christ, Types
     of, in Anticipation;
     Symbolism.
  c John 3:14; Hel. 8:14.
20a Hosea 11:3;
     1 Ne. 17:41 (40–41).
21a TG Doubt; Unbelief.
  b TG Apathy; Laziness.

22a Alma 25:16;
     37:46 (45–46).
  b 2 Ne. 2:10;
     Alma 22:14; 34:9 (8–16).
  c TG Jesus Christ,
     Resurrection.
  d Alma 11:44.
     TG Resurrection.
  e TG Jesus Christ, Judge.
  f TG Good Works.
23a Alma 33:1; 34:4.
  b Alma 32:41;
     D&C 63:23.
  c Alma 32:43.

life. And then may God grant unto you that your *d*burdens may be light, through the joy of his Son. And even all this can ye do if ye *e*will. Amen.

CHAPTER 34

Amulek testifies that the word is in Christ unto salvation—Unless an atonement is made, all mankind must perish—The whole law of Moses points toward the sacrifice of the Son of God—The eternal plan of redemption is based on faith and repentance—Pray for temporal and spiritual blessings—This life is the time for men to prepare to meet God—Work out your salvation with fear before God. About 74 B.C.

AND now it came to pass that after Alma had spoken these words unto them he sat down upon the ground, and *a*Amulek arose and began to teach them, saying:

2 My brethren, I think that it is impossible that ye should be ignorant of the things which have been spoken concerning the coming of Christ, who is taught by us to be the Son of God; yea, I know that *a*these things were taught unto you bountifully before your dissension from among us.

3 And as ye have desired of my beloved brother that he should make known unto you *a*what ye should do, because of your afflictions; and he hath spoken somewhat unto you to prepare your minds; yea, and he hath exhorted you unto faith and to patience—

4 Yea, even that ye would have so much faith as even to *a*plant the word in your hearts, that ye may try the experiment of its goodness.

5 And we have beheld that the great question which is in your minds is whether the word be in the Son of God, or whether there shall be *a*no Christ.

6 And ye also beheld that my brother has proved unto you, in many instances, that the *a*word is in Christ unto salvation.

7 My brother has called upon the words of *a*Zenos, that redemption cometh through the Son of God, and also upon the words of *b*Zenock; and also he has appealed unto *c*Moses, to prove that these things are true.

8 And now, behold, I will *a*testify unto you of myself that these things are true. Behold, I say unto you, that I do know that Christ shall come among the children of men, to take upon him the *b*transgressions of his people, and that he shall *c*atone for the sins of the world; for the Lord God hath spoken it.

9 For it is expedient that an *a*atonement should be made; for according to the great *b*plan of the Eternal God there must be an atonement made, or else all mankind must unavoidably perish; yea, all are hardened; yea, all are *c*fallen and are lost, and must perish except it be through the atonement which it is expedient should be made.

10 For it is expedient that there should be a great and last *a*sacrifice; yea, not a *b*sacrifice of man, neither of beast, neither of any manner of fowl; for it shall not be a human sacrifice; but it must be an *c*infinite and *d*eternal *e*sacrifice.

23 *d* Mosiah 24:15 (13–15);
        Alma 31:38.
     e TG Agency.
34 1 *a* Alma 8:21; 31:32.
     2 *a* Alma 16:15 (13–21).
     3 *a* Alma 32:5.
     4 *a* Alma 33:23.
     5 *a* Jacob 7:2 (2, 9);
        Alma 30:12 (12, 22);
        31:16 (16, 29).
     6 *a* John 1:14 (1, 14).
     7 *a* Alma 33:13;

Hel. 8:19.
     b Alma 33:15;
        Hel. 8:20 (19–20).
     c Alma 33:19.
     8 *a* TG Testimony;
        Witness.
     b TG Jesus Christ,
        Redeemer.
     c TG Jesus Christ,
        Atonement through.
     9 *a* 2 Ne. 2:10; 9:7 (7–9);
        Alma 22:14; 33:22.

b Alma 12:26 (22–33);
        42:8 (6–28);
        Moses 6:62.
     c TG Fall of Man.
     10 *a* 1 Chr. 6:49;
        Moses 5:7 (6–7).
     b TG Blood,
        Symbolism of.
     c 2 Ne. 9:7.
     d Isa. 45:17;
        Heb. 5:9.
     e TG Sacrifice.

11 Now there is not any man that can sacrifice his own blood which will atone for the sins of another. Now, if a man murdereth, behold will our law, which is ^ajust, take the life of his brother? I say unto you, Nay.

12 But the law requireth the ^alife of him who hath ^bmurdered; therefore there can be nothing which is short of an infinite atonement which will suffice for the sins of the world.

13 Therefore, it is expedient that there should be a great and last sacrifice, and then shall there be, or it is expedient there should be, a ^astop to the shedding of ^bblood; then shall the ^claw of Moses be fulfilled; yea, it shall be all fulfilled, every jot and tittle, and none shall have passed away.

14 And behold, this is the whole ^ameaning of the ^blaw, every whit ^cpointing to that great and last ^dsacrifice; and that great and last ^esacrifice will be the Son of God, yea, ^finfinite and eternal.

15 And thus he shall bring ^asalvation to all those who shall believe on his name; this being the intent of this last sacrifice, to bring about the bowels of mercy, which overpowereth justice, and bringeth about means unto men that they may have faith unto repentance.

16 And thus ^amercy can satisfy the demands of ^bjustice, and encircles them in the arms of safety, while he that exercises no faith unto repentance is exposed to the whole law of the demands of ^cjustice; therefore only unto him that has faith unto repentance is brought about the great and eternal ^dplan of ^eredemption.

17 Therefore may God grant unto you, my brethren, that ye may begin to exercise your ^afaith unto repentance, that ye begin to ^bcall upon his holy name, that he would have mercy upon you;

18 Yea, cry unto him for mercy; for he is ^amighty to save.

19 Yea, humble yourselves, and continue in ^aprayer unto him.

20 Cry unto him when ye are in your ^afields, yea, over all your flocks.

21 ^aCry unto him in your houses, yea, over all your household, both morning, mid-day, and evening.

22 Yea, cry unto him against the power of your ^aenemies.

23 Yea, ^acry unto him against the ^bdevil, who is an enemy to all ^crighteousness.

24 Cry unto him over the crops of your fields, that ye may prosper in them.

25 Cry over the flocks of your fields, that they may increase.

26 But this is not all; ye must ^apour out your souls in your ^bclosets, and your secret places, and in your wilderness.

27 Yea, and when you do not cry unto the Lord, let your ^ahearts be ^bfull, drawn out in prayer unto him continually for your ^cwelfare, and also for the welfare of ^dthose who are around you.

11a Deut. 24:16;
    Mosiah 29:25.
12a TG Blood, Shedding of;
    Life, Sanctity of.
  b TG Capital Punishment;
    Murder.
13a 3 Ne. 9:19.
  b TG Blood, Symbolism of.
  c 3 Ne. 1:24; 15:5.
14a 2 Ne. 25:24;
    Jarom 1:5;
    Mosiah 2:3;
    Alma 30:3.
  b TG Law of Moses.
  c TG Jesus Christ, Types
    of, in Anticipation.

  d Ex. 12:21 (1–30).
  e D&C 138:35.
  f D&C 20:17 (17, 28).
15a TG Salvation.
16a TG Mercy.
  b TG God, Justice of.
  c Mosiah 15:27;
    Alma 12:32.
  d TG Salvation, Plan of.
  e TG Redemption.
17a TG Faith.
  b TG God, Access to;
    Prayer.
18a Heb. 7:25 (24–25).
19a TG Prayer.
20a Alma 33:5 (4–5).

21a Ps. 5:3 (1–3);
    Dan. 6:10;
    3 Ne. 18:21.
22a TG Enemies.
23a 3 Ne. 18:15 (15, 18).
  b TG Devil.
  c TG Righteousness.
26a 1 Sam. 1:15;
    Enos 1:9.
  b Matt. 6:6 (5–6);
    Alma 33:7 (4–11).
27a TG Heart.
  b TG Meditation.
  c 2 Ne. 32:9.
    TG Welfare.
  d D&C 108:7.

28 And now behold, my beloved brethren, I say unto you, do not suppose that this is all; for after ye have done all these things, if ye ᵃturn away the ᵇneedy, and the ᶜnaked, and visit not the sick and afflicted, and ᵈimpart of your substance, if ye have, to those who stand in need—I say unto you, if ye do not any of these things, behold, your ᵉprayer is ᶠvain, and availeth you nothing, and ye are as ᵍhypocrites who do deny the faith.

29 Therefore, if ye do not remember to be ᵃcharitable, ye are as dross, which the refiners do cast out, (it being of no worth) and is trodden under foot of men.

30 And now, my brethren, I would that, after ye have ᵃreceived so many witnesses, seeing that the holy scriptures testify of these things, ye come forth and bring ᵇfruit unto repentance.

31 Yea, I would that ye would come forth and ᵃharden not your hearts any longer; for behold, now is the time and the ᵇday of your ᶜsalvation; and therefore, if ye will repent and ᵈharden not your hearts, immediately shall the great plan of redemption be brought about unto you.

32 For behold, this ᵃlife is the time for men to ᵇprepare to meet God; yea, behold the day of ᶜthis life is the day for men to perform their ᵈlabors.

33 And now, as I said unto you before, as ye have had so many ᵃwitnesses, therefore, I beseech of you that ye do not ᵇprocrastinate the day of your ᶜrepentance until the end; for after this day of life, which is given us to prepare for eternity, behold, if we do not improve our time while in this life, then cometh the ᵈnight of ᵉdarkness wherein there can be no labor performed.

34 Ye cannot say, when ye are brought to that awful ᵃcrisis, that I will repent, that I will return to my God. Nay, ye cannot say this; for that same spirit which doth ᵇpossess your bodies at the time that ye go out of this life, that same spirit will have power to possess your body in that eternal world.

35 For behold, if ye have procrastinated the day of your repentance even until death, behold, ye have become ᵃsubjected to the spirit of the devil, and he doth ᵇseal you his; therefore, the Spirit of the Lord hath withdrawn from you, and hath no place in you, and the devil hath all power over you; and this is the final state of the wicked.

36 And this I know, because the Lord hath said he dwelleth not in ᵃunholy temples, but in the ᵇhearts of the ᶜrighteous doth he dwell; yea, and he has also said that the righteous shall sit down in his kingdom, to go no more out; but their garments should be made white through the ᵈblood of the Lamb.

37 And now, my beloved brethren, I desire that ye should remember

28a TG Apathy.
  b TG Poor.
  c Ezek. 18:7 (5–9).
  d TG Almsgiving;
    Good Works.
  e Ezek. 33:31;
    Matt. 15:8 (7–8).
  f Isa. 58:3;
    Moro. 7:6 (6–8).
  g TG Hypocrisy.
29a TG Charity;
    Generosity.
30a TG Witness.
  b Matt. 3:8;
    Alma 13:13.
31a TG Self-Mastery.
  b Rom. 13:12 (11–12).
  c Matt. 11:20;

3 Ne. 9:3;
    D&C 84:114.
  d TG Hardheartedness.
32a TG Mortality.
  b 2 Cor. 6:2;
    2 Ne. 2:21;
    Alma 12:24; 42:4 (4–6).
    TG Self-Mastery.
  c D&C 138:57.
  d TG Good Works;
    Industry.
33a TG Witness.
  b Job 27:8;
    Hel. 13:38;
    D&C 45:2.
    TG Apathy;
    Idleness;
    Procrastination.

c TG Repent.
  d Eccl. 9:10;
    John 9:4.
  e TG Darkness, Spiritual.
34a Alma 40:14 (13–14);
    Ether 9:34.
  b Rom. 6:16 (14–18).
35a 2 Ne. 28:19 (19–23).
  b 2 Ne. 9:9;
    3 Ne. 2:10.
    TG Devil; Sealing.
36a Mosiah 2:37;
    Alma 7:21;
    Hel. 4:24.
    TG Cleanliness.
  b D&C 130:3.
  c TG Righteousness.
  d Rev. 12:11.

these things, and that ye should
^awork out your salvation with fear
before God, and that ye should no
more deny the coming of Christ;

38 That ye ^acontend no more
against the Holy Ghost, but that ye
receive it, and take upon you the
^bname of Christ; that ye humble your-
selves even to the dust, and ^cworship
God, in whatsoever place ye may be
in, in spirit and in truth; and that
ye live in ^dthanksgiving daily, for
the many ^emercies and blessings
which he doth bestow upon you.

39 Yea, and I also ^aexhort you, my
brethren, that ye be ^bwatchful unto
prayer continually, that ye may not
be led away by the ^ctemptations
of the devil, that he may not overpower you, that ye may not become
his subjects at the last day; for behold, he rewardeth you ^dno good
thing.

40 And now my beloved brethren, I
would exhort you to have ^apatience,
and that ye bear with all manner
of ^bafflictions; that ye do not ^crevile
against those who do cast you out
because of your ^dexceeding poverty, lest ye become sinners like
unto them;

41 But that ye have ^apatience, and
bear with those ^bafflictions, with a
firm hope that ye shall one day rest
from all your afflictions.

CHAPTER 35

*The preaching of the word destroys
the craft of the Zoramites—They expel
the converts, who then join the people
of Ammon in Jershon—Alma sorrows
because of the wickedness of the people.
About 74* B.C.

Now it came to pass that after
Amulek had made an end of these
words, they withdrew themselves
from the multitude and came over
into the land of ^aJershon.

2 Yea, and the rest of the brethren,
after they had preached the word
unto the ^aZoramites, also came over
into the land of Jershon.

3 And it came to pass that after
the more popular part of the Zoramites had consulted together concerning the words which had been
preached unto them, they were angry because of the word, for it did
destroy their ^acraft; therefore they
would not hearken unto the words.

4 And they sent and gathered
together throughout all the land
all the people, and consulted with
them concerning the words which
had been spoken.

5 Now their rulers and their priests
and their teachers did not let the
people know concerning their
desires; therefore they found out
privily the minds of all the people.

6 And it came to pass that after
they had found out the minds of
all the people, those who were in
favor of the words which had been
spoken by Alma and his brethren
were cast out of the land; and they
were ^amany; and they came over
also into the land of Jershon.

7 And it came to pass that Alma
and his brethren did minister unto
them.

8 Now the people of the Zoram-
ites were angry with the ^apeople of
Ammon who were in Jershon, and
the ^bchief ruler of the Zoramites,
being a very wicked man, sent over
unto the people of Ammon desiring
them that they should cast out of
their land all those who came over
from them into their land.

9 And he breathed out many

37a Philip. 2:12 (12–16).
38a TG Holy Ghost, Loss of.
  b Mosiah 5:8;
    Alma 5:38.
    TG Jesus Christ, Taking
    the Name of.
  c TG Worship.
  d Ps. 69:30 (30–31);
    D&C 46:7.
    TG Thanksgiving.

  e Gen. 32:10;
    1 Ne. 1:20;
    D&C 46:15.
39a Heb. 3:13.
  b TG Watch.
  c TG Temptation.
  d Alma 30:60.
40a TG Patience;
    Steadfastness.
  b TG Affliction.

  c TG Reviling.
  d Alma 32:3.
41a TG Patience.
  b Job 23:2 (2–5).
35 1a Alma 28:1.
  2a Alma 30:59.
  3a TG Priestcraft.
  6a Alma 35:14.
  8a Alma 27:26.
  b Alma 30:59.

threatenings against them. And now the people of Ammon did not fear their words; therefore they did not cast them out, but they did receive all the poor of the Zoramites that came over unto them; and they did *a*nourish them, and did clothe them, and did give unto them lands for their inheritance; and they did administer unto them according to their wants.

10 Now this did *a*stir up the Zoramites to *b*anger against the people of Ammon, and they began to mix with the Lamanites and to stir them up also to anger against them.

11 And thus the Zoramites and the Lamanites began to make preparations for war against the people of Ammon, and also against the Nephites.

12 And thus ended the seventeenth year of the reign of the judges over the people of Nephi.

13 And the people of Ammon departed out of the land of Jershon, and came over into the land of Melek, and gave place in the land of Jershon for the armies of the Nephites, that they might contend with the armies of the Lamanites and the armies of the Zoramites; and thus commenced a war betwixt the Lamanites and the Nephites, in the eighteenth year of the reign of the judges; and an *a*account shall be given of their wars hereafter.

14 And Alma, and Ammon, and their brethren, and also the *a*two sons of Alma returned to the land of Zarahemla, after having been instruments in the hands of God of bringing *b*many of the *c*Zoramites to repentance; and as many as were brought to repentance were driven out of their land; but they have lands for their inheritance in the land of Jershon, and they have taken up arms to defend themselves,

and their wives, and children, and their lands.

15 Now Alma, being *a*grieved for the iniquity of his people, yea for the wars, and the bloodsheds, and the contentions which were among them; and having been to declare the word, or sent to declare the word, among all the people in every city; and seeing that the hearts of the people began to wax hard, and that they began to be *b*offended because of the strictness of the word, his heart was exceedingly sorrowful.

16 Therefore, he caused that his sons should be gathered together, that he might give unto them every one his *a*charge, separately, concerning the things pertaining unto righteousness. And we have an account of his commandments, which he gave unto them according to his own record.

The commandments of Alma to his son Helaman.

Comprising chapters 36 and 37.

CHAPTER 36

Alma testifies to Helaman of his conversion after seeing an angel—He suffered the pains of a damned soul; he called upon the name of Jesus, and was then born of God—Sweet joy filled his soul—He saw concourses of angels praising God—Many converts have tasted and seen as he has tasted and seen. About 74 B.C.

MY *a*son, give ear to my words; for I swear unto you, that inasmuch as ye shall keep the commandments of God ye shall prosper in the land.

2 I would that ye should do as I have done, in remembering the captivity of our fathers; for they were in *a*bondage, and none could

---

9a Mosiah 4:26;
   D&C 42:43.
   TG Nourish;
   Welfare.
10a Alma 47:1;
   Hel. 1:17.
 b TG Anger; War.

13a Alma 43:3.
14a Alma 31:7.
 b Alma 35:6.
 c Alma 30:59.
15a Alma 31:1.
 b TG Prophets,
   Rejection of.

16a TG Stewardship.
36 1a Hel. 5:13 (1–13);
   Moses 6:58.
 2a Mosiah 23:23;
   24:17 (17–21).
   TG Israel, Bondage of,
   in Egypt.

ᵇdeliver them except it was the ᶜGod of Abraham, and the God of Isaac, and the God of Jacob; and he surely did deliver them in their afflictions.

3 And now, O my son Helaman, behold, thou art in thy youth, and therefore, I beseech of thee that thou wilt hear my words and learn of me; for I do know that whosoever shall put their ᵃtrust in God shall be supported in their ᵇtrials, and their troubles, and their afflictions, and shall be ᶜlifted up at the last day.

4 And I would not that ye think that I ᵃknow of myself—not of the temporal but of the spiritual, not of the ᵇcarnal mind but of God.

5 Now, behold, I say unto you, if I had not been ᵃborn of God I should ᵇnot have known these things; but God has, by the mouth of his holy ᶜangel, made these things known unto me, not of any ᵈworthiness of myself;

6 For I went about with the sons of Mosiah, seeking to ᵃdestroy the church of God; but behold, God sent his holy angel to stop us by the way.

7 And behold, he spake unto us, as it were the voice of thunder, and the whole earth did ᵃtremble beneath our feet; and we all fell to the earth, for the ᵇfear of the Lord came upon us.

8 But behold, the voice said unto me: Arise. And I arose and stood up, and beheld the angel.

9 And he said unto me: If thou wilt of thyself be destroyed, seek no more to destroy the church of God.

10 And it came to pass that I fell to the earth; and it was for the space of ᵃthree days and three nights that I could not open my mouth, neither had I the use of my limbs.

11 And the angel spake more things unto me, which were heard by my brethren, but I did ᵃnot hear them; for when I heard the words— If thou wilt be destroyed of thyself, seek no more to destroy the church of God—I was struck with such great fear and amazement lest perhaps I should be destroyed, that I fell to the earth and I did hear no more.

12 But I was racked with ᵃeternal ᵇtorment, for my soul was ᶜharrowed up to the greatest degree and racked with all my sins.

13 Yea, I did remember all my sins and iniquities, for which I was ᵃtormented with the ᵇpains of hell; yea, I saw that I had ᶜrebelled against my God, and that I had not kept his holy commandments.

14 Yea, and I had ᵃmurdered many of his children, or rather led them away unto destruction; yea, and in fine so great had been my iniquities, that the very thought of coming into the presence of my God did rack my soul with inexpressible horror.

15 Oh, thought I, that I ᵃcould be banished and become extinct both soul and body, that I might not be brought to stand in the presence of my God, to be judged of my ᵇdeeds.

16 And now, for three days and for three nights was I racked, even with the ᵃpains of a ᵇdamned soul.

17 And it came to pass that as I was thus ᵃracked with torment, while I

2b Deut. 26:8.
  c Ex. 3:6;
    Alma 29:11.
3a TG Trust in God.
  b Rom. 8:28.
  c Mosiah 23:22 (21–22).
4a 1 Cor. 2:11;
    Alma 5:45 (45–46).
    TG Knowledge.
  b TG Carnal Mind.
5a TG Man, New, Spiritually
    Reborn.
  b Alma 26:21 (21–22).
  c Mosiah 27:11 (11–18).

  d TG Worthiness.
6a Mosiah 27:10; 28:4 (3–4).
7a Isa. 6:4;
    Mosiah 27:18.
  b Prov. 2:5.
    TG Fear of God.
10a Mosiah 27:23 (19–23);
    Alma 38:8.
11a Dan. 10:7;
    Acts 9:7 (3–7).
12a D&C 19:11 (11–15).
  b TG Despair.
  c TG Poor in Spirit;
    Repent;

    Sorrow.
13a TG Guilt.
  b Moses 1:20.
  c TG Disobedience.
14a Matt. 10:28.
15a Rev. 6:16 (15–17);
    Alma 12:14.
  b Isa. 59:18;
    Alma 41:3 (2–5); 42:27;
    D&C 1:10 (9–10).
16a TG Pain.
  b TG Damnation.
17a Ps. 119:67.

was ᵇharrowed up by the ᶜmemory of my many sins, behold, I ᵈremembered also to have heard my father prophesy unto the people concerning the coming of one Jesus Christ, a Son of God, to atone for the sins of the world.

18 Now, as my mind caught hold upon this thought, I cried within my heart: O Jesus, thou Son of God, ᵃhave mercy on me, who am ᵇin the ᶜgall of bitterness, and am encircled about by the everlasting ᵈchains of ᵉdeath.

19 And now, behold, when I thought this, I could remember my ᵃpains ᵇno more; yea, I was harrowed up by the memory of my sins no more.

20 And oh, what ᵃjoy, and what marvelous light I did behold; yea, my soul was filled with joy as exceeding as was my pain!

21 Yea, I say unto you, my son, that there could be nothing so exquisite and so bitter as were my pains. Yea, and again I say unto you, my son, that on the other hand, there can be nothing so exquisite and sweet as was my joy.

22 Yea, methought I saw, even as our father ᵃLehi saw, God sitting upon his throne, surrounded with numberless concourses of angels, in the attitude of singing and ᵇpraising their God; yea, and my soul did long to be there.

23 But behold, my limbs did receive their ᵃstrength again, and I stood upon my feet, and did manifest unto the people that I had been ᵇborn of God.

24 Yea, and from that time even until now, I have labored without ceasing, that I might bring souls unto ᵃrepentance; that I might bring them to ᵇtaste of the exceeding joy of which I did taste; that they might also be ᶜborn of God, and be ᵈfilled with the Holy Ghost.

25 Yea, and now behold, O my son, the Lord doth ᵃgive me exceedingly great joy in the fruit of my ᵇlabors;

26 For because of the ᵃword which he has imparted unto me, behold, many have been born of God, and have ᵇtasted as I have tasted, and have seen eye to eye as I have seen; therefore they do know of these things of which I have spoken, as I do know; and the knowledge which I have is of God.

27 And I have been supported under trials and troubles of every kind, yea, and in all manner of afflictions; yea, God has ᵃdelivered me from prison, and from bonds, and from death; yea, and I do put my trust in him, and he will still ᵇdeliver me.

28 And I know that he will ᵃraise me up at the last day, to dwell with him in ᵇglory; yea, and I will ᶜpraise him forever, for he has ᵈbrought our fathers out of Egypt, and he has swallowed up the ᵉEgyptians in the Red Sea; and he led them by his power into the promised land; yea, and he has delivered them out of

---

17b 2 Cor. 7:10 (8–11).
  c Alma 11:43;
    D&C 18:44.
  d 1 Ne. 10:17 (17–19);
    Enos 1:3.
18a Matt. 15:22.
  b IE in extreme remorse.
  c Jonah 2:2;
    Acts 8:23.
  d Prov. 5:22;
    2 Ne. 9:45; 28:22;
    Alma 12:11 (10–11);
    Moses 7:26.
  e TG Death, Spiritual,
    First.
19a TG Peace of God.
  b Jer. 31:34;
    D&C 19:16.

20a Moses 5:11.
    TG Forgive; Joy.
22a 1 Ne. 1:8.
    TG God, Manifesta-
    tions of.
  b Isa. 6:3 (1–4).
23a Moses 1:10.
  b Alma 22:15; 38:6.
    TG Conversion.
24a Alma 19:29.
  b Ps. 34:8;
    1 Ne. 8:12;
    Mosiah 4:11.
  c TG Holy Ghost,
    Baptism of.
  d 2 Ne. 32:2 (2, 5);
    3 Ne. 9:20.
    TG Holy Ghost,

Mission of.
25a TG Reward.
  b TG Work, Value of.
26a Prov. 10:11;
    Jacob 2:8;
    Alma 31:5;
    D&C 108:7.
  b 1 Pet. 2:3 (1–3).
27a Alma 14:28 (26–29).
  b Ps. 34:17.
28a Alma 26:7;
    3 Ne. 15:1.
  b TG Exaltation.
  c Ezra 3:11 (11–13);
    2 Ne. 9:49.
  d Mosiah 12:34;
    D&C 103:16.
  e Ex. 14:27 (26–27).

bondage and captivity from time to time.

29 Yea, and he has also brought our fathers out of the land of Jerusalem; and he has also, by his everlasting power, delivered them out of ªbondage and captivity, from time to time even down to the present day; and I have always retained in remembrance their captivity; yea, and ye also ought to retain in remembrance, as I have done, their captivity.

30 But behold, my son, this is not all; for ye ought to know as I do know, that ªinasmuch as ye shall keep the commandments of God ye shall ᵇprosper in the land; and ye ought to know also, that inasmuch as ye will not keep the commandments of God ye shall be cut off from his presence. Now this is according to his word.

CHAPTER 37

The plates of brass and other scriptures are preserved to bring souls to salvation—The Jaredites were destroyed because of their wickedness—Their secret oaths and covenants must be kept from the people—Counsel with the Lord in all your doings—As the Liahona guided the Nephites, so the word of Christ leads men to eternal life. About 74 B.C.

AND now, my son Helaman, I command you that ye take the ªrecords which have been ᵇentrusted with me;

2 And I also command you that ye keep a ªrecord of this people, according as I have done, upon the plates of Nephi, and keep all these things

sacred which I have kept, even as I have kept them; for it is for a ᵇwise purpose that they are kept.

3 And these ªplates of brass, which contain these engravings, which have the records of the holy scriptures upon them, which have the ᵇgenealogy of our forefathers, even from the beginning—

4 Behold, it has been prophesied by our fathers, that they should be kept and ªhanded down from one generation to another, and be kept and preserved by the hand of the Lord until they should go forth unto every nation, kindred, tongue, and people, that they shall know of the ᵇmysteries contained thereon.

5 And now behold, if they are kept they must retain their brightness; yea, and they will retain their brightness; yea, and also shall all the plates which do contain that which is holy writ.

6 Now ye may suppose that this is ªfoolishness in me; but behold I say unto you, that by ᵇsmall and simple things are great things brought to pass; and small means in many instances doth confound the wise.

7 And the Lord God doth work by ªmeans to bring about his great and eternal purposes; and by very ᵇsmall means the Lord doth ᶜconfound the wise and bringeth about the salvation of many souls.

8 And now, it has hitherto been wisdom in God that these things should be preserved; for behold, ªthey have ᵇenlarged the memory of this people, yea, and convinced many of the error of their ways, and brought them to the ᶜknowledge of

29a Mosiah 24:17;
    25:10; 27:16;
    Alma 5:5 (5–6);
    29:12 (11–12).
30a 2 Ne. 1:20.
  b Mosiah 1:7;
    Alma 37:13; 50:20.
37 1a Alma 45:2 (2–8);
    50:38; 63:1.
  b Mosiah 28:20.
 2a TG Record Keeping.
  b Enos 1:13 (13–18);
    W of M 1:7 (6–11);

Alma 37:12.
  TG Restoration of the
  Gospel.
3a Mosiah 28:20;
    Alma 63:12 (1, 11–14).
  b 1 Ne. 5:14.
4a 1 Ne. 5:19 (16–19);
    Alma 63:13;
    Hel. 3:16.
  b TG Mysteries of
    Godliness.
6a 1 Cor. 2:14.
  b 1 Ne. 16:29;

D&C 64:33; 123:16.
7a Isa. 55:8 (8–9);
    Alma 24:27.
  b 2 Kgs. 5:13;
    Alma 37:41.
  c 1 Cor. 1:27;
    D&C 133:58 (58–59).
8a Mosiah 2:34;
    Alma 33:2.
  b Mosiah 1:3 (3–5).
  c TG Education;
    Scriptures, Value of.

their God unto the salvation of their souls.

9 Yea, I say unto you, ^awere it not for these things that these records do contain, which are on these plates, Ammon and his brethren could not have ^bconvinced so many thousands of the Lamanites of the incorrect tradition of their fathers; yea, these records and their ^cwords brought them unto repentance; that is, they brought them to the knowledge of the Lord their God, and to rejoice in Jesus Christ their Redeemer.

10 And who knoweth but what they will be the ^ameans of bringing many thousands of them, yea, and also many thousands of our ^bstiff-necked brethren, the Nephites, who are now hardening their hearts in sin and iniquities, to the knowledge of their Redeemer?

11 Now these mysteries are not yet fully made known unto me; therefore I shall forbear.

12 And it may suffice if I only say they are preserved for a ^awise purpose, which purpose is known unto God; for he doth ^bcounsel in wisdom over all his works, and his paths are straight, and his course is ^cone eternal round.

13 O remember, remember, my son Helaman, how ^astrict are the commandments of God. And he said: ^bIf ye will keep my commandments ye shall ^cprosper in the land—but if ye keep not his commandments ye shall be cut off from his presence.

14 And now remember, my son, that God has ^aentrusted you with these things, which are ^bsacred, which he has kept sacred, and also which he will keep and ^cpreserve for a ^dwise purpose in him, that he

may show forth his power unto future generations.

15 And now behold, I tell you by the spirit of prophecy, that if ye transgress the commandments of God, behold, these things which are sacred shall be taken away from you by the power of God, and ye shall be delivered up unto Satan, that he may sift you as chaff before the wind.

16 But if ye keep the commandments of God, and do with these things which are sacred according to that which the Lord doth command you, (for you must appeal unto the Lord for all things whatsoever ye must do with them) behold, no power of earth or hell can ^atake them from you, for God is powerful to the fulfilling of all his words.

17 For he will fulfil all his ^apromises which he shall make unto you, for he has fulfilled his promises which he has made unto our fathers.

18 For he promised unto them that he would ^apreserve these things for a wise purpose in him, that he might show forth his power unto future generations.

19 And now behold, one purpose hath he fulfilled, even to the restoration of ^amany thousands of the Lamanites to the knowledge of the truth; and he hath shown forth his power in them, and he will also still show forth his power in them unto ^bfuture generations; therefore they shall be preserved.

20 Therefore I command you, my son Helaman, that ye be diligent in fulfilling all my words, and that ye be diligent in keeping the commandments of God as they are written.

21 And now, I will speak unto

9a Mosiah 1:5.
  b Alma 18:36; 22:12.
  c TG Gospel.
10a 2 Ne. 3:15.
  b TG Stiffnecked.
12a Alma 37:2.
  b Prov. 15:22;
    2 Ne. 9:28;
    Jacob 4:10.
  c 1 Ne. 10:19;

    Alma 7:20.
13a Luke 13:24 (22–30).
  b Alma 9:13 (13–14);
    3 Ne. 5:22.
  c Ps. 122:6;
    Mosiah 1:7;
    Alma 36:30; 50:20.
14a D&C 3:5.
  b TG Sacred.
  c TG Scriptures,

    Preservation of.
  d 1 Ne. 9:5 (3–6).
16a JS—H 1:59.
17a 2 Kgs. 10:10.
    TG Promise.
18a D&C 5:9.
19a Alma 23:5 (5–13).
  b 2 Ne. 3:15;
    Enos 1:13 (12–18);
    Morm. 7:9 (8–10).

you concerning those ᵃtwenty-four plates, that ye keep them, that the ᵇmysteries and the works of darkness, and their secret works, or the secret works of those people who have been destroyed, may be made ᶜmanifest unto this people; yea, all their murders, and robbings, and their plunderings, and all their wickedness and abominations, may be made manifest unto this people; yea, and that ye preserve these ᵈinterpreters.

22 For behold, the Lord saw that his people began to work in darkness, yea, work secret murders and abominations; therefore the Lord said, if they did not repent they should be destroyed from off the face of the earth.

23 And the Lord said: I will prepare unto my servant Gazelem, a ᵃstone, which shall shine forth in darkness unto light, that I may ᵇdiscover unto my people who serve me, that I may discover unto them the works of their brethren, yea, their secret works, their works of darkness, and their wickedness and abominations.

24 And now, my son, these ᵃinterpreters were prepared that the word of God might be fulfilled, which he spake, saying:

25 I will ᵃbring forth out of darkness unto light all their secret works and their abominations; and except they repent I will ᵇdestroy them from off the face of the earth; and I will bring to light all their secrets and abominations, unto every nation that shall hereafter possess the land.

26 And now, my son, we see that they did not repent; therefore they have been destroyed, and thus far the word of God has been fulfilled;

yea, their ᵃsecret abominations have been brought out of darkness and made known unto us.

27 And now, my son, I command you that ye retain all their oaths, and their covenants, and their agreements in their secret abominations; yea, and all their ᵃsigns and their wonders ye shall ᵇkeep from this people, that they know them not, lest peradventure they should fall into darkness also and be destroyed.

28 For behold, there is a ᵃcurse upon all this land, that destruction shall come upon all those workers of darkness, according to the power of God, when they are fully ripe; therefore I desire that this people might not be destroyed.

29 Therefore ye shall keep these secret plans of their ᵃoaths and their covenants from this people, and only their wickedness and their murders and their abominations shall ye make known unto them; and ye shall teach them to ᵇabhor such wickedness and abominations and murders; and ye shall also teach them that these people were destroyed on account of their wickedness and abominations and their murders.

30 For behold, they ᵃmurdered all the prophets of the Lord who came among them to declare unto them concerning their iniquities; and the blood of those whom they murdered did cry unto the Lord their God for vengeance upon those who were their murderers; and thus the judgments of God did come upon these workers of darkness and secret ᵇcombinations.

31 Yea, and ᵃcursed be the land forever and ever unto those workers of

21a Mosiah 8:9; 21:27; 28:11;
    Ether 1:2 (1–5); 15:33.
  b TG Secret Combinations.
  c Prov. 26:26;
    Alma 14:3 (2–3).
  d TG Urim and Thummim.
23a Mosiah 8:13.
  b IE reveal, make known.
24a TG Urim and Thummim.

25a Ps. 64:5 (4–6);
    D&C 88:108 (108–9).
  b Mosiah 21:26.
26a 2 Ne. 10:15.
27a Hel. 6:22.
    TG Signs.
  b Alma 63:12.
28a Ether 2:8 (7–12).
29a Hel. 6:25.

  b Deut. 32:19;
    Alma 13:12.
    TG Hate.
30a TG Prophets,
    Rejection of.
  b TG Secret Combinations.
31a Alma 45:16.
    TG Earth, Curse of.

darkness and secret combinations, even unto destruction, except they repent before they are fully ᵇripe.

32 And now, my son, remember the words which I have spoken unto you; trust not those secret plans unto this people, but teach them an everlasting ᵃhatred against sin and iniquity.

33 ᵃPreach unto them repentance, and faith on the Lord Jesus Christ; teach them to humble themselves and to be ᵇmeek and lowly in heart; teach them to ᶜwithstand every ᵈtemptation of the devil, with their faith on the Lord Jesus Christ.

34 Teach them to never be weary of good works, but to be meek and lowly in heart; for such shall find ᵃrest to their souls.

35 O, remember, my son, and ᵃlearn ᵇwisdom in thy ᶜyouth; yea, learn in thy youth to keep the commandments of God.

36 Yea, and ᵃcry unto God for all thy support; yea, let all thy ᵇdoings be unto the Lord, and whithersoever thou goest let it be in the Lord; yea, let all thy ᶜthoughts be directed unto the Lord; yea, let the affections of thy heart be placed upon the Lord forever.

37 ᵃCounsel with the Lord in all thy doings, and he will direct thee for ᵇgood; yea, when thou liest down at night lie down unto the Lord, that he may watch over you in your sleep; and when thou risest in the ᶜmorning let thy heart be full of thanks unto God; and if ye do these things, ye shall be lifted up at the last day.

38 And now, my son, I have somewhat to say concerning the thing which our fathers call a ball, or director—or our fathers called it ᵃLiahona, which is, being interpreted, a compass; and the Lord prepared it.

39 And behold, there cannot any man work after the manner of so curious a workmanship. And behold, it was prepared to show unto our fathers the course which they should travel in the wilderness.

40 And it did work for them according to their ᵃfaith in God; therefore, if they had faith to believe that God could cause that those spindles should point the way they should go, behold, it was done; therefore they had this miracle, and also many other miracles wrought by the power of God, day by day.

41 Nevertheless, because those miracles were worked by ᵃsmall means it did show unto them marvelous works. They were ᵇslothful, and forgot to exercise their faith and diligence and then those marvelous works ceased, and they did not progress in their journey;

42 Therefore, they tarried in the wilderness, or did ᵃnot travel a direct course, and were afflicted with hunger and thirst, because of their transgressions.

43 And now, my son, I would that ye should understand that these things are not without a ᵃshadow; for as our fathers were slothful to give heed to this compass (now these things were temporal) they

31 b Gen. 15:16;
    Hel. 13:14;
    D&C 61:31; 101:11.
32 a 2 Ne. 4:31;
    Alma 43:7.
33 a TG Mission of Early
    Saints; Preaching.
  b TG Meek.
  c TG Perseverance;
    Self-Mastery.
  d TG Temptation.
34 a Matt. 11:29 (28–30).
35 a TG Education; Learn.
  b TG Wisdom.

  c Eccl. 12:1;
    Lam. 3:27.
36 a TG Prayer.
  b Ps. 37:5 (4–7).
  c D&C 6:36.
    TG Motivations.
37 a Josh. 9:14;
    Ps. 34:4 (4, 6, 10);
    Prov. 3:5 (5–6);
    Lam. 3:25;
    Heb. 11:6;
    Jacob 4:10;
    D&C 3:4.
  b TG Abundant Life.

  c 1 Chr. 16:8 (7–36);
    Ps. 5:3; Ether 6:9;
    D&C 46:32.
38 a 1 Ne. 16:10 (10, 16, 26);
    18:12 (12, 21);
    2 Ne. 5:12;
    D&C 17:1.
40 a 1 Ne. 16:28.
41 a 1 Ne. 16:29;
    Alma 37:7 (6–8).
  b TG Apathy; Laziness.
42 a 1 Ne. 16:28.
43 a Col. 2:17; Heb. 8:5;
    Mosiah 3:15.

did not prosper; even so it is with things which are spiritual.

44 For behold, it is as easy to give heed to the ^aword of Christ, which will point to you a straight course to eternal bliss, as it was for our fathers to give heed to this compass, which would point unto them a straight course to the promised land.

45 And now I say, is there not a ^atype in this thing? For just as surely as this director did bring our fathers, by following its course, to the promised land, shall the words of Christ, if we follow their course, carry us beyond this vale of sorrow into a far better land of promise.

46 O my son, do not let us be ^aslothful because of the ^beasiness of the ^cway; for so was it with our fathers; for so was it prepared for them, that if they would ^dlook they might ^elive; even so it is with us. The way is prepared, and if we will look we may live forever.

47 And now, my son, see that ye take ^acare of these sacred things, yea, see that ye ^blook to God and live. Go unto this people and declare the word, and be sober. My son, farewell.

The commandments of Alma to his son Shiblon.

Comprising chapter 38.

CHAPTER 38

Shiblon was persecuted for righteousness' sake—Salvation is in Christ, who

is the life and the light of the world—Bridle all your passions. About 74 B.C.

MY ^ason, give ear to my words, for I say unto you, even as I said unto Helaman, that ^binasmuch as ye shall keep the commandments of God ye shall prosper in the land; and inasmuch as ye will not keep the commandments of God ye shall be ^ccut off from his ^dpresence.

2 And now, my son, I trust that I shall have great joy in you, because of your ^asteadiness and your faithfulness unto God; for as you have commenced in your youth to look to the Lord your God, even so I hope that you will continue in keeping his commandments; for blessed is he that ^bendureth to the end.

3 I say unto you, my son, that I have had great joy in thee already, because of thy faithfulness and thy diligence, and thy patience and thy long-suffering among the people of the ^aZoramites.

4 For I know that thou wast in bonds; yea, and I also know that thou wast stoned for the word's sake; and thou didst bear all these things with ^apatience because the Lord was ^bwith thee; and now thou knowest that the Lord did deliver thee.

5 And now my son, Shiblon, I would that ye should remember, that as much as ye shall put your ^atrust in God even so much ye shall be ^bdelivered out of your trials, and your ^ctroubles, and your afflictions, and ye shall be lifted up at the last day.

6 Now, my son, I would not that ye should think that I know these

44a Ps. 119:105.
45a TG Jesus Christ, Types of, in Anticipation.
46a Luke 6:46 (46–49);
  1 Ne. 17:41 (40–41).
 b Matt. 11:30.
 c Ex. 33:13 (12–13);
  2 Ne. 9:41; 31:21 (17–21);
  D&C 132:22 (22, 25).
 d Alma 25:16;
  33:22 (19–23).
 e John 11:25;
  Hel. 8:15;
  3 Ne. 15:9.

47a TG Scriptures, Preservation of.
 b Amos 5:6;
  Ether 12:41.
38 1a Alma 37:7; 63:1.
 b Alma 36:30.
 c 1 Ne. 2:21;
  2 Ne. 5:20 (20–24);
  Alma 9:14 (13–15).
 d TG God, Presence of.
2a TG Commitment.
 b Matt. 10:22;
  Mark 13:13;
  2 Ne. 31:16 (15–20);

Alma 32:13 (13–15);
 3 Ne. 15:9; 27:6 (6–17);
 D&C 20:29; 53:7.
3a Alma 31:7; 39:2.
4a TG Patience.
 b Ex. 3:12;
  1 Ne. 17:55;
  Mosiah 24:17.
5a Ps. 50:15;
  D&C 100:17.
 b Matt. 11:28 (28–30).
 c Ps. 81:7;
  Alma 9:17;
  D&C 3:8.

things of myself, but it is the Spirit of God which is in me which maketh these things known unto me; for if I had not been ᵃborn of God I should not have known these things.

7 But behold, the Lord in his great mercy sent his ᵃangel to declare unto me that I must stop the work of ᵇdestruction among his people; yea, and I have seen an angel face to face, and he spake with me, and his voice was as thunder, and it shook the whole earth.

8 And it came to pass that I was ᵃthree days and three nights in the most bitter ᵇpain and ᶜanguish of soul; and never, until I did cry out unto the Lord Jesus Christ for mercy, did I receive a ᵈremission of my sins. But behold, I did cry unto him and I did find peace to my soul.

9 And now, my son, I have told you this that ye may learn wisdom, that ye may learn of me that there is ᵃno other way or means whereby man can be saved, only in and through Christ. Behold, he is the life and the ᵇlight of the world. Behold, he is the word of truth and ᶜrighteousness.

10 And now, as ye have begun to teach the word even so I would that ye should continue to teach; and I would that ye would be diligent and ᵃtemperate in all things.

11 See that ye are not lifted up unto pride; yea, see that ye do not ᵃboast in your own wisdom, nor of your much strength.

12 Use ᵃboldness, but not overbearance; and also see that ye ᵇbridle all your passions, that ye may be filled with love; see that ye refrain from idleness.

13 Do not ᵃpray as the Zoramites do, for ye have seen that they pray to be heard of men, and to be praised for their wisdom.

14 Do not say: O God, I thank thee that we are ᵃbetter than our brethren; but rather say: O Lord, forgive my ᵇunworthiness, and remember my brethren in mercy—yea, acknowledge your unworthiness before God at all times.

15 And may the Lord bless your soul, and receive you at the last day into his kingdom, to sit down in peace. Now go, my son, and teach the word unto this people. Be ᵃsober. My son, farewell.

The commandments of Alma to his son Corianton.

Comprising chapters 39 through 42.

CHAPTER 39

Sexual sin is an abomination—Corianton's sins kept the Zoramites from receiving the word—Christ's redemption is retroactive in saving the faithful who preceded it. About 74 B.C.

AND now, my ᵃson, I have somewhat more to say unto thee than what I said unto thy brother; for behold, have ye not observed the steadiness of thy brother, his faithfulness, and his diligence in keeping the commandments of God? Behold, has he not set a good ᵇexample for thee?

2 For thou didst not give so much heed unto my words as did thy brother, among the people of the ᵃZoramites. Now this is what I have against thee; thou didst go on unto

---

6a Alma 36:23 (23, 26);
　　D&C 5:16.
　　TG Holy Ghost,
　　Baptism of;
　　Man, Natural, Not
　　Spiritually Reborn;
　　Man, New, Spiritually
　　Reborn.
7a Mosiah 27:11 (11–17).
　b Mosiah 28:4 (3–4);
　　Alma 26:18 (17–18);
　　36:6 (6–11).

8a Alma 36:10 (10, 16).
　b TG Pain.
　c TG Sorrow.
　d TG Remission of Sins.
9a Alma 21:9.
　b TG Jesus Christ, Light of
　　the World.
　c Ether 4:12.
10a TG Temperance.
11a TG Boast; Pride.
12a Alma 18:24.
　b TG Priesthood,

Magnifying Callings
　　within;
　　Self-Mastery.
13a TG Hypocrisy.
14a Alma 31:16.
　b Luke 18:13 (10–14).
　　TG Ingratitude;
　　Poor in Spirit.
15a 1 Pet. 5:8.
39 1a Alma 31:7.
　b TG Example.
2a Alma 38:3.

boasting in thy strength and thy wisdom.

3 And this is not all, my son. Thou didst do that which was grievous unto me; for thou didst forsake the ministry, and did go over into the land of Siron among the borders of the Lamanites, after the [a]harlot Isabel.

4 Yea, she did [a]steal away the hearts of many; but this was no excuse for thee, my son. Thou shouldst have tended to the ministry wherewith thou wast entrusted.

5 Know ye not, my son, that these things are an abomination in the sight of the Lord; yea, most [a]abominable above all sins save it be the shedding of innocent [b]blood or denying the Holy Ghost?

6 For behold, if ye [a]deny the Holy Ghost when it once has had place in you, and ye know that ye deny it, behold, this is a sin which is [b]unpardonable; yea, and whosoever murdereth against the light and knowledge of God, it is not easy for him to obtain [c]forgiveness; yea, I say unto you, my son, that it is not easy for him to obtain a forgiveness.

7 And now, my son, I would to God that ye had not been [a]guilty of so great a crime. I would not dwell upon your crimes, to harrow up your soul, if it were not for your good.

8 But behold, ye cannot [a]hide your crimes from God; and except ye repent they will stand as a testimony against you at the last day.

9 Now my son, I would that ye should repent and forsake your sins, and go no more after the [a]lusts of your eyes, but [b]cross yourself in all these things; for except ye do this ye can in nowise inherit the kingdom of God. Oh, remember, and take it upon you, and [c]cross yourself in these things.

10 And I command you to take it upon you to counsel with your elder brothers in your undertakings; for behold, thou art in thy youth, and ye stand in need to be nourished by your brothers. And give heed to their counsel.

11 Suffer not yourself to be led away by any vain or foolish thing; suffer not the devil to lead away your heart again after those wicked harlots. Behold, O my son, how great [a]iniquity ye brought upon the [b]Zoramites; for when they saw your [c]conduct they would not believe in my words.

12 And now the Spirit of the Lord doth say unto me: [a]Command thy children to do good, lest they [b]lead away the hearts of many people to destruction; therefore I command you, my son, in the fear of God, that ye [c]refrain from your iniquities;

13 That ye turn to the Lord with all your mind, might, and strength; that ye lead away the hearts of no more to do wickedly; but rather return unto them, and [a]acknowledge your faults and that wrong which ye have done.

14 [a]Seek not after riches nor the vain things of this world; for behold, you cannot carry them with you.

3a 1 Sam. 2:22 (22–25);
   Prov. 5:3.
   TG Sensuality.
4a Prov. 7:18 (6–27).
5a TG Adulterer;
   Fornication;
   Sexual Immorality.
 b TG Life, Sanctity of.
6a Moro. 8:28;
   D&C 76:35.
   TG Holy Ghost, Loss of.
 b TG Holy Ghost,
   Unpardonable Sin
   against.
 c Rom. 9:18;

D&C 64:10.
   TG Forgive.
7a TG Guilt.
8a TG God, Omniscience of.
9a Prov. 5:8.
   TG Carnal Mind;
   Chastity; Covet; Lust.
 b TG Self-Mastery.
 c 3 Ne. 12:30.
11a 1 Sam. 2:24 (22–25).
 b Alma 35:14 (2–14);
   43:4 (4–6, 13).
 c 2 Sam. 12:14;
   Ezek. 5:5;
   Rom. 2:21 (21–23); 14:13;

1 Cor. 9:14 (13–14);
   1 Ne. 21:6;
   Alma 4:11;
   D&C 103:9 (8–9).
   TG Example.
12a TG Commandments of
   God; Teaching.
 b TG Peer Influence.
 c TG Abstain.
13a Mosiah 27:35.
14a Matt. 6:33 (25–34);
   Jacob 2:18 (18–19);
   D&C 6:7 (6–7);
   68:31 (31–32).
   TG Treasure.

15 And now, my son, I would say somewhat unto you concerning the ^acoming of Christ. Behold, I say unto you, that it is he that surely shall come to take away the sins of the world; yea, he cometh to declare glad tidings of salvation unto his people.

16 And now, my son, this was the ministry unto which ye were called, to declare these glad tidings unto this people, to prepare their minds; or rather that salvation might come unto them, that they may prepare the minds of their ^achildren to hear the word at the time of his coming.

17 And now I will ease your mind somewhat on this subject. Behold, you marvel why these things should be known so long beforehand. Behold, I say unto you, is not a soul at this time as precious unto God as a soul will be at the time of his coming?

18 Is it not as necessary that the plan of redemption should be ^amade known unto this people as well as unto their children?

19 Is it not as easy at this time for the Lord to ^asend his angel to declare these glad tidings unto us as unto our children, or as after the time of his coming?

CHAPTER 40

Christ brings to pass the resurrection of all men—The righteous dead go to paradise and the wicked to outer darkness to await the day of their resurrection—All things will be restored to their proper and perfect frame in the Resurrection. About 74 B.C.

Now my son, here is somewhat more I would say unto thee; for I perceive that thy mind is worried concerning the resurrection of the dead.

2 Behold, I say unto you, that there is no resurrection—or, I would say, in other words, that this mortal does not put on ^aimmortality, this corruption does not ^bput on incorruption—^cuntil after the coming of Christ.

3 Behold, he bringeth to pass the ^aresurrection of the dead. But behold, my son, the resurrection is not yet. Now, I unfold unto you a mystery; nevertheless, there are many ^bmysteries which are ^ckept, that no one knoweth them save God himself. But I show unto you one thing which I have inquired diligently of God that I might know—that is concerning the resurrection.

4 Behold, there is a time appointed that all shall ^acome forth from the dead. Now when this time cometh no one knows; but God knoweth the time which is appointed.

5 Now, whether there shall be one time, or a ^asecond time, or a third time, that men shall come forth from the dead, it mattereth not; for God ^bknoweth all these things; and it sufficeth me to know that this is the case—that there is a time appointed that all shall rise from the dead.

6 Now there must needs be a space betwixt the time of death and the time of the resurrection.

7 And now I would inquire what becometh of the ^asouls of men ^bfrom this time of death to the time appointed for the resurrection?

8 Now whether there is more than one ^atime appointed for men to rise it mattereth not; for all do not die at once, and this mattereth not; all is

15a TG Jesus Christ,
    Mission of.
16a TG Family, Children,
    Responsibilities
    toward.
18a Jacob 4:4 (4–6).
19a Mosiah 3:2 (2–3).
40 2a Mosiah 16:10 (10–13).
    TG Immortality.

b 1 Cor. 15:53 (42–54).
c 1 Cor. 15:20 (20–23).
3a TG Resurrection.
b TG Mysteries of
    Godliness.
c D&C 25:4; 121:26; 124:41.
4a John 5:29 (28–29).
5a 1 Thes. 4:16;
    Mosiah 26:25 (24–25);

D&C 43:18; 76:85.
b TG God, Omniscience of.
7a Alma 40:21;
    D&C 138.
TG Soul.
b TG Spirits, Disembodied.
8a 2 Pet. 3:8.
TG Time.

as one day with God, and time only is measured unto men.

9 Therefore, there is a time appointed unto men that they shall rise from the dead; and there is a space between the time of death and the resurrection. And now, concerning this space of time, what becometh of the souls of men is the thing which I have inquired diligently of the Lord to know; and this is the thing of which I do know.

10 And when the time cometh when all shall rise, then shall they know that God ᵃknoweth all the ᵇtimes which are appointed unto man.

11 Now, concerning the ᵃstate of the soul between ᵇdeath and the resurrection—Behold, it has been made known unto me by an angel, that the spirits of all men, as soon as they are departed from this mortal body, yea, the spirits of all men, whether they be good or evil, are ᶜtaken ᵈhome to that God who gave them life.

12 And then shall it come to pass, that the spirits of those who are righteous are received into a state of ᵃhappiness, which is called ᵇparadise, a state of rest, a state of ᶜpeace, where they shall rest from all their troubles and from all care, and sorrow.

13 And then shall it come to pass, that the ᵃspirits of the wicked, yea, who are evil—for behold, they have no part nor portion of the Spirit of the Lord; for behold, they chose evil works rather than good; therefore the spirit of the ᵇdevil did enter into them, and take possession of their house—and these shall be cast out into ᶜouter darkness; there shall be ᵈweeping, and wailing, and gnashing of teeth, and this because of their own iniquity, being led captive by the will of the devil.

14 Now this is the state of the ᵃsouls of the ᵇwicked, yea, in darkness, and a state of awful, ᶜfearful looking for the fiery ᵈindignation of the wrath of God upon them; thus they remain in this ᵉstate, as well as the righteous in paradise, until the time of their resurrection.

15 Now, there are some that have understood that this state of happiness and this state of misery of the soul, before the resurrection, was a first resurrection. Yea, I admit it may be termed a resurrection, the ᵃraising of the spirit or the soul and their consignation to happiness or misery, according to the words which have been spoken.

16 And behold, again it hath been spoken, that there is a ᵃfirst ᵇresurrection, a resurrection of all those who have been, or who are, or who shall be, down to the resurrection of Christ from the dead.

17 Now, we do not suppose that this first resurrection, which is spoken of in this manner, can be the resurrection of the souls and their ᵃconsignation to happiness or misery. Ye cannot suppose that this is what it meaneth.

18 Behold, I say unto you, Nay; but it meaneth the ᵃreuniting of the

10a TG God, Foreknowl-
    edge of.
  b Acts 17:26.
11a John 20:17.
  b Job 14:10;
    Luke 16:22 (22–26);
    1 Ne. 15:31 (31–36);
    Alma 11:45;
    D&C 76:73 (71–74).
  c Alma 40:15.
  d Eccl. 12:7;
    2 Ne. 9:38;
    Alma 24:16;
    Hel. 8:23.
12a Isa. 51:11;

    Luke 16:22;
    D&C 138:15.
    TG Happiness.
  b TG Paradise.
  c 2 Kgs. 22:20;
    Alma 7:27;
    D&C 45:46.
    TG Peace of God.
13a TG Spirits in Prison.
  b TG Bondage, Spiritual.
  c TG Damnation;
    Darkness, Spiritual;
    Hell.
  d Matt. 8:12;
    Mosiah 16:2.

14a TG Spirits in Prison.
  b D&C 138:20.
  c Jacob 6:13;
    Moses 7:1.
  d TG God, Indignation of.
  e Alma 34:34.
15a Alma 40:11.
16a Jacob 4:11;
    Mosiah 15:21 (21–23);
    18:9.
  b TG Jesus Christ,
    Resurrection.
17a D&C 76:17 (17, 32, 50).
    TG Judgment, the Last.
18a Matt. 27:52.

soul with the body, of those from the days of Adam down to the resurrection of Christ.

19 Now, whether the souls and the bodies of those of whom has been spoken shall all be reunited at once, the wicked as well as the righteous, I do not say; let it suffice, that I say that they all come forth; or in other words, their resurrection cometh to pass ^abefore the resurrection of those who die after the resurrection of Christ.

20 Now, my son, I do not say that their resurrection cometh at the resurrection of Christ; but behold, I give it as my opinion, that the souls and the bodies are reunited, of the righteous, at the resurrection of Christ, and his ^aascension into heaven.

21 But whether it be at his resurrection or after, I do not say; but this much I say, that there is a ^aspace between death and the resurrection of the body, and a state of the soul in ^bhappiness or in ^cmisery until the time which is appointed of God that the dead shall come forth, and be reunited, both soul and body, and be ^dbrought to stand before God, and be judged according to their works.

22 Yea, this bringeth about the restoration of those things of which has been spoken by the mouths of the prophets.

23 The ^asoul shall be ^brestored to the ^cbody, and the body to the soul; yea, and every limb and joint shall be restored to its body; yea, even a ^dhair of the head shall not be lost; but all things shall be restored to their proper and ^eperfect frame.

24 And now, my son, this is the restoration of which has been ^aspoken by the mouths of the prophets—

25 And then shall the ^arighteous shine forth in the kingdom of God.

26 But behold, an awful ^adeath cometh upon the wicked; for they die as to things pertaining to things of righteousness; for they are unclean, and ^bno unclean thing can inherit the kingdom of God; but they are cast out, and consigned to partake of the fruits of their labors or their works, which have been evil; and they drink the dregs of a bitter ^ccup.

CHAPTER 41

In the Resurrection men come forth to a state of endless happiness or endless misery—Wickedness never was happiness—Carnal men are without God in the world—Every person receives again in the Restoration the characteristics and attributes acquired in mortality. About 74 B.C.

AND now, my son, I have somewhat to say concerning the restoration of which has been spoken; for behold, some have ^awrested the scriptures, and have gone far ^bastray because of this thing. And I perceive that thy mind has been ^cworried also concerning this thing. But behold, I will explain it unto thee.

2 I say unto thee, my son, that the plan of restoration is requisite with the justice of God; for it is requisite that all things should be restored to their proper order. Behold, it is requisite and just, according to the power and resurrection of Christ,

19a Mosiah 15:26.
20a TG Jesus Christ,
    Ascension of.
21a Luke 23:43 (39–43).
   b TG Paradise.
   c TG Spirits in Prison.
   d Alma 42:23.
23a Ezek. 37:14 (6–14);
    D&C 88:15 (15–17).
    TG Soul.
   b 2 Ne. 9:13;
    Alma 11:45 (40–45).
   c TG Body, Sanctity of.

 d Luke 21:18;
   Alma 41:2;
   D&C 29:25.
 e Philip. 3:21.
   TG Perfection.
24a Isa. 26:19.
   TG Resurrection.
25a Dan. 12:3;
   Matt. 13:43.
26a Ps. 94:3 (1–11);
   1 Cor. 6:9 (9–10);
   1 Ne. 15:33;
   Alma 12:16;

   D&C 29:41.
   TG Hell.
 b Eph. 5:5;
   Alma 11:37.
   TG Uncleanness.
 c Ps. 75:8.
41 1a 2 Pet. 1:20; 3:16;
   Alma 13:20.
   b TG Apostasy of
   Individuals.
   c TG Problem-Solving.

that the soul of man should be restored to its body, and that every ᵃpart of the body should be restored to itself.

3 And it is requisite with the ᵃjustice of God that men should be ᵇjudged according to their ᶜworks; and if their works were good in this life, and the desires of their hearts were good, that they should also, at the last day, be ᵈrestored unto that which is good.

4 And if their works are evil they shall be ᵃrestored unto them for evil. Therefore, all things shall be ᵇrestored to their proper order, every thing to its natural frame—ᶜmortality raised to ᵈimmortality, ᵉcorruption to incorruption—raised to ᶠendless happiness to ᵍinherit the kingdom of God, or to endless misery to inherit the kingdom of the devil, the one on one hand, the other on the other—

5 The one raised to ᵃhappiness according to his desires of happiness, or good according to his desires of good; and the other to evil according to his desires of evil; for as he has desired to do evil all the day long even so shall he have his reward of evil when the night cometh.

6 And so it is on the other hand. If he hath repented of his sins, and desired righteousness until the end of his days, even so he shall be rewarded unto righteousness.

7 ᵃThese are they that are redeemed of the Lord; yea, these are they that are taken out, that are delivered from that endless night of darkness; and thus they stand or fall; for behold, they are their own ᵇjudges, whether to do good or do evil.

8 Now, the decrees of God are ᵃunalterable; therefore, the way is prepared that ᵇwhosoever will may ᶜwalk therein and be saved.

9 And now behold, my son, do not risk ᵃone more offense against your God upon those points of doctrine, which ye have hitherto risked to commit sin.

10 Do not suppose, because it has been spoken concerning restoration, that ye shall be restored from sin to happiness. Behold, I say unto you, ᵃwickedness never was ᵇhappiness.

11 And now, my son, all men that are in a state of ᵃnature, or I would say, in a ᵇcarnal state, are in the ᶜgall of bitterness and in the ᵈbonds of iniquity; they are ᵉwithout God in the world, and they have gone ᶠcontrary to the nature of God; therefore, they are in a state contrary to the nature of happiness.

12 And now behold, is the meaning of the word restoration to take a thing of a natural state and place it in an unnatural state, or to place it in a state opposite to its nature?

13 O, my son, this is not the case; but the meaning of the word restoration is to bring back again ᵃevil for evil, or carnal for carnal, or devilish for devilish—good for that which is good; righteous for that which is righteous; just for that which is just; merciful for that which is merciful.

2a Alma 40:23.
3a TG God, Justice of;
   Justice.
   b TG Accountability;
   Judgment, the Last.
   c Isa. 59:18;
   Alma 36:15; 42:27;
   D&C 1:10 (9–10).
   d Hel. 14:31.
4a Alma 42:28.
   b 2 Ne. 9:13 (10–13);
   D&C 138:17.
   TG Resurrection.
   c TG Mortality.
   d TG Immortality.
   e 1 Cor. 15:50 (50–53).

f TG Eternal Life.
g TG Exaltation.
5a TG Happiness.
7a D&C 76:65.
   b 2 Ne. 2:26; Alma 42:27;
   Hel. 14:30.
   TG Agency.
8a Morm. 9:19.
   b Alma 42:27.
   c TG Walking with God.
9a Prov. 26:11;
   Matt. 12:45 (43–45);
   D&C 42:26 (23–28).
10a Ps. 32:10; Isa. 57:21;
   Hel. 13:38.
   TG Evil; Wickedness.

b Alma 50:21;
   Morm. 2:13.
   TG Happiness;
   Peace of God.
11a Mosiah 3:19.
   TG Man, Natural, Not
   Spiritually Reborn.
   b TG Carnal Mind;
   Fall of Man.
   c Acts 8:23; Morm. 8:31.
   d TG Bondage, Spiritual.
   e Eph. 2:12;
   Mosiah 27:31.
   f Hel. 13:38.
13a Dan. 12:10;
   Rev. 22:12 (6–16).

14 Therefore, my son, see that you are merciful unto your brethren; deal ^ajustly, ^bjudge righteously, and do ^cgood continually; and if ye do all these things then shall ye receive your ^dreward; yea, ye shall have ^emercy restored unto you again; ye shall have justice restored unto you again; ye shall have a righteous judgment restored unto you again; and ye shall have good rewarded unto you again.

15 For that which ye do ^asend out shall return unto you again, and be restored; therefore, the word restoration more fully condemneth the sinner, and justifieth him not at all.

CHAPTER 42

Mortality is a probationary time to enable man to repent and serve God—The Fall brought temporal and spiritual death upon all mankind—Redemption comes through repentance—God Himself atones for the sins of the world—Mercy is for those who repent—All others are subject to God's justice—Mercy comes because of the Atonement—Only the truly penitent are saved. About 74 B.C.

AND now, my son, I perceive there is somewhat more which doth worry your mind, which ye cannot understand—which is concerning the ^ajustice of God in the ^bpunishment of the sinner; for ye do try to suppose that it is ^cinjustice that the sinner should be consigned to a state of misery.

2 Now behold, my son, I will explain this thing unto thee. For behold, after the Lord God sent our first parents forth from the garden of ^aEden, to till the ^bground, from whence they were taken—yea, he drew out the man, and he placed at the east end of the garden of Eden, ^ccherubim, and a flaming sword which turned every way, to keep the tree of life—

3 Now, we see that the man had become as God, knowing good and evil; and lest he should put forth his hand, and take also of the tree of life, and eat and live forever, the Lord God placed ^acherubim and the flaming sword, that he should not partake of the fruit—

4 And thus we see, that there was a ^atime granted unto man to repent, yea, a ^bprobationary time, a time to repent and serve God.

5 For behold, if Adam had put forth his hand immediately, and ^apartaken of the ^btree of life, he would have lived forever, according to the word of God, having no space for repentance; yea, and also the word of God would have been void, and the great plan of salvation would have been frustrated.

6 But behold, it was appointed unto man to ^adie—therefore, as they were cut off from the tree of life they should be cut off from the face of the earth—and man became ^blost forever, yea, they became ^cfallen man.

7 And now, ye see by this that our first parents were ^acut off both temporally and spiritually from the ^bpresence of the Lord; and thus we see they became subjects to follow after their own ^cwill.

8 Now behold, it was not expedient

14a TG Honesty.
  b Matt. 7:1 (1–5);
    D&C 11:12.
  c TG Benevolence.
  d TG Reward.
  e TG Mercy.
15a Prov. 19:17;
    Eccl. 11:1;
    Alma 42:27 (27–28).
42 1a Mosiah 15:27.
    TG God, Justice of.
  b TG Punish.
  c Rom. 3:5; 2 Ne. 26:7.

    TG Injustice.
2a TG Eden.
  b Jacob 2:21;
    Mosiah 2:25;
    Morm. 9:17.
  c Gen. 3:24;
    Alma 12:21;
    Moses 4:31.
3a TG Cherubim.
4a Jacob 5:27.
  b Alma 34:32.
    TG Earth, Purpose of;
    Probation.

5a Alma 12:23; Moses 4:28.
  b Gen. 2:9; 3:24 (22–24);
    1 Ne. 8:10 (10–12);
    Moses 3:9.
6a TG Death.
  b 2 Ne. 9:7;
    Mosiah 16:4 (4–7);
    Alma 11:45; 12:36.
  c TG Fall of Man.
7a 2 Ne. 2:5; 9:6 (6–15);
    Hel. 14:16 (15–18).
  b TG God, Presence of.
  c TG Agency.

that man should be reclaimed from this ᵃtemporal death, for that would destroy the great ᵇplan of happiness.

9 Therefore, as the soul could never die, and the ᵃfall had brought upon all mankind a spiritual ᵇdeath as well as a temporal, that is, they were cut off from the presence of the Lord, it was expedient that mankind should be reclaimed from this spiritual death.

10 Therefore, as they had become ᵃcarnal, sensual, and devilish, by ᵇnature, this ᶜprobationary state became a state for them to prepare; it became a preparatory state.

11 And now remember, my son, if it were not for the plan of redemption, (laying it aside) as soon as they were dead their souls were ᵃmiserable, being cut off from the presence of the Lord.

12 And now, there was no means to reclaim men from this fallen state, which ᵃman had brought upon himself because of his own ᵇdisobedience;

13 Therefore, according to justice, the ᵃplan of ᵇredemption could not be brought about, only on conditions of repentance of men in this probationary state, yea, this preparatory state; for except it were for these conditions, mercy could not take effect except it should destroy the work of justice. Now the work of justice could not be destroyed; if so, God would ᶜcease to be God.

14 And thus we see that all mankind were ᵃfallen, and they were in the grasp of ᵇjustice; yea, the justice of God, which consigned them forever to be cut off from his presence.

15 And now, the plan of mercy could not be brought about except an atonement should be made; therefore God himself ᵃatoneth for the sins of the world, to bring about the plan of ᵇmercy, to appease the demands of ᶜjustice, that God might be a ᵈperfect, just God, and a ᵉmerciful God also.

16 Now, repentance could not come unto men except there were a ᵃpunishment, which also was ᵇeternal as the life of the soul should be, affixed ᶜopposite to the plan of happiness, which was as ᵈeternal also as the life of the soul.

17 Now, how could a man repent except he should ᵃsin? How could he sin if there was no ᵇlaw? How could there be a law save there was a punishment?

18 Now, there was a punishment affixed, and a just law given, which brought remorse of ᵃconscience unto man.

19 Now, if there was no law given—if a man ᵃmurdered he should ᵇdie—would he be afraid he would die if he should murder?

20 And also, if there was no law given against sin men would not be afraid to sin.

21 And if there was ᵃno law given, if men sinned what could justice do, or mercy either, for they would have no claim upon the creature?

22 But there is a law given, and a

8a Gen. 3:22 (22–24).
  b Alma 12:26 (22–33);
    34:9 (8–16);
    Moses 6:62.
9a TG Fall of Man.
  b Moses 5:4.
    TG Death, Spiritual,
    First.
10a TG Carnal Mind.
  b TG Man, Natural, Not
    Spiritually Reborn.
  c TG Mortality; Probation.
11a 2 Ne. 9:9 (7–9).
12a 1 Cor. 15:22.
  b TG Disobedience.
13a TG Salvation, Plan of.

  b TG Redemption;
    Repent.
  c 2 Ne. 2:13 (13–14).
14a Eph. 2:8 (8–9);
    Alma 22:14 (13–14).
  b Rom. 7:5;
    2 Ne. 2:5 (4–10); 25:23.
15a 2 Ne. 9:10;
    Mosiah 16:8 (7–8).
    TG Jesus Christ,
    Atonement through;
    Jesus Christ, Redeemer.
  b TG Jesus Christ,
    Mission of.
  c Alma 12:32.
    TG Justice.

  d TG God, Perfection of.
  e TG God, Mercy of.
16a TG Punish.
  b D&C 19:11 (10–12).
  c TG Opposition.
  d TG Eternity.
17a Rom. 7:8 (1–25).
    TG Sin.
  b Rom. 4:15; 5:13;
    2 Ne. 9:25.
18a TG Conscience.
19a TG Murder.
  b TG Blood, Shedding of.
21a 2 Ne. 9:26 (25–26);
    Mosiah 3:11;
    Alma 9:16 (15–16).

*a*punishment affixed, and a *b*repentance granted; which repentance, mercy claimeth; otherwise, justice claimeth the creature and executeth the *c*law, and the law inflicteth the punishment; if not so, the works of justice would be destroyed, and God would cease to be God.

23 But God ceaseth not to be God, and *a*mercy claimeth the penitent, and mercy cometh because of the *b*atonement; and the atonement bringeth to pass the *c*resurrection of the dead; and the *d*resurrection of the dead bringeth *e*back men into the presence of God; and thus they are restored into his presence, to be *f*judged according to their works, according to the law and justice.

24 For behold, justice exerciseth all his demands, and also *a*mercy claimeth all which is her own; and thus, none but the truly penitent are saved.

25 What, do ye suppose that *a*mercy can rob *b*justice? I say unto you, Nay; not one whit. If so, God would cease to be God.

26 And thus God bringeth about his great and eternal *a*purposes, which were prepared *b*from the foundation of the world. And thus cometh about the salvation and the redemption of men, and also their destruction and misery.

27 Therefore, O my son, *a*whosoever will come may come and partake of the waters of life freely; and whosoever will not come the same is not compelled to come; but in the last day it shall be *b*restored unto him according to his *c*deeds.

28 If he has desired to do *a*evil, and has not repented in his days, behold, evil shall be done unto him, according to the restoration of God.

29 And now, my son, I desire that ye should let these things *a*trouble you no more, and only let your sins trouble you, with that trouble which shall bring you down unto repentance.

30 O my son, I desire that ye should deny the *a*justice of God no more. Do not endeavor to excuse yourself in the least point because of your sins, by denying the justice of God; but do you let the justice of God, and his *b*mercy, and his long-suffering have full sway in your heart; and let it bring you down to the dust in *c*humility.

31 And now, O my son, ye are called of God to *a*preach the word unto this people. And now, my son, go thy way, declare the word with truth and soberness, that thou mayest *b*bring souls unto repentance, that the great plan of mercy may have claim upon them. And may God grant unto you even according to my words. Amen.

CHAPTER 43

Alma and his sons preach the word—The Zoramites and other Nephite dissenters become Lamanites—The Lamanites come against the Nephites in war—Moroni arms the Nephites with defensive armor—The Lord

22 *a* TG Punish.
  b TG Repent.
  c Gal. 3:13;
     D&C 76:48.
23 *a* TG God, Mercy of.
  b TG Jesus Christ,
     Atonement through.
  c 2 Ne. 2:8;
     Alma 7:12; 12:25 (24–25).
  d 2 Ne. 9:4;
     Alma 11:41 (41–45);
     Hel. 14:15 (15–18);
     Morm. 9:13.
  e Alma 40:21 (21–24).

  f TG Jesus Christ, Judge.
24 *a* TG God, Mercy of.
25 *a* TG Mercy.
  b TG Justice.
26 *a* Matt. 5:48;
     Rom. 8:17 (14–21);
     2 Ne. 2:15 (14–30);
     D&C 29:43 (42–44);
     Moses 1:39.
     TG Earth, Purpose of.
  b Alma 13:3 (3, 5, 7–8);
     3 Ne. 1:14.
27 *a* Alma 5:34; 41:7 (7–8);
     Hel. 14:30.

     TG Agency.
  b Alma 41:15.
  c Isa. 59:18;
     Alma 36:15;
     D&C 1:10 (9–10).
28 *a* Alma 41:4 (2–5).
29 *a* 2 Cor. 7:10 (8–11);
     Morm. 2:13.
30 *a* TG Justice.
  b TG God, Mercy of.
  c TG Humility.
31 *a* D&C 11:15.
  b TG Mission of Early
     Saints.

*reveals to Alma the strategy of the La-
manites—The Nephites defend their
homes, liberties, families, and religion—The armies of Moroni and Lehi
surround the Lamanites. About 74 B.C.*

AND now it came to pass that the
sons of Alma did go forth among
the people, to declare the word
unto them. And Alma, also, himself,
could not *a*rest, and he also went
forth.

2 Now *a*we shall say no more concerning their preaching, except
that they preached the word, and
the truth, according to the spirit
of prophecy and revelation; and
they preached after the *b*holy order
of God by which they were called.

3 And now *a*I return to an *b*account
of the wars between the Nephites
and the Lamanites, in the eighteenth
year of the reign of the judges.

4 For behold, it came to pass that
the *a*Zoramites became Lamanites;
therefore, in the commencement
of the eighteenth year the people of
the Nephites saw that the Lamanites
were coming upon them; therefore
they made preparations for war;
yea, they gathered together their
armies in the land of Jershon.

5 And it came to pass that the
Lamanites came with their thousands; and they came into the land
of *a*Antionum, which is the land of
the Zoramites; and a man by the
name of *b*Zerahemnah was their
leader.

6 And now, as the *a*Amalekites
were of a more wicked and murderous disposition than the Lamanites were, in and of themselves,
therefore, Zerahemnah appointed
chief *b*captains over the Lamanites,

and they were all Amalekites and
*c*Zoramites.

7 Now this he did that he might
preserve their *a*hatred towards the
Nephites, that he might bring them
into subjection to the accomplish-
ment of his designs.

8 For behold, his *a*designs were
to *b*stir up the Lamanites to anger
against the Nephites; this he did
that he might usurp great power
over them, and also that he might
gain power over the Nephites by
bringing them into *c*bondage.

9 And now the design of the Nephites was to support their lands, and
their houses, and their *a*wives,
and their children, that they might
preserve them from the hands of
their enemies; and also that they
might preserve their *b*rights and
their privileges, yea, and also their
*c*liberty, that they might worship
God according to their desires.

10 For they knew that if they
should fall into the hands of the
Lamanites, that whosoever should
*a*worship God in *b*spirit and in truth,
the true and the living God, the Lamanites would *c*destroy.

11 Yea, and they also knew the
extreme hatred of the Lamanites
towards their *a*brethren, who were
the *b*people of Anti-Nephi-Lehi,
who were called the people of Ammon—and they would not take up
arms, yea, they had entered into a
covenant and they would not break
it—therefore, if they should fall
into the hands of the Lamanites
they would be destroyed.

12 And the Nephites would not suffer that they should be destroyed;
therefore they gave them lands for
their inheritance.

43 1*a* Ether 12:2 (2–3).
    2*a* W of M 1:9 (1–9).
     b Alma 30:20 (20–23, 31);
      46:38.
     TG Priesthood.
    3*a* Morm. 5:9.
     b Alma 35:13.
    4*a* Alma 30:59; 35:14 (2–14);
      52:33 (20, 33).
    5*a* Alma 31:3.

     b Alma 44:1.
    6*a* Alma 21:4 (2–16).
     b Alma 48:5.
     c Alma 43:44.
    7*a* Alma 37:32.
    8*a* Alma 43:29.
     b Alma 27:12; 47:1.
     c Alma 44:2.
    9*a* Alma 44:5; 46:12;
      48:10 (10, 24).

     b TG Citizenship.
     c TG Liberty.
   10*a* TG Worship.
     b John 4:23 (23–24).
     c Dan. 6:7 (4–17).
  11*a* Alma 23:17;
     24:1 (1–3, 5, 20);
     25:13 (1, 13);
     27:2 (2, 21–26).
     b Alma 47:29.

13 And the people of Ammon did give unto the Nephites a large portion of their substance to ^asupport their armies; and thus the Nephites were compelled, alone, to withstand against the Lamanites, who were a compound of Laman and Lemuel, and the sons of Ishmael, and all those who had dissented from the Nephites, who were Amalekites and Zoramites, and the ^bdescendants of the priests of Noah.

14 Now those descendants were as numerous, nearly, as were the Nephites; and thus the Nephites were obliged to contend with their brethren, even unto bloodshed.

15 And it came to pass as the armies of the Lamanites had gathered together in the land of Antionum, behold, the armies of the Nephites were prepared to meet them in the ^aland of Jershon.

16 Now, the leader of the Nephites, or the man who had been ^aappointed to be the ^bchief captain over the Nephites—now the chief captain took the command of all the armies of the Nephites—and his name was Moroni;

17 And Moroni took all the command, and the government of their wars. And he was only twenty and five years old when he was appointed chief captain over the armies of the Nephites.

18 And it came to pass that he met the Lamanites in the borders of Jershon, and his people were armed with swords, and with cimeters, and all manner of ^aweapons of war.

19 And when the armies of the Lamanites saw that the people of Nephi, or that Moroni, had ^aprepared his people with ^bbreastplates and with arm-shields, yea, and also shields to defend their heads, and also they were dressed with thick clothing—

20 Now the army of Zerahemnah was not prepared with any such thing; they had only their ^aswords and their cimeters, their bows and their arrows, their ^bstones and their slings; and they were ^cnaked, save it were a skin which was girded about their loins; yea, all were naked, save it were the Zoramites and the Amalekites;

21 But they were not armed with breastplates, nor shields—therefore, they were exceedingly afraid of the armies of the Nephites because of their armor, notwithstanding their number being so much greater than the Nephites.

22 Behold, now it came to pass that they durst not come against the Nephites in the borders of Jershon; therefore they departed out of the land of Antionum into the wilderness, and took their journey round about in the wilderness, away by the head of the river Sidon, that they might come into the land of ^aManti and take possession of the land; for they did not suppose that the armies of Moroni would know whither they had gone.

23 But it came to pass, as soon as they had departed into the wilderness Moroni sent spies into the wilderness to watch their camp; and Moroni, also, knowing of the prophecies of Alma, sent certain men unto him, desiring him that he should ^ainquire of the Lord ^bwhither the armies of the Nephites should go to defend themselves against the Lamanites.

24 And it came to pass that the ^aword of the Lord came unto Alma, and Alma informed the messengers of Moroni, that the armies of the

13a Alma 56:27.
  b Alma 25:4.
15a Alma 27:26.
16a Alma 46:34.
  b Alma 46:11.
18a TG Weapon.
19a TG Skill.
  b Alma 49:24.

20a Mosiah 10:8;
    Alma 3:5 (4–5); 44:8.
  b 1 Ne. 16:15;
    Alma 49:2.
  c Enos 1:20.
22a Alma 22:27; 56:14.
23a Ex. 18:15;
    2 Kgs. 6:12 (8–18);

    Mosiah 28:6.
  b Alma 16:6 (5–8); 48:16;
    3 Ne. 3:20 (18–21).
24a Isa. 31:5;
    Alma 43:47;
    D&C 134:11.
    TG Guidance, Divine.

Lamanites were marching round about in the wilderness, that they might come over into the land of Manti, that they might commence an attack upon the weaker part of the people. And those messengers went and delivered the message unto Moroni.

25 Now Moroni, leaving a part of his army in the land of Jershon, lest by any means a part of the Lamanites should come into that land and take possession of the city, took the remaining part of his army and marched over into the land of Manti.

26 And he caused that all the people in that quarter of the land should gather themselves together to battle against the Lamanites, to defend their lands and their country, their rights and their liberties; therefore they were prepared against the time of the coming of the Lamanites.

27 And it came to pass that Moroni caused that his army should be secreted in the valley which was near the bank of the river Sidon, which was on the west of the river Sidon in the wilderness.

28 And Moroni placed spies round about, that he might know when the camp of the Lamanites should come.

29 And now, as Moroni knew the ᵃintention of the Lamanites, that it was their intention to destroy their brethren, or to ᵇsubject them and bring them into bondage that they might establish a kingdom unto themselves over all the land;

30 And he also knowing that it was the ᵃonly desire of the Nephites to preserve their lands, and their ᵇliberty, and their church, therefore he thought it no sin that he should defend them by ᶜstratagem; therefore, he found by his spies which course the Lamanites were to take.

31 Therefore, he divided his army and brought a part over into the valley, and ᵃconcealed them on the east, and on the south of the hill Riplah;

32 And the remainder he concealed in the west ᵃvalley, on the west of the river Sidon, and so down into the borders of the land Manti.

33 And thus having placed his army according to his desire, he was prepared to meet them.

34 And it came to pass that the Lamanites came up on the north of the hill, where a part of the army of Moroni was concealed.

35 And as the Lamanites had passed the hill Riplah, and came into the valley, and began to cross the river Sidon, the army which was concealed on the south of the hill, which was led by a man whose name was ᵃLehi, and he led his army forth and encircled the Lamanites about on the east in their rear.

36 And it came to pass that the Lamanites, when they saw the Nephites coming upon them in their rear, turned them about and began to contend with the army of Lehi.

37 And the work of death commenced on both sides, but it was more dreadful on the part of the Lamanites, for their ᵃnakedness was exposed to the heavy blows of the Nephites with their swords and their cimeters, which brought death almost at every stroke.

38 While on the other hand, there was now and then a man fell among the Nephites, by their swords and the loss of blood, they being shielded from the more vital parts of the body, or the more vital parts of the body being shielded from the strokes of the Lamanites, by their ᵃbreastplates, and their armshields, and their head-plates; and thus the Nephites did carry on the work of death among the Lamanites.

29a Alma 43:8.
  b Alma 49:7.
30a Alma 44:5;
   46:12 (12–20);
   48:10 (10–16).
  b Alma 46:35.
  c Judg. 7:16 (15–25).
31a Josh. 8:13;
   Alma 52:21 (21–31);
   58:16 (15–21).
32a Alma 43:41.
35a Alma 49:16.
37a Alma 3:5.
38a Alma 44:9.

39 And it came to pass that the Lamanites became frightened, because of the great destruction among them, even until they began to flee towards the river Sidon.

40 And they were pursued by Lehi and his men; and they were driven by Lehi into the waters of Sidon, and they crossed the waters of Sidon. And Lehi retained his armies upon the bank of the river Sidon that they should not cross.

41 And it came to pass that Moroni and his army met the Lamanites in the ^avalley, on the other side of the river Sidon, and began to fall upon them and to slay them.

42 And the Lamanites did flee again before them, towards the land of Manti; and they were met again by the armies of Moroni.

43 Now in this case the Lamanites did fight exceedingly; yea, never had the Lamanites been known to fight with such exceedingly great strength and courage, no, not even from the beginning.

44 And they were inspired by the ^aZoramites and the Amalekites, who were their chief captains and leaders, and by Zerahemnah, who was their chief captain, or their chief leader and commander; yea, they did fight like dragons, and many of the Nephites were slain by their hands, yea, for they did smite in two many of their head-plates, and they did pierce many of their breastplates, and they did smite off many of their arms; and thus the Lamanites did smite in their fierce anger.

45 Nevertheless, the Nephites were inspired by a ^abetter cause, for they were not ^bfighting for monarchy nor power but they were fighting for their homes and their ^cliberties, their wives and their children, and their all, yea, for their rites of worship and their church.

46 And they were doing that which they felt was the ^aduty which they owed to their God; for the Lord had said unto them, and also unto their fathers, that: ^bInasmuch as ye are not guilty of the ^cfirst offense, neither the second, ye shall not suffer yourselves to be slain by the hands of your enemies.

47 And again, the Lord has said that: Ye shall ^adefend your families even unto ^bbloodshed. Therefore for this cause were the Nephites contending with the Lamanites, to defend themselves, and their families, and their lands, their country, and their rights, and their religion.

48 And it came to pass that when the men of Moroni saw the fierceness and the anger of the Lamanites, they were about to shrink and flee from them. And Moroni, perceiving their intent, sent forth and inspired their hearts with these thoughts—yea, the thoughts of their lands, their liberty, yea, their freedom from bondage.

49 And it came to pass that they turned upon the Lamanites, and they ^acried with one voice ^bunto the Lord their God, for their ^cliberty and their freedom from bondage.

50 And they ^abegan to contend against the Lamanites with power; and in that selfsame hour that they cried unto the Lord for their freedom, the Lamanites began to flee before them; and they fled even to the waters of Sidon.

51 Now, the Lamanites were more ^anumerous, yea, by more than double the number of the Nephites; nevertheless, they were driven

41a Alma 43:32.
44a Alma 43:6.
45a Alma 44:1.
  b Mosiah 20:11;
    Alma 44:5.
  c TG Liberty.
46a TG Duty.
  b Alma 48:14 (14–16);
    D&C 98:33 (23–36).

  c Luke 6:29;
    3 Ne. 3:21 (20–21);
    Morm. 3:10 (10–11);
    D&C 98:23 (22–48).
47a Isa. 31:5;
    Alma 43:24; 61:14;
    Morm. 7:4;
    D&C 134:11.
  TG Family, Children,

    Responsibilities toward;
    War.
  b Josh. 1:18.
49a Ex. 2:23 (23–25);
    Mosiah 29:20.
  b Ps. 59:1 (1–5).
  c TG Liberty.
50a Ex. 17:11 (8–13).
51a Alma 46:30.

insomuch that they were gathered together in one body in the valley, upon the bank by the river Sidon.

52 Therefore the armies of Moroni encircled them about, yea, even on both sides of the river, for behold, on the east were the men of Lehi.

53 Therefore when Zerahemnah saw the men of Lehi on the east of the river Sidon, and the armies of Moroni on the west of the river Sidon, that they were encircled about by the Nephites, they were struck with terror.

54 Now Moroni, when he saw their *terror, commanded his men that they should stop shedding their blood.

CHAPTER 44

Moroni commands the Lamanites to make a covenant of peace or be destroyed—Zerahemnah rejects the offer, and the battle resumes—Moroni's armies defeat the Lamanites. About 74–73 B.C.

AND it came to pass that they did stop and withdrew a pace from them. And Moroni said unto *Zerahemnah: Behold, Zerahemnah, that we do *not desire to be men of blood. Ye know that ye are in our hands, yet we do not desire to slay you.

2 Behold, we have not come out to battle against you that we might shed your blood for power; neither do we desire to bring any one to the *yoke of bondage. But this is the *very cause for which ye have come against us; yea, and ye are angry with us because of our religion.

3 But now, ye behold that the Lord is with us; and ye behold that he has delivered you into our hands. And now I would that ye should understand that this is done unto us *because of our religion and our faith in Christ. And now ye see that ye cannot destroy this our faith.

4 Now ye see that this is the true faith of God; yea, ye see that God will support, and keep, and preserve us, so long as we are *faithful unto him, and unto our faith, and our religion; and never will the Lord suffer that we shall be destroyed except we should fall into transgression and deny our faith.

5 And now, Zerahemnah, I command you, in the name of that all-powerful God, who has strengthened our arms that we have gained power over you, *by our faith, by our religion, and by our *rites of worship, and by our church, and by the sacred support which we owe to our *wives and our children, by that *liberty which binds us to our lands and our country; yea, and also by the maintenance of the sacred word of God, to which we owe all our happiness; and by all that is most dear unto us—

6 Yea, and this is not all; I command you by all the desires which ye have for life, that ye *deliver up your weapons of war unto us, and we will seek not your blood, but we will *spare your lives, if ye will go your way and come not again to war against us.

7 And now, if ye do not this, behold, ye are in our hands, and I will command my men that they shall fall upon you, and *inflict the wounds of death in your bodies, that ye may become extinct; and then we will see who shall have power over this people; yea, we will see who shall be brought into bondage.

8 And now it came to pass that when Zerahemnah had heard these sayings he came forth and delivered up his *sword and his cimeter, and his bow into the hands of Moroni, and said unto him: Behold, here are

---

54a Alma 47:2.
44 1a Alma 43:5.
  b Alma 43:45.
  2a TG Bondage, Physical.
  b Alma 43:8.
  3a Alma 38:1.

TG Protection, Divine.
4a Mark 4:40 (35–41).
5a Alma 43:45 (9, 45);
  46:12 (12–20).
  b TG Ordinance.
  c Gen. 2:24 (23–24).

d TG Liberty.
6a Alma 52:25 (25, 32).
  b TG Benevolence.
7a Alma 62:11.
8a Alma 43:20.

our weapons of war; we will deliver them up unto you, but we will not suffer ourselves to take an ^boath unto you, which we know that we shall break, and also our children; but take our weapons of war, and suffer that we may depart into the wilderness; otherwise we will retain our swords, and we will perish or conquer.

9 Behold, we are ^anot of your faith; we do not believe that it is God that has delivered us into your hands; but we believe that it is your cunning that has preserved you from our swords. Behold, it is your ^bbreast-plates and your shields that have preserved you.

10 And now when Zerahemnah had made an end of speaking these words, Moroni returned the sword and the weapons of war, which he had received, unto Zerahemnah, saying: Behold, we will end the conflict.

11 Now I cannot recall the words which I have spoken, therefore as the Lord liveth, ye shall not depart except ye depart with an oath that ye will not return again against us to war. Now as ye are in our hands we will spill your blood upon the ground, or ye shall submit to the conditions which I have proposed.

12 And now when Moroni had said these words, Zerahemnah retained his sword, and he was angry with Moroni, and he rushed forward that he might slay Moroni; but as he raised his sword, behold, one of Moroni's soldiers smote it even to the earth, and it broke by the hilt; and he also smote Zerahemnah that he took off his scalp and it fell to the earth. And Zerahemnah withdrew from before them into the midst of his soldiers.

13 And it came to pass that the soldier who stood by, who smote off the scalp of Zerahemnah, took up the scalp from off the ground by the hair, and laid it upon the point of his sword, and stretched it forth unto them, saying unto them with a loud voice:

14 Even as this scalp has fallen to the earth, which is the scalp of your chief, so shall ye fall to the earth except ye will deliver up your weapons of war and depart with a covenant of peace.

15 Now there were many, when they heard these words and saw the scalp which was upon the sword, that were struck with fear; and many came forth and threw down their weapons of war at the feet of Moroni, and entered into a ^acovenant of peace. And as many as entered into a covenant they suffered to ^bdepart into the wilderness.

16 Now it came to pass that Zerahemnah was exceedingly wroth, and he did stir up the remainder of his soldiers to anger, to contend more powerfully against the Nephites.

17 And now Moroni was angry, because of the stubbornness of the Lamanites; therefore he commanded his people that they should fall upon them and slay them. And it came to pass that they began to slay them; yea, and the Lamanites did contend with their swords and their might.

18 But behold, their naked skins and their bare heads were exposed to the sharp swords of the Nephites; yea, behold they were pierced and smitten, yea, and did fall exceedingly fast before the swords of the Nephites; and they began to be swept down, even as the soldier of Moroni had prophesied.

19 Now Zerahemnah, when he saw that they were all about to be destroyed, cried mightily unto Moroni, promising that he would covenant and also his people with them, if they would spare the remainder of their lives, that they

ᵃnever would come to war again against them.

20 And it came to pass that Moroni caused that the work of death should ᵃcease again among the people. And he took the weapons of war from the Lamanites; and after they had entered into a ᵇcovenant with him of peace they were suffered to depart into the wilderness.

21 Now the number of their dead was not numbered because of the greatness of the number; yea, the number of their dead was exceedingly great, both on the Nephites and on the Lamanites.

22 And it came to pass that they did cast their dead into the waters of Sidon, and they have gone forth and are buried in the depths of the ᵃsea.

23 And the armies of the Nephites, or of Moroni, returned and came to their houses and their lands.

24 And thus ended the eighteenth year of the reign of the judges over the people of Nephi. And thus ended the record of Alma, which was written upon the plates of Nephi.

The account of the people of Nephi, and their wars and dissensions, in the days of Helaman, according to the record of Helaman, which he kept in his days.

Comprising chapters 45 through 62.

CHAPTER 45

Helaman believes the words of Alma— Alma prophesies the destruction of the Nephites—He blesses and curses the land—Alma may have been taken up by the Spirit, even as Moses—Dissension grows in the Church. About 73 B.C.

BEHOLD, now it came to pass that the people of Nephi were exceedingly rejoiced, because the Lord had again ᵃdelivered them out of the hands of their enemies; therefore they gave thanks unto the Lord their God; yea, and they did ᵇfast much and pray much, and they did worship God with exceedingly great joy.

2 And it came to pass in the nineteenth year of the reign of the judges over the people of Nephi, that Alma came unto his son Helaman and said unto him: Believest thou the words which I spake unto thee concerning those ᵃrecords which have been kept?

3 And Helaman said unto him: Yea, I ᵃbelieve.

4 And Alma said again: Believest thou in Jesus Christ, who shall come?

5 And he said: Yea, I believe all the words which thou hast spoken.

6 And Alma said unto him again: Will ye ᵃkeep my commandments?

7 And he said: Yea, I will keep thy commandments with all my heart.

8 Then Alma said unto him: Blessed art thou; and the Lord shall ᵃprosper thee in this land.

9 But behold, I have somewhat to ᵃprophesy unto thee; but what I prophesy unto thee ye shall not make known; yea, what I prophesy unto thee shall not be made known, even until the prophecy is fulfilled; therefore write the words which I shall say.

10 And these are the words: Behold, I perceive that this very people, the Nephites, according to the spirit of revelation which is in me, in ᵃfour hundred years from the time that Jesus Christ shall manifest himself unto them, shall dwindle in ᵇunbelief.

11 Yea, and then shall they see wars and pestilences, yea, famines and bloodshed, even until the

---

19a Alma 47:6.
20a Alma 46:7.
   b Alma 55:28;
      62:16 (16–17).
22a Alma 3:3.
45 1a TG Deliver.
   b TG Fast, Fasting.

2a Alma 37:1 (1–32); 50:38.
3a 1 Ne. 11:5.
6a TG Commandments
      of God;
      Obedience.
8a 1 Ne. 4:14;
      Alma 48:15, 25.

9a TG Prophecy.
10a 1 Ne. 12:12 (10–15);
      Hel. 13:9;
      Morm. 8:6.
   b TG Apostasy of
      Individuals.

people of Nephi shall become ^aextinct—

12 Yea, and this because they shall dwindle in unbelief and fall into the works of darkness, and ^alasciviousness, and all manner of iniquities; yea, I say unto you, that because they shall sin against so great light and knowledge, yea, I say unto you, that from that day, even the ^bfourth generation shall not all pass away before this great iniquity shall come.

13 And when that great day cometh, behold, the time very soon cometh that those who are now, or the seed of those who are now numbered among the people of Nephi, shall ^ano more be numbered among the people of Nephi.

14 But whosoever remaineth, and is not destroyed in that great and dreadful day, shall be ^anumbered among the ^bLamanites, and shall become like unto them, all, save it be a few who shall be called the disciples of the Lord; and them shall the Lamanites pursue even ^cuntil they shall become extinct. And now, because of iniquity, this prophecy shall be fulfilled.

15 And now it came to pass that after Alma had said these things to Helaman, he ^ablessed him, and also his other sons; and he also blessed the earth for the ^brighteous' sake.

16 And he said: Thus saith the Lord God—^aCursed shall be the land, yea, this land, unto every nation, kindred, tongue, and people, unto destruction, which do ^bwickedly, when they are fully ripe; and as I have said so shall it be; for this is the cursing and the ^cblessing of God upon the land, for the Lord cannot

look upon sin with the ^dleast degree of allowance.

17 And now, when Alma had said these words he blessed the ^achurch, yea, all those who should stand fast in the faith from that time henceforth.

18 And when Alma had done this he ^adeparted out of the land of Zarahemla, as if to go into the land of ^bMelek. And it came to pass that he was never heard of more; as to his death or burial we know not of.

19 Behold, this we know, that he was a righteous man; and the saying went abroad in the church that he was taken up by the ^aSpirit, or ^bburied by the hand of the Lord, even as Moses. But behold, the scriptures saith the Lord took Moses unto himself; and we suppose that he has also received Alma in the spirit, unto himself; therefore, for this cause we know nothing concerning his death and burial.

20 And now it came to pass in the commencement of the nineteenth year of the reign of the judges over the people of Nephi, that Helaman went forth among the people to declare the ^aword unto them.

21 For behold, because of their wars with the Lamanites and the many little dissensions and disturbances which had been among the people, it became expedient that the ^aword of God should be declared among them, yea, and that a ^bregulation should be made throughout the church.

22 Therefore, ^aHelaman and his brethren went forth to establish the church again in all the land, yea, in every city throughout all the land which was possessed by the people

11a Jarom 1:10;
   Hel. 13:6 (5–19).
12a TG Lust.
  b 2 Ne. 26:9;
   3 Ne. 27:32.
13a Hel. 3:16.
14a Moro. 9:24.
  b 1 Ne. 13:30;
   D&C 3:17.
  c Moro. 1:2 (1–3).
15a Gen. 49:1 (1–27);

   Alma 8:22.
  b Alma 46:10; 62:40.
16a 2 Ne. 1:7;
   Alma 37:31;
   Morm. 1:17;
   Ether 2:11 (8–12).
   TG Earth, Curse of.
  b Jer. 44:5 (5–6).
  c D&C 130:21.
  d D&C 1:31.
17a TG Church.

18a 3 Ne. 1:3 (2–3).
  b Alma 35:13.
19a 2 Kgs. 2:16.
  b Deut. 34:6 (5–6).
   TG Translated Beings.
20a Alma 46:1.
21a Alma 31:5.
  b Alma 6:7; 62:44 (44–47).
22a Alma 48:19.

of Nephi. And it came to pass that they did appoint *b*priests and *c*teachers throughout all the land, over all the churches.

23 And now it came to pass that after Helaman and his brethren had appointed priests and teachers over the churches that there arose a *a*dissension among them, and they would not give heed to the words of Helaman and his brethren;

24 But they grew proud, being lifted up in their hearts, because of their exceedingly great *a*riches; therefore they grew rich in their own eyes, and would not give heed to their words, to *b*walk uprightly before God.

CHAPTER 46

Amalickiah conspires to be king—Moroni raises the title of liberty—He rallies the people to defend their religion—True believers are called Christians—A remnant of Joseph will be preserved—Amalickiah and the dissenters flee to the land of Nephi—Those who will not support the cause of freedom are put to death. About 73–72 B.C.

AND it came to pass that as many as would not hearken to the *a*words of Helaman and his brethren were gathered together against their brethren.

2 And now behold, they were exceedingly wroth, insomuch that they were determined to slay them.

3 Now the leader of those who were wroth against their brethren was a large and a strong man; and his name was *a*Amalickiah.

4 And Amalickiah was desirous to be a *a*king; and those people who were wroth were also desirous that he should be their king; and they were the greater part of them the lower *b*judges of the land, and they were seeking for power.

5 And they had been led by the *a*flatteries of Amalickiah, that if they would support him and establish him to be their king that he would make them rulers over the people.

6 Thus they were led away by Amalickiah to dissensions, notwithstanding the preaching of Helaman and his brethren, yea, notwithstanding their exceedingly great care over the church, for they were *a*high priests over the church.

7 And there were many in the church who believed in the *a*flattering words of Amalickiah, therefore they *b*dissented even from the church; and thus were the affairs of the people of Nephi exceedingly precarious and dangerous, notwithstanding their great *c*victory which they had had over the Lamanites, and their great rejoicings which they had had because of their *d*deliverance by the hand of the Lord.

8 Thus we see how *a*quick the children of men do *b*forget the Lord their God, yea, how quick to do *c*iniquity, and to be led away by the evil one.

9 Yea, and we also see the great *a*wickedness one very wicked man can cause to take place among the children of men.

10 Yea, we see that Amalickiah, because he was a man of cunning device and a man of many flattering words, that he led away the hearts of many people to do wickedly; yea, and to seek to *a*destroy the church of God, and to destroy the foundation of *b*liberty which God had granted

22b TG Church
      Organization.
   c TG Teacher.
23a 3 Ne. 11:29 (28–29).
24a TG Treasure.
   b TG Pride;
      Walking in Darkness.
46 1a Alma 45:20.
   3a Alma 49:25.
   4a Alma 2:2.
   b Mosiah 29:11 (11–44).

5a Prov. 29:5.
6a Alma 46:38.
7a TG Flatter.
   b Alma 1:24.
   c Alma 44:20.
   d Josh. 21:44;
      1 Kgs. 5:3;
      Mosiah 9:17.
      TG Deliver.
8a Ex. 32:8;
   Judg. 2:17;

Hel. 4:26; 6:32;
   12:2 (2, 4–5).
   b Deut. 6:12.
   c Mosiah 13:29.
9a 2 Kgs. 10:29;
   Mosiah 29:17 (17–18).
10a TG Tyranny.
   b 2 Ne. 1:7;
      Mosiah 29:32.
      TG Liberty.

unto them, or which blessing God had sent upon the face of the land for the ^crighteous' sake.

11 And now it came to pass that when Moroni, who was the ^achief commander of the armies of the Nephites, had heard of these dissensions, he was angry with Amalickiah.

12 And it came to pass that he rent his coat; and he took a piece thereof, and wrote upon it—^aIn memory of our God, our religion, and freedom, and our peace, our wives, and our children—and he fastened it upon the end of a pole.

13 And he fastened on his head-plate, and his ^abreastplate, and his shields, and girded on his armor about his loins; and he took the pole, which had on the end thereof his rent coat, (and he called it the ^btitle of liberty) and he ^cbowed himself to the earth, and he prayed mightily unto his God for the blessings of liberty to rest upon his brethren, so long as there should a band of ^dChristians remain to possess the land—

14 For thus were all the true believers of Christ, who belonged to the church of God, called by those who did not belong to the church.

15 And those who did belong to the church were ^afaithful; yea, all those who were true believers in Christ ^btook upon them, gladly, the name of Christ, or ^cChristians as they were called, because of their belief in Christ who should come.

16 And therefore, at this time, Moroni prayed that the cause of the Christians, and the ^afreedom of the land might be favored.

17 And it came to pass that when he had poured out his soul to God, he named all the land which was ^asouth of the land ^bDesolation, yea, and in fine, all the land, both on the ^cnorth and on the south—A chosen land, and the land of ^dliberty.

18 And he said: Surely God shall not ^asuffer that we, who are despised because we take upon us the name of Christ, shall be trodden down and destroyed, until we bring it upon us by our own ^btransgressions.

19 And when Moroni had said these words, he went forth among the people, waving the ^arent part of his garment in the air, that all might see the writing which he had written upon the rent part, and crying with a loud voice, saying:

20 Behold, whosoever will maintain this title upon the land, let them come forth in the strength of the Lord, and ^aenter into a covenant that they will ^bmaintain their rights, and their religion, that the Lord God may bless them.

21 And it came to pass that when Moroni had proclaimed these words, behold, the people came running ^atogether with their armor girded about their loins, ^brending their garments in token, or as a ^ccovenant, that they would not forsake the Lord their God; or, in other words, if they should transgress the commandments of God, or fall into transgression, and be ^dashamed to take upon them the name of Christ, the Lord should rend them even as they had rent their garments.

10c Alma 45:15 (15–16); 62:40.
11a Alma 43:16.
12a 2 Sam. 10:12; Neh. 4:14 (10–14); Alma 44:5; 48:10 (10, 24).
13a Alma 44:9; 49:6 (6, 24).
  b Alma 51:20. TG Citizenship.
  c TG Reverence.
  d Alma 48:10.
15a TG Faithful;

Loyalty.
  b TG Jesus Christ, Taking the Name of.
  c Acts 11:26.
16a Alma 51:13.
17a 3 Ne. 3:24; Morm. 3:5.
  b Alma 22:30; 50:34.
  c Alma 22:31; 63:4.
  d 2 Ne. 1:7; Mosiah 29:32.
18a TG Protection, Divine.

  b TG Transgress.
19a TG Ensign.
20a Alma 48:13.
  b TG Citizenship.
21a 2 Sam. 20:14 (11–14).
  b TG Rend.
  c TG Commitment.
  d Jer. 17:13; Rom. 1:16; 2 Tim. 1:8; 1 Ne. 8:25; Morm. 8:38.

22 Now this was the covenant which they made, and they ᵃcast their garments at the feet of Moroni, saying: We ᵇcovenant with our God, that we shall be destroyed, even as our brethren in the land northward, if we shall fall into transgression; yea, he may cast us at the feet of our enemies, even as we have cast our garments at thy feet to be trodden under foot, if we shall fall into transgression.

23 Moroni said unto them: Behold, we are a ᵃremnant of the seed of Jacob; yea, we are a remnant of the seed of ᵇJoseph, whose ᶜcoat was rent by his brethren into many pieces; yea, and now behold, let us remember to keep the commandments of God, or our garments shall be rent by our brethren, and we be cast into prison, or be sold, or be slain.

24 Yea, let us preserve our liberty as a ᵃremnant of Joseph; yea, let us remember the words of Jacob, before his death, for behold, he saw that a ᵇpart of the ᶜremnant of the coat of Joseph was ᵈpreserved and had not decayed. And he said—Even as this remnant of garment of my son hath been preserved, so shall a ᵉremnant of the seed of my son be preserved by the hand of God, and be taken unto himself, while the remainder of the seed of Joseph shall perish, even as the remnant of his garment.

25 Now behold, this giveth my soul sorrow; nevertheless, my soul hath joy in my son, because of that part of his seed which shall be taken unto God.

26 Now behold, this was the language of Jacob.

27 And now who knoweth but what the remnant of the seed of Joseph, which shall perish as his garment, are those who have dissented from us? Yea, and even it shall be ourselves if we do not stand fast in the faith of Christ.

28 And now it came to pass that when Moroni had said these words he went forth, and also sent forth in all the parts of the land where there were dissensions, and gathered together all the people who were desirous to maintain their liberty, to stand against Amalickiah and those who had dissented, who were called Amalickiahites.

29 And it came to pass that when Amalickiah saw that the people of Moroni were more numerous than the Amalickiahites—and he also saw that his people were ᵃdoubtful concerning the justice of the cause in which they had undertaken—therefore, fearing that he should not gain the point, he took those of his people who would and departed into the ᵇland of Nephi.

30 Now Moroni thought it was not expedient that the Lamanites should have any more ᵃstrength; therefore he thought to cut off the people of Amalickiah, or to take them and bring them back, and put Amalickiah to death; yea, for he knew that he would stir up the Lamanites to anger against them, and cause them to come to battle against them; and this he knew that Amalickiah would do that he might obtain his purposes.

31 Therefore Moroni thought it was expedient that he should take his armies, who had gathered themselves together, and armed themselves, and entered into a covenant to keep the peace—and it came to pass that he took his army and marched out with his tents into the wilderness, to cut off the course of Amalickiah in the wilderness.

32 And it came to pass that he did

22a Acts 7:58; 22:20.
  b TG Commitment.
23a TG Israel, Remnant of.
  b TG Israel, Joseph,
    People of.
  c Gen. 37:3 (3, 31–36).

24a 2 Ne. 10:1;
    Jacob 5:45 (43–45).
  b Gen. 44:28.
  c 3 Ne. 5:23 (23–24); 10:17.
  d 2 Ne. 3:5 (5–24); 25:21;
    Ether 13:7.

  e Ether 13:6.
29a TG Doubt.
  b Alma 47:20.
30a Alma 43:51.

according to his desires, and marched forth into the wilderness, and headed the armies of Amalickiah.

33 And it came to pass that Amalickiah ^afled with a small number of his men, and the remainder were delivered up into the hands of Moroni and were taken back into the land of Zarahemla.

34 Now, Moroni being a man who was ^aappointed by the chief judges and the voice of the people, therefore he had power according to his will with the armies of the Nephites, to establish and to exercise authority over them.

35 And it came to pass that whomsoever of the Amalickiahites that would not enter into a covenant to support the ^acause of freedom, that they might maintain a free ^bgovernment, he caused to be put to death; and there were but few who denied the covenant of freedom.

36 And it came to pass also, that he caused the ^atitle of liberty to be hoisted upon every tower which was in all the land, which was possessed by the Nephites; and thus Moroni planted the standard of liberty among the Nephites.

37 And they began to have peace again in the land; and thus they did maintain peace in the land until nearly the end of the nineteenth year of the reign of the judges.

38 And Helaman and the ^ahigh priests did also maintain order in the church; yea, even for the space of four years did they have much peace and rejoicing in the church.

39 And it came to pass that there were many who died, firmly ^abelieving that their souls were redeemed by the Lord Jesus Christ; thus they went out of the world rejoicing.

40 And there were some who died

with fevers, which at some seasons of the year were very frequent in the land—but not so much so with fevers, because of the excellent qualities of the many ^aplants and roots which God had prepared to remove the cause of ^bdiseases, to which men were subject by the nature of the climate—

41 But there were many who died with ^aold age; and those who died in the faith of Christ are ^bhappy in him, as we must needs suppose.

CHAPTER 47

Amalickiah uses treachery, murder, and intrigue to become king of the Lamanites—The Nephite dissenters are more wicked and ferocious than the Lamanites. About 72 B.C.

Now we will return in our record to Amalickiah and those who had ^afled with him into the wilderness; for, behold, he had taken those who went with him, and went up in the ^bland of Nephi among the Lamanites, and did ^cstir up the Lamanites to anger against the people of Nephi, insomuch that the king of the Lamanites sent a proclamation throughout all his land, among all his people, that they should gather themselves together again to go to battle against the Nephites.

2 And it came to pass that when the proclamation had gone forth among them they were exceedingly afraid; yea, they ^afeared to displease the king, and they also feared to go to battle against the Nephites lest they should lose their lives. And it came to pass that they would not, or the more part of them would not, obey the commandments of the king.

3 And now it came to pass that

33a Alma 47:1.
34a Alma 43:16.
35a Alma 43:30.
  b TG Governments.
36a Alma 62:4.
38a Alma 43:2; 46:6; 49:30.
39a Moro. 7:41 (3, 41).
40a D&C 59:17 (17–20);

89:10.
  b Ezek. 47:12.
  TG Health;
  Sickness.
41a TG Old Age.
  b Rev. 14:13.
47 1a Alma 46:33.
  b 2 Ne. 5:8;

Omni 1:12;
  Alma 49:10.
  c Alma 27:12; 35:10; 43:8;
  Hel. 1:17.
  TG Provoking.
2a Alma 43:54 (49–54).

the king was wroth because of their disobedience; therefore he gave Amalickiah the command of that part of his army which was obedient unto his commands, and commanded him that he should go forth and ^acompel them to arms.

4 Now behold, this was the desire of Amalickiah; for he being a very ^asubtle man to do evil therefore he laid the plan in his heart to ^bdethrone the king of the Lamanites.

5 And now he had got the command of those parts of the Lamanites who were in favor of the king; and he sought to gain favor of those who were not obedient; therefore he went forward to the place which was called ^aOnidah, for thither had all the Lamanites fled; for they discovered the army coming, and, supposing that they were coming to destroy them, therefore they fled to Onidah, to the place of arms.

6 And they had appointed a man to be a king and a leader over them, being fixed in their minds with a determined resolution that they would ^anot be subjected to go against the Nephites.

7 And it came to pass that they had gathered themselves together upon the top of the mount which was called Antipas, in preparation to battle.

8 Now it was not Amalickiah's intention to give them battle according to the commandments of the king; but behold, it was his intention to gain favor with the armies of the Lamanites, that he might place himself at their head and dethrone the king and take possession of the kingdom.

9 And behold, it came to pass that he caused his army to pitch their tents in the valley which was near the mount Antipas.

10 And it came to pass that when it was night he sent a secret embassy into the mount Antipas, desiring that the leader of those who were upon the mount, whose name was Lehonti, that he should come down to the foot of the mount, for he desired to speak with him.

11 And it came to pass that when Lehonti received the message he durst not go down to the foot of the mount. And it came to pass that Amalickiah sent again the second time, desiring him to come down. And it came to pass that Lehonti would not; and he sent again the third time.

12 And it came to pass that when Amalickiah found that he could not get Lehonti to come down off from the mount, he went up into the mount, nearly to Lehonti's camp; and he sent again the fourth time his message unto Lehonti, desiring that he would come down, and that he would bring his guards with him.

13 And it came to pass that when Lehonti had come down with his guards to Amalickiah, that Amalickiah desired him to come down with his army in the night-time, and surround those men in their camps over whom the king had given him command, and that he would deliver them up into Lehonti's hands, if he would make him (Amalickiah) a second ^aleader over the whole army.

14 And it came to pass that Lehonti came down with his men and surrounded the men of Amalickiah, so that before they awoke at the dawn of day they were surrounded by the armies of Lehonti.

15 And it came to pass that when they saw that they were surrounded, they pled with Amalickiah that he would suffer them to fall in with their brethren, that they might not be destroyed. Now this was the very thing which Amalickiah desired.

16 And it came to pass that he delivered his men, ^acontrary to the commands of the king. Now this was the thing that Amalickiah

3a Alma 47:16 (16, 21).   5a Alma 32:4.   16a Alma 47:3.
4a 2 Sam. 13:3 (3–14).   6a Alma 44:19 (8, 19).
 b Alma 47:35 (8, 35).   13a Alma 49:10.

desired, that he might accomplish his designs in dethroning the king.

17 Now it was the custom among the Lamanites, if their chief leader was killed, to appoint the second leader to be their chief leader.

18 And it came to pass that Amalickiah caused that one of his servants should administer ªpoison by degrees to Lehonti, that he died.

19 Now, when Lehonti was dead, the Lamanites appointed Amalickiah to be their leader and their chief commander.

20 And it came to pass that Amalickiah marched with his armies (for he had gained his desires) to the ªland of Nephi, to the city of Nephi, which was the chief city.

21 And the king came out to meet him with his guards, for he supposed that Amalickiah had ªfulfilled his commands, and that Amalickiah had gathered together so great an army to go against the Nephites to battle.

22 But behold, as the king came out to meet him Amalickiah caused that his servants should go forth to meet the king. And they went and ªbowed themselves before the king, as if to reverence him because of his greatness.

23 And it came to pass that the king put forth his hand to raise them, as was the custom with the Lamanites, as a token of peace, which custom they had taken from the Nephites.

24 And it came to pass that when he had raised the first from the ground, behold he stabbed the king to the heart; and he fell to the earth.

25 Now the servants of the king fled; and the servants of Amalickiah raised a cry, saying:

26 Behold, the servants of the king have stabbed him to the heart, and he has fallen and they have fled; behold, come and see.

27 And it came to pass that Amalickiah commanded that his armies should march forth and see what had happened to the king; and when they had come to the spot, and found the king lying in his gore, Amalickiah pretended to be wroth, and said: Whosoever loved the king, let him go forth, and pursue his servants that they may be slain.

28 And it came to pass that all they who loved the king, when they heard these words, came forth and pursued after the servants of the king.

29 Now when the ªservants of the king saw an army pursuing after them, they were frightened again, and fled into the wilderness, and came over into the land of Zarahemla and joined the ᵇpeople of Ammon.

30 And the army which pursued after them returned, having pursued after them in vain; and thus Amalickiah, by his ªfraud, gained the hearts of the people.

31 And it came to pass on the morrow he entered the city Nephi with his armies, and took possession of the city.

32 And now it came to pass that the queen, when she had heard that the king was slain—for Amalickiah had sent an embassy to the queen informing her that the king had been slain by his servants, that he had pursued them with his army, but it was in vain, and they had made their escape—

33 Therefore, when the queen had received this message she sent unto Amalickiah, desiring him that he would spare the people of the city; and she also desired him that he should come in unto her; and she also desired him that he should bring ªwitnesses with him to testify concerning the death of the king.

34 And it came to pass that Amalickiah took the same servant that slew the king, and all them who

18ª Alma 54:7.
20ª Alma 46:29.
21ª Alma 47:3.

22ª Mosiah 7:12.
29ª Alma 55:5.
  ᵇ Alma 43:11; 62:17.

30ª Alma 55:1.
  TG Fraud.
33ª TG Witness.

were with him, and went in unto the queen, unto the place where she sat; and they all ªtestified unto her that the king was slain by his own servants; and they said also: They have fled; does not this testify against them? And thus they satisfied the queen concerning the death of the king.

35 And it came to pass that Amalickiah sought the ªfavor of the queen, and took her unto him to wife; and thus by his ᵇfraud, and by the assistance of his cunning servants, he ᶜobtained the kingdom; yea, he was acknowledged king throughout all the land, among all the people of the Lamanites, who were ᵈcomposed of the Lamanites and the Lemuelites and the Ishmaelites, and all the dissenters of the Nephites, from the reign of Nephi down to the present time.

36 Now these ªdissenters, having the same instruction and the same information of the Nephites, yea, having been instructed in the same ᵇknowledge of the Lord, nevertheless, it is strange to relate, not long after their dissensions they became more hardened and ᶜimpenitent, and more wild, wicked and ferocious than the Lamanites—drinking in with the ᵈtraditions of the Lamanites; giving way to ᵉindolence, and all manner of lasciviousness; yea, entirely forgetting the Lord their God.

CHAPTER 48

Amalickiah incites the Lamanites against the Nephites—Moroni prepares his people to defend the cause of the Christians—He rejoices in liberty and freedom and is a mighty man of God. About 72 B.C.

AND now it came to pass that, as soon as ªAmalickiah had obtained the kingdom he began to ᵇinspire the hearts of the Lamanites against the people of Nephi; yea, he did appoint men to speak unto the Lamanites from their ᶜtowers, against the Nephites.

2 And thus he did inspire their hearts against the Nephites, insomuch that in the latter end of the ªnineteenth year of the reign of the judges, he having accomplished his designs thus far, yea, having been made king over the Lamanites, he ᵇsought also to ᶜreign over all the land, yea, and all the people who were in the land, the Nephites as well as the Lamanites.

3 Therefore he had accomplished his design, for he had hardened the hearts of the Lamanites and blinded their minds, and stirred them up to anger, insomuch that he had gathered together a numerous host to go to battle against the Nephites.

4 For he was determined, because of the greatness of the number of his people, to ªoverpower the Nephites and to bring them into bondage.

5 And thus he did appoint ªchief captains of the ᵇZoramites, they being the most acquainted with the strength of the Nephites, and their places of resort, and the weakest parts of their cities; therefore he appointed them to be chief captains over his armies.

6 And it came to pass that they took their camp, and moved forth toward the land of Zarahemla in the wilderness.

7 Now it came to pass that while Amalickiah had thus been obtaining power by fraud and deceit, Moroni, on the other hand, had been ªpreparing

---

34a TG False;
    Lying.
35a Prov. 19:6 (6–7).
  b TG Conspiracy;
    Tyranny.
  c Alma 47:4.
  d Jacob 1:13 (13–14).
36a TG Apostasy of
    Individuals.

  b Heb. 10:26 (26–27);
    Alma 24:30.
  c Jer. 8:12.
  d TG Peer Influence.
  e 3 Ne. 4:5.
48 1a Alma 52:3 (1–3); 54:5.
  b Alma 62:35.
  c Mosiah 2:8.
2a Alma 48:21.

  b D&C 121:39.
  c Alma 54:24.
4a TG Tyranny.
5a Alma 43:6;
    49:5 (5, 23).
  b Alma 52:20 (20, 33).
7a Alma 49:8.

the minds of the people to be faithful unto the Lord their God.

8 Yea, he had been strengthening the armies of the Nephites, and erecting small ᵃforts, or places of resort; throwing up banks of earth round about to enclose his armies, and also building ᵇwalls of stone to encircle them about, round about their cities and the borders of their lands; yea, all round about the land.

9 And in their weakest fortifications he did place the greater number of men; and thus he did fortify and strengthen the land which was possessed by the Nephites.

10 And thus he was preparing to ᵃsupport their liberty, their lands, their wives, and their children, and their peace, and that they might live unto the Lord their God, and that they might maintain that which was called by their enemies the cause of ᵇChristians.

11 And Moroni was a ᵃstrong and a mighty man; he was a man of a perfect ᵇunderstanding; yea, a man that did not delight in bloodshed; a man whose soul did joy in the liberty and the freedom of his country, and his brethren from bondage and slavery;

12 Yea, a man whose heart did swell with thanksgiving to his God, for the many privileges and blessings which he bestowed upon his people; a man who did labor exceedingly for the ᵃwelfare and safety of his people.

13 Yea, and he was a man who was firm in the faith of Christ, and he had ᵃsworn with an oath to defend his people, his rights, and his country, and his religion, even to the loss of his blood.

14 Now the Nephites were taught to defend themselves against their enemies, even to the shedding of blood if it were necessary; yea, and they were also taught ᵃnever to give an offense, yea, and never to raise the sword except it were against an enemy, except it were to preserve their lives.

15 And this was their ᵃfaith, that by so doing God would ᵇprosper them in the land, or in other words, if they were faithful in keeping the commandments of God that he would prosper them in the land; yea, warn them to flee, or to prepare for war, according to their danger;

16 And also, that God would make it known unto them ᵃwhither they should go to defend themselves against their enemies, and by so doing, the Lord would deliver them; and this was the faith of Moroni, and his heart did glory in it; ᵇnot in the shedding of blood but in doing good, in preserving his people, yea, in keeping the commandments of God, yea, and resisting iniquity.

17 Yea, verily, verily I say unto you, if all men had been, and were, and ever would be, like unto ᵃMoroni, behold, the very powers of hell would have been shaken forever; yea, the ᵇdevil would never have power over the hearts of the children of men.

18 Behold, he was a man like unto ᵃAmmon, the son of Mosiah, yea, and even the other sons of Mosiah, yea, and also Alma and his sons, for they were all men of God.

19 Now behold, Helaman and his brethren were no less ᵃserviceable unto the people than was Moroni; for they did preach the word of God, and they did baptize unto

8 a Alma 49:13
      (2–13, 18–24).
   b Deut. 3:5.
10 a Alma 44:5; 46:12.
   b Alma 46:13.
11 a TG Strength.
   b Alma 18:22.
      TG Understanding.
12 a TG Welfare.
13 a Alma 46:20 (20–22).

      TG Dependability.
14 a Alma 43:46 (46–47);
      3 Ne. 3:21 (20–21);
      Morm. 3:10 (10–11);
      D&C 98:16.
15 a TG Steadfastness.
   b Alma 45:8.
16 a Alma 16:6 (5–8);
      43:23 (23–24);
      3 Ne. 3:20 (18–21).

      TG Guidance, Divine.
   b Alma 55:19.
17 a Alma 53:2.
   b 1 Ne. 22:26;
      3 Ne. 6:15;
      D&C 35:24.
18 a Alma 28:8.
19 a Alma 45:22.

repentance all men whosoever would hearken unto their words.

20 And thus they went forth, and the people did ^ahumble themselves because of their ^bwords, insomuch that they were highly ^cfavored of the Lord, and thus they were free from wars and contentions among themselves, yea, even for the space of four years.

21 But, as I have said, in the ^alatter end of the nineteenth year, yea, notwithstanding their peace amongst themselves, they were compelled reluctantly to contend with their brethren, the Lamanites.

22 Yea, and in fine, their wars never did cease for the space of many years with the Lamanites, notwithstanding their much reluctance.

23 Now, they were ^asorry to take up arms against the Lamanites, because they did not delight in the shedding of blood; yea, and this was not all—they were ^bsorry to be the means of sending so many of their brethren out of this world into an eternal world, ^cunprepared to meet their God.

24 Nevertheless, they could not suffer to lay down their lives, that their ^awives and their children should be ^bmassacred by the barbarous ^ccruelty of those who were once their brethren, yea, and had ^ddissented from their church, and had left them and had gone to destroy them by joining the Lamanites.

25 Yea, they could not bear that their brethren should rejoice over the blood of the Nephites, so long as there were any who should keep the commandments of God, for the promise of the Lord was, if they should keep his commandments they should ^aprosper in the land.

CHAPTER 49

The invading Lamanites are unable to take the fortified cities of Ammonihah and Noah—Amalickiah curses God and swears to drink the blood of Moroni—Helaman and his brethren continue to strengthen the Church. About 72 B.C.

AND now it came to pass in the eleventh month of the nineteenth year, on the tenth day of the month, the armies of the Lamanites were seen approaching towards the land of ^aAmmonihah.

2 And behold, the city had been rebuilt, and Moroni had stationed an army by the borders of the city, and they had ^acast up dirt round about to shield them from the arrows and the ^bstones of the Lamanites; for behold, they fought with stones and with arrows.

3 Behold, I said that the city of ^aAmmonihah had been rebuilt. I say unto you, yea, that it was in part rebuilt; and because the Lamanites had destroyed it once because of the iniquity of the people, they supposed that it would again become an easy prey for them.

4 But behold, how great was their disappointment; for behold, the Nephites had dug up a ^aridge of earth round about them, which was so high that the Lamanites could not cast their stones and their arrows at them that they might take effect, neither could they come upon them save it was by their place of ^bentrance.

5 Now at this time the chief ^acaptains of the Lamanites were astonished exceedingly, because of the wisdom of the Nephites in preparing their places of security.

6 Now the leaders of the Lamanites

20a TG Humility.
  b 1 Ne. 15:20;
    Hel. 6:5.
  c 1 Ne. 17:35.
21a Alma 48:2.
23a Alma 28:11 (11–12);
    D&C 42:45.
  b 3 Ne. 12:44.

  c Amos 4:12;
    Alma 20:17.
24a Alma 46:12.
  b TG Martyrdom.
  c TG Cruelty.
  d TG Apostasy of
    Individuals.
25a Alma 45:8.

49 1a Alma 8:6.
  2a Alma 48:8.
  b 1 Ne. 16:15;
    Alma 43:20.
  3a Alma 16:2 (2–3, 9, 11).
  4a Alma 48:8; 50:1.
  b Alma 49:20.
  5a Alma 52:19.

had supposed, because of the greatness of their numbers, yea, they supposed that they should be privileged to come upon them as they had hitherto done; yea, and they had also prepared themselves with shields, and with ªbreastplates; and they had also prepared themselves with garments of skins, yea, very thick garments to cover their nakedness.

7 And being thus prepared they supposed that they should easily overpower and ªsubject their brethren to the yoke of bondage, or slay and massacre them according to their pleasure.

8 But behold, to their uttermost astonishment, they were ªprepared for them, in a manner which never had been known among the children of Lehi. Now they were prepared for the Lamanites, to battle after the manner of the instructions of Moroni.

9 And it came to pass that the Lamanites, or the Amalickiahites, were exceedingly astonished at their manner of preparation for war.

10 Now, if king Amalickiah had come down out of the ªland of Nephi, at the head of his army, perhaps he would have caused the Lamanites to have attacked the Nephites at the city of Ammonihah; for behold, he did care not for the blood of his people.

11 But behold, Amalickiah did not come down himself to battle. And behold, his chief captains durst not attack the Nephites at the city of Ammonihah, for Moroni had altered the management of affairs among the Nephites, insomuch that the Lamanites were disappointed in their places of retreat and they could not come upon them.

12 Therefore they retreated into the wilderness, and took their camp and marched towards the land of ªNoah, supposing that to be the next best place for them to come against the Nephites.

13 For they knew not that Moroni had fortified, or had built ªforts of security, for every city in all the land round about; therefore, they marched forward to the land of Noah with a firm determination; yea, their chief captains came forward and took an ᵇoath that they would destroy the people of that city.

14 But behold, to their astonishment, the city of Noah, which had hitherto been a weak place, had now, by the means of Moroni, become strong, yea, even to exceed the strength of the city Ammonihah.

15 And now, behold, this was wisdom in Moroni; for he had supposed that they would be frightened at the city Ammonihah; and as the city of Noah had hitherto been the weakest part of the land, therefore they would march thither to battle; and thus it was according to his desires.

16 And behold, Moroni had appointed Lehi to be chief captain over the men of that city; and it was that ªsame Lehi who fought with the Lamanites in the valley on the east of the river Sidon.

17 And now behold it came to pass, that when the Lamanites had found that Lehi commanded the city they were again disappointed, for they feared Lehi exceedingly; nevertheless their chief captains had ªsworn with an oath to attack the city; therefore, they brought up their armies.

18 Now behold, the Lamanites could not get into their forts of security by any other way save by the entrance, because of the highness of the bank which had been thrown up, and the depth of the

6a Alma 46:13;
   Hel. 1:14.
7a Alma 43:29.
8a Alma 48:7 (7–10).
10a 2 Ne. 5:8;
    Omni 1:12;
    Alma 47:1 (1, 13–24).
12a Alma 16:3.
13a Alma 48:8; 50:10 (1–6, 10).
  b Alma 49:17.
16a Alma 43:35.
17a Alma 49:13.

ditch which had been dug round about, save it were by the entrance.

19 And thus were the Nephites prepared to destroy all such as should attempt to climb up to enter the fort by any other way, by casting over stones and arrows at them.

20 Thus they were prepared, yea, a body of their strongest men, with their swords and their slings, to smite down all who should attempt to come into their place of security by the place of ᵃentrance; and thus were they prepared to defend themselves against the Lamanites.

21 And it came to pass that the captains of the Lamanites brought up their armies before the place of entrance, and began to contend with the Nephites, to get into their place of security; but behold, they were driven back from time to time, insomuch that they were slain with an immense slaughter.

22 Now when they found that they could not obtain power over the Nephites by the pass, they began to dig down their banks of earth that they might obtain a pass to their armies, that they might have an equal chance to fight; but behold, in these attempts they were swept off by the stones and arrows which were thrown at them; and instead of filling up their ditches by pulling down the banks of earth, they were filled up in a measure with their dead and wounded bodies.

23 Thus the Nephites had all power over their enemies; and thus the Lamanites did attempt to destroy the Nephites until their ᵃchief captains were all slain; yea, and more than a thousand of the Lamanites were slain; while, on the other hand, there was not a single soul of the Nephites which was slain.

24 There were about fifty who were wounded, who had been ex-

posed to the arrows of the Lamanites through the pass, but they were shielded by their ᵃshields, and their breastplates, and their head-plates, insomuch that their wounds were upon their legs, many of which were very severe.

25 And it came to pass, that when the Lamanites saw that their chief captains were all slain they fled into the wilderness. And it came to pass that they returned to the land of Nephi, to inform their king, Amalickiah, who was a ᵃNephite by birth, concerning their great ᵇloss.

26 And it came to pass that he was exceedingly angry with his people, because he had not obtained his desire over the Nephites; he had not subjected them to the yoke of bondage.

27 Yea, he was exceedingly wroth, and he did ᵃcurse God, and also Moroni, swearing with an ᵇoath that he would drink his blood; and this because Moroni had kept the commandments of God in preparing for the safety of his people.

28 And it came to pass, that on the other hand, the people of Nephi did ᵃthank the Lord their God, because of his matchless power in delivering them from the hands of their enemies.

29 And thus ended the nineteenth year of the reign of the judges over the people of Nephi.

30 Yea, and there was continual peace among them, and exceedingly great prosperity in the church because of their heed and diligence which they gave unto the word of God, which was declared unto them by Helaman, and Shiblon, and Corianton, and Ammon and his brethren, yea, and by all those who had been ordained by the ᵃholy order of God, being baptized unto repentance, and sent forth to preach among the people.

20a Alma 49:4 (4, 18, 21, 24).
23a Alma 48:5.
24a Alma 43:19.
25a Alma 46:3.

b Alma 51:11.
27a TG Blaspheme.
 b Acts 23:12;
   Alma 51:9.

28a TG Thanksgiving.
30a Alma 30:20 (20–23, 31);
   43:2; 46:38.

CHAPTER 50

Moroni fortifies the lands of the Nephites—They build many new cities—Wars and destructions befell the Nephites in the days of their wickedness and abominations—Morianton and his dissenters are defeated by Teancum—Nephihah dies, and his son Pahoran fills the judgment seat. About 72–67 B.C.

AND now it came to pass that Moroni did not stop making preparations for war, or to defend his people against the Lamanites; for he caused that his armies should commence in the commencement of the twentieth year of the reign of the judges, that they should commence in digging up ᵃheaps of earth round about all the cities, throughout all the land which was possessed by the Nephites.

2 And upon the top of these ridges of earth he caused that there should be ᵃtimbers, yea, works of timbers built up to the height of a man, round about the cities.

3 And he caused that upon those works of timbers there should be a frame of pickets built upon the timbers round about; and they were strong and high.

4 And he caused towers to be erected that overlooked those works of pickets, and he caused places of security to be built upon those ᵃtowers, that the stones and the arrows of the Lamanites could not hurt them.

5 And they were prepared that they could cast stones from the top thereof, according to their pleasure and their strength, and slay him who should attempt to approach near the walls of the city.

6 Thus Moroni did prepare strongholds against the coming of their enemies, round about every city in all the land.

7 And it came to pass that Moroni caused that his armies should go forth into the east wilderness; yea, and they went forth and drove all the Lamanites who were in the east wilderness into their own lands, which were ᵃsouth of the land of Zarahemla.

8 And the land of ᵃNephi did run in a straight course from the east sea to the west.

9 And it came to pass that when Moroni had driven all the Lamanites out of the east wilderness, which was north of the lands of their own possessions, he caused that the inhabitants who were in the land of Zarahemla and in the land round about should go forth into the east wilderness, even to the borders by the seashore, and possess the land.

10 And he also placed armies on the south, in the borders of their possessions, and caused them to erect ᵃfortifications that they might secure their armies and their people from the hands of their enemies.

11 And thus he cut off all the strongholds of the Lamanites in the east wilderness, yea, and also on the west, fortifying the line between the Nephites and the Lamanites, between the land of Zarahemla and the land of Nephi, from the west sea, running by the head of the ᵃriver Sidon—the Nephites possessing all the land ᵇnorthward, yea, even all the land which was northward of the land Bountiful, according to their pleasure.

12 Thus Moroni, with his armies, which did increase daily because of the assurance of protection which his works did bring forth unto them, did seek to cut off the strength and the power of the Lamanites from off the lands of their possessions, that they should have no power upon the lands of their possession.

13 And it came to pass that the Nephites began the foundation of a

---

50 1a Alma 48:8; 49:4; 52:6.
  2a Alma 53:4.
  4a 2 Chr. 14:7 (7–8).
  7a Alma 22:32.

8a 2 Ne. 5:8;
   Omni 1:12 (12, 27);
   Mosiah 7:6 (6–7);
   9:1 (1, 3–4, 14).

10a Alma 49:13 (13, 18–24);
    53:3 (3–7).
11a Alma 2:15; 22:29.
  b Morm. 2:3.

city, and they called the name of the city ᵃMoroni; and it was by the east sea; and it was on the south by the line of the possessions of the Lamanites.

14 And they also began a foundation for a city between the city of Moroni and the city of Aaron, joining the borders of Aaron and Moroni; and they called the name of the city, or the land, ᵃNephihah.

15 And they also began in that same year to build many cities on the north, one in a particular manner which they called ᵃLehi, which was in the north by the borders of the seashore.

16 And thus ended the twentieth year.

17 And in these prosperous circumstances were the people of Nephi in the commencement of the twenty and first year of the reign of the judges over the people of Nephi.

18 And they did prosper ᵃexceedingly, and they became exceedingly rich; yea, and they did multiply and wax strong in the land.

19 And thus we see how merciful and just are all the dealings of the Lord, to the fulfilling of all his words unto the children of men; yea, we can behold that his words are verified, even at this time, which he spake unto Lehi, saying:

20 Blessed art thou and thy children; and they shall be blessed, inasmuch as they shall keep my ᵃcommandments they shall prosper in the land. But remember, inasmuch as they will not keep my commandments they shall be ᵇcut off from the presence of the Lord.

21 And we see that these promises have been verified to the people of Nephi; for it has been their quarrelings and their contentions, yea, their murderings, and their plunderings, their idolatry, their whoredoms, and their abominations, which were among themselves, which ᵃbrought upon them their wars and their destructions.

22 And those who were faithful in keeping the commandments of the Lord were delivered at all times, whilst thousands of their wicked brethren have been consigned to bondage, or to perish by the sword, or to dwindle in unbelief, and mingle with the Lamanites.

23 But behold there never was a ᵃhappier time among the people of Nephi, since the days of Nephi, than in the days of Moroni, yea, even at this time, in the twenty and first year of the reign of the judges.

24 And it came to pass that the twenty and second year of the reign of the judges also ended in peace; yea, and also the twenty and third year.

25 And it came to pass that in the commencement of the twenty and fourth year of the reign of the judges, there would also have been peace among the people of Nephi had it not been for a ᵃcontention which took place among them concerning the land of ᵇLehi, and the land of ᶜMorianton, which joined upon the borders of Lehi; both of which were on the borders by the seashore.

26 For behold, the people who possessed the land of Morianton did claim a part of the land of Lehi; therefore there began to be a warm ᵃcontention between them, insomuch that the people of Morianton took up arms against their brethren, and they were determined by the sword to slay them.

27 But behold, the people who possessed the land of Lehi fled to the camp of Moroni, and appealed unto

13a Alma 51:22 (22–24);
      62:32 (32, 34);
      3 Ne. 8:9.
14a Alma 51:24 (24–26);
      59:5; 62:18 (14, 18, 26).
15a Alma 51:26 (24–26);
      62:30.

18a Alma 1:29.
20a Lev. 25:18 (18–19);
      Ps. 1:3 (2–3);
      Alma 37:13; 62:48.
  b Ps. 37:2;
      D&C 1:14.
21a Alma 41:10.

23a 2 Ne. 5:27;
      Mosiah 2:41;
      4 Ne. 1:16 (15–18).
25a TG Contention.
  b Hel. 6:10.
  c Alma 51:26.
26a 3 Ne. 11:29.

him for assistance; for behold they were not in the wrong.

28 And it came to pass that when the people of Morianton, who were led by a man whose name was Morianton, found that the people of Lehi had fled to the camp of Moroni, they were exceedingly fearful lest the army of Moroni should come upon them and destroy them.

29 Therefore, Morianton put it into their hearts that they should flee to the land which was northward, which was covered with ªlarge bodies of water, and take possession of the land which was ᵇnorthward.

30 And behold, they would have carried this plan into effect, (which would have been a cause to have been lamented) but behold, Morianton being a man of much passion, therefore he was angry with one of his maid servants, and he fell upon her and beat her much.

31 And it came to pass that she fled, and came over to the camp of Moroni, and told Moroni all things concerning the matter, and also concerning their intentions to flee into the land northward.

32 Now behold, the people who were in the land Bountiful, or rather Moroni, feared that they would hearken to the words of Morianton and unite with his people, and thus he would obtain possession of those parts of the land, which would lay a foundation for serious consequences among the people of Nephi, yea, which ªconsequences would lead to the overthrow of their ᵇliberty.

33 Therefore Moroni sent an army, with their camp, to head the people of Morianton, to stop their flight into the land northward.

34 And it came to pass that they did not ªhead them until they had come to the borders of the land ᵇDesolation; and there they did head them, by the narrow pass which led by the sea into the land northward, yea, by the sea, on the west and on the east.

35 And it came to pass that the army which was sent by Moroni, which was led by a man whose name was Teancum, did meet the people of Morianton; and so stubborn were the people of Morianton, (being inspired by his wickedness and his ªflattering words) that a battle commenced between them, in the which Teancum did ᵇslay Morianton and defeat his army, and took them prisoners, and returned to the camp of Moroni. And thus ended the twenty and fourth year of the reign of the judges over the people of Nephi.

36 And thus were the people of Morianton brought back. And upon their ªcovenanting to keep the peace they were restored to the land of Morianton, and a union took place between them and the people of Lehi; and they were also restored to their lands.

37 And it came to pass that in the same year that the people of Nephi had peace restored unto them, that Nephihah, the ªsecond chief judge, died, having filled the judgment-seat with ᵇperfect uprightness before God.

38 Nevertheless, he had refused Alma to take possession of those ªrecords and those things which were esteemed by Alma and his fathers to be most sacred; therefore Alma had conferred ᵇthem upon his son, Helaman.

39 Behold, it came to pass that the son of Nephihah was appointed to fill the judgment-seat, in the stead of his father; yea, he was appointed

---

29a Mosiah 8:8;
    Hel. 3:4 (3–4).
  b Alma 22:31 (29–31); 51:30.
32a TG Contention;
    Division.
  b TG Liberty.
34a Hel. 1:28 (28–30).

  b Alma 46:17;
    Morm. 3:5 (5, 7).
35a Mosiah 27:8;
    Hel. 1:7; 2:5.
  b Alma 51:29.
36a 1 Ne. 4:37;
    Alma 44:15.

37a Alma 4:17 (16–18).
  b TG Perfection.
38a Alma 37:1 (1–5);
    45:2 (2–8).
  b 3 Ne. 1:2.

chief judge and ^agovernor over the people, with an ^boath and sacred ordinance to judge righteously, and to keep the peace and the ^cfreedom of the people, and to grant unto them their sacred privileges to worship the Lord their God, yea, to support and maintain the cause of God all his days, and to bring the wicked to justice according to their crime.

40 Now behold, his name was ^aPahoran. And Pahoran did fill the seat of his father, and did commence his reign in the end of the twenty and fourth year, over the people of Nephi.

CHAPTER 51

The king-men seek to change the law and set up a king—Pahoran and the freemen are supported by the voice of the people—Moroni compels the king-men to defend their country or be put to death—Amalickiah and the Lamanites capture many fortified cities—Teancum repels the Lamanite invasion and slays Amalickiah in his tent. About 67–66 B.C.

AND now it came to pass in the commencement of the twenty and fifth year of the reign of the judges over the people of Nephi, they having established peace between the people of Lehi and the people of Morianton concerning their lands, and having commenced the twenty and fifth year in ^apeace;

2 Nevertheless, they did not long maintain an entire peace in the land, for there began to be a contention among the people concerning the chief judge Pahoran; for behold, there were a part of the people who desired that a few particular points of the ^alaw should be altered.

3 But behold, Pahoran would not alter nor suffer the law to be altered;

therefore, he did not hearken to those who had sent in their voices with their petitions concerning the altering of the law.

4 Therefore, those who were desirous that the law should be altered were angry with him, and desired that he should no longer be chief judge over the land; therefore there arose a warm ^adispute concerning the matter, but not unto bloodshed.

5 And it came to pass that those who were desirous that Pahoran should be dethroned from the judgment-seat were called ^akingmen, for they were desirous that the law should be altered in a manner to overthrow the free government and to establish a ^bking over the land.

6 And those who were desirous that Pahoran should remain chief judge over the land took upon them the name of ^afreemen; and thus was the ^bdivision among them, for the freemen had sworn or ^ccovenanted to maintain their rights and the privileges of their religion by a free government.

7 And it came to pass that this matter of their contention was settled by the ^avoice of the people. And it came to pass that the voice of the people came in favor of the freemen, and Pahoran retained the judgment-seat, which caused much rejoicing among the brethren of Pahoran and also many of the people of liberty, who also put the king-men to silence, that they durst not oppose but were obliged to maintain the cause of freedom.

8 Now those who were in favor of kings were those of ^ahigh birth, and they sought to be ^bkings; and they were supported by those who sought power and authority over the people.

39a Alma 60:1.
  b TG Oath; Ordinance.
  c Alma 4:16 (16–17);
    Hel. 1:5 (3–5, 13).
40a Alma 59:3; 61:1;
    Hel. 1:2.
51 1a TG Peacemakers.

2a Alma 1:1.
4a TG Disputations.
5a Alma 60:16; 62:9.
  TG Kings, Earthly;
    Unrighteous Dominion.
  b 3 Ne. 6:30.
6a Alma 61:3 (3–4); 62:6.

  b 1 Kgs. 16:21 (21–22).
  c Alma 48:13;
    60:25 (25–27).
7a Alma 4:16;
    Hel. 1:5.
8a TG Haughtiness; Pride.
  b TG Tyranny.

9 But behold, this was a critical time for such contentions to be among the people of Nephi; for behold, Amalickiah had again *stirred up the hearts of the people of the Lamanites against the people of the Nephites, and he was gathering together soldiers from all parts of his land, and arming them, and preparing for war with all diligence; for he had *sworn to drink the blood of Moroni.

10 But behold, we shall see that his promise which he made was *rash; nevertheless, he did prepare himself and his armies to come to battle against the Nephites.

11 Now his armies were not so great as they had hitherto been, because of the many thousands who had been *slain by the hand of the Nephites; but notwithstanding their great loss, Amalickiah had gathered together a wonderfully great army, insomuch that he feared not to come down to the land of Zarahemla.

12 Yea, even Amalickiah did himself come down, at the head of the Lamanites. And it was in the twenty and fifth year of the reign of the judges; and it was at the same time that they had begun to settle the affairs of their contentions concerning the chief judge, Pahoran.

13 And it came to pass that when the men who were called kingmen had heard that the Lamanites were coming down to battle against them, they were glad in their hearts; and they refused to take up arms, for they were so wroth with the chief judge, and also with the *people of *liberty, that they would not take up arms to defend their country.

14 And it came to pass that when Moroni saw this, and also saw that the Lamanites were coming into the borders of the land, he was exceedingly wroth because of the *stubbornness of those people whom he had labored with so much diligence to preserve; yea, he was exceedingly wroth; his soul was filled with anger against them.

15 And it came to pass that he sent a petition, with the voice of the people, unto the governor of the land, desiring that he should read it, and give him (Moroni) power to compel those dissenters to defend their country or to put them to death.

16 For it was his first care to put an end to such contentions and dissensions among the people; for behold, this had been hitherto a cause of all their destruction. And it came to pass that it was granted according to the voice of the people.

17 And it came to pass that Moroni commanded that his army should go against those king-men, to pull down their pride and their nobility and level them with the earth, or they should take up arms and support the cause of liberty.

18 And it came to pass that the armies did march forth against them; and they did pull down their pride and their nobility, insomuch that as they did lift their weapons of war to fight against the men of Moroni they were hewn down and leveled to the earth.

19 And it came to pass that there were four thousand of those *dissenters who were hewn down by the sword; and those of their leaders who were not slain in battle were taken and *cast into prison, for there was no time for their trials at this period.

20 And the remainder of those dissenters, rather than be smitten down to the earth by the sword, yielded to the standard of liberty, and were compelled to hoist the *title of liberty upon their towers, and in their cities, and to take up arms in defence of their country.

9a Alma 63:14.
 b Acts 23:12;
   Alma 49:27 (26–27).
10a TG Rashness.
11a Alma 49:25 (22–25).
13a Alma 46:16 (10–16).
  b TG Liberty.
14a TG Stubbornness.
19a Alma 60:16.
  b Alma 62:9.
20a Alma 46:13 (12–13).

21 And thus Moroni put an end to those king-men, that there were not any known by the appellation of king-men; and thus he put an end to the stubbornness and the pride of those people who professed the blood of nobility; but they were brought down to humble themselves like unto their brethren, and to fight ^avaliantly for their freedom from bondage.

22 Behold, it came to pass that while Moroni was thus breaking down the wars and contentions among his own people, and subjecting them to peace and civilization, and making regulations to prepare for war against the Lamanites, behold, the Lamanites had come into the ^aland of Moroni, which was in the borders by the seashore.

23 And it came to pass that the Nephites were not sufficiently strong in the city of Moroni; therefore Amalickiah did drive them, slaying many. And it came to pass that Amalickiah took possession of the city, yea, possession of all their fortifications.

24 And those who fled out of the ^acity of Moroni came to the city of Nephihah; and also the people of the city of Lehi gathered themselves together, and made preparations and were ready to receive the Lamanites to battle.

25 But it came to pass that Amalickiah would not suffer the Lamanites to go against the city of Nephihah to battle, but kept them down by the seashore, leaving men in every city to maintain and defend it.

26 And thus he went on, taking possession of ^amany cities, the city of ^bNephihah, and the city of ^cLehi, and the city of ^dMorianton, and the city of Omner, and the city of ^eGid, and the city of ^fMulek, all of which were on the east borders by the seashore.

27 And thus had the Lamanites obtained, by the cunning of Amalickiah, so many cities, by their numberless hosts, all of which were strongly fortified after the manner of the ^afortifications of Moroni; all of which afforded strongholds for the Lamanites.

28 And it came to pass that they marched to the ^aborders of the land Bountiful, driving the Nephites before them and slaying many.

29 But it came to pass that they were met by Teancum, who had ^aslain Morianton and had ^bheaded his people in his flight.

30 And it came to pass that he headed Amalickiah also, as he was marching forth with his numerous army that he might take possession of the land Bountiful, and also the land ^anorthward.

31 But behold he met with a disappointment by being repulsed by Teancum and his men, for they were great warriors; for every man of Teancum did exceed the Lamanites in their strength and in their skill of war, insomuch that they did gain advantage over the Lamanites.

32 And it came to pass that they did harass them, insomuch that they did slay them even until it was dark. And it came to pass that Teancum and his men did pitch their tents in the borders of the land Bountiful; and Amalickiah did pitch his tents in the borders on the beach by the seashore, and after this manner were they driven.

33 And it came to pass that when the night had come, Teancum and his servant stole forth and went out by night, and went into the camp of Amalickiah; and behold, sleep

---

21a TG Courage.
22a Alma 50:13;
    62:32 (32, 34);
    3 Ne. 8:9.
24a Alma 50:14.
26a Alma 58:31.

b Alma 50:14;
   62:18 (14, 18, 26).
c Alma 50:15; 62:30.
d Alma 50:25; 55:33.
e Alma 55:7.
f Alma 52:2 (2, 16, 22);

53:6 (2, 6).
27a Alma 48:8 (8–9).
28a Alma 52:12.
29a Alma 50:35.
  b Hel. 1:28 (28–30).
30a Alma 50:29; 52:9.

had overpowered them because of their much fatigue, which was caused by the labors and heat of the day.

34 And it came to pass that Teancum stole privily into the tent of the king, and ^aput a javelin to his heart; and he did cause the ^bdeath of the king immediately that he did not awake his servants.

35 And he returned again privily to his own camp, and behold, his men were asleep, and he awoke them and told them all the things that he had done.

36 And he caused that his armies should stand in ^areadiness, lest the Lamanites had awakened and should come upon them.

37 And thus endeth the twenty and fifth year of the reign of the judges over the people of Nephi; and thus endeth the days of Amalickiah.

CHAPTER 52

Ammoron succeeds Amalickiah as king of the Lamanites—Moroni, Teancum, and Lehi lead the Nephites in a victorious war against the Lamanites—The city of Mulek is retaken, and Jacob the Zoramite is slain. About 66–64 B.C.

AND now, it came to pass in the twenty and sixth year of the reign of the judges over the people of Nephi, behold, when the Lamanites awoke on the first morning of the first month, behold, they found Amalickiah was dead in his own tent; and they also saw that Teancum was ^aready to give them battle on that day.

2 And now, when the Lamanites saw this they were affrighted; and they abandoned their design in marching into the land northward, and retreated with all their army into the city of ^aMulek, and sought protection in their fortifications.

3 And it came to pass that the ^abrother of Amalickiah was appointed king over the people; and his name was ^bAmmoron; thus king Ammoron, the brother of king Amalickiah, was appointed to reign in his stead.

4 And it came to pass that he did command that his people should maintain those cities, which they had taken by the shedding of blood; for they had not taken any cities save they had lost much blood.

5 And now, Teancum saw that the Lamanites were determined to maintain those cities which they had taken, and those parts of the land which they had obtained possession of; and also seeing the enormity of their number, Teancum thought it was not expedient that he should attempt to attack them in their forts.

6 But he kept his men round about, as if making preparations for war; yea, and truly he was preparing to defend himself against them, by ^acasting up walls round about and preparing places of resort.

7 And it came to pass that he kept thus preparing for war until Moroni had sent a large number of men to strengthen his army.

8 And Moroni also sent orders unto him that he should retain all the prisoners who fell into his hands; for as the Lamanites had taken many prisoners, that he should retain all the prisoners of the Lamanites as a ^aransom for those whom the Lamanites had taken.

9 And he also sent orders unto him that he should fortify the land ^aBountiful, and secure the ^bnarrow pass which led into the land ^cnorthward, lest the Lamanites should obtain that point and should have power to harass them on every side.

34a Alma 62:36.
  b Alma 54:16.
36a Alma 52:1.
52 1a Alma 51:36.
  2a Alma 51:26.
  3a Alma 48:1 (1–6); 54:5.

  b Alma 54:1;
    Hel. 1:16.
6a Alma 50:1; 53:3.
8a Alma 54:2 (1–2).
9a Alma 22:29;
    53:3 (3–4); 63:5;

    Hel. 1:23.
  b Alma 22:32;
    Morm. 2:29.
  c Alma 51:30.

10 And Moroni also sent unto him, desiring him that he would be ^afaithful in maintaining that quarter of the land, and that he would seek every opportunity to scourge the Lamanites in that quarter, as much as was in his power, that perhaps he might take again by stratagem or some other way those cities which had been taken out of their hands; and that he also would fortify and strengthen the cities round about, which had not fallen into the hands of the Lamanites.

11 And he also said unto him, I would come unto you, but behold, the Lamanites are upon us in the borders of the land by the west sea; and behold, I go against them, therefore I cannot come unto you.

12 Now, the king (Ammoron) had ^adeparted out of the land of Zarahemla, and had made known unto the queen concerning the death of his brother, and had gathered together a large number of men, and had marched forth against the Nephites on the borders by the west sea.

13 And thus he was endeavoring to harass the Nephites, and to draw away a part of their forces to that part of the land, while he had commanded those whom he had left to possess the cities which he had taken, that they should also harass the Nephites on the borders by the east sea, and should take possession of their lands as much as it was in their power, according to the power of their armies.

14 And thus were the Nephites in those dangerous circumstances in the ending of the twenty and sixth year of the reign of the judges over the people of Nephi.

15 But behold, it came to pass in the twenty and seventh year of the reign of the judges, that Teancum, by the command of Moroni—who had established armies to protect the south and the west borders of the land, and had begun his march towards the land Bountiful, that he might assist Teancum with his men in retaking the cities which they had lost—

16 And it came to pass that Teancum had received orders to make an attack upon the city of Mulek, and retake it if it were possible.

17 And it came to pass that Teancum made preparations to make an attack upon the city of Mulek, and march forth with his army against the Lamanites; but he saw that it was impossible that he could overpower them while they were in their fortifications; therefore he abandoned his designs and returned again to the city Bountiful, to wait for the coming of Moroni, that he might receive strength to his army.

18 And it came to pass that Moroni did arrive with his army at the land of Bountiful, in the latter end of the twenty and seventh year of the reign of the judges over the people of Nephi.

19 And in the commencement of the twenty and eighth year, Moroni and Teancum and many of the chief ^acaptains held a council of war—what they should do to cause the Lamanites to come out against them to battle; or that they might by some means flatter them out of their strongholds, that they might gain advantage over them and take again the city of Mulek.

20 And it came to pass they sent embassies to the army of the Lamanites, which protected the city of Mulek, to their leader, whose name was Jacob, desiring him that he would come out with his armies to meet them upon the plains between the two cities. But behold, Jacob, who was a ^aZoramite, would not come out with his army to meet them upon the plains.

21 And it came to pass that Moroni, having no hopes of meeting them upon fair grounds, therefore, he resolved upon a plan that he might

10a TG Trustworthiness.
12a Alma 51:28.
19a Alma 49:5; 55:23.
20a Alma 48:5.

[a]decoy the Lamanites out of their strongholds.

22 Therefore he caused that Teancum should take a small number of men and march down near the seashore; and Moroni and his army, by night, marched in the wilderness, on the west of the city [a]Mulek; and thus, on the morrow, when the guards of the Lamanites had discovered Teancum, they ran and told it unto Jacob, their leader.

23 And it came to pass that the armies of the Lamanites did march forth against Teancum, supposing by their numbers to overpower Teancum because of the smallness of his numbers. And as Teancum saw the armies of the Lamanites coming out against him he began to retreat down by the seashore, northward.

24 And it came to pass that when the Lamanites saw that he began to flee, they took courage and pursued them with vigor. And while Teancum was thus leading away the Lamanites who were pursuing them in vain, behold, Moroni commanded that a part of his army who were with him should march forth into the city, and take possession of it.

25 And thus they did, and slew all those who had been left to protect the city, yea, all those who would not [a]yield up their weapons of war.

26 And thus Moroni had obtained possession of the city Mulek with a part of his army, while he marched with the remainder to meet the Lamanites when they should return from the pursuit of Teancum.

27 And it came to pass that the Lamanites did pursue Teancum until they came near the city Bountiful, and then they were met by Lehi and a small army, which had been left to protect the city Bountiful.

28 And now behold, when the chief captains of the Lamanites had beheld Lehi with his army coming against them, they fled in much confusion, lest perhaps they should not obtain the city Mulek before Lehi should overtake them; for they were wearied because of their march, and the men of Lehi were fresh.

29 Now the Lamanites did not know that Moroni had been in their rear with his army; and all they feared was Lehi and his men.

30 Now Lehi was not desirous to overtake them till they should meet Moroni and his army.

31 And it came to pass that before the Lamanites had retreated far they were surrounded by the Nephites, by the men of Moroni on one hand, and the men of Lehi on the other, all of whom were fresh and full of strength; but the Lamanites were wearied because of their long march.

32 And Moroni commanded his men that they should fall upon them until they had given up their weapons of war.

33 And it came to pass that Jacob, being their leader, being also a [a]Zoramite, and having an unconquerable spirit, he led the Lamanites forth to battle with exceeding fury against Moroni.

34 Moroni being in their course of march, therefore Jacob was determined to slay them and cut his way through to the city of Mulek. But behold, Moroni and his men were more powerful; therefore they did not give way before the Lamanites.

35 And it came to pass that they fought on both hands with exceeding fury; and there were many slain on both sides; yea, and Moroni was wounded and Jacob was killed.

36 And Lehi pressed upon their rear with such fury with his strong men, that the Lamanites in the rear delivered up their weapons of war; and the remainder of them, being much confused, knew not whither to go or to strike.

37 Now Moroni seeing their confusion, he said unto them: If ye will

21a Josh. 8:13;
   Alma 43:31 (30–43);
      56:30.
22a Alma 51:26; 53:6 (2, 6).
25a Alma 44:6.
33a Alma 30:59.

bring forth your weapons of war and deliver them up, behold we will forbear shedding your blood.

38 And it came to pass that when the Lamanites had heard these words, their chief captains, all those who were not slain, came forth and threw down their weapons of war ᵃat the feet of Moroni, and also commanded their men that they should do the same.

39 But behold, there were many that would not; and those who would not deliver up their swords were taken and bound, and their weapons of war were taken from them, and they were compelled to march with their brethren forth into the land Bountiful.

40 And now the number of prisoners who were taken exceeded more than the number of those who had been slain, yea, more than those who had been slain on both sides.

CHAPTER 53

The Lamanite prisoners are used to fortify the city Bountiful—Dissensions among the Nephites give rise to Lamanite victories—Helaman takes command of the two thousand stripling sons of the people of Ammon. About 64–63 B.C.

AND it came to pass that they did set guards over the prisoners of the Lamanites, and did compel them to go forth and bury their dead, yea, and also the dead of the Nephites who were slain; and Moroni placed men over them to guard them while they should perform their labors.

2 And Moroni went to the city of Mulek with Lehi, and took command of the city and gave it unto Lehi. Now behold, this Lehi was a man who had been with Moroni in the more part of all his battles; and he was a man ᵃlike unto Moroni, and they rejoiced in each other's

safety; yea, they were beloved by each other, and also beloved by all the people of Nephi.

3 And it came to pass that after the Lamanites had finished burying their dead and also the dead of the Nephites, they were marched back into the land Bountiful; and Teancum, by the orders of Moroni, caused that they should commence laboring in ᵃdigging a ditch round about the land, or the city, ᵇBountiful.

4 And he caused that they should build a ᵃbreastwork of timbers upon the inner bank of the ditch; and they cast up dirt out of the ditch against the breastwork of timbers; and thus they did cause the Lamanites to labor until they had encircled the city of Bountiful round about with a strong wall of timbers and earth, to an exceeding height.

5 And this city became an exceeding stronghold ever after; and in this city they did guard the prisoners of the Lamanites; yea, even within a wall which they had caused them to ᵃbuild with their own hands. Now Moroni was compelled to cause the Lamanites to labor, because it was easy to guard them while at their labor; and he desired all his forces when he should make an attack upon the Lamanites.

6 And it came to pass that Moroni had thus gained a victory over one of the greatest of the armies of the Lamanites, and had obtained possession of the city of ᵃMulek, which was one of the strongest holds of the Lamanites in the land of Nephi; and thus he had also built a stronghold to retain his prisoners.

7 And it came to pass that he did no more attempt a battle with the Lamanites in that year, but he did employ his men in preparing for war, yea, and in making fortifications to guard against the Lamanites, yea, and also delivering their women and their children from famine and

---

38a Alma 55:23.
53 2a Alma 48:17.
   3a Alma 52:6.

b Alma 52:9 (9, 17, 27);
  63:5.
4a Alma 50:2 (2–3).

5a Alma 55:25 (25–26).
6a Alma 51:26; 52:22.

affliction, and providing food for their armies.

8 And now it came to pass that the armies of the Lamanites, on the west sea, south, while in the absence of Moroni on account of some intrigue amongst the Nephites, which caused ªdissensions amongst them, had gained some ground over the Nephites, yea, insomuch that they had obtained possession of a number of their cities in that part of the land.

9 And thus because of ªiniquity amongst themselves, yea, because of dissensions and intrigue among themselves they were placed in the most dangerous circumstances.

10 And now behold, I have somewhat to say concerning the ªpeople of Ammon, who, in the beginning, were Lamanites; but by Ammon and his brethren, or rather by the power and word of God, they had been ᵇconverted unto the Lord; and they had been brought down into the land of Zarahemla, and had ever since been protected by the Nephites.

11 And because of their oath they had been kept from taking up arms against their brethren; for they had taken an oath that they ªnever would shed blood more; and according to their oath they would have perished; yea, they would have suffered themselves to have fallen into the hands of their brethren, had it not been for the pity and the exceeding love which Ammon and his brethren had had for them.

12 And for this cause they were brought down into the land of Zarahemla; and they ever had been ªprotected by the Nephites.

13 But it came to pass that when they saw the danger, and the many ªafflictions and tribulations which the Nephites bore for them, they were moved with compassion and were ᵇdesirous to take up arms in the defence of their country.

14 But behold, as they were about to take their weapons of war, they were overpowered by the persuasions of Helaman and his brethren, for they were about to ªbreak the ᵇoath which they had made.

15 And Helaman feared lest by so doing they should lose their souls; therefore all those who had entered into this covenant were compelled to behold their brethren wade through their afflictions, in their dangerous circumstances at this time.

16 But behold, it came to pass they had many ªsons, who had not entered into a covenant that they would not take their weapons of war to defend themselves against their enemies; therefore they did assemble themselves together at this time, as many as were able to take up arms, and they called themselves Nephites.

17 And they entered into a covenant to fight for the liberty of the Nephites, yea, to protect the land unto the ªlaying down of their lives; yea, even they covenanted that they never would give up their ᵇliberty, but they would fight in all cases to protect the Nephites and themselves from bondage.

18 Now behold, there were two thousand of those young men, who entered into this covenant and took their weapons of war to defend their country.

19 And now behold, as they never had hitherto been a disadvantage to the Nephites, they became now at this period of time also a great support; for they took their weapons of war, and they would that Helaman should be their leader.

20 And they were all young men,

8ª Alma 31:8;
    Hel. 1:15.
9ª Josh. 7:4.
10ª Alma 27:26.
  ᵇ Alma 23:13 (8–13).
11ª Alma 24:18 (17–19).

12ª Alma 27:23.
13ª TG Affliction;
    Tribulation.
  ᵇ Alma 24:18 (17–19); 56:7.
14ª Num. 30:2.
  ᵇ TG Oath.

16ª Alma 57:6.
17ª TG Self-Sacrifice.
  ᵇ Alma 56:47.
    TG Liberty.

and they were exceedingly valiant for ^acourage, and also for strength and activity; but behold, this was not all—they were men who were true at all times in whatsoever thing they were entrusted.

21 Yea, they were men of truth and ^asoberness, for they had been taught to keep the commandments of God and to ^bwalk uprightly before him.

22 And now it came to pass that Helaman did march at the head of his ^atwo thousand stripling soldiers, to the support of the people in the borders of the land on the south by the west sea.

23 And thus ended the twenty and eighth year of the reign of the judges over the people of Nephi.

CHAPTER 54

Ammoron and Moroni negotiate for the exchange of prisoners—Moroni demands that the Lamanites withdraw and cease their murderous attacks—Ammoron demands that the Nephites lay down their arms and become subject to the Lamanites. About 63 B.C.

AND now it came to pass in the commencement of the twenty and ninth year of the judges, that ^aAmmoron sent unto Moroni desiring that he would exchange prisoners.

2 And it came to pass that Moroni felt to ^arejoice exceedingly at this request, for he desired the provisions which were imparted for the support of the Lamanite prisoners for the support of his own people; and he also desired his own people for the strengthening of his army.

3 Now the Lamanites had taken many women and children, and there was not a woman nor a child among all the prisoners of Moroni, or the prisoners whom Moroni had taken; therefore Moroni resolved

upon a stratagem to obtain as many prisoners of the Nephites from the Lamanites as it were possible.

4 Therefore he wrote an epistle, and sent it by the servant of Ammoron, the same who had brought an epistle to Moroni. Now these are the words which he wrote unto Ammoron, saying:

5 Behold, Ammoron, I have written unto you somewhat concerning this war which ye have waged against my people, or rather which thy ^abrother hath waged against them, and which ye are still determined to carry on after his death.

6 Behold, I would tell you somewhat concerning the ^ajustice of God, and the sword of his almighty wrath, which doth hang over you except ye repent and withdraw your armies into your own lands, or the land of your possessions, which is the land of Nephi.

7 Yea, I would tell you these things if ye were capable of hearkening unto them; yea, I would tell you concerning that awful ^ahell that awaits to receive such ^bmurderers as thou and thy brother have been, except ye repent and withdraw your murderous purposes, and return with your armies to your own lands.

8 But as ye have once rejected these things, and have fought against the people of the Lord, even so I may expect you will do it again.

9 And now behold, we are prepared to receive you; yea, and except you withdraw your purposes, behold, ye will pull down the ^awrath of that God whom you have rejected upon you, even to your utter destruction.

10 But, as the Lord liveth, our armies shall come upon you except ye withdraw, and ye shall soon be visited with ^adeath, for we will retain our cities and our lands; yea,

---

20a TG Courage;
    Dependability;
    Integrity.
21a TG Sobriety.
  b TG Walking with God.
22a Alma 56:3 (1–9).

54 1a Alma 52:3.
  2a Alma 52:8.
  5a Alma 48:1 (1–6);
    52:3 (1–3).
  6a TG God, Indignation of;
    God, Justice of.

7a TG Hell.
  b Alma 47:18 (18, 22–34).
    TG Murder.
9a TG Punish.
10a Alma 43:47.

and we will maintain our religion and the cause of our God.

11 But behold, it supposeth me that I talk to you concerning these things in vain; or it supposeth me that thou art a ^achild of hell; therefore I will close my epistle by telling you that I will not exchange prisoners, save it be on conditions that ye will deliver up a man and his wife and his children, for one prisoner; if this be the case that ye will do it, I will exchange.

12 And behold, if ye do not this, I will come against you with my armies; yea, even I will arm my women and my children, and I will come against you, and I will follow you even into your own land, which is the land of ^aour first inheritance; yea, and it shall be blood for blood, yea, life for life; and I will give you battle even until you are destroyed from off the face of the earth.

13 Behold, I am in my anger, and also my people; ye have sought to ^amurder us, and we have only sought to defend ourselves. But behold, if ye seek to destroy us more we will seek to destroy you; yea, and we will seek our land, the land of our first inheritance.

14 Now I close my epistle. I am Moroni; I am a leader of the people of the Nephites.

15 Now it came to pass that Ammoron, when he had received this epistle, was angry; and he wrote another epistle unto Moroni, and these are the words which he wrote, saying:

16 I am Ammoron, the king of the Lamanites; I am the brother of Amalickiah whom ye have ^amurdered. Behold, I will avenge his blood upon you, yea, and I will come upon you with my armies for I fear not your threatenings.

17 For behold, your fathers did wrong their brethren, insomuch that they did rob them of their ^aright to the ^bgovernment when it rightly belonged unto them.

18 And now behold, if ye will lay down your arms, and subject yourselves to be governed by those to whom the government doth rightly belong, then will I cause that my people shall lay down their weapons and shall be at war no more.

19 Behold, ye have breathed out many threatenings against me and my people; but behold, we fear not your threatenings.

20 Nevertheless, I will grant to exchange prisoners according to your request, gladly, that I may preserve my food for my men of war; and we will wage a war which shall be eternal, either to the subjecting the Nephites to our authority or to their eternal extinction.

21 And as concerning that God whom ye say we have rejected, behold, we ^aknow not such a being; neither do ye; but if it so be that there is such a being, we know not but that he hath made us as well as you.

22 And if it so be that there is a devil and a hell, behold will he not send you there to dwell with my brother whom ye have murdered, whom ye have hinted that he hath gone to such a place? But behold these things matter not.

23 I am Ammoron, and a descendant of ^aZoram, whom your fathers pressed and brought out of Jerusalem.

24 And behold now, I am a bold Lamanite; behold, this war hath been waged to avenge their wrongs, and ^ato maintain and to obtain their rights to the government; and I close my epistle to Moroni.

CHAPTER 55

Moroni refuses to exchange prisoners—The Lamanite guards are enticed

---

11a John 8:44 (43–44).
12a 2 Ne. 5:8 (5–8).
13a Alma 55:2.
16a Alma 51:34.

17a 2 Ne. 5:3 (1–4);
    Mosiah 10:15 (12–17).
b TG Governments.
21a TG Unbelief.

23a 1 Ne. 4:35;
    Jacob 1:13;
    4 Ne. 1:36 (36–37).
24a Alma 48:2 (1–4).

to become drunk, and the Nephite prisoners are freed—The city of Gid is taken without bloodshed. About 63–62 B.C.

Now it came to pass that when Moroni had received this epistle he was more angry, because he knew that Ammoron had a perfect knowledge of his ^afraud; yea, he knew that Ammoron knew that it was not a just cause that had caused him to wage a war against the people of Nephi.

2 And he said: Behold, I will not exchange prisoners with Ammoron save he will withdraw his ^apurpose, as I have stated in my epistle; for I will not grant unto him that he shall have any more power than what he hath got.

3 Behold, I know the place where the Lamanites do guard my people whom they have taken prisoners; and as Ammoron would not grant unto me mine epistle, behold, I will give unto him according to my words; yea, I will seek death among them until they shall sue for peace.

4 And now it came to pass that when Moroni had said these words, he caused that a search should be made among his men, that perhaps he might find a man who was a descendant of Laman among them.

5 And it came to pass that they found one, whose name was Laman; and he was ^aone of the servants of the king who was murdered by Amalickiah.

6 Now Moroni caused that Laman and a small number of his men should go forth unto the guards who were over the Nephites.

7 Now the Nephites were guarded in the city of ^aGid; therefore Moroni appointed Laman and caused that a small number of men should go with him.

8 And when it was evening Laman went to the guards who were over the Nephites, and behold, they saw him coming and they hailed him; but he saith unto them: Fear not; behold, I am a Lamanite. Behold, we have escaped from the Nephites, and they sleep; and behold we have taken of their wine and brought with us.

9 Now when the Lamanites heard these words they received him with joy; and they said unto him: Give us of your wine, that we may drink; we are glad that ye have thus taken wine with you for we are weary.

10 But Laman said unto them: Let us keep of our wine till we go against the Nephites to battle. But this saying only made them more desirous to drink of the wine;

11 For, said they: We are weary, therefore let us take of the wine, and by and by we shall receive wine for our rations, which will strengthen us to go against the Nephites.

12 And Laman said unto them: You may do according to your desires.

13 And it came to pass that they did take of the wine freely; and it was pleasant to their taste, therefore they took of it more freely; and it was strong, having been prepared in its ^astrength.

14 And it came to pass they did drink and were merry, and by and by they were all ^adrunken.

15 And now when Laman and his men saw that they were all drunken, and were in a ^adeep sleep, they returned to Moroni and told him all the things that had happened.

16 And now this was according to the design of Moroni. And Moroni had prepared his men with weapons of war; and he went to the city Gid, while the Lamanites were in a deep sleep and drunken, and cast in ^aweapons of war unto the prisoners, insomuch that they were all armed;

17 Yea, even to their women, and all those of their children, as many as were able to use a weapon of war,

55 1a Neh. 6:8;
      Alma 47:30 (12–35).
   2a Alma 54:13.
   5a Alma 47:29.

   7a Alma 51:26.
  13a Prov. 20:1.
      TG Wine.
  14a Mosiah 22:6 (6–11).

  15a 1 Sam. 26:12;
      Mosiah 24:19.
  16a Alma 62:22 (21–23).

when Moroni had armed all those prisoners; and all those things were done in a profound silence.

18 But had they awakened the Lamanites, behold they were drunken and the Nephites could have slain them.

19 But behold, this was not the desire of Moroni; he did not *a*delight in murder or bloodshed, but he delighted in the saving of his people from destruction; and for this cause he might not bring upon him injustice, he would not fall upon the Lamanites and destroy them in their drunkenness.

20 But he had obtained his desires; for he had armed those prisoners of the Nephites who were within the wall of the city, and had given them power to gain possession of those parts which were within the walls.

21 And then he caused the men who were with him to withdraw a pace from them, and surround the armies of the Lamanites.

22 Now behold this was done in the night-time, so that when the Lamanites awoke in the morning they beheld that they were surrounded by the Nephites without, and that their prisoners were armed within.

23 And thus they saw that the Nephites had power over them; and in these circumstances they found that it was not expedient that they should fight with the Nephites; therefore their chief *a*captains demanded their weapons of war, and they brought them forth and *b*cast them at the feet of the Nephites, pleading for mercy.

24 Now behold, this was the desire of Moroni. He took them prisoners of war, and took possession of the city, and caused that all the prisoners should be liberated, who were Nephites; and they did join the army of Moroni, and were a great strength to his army.

25 And it came to pass that he did cause the Lamanites, whom he had taken prisoners, that they should commence a *a*labor in strengthening the fortifications round about the city Gid.

26 And it came to pass that when he had fortified the city Gid, according to his desires, he caused that his prisoners should be taken to the city Bountiful; and he also guarded that city with an exceedingly strong force.

27 And it came to pass that they did, notwithstanding all the intrigues of the Lamanites, keep and protect all the prisoners whom they had taken, and also maintain all the ground and the advantage which they had retaken.

28 And it came to pass that the Nephites began *a*again to be victorious, and to reclaim their rights and their privileges.

29 Many times did the Lamanites attempt to encircle them about by night, but in these attempts they did lose many prisoners.

30 And many times did they attempt to administer of their wine to the Nephites, that they might destroy them with poison or with drunkenness.

31 But behold, the Nephites were not slow to *a*remember the Lord their God in this their time of affliction. They could not be taken in their snares; yea, they would not partake of their wine, save they had first given to some of the Lamanite prisoners.

32 And they were thus cautious that no poison should be administered among them; for if their wine would poison a Lamanite it would also poison a Nephite; and thus they did try all their liquors.

33 And now it came to pass that it was expedient for Moroni to make preparations to attack the city *a*Morianton; for behold, the Lamanites

---

19a Alma 48:16;
     55:30 (30–32).
23a Alma 52:19; 56:12.

b Alma 52:38.
25a Alma 53:5 (3–5).
28a Alma 44:20 (12–23).

31a Hosea 5:15;
     Alma 62:49 (49–51).
33a Alma 50:25; 51:26.

had, by their labors, fortified the city Morianton until it had become an exceeding stronghold.

34 And they were continually bringing new forces into that city, and also new supplies of provisions.

35 And thus ended the twenty and ninth year of the reign of the judges over the people of Nephi.

CHAPTER 56

Helaman sends an epistle to Moroni, recounting the state of the war with the Lamanites—Antipus and Helaman gain a great victory over the Lamanites—Helaman's two thousand stripling sons fight with miraculous power, and none of them are slain. Verse 1, about 62 B.C.; verses 2–19, about 66 B.C.; and verses 20–57, about 65–64 B.C.

AND now it came to pass in the commencement of the thirtieth year of the reign of the judges, on the second day in the first month, ªMoroni received an ᵇepistle from Helaman, stating the affairs of the people in ᶜthat quarter of the land.

2 And these are the words which he wrote, saying: My dearly beloved brother, Moroni, as well in the Lord as in the tribulations of our warfare; behold, my beloved brother, I have somewhat to tell you concerning our warfare in this part of the land.

3 Behold, ªtwo thousand of the sons of those men whom Ammon brought down out of the land of Nephi—now ye have known that these were descendants of Laman, who was the eldest son of our father Lehi;

4 Now I need not rehearse unto you concerning their traditions or their unbelief, for thou knowest concerning all these things—

5 Therefore it sufficeth me that I tell you that two thousand of these young men have taken their

weapons of war, and would that I should be their leader; and we have come forth to defend our country.

6 And now ye also know concerning the ªcovenant which their fathers made, that they would not take up their weapons of war against their brethren to shed blood.

7 But in the twenty and sixth year, when they saw our afflictions and our tribulations for them, they were about to ªbreak the covenant which they had made and take up their weapons of war in our defence.

8 But I would not suffer them that they should break this ªcovenant which they had made, supposing that God would strengthen us, insomuch that we should not suffer more because of the fulfilling the ᵇoath which they had taken.

9 But behold, here is one thing in which we may have great joy. For behold, in the twenty and sixth year, I, Helaman, did march at the head of these ªtwo thousand young men to the city of ᵇJudea, to assist Antipus, whom ye had appointed a leader over the people of that part of the land.

10 And I did join my two thousand ªsons, (for they are worthy to be called sons) to the army of Antipus, in which strength Antipus did rejoice exceedingly; for behold, his army had been reduced by the Lamanites because their forces had slain a vast number of our men, for which cause we have to mourn.

11 Nevertheless, we may console ourselves in this point, that they have died in the cause of their country and of their God, yea, and they are ªhappy.

12 And the Lamanites had also retained many prisoners, all of whom are chief ªcaptains, for none other have they spared alive. And we suppose that they are now at this

---

56 1a Alma 58:35.
   b Alma 59:1.
   c Alma 53:22 (8, 22).
   3a Alma 53:22.
   6a TG Covenants.

7a Alma 24:18 (17–19);
   53:13 (13–15).
8a TG Honesty.
   b TG Vow.
9a Alma 53:22.

   b Alma 57:11.
10a Alma 56:17.
11a Alma 28:12.
12a Alma 52:19.

time in the land of Nephi; it is so if they are not slain.

13 And now these are the cities of which the Lamanites have obtained possession by the shedding of the blood of so many of our valiant men:

14 The land of ᵃManti, or the city of Manti, and the city of Zeezrom, and the city of ᵇCumeni, and the city of Antiparah.

15 And these are the cities which they possessed when I arrived at the city of Judea; and I found Antipus and his men toiling with their might to fortify the city.

16 Yea, and they were depressed in body as well as in spirit, for they had fought valiantly by day and toiled by night to maintain their cities; and thus they had suffered great afflictions of every kind.

17 And now they were determined to conquer in this place or die; therefore you may well suppose that this little force which I brought with me, yea, those ᵃsons of mine, gave them great hopes and much joy.

18 And now it came to pass that when the Lamanites saw that Antipus had received a greater strength to his army, they were compelled by the orders of Ammoron to not come against the city of Judea, or against us, to battle.

19 And thus were we favored of the Lord; for had they come upon us in this our weakness they might have perhaps destroyed our little army; but thus were we preserved.

20 They were commanded by Ammoron to maintain those cities which they had taken. And thus ended the twenty and sixth year. And in the commencement of the twenty and seventh year we had prepared our city and ourselves for defence.

21 Now we were desirous that the Lamanites should come upon us; for we were not desirous to make an attack upon them in their strongholds.

22 And it came to pass that we kept spies out round about, to watch the movements of the Lamanites, that they might not pass us by night nor by day to make an attack upon our other cities which were on the northward.

23 For we knew in those cities they were not sufficiently strong to meet them; therefore we were desirous, if they should pass by us, to fall upon them in their rear, and thus bring them up in the rear at the same time they were met in the front. We supposed that we could overpower them; but behold, we were disappointed in this our desire.

24 They durst not pass by us with their whole army, neither durst they with a part, lest they should not be sufficiently strong and they should fall.

25 Neither durst they march down against the city of Zarahemla; neither durst they cross the head of Sidon, over to the city of Nephihah.

26 And thus, with their forces, they were determined to maintain those cities which they had taken.

27 And now it came to pass in the second month of this year, there was brought unto us many provisions from the fathers of those my two thousand sons.

28 And also there were sent two thousand men unto us from the land of Zarahemla. And thus we were prepared with ten thousand men, and provisions for them, and also for their wives and their children.

29 And the Lamanites, thus seeing our forces increase daily, and provisions arrive for our support, they began to be fearful, and began to sally forth, if it were possible to put an end to our receiving provisions and strength.

30 Now when we saw that the Lamanites began to grow uneasy on this wise, we were desirous to bring a stratagem into effect upon them; therefore Antipus ordered that I should march forth with my

---

14a Alma 43:22.   b Alma 57:7 (7–34).   17a Alma 56:10.

little sons to a neighboring city, [a]as if we were carrying provisions to a neighboring city.

31 And we were to march near the city of Antiparah, as if we were going to the city beyond, in the borders by the seashore.

32 And it came to pass that we did march forth, as if with our provisions, to go to that city.

33 And it came to pass that Antipus did march forth with a part of his army, leaving the remainder to maintain the city. But he did not march forth until I had gone forth with my little army, and came near the city Antiparah.

34 And now, in the city Antiparah were stationed the strongest army of the Lamanites; yea, the most numerous.

35 And it came to pass that when they had been informed by their spies, they came forth with their army and marched against us.

36 And it came to pass that we did flee before them, northward. And thus we did lead away the most powerful army of the Lamanites;

37 Yea, even to a considerable distance, insomuch that when they saw the army of Antipus pursuing them, with their might, they did not turn to the right nor to the left, but pursued their march in a straight course after us; and, as we suppose, it was their intent to slay us before Antipus should overtake them, and this that they might not be surrounded by our people.

38 And now Antipus, beholding our danger, did speed the march of his army. But behold, it was night; therefore they did not overtake us, neither did Antipus overtake them; therefore we did camp for the night.

39 And it came to pass that before the dawn of the morning, behold, the Lamanites were pursuing us. Now we were not sufficiently strong to contend with them; yea, I would not suffer that my little sons should fall into their hands; therefore we did continue our march, and we took our march into the wilderness.

40 Now they durst not turn to the right nor to the left lest they should be surrounded; neither would I turn to the right nor to the left lest they should overtake me, and we could not stand against them, but be slain, and they would make their escape; and thus we did flee all that day into the wilderness, even until it was dark.

41 And it came to pass that again, when the light of the morning came we saw the Lamanites upon us, and we did flee before them.

42 But it came to pass that they did not pursue us far before they halted; and it was in the morning of the third day of the seventh month.

43 And now, whether they were overtaken by Antipus we knew not, but I said unto my men: Behold, we know not but they have halted for the purpose that we should come against them, that they might catch us in their snare;

44 Therefore what say ye, my sons, will ye go against them to battle?

45 And now I say unto you, my beloved brother Moroni, that never had I seen [a]so great [b]courage, nay, not amongst all the Nephites.

46 For as I had ever called them my sons (for they were all of them very young) even so they said unto me: Father, behold our God is with us, and he will [a]not suffer that we should fall; then let us go forth; we would not slay our brethren if they would let us alone; therefore let us go, lest they should overpower the army of Antipus.

47 Now they never had fought, yet they did not fear death; and they did think more upon the [a]liberty of their [b]fathers than they did upon their lives; yea, they had

30a Alma 52:21; 58:1.
45a Alma 19:10.
  b TG Courage.
46a Alma 61:10 (10–11).
47a TG Birthright;
    Liberty.
    b Alma 53:17 (15–18).
    TG Honoring Father and Mother.

been taught by their ᶜmothers, that if they did not doubt, God would deliver them.

48 And they rehearsed unto me the words of their ᵃmothers, saying: We ᵇdo not doubt our mothers knew it.

49 And it came to pass that I did return with my two thousand against these Lamanites who had pursued us. And now behold, the armies of Antipus had overtaken them, and a terrible battle had commenced.

50 The army of Antipus being weary, because of their long march in so short a space of time, were about to fall into the hands of the Lamanites; and had I not returned with my two thousand they would have obtained their purpose.

51 For Antipus had fallen by the sword, and many of his leaders, because of their weariness, which was occasioned by the speed of their march—therefore the men of Antipus, being confused because of the fall of their leaders, began to give way before the Lamanites.

52 And it came to pass that the Lamanites took courage, and began to pursue them; and thus were the Lamanites pursuing them with great vigor when ᵃHelaman came upon their rear with his two thousand, and began to slay them exceedingly, insomuch that the whole army of the Lamanites halted and turned upon Helaman.

53 Now when the people of Antipus saw that the Lamanites had turned them about, they gathered together their men and came again upon the rear of the Lamanites.

54 And now it came to pass that we, the people of Nephi, the people of Antipus, and I with my two thousand, did surround the Lamanites, and did slay them; yea, insomuch that they were compelled to deliver up their weapons of war and also themselves as prisoners of war.

55 And now it came to pass that when they had surrendered themselves up unto us, behold, I numbered those young men who had fought with me, fearing lest there were many of them slain.

56 But behold, to my great joy, there had ᵃnot one soul of them fallen to the earth; yea, and they had fought as if with the ᵇstrength of God; yea, never were men known to have fought with such miraculous strength; and with such mighty power did they fall upon the Lamanites, that they did frighten them; and for this cause did the Lamanites deliver themselves up as prisoners of war.

57 And as we had no place for our prisoners, that we could guard them to keep them from the armies of the Lamanites, therefore we sent them to the land of Zarahemla, and a part of those men who were not slain of Antipus, with them; and the remainder I took and joined them to my stripling ᵃAmmonites, and took our march back to the city of Judea.

CHAPTER 57

Helaman recounts the taking of Antiparah and the surrender and later the defense of Cumeni—His Ammonite striplings fight valiantly; all are wounded, but none are slain—Gid reports the slaying and the escape of the Lamanite prisoners. About 63 B.C.

AND now it came to pass that I received an epistle from Ammoron, the king, stating that if I would deliver up those prisoners of war whom we had taken that he would deliver up the city of Antiparah unto us.

2 But I sent an epistle unto the king, that we were sure our forces were sufficient to take the city of

47c Alma 57:21.
  TG Marriage, Motherhood.
48a TG Family, Love within.
  b D&C 46:14.
52a Morm. 6:6.
  IE Mormon here abridges some of the material in the letter of Helaman.
56a Alma 57:25; 58:39.
  b TG Strength.
57a Alma 27:26.

Antiparah by our force; and by delivering up the prisoners for that city we should suppose ourselves unwise, and that we would only deliver up our prisoners on exchange.

3 And Ammoron refused mine epistle, for he would not exchange prisoners; therefore we began to make preparations to go against the city of Antiparah.

4 But the people of Antiparah did leave the city, and fled to their other cities, which they had possession of, to fortify them; and thus the city of Antiparah fell into our hands.

5 And thus ended the twenty and eighth year of the reign of the judges.

6 And it came to pass that in the commencement of the twenty and ninth year, we received a supply of provisions, and also an addition to our army, from the land of Zarahemla, and from the land round about, to the number of six thousand men, besides sixty of the ᵃsons of the Ammonites who had come to join their brethren, my little band of two thousand. And now behold, we were strong, yea, and we had also plenty of provisions brought unto us.

7 And it came to pass that it was our desire to wage a battle with the army which was placed to protect the city ᵃCumeni.

8 And now behold, I will show unto you that we soon accomplished our desire; yea, with our strong force, or with a part of our strong force, we did surround, by night, the city Cumeni, a little before they were to receive a supply of provisions.

9 And it came to pass that we did camp round about the city for many nights; but we did sleep upon our swords, and keep guards, that the Lamanites could not come upon us by night and slay us, which they attempted many times; but as many times as they attempted this their blood was spilt.

10 At length their provisions did arrive, and they were about to enter the city by night. And we, instead of being Lamanites, were Nephites; therefore, we did take them and their provisions.

11 And notwithstanding the Lamanites being cut off from their support after this manner, they were still determined to maintain the city; therefore it became expedient that we should take those provisions and send them to ᵃJudea, and our prisoners to the land of Zarahemla.

12 And it came to pass that not many days had passed away before the Lamanites began to lose all hopes of succor; therefore they yielded up the city unto our hands; and thus we had accomplished our designs in obtaining the city Cumeni.

13 But it came to pass that our prisoners were so numerous that, notwithstanding the enormity of our numbers, we were obliged to employ all our force to keep them, or to put them to death.

14 For behold, they would break out in great numbers, and would fight with stones, and with clubs, or whatsoever thing they could get into their hands, insomuch that we did slay upwards of two thousand of them after they had surrendered themselves prisoners of war.

15 Therefore it became expedient for us, that we should put an end to their lives, or guard them, sword in hand, down to the land of Zarahemla; and also our provisions were not any more than sufficient for our own people, notwithstanding that which we had taken from the Lamanites.

16 And now, in those critical circumstances, it became a very serious matter to determine concerning these prisoners of war; nevertheless, we did resolve to send them down to the land of Zarahemla; therefore we selected a part of our men, and gave them charge over our prisoners to go down to the land of Zarahemla.

57 6a Alma 53:16.   7a Alma 56:14.   11a Alma 56:9.

17 But it came to pass that on the morrow they did return. And now behold, we did not ^ainquire of them concerning the prisoners; for behold, the Lamanites were upon us, and they returned in season to save us from falling into their hands. For behold, Ammoron had sent to their support a new supply of provisions and also a numerous army of men.

18 And it came to pass that those men whom we sent with the prisoners did arrive in season to check them, as they were about to overpower us.

19 But behold, my little band of two thousand and sixty fought most desperately; yea, they were firm before the Lamanites, and did ^aadminister death unto all those who opposed them.

20 And as the remainder of our army were about to give way before the Lamanites, behold, those two thousand and sixty were firm and undaunted.

21 Yea, and they did ^aobey and observe to perform every word of command with exactness; yea, and even according to their faith it was done unto them; and I did remember the words which they said unto me that their ^bmothers had taught them.

22 And now behold, it was these my sons, and those men who had been selected to convey the prisoners, to whom we owe this great victory; for it was they who did beat the Lamanites; therefore they were driven back to the city of Manti.

23 And we retained our city Cumeni, and were not all destroyed by the sword; nevertheless, we had suffered great loss.

24 And it came to pass that after the Lamanites had fled, I immediately gave orders that my men who had been wounded should be taken from among the dead, and caused that their wounds should be dressed.

25 And it came to pass that there were two hundred, out of my two thousand and sixty, who had fainted because of the loss of blood; nevertheless, according to the goodness of God, and to our great astonishment, and also the joy of our whole army, there was ^anot one soul of them who did perish; yea, and neither was there one soul among them who had not received many wounds.

26 And now, their ^apreservation was astonishing to our whole army, yea, that they should be spared while there was a thousand of our brethren who were slain. And we do justly ascribe it to the miraculous ^bpower of God, because of their exceeding ^cfaith in that which they had been taught to believe—that there was a just God, and whosoever did not doubt, that they should be preserved by his marvelous power.

27 Now this was the ^afaith of these of whom I have spoken; they are young, and their minds are ^bfirm, and they do put their trust in God continually.

28 And now it came to pass that after we had thus taken care of our wounded men, and had buried our dead and also the dead of the Lamanites, who were many, behold, we did inquire of Gid concerning the ^aprisoners whom they had started to go down to the land of Zarahemla with.

29 Now Gid was the chief captain over the band who was appointed to guard them down to the land.

30 And now, these are the words which Gid said unto me: Behold, we did start to go down to the land of Zarahemla with our prisoners. And it came to pass that we did meet the spies of our armies, who

---

17a Alma 57:28.
19a Alma 62:11.
21a TG Trustworthiness.
  b Alma 56:47 (47–48).
25a Alma 56:56.
26a 1 Chr. 5:20 (18–22).
  b TG God, Power of.
  c TG Faith.
27a Alma 58:40.
  b Jacob 3:2.
28a Alma 57:17 (16–17).

had been sent out to watch the camp of the Lamanites.

31 And they cried unto us, saying—Behold, the armies of the Lamanites are marching towards the city of Cumeni; and behold, they will fall upon them, yea, and will destroy our people.

32 And it came to pass that our prisoners did hear their cries, which caused them to take courage; and they did rise up in rebellion against us.

33 And it came to pass because of their rebellion we did cause that our swords should come upon them. And it came to pass that they did in a body run upon our swords, in the which, the greater number of them were slain; and the remainder of them broke through and fled from us.

34 And behold, when they had fled and we could not overtake them, we took our march with speed towards the city Cumeni; and behold, we did arrive in time that we might assist our brethren in preserving the city.

35 And behold, we are again delivered out of the hands of our enemies. And blessed is the name of our God; for behold, it is he that has delivered us; yea, that has done this great thing for us.

36 Now it came to pass that when I, Helaman, had heard these words of Gid, I was filled with exceeding joy because of the goodness of God in preserving us, that we might not all perish; yea, and I trust that the souls of them who have been slain have *a*entered into the rest of their God.

CHAPTER 58

Helaman, Gid, and Teomner take the city of Manti by a stratagem—The Lamanites withdraw—The sons of the people of Ammon are preserved as they stand fast in defense of their liberty and faith. About 63–62 B.C.

AND behold, now it came to pass that our next object was to obtain the city of Manti; but behold, there was no way that we could lead them out of the city by our small bands. For behold, they remembered that which we had hitherto done; therefore we could not *a*decoy them away from their strongholds.

2 And they were so much more numerous than was our army that we durst not go forth and attack them in their strongholds.

3 Yea, and it became expedient that we should employ our men to the maintaining those parts of the land which we had regained of our possessions; therefore it became expedient that we should wait, that we might receive more strength from the land of Zarahemla and also a new supply of provisions.

4 And it came to pass that I thus did send an embassy to the governor of our land, to acquaint him concerning the affairs of our people. And it came to pass that we did wait to receive provisions and strength from the land of Zarahemla.

5 But behold, this did profit us but little; for the Lamanites were also receiving great strength from day to day, and also many provisions; and thus were our circumstances at this period of time.

6 And the Lamanites were sallying forth against us from time to time, resolving by stratagem to destroy us; nevertheless we could not come to battle with them, because of their *a*retreats and their strongholds.

7 And it came to pass that we did wait in these difficult circumstances for the space of many months, even until we were about to *a*perish for the want of food.

8 But it came to pass that we did receive food, which was guarded to us by an army of two thousand men to our assistance; and this is all the assistance which we did receive, to defend ourselves and our country

from falling into the hands of our enemies, yea, to contend with an enemy which was innumerable.

9 And now the cause of these our embarrassments, or the cause why they did not send more strength unto us, we knew not; therefore we were grieved and also filled with fear, lest by any means the judgments of God should come upon our land, to our overthrow and utter destruction.

10 Therefore we did pour out our souls in prayer to God, that he would strengthen us and deliver us out of the hands of our enemies, yea, and also give us strength that we might retain our cities, and our lands, and our possessions, for the support of our people.

11 Yea, and it came to pass that the Lord our God did visit us with assurances that he would deliver us; yea, insomuch that he did speak peace to our souls, and did grant unto us great faith, and did cause us that we should hope for our *a*deliverance in him.

12 And we did take courage with our small force which we had received, and were fixed with a determination to conquer our enemies, and to *a*maintain our lands, and our possessions, and our wives, and our children, and the cause of our *b*liberty.

13 And thus we did go forth with all our might against the Lamanites, who were in the city of Manti; and we did pitch our tents by the wilderness side, which was near to the city.

14 And it came to pass that on the morrow, that when the Lamanites saw that we were in the borders by the wilderness which was near the city, that they sent out their spies round about us that they might discover the number and the strength of our army.

15 And it came to pass that when they saw that we were not strong, according to our numbers, and fearing that we should cut them off from their support except they should come out to battle against us and kill us, and also supposing that they could easily destroy us with their numerous hosts, therefore they began to make preparations to come out against us to battle.

16 And when we saw that they were making preparations to come out against us, behold, I caused that Gid, with a small number of men, should *a*secrete himself in the wilderness, and also that Teomner and a small number of men should secrete themselves also in the wilderness.

17 Now Gid and his men were on the right and the others on the left; and when they had thus secreted themselves, behold, I remained, with the remainder of my army, in that same place where we had first pitched our tents against the time that the Lamanites should come out to battle.

18 And it came to pass that the Lamanites did come out with their numerous army against us. And when they had come and were about to fall upon us with the sword, I caused that my men, those who were with me, should retreat into the wilderness.

19 And it came to pass that the Lamanites did follow after us with great speed, for they were exceedingly desirous to overtake us that they might slay us; therefore they did follow us into the wilderness; and we did pass by in the midst of Gid and Teomner, insomuch that they were not discovered by the Lamanites.

20 And it came to pass that when the Lamanites had passed by, or when the army had passed by, Gid and Teomner did rise up from their secret places, and did cut off the spies of the Lamanites that they should not return to the city.

---

11 a TG Deliver.
12 a Alma 46:12;
         3 Ne. 2:12;

Morm. 2:23.
   b TG Liberty.
16 a Josh. 8:13;

Alma 43:31 (30–43);
52:21 (21–31).

21 And it came to pass that when they had cut them off, they ran to the city and fell upon the guards who were left to guard the city, insomuch that they did destroy them and did take possession of the city.

22 Now this was done because the Lamanites did suffer their whole army, save a few guards only, to be led away into the wilderness.

23 And it came to pass that Gid and Teomner by this means had obtained possession of their strongholds. And it came to pass that we took our course, after having traveled much in the wilderness towards the land of Zarahemla.

24 And when the Lamanites saw that they were marching towards the land of Zarahemla, they were exceedingly afraid, lest there was a plan laid to lead them on to destruction; therefore they began to retreat into the wilderness again, yea, even back by the same way which they had come.

25 And behold, it was night and they did pitch their tents, for the chief *captains of the Lamanites had supposed that the Nephites were weary because of their march; and supposing that they had driven their whole army therefore they took no thought concerning the city of Manti.

26 Now it came to pass that when it was night, I caused that my men should not sleep, but that they should march forward by another way towards the land of Manti.

27 And because of this our march in the night-time, behold, on the morrow we were beyond the Lamanites, insomuch that we did arrive before them at the city of Manti.

28 And thus it came to pass, that by this stratagem we did take possession of the city of Manti without the shedding of blood.

29 And it came to pass that when the armies of the Lamanites did arrive near the city, and saw that we were prepared to meet them, they were astonished exceedingly and struck with great fear, insomuch that they did *flee into the wilderness.

30 Yea, and it came to pass that the armies of the Lamanites did flee out of all this quarter of the land. But behold, they have carried with them many women and children out of the land.

31 And *those cities which had been taken by the Lamanites, all of them are at this period of time in our possession; and our fathers and our women and our children are returning to their homes, all save it be those who have been taken prisoners and carried off by the Lamanites.

32 But behold, our armies are small to maintain so great a number of cities and so great possessions.

33 But behold, we *trust in our God who has given us victory over those lands, insomuch that we have obtained those cities and those lands, which were our own.

34 Now we do not know the *cause that the government does not grant us more strength; neither do those men who came up unto us know why we have not received greater strength.

35 Behold, we do not know but what *ye are unsuccessful, and ye have drawn away the forces into that quarter of the land; if so, we do not desire to murmur.

36 And if it is not so, behold, we fear that there is some *faction in the government, that they do not send more men to our assistance; for we know that they are more numerous than that which they have sent.

37 But, behold, it mattereth not—we trust God will *deliver us, notwithstanding the weakness of our armies, yea, and deliver us out of the hands of our enemies.

25a Alma 59:12.
29a Alma 59:6.
31a Alma 56:14; 59:1.
33a TG Trust in God.
34a Alma 59:13.
35a Alma 56:1.
36a Alma 61:3.
37a 2 Kgs. 17:39.

38 Behold, this is the twenty and ninth year, in the latter end, and we are in the possession of our lands; and the Lamanites have fled to the land of Nephi.

39 And those sons of the people of Ammon, of whom I have so highly spoken, are with me in the city of Manti; and the Lord has supported them, yea, and kept them from falling by the sword, insomuch that even ^aone soul has not been slain.

40 But behold, they have received many wounds; nevertheless they ^astand fast in that ^bliberty wherewith God has made them free; and they are strict to remember the Lord their God from day to day; yea, they do observe to keep his statutes, and his judgments, and his commandments continually; and their faith is strong in the prophecies concerning that which is to come.

41 And now, my beloved brother, Moroni, may the Lord our God, who has redeemed us and made us free, keep you continually in his presence; yea, and may he favor this people, even that ye may have success in obtaining the possession of all that which the Lamanites have taken from us, which was for our support. And now, behold, I close mine epistle. I am Helaman, the son of Alma.

CHAPTER 59

Moroni asks Pahoran to strengthen the forces of Helaman—The Lamanites take the city of Nephihah—Moroni is angry with the government. About 62 B.C.

Now it came to pass in the thirtieth year of the reign of the judges over the people of Nephi, after Moroni had received and had read Helaman's ^aepistle, he was exceedingly rejoiced because of the welfare, yea, the exceeding success which Helaman had had, in obtaining ^bthose lands which were lost.

2 Yea, and he did make it known unto all his people, in all the land round about in that part where he was, that they might rejoice also.

3 And it came to pass that he immediately sent ^aan epistle to ^bPahoran, desiring that he should cause men to be gathered together to strengthen Helaman, or the armies of Helaman, insomuch that he might with ease maintain that part of the land which he had been so miraculously prospered in regaining.

4 And it came to pass when Moroni had sent this epistle to the land of Zarahemla, he began again to lay a plan that he might obtain the remainder of those possessions and cities which the Lamanites had taken from them.

5 And it came to pass that while Moroni was thus making preparations to go against the Lamanites to battle, behold, the people of ^aNephihah, who were gathered together from the city of Moroni and the city of Lehi and the city of Morianton, were attacked by the Lamanites.

6 Yea, even those who had been ^acompelled to flee from the land of Manti, and from the land round about, had come over and joined the Lamanites in this part of the land.

7 And thus being exceedingly numerous, yea, and receiving strength from day to day, by the command of Ammoron they came forth against the people of Nephihah, and they did begin to slay them with an exceedingly great slaughter.

8 And their armies were so numerous that the remainder of the people of ^aNephihah were ^bobliged to flee before them; and they came even and joined the army of Moroni.

---

39 *a* Alma 56:56.
40 *a* Alma 61:21.
 TG Trustworthiness.
 b TG Liberty.

59 1 *a* Alma 56:1.
 b Alma 58:31 (31, 41).
3 *a* Alma 60:1 (1–3).
 b Alma 50:40.

5 *a* Alma 50:14.
6 *a* Alma 58:29 (29–30).
8 *a* Alma 62:26.
 b Alma 60:17.

9 And now as Moroni had supposed that there ᵃshould be men sent to the city of Nephihah, to the assistance of the people to maintain that city, and knowing that it was easier to keep the city from falling into the hands of the Lamanites than to retake it from them, he supposed that they would easily maintain that city.

10 Therefore he retained all his force to maintain those places which he had recovered.

11 And now, when Moroni saw that the city of Nephihah was ᵃlost he was exceedingly sorrowful, and began to doubt, because of the wickedness of the people, whether they should not fall into the hands of their brethren.

12 Now this was the case with all his chief captains. They doubted and marveled also because of the wickedness of the people, and this because of the success of the Lamanites over them.

13 And it came to pass that Moroni was angry with the government, because of their ᵃindifference concerning the freedom of their country.

CHAPTER 60

Moroni complains to Pahoran of the government's neglect of the armies—The Lord suffers the righteous to be slain—The Nephites must use all of their power and means to deliver themselves from their enemies—Moroni threatens to fight against the government unless help is supplied to his armies. About 62 B.C.

AND it came to pass that he wrote ᵃagain to the governor of the land, who was Pahoran, and these are the words which he wrote, saying: Behold, I direct mine epistle to Pahoran, in the city of Zarahemla, who is the chief judge and the ᵇgovernor over the land, and also to all those who have been chosen by this people to govern and manage the affairs of this war.

2 For behold, I have somewhat to say unto them by the way of ᵃcondemnation; for behold, ye yourselves know that ye have been appointed to gather together men, and arm them with swords, and with cimeters, and all manner of weapons of war of every kind, and send forth against the Lamanites, in whatsoever parts they should come into our land.

3 And now behold, I say unto you that myself, and also my men, and also Helaman and his men, have suffered exceedingly great ᵃsufferings; yea, even hunger, thirst, and fatigue, and all manner of afflictions of every kind.

4 But behold, were this all we had suffered we would not murmur nor complain.

5 But behold, great has been the slaughter among our people; yea, thousands have fallen by the sword, while it might have otherwise been if ye had rendered unto our armies sufficient strength and succor for them. Yea, great has been your neglect towards us.

6 And now behold, we desire to know the cause of this exceedingly great neglect; yea, we desire to know the cause of your thoughtless state.

7 Can you think to sit upon your thrones in a state of thoughtless ᵃstupor, while your enemies are spreading the work of death around you? Yea, while they are murdering thousands of your brethren—

8 Yea, even they who have looked up to you for protection, yea, have placed you in a situation that ye might have succored them, yea, ye might have sent armies unto them, to have strengthened them, and have saved thousands of them from falling by the sword.

9a Alma 60:15.
11a Alma 62:14.
13a Alma 58:34; 61:3.
60 1a Alma 59:3.
    b Alma 50:39.
   2a TG Reproof.
3a Alma 61:2.
7a TG Apathy.

9 But behold, this is not all—ye have withheld your provisions from them, insomuch that many have fought and bled out their lives because of their great desires which they had for the welfare of this people; yea, and this they have done when they were about to ᵃperish with hunger, because of your exceeding great neglect towards them.

10 And now, my beloved brethren—for ye ought to be beloved; yea, and ye ought to have stirred yourselves more diligently for the welfare and the freedom of this people; but behold, ye have neglected them insomuch that the blood of thousands shall come upon your heads for vengeance; yea, for ᵃknown unto God were all their cries, and all their sufferings—

11 Behold, could ye suppose that ye could sit upon your thrones, and because of the exceeding goodness of God ye could do nothing and he would deliver you? Behold, if ye have supposed this ye have supposed in vain.

12 Do ye ᵃsuppose that, because so many of your brethren have been killed it is because of their wickedness? I say unto you, if ye have supposed this ye have supposed in vain; for I say unto you, there are many who have fallen by the sword; and behold it is to your condemnation;

13 For the Lord suffereth the ᵃrighteous to be slain that his justice and ᵇjudgment may come upon the wicked; therefore ye need not suppose that the righteous are lost because they are slain; but behold, they do enter into the rest of the Lord their God.

14 And now behold, I say unto you, I fear exceedingly that the judgments of God will come upon this people, because of their exceeding ᵃslothfulness, yea, even the slothfulness of our government, and their exceedingly great neglect towards their brethren, yea, towards those who have been slain.

15 For were it not for the wickedness which first commenced at our head, we ᵃcould have withstood our enemies that they could have gained no power over us.

16 Yea, had it not been for the war which broke out ᵃamong ourselves; yea, were it not for these ᵇking-men, who caused so much bloodshed among ourselves; yea, at the time we were contending among ourselves, if we had united our strength as we hitherto have done; yea, had it not been for the desire of power and authority which those king-men had over us; had they been true to the cause of our freedom, and united with us, and gone forth against our enemies, instead of taking up their swords against us, which was the cause of so much bloodshed among ourselves; yea, if we had gone forth against them in the strength of the Lord, we should have dispersed our enemies, for it would have been done, according to the ᶜfulfilling of his word.

17 But behold, now the Lamanites are coming upon us, taking ᵃpossession of our lands, and they are murdering our people with the sword, yea, our women and our children, and also carrying them away captive, causing them that they should suffer all manner of afflictions, and this because of the great wickedness of those who are seeking for power and authority, yea, even those king-men.

18 But why should I say much concerning this matter? For we know not but what ye yourselves are seeking for authority. We know not but what ye are also ᵃtraitors to your country.

9a Alma 58:7 (7–9).
10a Ex. 3:9; Ps. 9:12.
12a Luke 13:2 (1–2).
13a Lam. 4:13;
D&C 42:46.
b Alma 14:11 (10–11); D&C 103:3.
14a TG Laziness.
15a Alma 59:9.
16a Alma 51:19 (5–7, 13–27).
b Alma 62:9.
c Alma 38:1.
17a Alma 59:8 (5–8).
18a Alma 62:1.

19 Or is it that ye have neglected us because ye are in the heart of our country and ye are ^asurrounded by security, that ye do not cause food to be sent unto us, and also men to strengthen our armies?

20 Have ye forgotten the commandments of the Lord your God? Yea, have ye forgotten the captivity of our fathers? Have ye forgotten the many times we have been delivered out of the hands of our enemies?

21 Or do ye suppose that the Lord ^awill still deliver us, while we sit upon our thrones and do not make use of the means which the Lord has provided for us?

22 Yea, will ye sit in idleness while ye are surrounded with thousands of those, yea, and tens of thousands, who do also sit in idleness, while there are thousands round about in the borders of the land who are falling by the sword, yea, wounded and bleeding?

23 Do ye suppose that God will look upon you as guiltless while ye sit still and behold these things? Behold I say unto you, Nay. Now I would that ye should remember that God has said that the ^ainward vessel shall be ^bcleansed first, and then shall the outer vessel be cleansed also.

24 And now, except ye do repent of that which ye have done, and begin to be up and doing, and send forth food and men unto us, and also unto Helaman, that he may support those parts of our country which he has regained, and that we may also recover the remainder of our possessions in these parts, behold it will be expedient that we contend no more with the Lamanites until we have first cleansed our inward vessel, yea, even the great head of our government.

25 And except ye grant mine epistle, and come out and show unto me a true ^aspirit of freedom, and strive to strengthen and fortify our armies, and grant unto them food for their support, behold I will leave a part of my freemen to maintain this part of our land, and I will leave the strength and the blessings of God upon them, that none other power can operate against them—

26 And this because of their exceeding faith, and their patience in their ^atribulations—

27 And I will come unto you, and if there be any among you that has a desire for freedom, yea, if there be even a spark of freedom remaining, behold I will stir up insurrections among you, even until those who have desires to usurp power and authority shall become extinct.

28 Yea, behold I do not fear your power nor your authority, but it is my ^aGod whom I fear; and it is according to his commandments that I do take my sword to defend the cause of my country, and it is because of your iniquity that we have suffered so much loss.

29 Behold it is time, yea, the time is now at hand, that except ye do bestir yourselves in the defence of your country and your little ones, the ^asword of justice doth hang over you; yea, and it shall fall upon you and visit you even to your utter destruction.

30 Behold, I wait for assistance from you; and, except ye do administer unto our relief, behold, I come unto you, even in the land of Zarahemla, and smite you with the sword, insomuch that ye can have no more power to impede the progress of this people in the cause of our freedom.

31 For behold, the Lord will not suffer that ye shall live and wax strong in your iniquities to destroy his righteous people.

32 Behold, can you suppose that the Lord will spare you and come

19a TG Apathy.
21a 1 Ne. 17:23 (23–35).
23a Matt. 23:26 (25–26).
  b TG Purification.
25a Alma 51:6 (6–7); 61:15.
26a TG Tribulation.
28a Acts 5:29 (26–29).
29a Isa. 1:20 (19–20);
Hel. 13:5;
3 Ne. 2:19.

out in judgment against the Lamanites, when it is the *a*tradition of their fathers that has caused their hatred, yea, and it has been redoubled by those who have dissented from us, while your iniquity is for the cause of your love of glory and the vain things of the world?

33 Ye know that ye do transgress the laws of God, and ye do know that ye do trample them under your feet. Behold, the Lord saith unto me: If those whom ye have appointed your governors do not repent of their sins and *a*iniquities, ye shall *b*go up to battle against them.

34 And now behold, I, Moroni, am constrained, according to the covenant which I have made to keep the commandments of my God; therefore I would that ye should adhere to the word of God, and send speedily unto me of your provisions and of your men, and also to Helaman.

35 And behold, if ye will not do this I come unto you speedily; for behold, God will not suffer that we should perish with hunger; therefore he will give unto us of your food, even if it must be by the sword. Now see that ye fulfil the word of God.

36 Behold, I am Moroni, your chief captain. I *a*seek not for power, but to pull it down. I *b*seek not for honor of the world, but for the glory of my God, and the freedom and welfare of my country. And thus I close mine epistle.

CHAPTER 61

Pahoran tells Moroni of the insurrection and rebellion against the government—The king-men take Zarahemla and are in league with the Lamanites—Pahoran asks for military aid against the rebels. About 62 B.C.

BEHOLD, now it came to pass that soon after Moroni had sent his epistle unto the chief governor, he received an epistle from *a*Pahoran, the chief governor. And these are the words which he received:

2 I, Pahoran, who am the chief governor of this land, do send these words unto Moroni, the chief captain over the army. Behold, I say unto you, Moroni, that I do not joy in your great *a*afflictions, yea, it grieves my soul.

3 But behold, there are those who do joy in your afflictions, yea, insomuch that they have risen up in *a*rebellion against me, and also those of my people who are *b*freemen, yea, and those who have risen up are exceedingly numerous.

4 And it is those who have sought to take away the judgment-seat from me that have been the cause of this great iniquity; for they have used great *a*flattery, and they have *b*led away the hearts of many people, which will be the cause of sore affliction among us; they have withheld our provisions, and have daunted our *c*freemen that they have not come unto you.

5 And behold, they have driven me out before them, and I have fled to the land of Gideon, with as many men as it were possible that I could get.

6 And behold, I have sent a proclamation throughout this part of the land; and behold, they are *a*flocking to us *b*daily, to their arms, in the defence of their country and their *c*freedom, and to avenge our *d*wrongs.

7 And they have come unto us, insomuch that those who have risen up in rebellion against us are set at defiance, yea, insomuch that they do fear us and durst not come out against us to battle.

32a Alma 17:15.
33a Alma 61:18.
　b Alma 61:20.
36a Alma 61:9;
　　D&C 121:39.
　b TG Motivations.

61 1a Alma 50:40.
　2a Alma 60:3 (3–9).
　3a Alma 58:36; 59:13.
　　b Alma 51:6 (6–7).
　4a TG Flatter.
　　b TG Peer Influence.

　c Alma 51:6 (6–7); 62:6.
　6a Alma 62:5.
　　b Acts 2:47.
　　c TG Liberty.
　　d TG Injustice.

8 They have ᵃgot possession of the land, or the city, of Zarahemla; they have appointed a ᵇking over them, and he hath written unto the king of the Lamanites, in the which he hath joined an alliance with him; in the which alliance he hath agreed to maintain the city of Zarahemla, which maintenance he supposeth will enable the Lamanites to conquer the remainder of the land, and he shall be placed king over this people when they shall be conquered ᶜunder the Lamanites.

9 And now, in your epistle you have ᵃcensured me, but it mattereth not; I am not angry, but do rejoice in the greatness of your heart. I, Pahoran, do not ᵇseek for power, save only to retain my judgment-seat that I may preserve the rights and the liberty of my people. My soul standeth fast in that liberty in the which God hath made us ᶜfree.

10 And now, behold, we will resist wickedness even unto bloodshed. We would ᵃnot shed the blood of the Lamanites if they would stay in their own land.

11 We would not shed the blood of our brethren if they would not rise up in rebellion and take the sword against us.

12 We would subject ourselves to the ᵃyoke of bondage if it were requisite with the justice of God, or if he should command us so to do.

13 But behold he doth not command us that we shall subject ourselves to our enemies, but that we should put our ᵃtrust in him, and he will deliver us.

14 Therefore, my beloved brother, Moroni, let us resist evil, and whatsoever evil we cannot resist with our ᵃwords, yea, such as rebellions and dissensions, let us ᵇresist them with our swords, that we may retain our freedom, that we may rejoice in the great privilege of our church, and in the cause of our Redeemer and our God.

15 Therefore, come unto me speedily with a few of your men, and leave the remainder in the charge of Lehi and Teancum; give unto them power to conduct the ᵃwar in that part of the land, according to the ᵇSpirit of God, which is also the ᶜspirit of freedom which is in them.

16 Behold I have sent a few provisions unto them, that they may not perish until ye can come unto me.

17 Gather together whatsoever force ye can upon your march hither, and we will go speedily against those dissenters, in the strength of our God according to the faith which is in us.

18 And we will ᵃtake possession of the city of Zarahemla, that we may obtain more food to send forth unto Lehi and Teancum; yea, we will go forth against them in the strength of the Lord, and we will put an end to this great iniquity.

19 And now, Moroni, I do joy in receiving your epistle, for I was somewhat worried concerning what we should do, whether it should be just in us to go against our brethren.

20 But ye have said, except they repent the Lord ᵃhath commanded you that ye should go against them.

21 See that ye ᵃstrengthen Lehi and Teancum in the Lord; tell them to fear not, for God will deliver them, yea, and also all those who ᵇstand fast in that liberty wherewith God hath made them free. And now I close mine epistle to my beloved brother, Moroni.

8a Alma 61:18.
  b Alma 62:6.
    TG Tyranny.
  c Mosiah 7:21.
9a D&C 101:5.
    TG Reproof.
  b Alma 60:36;
    D&C 121:39.
  c John 8:36;

Gal. 5:1;
    D&C 88:86.
10a Alma 56:46.
12a TG Bondage, Physical;
    Submissiveness.
13a TG Trust in God.
14a TG Reproof.
  b Alma 43:47.
15a TG War.

  b 2 Cor. 3:17.
    TG God, Spirit of.
  c Alma 60:25.
18a Alma 61:8.
20a Alma 60:33.
21a Zech. 10:12.
  b Alma 58:40.

CHAPTER 62

Moroni marches to the aid of Pahoran in the land of Gideon—The king-men who refuse to defend their country are put to death—Pahoran and Moroni retake Nephihah—Many Lamanites join the people of Ammon—Teancum slays Ammoron and is in turn slain—The Lamanites are driven from the land, and peace is established—Helaman returns to the ministry and builds up the Church. About 62–57 B.C.

AND now it came to pass that when Moroni had received this epistle his heart did take courage, and was filled with exceedingly great joy because of the faithfulness of Pahoran, that he was not also a ᵃtraitor to the freedom and cause of his country.

2 But he did also mourn exceedingly because of the iniquity of those who had driven Pahoran from the judgment-seat, yea, in fine because of those who had rebelled against their country and also their God.

3 And it came to pass that Moroni took a small number of men, according to the desire of Pahoran, and gave Lehi and Teancum command over the remainder of his army, and took his march towards the land of Gideon.

4 And he did raise the ᵃstandard of ᵇliberty in whatsoever place he did enter, and gained whatsoever force he could in all his march towards the land of Gideon.

5 And it came to pass that thousands did ᵃflock unto his standard, and did take up their swords in the defence of their freedom, that they might not come into bondage.

6 And thus, when Moroni had gathered together whatsoever men he could in all his march, he came to the land of Gideon; and uniting his forces with those of Pahoran they became exceedingly strong, even stronger than the men of

Pachus, who was the ᵃking of those dissenters who had driven the ᵇfreemen out of the land of Zarahemla and had taken possession of the land.

7 And it came to pass that Moroni and Pahoran went down with their armies into the land of Zarahemla, and went forth against the city, and did meet the men of Pachus, insomuch that they did come to battle.

8 And behold, Pachus was slain and his men were taken prisoners, and Pahoran was restored to his judgment-seat.

9 And the men of Pachus received their trial, according to the law, and also those king-men who had been taken and ᵃcast into prison; and they were ᵇexecuted according to the law; yea, those men of Pachus and those ᶜking-men, whosoever would not take up arms in the defence of their country, but would fight against it, were put to death.

10 And thus it became expedient that this law should be strictly observed for the safety of their country; yea, and whosoever was found denying their freedom was speedily ᵃexecuted according to the law.

11 And thus ended the thirtieth year of the reign of the judges over the people of Nephi; Moroni and Pahoran having restored peace to the land of Zarahemla, among their own people, having ᵃinflicted death upon all those who were not true to the cause of freedom.

12 And it came to pass in the commencement of the thirty and first year of the reign of the judges over the people of Nephi, Moroni immediately caused that provisions should be sent, and also an army of six thousand men should be sent unto Helaman, to assist him in preserving that part of the land.

13 And he also caused that an

4a Alma 46:36 (12–13, 36).
  b TG Liberty.
5a Alma 61:6.
6a Alma 61:8 (4–8).
  b Alma 51:6 (6–7).
9a Alma 51:19.
  b TG Capital Punishment.
c Alma 51:5 (5, 17, 21); 60:16.
10a 1 Kgs. 2:46.
11a Alma 44:7; 57:19.

army of six thousand men, with a sufficient quantity of food, should be sent to the armies of Lehi and Teancum. And it came to pass that this was done to fortify the land against the Lamanites.

14 And it came to pass that Moroni and Pahoran, leaving a large body of men in the land of Zarahemla, took their march with a large body of men towards the land of Nephihah, being determined to ᵃoverthrow the Lamanites in that city.

15 And it came to pass that as they were marching towards the land, they took a large body of men of the Lamanites, and slew many of them, and took their provisions and their weapons of war.

16 And it came to pass after they had taken them, they caused them to enter into a ᵃcovenant that they would no more take up their weapons of war against the Nephites.

17 And when they had entered into this covenant they sent them to ᵃdwell with the people of Ammon, and they were in number about four thousand who had not been slain.

18 And it came to pass that when they had sent them away they pursued their march towards the land of ᵃNephihah. And it came to pass that when they had come to the city of Nephihah, they did pitch their tents in the plains of Nephihah, which is near the city of Nephihah.

19 Now Moroni was desirous that the Lamanites should come out to battle against them, upon the plains; but the Lamanites, knowing of their exceedingly great courage, and beholding the greatness of their numbers, therefore they durst not come out against them; therefore they did not come to battle in that day.

20 And when the night came, Moroni went forth in the darkness of the night, and came upon the top of the wall to spy out in what part of the city the Lamanites did camp with their army.

21 And it came to pass that they were on the east, by the entrance; and they were all asleep. And now Moroni returned to his army, and caused that they should prepare in haste strong cords and ladders, to be let down from the top of the ᵃwall into the inner part of the wall.

22 And it came to pass that Moroni caused that his men should march forth and come upon the top of the wall, and let ᵃthemselves down into that part of the city, yea, even on the west, where the Lamanites did not camp with their armies.

23 And it came to pass that they were all let down into the city by night, by the means of their strong cords and their ladders; thus when the morning came they were all within the walls of the city.

24 And now, when the Lamanites awoke and saw that the armies of Moroni were within the walls, they were affrighted exceedingly, insomuch that they did flee out by the pass.

25 And now when Moroni saw that they were fleeing before him, he did cause that his men should march forth against them, and slew many, and surrounded many others, and took them prisoners; and the remainder of them fled into the land of Moroni, which was in the borders by the seashore.

26 Thus had Moroni and Pahoran obtained the ᵃpossession of the city of Nephihah without the loss of one soul; and there were many of the Lamanites who were slain.

27 Now it came to pass that many of the Lamanites that were prisoners were desirous to ᵃjoin the people of Ammon and become a free people.

28 And it came to pass that as were desirous, unto them it was granted according to their desires.

29 Therefore, all the prisoners of

14a Alma 59:11 (5–11).
16a Alma 44:15, 20;
   3 Ne. 5:4.
17a Alma 47:29.
18a Alma 50:14; 51:26 (24–26).
21a Alma 49:13 (13, 18–24).
22a Alma 55:16.
26a Alma 59:8.
27a Alma 24:26 (25–27).

the Lamanites did join the people of Ammon, and did begin to labor exceedingly, tilling the ground, raising all manner of grain, and flocks and herds of every kind; and thus were the Nephites relieved from a great burden; yea, insomuch that they were relieved from all the prisoners of the Lamanites.

30 Now it came to pass that Moroni, after he had obtained possession of the city of Nephihah, having taken many prisoners, which did reduce the armies of the Lamanites exceedingly, and having regained many of the Nephites who had been taken prisoners, which did strengthen the army of Moroni exceedingly; therefore Moroni went forth from the land of Nephihah to the land of ªLehi.

31 And it came to pass that when the Lamanites saw that Moroni was coming against them, they were again frightened and fled before the army of Moroni.

32 And it came to pass that ªMoroni and his army did pursue them from city to city, until they were met by Lehi and Teancum; and the Lamanites fled from Lehi and Teancum, even down upon the borders by the seashore, until they came to the land of Moroni.

33 And the armies of the Lamanites were all gathered together, insomuch that they were all in one body in the land of Moroni. Now Ammoron, the king of the Lamanites, was also with them.

34 And it came to pass that Moroni and Lehi and Teancum did encamp with their armies round about in the borders of the land of Moroni, insomuch that the Lamanites were encircled about in the borders by the wilderness on the south, and in the borders by the wilderness on the east.

35 And thus they did encamp for the night. For behold, the Nephites and the Lamanites also were weary because of the greatness of the march; therefore they did not resolve upon any stratagem in the night-time, save it were Teancum; for he was exceedingly angry with Ammoron, insomuch that he considered that Ammoron, and Amalickiah his brother, had been the ªcause of this great and lasting war between them and the Lamanites, which had been the cause of so much war and bloodshed, yea, and so much famine.

36 And it came to pass that Teancum in his anger did go forth into the camp of the Lamanites, and did let himself down over the walls of the city. And he went forth with a cord, from place to place, insomuch that he did find the king; and he did ªcast a javelin at him, which did pierce him near the heart. But behold, the king did awaken his servants before he died, insomuch that they did pursue Teancum, and slew him.

37 Now it came to pass that when Lehi and Moroni knew that Teancum was dead they were exceedingly sorrowful; for behold, he had been a man who had ªfought valiantly for his country, yea, a true friend to liberty; and he had suffered very many exceedingly sore afflictions. But behold, he was dead, and had gone the way of all the earth.

38 Now it came to pass that Moroni marched forth on the morrow, and came upon the Lamanites, insomuch that they did slay them with a great slaughter; and they did drive them out of the land; and they did flee, even that they did not return at that time against the Nephites.

39 And thus ended the thirty and first year of the reign of the judges over the people of Nephi; and thus they had had wars, and bloodsheds, and famine, and affliction, for the space of many years.

40 And there had been murders,

30a Alma 50:15; 51:26 (24–26).
32a Alma 50:13; 51:22 (22–23);
     3 Ne. 8:9.
35a Alma 48:1.
36a Alma 51:34.
37a IE throughout the
     Amalickiah-Ammoron
     wars.
Alma 50:35;
51:29–34; 52; 61; 62:3–37.

and contentions, and dissensions, and all manner of iniquity among the people of Nephi; nevertheless for the *righteous' sake, yea, because of the prayers of the righteous, they were spared.

41 But behold, because of the exceedingly great length of the war between the Nephites and the Lamanites many had become hardened, because of the exceedingly great length of the war; and many were softened because of their *afflictions, insomuch that they did humble themselves before God, even in the depth of humility.

42 And it came to pass that after Moroni had fortified those parts of the land which were most exposed to the Lamanites, until they were sufficiently strong, he returned to the city of Zarahemla; and also Helaman returned to the place of his inheritance; and there was once more peace established among the people of Nephi.

43 And Moroni yielded up the *command of his armies into the hands of his son, whose name was *Moronihah; and he retired to his own house that he might spend the remainder of his days in peace.

44 And Pahoran did return to his judgment-seat; and Helaman did take upon him again to preach unto the people the word of God; for because of so many wars and contentions it had become expedient that a *regulation should be made again in the church.

45 Therefore, Helaman and his brethren went forth, and did declare the word of God with much power unto the *convincing of many people of their wickedness, which did cause them to repent of their sins and to be baptized unto the Lord their God.

46 And it came to pass that they did establish again the church of God, throughout all the land.

47 Yea, and regulations were made concerning the law. And their *judges, and their chief judges were chosen.

48 And the people of Nephi began to *prosper again in the land, and began to multiply and to wax exceedingly strong again in the land. And they began to grow exceedingly rich.

49 But notwithstanding their riches, or their strength, or their prosperity, they were not lifted up in the pride of their eyes; neither were they *slow to remember the Lord their God; but they did humble themselves exceedingly before him.

50 Yea, they did remember how great things the Lord had done for them, that he had *delivered them from death, and from bonds, and from prisons, and from all manner of *afflictions, and he had *delivered them out of the hands of their enemies.

51 And they did pray unto the Lord their God continually, insomuch that the Lord did bless them, according to his word, so that they did wax strong and *prosper in the land.

52 And it came to pass that all these things were done. And *Helaman died, in the thirty and fifth year of the reign of the judges over the people of Nephi.

CHAPTER 63

Shiblon and later Helaman take possession of the sacred records—Many Nephites travel to the land northward—Hagoth builds ships, which sail forth in the west sea—Moronihah defeats the Lamanites in battle. About 56–52 B.C.

40a Alma 45:15 (15–16);
   46:10.
41a TG Adversity;
   Affliction.
43a Hel. 4:16 (10, 16).
   b Alma 63:15.
44a Alma 45:21.
45a Alma 21:17;
   D&C 18:44.
47a Mosiah 29:39.
48a Alma 50:20.
49a Alma 55:31.
50a 2 Cor. 11:26 (24–33).
   b TG Adversity.
c TG Deliver.
51a Gen. 26:22.
   TG Prosper.
52a His great career spans
   Alma 31–62.

AND it came to pass in the commencement of the thirty and sixth year of the reign of the judges over the people of Nephi, that ªShiblon took possession of those ᵇsacred things which had been delivered unto Helaman by Alma.

2 And he was a just man, and he did walk uprightly before God; and he did observe to do good continually, to keep the commandments of the Lord his God; and also did his brother.

3 And it came to pass that ªMoroni died also. And thus ended the thirty and sixth year of the reign of the judges.

4 And it came to pass that in the thirty and seventh year of the reign of the judges, there was a large company of men, even to the amount of five thousand and four hundred men, with their wives and their children, departed out of the land of Zarahemla into the land which was ªnorthward.

5 And it came to pass that Hagoth, he being an ªexceedingly curious man, therefore he went forth and built him an exceedingly large ship, on the borders of the land ᵇBountiful, by the land Desolation, and launched it forth into the west sea, by the ᶜnarrow neck which led into the land northward.

6 And behold, there were many of the Nephites who did enter therein and did sail forth with much provisions, and also many women and children; and they took their course northward. And thus ended the thirty and seventh year.

7 And in the thirty and eighth year, this man built ªother ships. And the first ship did also return, and many more people did enter into it; and they also took much provisions, and set out again to the land northward.

8 And it came to pass that they were never heard of more. And we suppose that they were drowned in the depths of the sea. And it came to pass that one other ship also did sail forth; and whither she did go we know not.

9 And it came to pass that in this year there were many people who went forth into the land ªnorthward. And thus ended the thirty and eighth year.

10 And it came to pass in the thirty and ninth year of the reign of the judges, ªShiblon died also, and Corianton had gone forth to the land northward in a ship, to carry forth provisions unto the people who had gone forth into that land.

11 Therefore it became expedient for ªShiblon to confer those sacred things, before his death, upon the son of ᵇHelaman, who was called ᶜHelaman, being called after the name of his father.

12 Now behold, all those ªengravings which were in the possession of Helaman were written and sent forth among the children of men throughout all the land, save it were those parts which had been commanded by Alma should ᵇnot go forth.

13 Nevertheless, these things were to be kept sacred, and ªhanded down from one generation to another; therefore, in this year, they had been conferred upon Helaman, before the death of Shiblon.

14 And it came to pass also in this year that there were some dissenters

63 1ª Alma 38:1 (1–2); 49:30.
  ᵇ Mosiah 1:3;
    Alma 37:1 (1–12).
    TG Sacred.
  3ª See Alma 43–63 for his
    great contributions.
  4ª Alma 22:31; 46:17;
    Hel. 3:3.
  5ª Hel. 3:10 (10, 14).

    ᵇ Alma 53:3 (3–4);
    Hel. 1:23.
    ᶜ Alma 22:32;
    Morm. 2:29;
    Ether 10:20.
  7ª Hel. 3:10.
  9ª Hel. 3:12 (11–12); 6:6.
 10ª Alma 31:7.
 11ª Alma 63:1.

    ᵇ See heading to the book
    of Helaman.
    ᶜ Hel. 3:37.
 12ª Alma 18:36;
    3 Ne. 1:2.
    ᵇ Alma 37:27 (27–32).
 13ª Alma 37:4.

who had gone forth unto the Lamanites; and they were *a*stirred up again to anger against the Nephites.

15 And also in this same year they came down with a numerous army to war against the people of *a*Moronihah, or against the army of Moronihah, in the which they were beaten and driven back again to their own lands, suffering great loss.

16 And thus ended the thirty and ninth year of the reign of the judges over the people of Nephi.

17 And thus ended the account of *a*Alma, and Helaman his son, and also Shiblon, who was his son.

THE BOOK OF HELAMAN

An account of the Nephites. Their wars and contentions, and their dissensions. And also the prophecies of many holy prophets, before the coming of Christ, according to the records of Helaman, who was the son of Helaman, and also according to the records of his sons, even down to the coming of Christ. And also many of the Lamanites are converted. An account of their conversion. An account of the righteousness of the Lamanites, and the wickedness and abominations of the Nephites, according to the record of Helaman and his sons, even down to the coming of Christ, which is called the book of Helaman, and so forth.

CHAPTER 1

Pahoran the second becomes chief judge and is murdered by Kishkumen—Pacumeni fills the judgment seat—Coriantumr leads the Lamanite armies, takes Zarahemla, and slays Pacumeni—Moronihah defeats the Lamanites and retakes Zarahemla, and Coriantumr is slain. About 52–50 B.C.

AND now behold, it came to pass in the commencement of the fortieth year of the reign of the judges over the people of Nephi, there began to be a serious difficulty among the people of the Nephites.

2 For behold, *a*Pahoran had died, and gone the way of all the earth; therefore there began to be a serious contention concerning who should have the judgment-seat among the brethren, who were the sons of Pahoran.

3 Now these are their names who did contend for the judgment-seat, who did also cause the people to contend: Pahoran, Paanchi, and Pacumeni.

4 Now these are not all the sons of Pahoran (for he had many), but these are they who did contend for the judgment-seat; therefore, they did cause three *a*divisions among the people.

5 Nevertheless, it came to pass that Pahoran was appointed by the *a*voice of the people to be chief judge and a governor over the people of Nephi.

6 And it came to pass that Pacumeni, when he saw that he could not obtain the judgment-seat, he did *a*unite with the voice of the people.

7 But behold, Paanchi, and that part of the people that were desirous that he should be their governor, was exceedingly wroth; therefore,

---

14*a* Alma 51:9;
　　Hel. 4:4.
15*a* Alma 62:43.
17*a* Alma 1:2 (1–2).

[HELAMAN]
1 2*a* Alma 50:40.
　4*a* Matt. 12:25.

5*a* Mosiah 29:11;
　　Alma 51:7;
　　Hel. 5:2.
6*a* TG Unity.

he was about to ^a^flatter away those people to rise up in rebellion against their brethren.

8 And it came to pass as he was about to do this, behold, he was taken, and was tried according to the ^a^voice of the people, and condemned unto death; for he had raised up in rebellion and sought to destroy the ^b^liberty of the people.

9 Now when those people who were desirous that he should be their governor saw that he was condemned unto death, therefore they were angry, and behold, they sent forth one ^a^Kishkumen, even to the judgment-seat of Pahoran, and murdered Pahoran as he sat upon the judgment-seat.

10 And he was pursued by the servants of Pahoran; but behold, so speedy was the flight of Kishkumen that no man could overtake him.

11 And he went unto those that sent him, and they all entered into a covenant, yea, ^a^swearing by their everlasting Maker, that they would tell no man that Kishkumen had murdered Pahoran.

12 Therefore, Kishkumen was not known among the people of Nephi, for he was in disguise at the time that he murdered Pahoran. And Kishkumen and his band, who had covenanted with him, did mingle themselves among the people, in a manner that they all could not be found; but as many as were found were condemned unto ^a^death.

13 And now behold, Pacumeni was appointed, according to the ^a^voice of the people, to be a chief judge and a governor over the people, to reign in the stead of his brother Pahoran; and it was according to his right. And all this was done in the fortieth year of the reign of the judges; and it had an end.

14 And it came to pass in the forty and first year of the reign of the judges, that the Lamanites had gathered together an innumerable army of men, and ^a^armed them with swords, and with cimeters and with bows, and with arrows, and with head-plates, and with breastplates, and with all manner of shields of every kind.

15 And they came down again that they might pitch battle against the Nephites. And they were led by a man whose name was ^a^Coriantumr; and he was a descendant of Zarahemla; and he was a ^b^dissenter from among the Nephites; and he was a large and a mighty man.

16 Therefore, the king of the Lamanites, whose name was Tubaloth, who was the son of ^a^Ammoron, supposing that Coriantumr, being a mighty man, could stand against the Nephites, with his strength and also with his great ^b^wisdom, insomuch that by sending him forth he should gain power over the Nephites—

17 Therefore he did ^a^stir them up to anger, and he did gather together his armies, and he did appoint Coriantumr to be their leader, and did cause that they should march down to the land of Zarahemla to battle against the Nephites.

18 And it came to pass that because of so much contention and so much difficulty in the government, that they had not kept sufficient guards in the land of Zarahemla; for they had supposed that the Lamanites durst not come into the heart of their lands to attack that great city Zarahemla.

19 But it came to pass that Coriantumr did march forth at the head of his numerous host, and came upon the inhabitants of the city, and their march was with such exceedingly great speed that there

---

7a Mosiah 27:8;
   Alma 50:35;
   Hel. 2:5;
   Ether 8:2.
8a Alma 1:14 (10–15).
 b TG Liberty.

9a Hel. 2:3.
11a Gen. 24:3;
    Ether 8:14 (13–14).
12a TG Capital Punishment.
13a Hel. 1:5; 2:2.
14a Alma 2:12; 49:6 (6, 24).

15a Hel. 1:30.
  b Alma 31:8; 53:8;
    Hel. 4:8.
16a Alma 52:3.
  b Ezek. 28:5 (4–5).
17a Alma 35:10; 47:1.

was no time for the Nephites to gather together their armies.

20 Therefore Coriantumr did cut down the watch by the entrance of the city, and did march forth with his whole army into the city, and they did slay every one who did oppose them, insomuch that they did take possession of the whole city.

21 And it came to pass that Pacumeni, who was the chief judge, did flee before Coriantumr, even to the walls of the city. And it came to pass that Coriantumr did smite him against the wall, insomuch that he died. And thus ended the days of Pacumeni.

22 And now when Coriantumr saw that he was in possession of the city of Zarahemla, and saw that the Nephites had fled before them, and were slain, and were taken, and were cast into prison, and that he had obtained the possession of the strongest hold in all the land, his heart *took courage insomuch that he was about to go forth against all the land.

23 And now he did not tarry in the land of Zarahemla, but he did march forth with a large army, even towards the city of *Bountiful; for it was his determination to go forth and cut his way through with the sword, that he might obtain the north parts of the land.

24 And, supposing that their greatest strength was in the center of the land, therefore he did march forth, giving them no time to assemble themselves together save it were in small bodies; and in this manner they did fall upon them and cut them down to the earth.

25 But behold, this march of Coriantumr through the center of the land gave Moronihah great advantage over them, notwithstanding the greatness of the number of the Nephites who were slain.

26 For behold, Moronihah had supposed that the Lamanites durst not come into the center of the land, but that they would attack the cities round about in the borders as they had hitherto done; therefore Moronihah had caused that their strong armies should maintain those parts round about by the borders.

27 But behold, the Lamanites were not frightened according to his desire, but they had come into the center of the land, and had taken the capital city which was the city of Zarahemla, and were marching through the most capital parts of the land, slaying the people with a great slaughter, both men, women, and children, taking possession of many cities and of many strongholds.

28 But when Moronihah had discovered this, he immediately sent forth Lehi with an army round about to *head them before they should come to the land Bountiful.

29 And thus he did; and he did head them before they came to the land Bountiful, and gave unto them battle, insomuch that they began to retreat back towards the land of Zarahemla.

30 And it came to pass that Moronihah did head them in their retreat, and did give unto them battle, insomuch that it became an exceedingly bloody battle; yea, many were slain, and among the number who were slain *Coriantumr was also found.

31 And now, behold, the Lamanites could not retreat either way, neither on the north, nor on the south, nor on the east, nor on the west, for they were surrounded on every hand by the Nephites.

32 And thus had Coriantumr plunged the Lamanites into the midst of the Nephites, insomuch that they were in the power of the Nephites, and he himself was slain, and the Lamanites did *yield themselves into the hands of the Nephites.

22a TG Pride.
23a Alma 22:29.
28a Alma 50:34; 51:29 (29–30).
30a Hel. 1:15.
32a Hel. 4:3.

33 And it came to pass that Moronihah took possession of the city of Zarahemla again, and caused that the Lamanites who had been taken prisoners should depart out of the land in ᵃpeace.

34 And thus ended the forty and first year of the reign of the judges.

CHAPTER 2

Helaman, the son of Helaman, becomes chief judge—Gadianton leads the band of Kishkumen—Helaman's servant slays Kishkumen, and the Gadianton band flees into the wilderness. About 50–49 B.C.

AND it came to pass in the forty and second year of the reign of the judges, after Moronihah had established again peace between the Nephites and the Lamanites, behold there was no one to fill the judgment-seat; therefore there began to be a contention again among the people concerning who should fill the judgment-seat.

2 And it came to pass that ᵃHelaman, who was the son of Helaman, was appointed to fill the judgment-seat, by the ᵇvoice of the people.

3 But behold, ᵃKishkumen, who had murdered Pahoran, did lay wait to destroy Helaman also; and he was upheld by his band, who had entered into a covenant that no one should know his wickedness.

4 For there was one ᵃGadianton, who was exceedingly expert in many words, and also in his craft, to carry on the secret work of murder and of robbery; therefore he became the leader of the band of Kishkumen.

5 Therefore he did ᵃflatter them, and also Kishkumen, that if they would place him in the judgment-seat he would grant unto those who belonged to his band that they should be placed in power and authority among the people; therefore Kishkumen sought to destroy Helaman.

6 And it came to pass as he went forth towards the judgment-seat to destroy Helaman, behold one of the servants of Helaman, having been out by night, and having obtained, through disguise, a knowledge of those plans which had been laid by this band to destroy Helaman—

7 And it came to pass that he met Kishkumen, and he gave unto him a sign; therefore Kishkumen made known unto him the object of his desire, desiring that he would conduct him to the judgment-seat that he might murder Helaman.

8 And when the servant of Helaman had known all the heart of Kishkumen, and how that it was his ᵃobject to murder, and also that it was the object of all those who belonged to his band to murder, and to rob, and to gain power, (and this was their ᵇsecret plan, and their combination) the servant of Helaman said unto Kishkumen: Let us go forth unto the judgment-seat.

9 Now this did please Kishkumen exceedingly, for he did suppose that he should accomplish his design; but behold, the servant of Helaman, as they were going forth unto the judgment-seat, did stab Kishkumen even to the heart, that he fell dead without a groan. And he ran and told Helaman all the things which he had seen, and heard, and done.

10 And it came to pass that Helaman did send forth to take this band of robbers and ᵃsecret murderers, that they might be executed according to the law.

11 But behold, when Gadianton had found that Kishkumen did not return he feared lest that he should be destroyed; therefore he caused that his band should follow him. And they took their flight out of

33a Alma 44:15.
2 2a Hel. 3:20.
  b Hel. 1:13.
  3a Hel. 1:9.
  4a Hel. 3:23; 6:18 (18, 29).

5a Mosiah 27:8;
  Alma 50:35;
  Hel. 1:7;
  Ether 8:2.
  TG Flatter.

8a TG Conspiracy.
  b 2 Ne. 10:15;
  Moses 5:31 (18–31).
  TG Secret Combinations.
10a Hel. 3:23.

the land, by a secret way, into the wilderness; and thus when Helaman sent forth to take them they could nowhere be found.

12 And more of this Gadianton shall be spoken hereafter. And thus ended the forty and second year of the reign of the judges over the people of Nephi.

13 And behold, in the end of this book ye shall see that this ªGadianton did prove the overthrow, yea, almost the entire destruction of the people of Nephi.

14 Behold I do not mean the end of the ªbook of Helaman, but I mean the end of the book of Nephi, from which I have taken all the account which I have written.

CHAPTER 3

Many Nephites migrate to the land northward—They build houses of cement and keep many records—Tens of thousands are converted and baptized—The word of God leads men to salvation—Nephi the son of Helaman fills the judgment seat. About 49–39 B.C.

AND now it came to pass in the forty and third year of the reign of the judges, there was no contention among the people of Nephi save it were a little pride which was in the church, which did cause some little dissensions among the people, which affairs were settled in the ending of the forty and third year.

2 And there was no contention among the people in the forty and fourth year; neither was there much contention in the forty and fifth year.

3 And it came to pass in the forty and sixth, yea, there was much contention and many dissensions; in the which there were an exceedingly great many who departed out of the land of Zarahemla, and went forth unto the land ªnorthward to inherit the land.

4 And they did travel to an exceedingly great distance, insomuch that they came to ªlarge bodies of water and many rivers.

5 Yea, and even they did spread forth into all parts of the land, into whatever parts it had not been rendered desolate and without timber, because of the many inhabitants who had before inherited the land.

6 And now no part of the land was desolate, save it were for timber; but because of the greatness of the ªdestruction of the people who had before inhabited the land it was called ᵇdesolate.

7 And there being but little timber upon the face of the land, nevertheless the people who went forth became exceedingly ªexpert in the working of cement; therefore they did build houses of cement, in the which they did dwell.

8 And it came to pass that they did multiply and spread, and did go forth from the land southward to the land northward, and did spread insomuch that they began to cover the face of the whole earth, from the sea south to the sea north, from the ªsea west to the sea east.

9 And the people who were in the land northward did dwell in ªtents, and in houses of cement, and they did suffer whatsoever tree should spring up upon the face of the land that it should grow up, that in time they might have timber to build their houses, yea, their cities, and their temples, and their ᵇsynagogues, and their sanctuaries, and all manner of their buildings.

10 And it came to pass as timber was exceedingly scarce in the land northward, they did send forth much by the way of ªshipping.

13a Hel. 6:18;
    3 Ne. 4:1.
14a W of M 1:9;
    3 Ne. 5:10.
3 3a Alma 63:4.
    4a Mosiah 8:8;

Alma 50:29;
    Morm. 6:4.
6a Mosiah 8:8;
    21:26 (26–27).
  b Alma 22:31.
7a TG Skill.

8a Alma 22:27 (27, 32–33);
    Hel. 11:20.
9a Gen. 25:27;
    Ether 2:13.
  b Alma 16:13.
10a Alma 63:7 (5–8).

11 And thus they did enable the people in the land northward that they might build many cities, both of wood and of cement.

12 And it came to pass that there were many of the *a*people of Ammon, who were Lamanites by birth, did also go forth into this land.

13 And now there are many *a*records kept of the proceedings of this people, by many of this people, which are particular and very large, concerning them.

14 But behold, a *a*hundredth part of the proceedings of this people, yea, the account of the Lamanites and of the Nephites, and their wars, and contentions, and dissensions, and their preaching, and their prophecies, and their shipping and their building of ships, and their building of *b*temples, and of synagogues and their *c*sanctuaries, and their righteousness, and their wickedness, and their murders, and their robbings, and their plundering, and all manner of abominations and whoredoms, cannot be contained in this work.

15 But behold, there are many books and many *a*records of every kind, and they have been kept chiefly by the Nephites.

16 And they have been *a*handed down from one generation to another by the Nephites, even until they have fallen into transgression and have been murdered, plundered, and hunted, and driven forth, and slain, and *b*scattered upon the face of the earth, and mixed with the Lamanites until they are *c*no more called the Nephites, becoming wicked, and wild, and ferocious, yea, even becoming Lamanites.

17 And now I return again to mine account; therefore, what I have spoken had passed after there had been great contentions, and disturbances, and wars, and dissensions, among the people of Nephi.

18 The forty and sixth year of the reign of the judges ended;

19 And it came to pass that there was still great contention in the land, yea, even in the forty and seventh year, and also in the forty and eighth year.

20 Nevertheless *a*Helaman did fill the judgment-seat with justice and equity; yea, he did observe to keep the statutes, and the judgments, and the commandments of God; and he did do that which was right in the sight of God continually; and he did walk after the ways of his father, insomuch that he did prosper in the land.

21 And it came to pass that he had two sons. He gave unto the eldest the name of *a*Nephi, and unto the youngest, the name of Lehi. And they began to grow up unto the Lord.

22 And it came to pass that the wars and contentions began to cease, in a small degree, among the people of the Nephites, in the latter end of the forty and eighth year of the reign of the judges over the people of Nephi.

23 And it came to pass in the forty and ninth year of the reign of the judges, there was continual peace established in the land, all save it were the *a*secret combinations which *b*Gadianton the robber had established in the more settled parts of the land, which at that time were not known unto those who were at the head of government; therefore they were not destroyed out of the land.

24 And it came to pass that in this same year there was exceedingly great prosperity in the church, insomuch that there were thousands who did *a*join themselves unto the

12*a* Alma 27:26; 63:9 (4–9);
    Hel. 6:6.
13*a* W of M 1:3 (1–11).
14*a* 3 Ne. 5:8; 26:6 (6–11).
    b 2 Ne. 5:16;
    Jacob 1:17;
    3 Ne. 11:1.
c Alma 23:2.
15*a* 3 Ne. 5:9; 4 Ne. 1:48.
16*a* 1 Ne. 5:18 (16–19);
    Alma 37:4.
b Ezek. 36:19 (16–20).
c Alma 45:13 (12–14).
20*a* Hel. 2:2.
21*a* Hel. 3:37; 4:14; 5:4–5;
    3 Ne. 1:2.
23*a* 2 Ne. 10:15;
    Hel. 2:10 (8–10);
    7:25 (4–5, 21, 25).
b Hel. 2:4; 6:18.
24*a* Mosiah 25:23.

church and were baptized unto repentance.

25 And so great was the prosperity of the church, and so many the blessings which were poured out upon the people, that even the high priests and the teachers were themselves astonished beyond measure.

26 And it came to pass that the work of the Lord did prosper unto the baptizing and uniting to the church of God, many souls, yea, even tens of thousands.

27 Thus we may see that the Lord is merciful unto all who will, in the sincerity of their hearts, call upon his holy name.

28 Yea, thus we see that the *gate of heaven is open unto *ball, even to those who will believe on the name of Jesus Christ, who is the Son of God.

29 Yea, we see that whosoever will may lay hold upon the *word of God, which is *quick and powerful, which shall *divide asunder all the cunning and the snares and the wiles of the devil, and lead the man of Christ in a strait and *narrow course across that everlasting *gulf of misery which is prepared to engulf the wicked—

30 And land their souls, yea, their immortal souls, at the *right hand of God in the kingdom of heaven, to sit down with Abraham, and Isaac, and with Jacob, and with all our holy fathers, to go no more out.

31 And in this year there was continual rejoicing in the land of Zarahemla, and in all the regions round about, even in all the land which was possessed by the *Nephits.

32 And it came to pass that there was peace and exceedingly great joy in the remainder of the forty and ninth year; yea, and also there was continual peace and great joy in the fiftieth year of the reign of the judges.

33 And in the fifty and first year of the reign of the judges there was peace also, save it were the pride which began to enter into the church—not into the church of God, but into the hearts of the people who *professed to belong to the church of God—

34 And they were lifted up in *pride, even to the persecution of many of their brethren. Now this was a great evil, which did cause the more humble part of the people to suffer great persecutions, and to wade through much affliction.

35 Nevertheless they did *fast and *pray oft, and did wax stronger and stronger in their *humility, and firmer and firmer in the faith of Christ, unto the filling their souls with joy and consolation, yea, even to the *purifying and the *sanctification of their hearts, which sanctification cometh because of their *yielding their hearts unto God.

36 And it came to pass that the fifty and second year ended in peace also, save it were the exceedingly great pride which had gotten into the hearts of the people; and it was because of their exceedingly great *riches and their prosperity in the land; and it did grow upon them from day to day.

37 And it came to pass in the fifty and third year of the reign of the judges, *Helaman died, and his eldest son *Nephi began to reign in his stead. And it came to pass that he did fill the judgment-seat with justice and equity; yea, he did keep

28a Isa. 26:2.
    b Acts 10:28 (9–35, 44);
      Rom. 2:11 (10–11).
29a Micah 2:7;
      Jacob 2:8;
      D&C 11:2; 33:1.
    TG Gospel.
    b Heb. 4:12;
      D&C 27:1.
    c D&C 6:2.
    d 2 Ne. 9:41; 33:9.
    e 1 Ne. 12:18; 15:28 (28–30).
30a Matt. 25:34 (31–46).
33a D&C 112:26.
34a TG Pride.
35a TG Fast, Fasting.
    b TG Prayer.
    c TG Humility.
    d TG Cleanliness;
      Purification;
      Purity.
    e TG Sanctification.
    f 2 Chr. 30:8;
      Rom. 6:13 (12–14).
    TG Submissiveness;
      Teachable.
36a TG Treasure.
37a Alma 63:11;
      Hel. 16:25.
    b Hel. 3:21; 5:1.

the commandments of God, and did walk in the ways of his father.

CHAPTER 4

Nephite dissenters and the Lamanites join forces and take the land of Zarahemla—The Nephites' defeats come because of their wickedness—The Church dwindles, and the people become weak like the Lamanites. About 38–30 B.C.

AND it came to pass in the fifty and fourth year there were many dissensions in the church, and there was also a *a*contention among the people, insomuch that there was much bloodshed.

2 And the rebellious part were slain and driven out of the land, and they did go unto the king of the Lamanites.

3 And it came to pass that they did endeavor to stir up the Lamanites to *a*war against the Nephites; but behold, the Lamanites were *b*exceedingly afraid, insomuch that they would not hearken to the words of those dissenters.

4 But it came to pass in the fifty and sixth year of the reign of the judges, there were *a*dissenters who went up from the Nephites unto the Lamanites; and they succeeded with those others in *b*stirring them up to anger against the Nephites; and they were all that year preparing for war.

5 And in the fifty and seventh year they did come down against the Nephites to battle, and they did commence the work of death; yea, insomuch that in the fifty and eighth year of the reign of the judges they succeeded in obtaining *a*possession of the land of Zarahemla; yea, and also all the lands, even unto the land which was near the land Bountiful.

6 And the Nephites and the armies of Moronihah were driven even into the land of Bountiful;

7 And there they did fortify against the Lamanites, from the west sea, even unto the east; it being a *a*day's journey for a Nephite, on the line which they had fortified and stationed their armies to defend their north country.

8 And thus those *a*dissenters of the Nephites, with the help of a numerous army of the Lamanites, had obtained all the possession of the Nephites which was in the land southward. And all this was done in the fifty and eighth and ninth years of the reign of the judges.

9 And it came to pass in the sixtieth year of the reign of the judges, Moronihah did succeed with his armies in obtaining many parts of the land; yea, they regained many cities which had fallen into the hands of the Lamanites.

10 And it came to pass in the sixty and first year of the reign of the judges they succeeded in regaining even the half of all their possessions.

11 Now this great loss of the Nephites, and the great slaughter which was among them, *a*would not have happened had it not been for their *b*wickedness and their abomination which was among them; yea, and it was among those also who professed to belong to the church of God.

12 And it was because of the *a*pride of their hearts, because of their exceeding *b*riches, yea, it was because of their oppression to the *c*poor, withholding their food from the hungry, withholding their clothing from the naked, and smiting their humble brethren upon the cheek, making a *d*mock of that which was sacred, denying the spirit of prophecy and of revelation, murdering, plundering, lying, stealing,

4 1*a* 3 Ne. 11:29.
 3*a* Hel. 11:24.
  b Hel. 1:32 (30–33).
 4*a* Hel. 5:17.
  b Alma 63:14.
 5*a* Hel. 5:16, 52.
 7*a* Alma 22:32.

 8*a* Hel. 1:15.
 11*a* D&C 82:10.
  b Mosiah 27:13.
 12*a* Obad. 1:3 (3–4);
  2 Ne. 20:33;
  D&C 101:42.
  b 1 Tim. 6:17;

 2 Ne. 9:42;
 3 Ne. 6:12 (10–16).
 c Ezek. 18:12;
 Zech. 7:10;
 D&C 42:30 (30–39, 71).
 d TG Mocking;
 Sacrilege.

committing adultery, rising up in great contentions, and deserting away into the land of Nephi, among the Lamanites—

13 And because of this their great wickedness, and their ªboastings in their own strength, they were left in their own strength; therefore they did not prosper, but were afflicted and smitten, and driven before the Lamanites, until they had lost possession of almost all their lands.

14 But behold, Moronihah did ªpreach many things unto the people because of their iniquity, and also ᵇNephi and Lehi, who were the sons of Helaman, did preach many things unto the people, yea, and did prophesy many things unto them concerning their iniquities, and what should come unto them if they did not repent of their sins.

15 And it came to pass that they did repent, and inasmuch as they did repent they did begin to prosper.

16 For when Moronihah saw that they did repent he did venture to ªlead them forth from place to place, and from city to city, even until they had regained the one-half of their property and the one-half of all their lands.

17 And thus ended the sixty and first year of the reign of the judges.

18 And it came to pass in the sixty and second year of the reign of the judges, that Moronihah could obtain no more possessions over the Lamanites.

19 Therefore they did abandon their design to obtain the remainder of their lands, for so numerous were the Lamanites that it became impossible for the Nephites to obtain more power over them; therefore Moronihah did employ all his armies in maintaining those parts which he had taken.

20 And it came to pass, because of the greatness of the number of the Lamanites the Nephites were in great fear, lest they should be overpowered, and trodden down, and slain, and destroyed.

21 Yea, they began to remember the ªprophecies of Alma, and also the ᵇwords of Mosiah; and they saw that they had been a ᶜstiffnecked people, and that they had set at ᵈnaught the commandments of God;

22 And that they had altered and trampled under their feet the ªlaws of Mosiah, or that which the Lord commanded him to give unto the people; and they saw that their laws had become corrupted, and that they had become a wicked people, insomuch that they were wicked even like unto the Lamanites.

23 And because of their iniquity the church had begun to ªdwindle; and they began to disbelieve in the spirit of prophecy and in the spirit of revelation; and the judgments of God did stare them in the face.

24 And they saw that they had become ªweak, like unto their brethren, the Lamanites, and that the Spirit of the Lord did no more preserve them; yea, it had withdrawn from them because the Spirit of the Lord doth not ᵇdwell in ᶜunholy ᵈtemples—

25 Therefore the Lord did cease to preserve them by his miraculous and matchless power, for they had fallen into a state of ªunbelief and awful wickedness; and they saw that the Lamanites were exceedingly more numerous than they, and except they should ᵇcleave unto the Lord their God they must unavoidably perish.

26 For behold, they saw that the strength of the Lamanites was as

13a Ezek. 35:13.
    TG Boast;
    Trust Not in the Arm
    of Flesh.
14a Hel. 5:17 (14–20).
  b Hel. 3:21.
16a Alma 62:43.
21a Alma 5:53 (1–62).

  b Mosiah 29:27.
  c TG Stiffnecked.
  d Prov. 1:25.
22a Alma 1:1.
23a TG Apostasy of
    Individuals.
24a Jer. 46:15 (15–17);
    Mosiah 1:13.

  b TG Holy Ghost, Loss of.
  c Mosiah 2:37;
    Alma 7:21; 34:36.
  d TG Temple.
25a TG Unbelief.
  b Josh. 23:8;
    Jacob 6:5;
    D&C 11:19.

great as their strength, even man for man. And thus had they fallen into this great transgression; yea, thus had they become [a]weak, because of their transgression, in the space of [b]not many years.

CHAPTER 5

Nephi and Lehi devote themselves to preaching—Their names invite them to pattern their lives after their forebears—Christ redeems those who repent—Nephi and Lehi make many converts and are imprisoned, and fire encircles them—A cloud of darkness overshadows three hundred people—The earth shakes, and a voice commands men to repent—Nephi and Lehi converse with angels, and the multitude is encircled by fire. About 30 B.C.

AND it came to pass that in this same year, behold, [a]Nephi [b]delivered up the judgment-seat to a man whose name was [c]Cezoram.

2 For as their laws and their governments were established by the [a]voice of the people, and they who [b]chose evil were [c]more numerous than they who chose good, therefore they were [d]ripening for destruction, for the laws had become corrupted.

3 Yea, and this was not all; they were a [a]stiffnecked people, insomuch that they could not be governed by the law nor justice, save it were to their destruction.

4 And it came to pass that Nephi had become weary because of their iniquity; and he yielded up the judgment-seat, and took it upon him to preach the word of God all the remainder of his days, and his brother Lehi also, all the remainder of his days;

5 For they remembered the words which their [a]father Helaman spake unto them. And these are the words which he spake:

6 Behold, my sons, I desire that ye should remember to keep the commandments of God; and I would that ye should declare unto the people these words. Behold, I have given unto you the names of our first [a]parents who came out of the land of Jerusalem; and this I have done that when you remember your names ye may remember them; and when ye remember them ye may remember their works; and when ye remember their works ye may know how that it is said, and also written, that they were [b]good.

7 Therefore, my sons, I would that ye should do that which is good, that it may be said of you, and also written, even as it has been said and written of them.

8 And now my sons, behold I have somewhat more to desire of you, which desire is, that ye may not do these things that ye may boast, but that ye may do these things to lay up for yourselves a [a]treasure in heaven, yea, which is eternal, and which fadeth not away; yea, that ye may have that [b]precious gift of eternal life, which we have reason to suppose hath been given to our fathers.

9 O remember, remember, my sons, the [a]words which king Benjamin spake unto his people; yea, remember that there is no other way nor means whereby man can be saved, only through the [b]atoning blood of Jesus Christ, who shall come; yea, remember that he cometh to [c]redeem the [d]world.

26a Ezek. 19:8 (6–9).
  TG Weak.
  b Alma 46:8;
    Hel. 6:32; 7:6; 11:26; 12:2.
5 1a Hel. 3:37.
  b Alma 4:20 (15–20).
  c Hel. 6:15.
  2a Mosiah 29:25 (25–27);
    Hel. 1:5 (3–5, 13).
  b Alma 10:19.

  c 4 Ne. 1:40.
  d Hel. 6:40; 10:11;
    D&C 18:6; 61:31.
  3a TG Stiffnecked.
  5a Hel. 3:21 (21, 37).
  6a 1 Ne. 1:4 (1, 4).
  b 2 Ne. 4:12; 33:3 (1–15);
    Jacob 1:10 (9–12).
  8a Hel. 8:25;
    3 Ne. 13:20 (19–21).

    TG Treasure.
  b 1 Ne. 15:36.
  9a Mosiah 2:9.
  b Mosiah 3:18; 4:2.
    TG Jesus Christ,
    Atonement through.
  c TG Jesus Christ,
    Redeemer.
  d TG World.

10 And remember also the words which Amulek spake unto Zeezrom, ^ain the city of Ammonihah; for he said unto him that the Lord surely should come to redeem his people, but that he should not come to redeem them in their sins, but to redeem them from their sins.

11 And he hath power given unto him from the Father to redeem them from their sins because of repentance; therefore he hath ^asent his angels to declare the tidings of the conditions of repentance, which bringeth unto the power of the Redeemer, unto the salvation of their souls.

12 And now, my sons, remember, remember that it is upon the ^arock of our Redeemer, who is Christ, the Son of God, that ye must build your ^bfoundation; that when the devil shall send forth his mighty winds, yea, his shafts in the whirlwind, yea, when all his hail and his mighty ^cstorm shall beat upon you, it shall have no power over you to drag you down to the gulf of misery and endless wo, because of the rock upon which ye are built, which is a sure foundation, a foundation whereon if men build they cannot fall.

13 And it came to pass that these were the words which Helaman ^ataught to his sons; yea, he did teach them many things which are not written, and also many things which are written.

14 And they did remember his words; and therefore they went forth, keeping the commandments of God, to teach the word of God among all the people of Nephi, beginning at the city Bountiful;

15 And from thenceforth to the city of Gid; and from the city of Gid to the city of Mulek;

16 And even from one city to another, until they had gone forth ^aamong all the people of Nephi who were in the land southward; and from thence into the land of Zarahemla, among the Lamanites.

17 And it came to pass that they did ^apreach with great ^bpower, insomuch that they did confound many of those ^cdissenters who had gone over from the Nephites, insomuch that they came forth and did confess their sins and were baptized unto repentance, and immediately returned to the Nephites to endeavor to repair unto them the wrongs which they had done.

18 And it came to pass that Nephi and Lehi did preach unto the Lamanites with such great power and authority, for they had power and authority given unto them that they might ^aspeak, and they also had what they should speak given unto them—

19 Therefore they did speak unto the great astonishment of the Lamanites, to the convincing them, insomuch that there were eight thousand of the Lamanites who were in the land of Zarahemla and round about ^abaptized unto repentance, and were convinced of the ^bwickedness of the ^ctraditions of their fathers.

20 And it came to pass that Nephi and Lehi did proceed from thence to go to the ^aland of Nephi.

21 And it came to pass that they were taken by an army of the Lamanites and cast into ^aprison; yea, even in that same prison in which Ammon and his brethren were cast by the servants of Limhi.

10a Alma 11:34.
11a Alma 13:24 (24–25); 39:19.
12a Ps. 71:3;
    Matt. 7:24 (24–27);
    D&C 6:34;
    Moses 7:53.
    TG Cornerstone;
    Rock.
  b Isa. 28:16 (14–17);

Jacob 4:16.
  c Alma 26:6;
    3 Ne. 14:25 (25, 27).
13a Mosiah 1:4;
    Alma 18:36; 36:1;
    Moses 6:58.
16a Hel. 4:5.
17a Hel. 4:14.
  b TG Teaching with the Spirit.

  c Hel. 4:4 (2, 4).
18a D&C 24:6; 100:5 (5–8).
    TG Prophets, Mission of.
19a TG Missionary Work.
  b Mal. 2:6.
  c Hel. 15:4.
20a Alma 22:1.
21a Mosiah 7:7 (6–8); 21:23 (22–24).

22 And after they had been cast into prison many days without food, behold, they went forth into the prison to take them that they might slay them.

23 And it came to pass that Nephi and Lehi were encircled about *as if by *fire, even insomuch that they durst not lay their hands upon them for fear lest they should be burned. Nevertheless, Nephi and Lehi were not burned; and they were as standing in the midst of fire and were not burned.

24 And when they saw that they were encircled about with a *pillar of fire, and that it burned them not, their hearts did take courage.

25 For they saw that the Lamanites durst not lay their hands upon them; neither durst they come near unto them, but stood as if they were struck dumb with amazement.

26 And it came to pass that Nephi and Lehi did stand forth and began to speak unto them, saying: *Fear not, for behold, it is God that has shown unto you this marvelous thing, in the which is shown unto you that ye cannot lay your hands on us to slay us.

27 And behold, when they had said these words, the earth shook exceedingly, and the walls of the prison did shake as if they were about to tumble to the earth; but behold, they did not fall. And behold, they that were in the prison were Lamanites and Nephites who were dissenters.

28 And it came to pass that they were overshadowed with a cloud of *darkness, and an awful solemn fear came upon them.

29 And it came to pass that there came a *voice as if it were above the cloud of darkness, saying: Repent ye, repent ye, and seek no more to destroy my *servants whom I have sent unto you to declare good tidings.

30 And it came to pass when they heard this *voice, and beheld that it was not a voice of thunder, neither was it a voice of a great tumultuous noise, but behold, it was a *still voice of perfect mildness, as if it had been a whisper, and it did pierce even to the very soul—

31 And notwithstanding the mildness of the voice, behold the earth shook exceedingly, and the walls of the prison trembled again, as if it were about to tumble to the earth; and behold the cloud of darkness, which had overshadowed them, did not disperse—

32 And behold the voice came again, saying: *Repent ye, repent ye, for the kingdom of heaven is at hand; and seek no more to destroy my servants. And it came to pass that the earth shook again, and the walls trembled.

33 And also again the third time the voice came, and did speak unto them marvelous words which *cannot be uttered by man; and the walls did tremble again, and the earth shook as if it were about to divide asunder.

34 And it came to pass that the Lamanites could not flee because of the cloud of darkness which did overshadow them; yea, and also they were immovable because of the fear which did come upon them.

35 Now there was one among them who was a Nephite by birth, who had once belonged to the church of God but had dissented from them.

36 And it came to pass that he turned him about, and behold, he saw through the cloud of darkness the faces of Nephi and Lehi; and behold, they did *shine exceedingly,

23*a* Ex. 24:17;
      D&C 137:2.
   b Ex. 3:2;
      Dan. 3:25 (25, 27).
24*a* Ex. 14:24;
      1 Ne. 1:6;
      D&C 29:12;
      JS—H 1:16.

      TG Protection, Divine.
26*a* Dan. 10:12.
28*a* Ex. 14:20.
29*a* Deut. 4:33;
      3 Ne. 11:3 (3–14).
   b TG Servant.
30*a* Moses 1:25.
   b 1 Kgs. 19:12;

      D&C 85:6 (6–7).
32*a* Matt. 3:2 (2–3);
      Alma 7:9; 9:25 (25–26).
33*a* Rom. 8:26.
36*a* Ex. 34:29 (29–35);
      Acts 6:15.

even as the faces of angels. And he beheld that they did lift their eyes to heaven; and they were in the attitude as if talking or lifting their voices to some being whom they beheld.

37 And it came to pass that this man did cry unto the multitude, that they might turn and look. And behold, there was power given unto them that they did turn and look; and they did behold the faces of Nephi and Lehi.

38 And they said unto the man: Behold, what do all these things mean, and who is it with whom these men do converse?

39 Now the man's name was Aminadab. And Aminadab said unto them: They do converse with the angels of God.

40 And it came to pass that the Lamanites said unto him: ^aWhat shall we do, that this cloud of darkness may be removed from overshadowing us?

41 And Aminadab said unto them: You must ^arepent, and cry unto the voice, even until ye shall have ^bfaith in Christ, who was taught unto you by Alma, and ^cAmulek, and Zeezrom; and when ye shall do this, the cloud of darkness shall be removed from overshadowing you.

42 And it came to pass that they all did begin to cry unto the voice of him who had shaken the earth; yea, they did cry even until the cloud of darkness was dispersed.

43 And it came to pass that when they cast their eyes about, and saw that the cloud of darkness was dispersed from overshadowing them, behold, they saw that they were ^aencircled about, yea every soul, by a pillar of fire.

44 And ^aNephi and ^bLehi were in the midst of them; yea, they were encircled about; yea, they were as

if in the midst of a flaming fire, yet it did harm them not, neither did it take hold upon the walls of the prison; and they were filled with that ^cjoy which is unspeakable and full of glory.

45 And behold, the ^aHoly Spirit of God did come down from heaven, and did enter into their hearts, and they were filled as if with fire, and they could ^bspeak forth marvelous words.

46 And it came to pass that there came a voice unto them, yea, a pleasant voice, as if it were a whisper, saying:

47 ^aPeace, peace be unto you, because of your faith in my Well Beloved, who was from the foundation of the world.

48 And now, when they heard this they cast up their eyes as if to behold from whence the voice came; and behold, they saw the ^aheavens open; and angels came down out of heaven and ministered unto them.

49 And there were about three hundred souls who saw and heard these things; and they were bidden to go forth and marvel not, neither should they doubt.

50 And it came to pass that they did go forth, and did minister unto the people, declaring throughout all the regions round about all the things which they had heard and seen, insomuch that the more part of the Lamanites were ^aconvinced of them, because of the greatness of the evidences which they had received.

51 And as many as were ^aconvinced did lay down their weapons of war, and also their hatred and the tradition of their fathers.

52 And it came to pass that they did ^ayield up unto the Nephites the lands of their possession.

40a Acts 2:37 (37–39).
41a TG Repent.
  b TG Faith.
  c Alma 31:6 (5–38).
43a 3 Ne. 17:24; 19:14.
44a Hel. 6:6.

  b Hel. 11:19.
  c TG Joy.
45a 3 Ne. 9:20; 19:14 (13–14); Ether 12:14.
  b TG Holy Ghost, Gifts of.
47a TG Peace of God.

48a Acts 7:56 (55–56); 1 Ne. 1:8.
50a Ether 12:14.
51a Alma 31:5.
52a Hel. 4:5 (5, 18–19).

CHAPTER 6

The righteous Lamanites preach to the wicked Nephites—Both peoples prosper during an era of peace and plenty—Lucifer, the author of sin, stirs up the hearts of the wicked and the Gadianton robbers in murder and wickedness—The robbers take over the Nephite government. About 29–23 B.C.

AND it came to pass that when the sixty and second year of the reign of the judges had ended, all these things had happened and the Lamanites had become, the more part of them, a righteous people, insomuch that their ªrighteousness did exceed that of the Nephites, because of their firmness and their steadiness in the faith.

2 For behold, there were many of the Nephites who had become ªhardened and impenitent and grossly wicked, insomuch that they did reject the word of God and all the preaching and prophesying which did come among them.

3 Nevertheless, the people of the church did have great joy because of the conversion of the Lamanites, yea, because of the church of God, which had been established among them. And they did ªfellowship one with another, and did rejoice one with another, and did have great joy.

4 And it came to pass that many of the Lamanites did come down into the land of Zarahemla, and did declare unto the people of the Nephites the manner of their ªconversion, and did exhort them to faith and repentance.

5 Yea, and many did ªpreach with exceedingly great power and authority, unto the bringing down many

of them into the depths of humility, to be the humble followers of God and the Lamb.

6 And it came to pass that many of the Lamanites did go into the land northward; and also ªNephi and ᵇLehi went into the ᶜland northward, to preach unto the people. And thus ended the sixty and third year.

7 And behold, there was peace in all the land, insomuch that the Nephites did go into whatsoever part of the land they would, whether among the Nephites or the Lamanites.

8 And it came to pass that the Lamanites did also go whithersoever they would, whether it were among the Lamanites or among the Nephites; and thus they did have free intercourse one with another, to ªbuy and to sell, and to get gain, according to their desire.

9 And it came to pass that they became exceedingly rich, both the Lamanites and the Nephites; and they did have an exceeding plenty of ªgold, and of silver, and of all manner of precious metals, both in the land south and in the land north.

10 Now the land south was called ªLehi, and the land north was called ᵇMulek, which was after the ᶜson of Zedekiah; for the Lord did bring Mulek into the land north, and Lehi into the land south.

11 And behold, there was all manner of gold in both these lands, and of silver, and of precious ore of every kind; and there were also curious workmen, who did ªwork all kinds of ore and did refine it; and thus they did become rich.

12 They did raise grain in abundance, both in the north and in the south; and they did flourish exceedingly, both in the north and in the

6 1 a Hel. 13:1.
  2 a Rom. 1:28 (28–32);
        Hel. 6:21.
        TG Hardheartedness.
  3 a TG Fellowshipping.
  4 a TG Conversion.
  5 a 1 Ne. 15:20;
        Alma 48:20.
  6 a Hel. 7:1.

    b Hel. 5:44 (36–44); 11:19.
    c Alma 63:9 (4–9);
        Hel. 3:12 (11–12).
  8 a 3 Ne. 6:11.
  9 a 1 Ne. 18:25;
        2 Ne. 5:15 (14–16);
        Jacob 2:12 (12–13);
        Ether 9:17; 10:23 (12, 23).
 10 a Alma 50:25.

    b Omni 1:14;
        Mosiah 25:2 (2–4);
        Hel. 8:21.
    c Jer. 39:6; 52:10;
        Ezek. 17:22 (22–23);
        Alma 22:31.
 11 a TG Industry.

south. And they did multiply and wax exceedingly strong in the land. And they did raise many flocks and herds, yea, many fatlings.

13 Behold their women did toil and spin, and did ªmake all manner of ᵇcloth, of fine-twined linen and cloth of every kind, to clothe their nakedness. And thus the sixty and fourth year did pass away in peace.

14 And in the sixty and fifth year they did also have great joy and peace, yea, much preaching and many prophecies concerning that which was to come. And thus passed away the sixty and fifth year.

15 And it came to pass that in the sixty and sixth year of the reign of the judges, behold, ªCezoram was murdered by an unknown hand as he sat upon the judgment-seat. And it came to pass that in the same year, that his son, who had been appointed by the people in his stead, was also murdered. And thus ended the sixty and sixth year.

16 And in the commencement of the sixty and seventh year the people began to grow exceedingly wicked again.

17 For behold, the Lord had blessed them so long with the ªriches of the world that they had not been stirred up to anger, to wars, nor to bloodshed; therefore they began to set their hearts upon their riches; yea, they began to seek to get gain that they might be lifted up one above another; therefore they began to commit ᵇsecret murders, and to rob and to plunder, that they might get gain.

18 And now behold, those murderers and plunderers were a band who had been formed by Kishkumen and ªGadianton. And now it had come to pass that there were many, even among the Nephites, of Gadianton's

band. But behold, they were more numerous among the more wicked part of the Lamanites. And they were called Gadianton's robbers and murderers.

19 And it was they who did murder the chief judge ªCezoram, and his son, while in the judgment-seat; and behold, they were not found.

20 And now it came to pass that when the Lamanites found that there were robbers among them they were exceedingly sorrowful; and they did use every means in their power to destroy them off the face of the earth.

21 But behold, Satan did stir up the ªhearts of the more part of the Nephites, insomuch that they did unite with those bands of robbers, and did enter into their covenants and their oaths, that they would protect and preserve one another in whatsoever difficult circumstances they should be placed, that they should not suffer for their murders, and their plunderings, and their ᵇstealings.

22 And it came to pass that they did have their signs, yea, their ªsecret signs, and their ᵇsecret words; and this that they might distinguish a brother who had entered into the covenant, that whatsoever wickedness his brother should do he should not be injured by his brother, nor by those who did belong to his band, who had taken this covenant.

23 And thus they might murder, and plunder, and steal, and commit ªwhoredoms and all manner of wickedness, contrary to the laws of their country and also the laws of their God.

24 And whosoever of those who belonged to their band should reveal unto the world of their ªwickedness and their abominations, should be

---

13a TG Art.
  b Mosiah 10:5;
    Alma 1:29.
15a Hel. 5:1; 6:19.
17a TG Treasure.
  b 3 Ne. 6:23; 9:9.

18a Hel. 2:4 (4, 12–13); 3:23.
19a Hel. 6:15.
21a Hel. 6:2.
  b TG Stealing.
22a Alma 37:27.
    TG Secret Combinations.

  b Hel. 11:2;
    3 Ne. 3:7.
23a TG Whore.
24a TG Wickedness.

tried, not according to the laws of their country, but according to the laws of their wickedness, which had been given by Gadianton and Kishkumen.

25 Now behold, it is these secret *oaths and covenants which Alma commanded his son should not go forth unto the world, lest they should be a means of bringing down the people unto destruction.

26 Now behold, those *secret oaths and covenants did not come forth unto Gadianton from the *records which were delivered unto Helaman; but behold, they were put into the heart of *Gadianton by that *same being who did entice our first parents to partake of the forbidden fruit—

27 Yea, that same being who did plot with *Cain, that if he would murder his brother Abel it should not be known unto the world. And he did plot with Cain and his followers from that time forth.

28 And also it is that same being who put it into the hearts of the people to *build a tower sufficiently high that they might get to heaven. And it was that same being who led on the people who came from that tower into this land; who spread the works of darkness and abominations over all the face of the land, until he dragged the people down to an *entire destruction, and to an everlasting hell.

29 Yea, it is that same being who put it into the heart of *Gadianton to still carry on the work of darkness, and of secret murder; and he has brought it forth from the beginning of man even down to this time.

30 And behold, it is he who is the *author of all sin. And behold, he doth carry on his works of darkness

and secret murder, and doth hand down their plots, and their oaths, and their covenants, and their plans of awful wickedness, from generation to generation according as he can get hold upon the hearts of the children of men.

31 And now behold, he had got great hold upon the hearts of the Nephites; yea, insomuch that they had become exceedingly wicked; yea, the more part of them had turned out of the *way of righteousness, and did *trample under their feet the commandments of God, and did turn unto their own ways, and did build up unto themselves *idols of their gold and their silver.

32 And it came to pass that all these iniquities did come unto them in the space of *not many years, insomuch that a more part of it had come unto them in the sixty and seventh year of the reign of the judges over the people of Nephi.

33 And they did grow in their iniquities in the sixty and eighth year also, to the great sorrow and lamentation of the righteous.

34 And thus we see that the *Nephites did begin to dwindle in unbelief, and grow in wickedness and abominations, while the Lamanites began to grow exceedingly in the knowledge of their God; yea, they did begin to keep his statutes and commandments, and to walk in truth and uprightness before him.

35 And thus we see that the Spirit of the Lord began to *withdraw from the Nephites, because of the wickedness and the hardness of their hearts.

36 And thus we see that the Lord began to pour out his *Spirit upon the Lamanites, because of their

25a Alma 37:29 (27–32).
26a 3 Ne. 3:9;
   Ether 8:9 (9–19);
   Moses 5:29 (29, 49–52).
 b 3 Ne. 6:28.
 c Hel. 8:28.
 d Moses 4:6 (6–12).
27a Moses 5:25 (18–33).
28a Gen. 11:4 (1–4);

   Ether 1:3.
 b Ether 8:21 (9, 15–25).
29a Hel. 2:4 (4–13).
30a Alma 5:40 (39–42);
   Moro. 7:12 (12, 17);
   Moses 4:4.
31a Gen. 6:12;
   2 Ne. 28:11.
 b 1 Ne. 19:7.

 c Judg. 2:17; 2 Ne. 9:37;
   Alma 7:6.
32a Alma 46:8;
   Hel. 4:26; 7:6; 11:26.
34a Moro. 9:20.
35a Matt. 13:15;
   Mosiah 2:36;
   D&C 121:37.
36a TG God, Spirit of.

easiness and [b]willingness to believe in his words.

37 And it came to pass that the Lamanites did hunt the band of robbers of Gadianton; and they did preach the word of God among the more wicked part of them, insomuch that this band of robbers was utterly destroyed from among the Lamanites.

38 And it came to pass on the other hand, that the Nephites did build them up and support them, beginning at the more wicked part of them, until they had overspread all the land of the Nephites, and had seduced the more part of the righteous until they had come down to believe in their works and partake of their spoils, and to join with them in their secret murders and combinations.

39 And thus they did obtain the sole management of the government, insomuch that they did trample under their feet and smite and rend and turn their backs upon the [a]poor and the meek, and the humble followers of God.

40 And thus we see that they were in an awful state, and [a]ripening for an everlasting destruction.

41 And it came to pass that thus ended the sixty and eighth year of the reign of the judges over the people of Nephi.

———

THE PROPHECY OF NEPHI, THE SON OF HELAMAN—God threatens the people of Nephi that he will visit them in his anger, to their utter destruction except they repent of their wickedness. God smiteth the people of Nephi with pestilence; they repent and turn unto him. Samuel, a Lamanite, prophesies unto the Nephites.

Comprising chapters 7 through 16.

CHAPTER 7

Nephi is rejected in the north and returns to Zarahemla—He prays upon his garden tower and then calls upon the people to repent or perish. About 23–21 B.C.

BEHOLD, now it came to pass in the sixty and ninth year of the reign of the judges over the people of the Nephites, that Nephi, the son of Helaman, [a]returned to the land of Zarahemla from the land northward.

2 For he had been forth among the people who were in the land northward, and did preach the word of God unto them, and did prophesy many things unto them;

3 And they did [a]reject all his words, insomuch that he could not stay among them, but returned again unto the land of his nativity.

4 And seeing the people in a state of such awful wickedness, and those Gadianton robbers filling the judgment-seats—having [a]usurped the power and authority of the land; laying aside the commandments of God, and not in the least aright before him; doing no justice unto the children of men;

5 Condemning the righteous because of their righteousness; letting the guilty and the wicked go [a]unpunished because of their [b]money; and moreover to be held in office at the head of government, to rule and do according to their wills, that they might get gain and glory of the [c]world, and, moreover, that they might the more easily commit adultery, and steal, and kill, and do according to their own wills—

6 Now this great iniquity had come upon the Nephites, in the space of [a]not many years; and when Nephi saw it, his heart was swollen with sorrow within his breast; and he did exclaim in the agony of his soul:

36b Ex. 25:2 (1–7).
39a Ps. 109:16 (15–16);
       Ezek. 22:7 (7–13);
       Amos 5:12;
       Alma 5:55 (54–56);
       D&C 56:16.
40a Hel. 5:2; 11:37;

D&C 18:6; 61:31.
7 1a Hel. 6:6.
  3a TG Prophets,
        Rejection of.
  4a TG Tyranny;
        Unrighteous Dominion.
  5a Job 12:6; 21:7;

Ps. 73:12.
  b TG Bribe.
  c Matt. 13:22;
       D&C 39:9.
6a IE six years; see
       Hel. 4:26; 6:6, 32; 11:26.

7 Oh, that I could have had my days in the days when my father Nephi first came out of the land of Jerusalem, that I could have ªjoyed with him in the promised land; then were his people easy to be entreated, ᵇfirm to keep the commandments of God, and slow to be led to do iniquity; and they were quick to hearken unto the words of the Lord—

8 Yea, if my days could have been in those days, then would my soul have had joy in the righteousness of my brethren.

9 But behold, I am consigned that these are my days, and that my soul shall be filled with ªsorrow because of this the wickedness of my brethren.

10 And behold, now it came to pass that it was upon a tower, which was in the ªgarden of Nephi, which was by the highway which led to the chief market, which was in the city of Zarahemla; therefore, Nephi had bowed himself upon the tower which was in his garden, which tower was also near unto the garden gate by which led the highway.

11 And it came to pass that there were certain men passing by and saw Nephi as he was pouring out his soul unto God upon the ªtower; and they ran and told the people what they had seen, and the people came together in multitudes that they might know the cause of so great mourning for the wickedness of the people.

12 And now, when Nephi arose he beheld the multitudes of people who had gathered together.

13 And it came to pass that he opened his mouth and said unto them: Behold, ªwhy have ye gathered yourselves together? That I may tell you of your iniquities?

14 Yea, because I have got upon my tower that I might pour out my soul unto my God, because of the exceeding sorrow of my heart, which is because of your iniquities!

15 And because of my ªmourning and lamentation ye have gathered yourselves together, and do marvel; yea, and ye have great need to marvel; yea, ye ought to marvel because ye are given away that the devil has got so great hold upon your hearts.

16 Yea, how could you have given way to the enticing of him who is seeking to hurl away your souls down to ªeverlasting misery and endless wo?

17 O repent ye, repent ye! ªWhy will ye die? Turn ye, turn ye unto the Lord your God. Why has he forsaken you?

18 It is because you have hardened your hearts; yea, ye will not ªhearken unto the voice of the ᵇgood shepherd; yea, ye have ᶜprovoked him to anger against you.

19 And behold, instead of ªgathering you, except ye will repent, behold, he shall scatter you forth that ye shall become meat for dogs and wild beasts.

20 O, how could you have ªforgotten your God in the very day that he has delivered you?

21 But behold, it is to get ªgain, to be ᵇpraised of men, yea, and that ye might get gold and silver. And ye have set your hearts upon the ᶜriches and the vain things of this world, for the which ye do murder, and plunder, and steal, and bear ᵈfalse witness against your neighbor, and do all manner of iniquity.

22 And for this cause ªwo shall come unto you except ye shall repent.

7a 2 Ne. 5:27 (26–28).
  b D&C 5:22.
9a Jer. 9:1 (1–3).
10a Hel. 9:8.
11a Alma 50:4.
13a Matt. 3:7 (5–8).
15a TG Mourning.
16a Alma 26:20.
17a Isa. 1:5 (5–6);

    Ezek. 18:23 (23, 32).
18a TG Disobedience.
  b Ezek. 34:12; John 10:14;
    Alma 5:60 (38–60).
    TG Jesus Christ, Good
    Shepherd.
  c Num. 14:11 (11–12);
    1 Ne. 17:30 (23–31);
    Jacob 1:8;

    Alma 12:37 (36–37).
19a 3 Ne. 10:4 (4–7).
20a Isa. 17:10 (4–11).
21a TG Selfishness.
  b TG Peer Influence.
  c TG Treasure.
  d Matt. 15:19 (19–20).
    TG Slander.
22a Rev. 8:13; D&C 5:5.

For if ye will not repent, behold, this ᵇgreat city, and also all those great cities which are round about, which are in the land of our possession, shall be taken away that ye shall have no place in them; for behold, the Lord will not grant unto you ᶜstrength, as he has hitherto done, to withstand against your enemies.

23 For behold, thus saith the Lord: I will not show unto the wicked of my strength, to one more than the other, save it be unto those who repent of their sins, and hearken unto my words. Now therefore, I would that ye should behold, my brethren, that it shall be ᵃbetter for the Lamanites than for you except ye shall repent.

24 For behold, they are more righteous than you, for they have not sinned against that great knowledge which ye have received; therefore the Lord will be merciful unto them; yea, he will ᵃlengthen out their days and increase their seed, even when thou shalt be utterly ᵇdestroyed except thou shalt repent.

25 Yea, wo be unto you because of that great abomination which has come among you; and ye have united yourselves unto it, yea, to that ᵃsecret band which was established by Gadianton!

26 Yea, ᵃwo shall come unto you because of that pride which ye have suffered to enter your hearts, which has lifted you up beyond that which is good because of your exceedingly great riches!

27 Yea, wo be unto you because of your wickedness and abominations!

28 And except ye repent ye shall perish; yea, even your lands shall be taken from you, and ye shall be destroyed from off the face of the earth.

29 Behold now, I do not say that these things shall be, of myself, because it is not of myself that I ᵃknow these things; but behold, I ᵇknow that these things are true because the Lord God has made them known unto me, therefore I testify that they shall be.

CHAPTER 8

Corrupt judges seek to incite the people against Nephi—Abraham, Moses, Zenos, Zenock, Ezias, Isaiah, Jeremiah, Lehi, and Nephi all testified of Christ—By inspiration Nephi announces the murder of the chief judge. About 23–21 B.C.

AND now it came to pass that when Nephi had said these words, behold, there were men who were judges, who also belonged to the secret band of Gadianton, and they were angry, and they cried out against him, saying unto the people: Why do ye not seize upon this man and bring him forth, that he may be condemned according to the crime which he has done?

2 Why seest thou this man, and hearest him revile against this people and against our law?

3 For behold, Nephi had spoken unto them concerning the corruptness of their law; yea, many things did Nephi speak which cannot be written; and nothing did he speak which was contrary to the commandments of God.

4 And those judges were angry with him because he ᵃspake plainly unto them concerning their secret works of darkness; nevertheless, they durst not lay their own hands upon him, for they feared the people lest they should cry out against them.

5 Therefore they did cry unto the people, saying: Why do you suffer this man to revile against us? For

---

22b Hel. 8:5.
   c Mosiah 7:29.
23a Hel. 15:14 (11–15).
24a Ex. 20:12;
     1 Ne. 17:55;

Alma 9:16;
   D&C 5:33.
  b Alma 9:19;
   Hel. 10:14.
25a 2 Ne. 10:15;

Hel. 3:23.
26a Isa. 5:8 (8–25).
29a Hel. 8:8.
  b Hel. 8:12.
8 4a 1 Ne. 16:2 (2–3).

behold he doth condemn all this people, even unto destruction; yea, and also that these our *great cities shall be taken from us, that we shall have no place in them.

6 And now we know that this is impossible, for behold, we are *powerful, and our cities great, therefore our enemies can have no power over us.

7 And it came to pass that thus they did *stir up the people to anger against Nephi, and raised contentions among them; for there were some who did cry out: *Let this man alone, for he is a good man, and those things which he saith will surely come to pass except we repent;

8 Yea, behold, all the judgments will come upon us which he has testified unto us; for we know that he has testified aright unto us concerning our iniquities. And behold they are many, and he *knoweth as well all things which shall befall us as he knoweth of our iniquities;

9 Yea, and behold, if he had not been a prophet he could not have *testified concerning those things.

10 And it came to pass that those people who sought to destroy Nephi were compelled because of their fear, that they did not lay their hands on him; therefore he began again to speak unto them, seeing that he had gained favor in the eyes of some, insomuch that the remainder of them did fear.

11 Therefore he was constrained to speak more unto them saying: Behold, my brethren, have ye not read that God gave power unto one man, even Moses, to smite upon the waters of the *Red Sea, and they parted hither and thither, insomuch that the Israelites, who were our fathers, came through upon dry ground, and the waters closed upon the armies of the Egyptians and swallowed them up?

12 And now behold, if God gave unto this man such power, then why should ye dispute among yourselves, and say that he hath given unto me no power whereby I may *know concerning the judgments that shall come upon you except ye repent?

13 But, behold, ye not only deny my words, but ye also deny all the words which have been spoken by our fathers, and also the words which were spoken by this man, Moses, who had such great power given unto him, yea, the words which he hath spoken concerning the coming of the Messiah.

14 Yea, did he not bear record that the Son of God should come? And as he *lifted up the brazen serpent in the wilderness, even so shall he be lifted up who should come.

15 And as many as should look upon that serpent should *live, even so as many as should look upon the Son of God with faith, having a contrite spirit, might *live, even unto that life which is eternal.

16 And now behold, Moses did not only testify of these things, but also *all the holy prophets, from his days even to the days of Abraham.

17 Yea, and behold, *Abraham saw of his coming, and was filled with gladness and did rejoice.

18 Yea, and behold I say unto you, that Abraham not only knew of these things, but there were *many before the days of Abraham who were called by the *order of God;

5 a Hel. 7:22.
6 a Moses 8:21 (20–22).
7 a TG Provoking.
   b Acts 5:38 (37–40).
8 a Hel. 7:29.
   TG God, Foreknowl-
   edge of.
9 a TG Testimony.
11 a Ex. 14:16;
   Josh. 2:10;
   Neh. 9:11;

1 Ne. 17:26;
Mosiah 7:19;
D&C 8:3;
Moses 1:25.
12 a Hel. 7:29 (28–29).
14 a Num. 21:9 (6–9);
   2 Ne. 25:20;
   Alma 33:19 (19–22).
   TG Jesus Christ, Types
   of, in Anticipation.
15 a 1 Ne. 17:41;

Alma 37:46 (46–47);
3 Ne. 15:9.
   b John 11:25.
16 a Luke 24:27;
   Rev. 19:10;
   Jacob 4:4 (4–5); 7:11.
17 a Gen. 22:8 (8–14);
   John 8:56 (53, 56).
18 a Alma 13:19;
   D&C 84:14 (6–16); 136:37.
   b TG Priesthood.

yea, even after the order of his Son; and this that it should be shown unto the people, a great many thousand years before his coming, that even redemption should come unto them.

19 And now I would that ye should know, that even since the days of Abraham there have been many prophets that have testified these things; yea, behold, the prophet ᵃZenos did testify boldly; for the which he was slain.

20 And behold, also ᵃZenock, and also ᵇEzias, and also ᶜIsaiah, and ᵈJeremiah, (Jeremiah being that same prophet who testified of the destruction of ᵉJerusalem) and now we know that Jerusalem was destroyed according to the words of Jeremiah. O then why not the Son of God come, according to his prophecy?

21 And now will you dispute that ᵃJerusalem was destroyed? Will ye say that the ᵇsons of Zedekiah were not slain, all except it were ᶜMulek? Yea, and do ye not behold that the seed of Zedekiah are with us, and they were driven out of the land of Jerusalem? But behold, this is not all—

22 Our father Lehi was driven out of Jerusalem because he ᵃtestified of these things. Nephi also testified of these things, and also almost all of our fathers, even down to this time; yea, they have testified of the ᵇcoming of Christ, and have looked forward, and have rejoiced in his day which is to come.

23 And behold, he is God, and he is ᵃwith them, and he did manifest himself unto them, that they were redeemed by him; and they gave unto him glory, because of that which is to come.

24 And now, seeing ye know these things and cannot deny them except ye shall lie, therefore in this ye have sinned, for ye have rejected all these things, notwithstanding so many ᵃevidences which ye have received; yea, even ye have received ᵇall things, both things in heaven, and all things which are in the earth, as a witness that they are true.

25 But behold, ye have rejected the truth, and ᵃrebelled against your holy God; and even at this time, instead of laying up for yourselves ᵇtreasures in heaven, where nothing doth corrupt, and where nothing can come which is unclean, ye are heaping up for yourselves wrath against the day of ᶜjudgment.

26 Yea, even at this time ye are ripening, because of your murders and your ᵃfornication and wickedness, for everlasting destruction; yea, and except ye repent it will come unto you soon.

27 Yea, behold it is now even at your doors; yea, go ye in unto the judgment-seat, and search; and behold, your judge is murdered, and he ᵈlieth in his blood; and he hath been murdered ᵇby his brother, who seeketh to sit in the judgment-seat.

28 And behold, they both belong to your secret band, whose ᵃauthor is Gadianton and the evil one who seeketh to destroy the souls of men.

19a Alma 34:7;
    Hel. 15:11.
20a 1 Ne. 19:10;
    Alma 33:15; 34:7;
    3 Ne. 10:16 (15–16).
  b TG Scriptures, Lost.
  c Isa. 53:2 (1–12).
  d 1 Ne. 5:13; 7:14.
  e Jer. 26:18 (17–19);
    1 Ne. 1:4 (4–18);
    2 Ne. 6:8; 25:6.
21a Omni 1:15.
  b 2 Kgs. 25:7;

     Jer. 39:6; 52:10.
  c Ezek. 17:22 (22–23);
    Hel. 6:10;
    Morm. 7:2.
22a D&C 138:49.
  b TG Jesus Christ,
    Prophecies about.
23a Alma 40:11 (11–12).
24a 2 Kgs. 17:13;
    1 Ne. 10:5.
  b Alma 30:44;
    Moses 6:63.
25a Ps. 5:10;

     Mosiah 2:37 (36–38);
     3:12.
  b Hel. 5:8;
    3 Ne. 13:20 (19–21).
    TG Treasure.
  c Ps. 109:7 (3–7);
    D&C 10:23 (20–23);
    121:24 (23–25).
26a TG Fornication.
27a Hel. 9:3, 15.
  b Hel. 9:6 (6, 26–38).
28a Hel. 6:26 (26–30).

CHAPTER 9

*Messengers find the chief judge dead
at the judgment seat—They are imprisoned and later released—By inspiration
Nephi identifies Seantum as the murderer—Nephi is accepted by some as a
prophet. About 23–21 B.C.*

BEHOLD, now it came to pass that
when Nephi had spoken these
words, certain men who were among
them ran to the judgment-seat; yea,
even there were ᵃfive who went,
and they said among themselves, as
they went:

2 Behold, now we will know of a
surety whether this man be a prophet
and God hath commanded him to
prophesy such marvelous things
unto us. Behold, we do not ᵃbelieve
that he hath; yea, we do not believe
that he is a prophet; nevertheless,
if this thing which he has said concerning the chief judge be true, that
he be dead, then will we believe
that the other words which he has
spoken are true.

3 And it came to pass that they ran
in their might, and came in unto
the judgment-seat; and behold, the
chief judge had fallen to the earth,
and did ᵃlie in his blood.

4 And now behold, when they saw
this they were astonished exceedingly, insomuch that they fell to
the earth; for they had not believed
the words which Nephi had spoken
concerning the chief judge.

5 But now, when they saw they
believed, and fear came upon them
lest all the judgments which Nephi
had spoken ᵃshould come upon the
people; therefore they did quake,
and had fallen to the earth.

6 Now, immediately when the
judge had been murdered—he being
stabbed by his brother by a garb of
secrecy, and he fled, and the servants
ran and told the people, raising the
cry of murder among them;

7 And behold the people did gather
themselves together unto the place
of the judgment-seat—and behold,
to their astonishment they saw
those ᵃfive men who had fallen to
the earth.

8 And now behold, the people
knew nothing concerning the multitude who had gathered together
at the ᵃgarden of Nephi; therefore
they said among themselves: These
men are they who have murdered
the judge, and God has smitten them
that they could not flee from us.

9 And it came to pass that they laid
hold on them, and bound them and
cast them into prison. And there
was a proclamation sent abroad
that the judge was slain, and that
the murderers had been taken and
were cast into prison.

10 And it came to pass that on the
morrow the people did assemble
themselves together to ᵃmourn and
to ᵇfast, at the burial of the great
chief judge who had been slain.

11 And thus also those judges who
were at the garden of Nephi, and
heard his words, were also gathered
together at the burial.

12 And it came to pass that they
inquired among the people, saying:
Where are the five who were sent to
inquire concerning the chief judge
whether he was dead? And they answered and said: Concerning this
five whom ye say ye have sent, we
know not; but there are five who are
the murderers, whom we have cast
into prison.

13 And it came to pass that the
judges desired that they should be
brought; and they were brought,
and behold they were the five who
were sent; and behold the judges inquired of them to know concerning
the matter, and they told them all
that they had done, saying:

14 We ran and came to the place
of the judgment-seat, and when
we saw all things even as Nephi
had testified, we were astonished

9 1a Hel. 9:7 (7, 12).
2a Dan. 2:9.
3a Hel. 8:27.
5a 2 Kgs. 22:13 (8–20).
7a Hel. 9:1.
8a Hel. 7:10 (10–11, 14).
10a TG Mourning.
b TG Fast, Fasting.

insomuch that we fell to the earth; and when we were recovered from our astonishment, behold they cast us into ^aprison.

15 Now, as for the murder of this man, we know not who has done it; and only this much we know, we ran and came ^aaccording as ye desired, and behold he was dead, according to the words of Nephi.

16 And now it came to pass that the judges did expound the matter unto the people, and did cry out against Nephi, saying: Behold, we know that this Nephi must have agreed with some one to slay the judge, and then he might declare it unto us, that he might convert us unto his faith, that he might raise himself to be a great man, chosen of God, and a prophet.

17 And now behold, we will detect this man, and he shall confess his fault and make known unto us the true murderer of this judge.

18 And it came to pass that the five were liberated on the day of the burial. Nevertheless, they did rebuke the judges in the words which they had spoken against Nephi, and did contend with them one by one, insomuch that they did confound them.

19 Nevertheless, they caused that Nephi should be taken and bound and brought before the multitude, and they began to question him in divers ways that they might cross him, that they might accuse him to death—

20 Saying unto him: Thou art confederate; who is this man that hath done this murder? Now tell us, and acknowledge thy fault; saying, Behold here is ^amoney; and also we will grant unto thee thy life if thou wilt tell us, and acknowledge the agreement which thou hast made with him.

21 But Nephi said unto them: O ye ^afools, ye uncircumcised of heart, ye blind, and ye ^bstiffnecked people, do ye know how long the Lord your God will suffer you that ye shall go on in this your way of sin?

22 O ye ought to begin to howl and ^amourn, because of the great destruction which at this time doth await you, except ye shall repent.

23 Behold ye say that I have agreed with a man that he should murder Seezoram, our chief judge. But behold, I say unto you, that this is because I have testified unto you that ye might know concerning this thing; yea, even for a witness unto you, that I did know of the wickedness and abominations which are among you.

24 And because I have done this, ye say that I have agreed with a man that he should do this thing; yea, because I showed unto you this sign ye are angry with me, and seek to destroy my life.

25 And now behold, I will show unto you another sign, and see if ye will in this thing seek to destroy me.

26 Behold I say unto you: Go to the house of Seantum, who is the ^abrother of Seezoram, and say unto him—

27 Has Nephi, the pretended prophet, who doth prophesy so much evil concerning this people, agreed with thee, in the which ye have murdered Seezoram, who is your brother?

28 And behold, he shall say unto you, Nay.

29 And ye shall say unto him: Have ye murdered your brother?

30 And he shall stand with fear, and wist not what to say. And behold, he shall deny unto you; and he shall make as if he were astonished; nevertheless, he shall declare unto you that he is innocent.

31 But behold, ye shall examine

14a Gen. 39:20.
15a Hel. 8:27.
20a 1 Sam. 8:3 (1–4);
    Ether 9:11.

TG Bribe.
21a Ps. 75:4;
    Luke 24:25;
    Acts 7:51.

b TG Stiffnecked.
22a Ezek. 24:23;
    Mosiah 7:24.
26a Hel. 8:27.

him, and ye shall find blood upon the skirts of his cloak.

32 And when ye have seen this, ye shall say: From whence cometh this blood? Do we not know that it is the blood of your brother?

33 And then shall he tremble, and shall look pale, even as if death had come upon him.

34 And then shall ye say: Because of this fear and this paleness which has come upon your face, behold, we know that thou art guilty.

35 And then shall greater fear come upon him; and then shall he confess unto you, and deny no more that he has done this murder.

36 And then shall he say unto you, that I, Nephi, know nothing concerning the matter save it were given unto me by the power of God. And then shall ye know that I am an honest man, and that I am sent unto you from God.

37 And it came to pass that they went and did, even according as Nephi had said unto them. And behold, the words which he had said were true; for according to the words he did deny; and also according to the words he did confess.

38 And he was brought to prove that he himself was the very murderer, insomuch that the five were set at liberty, and also was Nephi.

39 And there were some of the Nephites who believed on the words of Nephi; and there were some also, who believed because of the testimony of the five, for they had been converted while they were in prison.

40 And now there were some among the people, who said that Nephi was a prophet.

41 And there were others who said: Behold, he is a god, for except he was a god he could not *know of all things. For behold, he has told

us the thoughts of our hearts, and also has told us things; and even he has brought unto our knowledge the true murderer of our chief judge.

CHAPTER 10

The Lord gives Nephi the sealing power—He is empowered to bind and loose on earth and in heaven—He commands the people to repent or perish— The Spirit carries him from multitude to multitude. About 21–20 B.C.

AND it came to pass that there arose a division among the people, insomuch that they divided hither and thither and went their ways, leaving Nephi alone, as he was standing in the midst of them.

2 And it came to pass that Nephi went his way towards his own house, *pondering upon the things which the Lord had shown unto him.

3 And it came to pass as he was thus pondering—being much cast down because of the wickedness of the people of the Nephites, their secret works of darkness, and their murderings, and their plunderings, and all manner of iniquities—and it came to pass as he was thus pondering in his heart, behold, a *voice came unto him saying:

4 *Blessed art thou, Nephi, for those things which thou hast done; for I have beheld how thou hast with *unwearyingness declared the word, which I have given unto thee, unto this people. And thou hast not feared them, and hast not sought thine *own life, but hast sought my *will, and to keep my commandments.

5 And now, because thou hast done this with such unwearyingness, behold, I will bless thee forever; and I will make thee mighty in word and in deed, in faith and in works; yea, even that *all things shall be *done

41a TG God, Omni-
      science of.
10 2a TG Meditation.
   3a TG Guidance, Divine.
   4a Acts 23:11.
    b Acts 20:31.

TG Dedication;
   Dependability;
   Priesthood, Magnifying
   Callings within;
   Steadfastness.
 c TG Self-Sacrifice.

 d Mosiah 24:15;
   3 Ne. 11:11.
 5a 3 Ne. 18:20;
   D&C 88:64 (63–65).
  b Ex. 33:17.

unto thee according to thy ᶜword, for thou shalt ᵈnot ask that which is contrary to my will.

6 Behold, thou art Nephi, and I am God. Behold, I declare it unto thee in the presence of mine angels, that ye shall have power over this people, and shall smite the earth with ᵃfamine, and with pestilence, and destruction, according to the wickedness of this people.

7 Behold, I give unto you ᵃpower, that whatsoever ye shall ᵇseal on earth shall be sealed in heaven; and whatsoever ye shall loose on earth shall be loosed in heaven; and thus shall ye have power among this people.

8 And thus, if ye shall say unto this temple it shall be rent in twain, it shall be done.

9 And if ye shall say unto this ᵃmountain, Be thou cast down and become smooth, it shall be done.

10 And behold, if ye shall say that God shall smite this people, it shall come to pass.

11 And now behold, I command you, that ye shall go and declare unto this people, that thus saith the Lord God, who is the Almighty: Except ye repent ye shall be smitten, even unto ᵃdestruction.

12 And behold, now it came to pass that when the Lord had spoken these words unto Nephi, he did stop and did not go unto his own house, but did return unto the multitudes who were scattered about upon the face of the land, and began to declare unto them the word of the Lord which had been spoken unto him, concerning their destruction if they did not repent.

13 Now behold, ᵃnotwithstanding that great miracle which Nephi had done in telling them concerning the death of the chief judge,

they did harden their hearts and did not hearken unto the words of the Lord.

14 Therefore Nephi did declare unto them the word of the Lord, saying: Except ye repent, thus saith the Lord, ye shall be ᵃsmitten even unto destruction.

15 And it came to pass that when Nephi had declared unto them the word, behold, they did still harden their hearts and would not hearken unto his words; therefore they did ᵃrevile against him, and did seek to lay their hands upon him that they might cast him into prison.

16 But behold, the power of God was with him, and they could not take him to cast him into prison, for he was taken by the Spirit and ᵃconveyed away out of the midst of them.

17 And it came to pass that thus he did go forth in the Spirit, from multitude to multitude, declaring the word of God, even until he had declared it unto them all, or sent it forth among all the people.

18 And it came to pass that they would not hearken unto his words; and there began to be contentions, insomuch that they were divided against themselves and began to slay one another with the sword.

19 And thus ended the seventy and first year of the reign of the judges over the people of Nephi.

CHAPTER 11

Nephi persuades the Lord to replace their war with a famine—Many people perish—They repent, and Nephi importunes the Lord for rain—Nephi and Lehi receive many revelations—The Gadianton robbers entrench themselves in the land. About 20–6 B.C.

5c 1 Kgs. 17:1;
  Enos 1:12.
  d James 4:3 (1–3);
  2 Ne. 4:35;
  D&C 46:30.
6a Hel. 11:4 (4–18).
  TG Drought.

7a Hel. 11:18.
  b Matt. 16:19.
  TG Priesthood,
  Authority.
9a Matt. 17:20;
  Jacob 4:6;
  Morm. 8:24;

Ether 12:30.
11a Hel. 5:2; 11:8.
13a Mark 6:6 (4–6).
14a Hel. 7:24.
15a TG Reviling.
16a Acts 8:39 (39–40).

AND now it came to pass in the seventy and second year of the reign of the judges that the contentions did increase, insomuch that there were wars throughout all the land among all the people of Nephi.

2 And it was this *secret band of robbers who did carry on this work of destruction and wickedness. And this war did last all that year; and in the seventy and third year it did also last.

3 And it came to pass that in this year Nephi did cry unto the Lord, saying:

4 O Lord, do not suffer that this people shall be destroyed by the sword; but O Lord, rather *let there be a *famine in the land, to stir them up in remembrance of the Lord their God, and perhaps they will repent and turn unto thee.

5 And so it was done, according to the words of Nephi. And there was a great famine upon the land, among all the people of Nephi. And thus in the seventy and fourth year the famine did continue, and the work of destruction did cease by the sword but became sore by famine.

6 And this work of destruction did also continue in the seventy and fifth year. For the earth was smitten that it was *dry, and did not yield forth grain in the season of grain; and the whole earth was smitten, even among the Lamanites as well as among the Nephites, so that they were smitten that they did perish by thousands in the more wicked parts of the land.

7 And it came to pass that the people saw that they were about to perish by famine, and they began to *remember the Lord their God; and they began to remember the words of Nephi.

8 And the people *began to plead with their chief judges and their leaders, that they would say unto Nephi: Behold, we know that thou art a man of God, and therefore cry unto the Lord our God that he turn away from us this famine, lest all the words which thou hast spoken concerning our *destruction be fulfilled.

9 And it came to pass that the judges did say unto Nephi, according to the words which had been desired. And it came to pass that when Nephi saw that the people had *repented and did humble themselves in sackcloth, he cried again unto the Lord, saying:

10 O Lord, behold this people repenteth; and they have swept away the band of Gadianton from amongst them insomuch that they have become extinct, and they have concealed their secret plans in the earth.

11 Now, O Lord, because of this their humility wilt thou turn away thine anger, and let thine anger be appeased in the destruction of those wicked men whom thou hast already destroyed.

12 O Lord, wilt thou turn away thine anger, yea, thy fierce anger, and cause that this famine may cease in this land.

13 O Lord, wilt thou hearken unto me, and cause that it may be done according to my words, and send forth *rain upon the face of the earth, that she may bring forth her fruit, and her grain in the season of grain.

14 O Lord, thou didst hearken unto *my words when I said, Let there be a famine, that the pestilence of the sword might cease; and I know that thou wilt, even at this time, hearken unto my words, for thou saidst that: If this people repent I will spare them.

15 Yea, O Lord, and thou seest that they have repented, because of the famine and the pestilence and

11 2a Hel. 6:22 (18–24);
        11:26 (25–26).
    4a Hel. 11:14.
     b 1 Kgs. 8:35;
        1 Chr. 21:12;

    Hel. 10:6.
    TG Famine.
   6a TG Drought.
   7a Amos 4:7 (6–10);
    Hel. 12:3.

   8a Ex. 10:7.
    b Hel. 10:11 (11–14).
   9a Morm. 2:12.
  13a 1 Kgs. 18:41 (1, 41–46).
  14a Hel. 11:4.

destruction which has come unto them.

16 And now, O Lord, wilt thou turn away thine anger, and try again if they will serve thee? And if so, O Lord, thou canst bless them according to thy words which thou hast said.

17 And it came to pass that in the seventy and sixth year the Lord did turn away his anger from the people, and caused that ªrain should fall upon the earth, insomuch that it did bring forth her fruit in the season of her fruit. And it came to pass that it did bring forth her grain in the season of her grain.

18 And behold, the people did rejoice and glorify God, and the whole face of the land was filled with rejoicing; and they did no more seek to destroy Nephi, but they did esteem him as a ªgreat prophet, and a man of God, having great power and authority given unto him from God.

19 And behold, Lehi, his brother, was not a ªwhit behind him as to things pertaining to righteousness.

20 And thus it did come to pass that the people of Nephi began to prosper again in the land, and began to build up their waste places, and began to multiply and spread, even until they did ªcover the whole face of the land, both on the northward and on the southward, from the sea west to the sea east.

21 And it came to pass that the seventy and sixth year did end in peace. And the seventy and seventh year began in peace; and the ªchurch did spread throughout the face of all the land; and the more part of the people, both the Nephites and the Lamanites, did belong to the church; and they did have exceedingly great peace in the land; and thus ended the seventy and seventh year.

22 And also they had peace in the seventy and eighth year, save it were a few contentions concerning the points of doctrine which had been laid down by the prophets.

23 And in the seventy and ninth year there began to be much strife. But it came to pass that Nephi and Lehi, and many of their brethren who knew concerning the true points of doctrine, having many ªrevelations daily, therefore they did preach unto the people, insomuch that they did put an end to their strife in that same year.

24 And it came to pass that in the eightieth year of the reign of the judges over the people of Nephi, there were a certain number of the dissenters from the people of Nephi, who had some years before gone over unto the Lamanites, and taken upon themselves the name of Lamanites, and also a certain number who were real descendants of the Lamanites, being stirred up to anger by them, or by those dissenters, therefore they commenced a ªwar with their brethren.

25 And they did commit murder and plunder; and then they would retreat back into the mountains, and into the wilderness and secret places, hiding themselves that they could not be discovered, receiving daily an addition to their numbers, inasmuch as there were dissenters that went forth unto them.

26 And thus in time, yea, even in the space of ªnot many years, they became an exceedingly great band of robbers; and they did search out all the ᵇsecret plans of Gadianton; and thus they became robbers of Gadianton.

27 Now behold, these robbers did make great havoc, yea, even great destruction among the people of Nephi, and also among the people of the Lamanites.

17a Deut. 11:14 (13–17);
    Ether 2:24;
    D&C 117:1.
18a Hel. 10:7 (5–11).
19a Hel. 5:44 (36–44); 6:6.
20a Jarom 1:6;

Alma 22:27 (27, 32–33);
    Hel. 3:8;
    3 Ne. 1:17.
21a TG Church;
    Peace.
23a Jarom 1:4;

Alma 26:22;
    D&C 107:19.
24a Hel. 4:3.
26a Hel. 4:26; 6:32; 7:6.
  b Hel. 11:2.

28 And it came to pass that it was expedient that there should be a stop put to this work of destruction; therefore they sent an army of strong men into the wilderness and upon the mountains to search out this band of robbers, and to destroy them.

29 But behold, it came to pass that in that same year they were driven back even into their own lands. And thus ended the eightieth year of the reign of the judges over the people of Nephi.

30 And it came to pass in the commencement of the eighty and first year they did go forth again against this band of robbers, and did destroy many; and they were also visited with much destruction.

31 And they were again obliged to return out of the wilderness and out of the *mountains unto their own lands, because of the exceeding greatness of the numbers of those robbers who infested the mountains and the wilderness.

32 And it came to pass that thus ended this year. And the robbers did still increase and wax strong, insomuch that they did defy the whole armies of the Nephites, and also of the Lamanites; and they did cause great fear to come unto the people upon all the face of the land.

33 Yea, for they did visit many parts of the land, and did do great destruction unto them; yea, did kill many, and did carry away others captive into the wilderness, yea, and more especially their women and their children.

34 Now this great evil, which came unto the people because of their iniquity, did stir them up again in *remembrance of the Lord their God.

35 And thus ended the eighty and first year of the reign of the judges.

36 And in the eighty and second year they began again to *forget the Lord their God. And in the eighty and third year they began to wax strong in iniquity. And in the eighty and fourth year they did not mend their ways.

37 And it came to pass in the eighty and fifth year they did wax stronger and stronger in their pride, and in their wickedness; and thus they were *ripening again for destruction.

38 And thus ended the eighty and fifth year.

CHAPTER 12

Men are unstable and foolish and quick to do evil—The Lord chastens His people—The nothingness of men is compared with the power of God—In the day of judgment, men will gain everlasting life or everlasting damnation. About 6 B.C.

AND thus we can behold how false, and also the unsteadiness of the hearts of the children of men; yea, we can see that the Lord in his great infinite goodness doth bless and *prosper those who put their *trust in him.

2 Yea, and we may see at the very *time when he doth *prosper his people, yea, in the increase of their fields, their flocks and their herds, and in gold, and in silver, and in all manner of *precious things of every kind and art; sparing their lives, and delivering them out of the hands of their enemies; softening the hearts of their enemies that they should not declare wars against them; yea, and in fine, doing all things for the welfare and happiness of his people; yea, then is the time that they do *harden their hearts, and do *forget the Lord their God, and do *trample under their feet the

---

31a 3 Ne. 1:27.
34a Hosea 5:15.
36a Mosiah 13:29.
37a Hel. 6:40.
12 1a 2 Chr. 26:5;
　　　 Ps. 1:3 (2–3).
　 b Ps. 36:7 (7–8);

2 Ne. 22:2;
　 Mosiah 4:6.
　 TG Trust in God.
2a Alma 46:8;
　 Hel. 4:26; 6:32.
 b Ps. 62:10.
 c TG Treasure.

d TG Apostasy of
　 Individuals.
e Deut. 8:11 (10–20).
f Alma 5:53;
　 3 Ne. 28:35.
　 TG Sacrilege.

Holy One—yea, and this because of their ease, and their exceedingly great prosperity.

3 And thus we see that except the Lord doth ªchasten his people with many afflictions, yea, except he doth visit them with ᵇdeath and with terror, and with famine and with all manner of pestilence, they will not ᶜremember him.

4 O how ªfoolish, and how vain, and how evil, and devilish, and how ᵇquick to do iniquity, and how slow to do good, are the children of men; yea, how quick to hearken unto the words of the evil one, and to set their ᶜhearts upon the vain things of the world!

5 Yea, how quick to be lifted up in ªpride; yea, how quick to ᵇboast, and do all manner of that which is iniquity; and how slow are they to remember the Lord their God, and to give ear unto his counsels, yea, how slow to ᶜwalk in wisdom's paths!

6 Behold, they do not desire that the Lord their God, who hath ªcreated them, should ᵇrule and reign over them; notwithstanding his great goodness and his mercy towards them, they do set at ᶜnaught his counsels, and they will not that he should be their guide.

7 O how great is the ªnothingness of the children of men; yea, even they are ᵇless than the dust of the earth.

8 For behold, the dust of the earth moveth hither and thither, to the dividing asunder, at the command of our great and everlasting God.

9 Yea, behold at his ªvoice do the hills and the mountains tremble and ᵇquake.

10 And by the ªpower of his voice they are broken up, and become smooth, yea, even like unto a valley.

11 Yea, by the power of his voice doth the ªwhole earth shake;

12 Yea, by the power of his voice, do the foundations rock, even to the very center.

13 Yea, and if he say unto the earth—Move—it is moved.

14 Yea, if he say unto the ªearth—Thou shalt ᵇgo back, that it ᶜlengthen out the day for many hours—it is done;

15 And thus, according to his word the ªearth goeth back, and it appeareth unto man that the ᵇsun standeth still; yea, and behold, this is so; for surely it is the earth that moveth and not the sun.

16 And behold, also, if he say unto the ªwaters of the great deep—ᵇBe thou dried up—it is done.

17 Behold, if he say unto this mountain—Be thou raised up, and ªcome over and fall upon that city, that it be buried up—behold it is done.

18 And behold, if a man ªhide up a treasure in the earth, and the Lord shall say—Let it be ᵇaccursed, because of the iniquity of him who hath hid it up—behold, it shall be accursed.

19 And if the Lord shall say—Be thou accursed, that no man shall find thee from this time henceforth and forever—behold, no man getteth it henceforth and forever.

3a Deut. 11:2 (1–8);
   Ezek. 20:26;
   Mosiah 23:21;
   D&C 98:21; 101:8.
 b Ps. 78:34.
 c Amos 4:6 (6–11);
   Jonah 2:7;
   Mosiah 1:17.
4a TG Foolishness.
 b Ex. 32:8; Judg. 2:17;
   Isa. 59:7; Jer. 4:22.
 c Gen. 6:5;
   Matt. 15:19;
   Heb. 3:12.
5a Prov. 29:23.

 b TG Boast.
 c TG Walking in Darkness;
   Walking with God.
6a Isa. 45:9 (9–10);
   D&C 58:30.
 b Judg. 8:23 (22–23);
   D&C 60:4.
 c Jer. 8:7.
7a Isa. 40:17 (15, 17);
   Dan. 4:35; Moses 1:10.
 b Gen. 18:27.
9a Ezek. 1:24.
 b Judg. 5:5; 3 Ne. 22:10.
10a 1 Ne. 17:46.
11a Morm. 5:23;

   Ether 4:9.
14a Josh. 10:12 (12–14).
 b Isa. 38:8 (7–8).
 c 2 Kgs. 20:9 (8–11).
15a Alma 30:44.
 b Hab. 3:11.
16a Matt. 8:27 (23–27);
   Jacob 4:9.
 b Isa. 44:27; 51:10.
17a 3 Ne. 8:10 (10, 25);
   9:8 (5–6, 8).
18a Hel. 13:18 (18–23);
   Morm. 1:18 (17–19);
   Ether 14:1.
 b Hel. 13:17.

20 And behold, if the Lord shall say unto a man—Because of thine iniquities, thou shalt be accursed ^aforever—it shall be done.

21 And if the Lord shall say—Because of thine iniquities thou shalt be ^acut off from my presence—he will cause that it shall be so.

22 And wo unto him to whom he shall say this, for it shall be unto him that will do iniquity, and he cannot be ^asaved; therefore, for this cause, that men might be saved, hath repentance been declared.

23 Therefore, blessed are they who will repent and hearken unto the voice of the Lord their God; for these are they that shall be saved.

24 And may God grant, in his great fulness, that men might be brought unto repentance and good works, that they might be restored unto grace for ^agrace, according to their works.

25 And I would that all men might be saved. But we read that in the ^agreat and last day there are some who shall be cast out, yea, who shall be cast off from the ^bpresence of the Lord;

26 Yea, who shall be consigned to a state of endless misery, fulfilling the words which say: They that have done good shall have ^aeverlasting life; and they that have done evil shall have everlasting ^bdamnation. And thus it is. Amen.

The prophecy of Samuel, the Lamanite, to the Nephites.

Comprising chapters 13 through 15.

CHAPTER 13

Samuel the Lamanite prophesies the destruction of the Nephites unless they repent—They and their riches are cursed—They reject and stone the prophets, are encircled about by demons, and seek for happiness in doing iniquity. About 6 B.C.

AND now it came to pass in the eighty and sixth year, the Nephites did still remain in wickedness, yea, in great wickedness, while the ^aLamanites did observe strictly to keep the commandments of God, according to the law of Moses.

2 And it came to pass that in this year there was one ^aSamuel, a ^bLamanite, came into the land of Zarahemla, and began to preach unto the people. And it came to pass that he did preach, many days, repentance unto the people, and they did ^ccast him out, and he was about to ^dreturn to his own land.

3 But behold, the ^avoice of the Lord came unto him, that he should return again, and prophesy unto the people whatsoever things should come into his ^bheart.

4 And it came to pass that they would not suffer that he should enter into the city; therefore he went and got upon the ^awall thereof, and stretched forth his hand and cried with a loud voice, and ^bprophesied unto the people whatsoever things the Lord put into his heart.

5 And he said unto them: Behold, I, Samuel, a Lamanite, do speak the words of the Lord which he doth put into my heart; and behold he hath put it into my heart to say unto this people that the ^asword of justice hangeth over this people; and four hundred years pass not away save the sword of justice falleth upon this people.

6 Yea, heavy ^adestruction awaiteth

20a Mosiah 27:31.
21a Jer. 23:39 (39–40);
    D&C 63:4.
22a TG Salvation.
24a TG Grace.
25a Mal. 4:5;
    3 Ne. 26:4.
  b TG God, Presence of.
26a Dan. 12:2 (2–3);
    D&C 19:7.

  b TG Damnation.
13 1a Hel. 6:1; 15:5.
  2a Hel. 14:1;
    3 Ne. 23:9 (9–10).
  b Hel. 16:7.
  c Hel. 14:10.
  d Alma 26:27.
  3a Gal. 2:2;
    Alma 8:16; 20:2;
    3 Ne. 1:12.

  b D&C 100:5.
  4a Hel. 14:11; 16:1.
  b TG Teaching with the
    Spirit.
  5a Alma 60:29;
    3 Ne. 2:19.
  6a Alma 45:11 (10–14);
    Hel. 15:17.

this people, and it surely cometh unto this people, and nothing can save this people save it be repentance and faith on the Lord Jesus Christ, who surely shall come into the world, and shall suffer many things and shall be slain for his people.

7 And behold, an ^aangel of the Lord hath declared it unto me, and he did bring ^bglad tidings to my soul. And behold, I was sent unto you to declare it unto you also, that ye might have glad tidings; but behold ye would ^cnot receive me.

8 Therefore, thus saith the Lord: Because of the hardness of the hearts of the people of the Nephites, except they repent I will take away my word from them, and I will ^awithdraw my Spirit from them, and I will suffer them no longer, and I will turn the hearts of their brethren against them.

9 And ^afour hundred years shall not pass away before I will cause that they shall be smitten; yea, I will visit them with the sword and with famine and with pestilence.

10 Yea, I will visit them in my fierce anger, and there shall be those of the ^afourth generation who shall live, of your enemies, to behold your utter destruction; and this shall surely come except ye repent, saith the Lord; and those of the fourth generation shall visit your destruction.

11 But if ye will repent and ^areturn unto the Lord your God I will turn away mine anger, saith the Lord; yea, thus saith the Lord, blessed are they who will repent and turn unto me, but wo unto him that repenteth not.

12 Yea, ^awo unto this great city of Zarahemla; for behold, it is because of those who are righteous that it

is saved; yea, wo unto this great city, for I perceive, saith the Lord, that there are many, yea, even the more part of this great city, that will harden their hearts against me, saith the Lord.

13 But blessed are they who will repent, for them will I spare. But behold, if it were not for the righteous who are in this great city, behold, I would cause that ^afire should come down out of heaven and ^bdestroy it.

14 But behold, it is for the righteous' sake that it is spared. But behold, the time cometh, saith the Lord, that when ye shall cast out the righteous from among you, then shall ye be ^aripe for destruction; yea, wo be unto this great city, because of the wickedness and abominations which are in her.

15 Yea, and wo be unto the city of Gideon, for the wickedness and abominations which are in her.

16 Yea, and wo be unto all the cities which are in the land round about, which are possessed by the Nephites, because of the wickedness and abominations which are in them.

17 And behold, a ^acurse shall come upon the land, saith the Lord of Hosts, because of the people's sake who are upon the land, yea, because of their wickedness and their abominations.

18 And it shall come to pass, saith the Lord of Hosts, yea, our great and true God, that whoso shall ^ahide up treasures in the earth shall find them again no more, because of the great curse of the land, save he be a righteous man and shall hide it up unto the Lord.

19 For I will, saith the Lord, that they shall hide up their ^atreasures

7a Alma 13:26;
   Hel. 14:26 (9, 26, 28).
  b Isa. 52:7.
  c TG Prophets,
   Rejection of.
8a Ex. 23:21 (20–21).
9a Alma 45:10.
10a 1 Ne. 12:12; 2 Ne. 26:9;

Alma 45:12;
   3 Ne. 27:32.
11a 1 Sam. 7:3;
   3 Ne. 10:6 (5–7).
12a 3 Ne. 8:24 (8, 24); 9:3.
13a 2 Kgs. 1:10 (9–16);
   3 Ne. 9:11.
  b Gen. 18:23; 1 Ne. 22:16;

D&C 64:24.
14a Gen. 15:16;
   Alma 37:31;
   D&C 61:31; 101:11.
17a Hel. 12:18.
18a Morm. 1:18 (17–19);
   Ether 14:1.
19a Prov. 13:11.

unto me; and cursed be they who hide not up their treasures unto me; for none hideth up their treasures unto me save it be the righteous; and he that hideth not up his treasures unto me, cursed is he, and also the treasure, and none shall redeem it because of the curse of the land.

20 And the day shall come that they shall hide up their treasures, because they have set their hearts upon riches; and because they have set their hearts upon their riches, and will hide up their treasures when they shall flee before their enemies; because they will not hide them unto me, cursed be they and also their treasures; and in that day shall they be smitten, saith the Lord.

21 Behold ye, the people of this great city, and hearken unto my words; yea, hearken unto the words which the Lord saith; for behold, he saith that ye are *a*cursed because of your riches, and also are your riches cursed because ye have set your hearts upon them, and have not *b*hearkened unto the words of him who gave them unto you.

22 Ye do not remember the Lord your God in the things with which he hath blessed you, but ye do always remember your *a*riches, not to thank the Lord your God for them; yea, your hearts are not drawn out unto the Lord, but they do swell with great pride, unto *b*boasting, and unto great *c*swelling, *d*envyings, strifes, malice, persecutions, and murders, and all manner of iniquities.

23 For this cause hath the Lord God caused that a curse should come upon the land, and also upon your riches, and this because of your iniquities.

24 Yea, wo unto this people, because of this time which has arrived, that ye do *a*cast out the prophets, and do mock them, and cast stones at them, and do slay them, and do all manner of iniquity unto them, even as they did of old time.

25 And now when ye talk, ye say: If our days had been in the days of our *a*fathers of old, we would not have *b*slain the prophets; we would not have stoned them, and cast them out.

26 Behold ye are worse than they; for as the Lord liveth, if a *a*prophet come among you and declareth unto you the word of the Lord, which testifieth of your *b*sins and iniquities, ye are *c*angry with him, and cast him out and seek all manner of ways to destroy him; yea, you will say that he is a *d*false *e*prophet, and that he is a sinner, and of the devil, because he *f*testifieth that your deeds are evil.

27 But behold, if a man shall come among you and shall say: Do this, and there is no iniquity; do that and ye shall not suffer; yea, he will say: *a*Walk after the pride of your own hearts; yea, walk after the pride of your eyes, and do whatsoever your heart desireth—and if a man shall come among you and say this, ye will receive him, and say that he is a *b*prophet.

28 Yea, ye will lift him up, and ye will give unto him of your substance; ye will give unto him of your gold, and of your silver, and ye will clothe him with costly apparel; and because he speaketh *a*flattering words unto you, and he saith that all is

---

21*a* TG Curse.
  b TG Disobedience.
22*a* Luke 12:34.
  b TG Boast.
  c Alma 30:31.
  d TG Envy.
24*a* 2 Chr. 36:16 (15–16);
    Neh. 9:26;
    Jer. 20:2;
    1 Ne. 1:20;

Hel. 16:6.
25*a* Matt. 23:32;
    Acts 7:51 (51–52).
  b TG Prophets,
    Rejection of.
26*a* 2 Chr. 18:7;
    Luke 16:31 (19–31).
  b Micah 3:8.
  c Isa. 30:9 (9–10).
  d Mosiah 12:14.

  e Luke 11:15 (14–22);
    Mosiah 3:9 (9–12).
  f Gal. 4:16.
27*a* TG Walking in Darkness.
  b Lam. 2:14; 4:13;
    Micah 2:11.
    TG False Prophets.
28*a* 2 Tim. 4:3 (3–4).

well, then ye will not find fault with him.

29 O ye wicked and ye perverse generation; ye hardened and ye ᵃstiffnecked people, how long will ye suppose that the Lord will suffer you? Yea, how long will ye suffer yourselves to be led by ᵇfoolish and ᶜblind guides? Yea, how long will ye ᵈchoose darkness rather than ᵉlight?

30 Yea, behold, the anger of the Lord is already kindled against you; behold, he hath cursed the land because of your iniquity.

31 And behold, the time cometh that he curseth your riches, that they become ᵃslippery, that ye cannot hold them; and in the days of your poverty ye cannot retain them.

32 And in the days of your poverty ye shall cry unto the Lord; and in vain shall ye cry, for your desolation is already come upon you, and your destruction is made sure; and then shall ye weep and howl in that day, saith the Lord of Hosts. And then shall ye lament, and say:

33 O ᵃthat I had repented, and had not killed the prophets, and ᵇstoned them, and cast them out. Yea, in that day ye shall say: O that we had remembered the Lord our God in the day that he gave us our riches, and then they would not have become slippery that we should lose them; for behold, our riches are gone from us.

34 Behold, we lay a tool here and on the morrow it is gone; and behold, our swords are taken from us in the day we have sought them for battle.

35 Yea, we have hid up our ᵃtreasures and they have slipped away from us, because of the curse of the land.

36 O that we had repented in the day that the word of the Lord came unto us; for behold the land is cursed, and all things are become slippery, and we cannot hold them.

37 Behold, we are surrounded by ᵃdemons, yea, we are encircled about by the angels of him who hath sought to destroy our souls. Behold, our iniquities are great. O Lord, canst thou not turn away thine anger from us? And this shall be your language in those days.

38 But behold, your ᵃdays of probation are past; ye have ᵇprocrastinated the day of your salvation until it is everlastingly too late, and your destruction is made sure; yea, for ye have sought all the days of your lives for that which ye could not obtain; and ye have sought for ᶜhappiness in doing iniquity, which thing is ᵈcontrary to the nature of that righteousness which is in our great and Eternal Head.

39 O ye people of the land, that ye would hear my words! And I pray that the anger of the Lord be turned away from you, and that ye would repent and be saved.

CHAPTER 14

Samuel predicts light during the night and a new star at Christ's birth—Christ redeems men from temporal and spiritual death—The signs of His death include three days of darkness, the rending of the rocks, and great upheavals of nature. About 6 B.C.

AND now it came to pass that ᵃSamuel, the Lamanite, did prophesy a great many more things which cannot be written.

2 And behold, he said unto them: Behold, I give unto you a sign; for ᵃfive years more cometh, and behold, then cometh the Son of God

---

29a TG Stiffnecked.
  b Ezek. 13:3; 2 Ne. 28:9.
  c Matt. 15:14; 23:16.
  d John 3:19.
  e Job 24:13 (2–16).
31a Jer. 48:36 (35–36);
    Morm. 1:18 (17–19).
33a Morm. 2:10 (10–15).

  b Matt. 23:37.
35a TG Treasure.
37a Mosiah 2:32.
38a Morm. 2:15 (10–15).
  TG Probation.
  b Alma 34:33 (33–34).
  TG Apathy;
    Procrastination.

  c Alma 41:10.
    TG Abundant Life;
    Happiness.
  d Alma 41:11 (10–12).
14 1a Hel. 13:2;
    3 Ne. 23:9 (9–10).
  2a Hel. 16:4;
    3 Ne. 1:5 (5–21).

to redeem all those who shall believe on his name.

3 And behold, this will I give unto you for a *a*sign at the time of his coming; for behold, there shall be great lights in heaven, insomuch that in the night before he cometh there shall be no darkness, insomuch that it shall appear unto man as if it was day.

4 Therefore, there shall be one *a*day and a night and a day, as if it were one day and there were no night; and this shall be unto you for a sign; for ye shall know of the rising of the sun and also of its setting; therefore they shall know of a surety that there shall be two days and a night; nevertheless the night shall not be darkened; and it shall be the night before he is *b*born.

5 And behold, there shall a new *a*star arise, such an one as ye never have beheld; and this also shall be a sign unto you.

6 And behold this is not all, there shall be many *a*signs and wonders in heaven.

7 And it shall come to pass that ye shall all be amazed, and wonder, insomuch that ye shall *a*fall to the earth.

8 And it shall come to pass that whosoever shall *a*believe on the Son of God, the same shall have everlasting life.

9 And behold, thus hath the Lord commanded me, by his angel, that I should come and tell this thing unto you; yea, he hath commanded that I should prophesy these things unto you; yea, he hath said unto me: Cry unto this people, repent and prepare the way of the Lord.

10 And now, because I am a Lamanite, and have spoken unto you the words which the Lord hath commanded me, and because it was hard against you, ye are angry with me and do seek to destroy me, and have *a*cast me out from among you.

11 And ye shall *a*hear my words, for, for this intent have I come up upon the walls of this city, that ye might hear and know of the judgments of God which do await you because of your iniquities, and also that ye might know the conditions of repentance;

12 And also that ye might know of the coming of Jesus Christ, the Son of God, the *a*Father of heaven and of earth, the Creator of all things from the beginning; and that ye might know of the signs of his coming, to the intent that ye might believe on his name.

13 And if ye *a*believe on his name ye will repent of all your sins, that thereby ye may have a remission of them through his *b*merits.

14 And behold, again, another sign I give unto you, yea, a sign of his *a*death.

15 For behold, he surely must die that *a*salvation may come; yea, it behooveth him and becometh expedient that he *b*dieth, to bring to pass the *c*resurrection of the dead, that thereby men may be brought into the *d*presence of the Lord.

16 Yea, behold, this death bringeth to pass the *a*resurrection, and *b*redeemeth all mankind from the first death—that spiritual death; for all mankind, by the *c*fall of Adam being *d*cut off from the presence of

---

3*a* Hel. 16:13;
    3 Ne. 1:15 (8–20).
4*a* 3 Ne. 1:8.
  b TG Jesus Christ, Birth of.
5*a* Matt. 2:2 (1–2);
    3 Ne. 1:21.
    TG Astronomy.
6*a* 3 Ne. 2:1.
7*a* 3 Ne. 1:16 (16–17).
8*a* John 3:16.
10*a* Hel. 13:2 (2–7).
11*a* Ezek. 2:7 (6–7).

12*a* Mosiah 3:8; 15:4;
    3 Ne. 9:15;
    Ether 4:7.
    TG Jesus Christ, Creator.
13*a* Acts 16:31 (30–31).
  b D&C 19:16 (16–20).
14*a* TG Jesus Christ,
    Death of.
15*a* TG Jesus Christ, Savior.
  b 1 Cor. 15:36.
  c 2 Ne. 9:4;
    Alma 42:23;

    Morm. 9:13.
    TG Resurrection.
  d TG God, Presence of.
16*a* John 20:9;
    D&C 18:12 (11–12).
  b TG Salvation, Plan of.
  c TG Fall of Man.
  d 2 Ne. 2:5; 9:6 (6–15);
    Alma 11:42 (40–45);
    12:16 (16, 24, 36);
    42:7 (6–11).

the Lord, are considered as ᵉdead, both as to things temporal and to things spiritual.

17 But behold, the resurrection of Christ ᵃredeemeth mankind, yea, even all mankind, and bringeth them back into the presence of the Lord.

18 Yea, and it bringeth to pass the condition of repentance, that whosoever repenteth the same is not ᵃhewn down and cast into the fire; but whosoever repenteth not is hewn down and cast into the fire; and there cometh upon them again a ᵇspiritual death, yea, a second death, for they are cut off again as to things pertaining to righteousness.

19 Therefore repent ye, repent ye, lest by knowing these things and not doing them ye shall suffer yourselves to come under condemnation, and ye are brought down unto this second death.

20 But behold, as I said unto you concerning another ᵃsign, a sign of his death, behold, in that day that he shall suffer death the sun shall be darkened and refuse to give his ᵇlight unto you; and also the moon and the stars; and there shall be no light upon the face of this land, even from the time that he shall suffer death, for the space of ᶜthree days, to the time that he shall rise again from the dead.

21 Yea, at the time that he shall yield up the ᵃghost there shall be ᵇthunderings and lightnings for the space of many hours, and the earth shall shake and tremble; and the ᶜrocks which are upon the face of this earth, which are both above the earth and beneath, which ye know at this time are solid, or the more

part of it is one solid mass, shall be ᵈbroken up;

22 Yea, they shall be rent in twain, and shall ever after be ᵃfound in seams and in cracks, and in broken fragments upon the face of the whole earth, yea, both above the earth and beneath.

23 And behold, there shall be great ᵃtempests, and there shall be many mountains laid low, like unto a valley, and there shall be many places which are now called ᵇvalleys which shall become mountains, whose height is great.

24 And ᵃmany highways shall be broken up, and many cities shall become desolate.

25 And many ᵃgraves shall be opened, and shall yield up many of their dead; and many saints shall appear unto many.

26 And behold, thus hath the ᵃangel spoken unto me; for he said unto me that there should be thunderings and lightnings for the space of many hours.

27 And he said unto me that while the thunder and the lightning lasted, and the tempest, that these things should be, and that ᵃdarkness should cover the face of the whole earth for the space of three days.

28 And the angel said unto me that many shall see greater things than these, to the intent that they might believe that ᵃthese signs and these wonders should come to pass upon all the face of this land, to the intent that there should be no cause for unbelief among the children of men—

29 And this to the intent that whosoever will believe might be saved, and that whosoever will not believe,

---

16e TG Death, Spiritual, First.
17a TG Redemption.
18a Luke 13:7.
   b TG Death, Spiritual, Second.
20a 3 Ne. 8:5 (5–25); 11:2.
   b Luke 23:44.
   c Mosiah 3:10.
21a Matt. 27:50 (50–54).
   b 1 Ne. 19:11;

   3 Ne. 8:6 (5–23).
   c 3 Ne. 10:9.
   d Gen. 7:11;
     1 Ne. 12:4.
22a 3 Ne. 8:18.
23a 3 Ne. 10:14.
   b Isa. 40:4;
     Luke 3:5;
     D&C 49:23; 109:74.
24a 3 Ne. 8:14 (8–10, 14);
     9:12 (3–12); 10:7.

25a Matt. 27:52 (52–53);
     3 Ne. 23:11 (7–13).
26a Alma 13:26;
     Hel. 13:7.
27a 1 Ne. 19:10;
     3 Ne. 8:3; 10:9.
28a 1 Ne. 12:4 (4–5);
     19:12 (10–12);
     3 Ne. 10:11.

a ᵃrighteous judgment might come upon them; and also if they are condemned they bring upon themselves their own condemnation.

30 And now remember, remember, my brethren, that whosoever perisheth, perisheth unto ᵃhimself; and whosoever doeth iniquity, doeth it unto himself; for behold, ye are ᵇfree; ye are permitted to act for yourselves; for behold, God hath given unto you a ᶜknowledge and he hath made you free.

31 He hath given unto you that ye might ᵃknow good from evil, and he hath given unto you that ye might ᵇchoose life or death; and ye can do good and be ᶜrestored unto that which is good, or have that which is good restored unto you; or ye can do evil, and have that which is evil restored unto you.

CHAPTER 15

The Lord chastened the Nephites because He loved them—Converted Lamanites are firm and steadfast in the faith—The Lord will be merciful unto the Lamanites in the latter days. About 6 B.C.

AND now, my beloved brethren, behold, I declare unto you that except ye shall repent your houses shall be left unto you ᵃdesolate.

2 Yea, except ye repent, your women shall have great cause to mourn in the day that they shall give suck; for ye shall attempt to flee and there shall be no place for ᵃrefuge; yea, and wo unto them which are ᵇwith child, for they shall be heavy and cannot flee; therefore, they shall be trodden down and shall be left to perish.

3 Yea, wo unto this ᵃpeople who

are called the ᵇpeople of Nephi except they shall repent, when they shall see all these signs and wonders which shall be showed unto them; for behold, they have been a chosen people of the Lord; yea, the people of Nephi hath he loved, and also hath he ᶜchastened them; yea, in the days of their iniquities hath he chastened them because he loveth them.

4 But behold my brethren, the ᵃLamanites hath he hated because their deeds have been evil continually, and this because of the iniquity of the ᵇtradition of their fathers. But behold, salvation hath come unto them through the preaching of the Nephites; and for this intent hath the Lord ᶜprolonged their days.

5 And I would that ye should behold that the ᵃmore part of them are in the path of their duty, and they do walk circumspectly before God, and they do observe to keep his commandments and his statutes and his judgments according to the law of Moses.

6 Yea, I say unto you, that the more part of them are doing this, and they are striving with ᵃunwearied diligence that they may bring the remainder of their brethren to the knowledge of the truth; therefore there are many who do add to their numbers daily.

7 And behold, ye do know of yourselves, for ye have witnessed it, that as many of them as are brought to the knowledge of the truth, and to know of the wicked and abominable traditions of their fathers, and are led to believe the holy scriptures, yea, the prophecies of the holy prophets, which are written, which

---

29a TG Judgment.
30a 3 Ne. 3:11.
  b Gal. 5:1;
    2 Ne. 2:27 (26–27);
    Alma 41:7;
    Moses 6:56.
    TG Agency.
  c TG Knowledge.
31a Moro. 7:16.
  b Rom. 6:16 (14–18);

Alma 3:27 (26–27).
  c Alma 41:3 (1–15).
15 1a Isa. 5:9;
    Matt. 23:38.
2a TG Refuge.
  b Matt. 24:19.
3a W of M 1:11.
  b Jacob 5:25.
  c Prov. 3:12;
    Heb. 12:6 (5–11);

D&C 95:1.
4a Jacob 5:40.
  b Ezek. 20:18;
    Hel. 5:19.
    TG Traditions of Men.
  c Alma 9:16.
5a Hel. 13:1; 16:6.
6a TG Dedication.

leadeth them to faith on the Lord, and unto repentance, which faith and repentance bringeth a [a]change of heart unto them—

8 Therefore, as many as have come to this, ye know of yourselves are [a]firm and steadfast in the faith, and in the thing wherewith they have been made free.

9 And ye know also that they have [a]buried their weapons of war, and they fear to take them up lest by any means they should sin; yea, ye can see that they fear to sin—for behold they will suffer themselves that they be trodden down and slain by their enemies, and will not lift their swords against them, and this because of their [b]faith in Christ.

10 And now, because of their [a]steadfastness when they do believe in that thing which they do believe, for because of their firmness when they are once enlightened, behold, the Lord shall bless them and prolong their days, notwithstanding their iniquity—

11 Yea, even if they should dwindle in unbelief the Lord shall [a]prolong their days, until the time shall come which hath been spoken of by our fathers, and also by the prophet [b]Zenos, and many other prophets, concerning the [c]restoration of our brethren, the Lamanites, again to the knowledge of the truth—

12 Yea, I say unto you, that in the latter times the [a]promises of the Lord have been extended to our brethren, the Lamanites; and notwithstanding the many afflictions which they shall have, and notwithstanding they shall be [b]driven to and fro upon the face of the earth, and be hunted, and shall be smitten and scattered abroad, having no

place for [c]refuge, the Lord shall be [d]merciful unto them.

13 And this is according to the prophecy, that they shall again be [a]brought to the true knowledge, which is the knowledge of their Redeemer, and their great and true [b]shepherd, and be numbered among his [c]sheep.

14 Therefore I say unto you, it shall be [a]better for them than for you except ye repent.

15 For behold, [a]had the mighty works been shown unto them which have been shown unto you, yea, unto them who have dwindled in unbelief because of the traditions of their fathers, ye can see of yourselves that they never would again have dwindled in unbelief.

16 Therefore, saith the Lord: I will not utterly destroy them, but I will cause that in the day of my wisdom they shall [a]return again unto me, saith the Lord.

17 And now behold, saith the Lord, concerning the people of the Nephites: If they will not repent, and observe to do my will, I will utterly [a]destroy them, saith the Lord, because of their unbelief notwithstanding the many mighty works which I have done among them; and as surely as the Lord liveth shall these things be, saith the Lord.

CHAPTER 16

The Nephites who believe Samuel are baptized by Nephi—Samuel cannot be slain with the arrows and stones of the unrepentant Nephites—Some harden their hearts, and others see angels—The unbelievers say it is not reasonable to believe in Christ and His coming in Jerusalem. About 6–1 B.C.

7a TG Conversion.
8a Alma 23:6; 27:27;
  3 Ne. 6:14.
9a Alma 24:17 (17–26).
  b Mark 5:34 (34–36).
10a TG Steadfastness.
11a Deut. 11:9 (8–9);
  Alma 9:16.
  b Hel. 8:19;

3 Ne. 10:16.
  c Morm. 5:12 (9, 12); 7:1.
12a Enos 1:13 (12–13).
  b Morm. 5:15.
  c TG Refuge.
  d 1 Ne. 13:31;
  2 Ne. 4:7; 10:18 (18–19);
  Jacob 3:6 (5–9);
  Morm. 5:20 (20–21).

13a 3 Ne. 16:12.
  b TG Jesus Christ, Good
    Shepherd.
  c TG Sheep.
14a Hel. 7:23.
15a Matt. 11:21 (20–24).
16a Enos 1:13.
17a Hel. 13:6 (5–10);
  Morm. 3:2.

AND now, it came to pass that there were many who heard the words of Samuel, the Lamanite, which he spake upon the ^awalls of the city. And as many as believed on his word went forth and sought for Nephi; and when they had come forth and found him they confessed unto him their sins and denied not, desiring that they might be ^bbaptized unto the Lord.

2 But as many as there were who did not believe in the words of Samuel were ^aangry with him; and they cast stones at him upon the wall, and also many shot arrows at him as he stood upon the wall; but the Spirit of the Lord was with him, insomuch that they could not hit him with their stones neither with their arrows.

3 Now when they saw that they could not hit him, there were many more who did believe on his words, insomuch that they went away unto Nephi to be baptized.

4 For behold, Nephi was baptizing, and prophesying, and preaching, crying repentance unto the people, showing signs and wonders, working ^amiracles among the people, that they might know that the Christ must ^bshortly come—

5 Telling them of things which must shortly come, that they might know and remember at the time of their coming that they had been made known unto them beforehand, to the intent that they might believe; therefore as many as believed on the words of Samuel went forth unto him to be baptized, for they came repenting and confessing their sins.

6 But the ^amore part of them did not believe in the words of Samuel; therefore when they saw that they could not hit him with their stones and their arrows, they cried unto their captains, saying: ^bTake this fellow and bind him, for behold

he ^chath a devil; and because of the power of the devil which is in him we cannot hit him with our stones and our arrows; therefore take him and bind him, and away with him.

7 And as they went forth to lay their hands on him, behold, he did cast himself down from the wall, and did flee out of their lands, yea, even unto his own country, and began to preach and to prophesy ^aamong his own people.

8 And behold, he was never heard of more among the Nephites; and thus were the affairs of the people.

9 And thus ended the eighty and sixth year of the reign of the judges over the people of Nephi.

10 And thus ended also the eighty and seventh year of the reign of the judges, the more part of the people remaining in their pride and wickedness, and the lesser part walking more circumspectly before God.

11 And these were the conditions also, in the eighty and eighth year of the reign of the judges.

12 And there was but little alteration in the affairs of the people, save it were the people began to be more hardened in iniquity, and do more and more of that which was ^acontrary to the commandments of God, in the eighty and ninth year of the reign of the judges.

13 But it came to pass in the ninetieth year of the reign of the judges, there were ^agreat signs given unto the people, and wonders; and the words of the prophets ^bbegan to be fulfilled.

14 And ^aangels did appear unto men, wise men, and did declare unto them glad tidings of great joy; thus in this year the scriptures began to be fulfilled.

15 Nevertheless, the people began to harden their hearts, all save it were the most believing part of them, both of the Nephites and also of the

16 1a Hel. 13:4.
   b Alma 9:27.
  2a Prov. 29:10.
  4a TG Miracle.
   b Hel. 14:2.
  6a Hel. 15:5;
     3 Ne. 1:22.
   b Hel. 13:24.
   c John 7:20.
  7a Hel. 13:2.
 12a TG Disobedience.
 13a 3 Ne. 1:4.
   b Hel. 14:3 (3–7).
 14a Alma 13:26.

Lamanites, and began to depend upon their *own strength and upon their own wisdom, saying:

16 Some things they may have guessed right, among so many; but behold, we know that all these great and marvelous works cannot come to pass, of which has been spoken.

17 And they began to reason and to contend among themselves, saying:

18 That it is *not reasonable that such a being as a Christ shall come; if so, and he be the Son of God, the Father of heaven and of earth, as it has been spoken, why will he not show himself unto us as well as unto them who shall be at Jerusalem?

19 Yea, why will he not show himself in this land as well as in the land of Jerusalem?

20 But behold, we know that this is a wicked *tradition, which has been handed down unto us by our fathers, to cause us that we should believe in some great and marvelous thing which should come to pass, but not among us, but in a land which is far distant, a land which we know not; therefore they can keep us in ignorance, for we cannot *witness with our own eyes that they are true.

21 And they will, by the cunning and the mysterious arts of the evil one, work some great mystery which we cannot understand, which will keep us down to be servants to their words, and also servants unto them, for we depend upon them to teach us the word; and thus will they keep us in ignorance if we will yield ourselves unto them, all the days of our lives.

22 And many more things did the people *imagine up in their hearts, which were foolish and *vain; and they were much disturbed, for Satan did stir them up to do iniquity continually; yea, he did go about spreading *rumors and contentions upon all the face of the land, that he might harden the hearts of the people against that which was good and against that which should come.

23 And notwithstanding the signs and the wonders which were wrought among the people of the Lord, and the many miracles which they did, Satan did get great hold upon the hearts of the people upon all the face of the land.

24 And thus ended the ninetieth year of the reign of the judges over the people of Nephi.

25 *And thus ended the book of Helaman, according to the record of Helaman and his sons.

THIRD NEPHI
THE BOOK OF NEPHI

THE SON OF NEPHI, WHO WAS THE SON OF HELAMAN

And Helaman was the son of Helaman, who was the son of Alma, who was the son of Alma, being a descendant of Nephi who was the son of Lehi, who came out of Jerusalem in the first year of the reign of Zedekiah, the king of Judah.

CHAPTER 1

Nephi, the son of Helaman, departs out of the land, and his son Nephi keeps the records—Though signs and wonders abound, the wicked plan to slay the righteous—The night of Christ's birth arrives—The sign is given, and a

---

15a Isa. 5:21.
18a Alma 30:53.
20a TG Traditions of Men.

b Alma 30:15;
   Ether 12:5 (5–6, 19).
22a Gen. 6:5.

b 4 Ne. 1:43.
c Prov. 6:18 (16–19).
25a Hel. 3:37.

new star arises—Lyings and deceivings increase, and the Gadianton robbers slaughter many. About A.D. *1–4.*

NOW it came to pass that the ninety and first year had passed away and it was ^asix hundred years from the time that Lehi left Jerusalem; and it was in the year that ^bLachoneus was the chief judge and the governor over the land.

2 And ^aNephi, the son of Helaman, had departed out of the land of Zarahemla, giving charge unto his son ^bNephi, who was his eldest son, concerning the ^cplates of brass, and ^dall the records which had been kept, and all those things which had been kept sacred from the departure of Lehi out of Jerusalem.

3 Then he ^adeparted out of the land, and ^bwhither he went, no man knoweth; and his son Nephi did keep the records in his stead, yea, the record of this people.

4 And it came to pass that in the commencement of the ninety and second year, behold, the prophecies of the prophets began to be fulfilled more fully; for there began to be ^agreater signs and greater miracles wrought among the people.

5 But there were some who began to say that the time was past for the words to be fulfilled, which were ^aspoken by Samuel, the Lamanite.

6 And they began to ^arejoice over their brethren, saying: Behold the time is past, and the words of Samuel are not fulfilled; therefore, your joy and your faith concerning this thing hath been vain.

7 And it came to pass that they did make a great uproar throughout the land; and the people who believed began to be very sorrowful, lest by any means those things which had been spoken might not come to pass.

8 But behold, they did watch steadfastly for ^athat day and that night and that day which should be as one day as if there were no night, that they might know that their faith had not been vain.

9 Now it came to pass that there was a day set apart by the ^aunbelievers, that all those who believed in those traditions should be ^bput to death except the ^csign should come to pass, which had been given by Samuel the prophet.

10 Now it came to pass that when Nephi, the son of Nephi, saw this wickedness of his people, his heart was exceedingly sorrowful.

11 And it came to pass that he went out and bowed himself down upon the earth, and cried mightily to his God in behalf of his people, yea, those who were about to be destroyed because of their faith in the tradition of their fathers.

12 And it came to pass that he cried mightily unto the Lord ^aall that day; and behold, the ^bvoice of the Lord came unto him, saying:

13 Lift up your head and be of good cheer; for behold, the time is at hand, and on this night shall the ^asign be given, and on the ^bmorrow come I into the world, to show unto the world that I will fulfil all that which I have caused to be ^cspoken by the mouth of my holy prophets.

14 Behold, I ^acome unto my own, to ^bfulfil all things which I have made known unto the children of men from the ^cfoundation of the

1 1a 2 Ne. 25:19;
        Alma 13:25.
    b 3 Ne. 3:1; 6:19.
  2a Hel. 3:21 (20–21).
    b 3 Ne. 7:15 (15, 20, 23).
    c Alma 37:3 (3–12);
        63:12 (1, 11–14).
    d Alma 50:38.
  3a Alma 45:18 (18–19).
    b 3 Ne. 2:9.
  4a Hel. 16:13 (13, 23).

  5a Hel. 14:2.
  6a TG Mocking.
  8a Hel. 14:4 (3–4).
  9a TG Unbelief.
    b 3 Ne. 1:16.
       TG Martyrdom.
    c Hel. 14:3 (2–7).
 12a Enos 1:4;
        Alma 5:46.
    b Alma 20:2;
        Hel. 13:3.

 13a Matt. 2:2.
    b Luke 2:11 (10–11).
    c TG Jesus Christ,
        Prophecies about.
 14a John 1:11.
    b Matt. 5:17 (17–18);
        Luke 24:44.
    c Alma 42:26;
        3 Ne. 26:5.

world, and to do the ^dwill, ^eboth ^fof the Father and of the Son—of the Father because of me, and of the Son because of my flesh. And behold, the time is at hand, and this night shall the sign be given.

15 And it came to pass that the words which came unto Nephi were fulfilled, according as they had been spoken; for behold, at the going down of the ^asun there was ^bno darkness; and the people began to be astonished because there was no darkness when the night came.

16 And there were many, who had not believed the words of the prophets, who ^afell to the earth and became as if they were dead, for they knew that the great ^bplan of destruction which they had laid for those who believed in the words of the prophets had been frustrated; for the sign which had been given was already at hand.

17 And they began to know that the Son of God must shortly appear; yea, in fine, all the people upon the face of the whole earth from the ^awest to the east, both in the land north and in the land south, were so exceedingly astonished that they fell to the earth.

18 For they knew that the prophets had testified of these things for many years, and that the sign which had been given was already at hand; and they began to fear because of their iniquity and their unbelief.

19 And it came to pass that there was no darkness in all that night, but it was as light as though it was mid-day. And it came to pass that the sun did rise in the morning again, according to its proper order; and they knew that it was the day that the Lord should be ^aborn, because of the ^bsign which had been given.

20 And it had come to pass, yea, all things, every whit, according to the words of the prophets.

21 And it came to pass also that a new ^astar did appear, according to the word.

22 And it came to pass that from this time forth there began to be ^alyings sent forth among the people, by Satan, to harden their hearts, to the intent that they might not believe in those ^bsigns and wonders which they had seen; but notwithstanding these lyings and deceivings the ^cmore part of the people did believe, and were converted unto the Lord.

23 And it came to pass that Nephi went forth among the people, and also many others, baptizing unto repentance, in the which there was a great ^aremission of sins. And thus the people began again to have peace in the land.

24 And there were no contentions, save it were a few that began to preach, endeavoring to prove by the ^ascriptures that it was no more expedient to observe the law of Moses. Now in this thing they did err, having not understood the scriptures.

25 But it came to pass that they soon became converted, and were convinced of the error which they were in, for it was made known unto them that the law was not yet ^afulfilled, and that it must be fulfilled in every whit; yea, the word came unto them that it must be fulfilled; yea, that one jot or tittle should not pass away till it should all be fulfilled; therefore in this same year were they brought to a knowledge of their error and did ^bconfess their faults.

26 And thus the ninety and second

14d TG God, Will of.
  e D&C 93:4 (4, 14).
  f Mosiah 15:3.
15a Josh. 10:13.
  b Hel. 14:3.
16a Hel. 14:7.
  b 3 Ne. 1:9 (9, 11).
17a Hel. 11:20.

19a TG Jesus Christ, Birth of.
  b Hel. 14:3.
21a Matt. 2:2 (1–2);
    Hel. 14:5.
22a Moses 5:13.
  b TG Signs.
  c Hel. 16:6.
23a TG Remission of Sins.

24a Alma 34:13.
25a Matt. 5:18;
    2 Ne. 25:24.
  b Num. 5:7 (6–10);
    Mosiah 26:29 (29, 35);
    Alma 17:4.

year did pass away, bringing ^aglad tidings unto the people because of the signs which did come to pass, according to the words of the prophecy of all the holy prophets.

27 And it came to pass that the ninety and third year did also pass away in peace, save it were for the Gadianton robbers, who dwelt upon the ^amountains, who did infest the land; for so strong were their holds and their secret places that the people could not overpower them; therefore they did commit many murders, and did do much slaughter among the people.

28 And it came to pass that in the ninety and fourth year they began to increase in a great degree, because there were many dissenters of the Nephites who did flee unto them, which did cause much sorrow unto those Nephites who did remain in the land.

29 And there was also a cause of much sorrow among the Lamanites; for behold, they had many children who did grow up and began to wax strong in years, that they became for themselves, and were ^aled away by some who were ^bZoramites, by their lyings and their flattering words, to join those Gadianton robbers.

30 And thus were the Lamanites afflicted also, and began to decrease as to their faith and righteousness, because of the wickedness of the ^arising generation.

CHAPTER 2

Wickedness and abominations increase among the people—The Nephites and Lamanites unite to defend themselves against the Gadianton robbers—Converted Lamanites become white and are called Nephites. About A.D. 5–16.

AND it came to pass that thus passed away the ninety and fifth year also, and the people began to forget those ^asigns and wonders which they had heard, and began to be less and less astonished at a sign or a wonder from heaven, insomuch that they began to be hard in their hearts, and blind in their minds, and began to disbelieve all which they had heard and seen—

2 ^aImagining up some vain thing in their hearts, that it was wrought by men and by the power of the devil, to lead away and ^bdeceive the hearts of the people; and thus did Satan get possession of the hearts of the people again, insomuch that he did blind their eyes and lead them away to believe that the doctrine of Christ was a ^cfoolish and a vain thing.

3 And it came to pass that the people began to wax strong in wickedness and abominations; and they did not believe that there should be any more signs or wonders given; and Satan did ^ago about, leading away the hearts of the people, tempting them and causing them that they should do great wickedness in the land.

4 And thus did pass away the ninety and sixth year; and also the ninety and seventh year; and also the ninety and eighth year; and also the ninety and ninth year;

5 And also an hundred years had passed away since the days of ^aMosiah, who was king over the people of the Nephites.

6 And six hundred and nine years had passed away since Lehi left Jerusalem.

7 And nine years had passed away from the time when the sign was given, which was spoken of by the prophets, that Christ should come into the world.

8 Now the Nephites began to ^areckon their time from this period

26*a* Luke 2:10.
27*a* Hel. 11:31 (25–31);
  3 Ne. 2:11.
29*a* TG Peer Influence.
  b Alma 30:59; 43:4.
30*a* Judg. 2:10.
2 1*a* Hel. 14:6.
  2*a* Heb. 3:12.
  b TG Deceit.
  c 1 Cor. 1:23 (23–25);
Alma 30:13 (12–18).
3*a* Job 1:7;
  D&C 10:27.
5*a* Mosiah 29:46 (46–47).
8*a* 3 Ne. 5:7; 8:2.

when the sign was given, or from the coming of Christ; therefore, nine years had passed away.

9 And Nephi, who was the father of Nephi, who had the charge of the records, ^adid not return to the land of Zarahemla, and could nowhere be found in all the land.

10 And it came to pass that the people did still ^aremain in wickedness, notwithstanding the much preaching and prophesying which was sent among them; and thus passed away the tenth year also; and the eleventh year also passed away in iniquity.

11 And it came to pass in the thirteenth year there began to be wars and contentions throughout all the land; for the ^aGadianton robbers had become so ^bnumerous, and did slay so many of the people, and did lay waste so many cities, and did spread so much death and carnage throughout the land, that it became expedient that all the people, both the Nephites and the Lamanites, should take up arms against them.

12 Therefore, all the Lamanites who had become converted unto the Lord did unite with their brethren, the Nephites, and were compelled, for the ^asafety of their lives and their women and their children, to take up arms against those Gadianton robbers, yea, and also to maintain their rights, and the privileges of their church and of their worship, and their freedom and their ^bliberty.

13 And it came to pass that before this thirteenth year had passed away the Nephites were threatened with utter destruction because of this war, which had become exceedingly sore.

14 And it came to pass that those Lamanites who had united with the Nephites were numbered among the Nephites;

15 And their ^acurse was taken from them, and their skin became ^bwhite like unto the Nephites;

16 And their young men and their daughters became exceedingly fair, and they were numbered among the Nephites, and were called Nephites. And thus ended the thirteenth year.

17 And it came to pass in the commencement of the fourteenth year, the war between the robbers and the people of Nephi did continue and did become exceedingly sore; nevertheless, the people of Nephi did gain some advantage of the robbers, insomuch that they did drive them back out of their lands into the mountains and into their secret places.

18 And thus ended the fourteenth year. And in the fifteenth year they did come forth against the people of Nephi; and because of the wickedness of the people of Nephi, and their many contentions and dissensions, the Gadianton robbers did gain many advantages over them.

19 And thus ended the fifteenth year, and thus were the people in a state of many afflictions; and the ^asword of destruction did hang over them, insomuch that they were about to be smitten down by it, and this because of their iniquity.

CHAPTER 3

Giddianhi, the Gadianton leader, demands that Lachoneus and the Nephites surrender themselves and their lands—Lachoneus appoints Gidgiddoni as chief captain of the armies—The Nephites assemble in Zarahemla and Bountiful to defend themselves. About A.D. 16–18.

AND now it came to pass that in the sixteenth year from the coming of Christ, ^aLachoneus, the governor of the land, received an epistle from

9a 3 Ne. 1:3 (2–3).
10a Alma 34:35.
11a 3 Ne. 1:27.
  b Morm. 2:8.
12a Alma 58:12;

3 Ne. 3:2.
  b TG Liberty.
15a Alma 17:15; 23:18.
  b 2 Ne. 5:21; 30:6;
Jacob 3:8.

19a Alma 60:29;
Hel. 13:5;
3 Ne. 3:3.
3 1a 3 Ne. 1:1; 6:6.

the leader and the governor of this band of robbers; and these were the words which were written, saying:

2 Lachoneus, most noble and chief governor of the land, behold, I write this epistle unto you, and do give unto you exceedingly great praise because of your firmness, and also the firmness of your people, in ªmaintaining that which ye suppose to be your right and ᵇliberty; yea, ye do stand well, as if ye were supported by the hand of a god, in the defence of your liberty, and your property, and your country, or that which ye do call so.

3 And it seemeth a pity unto me, most noble Lachoneus, that ye should be so foolish and vain as to suppose that ye can stand against so many brave men who are at my command, who do now at this time stand in their arms, and do await with great anxiety for the word— Go down upon the Nephites and ªdestroy them.

4 And I, knowing of their unconquerable spirit, having proved them in the field of battle, and knowing of their everlasting hatred towards you because of the many wrongs which ye have done unto them, therefore if they should come down against you they would visit you with utter destruction.

5 Therefore I have written this epistle, sealing it with mine own hand, feeling for your welfare, because of your firmness in that which ye believe to be right, and your noble spirit in the field of battle.

6 Therefore I write unto you, desiring that ye would yield up unto this my people, your cities, your lands, and your possessions, rather than that they should visit you with the sword and that destruction should come upon you.

7 Or in other words, yield your-

selves up unto us, and unite with us and become acquainted with our ªsecret works, and become our brethren that ye may be like unto us—not our slaves, but our brethren and partners of all our substance.

8 And behold, I ªswear unto you, if ye will do this, with an oath, ye shall not be destroyed; but if ye will not do this, I swear unto you with an oath, that on the morrow month I will command that my armies shall come down against you, and they shall not stay their hand and shall spare not, but shall slay you, and shall let fall the sword upon you even until ye shall become extinct.

9 And behold, I am ªGiddianhi; and I am the governor of this the ᵇsecret society of Gadianton; which society and the works thereof I know to be ᶜgood; and they are of ᵈancient date and they have been handed down unto us.

10 And I write this epistle unto you, Lachoneus, and I hope that ye will deliver up your lands and your possessions, without the shedding of blood, that this my people may recover their rights and ªgovernment, who have dissented away from you because of your wickedness in retaining from them their rights of government, and except ye do this, I will avenge their wrongs. I am Giddianhi.

11 And now it came to pass when Lachoneus received this epistle he was exceedingly astonished, because of the boldness of Giddianhi demanding the possession of the land of the Nephites, and also of threatening the people and avenging the wrongs of those that had received no wrong, save it were they had ªwronged themselves by dissenting away unto those wicked and abominable robbers.

12 Now behold, this Lachoneus,

2a 3 Ne. 2:12.
  b TG Liberty.
3a 3 Ne. 2:19.
7a Hel. 6:22 (22–26).
8a Hel. 1:11;

Ether 8:14 (13–14).
9a 3 Ne. 4:14.
  b TG Secret Combinations.
  c Alma 30:53.
  d Hel. 6:26 (26–30);

Ether 8:9 (9–19);
  Moses 5:29 (29, 49–52).
10a TG Governments.
11a Hel. 14:30.

the governor, was a just man, and could not be frightened by the demands and the threatenings of a ᵃrobber; therefore he did not hearken to the epistle of Giddianhi, the governor of the robbers, but he did cause that his people should cry unto the Lord for ᵇstrength against the time that the robbers should come down against them.

13 Yea, he sent a proclamation among all the people, that they should ᵃgather together their women, and their children, their flocks and their herds, and all their substance, save it were their land, unto one place.

14 And he caused that ᵃfortifications should be built round about them, and the strength thereof should be exceedingly great. And he caused that armies, both of the Nephites and of the Lamanites, or of all them who were numbered among the Nephites, should be placed as guards round about to watch them, and to guard them from the robbers day and night.

15 Yea, he said unto them: As the Lord liveth, except ye repent of all your iniquities, and cry unto the Lord, ye will in nowise be ᵃdelivered out of the hands of those Gadianton robbers.

16 And so great and marvelous were the words and prophecies of Lachoneus that they did cause fear to come upon all the people; and they did exert themselves in their might to do according to the words of Lachoneus.

17 And it came to pass that Lachoneus did appoint chief captains over all the armies of the Nephites, to command them at the time that the robbers should come down out of the wilderness against them.

18 Now the chiefest among all the chief captains and the great commander of all the armies of the Nephites was appointed, and his name was ᵃGidgiddoni.

19 Now it was the custom among all the Nephites to appoint for their chief captains, (save it were in their times of wickedness) some one that had the ᵃspirit of revelation and also prophecy; therefore, this Gidgiddoni was a great prophet among them, as also was the chief judge.

20 Now the people said unto Gidgiddoni: ᵃPray unto the Lord, and let us go up upon the mountains and into the wilderness, that we may fall upon the robbers and destroy them in their own lands.

21 But Gidgiddoni saith unto them: The Lord ᵃforbid; for if we should go up against them the Lord would ᵇdeliver us into their hands; therefore we will prepare ourselves in the center of our lands, and we will gather all our armies together, and we will not go against them, but we will wait till they shall come against us; therefore as the Lord liveth, if we do this he will deliver them into our hands.

22 And it came to pass in the seventeenth year, in the latter end of the year, the proclamation of Lachoneus had gone forth throughout all the face of the land, and they had taken their ᵃhorses, and their chariots, and their cattle, and all their flocks, and their herds, and their grain, and all their substance, and did march forth by thousands and by tens of thousands, until they had all gone forth to the ᵇplace which ᶜhad been appointed that they should gather themselves together, to defend themselves against their enemies.

23 And the ᵃland which was

12a 1 Kgs. 20:3 (2–3);
    Alma 54:7 (5–11).
  b TG Strength.
13a 3 Ne. 3:22; 4:1.
14a Morm. 2:4.
15a TG Deliver;
    Protection, Divine.

18a 3 Ne. 4:13 (13, 24, 26); 6:6.
19a TG Guidance, Divine.
20a Alma 16:6 (5–8);
    43:23 (23–24); 48:16.
21a Alma 43:46 (46–47);
    48:14;
    Morm. 3:10 (10–11).

  b 1 Sam. 14:12;
    2 Kgs. 3:18;
    1 Ne. 3:29.
22a 3 Ne. 4:4.
  b Morm. 2:7.
  c 3 Ne. 3:13.
23a 3 Ne. 4:16.

appointed was the land of Zarahemla, and the land which was between the land Zarahemla and the land *b*Bountiful, yea, to the line which was between the *c*land Bountiful and the land Desolation.

24 And there were a great many thousand people who were called Nephites, who did gather themselves together in this land. Now Lachoneus did cause that they should gather themselves together in the land *a*southward, because of the great curse which was upon the *b*land northward.

25 And they did fortify themselves against their enemies; and they did dwell in one land, and in one body, and they did fear the words which had been spoken by Lachoneus, insomuch that they did repent of all their sins; and they did put up their *a*prayers unto the Lord their God, that he would deliver them in the time that their enemies should come down against them to battle.

26 And they were exceedingly sorrowful because of their enemies. And Gidgiddoni did cause that they should make *a*weapons of war of every kind, and they should be strong with armor, and with shields, and with bucklers, after the manner of his instruction.

CHAPTER 4

The Nephite armies defeat the Gadianton robbers—Giddianhi is slain, and his successor, Zemnarihah, is hanged—The Nephites praise the Lord for their victories. About A.D. *19–22.*

AND it came to pass that in the latter end of the eighteenth year those armies of *a*robbers had prepared for battle, and began to come down and to sally forth from the hills, and out of the mountains, and the wilderness, and their strongholds, and their *b*secret places, and began to take possession of the lands, both which were in the land south and which were in the land north, and began to take possession of all the lands which had been *c*deserted by the Nephites, and the cities which had been left desolate.

2 But behold, there were no wild beasts nor *a*game in those lands which had been deserted by the Nephites, and there was no game for the robbers save it were in the wilderness.

3 And the robbers could not exist save it were in the wilderness, for the want of food; for the Nephites had left their lands desolate, and had gathered their flocks and their herds and all their substance, and they were in one body.

4 Therefore, there was no chance for the robbers to plunder and to obtain food, save it were to come up in open battle against the Nephites; and the Nephites being in one body, and having so great a number, and having reserved for themselves provisions, and *a*horses and cattle, and flocks of every kind, that they might subsist for the space of *b*seven years, in the which time they did hope to destroy the robbers from off the face of the land; and thus the eighteenth year did pass away.

5 And it came to pass that in the nineteenth year Giddianhi found that it was expedient that he should go up to battle against the Nephites, for there was *a*no way that they could subsist save it were to plunder and rob and murder.

6 And they durst not spread themselves upon the face of the land insomuch that they could raise grain, lest the Nephites should come upon

23b Alma 22:29;
   3 Ne. 11:1.
  c Morm. 3:7; 4:2.
24a Alma 46:17;
   Morm. 3:5.
  b Alma 22:31 (30–31).
25a TG Trust in God.

26a 2 Ne. 5:14; Jarom 1:8;
   Mosiah 10:8;
   Alma 2:12;
   Hel. 1:14.
4 1a Hel. 2:13 (11–13).
  b Alma 58:6.
  c 3 Ne. 3:13 (13–14, 22).

2a 1 Ne. 18:25;
   2 Ne. 5:24;
   3 Ne. 4:20.
4a 3 Ne. 3:22; 6:1 (1–2).
  b Gen. 41:36 (29–36);
   3 Ne. 4:18.
5a Alma 47:36.

them and slay them; therefore Giddianhi gave commandment unto his armies that in this year they should go up to battle against the Nephites.

7 And it came to pass that they did come up to battle; and it was in the sixth month; and behold, great and terrible was the day that they did come up to battle; and they were girded about after the manner of robbers; and they had a lamb-skin about their loins, and they were dyed in blood, and their heads were shorn, and they had head-plates upon them; and great and terrible was the appearance of the armies of Giddianhi, because of their armor, and because of their being dyed in blood.

8 And it came to pass that the armies of the Nephites, when they saw the appearance of the army of Giddianhi, had all fallen to the earth, and did lift their cries to the Lord their God, that he would spare them and deliver them out of the hands of their enemies.

9 And it came to pass that when the armies of Giddianhi saw this they began to shout with a loud voice, because of their joy, for they had supposed that the Nephites had fallen with fear because of the terror of their armies.

10 But in this thing they were disappointed, for the Nephites did not ^afear them; but they did fear their God and did supplicate him for ^bprotection; therefore, when the armies of Giddianhi did rush upon them they were prepared to meet them; yea, in the strength of the Lord they did receive them.

11 And the battle commenced in this the sixth month; and great and terrible was the battle thereof, yea, great and terrible was the ^aslaughter thereof, insomuch that there never was known so great a slaughter among all the people of Lehi since he left Jerusalem.

12 And notwithstanding the ^athreatenings and the oaths which Giddianhi had made, behold, the Nephites did beat them, insomuch that they did fall back from before them.

13 And it came to pass that ^aGidgiddoni commanded that his armies should pursue them as far as the borders of the wilderness, and that they should not spare any that should fall into their hands by the way; and thus they did pursue them and did slay them, to the borders of the wilderness, even until they had fulfilled the commandment of Gidgiddoni.

14 And it came to pass that Giddianhi, who had stood and fought with boldness, was pursued as he fled; and being weary because of his much fighting he was overtaken and slain. And thus was the end of Giddianhi the robber.

15 And it came to pass that the armies of the Nephites did return again to their place of security. And it came to pass that this nineteenth year did pass away, and the robbers did not come again to battle; neither did they come again in the twentieth year.

16 And in the twenty and first year they did not come up to battle, but they came up on all sides to lay siege round about the people of Nephi; for they did suppose that if they should cut off the people of Nephi from their ^alands, and should hem them in on every side, and if they should cut them off from all their outward privileges, that they could cause them to yield themselves up according to their wishes.

17 Now they had appointed unto themselves another leader, whose name was Zemnarihah; therefore it was Zemnarihah that did cause that this siege should take place.

18 But behold, this was an advantage to the Nephites; for it was impossible for the robbers to lay

---

10a TG Reverence.
  b Jer. 17:17 (17–18).

11a Alma 28:11 (8–12).
12a 3 Ne. 3:8 (4–10).

13a 3 Ne. 3:18.
16a 3 Ne. 3:23.

siege sufficiently long to have any effect upon the Nephites, because of their ^amuch ^bprovision which they had laid up in store,

19 And because of the scantiness of provisions among the robbers; for behold, they had nothing save it were meat for their subsistence, which meat they did obtain in the wilderness;

20 And it came to pass that the ^awild game became scarce in the wilderness insomuch that the robbers were about to perish with hunger.

21 And the Nephites were continually marching out by day and by night, and falling upon their armies, and cutting them off by thousands and by tens of thousands.

22 And thus it became the desire of the people of Zemnarihah to withdraw from their design, because of the great destruction which came upon them by night and by day.

23 And it came to pass that Zemnarihah did give command unto his people that they should withdraw themselves from the siege, and march into the furthermost parts of the land northward.

24 And now, Gidgiddoni being aware of their design, and knowing of their weakness because of the want of food, and the great slaughter which had been made among them, therefore he did send out his armies in the night-time, and did cut off the way of their retreat, and did place his armies in the way of their retreat.

25 And this did they do in the night-time, and got on their march beyond the robbers, so that on the morrow, when the robbers began their march, they were met by the armies of the Nephites both in their front and in their rear.

26 And the robbers who were on the south were also cut off in their places of retreat. And all these things were done by command of Gidgiddoni.

27 And there were many thousands who did yield themselves up prisoners unto the Nephites, and the remainder of them were slain.

28 And their leader, Zemnarihah, was taken and hanged upon a tree, yea, even upon the top thereof until he was dead. And when they had hanged him until he was dead they did fell the tree to the earth, and did cry with a loud voice, saying:

29 May the Lord preserve his people in righteousness and in holiness of heart, that they may cause to be felled to the earth all who shall seek to slay them because of power and secret combinations, even as this man hath been felled to the earth.

30 And they did rejoice and cry again with one voice, saying: May the ^aGod of Abraham, and the God of Isaac, and the God of Jacob, protect this people in righteousness, so long as they shall ^bcall on the name of their God for ^cprotection.

31 And it came to pass that they did break forth, all as one, in singing, and ^apraising their God for the great thing which he had done for them, in preserving them from falling into the hands of their enemies.

32 Yea, they did cry: Hosanna to the Most High God. And they did cry: Blessed be the name of the Lord God ^aAlmighty, the Most High God.

33 And their hearts were swollen with joy, unto the gushing out of many tears, because of the great goodness of God in delivering them out of the hands of their enemies; and they knew it was because of their repentance and their humility that they had been delivered from an everlasting destruction.

18a 3 Ne. 4:4.
  b Gen. 41:36 (33–57);
     D&C 4:4.
20a 1 Ne. 18:25;
     2 Ne. 5:24;

       3 Ne. 4:2.
30a Alma 29:11.
  b Gen. 4:26;
     Ether 4:15;
     Moro. 2:2.

         c TG Protection, Divine.
31a Alma 26:8.
     TG Thanksgiving.
32a 1 Ne. 1:14.

CHAPTER 5

The Nephites repent and forsake their sins—Mormon writes the history of his people and declares the everlasting word to them—Israel will be gathered in from her long dispersion. About A.D. 22–26.

AND now behold, there was not a living soul among all the people of the Nephites who did ^adoubt in the least the words of all the holy prophets who had spoken; for they knew that it must needs be that they must be fulfilled.

2 And they knew that it must be expedient that Christ had come, because of the many signs which had been given, according to the words of the prophets; and because of the things which had come to pass already they knew that it must needs be that all things should come to pass according to that which had been spoken.

3 Therefore they did forsake all their sins, and their abominations, and their whoredoms, and did serve God with all diligence day and night.

4 And now it came to pass that when they had taken all the robbers prisoners, insomuch that none did escape who were not slain, they did cast their prisoners into prison, and did cause the word of God to be preached unto them; and as many as would repent of their sins and ^aenter into a ^bcovenant that they would murder no more were set at ^cliberty.

5 But as many as there were who did not enter into a covenant, and who did still continue to have those ^asecret murders in their hearts, yea, as many as were found breathing out threatenings against their brethren were condemned and punished according to the law.

6 And thus they did put an end to all those wicked, and secret, and abominable combinations, in the which there was so much wickedness, and so many murders committed.

7 And thus had the ^atwenty and second year passed away, and the twenty and third year also, and the twenty and fourth, and the twenty and fifth; and thus had twenty and five years passed away.

8 And there had many things transpired which, in the eyes of some, would be great and marvelous; nevertheless, they cannot all be written in this book; yea, this book cannot contain even a ^ahundredth part of what was done among so many people in the space of twenty and five years;

9 But behold there are ^arecords which do contain ^ball the proceedings of this people; and a ^cshorter but true account was given by Nephi.

10 Therefore I have made my ^arecord of these things according to the record of Nephi, which was engraven on the plates which were called the ^bplates of Nephi.

11 And behold, I do make the record on plates which I have made with mine own hands.

12 And behold, I am called ^aMormon, being called after the ^bland of Mormon, the land in which Alma did establish the church among the people, yea, the first church which was established among them after their transgression.

13 Behold, I am a disciple of Jesus Christ, the Son of God. I have been ^acalled of him to declare his word among his people, that they might have everlasting life.

14 And it hath become expedient that I, according to the will of God, that the prayers of those who have

5 1*a* TG Doubt.
4*a* 3 Ne. 6:3.
  b Alma 44:15; 62:16 (16–17).
  c TG Liberty.
5*a* 2 Ne. 10:15.
7*a* 3 Ne. 2:8.
8*a* W of M 1:5;

3 Ne. 26:6 (6–12).
9*a* Hel. 3:15 (13–15).
  b W of M 1:5;
    Alma 13:31.
  c Morm. 2:18.
10*a* Hel. 2:14.
  b W of M 1:1;

Morm. 1:4 (1–4);
    2:17 (17–18);
    8:5 (1, 4–5, 14).
12*a* W of M 1:11.
  b Mosiah 18:4;
    Alma 5:3.
13*a* 3 Ne. 30:1; Moro. 7:2.

gone hence, who were the holy ones, should be fulfilled according to their faith, should make a ªrecord of these things which have been done—

15 Yea, a ªsmall record of that which hath taken place from the time that Lehi left Jerusalem, even down until the present time.

16 Therefore I do make my record from the accounts which have been given by those who were before me, until the commencement of my day;

17 And then I do make a ªrecord of the things which I have seen with mine own eyes.

18 And I know the record which I make to be a just and a true record; nevertheless there are many things which, according to our ªlanguage, we are not able to ᵇwrite.

19 And now I make an end of my saying, which is of myself, and proceed to give my account of the things which have been before me.

20 I am Mormon, and a pure ªdescendant of Lehi. I have reason to bless my God and my Savior Jesus Christ, that he brought our fathers out of the land of Jerusalem, (and ᵇno one knew it save it were himself and those whom he brought out of that land) and that he hath given me and my people so much knowledge unto the salvation of our souls.

21 Surely he hath ªblessed the house of ᵇJacob, and hath been ᶜmerciful unto the seed of Joseph.

22 And ªinsomuch as the children of Lehi have kept his commandments he hath blessed them and prospered them according to his word.

23 Yea, and surely shall he again bring a ªremnant of the seed of Joseph to the ᵇknowledge of the Lord their God.

24 And as surely as the Lord liveth, will he ªgather in from the four quarters of the earth all the remnant of the ᵇseed of Jacob, who are scattered abroad upon all the face of the earth.

25 And as he hath ªcovenanted with all the house of Jacob, even so shall the covenant wherewith he hath covenanted with the house of Jacob be fulfilled in his own due time, unto the ᵇrestoring all the house of Jacob unto the knowledge of the covenant that he hath covenanted with them.

26 And then shall they ªknow their Redeemer, who is Jesus Christ, the Son of God; and then shall they be gathered in from the four quarters of the earth unto their own lands, from whence they have been dispersed; yea, as the Lord liveth so shall it be. Amen.

CHAPTER 6

The Nephites prosper—Pride, wealth, and class distinctions arise—The Church is rent with dissensions—Satan leads the people in open rebellion—Many prophets cry repentance and are slain—Their murderers conspire to take over the government. About A.D. 26–30.

AND now it came to pass that the people of the Nephites did all return to their own lands in the twenty and sixth year, every man, with his family, his flocks and his herds, his ªhorses and his cattle, and all

14a Enos 1:16 (13–18);
    D&C 3:19;
    10:47 (46–50).
15a Morm. 7:9; 8:12.
17a W of M 1:5;
    Morm. 1:1.
18a TG Language.
  b 3 Ne. 19:32 (32–34);
    Morm. 9:33 (32–33);
    Ether 12:25 (24–25);
    D&C 76:116.
20a Morm. 1:5; 8:13.

  b 1 Ne. 4:36;
    3 Ne. 15:14.
21a TG Israel, Blessings of.
  b Gen. 32:28 (24–32);
    Ps. 135:4;
    D&C 49:24 (23–25).
  c Ps. 98:3.
22a 2 Ne. 1:20;
    Jarom 1:9;
    Omni 1:6;
    Mosiah 1:7;
    Alma 9:13 (13–14); 37:13.

23a Alma 46:24;
    3 Ne. 10:17.
  b 2 Ne. 3:12;
    Morm. 7:5 (5, 10).
24a TG Israel, Gathering of.
  b Gen. 46:8.
25a 3 Ne. 15:8; 16:5.
  b 2 Ne. 30:3 (1–6);
    3 Ne. 16:13 (6–13).
26a 2 Ne. 30:7 (7–8);
    3 Ne. 20:31 (29–34).
6 1a 3 Ne. 3:22 (21–23).

things whatsoever did belong unto them.

2 And it came to pass that they had *not eaten up all their provisions; therefore they did take with them all that they had not devoured, of all their grain of every kind, and their gold, and their silver, and all their precious things, and they did return to their own lands and their possessions, both on the north and on the south, both on the land northward and on the land southward.

3 And they granted unto those robbers who had *entered into a covenant to keep the peace of the land, who were desirous to remain Lamanites, lands, according to their numbers, that they might have, with their labors, wherewith to subsist upon; and thus they did establish peace in all the land.

4 And they began again to prosper and to wax great; and the twenty and sixth and seventh years passed away, and there was great *order in the land; and they had formed their laws according to equity and justice.

5 And now there was nothing in all the land to hinder the people from prospering continually, except they should fall into transgression.

6 And now it was *Gidgiddoni, and the judge, *Lachoneus, and those who had been appointed leaders, who had established this great peace in the land.

7 And it came to pass that there were many cities built anew, and there were many old cities repaired.

8 And there were many *highways cast up, and many roads made, which led from city to city, and from land to land, and from place to place.

9 And thus passed away the twenty and eighth year, and the people had continual peace.

10 But it came to pass in the twenty and ninth year there began to be some disputings among the people; and some were lifted up unto pride and *boastings because of their exceedingly great riches, yea, even unto great persecutions;

11 For there were many *merchants in the land, and also many *lawyers, and many officers.

12 And the people began to be distinguished by ranks, according to their *riches and their chances for learning; yea, some were *ignorant because of their poverty, and others did receive great *learning because of their riches.

13 Some were lifted up in pride, and others were exceedingly humble; some did return railing for railing, while others would receive railing and *persecution and all manner of *afflictions, and would not turn and *revile again, but were humble and penitent before God.

14 And thus there became a great inequality in all the land, insomuch that the church began to be broken up; yea, insomuch that in the thirtieth year the church was broken up in all the land save it were among a few of the Lamanites who were converted unto the true faith; and *they would not depart from it, for they were firm, and steadfast, and immovable, willing with all *diligence to keep the commandments of the Lord.

15 Now the cause of this iniquity of the people was this—*Satan had great *power, unto the stirring up of the people to do all manner of iniquity, and to the puffing them up

2a 3 Ne. 4:4.
3a 3 Ne. 5:4.
4a TG Order.
6a 3 Ne. 3:18.
  b 3 Ne. 3:1.
8a 3 Ne. 8:13.
10a TG Boast.
11a Hel. 6:8.
  b Alma 10:14 (14–17, 27);

14:5 (5, 18–27).
12a 1 Tim. 6:17;
  Hel. 4:12 (11–13).
  b TG Ignorance.
  c TG Learn.
13a TG Persecution.
  b TG Affliction.
  c 3 Ne. 12:39;
  4 Ne. 1:34;

D&C 98:23 (23–27).
  TG Reviling.
14a Alma 23:6; 27:27;
  Hel. 15:8 (5–16).
  b TG Dedication;
  Diligence.
15a Moses 6:15.
  b 1 Ne. 22:26;
  Alma 48:17.

with pride, tempting them to seek for power, and authority, and ^criches, and the vain things of the world.

16 And thus Satan did lead away the hearts of the people to do all manner of iniquity; therefore they had enjoyed peace but a few years.

17 And thus, in the commencement of the thirtieth year—the people having been ^adelivered up for the space of a long time to be carried about by the ^btemptations of the devil whithersoever he desired to carry them, and to do whatsoever iniquity he desired they should— and thus in the commencement of this, the thirtieth year, they were in a state of awful wickedness.

18 Now they did not sin ^aignorantly, for they knew the ^bwill of God concerning them, for it had been taught unto them; therefore they did wilfully ^crebel against God.

19 And now it was in the days of Lachoneus, the son of ^aLachoneus, for Lachoneus did fill the seat of his father and did govern the people that year.

20 And there began to be men ^ainspired from heaven and sent forth, standing among the people in all the land, preaching and testifying boldly of the sins and iniquities of the people, and testifying unto them concerning the redemption which the Lord would make for his people, or in other words, the resurrection of Christ; and they did testify boldly of his ^bdeath and sufferings.

21 Now there were many of the people who were exceedingly angry because of those who testified of these things; and those who were angry were chiefly the chief judges, and they who ^ahad been high priests and lawyers; yea, all those who were lawyers were angry with those who testified of these things.

22 Now there was no lawyer nor judge nor high priest that could have power to condemn any one to death save their condemnation was signed by the governor of the land.

23 Now there were many of those ^awho testified of the things pertaining to Christ who testified boldly, who were taken and put to death ^bsecretly by the judges, that the knowledge of their death came not unto the governor of the land until after their death.

24 Now behold, this was contrary to the laws of the land, that any man should be put to death except they had power from the governor of the land—

25 Therefore a complaint came up unto the land of Zarahemla, to the governor of the land, against these judges who had condemned the prophets of the Lord unto ^adeath, not according to the law.

26 Now it came to pass that they were taken and brought up before the judge, to be judged of the crime which they had done, according to the ^alaw which had been given by the people.

27 Now it came to pass that those judges had many friends and kindreds; and the remainder, yea, even almost all the lawyers and the high priests, did gather themselves together, and unite with the kindreds of those judges who were to be tried according to the law.

28 And they did enter into a ^acovenant one with another, yea, even into that covenant which was given by them of old, which covenant was given and administered by the ^bdevil, to combine against all righteousness.

15c TG Selfishness.
17a Moses 5:23.
  b TG Temptation.
18a Num. 15:27 (2–29);
    Mosiah 3:11.
    TG Ignorance.
  b TG God, Will of.
  c TG Rebellion.
19a 3 Ne. 1:1.

20a TG Inspiration;
    Prophets, Mission of.
  b TG Jesus Christ,
    Death of.
21a D&C 121:37.
    TG Apostasy of
    Individuals.
23a 3 Ne. 7:14.
  b Hel. 6:17 (17–38).

25a 3 Ne. 9:9.
26a Mosiah 29:25;
    Alma 1:14.
28a TG Secret
    Combinations.
  b Hel. 6:26;
    Ether 8:9 (9, 15–16).

29 Therefore they did combine against the people of the Lord, and enter into a covenant to destroy them, and to deliver those who were guilty of murder from the grasp of justice, which was about to be administered according to the law.

30 And they did set at defiance the law and the rights of their country; and they did covenant one with another to destroy the governor, and to establish a ^aking over the land, that the land should no more be at ^bliberty but should be subject unto kings.

CHAPTER 7

The chief judge is murdered, the government is destroyed, and the people divide into tribes—Jacob, an anti-Christ, becomes king of a secret combination—Nephi preaches repentance and faith in Christ—Angels minister to him daily, and he raises his brother from the dead—Many repent and are baptized. About A.D. 30–33.

Now behold, I will show unto you that they did not establish a king over the land; but in this same year, yea, the thirtieth year, they did destroy upon the judgment-seat, yea, did murder the chief judge of the land.

2 And the people were divided one against another; and they did ^aseparate one from another into tribes, every man according to his family and his kindred and friends; and thus they did destroy the government of the land.

3 And every tribe did appoint a chief or a leader over them; and thus they became tribes and leaders of tribes.

4 Now behold, there was no man among them save he had much family and many kindreds and friends; therefore their tribes became exceedingly great.

5 Now all this was done, and there were no wars as yet among them; and all this iniquity had come upon the people ^abecause they did ^byield themselves unto the power of Satan.

6 And the regulations of the government were destroyed, because of the ^asecret combination of the friends and kindreds of those who murdered the prophets.

7 And they did cause a great contention in the land, insomuch that the more righteous part of the people had nearly all become wicked; yea, there were but few righteous men among them.

8 And thus six years had not passed away since the more part of the people had turned from their righteousness, like the dog to his ^avomit, or like the sow to her wallowing in the mire.

9 Now this secret combination, which had brought so great iniquity upon the people, did gather themselves together, and did place at their head a man whom they did call Jacob;

10 And they did call him their king; therefore he became a king over this wicked band; and he was one of the chiefest who had given his voice against the prophets who testified of Jesus.

11 And it came to pass that they were not so strong in number as the tribes of the people, who were united together save it were their leaders did establish their laws, every one according to his tribe; nevertheless they were enemies; notwithstanding they were not a righteous people, yet they were united in the hatred of those who had entered into a covenant to ^adestroy the government.

12 Therefore, Jacob seeing that their enemies were more numerous than they, he being the king of the band, therefore he commanded his

---

30a 1 Sam. 8:5;
    Alma 51:5;
    3 Ne. 7:12.
    TG Tyranny.
  b TG Liberty.

7 2a TG Unity.
  5a Moses 4:6.
    b Rom. 6:16 (13–20);
    Alma 10:25.
  6a 2 Ne. 9:9.

8a Prov. 26:11;
  2 Pet. 2:22.
11a 3 Ne. 9:9.

people that they should take their flight into the northernmost part of the land, and there build up unto themselves a ^akingdom, until they were joined by dissenters, (for he flattered them that there would be many dissenters) and they become sufficiently strong to contend with the tribes of the people; and they did so.

13 And so speedy was their march that it could not be impeded until they had gone forth out of the reach of the people. And thus ended the thirtieth year; and thus were the affairs of the people of Nephi.

14 And it came to pass in the thirty and first year that they were divided into tribes, every man according to his family, kindred and friends; nevertheless they had come to an agreement that they would not go to war one with another; but they were not united as to their laws, and their manner of government, for they were established according to the minds of those who were their chiefs and their leaders. But they did establish very strict laws that one tribe should not trespass against another, insomuch that in some degree they had peace in the land; nevertheless, their hearts were turned from the Lord their God, and they did stone the ^aprophets and did cast them out from among them.

15 And it came to pass that ^aNephi—having been visited by angels and also the voice of the Lord, therefore having seen angels, and being eye-witness, and having had power given unto him that he might know concerning the ministry of Christ, and also being eye-witness to their quick return from righteousness unto their wickedness and abominations;

16 Therefore, being ^agrieved for the hardness of their hearts and the blindness of their minds—went forth among them in that same year, and began to testify, boldly, repentance and remission of sins through faith on the Lord Jesus Christ.

17 And he did minister many things unto them; and all of them cannot be written, and a part of them would not suffice, therefore they are not written in this book. And Nephi did minister with ^apower and with great authority.

18 And it came to pass that they were angry with him, even because he had greater power than they, for it were ^anot possible that they could disbelieve his words, for so great was his faith on the Lord Jesus Christ that angels did minister unto him daily.

19 And in the name of Jesus did he cast out devils and ^aunclean spirits; and even his ^bbrother did he ^craise from the dead, after he had been stoned and suffered death by the people.

20 And the people saw it, and did witness of it, and were angry with him because of his power; and he did also do ^amany more miracles, in the sight of the people, in the name of Jesus.

21 And it came to pass that the thirty and first year did pass away, and there were but few who were converted unto the Lord; but as many as were converted did truly signify unto the people that they had been ^avisited by the power and ^bSpirit of God, which was in Jesus Christ, in whom they believed.

22 And as many as had devils cast out from them, and were ^ahealed of their sicknesses and their infirmities, did truly manifest unto the

---

12a 3 Ne. 6:30.
14a 3 Ne. 6:23 (23–25).
15a 3 Ne. 1:2 (2–3, 10); 11:18.
16a Gen. 6:6;
    1 Ne. 2:18;
    Alma 31:24;
    Moses 8:25.

17a TG Priesthood,
    Power of.
18a Alma 4:19.
19a TG Spirits, Evil or
    Unclean.
  b 3 Ne. 19:4.
  c TG Death, Power over.

20a 3 Ne. 8:1.
21a TG God, Manifesta-
    tions of.
  b TG God, Spirit of.
22a Mark 2:11 (11–12);
    Acts 8:7.

people that they had been wrought upon by the Spirit of God, and had been healed; and they did show forth signs also and did do some miracles among the people.

23 Thus passed away the thirty and second year also. And Nephi did cry unto the people in the commencement of the thirty and third year; and he did preach unto them repentance and remission of sins.

24 Now I would have you to remember also, that there were none who were brought unto ᵃrepentance who were not baptized with water.

25 Therefore, there were ordained of Nephi, men unto this ministry, that all such as should come unto them should be ᵃbaptized with water, and this as a witness and a testimony before God, and unto the people, that they had repented and received a ᵇremission of their sins.

26 And there were many in the commencement of this year that were baptized unto repentance; and thus the more part of the year did pass away.

CHAPTER 8

Tempests, earthquakes, fires, whirlwinds, and physical upheavals attest the crucifixion of Christ—Many people are destroyed—Darkness covers the land for three days—Those who remain bemoan their fate. About A.D. *33–34.*

AND now it came to pass that according to our record, and we know our record to be ᵃtrue, for behold, it was a ᵇjust man who did keep the record—for he truly did ᶜmany ᵈmiracles in the ᵉname of Jesus; and

there was not any man who could do a miracle in the name of Jesus save he were cleansed every whit from his iniquity—

2 And now it came to pass, if there was no mistake made by this man in the reckoning of our time, the ᵃthirty and third year had passed away;

3 And the people began to look with great earnestness for the sign which had been given by the prophet Samuel, the Lamanite, yea, for the time that there should be ᵃdarkness for the space of three days over the face of the land.

4 And there began to be great ᵃdoubtings and ᵇdisputations among the people, notwithstanding so many signs had been given.

5 And it came to pass in the ᵃthirty and fourth year, in the first month, on the fourth day of the month, there arose a great ᵇstorm, such an one as never had been known in all the land.

6 And there was also a great and terrible tempest; and there was terrible ᵃthunder, insomuch that it did ᵇshake the whole earth as if it was about to divide asunder.

7 And there were exceedingly sharp lightnings, such as never had been known in all the land.

8 And the ᵃcity of Zarahemla did take fire.

9 And the city of ᵃMoroni did ᵇsink into the depths of the sea, and the inhabitants thereof were drowned.

10 And the earth was carried up upon the city of ᵃMoronihah, that in the place of the city there became a great ᵇmountain.

24a TG Baptism,
   Qualifications for.
25a TG Baptism.
   b D&C 20:37.
   TG Remission of Sins.
8 1a John 21:24.
   b 3 Ne. 23:7.
   c 3 Ne. 7:20 (19–20).
   d John 6:14;
   Morm. 9:18 (18–19).
   e Acts 3:6 (6–16);

Jacob 4:6.
2a 3 Ne. 2:8.
3a 1 Ne. 19:10;
   Hel. 14:27 (20, 27);
   3 Ne. 10:9.
   TG Darkness, Physical.
4a TG Doubt.
   b TG Disputations.
5a Hel. 14:20 (20–27);
   3 Ne. 11:2.
   b TG Jesus Christ,

Crucifixion of;
   Jesus Christ, Death of.
6a 1 Ne. 19:11;
   Hel. 14:21 (20–27).
   b Matt. 27:51 (45, 50–51).
8a 4 Ne. 1:7–8.
9a Alma 50:13.
   b 3 Ne. 9:4 (4–5).
10a 3 Ne. 8:25.
   b Hel. 12:17;
   3 Ne. 9:8 (6–8).

11 And there was a great and terrible destruction in the land southward.

12 But behold, there was a more great and terrible destruction in the land northward; for behold, the [a]whole face of the land was changed, because of the tempest and the whirlwinds, and the thunderings and the lightnings, and the exceedingly great quaking of the whole earth;

13 And the [a]highways were broken up, and the level roads were spoiled, and many smooth places became rough.

14 And many [a]great and notable cities were [b]sunk, and many were [c]burned, and many were shaken till the buildings thereof had fallen to the earth, and the inhabitants thereof were slain, and the places were left desolate.

15 And there were some cities which remained; but the damage thereof was exceedingly great, and there were many in them who were slain.

16 And there were some who were carried away in the [a]whirlwind; and whither they went no man knoweth, save they know that they were carried away.

17 And thus the face of the whole earth became deformed, because of the tempests, and the thunderings, and the lightnings, and the quaking of the earth.

18 And behold, the rocks were rent in twain; they were broken up upon the face of the whole earth, insomuch that they were [a]found in broken fragments, and in seams and in cracks, upon all the face of the land.

19 And it came to pass that when the thunderings, and the lightnings, and the storm, and the tempest, and the quakings of the earth did cease—for behold, they did last for about the space of [a]three [b]hours; and it was said by some that the time was greater; nevertheless, all these great and terrible things were done in about the space of three hours—and then behold, there was [c]darkness upon the face of the land.

20 And it came to pass that there was thick darkness upon all the face of the land, insomuch that the inhabitants thereof who had not fallen could [a]feel the [b]vapor of darkness;

21 And there could be no light, because of the darkness, neither candles, neither torches; neither could there be fire kindled with their fine and exceedingly dry wood, so that there could not be any light at all;

22 And there was not any light seen, neither fire, nor glimmer, neither the sun, nor the moon, nor the stars, for so great were the mists of darkness which were upon the face of the land.

23 And it came to pass that it did last for the space of three days that there was no light seen; and there was great mourning and [a]howling and weeping among all the people continually; yea, great were the groanings of the people, because of the darkness and the great destruction which had come upon them.

24 And in one place they were heard to cry, saying: O that we had repented [a]before this great and terrible day, and then would our brethren have been spared, and they would not have been [b]burned in that great city Zarahemla.

25 And in another place they were heard to cry and mourn, saying: O that we had repented before this great and terrible day, and had not killed and stoned the prophets, and cast them out; then would our

12a 3 Ne. 11:1.
13a Hel. 14:24;
     3 Ne. 6:8.
14a 3 Ne. 9:12; 10:4.
  b 1 Ne. 12:4.
  c 2 Ne. 26:4;
     3 Ne. 9:3 (3–9).
16a Dan. 11:40;
     3 Ne. 10:13 (13–14).
18a Hel. 14:22 (21–22).
19a Luke 23:44 (44–45).
  b Alma 18:14.
  c 1 Ne. 19:10;
     3 Ne. 10:9.
20a Ex. 10:21.
  b 1 Ne. 12:5; 19:11.
23a 3 Ne. 10:8 (2, 8).
24a TG Procrastination.
  b Hel. 13:12;
     3 Ne. 9:3.

mothers and our fair daughters, and our children have been spared, and not have been buried up in that great city ᵃMoronihah. And thus were the howlings of the people great and terrible.

CHAPTER 9

In the darkness, the voice of Christ proclaims the destruction of many people and cities for their wickedness—He also proclaims His divinity, announces that the law of Moses is fulfilled, and invites men to come unto Him and be saved. About A.D. 34.

AND it came to pass that there was a ᵃvoice heard among all the inhabitants of the earth, upon all the face of this land, crying:

2 Wo, wo, wo unto this people; wo unto the inhabitants of the whole earth except they shall ᵃrepent; for the devil ᵇlaugheth, and his angels rejoice, because of the slain of the fair sons and daughters of my people; and it is because of their iniquity and abominations that they are fallen!

3 Behold, that great city Zarahemla have I ᵃburned with fire, and the inhabitants thereof.

4 And behold, that great city Moroni have I caused to be ᵃsunk in the depths of the sea, and the inhabitants thereof to be drowned.

5 And behold, that great city ᵃMoronihah have I covered with earth, and the inhabitants thereof, to hide their iniquities and their abominations from before my face, that the blood of the prophets and the saints shall not come any more unto me against them.

6 And behold, the city of Gilgal have I caused to be sunk, and the inhabitants thereof to be buried up in the depths of the earth;

7 Yea, and the city of Onihah and the inhabitants thereof, and the city of Mocum and the inhabitants thereof, and the city of ᵃJerusalem and the inhabitants thereof; and ᵇwaters have I caused to come up in the stead thereof, to hide their wickedness and abominations from before my face, that the ᶜblood of the prophets and the saints shall ᵈnot come up any more unto me against them.

8 And behold, the city of Gadiandi, and the city of Gadiomnah, and the city of Jacob, and the city of Gimgimno, all these have I caused to be sunk, and made ᵃhills and valleys in the places thereof; and the inhabitants thereof have I ᵇburied up in the depths of the earth, to hide their wickedness and abominations from before my face, that the blood of the prophets and the saints should not come up any more unto me against them.

9 And behold, that great city Jacobugath, which was inhabited by the people of king Jacob, have I caused to be burned with fire because of their sins and their ᵃwickedness, which was above all the wickedness of the whole earth, because of their ᵇsecret murders and combinations; for it was they that did ᶜdestroy the peace of my people and the government of the land; therefore I did cause them to be burned, to ᵈdestroy them from before my face, that the blood of the prophets and the saints should not come up unto me any more against them.

25a 3 Ne. 8:10; 9:5.
9 1a 1 Ne. 19:11.
  2a TG Repent.
    b Moses 7:26.
  3a Matt. 11:20;
    Hel. 13:12;
    3 Ne. 8:14 (14–24).
  4a 3 Ne. 8:9;
    4 Ne. 1:9.
  5a 3 Ne. 8:25 (10, 25).
  7a Alma 21:1; 24:1.

    b Ezek. 26:19.
    c Rev. 16:6 (5–7).
    d Jonah 1:2.
  8a 1 Ne. 19:11;
    3 Ne. 10:13 (13–14);
    Moses 7:14.
    b Num. 16:32;
    Hel. 12:17;
    3 Ne. 8:10 (10, 25).
  9a Gen. 6:5 (5–6);
    Morm. 4:12 (10–12);

    D&C 112:23;
    Moses 7:36 (36–37);
    8:22 (22, 28–30).
    b Hel. 6:17 (17–38);
    3 Ne. 6:23.
    c 3 Ne. 7:11 (9–13).
    d Gen. 6:13;
    1 Ne. 17:31;
    2 Ne. 1:17;
    Mosiah 12:8.

10 And behold, the city of Laman, and the city of Josh, and the city of Gad, and the city of Kishkumen, have I caused to be burned with fire, and the inhabitants thereof, because of their wickedness in casting out the prophets, and stoning those whom I did send to declare unto them concerning their wickedness and their abominations.

11 And because they did cast them all out, that there were none righteous among them, I did send down *a*fire and destroy them, that their wickedness and abominations might be hid from before my *b*face, that the blood of the prophets and the saints whom I sent among them might not cry unto me *c*from the ground against them.

12 And *a*many great destructions have I caused to come upon this land, and upon this people, because of their wickedness and their abominations.

13 O all ye that are *a*spared because ye were more *b*righteous than they, will ye not now return unto me, and repent of your sins, and be converted, that I may *c*heal you?

14 Yea, verily I say unto you, if ye will *a*come unto me ye shall have *b*eternal life. Behold, mine *c*arm of mercy is extended towards you, and whosoever will come, him will I receive; and blessed are those who come unto me.

15 Behold, I am Jesus Christ the Son of God. I *a*created the heavens and the earth, and all things that in them are. I was with the Father from the beginning. *b*I am in the Father, and the Father in me; and in me hath the Father glorified his name.

16 I came unto my own, and my own *a*received me not. And the scriptures *b*concerning my coming are fulfilled.

17 And as many as have received me, to them have I *a*given to become the sons of God; and even so will I to as many as shall believe on my name, for behold, by me *b*redemption cometh, and *c*in me is the *d*law of Moses fulfilled.

18 I am the *a*light and the life of the world. I am *b*Alpha and Omega, the beginning and the end.

19 And ye shall offer up unto me *a*no more the shedding of blood; yea, your sacrifices and your burnt offerings shall be done away, for I will accept none of your sacrifices and your burnt offerings.

20 And ye shall offer for a *a*sacrifice unto me a broken heart and a contrite spirit. And whoso cometh unto me with a broken heart and a contrite spirit, him will I *b*baptize with fire and with the Holy Ghost, even as the Lamanites, because of their faith in me at the time of their conversion, were baptized with fire and with the Holy Ghost, and they knew it not.

21 Behold, I have come unto the world to bring *a*redemption unto the world, to save the world from sin.

11a 2 Kgs. 1:10 (9–16);
    Hel. 13:13.
  b Deut. 31:18.
  c Gen. 4:10.
12a Hel. 14:24;
    3 Ne. 8:14 (8–10, 14);
    10:7 (4–7).
13a 3 Ne. 10:6 (6, 12); 27:31.
  b Gen. 18:26.
  c Jer. 3:22; 17:14;
    Matt. 13:15;
    3 Ne. 18:32.
14a 1 Ne. 1:14;
    2 Ne. 26:25 (24–28);
    Alma 5:34 (33–36).
  b John 3:16.
  c Isa. 59:16;
    Alma 19:36.

15a John 1:3 (1–3);
    Col. 1:16;
    Heb. 1:2 (1–3);
    Mosiah 15:4;
    Hel. 14:12; Ether 4:7;
    D&C 14:9.
  b 3 Ne. 11:27 (7, 11, 27);
    19:23 (23, 29).
16a John 1:11; D&C 6:21.
  b 3 Ne. 15:5.
17a John 1:12.
    TG Man, Potential to
    Become like Heavenly
    Father; Sons and
    Daughters of God.
  b Ps. 107:2.
    TG Jesus Christ,
    Redeemer.

  c 3 Ne. 15:8 (2–8).
  d Heb. 8:13;
    3 Ne. 12:19 (19, 46–47).
18a TG Jesus Christ, Light of
    the World.
  b Rev. 1:8.
    TG Jesus Christ,
    Firstborn.
19a Mosiah 13:27;
    Alma 34:13;
    3 Ne. 15:4 (2–10).
20a Ps. 51:17; Omni 1:26;
    3 Ne. 12:19;
    D&C 64:34.
  b TG Holy Ghost,
    Baptism of.
21a TG Jesus Christ,
    Atonement through.

22 Therefore, whoso ªrepenteth and cometh unto me ᵇas a ᶜlittle child, him will I receive, for of such is the kingdom of God. Behold, for such I have ᵈlaid down my life, and have taken it up again; therefore repent, and come unto me ye ends of the earth, and be saved.

CHAPTER 10

There is silence in the land for many hours—The voice of Christ promises to gather His people as a hen gathers her chickens—The more righteous part of the people have been preserved. About A.D. 34–35.

AND now behold, it came to pass that all the people of the land did ªhear these sayings, and did witness of it. And after these sayings there was silence in the land for the space of many hours;

2 For so great was the astonishment of the people that they did cease lamenting and howling for the loss of their kindred which had been slain; therefore there was silence in all the land for the space of many hours.

3 And it came to pass that there came a voice again unto the people, and all the people did hear, and did witness of it, saying:

4 O ye people of these ªgreat cities which have fallen, who are descendants of Jacob, yea, who are of the house of Israel, how oft have I ᵇgathered you as a hen gathereth her chickens under her wings, and have ᶜnourished you.

5 And again, ªhow oft would I have gathered you as a hen gathereth her chickens under her wings, yea, O ye people of the house of Israel, who have fallen; yea, O ye people of the house of Israel, ye that dwell at Jerusalem, as ye that have fallen; yea, how oft would I have gathered you as a hen gathereth her chickens, and ye would not.

6 O ye house of Israel whom I have ªspared, how oft will I gather you as a hen gathereth her chickens under her wings, if ye will repent and ᵇreturn unto me with full purpose of ᶜheart.

7 But if not, O house of Israel, the places of your dwellings shall become ªdesolate until the time of the fulfilling of the ᵇcovenant to your fathers.

8 And now it came to pass that after the people had heard these words, behold, they began to weep and howl ªagain because of the loss of their kindred and friends.

9 And it came to pass that thus did the three days pass away. And it was in the morning, and the ªdarkness dispersed from off the face of the land, and the earth did cease to tremble, and the ᵇrocks did cease to rend, and the dreadful groanings did cease, and all the tumultuous noises did pass away.

10 And the earth did cleave together again, that it stood; and the ªmourning, and the weeping, and the wailing of the people who were spared alive did cease; and their mourning was turned into joy, and their lamentations into the ᵇpraise and thanksgiving unto the Lord Jesus Christ, their Redeemer.

11 And thus far were the ªscriptures ᵇfulfilled which had been spoken by the prophets.

12 And it was the ªmore righteous part of the people who were saved, and it was they who received the

---

22a TG Repent.
  b Mark 10:15.
  c Mosiah 3:19;
    3 Ne. 11:37 (37–38).
  d John 10:15 (15–18).
    TG Jesus Christ,
    Death of;
    Self-Sacrifice.
10 1a 1 Ne. 19:11.
  4a 3 Ne. 8:14 (8–16);
    9:12 (3–12).

  b Hel. 7:19.
  c Luke 16:29 (29–31);
    1 Ne. 17:3;
    Jacob 5:25.
  5a Matt. 23:37;
    D&C 43:24 (24–25).
  6a 3 Ne. 9:13.
  b 1 Sam. 7:3;
    Hel. 13:11;
    3 Ne. 24:7.
  c Ezek. 36:26.

7a Ezek. 26:19.
  b Enos 1:16 (12–18).
  8a 3 Ne. 8:23 (23–25).
  9a 3 Ne. 8:19 (3, 19–23).
  b Hel. 14:21.
10a TG Mourning.
  b Acts 16:25.
11a 1 Ne. 19:12 (10–12).
  b Acts 3:18 (18–21).
12a 2 Ne. 26:8;
    3 Ne. 9:13 (11–13); 27:31.

prophets and stoned them not; and it was they who had not shed the blood of the saints, who were spared—

13 And they were spared and were not sunk and buried up in the earth; and they were not drowned in the depths of the sea; and they were not burned by fire, neither were they fallen upon and crushed to death; and they were not carried away in the whirlwind; neither were they overpowered by the vapor of smoke and of darkness.

14 And now, whoso readeth, let him understand; he that hath the scriptures, let him *a*search them, and see and behold if all these deaths and destructions by fire, and by smoke, and by *b*tempests, and by whirlwinds, and by the *c*opening of the earth to receive them, and all these things are not unto the fulfilling of the prophecies of many of the holy prophets.

15 Behold, I say unto you, Yea, many have testified of these things at the coming of Christ, and were *a*slain because they testified of these things.

16 Yea, the prophet *a*Zenos did testify of these things, and also Zenock spake *b*concerning these things, because they testified particularly concerning us, who are the remnant of their seed.

17 Behold, our father Jacob also testified concerning a *a*remnant of the seed of Joseph. And behold, are not we a remnant of the seed of Joseph? And these things which testify of us, are they not written upon the plates of brass which our father Lehi brought out of Jerusalem?

18 And it came to pass that in the ending of the thirty and fourth year, behold, I will show unto you that the people of Nephi who were spared, and also those who had been called

*a*Lamanites, who had been spared, did have great favors shown unto them, and great *b*blessings poured out upon their heads, insomuch that soon after the *c*ascension of Christ into heaven he did truly manifest himself unto them—

19 *a*Showing his body unto them, and ministering unto them; and an account of his ministry shall be given hereafter. Therefore for this time I make an end of my sayings.

Jesus Christ did show himself unto the people of Nephi, as the multitude were gathered together in the land Bountiful, and did minister unto them; and on this wise did he show himself unto them.

Comprising chapters 11 through 26.

CHAPTER 11

The Father testifies of His Beloved Son—Christ appears and proclaims His Atonement—The people feel the wound marks in His hands and feet and side—They cry Hosanna—He sets forth the mode and manner of baptism—The spirit of contention is of the devil—Christ's doctrine is that men should believe and be baptized and receive the Holy Ghost. About A.D. *34.*

AND now it came to pass that there were a great multitude *a*gathered together, of the people of Nephi, round about the temple which was in the land *b*Bountiful; and they were marveling and wondering one with another, and were showing one to another the *c*great and marvelous change which had taken place.

2 And they were also conversing about this Jesus Christ, of whom the *a*sign had been given concerning his death.

14a TG Scriptures, Study of.
   b Hel. 14:23.
   c Num. 16:32;
     1 Ne. 19:11;
     2 Ne. 26:5.
15a TG Martyrdom.
16a Hel. 8:20 (19–20).

   b 1 Ne. 19:21.
17a Alma 46:24;
     3 Ne. 5:23 (23–24).
18a 4 Ne. 1:20.
   b TG Blessing.
   c Acts 1:9 (9–11).
19a 3 Ne. 11:12 (12–15).

11 1a Hel. 3:14 (9, 14).
    b Alma 22:29;
      3 Ne. 3:23.
    c 3 Ne. 8:12 (11–14).
  2a 3 Ne. 14:20 (20–27);
     3 Ne. 8:5 (5–25).

3 And it came to pass that while they were thus conversing one with another, they heard a ^avoice as if it came out of heaven; and they cast their eyes round about, for they understood not the voice which they heard; and it was not a harsh voice, neither was it a loud voice; nevertheless, and notwithstanding it being a ^bsmall voice it did ^cpierce them that did hear to the center, insomuch that there was no part of their frame that it did not cause to quake; yea, it did pierce them to the very soul, and did cause their hearts to burn.

4 And it came to pass that again they heard the voice, and they ^aunderstood it not.

5 And again the third time they did hear the voice, and did ^aopen their ears to hear it; and their eyes were towards the sound thereof; and they did look steadfastly towards heaven, from whence the sound came.

6 And behold, the third time they did understand the voice which they heard; and it said unto them:

7 Behold my ^aBeloved Son, ^bin whom I am well pleased, in whom I have glorified my name—hear ye him.

8 And it came to pass, as they understood they cast their eyes up again towards heaven; and behold, they ^asaw a Man ^bdescending out of heaven; and he was clothed in a white robe; and he came down and stood in the midst of them; and the eyes of the whole multitude were turned upon him, and they durst not open their mouths, even one to another, and wist not what it meant, for they thought it was an angel that had appeared unto them.

9 And it came to pass that he stretched forth his hand and spake unto the people, saying:

10 Behold, I am Jesus Christ, whom the prophets testified shall come into the world.

11 And behold, I am the ^alight and the life of the world; and I have drunk out of that bitter ^bcup which the Father hath given me, and have glorified the Father in ^ctaking upon me the sins of the world, in the which I have suffered the ^dwill of the Father in all things from the beginning.

12 And it came to pass that when Jesus had spoken these words the whole multitude ^afell to the earth; for they remembered that it had been ^bprophesied among them that Christ should ^cshow himself unto them after his ascension into heaven.

13 And it came to pass that the ^aLord spake unto them saying:

14 Arise and come forth unto me, that ye may ^athrust your hands into my side, and also that ye may ^bfeel the prints of the nails in my hands and in my feet, that ye may know that I am the ^cGod of Israel, and the God of the whole ^dearth, and have been slain for the sins of the world.

15 And it came to pass that the multitude went forth, and thrust their hands into his side, and ^adid feel the prints of the nails in his hands and in his feet; and this they

---

3a Deut. 4:33; Ezek. 1:24;
   Hel. 5:29 (28–36).
  b 1 Kgs. 19:12 (11–13);
   D&C 85:6.
  c 1 Sam. 3:11; Jer. 20:9.
4a Ezek. 1:24 (24–28);
   1 Cor. 14:2.
5a Job 36:15;
   D&C 101:92.
7a Matt. 3:17; 17:5;
   JS—H 1:17.
   TG Witness of the
   Father.
  b 3 Ne. 9:15.

8a 1 Ne. 12:6;
   2 Ne. 26:1 (1, 9);
   Alma 16:20;
   Ether 3:17 (17–18).
  b Acts 1:9 (9–11).
11a TG Jesus Christ, Light of
   the World.
  b John 18:11.
  c John 1:29.
  d Mark 14:36 (32–42);
   Luke 22:42;
   John 6:38; Hel. 10:4;
   D&C 19:2.
12a TG Reverence.

  b Alma 16:20.
  c 3 Ne. 10:19.
13a TG Jesus Christ, Lord.
14a John 20:27.
  b Luke 24:39 (36–39);
   D&C 129:2.
  c Isa. 45:3; 3 Ne. 15:5;
   D&C 36:1; 127:3.
  d Ex. 9:29;
   1 Ne. 11:6.
15a 3 Ne. 18:25.
   TG Jesus Christ,
   Appearances,
   Postmortal.

did do, going forth one by one until they had all gone forth, and did see with their eyes and did feel with their hands, and did know of a surety and did bear record, that it was he, of whom it was written by the prophets, that should come.

16 And when they had all gone forth and had witnessed for themselves, they did cry out with one accord, saying:

17 Hosanna! Blessed be the name of the Most High God! And they did fall down at the feet of Jesus, and did ªworship him.

18 And it came to pass that he spake unto ªNephi (for Nephi was among the multitude) and he commanded him that he should come forth.

19 And Nephi arose and went forth, and ªbowed himself before the Lord and did ᵇkiss his feet.

20 And the Lord commanded him that he should ªarise. And he arose and stood before him.

21 And the Lord said unto him: I give unto you ªpower that ye shall ᵇbaptize this people when I am again ascended into heaven.

22 And again the Lord called ªothers, and said unto them likewise; and he gave unto them power to baptize. And he said unto them: On this wise shall ye baptize; and there shall be ᵇno disputations among you.

23 Verily I say unto you, that whoso repenteth of his sins through your ªwords, and ᵇdesireth to be baptized in my name, on this wise shall ye baptize them—Behold, ye shall go down and ᶜstand in the water, and in my name shall ye baptize them.

24 And now behold, these are the words which ye shall say, calling them by name, saying:

25 Having ªauthority given me of Jesus Christ, I baptize you in the name of the ᵇFather, and of the Son, and of the Holy Ghost. Amen.

26 And then shall ye ªimmerse them in the water, and come forth again out of the water.

27 And after this manner shall ye ªbaptize in my name; for behold, verily I say unto you, that the Father, and the Son, and the Holy Ghost are ᵇone; and I am in the Father, and the Father in me, and the Father and I are one.

28 And according as I have commanded you thus shall ye baptize. And there shall be no ªdisputations among you, as there have hitherto been; neither shall there be disputations among you concerning the points of my doctrine, as there have hitherto been.

29 For verily, verily I say unto you, he that hath the spirit of ªcontention is not of me, but is of the ᵇdevil, who is the father of contention, and he stirreth up the hearts of men to contend with anger, one with another.

30 Behold, this is not my doctrine, to stir up the hearts of men with anger, one against another; but this

---

17a TG Worship.
18a 3 Ne. 1:2 (2–3, 10);
     7:15 (15, 20, 23).
19a Ex. 34:8;
     Ether 6:12.
   b 3 Ne. 17:10.
20a Josh. 7:10;
     Ezek. 2:1 (1–2).
21a TG Church Organization;
     Priesthood, Authority.
   b TG Baptism, Essential.
22a 1 Ne. 12:7;
     3 Ne. 12:1.
   b 1 Cor. 11:16 (16–19);
     3 Ne. 18:34.
   TG Disputations.
23a Mosiah 26:15 (15–16);

3 Ne. 12:2.
   b TG Baptism,
     Qualifications for.
   c 3 Ne. 19:11 (10–13).
25a Mosiah 18:13;
     Alma 5:3;
     D&C 20:73.
   TG Delegation of
     Responsibility;
     Priesthood, Authority.
   b TG Godhead.
26a Moses 6:52.
   TG Baptism, Immersion;
     Jesus Christ, Types of, in
     Memory.
27a TG Baptism.
   b Alma 11:44;

3 Ne. 28:10;
     Morm. 7:7;
     D&C 20:28.
28a Acts 4:32;
     1 Cor. 1:10 (10–13);
     Eph. 4:13 (11–14);
     D&C 38:27.
   TG Disputations.
29a 2 Tim. 2:24 (23–24);
     Mosiah 23:15.
   TG Contention.
   b Eph. 4:27 (26–27);
     Mosiah 2:32 (32–33);
     Alma 2:5; 45:23;
     Hel. 4:1.

is my doctrine, that such things ^ashould be done away.

31 Behold, verily, verily, I say unto you, I will declare unto you my ^adoctrine.

32 And this is my ^adoctrine, and it is the doctrine which the Father hath given unto me; and I bear ^brecord of the Father, and the Father beareth record of me, and the ^cHoly Ghost beareth record of the Father and me; and I bear record that the Father commandeth all men, everywhere, to repent and believe in me.

33 And whoso believeth in me, and is ^abaptized, the same shall be ^bsaved; and they are they who shall ^cinherit the kingdom of God.

34 And whoso believeth not in me, and is not ^abaptized, shall be damned.

35 Verily, verily, I say unto you, that this is my doctrine, and I bear record of it from the Father; and whoso ^abelieveth in me believeth in the Father also; and unto him will the Father bear record of me, for he will visit him ^bwith fire and with the ^cHoly Ghost.

36 And thus will the Father bear record of me, and the ^aHoly Ghost will bear record unto him of the Father and me; for the Father, and I, and the Holy Ghost are ^bone.

37 And again I say unto you, ye must repent, and ^abecome as a ^blittle child, and be baptized in my name, or ye can in nowise receive these things.

38 And again I say unto you, ye must repent, and be baptized in my name, and become as a little ^achild, or ye can in nowise inherit the kingdom of God.

39 Verily, verily, I say unto you, that this is my ^adoctrine, and whoso ^bbuildeth upon this buildeth upon my rock, and the ^cgates of hell shall not prevail against them.

40 And whoso shall ^adeclare more or less than this, and establish it for my doctrine, the same cometh of evil, and is not built upon my rock; but he buildeth upon a ^bsandy foundation, and the gates of hell stand open to receive such when the floods come and the winds beat upon them.

41 Therefore, go forth unto this people, and declare the words which I have spoken, unto the ends of the earth.

CHAPTER 12

Jesus calls and commissions the twelve disciples—He delivers to the Nephites a discourse similar to the Sermon on the Mount—He speaks the Beatitudes—His teachings transcend and take precedence over the law of Moses—Men are commanded to be perfect even as He and His Father are perfect—Compare Matthew 5. About A.D. 34.

^aAND it came to pass that when Jesus had spoken these words unto Nephi, and to those who had been called, (now the number of them who had been called, and received power and authority to ^bbaptize, was ^ctwelve) and behold, he stretched forth his hand unto the multitude,

---

30 a Mark 9:50;
   John 16:33.
31 a John 18:37;
   2 Ne. 31:21 (2–21).
32 a TG Jesus Christ,
   Teaching Mode of.
   b 1 Jn. 5:7 (6–9).
   TG Jesus Christ,
   Relationships with
   the Father.
   c 3 Ne. 28:11;
   Ether 5:4;
   Moses 1:24.
33 a Mark 16:16.
   TG Baptism, Essential.

b TG Salvation, Plan of.
   c TG Exaltation.
34 a TG Baptism.
35 a Ether 4:12.
   b 3 Ne. 9:20; 12:2.
   c TG Holy Ghost,
   Baptism of.
36 a TG Holy Ghost, Source
   of Testimony.
   b TG Godhead; Unity.
37 a Mark 10:15;
   Luke 18:17.
   b 3 Ne. 9:22.
38 a TG Baptism,
   Qualifications for.

39 a Mark 4:2.
   b Matt. 7:24 (24–29);
   1 Pet. 2:6 (4–8);
   1 Ne. 13:36.
   TG Rock.
   c Matt. 16:18;
   3 Ne. 18:13 (12–13);
   D&C 17:8.
40 a Rom. 16:17 (17–19);
   1 Tim. 1:3.
   b 3 Ne. 14:26 (24–27).
12 1 a Matt. 5:1 (1–48).
   b Mark 16:16 (15–16);
   John 4:2 (1–2).
   c 3 Ne. 11:22; 13:25.

and cried unto them, saying: [d]Blessed are ye if ye shall give heed unto the words of these twelve whom I have [e]chosen from among you to minister unto you, and to be your servants; and unto them I have given power that they may baptize you with water; and after that ye are baptized with water, behold, I will baptize you with fire and with the Holy Ghost; therefore blessed are ye if ye shall believe in me and be baptized, after that ye have seen me and know that I am.

2 And again, more blessed are they who shall [a]believe in your words because that ye shall testify that ye have seen me, and that ye know that I am. Yea, blessed are they who shall [b]believe in your [c]words, and [d]come down into the depths of humility and be baptized, for they shall be visited [e]with fire and with the Holy Ghost, and shall receive a remission of their sins.

3 Yea, blessed are the [a]poor in spirit who [b]come unto me, for theirs is the kingdom of heaven.

4 And again, blessed are all they that [a]mourn, for they shall be [b]comforted.

5 And blessed are the [a]meek, for they shall inherit the [b]earth.

6 And blessed are all they who do [a]hunger and [b]thirst after [c]righteousness, for they shall be [d]filled with the Holy Ghost.

7 And blessed are the [a]merciful, for they shall obtain mercy.

8 And blessed are all the [a]pure in heart, for they shall [b]see God.

9 And blessed are all the [a]peacemakers, for they shall be called the [b]children of God.

10 And blessed are all they who are [a]persecuted for my name's sake, for theirs is the kingdom of heaven.

11 And blessed are ye when men shall [a]revile you and persecute, and shall say all manner of evil against you falsely, for my sake;

12 For [a]ye shall have great joy and be exceedingly glad, for great shall be your [b]reward in heaven; for so [c]persecuted they the prophets who were before you.

13 Verily, verily, I say unto you, I give unto you to be the [a]salt of the earth; but if the salt shall lose its savor wherewith shall the earth be salted? The salt shall be thenceforth good for nothing, but to be cast out and to be trodden under foot of men.

14 Verily, verily, I say unto you, I give unto you to be the light of this people. A city that is set on a hill cannot be hid.

15 Behold, do men light a [a]candle and put it under a bushel? Nay, but on a candlestick, and it giveth light to all that are in the house;

16 Therefore let your [a]light so shine before this people, that they may see your good works and [b]glorify your Father who is in heaven.

17 Think not that I am come to destroy the law or the prophets.

1d TG Blessing.
  e TG Called of God.
2a TG Teachable.
  b Mosiah 26:15 (15–16);
    D&C 46:14.
  c 3 Ne. 11:23.
  d Ether 4:13.
  e 3 Ne. 11:35;
    19:13 (13–14).
3a Ps. 86:1;
    Eccl. 4:13 (13–14);
    Matt. 5:3;
    D&C 56:18 (17–18).
    TG Poor in Spirit.
  b Matt. 11:28 (28–30).
4a Morm. 2:11 (11–14).
    TG Mourning.
  b Matt. 5:4;
    Alma 28:6.

TG Comfort.
5a Zeph. 2:3 (1–3);
    Rom. 12:16.
    TG Meek.
  b TG Earth, Destiny of.
6a Matt. 5:6;
    2 Ne. 9:51;
    Enos 1:4.
  b Jer. 29:13.
  c Prov. 21:21.
  d TG Spirituality.
7a TG Mercy.
8a TG Purity.
  b TG God, Privilege of
    Seeing.
9a TG Peacemakers.
  b TG Sons and Daughters
    of God.
10a Matt. 5:10;

D&C 122:5 (5–9).
11a TG Reviling.
12a TG Matt. 5:12.
  b TG Reward.
  c 2 Cor. 7:4.
    TG Prophets,
    Rejection of.
13a 2 Chr. 13:5;
    Matt. 5:13;
    D&C 101:39 (39–40).
    TG Mission of Early
    Saints;
    Salt.
15a Luke 8:16.
16a 3 Ne. 18:24.
    TG Example.
  b John 11:4 (1–4);
    Ether 12:4.

I am not come to destroy but to fulfil;

18 For verily I say unto you, [a]one jot nor one tittle hath not passed away from the [b]law, but in me it hath all been fulfilled.

19 And behold, I have given you the law and the commandments of my Father, that ye shall believe in me, and that ye shall repent of your sins, and come unto me with a [a]broken heart and a contrite spirit. Behold, ye have the commandments before you, and the [b]law is fulfilled.

20 Therefore [a]come unto me and be ye saved; for verily I say unto you, that except ye shall keep my [b]commandments, which I have commanded you at this time, ye shall in no case enter into the kingdom of heaven.

21 Ye have heard that it hath been said by them of old time, and it is also written before you, that thou shalt not [a]kill, and whosoever shall kill shall be in danger of the judgment of God;

22 But I say unto you, that whosoever is [a]angry with his brother shall be in danger of his judgment. And whosoever shall say to his brother, Raca, shall be in danger of the council; and whosoever shall say, Thou fool, shall be in danger of hell fire.

23 Therefore, [a]if ye shall come unto me, or shall desire to come unto me, and rememberest that thy brother hath aught against thee—

24 Go thy way unto thy brother, and first be [a]reconciled to thy brother,

and then come unto me with full [b]purpose of heart, and I will receive you.

25 [a]Agree with thine adversary quickly while thou art in the way with him, lest at any time he shall get thee, and thou shalt be cast into prison.

26 Verily, verily, I say unto thee, thou shalt by no means come out thence until thou hast paid the uttermost senine. And while ye are in prison can ye pay even one [a]senine? Verily, verily, I say unto you, Nay.

27 Behold, it is written by them of old time, that thou shalt not commit [a]adultery;

28 But I say unto you, that whosoever looketh on a woman, to [a]lust after her, hath committed adultery already in his heart.

29 Behold, I give unto you a commandment, that ye suffer [a]none of these things to enter into your [b]heart;

30 For it is better that ye should deny yourselves of these things, wherein ye will take up your [a]cross, than that ye should be cast into hell.

31 It hath been written, that whosoever shall put away his wife, let him give her a writing of [a]divorcement.

32 Verily, verily, I say unto you, that whosoever shall [a]put away his wife, saving for the cause of [b]fornication, causeth her to commit [c]adultery; and whoso shall marry her who is divorced committeth adultery.

33 And again it is written, thou shalt not [a]forswear thyself, but

18a Matt. 5:18.
   b TG Law of Moses.
19a 3 Ne. 9:20.
   TG Contrite Heart.
   b 3 Ne. 9:17.
20a Isa. 55:3.
   b 3 Ne. 15:10.
21a Ex. 20:13 (13–17);
   Deut. 5:17 (17–21);
   Matt. 5:21;
   Mosiah 13:21 (21–24);
   D&C 42:18.
   TG Life, Sanctity of.

22a Matt. 5:22.
23a Matt. 5:23.
24a TG Forgive;
   Reconciliation.
   b 3 Ne. 18:29 (28–33);
   D&C 46:4.
25a Matt. 5:25 (25–26).
26a Alma 11:3; 30:33.
27a Matt. 5:27;
   2 Ne. 9:36;
   D&C 59:6.
28a TG Lust.
29a D&C 42:23.

   b Acts 8:22.
30a Matt. 10:38; 16:24;
   Luke 9:23; 14:27;
   D&C 23:6.
31a TG Divorce.
32a Matt. 5:32;
   Mark 10:11 (11–12);
   Luke 16:18.
   b TG Fornication.
   c TG Adulterer.
33a TG Swearing.

shalt [b]perform unto the Lord thine [c]oaths;

34 But verily, verily, I say unto you, [a]swear not at all; neither by heaven, for it is God's throne;

35 Nor by the earth, for it is his footstool;

36 Neither shalt thou swear by thy head, because thou canst not make one hair black or white;

37 But let your [a]communication be [b]Yea, yea; Nay, nay; for whatsoever cometh of more than these is evil.

38 And behold, it is written, an [a]eye for an eye, and a tooth for a tooth;

39 But I say unto you, that ye shall not [a]resist evil, but whosoever shall smite thee on thy right [b]cheek, [c]turn to him the other also;

40 And if any man will sue thee at the law and take away thy coat, [a]let him have thy cloak also;

41 And whosoever shall compel thee to [a]go a mile, go with him twain.

42 [a]Give to him that asketh thee, and from him that would [b]borrow of thee turn thou not away.

43 And behold it is written also, that thou shalt love thy neighbor and hate thine enemy;

44 But behold I say unto you, love your [a]enemies, bless them that curse you, do [b]good to them that hate you, and [c]pray for them who despitefully use you and persecute you;

45 That ye may be the children of your Father who is in heaven; for he maketh his sun to rise [a]on the evil and on the good.

46 Therefore those things which were of old time, which were under the law, in me are all [a]fulfilled.

47 [a]Old things are done away, and all things have become [b]new.

48 Therefore I would that ye should be [a]perfect even as I, or your Father who is in heaven is perfect.

CHAPTER 13

Jesus teaches the Nephites the Lord's Prayer—They are to lay up treasures in heaven—The twelve disciples in their ministry are commanded to take no thought for temporal things—Compare Matthew 6. About A.D. 34.

[a]VERILY, verily, I say that I would that ye should do alms unto the poor; but take heed that ye do not your alms before men to be seen of them; otherwise ye have no reward of your Father who is in heaven.

2 Therefore, when ye shall do your alms do not sound a trumpet before you, as will hypocrites do in the synagogues and in the streets, that they may have [a]glory of men. Verily I say unto you, they have their reward.

3 But when thou doest alms let not thy left hand know what thy right hand doeth;

4 That thine alms may be in secret; and thy Father who seeth in secret, himself shall reward thee openly.

5 And when thou [a]prayest thou shalt not do as the [b]hypocrites, for

33b TG Dependability.
  c TG Oath.
34a Lev. 5:4;
    Morm. 3:14.
    TG Profanity.
37a TG Communication.
  b TG Honesty.
38a Lev. 24:20;
    Matt. 5:38 (38–42).
    TG Punish.
39a 3 Ne. 6:13;
    4 Ne. 1:34;
    D&C 98:23 (23–27).
    TG Submissiveness.
  b Lam. 3:30.
  c TG Forbear;
    Patience.

40a TG Charity; Initiative.
41a TG Generosity.
42a Jacob 2:19 (17–19);
    Mosiah 4:26.
  b TG Borrow.
44a Prov. 24:17;
    25:21 (21–22);
    Alma 48:23.
    TG Enemies.
  b TG Benevolence.
  c Acts 7:60 (59–60);
    2 Tim. 4:16.
45a Matt. 5:45.
46a Heb. 8:13.
47a 3 Ne. 9:17; 15:2 (2, 7);
    D&C 22:1.
  b Jer. 31:31 (31–33);

    Ether 13:9.
48a Matt. 5:48;
    3 Ne. 19:29 (28–29);
    27:27.
    TG God, Perfection of;
    God, the Standard of
    Righteousness;
    Jesus Christ, Exemplar;
    Man, New, Spiritually
    Reborn; Man, Potential
    to Become like
    Heavenly Father.
13 1a Matt. 6:1 (1–34).
    TG Almsgiving.
  2a D&C 121:35 (34–35).
  5a TG Prayer.
  b TG Hypocrisy.

they love to pray, standing in the synagogues and in the corners of the streets, that they may be seen of men. Verily I say unto you, they have their reward.

6 But thou, when thou prayest, enter into thy closet, and when thou hast ªshut thy door, pray to thy Father who is in secret; and thy Father, who ᵇseeth in secret, shall reward thee openly.

7 But when ye pray, use not ªvain repetitions, as the ᵇheathen, for they think that they shall be heard for their much speaking.

8 Be not ye therefore like unto them, for your Father ªknoweth what things ye have need of before ye ᵇask him.

9 After this ªmanner therefore ᵇpray ye: Our ᶜFather who art in heaven, hallowed be thy name.

10 Thy will be done on earth as it is in heaven.

11 And forgive us our debts, as we forgive our debtors.

12 And ªlead us not into temptation, but deliver us from evil.

13 For thine is the kingdom, and the power, and the glory, forever. Amen.

14 For, if ye ªforgive men their trespasses your heavenly Father will also forgive you;

15 But if ye forgive not men their trespasses neither will your Father forgive your trespasses.

16 Moreover, when ye ªfast be not as the ᵇhypocrites, of a sad countenance, for they disfigure their faces that they may appear unto men to fast. Verily I say unto you, they have their reward.

17 But thou, when thou fastest, anoint thy head, and ªwash thy face;

18 That thou appear not unto men to fast, but unto thy Father, who is in ªsecret; and thy Father, who seeth in secret, shall reward thee openly.

19 Lay not up for yourselves treasures upon earth, where ªmoth and rust doth corrupt, and thieves break through and steal;

20 But lay up for yourselves ªtreasures in heaven, where neither moth nor rust doth corrupt, and where thieves do not break through nor steal.

21 For where your treasure is, there will your heart be also.

22 The ªlight of the body is the ᵇeye; if, therefore, thine eye be ᶜsingle, thy whole body shall be full of light.

23 But if thine eye be evil, thy whole body shall be full of darkness. If, therefore, the light that is in thee be darkness, how great is that darkness!

24 No man can ªserve ᵇtwo masters; for either he will hate the one and love the other, or else he will hold to the one and despise the other. Ye cannot serve God and Mammon.

25 And now it came to pass that when Jesus had spoken these words he looked upon the ªtwelve whom he had chosen, and said unto them: Remember the words which I have spoken. For behold, ye are they whom I have chosen to ᵇminister unto this people. Therefore I say unto you, ᶜtake no thought for your life, what ye shall eat, or what ye

6a 2 Kgs. 4:33.
  b TG God, Omniscience of.
7a TG Sincere.
  b TG Heathen.
8a D&C 84:83.
  b Ezek. 36:37.
9a Matt. 6:9 (9–13).
  b TG Prayer.
  c TG God the Father,
    Elohim.
12a JST Matt. 6:14
    (Matt. 6:13 note a).
14a Mosiah 26:31.

  TG Forgive.
16a Isa. 58:5 (5–7);
    Zech. 7:5 (5–6).
    TG Fast, Fasting.
  b TG Hypocrisy.
17a TG Wash.
18a Isa. 45:15;
    D&C 38:7.
19a 3 Ne. 27:32.
20a Hel. 5:8; 8:25.
    TG Treasure.
22a Ezra 9:8.
  b Matt. 6:22 (20–25).

  c D&C 88:67.
    TG Dedication.
24a 1 Sam. 7:3;
    Alma 5:41 (39–42);
    Moses 1:15.
  b Hosea 10:2.
25a Matt. 6:25;
    3 Ne. 12:1; 15:11.
  b TG Church Organization;
    Delegation of
    Responsibility.
  c Alma 31:37;
    D&C 84:81 (79–85).

shall drink; nor yet for your body, what ye shall put on. Is not the life more than meat, and the body than ᵈraiment?

26 Behold the ᵃfowls of the air, for they sow not, neither do they reap nor gather into barns; yet your heavenly Father feedeth them. Are ye not much better than they?

27 Which of you by taking thought can add one cubit unto his stature?

28 And why take ye thought for raiment? Consider the ᵃlilies of the field how they grow; they toil not, neither do they spin;

29 And yet I say unto you, that even Solomon, in all his glory, was not arrayed like one of these.

30 Wherefore, if God so clothe the grass of the field, which today is, and tomorrow is cast into the oven, even so will he clothe you, if ye are not of little faith.

31 Therefore take no thought, saying, What shall we eat? or, What shall we drink? or, Wherewithal shall we be clothed?

32 For your heavenly Father knoweth that ye have need of all these things.

33 But ᵃseek ye first the ᵇkingdom of God and his righteousness, and all these things shall be added unto you.

34 Take therefore no thought for the morrow, for the morrow shall take thought for the things of itself. ᵃSufficient is the day unto the evil thereof.

CHAPTER 14

Jesus commands: Judge not; ask of God; beware of false prophets—He promises salvation to those who do the will of the Father—Compare Matthew 7. About A.D. 34.

ᵃAND now it came to pass that when Jesus had spoken these words he turned again to the multitude, and did open his mouth unto them again, saying: Verily, verily, I say unto you, Judge not, that ye be not judged.

2 ᵃFor with what judgment ye judge, ye shall be judged; and with what measure ye mete, it shall be measured to you again.

3 And why beholdest thou the mote that is in thy brother's eye, but considerest not the beam that is in thine own eye?

4 Or how wilt thou say to thy brother: Let me pull the mote out of thine eye—and behold, a beam is in thine own eye?

5 Thou ᵃhypocrite, first cast the ᵇbeam out of thine own eye; and then shalt thou see clearly to cast the mote out of thy brother's eye.

6 Give not that which is ᵃholy unto the dogs, neither cast ye your pearls before swine, lest they trample them under their feet, and turn again and rend you.

7 ᵃAsk, and it shall be given unto you; ᵇseek, and ye shall find; knock, and it shall be opened unto you.

8 For every one that asketh, receiveth; and he that seeketh, findeth; and to him that knocketh, it shall be opened.

9 Or what man is there of you, who, if his son ask bread, will give him a stone?

10 Or if he ask a fish, will he give him a serpent?

11 If ye then, being evil, know how to give good gifts unto your children, how much more shall your Father who is in heaven give good things to them that ask him?

12 Therefore, all things whatsoever ye would that men should do to you, ᵃdo ye even so to them, for this is the law and the prophets.

25d Job 27:16 (16–17).
26a D&C 117:6.
28a TG Nature, Earth.
33a TG Commitment.
  b Luke 12:31 (22–34).
     TG Objectives.
34a Matt. 6:34.

14 1a Matt. 7:1 (1–27);
       JST Matt. 7:1–2
       (Matt. 7:1 note a).
  2a Morm. 8:19.
  5a TG Hypocrisy.
  b John 8:7 (3–11).
  6a TG Holiness.

7a 3 Ne. 27:29.
    TG Prayer.
  b TG Initiative;
     Objectives.
12a TG Benevolence;
     Compassion;
     Courtesy.

13 Enter ye in at the ^astrait gate; for wide is the gate, and ^bbroad is the way, which leadeth to destruction, and many there be who go in thereat;

14 Because strait is the ^agate, and ^bnarrow is the way, which leadeth unto life, and ^cfew there be that find it.

15 Beware of ^afalse prophets, who come to you in sheep's clothing, but inwardly they are ravening wolves.

16 Ye shall know them by their ^afruits. Do men gather grapes of thorns, or figs of thistles?

17 Even so every ^agood tree bringeth forth good fruit; but a corrupt tree bringeth forth evil fruit.

18 A good tree cannot bring forth evil fruit, neither a corrupt tree bring forth good fruit.

19 Every tree that ^abringeth not forth good fruit is hewn down, and cast into the fire.

20 Wherefore, by their ^afruits ye shall know them.

21 Not every one that saith unto me, Lord, Lord, shall ^aenter into the kingdom of heaven; but he that doeth the will of my Father who is in heaven.

22 Many will ^asay to me in that day: Lord, Lord, have we not prophesied in thy name, and in thy name have cast out devils, and in thy name done many wonderful works?

23 And then will ^aI profess unto them: I never ^bknew you; ^cdepart from me, ye that work iniquity.

24 Therefore, whoso heareth these sayings of mine and doeth them,

I will liken him unto a wise man, who built his house upon a ^arock—

25 And the ^arain descended, and the floods came, and the winds blew, and beat upon that house; and it ^bfell not, for it was founded upon a rock.

26 And every one that heareth these sayings of mine and doeth them not shall be likened unto a ^afoolish man, who built his house upon the ^bsand—

27 And the rain descended, and the floods came, and the winds blew, and beat upon that house; and it fell, and great was the fall of it.

CHAPTER 15

Jesus announces that the law of Moses is fulfilled in Him—The Nephites are the other sheep of whom He spoke in Jerusalem—Because of iniquity, the Lord's people in Jerusalem do not know of the scattered sheep of Israel. About A.D. 34.

AND now it came to pass that when Jesus had ended these sayings he cast his eyes round about on the multitude, and said unto them: Behold, ye have heard the things which I ^ataught before I ascended to my Father; therefore, whoso remembereth these sayings of mine and ^bdoeth them, him will I ^craise up at the last day.

2 And it came to pass that when Jesus had said these words he perceived that there were some among them who marveled, and wondered what he would concerning the law

13a Luke 13:24;
   3 Ne. 27:33.
  b D&C 132:25.
14a 2 Ne. 9:41; 31:9 (9, 17–18);
   D&C 22:4.
  b 1 Ne. 8:20.
  c Matt. 7:14;
   1 Ne. 14:12.
15a Jer. 23:21 (21–32);
   2 Ne. 28:12 (9, 12, 15).
  TG False Prophets.
16a Col. 1:6;
   Alma 32:42 (28–42);
   D&C 52:34 (18, 34).

17a Alma 5:41.
19a Matt. 3:10;
   Alma 5:36 (36–41);
   D&C 97:7.
20a Matt. 7:17 (16–20); 12:33;
   Luke 6:43 (43–45);
   Moro. 7:5.
21a 1 Jn. 2:17.
22a Matt. 7:23.
23a Matt. 7:23.
  b Mosiah 5:13;
   26:25 (24–27);
   D&C 112:26.
  c Ps. 119:115;

   Luke 13:27.
24a TG Rock.
25a Alma 26:6;
   Hel. 5:12.
  b Prov. 12:7.
26a TG Foolishness.
  b 3 Ne. 11:40.
15 1a IE in Galilee and Judea.
  b James 1:22 (22–24).
  c John 6:39;
   1 Ne. 13:37;
   Mosiah 23:22;
   Alma 26:7;
   D&C 5:35.

of Moses; for they understood not the saying that *old things had passed away, and that all things had become new.

3 And he said unto them: Marvel not that I said unto you that old things had passed away, and that all things had become *new.

4 Behold, I say unto you that the *law is fulfilled that was given unto Moses.

5 Behold, *I am he that gave the law, and I am he who covenanted with my people Israel; therefore, the law in me is fulfilled, for I have come to *fulfil the law; therefore it hath an end.

6 Behold, I do *not destroy the prophets, for as many as have not been fulfilled in me, verily I say unto you, shall all be fulfilled.

7 And because I said unto you that old things have passed away, I do not destroy that which hath been spoken concerning things which are to come.

8 For behold, the *covenant which I have made with my people is not all fulfilled; but the law which was given unto Moses hath an end in me.

9 Behold, I am the *law, and the *light. Look unto me, and endure to the end, and ye shall *live; for unto him that *endureth to the end will I give eternal life.

10 Behold, I have given unto you the *commandments; therefore keep my commandments. And this is the law and the prophets, for they truly *testified of me.

11 And now it came to pass that when Jesus had spoken these words, he *said unto those twelve whom he had chosen:

12 Ye are my *disciples; and ye are a *light unto this people, who are a remnant of the house of *Joseph.

13 And behold, this is the *land of your inheritance; and the Father hath given it unto you.

14 And not at any time hath the Father given me commandment that I should *tell it unto your brethren at Jerusalem.

15 Neither at any time hath the Father given me commandment that I should tell unto them concerning the *other tribes of the house of Israel, whom the Father hath led away out of the land.

16 This much did the Father *command me, that I should tell unto them:

17 That other sheep I have which are not of this fold; them also I must bring, and they shall hear my voice; and there shall be one fold, and one *shepherd.

18 And now, because of *stiff-neckedness and *unbelief they *understood not my word; therefore I was commanded to say no more of the *Father concerning this thing unto them.

19 But, verily, I say unto you that the Father hath commanded me, and I tell it unto you, that ye were *separated from among them because of their iniquity; therefore it

2 a 3 Ne. 12:47 (46–47).
3 a Heb. 8:13;
   Ether 13:9.
4 a Mosiah 13:27 (27–31);
   3 Ne. 9:17 (17–20).
5 a 1 Cor. 10:4 (1–4);
   3 Ne. 11:14.
   TG Jesus Christ, Jehovah.
 b Alma 34:13.
   TG Jesus Christ,
   Mission of.
6 a 3 Ne. 20:11 (11–12);
   23:3 (1–3).
8 a 3 Ne. 5:25 (24–26); 16:5.
   TG Covenants;
   Restoration of the
   Gospel.
9 a 2 Ne. 26:1.

 b TG Jesus Christ, Light of
   the World.
 c Lev. 18:5;
   John 11:25;
   D&C 84:44.
 d Matt. 10:22 (22–33);
   Mark 13:13;
   2 Ne. 31:20;
   Alma 32:13 (13–15);
   3 Ne. 27:6 (6–17).
10 a 3 Ne. 12:20.
 b Mosiah 13:33.
11 a 3 Ne. 13:25;
   Moro. 2:1.
12 a TG Church Organization.
 b TG Example;
   Leadership.
 c TG Israel, Joseph,

   People of.
13 a 1 Ne. 18:23;
   3 Ne. 16:16.
14 a 3 Ne. 5:20.
15 a 2 Ne. 21:12;
   3 Ne. 16:1 (1–4).
   TG Israel, Ten Lost
   Tribes of.
16 a John 15:15; 16:12.
17 a TG Shepherd.
18 a TG Stiffnecked.
 b TG Doubt;
   Unbelief.
 c D&C 10:59.
 d John 12:50.
19 a 1 Kgs. 8:53;
   John 17:6 (6–22).

is because of their iniquity that they know not of you.

20 And verily, I say unto you again that the other tribes hath the Father separated from them; and it is because of their iniquity that they know not of them.

21 And verily I say unto you, that ye are they of whom I said: ^aOther sheep I have which are not of this fold; them also I must bring, and they shall hear my voice; and there shall be one fold, and one ^bshepherd.

22 And they understood me not, for they supposed it had been the ^aGentiles; for they understood not that the Gentiles should be ^bconverted through their preaching.

23 And they understood me not that I said they shall hear my voice; and they understood me not that the ^aGentiles should not at any time hear my voice—that I should not manifest myself unto them save it were by the ^bHoly Ghost.

24 But behold, ye have both heard ^amy voice, and seen me; and ye are my sheep, and ye are numbered among those whom the Father hath ^bgiven me.

CHAPTER 16

Jesus will visit others of the lost sheep of Israel—In the latter days the gospel will go to the Gentiles and then to the house of Israel—The Lord's people will see eye to eye when He brings again Zion. About A.D. 34.

AND verily, verily, I say unto you that I have ^aother sheep, which are not of this land, neither of the land of Jerusalem, neither in any parts of that land round about whither I have been to minister.

2 For they of whom I speak are they who have not as yet heard my voice; neither have I at any time manifested myself unto them.

3 But I have received a ^acommandment of the Father that I shall go unto them, and that they shall ^bhear my voice, and shall be numbered among my sheep, that there may be one fold and one shepherd; therefore I go to show myself unto them.

4 And I command you that ye shall ^awrite these sayings after I am gone, that if it so be that my people at Jerusalem, they who have seen me and been with me in my ministry, do not ask the Father in my name, that they may receive a knowledge of you by the Holy Ghost, and also of the other tribes whom they know not of, that these sayings which ye shall write shall be kept and shall be manifested unto the ^bGentiles, that through the fulness of the Gentiles, the remnant of their seed, who shall be scattered forth upon the face of the earth because of their ^cunbelief, may be brought in, or may be brought to a ^dknowledge of me, their Redeemer.

5 And then will I ^agather them in from the four quarters of the earth; and then will I fulfil the ^bcovenant which the Father hath made unto all the people of the ^chouse of Israel.

6 And blessed are the ^aGentiles, because of their belief in me, in and of the Holy Ghost, which ^bwitnesses unto them of me and of the Father.

21a John 10:16 (14–16).
  b TG Jesus Christ, Good Shepherd.
22a TG Gentiles.
  b Acts 10:45 (34–48).
23a Matt. 15:24.
  b 1 Ne. 10:11.
  TG Holy Ghost, Mission of.
24a Alma 5:38;
  3 Ne. 16:3 (1–5); 18:31.
  b John 6:37;
  D&C 27:14.
16 1a 1 Ne. 19:10;

2 Ne. 21:12;
3 Ne. 15:15.
  TG Israel, Ten Lost Tribes of.
3a 3 Ne. 18:27.
  b 3 Ne. 17:4.
4a 2 Ne. 25:18.
  TG Scriptures to Come Forth.
  b 1 Ne. 10:14;
  3 Ne. 21:6 (1–11).
  c TG Unbelief.
  d Ezek. 20:42 (42–44);
  Micah 7:9 (8–9);

3 Ne. 20:13.
  TG Israel, Restoration of.
5a TG Israel, Gathering of.
  b 3 Ne. 5:25 (24–26); 15:8.
  c 1 Ne. 22:9;
  3 Ne. 21:27 (26–29).
6a 1 Ne. 13:39 (23, 30–42);
  2 Ne. 30:3;
  3 Ne. 20:27.
  b 2 Ne. 32:5;
  3 Ne. 11:32 (32, 35–36).
  TG Holy Ghost, Source of Testimony.

7 Behold, because of their belief in me, saith the Father, and because of the unbelief of you, O house of Israel, in the ^alatter day shall the truth come unto the ^bGentiles, that the fulness of these things shall be made known unto them.

8 But wo, saith the Father, unto the ^aunbelieving of the Gentiles—for notwithstanding they have come forth upon the face of this land, and have ^bscattered my people who are of the house of Israel; and my people who are of the house of Israel have been ^ccast out from among them, and have been trodden under feet by them;

9 And because of the mercies of the Father unto the Gentiles, and also the judgments of the Father upon my people who are of the house of Israel, verily, verily, I say unto you, that after all this, and I have caused my people who are of the house of Israel to be smitten, and to be afflicted, and to be ^aslain, and to be cast out from among them, and to become ^bhated by them, and to become a hiss and a byword among them—

10 And thus commandeth the Father that I should say unto you: At that day when the Gentiles shall ^asin against my gospel, and shall reject the fulness of my gospel, and shall be ^blifted up in the pride of their hearts above all nations, and above all the people of the whole earth, and shall be filled with all manner of lyings, and of deceits, and of mischiefs, and all manner

of hypocrisy, and ^cmurders, and ^dpriestcrafts, and whoredoms, and of secret abominations; and if they shall do all those things, and shall ^ereject the fulness of my gospel, behold, saith the Father, I will bring the fulness of my gospel from among them.

11 And then will I ^aremember my covenant which I have made unto my people, O house of Israel, and I will bring my gospel unto them.

12 And I will show unto thee, O house of Israel, that the Gentiles shall not have power over you; but I will remember my covenant unto you, O house of Israel, and ye shall come unto the ^aknowledge of the fulness of my gospel.

13 But if the Gentiles will repent and return unto me, saith the Father, behold they shall be ^anumbered among my people, O house of Israel.

14 And I will not suffer my people, who are of the house of Israel, to go through among them, and tread them down, saith the Father.

15 But if they will not turn unto me, and hearken unto my voice, I will suffer them, yea, I will suffer my people, O house of Israel, that they shall go through among them, and shall ^atread them down, and they shall be as salt that hath lost its savor, which is thenceforth good for nothing but to be cast out, and to be trodden under foot of my people, O house of Israel.

16 Verily, verily, I say unto you, thus hath the Father commanded

---

7a TG Restoration of the
    Gospel.
 b D&C 19:27; 107:33.
   TG Mission of Latter-day
    Saints.
8a 2 Ne. 6:15; 28:15 (15–32);
    Ether 2:9 (8–11).
 b 1 Ne. 13:14;
    2 Ne. 26:19;
    Morm. 5:9 (9, 15).
 c 3 Ne. 20:28.
9a Amos 9:1 (1–4).
 b Jer. 23:40;
    Lam. 2:16 (15–16);

    Joel 2:17;
    1 Ne. 19:14.
10a 3 Ne. 20:15.
 b Morm. 8:36 (35–41).
 c 3 Ne. 30:2;
    Morm. 8:31.
 d 2 Ne. 26:29.
   TG Priestcraft.
 e 3 Ne. 20:28 (27–28);
    D&C 6:31.
11a Isa. 44:21;
    3 Ne. 20:29 (28–31);
    21:4 (1–11);
    Morm. 5:20.

12a Hel. 15:13.
   TG Israel, Restoration of;
    Knowledge.
13a Gal. 3:7 (7, 29);
    1 Ne. 15:13 (13–17);
    22:9 (5–10);
    2 Ne. 10:18 (18–19);
    3 Ne. 30:2;
    Abr. 2:10 (9–11).
15a Micah 5:8 (8–15);
    3 Ne. 20:16;
    21:12 (12–21);
    D&C 87:5.

me—that I should give unto ^athis people this land for their inheritance.

17 And then the ^awords of the prophet Isaiah shall be fulfilled, which say:

18 ^aThy ^bwatchmen shall lift up the voice; with the voice together shall they sing, for they shall see eye to eye when the Lord shall bring again Zion.

19 Break forth into joy, sing together, ye waste places of Jerusalem; for the Lord hath comforted his people, he hath redeemed Jerusalem.

20 The Lord hath made bare his holy arm in the eyes of all the nations; and all the ends of the earth shall see the salvation of God.

CHAPTER 17

Jesus directs the people to ponder His words and pray for understanding— He heals their sick—He prays for the people, using language that cannot be written—Angels minister to and fire encircles their little ones. About A.D. 34.

BEHOLD, now it came to pass that when Jesus had spoken these words he looked round about again on the multitude, and he said unto them: Behold, my ^atime is at hand.

2 I ^aperceive that ye are weak, that ye cannot ^bunderstand all my words which I am commanded of the Father to speak unto you at this time.

3 Therefore, go ye unto your homes, and ^aponder upon the things which I have said, and ask of the Father, in my name, that ye may understand,

and ^bprepare your minds for the ^cmorrow, and I come unto you again.

4 But now I ^ago unto the Father, and also to ^bshow myself unto the lost tribes of Israel, for they are not ^clost unto the Father, for he knoweth whither he hath taken them.

5 And it came to pass that when Jesus had thus spoken, he cast his eyes round about again on the multitude, and beheld they were ^ain tears, and did look steadfastly upon him as if they would ask him to tarry a little longer with them.

6 And he said unto them: Behold, my bowels are filled with ^acompassion towards you.

7 Have ye any that are ^asick among you? Bring them hither. Have ye any that are lame, or blind, or halt, or maimed, or ^bleprous, or that are withered, or that are deaf, or that are afflicted in any manner? Bring them hither and I will ^cheal them, for I have compassion upon you; my bowels are filled with mercy.

8 For I perceive that ye desire that I should show unto you what I have done unto your brethren at Jerusalem, for I see that your ^afaith is ^bsufficient that I should heal you.

9 And it came to pass that when he had thus spoken, all the multitude, with one accord, did go forth with their sick and their afflicted, and their lame, and with their ^ablind, and with their dumb, and with all them that were afflicted in any manner; and he did heal them every one as they were brought forth unto him.

16*a* 3 Ne. 15:13.
17*a* 3 Ne. 20:11.
18*a* Isa. 52:8 (8–10);
 3 Ne. 20:32.
 b Ezek. 33:2 (2, 7);
 D&C 101:45 (45, 53–54).
 TG Watchman.
17 1*a* IE to return to the Father. See v. 4.
 2*a* TG Jesus Christ, Teaching Mode of.
 b John 16:12;
 D&C 50:40;
 78:18 (17–18).

3*a* TG Meditation.
 b Ezra 7:10;
 D&C 29:8; 132:3.
 c 3 Ne. 19:2.
4*a* 3 Ne. 18:39.
 b 3 Ne. 16:3.
 TG Jesus Christ, Appearances, Postmortal.
 c TG Israel, Ten Lost Tribes of.
5*a* TG God, Love of.
6*a* TG Compassion.
7*a* TG Sickness.

 b TG Leprosy.
 c TG Administrations to the Sick;
 Heal.
8*a* Matt. 8:10 (1–17);
 Luke 18:42.
 b 2 Ne. 27:23;
 Ether 12:12.
9*a* Matt. 9:28 (28–31);
 Mosiah 3:5;
 3 Ne. 26:15;
 D&C 84:69.

10 And they did all, both they who had been healed and they who were whole, bow down at his feet, and did worship him; and as many as could come for the multitude did *a*kiss his feet, insomuch that they did bathe his feet with their tears.

11 And it came to pass that he commanded that their *a*little children should be brought.

12 So they brought their little children and set them down upon the ground round about him, and Jesus stood in the midst; and the multitude gave way till they had all been brought unto him.

13 And it came to pass that when they had all been brought, and Jesus stood in the midst, he commanded the multitude that they should *a*kneel down upon the ground.

14 And it came to pass that when they had knelt upon the ground, Jesus groaned within himself, and said: Father, I am *a*troubled because of the wickedness of the people of the house of Israel.

15 And when he had said these words, he himself also *a*knelt upon the earth; and behold he *b*prayed unto the Father, and the things which he prayed cannot be written, and the multitude did bear record who heard him.

16 And after this manner do they bear record: The *a*eye hath never seen, neither hath the ear heard, before, so great and marvelous things as we saw and heard Jesus speak unto the Father;

17 And no *a*tongue can speak, neither can there be written by any man, neither can the hearts of men conceive so great and marvelous things as we both saw and heard

Jesus speak; and no one can conceive of the joy which filled our souls at the time we heard him pray for us unto the Father.

18 And it came to pass that when Jesus had made an end of praying unto the Father, he arose; but so great was the *a*joy of the multitude that they were overcome.

19 And it came to pass that Jesus spake unto them, and bade them arise.

20 And they arose from the earth, and he said unto them: Blessed are ye because of your faith. And *a*now behold, my joy is full.

21 And when he had said these words, he *a*wept, and the multitude bare record of it, and he took their little children, one by one, and *b*blessed them, and prayed unto the Father for them.

22 And when he had done this he wept again;

23 And he spake unto the multitude, and said unto them: Behold your little ones.

24 And as they looked to behold they cast their eyes towards heaven, and they saw the heavens open, and they saw angels descending out of heaven as it were in the midst of fire; and they came down and *a*encircled those little ones about, and they were encircled about with fire; and the angels did minister unto them.

25 And the multitude did see and *a*hear and bear record; and they know that their record is true for they all of them did see and hear, every man for himself; and they were in number about two thousand and five hundred souls; and they did consist of men, women, and children.

10*a* Luke 7:38 (38, 45);
　　　3 Ne. 11:19.
11*a* Matt. 19:13 (13–14);
　　　Mark 10:13;
　　　3 Ne. 26:14 (14, 16).
　　　TG Children.
13*a* Acts 9:40; 20:36;
　　　3 Ne. 19:6 (6, 16–17).
14*a* Mosiah 28:3;
　　　Alma 31:2;

　　　3 Ne. 17:20; 27:32;
　　　Moses 7:41.
15*a* 3 Ne. 19:19 (19, 27).
　　b TG Jesus Christ,
　　　Relationships with
　　　the Father.
16*a* Isa. 64:4; 1 Cor. 2:9;
　　　3 Ne. 19:32 (30–36);
　　　D&C 76:10, 116 (114–19).
17*a* 2 Cor. 12:4;

　　　3 Ne. 19:34 (32–34).
18*a* TG Joy.
20*a* 3 Ne. 17:14.
21*a* Hel. 5:43 (23–24, 43–45);
　　　3 Ne. 19:14.
　　b Mark 10:16 (14–16).
24*a* Hel. 5:43 (23–24, 43–45);
　　　3 Ne. 19:14.
　　　TG Transfiguration.
25*a* Ex. 19:9 (9–13).

CHAPTER 18

Jesus institutes the sacrament among the Nephites—They are commanded to pray always in His name—Those who eat His flesh and drink His blood unworthily are damned—The disciples are given power to confer the Holy Ghost. About A.D. 34.

AND it came to pass that Jesus commanded his disciples that they should bring forth some *a*bread and wine unto him.

2 And while they were gone for bread and wine, he commanded the multitude that they should sit themselves down upon the earth.

3 And when the disciples had come with *a*bread and wine, he took of the bread and brake and blessed it; and he gave unto the disciples and commanded that they should eat.

4 And when they had eaten and were filled, he commanded that they should give unto the multitude.

5 And when the multitude had eaten and were filled, he said unto the disciples: Behold there shall one be *a*ordained among you, and to him will I give power that he shall *b*break *c*bread and bless it and give it unto the people of my *d*church, unto all those who shall believe and be baptized in my name.

6 And this shall ye always observe to *a*do, even as I have done, even as I have broken bread and blessed it and given it unto you.

7 And this shall ye do in *a*remembrance of my *b*body, which I have shown unto you. And it shall be a testimony unto the Father that ye do always remember me. And if ye do always remember me ye shall have my Spirit to be with you.

8 And it came to pass that when he said these words, he commanded his disciples that they should take of the *a*wine of the cup and drink of it, and that they should also give unto the multitude that they might drink of it.

9 And it came to pass that they did so, and did drink of it and were filled; and they gave unto the multitude, and they did drink, and they were filled.

10 And when the disciples had done this, Jesus said unto them: Blessed are ye for this thing which ye have done, for this is fulfilling my commandments, and this doth witness unto the Father that ye are *a*willing to do that which I have commanded you.

11 And this shall ye always do to those who repent and are baptized in my name; and ye shall do it in *a*remembrance of my *b*blood, which I have shed for you, that ye may witness unto the Father that ye do always remember me. And if ye do always remember me ye shall have my Spirit to be with you.

12 And I give unto you a commandment that ye shall do these things. And if ye shall always do these things blessed are ye, for ye are built upon my *a*rock.

13 But whoso among you shall do *a*more or less than these are not built upon my rock, but are built upon a sandy foundation; and when the rain descends, and the floods come, and the winds blow, and beat upon them, they shall *b*fall, and the *c*gates of hell are ready open to receive them.

14 Therefore blessed are ye if ye shall keep my commandments, which the Father hath commanded me that I should give unto you.

---

18 1*a* Matt. 26:26;
      3 Ne. 20:3 (3–9); 26:13.
   3*a* TG Jesus Christ, Types
      of, in Memory.
   5*a* TG Church
      Organization.
    b Moro. 4:1.
    c Matt. 14:19 (19–21);
      3 Ne. 20:6 (6–7).
    d TG Church.

   6*a* TG Jesus Christ,
      Exemplar.
   7*a* 3 Ne. 20:8;
      Moro. 4:3.
      TG Sacrament.
    b TG Bread of Life.
   8*a* Matt. 26:27 (27–29).
      TG Jesus Christ, Types
      of, in Memory.
  10*a* TG Commitment.

  11*a* Moro. 5:1.
    b TG Blood, Symbolism of.
  12*a* TG Rock.
  13*a* Josh. 1:7;
      D&C 3:2.
    b TG Apostasy of
      Individuals.
    c Matt. 16:18;
      3 Ne. 11:39.

15 Verily, verily, I say unto you, ye must watch and ^apray always, lest ye be tempted by the devil, and ye be led away captive by him.

16 And as I have prayed among you even so shall ye pray in my ^achurch, among my people who do repent and are baptized in my name. Behold I am the ^blight; I have set an ^cexample for you.

17 And it came to pass that when Jesus had spoken these words unto his disciples, he turned again unto the multitude and said unto them:

18 Behold, verily, verily, I say unto you, ye must watch and pray always lest ye enter into temptation; for ^aSatan desireth to have you, that he may sift you as wheat.

19 Therefore ye must always pray unto the Father in my name;

20 And ^awhatsoever ye shall ask the Father in my name, which is right, believing that ye shall receive, behold it shall be given unto you.

21 ^aPray in your families unto the Father, always in my name, that your wives and your children may be blessed.

22 And behold, ye shall ^ameet together; and ye shall not forbid any man from coming unto you when ye shall meet together, but suffer them that they may come unto you and forbid them not;

23 But ye shall ^apray for them, and shall not cast them out; and if it so be that they come unto you oft ye shall pray for them unto the Father, in my name.

24 Therefore, hold up your ^alight that it may shine unto the world. Behold I am the ^blight which ye shall hold up—that which ye have seen me do. Behold ye see that I have prayed unto the Father, and ye all have witnessed.

25 And ye see that I have commanded that ^anone of you should go away, but rather have commanded that ye should come unto me, that ye might ^bfeel and see; even so shall ye do unto the world; and whosoever breaketh this commandment suffereth himself to be led into temptation.

26 And now it came to pass that when Jesus had spoken these words, he turned his eyes again upon the ^adisciples whom he had chosen, and said unto them:

27 Behold verily, verily, I say unto you, I give unto you another commandment, and then I must go unto my ^aFather that I may fulfil ^bother commandments which he hath given me.

28 And now behold, this is the commandment which I give unto you, that ye shall not suffer any one knowingly to ^apartake of my flesh and blood ^bunworthily, when ye shall minister it;

29 For whoso eateth and drinketh my flesh and ^ablood ^bunworthily eateth and drinketh damnation to his soul; therefore if ye know that a man is unworthy to eat and drink of my flesh and blood ye shall forbid him.

30 Nevertheless, ye shall not ^acast him out from among you, but ye

15a Alma 34:23;
    D&C 93:49.
16a TG Jesus Christ, Head of
    the Church.
  b TG Jesus Christ, Light of
    the World.
  c TG God, the Standard of
    Righteousness;
    Jesus Christ, Exemplar.
18a Luke 22:31;
    2 Ne. 2:18 (17–18);
    D&C 10:22 (22–27).
20a Isa. 58:9 (8–9);
    Matt. 21:22 (21–22);
    Mark 11:24; Hel. 10:5;
    Morm. 9:21;
    Moro. 7:26;
    D&C 88:64 (63–65).
21a Alma 34:21.
    TG Family, Children,
    Responsibilities toward.
22a TG Meetings.
23a 3 Ne. 18:30.
    TG Missionary Work.
24a TG Jesus Christ, Light of
    the World.
  b Matt. 5:16;
    Mark 4:21;
    3 Ne. 12:16.
25a Alma 5:33; 19:36.
  b 3 Ne. 11:15 (14–16).
26a 3 Ne. 13:25.
27a TG God the Father,
    Elohim.
  b 3 Ne. 16:3.
28a Ex. 12:43;
    1 Cor. 11:27 (27–30);
    4 Ne. 1:27.
  b Lev. 7:18;
    Morm. 9:29.
29a TG Blood,
    Symbolism of.
  b 3 Ne. 12:24 (23–26);
    D&C 46:4.
30a D&C 46:3.

shall *b*minister unto him and shall pray for him unto the Father, in my name; and if it so be that he repenteth and is baptized in my name, then shall ye receive him, and shall minister unto him of my flesh and blood.

31 But if he repent not he shall not be numbered among my people, that he may not destroy my people, for behold I *a*know *b*my sheep, and they are numbered.

32 Nevertheless, ye shall not cast him out of your *a*synagogues, or your places of worship, for unto such shall ye continue to minister; for ye know not but what they will return and repent, and come unto me with full purpose of heart, and I shall *b*heal them; and ye shall be the means of bringing salvation unto them.

33 Therefore, keep these sayings which I have commanded you that ye come not under *a*condemnation; for wo unto him whom the Father condemneth.

34 And I give you these commandments because of the disputations which have been among you. And blessed are ye if ye have *a*no disputations among you.

35 And now I go unto the Father, because it is expedient that I should go unto the Father *a*for your sakes.

36 And it came to pass that when Jesus had made an end of these sayings, he touched with his *a*hand the *b*disciples whom he had chosen, one by one, even until he had touched them all, and spake unto them as he touched them.

37 And the multitude heard not the words which he spake, therefore they did not bear record; but the disciples bare record that he gave

them *a*power to give the *b*Holy Ghost. And I will show unto you *c*hereafter that this record is true.

38 And it came to pass that when Jesus had touched them all, there came a *a*cloud and overshadowed the multitude that they could not see Jesus.

39 And while they were overshadowed he *a*departed from them, and ascended into heaven. And the disciples saw and did bear record that he ascended again into heaven.

CHAPTER 19

The twelve disciples minister unto the people and pray for the Holy Ghost— The disciples are baptized and receive the Holy Ghost and the ministering of angels—Jesus prays using words that cannot be written—He attests to the exceedingly great faith of these Nephites. About A.D. *34.*

AND now it came to pass that when Jesus had ascended into heaven, the multitude did disperse, and every man did take his wife and his children and did return to his own home.

2 And it was noised abroad among the people immediately, before it was yet dark, that the multitude had seen Jesus, and that he had ministered unto them, and that he would also show himself on the *a*morrow unto the multitude.

3 Yea, and even all the night it was noised abroad concerning Jesus; and insomuch did they send forth unto the people that there were many, yea, an exceedingly great number, did labor exceedingly all that night, that they might be on the morrow in the place where Jesus should show himself unto the multitude.

30*b* 3 Ne. 18:23.
31*a* D&C 27:14.
  b John 10:14; Alma 5:38;
    3 Ne. 15:24.
32*a* Alma 16:13;
    Moro. 7:1.
  b Jer. 3:22;
    3 Ne. 9:13 (13–14);
    D&C 112:13.
33*a* TG Condemnation.
34*a* 3 Ne. 11:28 (28–30).
    TG Disputations.
35*a* 1 Jn. 2:1; 2 Ne. 2:9;
    Moro. 7:28 (27–28);
    D&C 29:5.
36*a* TG Hands, Laying on of.
  b 1 Ne. 12:7;
    3 Ne. 15:11; 19:4 (4–12).
37*a* TG Holy Ghost, Gift of;
    Priesthood, Authority.
  b Alma 31:36.
  c 3 Ne. 26:17; 28:18;
    Moro. 2:2 (2–3).
38*a* Ex. 19:9 (9, 16);
    2 Chr. 5:14 (11–14).
39*a* 3 Ne. 17:4.
19 2*a* 3 Ne. 17:3.

4 And it came to pass that on the morrow, when the multitude was gathered together, behold, Nephi and his ^abrother whom he had raised from the ^bdead, whose name was Timothy, and also his son, whose name was Jonas, and also Mathoni, and Mathonihah, his brother, and Kumen, and Kumenonhi, and Jeremiah, and Shemnon, and Jonas, and Zedekiah, and Isaiah—now these were the ^cnames of the ^ddisciples whom Jesus had chosen— and it came to pass that they went forth and stood in the midst of the multitude.

5 And behold, the multitude was ^aso great that they did cause that they should be separated into twelve bodies.

6 And the twelve did teach the multitude; and behold, they did cause that the multitude should ^akneel down upon the face of the earth, and should pray unto the Father in the name of Jesus.

7 And the disciples did pray unto the Father also in the name of Jesus. And it came to pass that they arose and ministered unto the people.

8 And when they had ministered those same words which Jesus had spoken—nothing varying from the words which Jesus had spoken—behold, they knelt again and prayed to the Father in the name of Jesus.

9 And they did pray for that which they most desired; and they desired that the ^aHoly Ghost should be given unto them.

10 And when they had thus prayed they went down unto the water's edge, and the multitude followed them.

11 And it came to pass that Nephi went down ^ainto the water and was ^bbaptized.

12 And he came up out of the water and began to baptize. And he baptized all those whom Jesus had chosen.

13 And it came to pass when they were all baptized and had come ^aup out of the water, the ^bHoly Ghost did fall upon them, and they were filled with the Holy Ghost and with fire.

14 And behold, they were ^aencircled about as if it were by fire; and it came down from heaven, and the multitude did witness it, and did bear record; and angels did come down out of heaven and did minister unto them.

15 And it came to pass that while the angels were ministering unto the disciples, behold, Jesus came and stood in the midst and ministered unto them.

16 And it came to pass that he spake unto the multitude, and commanded them that they should kneel down again upon the earth, and also that his disciples should kneel down upon the earth.

17 And it came to pass that when they had all knelt down upon the earth, he commanded his disciples that they should pray.

18 And behold, they began to pray; and they did pray unto Jesus, calling him their Lord and their God.

19 And it came to pass that Jesus departed out of the midst of them, and went a little way off from them and ^abowed himself to the earth, and he said:

20 Father, I thank thee that thou hast given the Holy Ghost unto these whom I have ^achosen; and it is because of their belief in me that I have chosen them out of the world.

21 Father, I pray thee that thou wilt give the Holy Ghost unto all them that shall believe in their words.

4a 3 Ne. 7:19.
  b TG Death, Power over.
  c 3 Ne. 28:25.
  d 3 Ne. 18:36 (36–37);
    26:17.
5a Mosiah 2:7.
6a 3 Ne. 17:13.

9a 3 Ne. 9:20.
11a 3 Ne. 11:23.
  b Matt. 3:14 (13–15);
    JS—H 1:71 (70–71).
13a TG Baptism, Immersion.
  b 3 Ne. 12:2;
    Morm. 7:10.

    TG Holy Ghost,
    Baptism of.
14a Hel. 5:43 (23–24, 43–45);
    3 Ne. 17:24.
19a 3 Ne. 17:15.
20a TG Church Organization.

22 Father, thou hast given them the Holy Ghost because they believe in [a]me; and thou seest that they believe in me because thou hearest them, and they pray unto me; and they pray unto me because I am with them.

23 And now Father, I [a]pray unto thee for them, and also for all those who shall believe on their words, that they may believe in me, that I may be in them [b]as thou, Father, art in me, that we may be [c]one.

24 And it came to pass that when Jesus had thus prayed unto the Father, he came unto his disciples, and behold, they did still continue, without ceasing, to pray unto him; and they did not [a]multiply many words, for it was given unto them what they should [b]pray, and they were filled with desire.

25 And it came to pass that Jesus blessed them as they did pray unto him; and his [a]countenance did smile upon them, and the light of his [b]countenance did [c]shine upon them, and behold they were as [d]white as the countenance and also the garments of Jesus; and behold the whiteness thereof did exceed all the whiteness, yea, even there could be nothing upon earth so white as the whiteness thereof.

26 And Jesus said unto them: Pray on; nevertheless they did not cease to pray.

27 And he turned from them again, and went a little way off and bowed himself to the earth; and he prayed again unto the Father, saying:

28 Father, I thank thee that thou hast [a]purified those whom I have chosen, because of their faith, and

I pray for them, and also for them who shall believe on their words, that they may be purified in me, through faith on their words, even as they are purified in me.

29 Father, I pray not for the world, but for those whom thou hast given me [a]out of the world, because of their faith, that they may be purified in me, that I may be in them as thou, Father, art in me, that we may be one, that I may be glorified in them.

30 And when Jesus had spoken these words he came again unto his disciples; and behold they did pray steadfastly, without ceasing, unto him; and he did smile upon them again; and behold they were [a]white, even as Jesus.

31 And it came to pass that he went again a little way off and prayed unto the Father;

32 And tongue cannot speak the words which he prayed, neither can be [a]written by man the words which he prayed.

33 And the multitude did hear and do bear record; and their [a]hearts were open and they did understand in their hearts the words which he prayed.

34 Nevertheless, so great and marvelous were the words which he prayed that they cannot be written, neither can they be [a]uttered by man.

35 And it came to pass that when Jesus had made an end of praying he came again to the disciples, and said unto them: [a]So great [b]faith have I never seen among all the Jews; wherefore I could not show unto them so great [c]miracles, because of their [d]unbelief.

22a Acts 7:59.
23a TG Jesus Christ,
    Relationships with the
    Father.
  b 3 Ne. 9:15; 11:27.
  c John 17:22 (1–22);
    1 Cor. 6:17.
24a Matt. 6:7.
  b Hel. 10:5;
    D&C 46:30.
25a Num. 6:25 (23–27).
  b Ps. 4:6.

  c Dan. 9:17.
  d TG Transfiguration.
28a Neh. 12:30;
    Moro. 7:48;
    D&C 50:29 (28–29);
    88:74 (74–75).
    TG Purity.
29a John 17:6.
30a Matt. 17:2.
32a 3 Ne. 5:18;
    D&C 76:116.
33a Prov. 2:2; 8:5;

    Isa. 44:18;
    Mosiah 2:9; 12:27.
34a 2 Cor. 12:4;
    3 Ne. 17:17.
35a Matt. 8:10.
  b TG Faith.
  c John 11:47 (47–48).
  d Matt. 13:58.
    TG Doubt;
    Unbelief.

36 Verily I say unto you, there are none of them that have seen so great things as ye have seen; neither have they heard so great things as ye have heard.

CHAPTER 20

Jesus provides bread and wine miraculously and again administers the sacrament unto the people—The remnant of Jacob will come to the knowledge of the Lord their God and will inherit the Americas—Jesus is the prophet like unto Moses, and the Nephites are children of the prophets—Others of the Lord's people will be gathered to Jerusalem. About A.D. 34.

AND it came to pass that he commanded the multitude that they should ^acease to ^bpray, and also his disciples. And he commanded them that they should not cease to pray in their hearts.

2 And he commanded them that they should arise and stand up upon their feet. And they arose up and stood upon their feet.

3 And it came to pass that he ^abrake ^bbread again and blessed it, and gave to the disciples to eat.

4 And when they had eaten he commanded them that they should break bread, and give unto the multitude.

5 And when they had given unto the multitude he also gave them wine to drink, and commanded them that they should give unto the multitude.

6 Now, there had been no ^abread, neither wine, brought by the disciples, neither by the multitude;

7 But he truly ^agave unto them bread to eat, and also wine to drink.

8 And he said unto them: He that eateth this bread eateth of ^amy body to his soul; and he that drinketh of this wine drinketh of my blood to his soul; and his soul shall never hunger nor thirst, but shall be filled.

9 Now, when the multitude had all eaten and drunk, behold, they were filled with the Spirit; and they did cry out with one voice, and gave glory to Jesus, whom they both saw and heard.

10 And it came to pass that when they had all given glory unto Jesus, he said unto them: Behold now I finish the commandment which the Father hath commanded me concerning this people, who are a remnant of the house of Israel.

11 Ye remember that I spake unto you, and said that when the ^awords of ^bIsaiah should be fulfilled—behold they are written, ye have them before you, therefore search them—

12 And verily, verily, I say unto you, that when they shall be fulfilled then is the fulfilling of the ^acovenant which the Father hath made unto his people, O house of Israel.

13 And then shall the ^aremnants, which shall be ^bscattered abroad upon the face of the earth, be ^cgathered in from the east and from the west, and from the south and from the north; and they shall be brought to the ^dknowledge of the Lord their God, who hath redeemed them.

14 And the Father hath ^acommanded me that I should give unto you this ^bland, for your inheritance.

15 And I say unto you, that if the Gentiles do not ^arepent after

20 1 a 1 Sam. 7:8;
        2 Ne. 32:9.
      b Mosiah 24:12.
    3 a Mark 6:41 (36–44).
      b 3 Ne. 18:1; 26:13.
    6 a Matt. 14:19 (19–21).
    7 a John 6:14.
    8 a John 6:51 (50–58);
        1 Cor. 11:24 (20–26);
        3 Ne. 18:7;

        Moro. 4:3.
   11 a 3 Ne. 16:17 (17–20);
        23:3 (1–3).
      b 2 Ne. 25:5 (1–5);
        Morm. 8:23.
   12 a Gen. 17:11 (9–12);
        3 Ne. 15:7.
   13 a 3 Ne. 16:13 (6–13);
        21:3 (2–7).
      b TG Israel, Scattering of.

      c Jer. 46:27 (2–28);
        3 Ne. 22:7 (6–17).
        TG Israel, Gathering of.
      d Ezek. 20:42 (42–44);
        3 Ne. 16:4 (4–5).
   14 a TG Jesus Christ,
        Authority of.
      b TG Promised Lands.
   15 a 3 Ne. 16:10 (10–14).

the ᵇblessing which they shall receive, after they have scattered my people—

16 Then shall ye, who are a ᵃremnant of the house of Jacob, go forth among them; and ye shall be in the midst of them who shall be many; and ye shall be among them as a lion among the beasts of the forest, and as a young ᵇlion among the flocks of sheep, who, if he goeth through both ᶜtreadeth down and teareth in pieces, and none can deliver.

17 Thy hand shall be lifted up upon thine adversaries, and all thine enemies shall be cut off.

18 And I will ᵃgather my people together as a man gathereth his sheaves into the floor.

19 For I will make my ᵃpeople with whom the Father hath covenanted, yea, I will make thy ᵇhorn iron, and I will make thy hoofs brass. And thou shalt ᶜbeat in pieces many people; and I will consecrate their gain unto the Lord, and their substance unto the Lord of the whole earth. And behold, I am he who doeth it.

20 And it shall come to pass, saith the Father, that the ᵃsword of my justice shall hang over them at that day; and except they repent it shall fall upon them, saith the Father, yea, even upon all the nations of the Gentiles.

21 And it shall come to pass that I will establish my ᵃpeople, O house of Israel.

22 And behold, this ᵃpeople will I establish in this land, unto the fulfilling of the ᵇcovenant which I made with your father Jacob; and it shall be a ᶜNew Jerusalem. And the ᵈpowers of heaven shall be in the midst of this people; yea, even ᵉI will be in the midst of you.

23 Behold, I am he of whom Moses spake, saying: ᵃA prophet shall the Lord your God raise up unto you of your brethren, like unto me; him shall ye hear in all things whatsoever he shall say unto you. And it shall come to pass that every soul who will not hear that prophet shall be cut off from among the people.

24 Verily I say unto you, yea, and ᵃall the prophets from Samuel and those that follow after, as many as have spoken, have testified of me.

25 And behold, ye are the ᵃchildren of the prophets; and ye are of the house of Israel; and ye are of the ᵇcovenant which the Father made with your fathers, saying unto Abraham: And ᶜin thy seed shall all the kindreds of the earth be blessed.

26 The Father having raised me up unto you first, and sent me to ᵃbless you in ᵇturning away every one of you from his iniquities; and this because ye are the children of the covenant—

27 And after that ye were blessed then fulfilleth the Father the covenant which he made with Abraham, saying: ᵃIn thy seed shall all the kindreds of the earth be blessed— unto the pouring out of the Holy

15b 3 Ne. 20:27.
16a TG Israel, Remnant of.
   b Gen. 49:9;
     Morm. 5:24;
     D&C 87:5 (4–5);
     109:65 (65–67).
     TG Israel,
     Deliverance of.
   c Micah 5:8 (8–9);
     3 Ne. 16:15 (14–15);
     21:12 (11–21).
18a Micah 4:12.
19a Lev. 26:12;
     D&C 63:1 (1–6).
   b TG Last Days.
   c Micah 4:13.
20a 1 Ne. 14:17; 22:16 (15–16);

   3 Ne. 29:4.
21a 1 Kgs. 8:51;
     3 Ne. 16:8 (8–15);
     21:23 (12–24).
22a TG Israel, Joseph,
     People of.
   b Gen. 49:26 (22–26).
   c Isa. 2:3 (2–5);
     3 Ne. 21:23 (23–24);
     Ether 13:3 (1–12);
     D&C 84:2 (2–4).
     TG Jerusalem, New.
   d 3 Ne. 21:25.
   e Isa. 59:20 (20–21);
     3 Ne. 24:1.
23a Deut. 18:15 (15–19);
     Acts 3:22 (22–23);

   1 Ne. 22:20 (20–21);
     D&C 133:63.
24a Acts 3:24 (24–26);
     1 Ne. 10:5;
     Jacob 7:11.
25a Rom. 4:24 (23–24).
   b TG Abrahamic Covenant.
   c Gen. 12:3 (1–3);
     22:18 (9, 18).
     TG Seed of Abraham.
26a TG Israel, Blessings of.
   b Prov. 16:6;
     Alma 19:33.
27a Gen. 12:2 (1–3);
     Gal. 3:8 (7–29);
     2 Ne. 29:14;
     Abr. 2:9.

Ghost through me upon the Gentiles, which *b*blessing upon the *c*Gentiles shall make them mighty above all, unto the *d*scattering of my people, O house of Israel.

28 And they shall be a *a*scourge unto the people of this land. Nevertheless, when they shall have received the fulness of my gospel, then if they shall harden their hearts against me I will return their *b*iniquities upon their own heads, saith the Father.

29 And I will *a*remember the covenant which I have made with my people; and I have covenanted with them that I would *b*gather them together in mine own due time, that I would give unto them again the *c*land of their fathers for their inheritance, which is the land of Jerusalem, which is the promised land unto them forever, saith the Father.

30 And it shall come to pass that the time cometh, when the fulness of my gospel shall be preached unto them;

31 And they shall *a*believe in me, that I am Jesus Christ, the Son of God, and shall pray unto the Father in my name.

32 Then shall their *a*watchmen lift up their voice, and with the voice together shall they sing; for they shall see eye to eye.

33 Then will the Father gather them together again, and give unto them *a*Jerusalem for the *b*land of their inheritance.

34 Then shall they break forth into joy—*a*Sing together, ye waste places of Jerusalem; for the Father hath comforted his people, he hath redeemed Jerusalem.

35 The Father hath made bare his holy arm in the eyes of all the nations; and all the ends of the earth shall see the salvation of the Father; and the Father and I are one.

36 And then shall be brought to pass that which is written: *a*Awake, awake again, and put on thy strength, O Zion; put on thy beautiful garments, O Jerusalem, the holy city, for henceforth there shall no more come into thee the uncircumcised and the unclean.

37 Shake thyself from the dust; arise, sit down, O Jerusalem; loose thyself from the bands of thy neck, O captive daughter of Zion.

38 For thus saith the Lord: Ye have sold yourselves for naught, and ye shall be redeemed without money.

39 Verily, verily, I say unto you, that my people shall know my name; yea, in that day they shall know that I am he that doth speak.

40 And then shall they say: *a*How beautiful upon the mountains are the feet of him that bringeth good tidings unto them, that *b*publisheth peace; that bringeth good tidings unto them of good, that publisheth salvation; that saith unto Zion: Thy God reigneth!

41 And then shall a cry go forth: *a*Depart ye, depart ye, go ye out from thence, touch not that which is *b*unclean; go ye out of the midst of her; be ye *c*clean that bear the vessels of the Lord.

27*b* 3 Ne. 20:15.
   c 3 Ne. 16:6 (6–7);
      Morm. 5:19.
   d 3 Ne. 16:8 (8–9);
      Morm. 5:9.
28*a* Josh. 23:13;
   1 Ne. 2:24;
   3 Ne. 16:8 (8–10).
   b Isa. 51:23.
29*a* Isa. 44:21;
   3 Ne. 16:11 (11–12).
   b TG Israel, Gathering of.
   c Amos 9:15;
      Alma 7:10;

D&C 133:24.
   TG Israel, Land of.
31*a* 3 Ne. 5:26 (21–26);
   21:26 (26–29).
32*a* Isa. 52:8 (8–9);
   3 Ne. 16:18 (18–20).
   TG Watchman.
33*a* Isa. 18:7;
   D&C 84:2.
   TG Jerusalem.
   b Deut. 11:11.
   TG Israel, Land of;
      Lands of Inheritance.
34*a* Isa. 54:1.

36*a* Isa. 52:1 (1–3);
   D&C 113:7 (7–10).
   TG Priesthood,
      Power of.
40*a* Isa. 52:7;
   Nahum 1:15;
   Mosiah 15:18 (13–18);
   D&C 128:19.
   b Mark 13:10;
   1 Ne. 13:37.
41*a* Isa. 52:11 (11–15).
   b TG Uncleanness.
   c D&C 133:5.
   TG Cleanliness.

42 For ye shall ^anot go out with ^bhaste nor go by flight; for the Lord will go before you, and the God of Israel shall be your rearward.

43 Behold, my servant shall deal prudently; he shall be exalted and extolled and be very high.

44 As many were astonished at thee—his visage was so marred, more than any man, and his form more than the sons of men—

45 So shall he ^asprinkle many nations; the kings shall shut their mouths at him, for that which had not been told them shall they see; and that which they had not heard shall they ^bconsider.

46 Verily, verily, I say unto you, all these things shall surely come, even as the Father hath commanded me. Then shall this covenant which the Father hath covenanted with his people be fulfilled; and then shall ^aJerusalem be inhabited again with my people, and it shall be the land of their inheritance.

CHAPTER 21

Israel will be gathered when the Book of Mormon comes forth—The Gentiles will be established as a free people in America—They will be saved if they believe and obey; otherwise, they will be cut off and destroyed—Israel will build the New Jerusalem, and the lost tribes will return. About A.D. 34.

AND verily I say unto you, I give unto you a ^asign, that ye may know the ^btime when these things shall be about to take place—that I shall gather in, from their long dispersion, my people, O house of Israel, and shall establish again among them my Zion;

2 And behold, this is the thing which I will give unto you for a sign—for verily I say unto you that ^awhen these things which I declare unto you, and which I shall declare unto you hereafter of myself, and by the power of the Holy Ghost which shall be given unto you of the Father, shall be made known unto the Gentiles that they may know concerning this people who are a remnant of the house of Jacob, and concerning this my people who shall be scattered by them;

3 Verily, verily, I say unto you, when these things shall be made ^aknown unto them of the Father, and shall come forth of the Father, ^bfrom them unto you;

4 For it is wisdom in the Father that they should be established in this land, and be set up as a ^afree people by the power of the Father, that these things might come forth from them unto a remnant of your seed, that the ^bcovenant of the Father may be fulfilled which he hath covenanted with his people, O house of Israel;

5 Therefore, when these works and the works which shall be wrought among you hereafter shall come forth ^afrom the Gentiles, unto your ^bseed which shall dwindle in unbelief because of iniquity;

6 For thus it behooveth the Father that it should come forth from the ^aGentiles, that he may show forth his power unto the Gentiles, for this cause that the Gentiles, if they will not harden their hearts, that they

42a 3 Ne. 21:29.
  b TG Haste;
    Rashness.
45a Lev. 1:5;
    Isa. 52:15;
    Ezek. 36:25.
  b 3 Ne. 21:8;
    D&C 101:94.
46a Joel 2:18;
    Ether 13:5 (5, 11).
21 1a Isa. 66:19.
  b TG Last Days.

2a 1 Ne. 10:14;
    Ether 4:17;
    D&C 20:9 (8–11);
    JS—H 1:34.
3a TG Witness of the
    Father.
  b 3 Ne. 20:13;
    Morm. 5:15 (10–21).
4a John 8:32 (32–36);
    1 Ne. 13:19 (17–19);
    D&C 101:77 (77–80).
  b Ps. 89:35;

3 Ne. 16:11 (8–12);
    Morm. 5:20.
    TG Abrahamic Covenant.
5a 3 Ne. 26:8.
  b 2 Ne. 30:5;
    Morm. 5:15;
    D&C 3:18.
6a 1 Ne. 10:14;
    Jacob 5:54;
    3 Ne. 16:4 (4–7);
    21:24 (24–26);
    Morm. 5:15.

may repent and come unto me and be baptized in my name and know of the true points of my doctrine, that they may be ᵇnumbered among my people, O house of Israel;

7 And when these things come to pass that thy ᵃseed shall begin to know these things—it shall be a sign unto them, that they may know that the work of the Father hath already commenced unto the fulfilling of the covenant which he hath made unto the people who are of the house of Israel.

8 And when that day shall come, it shall come to pass that kings shall shut their mouths; for that which had not been told them shall they see; and that which they had not heard shall they ᵃconsider.

9 For in that day, for my sake shall the Father ᵃwork a work, which shall be a great and a ᵇmarvelous ᶜwork among them; and there shall be among them those who will not believe it, although a man shall declare it unto them.

10 But behold, the life of my servant shall be in my hand; therefore they shall not hurt him, although he shall be ᵃmarred because of them. Yet I will heal him, for I will show unto them that ᵇmy wisdom is greater than the cunning of the devil.

11 Therefore it shall come to pass that whosoever will not believe in my words, who am Jesus Christ, which the Father shall cause ᵃhim to bring forth unto the ᵇGentiles, and shall give unto him power that he shall bring them forth unto the Gentiles, (it shall be done even as

Moses said) they shall be ᶜcut off from among my people who are of the covenant.

12 And my people who are a remnant of Jacob shall be among the Gentiles, yea, in the midst of them as a ᵃlion among the beasts of the forest, as a young lion among the flocks of sheep, who, if he go through both treadeth down and teareth in pieces, and none can deliver.

13 Their hand shall be lifted up upon their ᵃadversaries, and all their enemies shall be cut off.

14 Yea, wo be unto the Gentiles except they ᵃrepent; for it shall come to pass in that day, saith the Father, that I will cut off thy horses out of the midst of thee, and I will destroy thy ᵇchariots;

15 And I will cut off the cities of thy land, and throw down all thy ᵃstrongholds;

16 And I will cut off ᵃwitchcrafts out of thy land, and thou shalt have no more soothsayers;

17 Thy ᵃgraven images I will also cut off, and thy standing images out of the midst of thee, and thou shalt no more worship the works of thy hands;

18 And I will pluck up thy ᵃgroves out of the midst of thee; so will I destroy thy cities.

19 And it shall come to pass that all ᵃlyings, and deceivings, and envyings, and strifes, and priestcrafts, and whoredoms, shall be done away.

20 For it shall come to pass, saith the Father, that at that ᵃday whosoever will not repent and come unto my Beloved Son, them will I

6b Gal. 3:7 (7, 29); 2 Ne. 30:3; 3 Ne. 16:13; Abr. 2:10 (9–11).
7a 3 Ne. 5:23 (21–26); 21:26.
8a 3 Ne. 20:45.
9a TG God, Works of.
 b 1 Ne. 22:8. TG Restoration of the Gospel.
 c Acts 13:41 (40–41).
10a D&C 135:1 (1–3).
 b D&C 10:43.
11a 2 Ne. 3:11 (6–15); Morm. 8:16 (16, 25);

Ether 3:28 (21–28).
 b 1 Ne. 21:6.
 c D&C 1:14; 133:63.
12a Isa. 5:29; Micah 5:8 (8–15); Mal. 4:3; 2 Ne. 15:29; 3 Ne. 16:15 (7–15); 20:16; 25:3; D&C 87:5.
13a 1 Ne. 21:17 (17–19).
14a Eph. 3:6 (1–7); 2 Ne. 10:18; 33:9.
 b Lev. 26:22 (21–22); Hel. 14:24.

15a 2 Ne. 12:15.
16a TG Sorcery; Superstitions.
17a Ex. 20:4 (3–4, 23); Isa. 41:29 (24, 29); Mosiah 13:12; D&C 1:16. TG Idolatry.
18a 1 Kgs. 16:33 (32–33).
19a 3 Ne. 30:2; D&C 109:30.
20a Amos 5:18; Alma 29:2; Morm. 9:27.

*b*cut off from among my people, O house of Israel;

21 And I will execute *a*vengeance and *b*fury upon them, even as upon the heathen, such as they have not heard.

22 But if they will repent and hearken unto my words, and *a*harden not their hearts, I will *b*establish my church among them, and they shall come in unto the covenant and be *c*numbered among this the remnant of Jacob, unto whom I have given this land for their *d*inheritance;

23 And they shall assist my *a*people, the remnant of Jacob, and also as many of the house of Israel as shall come, that they may build a city, which shall be called the *b*New Jerusalem.

24 And then shall *a*they assist my people that they may be gathered in, who are scattered upon all the face of the land, in unto the New Jerusalem.

25 And then shall the *a*power of heaven come down among them; and *b*I also will be in the midst.

26 And then shall the work of the Father commence at that day, even *a*when this gospel shall be preached among the remnant of *b*this people. Verily I say unto you, at that day shall the work of the Father commence among all the dispersed of my people, yea, even the tribes which have been *c*lost, which the Father hath led away out of Jerusalem.

27 Yea, the work shall commence among all the *a*dispersed of my people, with the Father to prepare the way whereby they may *b*come unto me, that they may call on the Father in my name.

28 Yea, and then shall the work commence, with the Father among all nations in preparing the way whereby his people may be *a*gathered home to the land of their inheritance.

29 And they shall go out from all nations; and they shall *a*not go out in *b*haste, nor go by flight, for I will go before them, saith the Father, and I will be their rearward.

CHAPTER 22

In the last days, Zion and her stakes will be established, and Israel will be gathered in mercy and tenderness— They will triumph—Compare Isaiah 54. About A.D. 34.

AND then shall that which is written come to pass: Sing, O *a*barren, thou that didst not bear; break forth into *b*singing, and cry aloud, thou that didst not travail with child; for more are the children of the *c*desolate than the children of the married wife, saith the Lord.

2 Enlarge the place of thy tent, and let them stretch forth the curtains of thy habitations; spare not, lengthen thy cords and strengthen thy *a*stakes;

3 For thou shalt break forth on the right hand and on the left, and thy seed shall *a*inherit the *b*Gentiles and make the desolate cities to be inhabited.

20*b* Jer. 44:8 (6–8).
21*a* Isa. 34:8; 61:2;
  Jer. 23:19 (19–20);
  Mal. 4:1 (1, 3);
  D&C 97:26 (25–28).
  b Ezek. 21:17 (14–17).
22*a* TG Hardheartedness.
  b 1 Ne. 14:12 (12, 14).
  TG Dispensations;
  Millennium, Preparing a
  People for.
  c 2 Ne. 10:18 (18–19);
  3 Ne. 16:13; 30:2.
  d TG Lands of Inheritance.

23*a* 3 Ne. 16:8 (8–15).
  b 3 Ne. 20:22 (21–22, 39);
  Ether 13:3 (1–12).
  TG Jerusalem, New.
24*a* 3 Ne. 21:6.
25*a* 1 Ne. 13:37;
  3 Ne. 20:22.
  b Isa. 2:2 (2–4);
  59:20 (20–21);
  3 Ne. 24:1.
26*a* 3 Ne. 20:31 (29–34);
  Morm. 5:14.
  b 1 Ne. 14:17;
  3 Ne. 21:6 (6–7).

  c TG Israel, Ten Lost
  Tribes of.
27*a* 3 Ne. 16:5 (4–5).
  b TG Israel,
  Restoration of.
28*a* TG Israel, Gathering of.
29*a* 3 Ne. 20:42.
  b Isa. 52:12 (11–12).
22 1*a* Isa. 54:1 (1–17).
  b TG Singing.
  c Isa. 49:21.
2*a* TG Stake.
3*a* Obad. 1:19 (19–21).
  b TG Gentiles.

4 Fear not, for thou shalt not be ashamed; neither be thou confounded, for thou shalt not be put to [a]shame; for thou shalt forget the [b]shame of thy youth, and shalt not remember the [c]reproach of thy youth, and shalt not remember the reproach of thy widowhood any more.

5 For thy maker, thy [a]husband, the Lord of Hosts is his name; and thy Redeemer, the Holy One of Israel— the God of the whole earth shall he be called.

6 For the Lord hath called thee [a]as a woman forsaken and grieved in spirit, and a wife of youth, when thou wast refused, saith thy God.

7 For a small moment have I [a]forsaken thee, but with great mercies will I gather thee.

8 In a little wrath I hid my face from thee for a moment, but with everlasting [a]kindness will I have [b]mercy on thee, saith the Lord thy Redeemer.

9 For [a]this, the [b]waters of Noah unto me, for as I have sworn that the waters of Noah should no more go over the earth, so have I sworn that I would not be wroth with thee.

10 For the [a]mountains shall depart and the hills be removed, but my [b]kindness shall not [c]depart from thee, neither shall the covenant of my peace be removed, saith the Lord that hath mercy on thee.

11 O thou afflicted, tossed with tempest, and not comforted! Behold, I will lay thy [a]stones with fair colors, and lay thy foundations with sapphires.

12 And I will make thy windows of agates, and thy gates of carbuncles, and all thy borders of pleasant stones.

13 And [a]all thy children shall be taught of the Lord; and great shall be the [b]peace of thy children.

14 In [a]righteousness shalt thou be established; thou shalt be far from oppression for thou shalt not fear, and from terror for it shall not come near thee.

15 Behold, they shall surely gather together [a]against thee, not by me; whosoever shall gather together against thee shall fall for thy sake.

16 Behold, I have created the smith that bloweth the coals in the fire, and that bringeth forth an instrument for his work; and I have created the waster to destroy.

17 No weapon that is formed against thee shall prosper; and every tongue that shall revile against thee in judgment thou shalt condemn. This is the heritage of the [a]servants of the Lord, and their righteousness is of me, saith the Lord.

CHAPTER 23

Jesus approves the words of Isaiah— He commands the people to search the prophets—The words of Samuel the Lamanite concerning the Resurrection are added to their records. About A.D. 34.

AND now, behold, I say unto you, that ye ought to [a]search these things. Yea, a commandment I give unto you that ye search these things diligently; for great are the words of [b]Isaiah.

2 For surely he spake as touching all things concerning my people which are of the house of Israel;

4a Joel 2:26 (26–27);
       2 Ne. 6:13 (7, 13).
  b TG Shame.
  c TG Reproach.
5a Hosea 3:5 (4–5).
6a Isa. 62:4.
7a Jer. 46:27 (2–28);
       3 Ne. 20:13 (11–13).
8a TG Kindness.
  b TG God, Mercy of.
9a Isa. 54:9.
  b Gen. 8:21;

Matt. 24:37 (36–38);
       Alma 10:22.
     TG Earth, Cleansing of.
10a Isa. 40:4 (4–5).
     TG Earth, Renewal of.
  b TG Israel, Blessings of.
  c Ps. 94:14;
       D&C 35:25.
11a Rev. 21:19 (18–21).
     TG Rock.
13a Isa. 60:21;
       Jer. 31:34 (33–34).

  b 1 Ne. 22:17 (15–22);
       2 Ne. 30:10;
       Moses 7:61.
14a TG Righteousness.
15a 1 Ne. 22:14.
17a TG Servant.
23 1a TG Scriptures, Study of.
  b 2 Ne. 25:5 (1–5);
       3 Ne. 20:11;
       Morm. 8:23.

[a]therefore it must needs be that he must speak also to the Gentiles.

3 And all things that he spake have been and [a]shall be, even according to the words which he spake.

4 Therefore give heed to my words; write the things which I have told you; and according to the time and the will of the Father [a]they shall go forth unto the Gentiles.

5 And whosoever will hearken unto my words and repenteth and is baptized, the same shall be saved. Search the [a]prophets, for many there be that testify of these things.

6 And now it came to pass that when Jesus had said these words he said unto them again, after he had expounded all the scriptures unto them which they had received, he said unto them: Behold, other scriptures I would that ye should write, that ye have not.

7 And it came to pass that he said unto [a]Nephi: Bring forth the record which ye have kept.

8 And when Nephi had brought forth the records, and laid them before him, he cast his eyes upon them and said:

9 Verily I say unto you, I commanded my servant [a]Samuel, the Lamanite, that he should testify unto this people, that at the day that the Father should glorify his name in me that there were [b]many [c]saints who should [d]arise from the dead, and should appear unto many, and should minister unto them. And he said unto them: Was it not so?

10 And his disciples answered him and said: Yea, Lord, Samuel did prophesy according to thy words, and they were all fulfilled.

11 And Jesus said unto them: How be it that ye have not [a]written this thing, that many [b]saints did arise and appear unto many and did minister unto them?

12 And it came to pass that Nephi remembered that this thing had not been written.

13 And it came to pass that Jesus commanded that it should be [a]written; therefore it was written according as he commanded.

14 And now it came to pass that when Jesus had [a]expounded all the scriptures in one, which they had written, he commanded them that they should [b]teach the things which he had expounded unto them.

CHAPTER 24

The Lord's messenger will prepare the way for the Second Coming—Christ will sit in judgment—Israel is commanded to pay tithes and offerings—A book of remembrance is kept—Compare Malachi 3. About A.D. 34.

AND it came to pass that he commanded them that they should write the words which the Father had given unto Malachi, which he should tell unto them. And it came to pass that after they were written he expounded them. And these are the words which he did tell unto them, saying: Thus said the Father unto Malachi—Behold, I will [a]send my [b]messenger, and he shall prepare the way before me, and the Lord whom ye seek shall suddenly [c]come to his temple, even the [d]messenger of the covenant, whom ye delight in; behold, he shall come, saith the Lord of Hosts.

2 But who may [a]abide the day of his coming, and who shall stand when he appeareth? For he is like

---

2a Isa. 49:6.
3a 3 Ne. 15:6; 20:11 (11–12).
4a Morm. 8:26.
5a Luke 24:27 (25–27).
7a 3 Ne. 8:1;
   4 Ne. 1:19.
9a Hel. 13:2.
  b Hel. 14:25 (1, 21–26).
  c TG Saints.

  d TG Resurrection.
11a TG Jesus Christ,
   Teaching Mode of.
  b Matt. 27:52 (52–53).
13a TG Record Keeping.
14a Luke 24:44 (27, 44).
  b TG Scriptures, Study of;
   Teaching.
24 1a Mal. 3:1 (1–18).

  b D&C 45:9.
  c Isa. 59:20 (20–21);
   3 Ne. 20:22; 21:25.
  d TG Jesus Christ,
   Messenger of the
   Covenant.
2a 3 Ne. 25:1.

a ᵇrefiner's fire, and like fuller's soap.

3 And he shall sit as a refiner and purifier of silver; and he shall ᵃpurify the ᵇsons of Levi, and purge them as gold and silver, that they may ᶜoffer unto the Lord an offering in righteousness.

4 Then shall the offering of Judah and Jerusalem be pleasant unto the Lord, as in the days of old, and as in former years.

5 And I will come ᵃnear to you to judgment; and I will be a swift witness against the ᵇsorcerers, and against the adulterers, and against false ᶜswearers, and against those that ᵈoppress the hireling in his wages, the widow and the ᵉfatherless, and that turn aside the ᶠstranger, and fear not me, saith the Lord of Hosts.

6 For ᵃI am the Lord, I change not; therefore ye sons of Jacob are not consumed.

7 Even from the days of your fathers ye are gone away from mine ᵃordinances, and have not kept them. ᵇReturn unto me and I will return unto you, saith the Lord of Hosts. But ye say: Wherein shall we return?

8 Will a man rob God? Yet ye have robbed me. But ye say: Wherein have we robbed thee? In ᵃtithes and ᵇofferings.

9 Ye are cursed with a curse, for ye have robbed me, even this whole nation.

10 Bring ye all the ᵃtithes into the storehouse, that there may be ᵇmeat in my house; and prove me now herewith, saith the Lord of Hosts, if I will not open you the ᶜwindows of heaven, and pour you out a ᵈblessing that there shall not be room enough to receive it.

11 And I will rebuke the ᵃdevourer for your sakes, and he shall not destroy the fruits of your ground; neither shall your vine cast her fruit before the time in the fields, saith the Lord of Hosts.

12 And all nations shall call you blessed, for ye shall be a delightsome land, saith the Lord of Hosts.

13 Your words have been stout against me, saith the Lord. Yet ye say: What have we spoken against thee?

14 Ye have ᵃsaid: It is ᵇvain to serve God, and what doth it profit that we have kept his ᶜordinances and that we have walked mournfully before the Lord of Hosts?

15 And now we call the proud happy; yea, they that work wickedness are set up; yea, they that tempt God are even delivered.

16 Then they that feared the Lord ᵃspake often one to another, and the Lord hearkened and heard; and a book of ᵇremembrance was written before him for them that feared the Lord, and that thought upon his name.

17 And they shall be ᵃmine, saith the Lord of Hosts, in that day when I ᵇmake up my jewels; and I will

2b Deut. 4:24; Zech. 13:9;
   D&C 128:24.
   TG Earth, Cleansing of;
   Jesus Christ, Second
   Coming.
3a TG Purification.
 b Deut. 10:8;
   D&C 84:31 (31–34);
   128:24.
 c D&C 13.
5a Ezek. 43:7 (1–7).
 b TG Sorcery.
 c Hosea 10:4;
   D&C 104:5 (4–5).
   TG Swearing.
 d Ps. 94:6.

   TG Oppression.
 e Ps. 10:14; 68:5;
   James 1:27;
   D&C 136:8.
 f TG Stranger.
6a 2 Ne. 6:7; Moses 1:6.
7a TG Ordinance.
 b 1 Sam. 7:3;
   Hel. 13:11;
   3 Ne. 10:6 (5–7);
   Moro. 9:22.
8a TG Tithing.
 b Neh. 10:32.
   TG Sacrifice.
10a D&C 64:23; 119:4 (1–7).
  b TG Food.

 c Gen. 7:11.
 d TG Blessing.
11a D&C 86:3.
14a Job 16:11 (11–17);
   Jer. 20:7 (7–8);
   Hab. 1:2 (1–4).
  b Mal. 3:14 (14–15).
  c TG Ordinance.
16a 4 Ne. 1:12;
   Moro. 6:5 (5–6).
  b D&C 85:9 (7–9);
   Moses 6:5.
   TG Book of
   Remembrance.
17a Lev. 20:26.
  b D&C 101:3.

spare them as a man spareth his own son that serveth him.

18 Then shall ye return and [a]discern between the righteous and the wicked, between him that serveth God and him that serveth him not.

CHAPTER 25

At the Second Coming, the proud and wicked will be burned as stubble—Elijah will return before that great and dreadful day—Compare Malachi 4. About A.D. 34.

[a]FOR behold, the day cometh that shall [b]burn as an oven; and all the [c]proud, yea, and all that do wickedly, shall be stubble; and the day that cometh shall burn them up, saith the Lord of Hosts, that it shall leave them neither root nor branch.

2 But unto you that fear my name, shall the [a]Son of Righteousness arise with healing in his wings; and ye shall go forth and [b]grow up as [c]calves in the stall.

3 And ye shall [a]tread down the wicked; for they shall be ashes under the soles of your feet in the day that I shall do this, saith the Lord of Hosts.

4 Remember ye the law of Moses, my servant, which I commanded unto him in [a]Horeb for all Israel, with the statutes and judgments.

5 Behold, I will send you [a]Elijah the prophet before the coming of the great and dreadful [b]day of the Lord;

6 And he shall [a]turn the heart of the [b]fathers to the children, and the heart of the children to their fathers, lest I come and [c]smite the earth with a curse.

CHAPTER 26

Jesus expounds all things from the beginning to the end—Babes and children utter marvelous things that cannot be written—Those in the Church of Christ have all things in common among them. About A.D. 34.

AND now it came to pass that when Jesus had told these things he expounded them unto the multitude; and he did expound all things unto them, both great and small.

2 And he saith: [a]These scriptures, which ye had not with you, the Father commanded that I should give unto you; for it was wisdom in him that they should be given unto future generations.

3 And he did expound all things, even from the beginning until the [a]time that he should come in his [b]glory—yea, even all things which should come upon the face of the earth, even until the [c]elements should melt with fervent heat, and the earth should be [d]wrapt together as a scroll, and the heavens and the earth should pass away;

4 And even unto the [a]great and last day, when all people, and all kindreds, and all nations and tongues shall [b]stand before God, to be judged

18a TG Discernment, Spiritual.
25 1a Mal. 4:1 (1–6).
  b Ps. 21:9 (8–10);
    Isa. 24:6; 66:16;
    1 Ne. 22:15;
    3 Ne. 24:2;
    D&C 29:9;
    64:23 (23–24); 133:64;
    JS—H 1:37.
    TG Earth, Cleansing of.
  c Ps. 18:27;
    2 Ne. 20:33.
    TG Pride.
  2a Ps. 84:11; Mal. 4:2;
    Ether 9:22.
  b D&C 45:58.

  c Amos 6:4; 1 Ne. 22:24.
  3a 3 Ne. 21:12.
  4a Ex. 3:1; 19:18 (9, 16–20);
    1 Kgs. 19:8;
    Neh. 9:13;
    Mosiah 12:33; 13:5.
  5a 2 Kgs. 2:2;
    D&C 2:1; 35:4; 110:13
    (13–16); 128:17 (17–18).
    TG Genealogy and
    Temple Work.
  b TG Day of the Lord.
  6a D&C 98:16 (16–17).
  b TG Family, Eternal;
    Salvation for the Dead.
  c Mal. 4:6;
    D&C 110:15 (13–16).

26 2a IE Mal. 3–4, quoted in
    3 Ne. 24–25.
  3a TG Day of the Lord.
  b Ps. 72:19.
    TG Jesus Christ, Glory of.
  c Amos 9:13;
    2 Pet. 3:10 (10, 12);
    Morm. 9:2.
    TG Earth, Cleansing of;
    Earth, Destiny of;
    World, End of.
  d Morm. 5:23.
  4a Mal. 4:5; Hel. 12:25;
    3 Ne. 28:31.
  b Mosiah 16:10
    (1–2, 10–11).
    TG Judgment, the Last.

of their works, whether they be good or whether they be evil—

5 If they be good, to the ªresurrection of everlasting life; and if they be evil, to the resurrection of damnation; being on a parallel, the one on the one hand and the other on the other hand, according to the mercy, and the ᵇjustice, and the holiness which is in Christ, who was ᶜbefore the world began.

6 And now there cannot be written in this book even a ªhundredth part of the things which Jesus did truly teach unto the people;

7 But behold the ªplates of Nephi do contain the more part of the things which he taught the people.

8 And these things have I written, which are a ªlesser part of the things which he taught the people; and I have written them to the intent that they may be brought again unto this people, ᵇfrom the Gentiles, according to the words which Jesus hath spoken.

9 And when they shall have received this, which is expedient that they should have first, to try their faith, and if it shall so be that they shall believe these things then shall the ªgreater things be made manifest unto them.

10 And if it so be that they will not believe these things, then shall the ªgreater things be ᵇwithheld from them, unto their condemnation.

11 Behold, I was about to write them, all which were engraven upon the plates of Nephi, but the Lord ªforbade it, saying: I will ᵇtry the faith of my people.

12 Therefore I, ªMormon, do write the things which have been commanded me of the Lord. And now I, ᵇMormon, make an end of my sayings, and proceed to write the things which have been commanded me.

13 Therefore, I would that ye should behold that the Lord truly did teach the people, for the space of three days; and after that he did ªshow himself unto them oft, and did break ᵇbread oft, and bless it, and give it unto them.

14 And it came to pass that he did teach and minister unto the ªchildren of the multitude of whom hath been spoken, and he did ᵇloose their ᶜtongues, and they did speak unto their fathers great and marvelous things, even greater than he had revealed unto the people; and he loosed their tongues that they could utter.

15 And it came to pass that after he had ascended into heaven—the second time that he showed himself unto them, and had gone unto the Father, after having ªhealed all their sick, and their lame, and opened the eyes of their blind and unstopped the ears of the deaf, and even had done all manner of cures among them, and raised a man from the ᵇdead, and had shown forth his power unto them, and had ascended unto the Father—

16 Behold, it came to pass on the morrow that the multitude gathered themselves together, and they both saw and heard these children; yea, even ªbabes did open their mouths

---

5a Dan. 12:2.
  b TG God, Justice of; Justice.
  c 3 Ne. 1:14; Ether 3:14. TG Man, Antemortal Existence of.
6a John 21:25; W of M 1:5; 3 Ne. 5:8 (8–11); Ether 15:33.
7a Jarom 1:14; 4 Ne. 1:19.
8a 3 Ne. 28:33; D&C 11:22.

  b 3 Ne. 21:5 (5–6).
9a John 16:12; 2 Ne. 27:8 (7–11, 21); Morm. 8:12; Ether 4:8 (4–10).
10a Ether 4:7 (1–8).
  b 2 Ne. 28:27; Alma 12:10 (9–11); D&C 6:26 (26–27).
11a 3 Ne. 26:18.
  b Ether 12:6.
12a 3 Ne. 28:24.
  b W of M 1:1 (1–2).
13a John 21:14;

3 Ne. 27:2.
  b 3 Ne. 18:1; 20:3 (3–9). TG Bread; Sacrament.
14a Luke 10:21; Alma 32:23; 3 Ne. 17:11; D&C 128:18.
  b D&C 23:3.
  c 3 Ne. 19:32; 28:14 (14, 16).
15a 3 Ne. 17:9. TG Administrations to the Sick; Heal.
  b TG Death, Power over.
16a Matt. 11:25.

and utter marvelous things; and the things which they did utter were *b*forbidden that there should not any man write them.

17 And it came to pass that the *a*disciples whom Jesus had chosen began *b*from that time forth to *c*baptize and to teach as many as did come unto them; and as many as were baptized in the name of Jesus were filled with the Holy Ghost.

18 And many of them saw and heard unspeakable things, which are *a*not lawful to be written.

19 And they taught, and did *a*minister one to another; and they had *b*all things *c*common among them, every man dealing justly, one with another.

20 And it came to pass that they did do all things even as Jesus had commanded them.

21 And they who were baptized in the name of Jesus were called the *a*church of Christ.

CHAPTER 27

Jesus commands them to call the Church in His name—His mission and atoning sacrifice constitute His gospel—Men are commanded to repent and be baptized that they may be sanctified by the Holy Ghost—They are to be even as Jesus is. About A.D. 34–35.

AND it came to pass that as the disciples of Jesus were journeying and were preaching the things which they had both heard and seen, and were baptizing in the name of Jesus, it came to pass that the disciples were gathered together and were *a*united in *b*mighty prayer and *c*fasting.

2 And Jesus again *a*showed himself unto them, for they were praying

unto the Father in his name; and Jesus came and stood in the midst of them, and said unto them: What will ye that I shall give unto you?

3 And they said unto him: Lord, we will that thou wouldst tell us the *a*name whereby we shall call this church; for there are disputations among the people concerning this matter.

4 And the Lord said unto them: Verily, verily, I say unto you, why is it that the people should murmur and dispute because of this thing?

5 Have they not read the scriptures, which say ye must take upon you the *a*name of Christ, which is my name? For by this name shall ye be called at the last day;

6 And whoso taketh upon him my name, and *a*endureth to the end, the same shall be saved at the last day.

7 Therefore, whatsoever ye shall do, ye shall do it in my name; therefore ye shall call the church in my name; and ye shall call upon the Father in my name that he will bless the church for my sake.

8 And how be it *a*my *b*church save it be called in my name? For if a church be called in Moses' name then it be Moses' church; or if it be called in the name of a man then it be the church of a man; but if it be called in my name then it is my church, if so be that they are built upon my gospel.

9 Verily I say unto you, that ye are built upon my gospel; therefore ye shall call whatsoever things ye do call, in my name; therefore if ye call upon the Father, for the church, if it be in my name the Father will hear you;

10 And if it so be that the church

16*b* 3 Ne. 27:23.
17*a* 3 Ne. 19:4 (4–12);
        4 Ne. 1:14.
    b Ether 12:31.
    c 4 Ne. 1:1.
18*a* 3 Ne. 26:11.
19*a* TG Benevolence.
    b 4 Ne. 1:3 (3, 25–26).
    c TG Consecration.
21*a* Mosiah 18:17;
        Alma 4:5 (4–5).

TG Church.
27 1*a* D&C 29:6; 84:1.
      b Alma 8:10;
          D&C 5:24; 29:2.
      c Mosiah 27:22;
          Alma 5:46; 6:6.
      TG Fast, Fasting.
    2*a* 3 Ne. 26:13.
        TG Jesus Christ,
        Appearances,
        Postmortal.

3*a* D&C 1:1; 20:1.
5*a* TG Jesus Christ, Taking
        the Name of.
6*a* Alma 32:13 (13–15); 38:2;
        3 Ne. 15:9.
8*a* 1 Cor. 1:12 (11–13);
        D&C 115:4.
    b TG Jesus Christ, Head of
        the Church.

is built upon my gospel then will the Father show forth his own works in it.

11 But if it be not built upon my gospel, and is built upon the works of men, or upon the works of the devil, verily I say unto you they have joy in their works for a season, and by and by the end cometh, and they are ªhewn down and cast into the ᵇfire, from whence there is no return.

12 For their works do ªfollow them, for it is because of their works that they are hewn down; therefore remember the things that I have told you.

13 Behold I have given unto you my ªgospel, and this is the gospel which I have given unto you—that I came into the world to do the ᵇwill of my Father, because my Father sent me.

14 And my Father sent me that I might be ªlifted up upon the ᵇcross; and after that I had been lifted up upon the ᶜcross, that I might ᵈdraw all men unto me, that as I have been lifted up by men even so should men be lifted up by the Father, to stand before me, to be ᵉjudged of their works, whether they be good or whether they be evil—

15 And for this cause have I been ªlifted up; therefore, according to the power of the Father I will draw all men unto me, that they may be judged according to their ᵇworks.

16 And it shall come to pass, that whoso ªrepenteth and is baptized in my ᵇname shall be filled; and if he ᶜendureth to the end, behold, him will I hold guiltless before my Father at that day when I shall stand to judge the world.

17 And he that endureth not unto the end, the same is he that is also hewn down and cast into the fire, from whence they can no more return, because of the ªjustice of the Father.

18 And this is the word which he hath given unto the children of men. And for this cause he fulfilleth the words which he hath given, and he lieth not, but fulfilleth all his words.

19 And ªno unclean thing can enter into his kingdom; therefore nothing entereth into his ᵇrest save it be those who have ᶜwashed their garments in my blood, because of their faith, and the repentance of all their sins, and their faithfulness unto the end.

20 Now this is the commandment: ªRepent, all ye ends of the earth, and come unto me and be ᵇbaptized in my name, that ye may be ᶜsanctified by the reception of the Holy Ghost, that ye may stand ᵈspotless before me at the last day.

21 Verily, verily, I say unto you, this is my ªgospel; and ye know the things that ye must ᵇdo in my church; for the works which ye have seen me do that shall ye also do; for that which ye have seen me do even that shall ye do;

11a Jacob 5:46; 6:7;
     Alma 5:52;
     D&C 132:13.
  b TG Hell.
12a Rev. 14:13;
     D&C 59:2.
13a Acts 10:36 (36–40);
     D&C 76:40 (40–42).
     TG Gospel.
  b John 6:39.
     TG Jesus Christ,
     Mission of.
14a 3 Ne. 15:1;
     Morm. 2:19.
  b Moses 7:55.
  c Luke 9:44 (44–45);
     1 Ne. 11:33.

  d John 6:44;
     2 Ne. 9:5;
     D&C 17:8; 27:18.
  e TG Jesus Christ, Judge.
15a TG Jesus Christ,
     Atonement through.
  b 1 Sam. 2:3.
16a TG Repent.
  b TG Baptism,
     Qualifications for.
  c 1 Ne. 13:37.
     TG Endure;
     Steadfastness.
17a TG God, Justice of.
19a Alma 11:37.
     TG Uncleanness.
  b D&C 84:24.

     TG Rest.
  c Rev. 1:5 (1–6); 7:14;
     1 Ne. 12:10;
     Alma 5:21 (21–27);
     13:11 (11–13).
20a Ether 4:18;
     Moro. 7:34.
  b TG Baptism, Essential.
  c TG Sanctification.
  d 1 Cor. 1:8;
     D&C 4:2.
21a 1 Ne. 13:36.
     TG Gospel;
     Salvation, Plan of.
  b TG Jesus Christ,
     Exemplar.

22 Therefore, if ye do these things blessed are ye, for ye shall be lifted up at the last day.

23 "Write the things which ye have seen and heard, save it be those which are *forbidden.

24 Write the works of this people, which shall be, even as hath been written, of that which hath been.

25 For behold, out of the books which have been written, and which shall be written, shall this people be "judged, for by them shall their *works be known unto men.

26 And behold, all things are "written by the Father; therefore out of the books which shall be written shall the world be judged.

27 And know ye that "ye shall be *judges of this people, according to the judgment which I shall give unto you, which shall be just. Therefore, what "manner of men ought ye to be? Verily I say unto you, even *as I am.

28 And now I "go unto the Father. And verily I say unto you, whatsoever things ye shall ask the Father in my name shall be given unto you.

29 Therefore, "ask, and ye shall receive; knock, and it shall be opened unto you; for he that asketh, receiveth; and unto him that knocketh, it shall be opened.

30 And now, behold, my joy is great, even unto fulness, because of you, and also this generation; yea, and even the Father rejoiceth, and also all the holy angels, because of you and this generation; for "none of them are lost.

31 Behold, I would that ye should

understand; for I mean them who are "now alive of *this generation; and none of them are lost; and in them I have fulness of "joy.

32 But behold, it "sorroweth me because of the *fourth generation from this generation, for they are led away captive by him even as was the "son of perdition; for they will sell me for silver and for gold, and for that which *moth doth corrupt and which thieves can break through and steal. And in that day will I visit them, even in turning their works upon their own heads.

33 And it came to pass that when Jesus had ended these sayings he said unto his disciples: Enter ye in at the "strait gate; for strait is the gate, and narrow is the way that leads to life, and few there be that find it; but wide is the gate, and broad the way which leads to death, and many there be that travel therein, until the night cometh, wherein no man can work.

CHAPTER 28

Nine of the twelve disciples desire and are promised an inheritance in Christ's kingdom when they die—The Three Nephites desire and are given power over death so as to remain on the earth until Jesus comes again—They are translated and see things not lawful to utter, and they are now ministering among men. About A.D. 34–35.

AND it came to pass when Jesus had said these words, he spake unto his disciples, one by one, saying unto them: What is it that ye "desire of

23a TG Record Keeping.
  b 3 Ne. 26:16 (16, 18).
25a 2 Ne. 33:15 (10–15);
    W of M 1:11.
  b Ps. 33:15 (13–15);
    1 Ne. 15:33 (26–36).
26a 3 Ne. 24:16.
    TG Book of Life.
27a 1 Ne. 12:10 (9–10);
    Morm. 3:19.
  b Rev. 20:4 (4–6).
  c 2 Pet. 3:11.
    TG Godliness;
    Jesus Christ, Exemplar;

Man, Potential to
  Become like Heavenly
  Father.
  d Matt. 5:48;
    3 Ne. 12:48.
28a John 16:10; 20:17.
29a Matt. 7:7;
    3 Ne. 14:7.
30a John 17:12.
31a 3 Ne. 9:13 (11–13); 10:12.
  b 3 Ne. 28:23.
  c TG Joy.
32a Gen. 6:6;
    3 Ne. 17:14.

  b 1 Ne. 12:11 (11–12);
    2 Ne. 26:9 (9–10);
    Alma 45:12 (10, 12);
    Hel. 13:6 (5–19).
  c John 17:12;
    3 Ne. 29:7.
  d Matt. 6:19;
    3 Ne. 13:19 (19–21).
33a Matt. 7:13 (13–14).
    Luke 13:24;
    3 Ne. 14:13;
    D&C 22:4 (1–4).
28 1a 2 Chr. 1:7 (7–12);
    D&C 7:1 (1–8).

me, after that I am gone to the Father?

2 And they all spake, save it were three, saying: We desire that after we have lived unto the age of man, that our ministry, wherein thou hast called us, may have an end, that we may speedily come unto thee in thy kingdom.

3 And he said unto them: Blessed are ye because ye desired this thing of me; therefore, after that ye are [a]seventy and two years old ye shall come unto me in my [b]kingdom; and with me ye shall find [c]rest.

4 And when he had spoken unto them, he turned himself unto the three, and said unto them: What will ye that I should do unto you, when I am gone unto the Father?

5 And they sorrowed in their hearts, for they durst not speak unto him the thing which they desired.

6 And he said unto them: Behold, I [a]know your thoughts, and ye have desired the thing which [b]John, my beloved, who was with me in my ministry, before that I was lifted up by the Jews, desired of me.

7 Therefore, more blessed are ye, for ye shall [a]never taste of [b]death; but ye shall live to behold all the doings of the Father unto the children of men, even until all things shall be fulfilled according to the will of the Father, when I shall come in my glory with the [c]powers of heaven.

8 And ye shall never endure the pains of death; but when I shall come in my glory ye shall be changed in the twinkling of an eye from [a]mortality to [b]immortality;

and then shall ye be blessed in the kingdom of my Father.

9 And again, ye shall not have pain while ye shall dwell in the flesh, neither sorrow save it be for the [a]sins of the world; and all this will I do because of the thing which ye have desired of me, for ye have desired that ye might [b]bring the souls of men unto me, while the world shall stand.

10 And for this cause ye shall have [a]fulness of joy; and ye shall sit down in the kingdom of my Father; yea, your joy shall be full, even as the Father hath given me fulness of joy; and ye shall be even as I am, and I am even as the Father; and the Father and I are [b]one;

11 And the [a]Holy Ghost beareth record of the Father and me; and the Father giveth the Holy Ghost unto the children of men, because of me.

12 And it came to pass that when Jesus had spoken these words, he touched every one of them with his finger save it were the [a]three who were to tarry, and then he departed.

13 And behold, the heavens were opened, and they were [a]caught up into heaven, and saw and heard unspeakable things.

14 And it was [a]forbidden them that they should utter; neither was it given unto them [b]power that they could utter the things which they saw and heard;

15 And whether they were in the body or out of the body, they could not tell; for it did seem unto them like a [a]transfiguration of them, that

3 a 4 Ne. 1:14.
  b TG Election.
  c TG Rest.
6 a Amos 4:13;
    Alma 18:32.
  b John 21:22 (21–23);
    D&C 7:3 (1–8).
7 a 4 Ne. 1:37 (14, 37);
    Morm. 8:10 (10–12);
    Ether 12:17.
  b Luke 9:27.
    TG Translated Beings.
  c 3 Ne. 20:22.
8 a 3 Ne. 28:36 (36–40).

TG Mortality.
  b TG Immortality.
9 a 4 Ne. 1:44;
    Morm. 8:10.
  b Philip. 1:24 (23–24);
    3 Ne. 28:27;
    D&C 7:5 (1–8).
10 a John 16:15;
    D&C 76:59;
    84:38 (37–38).
  b Deut. 6:4;
    Gal. 3:20;
    2 Ne. 31:21;
    3 Ne. 11:27 (27–28, 36);

Morm. 7:7;
    D&C 20:28.
11 a 2 Ne. 31:18 (17–21);
    3 Ne. 11:32;
    Ether 5:4;
    Moses 6:66.
12 a 4 Ne. 1:14 (14, 37);
    Morm. 1:13.
13 a 2 Cor. 12:4 (2–4).
14 a D&C 76:115.
  b 3 Ne. 19:32; 26:14.
15 a Moses 1:11.
    TG Transfiguration.

they were changed from this body of flesh into an immortal state, that they could behold the things of God.

16 But it came to pass that they did again minister upon the face of the earth; nevertheless they did not minister of the things which they had heard and seen, because of the commandment which was given them in heaven.

17 And now, whether they were mortal or immortal, from the day of their transfiguration, I know not;

18 But this much I know, according to the record which hath been given—they did go forth upon the face of the land, and did minister unto all the people, uniting as many to the church as would believe in their preaching; baptizing them, and as many as were baptized did receive the Holy Ghost.

19 And they were cast into prison by them who did not belong to the church. And the ªprisons could not hold them, for they were rent in twain.

20 And they were cast down into the earth; but they did smite the earth with the word of God, insomuch that by his ªpower they were delivered out of the depths of the earth; and therefore they could not dig pits sufficient to hold them.

21 And thrice they were cast into a ªfurnace and received no harm.

22 And twice were they cast into a ªden of wild beasts; and behold they did play with the beasts as a child with a suckling lamb, and received no harm.

23 And it came to pass that thus they did go forth among all the people of Nephi, and did preach the ªgospel of Christ unto all people upon the face of the land; and

they were converted unto the Lord, and were united unto the church of Christ, and thus the people of ᵇthat generation were blessed, according to the word of Jesus.

24 And now I, ªMormon, make an end of speaking concerning these things for a time.

25 Behold, I was about to write the ªnames of those who were never to taste of death, but the Lord forbade; therefore I write them not, for they are hid from the world.

26 But behold, ªI have seen them, and they have ministered unto me.

27 And behold they will be ªamong the Gentiles, and the Gentiles shall know them not.

28 They will also be among the Jews, and the Jews shall know them not.

29 And it shall come to pass, when the Lord seeth fit in his wisdom that they shall minister unto all the ªscattered tribes of Israel, and unto all nations, kindreds, tongues and people, and shall bring out of them unto Jesus many souls, that their desire may be fulfilled, and also because of the convincing power of God which is in them.

30 And they are as the ªangels of God, and if they shall pray unto the Father in the name of Jesus they can show themselves unto whatsoever man it seemeth them good.

31 Therefore, great and marvelous works shall be wrought by them, before the ªgreat and coming day when all people must surely stand before the judgment-seat of Christ;

32 Yea even among the Gentiles shall there be a ªgreat and marvelous work wrought by them, before that judgment day.

33 And if ye had ªall the scriptures which give an account of all the

---

19a Acts 16:26;
   Alma 14:27 (26–28);
   4 Ne. 1:30;
   Morm. 8:24.
20a 1 Ne. 7:17 (17–18);
   Jacob 4:6.
21a Dan. 3:25; 4 Ne. 1:32;
   Morm. 8:24.

22a Dan. 6:16 (16–27);
   4 Ne. 1:33.
23a TG Gospel.
   b 3 Ne. 27:31 (30–31).
24a 3 Ne. 26:12.
25a 3 Ne. 19:4.
26a Morm. 8:11.
27a 3 Ne. 28:9.

29a TG Israel, Scattering
   of; Israel, Ten Lost
   Tribes of.
30a TG Angels.
31a Mal. 4:5; Hel. 12:25;
   3 Ne. 26:4; Morm. 9:2.
32a 2 Ne. 25:17.
33a 3 Ne. 26:8 (6–12).

marvelous works of Christ, ye would, according to the words of Christ, know that these things must surely come.

34 And wo be unto him that will [a]not hearken unto the words of Jesus, and also to them whom he hath chosen and [b]sent among them; for whoso [c]receiveth not the words of Jesus and the words of those whom he hath sent receiveth not him; and therefore he will not receive them at the last day;

35 And it would be better for them if they had not been born. For do ye suppose that ye can get rid of the justice of an [a]offended God, who hath been [b]trampled under feet of men, that thereby salvation might come?

36 And now behold, as I spake concerning those whom the Lord hath chosen, yea, even three who were caught up into the heavens, that I knew not whether they were [a]cleansed from [b]mortality to immortality—

37 But behold, since I wrote, I have inquired of the Lord, and he hath made it manifest unto me that there must needs be a change wrought upon their bodies, or else it needs be that they must taste of death;

38 Therefore, that they might not taste of death there was a [a]change wrought upon their bodies, that they might not [b]suffer pain nor sorrow save it were for the sins of the world.

39 Now this change was not equal to that which shall take place at the last day; but there was a change wrought upon them, insomuch that Satan could have no power over them, that he could not [a]tempt them; and they were [b]sanctified in the flesh, that they were [c]holy, and

that the powers of the earth could not hold them.

40 And in this state they were to remain until the judgment day of Christ; and at that day they were to receive a greater change, and to be received into the kingdom of the Father to go no more out, but to dwell with God eternally in the heavens.

CHAPTER 29

The coming forth of the Book of Mormon is a sign that the Lord has commenced to gather Israel and fulfill His covenants—Those who reject His latter-day revelations and gifts will be cursed. About A.D. 34–35.

AND now behold, I say unto you that when the Lord shall see fit, in his wisdom, that these sayings shall [a]come unto the Gentiles according to his word, then ye may know that the [b]covenant which the Father hath made with the children of Israel, concerning their restoration to the [c]lands of their inheritance, is already beginning to be fulfilled.

2 And ye may know that the words of the Lord, which have been spoken by the holy prophets, shall all be fulfilled; and ye need not say that the Lord [a]delays his coming unto the children of Israel.

3 And ye need not imagine in your hearts that the words which have been spoken are vain, for behold, the Lord will remember his covenant which he hath made unto his people of the house of Israel.

4 And when ye shall see these sayings coming forth among you, then ye need not any longer spurn at the doings of the Lord, for the [a]sword of his [b]justice is in his right hand;

34a Ether 4:8 (8–12).
  b Matt. 10:5 (5–42).
  c TG Prophets,
    Rejection of.
35a TG Blaspheme.
  b Hel. 12:2.
36a TG Purification.
  b 3 Ne. 28:8 (8–9).
    TG Immortality;

Mortality.
38a TG Translated Beings.
  b TG Suffering.
39a TG Temptation;
    Test.
  b TG Sanctification.
  c TG Holiness.
29 1a 2 Ne. 30:3 (3–8);
    Morm. 3:17.

  b Ezek. 20:37;
    Morm. 5:14 (14, 20).
  c TG Lands of Inheritance.
2a Matt. 24:48;
    Luke 12:45.
4a 3 Ne. 20:20.
  b TG Justice.

and behold, at that day, if ye shall spurn at his doings he will cause that it shall soon overtake you.

5 ^aWo unto him that ^bspurneth at the doings of the Lord; yea, wo unto him that shall ^cdeny the Christ and his works!

6 Yea, ^awo unto him that shall deny the revelations of the Lord, and that shall say the Lord no longer worketh by revelation, or by prophecy, or by ^bgifts, or by tongues, or by healings, or by the power of the Holy Ghost!

7 Yea, and wo unto him that shall say at that day, to get ^again, that there can be ^bno miracle wrought by Jesus Christ; for he that doeth this shall become ^clike unto the son of perdition, for whom there was no mercy, according to the word of Christ!

8 Yea, and ye need not any longer ^ahiss, nor ^bspurn, nor make game of the ^cJews, nor any of the remnant of the house of Israel; for behold, the Lord remembereth his covenant unto them, and he will do unto them according to that which he hath sworn.

9 Therefore ye need not suppose that ye can turn the right hand of the Lord unto the left, that he may not execute judgment unto the fulfilling of the covenant which he hath made unto the house of Israel.

CHAPTER 30

The latter-day Gentiles are commanded to repent, come unto Christ, and be numbered with the house of Israel. About A.D. 34–35.

HEARKEN, O ye Gentiles, and hear the words of Jesus Christ, the Son of the living God, which he hath ^acommanded me that I should speak concerning you, for, behold he commandeth me that I should write, saying:

2 Turn, all ye ^aGentiles, from your wicked ways; and ^brepent of your evil doings, of your ^clyings and deceivings, and of your whoredoms, and of your secret abominations, and your idolatries, and of your ^dmurders, and your ^epriestcrafts, and your ^fenvyings, and your strifes, and from all your wickedness and abominations, and come unto me, and be baptized in my name, that ye may receive a remission of your sins, and be filled with the Holy Ghost, that ye may be ^gnumbered with my people who are of the house of Israel.

5a 2 Ne. 28:15; Morm. 9:26.
b Morm. 8:17; Ether 4:8 (8–10).
c Matt. 10:33 (32–33); Moro. 1:3.
6a Morm. 9:7 (7–11, 15).
b TG Holy Ghost, Gifts of.
7a TG Priestcraft.
b 2 Ne. 28:6 (4–6); Morm. 8:26; 9:15 (15–26).
c 2 Ne. 9:9; 3 Ne. 27:32. TG Sons of Perdition.
8a 1 Ne. 19:14.
b 2 Ne. 29:5 (4–5). TG Backbiting.
c TG Israel, Judah, People of.
30 1a 3 Ne. 5:13 (12–13).
2a Rom. 15:10 (8–21).
b TG Repent.
c Alma 16:18; 3 Ne. 21:19 (19–21).
d 3 Ne. 16:10; Morm. 8:31.
e TG Priestcraft.
f TG Envy.
g Gal. 3:29 (27–29); 2 Ne. 10:18 (18–19); 3 Ne. 21:22 (22–25); Abr. 2:10.

FOURTH NEPHI
THE BOOK OF NEPHI

WHO IS THE SON OF NEPHI—ONE OF THE
DISCIPLES OF JESUS CHRIST

An account of the people of Nephi, according to his record.

The Nephites and the Lamanites are all converted unto the Lord—They have all things in common, work miracles, and prosper in the land—After two centuries, divisions, evils, false churches, and persecutions arise—After three hundred years, both the Nephites and the Lamanites are wicked—Ammaron hides up the sacred records. About A.D. 35–321.

AND it came to pass that the thirty and fourth year passed away, and also the thirty and fifth, and behold the disciples of Jesus had formed a church of Christ in all the lands round about. And as many as did come unto them, and did truly repent of their sins, were *a*baptized in the name of Jesus; and they did also receive the Holy Ghost.

2 And it came to pass in the thirty and sixth year, the people were all converted unto the Lord, upon all the face of the land, both Nephites and Lamanites, and there were no contentions and disputations among them, and every man did deal justly one with another.

3 And they had *a*all things common among them; therefore there were not rich and poor, bond and free, but they were all made free, and partakers of the heavenly *b*gift.

4 And it came to pass that the thirty and seventh year passed away also, and there still continued to be *a*peace in the land.

5 And there were great and marvelous works wrought by the disciples of Jesus, insomuch that they did *a*heal the sick, and *b*raise the dead, and cause the lame to walk, and the blind to receive their sight, and the deaf to hear; and all manner of *c*miracles did they work among the children of men; and in nothing did they work miracles save it were in the name of Jesus.

6 And thus did the thirty and eighth year pass away, and also the thirty and ninth, and forty and first, and the forty and second, yea, even until forty and nine years had passed away, and also the fifty and first, and the fifty and second; yea, and even until fifty and nine years had passed away.

7 And the Lord did prosper them exceedingly in the land; yea, insomuch that they did build cities again where there had been cities burned.

8 Yea, even that great *a*city Zarahemla did they cause to be built again.

9 But there were many cities which had been *a*sunk, and waters came up in the stead thereof; therefore these cities could not be renewed.

10 And now, behold, it came to pass that the people of Nephi did wax strong, and did multiply exceedingly fast, and became an exceedingly *a*fair and delightsome people.

---

1 1*a* 3 Ne. 26:17.
  3*a* Jacob 2:19 (17–19);
      Mosiah 4:26;
      18:27 (19–29);
      Alma 16:16;
      3 Ne. 12:42; 26:19.

TG Consecration.
  b TG God, Gifts of.
4*a* TG Peace.
5*a* TG Heal.
  b TG Death, Power over.
  c John 14:12 (12–14).

TG Miracle.
8*a* 3 Ne. 8:8 (8, 24).
9*a* 3 Ne. 9:4 (4, 7).
10*a* 1 Ne. 13:15;
      2 Ne. 5:21;
      Morm. 9:6.

11 And they were married, and given in marriage, and were blessed according to the multitude of the ᵃpromises which the Lord had made unto them.

12 And they did not walk any more after the ᵃperformances and ᵇordinances of the ᶜlaw of Moses; but they did walk after the commandments which they had received from their Lord and their God, continuing in ᵈfasting and prayer, and in meeting together oft both to pray and to hear the word of the Lord.

13 And it came to pass that there was no contention among all the people, in all the land; but there were mighty miracles wrought among the disciples of Jesus.

14 And it came to pass that the seventy and first year passed away, and also the seventy and second year, yea, and in fine, till the seventy and ninth year had passed away; yea, even an hundred years had passed away, and the ᵃdisciples of Jesus, whom he had chosen, had all gone to the ᵇparadise of God, save it were the ᶜthree who should tarry; and there were other ᵈdisciples ᵉordained in their stead; and also many of that ᶠgeneration had passed away.

15 And it came to pass that there was no ᵃcontention in the land, because of the ᵇlove of God which did dwell in the hearts of the people.

16 And there were no ᵃenvyings, nor ᵇstrifes, nor ᶜtumults, nor whoredoms, nor lyings, nor murders, nor any manner of ᵈlasciviousness; and surely there could not be a ᵉhappier people among all the people who had been created by the hand of God.

17 There were no robbers, nor murderers, neither were there Lamanites, nor any manner of -ites; but they were in ᵃone, the children of Christ, and heirs to the kingdom of God.

18 And how blessed were they! For the Lord did bless them in all their doings; yea, even they were blessed and prospered until an hundred and ten years had passed away; and the first generation from Christ had passed away, and there was no contention in all the land.

19 And it came to pass that ᵃNephi, he that kept this last record, (and he kept it upon the ᵇplates of Nephi) died, and his son Amos kept it in his stead; and he kept it upon the plates of Nephi also.

20 And he kept it eighty and four years, and there was still peace in the land, save it were a small part of the people who had revolted from the church and taken upon them the name of Lamanites; therefore there began to be ᵃLamanites again in the land.

21 And it came to pass that ᵃAmos died also, (and it was an hundred and ninety and four years from the coming of Christ) and his son Amos kept the record in his stead; and he also kept it upon the plates of Nephi; and it was also written in the book of Nephi, which is this book.

22 And it came to pass that two hundred years had passed away; and the second generation had all passed away save it were a few.

23 And now I, Mormon, would that ye should know that the people had multiplied, insomuch that they were spread upon all the face of the land,

11a TG Promise.
12a 2 Ne. 25:30.
  b TG Ordinance.
  c 3 Ne. 9:19; 15:4 (2–8).
    TG Law of Moses.
  d Moro. 6:5;
    D&C 88:76.
14a 3 Ne. 28:3;
    Morm. 3:19.
  b TG Paradise.
  c 3 Ne. 28:12.

    TG Translated Beings.
  d TG Apostles.
  e TG Priesthood,
    History of.
  f 1 Ne. 12:12.
15a TG Contention.
  b TG God, Love of.
16a TG Envy.
  b TG Strife.
  c TG Rioting and Reveling.
  d TG Lust.

  e Prov. 14:34;
    Mosiah 2:41;
    Alma 50:23.
    TG Happiness.
17a John 17:21 (21–23).
    TG Zion.
19a 4 Ne. heading.
  b 3 Ne. 26:7.
20a 3 Ne. 10:18;
    Morm. 1:9.
21a 4 Ne. 1:47.

and that they had become exceedingly "rich, because of their prosperity in Christ.

24 And now, in this two hundred and first year there began to be among them those who were lifted up in "pride, such as the wearing of costly apparel, and all manner of fine pearls, and of the fine things of the world.

25 And from that time forth they did have their goods and their substance no more "common among them.

26 And they began to be divided into classes; and they began to build up "churches unto themselves to get "gain, and began to deny the true church of Christ.

27 And it came to pass that when two hundred and ten years had passed away there were many churches in the land; yea, there were many churches which professed to know the Christ, and yet they did "deny the more parts of his gospel, insomuch that they did receive all manner of wickedness, and did administer that which was sacred unto him to whom it had been "forbidden because of unworthiness.

28 And this church did multiply exceedingly because of iniquity, and because of the power of "Satan who did get hold upon their "hearts.

29 And again, there was another church which denied the Christ; and they did "persecute the true "church of Christ, because of their humility and their belief in Christ; and they did despise them because of the many miracles which were wrought among them.

30 Therefore they did exercise power and authority over the disciples of Jesus who did tarry with them, and they did cast them into "prison; but by the power of the word of God, which was in them, the prisons were rent in twain, and they went forth doing mighty miracles among them.

31 Nevertheless, and notwithstanding all these miracles, the people did harden their hearts, and did seek to kill them, even as the Jews at Jerusalem sought to kill Jesus, according to his word.

32 And they did cast them into "furnaces of "fire, and they came forth receiving no harm.

33 And they also cast them into "dens of wild beasts, and they did play with the wild beasts even as a child with a lamb; and they did come forth from among them, receiving no harm.

34 Nevertheless, the people did harden their hearts, for they were led by many priests and "false prophets to build up many churches, and to do all manner of iniquity. And they did "smite upon the people of Jesus; but the people of Jesus did not smite again. And thus they did dwindle in unbelief and wickedness, from year to year, even until two hundred and thirty years had passed away.

35 And now it came to pass in this year, yea, in the two hundred and thirty and first year, there was a great division among the people.

36 And it came to pass that in this year there arose a people who were called the "Nephites, and they were true believers in Christ; and among them there were those who were called by the Lamanites—Jacobites, and Josephites, and "Zoramites;

37 Therefore the true believers in Christ, and the true worshipers of

---

23 a TG Treasure.
24 a TG Pride;
   Selfishness.
25 a TG Consecration.
26 a 1 Ne. 22:23;
   2 Ne. 28:3 (3–32);
   Morm. 8:28 (28, 32–38).
   b Ezek. 22:27;
   D&C 10:56.

27 a TG Apostasy of
   Individuals.
   b 3 Ne. 18:28 (28–29).
28 a TG Devil, Church of.
   b TG Hardheartedness.
29 a TG Persecution.
   b TG Jesus Christ, Head of
   the Church.

30 a 3 Ne. 28:19 (19–20).
32 a 3 Ne. 28:21.
   b Dan. 3:27.
33 a 3 Ne. 28:22.
34 a TG False Prophets.
   b 3 Ne. 6:13; 12:39;
   D&C 98:23 (23–27).
36 a Morm. 1:8.
   b Jacob 1:13.

Christ, (among whom were the ᵃthree disciples of Jesus who should tarry) were called Nephites, and Jacobites, and Josephites, and Zoramites.

38 And it came to pass that they who rejected the gospel were called Lamanites, and Lemuelites, and Ishmaelites; and they did not dwindle in ᵃunbelief, but they did ᵇwilfully rebel against the gospel of Christ; and they did teach their children that they should not believe, even as their fathers, from the beginning, did dwindle.

39 And it was because of the wickedness and abomination of their fathers, even as it was in the beginning. And they were ᵃtaught to hate the children of God, even as the Lamanites were taught to ᵇhate the children of Nephi from the beginning.

40 And it came to pass that two hundred and forty and four years had passed away, and thus were the affairs of the people. And the ᵃmore wicked part of the people did wax strong, and became exceedingly more numerous than were the people of God.

41 And they did still continue to build up churches unto themselves, and adorn them with all manner of precious things. And thus did two hundred and fifty years pass away, and also two hundred and sixty years.

42 And it came to pass that the wicked part of the people began again to build up the secret oaths and ᵃcombinations of Gadianton.

43 And also the people who were called the people of Nephi began to be proud in their hearts, because of their exceeding riches, and become ᵃvain like unto their brethren, the Lamanites.

44 And from this time the disciples began to sorrow for the ᵃsins of the world.

45 And it came to pass that when three hundred years had passed away, both the people of Nephi and the Lamanites had become exceedingly wicked one like unto another.

46 And it came to pass that the robbers of ᵃGadianton did spread over all the face of the land; and there were none that were righteous save it were the disciples of Jesus. And gold and silver did they lay up in store in abundance, and did ᵇtraffic in all manner of traffic.

47 And it came to pass that after three hundred and five years had passed away, (and the people did still remain in wickedness) ᵃAmos died; and his brother, Ammaron, did keep the record in his stead.

48 And it came to pass that when three hundred and twenty years had passed away, ᵃAmmaron, being constrained by the Holy Ghost, did ᵇhide up the ᶜrecords which were ᵈsacred—yea, even all the sacred records which had been handed down from generation to generation, which were sacred—even until the three hundred and twentieth year from the coming of Christ.

49 And he did hide them up unto the Lord, that they might ᵃcome again unto the remnant of the house of Jacob, according to the prophecies and the promises of the Lord. And thus is the end of the record of Ammaron.

37a 3 Ne. 28:7;
  Morm. 8:10 (10–12).
38a TG Unbelief.
  b Josh. 22:18;
  Morm. 1:16.
39a Mosiah 10:17.
  b TG Hate;
  Malice.
40a Hel. 5:2.
42a TG Secret Combinations.
43a Hel. 16:22.
44a Eccl. 3:16 (16–17);
  3 Ne. 28:9;
  Morm. 8:10 (9–10).
46a Morm. 2:8;
  Ether 8:20.
  b Mosiah 24:7;
  Ether 10:22.
47a 4 Ne. 1:21.
48a Morm. 1:2.
  b Morm. 2:17.
  c TG Scriptures,
  Preservation of.
  d Hel. 3:15 (13, 15–16).
49a Enos 1:13;
  Morm. 5:9.

THE BOOK OF MORMON

CHAPTER 1

Ammaron instructs Mormon concerning the sacred records—War commences between the Nephites and the Lamanites—The Three Nephites are taken away—Wickedness, unbelief, sorceries, and witchcraft prevail. About A.D. 321–26.

AND now I, Mormon, make a ^arecord of the things which I have both seen and heard, and call it the ^bBook of Mormon.

2 And about the time that ^aAmmaron hid up the records unto the Lord, he came unto me, (I being about ten years of age, and I began to be ^blearned somewhat after the manner of the learning of my people) and Ammaron said unto me: I perceive that thou art a ^csober child, and art quick to observe;

3 Therefore, when ye are about twenty and four years old I would that ye should remember the things that ye have observed concerning this people; and when ye are of that age go to the ^aland Antum, unto a hill which shall be called ^bShim; and there have I deposited unto the Lord all the sacred engravings concerning this people.

4 And behold, ye shall take the ^aplates of Nephi unto yourself, and the remainder shall ye leave in the place where they are; and ye shall engrave on the plates of Nephi all the things that ye have observed concerning this people.

5 And I, Mormon, being a descendant of ^aNephi, (and my father's name was Mormon) I remembered the things which Ammaron commanded me.

6 And it came to pass that I, being eleven years old, was carried by my father into the land southward, even to the land of Zarahemla.

7 The whole face of the land had become covered with buildings, and the people were as numerous almost, as it were the sand of the sea.

8 And it came to pass in this year there began to be a war between the ^aNephites, who consisted of the Nephites and the Jacobites and the Josephites and the Zoramites; and this war was between the Nephites, and the Lamanites and the Lemuelites and the Ishmaelites.

9 Now the ^aLamanites and the Lemuelites and the Ishmaelites were called Lamanites, and the two parties were Nephites and Lamanites.

10 And it came to pass that the war began to be among them in the borders of Zarahemla, by the waters of Sidon.

11 And it came to pass that the Nephites had gathered together a great number of men, even to exceed the number of thirty thousand. And it came to pass that they did have in this same year a number of ^abattles, in which the Nephites did beat the Lamanites and did slay many of them.

12 And it came to pass that the Lamanites withdrew their design, and there was peace settled in the land; and peace did remain for the space of about four years, that there was no bloodshed.

13 But wickedness did prevail upon the face of the whole land, insomuch that the Lord did take away his ^abeloved disciples, and the work of miracles and of healing did cease because of the iniquity of the people.

14 And there were no ^agifts from

1 1 *a* 3 Ne. 5:11 (11–18);
   Morm. 8:5.
 b W of M 1:5; Morm. 5:9.
2 *a* 4 Ne. 1:48 (47–49).
 b Enos 1:1;
   Mosiah 1:3 (3–5).
 c TG Sobriety;

Trustworthiness.
3 *a* Morm. 2:17.
 b Morm. 4:23; Ether 9:3.
4 *a* W of M 1:1 (1, 11);
   3 Ne. 5:10 (9–12);
   Morm. 2:17 (17–18);
   8:5 (1, 4–5, 14).

5 *a* 3 Ne. 5:20 (12, 20).
8 *a* 4 Ne. 1:36.
9 *a* 4 Ne. 1:20.
11 *a* 2 Ne. 1:12;
   Morm. 4:1 (1–23).
13 *a* 3 Ne. 28:12 (2, 12).
14 *a* 1 Sam. 3:1.

the Lord, and the ^bHoly Ghost did not come upon any, because of their wickedness and ^cunbelief.

15 And I, being ^afifteen years of age and being somewhat of a ^bsober mind, therefore I was ^cvisited of the Lord, and ^dtasted and knew of the goodness of Jesus.

16 And I did endeavor to preach unto this people, but my mouth was shut, and I was forbidden that I should preach unto them; for behold they had ^awilfully rebelled against their God; and the beloved disciples were ^btaken away out of the land, because of their iniquity.

17 But I did remain among them, but I was forbidden to ^apreach unto them, because of the hardness of their hearts; and because of the hardness of their hearts the land was ^bcursed for their sake.

18 And these Gadianton robbers, who were among the Lamanites, did infest the land, insomuch that the inhabitants thereof began to ^ahide up their ^btreasures in the earth; and they became slippery, because the Lord had cursed the land, that they could not hold them, nor retain them again.

19 And it came to pass that there were ^asorceries, and witchcrafts, and magics; and the power of the evil one was wrought upon all the face of the land, even unto the fulfilling of all the words of Abinadi, and also ^bSamuel the Lamanite.

CHAPTER 2

Mormon leads the Nephite armies—Blood and carnage sweep the land—The Nephites lament and mourn with the sorrowing of the damned—Their day of grace is passed—Mormon obtains the plates of Nephi—Wars continue. About A.D. *327–50.*

AND it came to pass in that same year there began to be a war again between the Nephites and the Lamanites. And notwithstanding I being ^ayoung, was large in stature; therefore the people of Nephi appointed me that I should be their leader, or the leader of their armies.

2 Therefore it came to pass that in my sixteenth year I did go forth at the head of an army of the Nephites, against the Lamanites; therefore three hundred and twenty and six years had passed away.

3 And it came to pass that in the three hundred and twenty and seventh year the Lamanites did come upon us with ^aexceedingly great power, insomuch that they did frighten my armies; therefore they would not fight, and they began to retreat towards the ^bnorth countries.

4 And it came to pass that we did come to the city of Angola, and we did take possession of the city, and make preparations to defend ourselves against the Lamanites. And it came to pass that we did ^afortify the city with our might; but notwithstanding all our fortifications the Lamanites did come upon us and did drive us out of the city.

5 And they did also drive us forth out of the land of David.

6 And we marched forth and came to the land of Joshua, which was in the borders west by the seashore.

7 And it came to pass that we did gather in our people as fast as it were

---

14b TG Holy Ghost, Loss of.
  c TG Unbelief.
15a Morm. 2:1 (1–2).
  b TG Sobriety.
  c Ex. 3:16;
    2 Ne. 4:26;
    Alma 9:21.
  d Ps. 34:8.
16a 4 Ne. 1:38.
    TG Rebellion.

  b Morm. 8:10.
17a Micah 3:6 (5–7).
  b 2 Ne. 1:7;
    Alma 45:16 (10–14, 16);
    Ether 2:11 (8–12).
18a Hel. 12:18;
    Morm. 2:10 (10–14);
    Ether 14:1 (1–2).
  b Hel. 13:18–23, 30–37.
    TG Treasure.

19a TG Sorcery.
  b Morm. 2:10 (10–15).
2 1a Morm. 1:15 (12, 15–16).
  3a Morm. 4:13 (13–17); 5:6.
  b Alma 50:11;
    Morm. 2:29.
  4a 3 Ne. 3:14 (14, 25);
    Morm. 2:21.

possible, that we might get them together in ªone body.

8 But behold, the land was ªfilled with ᵇrobbers and with Lamanites; and notwithstanding the great destruction which hung over my people, they did not repent of their evil doings; therefore there was blood and carnage spread throughout all the face of the land, both on the part of the Nephites and also on the part of the Lamanites; and it was one complete revolution throughout all the face of the land.

9 And now, the Lamanites had a king, and his name was ªAaron; and he came against us with an army of forty and four thousand. And behold, I withstood him with forty and two thousand. And it came to pass that I beat him with my army that he fled before me. And behold, all this was done, and three hundred and thirty years had passed away.

10 And it came to pass that the Nephites began to repent of their iniquity, and began to cry even as had been prophesied by Samuel the prophet; for behold no man could ªkeep that which was his own, for the thieves, and the robbers, and the murderers, and the magic art, and the witchcraft which was in the land.

11 Thus there began to be a ªmourning and a lamentation in all the land because of these things, and more especially among the people of Nephi.

12 And it came to pass that when I, Mormon, saw their lamentation and their ªmourning and their sorrow before the Lord, my heart did begin to rejoice within me, knowing the mercies and the long-suffering of the Lord, therefore supposing that he would be merciful unto them that they would ᵇagain become a righteous people.

13 But behold this my joy was vain, for their ªsorrowing was not unto repentance, because of the goodness of God; but it was rather the ᵇsorrowing of the ᶜdamned, because the Lord would not always suffer them to take ᵈhappiness in sin.

14 And they did not come unto Jesus with broken ªhearts and contrite spirits, but they did ᵇcurse God, and wish to die. Nevertheless they would struggle with the sword for their lives.

15 And it came to pass that my sorrow did return unto me again, and I saw that the ªday of ᵇgrace ᶜwas passed with them, both temporally and spiritually; for I saw thousands of them hewn down in open ᵈrebellion against their God, and heaped up as ᵉdung upon the face of the land. And thus three hundred and forty and four years had passed away.

16 And it came to pass that in the three hundred and forty and fifth year the Nephites did begin to flee before the Lamanites; and they were pursued until they came even to the land of Jashon, before it was possible to stop them in their retreat.

17 And now, the city of Jashon was near the ªland where Ammaron had ᵇdeposited the records unto the Lord, that they might not be destroyed. And behold I had gone according to the word of Ammaron, and taken the ᶜplates of Nephi, and did make a record according to the words of Ammaron.

18 And upon the plates of Nephi I

7a 3 Ne. 3:22 (22–25).
8a 3 Ne. 2:11.
  b 4 Ne. 1:46;
     Morm. 8:9;
     Ether 8:20.
9a Moro. 9:17.
10a Hel. 12:18; 13:18 (17–23);
     Morm. 1:18 (17–19);
     Ether 14:1 (1–2).
11a 3 Ne. 12:4.

12a TG Mourning.
  b Hel. 11:9 (8–17).
13a 2 Cor. 7:10;
     Alma 42:29.
  b Hosea 7:14;
     Ether 8:7.
  c TG Damnation.
  d Alma 41:10.
14a TG Contrite Heart.
  b TG Blaspheme.

15a Hel. 13:38.
  b TG Grace.
  c Jer. 8:20.
  d TG Rebellion.
  e Jer. 8:2 (1–3).
17a Morm. 1:3 (1–4).
  b 4 Ne. 1:48 (48–49).
  c Morm. 8:5 (1, 4–5, 14).

did make a full account of all the wickedness and abominations; but upon *these plates I did forbear to make a full account of their wickedness and abominations, for behold, a continual scene of wickedness and abominations has been before mine eyes ever since I have been sufficient to behold the ways of man.

19 And wo is me because of their wickedness; for my heart has been filled with sorrow because of their wickedness, all my days; nevertheless, I know that I shall be *lifted up at the last day.

20 And it came to pass that in this year the people of Nephi again were hunted and driven. And it came to pass that we were driven forth until we had come northward to the land which was called Shem.

21 And it came to pass that we did *fortify the city of Shem, and we did gather in our people as much as it were possible, that perhaps we might save them from destruction.

22 And it came to pass in the three hundred and forty and sixth year they began to come upon us again.

23 And it came to pass that I did speak unto my people, and did urge them with great energy, that they would stand boldly before the Lamanites and *fight for their *wives, and their children, and their houses, and their homes.

24 And my words did arouse them somewhat to vigor, insomuch that they did not flee from before the Lamanites, but did stand with boldness against them.

25 And it came to pass that we did contend with an army of thirty thousand against an army of fifty thousand. And it came to pass that we did stand before them with such firmness that they did flee from before us.

26 And it came to pass that when they had fled we did pursue them with our armies, and did meet them again, and did *beat them; nevertheless the *strength of the Lord was not with us; yea, we were left to ourselves, that the Spirit of the Lord did not abide in us; therefore we had become weak like unto our brethren.

27 And my heart did sorrow because of this the great calamity of my people, because of their wickedness and their abominations. But behold, we did go forth against the Lamanites and the robbers of Gadianton, until we had again taken possession of the lands of our inheritance.

28 And the three hundred and forty and ninth year had passed away. And in the three hundred and fiftieth year we made a treaty with the Lamanites and the robbers of Gadianton, in which we did get the lands of our inheritance divided.

29 And the Lamanites did give unto us the land *northward, yea, even to the *narrow passage which led into the land southward. And we did give unto the Lamanites all the land southward.

CHAPTER 3

Mormon cries repentance unto the Nephites—They gain a great victory and glory in their own strength—Mormon refuses to lead them, and his prayers for them are without faith—The Book of Mormon invites the twelve tribes of Israel to believe the gospel. About A.D. 360–62.

AND it came to pass that the Lamanites did not come to battle again until ten years more had passed away. And behold, I had employed my people, the Nephites, in preparing their lands and their arms against the time of battle.

2 And it came to pass that the Lord did say unto me: Cry unto

18*a* 3 Ne. 5:15 (8–20).
19*a* Mosiah 23:22;
    Ether 4:19.
21*a* Morm. 2:4.

23*a* Alma 58:12.
  b Ether 14:2.
26*a* Morm. 3:8 (7–8, 13).
  b TG God, Spirit of;

    Strength.
29*a* Morm. 2:3.
  b Alma 22:32; 52:9; 63:5.

this people—Repent ye, and come unto me, and be ye baptized, and build up again my church, and ye shall be ^aspared.

3 And I did cry unto this people, but it was ^ain vain; and they did ^bnot realize that it was the Lord that had spared them, and granted unto them a chance for repentance. And behold they did harden their hearts against the Lord their God.

4 And it came to pass that after this tenth year had passed away, making, in the whole, three hundred and sixty years from the coming of Christ, the king of the Lamanites sent an epistle unto me, which gave unto me to know that they were preparing to come again to battle against us.

5 And it came to pass that I did cause my people that they should gather themselves together at the land ^aDesolation, to a city which was in the borders, by the narrow pass which led into the land ^bsouthward.

6 And there we did place our armies, that we might stop the armies of the Lamanites, that they might not get possession of any of our lands; therefore we did fortify against them with all our force.

7 And it came to pass that in the three hundred and sixty and first year the Lamanites did come down to the ^acity of Desolation to battle against us; and it came to pass that in that year we did beat them, insomuch that they did return to their own lands again.

8 And in the three hundred and sixty and second year they did come down ^aagain to battle. And we did beat them again, and did slay a great number of them, and their dead were cast into the sea.

9 And now, because of this great thing which my people, the Nephites, had done, they began to ^aboast in their own strength, and began to swear before the heavens that they would avenge themselves of the blood of their brethren who had been slain by their enemies.

10 And they did ^aswear by the heavens, and also by the throne of God, that they ^bwould go up to battle against their enemies, and would cut them off from the face of the land.

11 And it came to pass that I, Mormon, did utterly ^arefuse from this time forth to be a commander and a leader of this people, because of their wickedness and abomination.

12 Behold, I had led them, notwithstanding their wickedness I had led them many times to battle, and had loved them, according to the ^alove of God which was in me, with all my heart; and my soul had been poured out in prayer unto my God all the day long for them; nevertheless, it was ^bwithout faith, because of the ^chardness of their hearts.

13 And ^athrice have I delivered them out of the hands of their enemies, and they have repented not of their sins.

14 And when they had sworn by all that had been ^aforbidden them by our Lord and Savior Jesus Christ, that they would go up unto their enemies to battle, and avenge themselves of the blood of their brethren, behold the voice of the Lord came unto me, saying:

15 ^aVengeance is mine, and I will

---

3 2a Hel. 15:17 (16–17);
   Morm. 6:11 (11–15).
  3a Morm. 4:18.
   b TG Hardheartedness;
   Ingratitude.
  5a Alma 50:34;
   Morm. 4:3 (1–3).
   b Ether 9:31 (31–32); 10:21.
  7a 3 Ne. 3:23;
   Morm. 4:2 (2, 19).

  8a Morm. 2:26; 3:13.
  9a Prov. 14:16;
   2 Ne. 4:34;
   Morm. 4:8.
 10a TG Swearing.
   b Alma 43:46 (46–47);
   48:14;
   3 Ne. 3:21 (20–21);
   Morm. 4:4.
 11a Morm. 5:1.

 12a TG God, Love of.
   b James 1:6;
   Morm. 5:2.
   c Neh. 9:16 (16–17).
 13a Morm. 2:26;
   3:8 (7–8).
 14a 3 Ne. 12:34.
 15a Isa. 35:4;
   Rom. 12:19.
   TG Vengeance.

^brepay; and because this people repented not after I had delivered them, behold, they shall be cut off from the face of the earth.

16 And it came to pass that I utterly refused to go up against mine enemies; and I did even as the Lord had commanded me; and I did stand as an idle witness to manifest unto the world the things which I saw and heard, according to the manifestations of the Spirit which had testified of things to come.

17 Therefore I write ^aunto you, Gentiles, and also unto you, house of Israel, when the work shall commence, that ye shall be about to prepare to return to the land of your inheritance;

18 Yea, behold, I write unto all the ends of the earth; yea, unto you, twelve tribes of Israel, who shall be ^ajudged according to your works by the twelve whom Jesus chose to be his disciples in the land of Jerusalem.

19 And I write also unto the remnant of this people, who shall also be judged by the ^atwelve whom Jesus chose in this land; and they shall be judged by the other twelve whom Jesus chose in the land of Jerusalem.

20 And these things doth the Spirit manifest unto me; therefore I write unto you all. And for this cause I write unto you, that ye may know that ye must all stand before the ^ajudgment-seat of Christ, yea, every soul who belongs to the whole human ^bfamily of Adam; and ye must stand to be judged of your works, whether they be good or evil;

21 And also that ye may ^abelieve the gospel of Jesus Christ, which ye shall ^bhave among you; and also

that the ^cJews, the covenant people of the Lord, shall have other ^dwitness besides him whom they saw and heard, that Jesus, whom they slew, was the ^every Christ and the very God.

22 And I would that I could persuade ^aall ye ends of the earth to repent and prepare to stand before the judgment-seat of Christ.

CHAPTER 4

War and carnage continue—The wicked punish the wicked—Greater wickedness prevails than ever before in all Israel—Women and children are sacrificed to idols—The Lamanites begin to sweep the Nephites before them. About A.D. 363–75.

AND now it came to pass that in the three hundred and sixty and third year the Nephites did go up with their armies to ^abattle against the Lamanites, out of the land Desolation.

2 And it came to pass that the armies of the Nephites were driven back again to the land of Desolation. And while they were yet weary, a fresh army of the Lamanites did come upon them; and they had a sore battle, insomuch that the Lamanites did take possession of the ^acity Desolation, and did slay many of the Nephites, and did take many prisoners.

3 And the remainder did flee and join the inhabitants of the city Teancum. Now the city Teancum lay in the borders by the seashore; and it was also near the city ^aDesolation.

4 And it was ^abecause the armies of the Nephites went up unto the Lamanites that they began to be smitten; for were it not for that, the

---

15 *b* 2 Sam. 16:12 (9–12);
    D&C 82:23.
    TG God, Justice of.
17 *a* 2 Ne. 30:3 (3–8);
    3 Ne. 29:1.
18 *a* Matt. 19:28;
    Luke 22:30 (29–30);
    D&C 29:12.
19 *a* 1 Ne. 12:10 (9–10);

    3 Ne. 27:27.
20 *a* TG Jesus Christ, Judge;
    Judgment, the Last.
  b D&C 27:11.
21 *a* D&C 3:20.
  b 1 Ne. 13:23 (20–29, 41).
  c TG Israel, Judah,
    People of.
  d 2 Ne. 25:18.

  e 2 Ne. 26:12;
    Mosiah 7:27.
22 *a* Alma 29:1.
4 1 *a* 2 Ne. 1:12;
    Morm. 1:11 (11–19).
  2 *a* 3 Ne. 3:23;
    Morm. 3:7.
  3 *a* Morm. 3:5.
  4 *a* Morm. 3:10 (10–11).

Lamanites could have had no power over them.

5 But, behold, the judgments of God will overtake the ^awicked; and it is by the wicked that the wicked are ^bpunished; for it is the wicked that stir up the hearts of the children of men unto bloodshed.

6 And it came to pass that the Lamanites did make preparations to come against the city Teancum.

7 And it came to pass in the three hundred and sixty and fourth year the Lamanites did come against the city Teancum, that they might take possession of the city Teancum also.

8 And it came to pass that they were repulsed and driven back by the Nephites. And when the Nephites saw that they had driven the Lamanites they did again ^aboast of their own strength; and they went forth in their own might, and took possession again of the city Desolation.

9 And now all these things had been done, and there had been thousands slain on both sides, both the Nephites and the Lamanites.

10 And it came to pass that the three hundred and sixty and sixth year had passed away, and the Lamanites came again upon the Nephites to battle; and yet the Nephites repented not of the evil they had done, but persisted in their wickedness continually.

11 And it is impossible for the tongue to describe, or for man to write a perfect description of the horrible scene of the blood and carnage which was among the people, both of the Nephites and of the Lamanites; and every heart was hardened, so that they ^adelighted in the shedding of blood continually.

12 And there never had been so great ^awickedness among all the children of Lehi, nor even among all the house of Israel, according to the words of the Lord, as was among this people.

13 And it came to pass that the Lamanites did take possession of the city Desolation, and this because their ^anumber did exceed the number of the Nephites.

14 And they did also march forward against the city Teancum, and did drive the inhabitants forth out of her, and did take many prisoners both women and children, and did offer them up as ^asacrifices unto their idol gods.

15 And it came to pass that in the three hundred and sixty and seventh year, the Nephites being angry because the Lamanites had sacrificed their women and their children, that they did go against the Lamanites with exceedingly great anger, insomuch that they did beat again the Lamanites, and drive them out of their lands.

16 And the Lamanites did not come again against the Nephites until the three hundred and seventy and fifth year.

17 And in this year they did come down against the Nephites with all their powers; and they were not numbered because of the greatness of their number.

18 And ^afrom this time forth did the Nephites gain no power over the Lamanites, but began to be swept off by them even as a dew before the sun.

19 And it came to pass that the Lamanites did come down against the ^acity Desolation; and there was an exceedingly sore battle fought in the land Desolation, in the which they did beat the Nephites.

5a Nahum 1:3.
  b 2 Pet. 2:12;
    D&C 63:33.
8a Morm. 3:9.
11a Moro. 9:5 (5, 23).
  TG Blood, Shedding of.
12a Gen. 6:5 (5–6);

3 Ne. 9:9;
D&C 112:23;
Moses 7:36 (36–37);
  8:22 (22, 28–30).
13a Morm. 2:3; 5:6.
14a Jer. 19:5;
  Alma 17:15;

Abr. 1:8 (6–14).
TG Idolatry;
  Sacrifice.
18a Morm. 3:3.
19a Morm. 3:7.

20 And they fled again from before them, and they came to the city Boaz; and there they did stand against the Lamanites with exceeding boldness, insomuch that the Lamanites did not beat them until they had come again the second time.

21 And when they had come the second time, the Nephites were driven and slaughtered with an exceedingly great slaughter; their women and their ᵃchildren were again sacrificed unto idols.

22 And it came to pass that the Nephites did again flee from before them, taking all the inhabitants with them, both in towns and villages.

23 And now I, Mormon, seeing that the Lamanites were about to overthrow the land, therefore I did go to the hill ᵃShim, and did take up all the ᵇrecords which Ammaron had hid up unto the Lord.

CHAPTER 5

Mormon again leads the Nephite armies in battles of blood and carnage—The Book of Mormon will come forth to convince all Israel that Jesus is the Christ —Because of their unbelief, the Lamanites will be scattered, and the Spirit will cease to strive with them—They will receive the gospel from the Gentiles in the latter days. About A.D. 375–84.

AND it came to pass that I did go forth among the Nephites, and did repent of the ᵃoath which I had made that I would no more assist them; and they gave me command again of their armies, for they looked upon me as though I could deliver them from their afflictions.

2 But behold, I was ᵃwithout hope, for I knew the judgments of the Lord which should come upon them; for they repented not of their iniquities, but did struggle for their lives without calling upon that Being who created them.

3 And it came to pass that the Lamanites did come against us as we had fled to the city of Jordan; but behold, they were driven back that they did not take the city at that time.

4 And it came to pass that they came against us again, and we did maintain the city. And there were also other cities which were maintained by the Nephites, which strongholds did cut them off that they could not get into the country which lay before us, to destroy the inhabitants of our land.

5 But it came to pass that whatsoever lands we had passed by, and the inhabitants thereof were not gathered in, were destroyed by the Lamanites, and their towns, and villages, and cities were burned with fire; and thus three hundred and seventy and nine years passed away.

6 And it came to pass that in the three hundred and eightieth year the Lamanites did come again against us to battle, and we did stand against them boldly; but it was all in vain, for so ᵃgreat were their numbers that they did tread the people of the Nephites under their feet.

7 And it came to pass that we did again take to flight, and those whose flight was swifter than the Lamanites' did escape, and those whose flight did not exceed the Lamanites' were swept down and destroyed.

8 And now behold, I, Mormon, do not desire to harrow up the souls of men in casting before them such an awful scene of blood and carnage as was laid before mine eyes; but I, knowing that these things must surely be made known, and that all things which are hid must be ᵃrevealed upon the house-tops—

9 And also that a knowledge of these things must ᵃcome unto the remnant of these people, and also unto the Gentiles, who the Lord

---

21a 2 Kgs. 17:31.
   TG Idolatry.
23a Morm. 1:3;
   Ether 9:3.
  b W of M 1:3.

5 1a Morm. 3:11 (11, 16).
   TG Vow.
2a Morm. 3:12.
6a Morm. 2:3; 4:13 (13–17).
8a Matt. 10:26 (26–33);

Luke 12:3;
2 Ne. 27:11;
D&C 1:3; 88:108.
9a 4 Ne. 1:49.

hath said should *b*scatter this people, and this people should be counted as naught among them—therefore *c*I write a *d*small abridgment, daring not to give a full account of the things which I have seen, because of the commandment which I have received, and also that ye might not have too great sorrow because of the wickedness of this people.

10 And now behold, this I speak unto their seed, and also to the Gentiles who have care for the house of Israel, that realize and know from whence their blessings come.

11 For I know that such will sorrow for the calamity of the house of Israel; yea, they will sorrow for the destruction of this people; they will sorrow that this people had not repented that they might have been clasped in the arms of Jesus.

12 Now *a*these things are *b*written unto the *c*remnant of the house of Jacob; and they are written after this manner, because it is known of God that wickedness will not bring them forth unto them; and they are to be *d*hid up unto the Lord that they may come forth in his own due time.

13 And this is the commandment which I have received; and behold, they *a*shall come forth according to the commandment of the Lord, when he shall see fit, in his wisdom.

14 And behold, they shall go unto the *a*unbelieving of the *b*Jews; and for this intent shall they go—that they may be *c*persuaded that Jesus is the Christ, the Son of the living God; that the Father may bring about, through his most Beloved, his great and eternal purpose, in restoring the Jews, or all the house of Israel, to the *d*land of their inheritance, which the Lord their God hath given them, unto the fulfilling of his *e*covenant;

15 And also that the seed of *a*this people may more fully believe his gospel, which shall *b*go forth unto them from the Gentiles; for this people shall be *c*scattered, and shall *d*become a dark, a filthy, and a loathsome people, beyond the description of that which ever hath been amongst us, yea, even that which hath been among the Lamanites, and this because of their unbelief and idolatry.

16 For behold, the Spirit of the Lord hath already ceased to *a*strive with their fathers; and they are without Christ and God in the world; and they are driven about as *b*chaff before the wind.

17 They were once a delightsome people, and they had Christ for their *a*shepherd; yea, they were led even by God the Father.

18 But now, behold, they are *a*led about by Satan, even as chaff is driven before the wind, or as a vessel is tossed about upon the waves, without sail or anchor, or without anything wherewith to steer her; and even as she is, so are they.

19 And behold, the Lord hath reserved their blessings, which they

---

9*b* 3 Ne. 16:8 (8–9).
  c Alma 43:3.
  d Morm. 1:1.
12*a* 1 Ne. 19:19;
     Enos 1:16;
     Hel. 15:11 (11–13);
     Morm. 7:1 (1, 9–10).
  b TG Book of Mormon;
     Scriptures to Come
     Forth.
  c 2 Ne. 25:8; 27:6;
     Jarom 1:2;
     D&C 3:20 (16–20).
  d Morm. 8:4 (4, 13–14);
     Moro. 10:2 (1–2).
     TG Scriptures,

Preservation of.
13*a* 2 Ne. 3:18.
14*a* Rom. 11:20 (1–36);
     1 Ne. 10:11;
     Jacob 4:15 (15–18).
     TG Unbelief.
  b 2 Ne. 26:12; 29:13;
     30:7 (7–8).
     TG Israel, Judah,
     People of.
  c John 20:31;
     2 Ne. 25:16 (16–17).
     TG Israel, Restoration of.
  d TG Lands of Inheritance.
  e Ezek. 20:37;
     3 Ne. 29:1 (1–3).

15*a* 2 Ne. 30:5;
     3 Ne. 21:5 (3–7, 24–26).
  b 1 Ne. 13:38 (20–29, 38);
     Morm. 7:8 (8–9).
  c 1 Ne. 10:12 (12–14);
     3 Ne. 16:8.
  d 2 Ne. 26:33.
16*a* Gen. 6:3;
     Ether 2:15;
     Moro. 8:28.
  b Ps. 1:4 (1–4);
     Hosea 13:3 (1–4).
17*a* TG Jesus Christ, Good
     Shepherd.
18*a* 2 Ne. 28:21.

might have received in the land, for the ªGentiles who shall possess the land.

20 But behold, it shall come to pass that they shall be driven and scattered by the Gentiles; and after they have been driven and scattered by the Gentiles, behold, then will the Lord ªremember the ᵇcovenant which he made unto Abraham and unto all the house of Israel.

21 And also the Lord will remember the ªprayers of the righteous, which have been put up unto him for them.

22 And then, O ye Gentiles, how can ye stand before the power of God, except ye shall repent and turn from your evil ways?

23 Know ye not that ye are in the ªhands of God? Know ye not that he hath all power, and at his great command the ᵇearth shall be ᶜrolled together as a scroll?

24 Therefore, repent ye, and humble yourselves before him, lest he shall come out in justice against you—lest a ªremnant of the seed of Jacob shall go forth among you as a ᵇlion, and tear you in pieces, and there is none to deliver.

CHAPTER 6

The Nephites gather to the land of Cumorah for the final battles—Mormon hides the sacred records in the hill Cumorah—The Lamanites are victorious, and the Nephite nation is destroyed—Hundreds of thousands are slain with the sword. About A.D. 385.

AND now I finish my record concerning the ªdestruction of my people, the Nephites. And it came to pass

that we did march forth before the Lamanites.

2 And I, Mormon, wrote an epistle unto the king of the Lamanites, and desired of him that he would grant unto us that we might gather together our people unto the ªland of ᵇCumorah, by a hill which was called Cumorah, and there we could give them battle.

3 And it came to pass that the king of the Lamanites did grant unto me the thing which I desired.

4 And it came to pass that we did march forth to the land of Cumorah, and we did pitch our tents around about the hill Cumorah; and it was in a land of ªmany waters, rivers, and fountains; and here we had hope to gain advantage over the Lamanites.

5 And when ªthree hundred and eighty and four years had passed away, we had gathered in all the remainder of our people unto the land of Cumorah.

6 And it came to pass that when we had gathered in all our people in one to the land of Cumorah, behold I, Mormon, began to be old; and knowing it to be the last struggle of my people, and having been commanded of the Lord that I should not suffer the records which had been handed down by our fathers, which were ªsacred, to fall into the hands of the Lamanites, (for the Lamanites would ᵇdestroy them) therefore I made ᶜthis record out of the plates of Nephi, and ᵈhid up in the hill Cumorah all the records which had been entrusted to me by the hand of the Lord, save it were ᵉthese few plates which I gave unto my son ᶠMoroni.

19a 3 Ne. 20:27.
20a 1 Ne. 13:31;
  3 Ne. 16:11 (8–12).
 b TG Abrahamic Covenant.
21a Enos 1:12 (12–18);
  Morm. 8:25 (24–26);
  9:36 (36–37).
23a Ether 1:1;
  D&C 87:6 (6–7).
 b Hel. 12:11 (8–18);
  Morm. 9:2.
 c 3 Ne. 26:3.

24a TG Israel, Remnant of.
 b 3 Ne. 20:16 (15–16).
6 1a 1 Ne. 12:19 (19–20);
  Jarom 1:10;
  Alma 45:11 (9–14);
  Hel. 13:5 (5–11).
2a Ether 9:3.
 b Morm. 8:2;
  D&C 128:20.
4a Mosiah 8:8;
  Alma 50:29;
  Hel. 3:4 (3–4).

5a W of M 1:2.
6a TG Sacred.
 b 2 Ne. 26:17;
  Enos 1:14.
 c Morm. 2:18.
 d Ether 15:11.
 e Moro. 9:24; 10:2;
  D&C 17:1;
  JS—H 1:52.
 f Morm. 8:1.

7 And it came to pass that my people, with their wives and their children, did now behold the ªarmies of the Lamanites marching towards them; and with that awful ᵇfear of death which fills the breasts of all the wicked, did they await to receive them.

8 And it came to pass that they came to battle against us, and every soul was filled with terror because of the greatness of their numbers.

9 And it came to pass that they did fall upon my people with the sword, and with the bow, and with the arrow, and with the ax, and with all manner of weapons of war.

10 And it came to pass that my men were hewn down, yea, even my ªten thousand who were with me, and I fell wounded in the midst; and they passed by me that they did not put an end to my life.

11 And when they had gone through and hewn down ªall my people save it were twenty and four of us, (among whom was my son Moroni) and we having survived the dead of our people, did behold on the morrow, when the Lamanites had returned unto their camps, from the top of the hill Cumorah, the ten thousand of my people who were hewn down, being led in the front by me.

12 And we also beheld the ten thousand of my people who were led by my son Moroni.

13 And behold, the ten thousand of Gidgiddonah had fallen, and he also in the midst.

14 And Lamah had fallen with his ten thousand; and Gilgal had fallen with his ten thousand; and Limhah had fallen with his ten thousand; and Jeneum had fallen with his ten thousand; and Cumenihah, and Moronihah, and Antionum, and Shiblom, and Shem, and Josh, had fallen with their ten thousand each.

15 And it came to pass that there were ten more who did fall by the sword, with their ten thousand each; yea, even ªall my people, save it were those twenty and four who were with me, and also a ᵇfew who had escaped into the south countries, and a few who had deserted over unto the Lamanites, had fallen; and their flesh, and bones, and blood lay upon the face of the earth, being left by the hands of those who slew them to molder upon the land, and to crumble and to return to their mother earth.

16 And my soul was rent with ªanguish, because of the slain of my people, and I cried:

17 ªO ye fair ones, how could ye have departed from the ways of the Lord! O ye fair ones, how could ye have rejected that Jesus, who stood with open arms to receive you!

18 Behold, if ye had not done this, ye would not have fallen. But behold, ye are fallen, and I ªmourn your loss.

19 O ye ªfair sons and daughters, ye fathers and mothers, ye husbands and wives, ye fair ones, how is it that ye could have ᵇfallen!

20 But behold, ye are gone, and my sorrows cannot bring your return.

21 And the day soon cometh that your mortal must put on immortality, and these bodies which are now moldering in corruption must soon become ªincorruptible bodies; and then ye must stand before the judgment-seat of Christ, to be judged according to your works; and if it so be that ye are righteous, then are ye blessed with your fathers who have gone before you.

22 O that ye had repented before this great ªdestruction had come upon you. But behold, ye are gone,

---

7a 1 Ne. 12:15.
  b TG Fearful.
10a Judg. 1:4.
11a 1 Ne. 12:19 (19–20);
    Hel. 15:17 (16–17);
    Morm. 3:2.
15a Alma 9:24.
  b Morm. 8:2.
16a TG Despair;
    Mourning;
    Sorrow.
17a 2 Ne. 26:7.
18a Lam. 2:11.
19a Ether 13:17.
  b 1 Ne. 13:15.
21a 1 Cor. 15:53 (53–54).
22a 2 Sam. 1:27 (17–27).

and the Father, yea, the Eternal Father of heaven, ^bknoweth your state; and he doeth with you according to his ^cjustice and ^dmercy.

CHAPTER 7

Mormon invites the Lamanites of the latter days to believe in Christ, accept His gospel, and be saved—All who believe the Bible will also believe the Book of Mormon. About A.D. 385.

AND now, behold, I would speak somewhat unto the ^aremnant of this people who are spared, if it so be that God may give unto them my words, that they may know of the things of their fathers; yea, I speak unto you, ye remnant of the house of Israel; and these are the words which I speak:

2 Know ye that ye are of the ^ahouse of Israel.

3 Know ye that ye must come unto repentance, or ye cannot be saved.

4 Know ye that ye must lay down your weapons of war, and delight no more in the shedding of blood, and take them not again, save it be that God shall ^acommand you.

5 Know ye that ye must come to the ^aknowledge of your fathers, and repent of all your sins and iniquities, and ^bbelieve in Jesus Christ, that he is the Son of God, and that he was slain by the Jews, and by the power of the Father he hath risen again, whereby he hath gained the ^cvictory over the grave; and also in him is the sting of death swallowed up.

6 And he bringeth to pass the ^aresurrection of the dead, whereby man must be raised to stand before his ^bjudgment-seat.

7 And he hath brought to pass the ^aredemption of the ^bworld, whereby he that is found ^cguiltless before him at the judgment day hath it given unto him to ^ddwell in the presence of God in his kingdom, to sing ceaseless praises with the ^echoirs above, unto the Father, and unto the Son, and unto the Holy Ghost, which are ^fone God, in a state of ^ghappiness which hath no end.

8 Therefore repent, and be baptized in the name of Jesus, and lay hold upon the ^agospel of Christ, which shall be set before you, not only in this record but also in the record which shall come unto the Gentiles ^bfrom the Jews, which record shall come from the Gentiles ^cunto you.

9 For behold, ^athis is ^bwritten for the intent that ye may ^cbelieve that; and if ^dye believe that ye will believe this also; and if ye believe this ye will know concerning your fathers, and also the marvelous works which were wrought by the power of God among them.

10 And ye will also know that ye are a ^aremnant of the seed of Jacob; therefore ye are numbered among the people of the first covenant; and if it so be that ye believe in Christ, and are baptized, first ^bwith water, then with fire and with the Holy Ghost, following the ^cexample of our Savior, according to that which

---

22 b 2 Sam. 7:20;
        D&C 6:16.
     c TG God, Justice of.
     d Ps. 36:5 (5–6);
        Alma 26:16;
        D&C 97:6.
7 1 a Hel. 15:11 (11–13);
        Morm. 5:12 (9, 12).
  2 a 1 Ne. 5:14;
        Alma 10:3;
        Hel. 6:10; 8:21.
  4 a Alma 43:47.
  5 a 2 Ne. 3:12;
        3 Ne. 5:23.
     b TG Faith.
     c Isa. 25:8;
        Mosiah 16:8 (7–8);

Alma 24:23.
  6 a TG Resurrection.
     b TG Jesus Christ, Judge.
  7 a TG Redemption.
     b TG World.
     c Mosiah 13:15;
        D&C 58:30.
        TG Justification.
     d Ps. 27:4;
        1 Ne. 10:21;
        D&C 76:62 (50–62);
        Moses 6:57.
     e Mosiah 2:28.
     f Deut. 6:4; Gal. 3:20;
        D&C 20:28.
     g TG Happiness.
  8 a TG Gospel.

     b 2 Ne. 29:4 (4–13).
     c 1 Ne. 13:38 (20–29, 38);
        Morm. 5:15.
  9 a 1 Ne. 19:19;
        Enos 1:16 (12–18);
        3 Ne. 5:15 (12–17);
        Morm. 5:12.
        TG Israel, Restoration of.
     b TG Book of Mormon.
     c 1 Ne. 13:40 (38–42).
     d 2 Ne. 3:15 (12–15);
        Alma 37:19 (1–20).
10 a TG Israel, Remnant of.
     b 3 Ne. 19:13 (13–14);
        Ether 12:14.
     c TG God, the Standard of
        Righteousness.

he hath commanded us, it shall be well with you in the day of judgment. Amen.

CHAPTER 8

The Lamanites seek out and destroy the Nephites—The Book of Mormon will come forth by the power of God—Woes pronounced upon those who breathe out wrath and strife against the work of the Lord—The Nephite record will come forth in a day of wickedness, degeneracy, and apostasy. About A.D. 400–421.

BEHOLD I, ^aMoroni, do finish the ^brecord of my father, Mormon. Behold, I have but few things to write, which things I have been commanded by my father.

2 And now it came to pass that after the ^agreat and tremendous battle at Cumorah, behold, the Nephites who had escaped into the country southward were hunted by the ^bLamanites, until they were all destroyed.

3 And my father also was killed by them, and I even ^aremain ^balone to write the sad tale of the destruction of my people. But behold, they are gone, and I fulfil the commandment of my father. And whether they will slay me, I know not.

4 Therefore I will write and ^ahide up the records in the earth; and whither I go it mattereth not.

5 Behold, my father hath made ^athis record, and he hath written the intent thereof. And behold, I would write it also if I had room upon the ^bplates, but I have not; and ore I have none, for I am alone. My father hath been slain in battle, and all my kinsfolk, and I have not

friends nor whither to go; and ^chow long the Lord will suffer that I may live I know not.

6 Behold, ^afour hundred years have passed away since the coming of our Lord and Savior.

7 And behold, the Lamanites have hunted my people, the Nephites, down from city to city and from place to place, even until they are no more; and great has been their ^afall; yea, great and marvelous is the destruction of my people, the Nephites.

8 And behold, it is the hand of the Lord which hath done it. And behold also, the Lamanites are at ^awar one with another; and the whole face of this land is one continual round of murder and bloodshed; and no one knoweth the end of the war.

9 And now, behold, I say no more concerning them, for there are none save it be the Lamanites and ^arobbers that do exist upon the face of the land.

10 And there are none that do know the true God save it be the ^adisciples of Jesus, who did tarry in the land until the wickedness of the people was so great that the Lord would not suffer them to ^bremain with the people; and whether they be upon the face of the land no man knoweth.

11 But behold, my ^afather and I have seen ^bthem, and they have ministered unto us.

12 And whoso receiveth ^athis record, and shall not condemn it because of the imperfections which are in it, the same shall know of ^bgreater things than these. Behold, I am Moroni; and were it possible, I would make all things known unto you.

8 1*a* Morm. 6:6;
      Moro. 9:24.
   b TG Record Keeping.
 2*a* Morm. 6:15 (2–15).
   b D&C 3:18.
 3*a* Moro. 9:22.
   b Ether 4:3.
 4*a* Morm. 5:12;
      Moro. 10:2 (1–2).
 5*a* Morm. 2:17 (17–18).

   b Morm. 6:6.
   c Moro. 1:1; 10:1 (1–2).
 6*a* Alma 45:10.
 7*a* 1 Ne. 12:2 (2–3);
      Enos 1:24.
 8*a* 1 Ne. 12:21 (20–23).
 9*a* 4 Ne. 1:46;
      Morm. 2:8 (8, 28);
      Ether 8:20.
10*a* 3 Ne. 28:7;

      4 Ne. 1:37 (14, 37);
      Ether 12:17.
   b Morm. 1:16.
11*a* 3 Ne. 28:26.
   b TG Translated Beings.
12*a* 3 Ne. 5:15 (8–18).
   b John 16:12;
      3 Ne. 26:9 (6–11);
      D&C 42:15.

13 Behold, I make an end of speaking concerning this people. I am the son of Mormon, and my father was a *a*descendant of Nephi.

14 And I am the same who *a*hideth up this record unto the Lord; the plates thereof are of no worth, because of the commandment of the Lord. For he truly saith that no one shall have them *b*to get gain; but the record thereof is of *c*great worth; and whoso shall bring it to light, him will the Lord bless.

15 For none can have power to bring it to light save it be given him of God; for God wills that it shall be done with an *a*eye single to his glory, or the welfare of the ancient and long dispersed covenant people of the Lord.

16 And blessed be *a*he that shall bring this thing to light; for it shall be *b*brought out of darkness unto light, according to the word of God; yea, it shall be brought out of the earth, and it shall shine forth out of darkness, and come unto the knowledge of the people; and it shall be done by the power of God.

17 And if there be *a*faults they be the faults of a man. But behold, we know no fault; nevertheless God knoweth all things; therefore, he that *b*condemneth, let him be aware lest he shall be in danger of hell fire.

18 And he that saith: Show unto me, or ye shall be *a*smitten—let him beware lest he commandeth that which is forbidden of the Lord.

19 For behold, the same that *a*judgeth *b*rashly shall be judged rashly again; for according to his works shall his wages be; therefore, he that smiteth shall be smitten again, of the Lord.

20 Behold what the scripture says—man shall not *a*smite, neither shall he *b*judge; for judgment is mine, saith the Lord, and vengeance is mine also, and I will repay.

21 And he that shall breathe out *a*wrath and *b*strifes against the work of the Lord, and against the *c*covenant people of the Lord who are the house of Israel, and shall say: We will destroy the work of the Lord, and the Lord will not remember his covenant which he hath made unto the house of Israel—the same is in danger to be hewn down and cast into the fire;

22 For the eternal *a*purposes of the Lord shall roll on, until all his promises shall be fulfilled.

23 Search the prophecies of *a*Isaiah. Behold, I cannot write them. Yea, behold I say unto you, that those saints who have gone before me, who have possessed this land, shall *b*cry, yea, even from the dust will they cry unto the Lord; and as the Lord liveth he will remember the covenant which he hath made with them.

24 And he knoweth their *a*prayers, that they were in behalf of their brethren. And he knoweth their faith, for in his name could they remove *b*mountains; and in his name could they cause the earth to shake; and by the power of his word did they cause *c*prisons to tumble to the earth; yea, even the fiery furnace could not harm them, neither wild

13*a* Alma 10:3;
   3 Ne. 5:20.
14*a* Ether 4:3;
   Moro. 10:2 (1–2).
   b JS—H 1:53.
   TG Scriptures,
   Preservation of.
   c 2 Ne. 3:7 (6–9).
15*a* 3 Ne. 21:11 (8–11);
   D&C 4:5.
16*a* 3 Ne. 3:28 (21–28).
   b TG Scriptures to Come

Forth.
17*a* 1 Ne. 19:6;
   Morm. 9:31 (31, 33);
   Ether 12:23 (22–28, 35).
   b 3 Ne. 29:5 (1–9);
   Ether 4:8 (8–10).
18*a* JS—H 1:60 (60–61).
19*a* 3 Ne. 14:2;
   Moro. 7:14.
   TG Gossip.
   b TG Rashness.
20*a* TG Violence.
   b James 4:12 (11–12).

21*a* Prov. 19:19.
   b TG Strife.
   c 1 Ne. 14:17.
22*a* D&C 3:3.
23*a* Isa. 29:4;
   3 Ne. 20:11; 23:1 (1–3).
   b 2 Ne. 3:20; 26:16.
24*a* Enos 1:13 (12–18);
   Morm. 9:36 (34–37);
   D&C 10:46 (46–49).
   b Jacob 4:6;
   Hel. 10:9.
   c 3 Ne. 28:19 (19–21).

beasts nor poisonous serpents, because of the power of his word.

25 And behold, their *a*prayers were also in behalf of him that the Lord should suffer to bring these things forth.

26 And no one need say they shall not come, for they surely shall, for the Lord hath spoken it; for *a*out of the earth shall they come, by the hand of the Lord, and none can stay it; and it shall come in a day when it shall be said that *b*miracles are done away; and it shall come even as if one should speak *c*from the dead.

27 And it shall come in a day when the *a*blood of saints shall cry unto the Lord, because of secret *b*combinations and the works of darkness.

28 Yea, it shall come in a day when the power of God shall be *a*denied, and *b*churches become defiled and be *c*lifted up in the pride of their hearts; yea, even in a day when leaders of churches and teachers shall rise in the pride of their hearts, even to the envying of them who belong to their churches.

29 Yea, it shall come in a day when *a*there shall be heard of fires, and tempests, and *b*vapors of smoke in foreign lands;

30 And there shall also be heard of *a*wars, rumors of wars, and earthquakes in divers places.

31 Yea, it shall come in a day when there shall be great *a*pollutions upon the face of the earth; there shall be *b*murders, and robbing, and lying,

and deceivings, and whoredoms, and all manner of abominations; when there shall be many who will say, Do this, or do that, and it *c*mattereth not, for the Lord will *d*uphold such at the last day. But wo unto such, for they are in the *e*gall of bitterness and in the *f*bonds of iniquity.

32 Yea, it shall come in a day when there shall be *a*churches built up that shall say: Come unto me, and for your money you shall be forgiven of your sins.

33 O ye wicked and perverse and *a*stiffnecked people, why have ye built up churches unto yourselves to get *b*gain? Why have ye *c*transfigured the holy word of God, that ye might bring *d*damnation upon your souls? Behold, look ye unto the *e*revelations of God; for behold, the time cometh at that day when all these things must be fulfilled.

34 Behold, the Lord hath shown unto me great and marvelous things concerning that which must shortly come, at that day when these things shall come forth among you.

35 Behold, I speak unto you as if ye were present, and yet ye are not. But behold, Jesus Christ hath shown you unto me, and I know your doing.

36 And I know that ye do *a*walk in the pride of your hearts; and there are none save a few only who do not *b*lift themselves up in the pride of their hearts, unto the wearing of *c*very fine apparel, unto envying,

---

25*a* Morm. 5:21.
26*a* 3 Ne. 23:4.
  b 3 Ne. 29:7;
     Morm. 9:15 (15–26);
     Moro. 7:37 (27–37).
  c 2 Ne. 26:16 (15–16);
     33:13;
     Morm. 9:30;
     Moro. 10:27.
27*a* Gen. 4:10;
     Rev. 6:10 (1, 10);
     2 Ne. 28:10;
     Ether 8:22 (22–24);
     D&C 87:7.
  b TG Secret
     Combinations.
28*a* TG Unbelief.

  b 2 Tim. 3:1 (1–7);
     1 Ne. 14:10 (9–10);
     2 Ne. 28:3 (3–32);
     D&C 33:4.
  c 2 Kgs. 14:10;
     Jacob 2:13.
29*a* Joel 2:30 (28–32);
     2 Ne. 27:2 (1–3).
  b 1 Ne. 19:11;
     D&C 45:41 (40–41).
30*a* Matt. 24:6;
     1 Ne. 14:16 (15–17).
31*a* TG Pollution.
  b 3 Ne. 16:10; 30:2.
  c 2 Ne. 28:21;
     Alma 1:4; 30:17.
  d 2 Ne. 28:8.

  e Acts 8:23;
     Alma 41:11.
  f TG Bondage, Spiritual.
32*a* TG Devil, Church of.
33*a* D&C 5:8.
  b TG Priestcraft.
  c 1 Ne. 13:26 (20–41).
     TG Apostasy of the Early
     Christian Church.
  d TG Damnation.
  e 1 Ne. 14:23 (18–27);
     Ether 4:16.
36*a* TG Walking in Darkness.
  b Jacob 2:13;
     3 Ne. 16:10.
  c 2 Ne. 28:13 (11–14);
     Alma 5:53.

and strifes, and malice, and persecutions, and all manner of iniquities; and your churches, yea, even every one, have become polluted because of the pride of your hearts.

37 For behold, ye do love *a*money, and your substance, and your fine apparel, and the adorning of your churches, more than ye love the poor and the needy, the sick and the afflicted.

38 O ye pollutions, ye hypocrites, ye teachers, who sell yourselves for that which will canker, why have ye polluted the holy church of God? Why are ye *a*ashamed to take upon you the name of Christ? Why do ye not think that greater is the value of an endless happiness than that *b*misery which never dies—because of the *c*praise of the world?

39 Why do ye adorn yourselves with that which hath no life, and yet suffer the hungry, and the needy, and the naked, and the sick and the afflicted to pass by you, and notice them not?

40 Yea, why do ye build up your *a*secret abominations to get gain, and cause that widows should mourn before the Lord, and also orphans to mourn before the Lord, and also the blood of their fathers and their husbands to cry unto the Lord from the ground, for vengeance upon your heads?

41 Behold, the sword of vengeance hangeth over you; and the time soon cometh that he avengeth the *a*blood of the saints upon you, for he will not suffer their cries any longer.

CHAPTER 9

Moroni calls upon those who do not believe in Christ to repent—He proclaims

a God of miracles, who gives revelations and pours out gifts and signs upon the faithful—Miracles cease because of unbelief—Signs follow those who believe—Men are exhorted to be wise and keep the commandments. About A.D. 401–21.

AND now, I speak also concerning those who do not believe in Christ.

2 Behold, will ye believe in the day of your visitation—behold, when the Lord shall come, yea, even that *a*great day when the *b*earth shall be rolled together as a scroll, and the elements shall *c*melt with fervent heat, yea, in that great day when ye shall be brought to stand before the Lamb of God—then will ye say that there is no God?

3 Then will ye longer deny the Christ, or can ye behold the Lamb of God? Do ye suppose that ye shall dwell with him under a *a*consciousness of your guilt? Do ye suppose that ye could be happy to dwell with that holy Being, when your souls are racked with a consciousness of guilt that ye have ever abused his laws?

4 Behold, I say unto you that ye would be more miserable to dwell with a holy and just God, under a consciousness of your *a*filthiness before him, than ye would to dwell with the *b*damned souls in *c*hell.

5 For behold, when ye shall be brought to see your *a*nakedness before God, and also the glory of God, and the *b*holiness of Jesus Christ, it will kindle a flame of unquenchable fire upon you.

6 O then ye *a*unbelieving, *b*turn ye unto the Lord; cry mightily unto the Father in the name of Jesus, that perhaps ye may be found spotless,

37*a* Ezek. 34:8;
    1 Ne. 13:7;
    2 Ne. 28:13 (9–16).
38*a* Rom. 1:16;
    2 Tim. 1:8;
    1 Ne. 8:25;
    Alma 46:21.
  b Rom. 3:16;
    Mosiah 3:25.
  c 1 Ne. 13:9.

40*a* TG Secret Combinations.
41*a* 1 Ne. 22:14;
    D&C 136:36.
9 2*a* Mal. 4:5;
    3 Ne. 28:31.
  b Morm. 5:23;
    D&C 63:21 (20–21).
    TG World, End of.
  c Amos 9:13;
    3 Ne. 26:3.

3*a* TG Conscience; Guilt.
4*a* TG Filthiness.
  b TG Damnation.
  c TG Hell.
5*a* Ex. 32:25;
    2 Ne. 9:14.
  b TG Holiness.
6*a* TG Unbelief.
  b Ezek. 18:23, 32;
    D&C 98:47.

ᶜpure, fair, and white, having been cleansed by the blood of the ᵈLamb, at that great and last day.

7 And again I speak unto you who ᵃdeny the revelations of God, and say that they are done away, that there are no revelations, nor prophecies, nor gifts, nor healing, nor speaking with tongues, and the ᵇinterpretation of tongues;

8 Behold I say unto you, he that denieth these things knoweth not the ᵃgospel of Christ; yea, he has not read the scriptures; if so, he does not ᵇunderstand them.

9 For do we not read that God is the ᵃsame ᵇyesterday, today, and forever, and in him there is no ᶜvariableness neither shadow of changing?

10 And now, if ye have imagined up unto yourselves a god who doth vary, and in whom there is shadow of changing, then have ye imagined up unto yourselves a god who is not a God of miracles.

11 But behold, I will show unto you a God of ᵃmiracles, even the God of Abraham, and the God of Isaac, and the God of Jacob; and it is that same ᵇGod who created the heavens and the earth, and all things that in them are.

12 Behold, he created Adam, and by ᵃAdam came the ᵇfall of man. And because of the fall of man came Jesus Christ, even the Father and the Son; and because of Jesus Christ came the ᶜredemption of man.

13 And because of the redemption of man, which came by Jesus Christ, they are brought back into the ᵃpresence of the Lord; yea, this is wherein all men are redeemed, because the death of Christ bringeth to pass the ᵇresurrection, which bringeth to pass a redemption from an endless ᶜsleep, from which sleep all men shall be awakened by the power of God when the trump shall sound; and they shall come forth, both small and great, and all shall stand before his bar, being redeemed and loosed from this eternal ᵈband of death, which death is a temporal death.

14 And then cometh the ᵃjudgment of the Holy One upon them; and then cometh the time that he that is ᵇfilthy shall be filthy still; and he that is righteous shall be righteous still; he that is happy shall be happy still; and he that is unhappy shall be unhappy still.

15 And now, O all ye that have imagined up unto yourselves a god who can do ᵃno miracles, I would ask of you, have all these things passed, of which I have spoken? Has the end come yet? Behold I say unto you, Nay; and God has not ceased to be a God of miracles.

16 Behold, are not the things that God hath wrought marvelous in our eyes? Yea, and who can comprehend the marvelous ᵃworks of God?

17 Who shall say that it was not a miracle that by his ᵃword the heaven and the earth should be; and by the power of his word man was ᵇcreated of the ᶜdust of the earth; and by the power of his word have miracles been wrought?

6c TG Cleanliness; Purification.
  d TG Jesus Christ, Lamb of God.
7a 3 Ne. 29:6.
  b 1 Cor. 12:10; A of F 1:7.
8a TG Gospel.
  b Matt. 22:29.
9a Heb. 13:8; 1 Ne. 10:18 (18–19); Alma 7:20; Moro. 8:18; D&C 20:12.
  b TG God, Eternal Nature of.
  c TG God, Perfection of.

11a TG God, Power of.
  b Gen. 1:1; Mosiah 4:2; D&C 76:24 (20–24).
12a Mosiah 3:26; Moro. 8:8.
  b TG Fall of Man.
  c TG Jesus Christ, Redeemer.
13a TG God, Presence of.
  b Hel. 14:15 (15–18).
  c Dan. 12:2; D&C 43:18.
  d Alma 36:18; D&C 138:16.

14a TG Judgment, the Last.
  b Alma 7:21; D&C 88:35.
15a Morm. 8:26; Moro. 7:35; D&C 35:8.
  TG Miracle.
16a Ps. 40:5; 92:5; D&C 76:114; Moses 1:4 (3–5).
17a Jacob 4:9.
  b TG Man, Physical Creation of.
  c Gen. 2:7; Mosiah 2:25; D&C 77:12; 93:35 (33–35).

18 And who shall say that Jesus Christ did not do many mighty ^amiracles? And there were many ^bmighty miracles wrought by the hands of the apostles.

19 And if there were ^amiracles wrought then, why has God ceased to be a God of miracles and yet be an unchangeable Being? And behold, I say unto you he ^bchangeth not; if so he would cease to be God; and he ceaseth not to be God, and is a God of miracles.

20 And the reason why he ceaseth to do ^amiracles among the children of men is because that they dwindle in unbelief, and depart from the right way, and know not the God in whom they should ^btrust.

21 Behold, I say unto you that whoso believeth in Christ, doubting nothing, ^awhatsoever he shall ask the Father in the name of Christ it shall be granted him; and this ^bpromise is unto all, even unto the ends of the earth.

22 For behold, thus said Jesus Christ, the Son of God, unto his disciples who should tarry, yea, and also to ^aall his disciples, in the hearing of the multitude: Go ye into all the world, and preach the gospel to every creature;

23 And he that ^abelieveth and is baptized shall be saved, but he that believeth not shall be ^bdamned;

24 And ^athese signs shall follow them that believe—in my name shall they cast out ^bdevils; they shall speak with new tongues; they shall take up serpents; and if they drink any deadly thing it shall not hurt them; they shall lay ^chands on the sick and they shall recover;

25 And whosoever shall believe in my name, doubting nothing, unto him will I ^aconfirm all my words, even unto the ends of the earth.

26 And now, behold, who can stand ^aagainst the works of the Lord? ^bWho can deny his sayings? Who will rise up against the almighty power of the Lord? Who will despise the works of the Lord? Who will despise the children of Christ? Behold, all ye who are ^cdespisers of the works of the Lord, for ye shall wonder and perish.

27 O then despise not, and wonder not, but hearken unto the words of the Lord, and ask the Father in the name of Jesus for what things soever ye shall stand in need. ^aDoubt not, but be believing, and begin as in times of old, and ^bcome unto the Lord with all your ^cheart, and ^dwork out your own salvation with fear and trembling before him.

28 Be ^awise in the days of your ^bprobation; strip yourselves of all uncleanness; ask not, that ye may consume it on your ^clusts, but ask with a firmness unshaken, that ye will yield to no temptation, but that ye will serve the true and ^dliving God.

29 See that ye are not baptized ^aunworthily; see that ye partake not of the sacrament of Christ ^bunworthily; but see that ye do all

18a John 6:14;
　　3 Ne. 8:1.
　b Mark 6:5.
19a Rom. 15:19 (18–19);
　　D&C 63:10 (7–10).
　b TG God, Perfection of.
20a Judg. 6:13 (11–13);
　　Ether 12:12 (12–18);
　　Moro. 7:37.
　b TG Trust in God.
21a Matt. 21:22 (18–22);
　　3 Ne. 18:20.
　b TG Promise.
22a Mark 16:15.
　　TG Missionary Work;
　　World.

23a Mark 16:16.
　b TG Damnation.
24a Mark 16:17 (17–18).
　　TG Signs.
　b Mark 5:15 (15–20);
　　1 Ne. 11:31.
　c TG Administrations to
　　the Sick;
　　Hands, Laying on of.
25a TG Testimony.
26a 2 Ne. 26:20; 28:5 (4–6, 15).
　b 3 Ne. 29:5 (4–7).
　c Prov. 13:13.
27a TG Doubt.
　b 3 Ne. 21:20;
　　Ether 5:5;

Moro. 10:30 (30–32).
　c Josh. 22:5;
　　D&C 64:34 (22, 34).
　　TG Commitment.
　d Philip. 2:12 (12–16).
28a Matt. 10:16;
　　Jacob 6:12.
　b TG Probation.
　c TG Covet;
　　Lust.
　d Alma 5:13.
29a TG Baptism,
　　Qualifications for.
　b Lev. 22:3;
　　1 Cor. 11:27 (27–30);
　　3 Ne. 18:29 (28–32).

things in ᶜworthiness, and do it in the name of Jesus Christ, the Son of the living God; and if ye do this, and endure to the end, ye will in nowise be cast out.

30 Behold, I speak unto you as though I ᵃspake from the dead; for I know that ye shall have my words.

31 Condemn me not because of mine ᵃimperfection, neither my father, because of his imperfection, neither them who have written before him; but rather give thanks unto God that he hath made manifest unto you our imperfections, that ye may learn to be more wise than we have been.

32 And now, behold, we have written this record according to our knowledge, in the characters which are called among us the ᵃreformed Egyptian, being handed down and altered by us, according to our manner of speech.

33 And if our plates had been ᵃsufficiently large we should have written in Hebrew; but the Hebrew hath been altered by us also; and if

we could have written in Hebrew, behold, ye would have had no ᵇimperfection in our record.

34 But the Lord knoweth the things which we have written, and also that none other people knoweth our language; and because that none other people knoweth our language, therefore he hath prepared ᵃmeans for the interpretation thereof.

35 And these things are written that we may rid our garments of the blood of our ᵃbrethren, who have dwindled in unbelief.

36 And behold, these things which we have ᵃdesired concerning our brethren, yea, even their restoration to the knowledge of Christ, are according to the prayers of all the saints who have dwelt in the land.

37 And may the Lord Jesus Christ grant that their prayers may be answered according to their faith; and may God the Father remember the covenant which he hath made with the house of Israel; and may he bless them forever, through faith on the name of Jesus Christ. Amen.

THE BOOK OF ETHER

The record of the Jaredites, taken from the twenty-four plates found by the people of Limhi in the days of King Mosiah.

CHAPTER 1

Moroni abridges the writings of Ether—Ether's genealogy is set forth—The language of the Jaredites is not confounded at the Tower of Babel—The Lord promises to lead them to a choice land and make them a great nation.

AND now I, Moroni, proceed to give an ᵃaccount of those ancient inhabitants who were destroyed by the ᵇhand of the Lord upon the face of this north country.

2 And I take mine account from the ᵃtwenty and four plates which

---

29c TG Worthiness.
30a Morm. 8:26;
    Moro. 10:27.
31a Morm. 8:17;
    Ether 12:23 (22–28, 35).
32a 1 Ne. 1:2;
    Mosiah 1:2 (2–4).
33a Jarom 1:14 (2, 14).

b 3 Ne. 5:18.
34a Mosiah 8:13 (13–18);
    Ether 3:23 (23, 28);
    D&C 17:1.
35a 2 Ne. 26:15.
36a Morm. 5:21;
    8:24 (24–26);
    D&C 10:46 (46–49).

[ETHER]

1 1a Mosiah 28:19.
   b 1 Sam. 5:9;
    Morm. 5:23;
    D&C 87:6 (6–7).
2a Alma 37:21 (21–31);
    Ether 15:33.

were found by the people of Limhi, which is called the Book of Ether.

3 And as I suppose that the ªfirst part of this record, which speaks concerning the creation of the world, and also of Adam, and an account from that time even to the great ᵇtower, and whatsoever things transpired among the children of men until that time, is had among the Jews—

4 Therefore I do not write those things which transpired from the ªdays of Adam until that time; but they are had upon the plates; and whoso findeth them, the same will have power that he may get the full account.

5 But behold, I give not the full account, but a ªpart of the account I give, from the tower down until they were destroyed.

6 And on this wise do I give the account. He that wrote this record was ªEther, and he was a descendant of Coriantor.

7 Coriantor was the son of Moron.

8 And Moron was the son of Ethem.

9 And Ethem was the son of Ahah.

10 And Ahah was the son of Seth.

11 And Seth was the son of Shiblon.

12 And Shiblon was the son of Com.

13 And Com was the son of Coriantum.

14 And Coriantum was the son of Amnigaddah.

15 And Amnigaddah was the son of Aaron.

16 And Aaron was a descendant of Heth, who was the son of Hearthom.

17 And Hearthom was the son of Lib.

18 And Lib was the son of Kish.

19 And Kish was the son of Corom.

20 And Corom was the son of Levi.

21 And Levi was the son of Kim.

22 And Kim was the son of Morianton.

23 And Morianton was a descendant of Riplakish.

24 And Riplakish was the son of Shez.

25 And Shez was the son of Heth.

26 And Heth was the son of Com.

27 And Com was the son of Coriantum.

28 And Coriantum was the son of Emer.

29 And Emer was the son of Omer.

30 And Omer was the son of Shule.

31 And Shule was the son of Kib.

32 And ªKib was the son of ᵇOrihah, who was the son of Jared;

33 Which ªJared came forth with his brother and their families, with some others and their families, from the great tower, at the time the Lord ᵇconfounded the language of the people, and swore in his wrath that they should be scattered upon all the ᶜface of the earth; and according to the word of the Lord the people were scattered.

34 And the ªbrother of Jared being a large and mighty man, and a man highly favored of the Lord, Jared, his brother, said unto him: Cry unto the Lord, that he will not confound us that we may not ᵇunderstand our words.

35 And it came to pass that the brother of Jared did cry unto the Lord, and the Lord had compassion upon Jared; therefore he did not confound the ªlanguage of Jared; and Jared and his brother were not confounded.

36 Then Jared said unto his brother: Cry again unto the Lord, and it may be that he will turn away his anger from them who are our ªfriends, that he confound not their language.

37 And it came to pass that the brother of Jared did cry unto the Lord, and the Lord had compassion

---

3 a Ether 8:9.
  b Gen. 11:4 (1–9);
    Omni 1:22;
    Mosiah 28:17;
    Hel. 6:28.
4 a IE covering same period
    as Genesis 1–10.

5 a Ether 3:17; 15:33.
6 a Ether 11:23; 12:2; 15:34.
32 a Ether 7:3.
  b Ether 6:27.
33 a Gen. 11:9 (6–9).
  b Omni 1:22.
  c Mosiah 28:17.

34 a Ether 2:13; 6:1.
  b TG Communication.
35 a Zeph. 3:9;
    Ether 3:24;
    Moses 6:6 (5–6).
36 a Ether 2:1.

upon their friends and their families also, that they were not confounded.

38 And it came to pass that Jared spake again unto his brother, saying: Go and ªinquire of the Lord whether he will drive us out of the land, and if he will drive us out of the land, cry unto him whither we shall go. And who knoweth but the Lord will carry us forth into a land which is ᵇchoice above all the earth? And if it so be, let us be faithful unto the Lord, that we may receive it for our inheritance.

39 And it came to pass that the brother of Jared did cry unto the Lord according to that which had been spoken by the mouth of Jared.

40 And it came to pass that the Lord did hear the brother of Jared, and ªhad compassion upon him, and said unto him:

41 Go to and gather together thy ªflocks, both male and female, of every kind; and also of the ᵇseed of the earth of every kind; and ᶜthy ᵈfamilies; and also Jared thy brother and his family; and also thy ᵉfriends and their families, and the friends of Jared and their families.

42 And when thou hast done this thou shalt ªgo at the head of them down into the valley which is northward. And there will I meet thee, and I will go ᵇbefore thee into a land which is ᶜchoice above all the lands of the earth.

43 And there will I bless thee and thy seed, and raise up unto me of thy seed, and of the seed of thy brother, and they who shall go with thee, a great nation. And ªthere shall be none ᵇgreater than the nation which I will raise up unto me of thy seed, upon all the face of the earth. And

thus I will do unto thee because this long time ye have cried unto me.

CHAPTER 2

The Jaredites prepare for their journey to a promised land—It is a choice land whereon men must serve Christ or be swept off—The Lord talks to the brother of Jared for three hours—The Jaredites build barges—The Lord asks the brother of Jared to propose how the barges will be lighted.

AND it came to pass that Jared and his brother, and their families, and also the ªfriends of Jared and his brother and their families, went down into the valley which was northward, (and the name of the valley was ᵇNimrod, being called after the mighty hunter) with their ᶜflocks which they had gathered together, male and female, of every kind.

2 And they did also lay snares and catch ªfowls of the air; and they did also prepare a vessel, in which they did carry with them the fish of the waters.

3 And they did also carry with them deseret, which, by interpretation, is a honey bee; and thus they did carry with them ªswarms of bees, and all manner of that which was upon the face of the land, ᵇseeds of every kind.

4 And it came to pass that when they had come down into the valley of Nimrod the Lord came down and talked with the brother of Jared; and he was in a ªcloud, and the brother of Jared saw him not.

5 And it came to pass that the Lord commanded them that they should ªgo forth into the wilderness, yea,

---

38a 2 Chr. 18:4 (4–7).
  b 1 Ne. 2:20.
    TG Lands of Inheritance.
40a Ether 3:3.
41a Ether 2:1 (1–3).
  b 1 Ne. 8:1; 16:11;
    Ether 9:17.
  c Ether 6:20.
  d Num. 1:2; Mosiah 6:3;
    D&C 48:6.
  e Ether 6:16.

42a Gen. 12:1; Num. 9:17;
    1 Ne. 2:2; Ether 2:5;
    Abr. 2:3.
  b Judg. 4:14;
    D&C 84:88 (87–88).
  c 1 Ne. 13:30.
43a Gen. 26:3;
    Deut. 28:8.
  b Ether 15:2.
2 1a Ether 1:36.
  b Gen. 10:8;

1 Chr. 1:10.
  c Ether 1:41; 6:4;
    9:18 (18–19).
2a Gen. 7:3 (1–3).
3a 1 Ne. 17:5; 18:6.
  b 1 Ne. 16:11.
4a Num. 11:25;
    D&C 34:7 (7–9);
    JS—H 1:68 (68–71).
5a Num. 9:17;
    Ether 1:42.

into that quarter where there never had man been. And it came to pass that the Lord did go before them, and did talk with them as he stood in a [b]cloud, and gave [c]directions whither they should travel.

6 And it came to pass that they did travel in the wilderness, and did [a]build [b]barges, in which they did cross many waters, being directed continually by the hand of the Lord.

7 And the Lord would not suffer that they should stop beyond the sea in the wilderness, but he would that they should come forth even unto the [a]land of promise, which was choice above all other lands, which the Lord God had [b]preserved for a righteous people.

8 And he had sworn in his wrath unto the brother of Jared, that whoso should possess this land of promise, from that time henceforth and forever, should [a]serve him, the true and only God, or they should be [b]swept off when the fulness of his wrath should come upon them.

9 And now, we can behold the decrees of God concerning this land, that it is a land of promise; and whatsoever nation shall possess it shall serve God, or they shall be [a]swept off when the fulness of his [b]wrath shall come upon them. And the fulness of his wrath cometh upon them when they are [c]ripened in iniquity.

10 For behold, this is a land which is choice above all other lands; wherefore he that doth possess it shall serve God or shall be [a]swept off; for it is the everlasting decree of God. And it is not until the [b]fulness of iniquity among the children of the land, that they are [c]swept off.

11 And this cometh unto you, O ye [a]Gentiles, that ye may know the decrees of God—that ye may repent, and not continue in your iniquities until the fulness come, that ye may not bring down the fulness of the [b]wrath of God upon you as the inhabitants of the land have hitherto done.

12 Behold, this is a choice land, and whatsoever nation shall possess it shall be [a]free from bondage, and from captivity, and from all other nations under heaven, if they will but [b]serve the God of the land, who is Jesus Christ, who hath been manifested by the things which we have written.

13 And now I proceed with my record; for behold, it came to pass that the Lord did bring Jared and his brethren forth even to that great sea which divideth the lands. And as they came to the sea they pitched their tents; and they called the name of the place [a]Moriancumer; and they dwelt in [b]tents, and dwelt in tents upon the seashore for the space of four years.

14 And it came to pass at the end of four years that the Lord came again unto the brother of Jared, and stood in a cloud and [a]talked with him. And for the space of three hours did the Lord talk with the brother of Jared, and [b]chastened him because he remembered not to [c]call upon the name of the Lord.

15 And the brother of Jared repented of the evil which he had done, and did call upon the name of the Lord for his brethren who were with him. And the Lord said unto him: I will forgive thee and thy brethren of their sins; but thou shalt not sin

5 b Ex. 13:21.
  c TG Guidance, Divine.
6 a TG Skill.
  b Gen. 6:14 (14–15);
    Ether 2:16.
7 a TG Promised Lands.
  b 1 Ne. 4:14.
8 a Ether 13:2.
  b Jarom 1:3 (3, 10);
    Alma 37:28;
    Ether 9:20.

9 a 2 Ne. 6:15.
  b TG God, Indignation of.
  c Gen. 15:16;
    1 Ne. 14:6.
10 a Jarom 1:12.
  b 2 Ne. 28:16.
  c 1 Ne. 17:37.
11 a 1 Ne. 14:6;
    2 Ne. 28:32.
  b Alma 45:16 (10–14, 16);
    Morm. 1:17.

12 a 1 Ne. 13:19.
    TG Liberty.
  b Isa. 60:12.
13 a Alma 8:7;
    Ether 1:34.
  b Gen. 25:27;
    Hel. 3:9.
14 a Ex. 25:22.
  b 1 Ne. 16:25.
    TG Chastening; Reproof.
  c TG Prayer.

any more, for ye shall remember that my *Spirit will not always *strive with man; wherefore, if ye will sin until ye are fully ripe ye shall be cut off from the presence of the Lord. And these are my *thoughts upon the land which I shall give you for your inheritance; for it shall be a land *choice above all other lands.

16 And the Lord said: Go to work and build, after the manner of *barges which ye have hitherto built. And it came to pass that the brother of Jared did go to work, and also his brethren, and built barges after the manner which they had built, according to the *instructions of the Lord. And they were small, and they were light upon the water, even like unto the lightness of a fowl upon the water.

17 And they were built after a manner that they were exceedingly *tight, even that they would hold water like unto a dish; and the bottom thereof was tight like unto a dish; and the sides thereof were tight like unto a dish; and the ends thereof were peaked; and the top thereof was tight like unto a dish; and the length thereof was the length of a tree; and the door thereof, when it was shut, was tight like unto a dish.

18 And it came to pass that the brother of Jared cried unto the Lord, saying: O Lord, I have performed the work which thou hast commanded me, and I have made the barges according as thou hast directed me.

19 And behold, O Lord, in them there is no light; whither shall we steer? And also we shall perish, for in them we cannot breathe, save it is the air which is in them; therefore we shall perish.

20 And the Lord said unto the brother of Jared: Behold, thou shalt make a hole in the top, and also in the bottom; and when thou shalt suffer for air thou shalt unstop the hole and receive air. And if it be so that the water come in upon thee, behold, ye shall stop the hole, that ye may not perish in the flood.

21 And it came to pass that the brother of Jared did so, according as the Lord had commanded.

22 And he cried again unto the Lord saying: O Lord, behold I have done even as thou hast commanded me; and I have prepared the vessels for my people, and behold there is no light in them. Behold, O Lord, wilt thou suffer that we shall cross this great water in darkness?

23 And the Lord said unto the brother of Jared: What will ye that I should do that ye may have light in your vessels? For behold, ye cannot have *windows, for they will be dashed in pieces; neither shall ye take fire with you, for ye shall not go by the light of fire.

24 For behold, ye shall be as a *whale in the midst of the sea; for the mountain waves shall dash upon you. Nevertheless, I will bring you up again out of the depths of the sea; for the *winds have gone forth *out of my mouth, and also the *rains and the floods have I sent forth.

25 And behold, I prepare you against these things; for ye cannot cross this great deep save I prepare you against the waves of the sea, and the winds which have gone forth, and the floods which shall come. Therefore what will ye that I should prepare for you that ye may have light when ye are swallowed up in the depths of the sea?

15a TG God, Spirit of.
  b Gen. 6:3;
    2 Ne. 26:11;
    Morm. 5:16;
    Moses 8:17.
  c TG Earth, Purpose of.
  d Ether 9:20.

16a Ether 2:6.
  b Ex. 25:40;
    Prov. 16:9;
    1 Ne. 17:51 (50–51).
17a Ether 6:7.
23a Gen. 6:16.
24a Gen. 1:21;

    Ether 6:10.
  b Ether 6:5.
  c Job 37:2 (2–13).
  d Ps. 148:8;
    D&C 117:1.

CHAPTER 3

The brother of Jared sees the finger of the Lord as He touches sixteen stones—Christ shows His spirit body to the brother of Jared—Those who have a perfect knowledge cannot be kept from within the veil—Interpreters are provided to bring the Jaredite record to light.

AND it came to pass that the brother of Jared, (now the number of the vessels which had been prepared was eight) went forth unto the ᵃmount, which they called the mount ᵇShelem, because of its exceeding height, and did ᶜmolten out of a rock sixteen small stones; and they were white and clear, even as transparent ᵈglass; and he did carry them in his hands upon the top of the mount, and cried again unto the Lord, saying:

2 O Lord, thou hast said that we must be encompassed about by the floods. Now behold, O Lord, and do not be ᵃangry with thy servant because of his weakness before thee; for we know that thou art holy and dwellest in the heavens, and that we are ᵇunworthy before thee; because of the ᶜfall our ᵈnatures have become evil continually; nevertheless, O Lord, thou hast given us a commandment that we must call upon thee, that from thee we may receive according to our desires.

3 Behold, O Lord, thou hast smitten us because of our iniquity, and hast driven us forth, and for these many years we have been in the wilderness; nevertheless, thou hast been ᵃmerciful unto us. O Lord, look upon me in pity, and turn away thine anger from this thy people, and suffer not that they shall go forth across this raging deep in darkness; but behold these ᵇthings which I have molten out of the rock.

4 And I know, O Lord, that thou hast all ᵃpower, and can do whatsoever thou wilt for the benefit of man; therefore touch these stones, O Lord, with thy ᵇfinger, and prepare them that they may shine forth in darkness; and they shall shine forth unto us in the vessels which we have prepared, that we may have ᶜlight while we shall cross the sea.

5 Behold, O Lord, thou canst do this. We know that thou art able to show forth great power, which ᵃlooks small unto the understanding of men.

6 And it came to pass that when the brother of Jared had said these words, behold, the ᵃLord stretched forth his hand and touched the stones one by one with his ᵇfinger. And the ᶜveil was taken from off the eyes of the brother of Jared, and he saw the finger of the Lord; and it was as the finger of a man, like unto flesh and blood; and the brother of Jared ᵈfell down before the Lord, for he was struck with ᵉfear.

7 And the Lord saw that the brother of Jared had fallen to the earth; and the Lord said unto him: Arise, why hast thou fallen?

8 And he saith unto the Lord: I saw the finger of the Lord, and I feared lest he should ᵃsmite me; for I knew not that the Lord had flesh and blood.

9 And the Lord said unto him: Because of thy faith thou hast seen that I shall take upon me ᵃflesh and blood; and never has man come before me with ᵇsuch exceeding faith as thou hast; for were it not so ye

---

3 1*a* Ex. 24:13 (12–13);
    Deut. 10:1;
    1 Ne. 11:1.
  b Ether 4:1.
  c TG Skill.
  d Rev. 21:21.
2*a* Gen. 18:32 (25–33).
  b Moses 1:10.
  c TG Fall of Man.
  d Mosiah 3:19.

3*a* Ether 1:40 (34–43).
  b Ether 6:2 (2–3, 10).
4*a* TG God, Power of.
  b Ether 12:20 (19–21).
  c TG Light [noun].
5*a* Isa. 55:8 (8–9).
6*a* TG Jesus Christ, Lord.
  b Dan. 5:5;
    Abr. 3:12 (11–12).
  c Ether 12:19 (19, 21).

  d Ezek. 1:28;
    Acts 9:4 (3–5).
  e Ex. 3:6;
    JS—H 1:32.
8*a* Moses 1:11.
9*a* TG Flesh and Blood;
    Jesus Christ,
    Condescension of.
  b Matt. 8:10;
    Alma 19:10.

could not have seen my finger. Sawest thou more than this?

10 And he answered: Nay; Lord, [a]show thyself unto me.

11 And the Lord said unto him: [a]Believest thou the words which I shall speak?

12 And he answered: Yea, Lord, I know that thou speakest the truth, for thou art a God of truth, and [a]canst not lie.

13 And when he had said these words, behold, the Lord [a]showed himself unto him, and said: [b]Because thou knowest these things ye are redeemed from the fall; therefore ye are brought back into my [c]presence; therefore I [d]show myself unto you.

14 Behold, I am he who was [a]prepared from the foundation of the world to [b]redeem my people. Behold, I am Jesus Christ. I am the [c]Father and the Son. In me shall all mankind have [d]life, and that eternally, even they who shall believe on my name; and they shall become my [e]sons and my daughters.

15 And never have I [a]showed myself unto man whom I have created, for never has man [b]believed in me as thou hast. Seest thou that ye are created after mine own [c]image? Yea, even all men were created in the beginning after mine own image.

16 Behold, this [a]body, which ye now [b]behold, is the [c]body of my [d]spirit; and man have I created after the body of my spirit; and even as I appear unto thee to be in the

spirit will I appear unto my people in the flesh.

17 And now, as I, Moroni, said I could [a]not make a full account of these things which are written, therefore it sufficeth me to say that Jesus showed himself unto this man in the spirit, even after the manner and in the likeness of the same body even as he [b]showed himself unto the Nephites.

18 And he ministered unto him even as he ministered unto the Nephites; and all this, that this man might know that he was God, because of the many great works which the Lord had showed unto him.

19 And because of the [a]knowledge of this man he could not be kept from beholding within the [b]veil; and he saw the finger of Jesus, which, when he saw, he fell with fear; for he knew that it was the finger of the Lord; and he had [c]faith no longer, for he knew, nothing [d]doubting.

20 Wherefore, having this perfect knowledge of God, he could [a]not be kept from within the veil; therefore he [b]saw Jesus; and he did minister unto him.

21 And it came to pass that the Lord said unto the brother of Jared: Behold, thou shalt not suffer these things which ye have seen and heard to go forth unto the world, until the [a]time cometh that I shall glorify my name in the flesh; wherefore, ye shall [b]treasure up the things which ye have seen and heard, and show it to no man.

10a Ex. 33:18 (17–18).
11a 1 Ne. 11:4 (4–5).
12a Num. 23:19;
  Heb. 6:18.
13a 1 Sam. 3:21;
  D&C 67:11 (11–12).
  b Enos 1:8 (6–8).
  c TG God, Presence of;
  God, Privilege of Seeing.
  d TG Jesus Christ,
  Appearances, Antemortal.
14a TG Jesus Christ,
  Foreordained.
  b TG Jesus Christ,
  Redeemer.
  c Mosiah 15:2.
  d Mosiah 16:9;

  D&C 88:13 (7–13).
  e TG Sons and Daughters
  of God.
15a Ex. 3:6; 33:20 (11–23);
  John 1:18;
  D&C 107:54;
  Moses 1:2.
  TG God, Privilege of
  Seeing.
  b TG Faith.
  c Gen. 1:26 (26–28);
  Mosiah 7:27;
  D&C 20:18 (17–18).
  TG God, Body of,
  Corporeal Nature.
16a TG God, Manifestations of.

  b D&C 17:1.
  c TG Spirit Body.
  d TG Man, Antemortal
  Existence of.
17a Ether 1:5; 15:33.
  b 3 Ne. 11:8 (8–16).
19a TG Knowledge.
  b TG Veil.
  c Alma 32:34.
  d TG Doubt.
20a Ether 12:21 (19–21).
  b TG Jesus Christ,
  Appearances, Antemortal.
21a Ether 4:1.
  b Luke 2:19 (17–20).

22 And behold, when ye shall come unto me, ye shall write them and shall seal them up, that no one can interpret them; for ye shall write them in a ªlanguage that they cannot be read.

23 And behold, these ªtwo stones will I give unto thee, and ye shall seal them up also with the things which ye shall write.

24 For behold, the ªlanguage which ye shall write I have confounded; wherefore I will cause in my own due time that these stones shall magnify to the eyes of men these things which ye shall write.

25 And when the Lord had said these words, he ªshowed unto the brother of Jared ᵇall the inhabitants of the earth which had been, and also all that would be; and he ᶜwithheld them not from his sight, even unto the ends of the earth.

26 For he had said unto him in times before, that ªif he would ᵇbelieve in him that he could show unto him ᶜall things—it should be shown unto him; therefore the Lord could not withhold anything from him, for he knew that the Lord could show him all things.

27 And the Lord said unto him: Write these things and ªseal them up; and I will show them in mine own due time unto the children of men.

28 And it came to pass that the Lord commanded him that he should seal up the two ªstones which he had received, and show them not, until the Lord should show them unto the children of ᵇmen.

CHAPTER 4

Moroni is commanded to seal up the writings of the brother of Jared—They will not be revealed until men have faith even as the brother of Jared—Christ commands men to believe His words and those of His disciples—Men are commanded to repent, believe the gospel, and be saved.

AND the Lord commanded the brother of Jared to go down out of the ªmount from the presence of the Lord, and ᵇwrite the things which he had seen; and they were forbidden to come unto the children of men ᶜuntil after that he should be lifted up upon the cross; and for this cause did king Mosiah keep them, that they should not come unto the world until after Christ should show himself unto his people.

2 And after Christ truly had showed himself unto his people he commanded that they should be made manifest.

3 And now, after that, they have all dwindled in unbelief; and there is ªnone save it be the Lamanites, and they have rejected the gospel of Christ; therefore I am commanded that I should ᵇhide them up again in the earth.

4 Behold, I have written upon these plates the ªvery things which the brother of Jared saw; and there never were ᵇgreater things made manifest than those which were made manifest unto the brother of Jared.

5 Wherefore the Lord hath commanded me to write them; and I have written them. And he commanded

22ª Mosiah 8:11 (11–12).
    TG Language.
23ª Mosiah 8:13 (13–18);
    Morm. 9:34;
    D&C 17:1.
    TG Urim and Thummim.
24ª Ether 1:35.
25ª 2 Ne. 27:7.
    TG God, Omniscience of;
    Revelation.
  ᵇ Moses 1:8.
  ᶜ Luke 24:16 (10–24);

    D&C 25:4.
26ª Ether 3:11–13.
  ᵇ TG Believe.
  ᶜ 2 Ne. 27:7 (7–8, 10–11);
    Mosiah 8:19;
    Ether 4:4 (1–8).
27ª 2 Ne. 27:7 (6–23).
28ª D&C 17:1.
  ᵇ 2 Ne. 3:6;
    3 Ne. 21:11 (8–11);
    Morm. 8:16 (16, 25).
4 1ª Ether 3:1.

  ᵇ Ether 12:24.
    TG Record Keeping;
    Scriptures, Writing of.
  ᶜ Ether 3:21.
3ª Morm. 8:3 (2–3).
  ᵇ Morm. 8:14.
    TG Scriptures,
    Preservation of.
4ª Ether 5:1.
  ᵇ 2 Ne. 27:7 (7–8, 10–11);
    Mosiah 8:19;
    Ether 3:26 (21–28).

me that I should ^aseal them up; and he also hath commanded that I should seal up the interpretation thereof; wherefore I have sealed up the ^binterpreters, according to the commandment of the Lord.

6 For the Lord said unto me: They shall not go forth unto the Gentiles until the day that they shall repent of their iniquity, and become clean before the Lord.

7 And in that day that they shall exercise ^afaith in me, saith the Lord, even as the brother of Jared did, that they may become ^bsanctified in me, then will I ^cmanifest unto them the things which the brother of Jared saw, even to the unfolding unto them all my ^drevelations, saith Jesus Christ, the Son of God, the ^eFather of the heavens and of the earth, and all things that in them are.

8 And he that will ^acontend against the word of the Lord, let him be accursed; and he that shall ^bdeny these things, let him be accursed; for unto them will I show ^cno greater things, saith Jesus Christ; for I am he who speaketh.

9 And at my command the heavens are opened and are ^ashut; and at my word the ^bearth shall shake; and at my command the inhabitants thereof shall pass away, even so as by fire.

10 And he that believeth not my words believeth not my disciples; and if it so be that I do not speak, judge ye; for ye shall know that it is I that speaketh, at the ^alast day.

11 But he that ^abelieveth these

things which I have spoken, him will I visit with the manifestations of my Spirit, and he shall ^bknow and bear record. For because of my Spirit he shall ^cknow that these things are ^dtrue; for it persuadeth men to do good.

12 And whatsoever thing persuadeth men to do good is of me; for ^agood cometh of none save it be of me. I am the same that leadeth men to all good; he that will ^bnot believe my words will not believe me—that I am; and he that will not believe me will not believe the Father who sent me. For behold, I am the Father, I am the ^clight, and the ^dlife, and the ^etruth of the world.

13 ^aCome unto me, O ye Gentiles, and I will show unto you the greater things, the knowledge which is hid up because of unbelief.

14 Come unto me, O ye house of Israel, and it shall be made ^amanifest unto you how great things the Father hath laid up for you, from the foundation of the world; and it hath not come unto you, because of unbelief.

15 Behold, when ye shall rend that veil of unbelief which doth cause you to remain in your awful state of wickedness, and hardness of heart, and blindness of mind, then shall the great and marvelous things which have been ^ahid up from the foundation of the world from you— yea, when ye shall ^bcall upon the Father in my name, with a broken heart and a contrite spirit, then shall ye know that the Father hath

---

5a Dan. 12:9;
   3 Ne. 26:9 (7–12, 18);
   Ether 5:1;
   D&C 17:6; 35:18;
   JS—H 1:65.
 b Morm. 6:6;
   D&C 17:1;
   JS—H 1:52.
   TG Urim and Thummim.
7a D&C 5:28.
 b TG Sanctification.
 c 2 Ne. 30:16; Alma 12:9;
   3 Ne. 26:10 (6–11).
 d 2 Ne. 27:22.
 e Mosiah 3:8.

8a Job 9:3 (1–4);
   3 Ne. 29:5 (1–9);
   Morm. 8:17.
 b 2 Ne. 27:14; 28:29 (29–31);
   3 Ne. 28:34.
 c Alma 12:10 (10–11);
   3 Ne. 26:10 (9–10).
9a 1 Kgs. 8:35;
   D&C 77:8.
 b Hel. 12:11 (8–18);
   Morm. 5:23.
10a 2 Ne. 25:22; 33:15 (10–15);
   3 Ne. 27:25 (23–27).
11a D&C 5:16.
 b 2 Ne. 32:5; 3 Ne. 16:6.

 c TG Testimony.
 d TG Alma 3:12;
   Ether 5:3 (1–4);
   Moro. 10:4 (1–5).
12a Omni 1:25; Alma 5:40;
   Moro. 7:16 (12–17).
 b 3 Ne. 11:35; 28:34.
 c TG Jesus Christ, Light
   of the World.
 d Col. 3:4.
 e Alma 38:9.
13a 3 Ne. 12:2 (2–3).
14a D&C 121:26 (26–29).
15a 2 Ne. 27:10.
 b Gen. 4:26; Moro. 2:2.

remembered the covenant which he made unto your fathers, O house of Israel.

16 And then shall my ^arevelations which I have caused to be written by my servant John be unfolded in the eyes of all the people. Remember, when ye see these things, ye shall know that the time is at hand that they shall be made manifest in very deed.

17 Therefore, ^awhen ye shall receive this record ye may know that the work of the Father has commenced upon all the face of the land.

18 Therefore, ^arepent all ye ends of the earth, and come unto me, and believe in my gospel, and be ^bbaptized in my name; for he that believeth and is baptized shall be saved; but he that believeth not shall be damned; and ^csigns shall follow them that believe in my name.

19 And blessed is he that is found ^afaithful unto my name at the last day, for he shall be ^blifted up to dwell in the kingdom prepared for him ^cfrom the foundation of the world. And behold it is I that hath spoken it. Amen.

CHAPTER 5

Three witnesses and the work itself will stand as a testimony of the truthfulness of the Book of Mormon.

AND now I, Moroni, have written the words which were commanded me, according to my memory; and I have told you the things which I have ^asealed up; therefore touch them not in order that ye may translate; for that thing is forbidden you, except by and by it shall be wisdom in God.

2 And behold, ye may be privileged that ye may show the plates unto ^athose who shall assist to bring forth this work;

3 And unto ^athree shall they be shown by the power of God; wherefore they shall ^bknow of a surety that these things are ^ctrue.

4 And in the mouth of three ^awitnesses shall these things be established; and the ^btestimony of three, and this work, in the which shall be shown forth the power of God and also his word, of which the Father, and the Son, and the Holy Ghost bear record—and all this shall stand as a testimony against the world at the last day.

5 And if it so be that they repent and ^acome unto the Father in the name of Jesus, they shall be received into the kingdom of God.

6 And now, if I have no authority for these things, judge ye; for ye shall know that I have authority when ye shall see me, and we shall stand before God at the last day. Amen.

CHAPTER 6

The Jaredite barges are driven by the winds to the promised land—The people praise the Lord for His goodness—Orihah is appointed king over them—Jared and his brother die.

AND now I, Moroni, proceed to give the record of ^aJared and his brother.

2 For it came to pass after the Lord had prepared the ^astones which the brother of Jared had carried up into the mount, the brother of Jared

16a Rev. 1:1;
       1 Ne. 14:23 (18–27).
17a 3 Ne. 21:2 (1–11, 28).
18a 3 Ne. 27:20;
       Moro. 7:34.
   b John 3:5 (3–5).
     TG Baptism, Essential.
   c TG Holy Ghost, Gifts of.
19a Ps. 31:23;
       Mosiah 2:41;
       D&C 6:13; 63:47.
     TG Jesus Christ, Taking

       the Name of.
   b Morm. 2:19.
   c 2 Ne. 9:18;
       Alma 42:26;
       Ether 3:14.
5 1a 2 Ne. 27:8 (7–11, 21);
       Ether 4:5 (4–7);
       D&C 17:6.
   2a 2 Ne. 27:14 (13–14);
       D&C 5:15 (1–16).
   3a 2 Ne. 11:3; 27:12 (12–14);
       D&C 17:3 (3–5).

   b D&C 5:25.
   c Ether 4:11 (6–11);
       Moro. 10:4 (1–4).
   4a 2 Ne. 27:12 (12–14);
       D&C 14:8; 17:1.
   b 2 Ne. 25:18; 29:11.
   5a Morm. 9:27;
       Moro. 10:30 (30–32).
6 1a Ether 1:34.
   2a Ether 3:3.

came down out of the mount, and he did put forth the stones into the vessels which were prepared, one in each end thereof; and behold, they did give light unto the vessels.

3 And thus the Lord caused stones to shine in darkness, to give light unto men, women, and children, that they might not cross the great waters in darkness.

4 And it came to pass that when they had prepared all manner of ^afood, that thereby they might subsist upon the water, and also food for their flocks and herds, and ^bwhatsoever beast or animal or fowl that they should carry with them—and it came to pass that when they had done all these things they got aboard of their vessels or barges, and set forth into the sea, commending themselves unto the Lord their God.

5 And it came to pass that the Lord God caused that there should be a ^afurious wind blow upon the face of the waters, ^btowards the promised land; and thus they were tossed upon the waves of the sea before the wind.

6 And it came to pass that they were many times buried in the depths of the sea, because of the mountain waves which broke upon them, and also the great and terrible tempests which were caused by the fierceness of the wind.

7 And it came to pass that when they were buried in the deep there was no water that could hurt them, their vessels being ^atight like unto a dish, and also they were tight like unto the ^bark of Noah; therefore when they were encompassed about by many waters they did cry unto the Lord, and he did bring them forth again upon the top of the waters.

8 And it came to pass that the wind did never cease to blow towards the promised land while they were upon the waters; and thus they were ^adriven forth before the wind.

9 And they did ^asing praises unto the Lord; yea, the brother of Jared did sing praises unto the Lord, and he did ^bthank and praise the Lord all the day long; and when the night came, they did not cease to praise the Lord.

10 And thus they were driven forth; and no monster of the sea could break them, neither ^awhale that could mar them; and they did have light continually, whether it was above the water or under the water.

11 And thus they were driven forth, ^athree hundred and forty and four days upon the water.

12 And they did ^aland upon the shore of the ^bpromised land. And when they had set their feet upon the shores of the promised land they bowed themselves down upon the face of the land, and did humble themselves before the Lord, and did shed tears of joy before the Lord, because of the multitude of his ^ctender mercies over them.

13 And it came to pass that they went forth upon the face of the land, and began to till the earth.

14 And Jared had four ^asons; and they were called Jacom, and Gilgah, and Mahah, and Orihah.

15 And the brother of Jared also begat sons and daughters.

16 And the ^afriends of Jared and his brother were in number about twenty and two souls; and they also begat sons and daughters before they came to the promised land; and therefore they began to be many.

17 And they were taught to ^awalk

4a TG Food.
  b Ether 2:1; 9:18 (18–19).
5a Ether 2:24 (24–25).
  b 1 Ne. 18:8.
7a Ether 2:17.
  b Gen. 6:14;
     Moses 7:43.
8a 1 Ne. 18:13 (8–13).

9a TG Singing.
  b 1 Chr. 16:8 (7–36);
     Ps. 34:1 (1–3);
     Alma 37:37;
     D&C 46:32.
10a Gen. 1:21;
     Ether 2:24.
11a Gen. 7:11; 8:13.

12a Ether 7:16.
  b Alma 22:30 (29–34);
     Ether 7:6.
  c Ether 7:27; 10:2.
14a Ether 6:27.
16a Ether 1:41.
17a TG Walking with God.

humbly before the Lord; and they were also [b]taught from on high.

18 And it came to pass that they began to spread upon the face of the land, and to multiply and to till the earth; and they did wax strong in the land.

19 And the brother of Jared began to be old, and saw that he must soon go down to the grave; wherefore he said unto Jared: Let us gather together our people that we may number them, that we may know of them what they will desire of us before we go down to our graves.

20 And accordingly the people were gathered together. Now the number of the sons and the daughters of the brother of Jared were twenty and two souls; and the number of sons and daughters of Jared were twelve, he having four sons.

21 And it came to pass that they did number their people; and after that they had numbered them, they did desire of them the things which they would that they should do before they went down to their graves.

22 And it came to pass that the people desired of them that they should [a]anoint one of their sons to be a king over them.

23 And now behold, this was grievous unto them. And the brother of Jared said unto them: Surely this thing [a]leadeth into captivity.

24 But Jared said unto his brother: Suffer them that they may have a king. And therefore he said unto them: Choose ye out from among our sons a king, even whom ye will.

25 And it came to pass that they chose even the firstborn of the brother of Jared; and his name was Pagag. And it came to pass that he refused and would not be their [a]king. And the people would that his father should constrain him, but his father would not; and he

commanded them that they should constrain no man to be their king.

26 And it came to pass that they chose all the brothers of Pagag, and they would not.

27 And it came to pass that neither would the [a]sons of Jared, even all save it were one; and [b]Orihah was anointed to be king over the people.

28 And he began to reign, and the people began to [a]prosper; and they became exceedingly rich.

29 And it came to pass that Jared died, and his brother also.

30 And it came to pass that Orihah did walk humbly before the Lord, and did remember how great things the Lord had done for his father, and also taught his people how great things the Lord had done for their fathers.

CHAPTER 7

Orihah reigns in righteousness—Amid usurpation and strife, the rival kingdoms of Shule and Cohor are set up— Prophets condemn the wickedness and idolatry of the people, who then repent.

AND it came to pass that Orihah did execute judgment upon the land in righteousness all his days, whose days were exceedingly many.

2 And he begat sons and daughters; yea, he begat thirty and one, among whom were twenty and three sons.

3 And it came to pass that he begat [a]Kib in his [b]old age. And it came to pass that Kib reigned in his stead; and Kib begat Corihor.

4 And when Corihor was thirty and two years old he rebelled against his father, and went over and dwelt in the land of Nehor; and he begat sons and daughters, and they became exceedingly fair; wherefore Corihor drew away many people after him.

5 And when he had gathered together an army he came up unto the

17b TG Guidance, Divine;
    Revelation.
22a TG Anointing.
23a 1 Sam. 8:11 (10–18);
    Mosiah 29:18 (16–23);

Ether 7:5.
25a TG Kings, Earthly.
27a Ether 6:14.
  b Ether 1:32.
28a TG Prosper.

7 3a Ether 1:32 (31–32).
  b Gen. 18:12 (11–12);
    Ether 7:26; 9:23.

land of ^aMoron where the king dwelt, and took him captive, which ^bbrought to pass the saying of the brother of Jared that they would be brought into captivity.

6 Now the ^aland of Moron, where the king dwelt, was near the land which is called Desolation by the Nephites.

7 And it came to pass that Kib dwelt in ^acaptivity, and his people under Corihor his son, until he became exceedingly old; nevertheless Kib begat Shule in his old age, while he was yet in captivity.

8 And it came to pass that Shule was angry with his brother; and Shule waxed strong, and became mighty as to the strength of a man; and he was also mighty in judgment.

9 Wherefore, he came to the hill Ephraim, and he did molten out of the hill, and made swords out of ^asteel for those whom he had drawn away with him; and after he had armed them with swords he returned to the city Nehor, and gave battle unto his brother Corihor, by which means he obtained the kingdom and restored it unto his father Kib.

10 And now because of the thing which Shule had done, his father bestowed upon him the kingdom; therefore he began to reign in the stead of his father.

11 And it came to pass that he did execute judgment in righteousness; and he did spread his kingdom upon all the face of the land, for the people had become exceedingly numerous.

12 And it came to pass that Shule also begat many sons and daughters.

13 And Corihor repented of the many evils which he had done; wherefore Shule gave him power in his kingdom.

14 And it came to pass that Corihor had many sons and daughters. And among the sons of Corihor there was one whose name was Noah.

15 And it came to pass that Noah rebelled against Shule, the king, and also his father Corihor, and drew away Cohor his brother, and also all his brethren and many of the people.

16 And he gave battle unto Shule, the king, in which he did obtain the land of their ^afirst inheritance; and he became a king over that part of the land.

17 And it came to pass that he gave battle again unto Shule, the king; and he took Shule, the king, and carried him away captive into Moron.

18 And it came to pass as he was about to put him to death, the sons of Shule crept into the house of Noah by night and slew him, and broke down the door of the prison and brought out their father, and placed him upon his throne in his own kingdom.

19 Wherefore, the son of Noah did build up his kingdom in his stead; nevertheless they did not gain power any more over Shule the king, and the people who were under the reign of Shule the king did prosper exceedingly and wax great.

20 And the country was ^adivided; and there were two kingdoms, the kingdom of Shule, and the kingdom of Cohor, the son of Noah.

21 And Cohor, the son of Noah, caused that his people should give battle unto Shule, in which Shule did beat them and did slay Cohor.

22 And now Cohor had a son who was called Nimrod; and Nimrod gave up the kingdom of Cohor unto Shule, and he did gain favor in the eyes of Shule; wherefore Shule did bestow great favors upon him, and he did do in the kingdom of Shule according to his desires.

23 And also in the reign of Shule there came ^aprophets among the people, who were sent from the Lord, prophesying that the wickedness and ^bidolatry of the people was bringing a curse upon the land, and they should be destroyed if they did not repent.

5a Ether 14:6 (6, 11).
 b Ether 6:23.
6a Ether 6:12.
7a Ether 8:4 (3–4); 10:14.
9a 1 Ne. 16:18.
16a Ether 6:12.
20a 2 Ne. 5:7 (1–14).
23a Ether 9:28;
11:1 (1, 12, 20).
 b TG Idolatry.

24 And it came to pass that the people did ^arevile against the prophets, and did mock them. And it came to pass that king Shule did execute judgment against all those who did revile against the prophets.

25 And he did execute a law throughout all the land, which gave power unto the prophets that they should go whithersoever they would; and by this cause the people were brought unto repentance.

26 And because the people did repent of their iniquities and idolatries the Lord did spare them, and they began to prosper again in the land. And it came to pass that Shule ^abegat sons and daughters in his old age.

27 And there were no more wars in the days of Shule; and he remembered the great things that the Lord had done for his fathers in bringing them ^aacross the great deep into the promised land; wherefore he did execute judgment in righteousness all his days.

CHAPTER 8

There is strife and contention over the kingdom—Akish forms an oath-bound secret combination to slay the king—Secret combinations are of the devil and result in the destruction of nations—Modern Gentiles are warned against the secret combination that will seek to overthrow the freedom of all lands, nations, and countries.

AND it came to pass that he begat Omer, and Omer reigned in his stead. And Omer begat Jared; and Jared begat sons and daughters.

2 And Jared rebelled against his father, and came and dwelt in the land of Heth. And it came to pass that he did ^aflatter many people, because of his cunning words, until he had gained the half of the kingdom.

3 And when he had gained the half of the kingdom he gave battle unto his father, and he did carry away his father into captivity, and did make him serve in captivity;

4 And now, in the days of the reign of Omer he was in ^acaptivity the half of his days. And it came to pass that he begat sons and daughters, among whom were Esrom and Coriantumr;

5 And they were exceedingly angry because of the doings of Jared their brother, insomuch that they did raise an army and gave battle unto Jared. And it came to pass that they did give battle unto him by night.

6 And it came to pass that when they had slain the army of Jared they were about to slay him also; and he pled with them that they would not slay him, and he would give up the kingdom unto his father. And it came to pass that they did grant unto him his life.

7 And now Jared became exceedingly ^asorrowful because of the loss of the kingdom, for he had set his heart upon the kingdom and upon the glory of the world.

8 Now the daughter of Jared being exceedingly expert, and seeing the sorrows of her father, thought to devise a plan whereby she could redeem the kingdom unto her father.

9 Now the daughter of Jared was exceedingly fair. And it came to pass that she did talk with her father, and said unto him: Whereby hath my father so much sorrow? Hath he not read the ^arecord which our fathers brought across the great deep? Behold, is there not an ^baccount concerning them of ^cold, that they by their ^dsecret plans did obtain kingdoms and great glory?

10 And now, therefore, let my father send for Akish, the son of

---

24a Mosiah 27:2 (1–3).
   TG Prophets,
   Rejection of;
   Reviling.
26a Ether 7:3 (3, 7); 9:23.
27a Ether 6:12 (1–12).

8 2a Hel. 1:7; 2:5.
  4a Ether 7:7 (5–7); 10:14.
  7a Morm. 2:13.
  9a Ether 1:3.
   b 3 Ne. 6:28.
   c Hel. 6:26 (26–30);

3 Ne. 3:9.
   d Hel. 6:27;
   Ether 13:18;
   Moses 5:30 (18–52).

Kimnor; and behold, I am fair, and I will dance before him, and I will please him, that he will desire me to wife; wherefore if he shall desire of thee that ye shall give unto him me to wife, then shall ye say: I will give her if ye will bring unto me the ^ahead of my father, the king.

11 And now Omer was a friend to Akish; wherefore, when Jared had sent for Akish, the daughter of Jared danced before him that she pleased him, insomuch that he desired her to wife. And it came to pass that he said unto Jared: Give her unto me to wife.

12 And Jared said unto him: I will give her unto you, if ye will bring unto me the head of my father, the king.

13 And it came to pass that Akish gathered in unto the house of Jared all his kinsfolk, and said unto them: Will ye swear unto me that ye will be faithful unto me in the thing which I shall desire of you?

14 And it came to pass that they all ^asware unto him, by the God of heaven, and also by the heavens, and also by the earth, and by their heads, that whoso should vary from the assistance which Akish desired should lose his head; and whoso should divulge whatsoever thing Akish made known unto them, the same should lose his life.

15 And it came to pass that thus they did agree with ^aAkish. And Akish did administer unto them the oaths which were given by them of old who also sought power, which had been handed down even from ^bCain, who was a murderer from the beginning.

16 And they were kept up by the ^apower of the devil to administer these oaths unto the people, to keep them in darkness, to help such as sought power to gain power, and to murder, and to plunder, and to lie, and to commit all manner of wickedness and whoredoms.

17 And it was the daughter of Jared who put it into his heart to search up these things of old; and Jared put it into the heart of Akish; wherefore, Akish administered it unto his kindred and friends, leading them away by fair promises to do whatsoever thing he desired.

18 And it came to pass that they formed a ^asecret combination, even as they of old; which combination is most abominable and wicked above all, in the sight of God;

19 For the Lord worketh not in secret combinations, neither doth he will that man should shed blood, but in all things hath forbidden it, from the beginning of man.

20 And now I, Moroni, do not write the manner of their oaths and combinations, for it hath been made known unto me that they are had ^aamong all people, and they are had among the Lamanites.

21 And they have caused the ^adestruction of this people of whom I am now speaking, and also the destruction of the people of Nephi.

22 And whatsoever ^anation shall uphold such secret combinations, to get power and gain, until they shall spread over the nation, behold, they shall be destroyed; for the Lord will not suffer that the ^bblood of his saints, which shall be shed by them, shall always cry unto him from the ground for ^cvengeance upon them and yet he avenge them not.

23 Wherefore, O ye Gentiles, it is wisdom in God that these things should be shown unto you, that thereby ye may repent of your sins, and suffer not that these murderous combinations shall get above you,

---

10 a Mark 6:24 (22–28).
14 a Hel. 1:11;
        3 Ne. 3:8.
        TG Swearing.
15 a Ether 9:1.
      b Gen. 4:7 (7–8);
        Moses 5:25.

16 a Moses 4:6; 5:13.
18 a TG Secret Combinations.
20 a 4 Ne. 1:46;
        Morm. 2:8; 8:9.
21 a Hel. 6:28;
        D&C 38:13 (13–16).
22 a TG Governments.

b Rev. 6:10 (1–11); 19:2;
    2 Ne. 28:10;
    Morm. 8:27 (27, 40–41);
    D&C 87:7.
c TG God, Justice of;
    Vengeance.

which are built up to get *power and gain—and the work, yea, even the work of *destruction come upon you, yea, even the sword of the justice of the Eternal God shall fall upon you, to your overthrow and destruction if ye shall suffer these things to be.

24 Wherefore, the Lord commandeth you, when ye shall see these things come among you that ye shall awake to a sense of your awful situation, because of this *secret combination which shall be among you; or wo be unto it, because of the blood of them who have been slain; for they cry from the dust for vengeance upon it, and also upon those who built it up.

25 For it cometh to pass that whoso buildeth it up seeketh to overthrow the *freedom of all lands, nations, and countries; and it bringeth to pass the destruction of all people, for it is built up by the devil, who is the father of all lies; even that same liar who *beguiled our first parents, yea, even that same liar who hath caused man to commit murder from the beginning; who hath *hardened the hearts of men that they have *murdered the prophets, and stoned them, and cast them out from the beginning.

26 Wherefore, I, Moroni, am commanded to write these things that evil may be done away, and that the time may come that Satan may have *no power upon the hearts of the children of men, but that they may be *persuaded to do good continually, that they may come unto the fountain of all *righteousness and be saved.

CHAPTER 9

The kingdom passes from one to another by descent, intrigue, and murder—

Emer saw the Son of Righteousness— Many prophets cry repentance—A famine and poisonous serpents plague the people.

AND now I, Moroni, proceed with my record. Therefore, behold, it came to pass that because of the *secret combinations of Akish and his friends, behold, they did overthrow the kingdom of Omer.

2 Nevertheless, the Lord was merciful unto Omer, and also to his sons and to his daughters who did not seek his destruction.

3 And the Lord *warned Omer in a dream that he should depart out of the land; wherefore Omer *departed out of the land with his family, and traveled many days, and came over and passed by the hill of *Shim, and came over by the place *where the Nephites were destroyed, and from thence eastward, and came to a place which was called Ablom, by the seashore, and there he pitched his tent, and also his sons and his daughters, and all his household, save it were Jared and his family.

4 And it came to pass that Jared was anointed king over the people, by the hand of wickedness; and he gave unto Akish his daughter to wife.

5 And it came to pass that Akish *sought the life of his father-in-law; and he applied unto those whom he had sworn by the *oath of the ancients, and they obtained the head of his father-in-law, as he sat upon his throne, giving audience to his people.

6 For so great had been the spreading of this wicked and secret society that it had corrupted the hearts of all the people; therefore Jared was murdered upon his throne, and Akish reigned in his stead.

23a Moses 6:15.
  b Luke 13:3 (1–5).
24a D&C 42:64.
25a TG Liberty.
  b Gen. 3:13 (1–13);
    2 Ne. 9:9;
    Mosiah 16:3;
    Moses 4:19 (5–19).

  c TG Hardheartedness.
  d TG Prophets,
    Rejection of.
26a 2 Ne. 30:18.
  b 2 Ne. 33:4;
    Moro. 7:13 (12–17).
  c TG Righteousness.
9 1a Ether 8:15 (13–17).

3a TG Dream;
    Warn.
  b Ether 9:13.
  c Morm. 1:3; 4:23.
  d Morm. 6:2 (1–15).
5a Esth. 2:21.
  b TG Oath.

503 ETHER 9:7–23

7 And it came to pass that Akish began to be ᵃjealous of his son, therefore he shut him up in prison, and kept him upon little or no food until he had suffered death.

8 And now the brother of him that suffered death, (and his name was Nimrah) was angry with his father because of that which his father had done unto his brother.

9 And it came to pass that Nimrah gathered together a small number of men, and fled out of the land, and came over and dwelt with Omer.

10 And it came to pass that Akish begat other sons, and they won the hearts of the people, notwithstanding they had sworn unto him to do all manner of iniquity according to that which he desired.

11 Now the people of Akish were desirous for gain, even as Akish was desirous for ᵃpower; wherefore, the sons of Akish did offer them ᵇmoney, by which means they drew away the more part of the people after them.

12 And there began to be a war between the sons of Akish and Akish, which lasted for the space of many years, yea, unto the destruction of nearly all the people of the kingdom, yea, even all, save it were thirty souls, and they who fled with the house of Omer.

13 Wherefore, Omer was restored again to the ᵃland of his inheritance.

14 And it came to pass that Omer began to be old; nevertheless, in his old age he begat Emer; and he anointed Emer to be king to reign in his stead.

15 And after that he had anointed Emer to be king he saw peace in the land for the space of two years, and he died, having seen exceedingly many days, which were full of sorrow. And it came to pass that Emer did reign in his stead, and did fill the steps of his father.

16 And the Lord began again to take the curse from off the land, and the house of Emer did prosper exceedingly under the reign of Emer; and in the space of sixty and two years they had become exceedingly strong, insomuch that they became exceedingly rich—

17 Having ᵃall manner of fruit, and of grain, and of ᵇsilks, and of fine linen, and of ᶜgold, and of silver, and of precious things;

18 And also ᵃall manner of cattle, of oxen, and cows, and of sheep, and of swine, and of goats, and also many other kinds of animals which were useful for the food of man.

19 And they also had ᵃhorses, and asses, and there were elephants and cureloms and cumoms; all of which were useful unto man, and more especially the elephants and cureloms and cumoms.

20 And thus the Lord did pour out his blessings upon this land, which was ᵃchoice above all other lands; and he commanded that whoso should possess the land should possess it unto the Lord, or they should be ᵇdestroyed when they were ripened in iniquity; for upon such, saith the Lord: I will pour out the fulness of my wrath.

21 And Emer did execute judgment in righteousness all his days, and he begat many sons and daughters; and he begat Coriantum, and he anointed Coriantum to reign in his stead.

22 And after he had anointed Coriantum to reign in his stead he lived four years, and he saw peace in the land; yea, and he even saw the ᵃSon of Righteousness, and did rejoice and glory in his day; and he died in peace.

23 And it came to pass that Coriantum did walk in the steps of his father, and did build many mighty

7a TG Jealous.
11a TG Tyranny.
  b 1 Sam. 8:3 (1–4);
    Hel. 9:20.
    TG Bribe.
13a Ether 9:3.
17a Ether 1:41.
  b Ether 10:24.
  c Hel. 6:9 (9–11);
    Ether 10:12 (12, 23).
18a Ether 6:4.
19a 1 Ne. 18:25;
Enos 1:21;
  3 Ne. 6:1.
20a Ether 2:15.
  b Deut. 31:4 (4–5);
    Ether 2:8 (8–11).
22a 3 Ne. 25:2.

cities, and did administer that which was good unto his people in all his days. And it came to pass that he had no children even until he was exceedingly [a]old.

24 And it came to pass that his wife died, being an hundred and two years old. And it came to pass that Coriantum took to wife, in his old age, a young maid, and begat sons and daughters; wherefore he lived until he was an hundred and forty and two years old.

25 And it came to pass that he begat Com, and Com reigned in his stead; and he reigned forty and nine years, and he begat Heth; and he also begat other sons and daughters.

26 And the people had spread again over all the face of the land, and there began again to be an exceedingly great wickedness upon the face of the land, and [a]Heth began to embrace the secret plans again of old, to destroy his father.

27 And it came to pass that he did dethrone his father, for he slew him with his own sword; and he did reign in his stead.

28 And there came prophets in the land [a]again, crying repentance unto them—that they must prepare the way of the Lord or there should come a curse upon the face of the land; yea, even there should be a great famine, in which they should be destroyed if they did not repent.

29 But the people believed not the words of the prophets, but they cast them out; and some of them they cast into [a]pits and left them to perish. And it came to pass that they did all these things according to the commandment of the king, Heth.

30 And it came to pass that there began to be a great [a]dearth upon the land, and the inhabitants began to be destroyed exceedingly fast because of the dearth, for there was no rain upon the face of the earth.

31 And there came forth [a]poisonous serpents also upon the face of the land, and did poison many people. And it came to pass that their flocks began to flee before the poisonous serpents, towards the land [b]southward, which was called by the Nephites [c]Zarahemla.

32 And it came to pass that there were many of them which did perish by the way; nevertheless, there were some which fled into the land southward.

33 And it came to pass that the Lord did cause the [a]serpents that they should pursue them no more, but that they should hedge up the way that the people could not pass, that whoso should attempt to pass might fall by the poisonous serpents.

34 And it came to pass that the people did follow the course of the beasts, and did devour the [a]carcasses of them which fell by the way, until they had devoured them all. Now when the people saw that they must [b]perish they began to [c]repent of their iniquities and cry unto the Lord.

35 And it came to pass that when they had [a]humbled themselves sufficiently before the Lord he did send rain upon the face of the earth; and the people began to revive again, and there began to be fruit in the north countries, and in all the countries round about. And the Lord did show forth his power unto them in preserving them from famine.

CHAPTER 10

One king succeeds another—Some of the kings are righteous; others are wicked—When righteousness prevails, the people are blessed and prospered by the Lord.

AND it came to pass that Shez, who was a descendant of Heth—for

---

23a Ether 7:3 (3, 7).
26a Ether 10:1.
28a Ether 7:23;
    11:1 (1, 12, 20).
29a Jer. 38:6 (4–13).
30a TG Drought;
    Famine.
31a Ether 10:19.
  b Morm. 3:5;
    Ether 10:21.
  c Omni 1:13.
33a Deut. 8:15;
1 Ne. 17:41.
    TG Plague.
34a Jer. 7:33 (32–33).
  b Alma 34:34.
  c D&C 101:8.
35a D&C 5:24.

ªHeth had perished by the famine, and all his household save it were Shez—wherefore, Shez began to build up again a broken people.

2 And it came to pass that Shez did remember the destruction of his fathers, and he did build up a righteous kingdom; for he remembered what the Lord had done in bringing Jared and his brother ªacross the deep; and he did walk in the ways of the Lord; and he begat sons and daughters.

3 And his eldest son, whose name was Shez, did ªrebel against him; nevertheless, Shez was smitten by the hand of a robber, because of his exceeding riches, which brought peace again unto his father.

4 And it came to pass that his father did build up many cities upon the face of the land, and the people began again to spread over all the face of the land. And Shez did live to an exceedingly old age; and he begat Riplakish. And he died, and Riplakish reigned in his stead.

5 And it came to pass that Riplakish did not do that which was right in the sight of the Lord, for he did have many wives and ªconcubines, and did lay that upon men's shoulders which was grievous to be borne; yea, he did ᵇtax them with heavy taxes; and with the taxes he did build many spacious buildings.

6 And he did erect him an exceedingly beautiful throne; and he did build many prisons, and whoso would not be subject unto taxes he did ªcast into prison; and whoso was not able to pay taxes he did cast into prison; and he did cause that they should labor continually for their support; and whoso refused to labor he did cause to be put to death.

7 Wherefore he did obtain all his fine work, yea, even his fine ªgold he did cause to be refined in prison; and all manner of fine ᵇworkmanship he did cause to be wrought in prison. And it came to pass that he did afflict the people with his whoredoms and abominations.

8 And when he had reigned for the space of forty and two years the people did rise up in rebellion against him; and there began to be war again in the land, insomuch that Riplakish was killed, and his descendants were driven out of the land.

9 And it came to pass after the space of many years, Morianton, (he being a descendant of Riplakish) gathered together an army of outcasts, and went forth and gave battle unto the people; and he gained power over many cities; and the war became exceedingly sore, and did last for the space of many years; and he did gain power over all the land, and did establish himself king over all the land.

10 And after that he had established himself king he did ease the burden of the people, by which he did gain favor in the eyes of the people, and they did anoint him to be their king.

11 And he did do justice unto the people, but not unto himself because of his many ªwhoredoms; wherefore he was cut off from the presence of the Lord.

12 And it came to pass that Morianton built up many cities, and the people became exceedingly rich under his reign, both in buildings, and in ªgold and silver, and in raising grain, and in flocks, and herds, and such things which had been restored unto them.

13 And Morianton did live to an exceedingly great age, and then he begat Kim; and Kim did reign in the stead of his father; and he did reign eight years, and his father died. And it came to pass that Kim did ªnot reign in righteousness,

---

10 1ª Ether 9:26 (25–29).
2ª Ether 6:12 (1–12).
3ª Mosiah 10:6.
5ª Esth. 2:14;
  Jacob 3:5;

Mosiah 11:2 (2–14).
  ᵇ Gen. 47:24.
6ª TG Oppression;
  Tyranny.
7ª Esth. 1:4.

ᵇ TG Art.
11ª TG Whore.
12ª Ether 9:17 (17–18).
13ª 1 Ne. 17:35 (34–35).

wherefore he was not favored of the Lord.

14 And his brother did rise up in rebellion against him, by which he did bring him into ªcaptivity; and he did remain in captivity all his days; and he begat sons and daughters in captivity, and in his old age he begat Levi; and he died.

15 And it came to pass that Levi did serve in captivity after the death of his father, for the space of forty and two years. And he did make war against the king of the land, by which he did obtain unto himself the kingdom.

16 And after he had obtained unto himself the kingdom he did that which was right in the sight of the Lord; and the people did prosper in the land; and he did live to a good ªold age, and begat sons and daughters; and he also begat Corom, whom he anointed king in his stead.

17 And it came to pass that Corom did that which was good in the sight of the Lord all his days; and he begat many sons and daughters; and after he had seen many days he did pass away, even like unto the rest of the earth; and Kish reigned in his stead.

18 And it came to pass that Kish passed away also, and Lib reigned in his stead.

19 And it came to pass that Lib also did that which was good in the sight of the Lord. And in the days of Lib the ªpoisonous serpents were destroyed. Wherefore they did go into the land southward, to hunt food for the people of the land, for the land was covered with animals of the forest. And Lib also himself became a great ᵇhunter.

20 And they built a great city by the ªnarrow neck of land, by the place where the sea divides the land.

21 And they did preserve the land ªsouthward for a wilderness, to get game. And the whole face of the land northward was covered with inhabitants.

22 And they were exceedingly ªindustrious, and they did buy and sell and ᵇtraffic one with another, that they might get gain.

23 And they did ªwork in all manner of ᵇore, and they did make gold, and silver, and ᶜiron, and ᵈbrass, and all manner of metals; and they did dig it out of the earth; wherefore, they did cast up mighty heaps of earth to get ore, of gold, and of silver, and of iron, and of copper. And they did ᵉwork all manner of fine work.

24 And they did have ªsilks, and fine-twined ᵇlinen; and they did work all manner of ᶜcloth, that they might clothe themselves from their nakedness.

25 And they did make all manner of tools to till the earth, both to plow and to sow, to reap and to hoe, and also to thrash.

26 And they did make all manner of tools with which they did work their beasts.

27 And they did make all manner of ªweapons of war. And they did work all manner of work of exceedingly curious workmanship.

28 And never could be a people more blessed than were they, and more prospered by the hand of the Lord. And they were in a land that was choice above all lands, for the Lord had spoken it.

29 And it came to pass that Lib did live many years, and begat sons and daughters; and he also begat Hearthom.

14a Ether 7:7; 8:4 (3–4);
      10:30 (30–31).
16a TG Old Age.
19a Ether 9:31.
   b Gen. 25:27; Ether 2:1.
20a Alma 63:5.
21a Morm. 3:5;
      Ether 9:31 (31–32).

22a TG Industry.
   b Gen. 34:10 (10–21);
      Mosiah 24:7;
      4 Ne. 1:46.
23a TG Skill.
   b Hel. 6:9 (9–11);
      Ether 9:17.
   c 2 Ne. 5:15; Moses 5:46.

      d Gen. 4:22;
         Mosiah 8:10.
      e TG Art.
24a Ether 9:17.
   b Ex. 25:4 (4–5);
      1 Ne. 13:7 (7–8).
   c TG Clothing.
27a Ether 15:15.

30 And it came to pass that Hearthom reigned in the stead of his father. And when Hearthom had reigned twenty and four years, behold, the kingdom was taken away from him. And he served many years in ªcaptivity, yea, even all the remainder of his days.

31 And he begat Heth, and Heth lived in captivity all his days. And Heth begat Aaron, and Aaron dwelt in captivity all his days; and he begat Amnigaddah, and Amnigaddah also dwelt in captivity all his days; and he begat Coriantum, and Coriantum dwelt in captivity all his days; and he begat Com.

32 And it came to pass that Com drew away the half of the kingdom. And he reigned over the half of the kingdom forty and two years; and he went to battle against the king, Amgid, and they fought for the space of many years, during which time Com gained power over Amgid, and obtained power over the remainder of the kingdom.

33 And in the days of Com there began to be robbers in the land; and they adopted the old plans, and administered ªoaths after the manner of the ancients, and sought again to destroy the kingdom.

34 Now Com did fight against them much; nevertheless, he did not prevail against them.

CHAPTER 11

Wars, dissensions, and wickedness dominate Jaredite life—Prophets predict the utter destruction of the Jaredites unless they repent—The people reject the words of the prophets.

AND there came also in the days of Com many ªprophets, and prophesied of the destruction of that great people except they should repent, and turn unto the Lord, and forsake their murders and wickedness.

2 And it came to pass that the prophets were ªrejected by the people, and they fled unto Com for protection, for the people sought to destroy them.

3 And they prophesied unto Com many things; and he was blessed in all the remainder of his days.

4 And he lived to a good old age, and begat Shiblom; and Shiblom reigned in his stead. And the brother of Shiblom rebelled against him, and there began to be an exceedingly great war in all the land.

5 And it came to pass that the brother of Shiblom caused that all the prophets who prophesied of the destruction of the people should be put to ªdeath;

6 And there was great calamity in all the land, for they had testified that a great curse should come upon the land, and also upon the people, and that there should be a great destruction among them, such an one as never had been upon the face of the earth, and their bones should become as ªheaps of earth upon the face of the land except they should repent of their wickedness.

7 And they hearkened not unto the voice of the Lord, because of their wicked combinations; wherefore, there began to be wars and ªcontentions in all the land, and also many famines and pestilences, insomuch that there was a great destruction, such an one as never had been known upon the face of the earth; and all this came to pass in the days of Shiblom.

8 And the people began to repent of their iniquity; and inasmuch as they did the Lord did have ªmercy on them.

9 And it came to pass that Shiblom was slain, and Seth was brought into ªcaptivity, and did dwell in captivity all his days.

10 And it came to pass that Ahah,

30a Ether 10:14; 11:9.
33a TG Secret Combinations.
11 1a Ether 7:23; 9:28.
2a TG Prophets,

Rejection of.
5a TG Persecution.
6a Omni 1:22; Ether 14:21.
7a TG Contention.

8a TG Mercy.
9a Ether 10:30; 11:18 (18–19).

his son, did obtain the kingdom; and he did reign over the people all his days. And he did do all manner of iniquity in his days, by which he did cause the shedding of much blood; and few were his days.

11 And Ethem, being a descendant of Ahah, did obtain the kingdom; and he also did do that which was wicked in his days.

12 And it came to pass that in the days of Ethem there came many prophets, and prophesied again unto the people; yea, they did prophesy that the Lord would utterly ^adestroy them from off the face of the earth except they repented of their iniquities.

13 And it came to pass that the people hardened their hearts, and would not ^ahearken unto their words; and the prophets ^bmourned and withdrew from among the people.

14 And it came to pass that Ethem did execute judgment in wickedness all his days; and he begat Moron. And it came to pass that Moron did reign in his stead; and Moron did that which was wicked before the Lord.

15 And it came to pass that there arose a ^arebellion among the people, because of that secret ^bcombination which was built up to get power and gain; and there arose a mighty man among them in iniquity, and gave battle unto Moron, in which he did overthrow the half of the kingdom; and he did maintain the half of the kingdom for many years.

16 And it came to pass that Moron did overthrow him, and did obtain the kingdom again.

17 And it came to pass that there arose another mighty man; and he was a descendant of the brother of Jared.

18 And it came to pass that he did overthrow Moron and obtain the kingdom; wherefore, Moron dwelt in ^acaptivity all the remainder of his days; and he begat Coriantor.

19 And it came to pass that Coriantor dwelt in captivity all his days.

20 And in the days of Coriantor there also came many prophets, and prophesied of great and marvelous things, and cried repentance unto the people, and except they should repent the Lord God would execute ^ajudgment against them to their utter destruction;

21 And that the Lord God would send or bring forth ^aanother people to possess the ^bland, by his power, after the manner by which he brought their fathers.

22 And they did ^areject all the words of the prophets, because of their ^bsecret society and wicked abominations.

23 And it came to pass that Coriantor begat ^aEther, and he died, having dwelt in captivity all his days.

CHAPTER 12

The prophet Ether exhorts the people to believe in God—Moroni recounts the wonders and marvels done by faith—Faith enabled the brother of Jared to see Christ—The Lord gives men weakness that they may be humble—The brother of Jared moved Mount Zerin by faith—Faith, hope, and charity are essential to salvation—Moroni saw Jesus face to face.

AND it came to pass that the days of Ether were in the days of ^aCoriantumr; and Coriantumr was king over all the land.

2 And ^aEther was a prophet of the Lord; wherefore Ether came forth

---

12a Ether 12:3.
13a Jer. 44:16;
  Mosiah 16:2.
  b TG Mourning.
15a TG Rebellion.
  b TG Secret
    Combinations.
18a Ether 11:9.

20a TG Judgment.
21a Omni 1:21;
  Ether 13:21 (20–21).
  b Deut. 29:28.
22a TG Prophets,
    Rejection of.
  b TG Secret
    Combinations.

23a Ether 1:6; 12:2;
    15:34 (33–34).
12 1a Omni 1:21;
    Ether 13:20 (13–31).
  2a Ether 1:6; 11:23;
    15:34 (33–34).

in the days of Coriantumr, and began to prophesy unto the people, for he could not be ᵇrestrained because of the Spirit of the Lord which was in him.

3 For he did ᵃcry from the ᵇmorning, even until the going down of the sun, exhorting the people to believe in God unto repentance lest they should be ᶜdestroyed, saying unto them that ᵈby ᵉfaith all things are fulfilled—

4 Wherefore, whoso believeth in God might with ᵃsurety ᵇhope for a better world, yea, even a place at the right hand of God, which ᶜhope cometh of ᵈfaith, maketh an ᵉanchor to the souls of men, which would make them sure and steadfast, always abounding in ᶠgood works, being led to ᵍglorify God.

5 And it came to pass that Ether did prophesy great and marvelous things unto the people, which they did not believe, because they ᵃsaw them not.

6 And now, I, Moroni, would speak somewhat concerning these things; I would show unto the world that ᵃfaith is things which are ᵇhoped for and ᶜnot seen; wherefore, dispute not because ye see not, for ye receive no ᵈwitness until after the ᵉtrial of your faith.

7 For it was by faith that Christ showed himself unto our fathers, after he had risen from the dead; and he showed not himself unto them until after they had faith in him; wherefore, it must needs be that some had faith in him, for he showed himself ᵃnot unto the world.

8 But because of the faith of men he has shown himself unto the world, and glorified the name of the Father, and prepared a way that thereby others might be partakers of the heavenly gift, that they might hope for those things which they have not seen.

9 Wherefore, ye may also have hope, and be partakers of the gift, if ye will but have faith.

10 Behold it was by faith that they of old were ᵃcalled after the holy order of God.

11 Wherefore, by faith was the law of Moses given. But in the ᵃgift of his Son hath God prepared a more ᵇexcellent way; and it is by faith that it hath been fulfilled.

12 For if there be no ᵃfaith among the children of men God can do no ᵇmiracle among them; wherefore, he showed not himself until after their faith.

13 Behold, it was the faith of Alma and Amulek that caused the ᵃprison to tumble to the earth.

14 Behold, it was the faith of Nephi and Lehi that wrought the ᵃchange upon the Lamanites, that they were baptized with fire and with the ᵇHoly Ghost.

15 Behold, it was the faith of ᵃAmmon and his brethren which ᵇwrought so great a miracle among the Lamanites.

16 Yea, and even all they who

2b Jer. 20:9; Enos 1:26;
    Alma 43:1.
3a D&C 112:5.
  b Jer. 26:5.
  c Ether 11:12 (12, 20–22).
  d Heb. 11:7 (1–40).
  e 1 Cor. 13:13 (1–13);
    Moro. 7:1; 8:14;
    10:20 (20–23).
4a Heb. 7:22.
  b Alma 7:16; 22:16;
    Moro. 7:3;
    D&C 25:10; 138:14.
  c Heb. 11:1; Moro. 7:40.
  d Luke 7:50.
  e Heb. 6:19.

  f 1 Cor. 15:58;
    1 Tim. 2:10.
  g John 11:4 (1–4);
    3 Ne. 12:16.
5a Heb. 11:3;
    Alma 30:15;
    Hel. 16:20.
6a Ps. 78:41.
  b Rom. 8:25 (24–25).
  c Alma 32:21.
  d Lev. 9:6 (6, 23);
    2 Ne. 1:15.
    TG Sign Seekers.
  e 3 Ne. 26:11.
    TG Test.
7a Acts 10:41.

10a Alma 13:4 (3–4).
    TG Authority.
11a TG God, Gifts of.
  b 1 Cor. 12:31.
12a Luke 16:30 (27–31);
    Alma 32:18 (17–18);
    Moro. 7:37.
  b Ps. 78:41;
    Matt. 13:58;
    Morm. 9:20.
13a Alma 14:27 (26–29).
14a Hel. 5:50 (50–52).
  b Hel. 5:45;
    3 Ne. 9:20.
15a Alma 17:29 (29–39).
  b IE as told in Alma 17–26.

wrought *miracles wrought them by *faith, even those who were before Christ and also those who were after.

17 And it was by faith that the three disciples obtained a promise that they should *not taste of death; and they obtained not the promise until after their faith.

18 And neither at any time hath any wrought miracles until after their faith; wherefore they first believed in the Son of God.

19 And there were many whose faith was so exceedingly strong, even *before Christ came, who could not be kept from within the *veil, but truly saw with their eyes the things which they had beheld with an eye of faith, and they were glad.

20 And behold, we have seen in this record that one of these was the brother of Jared; for so great was his faith in God, that when God put forth his *finger he could not hide it from the sight of the brother of Jared, because of his word which he had spoken unto him, which word he had obtained by faith.

21 And after the brother of Jared had beheld the finger of the Lord, because of the *promise which the brother of Jared had obtained by faith, the Lord could not withhold anything from his sight; wherefore he showed him all things, for he could no longer be kept without the *veil.

22 And it is by faith that my fathers have obtained the *promise that these things should come unto their brethren through the Gentiles; therefore the Lord hath commanded me, yea, even Jesus Christ.

23 And I said unto him: Lord, the Gentiles will *mock at these things, because of our *weakness in writing; for Lord thou hast made us *mighty in word by faith, but thou hast not made us mighty in writing; for thou hast made all this people that they could speak much, because of the Holy Ghost which thou hast given them;

24 And thou hast made us that we could write but little, because of the *awkwardness of our hands. Behold, thou hast not made us mighty in *writing like unto the brother of Jared, for thou madest him that the things which he *wrote were mighty even as thou art, unto the overpowering of man to read them.

25 Thou hast also made our words powerful and great, even that we *cannot write them; wherefore, when we write we behold our *weakness, and stumble because of the placing of our words; and I fear lest the Gentiles shall *mock at our words.

26 And when I had said this, the Lord spake unto me, saying: *Fools *mock, but they shall mourn; and my grace is sufficient for the meek, that they shall take no advantage of your weakness;

27 And if men come unto me I will show unto them their *weakness. I *give unto men weakness that they may be humble; and my *grace is sufficient for all men that *humble themselves before me; for if they humble themselves before me, and have faith in me, then will I make *weak things become strong unto them.

16a TG Miracle.
  b Heb. 11:7 (7–40).
17a 3 Ne. 28:7;
    4 Ne. 1:37 (14, 37);
    Morm. 8:10 (10–12).
19a 2 Ne. 11:4; Jacob 4:5;
    Jarom 1:11;
    Alma 25:16 (15–16).
  b Ether 3:6.
    TG Veil.
20a Ether 3:4.
21a Ether 3:26 (25–26).
  b Ether 3:20;
    D&C 67:10 (10–13).

22a Enos 1:13.
23a Ether 12:36.
  b 1 Cor. 2:3 (1–5);
    1 Ne. 19:6;
    Morm. 8:17 (13–17);
    9:31 (31, 33).
  c 2 Ne. 33:1.
24a Jacob 4:1.
  b TG Language.
  c Ether 4:1.
25a 3 Ne. 5:18.
  b Ether 12:37.
  c 1 Cor. 2:14.
26a Prov. 14:9; 20:3.

  b Gal. 6:7; D&C 124:71.
    TG Mocking; Offense.
27a Jacob 4:7.
  b Ex. 4:11;
    1 Cor. 1:27 (26–31).
  c TG Grace.
  d D&C 1:28.
    TG Humility; Teachable.
  e Deut. 11:8; Joel 3:10;
    Luke 9:48 (46–48);
    18:14 (10–14);
    2 Cor. 12:9 (7–10);
    Heb. 11:34;
    1 Ne. 14:1.

28 Behold, I will show unto the Gentiles their weakness, and I will show unto them that ªfaith, hope and charity bringeth unto me—the fountain of all ᵇrighteousness.

29 And I, Moroni, having heard these words, was ªcomforted, and said: O Lord, thy righteous will be done, for I know that thou workest unto the children of men according to their faith;

30 For the brother of Jared said unto the mountain Zerin, ªRemove—and it was removed. And if he had not had faith it would not have moved; wherefore thou workest after men have faith.

31 For thus didst thou manifest thyself unto thy disciples; for ªafter they had ᵇfaith, and did speak in thy name, thou didst show thyself unto them in great power.

32 And I also remember that thou hast said that thou hast prepared a house for man, yea, even among the ªmansions of thy Father, in which man might have a more excellent ᵇhope; wherefore man must hope, or he cannot receive an inheritance in the place which thou hast prepared.

33 And again, I remember that thou hast said that thou hast ªloved the world, even unto the laying down of thy life for the world, that thou mightest take it again to prepare a place for the children of men.

34 And now I know that this ªlove which thou hast had for the children of men is charity; wherefore, except men shall have charity they cannot inherit that place which thou

hast prepared in the mansions of thy Father.

35 Wherefore, I know by this thing which thou hast said, that if the Gentiles have not ªcharity, because of our weakness, that thou wilt prove them, and ᵇtake away their ᶜtalent, yea, even that which they have received, and give unto them who shall have more abundantly.

36 And it came to pass that I prayed unto the Lord that he would give unto the Gentiles ªgrace, that they might have charity.

37 And it came to pass that the Lord said unto me: If they have not charity it mattereth not unto thee, thou hast been faithful; wherefore, thy garments shall be made ªclean. And because thou hast seen thy ᵇweakness thou shalt be made strong, even unto the sitting down in the place which I have prepared in the mansions of my Father.

38 And now I, Moroni, bid farewell unto the Gentiles, yea, and also unto my brethren whom I love, until we shall meet before the ªjudgment-seat of Christ, where all men shall know that my ᵇgarments are not spotted with your blood.

39 And then shall ye know that I have ªseen Jesus, and that he hath talked with me ᵇface to face, and that he told me in ᶜplain humility, even as a man telleth another in mine own language, concerning these things;

40 And only a few have I written, because of my weakness in writing.

41 And now, I would commend you to ªseek this Jesus of whom the

28 a Alma 7:24.
  b TG God, the Standard of Righteousness.
29 a TG Comfort.
30 a Matt. 17:20; Jacob 4:6; Hel. 10:9.
  TG God, Power of.
31 a 3 Ne. 26:17 (17–21).
  b 1 Cor. 13:13 (1–13); Moro. 7:44 (33–48).
32 a John 14:2; Enos 1:27; D&C 72:4; 98:18.
  b TG Hope.
33 a John 3:16 (16–18).
34 a Moro. 7:47. TG Love.
35 a 1 Cor. 13:2 (1–2).
  b Matt. 25:28 (14–30).
  c TG Talents.
36 a Ether 12:23. TG Grace.
37 a Job 15:14; 25:4; D&C 38:42; 88:74 (74–75); 135:5 (4–5). TG Cleanliness; Purification.
  b Ether 12:25 (25–27).
38 a TG Jesus Christ, Judge.
  b Acts 20:26; Jacob 1:19.
39 a TG Jesus Christ, Appearances, Postmortal.
  b Gen. 32:30; Ex. 33:11; Num. 12:8.
  c 2 Ne. 32:7; Alma 13:23.
41 a Ezra 8:22 (22–23); Ps. 27:8; Amos 5:6; Alma 37:47; D&C 88:63; 101:38.

prophets and apostles have written, that the grace of God the Father, and also the Lord Jesus Christ, and the Holy Ghost, which beareth [b]record of them, may be and abide in you forever. Amen.

CHAPTER 13

Ether speaks of a New Jerusalem to be built in America by the seed of Joseph—He prophesies, is cast out, writes the Jaredite history, and foretells the destruction of the Jaredites—War rages over all the land.

AND now I, Moroni, proceed to finish my record concerning the destruction of the people of whom I have been writing.

2 For behold, they rejected all the words of Ether; for he truly told them of all things, from the beginning of man; and that after the waters had [a]receded from off the face of this [b]land it became a choice land above all other lands, a chosen land of the Lord; wherefore the Lord would have that all men should [c]serve him who dwell upon the face thereof;

3 And that it was the place of the [a]New Jerusalem, which should [b]come down out of heaven, and the holy sanctuary of the Lord.

4 Behold, Ether saw the days of Christ, and he spake concerning a [a]New Jerusalem upon this land.

5 And he spake also concerning the house of Israel, and the [a]Jerusalem from whence [b]Lehi should come—after it should be destroyed it should be built up again, a [c]holy city unto the Lord; wherefore, it could not be a new Jerusalem for it had been in a time of old; but it should be built up again, and become a holy city of the Lord; and it should be built unto the house of Israel—

6 And that a [a]New Jerusalem should be built up upon this land, unto the remnant of the seed of [b]Joseph, for which things there has been a [c]type.

7 For as Joseph brought his father down into the land of [a]Egypt, even so he died there; wherefore, the Lord brought a remnant of the seed of Joseph out of the land of Jerusalem, that he might be merciful unto the seed of Joseph that they should [b]perish not, even as he was merciful unto the father of Joseph that he should perish not.

8 Wherefore, the remnant of the house of Joseph shall be built upon this [a]land; and it shall be a land of their inheritance; and they shall build up a holy [b]city unto the Lord, like unto the Jerusalem of old; and they shall [c]no more be confounded, until the end come when the earth shall pass away.

9 And there shall be a [a]new heaven and a new earth; and they shall be like unto the old save the old have passed away, and all things have become new.

10 And then cometh the New Jerusalem; and blessed are they who dwell therein, for it is they whose garments are [a]white through the blood of the Lamb; and they are they who are numbered among the remnant of the seed of Joseph, who were of the house of Israel.

11 And then also cometh the [a]Jerusalem of old; and the inhabitants thereof, blessed are they, for

41b 3 Ne. 11:32 (32, 36).
13 2a Gen. 7:19 (11–24); 8:3.
   b TG Earth, Dividing of.
   c Ether 2:8.
  3a 3 Ne. 20:22;
    21:23 (23–24).
   TG Jerusalem, New.
   b Rev. 3:12; 21:2.
  4a TG Zion.
  5a TG Jerusalem.
   b 1 Ne. 1:18 (18–20); 2:2.
   c Joel 2:18;
    Rev. 21:10 (10–27);

    3 Ne. 20:46 (29–36, 46).
  6a D&C 42:9; 45:66 (66–67);
    84:2 (2–5);
    A of F 1:10.
   b Ezek. 48:5 (4–5);
    D&C 28:8.
   TG Israel, Joseph,
    People of.
   c Alma 46:24 (24–26).
   TG Symbolism.
  7a Gen. 46:6 (2–7); 47:6.
   b 2 Ne. 3:5 (5–24).
  8a TG Promised Lands.

   b Rev. 21:10 (10–27).
   c Moro. 10:31.
  9a Heb. 8:13;
    2 Pet. 3:13 (10–13);
    Rev. 21:1;
    3 Ne. 12:47 (46–47);
    15:3 (2–10);
    D&C 101:25 (23–25).
  10a Rev. 7:14.
  11a TG Israel, Gathering of;
    Israel, Land of;
    Jerusalem.

they have been washed in the blood of the Lamb; and they are they who were scattered and gathered in from the four quarters of the earth, and from the *b*north countries, and are partakers of the fulfilling of the covenant which God made with their father, *c*Abraham.

12 And when these things come, bringeth to pass the scripture which saith, there are they who were *a*first, who shall be last; and there are they who were last, who shall be first.

13 And I was about to write more, but I am forbidden; but great and marvelous were the prophecies of Ether; but they esteemed him as naught, and cast him out; and he *a*hid himself in the cavity of a rock by day, and by night he went forth viewing the things which should come upon the people.

14 And as he dwelt in the cavity of a rock he made the *a*remainder of this record, viewing the destructions which came upon the people, by night.

15 And it came to pass that in that same year in which he was cast out from among the people there began to be a great war among the people, for there were many who rose up, who were mighty men, and sought to destroy Coriantumr by their secret plans of wickedness, of which hath been spoken.

16 And now Coriantumr, having studied, himself, in all the arts of war and all the cunning of the world, wherefore he gave battle unto them who sought to destroy him.

17 But he repented not, neither his *a*fair sons nor daughters; neither the fair sons and daughters of Cohor; neither the fair sons and daughters of Corihor; and in fine, there were none of the fair sons and daughters

upon the face of the whole earth who repented of their sins.

18 Wherefore, it came to pass that in the first year that Ether dwelt in the cavity of a rock, there were many people who were slain by the sword of those *a*secret combinations, fighting against Coriantumr that they might obtain the kingdom.

19 And it came to pass that the sons of Coriantumr fought much and bled much.

20 And in the second year the word of the Lord came to Ether, that he should go and *a*prophesy unto *b*Coriantumr that, if he would repent, and all his household, the Lord would give unto him his kingdom and spare the people—

21 Otherwise they should be destroyed, and all his household save it were himself. And he should only live to see the fulfilling of the prophecies which had been spoken concerning *a*another people receiving the land for their inheritance; and Coriantumr should receive a burial by them; and every soul should be destroyed save it were *b*Coriantumr.

22 And it came to pass that Coriantumr repented not, neither his household, neither the people; and the wars ceased not; and they sought to *a*kill Ether, but he fled from before them and hid again in the cavity of the rock.

23 And it came to pass that there arose up Shared, and he also gave battle unto Coriantumr; and he did beat him, insomuch that in the third year he did bring him into captivity.

24 And the sons of Coriantumr, in the fourth year, did beat Shared, and did obtain the kingdom again unto their father.

25 Now there began to be a war

11*b* D&C 133:26 (26–35).
  TG Israel, Ten Lost
     Tribes of.
  c Isa. 27:6.
12*a* Mark 10:31;
     Luke 13:30;
     1 Ne. 13:42;
     Jacob 5:63;

      D&C 18:26 (26–27); 90:9.
13*a* 1 Kgs. 17:3 (1–16);
     1 Ne. 3:27;
     Mosiah 17:4 (1–4).
14*a* Ether 15:33 (13, 33).
17*a* Morm. 6:19 (16–22).
18*a* Ether 8:9 (9–26).
20*a* Ether 15:1.

  b Omni 1:21;
     Ether 12:1 (1–2).
21*a* Ether 11:21.
  b Ether 14:24;
     15:29 (29–32).
22*a* Prov. 29:10.

upon all the face of the land, ^aevery man with his band fighting for that which he desired.

26 And there were robbers, and in fine, all manner of wickedness upon all the face of the land.

27 And it came to pass that Coriantumr was exceedingly angry with Shared, and he went against him with his armies to battle; and they did meet in great anger, and they did meet in the valley of Gilgal; and the battle became exceedingly sore.

28 And it came to pass that Shared fought against him for the space of three days. And it came to pass that Coriantumr beat him, and did pursue him until he came to the plains of Heshlon.

29 And it came to pass that Shared gave him battle again upon the plains; and behold, he did beat Coriantumr, and drove him back again to the valley of Gilgal.

30 And Coriantumr gave Shared battle again in the valley of Gilgal, in which he beat Shared and slew him.

31 And Shared wounded Coriantumr in his thigh, that he did not go to battle again for the space of two years, in which time all the people upon the face of the land were shedding blood, and there was none to restrain them.

CHAPTER 14

The iniquity of the people brings a curse upon the land—Coriantumr engages in warfare against Gilead, then Lib, and then Shiz—Blood and carnage cover the land.

AND now there began to be a great ^acurse upon all the land because of the iniquity of the people, in which, if a man should lay his tool or his sword upon his shelf, or upon the place whither he would keep it, behold, upon the morrow, he could not find it, so great was the curse upon the land.

2 Wherefore every man did cleave unto that which was his own, with his hands, and would not borrow neither would he lend; and every man kept the hilt of his sword in his right hand, in the ^adefence of his property and his own life and of his wives and children.

3 And now, after the space of two years, and after the death of Shared, behold, there arose the brother of Shared and he gave battle unto Coriantumr, in which Coriantumr did beat him and did pursue him to the wilderness of Akish.

4 And it came to pass that the brother of Shared did give battle unto him in the wilderness of Akish; and the battle became exceedingly sore, and many thousands fell by the sword.

5 And it came to pass that Coriantumr did lay siege to the wilderness; and the brother of Shared did march forth out of the wilderness by night, and slew a part of the army of Coriantumr, as they were drunken.

6 And he came forth to the land of ^aMoron, and placed himself upon the throne of Coriantumr.

7 And it came to pass that Coriantumr dwelt with his army in the wilderness for the space of two years, in which he did receive great strength to his army.

8 Now the brother of Shared, whose name was Gilead, also received great strength to his army, because of secret combinations.

9 And it came to pass that his high priest murdered him as he sat upon his throne.

10 And it came to pass that one of the secret combinations murdered him in a secret pass, and obtained unto himself the kingdom; and his name was Lib; and Lib was a man of great stature, more than any other man among all the people.

11 And it came to pass that in the first year of Lib, Coriantumr came up unto the land of Moron, and gave battle unto Lib.

25*a* TG Covet;
     Selfishness.
14 1*a* Hel. 12:18;

13:18 (17–23);
Morm. 1:18 (17–19);
2:10 (10–14).

2*a* Morm. 2:23.
6*a* Ether 7:5.

12 And it came to pass that he fought with Lib, in which Lib did smite upon his arm that he was wounded; nevertheless, the army of Coriantumr did press forward upon Lib, that he fled to the borders upon the seashore.

13 And it came to pass that Coriantumr pursued him; and Lib gave battle unto him upon the seashore.

14 And it came to pass that Lib did smite the army of Coriantumr, that they fled again to the wilderness of Akish.

15 And it came to pass that Lib did pursue him until he came to the plains of Agosh. And Coriantumr had taken all the people with him as he fled before Lib in that quarter of the land whither he fled.

16 And when he had come to the plains of Agosh he gave battle unto Lib, and he smote upon him until he died; nevertheless, the brother of Lib did come against Coriantumr in the stead thereof, and the battle became exceedingly sore, in the which Coriantumr fled again before the army of the brother of Lib.

17 Now the name of the brother of Lib was called Shiz. And it came to pass that Shiz pursued after Coriantumr, and he did overthrow many cities, and he did slay both women and children, and he did burn the cities.

18 And there went a fear of Shiz throughout all the land; yea, a cry went forth throughout the land— Who can stand before the army of Shiz? Behold, he sweepeth the earth before him!

19 And it came to pass that the people began to flock together in armies, throughout all the face of the land.

20 And they were divided; and a part of them fled to the army of Shiz, and a part of them fled to the army of Coriantumr.

21 And so great and lasting had been the war, and so long had been the scene of bloodshed and carnage, that the whole face of the land was covered with the ªbodies of the ᵇdead.

22 And so swift and speedy was the war that there was none left to bury the dead, but they did march forth from the shedding of ªblood to the shedding of blood, leaving the bodies of both men, women, and children strewed upon the face of the land, to become a prey to the ᵇworms of the flesh.

23 And the ªscent thereof went forth upon the face of the land, even upon all the face of the land; wherefore the people became troubled by day and by night, because of the scent thereof.

24 Nevertheless, Shiz did ªnot cease to pursue Coriantumr; for he had sworn to avenge himself upon Coriantumr of the blood of his brother, who had been slain, and the word of the Lord which came to Ether that Coriantumr should not fall by the sword.

25 And thus we see that the Lord did visit them in the fulness of his ªwrath, and their wickedness and abominations had prepared a way for their everlasting destruction.

26 And it came to pass that Shiz did pursue Coriantumr eastward, even to the borders by the seashore, and there he gave battle unto Shiz for the space of three days.

27 And so terrible was the destruction among the armies of Shiz that the people began to be frightened, and began to flee before the armies of Coriantumr; and they fled to the land of Corihor, and swept off the inhabitants before them, all them that would not join them.

28 And they pitched their tents in the valley of Corihor; and Coriantumr pitched his tents in the valley of Shurr. Now the valley of Shurr was near the hill Comnor;

21a Ether 11:6.
  b Ezek. 35:8.
22a Hosea 4:2 (1–3).

  b Isa. 14:11 (9–11).
23a Alma 16:11 (9–11).
24a Ether 13:21.

25a TG God, Indignation of.

wherefore, Coriantumr did gather his armies together upon the hill Comnor, and did sound a trumpet unto the armies of Shiz to invite them forth to battle.

29 And it came to pass that they came forth, but were driven again; and they came the second time, and they were driven again the second time. And it came to pass that they came again the third time, and the battle became exceedingly sore.

30 And it came to pass that Shiz smote upon Coriantumr that he gave him many deep wounds; and Coriantumr, having lost his blood, fainted, and was carried away as though he were dead.

31 Now the loss of men, women and children on both sides was so great that Shiz commanded his people that they should not pursue the armies of Coriantumr; wherefore, they returned to their camp.

CHAPTER 15

Millions of the Jaredites are slain in battle—Shiz and Coriantumr assemble all the people to mortal combat—The Spirit of the Lord ceases to strive with them—The Jaredite nation is utterly destroyed—Only Coriantumr remains.

AND it came to pass when Coriantumr had recovered of his wounds, he began to remember the ªwords which Ether had spoken unto him.

2 He saw that there had been slain by the sword already nearly ªtwo millions of his people, and he began to sorrow in his heart; yea, there had been slain two millions of mighty men, and also their wives and their children.

3 He began to repent of the evil which he had done; he began to remember the words which had been spoken by the mouth of all the prophets, and he saw them that they were fulfilled thus far, every whit; and his soul ªmourned and refused to be ᵇcomforted.

4 And it came to pass that he wrote an epistle unto Shiz, desiring him that he would spare the people, and he would give up the kingdom for the sake of the lives of the people.

5 And it came to pass that when Shiz had received his epistle he wrote an epistle unto Coriantumr, that if he would give himself up, that he might slay him with his own sword, that he would spare the lives of the people.

6 And it came to pass that the people repented not of their iniquity; and the people of Coriantumr were stirred up to anger against the people of Shiz; and the people of Shiz were stirred up to anger against the people of Coriantumr; wherefore, the people of Shiz did give battle unto the people of Coriantumr.

7 And when Coriantumr saw that he was about to fall he fled again before the people of Shiz.

8 And it came to pass that he came to the waters of Ripliancum, which, by interpretation, is large, or to exceed all; wherefore, when they came to these waters they pitched their tents; and Shiz also pitched his tents near unto them; and therefore on the morrow they did come to battle.

9 And it came to pass that they fought an exceedingly sore battle, in which Coriantumr was wounded again, and he fainted with the loss of blood.

10 And it came to pass that the armies of Coriantumr did press upon the armies of Shiz that they beat them, that they caused them to flee before them; and they did flee southward, and did pitch their tents in a place which was called Ogath.

11 And it came to pass that the army of Coriantumr did pitch their tents by the hill Ramah; and it was that same hill where my father Mormon did ªhide up the records unto the Lord, which were sacred.

---

15 1ª Ether 13:20 (20–21).
2ª Ether 1:43.
3ª TG Mourning.

b Gen. 37:35;
Moses 7:44.
TG Comfort.

11ª Morm. 6:6.

12 And it came to pass that they did gather together all the people upon all the face of the land, who had not been slain, save it was Ether.

13 And it came to pass that Ether did *behold all the doings of the people; and he beheld that the people who were for Coriantumr were gathered together to the army of Coriantumr; and the people who were for Shiz were gathered together to the army of Shiz.

14 Wherefore, they were for the space of four years gathering together the people, that they might get all who were upon the face of the land, and that they might receive all the strength which it was possible that they could receive.

15 And it came to pass that when they were all gathered together, every one to the army which he would, with their wives and their children—both men, women and children being armed with *weapons of war, having shields, and *breastplates, and head-plates, and being clothed after the manner of war—they did march forth one against another to battle; and they fought all that day, and conquered not.

16 And it came to pass that when it was night they were weary, and retired to their camps; and after they had retired to their camps they took up a howling and a *lamentation for the loss of the slain of their people; and so great were their cries, their howlings and lamentations, that they did rend the air exceedingly.

17 And it came to pass that on the morrow they did go again to battle, and great and terrible was that day; nevertheless, they conquered not, and when the night came again they did rend the air with their cries, and their howlings, and their mournings, for the loss of the slain of their people.

18 And it came to pass that Corian-tumr wrote again an epistle unto Shiz, desiring that he would not come again to battle, but that he would take the kingdom, and spare the lives of the people.

19 But behold, the *Spirit of the Lord had ceased striving with them, and *Satan had full power over the *hearts of the people; for they were given up unto the hardness of their hearts, and the blindness of their minds that they might be destroyed; wherefore they went again to battle.

20 And it came to pass that they fought all that day, and when the night came they slept upon their swords.

21 And on the morrow they fought even until the night came.

22 And when the night came they were *drunken with anger, even as a man who is drunken with wine; and they slept again upon their swords.

23 And on the morrow they fought again; and when the night came they had all fallen by the sword save it were fifty and two of the people of Coriantumr, and sixty and nine of the people of Shiz.

24 And it came to pass that they slept upon their swords that night, and on the morrow they fought again, and they contended in their might with their swords and with their shields, all that day.

25 And when the night came there were thirty and two of the people of Shiz, and twenty and seven of the people of Coriantumr.

26 And it came to pass that they ate and slept, and prepared for death on the morrow. And they were large and mighty men as to the strength of men.

27 And it came to pass that they fought for the space of three hours, and they fainted with the loss of blood.

28 And it came to pass that when

13a Ether 13:14.
15a Ether 10:27.
   b Mosiah 8:10.
16a TG Mourning.
19a TG God, Spirit of;
   Holy Ghost, Loss of.
   b TG Devil.
   c TG Hardheartedness.
22a Moro. 9:23.

the men of Coriantumr had received sufficient strength that they could walk, they were about to flee for their lives; but behold, Shiz arose, and also his men, and he swore in his wrath that he would slay Coriantumr or he would perish by the sword.

29 Wherefore, he did pursue them, and on the morrow he did overtake them; and they fought again with the sword. And it came to pass that when they had *all fallen by the sword, save it were Coriantumr and Shiz, behold Shiz had fainted with the loss of blood.

30 And it came to pass that when Coriantumr had leaned upon his sword, that he rested a little, he smote off the head of Shiz.

31 And it came to pass that after he had smitten off the head of Shiz, that Shiz raised up on his hands and *fell; and after that he had struggled for breath, he died.

32 And it came to pass that *Coriantumr fell to the earth, and became as if he had no life.

33 And the Lord spake unto Ether, and said unto him: Go forth. And he went forth, and beheld that the words of the Lord had all been fulfilled; and he *finished his *record; (and the *hundredth part I have not written) and he hid them in a manner that the people of Limhi did find them.

34 Now the last words which are written by *Ether are these: Whether the Lord will that I be translated, or that I suffer the will of the Lord in the flesh, it mattereth not, if it so be that I am *saved in the kingdom of God. Amen.

THE BOOK OF MORONI

CHAPTER 1

Moroni writes for the benefit of the Lamanites—The Nephites who will not deny Christ are put to death. About A.D. 401–21.

NOW I, Moroni, after having made an end of abridging the account of the people of Jared, I had supposed *not to have written more, but I have not as yet perished; and I make not myself known to the Lamanites lest they should destroy me.

2 For behold, their *wars are exceedingly fierce among themselves; and because of their *hatred they *put to death every Nephite that will not deny the Christ.

3 And I, Moroni, will not *deny the Christ; wherefore, I wander whithersoever I can for the safety of mine own life.

4 Wherefore, I write a few more things, contrary to that which I had supposed; for I had supposed not to have written any more; but I write a few more things, that perhaps they may be of *worth unto my brethren, the Lamanites, in some future day, according to the will of the Lord.

CHAPTER 2

Jesus gave the twelve Nephite disciples power to confer the gift of the Holy Ghost. About A.D. 401–21.

29a Ether 13:21.
31a Judg. 5:27 (26–27).
32a Omni 1:21 (20–22).
33a Ether 13:14.
   b Mosiah 8:9; 21:27; 28:11;
     Alma 37:21 (21–31);
     Ether 1:2 (1–5).

c 3 Ne. 26:6;
  Ether 3:17.
34a Ether 1:6; 11:23; 12:2.
   b Mosiah 13:9.

[Moroni]
1 1a Morm. 8:5;

Moro. 10:1 (1–2).
2a 1 Ne. 12:21 (20–23).
  b TG Hate.
  c Alma 45:14.
3a Matt. 10:33 (32–33);
  3 Ne. 29:5.
4a 2 Ne. 3:12 (11–12, 19).

THE words of Christ, which he spake unto his *disciples, the twelve whom he had chosen, as he laid his hands upon them—

2 And he called them by name, saying: Ye shall *call on the Father in my name, in mighty prayer; and after ye have done this ye shall have *power that to him upon whom ye shall lay your *hands, *ye shall give the Holy Ghost; and in my name shall ye give it, for thus do mine apostles.

3 Now Christ spake these words unto them at the time of his first appearing; and the multitude heard it not, but the disciples heard it; and on as many as they *laid their hands, fell the Holy Ghost.

CHAPTER 3

Elders ordain priests and teachers by the laying on of hands. About A.D. 401–21.

THE manner which the disciples, who were called the *elders of the church, *ordained *priests and teachers—

2 After they had prayed unto the Father in the name of Christ, they *laid their hands upon them, and said:

3 In the name of Jesus Christ I ordain you to be a priest (or if he be a *teacher, I ordain you to be a teacher) to preach repentance and *remission of sins through Jesus Christ, by the endurance of faith on his name to the end. Amen.

4 And after this manner did they *ordain priests and teachers, according to the *gifts and callings of God

unto men; and they ordained them by the *power of the Holy Ghost, which was in them.

CHAPTER 4

How elders and priests administer the sacramental bread is explained. About A.D. 401–21.

THE *manner of their *elders and priests administering the flesh and blood of Christ unto the church; and they administered it *according to the commandments of Christ; wherefore we know the manner to be true; and the elder or priest did minister it—

2 And they did kneel down with the *church, and pray to the Father in the name of Christ, saying:

3 O God, the Eternal Father, we ask thee in the name of thy Son, Jesus Christ, to bless and *sanctify this *bread to the souls of all those who partake of it; that they may eat in *remembrance of the body of thy Son, and witness unto thee, O God, the Eternal Father, that they are willing to take upon them the *name of thy Son, and always remember him, and keep his commandments which he hath given them, that they may always have his *Spirit to be with them. Amen.

CHAPTER 5

The mode of administering the sacramental wine is set forth. About A.D. 401–21.

THE *manner of administering the wine—Behold, they took the cup, and said:

2 O God, the Eternal Father, we

---

2 1*a* 3 Ne. 13:25; 15:11.
  2*a* Gen. 4:26;
       Ether 4:15.
    b Matt. 10:1.
       TG Priesthood,
       Melchizedek.
    c TG Hands, Laying on of.
    d 3 Ne. 18:37.
  3*a* Acts 19:6.
3 1*a* Alma 6:1.
       TG Elder.
    b TG Church Organization.

  c Mosiah 6:3.
2*a* TG Hands, Laying on of.
3*a* TG Teacher.
  b TG Remission of Sins.
4*a* D&C 18:32;
     20:39 (39, 60).
     TG Priesthood;
     Priesthood, History of.
  b TG God, Gifts of.
  c 1 Ne. 13:37;
     Moro. 6:9.
4 1*a* 3 Ne. 18:5 (1–7).

  b TG Elder.
  c D&C 20:76.
2*a* TG Church.
3*a* 1 Sam. 21:4.
  b TG Sacrament.
  c Luke 22:19;
     3 Ne. 18:7; 20:8.
  d TG Jesus Christ, Taking
     the Name of.
  e TG God, Spirit of.
5 1*a* 3 Ne. 18:11 (8–11);
       D&C 20:78.

ask thee, in the name of thy Son, Jesus Christ, to bless and sanctify this *a*wine to the souls of all those who drink of it, that they may do it in *b*remembrance of the *c*blood of thy Son, which was shed for them; that they may witness unto thee, O God, the Eternal Father, that they do always remember him, that they may have his *d*Spirit to be with them. Amen.

CHAPTER 6

Repentant persons are baptized and fellowshipped—Church members who repent are forgiven—Meetings are conducted by the power of the Holy Ghost. About A.D. 401–21.

AND now I speak concerning baptism. Behold, elders, priests, and teachers were baptized; and they were not baptized save they brought forth *a*fruit meet that they were *b*worthy of it.

2 Neither did they receive any unto baptism save they came forth with a *a*broken *b*heart and a contrite spirit, and witnessed unto the church that they truly repented of all their sins.

3 And none were received unto baptism save they *a*took upon them the name of Christ, having a determination to serve him to the end.

4 And after they had been received unto baptism, and were wrought upon and *a*cleansed by the power of the Holy Ghost, they were numbered among the people of the *b*church of Christ; and their *c*names were taken, that they might be remembered and nourished by the good word of God, to keep them in the right way, to keep them continually *d*watchful unto prayer, *e*relying alone upon the merits of Christ, who was the author and the finisher of their faith.

5 And the *a*church did meet together *b*oft, to *c*fast and to pray, and to speak one with another concerning the welfare of their souls.

6 And they did *a*meet together oft to partake of bread and wine, in *b*remembrance of the Lord Jesus.

7 And they were strict to observe that there should be *a*no iniquity among them; and whoso was found to commit iniquity, and *b*three witnesses of the church did condemn them before the *c*elders, and if they repented not, and *d*confessed not, their names were *e*blotted out, and they were not *f*numbered among the people of Christ.

8 But *a*as oft as they repented and sought forgiveness, with real *b*intent, they were *c*forgiven.

9 And their meetings were *a*conducted by the church after the manner of the workings of the Spirit, and by the *b*power of the Holy Ghost; for as the power of the Holy Ghost led them whether to preach, or to exhort, or to pray, or to supplicate, or to sing, even so it was done.

2*a* TG Sacrament.
  b Luke 22:20;
     1 Cor. 11:25.
  c D&C 27:2 (2–4).
  d TG Spirituality.
6 1*a* TG Baptism,
     Qualifications for.
  b TG Worthiness.
2*a* TG Poor in Spirit.
  b TG Contrite Heart.
3*a* 2 Ne. 9:23.
     TG Jesus Christ, Taking
     the Name of.
4*a* TG Purification.
  b TG Jesus Christ, Head of
     the Church.
  c D&C 20:82; 47:1 (1–4).

  d D&C 20:53.
     TG Watch.
  e 2 Ne. 31:19;
     D&C 3:20.
5*a* Acts 1:14 (13–14).
     TG Church.
  b 3 Ne. 24:16.
  c 4 Ne. 1:12;
     D&C 88:76.
6*a* TG Assembly for
     Worship;
     Meetings.
  b TG Sacrament.
7*a* D&C 20:54.
  b D&C 42:80 (80–81).
     TG Witness.
  c Ex. 4:29;

     Josh. 20:4;
     Alma 6:1.
     TG Elder.
  d TG Confession.
  e Ex. 32:33;
     D&C 20:83.
     TG Excommunication.
  f TG Book of Life.
8*a* Mosiah 26:30 (30–31).
  b TG Sincere.
  c TG Forgive.
9*a* D&C 20:45; 46:2.
  b 1 Ne. 13:37;
     Moro. 3:4.
     TG Holy Ghost, Gifts of;
     Teaching with the
     Spirit.

CHAPTER 7

An invitation is given to enter into the rest of the Lord—Pray with real intent—The Spirit of Christ enables men to know good from evil—Satan persuades men to deny Christ and do evil—The prophets manifest the coming of Christ—By faith, miracles are wrought and angels minister—Men should hope for eternal life and cleave unto charity. About A.D. 401–21.

AND now I, Moroni, write a few of the words of my father Mormon, which he spake concerning ^afaith, hope, and charity; for after this manner did he speak unto the people, as he taught them in the ^bsynagogue which they had built for the place of worship.

2 And now I, Mormon, speak unto you, my beloved brethren; and it is by the ^agrace of God the Father, and our Lord Jesus Christ, and his holy will, because of the gift of his ^bcalling unto me, that I am permitted to speak unto you at this time.

3 Wherefore, I would speak unto you that are of the ^achurch, that are the ^bpeaceable followers of Christ, and that have obtained a sufficient ^chope by which ye can enter into the ^drest of the Lord, from this time henceforth until ye shall rest with him in heaven.

4 And now my brethren, I judge these things of you because of your peaceable ^awalk with the children of men.

5 For I remember the word of God which saith by their ^aworks ye shall know them; for if their works be good, then they are good also.

6 For behold, God hath said a man being ^aevil cannot do that which is good; for if he ^boffereth a gift, or ^cprayeth unto God, except he shall do it with real ^dintent it profiteth him nothing.

7 For behold, it is not counted unto him for righteousness.

8 For behold, if a man being ^aevil giveth a gift, he doeth it ^bgrudgingly; wherefore it is counted unto him the same as if he had retained the gift; wherefore he is counted evil before God.

9 And likewise also is it counted evil unto a man, if he shall pray and not with ^areal intent of heart; yea, and it profiteth him nothing, for God receiveth none such.

10 Wherefore, a man being evil cannot do that which is good; neither will he give a good gift.

11 For behold, a bitter ^afountain cannot bring forth good water; neither can a good fountain bring forth bitter water; wherefore, a man being a servant of the devil cannot follow Christ; and if he ^bfollow Christ he cannot be a ^cservant of the devil.

12 Wherefore, all things which are ^agood cometh of God; and that which is ^bevil cometh of the devil; for the devil is an enemy unto God, and fighteth against him continually, and inviteth and enticeth

---

7 1a 1 Cor. 13:13 (1–13);
    Ether 12:3 (3–37);
    Moro. 8:14; 10:20 (20–23).
    b Alma 16:13;
    3 Ne. 18:32.
  2a TG Grace.
    b 3 Ne. 5:13.
    TG Called of God.
  3a TG Jesus Christ, Head of the Church.
    b Acts 13:16;
    Rom. 16:20.
    c Alma 7:16;
    Ether 12:4;
    D&C 138:14.
    d TG Rest.
  4a 1 Jn. 2:6;

    D&C 19:23.
  5a 3 Ne. 14:20 (15–20).
  6a Matt. 7:16 (15–18).
    b Lev. 17:8 (8–9);
    D&C 132:9.
    c Prov. 28:9;
    Alma 34:28.
    TG Prayer.
    d Lev. 19:5.
    TG Hypocrisy;
    Motivations;
    Sincere.
  8a Prov. 15:8.
    b 1 Chr. 29:9;
    D&C 64:34.
  9a James 1:6 (6–7); 5:16;
    Moro. 10:4.

    TG Sincere.
 11a Prov. 13:14;
    James 3:11.
    b Matt. 6:24; 8:19;
    2 Ne. 31:10 (10–13);
    D&C 56:2.
    c TG Servant.
 12a Gen. 1:31;
    James 1:17 (17–21);
    1 Jn. 4:1 (1–6);
    3 Jn. 1:11 (1–14);
    Ether 4:12;
    D&C 59:17 (16–20);
    Moses 2:31.
    b Isa. 45:7;
    2 Cor. 4:4.
    TG Evil.

to ^csin, and to do that which is evil continually.

13 But behold, that which is of God inviteth and enticeth to do ^agood continually; wherefore, every thing which inviteth and ^benticeth to do ^cgood, and to love God, and to serve him, is ^dinspired of God.

14 Wherefore, take heed, my beloved brethren, that ye do not judge that which is ^aevil to be of God, or that which is good and of God to be of the devil.

15 For behold, my brethren, it is given unto you to ^ajudge, that ye may know good from evil; and the way to judge is as plain, that ye may know with a perfect knowledge, as the daylight is from the dark night.

16 For behold, the ^aSpirit of Christ is given to every ^bman, that he may ^cknow good from evil; wherefore, I show unto you the way to judge; for every thing which inviteth to do good, and to persuade to believe in Christ, is sent forth by the power and gift of Christ; wherefore ye may know with a perfect knowledge it is of God.

17 But whatsoever thing persuadeth men to do ^aevil, and believe not in Christ, and deny him, and serve not God, then ye may know with a perfect knowledge it is of the devil; for after this manner doth the devil work, for he persuadeth no man to do good, no, not one; neither do his angels; neither do they who subject themselves unto him.

18 And now, my brethren, seeing that ye know the ^alight by which ye may judge, which light is the light of Christ, see that ye do not judge wrongfully; for with that same ^bjudgment which ye judge ye shall also be judged.

19 Wherefore, I beseech of you, brethren, that ye should search diligently in the ^alight of Christ that ye may know good from evil; and if ye will lay hold upon every good thing, and condemn it not, ye certainly will be a ^bchild of Christ.

20 And now, my brethren, how is it possible that ye can lay hold upon every good thing?

21 And now I come to that faith, of which I said I would speak; and I will tell you the way whereby ye may lay hold on every good thing.

22 For behold, God ^aknowing all things, being from ^beverlasting to everlasting, behold, he sent ^cangels to minister unto the children of men, to make manifest concerning the coming of Christ; and in Christ there should come every good thing.

23 And God also declared unto prophets, by his own mouth, that Christ should come.

24 And behold, there were divers ways that he did manifest things unto the children of men, which were good; and all things which are good cometh of Christ; otherwise men were ^afallen, and there could no good thing come unto them.

12*c* Alma 5:40 (39–42);
    Hel. 6:30.
    TG Sin.
13*a* D&C 35:12; 84:47 (47–51).
  b 2 Ne. 33:4;
    Ether 8:26.
  c TG Benevolence.
  d TG Inspiration.
14*a* Isa. 5:20;
    2 Ne. 15:20;
    D&C 64:16; 121:16.
15*a* Ezek. 44:24.
    TG Discernment,
    Spiritual.
16*a* TG Conscience;
    God, Spirit of;
    Light of Christ.

  b TG Mortality.
  c Gen. 3:5;
    Amos 5:14 (14–15);
    Matt. 12:33 (33–37);
    2 Ne. 2:5 (5, 18, 26);
    Mosiah 16:3;
    Alma 29:5;
    Hel. 14:31;
    Ether 4:12 (11–12).
17*a* TG Sin.
18*a* Mosiah 16:9;
    Ether 3:14;
    D&C 50:24; 88:13 (7–13).
    TG Light of Christ.
  b Luke 6:37.
19*a* D&C 84:45; 88:7 (6–13).
  b Mosiah 15:10; 27:25.

    TG Sons and Daughters
    of God.
22*a* TG God, Foreknowl-
    edge of;
    God, Omniscience of.
  b 2 Ne. 19:6; 26:12;
    Mosiah 3:5;
    Alma 11:39 (38–39, 44);
    Moro. 8:18.
    TG God, Eternal
    Nature of.
  c Acts 10:3 (3, 22);
    2 Ne. 10:3; 11:3;
    Jacob 7:5.
24*a* 2 Ne. 2:5.

25 Wherefore, by the ministering of [a]angels, and by every word which proceeded forth out of the mouth of God, men began to exercise faith in Christ; and thus by faith, they did lay hold upon every good thing; and thus it was until the coming of Christ.

26 And after that he came men also were [a]saved by faith in his name; and by faith, they become the [b]sons of God. And as surely as Christ liveth he spake these words unto our fathers, saying: [c]Whatsoever thing ye shall ask the Father in my name, which is good, in faith believing that ye shall receive, behold, it shall be done unto you.

27 Wherefore, my beloved brethren, have [a]miracles ceased because Christ hath ascended into heaven, and hath sat down on the right hand of God, to [b]claim of the Father his rights of mercy which he hath upon the children of men?

28 For he hath answered the ends of the law, and he claimeth all those who have faith in him; and they who have faith in him will [a]cleave unto every good thing; wherefore he [b]advocateth the cause of the children of men; and he dwelleth eternally in the heavens.

29 And because he hath done this, my beloved brethren, have miracles ceased? Behold I say unto you, Nay; neither have [a]angels ceased to minister unto the children of men.

30 For behold, they are subject unto him, to minister according to the word of his command, showing themselves unto them of strong faith and a firm mind in every form of [a]godliness.

31 And the office of their ministry is to call men unto repentance, and to fulfil and to do the work of the covenants of the Father, which he hath made unto the children of men, to prepare the way among the children of men, by declaring the word of Christ unto the [a]chosen vessels of the Lord, that they may bear testimony of him.

32 And by so doing, the Lord God prepareth the way that the [a]residue of men may have [b]faith in Christ, that the Holy Ghost may have place in their hearts, according to the power thereof; and after this manner bringeth to pass the Father, the covenants which he hath made unto the children of men.

33 And Christ hath said: [a]If ye will have [b]faith in me ye shall have power to do whatsoever thing is [c]expedient in me.

34 And he hath said: [a]Repent all ye ends of the earth, and come unto me, and be baptized in my name, and have faith in me, that ye may be saved.

35 And now, my beloved brethren, if this be the case that these things are true which I have spoken unto you, and God will show unto you, with [a]power and great glory at the last [b]day, that they are true, and if they are true has the day of miracles ceased?

36 Or have angels ceased to appear unto the children of men? Or has he [a]withheld the power of the Holy Ghost from them? Or will he, so

25 a Alma 12:29 (28–30);
   Moses 5:58.
26 a D&C 3:20.
   b TG Sons and Daughters
     of God.
   c 3 Ne. 18:20.
   TG Prayer.
27 a TG Miracle.
   b Isa. 53:12 (11–12);
     2 Ne. 2:9.
28 a TG Motivations.
   b 1 Jn. 2:1;
     2 Ne. 2:9;
     Mosiah 14:12; 15:8;

3 Ne. 18:35.
   TG Jesus Christ,
     Relationships with the
     Father.
29 a Judg. 13:3;
     Luke 1:26;
     Acts 5:19 (19–20).
   TG Angels;
     Miracle.
30 a TG Godliness.
31 a D&C 20:10.
32 a Acts 15:17;
     Moses 7:28.
   b Acts 16:5;

D&C 46:14.
33 a Moro. 10:23.
   b Gal. 2:16.
   TG Faith.
   c D&C 88:64 (64–65).
34 a 3 Ne. 27:20;
     Ether 4:18.
35 a 2 Ne. 33:11;
     Ether 5:4 (4–6).
   b Morm. 9:15;
     D&C 35:8.
36 a 1 Ne. 10:17 (17–19);
     Moro. 10:7 (4–5, 7, 19).

long as time shall last, or the earth shall stand, or there shall be one man upon the face thereof to be saved?

37 Behold I say unto you, Nay; for it is by faith that ^amiracles are wrought; and it is by faith that angels appear and minister unto men; wherefore, if these things have ceased wo be unto the children of men, for it is because of ^bunbelief, and all is vain.

38 For no man can be saved, according to the words of Christ, save they shall have faith in his name; wherefore, if these things have ceased, then has faith ceased also; and awful is the state of man, for they are as though there had been no redemption made.

39 But behold, my beloved brethren, I judge better things of you, for I judge that ye have faith in Christ because of your meekness; for if ye have not faith in him then ye are not ^afit to be numbered among the people of his church.

40 And again, my beloved brethren, I would speak unto you concerning ^ahope. How is it that ye can attain unto faith, save ye shall have hope?

41 And what is it that ye shall ^ahope for? Behold I say unto you that ye shall have ^bhope through the atonement of Christ and the power of his resurrection, to be raised unto life ^ceternal, and this because of your faith in him according to the promise.

42 Wherefore, if a man have ^afaith he ^bmust needs have hope; for without faith there cannot be any hope.

43 And again, behold I say unto you that he cannot have faith and hope, save he shall be ^ameek, and lowly of heart.

44 If so, his ^afaith and hope is vain, for none is ^bacceptable before God, save the ^cmeek and lowly in heart; and if a man be meek and lowly in heart, and ^dconfesses by the power of the Holy Ghost that Jesus is the Christ, he must needs have charity; for if he have not charity he is nothing; wherefore he must needs have charity.

45 And ^acharity suffereth long, and is ^bkind, and ^cenvieth not, and is not puffed up, seeketh not her own, is not easily ^dprovoked, thinketh no evil, and rejoiceth not in iniquity but rejoiceth in the truth, beareth all things, believeth all things, hopeth all things, endureth all things.

46 Wherefore, my beloved brethren, if ye have not charity, ye are nothing, for charity never faileth. Wherefore, cleave unto charity, which is the greatest of all, for all things must fail—

47 But ^acharity is the pure ^blove of Christ, and it endureth ^cforever; and whoso is found possessed of it at the last day, it shall be well with him.

48 Wherefore, my beloved brethren, ^apray unto the Father with all the energy of heart, that ye may be filled with this love, which he hath bestowed upon all who are true ^bfollowers of his Son, Jesus Christ; that ye may become the sons of God; that when he shall appear we

37a Matt. 13:58;
  Morm. 8:26; 9:20;
  Ether 12:12 (12–18).
 b Moro. 10:19 (19–27).
39a TG Worthiness.
40a Heb. 11:1;
  Ether 12:4.
  TG Hope.
41a D&C 138:14.
 b Zech. 9:12 (11–12);
  Titus 1:2;
  Jacob 2:19;
  Alma 46:39.
 c TG Eternal Life.

42a TG Faith.
 b Moro. 10:20.
43a TG Humility.
44a 1 Cor. 13:13 (1–13);
  Alma 7:24;
  Ether 12:31 (28–35).
 b Lev. 10:19.
 c TG Meek.
 d Luke 12:8 (8–9).
  TG Holy Ghost, Gifts of;
  Testimony.
45a 1 Cor. 13:4 (1–13).
 b TG Kindness.
 c TG Envy.

 d TG Provoking.
47a Rom. 13:10;
  2 Ne. 26:30.
  TG Charity.
 b Josh. 22:5;
  Ether 12:34;
  Moro. 7:48.
  TG Love.
 c TG Eternity.
48a TG Communication;
  Prayer.
 b TG Jesus Christ,
  Exemplar.

shall ^cbe like him, for we shall see him as he is; that we may have this hope; that we may be ^dpurified even as he is pure. Amen.

CHAPTER 8

The baptism of little children is an evil abomination—Little children are alive in Christ because of the Atonement—Faith, repentance, meekness and lowliness of heart, receiving the Holy Ghost, and enduring to the end lead to salvation. About A.D. 401–21.

AN epistle of my ^afather Mormon, written to me, Moroni; and it was written unto me soon after my calling to the ministry. And on this wise did he write unto me, saying:

2 My beloved son, Moroni, I rejoice exceedingly that your Lord Jesus Christ hath been mindful of you, and hath called you to his ministry, and to his holy work.

3 I am mindful of you always in my prayers, continually praying unto God the Father in the name of his Holy Child, Jesus, that he, through his infinite ^agoodness and ^bgrace, will keep you through the endurance of faith on his name to the end.

4 And now, my son, I speak unto you concerning that which grieveth me exceedingly; for it grieveth me that there should ^adisputations rise among you.

5 For, if I have learned the truth, there have been disputations among you concerning the baptism of your little children.

6 And now, my son, I desire that ye should labor diligently, that this gross error should be removed from among you; for, for this intent I have written this epistle.

7 For immediately after I had learned these things of you I inquired of the Lord concerning the matter. And the ^aword of the Lord came to me by the power of the Holy Ghost, saying:

8 ^aListen to the words of Christ, your Redeemer, your Lord and your God. Behold, I came into the world not to call the righteous but sinners to repentance; the ^bwhole need no physician, but they that are sick; wherefore, little ^cchildren are ^dwhole, for they are not capable of committing ^esin; wherefore the curse of ^fAdam is taken from them in me, that it hath no power over them; and the law of ^gcircumcision is done away in me.

9 And after this manner did the Holy Ghost manifest the word of God unto me; wherefore, my beloved son, I know that it is solemn ^amockery before God, that ye should baptize little children.

10 Behold I say unto you that this thing shall ye teach—repentance and baptism unto those who are ^aaccountable and capable of committing sin; yea, teach parents that they must repent and be baptized, and humble themselves as their little ^bchildren, and they shall all be saved with their little children.

11 And their little ^achildren need no repentance, neither baptism. Behold, baptism is unto repentance to the fulfilling the commandments unto the ^bremission of sins.

12 But little ^achildren are alive in Christ, even from the foundation of the world; if not so, God is a partial

---

48c 1 Jn. 3:2 (1–3);
    3 Ne. 27:27.
  d 3 Ne. 19:28 (28–29).
    TG Cleanliness;
    Purity.
8 1 a W of M 1:1.
  3 a Ex. 34:6 (5–7);
    Mosiah 4:11.
  b TG Grace.
  4 a TG Disputations.
  7 a TG Word of the Lord.

8 a D&C 15:1.
  b Mark 2:17.
  c Mark 10:14 (13–16).
    TG Conceived in Sin.
  d Mosiah 3:16;
    D&C 29:46; 74:7.
  e TG Sin.
  f Mosiah 3:16;
    Morm. 9:12.
  g Gen. 17:11 (10–27);
    Acts 15:24.

  TG Circumcision.
9 a 2 Ne. 31:13.
10 a TG Accountability.
  b TG Family, Children,
    Responsibilities toward;
    Family, Love within.
11 a TG Baptism,
    Qualifications for;
    Children.
  b TG Remission of Sins.
12 a D&C 29:46; 93:38.

God, and also a changeable God, and a *b*respecter to persons; for how many little children have died without baptism!

13 Wherefore, if little children could not be saved without baptism, these must have gone to an endless hell.

14 Behold I say unto you, that he that supposeth that little children need baptism is in the gall of bitterness and in the bonds of iniquity; for he hath neither *a*faith, hope, nor charity; wherefore, should he be cut off while in the thought, he must go down to hell.

15 For awful is the wickedness to suppose that God saveth one child because of baptism, and the other must perish because he hath no baptism.

16 Wo be unto them that shall pervert the ways of the Lord after this manner, for they shall perish except they repent. Behold, I speak with boldness, having *a*authority from God; and I fear not what man can do; for *b*perfect *c*love *d*casteth out all fear.

17 And I am filled with *a*charity, which is everlasting love; wherefore, all children are alike unto me; wherefore, I love little children with a perfect love; and they are all alike and *b*partakers of salvation.

18 For I know that God is not a partial God, neither a changeable being; but he is *a*unchangeable from *b*all eternity to all eternity.

19 Little *a*children cannot repent; wherefore, it is awful wickedness to deny the pure mercies of God unto them, for they are all alive in him because of his *b*mercy.

20 And he that saith that little children need baptism denieth the mercies of Christ, and setteth at naught the *a*atonement of him and the power of his redemption.

21 Wo unto such, for they are in danger of death, *a*hell, and an *b*endless torment. I speak it boldly; God hath commanded me. Listen unto them and give heed, or they stand against you at the *c*judgment-seat of Christ.

22 For behold that all little children are *a*alive in Christ, and also all they that are without the *b*law. For the power of *c*redemption cometh on all them that have *d*no law; wherefore, he that is not condemned, or he that is under no condemnation, cannot repent; and unto such baptism availeth nothing—

23 But it is mockery before God, denying the mercies of Christ, and the power of his Holy Spirit, and putting trust in *a*dead works.

24 Behold, my son, this thing ought not to be; for *a*repentance is unto them that are under condemnation and under the curse of a broken law.

25 And the first fruits of *a*repentance is *b*baptism; and baptism cometh by faith unto the fulfilling the commandments; and the fulfilling the commandments bringeth *c*remission of sins;

26 And the remission of sins bringeth *a*meekness, and lowliness of heart; and because of meekness and lowliness of heart cometh the

---

12*b* Eph. 6:9;
    D&C 38:16.
14*a* 1 Cor. 13:13 (1–13);
    Ether 12:3 (3–37);
    Moro. 7:1; 10:20 (20–23).
16*a* TG Authority.
   b TG Perfection.
   c TG Love.
   d 1 Jn. 4:18.
17*a* TG Charity.
   b Mosiah 3:16 (16–19).
18*a* Alma 7:20;
    Morm. 9:9.

TG God, Perfection of.
  b Moro. 7:22.
19*a* TG Jesus Christ,
    Atonement through;
    Salvation, Plan of.
21*a* TG Hell.
   b Jacob 6:10;
    Mosiah 28:3;
    D&C 19:12 (10–12).
   c TG Jesus Christ, Judge.
22*a* TG Salvation of Little

Children.
  b Acts 17:30.
  c TG Redemption.
  d TG Accountability.
23*a* D&C 22:2.
24*a* TG Repent.
25*a* TG Baptism,
    Qualifications for.
  b Moses 6:60.
  c D&C 76:52.
    TG Remission of Sins.
26*a* TG Meek.

visitation of the ᵇHoly Ghost, which ᶜComforter ᵈfilleth with hope and perfect ᵉlove, which love endureth by ᶠdiligence unto ᵍprayer, until the end shall come, when all the ʰsaints shall dwell with God.

27 Behold, my son, I will write unto you again if I go not out soon against the Lamanites. Behold, the ᵃpride of this nation, or the people of the Nephites, hath proven their destruction except they should repent.

28 Pray for them, my son, that repentance may come unto them. But behold, I fear lest the Spirit hath ᵃceased ᵇstriving with them; and in this part of the land they are also seeking to put down all power and authority which cometh from God; and they are ᶜdenying the Holy Ghost.

29 And after rejecting so great a knowledge, my son, they must perish soon, unto the fulfilling of the prophecies which were spoken by the prophets, as well as the words of our Savior himself.

30 Farewell, my son, until I shall write unto you, or shall meet you again. Amen.

––––––––––

The second epistle of Mormon to his son Moroni.

Comprising chapter 9.

CHAPTER 9

Both the Nephites and the Lamanites are depraved and degenerate—They torture and murder each other—Mormon prays that grace and goodness may rest upon Moroni forever. About A.D. *401.*

My beloved son, I write unto you again that ye may know that I am yet alive; but I write somewhat of that which is grievous.

2 For behold, I have had a sore battle with the Lamanites, in which we did not conquer; and Archeantus has fallen by the sword, and also Luram and Emron; yea, and we have lost a great number of our choice men.

3 And now behold, my son, I fear lest the Lamanites shall destroy this people; for they do not repent, and Satan stirreth them up continually to ᵃanger one with another.

4 Behold, I am laboring with them continually; and when I speak the word of God with ᵃsharpness they tremble and anger against me; and when I use no sharpness they ᵇharden their hearts against it; wherefore, I fear lest the Spirit of the Lord hath ceased ᶜstriving with them.

5 For so exceedingly do they anger that it seemeth me that they have no fear of death; and they have lost their love, one towards another; and they ᵃthirst after blood and revenge continually.

6 And now, my beloved son, notwithstanding their hardness, let us labor ᵃdiligently; for if we should cease to ᵇlabor, we should be brought under condemnation; for we have a labor to perform whilst in this tabernacle of clay, that we may conquer the enemy of all righteousness, and rest our souls in the kingdom of God.

7 And now I write somewhat concerning the sufferings of this people.

26b ᴛɢ Holy Ghost,
   Baptism of.
 c ᴛɢ Holy Ghost,
   Comforter;
   Holy Ghost, Mission of.
 d 1 Ne. 11:22 (22–25).
   ᴛɢ Hope.
 e 1 Pet. 1:22.
 f ᴛɢ Diligence;
   Perseverance.
 g ᴛɢ Prayer.
 h ᴛɢ Saints.
27a D&C 38:39.

   ᴛɢ Pride.
28a ᴛɢ Holy Ghost, Loss of.
 b Morm. 5:16;
   Moro. 9:4.
 c Alma 39:6.
   ᴛɢ Holy Ghost,
   Unpardonable Sin
   against.
9 3a ᴛɢ Anger.
 4a 2 Ne. 1:26 (26–27);
   W of M 1:17;
   D&C 121:43 (41–43).
 b ᴛɢ Hardheartedness.

   c Moro. 8:28;
     D&C 1:33.
 5a Morm. 4:11 (11–12).
 6a ᴛɢ Dedication;
     Diligence;
     Perseverance.
 b 1 Sam. 8:9;
   2 Cor. 5:9;
   Jacob 1:19;
   Enos 1:20.
   ᴛɢ Duty;
   Priesthood, Magnifying
   Callings within.

For according to the knowledge which I have received from Amoron, behold, the Lamanites have many prisoners, which they took from the tower of Sherrizah; and there were men, women, and children.

8 And the husbands and fathers of those women and children they have slain; and they feed the women upon the ᵃflesh of their husbands, and the children upon the flesh of their fathers; and no water, save a little, do they give unto them.

9 And notwithstanding this great ᵃabomination of the Lamanites, it doth not exceed that of our people in Moriantum. For behold, many of the daughters of the Lamanites have they taken prisoners; and after ᵇdepriving them of that which was most dear and precious above all things, which is ᶜchastity and ᵈvirtue—

10 And after they had done this thing, they did murder them in a most ᵃcruel manner, torturing their bodies even unto death; and after they have done this, they devour their flesh like unto wild beasts, because of the hardness of their hearts; and they do it for a token of bravery.

11 O my beloved son, how can a people like this, that are without civilization—

12 (And only a few years have passed away, and they were a civil and a delightsome people)

13 But O my son, how can a people like this, whose ᵃdelight is in so much abomination—

14 How can we expect that God will ᵃstay his hand in judgment against us?

15 Behold, my heart cries: Wo unto this people. Come out in judgment, O God, and hide their sins, and wickedness, and abominations from before thy face!

16 And again, my son, there are many ᵃwidows and their daughters who remain in Sherrizah; and that part of the provisions which the Lamanites did not carry away, behold, the army of Zenephi has carried away, and left them to wander whithersoever they can for food; and many old women do faint by the way and die.

17 And the army which is with me is weak; and the armies of the Lamanites are betwixt Sherrizah and me; and as many as have fled to the army of ᵃAaron have fallen victims to their awful brutality.

18 O the depravity of my people! They are without ᵃorder and without mercy. Behold, I am but a man, and I have but the ᵇstrength of a man, and I cannot any longer enforce my commands.

19 And they have become strong in their perversion; and they are alike brutal, sparing none, neither old nor young; and they delight in everything save that which is good; and the suffering of our women and our children upon all the face of this land doth exceed everything; yea, tongue cannot tell, neither can it be written.

20 And now, my son, I dwell no longer upon this horrible scene. Behold, thou knowest the wickedness of this people; thou knowest that they are without principle, and past feeling; and their wickedness doth ᵃexceed that of the Lamanites.

21 Behold, my son, I cannot recommend them unto God lest he should smite me.

22 But behold, my son, I recommend thee unto God, and I trust in Christ that thou wilt be saved; and I ᵃpray unto God that he will ᵇspare thy life, to witness the return of his

---

8a Lev. 26:29;
  1 Ne. 21:26.
9a TG Body, Sanctity of.
  b TG Sensuality.
  c TG Chastity.
  d TG Virtue.
10a TG Cruelty.

13a 2 Ne. 9:9 (8–9);
  Jacob 3:11.
14a 2 Sam. 24:16;
  Alma 10:23.
16a Mosiah 21:10 (10, 17).
  TG Widows.
17a Morm. 2:9.

18a TG Order.
  b TG Strength.
20a Hel. 6:34 (18–35).
22a W of M 1:8.
  b Morm. 8:3.

people unto him, or their utter destruction; for I know that they must perish except they ᶜrepent and return unto him.

23 And if they perish it will be like unto the ᵃJaredites, because of the wilfulness of their hearts, ᵇseeking for blood and ᶜrevenge.

24 And if it so be that they perish, we know that many of our brethren have ᵃdeserted over unto the Lamanites, and many more will also desert over unto them; wherefore, write somewhat a few things, if thou art spared and I shall perish and not see thee; but I trust that I may see thee soon; for I have sacred records that I would ᵇdeliver up unto thee.

25 My son, be faithful in Christ; and may not the things which I have written grieve thee, to weigh thee down unto ᵃdeath; but may Christ lift thee up, and may his sufferings and death, and the showing his body unto our fathers, and his mercy and ᵇlong-suffering, and the hope of his glory and of eternal life, rest in your ᶜmind forever.

26 And may the grace of God the Father, whose throne is high in the heavens, and our Lord Jesus Christ, who sitteth on the ᵃright hand of his power, until all things shall become subject unto him, be, and abide with you forever. Amen.

CHAPTER 10

A testimony of the Book of Mormon comes by the power of the Holy Ghost—

The gifts of the Spirit are dispensed to the faithful—Spiritual gifts always accompany faith—Moroni's words speak from the dust—Come unto Christ, be perfected in Him, and sanctify your souls. About A.D. 421.

Now I, Moroni, write somewhat as seemeth me good; and I write unto my brethren, the ᵃLamanites; and I would that they should know that more than ᵇfour hundred and twenty years have passed away since the sign was given of the coming of Christ.

2 And I ᵃseal up ᵇthese records, after I have spoken a few words by way of exhortation unto you.

3 Behold, I would exhort you that when ye shall read these things, if it be wisdom in God that ye should read them, that ye would remember how ᵃmerciful the Lord hath been unto the children of men, from the creation of Adam even down until the time that ye shall receive these things, and ᵇponder it in your ᶜhearts.

4 And when ye shall receive these things, I would exhort you that ye would ᵃask God, the Eternal Father, in the name of Christ, if these things are not ᵇtrue; and if ye shall ask with a ᶜsincere heart, with ᵈreal intent, having ᵉfaith in Christ, he will ᶠmanifest the ᵍtruth of it unto you, by the power of the Holy Ghost.

5 And by the power of the Holy Ghost ye may ᵃknow the ᵇtruth of all things.

6 And whatsoever thing is good is

22c 1 Sam. 7:3;
      Hel. 13:11;
      3 Ne. 10:6 (5–7); 24:7.
23a Jacob 5:44.
   b Morm. 4:11 (11–12).
   c Ether 15:22 (15–31).
24a Alma 45:14.
   b Morm. 6:6; 8:1.
25a TG Jesus Christ,
      Death of.
   b TG Forbear.
   c TG Mind.
26a TG Jesus Christ,
      Relationships with the
      Father.
10 1a D&C 10:48.
    b Morm. 8:5;

Moro. 1:1.
2a Morm. 5:12; 8:4 (4, 13–14).
    TG Scriptures,
      Preservation of;
      Seal.
   b Morm. 6:6.
3a Gen. 19:16.
   b Deut. 11:18.
      TG Meditation;
      Study.
   c Deut. 6:6.
4a TG Prayer.
   b 1 Ne. 13:39; 14:30;
      Mosiah 1:6;
      Alma 3:12;
      Ether 4:11 (6–11);
      5:3 (1–4).

TG Book of Mormon.
   c TG Honesty;
      Sincere.
   d James 1:5 (5–7);
      Moro. 7:9.
   e TG Faith.
   f TG Revelation.
   g Ps. 145:18.
      TG Guidance, Divine;
      Truth.
5a D&C 35:19.
      TG Discernment,
      Spiritual;
      Holy Ghost, Source of
      Testimony.
   b John 8:32.

just and true; wherefore, nothing that is good denieth the Christ, but acknowledgeth that he is.

7 And ye may ^aknow that he is, by the power of the Holy Ghost; wherefore I would exhort you that ye deny not the power of God; for he worketh by power, ^baccording to the faith of the children of men, the same today and tomorrow, and forever.

8 And again, I exhort you, my brethren, that ye deny not the ^agifts of God, for they are many; and they come from the same God. And there are ^bdifferent ways that these gifts are administered; but it is the same God who worketh all in all; and they are given by the manifestations of the ^cSpirit of God unto men, to profit them.

9 ^aFor behold, to one is given by the Spirit of God, that he may ^bteach the word of wisdom;

10 And to another, that he may ^ateach the word of ^bknowledge by the same Spirit;

11 And to another, exceedingly great ^afaith; and to another, the gifts of ^bhealing by the same Spirit;

12 And again, to another, that he may work mighty ^amiracles;

13 And again, to another, that he may prophesy concerning all things;

14 And again, to another, the beholding of angels and ministering spirits;

15 And again, to another, all kinds of tongues;

16 And again, to another, the interpretation of ^alanguages and of divers kinds of tongues.

17 And all these gifts come by the Spirit of Christ; and they come unto every man severally, according as he will.

18 And I would exhort you, my beloved brethren, that ye remember that ^aevery good ^bgift cometh of Christ.

19 And I would exhort you, my beloved brethren, that ye remember that he is the ^asame yesterday, today, and forever, and that all these gifts of which I have spoken, which are spiritual, never will be done away, even as long as the world shall stand, only according to the ^bunbelief of the children of men.

20 Wherefore, there must be ^afaith; and if there must be faith there must also be hope; and if there must be hope there must also be charity.

21 And except ye have ^acharity ye can in nowise be saved in the kingdom of God; neither can ye be saved in the kingdom of God if ye have not faith; neither can ye if ye have no hope.

22 And if ye have no hope ye must needs be in ^adespair; and despair cometh because of iniquity.

23 And Christ truly said unto our fathers: ^aIf ye have faith ye can do all things which are expedient unto me.

24 And now I speak unto all the ends of the earth—that if the day cometh that the power and gifts of God shall be done away among you, it shall be ^abecause of ^bunbelief.

25 And wo be unto the children of men if this be the case; for there shall be ^anone that doeth good among you, no not one. For if there

---

7a TG Testimony.
  b 1 Ne. 10:17 (17–19);
    Moro. 7:36.
8a TG God, Gifts of;
    Holy Ghost, Gifts of.
  b D&C 46:15.
  c TG God, Spirit of.
9a 1 Cor. 12:8 (8–11);
    D&C 46:12 (8–30).
  b Ex. 35:34;
    D&C 38:23;
    88:77 (77–79, 118);
    107:85 (85–89).

10a TG Education.
  b 1 Cor. 12:8.
    TG Learn.
11a TG Faith.
  b TG Heal.
12a TG Miracle.
16a TG Language.
18a James 1:17.
  b TG Talents.
19a Heb. 13:8.
  b Moro. 7:37.
    TG Doubt.
20a 1 Cor. 13:13 (1–13);

Ether 12:3 (3–37);
    Moro. 7:1, 42 (42–44);
    8:14.
21a TG Charity.
22a TG Despair.
23a Moro. 7:33.
24a Moro. 7:37.
  b TG Doubt;
    Unbelief.
25a Ps. 14:3;
    Rom. 3:12.

be one among you that doeth good, he shall work by the power and gifts of God.

26 And wo unto them who shall do these things away and die, for they ᵃdie in their ᵇsins, and they cannot be saved in the kingdom of God; and I speak it according to the words of Christ; and I lie not.

27 And I exhort you to remember these things; for the time speedily cometh that ye shall know that I lie not, for ye shall see me at the bar of God; and the Lord God will say unto you: Did I not declare my ᵃwords unto you, which were written by this man, like as one ᵇcrying from the dead, yea, even as one speaking out of the ᶜdust?

28 I declare these things unto the fulfilling of the prophecies. And behold, they shall proceed forth out of the mouth of the everlasting God; and his word shall ᵃhiss forth from generation to generation.

29 And God shall show unto you, that that which I have written is ᵃtrue.

30 And again I would exhort you that ye would ᵃcome unto Christ, and lay hold upon every good ᵇgift, and ᶜtouch not the evil gift, nor the ᵈunclean thing.

31 And ᵃawake, and arise from the dust, O Jerusalem; yea, and put on thy beautiful garments, O daughter of ᵇZion; and ᶜstrengthen thy ᵈstakes and enlarge thy borders forever, that thou mayest ᵉno more be confounded, that the covenants of the Eternal Father which he hath made unto thee, O house of Israel, may be fulfilled.

32 Yea, ᵃcome unto Christ, and be ᵇperfected in him, and ᶜdeny yourselves of all ungodliness; and if ye shall deny yourselves of all ungodliness, and ᵈlove God with all your might, mind and strength, then is his grace sufficient for you, that by his grace ye may be ᵉperfect in Christ; and if by the grace of God ye are perfect in Christ, ye can in nowise deny the power of God.

33 And again, if ye by the grace of God are perfect in Christ, and deny not his power, then are ye ᵃsanctified in Christ by the grace of God, through the shedding of the ᵇblood of Christ, which is in the covenant of the Father unto the remission of your ᶜsins, that ye become ᵈholy, without spot.

34 And now I bid unto all, farewell. I soon go to ᵃrest in the ᵇparadise of God, until my ᶜspirit and body shall again ᵈreunite, and I am brought forth triumphant through the ᵉair, to meet you before the ᶠpleasing bar of the great ᵍJehovah, the Eternal ʰJudge of both quick and dead. Amen.

26a Ezek. 18:26;
    1 Ne. 15:33 (32–33);
    Mosiah 15:26.
   b John 8:21 (21–24).
27a Isa. 51:16;
    2 Ne. 33:10 (10–11);
    D&C 1:24.
   b 2 Ne. 3:19 (19–20);
    27:13; 33:13 (13–15);
    Morm. 9:30.
   c Isa. 29:4.
28a 2 Ne. 29:2.
29a TG Book of Mormon.
30a 1 Ne. 6:4;
    Morm. 9:27;
    Ether 5:5.
   b TG Talents.
   c 2 Ne. 18:19.
   d TG Uncleanness.

31a Isa. 52:1 (1–2).
    TG Israel, Restoration of.
   b TG Zion.
   c Isa. 54:2.
    TG Priesthood,
    Power of.
   d TG Stake.
   e Ether 13:8.
32a Rev. 22:17 (17–21);
    Jacob 1:7;
    Omni 1:26.
    TG Teachable.
   b Gal. 3:24;
    Philip. 3:15 (14–15).
    TG Man, New, Spiritually
    Reborn; Worthiness.
   c Rom. 12:1 (1–3).
    TG Perseverance.
   d Deut. 11:1;

    Mosiah 2:4;
    D&C 20:19; 59:5 (5–6).
    TG Commitment;
    Dedication.
   e Rom. 6:6 (1–7).
    TG Perfection.
33a TG Sanctification.
   b TG Jesus Christ,
    Atonement through.
   c Ex. 34:7.
   d TG Holiness.
34a TG Rest.
   b TG Paradise.
   c TG Spirit Body.
   d TG Resurrection.
   e 1 Thes. 4:17.
   f Jacob 6:13.
   g TG Jesus Christ, Jehovah.
   h TG Jesus Christ, Judge.

THE END